The New York Times
COMPLETE
WORLD
WAR II

The New York Times

COMPLETE WORLD WAR II

1939-1945

The Coverage from the Battlefields to the Home Front

EDITED BY RICHARD OVERY • FOREWORD BY TOM BROKAW

BLACK DOG
& LEVENTHAL
PUBLISHERS
NEW YORK

Published by
Black Dog & Leventhal Publishers, Inc.
151 West 19th Street
New York, NY 10011

Distributed by
Workman Publishing Company
225 Varick Street
New York, NY 10014

Manufactured in China

Cover design by Liz Driesbach
Interior design by Sheila Hart Design
Cover photograph/illustration ©Corbis

All interior photographs courtesy of Getty Images
ISBN-13: 978-1-57912-9446

h g f e d c b a

Library of Congress Cataloging-in-Publication Data on file.

Contents

Foreword
By Tom Brokaw

A hundred years from now, five hundred, a thousand, historians will be studying World War II and wondering, "How did it come to this? This madness of all out war in the heart of Western civilization and across the vast Pacific ocean, a war so lethal and so ambitious it would be described by John Keegan, the noted British military historian, as "the greatest event in the history of mankind."

As you will see in these dispatches from reporters from The New York Times at home and abroad— from 1939 to the end of the war in 1945—it was at the beginning a confusing, complex time of duplicity, denial, wishful thinking. Adolf Hitler aroused Germany with maniacal fervor and Japan began to plant its flag well beyond its small island boundaries.

Germany invades Poland and on September 1, 1939, The Times reported in bold print "WASHINGTON VIEWS THE CRISIS GRAVELY," describing how President Franklin D. Roosevelt spent the day reading press dispatches and listening to radio broadcasts from Europe. The following day France mobilizes eight million for military duty and the day after that Great Britain declares war on Germany.

Yet on September 3 Harold B. Hinton of The New York Times publishes a long, analytical piece headlined, "CAN THE UNITED STATES KEEP OUT OF WAR?" He describes President Roosevelt's apprehensions about Hitler and his subtle preparations for war but he quotes the President as saying he hoped and believed the country could stay clear and his Administration would do all it could to keep it out of war.

That is how it began, this greatest event in the history of mankind, with ominous German overtures, alarmed European reaction and now you see it, now you don't denial from America's commander in chief.

From that date forward the reporters and editors of The New York Times were in a quick step march to keep pace with the unfolding events.

Canada and Australia, British Commonwealth countries, jump in; James Reston in London for The Times describes a city hunkered down against German air raids and then later chronicles the rise of Winston Churchill. In prescient terms: "War is Mr. Churchill's natural element. Like a happy old tugboat captain with a battered sailor's cap on his head and a dead cigar between his teeth he has looked and sounded like s real war leader."

And so he was.

The news kept on coming, from East and West:

"BRITISH CHILDREN EVACUATED FROM CITIES"

"FABLED RUSSIAN WINTER
CLOSING IN ON INVADER"

"SINGAPORE DOUBTS JAPANESE THREATS"

"U-BOAT SINKS BRITISH BATTLESHIP"

Charles Lindbergh continues to speak out against the United States getting involved in the war and American mothers of sons storm Congress, demanding the U.S. not get involved .

But by the fall of 1941 FDR's private concerns have turned into a roaring war weapons program he calls "The Arsenal of Democracy" and Hanson Baldwin writes in The Times "the Arsenal of Democracy has commenced to bristle with arms."

A month and a week later, December 7, 1941, the United States is stunned, attacked on a sunny Sunday morning at Pearl Harbor by the Japanese. It is, as FDR would tell the world, "a day that will live in infamy," a day that catapulted the United States into the war.

In the last great naval battles of modern history, the U.S. and Japan fight across the Pacific and on the tiny islands no one had heard of before—Tarawa, Iwo Jima, Guadalcanal—American and Japanese fight hand to hand, face to face in utter savagery.

A World War unlike any other. In North Africa, Italy, throughout Europe and in western Russian, in all the seas and the skies above.

Sixteen million Americans are in uniform doing everything from penetrating deep behind enemy lines to baking bread and packing parachutes, from jumping out of airplanes and taking submarines to great depths.

Russia advances from the east. Allied forces gather in England for the greatest military invasion ever under the command of a genial Kansas farm boy who had been a colonel as late as 1941.

D-Day, June 6, 1944, the emblematic battle of the war. It was a massive sea, air and land operation and it was the beginning of the end of the Third Reich and the madness of Adolf Hitler.

Yet, news of the invasion didn't reach New York Times reporters and other journalists in Washington until three hours after it began.

From that day on the news began to be more hopeful. Headlines in The Times:

"NAZIS CONTINUE TO GUESS ABOUT GENERAL PATTON'S ARMY"

"JAPANESE CRUSHED" (in Saipan)

"B-29s MAKE THEIR DEBUT"

"RED ARMY DRIVE SHOWS NO SIGN OF FLAGGING"

Caught in the pincers of Russia advancing from the east and the Allies from the West, the Germans fight on but the wounds are fatal. Adolf Hitler, history's despot, puts a gun to his head in a Berlin bunker, his malignant dreams of a thousand-year empire, at an end in less than a decade.

In the Pacific, the Allied spear is now pointed at the Japanese homeland, an invasion that no one welcomes but unless the Japanese surrender, it cannot be avoided.

But it is, called off by the devastating impact of two bombs, new weapons created out of the terrifying effect of nuclear fusion.

The madness ends in August 1945. A world war in every sense of the phrase gives way to a difficult peace with unprecedented re-building and re-alignment required, with a new kind of war, a Cold War between the Soviet Union and the West, with the creation of a new nation in the Middle East as a partial tribute to the horrors of the Holocaust.

An uneasy peace, but a welcome one. Men came home to go to college or go to work in a peacetime economy that had been dormant too long. Women gave birth to a new generation with its own distinctive title. Detroit began to build civilian cars again. Meat was available in the supermarkets, and butter. New cities arose in the southeast, southwest and west.

Those who had borne the battle left the terrible memories deep in an emotional vault and got on with their lives, determined to make up for all they and their families and friends had sacrificed.

In these reports from The New York Times you can trace the origins of that chaotic time, share in the momentous decision making, be inspired by the greatness of the leaders of the victors and enraged by the mendacity of the war mongers.

This is timeless journalism and a gift to those of us who lived through it and those who want to know history's great question: how did this happen, and how did we prevail.

Introduction

"HISTORY IN THE RAW"

World War II represented a profound challenge to every major newspaper in the democratic world because of its sheer scale, length and complexity. No one in 1939 could possibly have foreseen a war that was to last for six years and cost at least 55 million people their lives. No one in 1939 could have predicted that a war that began with the German invasion of Poland, a conflict confined at first to eastern Europe, would engulf the entire globe, from the Aleutian Islands in the far north of the Pacific to Madagascar in the southern Indian Ocean, from the sea lanes of the Caribbean to the icy waters of northern Norway.

The complexity of the war derives from the many conflicts now known unsatisfactorily by the single label of World War II. In Asia the Japanese began a war in 1937 against China and then undertook another one in 1941 across the Pacific, and a further campaign into Southeast Asia and toward India. In the Mediterranean, Italian dictator Benito Mussolini began war against Britain and France in June 1940 and then turned to Greece and Africa to try to carve out a new Roman Empire while the West was in crisis. The main threat came from the militarily and industrially powerful Germany. Hitler also found himself fighting two wars, one against the Western democracies, including by 1941 the United States, and a second one of imperial conquest in the Soviet Union. Against the West, at sea and in the air, Germany fought a war based on the most modern science and technology; against the Soviet Union it was more traditional, a clash of mass armies. Descriptions of the German soldiers at Stalingrad read like accounts of the Grand Army of Napoleon that froze to death in Russia 130 years earlier.

To make sense of these many conflicts, the fighting powers reduced the issue to one of life and death. For the democracies, the whole western tradition and democratic way of life seemed under mortal threat from the menace of militarism and modern authoritarianism. For Germany, Italy and Japan, the world dominated by the democracies and their empires (which were certainly not democratic) seemed to be based on outworn liberal values and a hypocritical defense of political freedom and open trade, which the West failed to honor in practice. They saw their own national futures blighted by Western domination. The Axis powers, as they became known, were ruled by aggressive nationalist regimes that wanted to replace the West's historical self-importance with what they called a "New Order" in Asia, in the Mediterranean and in Europe. It was against this rising ambition that the rest of the world rallied to support the Allies, who in January 1942 adopted the title United Nations in recognition of the growing number of states who opposed the Axis.

The major Allies—Britain, the United States, the

Soviet Union and China—had very different regimes and antagonistic agendas, but they were united by the single desire to defeat their common enemies as the first step to building a more rational and peaceable world system. It was easy for them to reduce the conflict to a simple right versus wrong, even though from the democracies' point of view there was a great deal that was wrong with the dictatorships that ruled China and the Soviet Union. The commitment to victory that held the alliance together until 1945 gradually gave way to a new crisis in which wartime friends soon became post-war enemies.

Through all the years of war The New York Times was dedicated to reporting, without "fear or favor," as much military and political news as possible. This meant filling the paper with articles and reports and editorials that were devoted to places and issues often remote from American interests. The Times publisher, Arthur Hays Sulzberger, and his editorial staff were committed during the war to making sure their readers were aware of the wider story of the conflict. More than 160 Times correspondents worldwide found themselves in distant geographical areas, following events rather than sitting in The Times bureau in a more familiar capital city. The Times printed more words on the war than any other newspaper, an average of 125,000 every weekday, and 240,000 in the Sunday edition. A million words a day flooded in to New York by radio, telephone or wire, and valuable advertising space was surrendered to make sure all the news was covered. The number of readers increased during the wartime period, from an average 1.26 million (weekday and Sunday) in 1941 to an average 1.47 million in 1945.[1] Despite limitations imposed by the wartime scarcity of newsprint, this does not seem to have unduly affected The Times. In late 1942 Sulzberger was invited to join the Publishers Newsprint Committee, which then fixed the allotment of paper at the average consumption in 1941. Under Order L-240, a scheme was established to ensure that every newspaper got its quota of supply. The Times printed more news, particularly world news, than other

papers, and those extra pages came at the expense of advertising revenue.[2]

Many problems arose in seeking out the news and making sure that it got into print. There was nothing straightforward about wartime reporting and wartime publishing. The first problem was official silence, the second censorship. Military operations were highly secret and the course of battle often shrouded by a deliberate veil of misinformation, or no information at all. The Battle of France in 1940 and the invasion of Normandy in 1944 had to be guessed at by correspondents on the basis of what few reliable communiqués were available. On the Eastern Front and the war in China, there were regular difficulties in getting any worthwhile material. German press conferences in the six months following the Barbarossa campaign launched against the Soviet Union on June 22, 1941 were contrived events with little hard news about the course of war. A major press conference held in early October in Berlin reported that the Soviets were now defeated, a claim that aroused a natural skepticism among the few American correspondents present, and was soon shown to be nonsense.[3]

Even when there was news to report, every country practiced censorship to avoid compromising security. This could take many forms, and correspondents became adept at writing copy that skirted what was known of censorship rules, which affected not only text but also images. American newspapers were not permitted to show pictures of dead soldiers or of people weeping. Britain permitted no images of the dead or badly injured from bombing raids.[4] Censorship could be a source of real frustration. Raymond Daniell, head of The Times London bureau during the London Blitz of 1940-41, curtly explained how newsmen felt about it:

"And always there is the censor to deal with. He often is a well-intentioned blunderer who either hopelessly slows things up or is so obtuse about differentiating between military information and harmless speculation that he drives correspondents to the verge of nervous breakdowns."[5]

Daniell thought that censorship, like Prohibition, was "noble in purpose," but a failure in practice. In dictatorships, censorship was taken for granted as a risk run by all foreign reporters. When The Times' Austrian correspondent, George E. Gedye, was expelled from Vienna in 1938 for publishing unflattering reports after the German takeover in March, he was told that no reason had to be given. He left the country accompanied by a detective and was searched thoroughly by customs men who stuck needles into his soap and inspected the cuffs of his trousers.[6] Times reporter Otto Tolischus was expelled from Germany in 1941 for articles defying censorship (for which he won a Pulitzer Prize), but then a few months later was imprisoned in Japan for writing articles that the censor had in fact passed.[7]

The war exposed The Times overseas' correspondents to frequent dangers, often in the most remote parts of the world. The dangers were seldom evident in the final reports in the paper, or appreciated by the public that read them. The British novelist W. Somerset Maugham, in a preface to Daniell's book, gave an honest assessment of their unsung risks:

"It is not a very safe profession that the newspaper man follows in wartime. Where there is trouble they must get into it if they can. They must have courage and endurance; they must undergo discomfort and often hardship; they must face danger and sometimes death to provide you with the news. But there is no mention in despatches for them; there are no medals or orders; they may show heroism but it will pass unnoticed."[8]

Correspondents wore a military uniform and a helmet at the front line, and the risks they ran were considerable. Two Times correspondents were killed. Byron Darnton was the victim of "friendly fire" from a B-25 light bomber that mistakenly attacked his landing craft on the way to Buna in New Guinea. Robert Post of the London bureau was lost in one of the first Eighth Air Force missions over Germany against the port of Wilhelmshaven in February 1943. Richard Johnston was wounded in an American attack on the French port of Brest, and

Hal Denny, who had already been captured in North Africa and interrogated (in this case painlessly) by the Gestapo, was hit by bomb fragments in Belgium. Out of the Times staff, 910 served in the three services, and nineteen of them died.[9]

One of the most remarkable stories involved the diminutive theater critic Brooks Atkinson, who became impatient to report on the war rather than Broadway shows. In late 1942 he traveled to Africa where he filed his first war report, and then on to China as correspondent in the China-Burma theater. Atkinson was the first to hear in October 1944 that Chiang Kai-shek had asked for General Stilwell to be recalled as his American adviser, and to avoid the censor he took a difficult route all the way back to New York to file the story. He had become so ill in China that he was immediately hospitalized on his return, his weight reduced to a fraction of his already meager body by the harsh conditions he had faced in Asia.[10]

The Times was keen during the war to show that it could maintain its political independence, demonstrated by its support for the Republican, Wendell Wilkie, in the 1940 election and for Franklin Roosevelt, a Democrat, four years later. It was difficult both before the war and during it to remain indifferent to Axis aggression. Only an automaton, "a journalistic robot," wrote Daniell, "could remain neutral in such circumstances". He thought that what was still possible was "journalistic objectivity" in the face of the barrage of misinformation and propaganda to which correspondents were subjected everywhere.[11] If The Times followed a line at all, it was to support internationalism. Sulzberger had been anti-war in the earlier 1930s, but both he and Charles Merz, the new editor appointed in November 1938, came to see the importance of greater American involvement in the wider world. Ferdinand Kuhn, the veteran correspondent in London before Daniell, predicted in 1939 that British weakness in the face of Germany would bring an inevitable doom of economic decline and apocalyptic bombing, while the United States seemed Britain's natural successor in the world, thanks to the "virility and youthfulness" of its population and the opportunities to "use our democracy wisely."[12]

The Times remained a strong advocate throughout the war of the idea that the United States should assume its proper share of post-war responsibilities. The Times diplomatic correspondent, Harold Callender, in A Preface to Peace published in 1944, warned that the United States now faced "an essentially smaller and tighter world in which no great power can be neutral or isolated."[13] Sulzberger remained anxious through the discussions that led to the formation of the United Nations Organization that somehow the public would fail to see that internationalism was now in its interest. In August 1945 The Times claimed, not without reason, that "we have become the most powerful nation in the world." But the message was intended to make sure that the American leadership and public understood that this meant an end forever to isolationism.[14]

The influence of The Times is hard to judge, though editorials were clearly read with interest and concern in the White House and by leaders abroad. But when it came to direct involvement, the opportunities were limited. The Japanese procurator, summing up the case against Otto Tolischus after his arrest, told Tolischus that because in a democracy the press affects public opinion, and public opinion affects the government, the things he had written contributed to a policy that "led to war between Japan and the United States," and that Tolischus was therefore "responsible for the war."[15] In truth, that kind of influence was far removed from reality. The Times occasionally provided a platform to prominent soldiers or politicians to explain their case. British Air Chief Marshal Arthur Harris was given several pages in 1944 to describe in great detail what the bomber offensive was accomplishing, the fruit of an earlier correspondence between Sulzberger and Harris about promoting bombing strategy in the American press.[16] In the summer of 1943, Sulzberger, accompanied by James Reston, visited Moscow to meet Soviet leaders. His objective, with Roosevelt's

personal approval, was to try to show the Soviet leadership that the American press understood that Russia was an important part of the war effort. He was shown the Pravda offices and was puzzled that there was no news room (news was handed down from above) and he met Soviet Foreign Commissar Vyacheslav Molotov, who smiled and said little. Sulzberger concluded that "Russia did not want to be known," and The Times ran many fewer Soviet stories later in the war than it had in 1941.[17] Soviet attitudes toward the paper can perhaps be summed up by a hostile profile of The Times' defense correspondent, Hanson Baldwin, published in Pravda in April 1944, in which Baldwin was called "an admiral of the ink pool" and accused of writing misleading and patronizing military analysis.[18] The Times' greatest influence was undoubtedly its unstinting support for the United Nations project and American world policy. In October 1944 The Times condemned both "nationalistic isolationists" and those pure idealists who wanted a genuine "Parliament of Man" for undermining the search for a new world organization, which for all its faults would still be better than a return to the pre-war world.[19]

The Times was progressive on many issues that were important to wartime America. There were anxieties about the large extension of presidential powers brought about by the war, which explains Roosevelt's often awkward relationship with the paper. On the right of blacks to join the war effort and to fight and work on equal terms, The Times ran regular reports and campaigned for greater integration. Special mention was made of the black unit that fought in the embattled enclave at Bastogne in December 1944 during the Battle of the Bulge.[20] There were regular features and editorials highlighting the work that women were doing and the paper provided a platform for the argument that after the war more women would want to continue with a career rather than accept the role of unpaid housekeeper. Neither American blacks nor American women got what they wanted in 1945. The Times' description of the disembarkation of demobilized soldiers in New York failed to comment on the segregation of white and black soldiers as they came down the gangplank.

The Times was not shy on exposing wartime atrocity, whether in the Czech village of Lidice or by the Japanese in the Chinese city of Nanjing. And the paper was a force in exposing injustice, evident in its regular coverage of the British failure to offer independence to India. The Times has been criticized, however, for failing to influence opinion on the biggest horror of them all, the persecution and extermination of six million European Jews by Adolf Hitler's Third Reich. It is nevertheless misleading to suggest that The Times ignored the subject. Throughout the 1930s and into the war, it published reports on German policy against the Jews. It reported on Kristallnacht in November 1938, and in November 1942 on Heinrich Himmler's systematic slaughter of Polish Jews.[21] But Arthur Sulzberger was conflicted about his own Jewishness, hostile to Zionism, and at great pains to ensure that American anti-Semitism would not identify The Times as a "Jewish paper."[22] In his determination to achieve that end, as Susan E. Tifft and Alex S. Jones wrote in "The Trust," their history of The Times, "he missed an opportunity to use the considerable power of the paper to focus a spotlight on one of the greatest crimes the world has ever known." Articles about the murder of the Jews rarely made it to page one of the paper. The description of the operations of the death camp at Treblinka appeared on page 11. In "Buried by the Times" Laurel Leff wrote that the destruction of Europe's Jews "remained below the surface, only emerging now and then in a diluted and fractured form."[23]

What The Times did in the wartime years was to publish what Hanson Baldwin called "history in the raw," different from the "precise, emotionless chronology of school books." This was the view of history as it happened, with all its limitations, and it was possible to get many things wrong, since reporters were always looking to an uncertain future, unlike historians who look back on a certain past. The Times published articles in late 1932 and early

1933 suggesting that there would never be a Hitler dictatorship. In April 1940, four weeks before British Primes Minister Neville Chamberlain resigned, the paper reported that he seemed more secure than ever as British leader. On June 12, 1941, ten days before the Barbarossa campaign, The Times ran Walter Duranty's special report that renewed agreement was much more likely between Germany and the Soviet Union than war.[24] Duranty, a longtime Moscow correspondent for The Times and Pulitzer Prize winner, was later severely criticized for underplaying Bolshevik brutalities and ignoring the Ukrainian famine in the early 1930's, causing the paper to renounce the award.

But The Times also got many things right, and often told the story before its major competitors. Both the good and the bad are reproduced in this selection of wartime articles culled from tens of thousands published throughout the whole period of war from 1939 to 1945. Since many of the articles were very long in the original, some, though not all, of this selection have been edited down from their original length. All the articles on the war can be found in full on the CD that accompanies this volume. They have been chosen because they reflect the main narrative of the war seen from the perspective of New York, including war on the home front and some of the strange quirks that the war provoked in American and European daily life. Articles also appear that describe the tough daily routine of service life in the field, which many correspondents shared. The narrative moves from crisis and uncertainty for the Allies, through a tense period in 1942 and 1943 when everything still seemed poised in the balance, to a final rush for victory which a stubborn Axis defense made more costly and lengthier than the public had been led to expect. It ends with the advent of a new nuclear age in which the certainty of unconditional victory brought with it the uncertainties of a nuclear future. That victory is now often taken for granted as the product of the natural triumph of virtue over crime. But it did not always seem so to those dictating the news to correspondents eager for something to lighten the grim images of war and death. All the more remarkable that a Times editor, Robert Duffus, could write in June 1940 after the British evacuation from Dunkirk, "It is the great tradition of democracy. It is the future. It is victory." On this prediction, The Times proved in the long run unassailably right.[25]

1   Meyer Berger *The Story of The New York Times 1851-1951* (New York: Simon & Schuster, 1951), pp. 447-8 and 570, Appendix II

2   Ibid., p. 476.

3   Howard Smith *Last Train from Berlin* (London: Cresset Press, 1942), pp. 62-3. Smith worked for the United Press in Berlin.

4   On America see G. H. Roeder *The Censored War: American Visual Experience during World War II* (New Haven: Yale University Press, 1993), pp. 20-1, 25; Aaron William Moore, *Writing War: Soldiers Record the Japanese Empire* (Cambridge, MA: Harvard University Press, 2013) pp. 183-5.

5   Raymond Daniell *Civilians Must Fight* (New York: Doubleday, 1941), p. 17.

6   George Gedye 'Vienna Waltz' in Hanson Baldwin and Shepard Stone (eds.) *We Saw It Happen: The News Behind the News That's Fit to Print* (New York: Simon & Schuster, 1939), p. 34.

7   Otto Tolischus *Tokyo Record* (London: Hamish Hamilton, 1943), pp. 254-5.

8   Daniell, *Civilians Must Fight*, preface by W. Somerset Maugham, p. viii.

9   Berger *The Story of The New York Times*, pp. 462-6, 503.

10 Ibid., pp. 489-92

11 Daniell *Civilians Must Fight*, pp. 13-14, 15.

12 Baldwin, Shepard (eds) *We Saw It Happen*, pp. 200-1. See too Berger *The Story of The New York Times*, pp. 531-2.

13 Harold Callender *A Preface to Peace* (London: George Allen & Unwin, 1944), p. 247.

14 "Eigjhteen Fateful Days", *The New York Times*, 19 August 1945.

15 Tolischus *Tokyo Record*, p 257.

16 RAF Museum, London, Harris Papers H28, Sulzberger to Harris, 21 Sept 1942. Harris wrote at the foot of the letter 'The publicity and technical quality of the N.Y. Times is grand'.

17 Berger *The Story of The New York Times*, pp. 469-71.

18 "Pravda Ridicules Times War Writer", *The New York Times*, 10 April 1944.

19 "New League Starting with Good Prospects", *The New York Times*, 15 October 1944.

20 "Negro Unit at Bastogne", *The New York Times*, 29 January 1945.

21 "Himmler Program Kills Polish Jews", *The New York Times*, 18 December 1942.

22 Susan Tifft and Alex Jones *The Trust: The Private and Powerful Family Behind The New York Times* (New York: Little, Brown & Co, 1999), pp. 216-18.

23 Laurel Leff *Buried by The Times: The Holocaust and America's Most Important Newspaper* (Cambridge: Cambridge University Press, 2005), pp. 164, 358

24 "Soviet-Nazi Deal Held More Likely than Clash", *The New York Times*, 12 June 1941.

25 Berger *The Story of the New York Times*, p. 437.

Prologue

"REICH TROOPS JAM ROAD TO POLAND"

1919–1939

On June 28, 1919 in the Hall of Mirrors in the French Palace of Versailles, outside Paris, a treaty was signed between the victorious Allied powers and Germany, bringing World War I to an end. American President Woodrow Wilson hoped that the treaty would pave the way for a new world order based on peace, disarmament and the freedom for peoples to choose their own destiny. Only twenty years separated the end of the first war and the start of a second war that was even more destructive and global. The roots of that second conflict can be found in the settlement reached in 1919. Alongside the idealistic ambitions for a new, peaceful world order were sown the seeds of a narrow nationalism that spawned a violent, intolerant politics. Even Wilson's idealism proved short-lived when, in 1920, the Senate rejected ratification of the treaty and effectively took the United States out of the new League of Nations. The League had been established to try to resolve international disputes by rational, peaceable means. Throughout the twenty years that followed, the United States stood aside from any formal commitment to the international order, just as the newly founded Soviet Union, emerging from the wartime Communist revolution of 1917, remained on the international margins. Britain chose to be semidetached from the crises inside and outside Europe, seeking the self-preservation of the Empire and unwilling to run risks that might undermine Britain's worldwide interests.

This situation was fertile ground for those forces in world politics that had not been satisfied by Wilsonian idealism. Economic downturns and political instability after the war plunged Italy into crisis and prompted a nationalist backlash expressed in the rise to power of Benito Mussolini and his Fascist blackshirts. Appointed prime minister in October 1922, Mussolini had established a tough dictatorship by 1926, with himself as self-proclaimed Duce, or leader. In Germany a postwar crisis was brought on by defeat and the humiliating Versailles Treaty that blamed Germans for the war and made them pay reparations for starting it, stripped away German territory in Poland and France, and forced Germany to disarm. All this generated a hyperinflation that destroyed all savings and at the same time prompted the rise of violent, ultranationalist movements that rejected the peace imposed by the West and pursued the politics of revenge. Adolf Hitler's National Socialist Party was among their number, though Hitler was not yet the prominent political figure he was to become. In November 1923 he staged a coup in imitation of Mussolini but it ended in farce with his arrest and imprisonment. It took him almost ten years to establish a broad nationalist movement, animated by a hatred of the Versailles Treaty and the Jews, and a desire to reestablish German military power. In 1933, in the midst of a major economic crisis and political chaos, Hitler was appointed chancellor of Germany, and within months had enacted legislation designed to exclude Germany's Jewish population from the new "national revolution." By 1934 he too had become dictator, Germany's Führer; in 1938 he appointed himself commander-in-chief of the armed forces.

On the other side of the world, Japan also came to reject the settlement arrived at in 1919. Japanese military leaders resented the second-class status accorded to Japan by the other major powers. They saw Japan's destiny as the leader of a major empire, like that of Britain and France, in a reinvigorated Asia. Frustrated by economic crisis and closed markets abroad, the Japanese Army invaded Manchuria in 1931, and moved on to attack northern China the following year. Step by step, Japan consolidated its position in Asia and when a full-scale war broke out in July 1937 between Japan and Chiang Kai-shek's Nationalist China, the Japanese declared a "new order" in Asia and tried to compel Europe and the United States to accept the altered balance of power in the region.

Mussolini and Hitler also were attracted to the idea of "new orders" in Europe and Africa, and since none of the League powers had prevented Japanese aggression, they began to undertake their own programs of territorial expansion. In 1935 Italy attacked the African nation of Ethiopia and conquered it by May 1936. In July 1936 Mussolini, together with Hitler, agreed to help the nationalist general Francisco Franco in his bid to seize power in Spain. Later, in the spring of 1939, Mussolini occupied Albania and began to think about further wars to build an Italian empire in the Mediterranean. Hitler tore up the Versailles Treaty by rearming Germany, remilitarizing the Rhineland and repudiating reparations. In March 1938 German troops were ordered into Austria and a so-called "Greater Germany" was created. In the summer of 1938 pressure was put on the Czech government to hand over territory where the majority of the population was German, and on September 30 at Munich, Britain and France accepted German arguments and agreed to transfer the "Sudeten" Germans to German rule, dismembering the Czech state.

Throughout the period when the "new order" states were disrupting the international order, the only states committed to upholding the international order—Britain and France—found their options limited. Neither wanted to risk all-out war because of the terrible human and material cost already revealed in the horrors of WWI. Both had unstable empires, full of nationalists demanding liberation from colonial rule. Both faced economic crises in the 1930s that increased the political risks for democracies if they chose to rearm. But in the end these multiple crises forced the democracies to begin large-scale rearmament, while trying to figure out ways of preserving peace. This strategy of appeasement might have worked if Britain and France had faced reasonable opponents. It was clear by 1939 that there was no possibility of appeasing Hitler, Mussolini and the Japanese Army and that war was now likely.

After the occupation of Prague by the Germans in March 1939, the British and French gave a guarantee to Poland that shaped the coming conflict. Hitler wanted Poland to give back the territory the Germans had lost in 1919, and to agree that the city of Danzig (which was under League supervision) should become German again. The Poles rejected this, fearful that they would suffer the fate of Czechoslovakia. Throughout the summer the British made it clear that any aggressive move by Germany would be met with force. On August 23 Hitler suddenly signed a pact with the Soviet Union guaranteeing non-aggression between the two countries. He was convinced that this freed him to attack Poland and seize the territory he wanted. He was also convinced that the West would back down. His war was a gamble on the timidity of the democracies. Though he could not know it, when he ordered the attack on Poland on September 1, he had launched World War II.

SIGNING PROVIDES BRILLIANT PAGEANT
Ceremony Staged in Gorgeous Setting of "All the Glories of France."

STORM OF CHEERS FOR FOCH
Wilson Received with Enthusiasm— Doughboys and Tommies In the Vast Throng.

By WALTER DURANTY

VERSAILLES, June 29.—There could have been found no nobler setting for the signing of peace than the palace of the greatest of French kings, on the hillcrest of Versailles. To reach it the plenipotentiaries and distinguished guests from all parts of the world, who motored to their places in the Hall of Mirrors, drove down the magnificent, tree-lined Avenuedu Chateau, then across the huge square—the famous Place d'Armes of Versailles—and up through the gates and over the cobblestones of the Court of Honor to the entrance, where officers of the Garde Republicaine, in picturesque uniform, were drawn up to receive them.

It was a few minutes after 2 when the first automobile made its way between dense lines of cavalry backed by a double rank of infantry with bayonets fixed— there were said to be 20,000 soldiers altogether guarding the route—that held back the cheering crowds.

The scene from the Court of Honor where I was standing was impressive to a degree. The Place d'Armes was a lake of white faces, dappled everywhere by the bright colors of flags and fringed with the horizon blue of troops whose bayonets shone like flames as the sun peeped for a moment from behind heavy clouds. Above airplanes—a dozen or more— wheeled and curvetted.

The entrance to the palace courtyard is usually barred by great gilded gates. Today, in the words of the hymn, it was "flung open wide the golden gates and let the victors in," Up that triumphal passage, fully a quarter of a mile long, between the wings of the palace and the entrance to the Hall of Mirrors, representatives of the victorious nations passed in flag-decked limousines—hundreds, one after another, without intermission—for fifty minutes.

Midway down the courtyard is a big bronze statue of Louis XIV on horseback, and all along its sides are statues of the Princes and Governors, Admirals and Generals, that made him Grande Monarque of France.

At the entrance, just inside the gates, General Bricker, commander of the Sixth Cavalry Division, was sitting on a splendid chestnut, hardly less immobile than the Great King, save when he flashed his sword up to salute a guest of especial distinction. And, as if to typify the whole scene, there were the inscriptions on the facade of the twin temple-like structures on either side of Louis XIV's statue: "To All the Glories of France." It was the supreme dedication of the palace to the greatest day that all its glorious history has known.

TORRENT OF CHEERS FOR FOCH

One of the earliest to arrive was Marshal Foch, amid a torrent of cheering, which broke out even louder a few moments later when the massive head of Premier Clemenceau—for once with a smile on the Tiger's face—was seen through the windows of a French military car. To both, as to other chiefs, including Wilson, Pershing, and Lloyd George, the troops paid the honor of presenting arms all around the courtyard.

After Clemenceau they came thick and fast, diplomats, soldiers, Princes of India in gorgeous turbans, Japanese in immaculate Western dress, Admirals, flying men, Arabs, and a thousand and one picturesque uniforms of the French, British, and Colonial Armies.

Once amidst terrific enthusiasm a whole wagonload of doughboys, themselves yelling "their heads off," drove up the sacred slope of victory, but instead of proceeding right to the entrance swung around the Louis statue in the middle of the courtyard and went out by a side gateway, where the rest of the automobiles also went after depositing their passengers. Ten minutes later a camion laden with British Tommies arrived and got a cordial reception.

Whoever was responsible for it had a good thought, that the rank and file who had suffered and sweated most should share in the glorious finale, and it was everyone's regret that a load or two of poilus had not equally participated.

It was 2:45 o'clock when Balfour, bowing and smiling, heralded the arrival of the British delegates. Lloyd George was just behind him, for once in the conventional high hat instead of his usual felt.

WARM WELCOME FOR WILSON.

At ten minutes of 3 came President Wilson in a big black limousine, with his flag, a white eagle on a dark blue ground.

Jubilant Parisians take to the streets on the day the Treaty of Versailles was signed, June 28, 1919.

The warmth of welcome accorded him bore witness to the place he still holds in French hearts and the people's appreciation of the stand he took in the past few weeks against altering the treaty in Germany's favor.

By 3 o'clock the last visitor had arrived, and the broad ribbon road stretched empty between the lines of troops from the gates of the palace courtyard. The Germans had already taken their places—to avoid a possible unpleasant incident they had been conveyed from the Hotel des Reservoirs Annex through the park.

It is impossible to tell what the day meant to the people of Versailles. To them, even more than to the rest of France, it was the wiping out of the ancient stain whose shame they had felt more deeply than any other. At the entrance of the crowded dining hall of the Hotel des Reservoirs the old aunt of the proprietor stood with swimming eyes.

"I saw them dine here," she said, "on the night before the other treaty. And now this—thank God I have lived for it!" At the ride entrance to the courtyard there was a pathetic incident. An old woman, supported by two sons, one in the uniform of a Major of Chasseurs, the other in civilian clothes, but with an armless sleeve and the Legion of Honor and War Cross ribbons in his buttonhole, came up to the stern guardians and begged admittance, although without a ticket.

Just let me inside the courtyard," she pleaded. "When the Germans were here a General was quartered in my house. I shared the defeat; let me share the victory."

The orders were strict and absolute, but for her they made an exception. ◇

JUNE 29, 1919

Wilson Says Treaty Will Furnish the Charter for a New Order of Affairs in the World

WASHINGTON, June 28—The following address by President Wilson to the American people on the occasion of the signing of the Peace Treaty was given out here today by Secretary Tumulty:

My Fellow Countrymen: The treaty of peace has been signed. If it is ratified and acted upon in full and sincere execution of its terms it will furnish the charter for a new order of affairs in the world. It is a severe treaty in the duties and penalties it imposes upon Germany; but it is severe only because great wrongs done by Germany are to be righted and repaired; it imposes nothing that Germany cannot do; and she can regain her rightful standing in the world by the prompt and honorable fulfillment of its terms.

And it is much more than a treaty of peace with Germany. It liberates great peoples who have never before been able to find the way to liberty. It ends, once and for all, an old and intolerable order under which small groups of selfish men could use the peoples of great empires to·serve their ambition for power and dominion. It associates the free governments of the world in a permanent League in which they are pledged to use their united power to maintain peace by maintaining right and justice.

It makes international law a reality supported by imperative sanctions. It does away with the right of conquest and rejects the policy of annexation and substitutes a new order under which backward nations—populations which have not yet come to political consciousness and peoples who are ready for independence but not yet quite prepared to dispense with protection and guidance—shall no more be subjected to the domination and exploitation of a stronger nation, but shall be put under the friendly direction and afforded the helpful assistance of governments which undertake to be responsible to the opinion of mankind in the execution of their task by accepting the direction of the League of Nations.

It recognizes the inalienable rights of nationality, the rights of minorities and the sanctity of religious belief and practice. It lays the basis for conventions which shall free the commercial intercourse of the world from unjust and vexatious restrictions and for every sort of international co-operation that will serve to cleanse the life of the world and facilitate its common action in beneficent service of every kind. It furnishes guarantees such as were never given or even contemplated for the fair treatment of all who labor at the daily tasks of the world.

It is for this reason that I have spoken of it as a great charter for a new order of affairs. There is ground here for deep satisfaction universal reassurance, and confident hope.

WOODROW WILSON. ◇

'BLACK SHIRTS' HOLD A ROMAN TRIUMPH IN ASSUMING POWER
100,000 Fascisti March Through the City As Mussolini Becomes Premier.

IRON RULE IS PROMISED

ROME, Oct. 31—The new Cabinet of Premier Mussolini took the oath of office today before the King, thereby becoming the official Government of Italy, and the Fascisti army, the Black Shirts, commanded by Mussolini, which has surrounded Rome, paraded through the city, 100,000 strong.

A fact which is everywhere favorably commented upon is that Mussolini and his Ministers all wore frock coats and silk hats at the ceremony of taking the oath. It was recalled in this connection that when the Socialists, Turati and Bissolati, visited the King recently they wore soft hats and rough sporting jackets. Mussolini's action is considered all the more interesting when it is remembered that up to a few years ago he also was a Socialist and a rabid revolutionary. He, however, decided that as he had accepted the monarchy the King should be treated with all the pomp appertaining to the office.

The scene when the ex-Socialist and ex-idol of the revolutionary masses took the oath of allegiance to the King was dramatic. The King greeted each Minister, saying: "I feel that I can hardly congratulate you, as you have a stiff, arduous task before you, but I congratulate the country for having you as Ministers."

SONOROUSLY ACCEPTS OATH
The King read the formula of the oath as follows:

"I swear to be faithful to my King and his legal descendants. I swear to be true to the Constitution and fundamental laws of the State for the inseparable welfare of my King and my country."

Mussolini, who was standing with the Ministers in a group around him, immediately stepped forward and, ❯

raising his outstretched arms, said with a booming voice:

"Your Majesty, I swear it."

The King was so deeply moved that he embraced Mussolini. Afterward each Minister went through the formality.

When all had taken the oath the King remained for a few moments in conversation with Mussolini, who afterward drove back to his office at the Ministry of the Interior. The Fascisti militia had a hard task restraining an enthusiastic crowd which wished to carry him in triumph through the streets.

'DOUBLE HAT' SYSTEM ENDED

Mussolini was early at his office this morning. Exactly at 8 o'clock, the hour at which all Government clerks are supposed to be at their posts, he telephoned to all his Ministers instructing them to have a roll call. Anyone who was not at his desk was severely reprimanded and warned that he would be dismissed at the next offense.

This is the first foretaste of a regime of strict discipline which Mussolini intends to institute throughout Italy. Up to the present time most of the Government offices have been worked on the "double hat" system, whereby each clerk possesses two hats, one of which remains permanently hung on a nail in his office, the other being worn going to and from the office. Whenever anyone went into a Government office

in search of a clerk, even two or three hours after the regular opening time, an usher would point out the hat hanging on a nail and say: "He is obviously in the office somewhere because his hat is here. You would better wait." The authorities have winked at this practice, but Mussolini does not propose to tolerate it. He said to The New York Times correspondent today:

"Italy must wake up to the fact that only hard work can save us from financial and economic ruin. I propose that the Government should begin in showing a good example, and Government clerks will be treated just like any clerk working for a private concern would be treated. If they work and do their duty they will be well treated, but if they are not ready to do what is expected of them they will be dismissed. This new regime will be hard for many of them, but they must realize that times have changed."

Mussolini also outlined the main points of his policy. As to internal affairs, it may be summed up in three words:

"Discipline, economy, sacrifice," Mussolini said.

"I have not reached my present position by holding forth visions of an easy paradise, as the Socialists did. All will be ruled with an iron hand. It must be a wonderful testimonial to the patriotism and common sense of Italians that the Fascisti with such a program have the backing of an overwhelming major-

ity of the country. Of course, they will be better off in the end, but our policy will not bear fruit for some time, and in the meanwhile there is going to be suffering."

LEGIONS ENTER IN TRIUMPH

Rome, Oct. 31—Associated Press—One hundred thousand well-disciplined Fascisti marched through Rome from north to south today to the plaudits of a million Italian citizens gathered in the capital from all parts of the kingdom.

Their commander, Mussolini, was the central figure of the procession. Like the others who walked behind, the leader wore the black shirt of the organization. He was bare-headed and in a buttonhole was the Fascisti badge, while on his sleeve were several stripes showing that he had been wounded in the war. Mussolini was surrounded by his general staff, including Signor Bianchi, de Vecchi, a number of generals and several Fascisti Deputies. He walked with a firm step the entire four miles to the disbanding point.

The day broke clear and fine, with one of Italy's brightest suns lighting the way to Borghese Park as the Fascisti troops, abroad early, proceeded up the Pincian Hill, from Tivoli, Santa Marinella and other places on the outskirts of the city, where they had been camping the last three days.

BIG PARADE FORMS IN PARK

"It is a Fascismo sun," said a sturdy young black-shirted peasant from the plains of Piedmont as he led the Piedmont contingent into Borghese Park, where 15,000 Fascisti, representing all the province of the kingdom, from Northern Venetia and Lombardy to Southern Calabria and Sicily, assembled.

With military precision they formed and automatically fell into the places assigned to them—dark-visaged youths, with set, determined faces, upon which shone the light of victory, all wearing the black shirt. The rest of their equipment varied from skull caps to soft felt hats and steel helmets—some of them were

Italian dictator Benito Mussolini (center, with a sash), leading his first cabinet through Rome's main thoroughfare, Via del Popolo, during the March of Rome, signifying the onset of fascism, November 1922.

without hats—and nondescript trousers, multi-colored socks and shoes that ranged from topboots to dancing pumps. They were armed only with riding crops and bludgeons, one man from Ancona swinging a baseball bat.

Briskly they swung into line to the tunes of innumerable bands, the Roman contingent leading the way along the Pincian Hill Road to the Piazza del Popolo and to the Porta del Popolo, through the Gate of the People into the People's Square, then marching down the Corso Umberto, Rome's main street, lined with flags.

Every window was filled with Romans cheering, some showering flowers upon the passing blackshirts, while those in the streets saluted straight-armed from the shoulder, with hands extended toward the west.

Through the heart of the city the process continued, the youths never looking to the right or left, and acknowledging the acclamations and cheers only by singing Fascisti marching songs. Thus they reached the monument of Victor Emmanuel and the tomb of the unknown soldier.

At the tomb each contingent, with banners flying, halted before the imposing monument; then two men from each contingent, one bearing a huge palm, the other a bouquet of flowers, ascended the steps leading to the tomb and deposited them upon it until it was lost to sight beneath the mass of bloom. The first wreath placed on the tomb was earned by a veteran Garibaldian, nearly a hundred years old, who was assisted up the steps by two youths whose combined ages totalled less than half his own.

PARADED BEFORE THE KING
On departing from the tomb the Fascisti proceeded at double-quick up the steep Cesare Battlisti Hill to the Quirinal, where the king appeared on the balcony. He stood at salute, and as each continent arrived the flag was dipped, as before the tomb of the unknown soldier. The King received a great ovation from the assembled multitude.

The Fascisti reformed and marched directly to the station, where fifty trained men capable of transporting from 500 to 1,000 soldiers each, had been held in readiness since morning in accordance with the demobilization order that "every soldier must be on his way home before nightfall."

A feature of the day was the absence of speeches, the Fascisti leaders having decided, as one of them put it, that they are men of action, not words. ◈

HOLD-UP MEN ESCHEW GERMAN PAPER MARKS
They Return Paper to Victims After Taking Foreign Currency—Suitcase for Car Fare.

BERLIN, Nov. 10 (Associated Press)— Holdup men in Berlin now disdain to take paper marks from their victims.

Max Weisse, who was recently held up in the Tiergarten district, was robbed of the money he carried in dollars and pounds sterling, but the holdup man gave the victim back his marks with a "Thank you; we don't bother ourselves with those any more."

A German who entered a street car carrying a large suitcase was asked for two fares by the conductor on the ground that he must pay for the case.

"But I can't carry enough paper money for one fare without it," the passenger protested as he produced several bundles of paper marks in small denominations from the case.

The conductor did not insist upon the extra fare. ◈

HITLER SEIZED NEAR MUNICH
Found in Home of E. F. Hanfstaengl, Ex–New York Art Dealer

*MUNICH, Nov. 12.—*Adolf Hitler, leader of the recent revolt, was arrested last night at Essina, forty miles from Munich. His only injury is a grazed shoulder, said to have been suffered by throwing himself on the ground too energetically in his desire to take cover when the Nationalist forces were fired on by Reichswehr troops in Odeonsplatz on Friday.

The news was common property in Munich this morning, but Dr. von Kahr's newspaper, the Münchner Zeitung, has issued a denial, stating that the Government has no official knowledge of the arrest.

General Ludendorff has issued a statement today to the effect that the oath he gave when he was released on parole only binds him to refrain from any political activity against the existing Government of Bavaria. While this particular incident is under consideration. Beyond this he still considers himself free to work for and to support the program outlined by the Nationalist fighting organization at Nuremberg on Sept. 1, when Hitler was present.

There have been practically no further demonstrations in the town, and curfew hour has been extended until 10 o'clock. Tomorrow the theatres are to reopen. ◈

BERLIN SHOPS CLOSE AS NEW RIOTS START
Two Million Trillion Paper Marks Turned Out By the Presses for Week Ended Oct. 31.

By CYRIL BROWN
By Wireless to The New York Times.

*BERLIN, Nov. 19—*Food rioting and plundering have been resumed in Greater Berlin and the stores so far unplundered remain closed. If you succeed in slipping in by the back door it is only to find the shopkeepers unwilling to sell anything, particularly the butchers, who meet the world-be customer with the stereotyped answer. "We have no meat." This shortage is largely due to the expectation that the price of meat as well as other food prices will be many hundred per cent higher in a day or two.

A prospective meat price for to- ◗

morrow of 7,000,000,000,000 marks per pound was quoted today, which at the best bootlegger rates for a dollar is nearly per pound. Bread was unbuyable either yesterday or today. It is learned that the military dictator, General von Seeckt, is considering some sort of food rationing system, the details of which are being worked out. These provide that the fashionable restaurants, semi-empty hotels, dance halls and other places known as "luxury enterprises" shall, when the necessity becomes acute, be converted into mass feeding stations and "warming rooms." ◇

AUGUST 5, 1932

JAPAN THREATENS DRIVE INTO CHINA

CHINESE READY TO FIGHT

By HALLETT ABEND
Wireless to The New York Times.

SHANGHAI, Friday, Aug. 5—The situation in Manchuria and North China grew more grave today as the Japanese concentrated more troops at Chinchow, whence they are in a position to strike either at Jehol Province or North China, and the renewed widespread attacks on South Manchurian cities by irregulars continued unabated.

The tension also increased greatly at Shanghai, where the Japanese naval patrol was more than doubled, the commander condemning the "terrorizing tactics" of boycott organizations.

Furthermore, expressions by both, Japanese and Chinese leaders showed determination to settle the Manchurian issue by the strongest measures. General Shigeru Honjo, the commander of the united Japanese armies in Manchuria, said that he had decided to resort to "last measures" because Gonshiro Ishimoto, the kidnapped Japanese head of an official mission in Jehol, was ill and there was little prospect of his rescue.

At the same time, the Nanking Government approved the agreements reached at the Peiping Politico-Military Conference, which were understood to call for a strong policy, and Governor Han Fu-chu of Shantung issued a statement from Tsinan expressing willingness to lead his own troops in an attempt to recover Manchuria—regardless of the prospects of success.

GEN WU URGES RESISTANCE
General Wu Pei-fu, the former North China war lord, also announced in Peiping that he favored a campaign against Manchukuo.

Military observers believe the increased activity of the Chinese irregulars between the South Manchuria Railway zone and the Gulf of Liaotung constitutes part of a carefully prearranged plan for a campaign to harass the Japanese and increase the prospects for success of a drive from Jehol against Mukden and Changchun, the capital of Manchu-kuo.

In Peiping the nervousness has mounted to new heights and the directors of the museum located in the Forbidden City rented a warehouse today in the legations quarters in order to be able to safeguard the palace treasures from possible looting. They appropriated $100,000 to pay for a rush order for packing cases in which to store the jewels and art treasures valued at tens of millions of dollars and appropriated an additional $30,000 to take out war risk insurance on the irreplaceable objects of art.

DEFENSE PLAN ABANDONED
These steps were taken after the directors discarded a tentative plan for surrounding the museum with machine guns, electrically charged barbed wire and a trench system.

The Japanese commander of the patrol forces in Shanghai, in announcing his decision to increase the number of the patrol units from eight to twenty-two, assured the Japanese residents of the city of the Japanese Government's readiness to afford them adequate protection.

"The Japanese residents are hereby notified," he said, "that if their business is interfered with or they are terrorized by anti-Japanese groups, to report to the landing party immediately. Protection of the interests of the Japanese here is my paramount duty. Our reviving trade has been damaged and the situation is becoming worse through illegal interference with the transportation of Japanese goods and the terrorizing tactics of the so-called Bloody Group for the Extermination of Traitors.

"Really, no words are too strong against the activities of the Chinese people," he added. ◇

AUGUST 8, 1932

SCHLEICHER WARNS GERMANY CAN'T WAIT FOR ARMS EQUALITY

Says Reich Will Support Every Measure Of Disarmament, but Must Have Security.

By FREDERICK T. BIRCHALL
Special Cable to The New York Times

BERLIN, Aug. 7—The busiest of the Ministerial buildings that house the German Government these days is a solid structure of gray granite away from all the rest of the pleasant tree-lined streets where the Landwehr Canal cuts through the city's heart.

It was formerly the War Department, but war is a word that has fallen into disfavor in present-day Germany. Besides, all the nations have signed the Kellogg Pact. So the building is now the Reichswehr-ministerium, the home of the German Ministry of Defense.

It used to swarm with heel-clicking, brilliantly uniformed officers smartly tailored to the last button, and on the whole it was not the most comfortable place for a civilian to visit. Nowadays, however, there is as much mufti as uniform among the occupants.

A white marble bust of the von Moltke who carried the German armies to Paris in 1870 and brought them back triumphant still stands in the entrance hall, and once daily a slim platoon of the Reichswehr, which furnishes the sentries on duty here, at the Presidential Palace and at a few other government buildings, marches in through the heavy arched gateway and passes out again.

ATMOSPHERE DIFFERENT NOW
But the atmosphere is generally quite different from the old days and just now the building's principal distinction is that it covers the activities, military and political, of Generalleutnant Kurt von Schleicher, Minister of Defense in the von Papen Cabinet and the most talked of man in Germany.

Half of Berlin speaks of General von Schleicher with bated breath. He is the "iron man" dear to the German heart, the "man behind the Cabinet"—

he is actually in it—the "real ruler of Germany," and so on.

General von Schleicher himself speaks little, but when he does he usually has something to say, as France discovered quite recently when for the first time in his life he talked over the radio.

So his fame has grown. When the Communists become quiescent it is because they fear von Schleicher; when the Nazis milden their truculence it is because the General has given a quiet tip to Adolf Hitler that things have gone far enough.

Nobody ever credits the rather kindly von Papen with any of these things. It is von Schleicher who has temporarily taken the place in German legend that the former Kaiser and President von Hindenburg have held in turn.

I sought out General von Schleicher in his office to ask him to elaborate somewhat on the views that he recently expressed regarding Germany's present handicap among the nations and her determination immediately to set about making her future worth while.

AN ORDINARY OFFICE

It was an ordinary office such as might have been occupied by any German business man. The only uniforms visible were those of the unteroffizier orderly at the building's portal who took in my name and the General's Adjutant, who listened to the interview.

The man who rose at his desk in greeting was clad in a gray business suit, and I should say that shrewdness rather than sternness was the prevailing characteristic of his rather genial face. They say that no man knows better and estimates more correctly the political currents in Germany. Probably he could bang the desk to good effect, but certainly he did not look half as truculent as our own General Dawes.

General von Schleicher, it had previously developed, had become gunshy regarding interviewers after several rather disastrous experiences. He had therefore requested that the questions put to him be previously submitted in writing. He does not speak English, although a rather understanding twinkle in his eye seemed to indicate that he comprehended at least the drift of what was said in that language. His answers are here translated from the German.

"How does the Minister of Defense view the internal state of Germany?" was the first question.

"I can answer the question only so far as it concerns my official capacity as Reichswehr Minister" was the General's cautious reply. "I object to the Reichswehr being thrown into the struggle of internal politics. That I reject any sort of military dictatorship I made clear in my recent radio talk."

OBEDIENCE TO PRESIDENT FIRST

"The commander in chief of the Reichswehr is the Reichspresident. The Reichswehr is a non-political instrument of force which on given occasions the President has used to enforce his orders. The Reichs president is elected by the people. He alone in the scheme of German Government can claim the authority of a clear popular majority. The Reichs-wehr's service to the people can therefore be no better performed than by obeying the President' s orders.

"For a few days in July it was necessary to confer executive power on the commandant of the Berlin military district. By this means the President's will was enforced without the Reichswehr having to intervene with its arms. I am convinced it will be so also in the future.

"The Reichstag elections show no difficulties in the government of Germany nowadays. The greatest success was attained by the radical parties, not only by the National Socialists but also on the other wing by the Communists. The outside world has ground for wondering at that. More than 60,000,000,000 marks (about $14,280,000,000) of our national wealth has been taken from us. Can anyone then really expect the German people to be content with existing conditions?

"On the contrary, there is reason for wondering that the German people bear their terrible distress so calmly and with such discipline.

SEES AUTHORITY UNDERMINED

"Neither must there be astonishment abroad at the rise everywhere in Germany of party organizations that violently battle against each other. This has been made possible not only by the fact that the authority of our sovereign State was undermined by the Treaty of Versailles. A country treated for thirteen years as a pariah by the outside world, a country to whom equality is denied to this very day, simply had to forfeit the respect of its own people.

"Only when the German Government can demonstrate to its people that it possesses equal rights with any other country in the world—only then shall we again have fully stable conditions in Germany, only then shall we be able to subject the parties and their organizations unquestionably to the State "There is therefore no question of German policy more important both with respect to domestic affairs and foreign relations than that of equality of rights. The German Government is determined to solve this question in the very near future.

"This leads to the second question you have asked me to answer—concerning my attitude on foreign policy." (General von Schleicher had been asked to voice his views on the foreign situation, especially on the course of the disarmament conference and its results thus far.) "To me, as the Minister of Defense, the question of disarmament is in the very centre of foreign policy.

EMPHASIZES RIGHTS

"Consider our position. By the treaties of 1919 we have the right to have the other signatories disarm according to the same methods that govern our own disarming. As a member of the League of Nations we have, moreover, the right to a degree of security equal to that of any other country.

"Thirteen years have passed since 1919 and our right is still unrealized. The disarmament conference sat for six months and adopted a resolution that neither achieves disarmament nor acknowledges equality of rights. What has become of all the nine principles formulated by all the governments at the beginning of the conference? They have found their graves in the debates in the technical committees.

"About President Hoover's proposals, calculated to carry disarmament a long way forward, there was amiable talk, but none of their more important provisions was included in the final resolutions. Germany's own self-explanatory demand for equal rights received no consideration, even though any disarmament convention can be worth something only when signed voluntarily by partners having equal rights. Germany therefore rejected the resolution.

"The German people have waited thirteen years for their due. They can wait no longer. Germany will not again send its representatives to Geneva unless the question of equal rights has been previously solved in conformity with the German position.

"On this question there are among us no party differences. No German Government could sign a disarmament convention that in all things does not accord Germany the same rights as any other country.

"If submarines, bombing planes, heavy artillery and tanks are now designated as a means of defense, by what justification can one deny Germany this protection?

"That Germany alone among the great powers is unable to provide for ❯

‹ her national security constitutes an immoral condition that we can no longer tolerate. Either the disarmament provision of the Treaty of Versailles must be applied to all the powers or the right to rebuild her system of defense and make it equal to the needs of national security must be conceded to Germany.

"We want no armament competition. For financial reasons alone we are unusual in that respect. But just because of our distressed financial position we ought not to be spending money on the costliest and at the same time the least productive system of defense, forced on us by the Treaty of Versailles, but should spend every penny to the best advantage.

"We are dreaming neither of establishing a peace-time army of 600,000 men—such as France now maintains—or of competing with the great naval powers. We do not wish to threaten the security of our neighbors. We support every measure of disarmament. But we do demand for ourselves also security, equal rights and freedom." ◊

AUGUST 16, 1932

HITLER DICTATOR-SHIP IN REICH HELD UNLIKELY
Woodbridge Thinks Nazi Leader Cannot Seize Power—Sees Steadying Force in People.

Professor Frederick J. E. Woodbridge, Theodore Roosevelt Professor of American History at the University of Berlin for the last year, returned on the Holland-American liner Volendam yesterday and said the probability of Adolf Hitler and the National Socialists gaining power in Germany was not strong. He said he did not think it possible for Hitler to seize power and that the Nazis would have to wait for a majority in the Reichstag.

"All coalitions are very doubtful," Professor Woodbridge said. "The present government, which does not depend on a coalition, is in a strong position and can keep up indefinitely because vast numbers of people do not want a disturbance.

"The present government is giving a sense of authority, control and progress. Hitler has undoubtedly proved a success as a leader of his movement. About his executive ability nobody as yet knows anything.

"I left Germany with the conviction that the German people, in spite of intense party differences and sentiments, would come through their present political difficulties with a genuinely constructive program and without civil war. When one looks at the political situation from the point of view of the strife of parties and partisan propaganda, one seems to see only chaos, disorder and peril; but as one observes what actually goes on from day to day and as one talks with people of different parties, one gets a profound sense of steadying forces that are firmly holding excesses in restraint." ◊

JANUARY 31, 1933

HITLER PUTS ASIDE AIM TO BE DICTATOR
Imprisoned For Munich Revolt In 1923

Adolf Hitler's acceptance of the German Chancellorship in a coalition with conservatives and nonpartisans marks a radical departure from his former demand that he be made "the Mussolini of Germany" as a condition to his assumption of government responsibility. It represents at the same time a recession from their former position by President Hindenburg and the Conservatives, who hitherto had been set against entrusting the Chancellorship to Hitler although willing to permit him to participate in the government. The net result is not altered thereby.

For the first time in his spectacular and tempestuous career Hitler is now called upon to prove in deed what he has been promising in word to the many millions of his supporters. He takes of-fice at a time when his own party is passing through a severe internal crisis, expressed in a bitter factional struggle between extremists who have insisted on extra-constitutional action and the more moderate elements who have maintained that the party could not continue in the Opposition forever and could survive only through constructive participation in the government.

This factional struggle, in which the Nazi leader had tried to placate both sides, assumed acute form last December with the resignation of the leaders of the more moderate faction, Gregor Strasser and Gottfried Feder. Strasser was Hitler's chief executive. Feder was the party ideologist credited as being the real founder of the party.

Both resigned in protest against their chief's refusal to participate in the government unless the powers of a dictator were given to him. This position, critics in the Nationalist Socialist party argued, was responsible for the loss of about 2,000,000 votes in the Reichstag elections last November.

PARTY DECLINED SINCE AUGUST

Ever since Hitler first refused the Chancellorship in a Coalition Cabinet in August, 1932, there has been a constant dribbling away from his party.

Adolf Hitler (right) rides with German President Paul von Hindenburg after Hitler's appointment as chancellor of Germany in January 1933.

FRENCH BLAME NAZIS FOR REICHSTAG FIRE
Papers Regard It as A Crude Excuse to Crush Opposition Before the Election.

Wireless to The New York Times.

PARIS, March 1.—With growing anxiety the French are watching events across the Rhine and Chancellor Hitler's repressive measures, in which they see a determined intention to achieve a Fascist dictatorship.

France, judging by today's press, even seems distinctly inclined to blame the Nazis themselves for the fire that wrecked the Reichstag Building, and sees in it simply a crude excuse on Herr Hitler's part to crush the Opposition just before the elections.

Leon Blum, the Socialist leader, is particularly outspoken. He calls the fire "a gross, cynical camouflage that could not fool the public in any other country but Germany,"

The semi-official Temps likewise throws considerable doubt on the authenticity of the charges against the Communists concerning the fire. It points out certain weaknesses in the story, as well as the Nazi's interest in making the most of it. The paper particularly expresses worry over the similarities that it sees between Herr Hitler's actions now and those of Premier Mussolini of Italy in 1922, and states that the German Chancellor has the same policies, ideas and methods.

"All that can be clearly said is that the German crisis, which has been developing for months, is now degenerating into civil war and pushing a great nation more and more toward anarchy and political chaos," the Temps concludes. "No one in history has yet been able to succeed in achieving a durable State and order by means of disorder." ◇

WEIZMANN ASSAILS REICH ANTI-SEMITES
Jewish Leader Tells London Friends of Palestine Of 'Barbarism' In Germany.

Wireless to The New York Times.

LONDON, March 2.—The plight of Jews in Germany was emphasized tonight by Dr. Chaim Weizmann, presiding at a dinner to the "friends of Palestine in the British Parliament" given by the British section of the Jewish Agency.

No unbiased observer with any respect for justice and fair play, Dr. Weizmann declared, could remain indifferent to the situation in Germany, where the "eco- ➤

The elections in Thuringia, which followed the losses suffered by the party in the last Reichstag elections, served to emphasize this point.

A powerful group of industrialists in the Federation of German Industries recently gave indications of a sharp change of attitude toward the National Socialists because of their radical trend. This group in the Federation of German Industries has been inclined in recent months to withdraw its support from the party and return to a policy of understanding with the German trade unions.

At the same time, however, a group of Nazi industrialists in the Rhineland and the Ruhr, who have been among Hitler's chief financial backers, have urged him to drop his uncompromising attitude and join the government. According to recent dispatches from Berlin, former Chancellor von Papen was the "friendly broker" between the National Socialists and this group of industrialists.

Recent Berlin dispatches indicate also a deal between Papen and Hitler for the overthrow of General von Schleicher, who roused the displeasure of the Rhineland-Ruhr industrialists by his inclination to deal leniently with labor and to seek the support of the trade unions. In this policy, these industrialists foresaw the abandonment of the economic program laid down by Papen

as Schleicher's predecessor in the Chancellorship.

LONG WITHOUT CITIZENSHIP
Outstanding is the dramatic element of Hitler's accession to power at the age of 43. The new Chancellor began as the son of poor parents in Austria. For a long time he was not even a German citizen, but a man without a country. His political career began in a very unpromising manner in 1921.

The Nazi leader went to Germany in 1914 at the outbreak of the war and enlisted in the German Army. By this act he sacrificed his Austrian citizenship. He had a good war record, being gassed, wounded and winning a silver war service medal.

The advent of the German Revolution with the military collapse of Germany in 1918 found him a bitter opponent of the revolutionary upheaval. He hated the republic from the day it was born and vowed that he would never rest until he had brought about a counterrevolution against the men and the parties whom he considered responsible for the downfall of the empire.

With General Erich von Ludendorff, who was one of his early supporters but with whom he parted company in later years, he attempted a revolution in Munich, which was easily

suppressed by the Bavarian Government on Nov. 8, 1923.

The uprising was to have been the signal for a general monarchist revolution. The collapse of the movement led to the sentencing of Hitler to five years in prison. He was liberated after serving a year in a Bavarian fortress.

He resumed activities on a large scale in 1928. From that time his movement, stimulated by the economic depression, progressed fast. By 1930 the National Socialist party had won 107 seats in the Reichstag. In July, 1931, this number was increased to 230.

Hitler received his first official political recognition in 1932 when Chancellor Heinrich Bruening consulted him on a proposal to extend the term of President von Hindenburg by act of Parliament to avoid the disturbance of a Presidential contest. The Nazi flatly refused. He became a candidate against von Hindenburg but was defeated by more than 6,000,000 votes.

In that election Hitler reached the peak of his strength, polling more than 13,000,000 votes. The reversal of the tide came with the Reichstag elections a few months later, when the National Socialists suffered a loss of about 2,000,000 votes. ◇

nomic and political existence of all Jews is imperiled by the policy which had inscribed anti-Semitism in its most primitive form as an essential part of its program."

It has been only a few days, he added, since Captain Hermann Wilhelm Goering, Minister without portfolio, accused the Jews of "organizing the cultural disruption of Germany" and it was a severe shock to civilized people to discover that it was possible for a great people like the Germans to relapse into barbarism in its attitude toward a small, law-abiding minority of its citizens.

"To our people in Germany, whose position, by all accounts, is becoming daily more intolerable," declared Dr. Weizmann, "we can only counsel courage and endurance. I feel our sympathy is shared by all friends of progress, worldwide. In the hour of their trial it is well that our fellow-Jews in Germany should know they do not stand alone but that the full weight of enlightened opinion in all civilized countries, especially in England, is behind them in their struggle against the forces of reaction."

There were 500 guests at the dinner, including 100 members of Parliament. ◊

MARCH 6, 1933

HITLER'S VICTORY SHOCK TO FRENCH
They Hoped for Repudiation of Dictatorship by Germans In Yesterday's Elections.

Wireless to The New York Times.

PARIS, March 5—Frenchmen eagerly snatched the special editions of the Paris dailies from the hands of shouting news vendors late tonight, then in most cases threw down the papers with expressions of disgust. It was obvious they expected or at least hoped for a popular electoral reaction against the Hitler dictatorship in Germany.

A few hundred Communists began a march down the grand boulevards, singing the "Internationale." When they reached the offices of Le Matin police reinforcements were waiting for them and broke up the demonstration. The crowd reading newspaper bulletins was left unmolested. Reflecting the attitude of many Frenchmen, Leon Blum, the Socialist leader, declared in a speech tonight:

"The Fascist activities of the Hitlerites hold for France no immediate danger of war. These activities will logically be directed toward the rearmament of Germany, which will constitute for her a symbol of revival and liberation. The danger then will lie with the counter-measures of the neighboring States, which are capable of dragging all of us into an armament race, and we know where that will lead.

"We must forbid the rearmament of Germany and push to a successful conclusion the work of the Disarmament Conference. But I fear first war, then ensuing misery, will be required to reforge the unity of the workers." ◊

MARCH 28, 1933

JAPAN QUITS LEAGUE TO 'INSURE PEACE'
Emperor and Premier Promise Continued Cooperation in International Affairs.

By HUGH BYAS
Wireless to The New York Times.

TOKYO, March 27—Count Ya-suya Uchida, the Foreign Minister, notified the League of Nations today of Japan's decision to withdraw because of "irreconcilable" differences with the League over Manchuria.

But in announcing the decision to the nation the government, through the lips of Emperor Hirohito and the Premier, Admiral Viscount Ma-koto Saito, repudiated the "Back to Asia" policy and solemnly assured the people that Japan did not seek to isolate herself in the Far East and would continue to cultivate the friendship of Western powers and to cooperate with them.

The note addressed to the League tersely repeated the contention so often heard at Geneva that, as China was not an organized State, the instruments governing the relations between ordinary countries must be modified in application to her.

The report adopted by the Assembly on Feb. 24, it is declared, besides misapprehending Japan's aims, contained gross errors of fact and the false deduction that the Japanese seizure of Mukden in September, 1931, was not defensive. Failure to take into account the tension which preceded and the aggravations which followed the seizure was alleged.

While this was being cabled to Geneva an imperial rescript was promulgated informing the nation that Japan's attitude toward enterprises intended to promote international peace had not changed. The official translation continues:

By quitting the League and embarking on a course of its own, our empire does not mean that it will stand aloof in the Far East nor isolate itself from the fraternity of nations."

The same note is struck in Premier Saito's message to the nation. As it is Japan's traditional policy, he says, to contribute to the promotion of international peace, the government will continue to cooperate in international enterprises designed to further the welfare of mankind.

"Nor does this country propose to shut itself up in the Far East, but will endeavor to strengthen the ties of friendship with other powers," he adds.

This double repudiation of the "Back to Asia" doctrine probably is correctly interpreted as a result, of views expressed by the Privy Council. Many of the wisest statesmen regret the course which has left Japan alone. Believing, however, in the essential justice of her cause they could but acquiesce in secession.

Lieut. Gen. Sadao Arakl, the War Minister, issued a statement declaring the nation had been reborn in moral principles. The empire's positive policy had been definitely established, giving an opportunity for national expansion. ◊

MARCH 30, 1933

EINSTEIN TO ALTER STATUS
Scientist Takes Steps to Renounce His Prussian Citizenship.

BERLIN, March 29 (AP)—Professor Albert Einstein has taken steps to renounce his Prussian citizenship.

Professor Einstein, who is a Jew, became a citizen in 1914 when he accepted a position with the Prussian Academy of Sciences. Upon landing at Brussels after his recent trip to the United States, he wrote to the German Consulate there for information about the steps necessary to end his citizenship. He pointed out that he formerly was Swiss.

Professsor Einstein was born in Ulm, Germany, but subsequently his family moved to Switzerland and he became a Swiss citizen.

Before sailing recently for Europe the professor said:

"I do not intend to put my foot on German soil again as long as conditions in Germany are as they are." ◇

OCTOBER 2, 1935

BERLIN WORKS OUT ANTI-JEWISH RULES

Wireless to The New York Times.

BERLIN, Oct. 1—The regulations governing the enforcement of the so-called Nurcmberg laws adopted by the National Socialist Reichstag Sept. 15 are still being worked out at the Ministry of the Interior, and no date has been set for their promulgation.

Fundamentally these laws are in force, however, and an official communiqué today sought to correct the prevalent impression that all mixed marriages, that is, marriages between "Aryans" and Jews would be decreed void. The new statute, it was stated, outlaws only such unions as have been consummated since last Sept. 17.

Meanwhile Jewry is anxiously awaiting the final implications of the laws, which were announced only in skeleton form in Nuremberg, and it is especially with reference to their effect on Jewish economic life that definitive clarification is awaited.

The draft decree adopted by the Reichstag confined itself to the purely racial and political aspects of the situation and omitted all reference to the limits that would be allowed Jews for business and economic activities.

MODEST HOPE AROUSED

Subsequent warnings from authoritative quarters against individual anti-Jewish boycott activities have stimulated a modest measure of hope in Jewish circles of a possible moderation of the hitherto silently condoned policy of economic persecution, which is being waged with almost unrelenting fury against the Jews in rural sections although it has not yet invaded the big cities in virulent form.

Meanwhile the Jews throughout Germany are passing through a transitional period that cannot fail to fill them with the deepest apprehension, and until their economic fate has been decreed in finality they will be compelled to defer all consideration of plans calculated to meet any fresh emergency.

The Ministry of the Interior today reminded all Germans of the flag law adopted in Nuremberg, which makes the swastika banner the sole authorized flag of the Reich. Not only will it now be flown exclusively from official flagstaffs but citizens are admonished to discard their old black-white-red colors and the various flags of the now obsolete States and provinces.

If a nationalist diehard in a fit of nostalgia cannot resist showing the old imperial flag his lapse will be condoned, but the Ministry expresses the hope that the populace will make its choice of flags unanimous.

JEWS WARNED ON BANNERS

As the new flag law forbids Jews to exhibit the Nazi banner, the Ministry reminds them that they are not allowed by law to compromise by displaying the black-white-red emblem on official occasions but are restricted in their choice to the Zionist colors.

Discussing the national implications of the Nuremberg laws in the German Jurists' Gazette, Professor Carl Schmitt, well-known juridical authority, asserts that these statutes after a lapse of centuries again constitute a "German constitutional freedom."

"For the first time our conception of constitutional principles is again German and today the German people once more are a German nation with respect to their Constitution, and statutory law," says Professor Schmitt.

German blood and German honor, he adds, have become the basic principles of German law, while the State has become an expression of racial strength and unity. "Another momentous constitutional decision was proclaimed at Nuremberg when the Fuehrer announced that if the present solution of the Jewish problem fails to achieve its purpose re-examination of the situation will come up for consideration and the solution of the Jewish problem will then be left to the party's judgment," he continues. "That statement must be accepted as a grave warning, for it makes the party not alone the guarantee of our racial sanctuary but also the defender of our Constitution." ◇

OCTOBER 13, 1935

ROOSEVELT SITS TIGHT ON NEUTRALITY TERMS

By TURNER CATLEDGE.

WASHINGTON, Oct. 12—Events revolving around the Italo-Ethiopian unpleasantness, as they occurred during the last week on this side of the water, left a clear indication with official Washington of the possible difficulties ahead in our attempt to wear the tailor-made mantle of neutrality which a tired Congress cut out, altered slightly and pieced together in the closing hours of the last session.

One week ago tonight, Oct. 5, acting upon a direct mandate of Congress, President Roosevelt issued an embargo against American exportation of weapons and ammunition to both Italy and Ethiopia. He was following the very letter of Section 1 of Senate Joint Resolution 173. At the same time, in connection with the same proclamation, he put the American business public on notice that any trade with the belligerent nations would be at the risk of the traders. In this he went beyond the Congressional mandate, but was still within the clear intent of the authors of the resolution.

The next day, Sunday, Oct. 6, the President, by proclamation wirelessed from the cruiser Houston in the Pacific, issued a warning to all United States citizens against traveling on Italian or Ethiopian ships except at their own risk. Here he was using the discretionary authority granted by Section 6 of the resolution.

PROTEST OF TRADERS

The following day, Monday, the first business day after our new and fixed neutrality policy became effective, a protest was raised by the Conference on Port Development of the City of New York. In a cable sent directly to the President at Cocos Island the conference branded his action as "ill-advised" and a "serious blow" to the commerce of the port of New York.

On Tuesday the members of the Export Managers Club of New York rose over their coffee cups at a luncheon at the Pennsylvania Hotel to declare their intention of trading with belligerent Italy and possibly with besieged Ethiopia, regardless of the President's proclamation.

The next day Secretary of Commerce Roper, noted for his readiness to reassure business and industry in their dealings with the unpredictable administration in Washington, sought to assure American exporters that the government had no real objections to their trading with the warring countries. In effect, he told the exporters that the President had his fingers crossed when he issued the warnings as to trade and travel except as to trade in arms, for, as a practical matter, there could be no physical risks in trading with Italy, the only one of the two with any commercial attractiveness.

REJOINDER BY HULL

On Thursday Secretary of State Hull took occasion to re-emphasize the warnings to American traders against engaging in transactions of any character with either Italy or Ethiopia. He pointed to the greater purposes of the administration.

"I repeat that our objective is to keep this country out of war," he said.

His statement and the deliberation with which he issued it were interpreted as a practical rebuke to Secretary Roper, as well as a redeclaration to the American people that the administration intends to follow the spirit as well as the letter of the neutrality resolution—at least for the present.

While these developments show the troubles which responsible officials already have encountered in following a non-discretionary method in keeping this country out of international involvements, they were much more significant from the standpoint of what they indicated for the future.

For the present, then, it can be safely predicted that the President will follow the course laid down or indicated by the neutrality resolution, regardless of the protests of exporters or shipping interests.

The phrase "for the present" is used advisedly. The test of this fixed method of keeping us out of war has not come. So long as the present conflict is confined to Italy and Ethiopia it may never come.

To date neither Mr. Roosevelt nor anyone else has had any definite indication that the neutrality resolution was not a generally popular act. It represented the sincere desire of the American people to stay out of the next war and the methods it prescribed were popular, so far as they were understood.

CHANGE POSSIBLE

Officials in Washington wonder, however, if that popular mind might not be changed under stress as it was changed in 1916–17. They wonder what would happen, for instance, if other and more powerful nations should become involved and soon thereafter some of our commerce should be stopped on the high seas or some of our nationals should be killed.

These officials answer their own questions with the frank intimation that the United States is following a day-to-day policy under the neutrality resolution, but with every apprehension that this will not suffice in a real test. They pray that the test may not come before Congress reconvenes, when, with a more enlightened public sentiment to support its action, it might give the Executive a better device for keeping us out of war.

BACKED BY LAW

So long as he follows his present course and throws himself completely on the law, the President can make short answer to those who would enlist this country in international action.

Importunings are heard on every hand for America's assistance in stifling the present outbreak. Former Secretary of State Stimson joined in the chorus during the week. In a letter to the editor of The New York Times, published on Friday, Mr. Stimson pointed out that the President, by affirming that war existed between Italy and Ethiopia, had inferentially called attention to the fact that these nations had broken the Kellogg-Briand pact.

That agreement, Mr. Stimson insisted, was a promise by Italy and Ethiopia to the United States and other signatories that they would not resort to war for the solution of international controversies. The League, he said, had fixed the blame, and so it was within the province of the United States to act.

Mr. Stimson insisted that "all the elements for moral leadership in this crisis lie in the hands of the President." But the President has been bound, or for self-protection has bound himself, with a law—Senate Joint Resolution 173. ◆

President Franklin D. Roosevelt in the Oval Office, 1935.

OCTOBER 13, 1935

ITALIANS DEFIANT OF WORLD CENSURE

WHOLE NATION IS UNIFIED

By ANNE O'HARE McCORMICK
Wireless to The New York Times.

ROME, Oct. 12—For the capital of a country at war against Ethiopia and against the world, Rome is strangely apathetic. Premier Benito Mussolini's new Italy is very old, after all, and it never seemed older than in these high-tension hours.

Behind the Fascist front is an older nation, careworn and warworn and with a long perspective. This Italy watches current events with a blasé somberness. The Romans, especially, have the attitude of stoical spectators at a drama of fate. Eager New York crowds may gather in Times Square to read bulletins from the war zone, but no such crowds gather in Rome. An Englishman arriving several days ago was amazed to find the atmosphere here less tense than in London. Outsiders cannot imagine how completely Italy is shut in with her own thoughts. She is shut in with history, too. World opinion is filtered and colored before reaching the people. What does strike home is that they have seen so many things pass that all, from Mussolini to the oldest cabman, believe that the cloud of opprobrium will dissolve quickly, just as world sentiment softened toward Japan, Germany and other lawbreakers.

FOREIGN REACTION DISTORTED

How much does Italy care for the moral and material reprobation of other nations? Judging by outward signs, not much. How much do the people know? The masses, reading only the Italian press, have little idea of the extent of the condemnation over the invasion of Ethiopia. External reactions are employed here as an instrument of internal policy. Thus the most virulent anti-Fascist attacks from abroad are headlined or suppressed as national feeling needs to be stirred up or toned down, while what opinion there is supporting the Italian stand is, of course, always featured. Quotations published in the past few days—from J. L. Garvin of The Observer, London; Frank Simonds, In the Nation, New York, and selected excerpts from editorials and letters in the French, British, American and German press—might easily convince the reader that the great body of foreign sentiment recognizes the justice of the Italian case.

Educated Italians know what the world thinks. Virtually all read French and Swiss newspapers circulating in every city by the thousands. Mussolini knows; a member of his clipping bureau reports Il Duce insists these days on seeing only the unfavorable criticism, particularly from the English-language press. He cares enormously about foreign opinion. That his delegate submitted to the humiliation of sitting at Geneva to be condemned proves how much Mussolini desires to remain in the League, not only to fulfill the pledge made to France a month ago, but also to maintain his influence in Europe. Italy wants to be quartered but not quarantined in Africa.

LEAGUE VOTE DEPRESSING

The implication of events does not escape even the cabman. The League vote, though expected, had a depressing effect. So had President Roosevelt's action anticipating Geneva in declaring a state of war and imposing the first official penalties. The League phalanx, however unreliable it may be in action, casts a rather black shadow over this peninsula. The American move was officially played down here as a measure assuring neutrality, but the people instinctively recognize in the President's swift asperity a judgment on Italy and a reinforcement of the British determination to make sanctions work.

The Italians know more than to care about world indignation, but the weight of the censure presses, and to one on the move they are an abnormally sensitive people. The mobilization against them, instead of dividing the nation and wrecking the regime responsible, has solidified Fascists and non-Fascists into 100 per cent Italians. Former Premier Vittorio Orlando, Italian member of the "big four" at the peace conference, is one of the many politicians of democratic Italy issuing from retirement their offers of services in a time of national emergency to the man who destroyed them.

SENSE OF GUILT ABSENT

To understand this it must be remembered that few among the vocal masses feel any sense of guilt at the aggression in Ethiopia. Questioning hundreds of persons in recent weeks the writer met only three—a young intellectual, an old liberal and a woman artist—suffering moral scruples over the breaking of pledges and the war.

Many quite honestly sympathize with "those poor Ethiopians," bombed and invaded, but only because they had been left so long to fall ill and starve under brutal masters!

The Italians feel misgivings, fear and deep pessimism as to the future, but they are not conscience-stricken. In their own eyes it is they who suffer an injustice. Admitting freely they fight for "vital national interests" because they are convinced war is the only way out, they refuse to believe any other nation blocks their way for reasons more moral than opposing interests. In this Mediterranean of misunderstandings, British battleships frighten Italy, and Italian submarines exasperate the British by popping up to salute, it is said, in the most unexpected places. Neither side can see the other's point. It is difficult, because the outlooks inside and outside Italy are as different as views through a window pane and a mirror.

NO CHEERS FOR TROOPS

The night after the news of Adowa troops in action were shown marching across a movie screen the audience neither applauded nor cheered. As it watched in silence the mind of one spectator traveled back to a Berlin theatre after conscription was proclaimed last March. The German audience went into a delirium at the sight of goose-stepping Reichswehr units. But the Italian mood is unlike the German. Between the Italians' organized mass meetings, with their flares of joy or anger, the everyday pitch is one of grim resignation. It is a new note, more formidable than the old. Too many are veterans who think this country lost the lasts war and are resolved to "finish the job." Too many are peasants, like the Tuscan farmer with two sons at the front.

"I want the other two to go," he said. "Rotting at home is worse than war."

This Italy does not care whether she pleases the world or not. Like all rebels against the established order, she has little to lose and is fatalistically prepared to lose it. Sanctions are dangerous because they will not stop the smoldering resentment of the penalized. The sunny Italy of yesterday is of darker mien today. It would be a fatal mistake to interpret this explosion as merely Fascist, as the imperial lust of Mussolini. In reality, it is the newest phase of world revolution—a poor nation organized to bait the rich. It can be interrupted, but with or without Il Duce it will go on. ◆

JULY 15, 1936

BRITAIN WILL GIVE GAS MASKS TO ALL
Mass Production Of New Type Of Respirator Is Ordered to Be Ready For Emergency.

Wireless to The New York Times.

LONDON, July 14—The goal of a perfect gas mask for every man, woman and child in Britain came nearer realization today. An official announcement spread the tidings that after long experiments government scientists had evolved a respirator that would give all necessary protection during a gas attack. Production will begin immediately on a huge scale, less than two decades after the war that was to end war forever.

As the first step toward providing millions of masks free of charge, the Home Office today submitted a supplementary estimate of £887,000 in the House of Commons. Previous estimates for the army, navy and air force had reached the colossal total of £188,000,000 and there is every prospect that Britain's defense expenditure will reach £200,000,000 during the present budget year.

The government does not intend to issue the new masks to the public, it was explained today, "unless this becomes necessary," but every effort will be made to have them ready for any emergency. The masks will be stored in convenient centers throughout the country. Arrangements will be made for citizens to try them on. Authorities today expressed hope that the public would "take advantage of the opportunity."

Today's gas mask estimate included provision of £25,000 for purchasing and equipping two factories near Manchester, £7,000 for additional staff in the Air Raid Precautions Department of the Home Office, and £5.000 for a civilian anti-gas school at Falfield, Gloucestershire.

In addition, the Commons will be asked to appropriate £100,000 extra for the secret service, bringing the total for the year to £350,000, while the biggest item of all is an additional £2,930,000 needed for a cattle subsidy to British farmers.

JULY 19, 1936

LEFTIST CABINET QUITS

SEVILLE REVOLT CRUSHED
But All Spanish Morocco Is Held by Revolutionary Force Numbering 20,000.

By The Associated Press

MADRID, July 19—The Leftist Cabinet of Premier Santiago Casares Quiroga, harassed by a military revolt in Spanish Morocco and the Canary Islands and outbreaks in Spain itself, resigned early today. It took office last May 13.

By WILLIAM P. CARNEY
Wireless to The New York Times.

MADRID, July 18 (Passed by the Censor)—The Spanish Government announces that an extensive plot against the republic has broken out. It is now learned from the government that rebels seized the radio station in Ceuta, Spanish Morocco, and broadcast an announcement purporting to have been issued by the Seville radio station stating that all government buildings in Madrid had been seized.

The government also announces that the Morocco operations were connected with a similar plot in Spain.

The plot was quickly suppressed, according to the government by promptly arresting many army officers, including General Barrera, who entered the Guadalajara military prison this morning.

MOROCCAN TOWNS BOMBED
The government further states that the military aviation remained loyal to it and that bombing planes sent from Spain bombarded Ceuta and Melilla, also in Spanish Morocco.

[A rebel force of 20,000 held complete control over Spanish Morocco last night, refugees reaching Tangier said, according to an Associated Press dispatch.]

It was learned from official sources that General Queipo de Llano had illegally declared martial law in Seville and had attempted to start a rebellion, which was quickly smothered by loyal troops there.

[From French border points came reports of fighting in various Spanish cities, including Cadiz, Burgos and Barcelona, according to The Associated Press, and at Hendaye it was rumored that all the garrisons in Andalusia had risen.]

A telegram from the Civil Governor at Las Palmas, the Canary Islands, said that he and the commanding officer of the Civil Guards there were barricaded in the Governor's palace, which was surrounded and besieged by rebel troops. The Socialist workers' union at Las Palmas has declared a general strike to show its sympathy with the government.

SITUATION IN MADRID NORMAL
Madrid presented a perfectly normal aspect today. It was officially denied that the rebels' plan was gradually to close in on the capital and strike here last. The government said in an official statement broadcast repeatedly today from the Ministry of the Interior, "Public order has not been disturbed in Madrid or anywhere in the provinces."

Coincident with news of the anti-gas precautions there were more signs today of the deadly seriousness with which Britain is rearming. Alfred Duff Cooper, the Secretary for War. told the Commons that he had decided to appoint Vice Admiral Sir Harold Brown, the engineer-in-chief of the fleet, as Director General of Munitions Production, with a seat on the Army Council. The new official will be responsible to Mr. Cooper for coordinating and speeding the production of munitions.

The appointment is regarded as another step toward a Ministry of Munitions, which Winston Churchill and others with war-time experience have been demanding for a year or more. ◇

Cyclists of the London police unit wearing gas masks and protective suits during an exercise, 1936.

The government categorically repudiated rumors that troops had crossed the straits from Morocco and landed at Algeciras or that General Francisco Franco, military Governor of the Canary Islands, had joined the rebellion.

[Reports from North Africa said General Franco was heading the revolt in Morocco.]

Rumors of a military uprising in the Balearic Islands were also officially refuted.

It was officially announced that a "foreign airplane," intended to bring the revolt's leader to Madrid from Morocco had been seized.

A joint note issued by the Socialist and Communist labor organizations was broadcast by a union radio station in Madrid tonight. It said that the Marxist trade unions would declare general strikes wherever martial law has been declared by military governors without the government's authorization.

All the higher army officers in Madrid called on the War Minister last night to assure him of their loyalty and readiness to fight for the defense of the republic.

A statement broadcast by the government early this morning said:

"Enemies of the State are still indulging in spreading false news, but the loyalty of all the forces in Spain to the government is general. Only in Morocco are there still parts of our army that are showing a hostile attitude toward the republic.

"The Ceuta radio station is trying to create alarm by broadcasting the announcement that some ships have been seized by rebel troops and are heading for the peninsula. The news is completely false.

"At the present moment our fleet is making for Spanish Morocco ports and is encountering no opposition in its efforts to restore peace. Peace and order will be completely restored very shortly.

"The government wishes to make known once more that the rumor in connection with the proposed declaration of martial law in Spain is absolutely baseless. There is no power in Spain other than the civil one and all other institutions in Spain are subordinate to the civil power, which is the one power in command."

The Socialist party's official newspaper, El Socialista, with bold headlines today urged the workers to "close up the guard with the necessary rigor for the decisive occasion."

"The regime now faces the difficult test with which it has been threatened for some time," it added. "But the regime has at its disposal reinforcements as reliable as they are considerable. These reinforcements have been offered unconditionally to the government by Leftist parties and organizations.

"As they mount guard, the workers still have not forgotten the repression they suffered in Asturias [chief scene of the 1934 revolt]. The workers know well what they could expect if the regime's adversaries triumphed and succeeded in establishing a Fascist corporative State." ◇

MAY 2, 1937

NEUTRALITY QUEST IN A THIRD PHASE

By HAROLD B. HINTON

WASHINGTON, May 1—The latest step the country has taken in its quest for peace, via the so-called neutrality route, is plainly derived from the experiences of the United States in the World War. The new legislation, dramatically enacted to replace the law expiring at midnight tonight, is designed to avoid such pitfalls as the nation faced from 1914 to 1917.

To realize how the whole neutrality movement has grown from the experiences of President Wilson and his advisers, one has only to recall the principal difficulties the United States suffered in those days.

American merchantmen were detained by British and French warships, taken into port and searched for contraband. Under the new neutrality law, the American Government would guarantee that no American ships would carry contraband.

Other American merchant vessels were sunk by German submarines for the reason, as the Germans argued the case, that they might be armed and ›

◀ a submarine could not risk coming to the surface to visit and search them. Under the new law, American merchantmen will be forbidden to carry armament.

PASSENGERS AFFECTED

American citizens lost their lives on the Lusitania, the Sussex and other passenger vessels of the warring countries. If another war should come American citizens would be breaking the laws of their own country by traveling on such vessels.

American goods carried as cargoes to belligerents were captured by other belligerents, and American merchants demanded that their country protest what they considered illegal seizures. The "cash and carry" policy of the new law requires that no American hold any right, title or interest in any cargo destined for any belligerent.

In the World War, the belligerents, principally the Allies, borrowed large sums in this country to purchase munitions here, thereby working up, in the opinion of some neutrality champions, a vested interest on the part of some manufacturers and bankers in the success of the allied arms. The new law forbids any export of arms, ammunition or implements of war to any belligerent, as well as all loans.

To understand the criticism which such international lawyers as John Bassett Moore, Edwin M. Borchard and others direct at the whole program, it must be realized that, under international law, none of these steps is needed to preserve the official neutrality of the United States. They are intended solely to keep this country from involvement through a repetition of the inflammatory incidents of World War days.

A nation, to be neutral, has only to avoid helping either side in a conflict by its governmental agencies. It need not forbid its citizens to perform such acts as running blockade, trading in contraband, or other unneutral adventures. Obviously, those citizens would perform such acts at their own risk.

But the United States has gone beyond this conception. In the three neutrality acts Congress has thus far adopted, there has been a steady progression toward isolation in time of foreign war. ◆

MARCH 12, 1938

The Austrian Situation

Following an ultimatum from Berlin, the Schuschnigg government in Austria retired yesterday evening and was succeeded by one headed by the Nazi leader, Arthur Seyss-Inquart, as Chancellor. He immediately asked Germany to send troops to help in preserving order. Some 50,000 highly armed and mechanized forces marched to the border. Both Munich and Vienna report some crossed into Austria. Berlin denies this. Nazi mobs took possession of Vienna and raided the Jewish quarter. The swastika was flown over public buildings, and Fatherland Front forces were disarmed. There were similar demonstrations in other cities.

Europe was aghast at the coup of Hitler. His action struck Italy with the force of an exploding bomb. The impression was that Italy would not retort with force, but it was believed the Rome-Berlin axis had been shaken and that Hitler's visit to Rome might be canceled. No advance notice of Germany's intention is believed to have been given to Mussolini.

Britain delivered a sharp protest to Berlin, saying Germany's action was bound to produce "the gravest reactions, of which it is impossible to foretell the issue." Other warnings were delivered earlier, but Foreign Minister von Ribbentrop retorted that Germany saw no reason to confer with Britain until her purposes had been achieved elsewhere.

In Paris it was understood Italy had been asked if she would join in a united effort to save Austria, but had refused. France, however, took action similar to that of Britain in protesting the Reich's action. The parties tried to get together to form a new Cabinet to deal with the situation, but they were still too deeply divided to make that accomplishment possible. It was believed Léon Blum would not be able to gain sufficient support to head a government.

Premier Negrin of Spain announced that Italy and Germany had made unofficial proposals for some agreement with the Loyalists, but they were determined not to enter on negotiations. ◆

SEPTEMBER 26, 1938

The Hitler Memorandum

By The Associated Press.

LONDON, Sept. 25—The text of the "final" memorandum of Chancellor Adolf Hitler of Germany given to Prime Minister Neville Chamberlain of Britain Friday for presentation to Czechoslovakia, as disclosed by authoritative sources in London, follows:

Reports increasing in number from hour to hour regarding incidents in the Sudetenland show that the situation has become completely intolerable for the Sudeten German people and, in consequence dangerous to the peace of Europe.

It is, therefore, essential that the separation of the Sudetenland, agreed to by Czechoslovakia, should be effected without any further delay.

On the attached map the Sudeten German area which is to be ceded is shaded in red. Areas in which a plebiscite also is to be held, over and above the areas to be occupied, are drawn in and shaded in green.

Final delimitation of the frontier must correspond to the wishes of those concerned. In order to determine these wishes a certain period is necessary for the preparation of a plebiscite during which disturbances must in all circumstances be prevented.

A situation of parity must be created. The area designated on the attached map as German is to be occupied by German troops without taking into account whether in a plebiscite it may prove to be in this or that part of an area with a Czech majority.

On the other hand, Czech territory is to be occupied by Czech troops without taking into account whether in this area there lie large German language islands in which in a plebiscite a majority will,

---

WHAT CHANCELLOR HITLER DEMANDS FROM CZECHOSLOVAKIA

This map was drawn from one obtained by The Associated Press from Czech sources and wirelessed from London last night. It purports to be a copy of the one given by Herr Hitler to Prime Minister Chamberlain representing his final demands. The heavily shaded area shows the territory whose surrender is demanded outright, with all property in it, by Oct. 1. The light shading shows the territory in which he demands a plebiscite by Nov. 25.

without doubt give expression to its German national feeling.

With a view to bringing about an immediate and final solution of the Sudeten German problem the following proposals are submitted by the German Government:

I

Withdrawal of the whole Czech armed forces, police, gendarmerie, customs officials and frontier guards from the area to be evacuated as designated on the attached map, this area to be handed over to Germany on Oct. 1.

II

Evacuated territory is to be handed over in its present condition (see further details in Appendix). The German Government agrees that plenipotentiary representatives of the Czech Government and of the Czech Army should be attached to headquarters of the Germany military forces to deal with details of modalities (methods of making effective) of the evacuation.

The Czech Government to discharge at once all Sudeten Germans serving in the military forces or police anywhere in Czech State territory and permit them to return home.

The Czech Government to liberate all political prisoners of the German race.

III

The German Government agrees to permit a plebiscite to take place in those areas—to be more definitely defined—before Nov. 25 at the latest.

The plebiscite itself will be carried out under control of an international commission. All persons who resided in the areas in question on Oct. 28, 1918, or who were born in those parts prior to this date will be eligible to vote.

A simple majority of all eligible male and female voters will determine the desire of the population to belong either to the German Reich or the Czech. State.

During the plebiscite both parties will withdraw their military forces out of the area to be defined more precisely. The date and duration will be settled mutually by the German and Czech Governments.

IV

The German Government proposes that an authoritative German-Czech commission should be set up to settle all further details.

APPENDIX

The evacuated Sudeten German area is to be handed over without destroying or rendering unusable in any way the military, economic or traffic establishment (plants). These include ground organization of air service and all wireless stations.

All economic and traffic materials especially rolling stock of the railway system in the designated areas are to be handed over undamaged. The same applies to all utility services (gas works, power stations, etc.).

Finally, no foodstuffs, goods, cattle, raw materials, etc., are to be moved. ◊

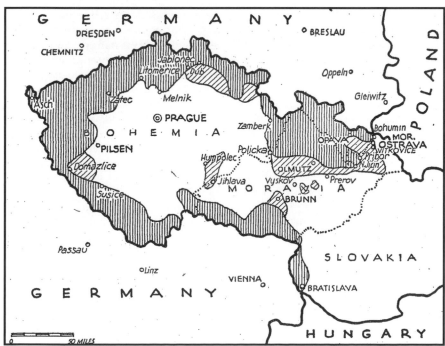

KELLOGG PACT CITED
President Asks Solution by Mediation— Notes the Horrors Of War

SEES NO NEED FOR FORCE
Convinced People of Europe Want Peace, He Asserts in a Dramatic Plea to Rulers

President Roosevelt made a personal appeal early today to Chancellor Hitler and President Benes to settle the German-Czech controversy by negotiation. He pointed to their countries' obligations under the Kellogg-Briand pact.

Britain and France were expected to send a joint appeal to Herr Hitler today, warning him that insistence on his demands to Prague would almost certainly mean a European war unless they were modified. Chiefs of the British and French Governments met last night and are to meet again this morning.

The text of the German demands, showing claims for Czechoslovak territory and property, was made public.

The French Cabinet unanimously approved Premier Daladier's proposal to warn Herr Hitler that he must guarantee to respect Czechoslovakia after the cession of the Sudetenland or risk war.

Prague received the German demands and it was indicated no government could accept them. Reports in other capitals said they had been declared unacceptable. An official broadcast said the mobilization was not provocative but had been ordered after Britain and France had indicated they could not approve Herr Hitler's terms.

Herr Hitler became incensed over the Czech broadcast and decided to address the nation tonight as part of a "historic manifestation" on the subject of Czechoslovakia. An uncompromising stand was forecast.

❮ Warsaw received a note from Prague indicating the Teschen district would be added to Poland if Germany got the Sudeten district. Geneva heard the cession of territory to Hungary also was contemplated. ◇

DOUBTS FELT IN LONDON
Roosevelt's Appeal Is Praised But Does Not Raise Hopes

Special Cable to The New York Times.

LONDON, Monday, Sept. 26.— The effectiveness of President Roosevelt's appeal was strongly doubted here this morning although its motives were appreciated wherever the news was read.

The British Government and people would be thankful if the President's intervention averted war, which all are dreading. But there is little belief here that Chancellor Adolf Hitler will pay much attention to a democratic President who has so often denounced his methods but who now appeals to his reasonableness in an emergency.

Moreover, the British can see little more logic in President Roosevelt's message to Herr Hitler and President Eduard Benes than in the United States Neutrality Act which makes no distinction between aggressor and victim.

One comment this morning was that it would have been just as sensible to have appealed to King Albert of Belgium to avert the War of 1914 as to ask President Benes to do so now. What Britain would like, of course, is a declaration by President Roosevelt expressing moral support for Britain, France and the Czechs in the present crisis. ◇

People Stand Outside Hotel for Hours to Get Glimpse of Him And Cheer Him

By The Associated Press

MUNICH, Germany, Sept. 29—Men and women of Munich stood cheerfully for hours today for a glimpse of the 69-year-old man who started this business of man-to-man talks for peace.

That man was Britain's Prime Minister, Neville Chamberlain, a strange figure in black amid the patriotic panorama of this cradle of Nazism.

Every second man who stood and waited and cheered wore a swastika lapel button. Every second woman was of the handsome, well-turned-out sort of which Munich is proud.

Roosevelt Makes Appeal

By LUTHER HUSTON
Special to The New York Times.

WASHINGTON, Sept. 26—President Roosevelt today made a direct personal appeal to Chancellor Adolf Hitler of Germany and President Eduard Benes of Czechoslovakia to settle their controversies by negotiation and preserve the peace of the world.

In a message sent to the German and Czechoslovak leaders, and forwarded also, through Secretary of State Cordell Hull, to the Prime Ministers of France and Great Britain, the President voiced the hope of 130,000,000 Americans that the controversies of Europe would be settled without resort to arms. He called the attention of the nations involved to their obligations under the Kellogg-Briand pact and other treaties and reminded them that even should these avenues of settlement become obstructed other methods of arbitration were available.

NO SOLUTION BY FORCE

As long as the parties to the dispute continue negotiations no differences are irreconcilable, the President said, but, once negotiations "are "broken off, reason is banished and force asserts itself." "And force," said Mr. Roosevelt, "produces no solution for the future good of humanity."

The President said that he was convinced that the problems faced by the European nations were not so difficult that they could not be solved by reason rather than by force. He asserted the conviction that all people in the troubled nations of Europe want peace to be made before instead of after war.

Mr. Roosevelt said that the consequences of an outbreak of war are "incalculable." He said that war would plunge the people of every country into "unspeakable horror," and that the economic system of every country that was drawn into the struggle would be shattered and its social structures "completely wrecked."

He called the attention of the leaders of Europe to the fact that the hatreds that motivated many factions in European nations did not exist in this country, that our civilization was formed of all the elements in Europe, and that this country was enmeshed in no political entanglements.

The sole desire of the American people is for peace, the President said, but they are not unmindful of the fact that this nation could not escape some of the consequences of war. For the sake of all humanity Mr. Roosevelt appealed to the statesmen who held in their hands the question of war or peace not to break off negotiations that would lead to "a peaceful, fair and constructive settlement of the questions at issue."

The President's dramatic effort to avert a European war that he obviously feared would eventually involve the United States was made without any previous indication that such a step was in contemplation. ◇

They packed lawns in front of the old-fashioned Regina Palace Hotel, headquarters of the British delegation to the four-power conference. The crowd was packed eight and ten feet deep around a square formed by brown-shirted Storm Troopers before the hotel entrance.

Inside additional dozens were camped on the hotel's twin stairways and in every conceivable spot in the tiny red, white and gold lobby.

LITTLE TO SEE MOST OF THE TIME

Most of the time there wasn't anything to see.

Every half-hour two steel-helmeted, black-coated honor guards with bayonets on shoulders snapped through the manual of arms on a hasty signal. Every now and then new black-shirted guards stamped to posts in front of the hotel's baroque marble pillars and the preceding guard goose-stepped away.

There were exciting intervals when Brownshirts filed in and out and the crowd held its breath in anticipation.

There were real cheers, like the kind one hears in an American football stadium, when the slim, black-coated Chamberlain, with a smile and a careful walk, came out. There were Hitler salutes, it is true, but many of the throng kept their hands at their sides and there was lots of noise of the kind one might hear anywhere where people are glad.

After Mr. Chamberlain had driven away in the sticky Munich afternoon for the conference of the statesmen beneath the gorgeous pagan panels of the Fueh-

rerhaus, the palace Herr Hitler built to glorify the birth here of the Nazi movement, the same people stood into the night, joking and waiting.

They were still waiting when the British Prime Minister came downstairs again for the third meeting with Chancellor Adolf Hitler, Premier Benito Mussolini of Italy and Premier Edouard Daladier of France. Then there was a thunder of "hochs" that must have reached all the way down the line of guards on both sides of the street leading from the hotel to the Fuehrerhaus. And downstairs a dance band was blaring that all-English rage of the year, "The Lambeth Walk," while Bavarian dancers linked arms and shouted the Cockney "Oy!"

EACH GROUP IS CHEERED

The street crowds roared acclaim for each group as automobiles bearing delegates back to the Feuhrerhaus whizzed tnrough the streets, but the loudest applause was that for Mr. Chamberlain.

Four times the crowds roared as one by one, M. Daladier, Mr. Chamberlain, Herr Hitler and finally Signor Mussolini and their escorts sped back to the scene of the conference.

The cheers for Mr. Chamberlain rolled along, block after block. Spectators knew well ahead that he was coming for they could hear shouts of "Chamberlain! Chamberlain!" as his car approached.

The Prime Minister waved his black hat to the crowds of Southern Germans, who cheered louder when they saw his broad smile.

"Things must be going better," was the frequent comment.

As Chancellor Hitler passed he seemed too busy with his own thoughts to give more than a preoccupied smile and stiff salute to his people. ◊

British Prime Minister Neville Chamberlain (front row, second from right) walks past a Nazi honor guard at his reception upon arriving at Oberwiesenfeld airport in Munich on the way to a meeting with Adolf Hitler over the latter's threats to invade Czechoslovakia, September 28, 1938.

Powers Make Accord

By FREDERICK T. BIRCHALL
Wireless to The New York Times.

MUNICH, Germany, Sept. 30—The four-power conference to decide the fate of Czechoslovakia and avert a general European war by bringing pressure to bear on her to accept its decisions has met here, reached an agreement and adjourned.

In something less than nine hours of actual conversation time it has settled everything to the satisfaction—more or less—of the conferees.

It may be said at once that the decisions give Germany just about all she has demanded except the total extinction of Czechoslovakia as an independent State, which has never in fact been among her formulated demands, although that has been implied.

The decisions indicate, moreover, that the Poles and Hungarians will receive their shares of the spoils of Czechoslovak dismemberment.

The only change discernible from Chancellor Adolf Hitler's Godesberg memorandum is in the period allowed for the fulfillment of the demand. That has been slightly extended and beginning tomorrow the predominantly German territories are to be evacuated and occupied progressively until Oct. 10.

PROPERTY MUST BE LEFT

The four governments—Britain, France, Germany and Italy—agree that the evacuation must be completed "without any existing installations being destroyed." This covers the German demand, previously objected to by the British, that Czech farmers in Sudeten territory must leave their farms, stock and crops intact behind them when they evacuate, without compensation for them.

The territories to be evacuated are divided into four categorres designated on maps appended to the agreement The first category will be occupied on Oct. 1 and 2, the second category on Oct. 2 and 3, the third category on Oct. 3, 4 and 5, the fourth category on Oct. 6 and 7 and the remainder, to be determined by an international commission that will lay down the conditions governing the evacuation, by Oct. 10.

This indicates that the incoming German troops will not reach the Czech border fortifications until several days after the beginning of the occupation. ⟩

CZECHS TO GET GUARANTEE

All that Czechoslovakia gains, provided she makes the sacrifices demanded from her, is an immediate guarantee by France and Great Britain of the integrity and frontiers of the territory she has left. This guarantee is to be supplemented by Germany and Italy after the demands by the Poles and Hungarians have been met. A new four-power meeting will be called if those demands are not settled within three months.

An international commission is to decide in doubtful territories whether plebiscites are necessary to determine their future, and if plebiscites are held they will be under international control. In the meantime, international "bodies" will hold the disputed territories.

The final determination of frontiers is also to be carried out by the international commission and the right of option into and out of the transferred territories shall be granted to the inhabitants.

Within four weeks all Sudeten Germans shall be released by the Czech Government from further military or police service and the Czech Government shall also agree to release all Sudeten prisoners.

LEAVE-TAKING IS CORDIAL

The agreement to this effect was signed by the four powers in the conference room at the Fuehrerhaus, Chancellor Hitler's personal headquarters in Munich, at 1 o'clock this morning [7 P.M. Thursday, Eastern standard time]. The leave-taking afterward was most cordial.

Herr Hitler, "on behalf of the German people," thanked Prime Minister Neville Chamberlain of Britain and Premier Edouard Daladier of France for their efforts for European peace. They responded in kind and will return home by air later today. Premier Benito Mussolini of Italy has already departed by special train.

Mr. Chamberlain spent an hour in the early morning discussing the agreement with two Czech representatives sent from Prague at his suggestion to receive it.

Much stress is laid on the unanimity obtained in the conference and the mutual friendliness exhibited by the conferees.

"I am not going to quibble about a village," Herr Hitler is said to have told the others when doubtful areas were being discussed and the main points of his demands had been conceded.

A duplicate of the agreement has been prepared for the Czechs and their two representatives will carry it to Prague by air this morning. No doubt seems to exist about their accepting it. What else could they do? ◊

SEPTEMBER 30, 1938

NAZI DEMANDS MET
Hitler Gets Almost All He Asked as Munich Conferees Agree

The war for which Europe had been feverishly preparing was averted early this morning when the leading statesmen of Britain, France, Germany and Italy, meeting in Munich, reached an agreement to allow Reich troops to occupy predominantly German portions of Czechoslovakia's Sudetenland progressively over a ten-day period beginning tomorrow. Most of Chancellor Hitler's demands were met. Prime Minister Chamberlain, whose peace efforts were finally crowned with success, received the loudest applause of Munich's crowds.

Before the start of the conference the Czech Government sent to the British Government a memorandum on its position with regard to the Anglo-French proposals. The Czechs felt that whatever agreement was reached would be at their expense and public opinion was deeply depressed.

Italians shouted their joy in Rome and elsewhere at the announcement of the Munich agreement. They regarded the solution as a victory for the dictatorships over the democracies

Paris was relieved at the Munich agreement, but continued its war preparations. Likewise in London, where the tension was relaxed, precautions went forward.

Pope Pius broke down and sobbed as he appealed in a world radio broadcast for prayers for peace. President Roosevelt urged the people of this country to offer such prayers. ◊

OCTOBER 1, 1938

PARIS NEWSPAPERS HAIL PEACE ACCORD
'World Can Breathe Again; Still Can Live,' Says Provost in Paris-Soir

Wireless to The New York Times

PARIS, Oct. 1—One word, "Peace," completely summarizes expressions on yesterdays's events in the French press, and the same word fell from the lip of every one in the streets, in camps and in homes.

Jean Prouvost, in his front-page editorial in Paris-Soir, could do nothing so appropriate as to repeat it three successive times in opening sentence, "Peace, Peace Peace."

Some of yesterday's headlines were:

L'Information, "A Great Victory for Peace."

La Liberte, which had steadfastly demanded peace, "We were right: Long Live Peace!" L'Intransigeant, "The Miracle of Union."

Ce Soir, organ of the extreme Left, which has been the only element in France demanding war, writes on the four-power pact and its lessons.

"Peace has been saved," it says, "but it is the fruit of the terrible blackmail threat of war, which Chamberlain himself appraised when he said: 'Rather than wait, Hitler is ready to risk a world war.'"

The Munich conference, says Le Temps, had a considerable bearing on the moral and political situation of Europe, and continues: "The fact that the Reich Fuehrer, the Italian Duce, the British Prime Minister and the French Premier have sat together and reached an accord capable of producing a new spirit in international affairs. What should certainly be said is that the Franco-British accord played its role under tragic circumstances and achieved its end, the maintenance of peace, by closer European cooperation. With Chamberlain, Daladier and Bonnet were active makers of this spirit of conciliation and are entitled to the gratitude of the friends of peace.

"France, in spite of all that was done to bewilder and disturb it, displayed calm and resolution. The army did its entire duty, from the high command to those who were called.

"In coming days, as long as matters have not been completely settled, there is need of observing the same discipline. It is not all over yet but has started on the right track. The improvement will enlarge itself little by little."

Gallus, in L'Intransigeant, says the joy felt by all French people does not arise solely from relief, but contains an element of hope. ◊

NAZIS SMASH, LOOT AND BURN JEWISH SHOPS AND TEMPLES UNTIL GOEBBELS CALLS HALT

Thousands Arrested for 'Protection' as Gangs Avenge Paris Death

By OTTO D. TOLISCHUS
Wireless to THE NEW YORK TIMES

BERLIN, Nov. 10.–A wave of destruction, looting and incendiarism unparalleled in Germany since the Thirty Years War and in Europe generally since the Bolshevist revolution, swept over Great Germany today as National Socialist cohorts took vengeance on Jewish shops, offices and synagogues for the murder by a young Polish Jew of Ernst vom Rath, third secretary of the German Embassy in Paris.

Beginning systematically in the early morning hours in almost every town and city in the country, the wrecking, looting and burning continued all day. Huge but mostly silent crowds looked on and the police confined themselves to regulating traffic and making wholesale arrests of Jews "for their own protection."

All day the main shopping districts as well as the side streets of Berlin and innumerable other places resounded to the shattering of shop windows falling to the pavement, the dull thuds of furniture and fittings being pounded to pieces and the clamor of fire brigades rushing to burning shops and synagogues. Although shop fires were quickly extinguished, synagogue fires were merely kept from spreading to adjoining buildings.

TWO DEATHS REPORTED

As far as could be ascertained the violence was mainly confined to property. Although individuals were beaten, reports so far tell of the death of only two persons—a Jew in Polzin, Pomerania, and another in Bunzdorf.

In extent, intensity and total damage, however, the day's outbreaks exceeded even those of the 1918 revolution and by nightfall there was scarcely a Jewish shop, cafe, office or synagogue in the country that was not either wrecked, burned severely or damaged.

Thereupon Propaganda Minister Joseph Goebbels issued the following proclamation:

"The justified and understandable anger of the German people over the cowardly Jewish murder of a German diplomat in Paris found extensive expression during last night. In numerous cities and towns of the Reich retaliatory action has been undertaken against Jewish buildings and businesses.

"Now a strict request is issued to the entire population to cease immediately all further demonstrations and actions against Jewry, no matter what kind. A final answer to the Jewish assassination in Paris will be given to Jewry by way of legislation and ordinance."

What this legal action is going to be remains to be seen. It is known, however, that measures for the extensive expulsion of foreign Jews are already being prepared in the Interior Ministry, and some towns, like Munich, have ordered all Jews to leave within forty-eight hours. All Jewish organizational, cultural and publishing activity has been suspended. It is assumed that the Jews, who have now lost most of their possessions and livelihood, will either be thrown into the streets or put into ghettos and concentration camps, or impressed into labor I brigades and put to work for the Third Reich, as the children of Israel were once before for the Pharaohs.

THOUSANDS ARE ARRESTED

In any case, all day in Berlin, as throughout the country, thousands of Jews, mostly men, were being taken from their homes and arrested—in particular prominent Jewish leaders, who in some cases, it is understood, were told they were being held as hostages for the good behavior of Jewry outside Germany.

In Breslau they were hunted out even in the homes of non-Jews where they might have been hiding.

Foreign embassies in Berlin and consulates throughout the country were besieged by frantic telephone calls and by persons, particularly weeping women and children, begging help that could not be given them. Incidentally, in Breslau the United States Consulate had to shut down for some time during the day because of fumes coming from a burn-

ing synagogue near by.

All pretense maintained during previous minor Jewish outbreaks—to the effect that the day's deeds had been the work of irresponsible, even Communist elements was dropped this time and the official German News Bureau, as well as newspapers that hitherto had ignored such happenings, frankly reported on them. The bureau said specifically:

"Continued anti-Jewish demonstrations occurred in numerous places. In most cities the synagogue was fired by the population. The fire department in many cases was able merely to save adjoining buildings. In addition, in many cities the windows of Jewish shops were smashed.

"Occasionally fires occurred and because of the population's extraordinary excitement the contents of shops were partly destroyed. Jewish shop owners were taken into custody by the police for their own." ◈

REICH IS REBUFFED BY POLES ON DANZIG

Warsaw, Politely But Firmly, Rejects Berlin's Bid to Talk Over Free City's Status

WARSAW, Poland, March 26—It was learned today that the Polish Government had politely but firmly declined German suggestions for negotiations on Danzig. These suggestions were communicated to the government by Ambassador Josef Lipski, who arrived here from Berlin Thursday after a conversation with Joachim von Ribbentrop, the German Foreign Minister.

Herr von Ribbentrop wanted to learn whether Poland was ready to discuss a final settlement of the Danzig problem.

This was not the first German proposal for talks on Danzig. In the past the Poles have declined all such proposals without much harm to Polish-German relations. It was understood that after President Ignaz Moscicki conferred with Marshal Edward Rydz-Smigly and Foreign Minister ▸

◄ Josef Beck it was decided to give a negative reply this time too.

It is pointed out that the treaty and conventions governing Danzig adequately safeguard Polish Interests and that the situation there is quite satisfactory. The Germans in the Free City enjoy full national rights and the National Socialists are in power.

Political circles here are confident that Poland's answer, though negative, will close the exchange of views about Danzig for the time being. However, in the present circumstances and the tense international situation the government has taken certain precautionary military measures.

INTERNATIONAL UNITY SOUGHT

WARSAW, Poland, March 26 (AP).—Poland, delicately poised between expanding Germany and Soviet Russia, moved today to meet a potential Nazi threat from the west by taking steps toward internal solidarity.

One major step in this direction came with a report that the government had permitted the famed peasant leader and ex-Premier, Wincenty Witos, and his aide, onetime Interior Minister Vladlslas Kiernik, to return to their homeland after a nine-year exile in Czecho-Slovakla.

It was reported reliably that M. Witos already was in Polish territory and his submission to the government's authority would be announced simultaneously with amnesty for him.

The anticipated repatriation of the two prominent political exiles was interpreted here as illustrating the internal consolidation now in process in Poland. ◇

MARCH 27, 1939

Coughlin Denounces 'Mongerers of War'

Calls Paraders Here the Dupes of Leftist Foes of Germany

DETROIT, March 26—Americans should express anxiety, the Rev. Charles E. Coughlin said today, because "uninformed thousands are prone to follow a warmongering leadership in New York and elsewhere" instead of working themselves to a point of frenzy in behalf of European democracies.

The cry to save democracy, he said in his weekly radio broadcast, "is raised by those who are more interested in destroying Germany than they are in restoring Czechoslovakia."

Yesterday's parade of protest in New York against Germany's acquisition of Czecho-Slovakia, the priest asserted, was participated in by many innocent people, "duped by propaganda and Leftist leadership."

"For these persons," he said, "the dissolution of Czecho-Slovakia is but a convient occasion to further the cause of tyranny and aggression under the name of liberty and democracy; to sound the drums of international war with the hope of stimulating the wicked passion of hate in the breasts of innocent citizens."

Czecho-Slovakia was born in Pittsburgh, the priest went on, and the "republic was doomed to dissolution from the outset because it was established upon the false principle of racial conflict within the precincts of one nation."

"If the conscience of Americans is offended because the principles of real democracy, of self-determination, of home rule have been crushed to earth by the Iron heel of the German Storm Troopers, let our indignation be impartial and therefore virtuous," he said.

"Let us lament over the plight of the British, French and Russian victims of conquest who, since the battle of Plassey in 1757 to the massacre of Moscow in 1923, have been appealing for liberty and justice and sympathy to the deafened ears of civilization."

About 500 persons yesterday picketed in front of radio stations WMCA, at 1,657 Broadway, and WJZ in the RCA building, 49 West Forty-ninth Street in demonstrations against failure of the stations in the past to carry broadcasts by the Rev. Charles E. Coughlin. ◇

MARCH 30, 1939

FRANCO COMPLETES CONQUEST OF SPAIN; LAST 10 CITIES BOW

Wireless to The New York Times.

HENDAYE, France (at the Spanish frontier), March 29—Events have moved swiftly since last night and Republican resistance has crumbled at all points in Spain.

Valencia, Almeria, Murcia, Ciu-dad Real, Jaen, Cuenca, Albacete, Guadalajara and Alicante, all in Republican hands last night, today are pledging allegiance to the Nationalists. These last nine of Spain's fifty-two provincial capitals were either occupied by advancing columns of Generalissimo Francisco Franco's army or seized by his sympathizers inside.

Burgos has been learning by radio during the day of the capitulation of Republican towns and villages along the Mediterranean coast and in the interior. The station at Palma, Majorca, after

---

MARCH 30, 1939

Madrid Hears of Collapse

Wireless to The New York Times.

MADRID, March 29—From all sides reports reached Madrid today of the complete collapse of Republican authority throughout Spain.

Travelers coming from Valencia reported the whole road was choked with traffic, and thousands of soldiers, who had thrown away their arms, were returning wearily to their villages. Hundreds of trucks passed down the road to Valencia loaded with refugees hoping to escape by sea. However, no steamer was in the harbor. The port was crowded to overflowing with refugees without means of escape.

Lieut. Col. Segismundo Casado of the National Defense Council, who arrived at Valencia yesterday, announced that he intended to stay to supervise the

Francisco Franco leading his staff on the Mediterranean front during the Spanish civil war, 1939.

short-wave conversations with Murcia and other former Republican strongholds, passed on messages of surrender to headquarters.

WIDE RADIO CONTACTS

It seems fairly obvious that Nationalist and Republican radio announcers have reached some agreement, for in places still well within the Republican lines operators have been in friendly conversation with Nationalist stations.

At Palma and Malaga are the chief Nationalist high-frequency stations on the Mediterranean. All day long they have been tutoring Republican stations at Murcia, Valencia and other points in collecting and relaying messages from mobile propaganda stations in the field to General Franco's headquarters. Republican stations were being gently admonished to add "Viva Franco!" to the orthodox "Ariba España" ["Up Spain!"]

In the field General Gonzalo Queipo de Llano's southern army and General Saliquet's central army were advancing rapidly last night in all sectors toward the last coast.

Ramon Serrano Suner, Minister of the Interior at Burgos, gave some idea of the strength of the Nationalist armies operating since Monday. In Central Spain, he said last night, there were about 300,000 men, under command of General Saliquet, assisted by twenty-five other generals. This army included General Gastone Gambara's Italian divisions—the Littorio, Blue Arrows, Black Arrows and Green Arrows—all with mechanized units, tanks, artillery and airplanes. ◇

task of handing over the city to the Nationalist armies.

As soon as his proclamation became known vast crowds assembled in the streets with Nationalist flags, shouting Nationalist slogans.

As in Madrid, the overthrow of the Republican authorities was achieved by the townspeople themselves. They took command to assure continuation of public services and law and order until the arrival of Nationalist troops.

Nationalist military authorities are fully installed here and beginning to function. Many high officers have arrived, including Generals Emilio Solchaga, Garcia Valino and Milan Astray, the last the founder of the Foreign Legion. Civil Guards and Assault Guards also entered during the day.

Fifteen hundred trucks loaded with foodstuffs poured into the city, where 600,000 rations were distributed today. It is hoped the distribution of white bread and tobacco will begin tomorrow.

It is now clear how great was the strength of Generalissimo Francisco Franco's "fifth column" in Madrid. It is estimated the fascist Falange Español had 40,000 members in the capital. Its leader, Dr. Manuel Valdes, a physician, says it was the Falange that took Madrid.

He said Falange members who had suffered untold misery for two years seized the city yesterday morning and held it for several hours until the arrival of troops. They took charge of public services and maintained law and order, he explained.

General Joaquin Rios Capape, who previously commanded troops in the University City sector and then in the Cerro de los Angeles, just south of the capital, entered and contacted Falange leaders, who appeared to be completely in command of the situation and gradually assumed all public offices, reflecting careful preparation.

Reorganization of the Falange in Madrid is now going ahead. Men of military experience and rank are being placed in responsible positions to mold a new party on the model hitherto obtaining in Nationalist Spain. ◇

APRIL 1, 1939

Chamberlain's Statement

By The Associated Press.

LONDON, March 31—The text of Prime Minister Neville Chamberlain's statement on the international situation in the House of Commons today follows:

I am glad to take this opportunity of stating again the general policy of His Majesty's Government. They have constantly advocated the adjustment by way of free negotiation between the parties concerned of any differences that may arise between them. They consider that this is the natural and proper course where differences exist.

In their opinion there should be no question incapable of solution by peaceful means and they would see no justification for the substitution of force or threats of force for the method of negotiation.

As the House is aware, certain consultations are now proceeding with other governments. In order to make perfectly clear the position of His Majesty's Government, in the meantime, before those consultations are concluded, I now have to inform the House that during that period, in the event of any action which clearly threatened Polish independence and which the Polish Government accordingly considered it vital to resist with their national forces, His Majesty's Government would feel themselves bound at once to lend the Polish Government all support in their power.

They have given the Polish Government an assurance to this effect.

I may add that the French Government have authorized me to make it plain that they stand in the same position in this matter as do His Majesty's Government.

The Foreign Secretary saw the Soviet Ambassador this morning and had a very full discussion with him on the subject. I have no doubt the principles on which we are acting are fully understood and appreciated by that government.

The visit of Colonel Beck [Foreign Minister Josef Beck of Poland] will provide an opportunity of discussing with him the various further measures that may be taken in order to accumulate the maximum amount of cooperation in any efforts that may be made to put an end to aggression—if aggression were intended—and to substitute for it the more reasonable and orderly method of discussion. ▸

◀ The question of a conference is simply a matter of expediency. We have no theoretical views about conferences if they prove to be the best way.

If there are other and more effective ways of achieving our object we might dispense with conferences.

The Dominions are being kept fully informed. ◇

AUGUST 21, 1939

REICH TROOPS JAM ROUTES TO POLAND

Gleiwitz, on Border, Bristles with Guns— Ambulance Units Are Ready for Action

GLEIWITZ, Germany, Aug. 22 (AP)— Four of Germany's famous motorized "super guns" and an attendant ammunition train rolled through Gleiwitz at 2:50 A.M.

Each sixteen-foot, 10-inch caliber barrel was carried on three sets of trucks and the ground and firing mechanism on three other sets of trucks drawn before them.

From the direction of the railroad station the half-mile column approached and disappeared into the dark headed toward this city's military garrison. The Polish border lies within two miles of these barracks.

The group going through the town this morning is the second artillery section to be seen here within the last week. The other, heavy mortars, took the same route at 3:45 P.M. yesterday.

Following the heavy pieces, the short muzzles of anti-aircraft machine guns jutted above the helmeted heads of soldiers.

Twenty-man motor trucks clattered rapidly through the streets on caterpillar treads. One was entirely filled with hawsers and inch-thick towing ropes. Another carried iron strips suitable for tracks for wide-tread motor carriages.

Many trucks carried square boxes covered with tar paper. There were also some rolling field kitchens. Ambulances crisscrossed Gleiwitz streets this afternoon.

Besides the regular army ambulances, civilian and Red Cross units were observed. ◇

AUGUST 22, 1939

Baltic Activities Reported

*BERLIN, Aug. 21 (AP)—*Berliners who spent Sunday near the Baltic said today that train after train had rushed past them in a northeasterly direction carrying soldiers, cannons, anti-aircraft equipment and field kitchens.

Others who drove in the direction of Dessau, seat of the Junkers airplane works, said they could not get near the city because it was designated as a military area.

They also said they had a difficult time obtaining gasoline. Filling station after filling station was empty.

At the War Department in Berlin today there was an endless coming and going of smart cars bearing high-ranking officers. Overhead more military planes roared by than has been the case in days.

The city otherwise seemed to be devoid of military activity, the inference being that everybody was on duty at the Polish frontier. ◇

AUGUST 22, 1939

Troops Pass Through Vienna

Wireless to The New York Times.

*VIENNA, Aug. 21—*From an early hour this morning and at regular intervals large contingents of motorized military units left this city by way of the Danube Bridge proceeding in a northeasterly direction toward the German-Slovak frontier.

Military trucks filled with soldiers as well as light artillery, full of camp equipment, Red Cross ambulances and truckloads of powder kegs and oil barrels, passed through the city.

Meanwhile there were visible demonstrations of joy when the newspapers containing reports of the successful termination of the Russo-German trade treaty appeared on the streets. ◇

AUGUST 24, 1939

GERMANY AND RUSSIA SIGN 10-YEAR NON-AGGRESSION PACT

BIND EACH OTHER NOT TO AID OPPONENTS IN WAR ACTS

By The Associated Press

MOSCOW, Aug. 24—Germany and Soviet Russia early today signed a non-aggression pact binding each of them for ten years not to "associate itself with any other groupings of powers which directly or indirectly is aimed at the other party."

By the pact they also agreed to "constantly remain in consultation with one another" on their common interests and to adjust difference by arbitration.

The non-aggression clauses bound each power to refrain from any act of force against the other and if either party is "the object of warlike acts by a third power" to refrain from supporting the third power.

The pact did not include the usual escape clause providing for its denunciation in case one of the contracting parties attacked a third power. This provision has been written into most non-aggression pacts in the past by Moscow.

ARRIVES BY PLANE
By. G.E.R. Gedye
Special cable to The New York Times

MOSCOW, Aug. 24—With the meticulous punctuality of a perfectly staged arrival, two huge Focke-Wulf Condor planes conveying Joachim von Ribbentrop, the German Prime Minister, and his thirty-two assistants, landed at the Moscow airdrome on the stroke of 1 p.m. yesterday.

Adequate but not excessive policy precautions were taken at the airdrome. For the first time the Soviet authorities displayed the swastika banner, five of which flew from the front of the airdrome building, but were placed so as not to be visible from the outside.

Vyacheslaff M. Molotoff was not present to welcome Herr von Ribbentrop but almost the entire staff of the huge German Embassy, headed by the Ambassador, Count Friedrich Werncr von del Schulenburg, with the military, naval and air attaches in uniform, was present. The German civilians mostly wore top hats and cutaway coats.

From the airdrome the party drove to the city through streets where police in their white summer jackets stood every ten paces.

The party drove directly to the former Austrian Embassy where they are being housed. Subsequently Herr von Ribbentrop and leading members of his mission had luncheon at the embassy with Count von del Schulenburg.

At about 3:30 P. M. Herr von Ribbentrop, accompanied by Count von del Schulenburg and an expert translator whom the Germans brought from Berlin, drove through the gates of the Kremlin.

Despite the diplomatic triumph which he believes he has won the father of the anti-Comintern pact must have experienced strange emotions as he drove across the world famed Red Square to the citadel of the Russian Communist Government on a mission that many foreigners in Moscow considered a last desperate effort by Germany to prevent the conclusion of a three-power pact of mutual assistance between Russia and the Western democracies that would have blocked completely Germany's dreams of European hegemony.◊

AUGUST 24, 1939

NEUTRALITY STEPS ARE READIED BY U. S.

Special to The New York Times.

WASHINGTON, Aug. 23—As President Roosevelt rushed back to Washington to meet the problems created for this country by a constantly deepening danger of war in Europe, high officials of the government, including Secretary of State Cordell Hull, who returned from a vacation, met today in the State and Treasury Departments and prepared plans and measures for the President's approval.

The feeling in official circles here that the danger of conflict is increasing hourly was in no wise allayed by the announcement from Berlin and Moscow that the Soviet-German anti-aggression pact had been signed, since this had been discounted here, and the exchanges between the British and German Governments today were regarded as more serious.

Feverish activity developed even before the White House announced at noon that the President had decided to hasten back to the capital, and tonight everything had been prepared for the Chief Executive to take whatever steps he deems necessary to meet the threatening situation.

Sumner Welles, Under-Secretary of State, announced that a meeting of officials from five government departments and high ranking army and navy officers would be held at 3 P.M. tomorrow, an hour after the President is scheduled to arrive here.

Among the problems dealt with at meetings held in the morning in the office of John W. Hanes, Under-Secretary of the Treasury, and in the afternoon in that of Adolf A. Berle, Assistant Secretary of State, were technical ones dealing with the shock upon money and export markets if war should develop in Europe. Also studied was cooperation of the navy in evacuating Americans from Europe, an undertaking to which, in case it is necessary, the Maritime Commission will lend its ships.

DATA FOR DECLARATION READY

In addition, material has been gathered for a comprehensive neutrality declaration, including all aspects of this country's position as a neutral, the rights of United States ships and those of belligerents and, in fact, all the data available from United States experience as a neutral during the last war. This will be available for the President should he care to use it.

Officials were confident that measures devised for the use of the President in the event of war would enable this country to meet an outbreak of hostilities without undue shock. ◊

AUGUST 24, 1939

FRANCE MOBILIZES; NOW EXPECTS WAR

People Confident Of Strength to Meet Aggressor as Hopes Of Peace Diminish

By P. J. PHILIP
Wireless to The New York Times.

PARIS, Aug. 24—Convinced by a report from French Ambassador Robert Coulondre at Berlin and by a reply that

Chancellor Adolf Hitler gave yesterday to Prime Minister Nevile Chamberlain's message through British Ambassador Sir Neville Henderson at Berchtesgaden that an invasion of Poland is intended by the German Government within the next few days, the French Government last night decided to call up a further contingent of reservists today.

This decision was communicated to the press in an official statement from Premier Edouard Daladier's office as follows:

"On account of the international situation the French Government has decided to complete military measures already taken by calling up an additional contingent of reserve soldiers."

During last night notices were posted on the walls of town halls and public buildings throughout the country calling up men whose mobilization number is 3 or 4. It is estimated that about 600,000 men of varying age and trained for dif-

ferent military work will be affected. These little notices are printed on white paper bordered by red, white and blue and under crossed flags of the republic.

Another notice posted during the night and also signed by the Minister of War, who is also Premier Daladier, announced that from today requisition of automobiles and other military requirements would be made.

Paris is still largely deserted, many families not having as yet returned from vacation, and the news that categories 3 and 4 are being called up and subsequent posting of notices attracted very little attention. Heavy rain kept the people off the streets and the city was unusually quiet all last evening.

It was expected that further measures of mobilization would be deferred until after today's Cabinet meeting, for which President Albert Lebrun returned from his vacation last night, but reports of the French and British ❯

❨ Ambassadors in Berlin confirmed the need for the greatest urgency.

FRAIL HOPES FOR PEACE

Despite the apparent gravity of the situation it should be added that all hope has not yet been abandoned that war can be avoided. This hope may be based on frail foundations, but these are not in official circles considered entirely unsubstantial.

The first among them is the fact that the German Government, army and people must know that annexation of Danzig and all the rest that Germany is now claiming from Poland cannot be expected without war—as Chancellor Hitler promised his people would be the case. The Polish Government has given assurances again to France that she intends to stand firm against invaders, and the French and British Governments have repeated their promise to Warsaw that, if the Poles resist, these governments will keep their promise.

Second, although an uncertain element in the situation that may make for peace is the attitude of Soviet Russia. It was believed here by many that the So-

viet Government's real aim in getting Foreign Minister Joachim von Rippentrop to Moscow while continuing conversations with the British and French military and naval missions was to try to stage a "Soviet Munich" and take a dominant diplomatic position in the world as a peacemaker.

If Russia succeeded, it was argued, she would have a great measure of popular opinion in the world behind her. If she failed she would be able to draw profit from the aftermath of a war between "capitalist countries" from which she would remain aloof.

French Ambassador Andre Francois-Poncet had a long interview yesterday in Rome with Foreign Minister Count Ciano of Italy. His report has not been received.

Contradicting whatever frail hopes may be founded on this diplomatic activity, are reports confirming the steady massing of German troops on the Polish frontier and elsewhere, and multiplication and exaggeration of frontier "incidents" in the German press. It is probable that more people here now believe that war cannot be avoided than that it

can, and the government is necessarily acting on the supposition that it cannot. What is obvious is that there is going to be no hesitancy and no weakness on the part of France.

If Herr Hitler still expects to obtain another conquest without war it is clear that he is mistaken.

The two categories of reservists called up will be at their posts along the whole of the frontier by Saturday and ready, under the command of General Gamelin, to meet any situation.

FRANCE NOW IS CONFIDENT

It is well worth remarking that there has been no general exodus of the civil population as yet from the east and north of France, such as there was last September. Among the public there was a feeling last September—which was not unfounded—that in the air, especially, France was not ready to meet a German attack. This year there is complete confidence in the efficacy of all arms and not only in the ultimate outcome if the test comes, but even in the initial repulse of the aggressor. ◆

SEPTEMBER 1, 1939

Border Clashes Increase

Wireless to The New York Times.

BERLIN, Sept. 1—An increasing number of border incidents involving shooting and mutual Polish-German casualties are reported by the German press and radio. The most serious is reported from Gleiwitz, a German city on the line where the southwestern portion of Poland meets the Reich.

At 8 P.M., according to the semiofficial news agency, a group of Polish insurrectionists forced an entrance into the Gleiwitz radio station, overpowering the watchmen and beating and generally mishandling the attendants. The Gleiwitz station was relaying a Breslau station's program, which was broken off by the Poles.

They proceeded to broadcast a prepared proclamation, partly in Polish and partly in German, announcing themselves as "the Polish Volunteer Corps of Upper Silesia speaking from the Polish

station in Gleiwitz." The city, they alleged, was in Polish hands.

Gleiwitz's surprised radio listeners notified the police, who halted the broadcast and exchanged fire with the insurrectionists, killing one and capturing the rest. The police are said to have discovered that the attackers were assisted by regular Polish troops.

The Gleiwitz incident is alleged here to have been the signal "for a general attack by Polish franc-tireurs on German territory."

Two other points—Pitschen, near Kreuzburg, and Hochlinden, northeast of Ratibor, both in the same vicinity as Gleiwitz, were the scenes of violations of the German boundary, it is claimed,

German troops entering Poland on September 1, 1939.

SEPTEMBER 1, 1939

HITLER GIVES WORD
In a Proclamation
He Accuses Warsaw
Of Appeal to Arms

By OTTO D. TOLISCHUS
Special Cable to The New York Times.

BERLIN, Sept. 1—Charging that Germany had been attacked, Chancellor Hitler at 5:11 o'clock this morning issued a proclamation to the army declaring that from now on force will be met with force and calling on the armed forces "to fulfill their duty to the end."

The text of the proclamation reads:

To the defense forces: The Polish nation refused my efforts for a peaceful regulation of neighborly relations; instead it has appealed to weapons.

Germans in Poland are persecuted with a bloody terror and are driven from their homes. The series of border violations, which are unbearable to a great power, prove that the Poles no longer are willing to respect the German frontier. In order to put an end to this frantic activity no other means is left to me now than to meet force with force.

'BATTLE FOR HONOR'

German defense forces will carry on the battle for the honor of the living rights of the reawakened German people with firm determination. I expect every German soldier, in view of the great tradition of eternal German soldiery, to do his duty until the end.

Remember always in all situations you are the representatives of National Socialist Greater Germany!

Long live our people and our Reich!
Berlin, Sept. 1, 1939.
ADOLF HITLER

The commander-in-chief of the air force issued a decree effective immediately prohibiting the passage of any airplanes over German territory excepting those of the Reich air force or the government.

This morning the naval authorities ordered all German mercantile ships in the Baltic Sea not to run to Danzig or Polish ports. Anti-air raid defenses were mobilized throughout the country early this morning.

A formal declaration of war against Poland had not yet been declared up to 8 o'clock [3 A.M. New York time] this morning and the question of whether the two countries are in a state of active belligerency is still open.

REICHSTAG WILL MEET TODAY

Foreign correspondents at an official conference at the Reich Press Ministry at 8:30 o'clock [3:30 A.M. New York time] were told that they would receive every opportunity to facilitate the transmission of dispatches. Wireless stations have been instructed to speed up communications and the Ministry is installing additional batteries of telephones.

The Reichstag has been summoned to meet at 10 o'clock [5 A.M. New York time] to receive a more formal declaration from Herr Hitler.

When Herr Hitler made his announcement Berlin's streets were still deserted except for the conventional early traffic, and there were no outward signs that the nation was finding itself in the first stages of war.

The government area was completely deserted, and the two guards doing sentry duty in front of the Chancellery remained their usual mute symbol of authority. It was only when official placards containing the orders to the populace began to appear on the billboards that early workers became aware of the situation. ◇

with fighting at both places still under way.

The attackers were all said to be heavily armed and supported by details of the regular Polish Army.

But it is further reported that German border guards repulsed all the attempts.

Polish insurrectionists and soldiers are alleged to have stormed the Hochlinden Custom House, which was recaptured by Germans after a battle lasting for an hour and a half. The number of dead and wounded was not determined because of darkness, but fourteen Poles, including six soldiers, were captured.

MANY CASUALTIES REPORTED

In the Pitschen incident a band of 100 Poles, including soldiers, were said to have been surprised two kilometers on the German side of the frontier. They are accused of opening the fire, which was returned, resulting in the death of two Poles and the capture of fifteen, while the Germans lost one dead and many wounded.

Since Saturday Neuberstisch, near Gleiwitz, is said to have been subjected daily to Polish rifle and grenade attacks. These have seriously damaged property and communications.

Polish bands assisted by soldiers are also said to have attacked the railroad station in the Alt Eiche district of Rosenberg in East Prussia. They were repulsed by German machine gunners, the Poles losing an unknown number of men, the Germans one dead and one wounded, says the report.

In Katowice a Polish customs official is accused of forcing a German woman into Polish territory, although her companion escaped. Nothing is known of the whereabouts of the supposedly kidnapped woman.

Poles are accused also of endeavoring to cross the border and attempting to set fire to German houses. Germans report many attacks against Germans within Poland. ◇

Chapter 1

"CAN THE UNITED STATES KEEP OUT OF WAR?"

September–October 1939

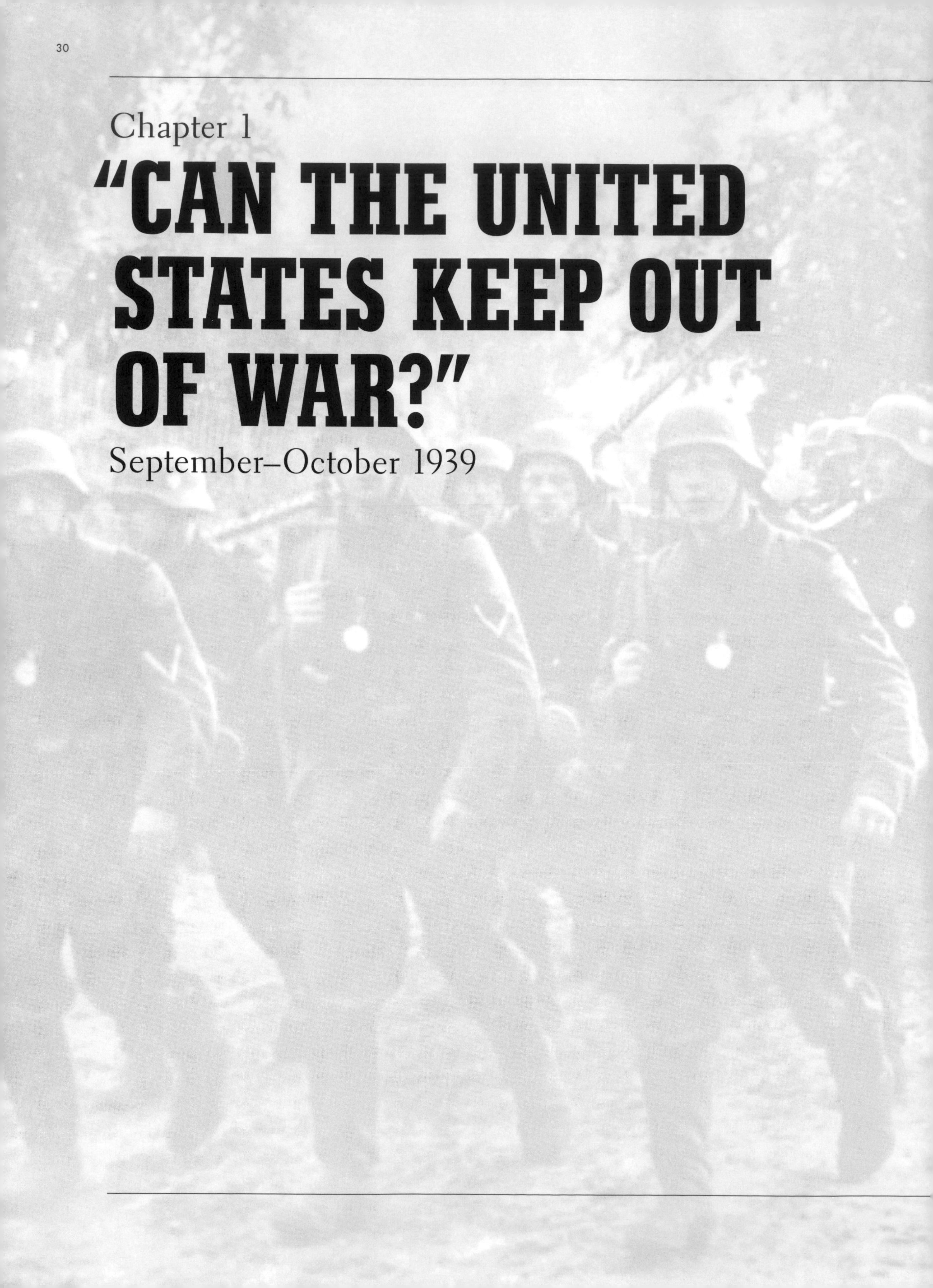

In the early morning on September 1, 1939 German forces began a carefully planned campaign to destroy the Polish armed forces in a series of rapid and destructive operations. The news, when it came, had not been unexpected, for the European crisis had intensified in the last days of August. In New York it was just after midnight and The Times rushed out an extra edition under the front-page headline "German Army Attacks Poland." Details were sent through by Otto Tolischus in Berlin (soon to be expelled by the Germans) and confirmed by The Times's Polish correspondent Jerzy Szapiro, who found himself under bombardment in Warsaw. The German campaign made rapid progress, but in London and Paris, already being evacuated in case of bombing, Hitler was being asked to withdraw his forces and avoid further war. His refusal resulted in two ultimatums. The British one ran out at 11 a.m. on September 3, the French one at 5 p.m. the same day. Prime Minister Neville Chamberlain solemnly announced over the radio that Britain was at war and his broadcast was reprinted in full on the front page of The Times that same day. Neither of the Western powers took immediate action to help the Poles, whose forces were swept aside in four weeks of bitter fighting. On September 17 the Soviet armed forces moved into eastern Poland under their agreement with Hitler and by September 27 all Polish resistance had ended

For the United States the crisis in Europe posed many dangers. Neutrality legislation, which had been signed into law in 1937, insured that the United States would not become involved in any war by taking sides or supplying arms. President Franklin D. Roosevelt was under strong pressure to declare U.S. neutrality formally in September 1939, and although he did so, he wanted to keep open the possibility of selling resources to the democracies. The isolationist mood in the United States, which The Times campaigned against, was strong. When The Times asked on September 3 "Can the United States Keep Out of War?," the overwhelming answer from the public would have been "yes." For Americans there was not just anxiety over German ambitions, but fear of what Japan might do in Asia and uncertainty over Soviet intentions following Stalin's decision to throw in his lot with Hitler. There was also widespread fascination in America with the war, evident in the extensive news coverage devoted by The Times to the opening weeks of the conflict.

The historian Allan Nevins asked whether civilization could survive a second war, a question widely debated in Europe in the 1930s. Nevins concluded that it might, but only because civilization somehow always had survived in the past. The Times published the assertion by the exiled Communist Leon Trotsky that sooner or later the United States would have to join in the war; though Trotsky was an unlikely ally for America's interventionists. Nevertheless, there still existed the possibility that the war might end as suddenly as it had begun. In October Hitler made veiled offers to the West to abandon the conflict now that he had seized his Polish prize. Demands that the West should make peace came from Francisco Franco, recent victor in the Spanish Civil War, the pope, Queen Wilhelmina of The Netherlands, even from Moscow. For all the popular hostility to Chamberlain as an appeaser, then and now, he was adamant in October 1939 that there should be no negotiating with Hitler. By late October American public opinion held that U.S. involvement in the war could be avoided altogether. A Gallup Poll showed that 54 percent were sure the United States could keep out of the conflict. This was not yet world war. If Britain and France had made peace, there would have been no world war at all.

GERMAN ARMY ATTACKS POLAND

HOSTILITIES BEGUN
Warsaw Reports German Offensive Moving on Three Objectives

By Jerzy Szapiro
Wireless to The New York Times.

WARSAW, Poland, Sept. 1—War began at 5 o'clock this morning with German planes attacking Gdynia, Cracow and Katowice.

At Gdynia three bombs exploded in the sea.

The regular German Army started an offensive in the direction of Dzialdowka—in Upper Silesia and Czestochowa. The German plan apparently is to cut off Western Poland along the line of Dzialdowka-Lodz-Czestochowa.

The offensive is developing from East Prussia, toward Silesia and northwards from Slovakia.

At 9 o'clock an attempt was made to bombard Warsaw. The planes, however, did not reach even the suburbs.

A military attack on the garrison at Westerplatte in the Danzig area was repulsed.

The Foreign Office at 8:45 A.M. issues a communiqué saying that military action had begun in Westerplatte in the Danzig area as well as in Buschkowa near Gdynia, and in Dzialowka, Chojnice and Lowa.

Hostilities have begun and Poland has been attacked, said the communiqué.

Three cities in Upper Silesia suffered artillery bombardment, particulars of which are lacking, it was said.

While this dispatch was being telephoned, the air-raid sirens sounded in Warsaw.

DANZIG FIGHTING REPORTED
WARSAW, Poland, Sept. 1 (AP)—It was reported today that Tczew and Czestochowa were bombed by German airplanes early this morning.

There was no official confirmation of the bombing.

Fighting was reported at Danzig.

It was reported officially that German troops had attacked Polish defenses near Mlawa, bordering the southern part of East Prussia. There was no announcement of the damage resulting from the bombing.

Mist and clouds were overhanging the city. A light drizzle apparently afforded momentary protection against air raids. Warsaw went to work as usual.

ROOSEVELT WARNS NAVY
WASHINGTON, Sept. 1 (AP)—President Roosevelt directed today that all naval ships and army commands be notified at once by radio of German-Polish hostilities.

The White House issued the following announcement:

"The President received word at 2:50 A.M. Eastern standard time by telephone from Ambassador Biddle at Warsaw and through Ambassador Bullitt in Paris that Germany has invaded Poland and that four Polish cities are being bombed.

"The President directed all naval ships and army commands be notified by radio at once.

"There probably will be a further announcement by the State Department in a few hours."

The announcement was issued by William Hassett, acting White House press secretary, after the President telephoned him at his home.

White House offices had been dark during the night, but Mr. Roosevelt himself was keeping in constant touch with European developments. Across the street from the Executive Mansion there were few lights burning in the rambling State Department Building.

One factor creating immediate concern in the capital was the presence of many Americans in Europe who have been unable to obtain passenger space on transatlantic liners.

There was speculation that naval vessels in European waters might be ordered to lend a hand to merchant ships in evacuating Americans.

Preparations were going forward, too, to keep American industry stable in event of a general European war. ◊

BRITISH MOBILIZING
Navy Raised to Its Full Strength, Army And Air Reserves Called Up

PARLIAMENT IS CONVOKED

By FERDINAND KUHN Jr.
Special Cable to The New York Times.

LONDON, Sept. 1—All attempts to bring about direct negotiations between Germany and Poland appeared to have broken down tonight as Great Britain mobilized her fleet to full strength, stretched her other defensive preparations close to the limit and began moving 3,000,000 school children and invalids from the crowded cities into the safety of the countryside.

Censorship was established over cables after London had been cut off for hours from communication with the Continent.

It was the peak of the crisis, but a day of rumors had not shifted the fundamental issue nor given a conclusive answer to the question of peace or war.

At midnight the British Government was not yet convinced that Germany really intended to attack Poland and provoke a world war.

TERMS CALLED SMOKE SCREEN
All that had happened during yesterday, including the sudden broadcasting of Chancellor Hitler's sixteen-point demands, was interpreted here as a smoke screen rather than as the flash of guns.

After hearing Herr Hitler's "terms" officials here quietly announced tonight that "the government primarily interested in the proposals is, of course, the Polish Government."

Until the Polish Government has had time to consider them, it was said in Whitehall that "it would be highly undesirable for any comment to be made."

It was fully expected that Poland would reject them later today; indeed, Polish circles here were describing them tonight as utterly unacceptable," for they would involve dismemberment of Poland and loss of Poland's capacity to defend her independence. In any event, there was no sign of any intention here to put pressure on Warsaw to accept.

Much might have been said about the German "proposals" here tonight if the government had not been so anxious to leave the first decision to Warsaw without any prompting. That the British regarded them as artful went without saying, since they conveyed a first impression of reasonableness that was not borne out by the terms themselves.

Until the announcement on the German wireless tonight, the British Government had not been told about them officially, and the Polish Government was not informed until Josef Lipski, Polish Ambassador to Berlin, visited Foreign Minister Joachim von Ribbentrop a few minutes before the broadcast took place.

Shortly after midnight last night, Sir Nevile Henderson, the British Ambassador in Berlin, had heard the "points" read to him by Herr von Ribbentrop, but the reading was so fast that the Ambassador could not even take notes of them in detail. In any event, he was told Herr Hitler's "points" were not being given to him or his government officially, on the ground that it was already too late.

TIME LIMIT EXPIRED

On Tuesday Herr Hitler had asked that a Polish negotiator should arrive in Berlin within twenty-four hours; and as nobody had arrived from Warsaw when the time limit expired, Sir Nevile was told that the "points" could not even be communicated officially to London.

The German time table with the Polish Government was even more unusual. About 9 o'clock yesterday morning M. Lipski had asked to see Herr von Ribbentrop. The Ambassador had no response until afternoon, when he was asked by telephone if he were coming as Ambassador or as a plenipotentiary to negotiate. He said "as Ambassador." He heard nothing more until evening, when he was summoned and was told it was already too late, as the time limit had expired.

Tonight, after midnight talks in Downing Street, it was said here that Herr Hitler's "points" had not come in any way as a reply to the British proposals. Great Britain's whole effort in the past few days has been concerned with the conditions in which direct negotiations between the Germans and Poles might take place.

In all the diplomatic interchanges of the last week, the British contention has been that the discussions must be on terms of equality, that a settlement should safeguard the essential interests of Poland and that its observance should be secured by effective guarantees.

If there was any optimism in London yesterday—and one could sense it in spite of all the alarms of the last twenty-four hours—it sprang from a feeling that Great Britain and France were strong enough to face any test.

Opinion in Downing Street was "tough" as never before. It was being said that "appeasement" was nowhere in evidence and that, far from allowing Germany to overrun Poland, the British and French were ready to hit hard on the very first day.

Much was being made of alleged deficiencies in the German Army's equipment and in the condition of German airplanes, which, according to a source close to the government, is far from what "German propaganda" has represented. ◈

SEPTEMBER 1, 1939

BRITISH CHILDREN TAKEN FROM CITIES
3,000,000 Persons Are in First Evacuation Group, Which Is to Be Moved Today

By FREDERICK T. BIRCHALL
Special Cable to The New York Times.

Children from Myrdle School, Stepney, London, being escorted to the station to be evacuated (the first school to do so), on September 1, 1939.

LONDON, Sept. 1—The greatest mass movement of population at short notice in the history of Great Britain is under way. It is an evacuation, under government order, of little children, invalids, women and old men from congested areas.

From London, Birmingham, Manchester, Liverpool, Edinburgh, Glasgow and twenty-three other cities the great exodus is going on as this dispatch is being written. The numbers are stupendous. More than 3,000,000 of these helpless human beings are being taken out of danger of German bombs.

Nothing like it has ever been attempted anywhere; yet it is going on without mishap—so far, indeed, without serious confusion.

Scenes everywhere were much the same whether in the aristocratic West End or the proletarian East Side, but one that this correspondent witnessed was typical both of the method and the neighborhood. This was in Myrtle Street, Whitechapel. Its school had 180 children to be evacuated. They ranged in age from 5 to 16. A large proportion was Jewish.

The children arrived at the school, most of them with mothers or elder sisters, just as the sun came over the eastern horizon about 5:30 this morning. The teachers were already waiting for them outside the school. One teacher at the gate kept the relatives outside it. Only the children were passed through.

All apparently were children of ▶

‹ poor families, but for this exodus they had been spruced up so that all were neat and clean. Every one, boy and girl alike, carried a knapsack over the shoulders, but the quality of the haversacks varied. Some were of real leather or rubberoid. Some were made out of pillowslips. In each were a change of clothes, toilet articles and a food package sufficient for the day. But there was one invariable piece of equipment. Each child carried a gas mask.

As they arrived in the school yard the teacher fastened onto each child a stout label on which were the child's name, number and school. When they were duly labeled they were marshaled into the assembly hall. There the headmistress told them that they were going on a holiday and that it would be nice to begin it with a little prayer. This was the prayer solemnly chanted in the treble child voices:

"May God take us all in His keeping and bring us safe back to our mummies."

At 7 o'clock came the evacuation order with a male guide who was to see the children safely to the station and onto the train. The teachers marshaled the children out and they went along in a ragged procession, the smallest ones hand in hand, with the bigger ones interspersed among them.

It was only four blocks to the station, but every block was lined with anxious mothers who ran alongside with cautions and last messages, which again threatened to upset decorum. So after one block the headmistress called a halt and primly told the disturbers to leave because the children were getting excited. Some obeyed, but others just couldn't.

All along the street windows were opened and faces leaned out, the women weeping and the men calling out: "Keep smiling! Keep your head up and keep your feet dry!" The children began to feel that this was a really good joke and forgot their tears.

Nevertheless, it took fifteen minutes to traverse those four blocks to the station, and there the little scene was soon ended. The children lined up along the platform. There were no more tears, for the weeping mothers had been left outside.

In a few minutes along came a cheerfully lighted train. The children were shepherded aboard and the train went off to collect more elsewhere. When it departed the children were happily singing. This excursion was really turning out to be a grand holiday.

There is no panic, no terror about this evacuation. The government has been anxious from the outset to have it understood it did not imply that war was inevitable; it would rather be in the nature of a rehearsal.

In that spirit it is being taken. Never

SEPTEMBER 1, 1939

FREE CITY IS SEIZED
Forster Notifies Hitler of Order Putting Danzig Into the Reich

Special Cable to The New York Times.

DANZIG, Sept. 1—By a decree issued early this morning Albert Forster, Nazi Chief of State, proclaimed the annexation of the Free City to the Reich, thus settling by a fell stroke the original point of contention in the international crisis.

In a telegram to Chancellor Hitler Herr Forster explained his action as necessary to remove "the pressing necessity of our people and State." Herr Forster also issued a proclamation to the people of Danzig saying the hour awaited for twenty years had arrived because "our Fuehrer, Adolf Hitler, has freed us."

[A New York Times dispatch from Berlin this morning said Herr Hitler telegraphed Herr Forster today thanking him and all Danzigers, and stating:

"The law for reannexation is in effect immediately."

The Chancellor stated furthermore, that Herr Forster was appointed head of the civil administration of the Danzig area.]

In a four-article decree Herr Forster declared the Constitution of Danzig no longer valid. He declared himself sole administrator of the Danzig part of the German Reich, and he declared that until the Reich's legal system had been introduced by command of Herr Hitler all laws except the Constitution remained in effect. Then Herr Forster immediately wired Herr Hitler of his action, begged the Chancellor to give his approval of the move and through Reich law complete the annexation.

The German flag is now flying everywhere over Danzig, Herr Forster said, and all church bells resound to the event. "We thank God," he declared, "that He gave the Fuehrer the strength and the possibility to free also us from the evil Versailles treaty."

'REPUBLIC IS MENACED'
By JERZY SZAPIRO
Wireless to The New York Times.

WARSAW, Poland, Sept. 1—"The republic is menaced!" This war cry was splashed over all the front pages of Warsaw newspapers yesterday, including the official Gazeta Polska. The gravest view of the situation is taken here in government circles. The occupation by the Gestapo [German secret police] of Danzig's main railroad station and of the vital junction to Polish-owned railroads in the Free City was regarded as a challenge that could not be tolerated any longer.

Control of the railroads is one of Poland's most important prerogatives in Danzig. It is gone by the seizure of the station, through the requisitioning of freight trains and the stoppage of traffic. Other prerogatives like customs control and the free use of the port now exist only on paper. Short of actual occupation of Free City territory by German troops the Nazis already have achieved their aims of Danzig's incorporation in the Reich.

Poland is seen here as nearing the limits of her patience and calm. There are already signs of impatience among the people, who are wondering why the war has not begun yet in spite of German provocations and Poland's preparedness. The semi-official Gazeta Polska for the first time uses the word "war" in its editorial commenting on mobilization.

REICH HELD RESPONSIBLE

"Poland's security is menaced," it says, "by Germany's demands and aggressive acts. We have made no demands, territorial or other. We want peace with all our neighbors. We do not want war and hope it will not break out. If it comes, Germany will be responsible for the worst cataclysm in the history of mankind."

"With superhuman patience," says the independent Wieczor, "we have tolerated various aggressive acts in the Reich and Danzig; Hitler's threats, the concentration of German troops on all frontiers, the occupation of Slovakia, the violation of our rights in Danzig, the territorial claims, the inhuman treatment of the Polish minority in Germany, frontier terrorism—these can last no longer."

Yesterday was very critical. When the news of the occupation of Danzig's station and the hoisting of swastikas in the Free City reached Warsaw after

did the stout souls of British plain folk show to better advantage. Never did the innate courtesy and kindness of the whole populace and the generous hospitality and readiness to help of the well-to-do shine more clearly. It is typical of that spirit and of the real piety of this land that the British Broadcasting Company held over the radio tonight a short religious service in which God was besought to comfort parents separated from their children and give courage to children and invalids, many of whom are leaving home for the first time.

No American could hear that or could witness the scenes of cheerful fortitude at schools, in little homes, in streets and at railway stations unmoved. This is a staunch and true people. In any "war of nerves" it is not they who will falter. ◊

---

midnight, it was feared a coup would come this morning. Everything was prepared on the Polish side to strike.

The situation is both tragic and grotesque, it is pointed out here. All Europe is mobilized and prepared for war, but the man responsible for the crisis cannot take the decision of peace or war. Chancellor Hitler's chances of victory in war or an advantageous agreement lessen daily, it is felt—and yet he hesitates.

War preparations here were speeded yesterday. Railroads were placed on a war basis and taken over by military authorities. Passenger traffic was greatly reduced. Beginning today special passes will be needed for traveling by private persons. Newspapers are full of descriptions of scenes of unparalleled enthusiasm from all parts of the country after the proclamation of general mobilization.

Hundreds of thousands of reservists hurried yesterday to join their units. The first day of full mobilization outwardly differed but little from all the other crisis days. Tram and bus services to Warsaw were slightly reduced, but the streets of the capital were still alive with cars and taxicabs, no restrictions having yet been imposed on gasoline consumption. The food situation is unchanged, which means it is satisfactory apart from the milk shortage in the morning owing to the disturbances of suburban traffic.

In all railroad stations cloakrooms were closed and cleared of trunks and other objects. The reason was the discovery in Warsaw of a German terrorist gang which planned to blow up several public buildings at the outbreak of war. ◊

WASHINGTON VIEWS THE CRISIS GRAVELY

Outbreak of Hostilities Now Only Matter of Hours, Some Officials Believe

By HAROLD B. HINTON
Special to The New York Times.

WASHINGTON, Aug. 31—Officials, guided only by incomplete and delayed dispatches from Europe, were inclined today to take the gravest view of the situation abroad, some of them fearing war was merely a matter of hours. Only private and confidential opinions were expressed, as both the State Department and the White House maintained official silence.

President Roosevelt spent most of his day reading press bulletins which were relayed to him and listening to radio news broadcasts. Late in the afternoon, he motored to Carderock, Md., a few miles from Washington, to inspect the Navy Department's new testing tank there, where large-scale ship models are put through their paces under various conditions. On his return he detoured a short distance to look at the site of the new Naval Hospital under construction at Bethesda, Md.

The terms for a peaceful solution of the crisis outlined in a Berlin broadcast

Hitler acts against Poland: The port of Gydnia, north of Danzing (toward top of the map) was blockaded this morning. At Glewitz (shown by cross) artillery fire was heard after a Polish-German skirmish had been reported there. Cracow, to the east, was among Polish cities said to have been bombed.

were felt to leave little hope of averting conflict, because they were considered obviously unacceptable to Poland.

EXPECT POLAND TO FIGHT

The general belief here is that Poland will fight if Germany makes any move into Danzig and that Great Britain and France will at once join as belligerents. The continued German intransigence on the Danzig question, despite the repeated appeals and representations from almost every quarter of the globe, has tended in the past few days to diminish official optimism that war will be averted. ◊

ROOSEVELT PLEDGE
He Promises Efforts to Keep U. S. Out of War—Thinks It Can Be Done

By FELIX BELAIR Jr.
Special to The New York Times.

WASHINGTON, Sept. 1—President Roosevelt pledged the nation today to make every effort to keep this country out of war. He said he hoped and believed it could be done.

Then he made a final check-up on the machinery already set up for pre-serving American neutrality, as well as for swinging military, naval and industrial forces into action in event of any unexpected emergency.

The President's promise to do all in his power to keep the nation at peace was given as he gravely faced his ▶

regular Friday morning press conference. There was little he could say at this critical period in the world's history, he remarked, except to appeal to the newspapermen present for their full cooperation in adhering as closely as possible to the facts, since this was best not only for this nation but for civilization as a whole.

In this regard, the President set an example for his auditors. He said what he had to say without attempting to minimize or exaggerate the gravity of the European situation. He appeared to be neither exuberant nor depressed by the turn of events that kept him from his bed for all but a few hours last night. Occasionally he was humorous, but throughout his manner was calm.

WOULD "ALLAY ANXIETY"

Later in the day the President let it be known that he would address the nation over the three major broadcasting networks on Sunday night from 10 to 10:15 o'clock, Eastern daylight time, in an effort "to allay anxiety and relieve suspense." Stephen T. Early, his secretary, who hurried back to Washington from a brief vacation today, said Mr. Roosevelt would speak on international affairs in a manner that would "clearly state our position" and would be of international interest.

The President began his memorable press conference with the explanation that there was little if anything he could say on such anticipated questions as when he would call a special session of Congress and issue a neutrality proclamation. These things, he explained, would have to await developments "over there" during the day, and possibly tomorrow, which would have a direct bearing on any American action.

But if any one had any questions that he was able to answer, Mr. Roosevelt said, he would answer gladly. A reporter observed that the question uppermost in everyone's mind just now was: "Can we keep out of it?" The President cast his eyes downward for a moment as he pondered the request for comment. Then he replied:

"Only this—that I not only sincerely hope so, but I believe we can, and that every effort will be made by the Administration to so do."

The President consented readily when permission was asked to quote him directly on his statement. ◆

FRANCE MOBILIZES; 8,000,000 ON CALL
Martial Law Declared Over Entire Country—Daladier Meets Deputies Today

By P. J. PHILIP
Wireless to The New York Times.

PARIS, Sept. 2 (Passed by Censor)— France's reply to Germany's violation of Poland was to decree general mobilization for this morning, establish martial law throughout the country and convoke Parliament for 3 P.M. today so as legally to carry out whatever must be done.

These decrees were approved at a Cabinet council held during yesterday morning without midnight secrecy or undue haste.

ULTIMATUM ORDERED

In the evening the government gave instructions to Ambassador Robert Coulondre in Berlin to hand to the Wilhelmstrasse an ultimatum in terms analogous to and in the same sense as the British note which, Prime Minister Chamberlain announced during the afternoon, had been handed in by the British Ambassador.

Only cessation of hostilities in Poland at this time could enable an international conference such as has been suggested to be set up, and hope of such a happening is frail.

There was much speculation tonight as to whether Premier Daladier will alter and enlarge his Cabinet, but the Premier has taken no one into his confidence. It is not possible now to predict that any "Sacred Union" Cabinet will be formed as was done in 1914.

RELIED UPON BY POLES

From the Polish Ambassador, Julius Lukasiewicz, Foreign Minister Georges Bonnet learned officially that fire had been opened by German troops along the Polish frontier at 5:45 o'clock yesterday morning, that airplanes had attacked several centers and that Poland, feeling her independence endangered, placed her reliance on France to fulfill her engagements.

This information and request confirmed news that had been pouring out from the German radio since before 8 A.M. when Albert Forster, Danzig's chief of state, handed over the Free City to Germany, an event followed by the Reichstag meeting and Chancellor Hitler's speech.

FORMALITIES OBSERVED

Even as early as that there was no doubt

Nazi Efforts Centered on Preventing Spread of Conflict to the Rest of Europe
HITLER EXPECTED TO REJECT TERMS

Acceptance of Ultimatum of Britain and France Said to Be Out of the Question
'LITTLE WAR' IS NAZI AIM

Wireless to The New York Times.

BERLIN, Saturday, Sept. 2— That Chancellor Hitler will accept the Anglo-French ultimatum is regarded here early this morning as out of the question.

In semi-official quarters it is regarded as out of the question because first, all efforts at peaceful solution have failed, even Prime Minister Chamberlain's own mediation effort, and, second, it is not Herr Hitler's way to leave "appeals" from Germans in Poland unheeded.

Thus Europe is plunged into a new if undeclared war which, for the moment, is still between Germany and Poland but which has already paralyzed the whole Continent, where more than

about the French retort, but formalities must be satisfied in a democratic country, which is not ruled by any personal pronoun. So diplomatic activity continued all during the day and Parliament must have its say simultaneously with the preparations being made by the military command.

General Marie Gustave Gamelin, supreme commander of French defense forces, was indeed the first at work yesterday morning, calling on Premier Daladier at 8:45. That was only the first of many meetings during the day. At the Ministry of Marine the Minister, Cesar Campinchi, was in conference with Vice Admiral Jean Darlan, commander of the navy.

It will not be until today, when certain diplomatic situations will have been cleared up and the Chamber of Deputies given its approval that the irrevocable choice between peace and war will be taken.

Meanwhile there is much insistence on what is described as the duplicity of Herr Hitler's presentation of his case. As on so many previous occasions both in internal and external relations, it is claimed he misrepresented facts and disregarded what did not suit his plans.

POINTS NEVER DELIVERED
In Thursday's broadcast of his sixteen points, which it is asserted he proposed for a settlement with Poland, it was stated that no answer had been received. Here it is said that unless they were contained in a document which Foreign Minister Joachim von Ribbentrop read hurriedly to British Ambassador Sir Nevile Henderson and of which he did not hand over a copy, they were never delivered.

Nevertheless on Wednesday evening the French Ambassador to Poland, Leon Noel, at the request of his government, asked Foreign Minister Josef Beck if he would make another effort at a direct settlement. M. Beck replied that he would and ordered his Ambassador in Berlin, Josef Lipski, to ask for an interview with Herr von Ribbentrop.

When M. Lipski did so he was asked whether he made this request as a plenipotentiary or as Ambassador, and at 7 o'clock Thursday evening he was received by Herr von Ribbentrop. It was only an hour and a half later that the German radio announced the German terms, which it declared had been rejected before they had been discussed and which were, in so far as the Polish Corridor was concerned, much more moderate than anything that had been proposed previously.

Herr Hitler's evident if not avowed demand, it is said, was that M. Beck should come hat in hand even more humbly than Chancellor Kurt Schuschnigg of Austria and Premier Milan Hodza of Czecho-Slovakia, and should be treated in an even more cavalier manner. Not having had his own way, Herr Hitler opened fire.

The intense diplomatic activity of the last few days here continued at increased pressure as Ambassadors and Ministers sought the latest information for their governments. The United States Ambassador, William C. Bullitt, was among the most active. He made several visits to the Foreign Office, on the second of which, at 1 o'clock, he transmitted President Roosevelt's strongly worded appeal to Germany and Poland.

Today's meeting of the Chamber of Deputies and Senate will be "for discussion of an important communication from the government." It is the second time within living memory that a decision will have to be taken by the elected representatives of France whether or not to go to war with Germany.

Today there will be the same union as there was in 1914. All party meetings which have been held have expressed approval of every step the government has taken.

Hope that peace could be and the belief that it might be arranged have died hard in many hearts. There are still some that think it can, in a sense, be limited to one front only, but there is not a doubt in any one's mind that in dealing with Hitlerian Germany there is now no alternative for France than to accept the challenge which has been thrown down in Poland. ◇

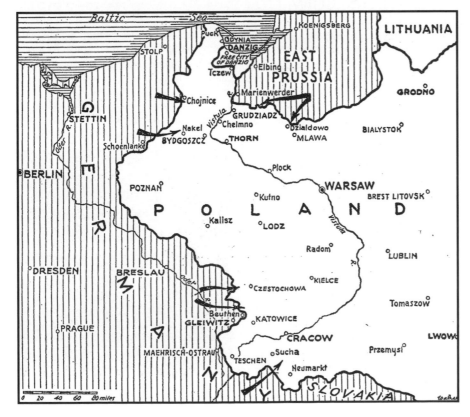

10,000,000 men are under arms, and which is rapidly expanding into a test of strength between resurgent Germany and the Western powers.

LOCAL WAR HELD AIM
At the moment, therefore, all German diplomatic efforts are now concentrated in localizing the conflict to keep it down to a "little war" and preventing its expansion into a big war. For that purpose, while emphasizing Herr Hitler's determination as expressed in his Reichstag speech to "win or die" in his struggle to revise the Versailles settlement in the East, all diplomatic quarters also stress the thesis that Germany does not want anything from the Western powers, least of all war with them.

With that end in view neither mobilization nor war has been declared so far and diplomatic contacts have continued in London throughout the day. ❯

Arrows indicate the advances of the Reich's forces in the north and south of Poland. The Germans hoped to crush Polish resistance before Western powers could interfere.

◀ Even the "theoretical" possibilities of further negotiations are held open, especially since Josef Lipski, the Polish envoy, is still in town, though assurances that Herr Hitler's sixteen points, announced Thursday, are still valid are declared to be impossible in view of the Polish rejection of them and military developments.

There is every indication that the possibility of localizing the conflict and keeping the western powers out is seriously entertained in German quarters, which hope to crush Poland's military resistance before the western powers intervene with force. And the press published yesterday many appeals to western statesmen to understand the meaning of the historic hour and to make right decisions that will create a better and more just peace.

But these hopes dimmed to the vanishing point when late yesterday afternoon Mr. Chamberlain's speech in the House of Commons became known with its virtual ultimatum to Germany to evacuate Poland or face the alternative of force being met with force in conformity with the doctrine proclaimed by Herr Hitler yesterday morning. Almost simultaneously with that speech Sir Nevile Henderson and Robert Coulondre, the British and French Ambassadors, called on Foreign Minister Joachim von Ribbentrop separately and delivered similar notes, which are believed to be in the same terms as Mr. Chamberlain's speech.

PREPARED FOR EVENTUALITIES
Semi-official quarters and the press declared Germany was prepared for all eventualities and trusted in Herr Hitler and the Germany Army implicitly. But it goes without saying that the entry of the Western powers would completely change the nature of the present conflict and put a strain on Germany's military and economic capacity, a test of which has yet to be made.

MANY RUSH TO SHELTER
The grim reality of the war was brought home to Germans shortly before 7 o'clock last night when sirens sent thousands scurrying to cover. In a few minutes the streets were completely deserted. There was no way for German residents or any one else to determine whether this was merely a trial or an attack. Natural anxiety was evident, but the regulations apparently were carried out to the letter. Less than half an hour later the lengthy wail of the siren announced that the danger had passed.

Berlin and other German cities will be blacked out indefinitely, by official order. Residents shout warnings to forgetful fellow-citizens who have neglected to cover their windows. A courteous German last night rang the bell of the American Church to inform the pastor that the interior rectory light was visible without suggesting that he cover the window or extinguish the light.

The Reich Civilian Air-Raid Defense Corps was fully mobilized for emergency service. The elevated trains used lights so dim that it was barely possible to discern the features of fellow-passengers. All street lights were extinguished. Fire apparatus, moreover, was stationed at key points.

CAFES DO BIG BUSINESS
Cafes did a rousing business all yesterday. The crowds were quiet and last night small groups were seen standing in the darkened streets eagerly conversing in hushed voices. Yesterday was the first "fish day" which, in the future, will be every Tuesday and Friday. Menus in even the larger hotels frequented by government, party and military leaders were reduced and the rationing system for most essentials is now in full force.

Vehicle owners fortunate enough to have received fuel for their cars were informed that the cars could be used only in life-or-death cases. Pleasure rides are forbidden. Taxis can be obtained only when necessity obviates other means of transportation.

Work clothes were removed from the restricted list and are now purchasable without ration cards. ◆

SEPTEMBER 3, 1939

NEUTRALITY VOTED BY DAIL AT DUBLIN
De Valera Gives Partition as Reason but Hears Strong Opposition In Session

By HUGH SMITH
Special Cable to The New York Times.

DUBLIN, Sept. 2—The Dail Eireann tonight approved Prime Minister Eamon de Valera's policy of neutrality in the event of a European war and gave his government the sweeping wartime powers that have been asked.

In his speech to the Dail, Mr. de Valera hinted that it might be necessary to reshuffle his Cabinet and create a special Ministry to control supplies. Arrangements were also being made tonight to establish a press censorship forthwith. For a State that proposes to remain neutral the Administration is abrogating ordinary constitutional rights to a degree equal to that of a country engaged in actual warfare.

Despite Ireland's remoteness from Central Europe, Dublin, Cork and other large centers here were blacked out tonight, while armed military guards were placed on railways and public buildings.

Even in the face of these official precautions and the calling up of army reserves, the people here refuse to believe that there is any immediate danger that Ireland will come within the war zone. In fact, ships from England today were again heavily laden with women and children coming to find sanctuary here.

FOOD SUPPLY A PARADOX
Just how far Ireland can maintain her neutrality and send food supplies to Britain is a question that is exercising many minds here. If hostilities with Germany develop on a large scale it is recognized that the export of farm produce from Ireland to Britain and the importation of supplies for Ireland industries from England could be carried on only under the protection of the British fleet. Mr. de Valera himself admitted in the Dail that the preservation of neutrality while having close trade relations with Britain would present many difficult and delicate problems.

OPPOSITION IS EXPRESSED
In the Senate tonight Mr. de Valera heard opposition to his neutrality policy. Sena-

Eamon De Valera

SEPTEMBER 3, 1939

CAN THE UNITED STATES KEEP OUT OF THE WAR?

By HAROLD B. HINTON

WASHINGTON, Sept. 2—The questioner who asked President Roosevelt at his press conference yesterday whether the United States can stay out of the European war was demanding of the Chief Executive the powers of a soothsayer. The President made the oracular response—which is the only one possible—that he hoped and believed the country could stay clear and that his Administration would do all that lay in its power to keep it clear.

There is no secret about which side in the conflict enjoys the sympathy of President Roosevelt, Secretary of State Hull, the entire Administration, nearly all of Congress and the overwhelming majority of the American public. The President's job in the difficult days to come will resemble that of Woodrow Wilson in 1914, 1915 and 1916 in that he must, to carry out his promise of yesterday, try to curb the natural sentimental reactions of public opinion in order to follow a pragmatic course of conduct that will have as its goal only the enlightened self-interest of the United States.

QUESTION OF WAR GUILT

So far as public opinion can be gauged here, there is every indication that the American people do not want to be involved in the European war as it stands at this writing.

Professional feelers of pulses believe that this frame of public mind will continue for some time—perhaps for a year or more. Then, the accumulation of dislikes (likes are not very important in determining mass psychology in wartime, experts believe) will bring national reaction to a focal point.

The question of war guilt has already been argued, and it will be a subject for argument in the free forums of American public opinion for a long time. Chancellor Hitler, replying to President Roosevelt's peace appeals, asserted that he had tried in every conceivable manner, including an acceptance of the British offer of mediation, to arrive at a peaceable solution, but that the Poles were too determined on armed arbitrament.

Prime Minister Chamberlain, in his speech to the House of Commons yesterday, was equally certain that the German Chancellor had done nothing of the kind and that on the Fuehrer's shoulders rested the responsibility for the catastrophe that seemed about to engulf Europe.

FINGER POINTED AT HITLER

Even those who have disagreed with Mr. Roosevelt's foreign policy concede that he has consistently pointed to Chancellor Hitler as the potential aggressor who might plunge the whole world into war. The President's conviction on this score, which has been fully shared by Mr. Hull, has been expressed on repeated occasions in language that was not even veiled by the niceties of official usage.

In his struggles with Congress the President has tried to keep before the eyes of the legislators the spectacle he envisaged of a growth in aggression, whether military, political or economic, which would eventually involve the interests of the United States. That is to say, he foresaw a time, even if that should be years and years ahead, when the United States would have to decide, perhaps all alone, whether it could live in a world where brute force was the only determinant.

Believing that this country's answer would be in the negative, when and if the issue were directly posed, the President has tried to lead the nation into taking part in the prevention of the very situation which has now arisen. He has had little success.

The United States Government has undoubtedly taken greater precautions than were dreamed of in 1914 to cushion the impact of European war on this country's national life. Plans drawn in advance (largely as a result of the war scare preceding the Munich agreement of last September) have thus far worked efficiently to promote the evacuation of American citizens from danger zones, to keep the financial structure of the country, including the Stock Exchanges, functioning as nearly normally as possible, and to approach closely as that can be done to "business as usual."

There has been complete absence of hysteria on the part of hard-worked and sleepless officials. Each one appeared to know in advance what he was supposed to do and has done it. The advent of the current European situation undoubtedly found the United States in a much better state of preparation than was the case twenty-five years ago.

Even under these favorable conditions, however, there has been an appreciable upset in the nation's normal routine in the two days that hostilities have been actually under way. Stock and bond quotations fluctuated up and down. Investors and speculators were trying to divine what the value of these securities would be in a world pretty generally involved in war.

UPSET TO NATION

The mere fact of cutting off telephonic communication with most of the continent of Europe, for private users, had an unsettling social and economic effect. Distressed Americans were unable to talk with relatives traveling or living in Europe. Merchants and bankers were unable to conclude quick deals involving profits to be made only with dispatch.

Thus, if Congress should come into session immediately the isolationists would be in a confused situation. They would have to admit that the war makes some difference to the United States. On the other hand, ›

---

tor Sir John Keane, Deputy Governor of the Bank of Ireland, declared that the Conservative and property-owning classes were much dissatisfied with the attitude of neutrality. If Ireland, he said, came out openly with the other Dominions of the British Commonwealth on the side of the democracies that act would do much to unite the country and break down the barriers dividing it.

Also opposing neutrality was Senator Frank MacDermott, who said:

"There is not a single country in the world whose spiritual and material interests are so immediately affected by this war as our own. If Britain, France and Poland are defeated everything the Irish race has stood for spiritually will go down and this country will be reduced to a state of rags and beggary that it has not known for centuries."

PARTITION IS EMPHASIZED

In his speech Mr. de Valera stressed that the partition of Ireland was a stumbling block to any whole-hearted cooperation with Britain.

"I know," he said, "that there are strong sympathies in this country with regard to the present issue, but I do not think that any one would suggest that the official policy of this State should be other than neutrality."

So many American citizens have been left here awaiting ships home that United States Consul William Small at Cork has found it necessary to issue a public appeal asking for lodgings for them. This announcement suggests that Americans returning home from Europe may find Ireland a suitable place to await transport across the Atlantic. ◇

they would be prodded by a measurable segment of public opinion at home urging them to keep out of "that mess" at all costs, the implication to them being that the best thing to do would be to do nothing.

FLUIDITY IN OUR POLICY

All of these divergent thoughts must course through President Roosevelt's mind as he weighs the best path to follow in these early days of the conflict. In this time of lightning developments he has resolved, and has told his helpers to resolve, that fluidity of policy is of the essence. Every department and agency in Washington is on an hour-to-hour basis for an indeterminate period.

For the moment the war news naturally outweighs all else in importance here. For the moment the 1940 Presidential campaign has been forgotten, but that situation will not last long. The President will have to appease fears that he will exploit the situation in favor of a third-term candidacy, or for the purpose of perpetuating the Democratic party in power, as time goes on.

Just now it can be reported that national anxiety has produced at least a semblance of national unity behind the President's declared policy of keeping the country out of war. That is not to say that there will be lacking, a little later, tedious and tendentious arguments about the best way to realize that aim. ◇

SEPTEMBER 3, 1939

SOUTH AMERICANS SEE GAINS
They Hope Sale of Surpluses to Warring Nations Will Give Them Prosperity

By JOHN H. WHITE
Special Cable to The New York Times.

BUENOS AIRES, Argentina, Sept. 2— South America's reaction to the European conflict has been almost exclusively commercial. War means immediate wealth for virtually all South American countries by creating a heavy demand for their raw materials.

At present there are huge unsold stocks of almost all these raw materials in all South American countries. War in Europe, therefore, offers an easy, painless remedy for existing serious economic ills.

This would react favorably on more than one shaky government, as political troubles in South America are closely linked with economic troubles. When

times are good and prices stationary, almost any kind of government can stay in power. When prices fall and banks begin closing on notes and mortgages, it is difficult for any government to remain in office except by force.

BUSINESS MEN WANT WAR

It is no exaggeration to say business men—Britons, Americans and other foreigners, as well as Argentinians— welcome war. They make no attempt to hide their eagerness.

It is also true than many economists in government positions welcome war in Europe as an opportunity to get themselves and their governments out of some of the monetary and other financial and economic messes into which they have got themselves. But they are not openly expressing their hopes, as are business men.

With very few exceptions the economic ills of virtually all South American countries have been aggravated rather than alleviated by the remedies applied. In most cases these remedies have consisted of South American versions of directed economy measures designed in the United States, Great Britain and elsewhere to cure industrial ills. They have not worked when applied to non-industrial new countries that depend almost exclusively on agriculture and mining.

SEPTEMBER 3, 1939

London Kills Zoo Snakes Lest Air Raid Free Them

Wireless to The New York Times.

*LONDON, Sept. 2—*All poisonous snakes and insects and the deadly black widow spider at the London Zoo have been destroyed in case they should obtain their freedom during an air raid.

All the zoo's valuable animals are being evacuated to the Whipsnade Zoo in Bedfordshire. Ba-Bar, the baby elephant, made the journey there today. Two giant pandas, four of the eight chimpanzees who amuse children with their daily tea party, the rare zebras and the orangutans are already safely in their new home.

Thousands of Londoners are having pets destroyed at clinics, particularly dogs which would be terrified by gunfire. ◇

SEPTEMBER 4, 1939

Chamberlain Talk Announcing War

By The Associated Press.

*LONDON, Sept. 3—*Following is the text of the address by Prime Minister Chamberlain this morning:
I am speaking to you from the Cabinet Room from 10 Downing Street.

This morning the British Ambassador in Berlin handed to the German Government a final note stating that unless we heard from them by 11 o'clock that they were preparing at once to withdraw their troops from Poland a state of war would exist between us.

I have to tell you now that no such undertaking has been received and in consequence this country is at war with Germany.

You can imagine what a bitter blow it is to me that all my long struggle to win peace has failed.

Yet I cannot believe that there is anything more or anything different that I

could have done that would have been more successful.

Up to the very last it would have been quite possible to arrange a peaceful and honorable settlement between Germany and Poland but Chancellor Hitler would not have it.

He had evidently made up his mind to attack Poland whatever happened, although he now says that he put forward reasonable proposals which were rejected

British Prime Minister Nevile Chamberlain.

To say that business men greet with glee a war to put an end to such a situation is to put it mildly—provided the war occurs in Europe, of course.

With the exception of the Chaco war between Bolivia and Paraguay and several serious civil wars in Brazil, the present generation in South American countries does not know what war means. Even those that followed the United States into the World War on the side of the Allies felt none of war's suffering or hardships. They have no direct political interest in the present conflict in Europe and contemplate no trouble in maintaining a detached and profitable neutrality, unless the United States should be dragged in.

In that case several South American republics would undoubtedly join the same side as the United States, although probably not in an active role.

PREFER ITALIAN FASCISM

The ideology of Premier Mussolini and Generalissimo Francisco Franco of Spain has a much stronger appeal to South Americans than Chancellor Hitler's. Unless Italy or Spain becomes seriously involved, South American countries probably will have little difficulty in maintaining a purely academic interest in the political issues at stake. ◆

SEPTEMBER 4, 1939

ITALY FAILS TO ACT AS HER ALLY FIGHTS
Rome Plans to Stay Neutral Unless Attacked—Fascist Moves Kept Secret

By HERBERT L. MATTHEWS
Special Cable to The New York Times.

ROME, Sept. 4—Although Great Britain and France are at war with Germany, Italy has taken no step to join her Axis partner. She remains friendly to Germany but neutral, and she will make no move against the French and British unless attacked. This was made clear in Premier Mussolini's newspaper, the Popolo d'Italia, this morning, which reaffirmed the declaration of neutrality contained in the Council of Ministers' communiqué Friday.

Whether there is any possibility of Italy going beyond that attitude toward one side or the other cannot be stated yet, for the Italians continue to be completely secret. Since history always repeats itself, one may well suppose that the French and British are doing everything they can to win Italian benevolence, if not aid. That is the normal and natural thing for them to do whether they have hopes for success or not. After all, diplomatic relations between Rome and Paris and London continue on a friendly basis, and none need be surprised if André François-Poncet and Sir Percy Loraine, the French and British Ambassadors, who see Count Ciano, the Foreign Minister, so often these days, should be exerting their greatest efforts to win Italy away from Germany. It is their business to do so.

ATTITUDE IS NOT CHANGING

None can say yet what success, if any, they are having. So far as today is concerned there is that Popolo d'Italia article to go upon, which indicates clearly enough that Italy is not changing her attitude because Britain and France have entered the conflict. Although it was printed before those countries acted it was written at a time when there could be no doubt of what was going to happen.

The editorial begins by saying that the Council of Ministers' communiqué should be "re-read and meditated." Its words were "sculpted in stone," says the editorial, meaning that it was meant to last.

From Premier Mussolini's efforts for "peace with justice," two things are to be deduced. It continues:

First, that notwithstanding certain foreign interpretations which are too hasty or ingenuous nothing is changed on the plane of Italo-German friendship.

Second, that Signor Mussolini has worked not only for the solution of the German-Polish problem but for all other problems which like this one now being solved by arms, have their origin in the Versailles Treaty.

"It is therefore natural," the article goes on, "that whatever happens, whether the German-Polish conflict remains localized or spreads to a catastrophe, the Duce's work—that is to say the work that will give a just peace to the Italian people and Europe—continues."

There are two things about that editorial that should not be missed. One is insistence on the revising of the Versailles Treaty. The idea first cropped out August 30 in another Popolo d'Italia editorial, thought to have been written by Signor Mussolini himself. It was repeated in the Ministerial Council's communiqué and all Italian comment ▸

---

by the Poles. That is not a true statement.

The proposals were never shown to the Poles nor to us and although they were announced in the German broadcast on Thursday night Herr Hitler did not wait to hear comment on them but ordered his troops to cross the Polish frontier next morning.

His action shows convincingly that there is no chance of expecting that this man will ever give up his intention of using force to gain his will.

And he can only be stopped by force.

We and France are today, in fulfillment of our obligations, going to the aid of Poland, who is so bravely resisting this wicked and unprovoked attack on her people.

We have a clear conscience.

We have done all that any country could do to establish peace. But a situation in which no word given by Germany's ruler could be trusted and no people or country could feel itself safe has become intolerable.

And now we have resolved to finish it. I know you will all play your part with calm courage. At such a moment as this the assurances of support we have received from the empire are a source of profound encouragement to us.

When I have finished speaking certain detailed announcements will be made on behalf of the government. These need your close attention.

The government have made plans under which it will be possible to carry on the work of the nation in the days of stress and strain which may be ahead of us.

These plans need your help. You may be taking your part in the fighting services or as a volunteer in one of the branches of civil defense. If so, you will report for duty in accordance with the instructions you receive.

You may be engaged in work essential to the prosecution of the war, for maintenance of the life of people in factories, in transport and public utility concerns and in the supply of the other necessaries of life.

If so, it is of vital importance that you should carry on with your job.

Now may God bless you all and may He defend the right. For it is evil things that we shall be fighting against, brute force, bad faith, injustice, oppression and persecution. And against them I am certain that right will prevail. ◆

Benito Mussolini with Adolf Hitler, ca. 1939.

〈 yesterday, while today it is again emphasized. One should, therefore, feel entitled to believe that so far as Italy is concerned revision of the Versailles Treaty (by which Italians really mean the granting of what was promised to them in the Treaty of London) would satisfy her demands for "justice with peace." If she could get that "justice with peace" without fighting or by going with one or the other side, one must also suppose she would act accordingly.

Premier Edouard Daladier of France in his speech before the Chamber of Deputies Saturday made clear the overtures to Italy. After paying homage to the "noble efforts" of the Italian Government on behalf of peace he said "if the attempt at conciliation were renewed we are ready to associate ourselves with it."

Italy's claims are chiefly against France and if the French were now willing to rectify them there is little doubt that M. Francois-Poncet has been telling Count Ciano that in the last few days. However, both French and British embassies deny that there was any contact with the Foreign Minister today.

The other thing to note in the Popolo d'Italia's editorial is its insistence that Signor Mussolini is continuing his peace work. Signor Mussolini's first openly mentioned peace work was the cessation of hostilities and the five-power conference, to which Viscount Halifax, British Foreign Secretary, referred Saturday. It was turned down regretfully and no mention that it was an Italian peace move has appeared in this country's press.

However, it is important to note that this was not an Axis move, it was an Italian move. Italy did not intervene to give Germany what she wanted; Italy intervened for peace. In so doing Italy took a stand at variance with Germany's.

Further than that one cannot go, and, indeed, the official attitude is that "nothing is changed on the plane of Italo-German friendship." The press continues its violent support of Germany, although at the same time it prints Polish official communiqués in full. The Polish diplomatic staff incidentally remains here and continues, apparently, on friendly relations with the Ministry of Foreign Affairs.

There has been one war measure announced here today—starting today dance halls will be closed. ◊

SEPTEMBER 4, 1939

CANADA DECLARES AUTOMATIC ENTRY
Prime Minister King on Radio Asserts Necessity of Step— Arrest of Nazis Begun

By JOHN MacCORMAC
Special to The New York Times.

OTTAWA, Sept. 3—On the principle that "when Britain is at war, Canada is at war," first laid down by the great French-Canadian Prime Minister, Sir Wilfred Laurier, Canada automatically entered the struggle against Hitlerism at 6 o'clock this morning when the British ultimatum to Berlin expired.

Canada's entry had been a foregone conclusion since French-Canada's chief representative in the present government, Minister of Justice Ernest Lapointe, had told Parliament last March that neutrality would be impossible for the Dominion in practice if the mother country were engaged.

It became certain on Friday when Prime Minister Mackenzie King cabled Prime Minister Neville Chamberlain that his government would recommend effective wartime cooperation with Britain to the Dominion Parliament.

Today nothing still remained to be decided but the degree of Canadian participation. Events and the wishes of the British Government are likely to play so large a part in this that it is quite likely Mr. King's recommendations to the special session of Parliament, called for Thursday, may not include the immediate dispatch of even a volunteer expeditionary force.

"Our first concern," said Prime Minister King in a broadcast speech late in the afternoon, "is with the defense of Canada. To be helpful to others we must ourselves be strong, secure and united. Our effort will be voluntary."

SUPPLY ORGANIZATION SPED

In the process of defending herself Canada will recruit new soldiers and train them. Later, if and when the British Government indicates the need for an expeditionary force and it becomes apparent that Canada is in no great danger of attack, there is no doubt that such a force will be sent.

Meanwhile, the Dominion will organize herself as a source of supply of food and war essentials.

At 9 A.M. the Canadian Cabinet met to put Canada for the second time in twenty-five years on a war footing. A

SEPTEMBER 4, 1939

AUSTRALIA AT WAR, RESOLVED TO WIN
Many Volunteer For Service in Commonwealth Forces as Units Are Called

Wireless to The New York Times.

MELBOURNE, Australia, Sept. 3— Prime Minister Robert G. Menzies announced tonight that Australia was at war with Germany.

The Prime Minister acted after he had broadcast a statement announcing that the Commonwealth would join Britain in war on the Reich. The proclamation declaring Australia in a state of war with Germany was signed by the Governor General, Lord Gowrie, at an urgent meeting of the Executive Council tonight.

Brigadier Geoffrey A. Street, Defense Minister, announced that the navy air force had been fully mobilized on a war basis and that a number of militia units had been called up for special duty, but that no immediate call would be made for recruits.

WAR PLANS ARE RUSHED

The Ministers, who had gone to Canberra for a meeting of Parliament Wednesday, immediately set in motion the last phases of the Commonwealth's war plans.

Speaking over 125 national and commercial stations at 9:15 P.M., Mr. Menzies said:

"It is my melancholy duty to announce officially that in consequence of Germany's persistence in her invasion of Poland, Britain has declared war, and as a result Australia also is at war.

"Britain and France with the cooperation of the dominions struggled to avoid this tragedy. They have patiently kept the door to negotiation open and have given no cause for aggression, but their efforts failed. We, therefore, as a great family of nations involved in the struggle must at all costs win, and we believe in our hearts that we will win."

Mr. Menzies outlined the course of recent events in Europe and declared it would exhibit the history of some of the most remarkable instances of ruthlessness and indifference to common humanity that the darkest centuries of European history could scarcely parallel and demonstrate that Adolf Hitler had steadily pursued a policy deliberately designed to produce either war or the subjugation of one country after another by the threat of war.

"Bitter as we all feel at this wanton crime," Mr. Menzies concluded, "this moment is not for rhetoric but for quiet thinking and that calm fortitude which rests on the unconquerable spirit of man created by God in His image. The truth is with us in the battle; truth must win. In the bitter months ahead, calmness, resoluteness, confidence and hard work will be required as never before.

"Our staying power, particularly that of the mother country, will be best assisted by keeping production going as fully as we can and maintaining our strength. Australia is ready to see it through. May God in His mercy and compassion grant that the world will soon be delivered from this agony."

A steady stream of men is calling at military headquarters offering their services, but so far only militia personnel, coast defenses, anti-aircraft batteries and other units required to protect vulnerable areas have been called. Members of the citizen air force have been called and also certain members of the Royal Australian Air Force Reserve.

While German citizens will be liable to internment a large proportion of the refugees will be allowed liberty, subject to strict surveillance.

NEW ZEALAND COME IN

Wireless to The New York Times.

*WELLINGTON, N. Z., Sept. 4—*Governor General Viscount Galway this morning proclaimed that New Zealand was at war with Germany and would give the fullest consideration to British suggestions as to the methods by which the common cause might best be aided.

DIVISION IN SOUTH AFRICA

Special Cable to The New York Times.

CAPE TOWN, South Africa, Sept. 4— The Union Cabinet, scheduled to meet this morning, is reported to be split over the question of supporting Britain in the war with Germany.

There was a prolonged Cabinet meeting last night and it is understood that the members were divided seven to six in favor of cooperation with the British Commonwealth as opposed to neutrality. ◆

6-year-old girl leading a spotted dog was the only lay spectator. But as the hours passed crowds and camera men gathered.

ARMY CHIEF ARRIVES

They saw Major Gen. T. V. Anderson, Chief of the General Staff, in civilian clothes but with an empty coat sleeve to proclaim his trade, dash up in a motor car to join the Cabinet conclave.

Not until he had listened to King George's speech to the Empire did Prime Minister King emerge. He returned in the afternoon to make his broadcast appeal to Canadians for a united war effort.

Already the streets of this capital were echoing with bugle calls, but they were a call to the colors by a local militia unit. From all over Canada come reports of active recruiting. The young men are joining up with as much readiness as in 1914.

The end of Hitlerism was the only issue in this war, Prime Minister King told the Canadian people.

ACTIVE NAZIS ARRESTED

The Canadian Mounted Police, reinforced by 500 former members, have started arresting active Nazis in Canada. They will be sent to internment camps if their numbers require such action.

The government reiterated, however, that the war would not be allowed to make any differences to United States citizens who wish to come to Canada, either on business or as tourists. Commenting on a report that Colonial Airways had asked New Yorkers flying to Canada to bring their passports, F. C. Blair, director of immigration, said this was totally unnecessary.

An appointment which met wide approval was that of Walter Thompson, publicity chief of the Canadian National Railways and chief press officer on the royal pilot train during the recent royal visit, as chief press censor.

Press censorship, delayed while the government awaited Britain's declaration of war, goes into effect tomorrow and the partial radio censorship will become more stringent and widespread. ◆

Editorial
WAR GUILT

The publication of the full exchange of messages between the British and German Governments from Aug. 22 and the terrible events of the last few days only serve to make it clearer than ever that the sole responsibility for the present catastrophe rests on the shoulders of one man—Adolf Hitler.

If this correspondence is published in Germany—and especially if, as seems more likely, the German end of the correspondence alone is published there— no doubt millions of Germans, with no outside sources of information, may continue to think that Hitler's course was justified. They can do so only if their memories have forgotten the events of the last few years and wiped out the trail of broken pledges that Hitler left behind him in his series of diplomatic advances.

The correspondence reveals an ever patient and persistent Chamberlain, seizing upon every hope of pacific adjustment, and a Hitler finally determined to carry his threats to the point of actual war and stooping to new depths of brazen mendacity for the effect upon his own people. So reasonable and patient were the messages of Chamberlain and of the British Ambassador, that Hitler was driven to pretend that it was vital for Germany that the questions at issue should be settled, not merely in a matter of weeks, or even days, but of hours. To make this pretext look anything but ridiculous he coolly invented "killings" and "barbaric actions of maltreatment" (of the German population in Poland) "which cry to heaven." It was precisely the technique adopted in alleging Czech persecutions a year before.

The only message from the German Government that is written in a tone of reason—though it still demanded return of Danzig and a German corridor through the Corridor—is the proposed "sixteen-point" settlement of the Polish question which the German Foreign Minister read to the British Ambassador at top speed at midnight on Aug. 30. It is now entirely obvious that this "offer" was never intended for serious two-sided discussion, but was merely framed as a propaganda document for the benefit of a German people already plunged into war. When the British Ambassador, hearing it for the first time, asked for the text, he was told that it was already too late, as a Polish plenipotentiary had not arrived in Berlin by that midnight as had been demanded by the German Government.

This demand had been handed to the British Ambassador only the evening before. The British, in their note two days previously (Aug. 28) had already informed the German Government that they had "received definite assurance from the Polish Government that they are prepared to enter into discussions." The German Government could then have sent for the Polish Ambassador; but it demanded instead that within twenty-four hours after its note to the British (which made no mention of the later announced sixteen points) the Poles send an emissary "empowered not only to discuss but to conduct and conclude negotiations." No doubt if the Poles had been willing or able to comply, this emissary would have been treated as Schuschnigg and others had been before him. This technique could not be used on a mere Ambassador, and Hitler apparently had little hope that he could work it again in any case, for he set a time schedule with which it was virtually impossible for the British or Poles to comply.

One internal evidence of the fraudulent character of the whole German negotiations is significant. In the sixteen-point proposal Hitler and von Ribbentrop declare their willingness to wait as long as twelve months—in fact, insist on at least that period—before the plebiscite to settle the fate of the Corridor. Yet in their messages to the British they declare that it is impossible to wait more than two days for the arrival of the Polish negotiator they had demanded!

Even after Hitler had launched his attack on Poland and bombarded open towns, the British and French held off from announcing a state of war for two days, advising the German Government that if it would agree to withdraw its forces Great Britain "would be willing to regard the position as being the same as it was before the German forces crossed the frontier" and would be open to discussion on the matters between the German and Polish Governments.

This time the record could hardly be clearer than it is. ◇

HULL ISSUES ORDER

NEUTRALITY EDICTS
Proclamations of Our Status and Arms Ban to Be Issued Today

Special to The New York Times.

WASHINGTON, Sept. 4—Following upon the heels of the sinking of the Athenia yesterday the United States took its first sweeping step to insure neutrality in the European war when Secretary Hull tonight issued an order drastically restricting travel by Americans to and

HITLER 'REPORTED' AS MENTALLY ILL
Professor H. C. Steinmetz Says This Statement Was Made by a 'Leading Physician'

By The Associated Press.

PALO ALTO, Calif., Sept. 6—Before a group of social psychologists, Professor Harry C. Steinmetz of San Diego State College repeated today what he termed "a report or calumny" that Adolf Hitler was suffering from a severe mental disorder and was under the almost constant care of an physician.

Professor Steinmetz said that the statement was made to him by "a leading American research physician, recently returned from Germany." He did not name the physician.

Secretary Cordell Hull, signing the Neutrality Proclamation, 1939.

from Europe.

Under the order, issued unexpectedly this evening, "imperative necessity" must be proved by any prospective traveler to Europe before a passport can be obtained. On return to this country the passport will be taken up and locked in the State Department. In no case shall a passport be granted for more than a six-month visit.

Minute details of the reason for a journey to Europe must be supplied, as well as of the identity of the applicant. Documentary evidence must be furnished as to the imperativeness of the trip. False or misleading statements will be punished by a fine up to $2,000, imprisonment up to five years, or both.

DECISION MADE ON PROCLAMATIONS

Meanwhile President Roosevelt and his Cabinet decided that the United States Government would declare its neutrality in the war tomorrow in two proclamations, one setting forth the status of this nation as a neutral under international law and the other establishing an arms embargo against present belligerents as required by our neutrality statute.

The decision to this effect was reached at a specially called Cabinet meeting this afternoon, at which means for convoying American nationals safely home and for putting a ban on war-profiteering in this country were also discussed.

The order by Secretary Hull in regard to travel by Americans came after he had conferred with President Roosevelt. The restriction on Americans traveling to Europe was regarded here as a far-reaching move to prevent this country being drawn into the conflict through the presence of her citizens on foreign flag ships attacked by a belligerent.

That part of the departmental order requiring the return of passports to the State Department was taken as a definite step to prevent these valuable identification documents from finding their way into the hands of spies or other agents of foreign governments. ◊

The report "or calumny" said that Hitler's affliction was paranoid manic depression. It is a supposedly incurable mental disease which causes its victims to have alternate fits of depression and elation, complicated by delusions that they are being persecuted.

Professor Steinmetz, addressing a division of the American Psychological Association, made the remark in a technical discussion of what he termed increasing paranoid conditions.

He asserted that whole peoples or groups were being subjected to a sort of national paranoid infection—that is, in their collective thinking and acting, particularly under prolonged, unusual stress.

Erroneous beliefs, he said, became a center of paranoid infection, especially under social disorganization and tension. Such stresses, he added, might cause people to take refuge in delusions, in "rationalizations" or excuse making, or in "defense mechanisms," described as mental tendencies designed to thwart expected trouble.

Such centers of infection, he added, could facilitate the spread of paranoid conditions among individuals, making their social organization progressively more dependent upon the very persons affected.

Features of paranoid conditions which he named included delusions of grandeur as well as of persecution; "retrospective falsification," a chronic course through suspicion, retreat and defense to delusion, illusion and attack.

Discussing recent potential modifications of the definition of "paranoia," Professor Steinmetz referred to the Oxford Group and "the bourgeois moral rearmament craze" as being "within the hypothetical classification of euphoric paranoidal delusion." ◊

SEPTEMBER 7, 1939

GERMAN INDUSTRIES PUT ON A WAR BASIS

Long Lists of Regulations Are Being Issued Daily

Wireless to The New York Times.

BERLIN, Sept. 6—The mobilization of Germany's industrial organization is proceeding at top speed. Long lists of specific regulations for different industries are published daily. They are designed to turn German business life into a unified mechanism for the most efficient carrying on of the war.

Workers who will be forced to change jobs, leaving unessential industries to augment labor in the essential ones, will no longer receive the same wages that they received in their original jobs as they have in the past. They must accept the wage scale of the new industry in which they are placed. The Reich Labor Organization will give weekly allowances up to 19 marks for those whose new jobs necessitate their living away from home.

Those who have incurred special obligations, which the wage scale of their new jobs makes them unable to meet, will receive financial assistance in order to meet these obligations.

The new impost of 50 per cent of one's income is meant to apply to all income whether derived from wages, salary or otherwise, according to the newly issued explanation of the original "war economy" decree issued Monday. This means that in addition to having to take a reduction in wages, workers must also pay a higher tax on earnings.

The new "Reich compulsory service law" issued today obligates manufacturers to operate their businesses as directed by the government in the best interests of the nation as decreed by the latter's agencies.

Berliners already are being deprived of their little luxuries on a scale un- ❯

known hitherto even under the Nazi régime. Tobacco and cigars are more expensive and unobtainable in some districts where would-be purchasers found all tobacconists "closed for stock-taking."

Berlin beer, never the stoutest of brews, is 20 per cent thinner. ◆

SEPTEMBER 10, 1939

PLEDGE AT LONDON
Ministry's Declaration Sets Plans for Britain To Fight to End

By FREDERICK T. BIRCHALL
Special Cable to The New York Times.

LONDON, Sept. 9—This highly significant official statement of government policy, the most important made for Great Britain since Prime Minister Neville Chamberlain announced that this country was at war, was issued tonight:

At their meeting this morning the War Cabinet decided to base their policy on the assumption that the war will last three years or more.

Instructions are being issued to all government departments to insure that plans for the future shall at once be prepared on this assumption.

In the meantime all measures for which preparation has already been made are being brought fully into active operation.

In furtherance of the expanded defense programs already operating, the Minister of Supply will forthwith take the necessary steps to insure that productive capacity for munitions of all kinds is increased on the scale required to meet every possible issue.

Corresponding arrangements are being made at the Admiralty and the Air Ministry.

In the great national interest, however, the civil needs of the country will be borne in mind as well as the importance of maintaining the export trade.

The War Cabinet are confident that this significant decision will meet with the whole-hearted support of the British people and will be welcomed by their allies and friends.

A REPLY OF DOUBLE FORCE

This is the British Government's emphatic and unmistakable answer to suggestions thrown out in the day's speech by Field Marshal Hermann Goering, published here, that in the light of German successes to date, Great Britain might be prepared to reconsider her position with regard to peace or war.

It is also a reply to certain wishful thinkers here who have been taking at face value the well-promulgated rumors of discontent inside the German lines, of food riots and strikes of women in the German cities, which inner official circles in London appraise at their actual worthlessness.

It is an answer, in fact, that once more carries mature men with good memories back to the somewhat analogous situation in 1914, when the wishful thinkers of that day were confidently asserting that the war would be finished in six months, until Earl Kitchener, rising in his place in the House of Lords, electrified the nation by soberly announcing that it would be, not a short, but a long war, carried on to the finish, "if not by us, then by those who come after us and take our place in the conflict."

In official quarters the emphasis is being laid, not so much on the assumption in the Cabinet statements that the war will last three years or more, but on the pledge that Great Britain is determined to see it through. In this there is not the slightest doubt that the government expresses the firm resolve of the nation as a whole.

The answer to Field Marshal Goering is a quite secondary matter. His speech, which, apart from his appeal to Britain to reconsider her position, is regarded here as a curious mixture of braggadocio and reasonableness, has happened to come at a time when an unequivocal declaration of the British position was needed. Goering's speech furnished an excuse for making it.

Obviously, as it seems here, Field Marshal Goering was making, none too skillfully, another attempt to divide Britain and France, a manoeuvre that has cropped out frequently in recent German propaganda.

His exaggerations of the undoubted success which has so far attended the overwhelming and wonderfully well equipped German attack on Poland and his deliberate minimizing of the powers of resistance still inherent in the still unbroken Polish Army is regarded as characteristic of the man and his party and not worth a serious effort at refutation.

The real point of the Goering speech, it is felt, lies in its appeal to Prime Minister Chamberlain.

GERMAN HOPES CALLED MISTAKEN

Evidently the German leaders are still hoping against hope that the Franco-British resolution to fight Nazism to the bitter end is not irrevocable. They will soon learn how mistaken that hope is.

As to the war operations thus far, the preliminary moves on the Western Front can scarcely be intelligently analyzed here, because so little that is really authoritative is known about them.

For the moment the real center of activity is still Poland; and the situation there is not yet so desperate as the German propagandists—who yesterday were professing that Warsaw was already in their possession when it wasn't—would have it.

The facts to date seem to be that the Germans invaded Poland with some fifty or sixty divisions. Of this huge and marvelously equipped force, some ten divisions were completely mechanized and therefore able to move extremely fast. The German success is regarded here as largely due to this factor.

Another factor largely in the Germans' favor was their overwhelming superiority in the air, which enabled their planes to break up Polish counter-attacks before they had time to develop and to paralyze the valuable efforts developing in the back areas.

By using thirty of their divisions there, the Germans were able almost at the outset to seize the great Silesian area containing the richest supply of Poland's raw materials.

Meanwhile their mechanized divisions from Pomerania drove eastward across the Corridor, while from East Prussia ten divisions advanced southwest. The big pincers move was aimed to lop off the great manufacturing area west of Warsaw.

But it is not over yet. Warsaw has been holding out; and Poland is likely to keep the German armies busy for some time to come, while the French press the advantages they have already gained on the Western Front.

And meanwhile the German leaders—and the German public, if it is ever permitted to know the facts—have something to think about in the firm expression of Britain's high resolve, just made. ◆

SEPTEMBER 10, 1939

ALL OF LIFE IN BRITAIN TRANSFORMED BY WAR
A Theatreless London Goes Black at Night and the Country, Filled With Refugees, Experiences a Rebirth

By JAMES B. RESTON
Wireless to The New York Times.

LONDON, Sept. 9—The world's largest city folds up every night now just like London, Ohio. After a week of war there is not a single play or movie in town; there is not a chink of light in Piccadilly Circus; the big restaurants arc deserted, and the boys didn't even play football in London today.

The only establishment that seems to have gained by the government's decision to keep theatres and sports events closed—the theory is that a single bomb might kill hundreds if they were packed together—is the "pub." There is definitely a boom in the drink business and already some persons are worried.

"Drink in excess may be an ally of the enemy," warns The Evening Standard darkly, and adds:

"The open door at the public house is partly due to the closed entrance at the cinema and the locked turnstiles at Chelsea and Highbury. The cinemas are still open in Warsaw and Paris. Madrid watched Charlie Chaplin when Franco was beating at the gates of the city....We don't want to fiddle while Europe burns. But we will fight none the worse for an occasional glimpse of Ginger Rogers."

George Bernard Shaw has been firing his merry shafts at the government for this theatre decision, too. He not only wants the theatres opened but more theatres built and all actors exempted from military service. He calls the government's decision "a masterstroke of unimaginative stupidity." This pressure forced slight modifications yesterday, and from now on Ginger Rogers will be fighting on the Allied side—at least in a few safe areas on the outskirts of the city.

TO IMAGINE NEW YORK–
The best way to understand what has happened to London this week is to imagine what New York would be like under similar conditions.

If you can possibly imagine all the youngsters from the lower East Side and Hell's Kitchen and Brooklyn and the Bronx suddenly thrown into every corner of every safe mansion in Westchester and upper New York State and New Jersey you will have a vague idea of what the evacuation was like....

If you can imagine those white New York ambulances rolling up to Gotham Hospital on East Seventy-sixth Street and to Bronx Maternity and Women's Hospital on the Concourse and to every other hospital in town, rolling up and carrying away every patient who could possibly be moved you will know something about this tragic exodus....

If you can see the people in those walk-ups on the river streets shoveling sand and dirt into burlap sacks and piling them up at their miserable windows....and see carpenters nailing boards over the windows of every store on every street in town you will know what has been going on in front of every door here all week....

If you could watch Manhattan suddenly fill up with thousands of young boys in uniform, young lads of 20 running for trains in Grand Central Station and manning anti-aircraft guns and digging trenches in Central Park you would understand what London is doing right now....

If you saw, like some fabulous picture on a popular science magazine cover, silver anti-aircraft balloons floating night and day above the skyscrapers....

And if at 9:30 o'clock it got darker than you had ever seen Manhattan and every light on the Great White Way went out and every movie and every single show closed, and cars crept along dark streets in second gear with only vague blue lights showing on the ground, you would have a glimmer of an idea of what a London blackout is like....

A STRAIN ON THE PEOPLE
For all these things are happening in London tonight and the people in the city are grim and strained.

From start to finish the business of buying and selling and living and dying and rearing children has changed in this first week of the war and the new routine has imposed a whole encyclopedia of new rules and duties on the average citizen.

Under penalty of a heavy fine he must not let a thread of light escape from his windows. He must not toot the horn of his car or ring bells or blow whistles or keep pigeons or take photographs in certain areas or hold certain foreign currency.

Even the ancient custom of going to bed is different. The average man not only goes to bed earlier, but he has several important chores to do before he goes. First he must turn off the gas at the main [a bomb may fracture the pipe and let the gas escape]. He must fill his bathtub with water for use against incendiary bombs. He must place buckets of water around the house and put his gas mask in the safest room where he can get it if there is a raid during the night.

On top of all that he usually lays aside a warm blanket and knows exactly where his shoes and trousers are. That's in case he has to run for the bomb-proof shelter at the end of the yard in the night.

NOT A WAR OF HATE
But in spite of all these inconveniences, though his family is split up and his gasoline rationed (ten gallons per month for a small car, at 32 cents a gallon) and his life is in danger, this average Briton is not fighting a war of hate. There is none of the old college spirit about this war. The people did not rush down to the palace to cheer when Prime Minister Chamberlain announced that they were at war with Germany. And one scarcely hears a word against the German people. This spirit of justice has been encouraged by the Government and over the Government-controlled radio stations.

A Government spokesman in the House of Commons, asked this week whether the Germans were bombing the civilian population in Poland, said frankly that the evidence showed that they were restricting their attacks to military objectives. Harold Nicholson, independent member of Parliament and one of the most popular British radio speakers, went on BBC the other night and said, "let's try to understand the German argument...let's don't be self-righteous."

Similarly Alfred Duff-Cooper wrote this week pleading for kindness to German Jews who are now refugees in this country. "It has been alleged," he ⟩

wrote, "that they are not all genuine refugees but that some have been sent in as agents…it is to be hoped that little credence will be attached to this kind of rumor."

What hatred there is—and there is a good deal of this kind—is personal hatred for Hitler and von Ribbentrop and Goebbels. The English, noted for their understatement, have paraded their gutter adjectives in Hitler's name and cartoonists have drawn him in the guise of everything from a snake to a dragon.

SEEN AS "HITLER'S WAR"

One man expressed the feeling of the public pretty well yesterday when he wrote to The Times of London suggesting that everybody agree to call this "Hitler's war." So many people recently have been talking about the Fuehrer and condemning him that one restaurant off Fleet Street felt obliged to post a sign reading "Don't mention Hitler during meals; it is bad for your digestion."

The past few days have confirmed the Government's fears that there are just as many rumor-mongers in the world in 1939 as there were in 1914 and officials and newspapers are taking every possible opportunity to ridicule them into silence. The first two commandments on how to behave during a war appear to be, first,

don't get spy fever, and, second, don't believe or spread rumors. After the first flight of German bombers near the English coast stories circulated rapidly that the bombers had penetrated far inland and Chamberlain had to issue a denial in the House of Commons.

LIFE IN THE COUNTRY

Life in the countryside has changed incredibly. In fact for the first time since before the Industrial Revolution, the center of the islands' social activity is back in the small town and country village. The village tavern naturally seems to attract adults who have fled from the cities and this is the only place where any kind of dramatic performances are being given. Several years ago an organization was formed in England to present poetry readings and simple plays in the nation's pubs and it is not at all unusual to go into a country tavern now and find a lad standing on a box reciting Shakespeare's sonnets to an appreciative audience.

For the children evacuated to the country, the war so far has been a windfall. They have had no classes and they have had a week of remarkably good weather; and while the quick young Cockneys from the East Side of London think the picturesque villages are "a bloomin' wilderness" their school

teachers report that most of them are beginning to settle down. The Ministry of Education hopes that classes can be resumed in some sections next week but it is bound to take months to find adequate accommodations for all classes and even then teachers plan to hold school in two shifts.

As usual a new routine of life produces a few ingenious devices. The Mens Wear Council, for example, has produced already a special white jacket to be worn during blackouts and one manufacturer has marketed a small red light which hooks on your clothes. Working hours are also being changed to meet the new early-to-bed-early-to-rise habit, some shops opening as early as 7:30 A.M. and all closing early enough to enable people to get home before the blackout.

In other words Britain has set about the task of meeting with fine patience her new task and, while bombs have not started falling yet on English soil, the people seem to agree with a barricaded shopkeeper in Charing Cross Row who posted a sign reading "business as usual during alterations." ◆

Nighttime view of Regent Street in London's Piccadilly Circus, 1939.

SEPTEMBER 10, 1939

CAN CIVILIZATION SURVIVE A WORLD WAR?

By ALLAN NEVINS
Professor of History, Columbia University.

In an eloquent passage written at the beginning of the first World War Romain Rolland spoke of it as "a sacrilegious conflict which shows a maddened Europe ascending its funeral pyre, and, like Hercules, destroying itself with its own hands." We are reminded of the figure as a new conflict begins. Each nation cries aloud that it is fighting for self-preservation; but for the continent as a whole the struggle seems rather self-destructive. Nor are the neutrals across the seas spared. Sir Edward Grey said on Aug. 3, 1914, that "if we are engaged in war we shall suffer but little more than if we stand aside." This was an overstatement, yet what nation escaped the devastating effects and repercussions of the World War?

If this second Armageddon endures and spreads, the damage wrought may be equally titanic. The whole world, as if mined for destruction, is contemplating the possibility of an explosion which will involve its costliest possessions, material, intellectual and spiritual, and do incalculable damage not merely to every human being on the planet but to long generations yet unborn.

In recent years men, facing the possibility of such a cataclysm, have frequently said that a new world war would be "the end of civilization." They have declared that, partly through the subsequent crises it would provoke, it would "destroy human culture." The idea has just been emphatically repudiated by Dr. Eduard Benes, the former President of Czecho-Slovakia, who better than most men knows the meaning of the word destruction. But it has been put forward so frequently and with such emphatic pessimism that it is worth a brief examination. Conceive of another four years' war, setting the whole world aflame, and piling new destruction on old ruins, adding vast new graveyards to those already dotting Europe. Would civilization or even great parts of it be extinguished?

Let it be said at once that the part of civilization represented by great monuments of art and architecture can—and all too easily may—be destroyed. Europe is filled with these monuments and filled also with fleets of bombers. A single air raid might wipe out all Oxford University, and with it a source of beauty, graciousness and inspiration which it took seven centuries to build. One well-planted shell would reduce Sainte Chapelle to a memory over which artists would grieve a thousand years hence. Italy is one of the treasure-houses of the human race. It would take but a few weeks' bombardment by fleets of racing planes to leave Florence a rubble heap, Rome a few square miles of smoking ashes, Venice some ruins sliding into the Adriatic; their towers, temples, palaces and museums forever vanished. New buildings could be erected, new galleries stocked with new works of art. But the human race would be permanently the poorer for what it had lost; life would be thinner and bleaker, and one important element of civilization would be irremediably weakened.

Let it be said also that if by the phrase "destruction of civilization" it is meant that one phase or cycle of civilization may be terminated, that also is possible. It is more than that; it can now be called inevitable. We are doubtless face to face with a new era in human culture. The first World War put an end to the century of comparative peace that had followed the Napoleonic conflicts, to the swift material and scientific advance of that hundred years, to the lurching but nevertheless seemingly irresistible advance toward democratic self-government throughout the world. It ushered in a period of moral lassitude, political chaos, economic storm, religious and racial persecution that would have seemed incredible to advance residents of the Western Hemisphere in 1900. After the French Revolution, the age of reason; after the World War, the age of unreason—and the new conflict cannot but add new and darker mazes to the Temple of Confusion.

These two terrible struggles, which future historians may well call the beginning and end of a thirty years' war—for fighting has never really ceased since 1914—are undoubtedly compelling mankind to turn not a new page but a new chapter. They mean the end of one civilization and the emergence of another, which at least in its beginnings will be baser, harder and darker.

But fortunately the talk of destroying civilization does not need to be taken literally and completely. Civilization is now a many-rooted, widely ramifying growth, indestructible by anything short of a planetary disaster. If it survived the downfall of Athens, the barbarian conquest of Rome, the so-called Dark Ages, the endless religious and dynastic conflicts, it can survive even two world wars.

The real danger is not that civilization will be destroyed, but that it will be crippled for generations and perhaps centuries. If this new war lasts long, an iron age will be inaugurated when it closes.

Europe as a continent may no longer hold the easy primacy which has been hers in the past. And it may not be merely the New World which will gain ground. There is danger that the depletion of European manhood, if pushed much further, will permanently weaken the Caucasian stock in its competition with black and yellow races; that Asia and Africa by sheer default of the present leaders will take a new rank in world affairs. European strength cannot withstand the drain of successive periods of butchery without exhaustion, and some of the resulting changes may go further than peoples of European blood will like to contemplate.

The next great lines in the history of civilization are to be written in blood. When the battle has been fought and its successful outcome assured, then it will be time to think of a new world order for strengthening and protecting civilization; an order in which, it is to be hoped, the United States will play a more courageous part than it did after the war of 1914-18, a role befitting its strength, its culture and its concern for the destinies of the human race. ◊

SEPTEMBER 10, 1939

Sales of Maps Soar Here

Rand McNally & Co., publishers, announced yesterday that more maps had been sold at its store at 7 West Fiftieth Street in the first twenty-four hours of the European war than during all the years since 1918. The announcement said fresh supplies of maps were being rushed daily by planes from factories working on a day-and-night schedule. ◊

SEPTEMBER 12, 1939

POLES UNPREPARED FOR BLOW SO HARD

The following dispatch is by a member of the Berlin staff of The New York Times who was allowed to visit the German armies in the field in Poland and to send this account:

By OTTO D. TOLISCHUS
Wireless to The New York Times.

WITH THE GERMAN ARMIES IN POLAND, Sept. 11—Having hurled against Poland their mighty military machine, the Germans are today crushing Poland like a soft-boiled egg.

After having broken through the shell of Polish border defenses, the Germans found inside, in comparison with their own forces, little more than a soft yolk, and they have penetrated that in many directions without really determined general resistance by the Polish Army.

That is the explanation of the apparent Polish military collapse in so short a time as it was gathered on a tour of the Polish battlefields made by this correspondent in the wake of the German Army and, sometimes, in the backwash of a day's battle while scattered Polish troops and snipers were still taking potshots at motor vehicles on the theory that they must be German. But such is the firm confidence of the Germans that a cocked pistol in front of the army driver is held to be sufficient protection for the foreign correspondents in their charge.

STAND MADE AT BORDER

Even a casual glance at the battlefields, gnarled by trenches, barbed-wire entanglements, shell holes, blown-up roads and bridges and shelled and gutted towns, indicates that the Poles made determined resistance at the border. But even these border defenses seem weak, and beyond them there is nothing.

It is a mystery to both Germans and neutral military experts on the tour with the writer that the Poles made no provisions for second or third lines and that in retreat they did not make any attempt to throw up earthworks or dig trenches such as helped the Germans stop the Allies after the Marne retreat in 1914.

In fact, the only tactics the Poles seemed to have pursued in the retreat were to fall back on towns from which, later, they were either easily driven out by artillery fire or just as easily flanked. But presumably neither their number nor their equipment, which, judging from the remnants thrown along the road of retreat, was pitifully light as compared with the Germans', permitted them to do anything else in view of the enormous length of the border they had to defend.

Again God has been with the bigger battalions, for the beautiful, dry weather, while converting Polish roads into choking dust clouds on the passage of motor vehicles, has kept them from turning into mud as would be normal at this time of year; this has permitted the German motorized divisions to display the speed they have.

But the Germans have proceeded not only with might and speed, but with method, and this bids fair to be the first war to be decided not by infantry, "the queen of all arms," but by fast motorized divisions and, especially, by the air force.

The first effort of the Germans was concentrated on defeating the hostile air fleet, which they did not so much by air battle but by consistent bombing of airfields and destruction of the enemy's ground organization. Having accomplished this, they had obtained domination of the air, which in turn enabled them, first, to move their own vast transports ahead without danger from the air and, second, to bomb the Poles' communications to smithereens, thereby reducing their mobility to a minimum.

NO BLACKOUT IN CONQUERED ZONE

Today the German rule of the air is so complete that, although individual Polish planes may still be seen flying at a high altitude, the German Army has actually abandoned the blackout in Poland. It is a strange sensation to come from a Germany thrown into Stygian darkness at night to a battlefront town like Lodz, as this correspondent did the night after the Germans announced its occupation, and find it illuminated although the enemy is only a few miles from the city.

With control of the air, the Germans moved forward not infantry but their tanks, armored cars and motorized artillery, which smashed any Polish resistance in the back. This is easy to understand when one has seen the methods of open warfare attempted by the Poles and an almost amateurish attempt at digging earthworks for machine-gun nests.

To German and neutral experts the Poles seem to have clung to eighteenth century war methods, which, in view of modern firing volume and weight, are not only odd but also futile. This does not mean that the Poles have not put up a brave fight. They have, and the Germans themselves freely admit it.

As a purely military matter, the German Army is the height of efficiency. It moves like clockwork, without hurry and apparently almost in a leisurely manner. Yet that army moves with inexorable exactitude. The roads into Poland are jammed but not choked with heavy vans and motor trucks carrying food and munitions, while the Poles have to depend mainly on their smashed railroads or on horse carts. Bombed bridges are soon passable for the Germans and they move forward quickly. Communication lines follow them almost automatically.

Poland may not be lost yet and may be even able to offer further resistance by withdrawing into the eastern swamp. But as long as the present disparity between the military resources and her will to fight exists she faces terrible odds.
◆

Polish prisoners of war captured in September, 1939.

SEPTEMBER 13, 1939

W. & J. Starts Courses on 'Second World War'

By The Associated Press.

WASHINGTON, Pa., Sept. 12—President Ralph C. Hutchison announced today that Washington and Jefferson College had started studies of the "second world war" designed to help prevent the "mass hysteria" which he said had characterized the conflict of 1914-18.

Dr. Hutchison expressed the belief that Washington and Jefferson having an enrollment of about 500, was the first college to offer such studies "to help this generation understand better than did their fathers when they entered the first World War."

Three faculty members will teach four war courses bearing full college credit and ranging from the cause of the hostilities to the accompanying propaganda. ◇

SEPTEMBER 16, 1939

LINDBERGH URGES WE SHUN THE WAR

He Tells Nation That if We Fight for Democracy Abroad We May Lose It Here

By FRANK L. KLUCKHOHN
Special to The New York Times.

WASHINGTON, Sept. 15—An appeal to the American people to maintain this country's isolation from the European war, and from European struggles, was made tonight in a radio speech by Colonel Charles A. Lindbergh. "If we enter fighting for democracy abroad, we may end by losing it at home," he said.

It was the first formal speech made by the flier since Aug. 28, 1931, when he addressed Japanese dignitaries in Tokyo, and the National Broadcasting Company, the Columbia Broadcasting System and the Mutual Broadcasting System all carried his words.

Colonel Lindbergh followed in the steps of his father, the late Charles A. Lindbergh, Representative from Minnesota and one of the few to vote against the entry of the United States into the World War in 1917, when he said:

"I am speaking tonight to those people in the United States who feel that the destiny of this country does not call for our involvement in European wars."

SAYS OCEANS GIVE PROTECTION

Colonel Lindbergh declared that the Atlantic and Pacific Oceans were still barriers for the United States, even against modern aircraft, and added that "we must band together to prevent the loss of more American lives in these internal struggles of Europe."

"If we take part successfully," he asserted in speaking of the European war, "we must throw the entire resources of our entire nation into the conflict. Munitions alone will not be enough. We cannot count upon victory merely by shipping abroad several thousand airplanes and cannon.

"We are likely to lose a million men, possibly several million—the best of American youth. We will be staggering under the burden of recovery during the rest of our lives. And our children will be fortunate if they see the end in their lives even if, by some unlikely chance, we do not pass on another Polish Corridor to them."

The flier held that if war brought new dark ages to Europe, the best service this country could render humanity would be to act as the bulwark for the type of civilization Europe has known. He held that by staying out of war itself this country might even be able to bring peace to Europe more quickly.

DECLARES TROOP AID "MADNESS"

Our safety does not lie in fighting European wars, Colonel Lindbergh declared, but rather in the internal strength of the American people and their institutions. In this connection he asserted that "as long as we maintain an army, a navy and an air force worthy of the name, as long as America does not decay within, we need fear no invasion of this country."

There is no halfway policy possible for this country, he said. He held that if this country enters the quarrels of Europe during war, it must stay in them in peace as well. He characterized as madness "the sending of American soldiers to be killed as they were in the last war," if we turn the course of peace over to the "greed, the fear and the intrigue" of European nations.

This country was colonized by men and women who preferred the wilderness and the Indians to the problems of Europe, he stated, adding that "the colonization of this country grew from European troubles and our freedom sprang from European war."

George Washington clearly saw the danger ahead and warned the American people against becoming entangled in European alliances, the colonel said, noting that this policy was followed for over one hundred years. Then in 1917 we entered "a European war."

"The Great War ended before our full force reached the field," he said. "We measured our dead in thousands. Europe measured hers in millions. A generation has passed since the armistice of 1918, but even in America we are still paying for our part in victory—and we will continue to pay for another generation."

Colonel Lindbergh warned against propaganda "foreign and domestic," as well as "obvious" and "insidious" with which he said this country would be deluged.

Much of our news is already colored, the colonel asserted. Americans, he said, should not only inquire about the personality, interests and nationality of every writer and speaker, but should ask who owns and who influences the newspaper, the news picture and the radio.

He made no reference to the arms embargo in the Neutrality Act.

Colonel Lindbergh made his address into the microphones in a hotel room. ◇

Charles Lindbergh argued for American isolation in September, 1939.

DIPLOMATS CROSS THE POLISH BORDER
Envoys Say Refugee Conditions Are Desperate, With the Danger Of Famine

CERNAUTI, Rumania, Sept. 15 (AP)— Foreign diplomats fleeing war-torn Poland arrived here tonight with reports of a tremendous new German drive through Southeast Poland designed to cut off Poland from Rumania.

The new southern offensive was reported being built up with vast numbers of reserves pouring in from Germany, while the air attack was being accelerated.

Extensive fighting was reported in the region of Lwow, largest city in Southeastern Poland, which lies slightly more than 100 miles northeast of the Polish-Rumanian frontier.

The caravan of diplomats that arrived at this town just across the Polish border included the United States Ambassador to Poland, Anthony J. D. Biddle; Mrs. Biddle, their daughter, Peggy Thompson Schultz, and Mrs. Biddle's secretary, Mary McKenzie. It was their fourth move since leaving bomb-wrecked Warsaw.

Others in the party of sixty that reached here at 6 P.M. included Mme. Josef Beck, wife of the Polish Foreign Minister, and their three children, and diplomatic representatives of Brazil, Spain, Italy, Belgium, Sweden, Japan, the Netherlands and Switzerland.

Cernauti, already over-crowded, offered few accommodations and most of the diplomatic refugees arranged to leave quickly for Bucharest. Mme. Beck is on her way to Paris.

The diplomats said they had left Zaleszcyki, an emergency Polish Government headquarters, because of threatened raids by German planes. They reported planes flew over the town yesterday and there were numerous alarms, but no bombs were dropped.

The diplomats reported that refugee conditions in the vicinity of Zaleszcyki, a village on the Polish-Rumanian border, were becoming desperate, with indications of a possible famine among those fleeing before the Nazi war machine.

Members of the diplomatic group said Germany apparently now was determined to cut off Poland from Rumania, regardless of the price to be paid for a swift advance. A touch of the rainy season already appeared to spur the new offensive and complete it before operations were bogged in mud.

CERNAUTI, Rumania, Sept. 15—This city today became the headquarters for diplomats, newspapermen and Poles. All day long one diplomatic automobile after another crossed the border after an exciting journey through Polish territory.

All the automobiles were camouflaged and the flags of the respective countries were displayed. The machines were filled with everything from pillows to radios. When the automobile of Ambassador Anthony J. D. Biddle arrived with its American flag hundreds of curious gathered around. A small police detachment was necessary to keep order.

All hotels were filled completely. At the border Rumanian officials took strict measures, prohibiting completely the entry of refugees without visas.

Rumania tonight barred her frontiers to the bulk of the thousands of Polish refugees fleeing before invading German armies.

An official communiqué stated that "all private persons" from Poland, especially from Galicia, where the percentage of Jews is high, were barred from entrance into Rumania.

The communiqué dashed the hopes of most of some 10,000 Jewish refugees congesting the Polish side of the Rumanian border seeking entry. ◆

Polish refugees fleeing the approaching German army, September, 1939.

SEPTEMBER 17, 1939

MERCHANT CONVOYS SET UP BY BRITAIN

By The Associated Press.

LONDON, Sept. 16—The British Admiralty pressed into service tonight convoys for merchant shipping after it was disclosed authoritatively that enemy craft had sunk twenty-one British ships, involving a tonnage of 122,843, during the first two weeks of the war.

The use of convoys was not instituted by the British in the last war until 1917.

While slim cruisers and racing destroyers roved and struck on the shipping lanes, planes of the Royal Aircraft patrolled the skies around the United Kingdom in redoubled efforts to halt the persistent shipping losses to U-boats or mines.

Despite the casualties, naval quarters expressed optimism about the situation at sea.

UNDERSTATEMENT IN REPORTS

Increasing patrol activity and the Admiralty's cautious announcement that "a number of U boats have been destroyed," was taken by naval authorities to tell a story of far greater successes than the guarded statement indicated.

Britain placed responsibility on Germany for the sinking last night of the 8,000-ton Belgian motorship Alex Van Opstal in the Channel off Weymouth, asserting she was sunk by mine or torpedo in violation of international law.

A British communiqué said there were no British mines in the neighborhood, that Germany had sent no notification of German mines there and that attack without warning was in violation of the submarine protocol to which Germany subscribed.

[The Alex Van Opstal left New York on Sept. 6 for Antwerp with eight passengers and 3,400 tons of grain.]

Eight passengers and a crew of forty-nine escaped from the Alex Van Opstal, which, according to her captain, broke in two after a terrific explosion near her No. 2 hatch.

The crew of another British tanker, the Inverliffey, landed in England today and members of her crew told how the captain of the submarine had hauled them to safety when the tanker exploded and went up in flames. Third officer Albert Lang said men in boats were trapped by flames from their burning ship after the explosion.

"Flames and smoke from the ship went up 500 or 600 feet," he said. "We seemed almost under this wall of flames, and when we thought we were done for the commander of the submarine sailed his ship alongside and told us we could stand around the conning tower. No sooner had we got on the submarine than it got up speed and took us out of danger. The commander treated us decently and took us to our boats before he waved his hand and submerged." ◇

SEPTEMBER 17, 1939

GANDHI URGES BRITAIN TO 'LIBERATE' INDIA
Says Free Country Would Be an Ally To Defend Democracy

Wireless to The New York Times.

WARDHA, India, Sept. 16—Mohandas K. Gandhi told Britain tonight that she could gain a willing ally in the war by making India a "free and independent nation."

"The recognition of India," he said, "as a free and independent nation seems to me to be a natural corollary of the British profession of democracy."

Mr. Gandhi asked for a clear statement of Britain's war aims in relation to democracy and imperialism, but urged the working committee of the Congress party that whatever support they should give to Britain should be given unconditionally.

He asked Britain for "honest action to implement the declarations of faith in democracy made on the eve of the war," and said:

"The question is, will Great Britain have an unwilling India dragged into war or a willing ally cooperating with her in the prosecution of the defense of true democracy?" ◇

SEPTEMBER 18, 1939

JAPAN NOW DRIVES FOR CHINA VICTORY
Kwantung Army Being Shifted to South— Peace Deal With Chiang Not Ruled Out

TOKYO, Sept. 18 (UP)—Informants close to the War Office said today that "it was natural to assume" that large numbers of Japanese troops were being removed from the Soviet frontiers of Manchukuo to China.

Following the Russo-Japanese agreement to cease fighting on the Manchukuoan-Soviet borders, increased military activity in China may be expected at once, it was said, in line with Premier Nobuyuki Abe's announced decision to bring the long undeclared war with China to an early end.

So far the China war has been fought largely with second line reservists, many of them married men, but now, it was said, major units of the crack Kwantung army will be thrust into the China struggle in an effort to induce Chinese Nationalist Generalissimo Chiang Kaishek to surrender. ‣

◀ RETIREMENT NOT NECESSARY

Japan, it was said, will be willing to make peace with General Chiang and permit him to continue in power if he will come to an early "reasonable" agreement.

This government still is willing to make peace with China on the basis of the declaration made by Prince Fumimaro Konoye, then Premier, last December. The Konoye declaration, it was recalled, did not make General Chiang's retirement a necessary preliminary to peace.

Japanese units late last week started moving forward south of Nanchang, in the Hankow-Canton railway area, and it was believed that a first phase of the new push would be to clear this railway and break Chinese positions in General Chiang's Hengyang defense triangle.

The Japanese then would move into Yunnan Province and undertake to cut the Burma-Chungking highway, thus rendering untenable the whole Chinese defense system in the southwest.

It will be recalled that when General Chiang abandoned Hankow almost a year ago he set up two "final" defense areas—one in the southwest to be fed by the Burma-Chungking highway and railways and highways into French Indo-China, and another in the northwest around Lanchow, Kansu province, and munitioned by trucks operating on the motor truck highway from Sian, Shensi Province, through Lanchow, to Soviet Russia.

The informants believed that General Chiang "now realizes" that both these defense areas are hopeless since his supplies of munitions from abroad are being cut off.

FIGHT CONTINUES, SAYS CHIANG

CHUNG KING, China, Sept. 17—Generalissimo Chiang Kai-shek tonight made his first public pronouncement on foreign affairs since the outbreak of the European war in a speech before the People's Political Council, now in session here. Despite the war in Europe, he stated, China must consistently carry out a fixed policy of armed resistance against Japanese aggression.

"The European war will make us fight Japan with greater vigor," he said, "since we are confident of ultimate victory and of China's rightful place in reshaping a new world order."

General Chiang called Japan's policy of non-intervention in any European war tantamount to saying that she does not want any interference by Europe or America in the Chinese-Japanese conflict, since she is attempting to establish her so-called "new order in East Asia," which would place her in the predominant position in Asia to the exclusion of other powers.

Turning to the Chinese-Japanese war situation, General Chiang declared:

"I am now in a position to state that our present military strength, compared with that at the outbreak of the war, is more than doubled. * * * Japan has exhausted her manpower and is already defeated." ◆

Japanese troops in northern Hebei province, China during the Second Japan-China war, 1939.

SEPTEMBER 17, 1939

SOVIET TROOPS MARCHED INTO POLAND AT 11 P. M.; NAZIS DEMAND WARSAW GIVE UP OR BE SHELLED

FIERCE BATTLE IS RAGING ON WESTERN FRONT

By The United Press

BERLIN, Sept. 17—A spokesman for the Propaganda Ministry announced that Russian troops had marched into Poland today at 4 A. M. Moscow time, [11 P.M. Saturday in New York].

The Soviet troops entered Poland with the full knowledge and approval of the German Government, he said.

The spokesman made his statement after D. N. B., the official German news agency, had reported from Moscow that the Soviet Government had informed the Polish Ambassador, Dr. Waclaw Grzybowski, Saturday night that Soviet troops were about to cross the frontier.

The agency said that the note handed to the Ambassador informed the Poles that the troops would cross the frontier along its entire length from Polozk in the north to Kamenets-Podolski in the south "in order to protect our own interests and to protect the White Russian and Ukrainian minorities."

The Soviet Government, the agency said, told the Poles that it maintained its neutrality despite its military action, but added that its treaties with the Polish State could be regarded canceled because the Polish State could no longer be regarded as existing.

TO OCCUPY TWO DISTRICTS

MOSCOW, Sept. 17—Soviet Russia has decided to send her army across the Polish frontier today and to occupy the Polish Ukraine and White Russia.

The government was understood unofficially to have sent a note last night to the Polish Ambassador here saying that the Red Army would enter the Polish Ukraine and White Russia today from Polozk to Kamanets-Podolski.

Copies of this note were said also

to have been sent simultaneously to all diplomatic representatives here saying the action was taken because Poland no longer exists. It was said to have declared there no longer is a Polish Government because its whereabouts are unknown.

The note was said to have declared that "the Soviet Union will retain neutrality, but feels it necessary to protect White Russian and Ukrainian minorities in Poland and will do everything to keep peace and order."

[Poland not only has a non-aggression pact with Russia but in mutual assistance treaties by which the British and French are pledged to aid Poland in defense of her independence against any aggression. Polish invocation of this treaty brought Great Britain and France into war against Germany on Sept. 3, two days after a German army invaded Western Poland.]

COVERS ENTIRE FRONTIER

The scene of the Russian action would extend across the whole of Russia's Polish frontier.

It would increase considerably Russia's frontier with Rumania. Rumania holds Bessarabia, wrested from Russia after the World War, and the Soviet Government never has relinquished its claims on this territory.

Russia's decision to act came after she had sent a vast number of men to her western frontier in semi-mobilization and had followed with her "peace" with Japan.

It was believed here that the Polish Embassy in Moscow would leave and that, possibly the British also would leave, since they are allies of Poland.

MAN POWER IS THREAT

If necessary, Soviet Russia could throw nearly 2,000,000 trained soldiers against the struggling Poles.

The official Communist party newspaper Pravda this spring estimated Russia's peacetime army at 1,800,000. This estimate did not include the millions of semi-trained reserves who could be called up by conscription.

In addition to this manpower, the newspaper credited Russia with 9,000 airplanes, 30,000 light machine guns, 23,000 heavy machine guns, 1,600 pieces of heavy artillery and between 6,000 and 10,000 tanks.

During the past week Russia called up part of her army reserves in a mobilization move, and foreign observers said most of the troops were sent to the western frontier, facing Poland. ◆

SEPTEMBER 18, 1939

SOVIET 'NEUTRALITY' STRESSED IN MOVE

By G. E. R. GEDYE
Wireless to The New York Times

MOSCOW, Sept. 17—The totally unprepared population of the Soviet Union learned through loudspeakers on the streets at 11 o'clock this morning that its governmentm during the night had committed it to the invasion of a neighbor's territory. Warlike operations, which elsewhere are preceded by parliamentary debates and long newspaper: campaigns and even in Germany by a special session of the Reichstag, here were brought to the knowledge of an unprepared people hours after they had begun.

Little wonder that the Moscow population, recalling the reiterated declarations of leaders headed by Joseph Stalin that they did not desire a foot of anyone else's territory, went about today asking: "What has happened now?" "Are we at war; with whom and why?"

"What do we want in Poland?" "What has gone wrong with the neutrality pact signed with the express purpose of keeping us from war?"

The Soviet radio declared that special propaganda meetings in every part of the Union today revealed general support "for the noble act of the government." The only emotion revealed by the foreign observers with whom the writer spoke was one of utter bewilderment.

NEUTRALITY ASSURANCES GIVEN

As the Soviet forces marched into Poland representatives of Britain and France and of countries as far removed from European quarrels as the United States received notes assuring them that Russia would observe "neutrality" toward them.

The British and French Embassies are awaiting instructions from their governments as to the next steps. In British quarters there was at first a tendency to assume that unless the Poles called on Britain to fulfill the terms of the Anglo-Polish pact the case might be met for the moment by withdrawal of the British Ambassador to mark disapproval of-the Soviet attitude.

News that Polish troops were resisting the Soviet advance caused a rather graver view to be taken this evening. Diplomatic circles considered it possible that the British and the French might break off diplomatic relations and even declare war.

However, it is not believed that any precipitate step will be taken. Probably Russia will first be asked for an explanation of her action and assurances that no annexation is intended. Neutral diplomats question whether a declaration of war at this juncture would be of any advantage to the Western democracies; although it is obvious that the day will come when they will be obliged to insist that Russia restore the territory of their ally.

Meantime, it is felt, they are more likely to concentrate on their efforts on the Western front. Existing blockade regulations suffice to assure that Russia' as a neutral will not import anything that might aid Germany in the prosecution of the war.◆

SEPTEMBER 18, 1939

Editorial
THE RUSSIAN BETRAYAL

It is altogether probable that the Russian invasion of Poland, just at the moment when that country has been laid waste and rendered all but helpless, reveals at least part of the secret understanding that lay behind the German-Russian non-aggression pact. This, no doubt, is the deal that Hitler and Stalin arranged. This was the price for which Stalin was ready to betray the French and British with whom he had ostensibly been negotiating for an anti- Nazi alliance. Germany having killed the prey, Soviet Russia will seize that part of the carcass that Germany cannot use. It will play the noble role of hyena to the German lion.

This gross betrayal of the professions that Soviet Russia has been making for years is being defended in the manner with which the world has now grown sickeningly familiar. Because Poland has "virtually ceased to exist," Russia is free to break every treaty with it.

The Soviet Government deems it its "sacred duty" to "extend the hand of assistance" to its dear brother Ukrainians and brother white Russians. The Polish Government has denounced as having been "rotten" anyway, and of having "persecuted" its minori ‣

ties in contrast one supposes, to the well-known kindliness with which Soviet Russia treats minority opinion. The technique is established: just before you pillage your neighbor and kill his wife and children, you must denounce him as a scoundrel.

What further agreements and developments lie behind the ominous non-aggression pact—whether, for example, a re-partition of Poland is to be followed by a partition of Rumania or a more extended drive on the Balkan states, either to annex them or to reduce them to vassalage—we shall doubtless learn soon enough. It is possible that Russia does not intend to participate in warfare if she can help it, but merely to sit on her re-acquired territories or new possessions and hold them. In any case the outlook is hopeless for Poland and dark for England and France. The latter are more threatened in Asia by Japan, and Germany is in a position to get valuable supplies in particular, some of the oil that her motorized warfare so desperately needs.

But this virtual alliance of Germany and Russia, at least for temporary ends, will certainly not work altogether against the democracies, As Germany and Russia draw closer together, as buffer states shrink or disappear, the mutual distrust between the two Governments must grow. It is not likely that Hitler has changed the opinion he expressed in "Mein Kampf" that "The present rulers of Russia do not at all think of entering an alliance sincerely or of keeping one." He must still believe that the Russian leaders combine "a rare mixture of bestial horror with an inconceivable gift of lying," and the Russian leaders doubtless reciprocate the compliment. In such conditions no real or durable alliance is probable. The two Governments can act together only in dividing helpless intervening nations "between them, while quarrels over the division are always possible.

The most immediate effect is the complete moral and "ideological" change which this working alliance must bring. It clears the air. It will sweep illusions from millions of minds. For at least the last fifteen years communism and fascism have lived on each other. Each has declared itself to be the other's exact antithesis and only formidable enemy. Millions of Germans stomached Hitler in the belief that he was the only hope, as he himself repeatedly boasted, to save them from communism. He framed his anti-Comintern pacts and posed before the world as communism's arch-foe. Though Stalin has always held western democracy in contempt, he created and kept alive for years the pretense of an alliance with it against fascism; his satellites, tools and dupes in other countries formed their "popular fronts" and their leagues against war and fascism. All these pretenses and lies have collapsed together. The most squirming apologists now will not be able to convince anyone but idiots of their sincerity. At last the issue stands clear. Hitlerism is brown communism, Stalinism is red fascism. The world will now understand that the only real "ideological" issue is one between democracy, liberty and peace on the one hand and despotism, terror and war on the other. ◇

Even before Mr. Roosevelt left the White House the streets through which he was to pass were being patrolled, and the Capitol Building and grounds had taken on the appearance of an armed camp. The corridors of the House wing of the building where the President was to speak were barricaded at strategic points and a Secret Service agent guarded every entrance to the chamber.

Rarely if ever before had there been assembled a more formidable guard of uniformed, Capitol and metropolitan police, Federal operatives and city detectives. Such was the apprehension of those whose first duty is to protect the life of the President that a number of selected private detectives were brought to Washington for the occasion from other cities.

ALL WINDOWS ARE WATCHED

Their numbers suddenly enlarged by news of the assassination of Premier Calinescu of Rumania, plainclothes secret service agents and city detectives idled about the corridors and doorways leading to the House chamber. Every Treasury agent available for duty was pressed into service.

As the President entered and left the west wing of the Capitol, every window overlooking his waiting limousine was being watched and Secret Service men walked back and forth along the balustrade bordering the esplanade which separates the building from the surrounding lawns. There was not a nook or cranny that was not under constant surveillance.

When the President goes to the Capitol he always is accompanied by a motorcade of escorting policemen. Their number was increased today and a Secret Service car flanked the President's car on either side a little to the rear.

For the first time in the Capitol's history, the Secret Service took over the duties of the House doormen. Admission to the chamber was by card only, and trained eyes scrutinized the few lucky ones who held them, in search of anything unusual about their appearance and clothing.

No one was allowed to enter or leave the chamber once the President had gone inside. The huge inner doors at all entrances, ordinarily closed only when the House goes home for the Summer, were shut tightly as Mr. Roosevelt began his address.

PRECAUTIONS IN THE PRESS GALLERY

Nor was the press gallery overlooked

SEPTEMBER 22, 1939

HEAVY GUARD KEPT AROUND ROOSEVELT
Women in Peace Group From Philadelphia Try Vainly to Storm The House Wing

By FELIX BELAIR Jr.
Special to The New York Times.

WASHINGTON, Sept. 21—The most elaborate precautions taken to safeguard the life of the Chief Executive since World War days were employed here today when President Roosevelt went to the Capitol to address a joint session of the Senate and House of Representatives on the subject of American neutrality.

President Roosevelt at the White House, 1939.

in the preparations for the Presidential visit. In the inner gallery overlooking the House floor, Secret Service agents were posted as a precaution against unauthorized intrusion, while other agents roamed about the adjoining room where correspondents write their dispatches.

The unusual amount of advance planning for the day was apparent to reporters as they arrived early this morning at the White House executive offices. All gates were half closed so that they could be manned easily by one of the household guards. Those not readily recognized were asked to present their credentials. Sight-seers and other pedestrians were barred from the White House grounds.

Actually, wherever the President went from the time he left the White House until he re-entered it, he was surrounded with Secret Service agents. They were around his automobile when he appeared on the south lawn of the mansion to start out for the Capitol, and they were within quick reaching distance even after he had entered the House chamber.

Tension did not ease until the iron gates closed behind Mr. Roosevelt after the motor trip back from the Capitol that ended where it began—on the south lawn.

The task of policing the Capitol's interior was made no easier by the appearance of several hundred Philadelphians, purporting to represent the Committee for Defense of Constitutional Rights, who picketed members of the Senate as they proceeded in a body from the Senate wing of the Capitol to the House chamber.

One group attempted to storm the entrance to the House wing, and several women became enraged at Capitol policemen who barred their way.

"And me with a flag in my hand," one remarked.

"We're mothers," another shouted. "We don't want our boys to go to war. I have six; she has seven."

Eventually Representative Luther A. Patrick arrived on the scene.

"What did Congress do to you that wronged you?" he inquired.

"We don't want it to do anything to wrong us," one of the women exclaimed. "Are you a Communist?"

"No," he assured her.

"Well," said she, "you sure look like one." ◆

SEPTEMBER 26, 1939

Letters to The Times
VIEWS ON THE ARMS EMBARGO

MAJORITY OPINION EXPRESSED IN LETTERS TO THE TIMES FAVORS REPEAL

To the Editor of The New York Times:

It seems to me that the discussion of the embargo repeal issue, in your letter columns and elsewhere, has ignored a fact of basic importance to our policy— the overwhelming popular sentiment in favor of the Allies.

Both the Gallup poll and the Fortune survey reveal that our sentiment in favor of non-participation is based in the premise that the Allies can win without it. Both sources show a considerable bloc of opinion, potentially much larger, which favors our entering the war in the event that the Allies should begin to sink. It follows, I submit, that a neutrality policy designed to help the Allies win is the best conceivable policy to keep us out of war. For if the Allies begin to lose the pressure for our participation will become enormous, perhaps irresistible.

Since Germany has every interest

in keeping us out of war, I cannot take seriously the conceptualist arguments of those who suggest that, in the context of war, repeal of our arms embargo would be an unfriendly act toward Germany, likely to involve us in the struggle. The phrase "act of war" has only the concreteness which history has given it. Lesser events than the repeal of an embargo have in the past been "acts of war," and greater affronts have often been ignored.

If Germany in its sovereignty decided that repeal was an act of war against it, and followed by declaring war against us, then certainly the repeal would be such an act. If, on the contrary, Germany did nothing, then repeal would be repeal, and neither an act of war nor an unfriendly act likely to embroil us in Europe.

Eugene V. Rostow,
New Haven, Conn., Sept. 23, 1939. ▶

◀ **FAVORING INTERNATIONAL LAW**
To the Editor of The New York Times:

The majority of the American people want peace. They stand by President Roosevelt and support the views expressed by him in his speech before Congress.

It is to be noted, however, that this great majority is unorganized, whereas the minority, those who disagree with the President, or a substantial part of it, appears to be highly organized.

Under these circumstances it would be most unfortunate and regrettable if the President's proposals should be defeated by the pressure of the organized opposition. Therefore, those who support him should immediately take effective measures to offset or overcome the pressure of that opposition.

I want peace as much as any American, and no one wants it more than our President; we all want to avoid involvement. We can best protect ourselves by repealing the embargo and having our neutrality governed by international law, as it should be. At the same time, by repealing the embargo, we would return to England and France, with whom we have common vital interests, the advantages which they have over Germany, to whose policies almost all of us are opposed.

Jules Schnapper.
Brooklyn, Sept. 23, 1939. ◆

SEPTEMBER 29, 1939

Editorial
NEWS IN WARTIME

The need of caution in sifting truth from falsehood in reports of war moves is also indicated in assaying reports of peace moves. In recent days the British have flatly denied official German accounts of a Nazi air raid on the British fleet in the North Sea. A similar denial now has been given to a report from Rome stating that the Pope is working diplomatically through neutral countries to induce Britain and France to agree to a conference for peace based on the creation of a Polish buffer state. This unconfirmed story was current in Rome, our correspondent said, and had been repeated by an Italian correspondent in Berlin. Later the Vatican declared that no new efforts had been initiated by the Holy See, and that the report had originated in Germany.

These contradictions of fact are the daily by-product of a war being fought at the moment more fiercely with diplomatic bombshells and propaganda raids than with military weapons. They differ from the contradictory interpretations placed on the negotiations now in progress in Moscow. These are the product of deliberate mystification. Even when the secret conversations in the Kremlin are concluded, the full extent of agreement or disagreement between Stalin and Hitler will be revealed only by their subsequent moves on the Western Front no less than in the East.

Less and less, however, do conflicting reports or confusing intrigues becloud the judgment of the American public. Opinion in this country has become pretty expert in sifting evidence and appraising the credibility of the statements of governments that live by lying and chicanery. Seldom in our history has America shown itself so aware, so skeptical, so consciously responsible as during the present crises, and the chief reason for this sobriety and vigilance is that our information, though often contradictory, is more complete and reliable than that of any other people. We are in the unique position of hearing all the contradictions and therefore of basing conclusions on all the evidence available. It is not by accident that the United States is the object of every variety of appeal and propaganda. It is a recognition of and in a way a tribute to the fact that this is now the largest open forum of free report and uncensored opinion. ◆

SEPTEMBER 29, 1939

TALLINN GIVES WAY
Capitulates to Demands as Russian Planes Fly Over The City

By G. E. R. GEDYE
Special Cable to The New York Times.

MOSCOW, Sept. 29—Without its necessitating any immediate change in the uncertain map of Europe the Estonian Republic virtually ceased to exist in the early hours of today.

By the signature of two treaties, labeled "mutual assistance" and "trade agreement," the little Baltic republic passed under the full domination of the Soviet Union and yielded to Russia naval bases and airdromes and the right to maintain military forces in Estonian territory.

She fully accepted the implications of Soviet assertions about the operations of mysterious, unidentified submarines in Estonian waters and handed to Moscow the keys to her security and national existence, which she had held since the collapse of Russian Czarism and the formation of the Soviet Union.

The "mutual assistance" pact is to come into force upon the exchange of ratifications at Tallinn, the capital of Estonia, within six days. The pact is concluded for ten years. Unless it is denounced by either party within a year from the date of expiration, it is to continue for another five years.

It was signed by Premier and Foreign Commissar Vyacheslaff M. Molotoff of Russia and Foreign Minister Karl Selter of Estonia.

TERMS OF THE AGREEMENT

Article I of the Soviet-Estonian pact says the two contracting parties will give each other every assistance, including military, if direct aggression occurs on the part of any great European power against their respective frontiers in the Baltic Sea or their land frontiers or across the territory of the Latvian Republic, as well as against the bases in Estonia, that are granted to the Soviet Union, which are indicated in Article III.

Article II says the U.S.S.R. is to give the Estonians assistance in armaments and other military equipment on favorable terms.

Article III says the Estonian Republic assures the U.S.S.R. of the right to maintain naval bases and several airdromes on the stipulated terms at a reasonable leasing price on the Estonian islands of Faarenaa, Hiccunha, Taleiska and Baleiski. The exact sites of the bases are to be allotted and their boundaries defined by mutual agreement.

For the protection of the bases and airdromes, the U.S.S.R. is to maintain at its own expense Soviet land and sea forces of a strictly limited strength in Estonia. The maximum numbers are to be determined by special agreement.

Article IV provides that the two parties agree not to participate in any coalition directed against either party. The fifth article says the pact does not affect the sovereign rights of the contracting parties or their economic or State organization. ◆

OCTOBER 1, 1939

HITLER, POLES CRUSHED, WOULD HALT WAR NOW

He Will Offer 'Peace' To Britain and France, Hinting Russia Will Help Him if Answer Is 'No'

By EDWIN L. JAMES

German Chancellor Adolf Hitler at a 1939 Nazi rally.

Now that Poland has been crushed and divided between Germany and Russia, Hitler thinks Britain and France should halt their war against Germany. It is his argument that if London and Paris declared war on Berlin in order to carry out their pledges to protect Poland, it is henceforth useless to fight about that because Poland is gone. It is understood that Italy will probably propose peace and Hitler has called the Reichstag to meet next week.

It looks like Hitler expects Britain and France to turn a deaf ear to his proposals and that he is preparing to tell the German people that the democratic allies are really fighting to destroy Germany and that the war he will lead will be to save the Third Reich from that destruction.

Of course, there is a certain amount of logic in all this as the Germans state it. But there are imponderable considerations which affect that logic. When they gave their guarantee to Poland, London and Paris had more in mind than a simple wish to preserve Polish independence. Poland, in a way, had become a symbol. In other words, London and Paris sought to end the aggression of Hitler, which seemed without limits, or rather which did not conform to the limits Hitler set upon it. From this point of view, the destruction of Poland constitutes a reason for continuing the war rather than for stopping it.

WHAT WOULD PEACE BRING?

It is naturally an important matter which Hitler plans to bring to the attention of Chamberlain and Daladier. The war has really not started on the Western Front and Germany proposes that it not start and that those concerned for-get about it, demobilize their forces and go home. What the British and French leaders have got to consider is, "Where will that leave us?"

Hitler started out with a program of getting as many Germans as possible within the confines of the Third Reich, making a great deal of the point that he wanted only Germans. There was no little sympathy with this ambition in many quarters. But when he went to Prague and annexed millions of Czechs, he did much damage to that program; he caused people all over the world to think that it was only a cloak for imperialistic ambition.

Now the line drawn through Poland has brought under the German aegis millions on millions of Poles, who are not German by any stretch of the imagination. That puts a further dent in the program Hitler boasted.

THE GERMAN-RUSSIAN HOOK-UP

For years Hitler built up his position as the great knight defender of the world against communism. Now he is a partner with Stalin in the rape of Poland. That does further damage to his simple program of bringing Germans together in one happy family. It makes his Anti-Comintern Pact, for years the center of his foreign policy, look like a lost hope in a fog—a fog out of which no one knows what will come.

Furthermore, Berlin is now threatening that Russia will come to the active military help of Germany if Britain and France keep up the war and he has announced with enthusiasm the arrangements made by which Russia will become a base of supplies for Germany. Whether or not one believes that Ger-many will let a Russian army cross its soil to fight on the Western Front, there can be no doubt that Hitler is threatening, for what the threat is worth, to bring Russian military force to his aid.

Where does that prospect leave Britain and France if they agree now to take back the declaration of war on Germany? What future do they face? What would happen to the Continent of Europe if they agreed that Hitler could have his Polish spoils with impunity? On the other hand, it may be argued that they should ask the question as to where they would be if they fought Germany and lost.

If Britain and France call off the war now, it means that Germany would be free to go ahead with her plans of economic collaboration with Russia, becoming in the next two or three years immensely more powerful. It would mean that Hitler and Stalin would almost certainly continue their expansion in Central Europe and in the Baltic regions. In other words, it would mean that Britain and France would, in the comparatively near future, confront a much more serious peril unless Hitler changed all his spots, and that they do not believe will happen.

MUSSOLINI'S POSITION

As for Mussolini, he is on the anxious seat. When he suggests peace, if he does, it will be not only altruism which actuates him. It is doubtful indeed that in a prolonged war Italy would be able to remain neutral—especially as a friend and purveyor to Germany. It seems that a realization of this is percolating ❯

through the Peninsula. If some day, London and Paris told Rome it would have to take a more positive position, Mussolini would be in a very tough position. What he has to think about today is whether Italy will be given the six months she got the last time to decide which way she would go.

The coming week promises to bring some clarification to the situation. There will be the expected peace offer of Hitler, accompanied by the threats he will emit. There may be the intervention of Mussolini and then there would be the replies of London and Paris.

The best guess seems to be that a week from now the war will still be on. In fact, it seems something better than a ten to one bet. ◊

OCTOBER 4, 1939

FRANCO OFFERS AID TO RESTORE PEACE
Says 'This War Is Absurd' and Sees Little Hope for a Quick, Decisive Victory

Wireless to The New York Times.

MADRID, Oct. 3—Declaring that "this war is absurd" and "the hope of a quick, decisive victory does not exist," Generalissimo Francisco Franco today appealed to the belligerents to make peace so that Germany could be a bulwark against the ideas of Soviet Russia.

General Franco's statement, which was the first he has made since he enjoined the Spanish nation to observe the "strictest neutrality," was made in the course of an interview with Manuel Aznar, chief of the Madrid Press Association.

"Spain," said General Franco, "is disposed to do all within her power without limitation or reserve to conciliate the present belligerents. In this way we can best serve the historic destinies of our country and defend that Western civilization which for Spain is sacred."

Discussing the unexpected alliance of Russia, the great enemy of Nationalist Spain during the recent civil war, with Germany, General Franco declared:

"The Russians' incursion in Europe is a matter of the deepest gravity; nobody can hide that fact.

"In view of what has already happened, it is necessary to agree quickly on some step to avoid greater damage: the evil must be minimized so that from the East of Europe will not come newer, stronger dangers for the spirit of Europe.

"This will not be attained without peace in the West of Europe. Germany should be a sufficiently strong and solid barrier to oppose the orientation of Europe toward those political and social ends of a great and expanding Russia." ◊

OCTOBER 4, 1939

TROTSKY SAYS U. S. WILL JOIN CONFLICT
Asserts Only Washington Can Get Russia to Shift From Supporting Germany

By LEON TROTSKY
North American Newspaper Alliance, Inc.

MEXICO CITY, Oct. 3—The policy of the Soviet Union, full of surprises even for interested observers, flows in reality from the Kremlin's traditional estimation of international relations, which could be formulated approximately in the following manner:

Since a long time ago the economic importance not only of France, but of Britain, has ceased to correspond to the dimensions of their colonial possessions. A new war must overthrow those empires. Not by accident, they say in the Kremlin, the smart opportunist, Mohandas K. Gandhi, already has raised a demand for the independence of India.

This is only the beginning. To tie one's fate to the fate of Britain and France, if the United States does not stand behind them, means to doom one's self beforehand.

The "operations" on the Western Front during the first month of the war only strengthened Moscow in its estimation. France and Britain do not decide to violate the neutrality of Belgium and Switzerland—their violation is absolutely inevitable in case the real war develops—nor do they attack seriously the German Westwall. Apparently, they do not want to wage a war at all, not having in advance the guarantee that the United States will not acquiesce in their defeat.

Moscow thinks, consequently, that the actual confused and indecisive manner of acting of France and Great Britain is a kind of military strike "against the United States," but not a war against Germany.

In these conditions, the August pact of Joseph Stalin and Adolf Hitler was supplemented inevitably by the September agreement. The real meaning of the algebraic formulas of the new diplomatic instrument will be determined by the course of the war during the next week.

STALIN SEEKS TO AVOID WAR
It is very improbable that Moscow will not intervene on Herr Hitler's side against the colonial empires. Mr. Stalin entered the extremely unpopular bloc with Herr Hitler only to save the Kremlin from the risks and disturbances of a war. After that, he found himself involved in a small war in order to justify his bloc with Herr Hitler. In the crevices of a great war, Moscow will try, also, to attain some further new conquests in the Baltic Sea and in the Balkans.

It is necessary, however, to view these provincial conquests in the perspective of the World War. If Mr. Stalin wants to retain the new provinces, then, sooner or later, he will be forced to stake the existence of his power. All his policy is directed toward the postponement of this moment.

But, if it is difficult to expect the direct military cooperation of Moscow with Berlin on the Western Front, it would be sheer light-mindedness to underestimate the economic support that the Soviet, with the help of German

DALADIER REJECTS HITLER PROPOSALS
Declares France Will Fight To Establish 'Real Justice And Lasting Peace'

By P. J. PHILIP
Wireless to The New York Times.

PARIS, Oct. 6—To Chancellor Hitler's speech before the Reichstag Premier Edouard Daladier replied this afternoon: "We must go on with the war that has been imposed on us until victory, which will alone permit the establishment in Europe of a regime of real justice and lasting peace."

The Premier was speaking to the Senate Foreign Affairs Committee, which had asked for a full account of the diplomatic position of the country. Every member of the committee was present and at the end of the meeting the Premier was subjected to extensive questioning. His thesis was, as it was a few days ago before the Chamber of Deputies Foreign Affairs Committee, that France and Britain were making war to end the reign of aggression and to end the necessity of mobilizing every six months.

He said they wanted a lasting peace that would depend on respect for the given word and on honor and would guarantee the security of France and of all nations. Such a peace, he stressed, would exclude all domination in Europe and could be founded only on the right of peoples to their life and their liberty.

Neither France nor Britain, he declared, would lay down their arms until such a peace had been effectively secured.

UNCERTAINTIES STILL REMAIN

But millions of men are standing to arms all over Europe. Whether they will fight and where they will fight has still been left uncertain, just as it is uncertain where and how the Rome-Berlin Axis, the anti-Comintern pact and the Third International are in accord and disaccord.

That puzzlement is not confined to France. Every country is suffering from it. Amid the confusion the French have this firm faith to hold to: that their men and their Maginot Line will resist any attack, whether the war be a waiting war or a lightning war.

They know that they do not want for themselves or for any other peoples a Europe on the Hitler model and, whether they must stand still and wait for victory or fight for it, they are prepared. They are confident, too, that the British Government, people and army are equally determined to stand fast and keep cool while Herr Hitler alternates between promising peace on his own conditions and threatening to spread the war further. ◇

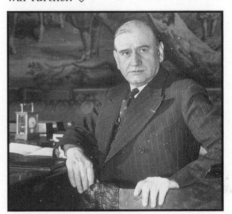

French War Minister Edouard Daladier.

technology, particularly in the means of transportation, can render the German Army. The importance of the Anglo-French blockage will certainly not be annihilated, but considerably weakened.

The German-Soviet pact will have, under these conditions, two consequences. It will greatly extend the duration of the war and bring closer the moment of intervention of the United States. By itself, this intervention is absolutely inevitable.

It is a question of the struggle for world domination, and America will not be able to stand aside.

The intervention of the United States, which would be capable of changing the orientation not only of Moscow but also of Rome, is, however, a song of the future. The empiricists of the Kremlin stand with both feet on the basis of the present. They do not believe in the victory of Britain and France, and consequently they stick to Germany.

To make the Kremlin change its policy there remains only one way, but a sure one. It is necessary to give Herr Hitler such a decisive blow that Mr. Stalin will cease to fear him. In this sense, it is possible to say that the most important key to the Kremlin's policy is now in Washington. ◇

CHURCHILL AWAKENS BRITONS
Of All Leaders He Best Rouses The Confidence Of the People and Their Fighting Spirit

By JAMES B. RESTON
Wireless to The New York Times.

LONDON, Oct. 7—Great Britain's First Lord of the Admiralty, Winston Churchill, who agreed with the poet Milton that it is "better to reign in hell than serve in heaven," has emerged from the first five weeks of war as the most inspiring figure in Great Britain and ultimate successor to the 71-year-old Prime Minister Neville Chamberlain.

War is Mr. Churchill's natural element. Like a happy old tugboat captain with a battered sailor's hat on his head and a dead cigar between his teeth he has looked and sounded like a war leader. And more than any other man he has spread a little confidence about the land.

In the newspapers and—what is probably more important—in pubs, the people are beginning to talk about him and smile approvingly at his chip-on-the-shoulder attitude. He is the Cabinet member who gives the impression that he is getting a big kick out of fighting Adolf Hitler. He has dropped the diplomatic double talk of the Front Bench and has spoken in simple, blunt language.

"THE PERFECT MAN"

When Mr. Churchill went to the United States to lecture in 1900, Mark Twain introduced him.

"Ladies and gentlemen," said the American humorist, "The lecturer tonight is Mr. Winston Churchill. By ❯

his father he is an Englishman; by his mother, an American. Behold the perfect man!"

That American connection is important. Mr. Churchill has inherited a deep vein of American candor from his mother, and while this very quality has made him many enemies and helped keep him out of No. 10 Downing Street, it is working definitely to his advantage today.

He has been condemned as a Russophobe and a Teutophobe, as an irresponsible genius, but even his old critics seem to agree now that he will make a great wartime leader. They read in Germany's tendency to vilify him a sign that Germans fear and respect him and many are beginning to believe that he and he alone has the drive and imagination to lead the British Empire through the greatest crisis in its history. ◇

Winston Churchill making a recruiting speech at London's mansion house for the territorial army in April, 1939.

U-BOAT SINKS BRITISH BATTLE-SHIP; 396 OF 1,200 ON ROYAL OAK RESCUED; SOVIET-FINNISH ACCORD HELD NEAR

By RAYMOND DANIELL
Special Cable to The New York Times.

LONDON, Oct. 14—A torpedo from a German submarine sent the battle-

---

Prime Minister Says Bar to Peace Is the Present German Government

By RAYMOND DANIELL
Wireless to The New York Times.

LONDON, Oct. 12—The answer of Great Britain to Chancellor Adolf Hitler's offer of a "white" peace was given by Prime Minister Neville Chamberlain today in the House of Commons. It was an emphatic "No!" delivered with all the vehemence at the Prime Minister's command and echoed by spokesmen for all parties.

Deeds, not words were necessary now, Mr. Chamberlain declared, to the accompaniment of cheers, if Herr Hitler hoped to convince the Allies that he wanted peace. Thus did the Birmingham business man who had tried to trade with the dictators return the onus for the final fateful decision of peace or war to the erstwhile Austrian house painter who is now German war lord.

Not by the slightest word or hint had Herr Hitler shown any intention or desire to right the wrongs done to Poland and Czecho-Slovakia, Mr. Chamberlain pointed out. Even if he had, his record of broken pledges was such that any further promise from him would require very substantial guarantees.

One thing and one thing alone, the Prime Minister declared, stood between the world and the peace so ardently desired by the people of all nations and that one thing was the present German Government.

Mr. Chamberlain spoke as an apostle of peace transformed by disillusionment into a man of action and of war. In some quarters it was felt that his blunt rejection of Herr Hitler's peace terms would be a signal for the unleashing of all the horrors of war by the Nazis. But bombs did not rain at once on British ports, nor was there any immediate assault on the Western Front.

In the distinguished strangers' gallery, as Mr. Chamberlain began speaking, sat August Zaleski, Foreign Minister of the new Polish Government established on French soil since the Nazi conquest. Before this afternoon's session of Parliament he had been received by King George and had read the parts of the Prime Minister's address dealing with the Allies' attitude toward restoration of his native land.

The Ambassadors of Argentina, Belgium, Brazil, China, Egypt, France, Russia, Spain and Poland listened intently to every word from their gallery. Near by were the Ministers of Norway, Sweden, Switzerland, Bulgaria, Iran, Yugoslavia, Latvia, the Netherlands, Rumania, Liberia, Denmark, Nepal and Finland and the High Commissioners for South Africa, Australia, Canada and Eire.

From the outset there was no doubt in the House of Commons about the tenor of Mr. Chamberlain's reply, which had been endorsed before its delivery by

France and by the British Dominions. The Prime Minister's demeanor was that which he reserved for occasions when he intends to be firm and uncompromising. His face was grim, and his voice was raised to an unusual degree for that British leader whose umbrella had become a symbol of the school of diplomacy known as appeasement of dictators. Instead of adopting his characteristic stance, leaning with one elbow on the Treasury table, he stood stiffly upright, away from the lectern on which his manuscript lay.

CHEERS GREET REFUSAL

At first the members listened eagerly like litigants waiting for some word in the judge's opinion that would show whether he had found for or against them. Before long that word came in the declaration that Britain could not accept Herr Hitler's terms without forfeiting her honor and abandoning her stand that international disputes should be settled by discussion and not by force.

Cheers greeted this firm refusal to surrender without fighting for the ideals for which Britain went to war. As the Prime Minister's speech proceeded in even more unequivocal terms, the enthusiasm of the Commons grew until at the end it was cheering every other phrase and leaders of the Opposition groups were outdoing each other in endorsing the rejection of Herr Hitler's terms, while expressing disappointment that this nation's war aims had not been more clearly enunciated. ◇

ship Royal Oak to the bottom of the sea today and struck grief into more than 800 British homes.

Of approximately 1,200 officers and men aboard, only 378 are known to have been saved and the Admiralty feared tonight that all the others are lost.

[Shortly before midnight the Admiralty gave out a list of eighteen names, bringing the list of survivors to 396 and indicating that 804 still were missing, The United Press reported.]

It was the second heavy blow Germany has struck at the navy of this island center of a far-flung empire since the war broke out on Sept. 3. Exactly a fortnight later the aircraft carrier Courageous was sunk by a submarine with a loss of 518 lives.

Such is Great Britain's superiority over Germany at sea, however, that it was human beings of flesh and blood instead of ships of steel that were mourned the most in government circles.

SPEEDY SINKING FEARED

Inquiry at the Admiralty regarding the probable cause of so heavy a loss of life elicited the opinion that the ship must

The British warship *Royal Oak* was torpedoed in Scapa Flow, an English naval base in the Northeast of Scotland, October 11, 1939.

have gone down rapidly after being hit. While British Navy ships carry lifebelts for every man and 30 per cent extra for emergencies, it was said these usually are stowed below. Probably few of the crew had time to get them. Most of those saved, it was believed, got off on carley floats or rafts.

Only the hardiest swimmers could live long in the icy waters of the North Sea even if they were wearing lifebelts, it was said.

Rescue work was complicated by a northeasterly gale. It is not known whether there was additional trouble, experienced in the case of the Courageous, of oil inches thick that covered the sea and is believed to have caused many drownings when the aircraft carrier went down.

The first list of survivors released by

the Admiralty contained only a handful of names. Later it was announced that 378 were saved, among them Captain W. G. Benn and Commander R. F. Nicholls, first and second in command. ◊

OCTOBER 16, 1939

ARMY AND NAVY ADD BILLIONS TO PLANS

HUGE NEW TONNAGE LIKELY

By HANSON W. BALDWIN
Special to The New York Times.

WASHINGTON, Oct. 15—Both the army and the navy are due to share in large-scale expansion within the next few months of plans prepared for submission to the President and to Congress are approved.

Most of these plans, which are expected to call for an extraordinary expenditure of perhaps several billions over and above the ordinary national defense annual budget for the next fiscal year, which may approximate another $2,000,000,000, are now ready and could be submitted to the present special ses-

sion of Congress after the debate on the Neutrality Act is finished.

It is more generally believed, however, that national defense legislation will await action by the next regular session of Congress opening in January.

Plans for further strengthening of the navy have been closely guarded and their details await announcement by the President or by Congress. There has been much talk about—and some public approval of—"two-ocean navy" to be attained by building enough ships to maintain in the Atlantic a fleet roughly as strong as the fleet in the Pacific, a program which would eventually cost billions of dollars.

"TWO-OCEAN" PROGRAM DOUBTED

Although the Navy Department's official spokesman has pointed out that any program to be offered will simply be responsive to the wishes of the President and of Congress, it is believed that the navy will not suggest any such tremendous expansion as that implied by the term "two-ocean navy."

Such a program would undoubtedly look not only toward further strengthening of our naval forces in the Atlantic, but to remedying certain deficiencies evident in our main forces in the Pacific.

The navy now has fifteen battleships in commission—twelve of them battle

line ships, the others in the Atlantic—and eight building. It is probable that two more 45,000-ton battleships will be requested at the next session, bringing to ten the number under construction. Today, we have five carriers built and two building; others may be requested. Submarines and destroyers will also be asked, and, of course, cruisers.

If any material addition is made to the fleet or to our present building program, additional manpower will be required by the navy over and above that already authorized by the President since the outbreak of war in Europe.

PROBABLE PERSONNEL INCREASES

The present authorized strength, as recently set by the President when he invoked his "limited emergency" powers—a strength which the navy hopes to reach before the start of the next fiscal year—is 145,000 enlisted men and 25,000 marines. These totals will probably be increased if a further expansion program is undertaken, since the navy is already feeling a severe shortage of petty officers and men because of the commissioning of forty old destroyers for duty with the neutrality patrol.

The army's plans, as published yesterday, contemplate an increase in the enlisted strength of the regular army to the full 280,000 authorized by the National Defense Act. The National ▸

Guard would be increased also to its full authorized quota as defined in the act, a force of approximately 420,000 enlisted men, bringing the strength of what is known as our "I. P. F." or "Initial Protective Force" to about 705,000, plus perhaps 30,000 to 40,000 officers.

The enlisted strength of the regular army, which is now about 210,000, including the Philippine Scouts, is being raised to 227,000 under the terms of the President's executive order issued soon after the start of the European war.

The further increase contemplated will mean, therefore, an addition of another 53,000 men to the regular forces, while the Guard would be almost doubled in strength. The Guard's strength today is somewhat short of 200,000, but it is being increased to 235,000 under the President's recent order. ◊

OCTOBER 18, 1939

BRITISH PREPARING FOR A 'BLITZKRIEG'
Motor Units Behind Lines Are Seen in Practice by Corps of Correspondents

By HAROLD DENNY
Wireless to The New York Times.

WITH THE BRITISH FORCES IN FRANCE, Oct. 16 [Delayed]—Though the war, which at any time may surge over the fields and villages about us, seems remote now, every element of the British Army, which is moving into position at a daily increasing pace, is on the alert as completely as if Chancellor Hitler's legions already were on the next ridge.

Behind the front line, where the infantry, formidably armed and strongly fortified, is on guard night and day, other elements are rehearsing daily the manoeuvres that they are likely to be called on to execute in battle conditions among these very hills and valleys.

Vital among these elements is the mechanized cavalry—a new development of modern war technique, and it was your correspondent's privilege today to participate in field exercises of this arm. These had many of the thrills of a real battle without, however, the annoyance of being shot at.

The unit that I visited was a squadron of this new horseless cavalry. It was composed of light but powerfully armored and armed tanks—which certainly will slow up if they do not themselves absolutely check any Hitlerian "Blitzkrieg" through here—and of "carriers."

ARMED BATTLE WAGONS

These "carriers" are well-armored battle wagons carrying machine guns and rifles of various types suitable for firing on anything, including infantry, tanks and airplanes. The speed with which these carriers can get into serious action is amazing.

We saw a squadron race across an open field, come to a sudden halt, and then the personnel of all but one leaped out with their guns and mounted them for anti-aircraft work. The one carrier covered them with its machine guns. Meanwhile, the carriers whose crews were mounting guns on the ground raced for cover and in a few seconds were so well camouflaged we, who knew where they were, had difficulty in finding them even with field glasses.

Then came a sham battle in which the correspondents participated, though as backseat drivers.

The function of motorized cavalry is much the same as that of cavalry in the earlier eras—to act as a screen for other arms, to feel out the enemy and make the initial contact, to seize and to hold ground when required until infantry can come up and take over. Officers and men who are in this branch know that it is one of the riskiest in all warfare, but those we met today displayed the same easy confidence that we have seen all along the British front.

CORRESPONDENTS IN TANKS

When the positions were taken for an advance by the tanks against a simulated enemy, the correspondents clumsily climbed into these weird vehicles and found themselves in the midst of a forest of mechanical implements arranged in an incredibly small space. It fell to the lot of this correspondent to sit in the place of the tank commander with eyeslits just in front of him in a tiny subturret that he could swing with almost no effort so as to see everything going on in front and at sides and even behind, had he chosen to swing his turret in that direction.

This little turret was like the conning-tower of a submarine. Everything was at hand to control the tank's movement. Just in front of my face was a speaking tube to the driver, who sat straight out in front before an instrument board as intricate as that on an airplane.

My own spot was tight and well-padded with rubber at places that might strike me. Below, at my left in the main turret, was another correspondent—Webb Miller of The United Press—manning a high-powered automatic gun and also fixed so fast in his place that he was almost immune to any injury from the progress of the tank itself. He did emerge, however, with a bruised leg as the result of one of our jumps over natural obstacles.

REPORT MADE BY WIRELESS

I frankly confess that I had only the faintest idea what was our objective, and in fact there was none—merely to make contact with the enemy, report his position by wireless, with which every tank is equipped, and scoot back for cover.

The squadron commander had instructed me to give orders through the speaking tube and I did so with excellent results, I thought. I commanded "forward" when I thought that appropriate and ordered the driver to veer off the path of a tank with which I thought we might collide.

He did these things and I felt quite pleased until he began going quite contrary to my directions. After hurdling a ditch and coming to rest on the edge of a potato field, I learned that the entire operating personnel had had full instructions before we started and we emerged as merely slightly seasick passengers. ◊

Troops of the British Expeditionary Force after disembarking the troopship 'Worthing' at Cherbourg in France, 1939.

OCTOBER 19, 1939

SHORTAGE FEARED OF SCOTCH WHISKY

231,000 CASES ON OCEAN
Loss of Two Ships With This Cargo Would Badly Deplete Supply of Aged Stocks

Special Cable to The New York Times.

LONDON, Oct. 18—There are two ships on the Atlantic tonight with 231,000 cases of eight-year-old Scotch whisky on board. If the Germans get it there is going to be a shortage of aged Scotch before long.

Distillers here say there is enough young whisky here to last at least two and a half years of a war, but all the really aged whisky available now is "depression whisky." In 1931, 1932 and 1933 the makers were hit hard and they did not lay down nearly the normal supply.

So, what with the war and depression, whiskies are likely to get younger and dearer all the time. The price is going up because British ships carrying them to New York are traveling in expensive convoys and insurance rates for both British and United States vessels have soared since the start of the war.

WAREHOUSE INSURANCE BARRED

Then, too, distillers over here are having plenty of trouble. They cannot get any insurance for their bonded warehouses, so that an air-raid like the few in Scotland the last couple of days might seriously diminish the supply. It is possible, for some unexplained reason, for distillers to get insurance on whisky not in warehouses, but that is not going to console the boys on Broadway if a stray bomb wipes out one of their favorite distilleries.

Before long nobody is likely to be permitted to grow barley or corn over here except for "human consumption." While there is evidence that whisky is actually consumed by human beings, there are other restrictions that prevent crops from being used for spirits.

The supply of gin also is likely to be reduced, but the same problem of an aged supply does not arise, because it is an immature spirit anyway.

EMBARGO ON DRINKING SEEN

The only immediate hope of increasing the supply of Scotch for the United States is that an embargo be placed on drinking in this country, as was done in the last war. So far, however, consumption of whisky has gone up since the blackout restricted many other forms of amusement. But if it keeps going up and the agitation for some wartime form of prohibition increases, consumption here may be reduced and so release some of the supply to the United States. ◇

OCTOBER 25, 1939

BELIEF RISING HERE U.S. WILL SHUN WAR
American Institute of Public Opinion Survey Shows 54% Hold to This View

The number of American voters who believe the United States will be drawn into the European war has decreased sharply since hostilities started, according to a survey made public yesterday by the American Institute of Public Opinion, of which Dr. George Gallup is director.

"Two weeks before the war broke out an institute survey found a large majority believing that the United States would be drawn into a war if it came," the institute said. "Today opinion is more evenly divided, with a small majority saying they think the country will avoid armed participation in the present war.

"The question on which a cross-section of voters throughout the country were asked to express their views read as follows:

"'Do you think the United States will go into the war in Europe, or do you think we will stay out of the war?'

"Those who expressed an opinion divided as follows:

> Will go in 46%
> Will stay out 54

"Approximately one voter in every eight (13 per cent) expressed no opinion.

"The fact that before the war a majority thought the United States would be involved, whereas today there is a tendency to believe it can stay out, may have several explanations. First, two months ago most voters thought of the next war in terms of the last, or, in other words, a 'war in earnest.' The first six weeks of the present war, however, with its cautious and perfunctory fighting and the absence of bombardments on open cities in France and England during that period, have apparently caused a reduction in fear of immediate American involvement.

"Second, the voters themselves, and many experts, apparently underestimated two months ago the intensity of desire throughout the country to avoid getting into war. Since the outbreak of hostilities this intensity has manifested itself in many surveys by the institute, in letters to Congress and in other ways.

"Third, President Roosevelt has on repeated occasions since early September solemnly assured the country that the United States is not going to join the conflict. These pronouncements may have had a quieting effect. ◇

Chapter 2

"FIGHTING IN THE WEST IS AT A STANDSTILL"

November 1939–March 1940

The months following the German victory over Poland were nicknamed the "Phony War" because there was very little military action between the Anglo-French Allies and the German Reich. Years later Cyrus Sulzberger, the lead foreign correspondent for The Times during the 1940s, wrote that the "British and French gave the appearance of being removed from the conflict they had accepted." The chief action was at sea and The Times gave full coverage to the battle off the Latin American coast, which led on December 18 to the scuttling of the German pocket battleship Graf Spee in Montevideo harbor.

The real fighting took place elsewhere, first in China, where the Japanese Army continued to press forward against crumbling Chinese resistance , but most important of all in the war begun by Stalin's Soviet Union against the small Scandinavian nation of Finland. This was an act of aggression prompted by the German-Soviet pact of August 1939, which put Finland into the Soviet sphere of influence. Stalin wanted to bolster Soviet security by establishing additional bases on Finnish territory. The Finns naturally refused. War began on November 30, 1939 and, to the astonishment of the wider world, the tiny Finnish Army resisted the Soviet assault. According to The Times, Finnish success partly stemmed from Soviet incompetence, but was chiefly a matter of Finnish tactical skill, with fast ski troops firing their submachine guns as they moved in and out of the snow-covered landscape. Soviet losses were heavy. "The bodies," wrote one eyewitness, "were frozen as hard as petrified wood."

In the end Finland had to give in and concede bases and territory to the Soviet giant. But all this time, as The Times headline put it, "Fighting in the West Is at a Standstill."

In China Japanese Army leaders were trying to patch up a peace with the Chinese warlords to ensure permanent domination of China. The Times was clear that even if Japanese civilians wanted to forge a better relationship with the United States, "The mentality of Japan's military commanders has not changed." The crisis in Asia remained at the forefront of much of the reporting during the Phony War. The Times's concern with the problem of India and the harsh British treatment of Mahatma Gandhi's independence movement was to be a feature throughout the wartime years. Oppression was also the key to reporting on the German occupation of Poland following defeat of the Polish forces in late September. The main focus was on the treatment of the large Polish Jewish community. Some two million Jews lived in the area of Poland under German control in the annexed territories and the so-called General-Government of Poland, set up under the National Socialist lawyer, Hans Frank. The Times ran articles alerting its readers to the establishment of ghettos for Jews in occupied Poland and the problems of famine faced by a Jewish population that was singled out for deliberate discrimination. In January Dr. Nahum Goldmann addressed the American Jewish Congress in Chicago with the news that as many as one million Jews would die in occupied Poland during 1940. The same month The Times ran a piece under the headline "Jews Lay Torture to Nazis in Poland."

In the United States attitudes toward the war were divided. Though many Americans sympathized with the Western Allies and disliked Hitlerism, Hitler still came out on top in a poll of college students, asking them who they felt were the world's most outstanding personalities. The American public had other concerns—the problem of Japanese aggression, the threat of communism—as well as the domestic problems of economic revival following the Great Depression. By March, however, there were signs that the Phony War was approaching an end. "War Seen Entering a New Phase of Violence" ran the headline. And indeed it was.

NOVEMBER 3, 1939

FINNS IN MOSCOW WITH FINAL OFFER

By G. E. R. GEDYE
Wireless to The New York Times.

MOSCOW, Nov. 2—The Finnish delegation returned to Moscow this morning—headed by Dr. Juho K. Paasikivi and composed as before, with the addition of R. Hakkarainen, Finnish Chief of Protocol. The members were met at the railroad station at 10:30 A. M. by Vladimir Barkoff, Soviet Chief of Protocol, and the Swedish, Norwegian and Danish Ministers.

It was decided that there would be no meeting with Joseph Stalin and Premier Vyacheslaff Molotoff today as the delegation was busy preparing a translation of final documents. The Finns this evening attended as spectators, accompanied by Mr. Barkoff, the session of the Supreme Soviet, which was devoted to a reception of the White Russian delegation from the former Polish White Russian region.

Information from Helsinki indicates that the Finns are bringing with them their final offer, and apparently they are now willing to meet the Soviet Union to a considerable extent concerning demands for the cession of territory that Moscow claims is essential for the defense of Leningrad.

FINNS NOT WHOLLY YIELDING

It is believed Finland is willing to cede Hogland and other islands off Kronstadt and further to meet the Soviet Union on the question of the cession of territory in the extreme north of Finland. What the Finns apparently feel unable to do—virtually destroy their independence—is to lease the port of Hangoe to the Soviet Government for the establishment of a Soviet base there. Rather than do this the Finns would prefer to fight.

[A Moscow broadcast intercepted in London this morning said that Finnish Foreign Minister Eljas Erkko in his speech Wednesday had "delivered an open threat of war against the Soviet Union," according to a United Press dispatch. The broadcast also said that comments in Finnish newspapers on Premier Molotoff's address to the Supreme Soviet were of a "hostile nature."]

Despite the alarming character of passages in Premier Molotoff's speech to the Supreme Soviet, in regard to Finland, the Finns seem to believe the Soviet Union will recognize the extent of their concessions as generous and conclude a peaceful agreement rather than proceed to extremes. ◇

NOVEMBER 12, 1939

THE REAL THREAT: NOT BOMBS, BUT IDEAS

By LIN YUTANG

In the progress of human civilization the arts of living and the arts of killing—artcraft and warcraft—have always existed side by side. No history of any nation shows that a period of peace without domestic or foreign wars ever existed for more than 300 years. This seems to derive from the fact that man is both a fighting and a peaceful animal. In him the fighting instinct and the instinct for peaceful living—which I call the carnivorous and the herbivorous instincts—are strangely mixed.

This is not to imply a state of human imperfection; it may be questioned whether the kind of civilization wherein man is so thoroughly tamed and domesticated that there is no more fight left in him would be worth having at all. Life is, or should be, accompanied by struggle, or else the racial fiber degenerates, which happens within the amazingly short period of a few generations in a well-provided family.

NOVEMBER 22, 1939

GANDHI WARNS BRITISH ON INDIA'S WAR ROLE
'Complete Freedom' for India Is Demanded as Price

BOMBAY, India, Nov. 21 (AP)—Mohandas K. Gandhi told Britain bluntly today that the resignation of eight of India's eleven provincial governments meant they could not participate in the war against Germany unless they obtained in return "complete freedom" for India.

The little leader of millions of Indians asserted that this was their "emphatic" answer to the British White Paper of Oct. 17 deferring discussion of India's status until after the war.

His statement was made as he met at Allahabad with a committee of the Congress party [Nationalists] to discuss the country's attitude toward the European conflict.

The Moslem League, second largest political party in India, has endorsed the British stand despite the protest resignations of the eight provincial governments dominated by the Congress party.

Two weeks after Britain declared war on Germany India committed herself officially to fight on the British side and M. Gandhi and his followers have criticized the Germans.

But the 70-year-old leader asserted today that the issue in his demands for a pledge of Indian independence is "purely a moral one, for owing to her material and military control, Britain is able to regulate garrisons and drain India's wealth at will."

The gist of the contention of the working committee of the Congress party with whom Gandhi conferred today is:

"If Britain fights for the maintenance and extension of democracy she must necessarily end imperialism in her own possessions and establish full democracy in India and the Indian people must have the right of self-determination to frame their own constitution through a constituent assembly." ◇

I am not trying to condone war, but am merely pointing out our biological heritage. In the world of nature the warring instinct and the instinct to live are different aspects of the same thing. Those primeval biological instincts go deeper than any temporary ideologies or political creeds. In the biological world merciless wars have always existed side by side with the most persistent displays of love for the young and all those manifestations of courtship which produce beauty and which we know as the charm and fragrance of the flower, the caroling of the lark and the song of the cricket.

It is somewhat disheartening to the student of nature that the most ruthless war is going on above ground and under ground day and night in what is apparently a peaceful forest, or to reflect that the kingfisher sitting on a branch so peacefully in a sunset has just returned from murder of an innocent minnow. It is also a source of comfort to know that nature's instinct to live is always overpowering and managed to stage a most impressive comeback after a natural disaster. Anybody who visited the coasts of the Long Island Sound last Spring and saw the green trees and peaceful landscape after the disastrous hurricane of the Autumn before cannot help being impressed by nature's persistent urge to live.

Today, once more, Europe is ravaged by war. To every observer war seemed inevitable after Munich, because peace was so much like war that, to the average Frenchman or Englishman a temporary peace seemed infinitely more devastating. To add to the confusion the fighting man still parades as a lover of peace, and aggressors accuse their victims as "warmongers." Hitler, returning red-handed from the murder of Poland, offered that same "outstretched hand" to Europe and asked innocently, "Why should there be war?" And Japan, plunging into a continental slaughter, claims only the desire to set up a "new order." Peace and war are worse confounded than ever.

What is the meaning of all this? Has man's instinct for peaceful living been temporarily inhibited, overshadowed and perhaps destroyed by the warring instinct? And will civilization—meaning the arts, the religions, the common faiths of mankind, the modern conquests of science and the arts of living—will this modern civilization be destroyed? Let us take up the second proposition first.

Many people are horrified by the thoughts of Paris or London demolished by air bombing, and many foremost thinkers of today are rather inclined to believe that modern civilization as we know it will be destroyed. I beg profoundly to differ.

Knowing that the warring instinct is but another aspect of the instinct for living, and believing that no man going to battle has ever renounced the desire to live. I think the instinct for living is the stronger of the two and hence cannot be destroyed. Since that instinct cannot be destroyed, civilization, too, or the arts of living, cannot be destroyed. What do we mean when we say that by this war modern civilization will be destroyed?

Physically the arts and sciences may receive a temporary setback, but I wager that after the war hens will still lay eggs and men will still not have forgotten how to make omelettes. Sheep will still grow wool and English mills will still turn out tweeds and homespuns. The physical features of a city may be altered under the most ruthless bombing, and conceivably some old manuscripts or even the Magna Carta, in the British Museum, may be lost or go up in flames. Some English poets and French scientists may be killed by shrapnel and some valuable laboratory equipment, or even all of Oxford, may be wiped out.

Still, the underground Bodleian Library cannot be destroyed. Still, the scientific method will survive: it is inconceivable that all treatises and textbooks of science will disappear. Gramophone records and Chopin's music will still be there, because the love for music will still be there. The quality of manhood may suffer perceptibly from the slaughter of the flower of the nation. But so long as a nation is not completely annihilated, and no nation can be annihilated with the worst aerial bombings, modern civilization and all the heritage of the arts and the sciences will be carried on. After war and destruction the generous instinct for peaceful living, the creative forces of human ingenuity will restore Europe in an amazingly short period.

This leads to the subtler, nonphysical aspects of the question and the positive side of human living. Modern civilization would be destroyed if the things we take for granted—freedom of belief, the rights and liberties of the individual, democracy and that now tottering faith in the common man—if these things were destroyed. Without war a totalitarian State which deprives men of these gifts of civilization and sets men as spies upon their fellow-men has already begun to destroy civilization. With a nation not so easily regimented, where the spirit of man still remains free, that civilization cannot be destroyed by a war.

It is, in fact, entirely possible for civilization to destroy itself by subordinating the instinct for peaceful living to the other instinct for killing. Civilization can be destroyed unless these simple values of human life are more jealously guarded and the simple liberties and privileges of living are more consciously appreciated. There is every sign of the danger that in contemporary thinking and contemporary life such common privileges of living are increasingly giving way to the claims of the State-monster. The citizen of a totalitarian State in Europe has already lost certain privileges and liberties of thinking and living which the savages of Africa have always enjoyed and are still enjoying.

In fact, we have already traveled a long way from civilization as ordinarily understood. All nature loafs. Then civilization came, offering man certain comforts of living in exchange for certain restrictions of liberty, generally called a sense of duty. No horse has a sense of duty, and every carrier-pigeon flies home just because he likes it. But man was put to work.

First he was told to work for a living. Next he was told to war for a living in defense of his right to work. And now we are told to put guns before butter and regard it as a nobler form of death to die with one's army boots on than with one's boots off in bed. We are going back to nature without the natural liberties of nature. Man has ration cards and a sense of duty. A million automatons, completely trained and regimented to think in one direction, either curse or praise the Soviet Union as their master tells them to do.

And so what threatens civilization today is not war itself or the destructions of war but the changing conceptions of life values entailed by certain types of political doctrines. These doctrines directly impinge upon man's ordinary, natural privileges of living and subordinate them to the needs of national killing. The importance of killing supersedes the importance of living, from the totalitarian standpoint.

It cannot be denied that from the point of view of the State, organized for war and conquest, totalitarianism has everything to be said for it, but from the standpoint of the individual as the ultimate aim served by civilization, and for the purpose of enjoying the ordinary blessings of living, it has nothing to be said on its side. It is neither the machine nor war that is destroying modern civilization but the tendency to surrender the rights of the individual to the State which is such a powerful factor in contemporary thinking. ◊

DECEMBER 1, 1939

SOVIET INVADERS SEIZE ARCTIC AREA

Wireless to The New York Times.

COPENHAGEN, Denmark, Dec. 1— Finland fought all day yesterday against the land, sea and air forces of Soviet Russia, which started an invasion of the neighboring country in the morning.

The Russians set cities and towns afire with aerial bombs, shelled ports from land and sea along the Gulf of Finland and captured the whole Finnish section of the Rybachi peninsula, including the port of Petsamo, in the far north on the Arctic Ocean.

Helsinki, Viborg, Kotka and Hangoe were among the many cities bombed. The dead were in the hundreds, with many wounded. The scenes in Helsinki were frightful; workers were still digging in the ruins in the heart of the city during the night.

[The Finnish High Command announced in the first war communiqué that the defending forces had halted the Russian attacks in stiff fighting, according to a United Press dispatch from Helsinki early this morning. A Soviet announcement early today said Russian forces had penetrated Finland 6¼ to about 10 miles, according to a United Press dispatch from Moscow.]

WAR BEGUN AT DAWN

Shortly after 9 A. M. yesterday the people of Finland realized that war with Russia was a fact. Not until then did it become known that at daybreak Russian forces had attacked three principal points on the Finnish-Soviet border north of Lake Ladoga, Finnish troops guarding the Karelian Isthmus between Lake Ladoga and the Gulf of Finland, and points on the Rybachi Peninsula on the Arctic Ocean.

Simultaneously Russian bombers swept over Finland, dropping incendiary bombs and high explosives on the main points and upon cities, and also whirling leaflets upon the Finnish people, telling them that Russia does not want war with the Finns but that they must get rid of "false leaders," naming Foreign Minister Eljas Erkko, Field Marshal Baron Carl Gustav Mannerheim, commander of the Finnish armed forces, and the whole government of Premier Aimo Cajander.

The Russian Baltic fleet took part in the invasion by bombarding the Karelian coast and further engaged in the occupation of the disputed islands in the Gulf of Finland—Seiskari, Tytarsaari and Hogland. Finally, the Russian fleet attacked Hangoe, strategic base west of Helsinki. In the extreme north the Russians invaded the Rybachi Peninsula and occupied the whole territory, including the port of Petsamo, in a few hours.

North of Lake Ladoga the Russian attack started near Suojaervi, beginning with artillery fire, and more than fifty shells fell upon Finnish territory in a short time. The chief Russian land attack was concentrated upon the Karelian Isthmus. At 9:15 A. M. heavy batteries near Leningrad opened fire against the border cities of Rajakoki, Vammelsuu and Terijoki, with units of the Russian Baltic fleet taking part in the bombardments.

The Russians later occupied Hyrsylae in the Suojaervi district.

Russian aerial squadrons struck yesterday morning at big power plants at Imatra Falls, near Viborg. At noon the industrial center of Enso, with Finland's biggest cellulose factories, was bombed, and a school and a hospital were hit. Many were killed or wounded. Details were not immediately obtainable.

Shortly after noon Russian planes bombed Viborg, chief eastern city of Finland, and Kotka, shipping center and a regular port of call of American Scantic Line vessels. Some buildings in Viborg were set afire. Details of the losses in the two cities were not made known. ◆

A rescue squad at work in the burning ruins of houses in Helsinki following a Russian bombing raid in 1939.

DECEMBER 1, 1939

FIGHTING IN WEST IS AT A STANDSTILL
French, for First Time Since War Began, Report Complete Quiet Along the Front

FINLAND HOLDS ATTENTION

Wireless to The New York Times.

PARIS, Nov. 30—With the Soviet aggression against Finland there is again an eastern front. Though at present it has no direct connection with the western theatre of the war this fact, nevertheless, dominates the entire military situation today. The development is so pregnant with possibilities that it may well mark a turning point.

Authorized circles here are reticent in view of the scanty and contradictory reports at hand. The recurring question today is: What new military combinations may develop and what new fronts?"

On the Western Front in the last twenty-four hours it has been the old story—bad weather, intermittent shelling and much patrolling. The visibility is so bad that for the first time since the war began the French air headquarters reported, "Activity: Nil."

In these conditions all reconnaissance work was left to ground patrols. On the outskirts of the Haardt forest the French ambushed an enemy patrol that lost four prisoners.

The major part of the artillery fire occurred in the sector near the Moselle River where German working parties were much harassed while strengthening their positions.

Today's French communiqués follow:

"No. 175 [morning]. Nothing to report."

"No. 176 [evening]. Customary activity on the part of our patrols.

"One of our torpedo boats successfully attacked an enemy submarine." ◊

DECEMBER 2, 1939

PRESIDENT IS STERN
Invasion Denounced In His Strongest Words Since War Began

By BERTRAM D. HULEN
Special to The New York Times.

WASHINGTON, Dec. 1—The Russian Government was taken sternly to task by President Roosevelt today in a statement condemning severely the invasion of Finland and the bombing of civilians.

Read by the President at his press conference this morning, as official reports were being received of continued Soviet bombings, the statement foreshadowed a prompt declaration of a moral embargo against the export of United States airplanes to Russia.

However, while Mr. Roosevelt in replying to questions left the door open to all possible future courses of action to mark the displeasure of the United States, it was understood that at his regular Friday Cabinet meeting this afternoon a decision was reached to reject any action so drastic as severing diplomatic relations with Russia, at least for the present.

In his statement, the President described the "profound shock to the government and the people of the United States" caused by Russia's resort to arms, said it was tragic to realize that "wanton disregard for law is still on the march," and declared that Russia's action menaces the security of small nations, and "jeopardizes the rights of mankind to self-government."

He closed with a fervent expression of the warm regard of the government and the people of the United States for Finland.

STRONGEST OF HIS STATEMENTS

The significance of the pointed phrasing was enhanced by the fact that this is the first time since the outbreak of the European war that the President has gone so far in expressing his disapproval of the politics of conquest. Even when Germany overran Poland, he did not issue such a statement, although to the last he pleaded for peace and left no doubt as to his concern over the course of events.

As the President was making his

President Roosevelt in 1939.

announcements at the press conference the United States legation in Helsinki reported to the State Department that it was evacuating many Americans from the capital to the legation's emergency quarters at Grankulla in private cars of members of the legation staff.

Still later the United States Minister to Finland, H. F. Arthur Achoenfeld, reported that the Minister of the Interior in a radio speech to the nation at noon said that there was calm throughout the whole country, and that evacuation from Helsinki was proceeding smoothly. He solicited continued public cooperation, praised the soldiers and appealed to the public to follow their example. He said that the Finnish people have chosen independence, and are unanimous, and that history will show whether their choice was right.

Hjalmar Procope, the Finnish Minister here, said today that the new government at Helsinki was truly representative of all political parties in Finland and had the unanimous support of the people, while the Communist-fostered government of Mr. Kuusinien consisted of a few Finnish Communists who lived in Russia.

"The appointment of this Communist government," he said, "shows the real value and meaning of the statements of Mr. Molotoff [Soviet Premier-Foreign Commissar Vyacheslojff M. Molotoff] and other Russian leaders that the aim of the action against Finland is to insure its independence and freedom. This shows that they intend the incorporation of Finland in the Soviet Union and the Bolshevik freedom." ◊

DECEMBER 3, 1939

POLAND PROTESTS GERMAN 'HORRORS'

Ambassador to Britain Says Country 'Has Become Sport of Bestial Hangmen'

Special Cable to The New York Times.

LONDON, Dec. 2—Count Edward Raczynski, the Polish Ambassador, handed to Viscount Halifax, the Foreign Secretary, today a strongly worded protest accusing the Germans of robbery and murder in Poland and charging that human life in that country "has become the sport of ferocious and bestial hangmen."

TEXT OF THE PROTEST

The text of the protest follows:

Reports reaching us every day during the whole month of September on the matter of the warfare employed by the Germans against Poland have shocked the whole world.

Never before and nowhere else has an enemy treated with such ruthlessness the whole of a defenseless population on whom in cities and even in villages there rained bombs, shells and machine-gun bullets. One would have thought that as soon as the whole country had been subjugated this lust for inflicting misery would have ceased.

However, the contrary has happened.

From all parts of the country occupied by Germany where, side by side with the military authorities, who declaim phrases about honor, and the administrative authorities, who talk so willingly and eloquently about culture, order and justice, there rule the Gestapo and Hitler Elite Guard detachments, reports are arriving which fill us with horror.

While the property of the population has become the object of unending robberies and is being seized on the spot from its owners, who together with their families are being evicted from their homes, so the entire population is being driven from vast and ancient Polish areas and human life has become the sport of ferocious and bestial hangmen.

Never before in modern history, not even during periods of the fiercest wars, have such gloomy events occurred as now occur daily in Poland.

In all districts of Western Poland leading citizens in the life of the nation are being shot, one after the other, and their names are whispered throughout the horrified country over their silent graves.

UNIVERSITY FACULTY JAILED

Within the space of a single day there were jailed and deported into the interior of Germany all professors of the ancient University of Cracow. These are only the most glaring of the acts of violence that are being perpetrated amid the incessant general oppression of millions of people.

The Polish Government is preparing an official publication containing a tabulation of the cruelties which have come to its cognizance. Before this White Book is published, however, it considers it its duty to declare without delay that the soil of Poland under German domination has become the soil of martyrdom.

National Socialist savagery is writing a new and ominous page in the history of German cruelty, which by its slaughter of the helpless outdoes the darkest memories of the past.

The spirit of conquest and robbery, which has marked in blood and destruction the march of Germany throughout the centuries, has come to life again and is sowing its seed amid ruin and crime.

The Germans will learn once more that by such acts one gains before the eyes of the world no greatness but contempt, no fame but infamy, no victory but defeat.

Poland will only fortify her will to resist and struggle. The world will raise the arm of justice and God will judge and chastise the criminals. ◈

Three Poles who were hung in a public square in Warsaw, 1940.

DECEMBER 8, 1939

FINNS OPEN DRIVE ON FOE IN KARELIA

HELSINKI, Finland, Dec. 7 (AP)—Finnish troops launched a strong counter-attack today in the Karelian Isthmus in an effort to halt a Red Army surge toward the eastern terminus of their Mannerheim Line.

The Russians bombarded the southern coast of Finland from the sea and renewed their land attacks on the central front.

Contrary to Russian assertions, a Finnish Army spokesman said, the invaders were not yet threatening the Mannerheim Line, a water defense system composed of an irregular chain of lakes extending almost across the narrow isthmus. The line begins at Sakkola on the east and follows a westward course through the town of Muolaa to Kuolema Lake, "The Lake of Death."

The heaviest fighting was reported along the Taipale River and along the southern edge of Lake Ladoga near Sakkola, which is twenty miles from the frontier, and at Uusikirkko, about twelve and a half miles from the frontier and fifteen miles southeast of the Mannerheim Line's eastern terminus.

DAMAGE BY RED FLEET DENIED

Despite the bad weather the Red Fleet bombarded undisclosed points along the southern coast, but the Finns declared the big guns had caused no damage. They said their famed coastal batteries, designed by Lieut. Gen. V. P. Nenonen, Chief of Finnish Artillery, had beaten off the attacks.

On the front in Central Finland the Finns reported they were holding their own against new Soviet attacks. Soviet fighters were aiming at Tolua Lake on this front.

A government spokesman said army physicians were treating eleven cases of gas poisoning at Salmi, on the northern shore of Lake Ladoga.

An army spokesman said papers taken from captured Russian officers indicated the Soviet forces were aiming at reaching the Atlantic. The prisoners had maps of the Aland Islands and Eastern Sweden on which certain objectives were marked for bombing, the spokesman asserted. He added that the papers indicated Russia had long planned her attack on Finland.

AWAIT RUSSIAN MOVE

With a rocky, ice-coated No Man's Land separating the two forces, the Finns were said to be leaving it to the Russians to take the initiative. The severe Winter weather—the temperature was reported at 20 degrees below zero—made both land and aerial activities extremely difficult there. The Russians were said to be awaiting long-overdue provisions and ammunition stocks.

Increasing cold and heavy snowstorms over the country led Finns to hope that the war might settle down to a long-drawn siege in which the Finnish troops might benefit to an even greater extent from their guerrilla type of warfare and in which the Russian troops, already reported to be suffering from inadequate clothing and food, would be handicapped by long lines of communication over trackless, snowbound territory.

Reports from the fighting fronts paid tribute to the effectiveness of the Finnish Army's anti-tank gun, a portable weapon easily carried by one man and said to be able to halt and cripple the light tanks that the Russians have been using.

Unofficial military quarters estimated that the Red Army had suffered at least 10,000 casualties, including dead and wounded, since the start of the invasion eight days ago. Finnish losses were said to be "amazingly small" by comparison. ◆

DECEMBER 11, 1939

'KEEP OUT OF WAR' KENNEDY ADVISES
He Warns Against Any Talk That We Can Make Things 'One Whit Better'

By The Associated Press.

BOSTON, Dec. 10—In his first speech since the start of the European war, Joseph P. Kennedy, Ambassador to Great Britain, strongly urged tonight that the United States "keep out" of the conflict.

"As you love America, don't let anything that comes out of any country in the world make you believe you can make a situation one whit better by getting into the war," he said.

"There is no place in this fight for us. It's going to be bad enough as it is."

He spoke extemporaneously at a reunion of parishioners of Our Lady of Assumption Church, where he served as an altar boy.

Smiling, but admittedly "not optimistic" concerning the world situation, he later declared in an interview:

"There is no reason—economic, financial or social—to justify the United States entering the war."

One of the chief influences that might bring such an involvement, he said, was the American people's "sporting spirit" in "not wanting to see an unfair or immoral thing done," but he reiterated that "this is not our fight."

Asked whether there was any possibility of peace in the near future, he replied that it was "anybody's guess."

"All want peace but all have their own ideas as to what peace should be," he asserted. "Under such circumstances, who can say when there will be peace?"

Emphasizing his feeling that the United States should "stay out," he declared:

"If anybody advocates our entering the war, the American public should demand a specific answer to the question: 'Why?'" ◆

Joseph P. Kennedy in 1939.

MOSCOW ACCEPTS EXPULSION QUIETLY
Geneva Body Is Said to Have Degenerated Into Organ of Allied Imperialism

By G. E. R. GEDYE
Wireless to The New York Times.

MOSCOW, Dec. 15—The Soviet Union has accepted with unexpected quiet its expulsion from the League of Nations. Apparently recent exuberance here has been subdued by the general condemnation of the invasion of Finland and by the slowness of the Finnish campaign. However, the only opportunity Soviet citizens have had to learn of Russia's expulsion was contained in an inconspicuous news item, the heading of which did not allude to that action but said noncommittally: "Session of the Council of the League of Nations." The message that follows, sent by the Tass Agency from Geneva, says briefly:

"The Council of the League acquainted itself with a resolution passed by the Assembly of the League of Nations and issued a decree on the expulsion of the U.S.S.R. from the League of Nations. The delegates of Greece, Yugoslavia and China refrained from voting. The delegates of Iran and Peru were not present at the session."

The item itself is tucked away in a corner under a long ironic dispatch from Geneva describing the degradation of the League, intended as a genuinely international body, into an auxiliary enterprise of the Anglo-French war bloc. ◊

RAIDER BLOWN UP

By JOHN W. WHITE
Wireless to The New York Times.

MONTEVIDEO, Uruguay, Dec. 17—The South Atlantic Odyssey of Germany's proud pocket battleship Admiral Graf Spee reached a dramatic and tragic end at sunset this evening when her commander, Captain Hans Langsdorff, stood in a launch and pressed an electric button that blew her up and caused her to burst into a roaring and exploding furnace as she sank in the mud in the mouth of the River Plate.

Standing at the salute with Captain Langsdorff in the launch were his officers. Floating near the doomed battleship were barges and launches into which the commander had loaded his crew of young, stern-faced Germans. A mile away stood the German cargo steamer Tacoma, which had followed the Graf Spee out of Montevideo Harbor to pick up the crew.

On board the Tacoma were all the married men of the crew. They had been transferred to the cargo ship a few minutes before the warship's departure.

TACOMA'S CAPTAIN ARRESTED
The captain of the Tacoma was arrested

The German pocket battleship Admiral Graf Spee in flames after being scuttled off Montevideo, Uruguay, December 17, 1939.

tonight because he took his ship out of the harbor without the customary permission of the port authorities. Members of the German crew aboard the Tacoma will be interned here. The rest of the crew has been taken to Buenos Aires where it is presumed they will deliver themselves to the Argentine authorities.

The crew was taken to Buenos Aires because, if it were returned to the shore here, its members would be interned. They expect Argentina to treat them as survivors of a sunken vessel.

The German Legation published a letter from Captain Langsdorff tonight in which he blamed Uruguay for the loss of his ship on the ground that insufficient time had been allowed to make the vessel seaworthy.

EXPLOSION IS TREMENDOUS

Captain Langsdorff pressed his electric button just as the top rim of the sun sank below the horizon, dyeing the sky a brilliant blood red. A dull, tremendous explosion followed. A great cloud of gray smoke hid the warship for a minute, then a light wind blew it toward the shore.

Overhead floated small, lazy clouds exactly the same color as the smoke. High in the blue sky, the half moon looked down completely unconcerned.

As this correspondent stood on a hotel roof and watched the breathtaking spectacle, it did not seem real. The setting was too perfect. But in three minutes the Graf Spee had settled on the bottom and flames had begun to burst up from her exploding magazines.

The electric button that the commander pressed was on the end of a long electric cable leading to a huge electric time mine that had been planted in the magazine. The effectiveness of that mine was terrific. In ten minutes the flames were roaring from the entire length of the warship, accompanied by constant explosions in the hold.

BURNS FOR SOME TIME

The Graf Spee burned steadily, and explosions of petroleum and shells continued. Fires later reached the petroleum stores and will probably burn all night. At 9:15 there was an unusual and heavy explosion that sent brightly colored rockets and great balls of flame high into the air in all directions.

As darkness settled down around the remains of the warship, on which Germany had pinned so many hopes, the bright Morse lights of an approaching warship signaled to Captain Langsdorff. Approaching the warship at 9:15, was the Argentine gunboat Libertad, which had come to take Captain Langsdorff

and his officers aboard for their journey up the River Plate to Buenos Aires.

The last short chapter of the Spee's history began at 6:20 P. M. when the warship started moving slowly from her anchorage toward the outer entrance of the harbor with a big red and black Nazi flag flying smartly from the mast behind the funnel and fighting top.

LARGE CROWD WATCHES

It was a bright, sunny afternoon and virtually the entire population of Montevideo was jammed along the seawalls and docks and on housetops, watching the Graf Spee's departure. For four days she had been an unwelcome visitor in Montevideo's pretty harbor and the city had talked or thought of little else. Now the unwelcome visitor was going.

Some of France's and Britain's greatest battleships were known to be assembled near the mouth of the River Plate, determined to hunt down and destroy the pocket battleship. For four months she had eluded her enemy and then been caught in a battle and forced to flee into Montevideo for refuge.

Any attempt to get through the Allied blockade seemed certain suicide, yet there were many who thought and said that that was what Captain Langsdorff was determined to do.

Hundreds of thousands of spectators actually held their breath in suspense as the Graf Spee's nose began to push through the narrow entrance between the two converging breakwaters here. If she turned southward she could be going only to Buenos Aires or to some other Argentine port. If she turned in any other direction undoubtedly she was planning to run for safety or to fight it out. The battle-scarred warship slipped through the harbor entrance and turned southward into the channel leading toward the middle of the river. It was the route to Buenos Aires.

As 8 o'clock approached there had been no movement for so long that spectators were beginning to get impatient. They thought that the Graf Spee would remain at anchor until after dark. They turned their attention to the brilliant sunset behind the gray warship. The stillness of twilight settled down.

Suddenly at 7:55 P. M. that stillness was shattered by a tremendous, deep, dull explosion. It could be heard all over Montevideo. A great cloud of gray smoke burst out of the ship and hid it.

Great sheets of brilliant flames then shot toward the sky and settled down to their task of destroying what had been one of Germany's proudest naval units. ◇

BRITISH RESTAURANTS WILL SERVE FREELY
Rations Coupons Won't Be Needed For Ham, Butter, Tea Orders

Special Cable to The New York Times.

LONDON, Jan. 4—People who have to buy meals away from home will be able to go into a restaurant, canteen, coffee stall or club and order ham, bacon, bread and butter and tea without parting with any ration coupons, it became known here yesterday. It had been announced earlier that half a coupon would have to be surrendered for each meal with bacon or ham.

The butter supply to caterers will be calculated on the basis of one-sixth of an ounce with each meal served. The best use of the allowance will be left to the judgment of caterers, and it is not proposed that they shall be required to divide it equally over each meal.

Two-sevenths of an ounce of sugar will be allotted to restaurants for each customer. Half the allowance is intended for cooking requirements and for service at table for sweetening purposes, and the other half for each cup of hot beverage, such as tea, coffee or cocoa.

One caterer thought that one-seventh of an ounce for tea would mean two lumps of sugar for a man who wanted a cup of tea, with perhaps three lumps for a man ordering a pot.

During the World War no butter was allowed for afternoon light tea or cups of hot beverage.

For home consumption the weekly ration of uncooked bacon or ham will be four ounces per head. ◇

JANUARY 5, 1940

JEWS LAY TORTURE TO NAZIS IN POLAND

PUBLIC FLOGGING ALLEGED

Special Cable to The New York Times.

LONDON, Jan. 4—Tales of Jews shot and tortured in Poland, as well as reports of fines amounting to impoverishment imposed by Nazis on Jews in sections of that country occupied by Germany, are reaching Jewish organizations here.

Some of these stories, which reach London through Paris, where Jewish relief headquarters for Poland are established, and through Baltic countries, repeat the familiar pattern of Nazi action when Chancellor Hitler occupied Austria and Czecho-Slovakia. As recounted

by the Jewish organizations, some of these stories follow.

In the neighborhood of Lodz, ac-

cording to one eyewitness, Jews are being treated with unusual harshness. At Zgierz, where there was a wealthy Jew-

---

JANUARY 7, 1940

WHY THE RUSSIAN ARMY HAS BOGGED IN FINLAND

By HAROLD DENNY
Wireless to The New York Times.

HELSINKI, Finland, Jan. 6—It is now a little more than a month since Soviet Russia invaded Finland and this model capital saw Soviet planes fly overhead and drop bombs on its streets and houses. Undoubtedly Joseph Stalin's design was for a "Blitzkrieg," in Russian "molnyenosnaya voina." It has not turned out to be one. In more than a month of fighting, in which Stalin has sacrificed many thousands of Russians, the Red Colossus, with a population of 180,000,000 persons and an area of one-sixth the land area of the globe, has only damaged the borders of this small country of fewer than 4,000,000.

The Russians have advanced a few miles on the Karelian isthmus and they

are held back below Viipuri (Viborg). Fighting is going on every day on the isthmian front, but to the best of our knowledge here there has only been a loss of men and equipment for the Russians. They have made incursions into the Far North, but these have brought no important military advantage and their offensive there seems to have been frozen up by the intense cold. On the "waist of Finland," they have just taken one of the severest beatings in history and hardly can attack there seriously again for some time. Further south, but north of Lake Ladoga, the Finns have carried the war into Soviet territory.

FINISH FIGHTERS TIRED

The Russians are doing badly in comparison with what might have been expected—and the Finns are doing astoundingly well. But though one finds an air of supreme confidence in all ranks of the Finnish Army, the country is still in deadly danger.

Front-line Finnish officers and men consider that on the basis of performance thus far a Finn is worth ten Russians and they estimate, probably with exaggeration, that casualties have been

in the ratio of twenty Russians to one Finn. But if it is a heroic army which still faces the Soviet troops across the frozen wastes in these Arctic and sub-Arctic regions, it is also a tired army. Most of all, the Finns need men for relief.

The bulk of the Finnish troops have been in the line for a month. There are units which have been on active service for thirty days without relief—under great hardship and with little sleep. Yet the Finnish leaders simply cannot let this front-line personnel go back to civilized comfort for a rest; its numbers are too few. They are providing what rest they can by transferring men who have had an overshare of hard fighting to quieter sectors and replacing them with others whose task has been less heavy. But front-line troops need more than that.

Volunteers are now arriving from Sweden. How many we are not told. There will be a place for all who can be sent.

IN NEED OF MUNITIONS

The Finns also need more munitions of every kind, especially airplanes (and they must have pilots also) and artillery. After a month of war, they are holding out at their fronts with remarkable ener-

Polish Jews being marched through a street in Warsaw by Gestapo troops in 1940.

ish community, all Jewish textile works and stores have been confiscated and turned over to Nazis. It is said one Jew named Zissman was buried alive for resisting the Nazis and another named Kalynski shot for resisting forced labor.

No Jews are allowed on the streets before 10 A. M. and a system of forced labor has been instituted. While at work the Jews are forced to sing their songs and shout "Jews are the cause of the present war." Both synagogues in the town were burned, it is said.

Jewish sources cite excerpts from reports by the German police in Lodz itself—excerpts, Jews say, that have been printed in the Schlesische Zeitung of Breslau. The police are quoted as saying there have been wholesale executions in Lodz and at least 100 Jews shot. The German police, it is added, reported that 1,000 Jews surrounded a synagogue when the police wanted to search it and hundreds were killed when the police opened fire. The synagogue was burned.

WHIPPED IN PUBLIC

In Sieradz, according to these reports, ten Jews, one a woman, were publicly whipped for not saluting storm troopers. In Kolo several Jews, including a rabbi and some of his students, were reported whipped for stealing. At Radom, the police are said to have reported that 3,600 Jews are awaiting trial for hiding arms.

According to Nazi police reports cited by Jews in London, an officer's job is simplified by the fact that many Jews commit suicide as soon as the police come to search their homes. There have been many killings because Jews resist with clubs and axes, the police are said to have reported.

According to Jewish reports that do not cite any German sources as authority, Chelm, second city in the province of Lublin, where there were estimated to be 25,000 Jews, has been the scene of repeated outbreaks. All Jews between the ages of 18 and 55 must register with the government and there have been many arrests, it is said here. Two Jewish physicians have been shot, according to information here.

In the Lublin area, according to these same circles, conditions are equally bad. The Germans are said to have announced their intention of making this area a ghetto. According to estimates here, 30,000 Jews have been added to the 35,000 who were there originally.

On all these people a collective fine of 620,000 zlotys in gold has been levied as a penalty for the maintenance of a secret wireless station, it is said.

All Jews in the area must wear a large six-pointed star and none is allowed to practice a profession or engage in trade. Synagogues are being used to house incoming Jews and the Jewish theological seminary is said to have been turned into a Storm Trooper barracks and made a center for anti-Semitism. Sixty per cent of the young Jews have fled from Lublin, London hears, and all Jews have been forced into the Jewish quarter.

400,000 NAZI FAMILIES FOR POLAND

BERLIN, Jan. 4 (UP)—The Reich Bureau for Settlement announced today that plans were being completed for the settlement of 400,000 German families from the old Reich in conquered Polish territories annexed by Germany.

These re-settlements will be in addition to 50,000 Germans re-settled from the Baltic States and 100,000 from the Russian share of Eastern Poland, who already are being "repatriated." ◆

gy and tenacity, but they also are hoping that help will reach them before they are overwhelmed by sheer numbers.

Now, what about the Russians? Why is it that the Red Army, with its million and half of regulars, its many millions of reserves and its great quantities of equipment, has now stalled against a country which is only a patch alongside the Soviet map?

Like several others here now who have had trips to the Finnish-Russian front, I have seen many parades in Moscow, and for the past five or six years the thrilling part of them has been the military spectacle. There were soldiers parading while fleets of bombing planes flew over them, and hundreds of tanks and other war machines rolling past. The troops that marched—we realized they were the pick of the Soviet Union, young men of the Communist party— were outstandingly smart. The tanks, ranging from whippets to gigantic land-battleships, looked unbeatable. The planes covered the whole city.

It never occurred to us that Russia would go to war with Finland or any other small Baltic country; yet it has, and thus far in every essential element it has met defeat.

What are the reasons for this defeat? One, of course, is the Finns' unexpected power of resistance. Another is the fantastically chaotic distribution system of the Soviet regime. Another is the childish Soviet reverence for anything mechanical. Another is the devastating effect of the 1937 purge in the Red Army and of the whole Soviet structure—in other words, a present shortage of brains.

TANKS HALTED

As for the tanks, they appeared so invincible in the Moscow Red Square and the Russians themselves thought they were. Yet they now seem thoroughly vulnerable to any enemy who is willing to stand his ground. The Finnish fronts are littered with these modern juggernauts, and to open the door of one of them is to encounter grinning skeletons of the crew burned to death.

There can be little doubt that Stalin much underrated the Finns when he ordered the march into their country. And so the first troops the Finns encountered were Russian colonial soldiers, the men of Central Asia. Better troops have since been put in—such poor devils as those who were massacred on the ice of Lake

Kyanta just before the New Year.

I have talked to some of these better troops, prisoners of the Finns on the isthmus front. They presented a convincing picture of an unwilling advance against an enemy who they had been told would torture them if they were captured; of action under the threats of officers who could shoot them if they failed to advance.

QUESTION OF BREAKDOWN

These men are not like the confident army we saw in Moscow. Their morale is so bad—even if one admits that they are only the poorest troops the Soviets had—and the letters found in their possession composed such a picture of discontent that one wonders how Stalin can put this adventure through without a breakdown.

No one, however, who has known Russia in the past believes it is likely to break down completely, for the simple reason that it has been in a chronic state of breakdown for years and yet nothing has happened. The Finns know this better than any people in the world outside Russia. ◆

JANUARY 14, 1940

CHAMBERLAIN'S GRIP FIRM AFTER SHAKE-UP
Remains in Full Command in Britain With No Formidable Rival in Sight—Social Upheaval Is Foreseen

By HAROLD CALLENDER
Wireless to The New York Times.

LONDON, Jan. 13—Soon after dismissing Leslie Hore-Belisha as War Secretary, Prime Minister Neville Chamberlain in a speech this week hinted that he intended to remain the head of the government until the war ended.

The Cabinet change resulting from a clash of personalities within the government and the army revealed the persistence of the criticism that is one aspect of the freedom for which the British believe they are fighting.

The Prime Minister's grim determination and confidence in his staying power were characteristic of his country.

The future of the government depends above all upon the progress of the war. If the struggle is prolonged there doubtless will be further shifts, even major crises, but they will be accompanied by discussion and debate.

This procedure is in accordance with a kind of traditional suspicion that no government can run the country properly unless it is constantly goaded, nagged and advised by the Opposition in Parliament and critics outside—a suspicion that forms the foundation of democracy as the British understand it.

WIDE FREEDOM OF EXPRESSION

The freedom of expression in Britain after four months of war is amazing when compared with that in France today or in the United States in 1917–18. Recently published articles have blamed the Chamberlain appeasement policy for the outbreak of the war, while many letters to the newspapers have dwelt more upon Britain's than upon Germany's faults.

In Left Wing publications there has even been considerable debate as to whether this war merits public support.

There has just appeared under the imprint of 1940 a new edition of Lord Ponsonby's book, "Falsehood in Wartime," which is a severe indictment of the veracity of British propaganda in the last war and inferentially of the veracity of all official propaganda.

Meanwhile, from Conservative quarters have come attacks on bureaucracy and suggestions that the government has not yet faced important strategic or economic problems.

If Mr. Hore-Belisha demands it, Mr. Chamberlain will be obliged to explain to the House of Commons why he dismissed a Minister who was energetic but a bit too showy and too ambitious to suit the army and some of his colleagues.

PREMIER'S RESPONSIBILITY

Whether or not he explains the lack of harmony between Mr. Hore Belisha and Viscount Gort, commander of the British Expeditionary Force, and General Sir Edmund Ironside, chief of the Imperial General Staff, the Prime Minister must assume the responsibility for the dropping of Mr. Hore-Belisha. This he feels competent to do. He has never run a war before, but feels confident of his ability in directing this one.

From determination to see it through Mr. Chamberlain seems to have gained a kind of rejuvenation. His voice is stronger and has a greater ring of self-assurance than formerly. He has not the slightest doubt about the rightness of the British cause or about Britain's ability to win.

His speeches are not very eloquent or inspiring and not so deftly phrased as Winston Churchill's and they reveal more than a trace of complacency.

But Mr. Chamberlain is in full command without a formidable rival as yet and enjoys greater support in the country than when he was striving for peace by Munich methods. The man who made so many concessions for appeasement has got the bit in his teeth and is now as determined to defeat Adolf Hitler as he once was to conciliate him.

Mr. Chamberlain's strength lies in the fact that in both these policies he has represented major currents of British opinion. Some would have had a showdown earlier. Some Conservatives now favor a negotiated peace with Herr Hitler. There has been and will be much criticism of Mr. Chamberlain, as there would be of any one in his place. But he seems to be firmly established in the saddle for the present. ◊

JANUARY 19, 1940

CHINESE REPORTED DRIVING FOR CANTON
One Force Said to Be Only 10 Miles North of City

HONG KONG, Jan. 19 (AP)—Chinese today reported fresh successes on the Kwangtung front in South China, where their accounts pictured Chinese forces driving spearheads from different directions toward Canton.

They said their troops had recaptured a station on the Canton-Hankow Railway, thirty-three miles north of Canton, and caused 500 Japanese casualties, while another force was heading toward Kongtsun, only ten miles north of Canton.

Japanese were silent on the Kwangtung situation, but said their soldiers were making rapid progress in a fresh offensive in the Tapieh Mountains of North Hupeh, Central Chinese province.

They reported Kaocheng, the principal Chinese stronghold in the region, had been captured and Chinese forces put to flight with Japanese in close pursuit.

PEIPING, Jan. 18 (AP)—A settlement was reported today to have ended an outbreak of fighting between the regular Chinese forces of General Yen Hsi-shan and his new communist-influenced volunteers. Frequent friction between these elements of the army in Southern Shansi Province had been reported, but foreign military advices discounted reports of a civil war or any widespread fighting. ◊

JANUARY 25, 1940

Editorial
JAPAN'S UNCHANGING AIMS

Embarrassed silence has been Tokyo's only reaction to the "peace terms" reported to have been signed by Wang Ching-wei, Japan's puppet leader in China. Mr. Wang's pro-Japanese friends

JANUARY 20, 1940

NORWAY, DENMARK TO DEFEND BORDERS
Two Scandinavian States Declare Neutrality but Will Fight if Freedom Is Threatened

Special Cable to The New York Times.

COPENHAGEN, Denmark, Jan. 19— Norway and Denmark today declared their absolute neutrality but added that if their independence was threatened they would employ all the military means at their command.

Premier Theodor Stauning, supported by six Danish party leaders, recommended that the nation restate its policy, and the neutrality proposal, backed by the threat of military measures in the event of an attack, was adopted by a vote of 135 to none. There was one abstention—the representative from Schleswig, a German.

The Communists as well as the National Socialists supported the proposal.

The Norwegian Premier, Johann Nygaardsvold, was supported when he introduced a similar proposal. He added that a coalition government would not be considered until there was an actual question of war.

During the debate on this issue the Liberal leader, Johann Ludwig Mow-inckel, compared Norway's position with that of Finland and added that in 1935 Russia had already made threats against Finland. He revealed conversations that he had had in Moscow and which in turn he had transmitted to his government.

NORDIC NATIONS ACT

COPENHAGEN, Denmark, Jan. 19 (AP)—Denmark struck out today with a firm declaration, adopted by a unanimous vote of the lower house of Parliament that her neutrality "must be maintained" and her independence defended.

The declaration was echoed in Norway, where Prime Minister Johann Nygaardsvold told Parliament that any attacks upon the nation would be met with resistance.

In neighboring Sweden, meanwhile, Stockholm authorities announced a new program of air raid defenses, including trenches in parks and additional shelters.

The Danish declaration was designed partly to correct impressions abroad that Denmark, because of limited armaments, would not resist an attack.

The pronouncement said:

"The Lower House decides to declare that all parts of the Danish people agree that the country's neutrality must be maintained and that all disposable means if necessary shall be used to keep order, preserve and protect the realm's peace and independence and promise the Cabinet support in its work in this direction."

Danes said that both foreign policy and domestic politics were involved in the decision to make the public declaration.

Political sources said that a precise pronouncement appeared required since there were suggestions abroad, based on a pessimistic New Year's broadcast by Premier Theodor Stauning, that Denmark might be unwilling to put up armed resistance in event of attack. ◆

FEBRUARY 4, 1940

REICH SMOKING BILL SOARS
47 Billion Cigarettes Used in 1939—War Strain Cited

Wireless to The New York Times.

BERLIN, Feb. 3—The strain on humanity of the international situation evidences itself in many ways. In Germany in the critical year of 1939 it brought about a strong increase in the use of tobacco in all its forms.

Reports state that 47,000,000,000 cigarettes, 9,000,000,000 cigars and 32,000,000 kilograms of pipe tobacco were smoked, while 7,000,000 kilograms were used as snuff. Of cigarettes alone, 15,000,000,000 more were smoked than during the pre-depression year of 1929. The total value of tobacco of all kinds sold last year amounted to about 3,000,000,000 marks. ◆

---

in Shanghai explain that a "gentleman's agreement" was signed on the Japanese side by "unofficial" representatives of the Japanese Government, "with the approval of the Japanese Army." Since no denial has come from the civilian leaders in Tokyo, it will be instructive for Americans to see what sort of "terms" Japan's agents in China say they have signed.

The reported agreement would permit Japanese troops to remain for two years in North and Central China, unless in the meantime "the new Government"—that is, the puppet Government—"demonstrates its ability to maintain peace and order." Permanent Japanese garrisons would be stationed in North China and Inner Mongolia; Inner Mongolia would be "governed jointly" by the Japanese Army and Chinese, and Japan would "supervise" railroads, customs and economic development in China. General Chiang Kaishek is abundantly right in saying that such a peace would make China a Japanese protectorate in all but name.

At a moment when Japan's civilian leaders would like to rebuild friendship with the United States, these "terms" remind us that the mentality of Japan's military commanders has not changed; and the absence of denial from Tokyo suggests that the army still controls the Japanese Government's policy. Was it not the "moderate" and "liberal" Admiral Yonai, the new Premier, who announced the other day that Japan's policy in China was "immutably fixed"? Apparently it is fixed in accordance with the army's unchanging ideas. There is every sign in the "peace terms" that Japan still aims at the complete domination of China, to the detriment of Chinese and foreign interests alike. There is no word in them about respect for the foreign rights which the Japanese have violated in their ruthless and unjustified invasion. ◆

FEBRUARY 12, 1940

WOMEN IN WAR

Winston Churchill's appeal for a million more women to work in British munition plants is another reminder that total warfare makes little distinction between the sexes. It is estimated that 4,000,000 women in England, Wales and Scotland will be drawn into industrial war work and millions more into the auxiliary services where men can be released. There has never been any such mass mobilization of women, not even toward the end of the World War. In the air raid precautions service alone 580,000 women have been enrolled and 35,000 are serving directly with the army. Feminine fliers have been found useful in transporting planes for the Royal Air Force, and 11,000 are registered as R. A. F. auxiliaries, with an equal number in training for the Women's Royal Naval Service. The arrest of a member of the women's aircraft service for desertion and her detention to await a court-martial emphasize the serious nature of the responsibilities women have assumed.

The same tendency pervades every warring nation of Europe. In Finland the courageous women of the Lotta Svard supplement the fighting forces and are encountered far up on the battle fronts. In France women keep the farms going. In Germany they are asked to make new sacrifices in the name of patriotism. When a nation goes to war today, everybody goes. Women are simply engulfed in the general catastrophe like drops in a tide. ◇

Members of the British Auxiliary Territorial Transport Service trundling lorry wheels across the barrack square at Eastern Command in Bedfordshire, England, in 1939.

FEBRUARY 25, 1940

Hitler Leads in Poll

Georgetown Students Vote on Leading Personalities

Special to The New York Times.

WASHINGTON, Feb. 24—Adolf Hitler was voted "the most outstanding personality in the world today" by students of the College of Arts and Sciences at Georgetown University in a campus poll undertaken by the Hoya, undergraduate weekly publication. Of 269 votes polled on this question, Hitler received 113. Pope Pius XII took second place with sixty-four, and President Roosevelt third with thirty-five.

President Roosevelt and Postmaster General Farley placed first and second in the "favorite political figure" class, with District Attorney Dewey and Al Smith running third and fourth. Mr. Roosevelt was picked by eighty-nine students as top Presidential choice, with Mr. Dewey and Paul V. McNutt trailing in that order.

FEBRUARY 25, 1940

SIX MONTHS' BLOCKADE TESTS NAZI AUTARCHY

By OTTO D. TOLISCHUS
Wireless to The New York Times.

BERLIN, Feb. 24—Although Germany bitterly complains about the new British "hunger blockade" which would starve her women and children and therefore justifies the most drastic counter-measures, her spokesmen also proclaim that by virtue of her own autarchy, her foresight and her remaining foreign trade—especially her political and economic rapprochement with Russia—Germany really has made herself blockade-proof. In fact, her spokesmen say, time is working not against Germany as in the last war, but for Germany, which day by day and in every way is getting stronger and stronger.

What is the truth about these apparently contradictory assertions?

Unfortunately, the truth is not so easy to obtain, for, in totalitarian warfare statisticians are joined to the propaganda forces so that statistics either are lacking or must be taken with a whole cellarful of salt, a safe way of reading them being to discount what they claim and accept only what they admit. But, with this qualification, an approximate estimate of the situation is still possible.

FINANCIAL CONDITION

The problem of material resources readily divides itself into three parts—finance, food and raw materials.

As regards finance, the government and its agencies already collect some 40 per cent of the national income in taxes and levies. In addition, the government also has mortgaged for its benefit all of the nation's savings and a good part of its remaining wealth. The declared public debt long since has passed 50,000,000,000 marks (it was 49,699,000,000 marks by the end of October, 1939). Methods of financing are causing so many headaches among financial experts that the projected additional tax and other financial measures still await the light of day.

As regards food, Germany claimed to be 82 per cent self-sufficient before the Polish conquest, and conquered territories rapidly are being converted into granaries with true German efficiency. But Germany was 80 per cent self-sufficient in food before the last war as well and had even larger conquered territories at her disposal during that war. Yet she was forced to her knees by a "hunger blockade." The Na-

The New York Times was ranked as the "favorite newspaper" by seventy-eight voters. Loyal to home products, thirty-nine put the Hoya in second place, and The New York Herald Tribune trailed in third position.

Mrs. Eleanor Roosevelt easily won the title of "most outstanding woman in the world today" with Queen Elizabeth nosing out Mme. Chiang Kai-Shek for second place.

One hundred forty-nine voters listed "Girls and Love" as the favorite "bull-session" topic. Sports finished a poor second with twenty-seven votes, and war was third with eighteen. ◆

tional Socialist regime blames her defeat on mismanagement and lack of foresight of the imperial regime, especially the great "pig murder" early in the last war, undertaken to save feed, and boasts that nothing like it can happen again. Its ration system, introduced even before hostilities began, and its agricultural "production battles," going on for years, are cited as proof of this.

STORE OF RAW MATERIALS

As regards raw materials, the German Institute for Business Research figured out as early as July, 1938, a self-sufficiency "of 65 per cent," which, theoretically, should be much higher now owing to the progress of the Four-Year plan. But the institute itself warned that "according to the 'law of minimum' even small gaps in the raw-material supply can exert a great influence on production possibilities if the lacking goods are absolutely necessary for the manufacture of certain commodities." In other words, lack of a few pounds of copper might stop a whole armament plant. And that the war has curtailed supply is evidenced by the fact that despite a drastic crack-down on all production for civilian use, stored stocks are rapidly being used up.

In both food and raw materials, therefore, Germany remains dependent upon her foreign trade.

All in all, it appears, therefore, that the blockade is unable to starve out Germany, and so far at least has been unable to cripple her war machine, which still is working at capacity. But it has definitely put Germany on short rations in every respect. And whether these rations cripple Germany's military might will depend largely on the conduct and duration of the war. ◆

Finnish Losses, Soviet Gains Under Pact

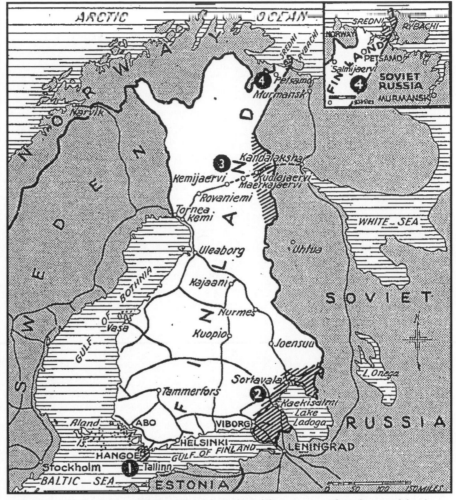

Russia is to get a lease on Hangoe (1), the entire Karelian Isthmus (2), territory east of Maerkaejaervi (3) and parts of the Sredni and Rybachi Peninsulas (4). The gains are shown approximately by the diagonal shading.

UNITY IS PARIS AIM

'Strong' Leader Is Called to Satisfy Critics of War Inaction

By P. J. PHILIP
Wireless to The New York Times.

PARIS, March 20—Dramatically in the last hours, but following a long series of incidents that steadily indicated the probability of that finale, Premier Edouard Daladier resigned today, and of course his entire Cabinet resigned with him.

Tonight Paul Reynaud is considering the invitation of President Albert Lebrun extended this afternoon that he should form another Cabinet. He has promised that tomorrow morning he will answer whether he is willing to undertake the task; that is to say, he considers that he will know by then whether he would be likely to succeed.

Opinion in many quarters tonight inclines to the belief that M. Reynaud will accept. He has certainly that energy of mind and purpose that first the Senate and then the Chamber of Deputies have asked for the conduct of the ❯

◄ war. Most probably, if he forms his Cabinet, he will himself take the Ministry of Foreign Affairs and keep M. Daladier at the Ministry of War if the latter will consent.

MAY INCLUDE TWO SOCIALISTS

He is credited also tonight with wishing to take two representative Socialists into the Cabinet. In the past he has always been a user of slogans, and his slogan just now seems to be that when one is in a war parties and personalities do not matter. The only thing that matters is winning. If he succeeds in getting the requisite support, this will be his first Premiership.

[The Socialists, the largest party, were not represented in the Daladier Cabinet. M. Daladier was reported last night to have changed his mind and agreed to enter a Reynaud Cabinet as Minister of Defense, according to The Associated Press. It also was reported that Georges Mandel would remain as Minister of Colonies.]

Meanwhile the effect on public opinion of Premier Daladier's resignation is what matters most of all. That it should have happened at the end of a secret session of the Chamber is considered unfortunate. The voters in this country like to know the reasons why their Deputies vote or abstain from voting the way they do.

It is admitted that there has been much criticism of the way the war was being conducted and that criticism has been principally that the Premier did not adapt his actions quickly enough to circumstances.

He has lacked initiative and imagination, his critics say, and the failure to support Finland quickly enough has been taken as an example, not because any one seriously believes that more could have been done directly for Finland, but as an indication of what might happen elsewhere if the same tempo of doing things were continued.

If these and other criticisms had been made in open session, it would undoubtedly have been better. That they were made secretly and ended in a very confused vote is not likely to help the formation of any other Daladier Cabinet. M. Reynaud may succeed. If he does not, others probably will be called, and if none of them can succeed, it seems inevitable that President Lebrun will turn again to the man who was not so much defeated as forced to resign because so many Deputies abstained from voting. ◆

MARCH 24, 1940

PARIS AND BERLIN: A REVEALING CONTRAST

By ANNE O'HARE McCORMICK
Paris (By Wireless).

At every turn Paris proclaims that it is the capital of a France at war. It is a city girded for battle, prepared for bombardment, ready with every form of succor for expected casualties. In a day here you meet more volunteer workers, hear of more "foyers" for this, that and the other service for soldiers, see more signs of behind-the-front war activity, than you encounter in a month in Berlin.

War is a leveling process and the face of war is singularly alike in all countries, but the first glimpse of Paris after Berlin illuminates the whole difference between two systems of government and two patterns of life. France at war has passed under a form of government control as complete in some respects as that prevailing at all times across the Rhine. Yet in the very aspect of the two capitals it is clear at once that in one the authorities attend to everything and in the other the habit of private enterprise and individual initiative is too strong to be smothered even under the iron mask of war.

An officer on leave from the front was describing yesterday a small engagement in which a French scouting party of nine men was suddenly confronted by a compact company of fifty-four Germans. By instinct, without orders he said, the French immediately fell apart and formed a long line while the Germans advanced in formation, all together, with the result that nine Frenchmen lost only two of their men and captured seven of the Germans.

The incident is typical of the contrast one immediately feels between the mass formation of Germany and the one-by-one march of France. Whether the self-regulated will win proportionate victories over the ordered mass when the opposing forces are multiplied by thousands is not only the supreme question of the war but its main issue. Daily it becomes plainer that the struggle in Europe is the Apocalypse of the long drawn-out fight of man to control the machine. For at its apogee the machine is a war machine, and Hitler is only that machine made flesh, utterly careless of the individual and especially contemptuous of

that private monopoly of himself and the use of his own mind which the Frenchman guards with peculiar obstinacy.

Two other contrasts between Berlin and Paris immediately hit the eye. Paris is not only the capital of France at war. It is the Allied war capital, the military center for both nations as obviously as London is the political center.

The animation of the city this week is partly due to the crowds of visitors who have crossed the Channel to spend the Easter holidays with British officers and men on leave from the front. The mingling of uniforms, the mixture of languages, the movement in the streets, the throngs in the cafes and theatres, create an atmosphere of gayety and vivacity belying the sandbags, the shuttered shops, the "abris" against air raids, the grim provisions on every side for the "defense passive."

They assure France that she is not alone. The fraternization of the French and British betokens an interdependence never felt in the last war. Even the gnarled old lady renting chairs in the Bois knows that it takes the armies and air fleets of both countries to match the German. "We must hang together or separately," she says, defining Allied policy in a phrase she thinks she has invented.

No war enthusiasms can be worked up among either people, but the Germans cannot really believe the worst will happen and the French think it can. They face open-eyed the horrors that may lie before them, profoundly pessimistic of the future yet determined to maintain a brave front and enjoy to the last minute the small pleasures of normal life—white bread, conversation, budding trees, a café on the terrasse in the first sunshine. France rises magnificently to emergencies, and this applies particularly to the women and the hard-eyed, tight-fisted peasants, above all to the peasants plowing this year the fields they have already seen devastated. "Will they come this way again?" they ask casually.

Berlin is strangely silent. Unter den Linden is a deserted thoroughfare compared to the Champs Elysées. Few restrictions on the use of petrol are imposed in France. Private automobiles and taxis dash around corners in almost the usual number and confusion.

In Berlin motor traffic is reduced to the minimum. Except for the buses burning synthetic oil, and laden trucks linked together in twos and threes to save fuel, the streets are empty. The people hurrying along the sidewalks seldom speak. They are all so preoccupied that even in company they seem to be walking alone. At night the silence deepens. To drive in the main streets in the blackout is like driving through a dark country lane. The buildings are completely blotted out and no sound issues from the invisible doors and windows. Groping along the tunnel-like streets you almost never hear a voice. Other gropers are shadows and footsteps.

Even the big shops, crowded though they are with people hunting for something to buy, are very quiet. Departments offering millinery, jewelry, novelties, silk and luxury goods are well stocked; others are sold out. Wearing apparel is marked with the price in marks and "points" and customers are more interested in the number of points the article will subtract from their hundred-point ration cards than in its cost in money.

The shop windows are filled with new goods in wide variety, but if you try to buy something so displayed you are told it is for "decoration." In Germany it is the authorities who are putting up the front, and the window dressing explains the suspicion of some Germans that war stocks aren't so plentiful as they are made to appear.

In Paris there is plenty of noise and enough light at night to make circulation easy. Street lamps are only turned down, many doors are illuminated and curtains are carelessly drawn over the windows. There is no rationing system and apparently no shortage of goods. Food restrictions are applied by the simple device of prohibiting the sale of certain goods on certain days. There are three days without meat, other days without pastry, alcohol, sweets.

Gourmets though they are, the French take their restrictions with a shrug while the Germans think and talk about eating all the time. The Hausfrau spends most of her time in the pursuit of food, and her scent is so sharp that if an enterprising merchant gets a supply of unrationed goods—nuts or oranges, for instance—a line a block long will form the instant he puts it on display.

The Germans are shut up with themselves. They have no allies with whom to fraternize. The Axis never made for comradeship and the Soviet pact induces no influx of Russians in Berlin. Today Germany is almost as completely cut off from the world as Russia is. Behind the Westwall she has had her own way with most of the neighboring peoples, but in all his coups de force or diplomacy Hitler has not made a single friend for his country. Germany fights her war alone, and this isolation produces an atmosphere as different from that of France as the air in a sealed room from that of a breeze-swept field. ◊

MARCH 31, 1940

JAPAN LOOKS TO WANG TO LAUNCH 'NEW ORDER'

By HUGH HYAS
Wireless to The New York Times.

TOKYO, March 30—Emerging from his fortress in the Shanghai French Concession, the only Chinese statesman who admits China has lost the war has assembled a government ready to sign a peace with Japan. One of the strongest political missions that ever left Japan will presently be in Nanking demonstrating to China and the world that Japan supports Wang Ching-wei.

Those elaborate performances appear to many merely the curtain raiser for another puppet play. To Japan they are a carefully prepared and long-pondered move. If the great experiment succeeds it will justify the policy which has cost Japan much in lives and money and will force foreign powers to realize that the new East Asia has been born. If it fails—but to assume failure is akin to lèse-majesté in Japan.

The outlook is wrapped in Yangtze mists but tell-tale signs to watch for are, first, the essential nature of the peace terms Japan is ready to sign with Wang when and if they are revealed; second, the amount of fighting power Chiang Kai-shek develops during the Summer. If the peace terms are such that sensible Chinese can feel that in losing the war they have not lost their country, peace will look very attractive to them. If next Summer Chiang Kai-shek can put fresh guerrilla armies all around Japan's over-extended front, if next Fall the fourth Winter of the war looms with peace still at the rainbow's end, Japan will have to review the situation.

JAPAN'S AIM UNCHANGED

In dividing China Japan does not admit that she is abandoning any of her objectives. Her aim still is to bring China as a unit into the "New Order" in East Asia under Japanese suzerainty. But three years of war have shown that China is too big to be swallowed at one mouthful and Japan bows to the logic of facts.

Wang Ching-wei's government offers what seems to Japan a solid basis for consolidating the gains already achieved. Chiang Kai-shek still has control of the larger part of the people and territory, but when material strengths are compared any semblance of equality is seen to be an illusion. The new Central Government dominates the entire coastline and its area includes 90 per cent of China's railroads; this area produces 90 per cent of the customs revenue, 100 per cent of the sales revenue, 78 per cent of the cotton, 75 per cent of the horses and includes high percentages of China's industrial, mineral and agricultural resources.

Conclusion of peace in this area will, according to Japanese blue prints, lead to a sudden improvement in trade. International investments will again earn returns, loan payments will be resumed. Even if guerrilla warfare surges around the frontiers, peace and prosperity will gradually return within them. The democracies may refuse recognition but virtually all their contacts with China will be in the region Wang controls. ◊

The Japanese-sponsored Wang regime in China began in March, 1939.

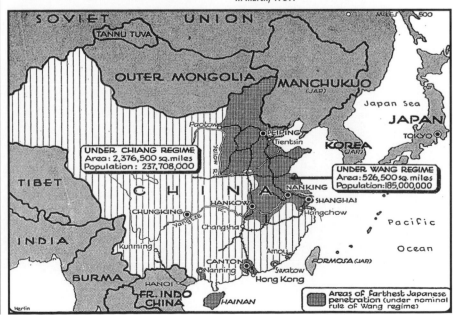

Chapter 3
"THE SUN ALSO SINKS"
April–June 1940

After months of waiting, the Phony War ended in a sudden flurry of military action, not a major conflict between the three great powers facing each other, but yet another small war in Scandinavia, this time against Denmark and Norway, which began on April 9 with a sudden German invasion. A combined British-French force was sent to Norway to boost Norwegian resistance, but it was small and inexperienced. The Times covered the campaign in detail but rightly predicted by April 26 that the "Ill-Armed British Face Disaster." As the world held its breath, the German armed forces finally launched an all-out attack in the West on May 10. For some days The Times treated the operation as yet another campaign against small nations, in this case The Netherlands and Belgium. By May 11 there was even talk of Allied victory in the Low Countries.

The same day The Times reported the fall of the Chamberlain government and the appointment of Churchill as the new prime minister. There followed a long report on a figure molded by his experience of war, a man later described by Times foreign correspondent Cyrus Sulzberger as "pudgy and not very large but somehow massive and indomitable," the right man for the moment. There was little that Churchill could do to prevent the onrush of German armies, which managed to overcome the problems of topography on the narrow roads of the Ardennes forest by sending the new armored (Panzer) divisions through the wooded gap in the French defenses. By the time the British and French realized what was happening, it was almost too late.

For reporters it was difficult to get a proper sense of what was happening, since official news reports were few and troop movements rapid and unpredictable. "Confusion Marks Battle of France" ran a headline on May 20, but the confusion soon gave way to a clearer picture. German forces raced toward the English Channel coast to encircle British forces and the left wing of the French army while the remainder of the French Army retreated south and west in disarray. Times reporter Harry Benny was with the British as they reached Dunkirk and watched the successful evacuation, "the one bright spot in the whole dark picture." But the British flight doomed France, whose government abandoned Paris on June 10 and sued for an armistice seven days later. It was, wrote Times correspondent Drew Middleton some years later, "the most decisive campaign in six years of war."

The effect in America was immediate. On May 12 The Times carried the headline "Army Corps Moves 600 Miles in 6 Days," but the story referred to troop movements in the United States, not Europe. A large U.S. army exercise tried to simulate what was happening in Europe using tanks and airplanes. The Times carried descriptions of German tactics and during June swung away from a long-term hostility to compulsory military service to throw its weight behind the idea of a proper "National Defense Program." Secretary of State Cordell Hull warned his fellow Americans that in the long run isolation was futile. The country waited to watch the fate of Britain—"David against Goliath" as Hanson Baldwin, The Times's military correspondent later put it.

On June 4 Churchill gave one of his many famous speeches rallying his people to fight to the end. Six days later Italian dictator Benito Mussolini declared war on Britain and France, stabbing them in the back, as Roosevelt claimed . The future looked bleak. On June 30 , in an editorial titled "The Sun Also Sinks," The Times reflected that in the end for all great conquerors, from Alexander the Great to Napoleon, "the curtain has fallen on tragedy," as it would do for Hitler, an optimism that was to be confirmed only after five long years of war.

OSLO APPREHENSIVE ON PLANS OF ALLIES

NAZI ACTION HELD SURE

By OTTO D. TOLISCHUS

OSLO, Norway, April 1—With grave apprehension but without any outward manifestation of alarm, Norway tonight awaited the speech of Prime Minister Chamberlain tomorrow, which is to elucidate the decisions of the Allied Supreme War Council regarding a strengthening of the Allied blockade and which, in doing so, may hold the issue of war or peace for Scandinavia.

The apprehension is based on announcements in part of the Allied press, backed by last Saturday's speech by Winston Churchill, British First Lord of the Admiralty, which are interpreted to mean that the Allies are determined to stop German shipments of Swedish iron ore from Narvik through Norwegian territorial waters at all costs, if necessary by sending the Allied fleet into Norwegian waters and policing them against what the Allies denounce as German abuse of Norwegian neutrality.

The German reaction to these intimations has left little doubt that Germany will take immediate counter-measures, and the recent flight of German planes over Norwegian territory is viewed here in the light of a German warning as to what might happen to the Scandinavian countries if they acquiesce in even a technical violation of their neutrality by Germany's enemies.

MOVE BY RUSSIA, TOO

If Germany moves against Scandinavia, Russia is not expected here to stay behind. The report that Russia has demanded an

CHAMBERLAIN GAINS POPULAR STRENGTH
Public Sees Him as Intent on Defeating Germany As He Was on Appeasing Her

By ANNE O'HARE McCORMICK
Special Cable to The New York Times.

LONDON, April 2—On March 31, 1939, a year ago almost to the day, this correspondent sat in the gallery when Prime Minister Chamberlain rose slowly in the House of Commons and in one brief declaration abandoned the policy of appeasement and shattered historic British precedent by pledging Great Britain to go to Poland's aid against aggression.

That day battle really was joined between England and Germany and the breathless crowd that filled the House instinctively felt it. The atmosphere was tense with a mixture of elation and foreboding. The Prime Minister was pale, grave, visibly shaken as he deliberately reversed the course he had followed until that moment with single-minded tenacity.

Today, after an eventful Easter recess, Mr. Chamberlain made another momentous declaration to the House. After the opening gun fired by First Lord of the Admiralty Winston Churchill in his Saturday broadcast, the Prime Minister officially launched the Allied offensive on the economic front. No one who has been in England as the decision to prosecute the economic war to the utmost was translated into action can doubt that today's declaration ushers in a struggle grimmer, more deadly, more full of hidden drama than the most spectacular military test. The British have chosen the line which they are sure they can fight hardest and hang on longest.

A year ago Mr. Chamberlain risked war without really believing it was unavoidable. Today he announced a conflict that must involve all neutrals and engage all forces to go on to the end. The man with blinders, as he is called, is as intent on war as he was on peace.

NEUTRAL DIPLOMATS ANXIOUS

Yet the atmosphere of the House was less tense today than a year ago. Except for diplomats from neutral States, who listened anxiously, the galleries were almost empty. The Cabinet members sat crowded on their long bench, more young men among them than in recent years. The Prime Minister himself was never more vigorous, more confident than he appeared as he got up to declare a war to the finish. His voice rang as he read the declaration of Franco-British resolution to fight together to a common victory and provide for continuous co-operation in the establishment of peace, reconstruction and international order.

REFLECTS AVERAGE MIND

The outstanding fact of today's session was its demonstration of the extent to which this rather commonplace figure, so lacking in showmanship or emotional appeal, dominates wartime England. If the British majority followed Mr. Chamberlain from appeasement to war and swing with him from the first uncertain phase of the conflict into its second phase, it must be because his movements accurately reflect the pace of the average British mind.

Certainly his tenaciousness, whether for peace or war, is typical. Tenacity in the British people is the quality that pushes to the top in an emergency.

"Old Neville's so frightfully all these," said a girl in the gallery after today's speech.

Mr. Churchill did not appear on the government bench today. The First Lord of the Admiralty supplies all the brilliance in the wartime Cabinet and

immediate demobilization in Finland and that she is rushing the fortification of Baltic Port, her naval base in Estonia, even in advance of the scheduled time, is taken as confirmation of this view.

As a result Norway finds herself in a fateful dilemma and prays that the bitter cup may pass her by once again. So delicate is the situation as regarded here that official quarters decline to make any comment until the Allied decisions are either announced or put into effect, and the Norwegian press is likewise abstaining from any expression of its opinion. Only the big headlines and the long reports from the Allied capitals testify to the importance of the issue, which is also the talk in all political and business circles, in clubs and at social gatherings. ◊

is now at the peak of popularity. There is less talk than there was a few months ago that he will displace the chief.

Despite his age, despite strong currents of dissatisfaction with the methods of the government, despite doubts that an economic war on neutrals can be carried out as successfully as the policy makers seem to believe, public opinion apparently still prefers Mr. Chamberlain to direct the risky experiments of war to any of his possible successors. ◊

Wreckage from Luftwaffe air raids that secured the Nazi occupation of Narvik, Norway, in April 1940.

APRIL 9, 1940

NAZIS IN NORWAY

NARVIK IS OCCUPIED

Sweden Is Mobilizing

Wireless to The New York Times.

LONDON, April 9—The Paris correspondent of Reuters, British news agency, reported this morning that the Oslo radio had announced that German troops had debarked in Norwegian ports at 3 A.M.

[Mrs. J. Borden Harriman, United States Minister to Norway, notified the State Department early this morning that she had been informed by the Foreign Minister that Norway considered herself at war with Germany.

[Mrs. Harriman also reported that at 5:30 A.M. Norwegian shore batteries were still engaged in battle with four invading German warships that were trying to force entry into Oslo Fjord.]

It was also announced that the Norwegian Government had left Oslo for Hamar, in Central Norway.

Reuters further reported that the Germans had occupied the cities of Bergen and Trondheim.

[The Oslo radio announced this morning that the Norwegian Government had ordered general mobilization after an all night session of the Cabinet, The Associated Press reported.]

Reuters also reported from Paris that

---

the Oslo radio announced this morning that the Germans had occupied Narvik.

The Norwegian legation here issued the following communiqué this morning:

"The German Minister in Oslo saw the Norwegian Foreign Secretary at 4:30 o'clock this morning and demanded that Norway should be handed over to the German administration. If this was not done all resistance would be defeated. This demand was refused and hostilities have started."

LONDON, April 9 (AP)—A Reuters, British news agency, dispatch from Paris, said there had been air raids on Oslo, capital of Norway, but that the Oslo radio was still in operation.

[The Oslo radio announced today that the Norwegian capital had been bombarded several times from the air and that the government had ordered that it be abandoned by the civilian population within two days, The Associated Press reported from Paris.]

KRISTIANSAND REPORTED BOMBED

STOCKHOLM, Sweden, April 9 (UP)—A flash picked up here from the Norwegian radio asserted that German planes had bombed Kristiansand, on the southern Norwegian coast, in the early hours of this morning.

The radio asserted that Kristiansand had been evacuated. Coastal batteries at Oskarsberg, near by, were said to be shelling German warships which were attempting to effect a landing.

REICH MINES SWEDISH PORTS

LONDON, April 9 (AP)—A German navigation service broadcast, intercepted by Reuters, British news agency, said ▸

◀ that all of Sweden's important harbors on the Skagerrak, arm of the North Sea, had been mined early today by Germany.

FOUR WARSHIPS REPULSED

STOCKHOLM, Sweden, April 9 (AP)— High authoritative quarters early today confirmed reports that four foreign warships had attempted to force an entrance into Oslo Fjord, water gateway to the Norwegian capital. The invaders were reported repulsed by shore batteries.

These quarters said that one of the attacking ships was a heavy cruiser. The attack took place about 12:30 A.M. and was over within a short time.

The engagement was marked by heavy bursts of cannon fire. Thereafter the invaders were said to have retired into the darkness.

Difficulties in obtaining details of the fighting were heightened by the fact that Norway snapped telephone communication with the rest of the world except for "state calls." Per sons who tried to place telephone calls to the Norwegian capital were told that only these official calls would be handled. ◊

OSLO ENTRY DESCRIBED
Witness Says Germans Bristled With Guns Ready for Instant Use

Wireless to The New York Times.

STOCKHOLM, Sweden, April 10—In an eyewitness account of the entry of a German column a thousand strong into the center of Oslo at 3 P.M. yesterday, a Reuters [British news agency] reporter who escaped over the frontier to Sweden writes that every man was armed with a formidable-looking rifle or machine gun and carried a bandolier, uncovered and glistening with bronzed machine-gun bullets, ready for immediate action.

But they met no resistance. The inhabitants, bewildered by the swift sequence of events and the incredible experience of the preceding eight hours, lined the streets to watch the invaders' entry.

The city had capitulated about an hour earlier, after a night and morning of terror during which German airplanes bombed all military objectives in the neighborhood and machine-gunned districts around the harbor defenses.

Already the Germans had taken over control of all military air fields, including Fornebo, just outside Oslo, where fifty German bombers landed. With these they had threatened to blow the populace of the city out of existence if any resistance was shown.

By noon the main railroad station in Oslo was packed with evacuées, hurriedly leaving the city. Women, children and elderly men carried all the possessions they could muster. All seemed dazed, but there was no outward sign of fear or panic.

DENMARK PROTESTS BUT YIELDS TO NAZIS

CAPITAL REPORTED QUIET
Occupation of Country Almost Complete, Germans Assert— Blackouts Are Ordered

Wireless to The New York Times.

STOCKHOLM, Sweden, April 9—Denmark surrendered to Germany under protest but without attempting any resistance, and today German soldiers were patrolling the streets of Copenhagen and other troops were moving into all parts of the country, especially along the Jutland coast, facing England.

King Christian and Premier Theodor Stauning issued a proclamation calling upon the army and the people not to offer any resistance, and latest reports from Copenhagen say that the occupation is proceeding peacefully, that everything is calm and that the German authorities are already organizing the country economically and politically.

BERLIN REPORTS PROCLAMATION

BERLIN, April 9 (AP)—A Copenhagen dispatch of D. N. B., the official German news agency, said tonight that King Christian and Premier Theodor Stauning had addressed a proclamation to the Danish people asking them to refrain from untoward acts and assuring them that Denmark was submitting to the German invasion under protest.

The text of the Danish proclamation, as released by D. N. B., follows:

To the Danish People:

German troops tonight crossed the Danish border. Some German troops will debark at various points in Denmark. The Danish Government has decided under protest to handle the affairs of the country with dispatch and in view of the occupation to communicate the following:

"German troops that are now in this country have come in contact with armed Danish forces. It is the further duty of the people to refrain from every resistance to these troops. The Danish Government will endeavor to insure the security of the people and of the Danish land in face of disastrous consequences resulting from the state of war, and consequently asks the population to maintain a calm, thoughtful attitude.

"May peace and order reign in the country. May all who have to do with the authorities observe an attitude of loyalty."

Copenhagen, April 9, 1940.

Christian Rex.

T. Stauning.

King Christian added the following personal message:

"In these circumstances, which are so grave to our country, I ask all of you inhabitants of the cities and country to maintain an attitude completely correct and dignified, since every inconsiderate act or word can draw in its wake most serious consequences." ◊

PLANES ROAR OVERHEAD

The air was filled with the roar of airplane engines as German fliers circled ceaselessly, hoping thereby to strike terror into the people. The streets were deserted. All offices and banks were closed.

From a hotel window a German fighting plane was seen power-diving over the harbor, its machine guns spitting amid desultory anti-aircraft fire. Toward late afternoon from the United States Legation, some distance from the city, the roar of airplane engines was heard again,

and three bombers were seen circling at a great height. While the people watched, unconcerned, there was a terrific roar as an explosion blew up a house only 200 yards away. As the wreckage disappeared in black smoke, five more bombs landed near by in quick succession.

KRISTIANSAND RAID PICTURED

STOCKHOLM, Sweden, April 10 (AP)—Eyewitness accounts of the attack by planes and warships on Kristiansand fortress, on the south coast of

Norway, said the streets were filled with granite splinters and the spire of the cathedral was shot down. Crying women and children filled the air raid shelters for three hours until the fortress fell. Three or four buildings were set on fire.

As many as 150 planes took part in the Oslo occupation, other eyewitnesses reported. Some of them ferried 400 German soldiers armed with machine guns and grenades. About 120 Norwegian soldiers were reported killed in this operation. ◇

APRIL 12, 1940

Editorial
THE BATTLE FOR NORWAY

When Winston Churchill refuses to "lift the veil" for the British Parliament, when the families of thousands of fighting men are told to wait still another day for definite news, the outer world must hold its breath a little longer as it reads the bulletins of the sea fighting around Norway. The outcome of these widely flung naval combats cannot yet be known; the greatest struggle of the war is still going on. In these circumstances the British and other admiralties are probably wise in keeping silent. After Jutland the British tried to satisfy the hunger for news but their premature reports gave the public a totally false picture of the great battle. Mr. Churchill himself told yesterday of one huge British battle cruiser, the Renown, which had her wireless apparatus shot away in a duel with two German ships and was cut off for hours from contact with London. The agonized suspense over the Renown may have its counterpart with other ships, in all the navies engaged; and there can be no conclusive report until the fate of the last ship has been reported.

But out of the mist that hangs over the North Countries there emerge two facts whose validity and importance are now established beyond question. The first is that Norway has chosen to fight and not to yield; to put no faith in German promises, to accept no regime of "protective custody" unless it is imposed on her by sheer overwhelming force of alien arms. With splendid courage Norway has mustered her small army in a desperate effort of resistance. The question now is whether aid from her allies can come to her in time.

The second fact is that the British fleet has struck with promptness and with power. Even a smashing victory at sea, if this is what we find when the curtain lifts, will still leave ahead the formidable problem of landing an ex-

peditionary force in Norway and driving the invader from that country. But the counter-attack has been begun with courage, dash and a full realization of the critical importance of the issue. ◇

APRIL 15, 1940

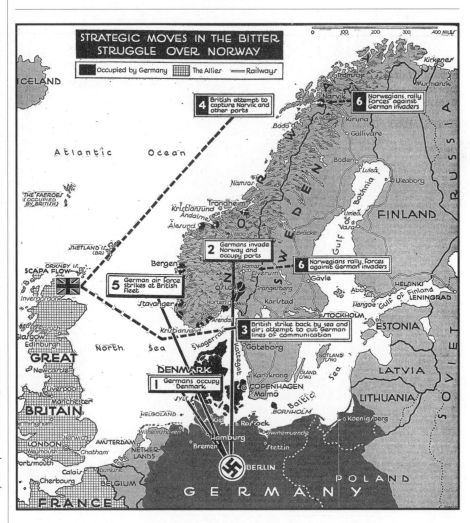

DEWEY SAYS ISSUE IS KEEP OUT OF WAR
Neutrality Safer If Change Is Made, He Adds—
Holds New Deal Broke Pledges

By JAMES C. HEGERTY
Special to The New York Times.

OKLAHOMA CITY, April 17—With a declaration that the record of the New Deal was "a record of covenants abandoned, pledges blithely cast aside," District Attorney Thomas E. Dewey, candidate for the Republican Presidential nomination, told a gathering here tonight that the continued neutrality of this nation toward the European war would be in "safer hands" under a Republican administration.

Mr. Dewey spoke at a rally in the Municipal Auditorium sponsored by the State Republican organization. While the primary problems facing the nation were those at home, he said, another inescapable issue was to safeguard American peace in a war-torn world and to keep a determination to stay out of the war.

"The pledge to keep the nation out of war is one which admits of no temporizing. It can be accepted only from men who have kept their pledged word in the past and will keep their pledged word in the future.

"We must judge this administration, not by its commitments for the future, but by its past conduct. The record of the New Deal is a record of covenants abandoned, pledges blithely cast aside. On the basis of that record, we as Americans must conclude that in the emergency of a world again at war the destiny of the nation would be safer in other hands." ◆

AP GIVES REPORT ON WAR COVERAGE
Kent Cooper Describes How Press Association Has Overcome Obstacles

The story of how The Associated Press has met the vast obligations imposed by the European war and its censorships— at the same time not permitting this "dislocation" to interfere with its coverage of this country—was told by Kent Cooper, general manager, in his annual report to the board of directors, made public yesterday.

"The management," he said, "takes pride in the record of news accomplishment during the year. At the same time it realizes that however high its standards are set, further improvement always is possible. Again it invites constructive criticisms and suggestions from the membership."

He recalled, too, that in pictures as well as news 1939 had brought extraordinary tasks, remarking that for AP's news photo service it was "the heaviest year in its history from a viewpoint of coverage, on both sides of the Atlantic."

PREPARATIONS MADE EARLY

Discussing the war coverage in detail "because of the unusual problems presented," Mr. Cooper mentioned the period of preparation that found the personnel abroad "reinforced materially long before the beginning of hostilities," and said this corps was able to "carry on with credit in reporting every major turn of affairs."

"The German march into Poland," he added, "found an Associated Press bureau, capably manned by American staff men, in readiness at Warsaw. Similarly, the first Soviet onrush into Finland was reported promptly and vividly because our own staff was on the ground well in advance.

"Meanwhile, in the less active sectors, at the capitals of belligerent and near-by neutral nations and along the Western Front, Associated Press men were reporting all there was to report. When the war came to American shores our bureaus at Buenos Aires and Montevideo distinguished themselves in turn with their accounts of the flight and destruction of the Admiral Graf Spee.

"Naturally, in such times, many important questions of news direction must be decided by the management. Rumors and speculation spring up prolifically in an atmosphere of war. Every censorship creates multitudinous problems of conduct for the correspondents caught in its grip.

TRUTH HARD TO OBTAIN

"Belligerency loosens all remaining restraint from the hand of propaganda, at the same time that it seeks to interpose every possible obstacle to disclosure of the real truth.

"We have tried to deal with these questions soundly and realistically. Where the truth was not ascertainable, Associated Press dispatches have not presented rumor in its stead. Particularly we have refrained from giving currency to fantastic reports, printed or otherwise circulated in one belligerent nation with respect to supposed happenings in an enemy country.

"Every correspondent and every editor has made it his concern to weed out propaganda, and to present official statements for what they are, and no more. These practices have been followed as being sound and proper. It is hoped they represent the overwhelming desire of the membership."

This description of the AP's war effort was but part of Mr. Cooper's summary of AP's world-wide operations in news, features and news pictures in 1939—of the growth of wirephoto to international scope and of the increase in the number of newspapers outside of the United States which now are participating in The Associated Press service. ◆

Ill-Armed British Face Disaster North of Trondheim, Writer Says

Remnants of Inexperienced Force of 1,500 Will Be Cut to Ribbons Unless They Are Strengthened, Witness Asserts

Unless the British expeditionary force seeking to advance in Norway from Namsos north of Trondheim receives adequate reinforcements and large supplies of anti-aircraft guns within a few days, it will be cut to ribbons, Leland Stowe, veteran war correspondent, reported yesterday in a copyrighted dispatch from Gaeddede, at the Norwegian-Swedish frontier, to The Chicago Daily News foreign service, which was published here by The New York Post.

The British force consisted of one battalion of Territorials [the equivalent of this country's National Guard] and one battalion of the King's Own Light Infantry, totaling fewer than 1,500 men, the majority of whom averaged only one year of military service, and who were without anti-aircraft, airplane or field artillery support, Mr. Stowe said.

"After only four days of fighting, nearly half of this initial B.E.F.F. contingent has been knocked out—either killed, wounded or captured," he reported. "On Monday these comparatively in-experienced and incredibly underarmed British troops were decisively defeated. They were driven back in precipitate disorder from Vist, three miles south of the bomb-ravaged town of Steinkjer."

Mr. Stowe told of having been the only newspaper correspondent to enter Steinkjer Monday evening and to pass beyond to the British advance headquarters and the edge of the heavy firing zone. He continued:

"A battalion of 600 Territorials were fighting desperately to hold Vist, the point of their farthest southward advance toward Trondheim. As twilight closed they were completely done in. For hours they had been torn and broken under the terrible triple onslaught of German infantry, tri-motored bombers and naval artillery firing from destroyers at the head of Breitstad Fjord."

Within two hours, Mr. Stowe said, the British troops were in flight, having no chance whatever with nothing but Brenn machine guns and rifles. Steinkjer was occupied by the Germans Tuesday. ◆

British troops pick through the ruins of Namsos, Norway after a German air raid, April 1940.

NAZIS INVADE HOLLAND, BELGIUM, LUXEMBOURG BY LAND AND AIR

Nazi Parachute Troops Land at Key Centers as Flooding Starts

First Bombing in France

Special Cable to The New York Times.

AMSTERDAM, The Netherlands, May 10—Germany invaded the Netherlands early today, land troops being preceded by widespread air attacks on airdromes and by the landing of parachute troops.

The Netherlands resisted and announced she was at war with Germany. Anti-aircraft batteries and fighter planes engaged swarms of German aircraft when they appeared simultaneously over a score of Netherland cities.

An official proclamation said:

"Since 3 A.M. German troops have crossed the Netherland frontier and German planes have tried to attack airports. Inundations are effective according to plans. The army anti-aircraft batteries were found prepared. So far as is known six German planes have been shot down."

(French, Belgian and British planes were sighted over the Netherlands this morning, a Reuters (British news agency) dispatch said in quoting the Netherland radio station at Hilversum, near Amsterdam.

German troops were first reported crossing the Netherland frontier near Roermond, eight miles north of the Belgian frontier. German planes landed troops by parachute at strategic points near Rotterdam, The Hague, Amsterdam and other large cities.

A large number of the German troops landed by parachute were said to be dressed in Netherland military uniforms.

Other Germans crossed the Maas River in rubber boats to Netherland territory. They were said to be reaching the Netherland side in "considerable numbers." ❯

A fierce air battle raged over Amsterdam as Netherland fighter planes dived repeatedly on German bombers and troop transport planes with chattering machine guns.

Schiphol Airdrome outside Amsterdam, the nation's largest, was heavily bombed. Military authorities immediately threw a heavy guard around the airdrome in an effort to defend it against German parachute troops.

Planes identified as German Heinkels bombed Schiphol Airdrome repeatedly, loosing some thirty heavy caliber bombs on the landing field between 5:15 and 5:30 A.M.

Reports poured in of planes in great numbers over a score of Netherland cities. Netherland authorities, hurriedly organizing defense, flashed orders to the whole country to be on the alert against parachute troops.

Fifty planes were over Nijmegen, sixty miles southeast of Amsterdam on the German border.

A number of parachute troops reportedly landed at Sliedrecht, Delft and several other points. Delft is twelve and a half miles from The Hague. About 100 parachute troops were landed near Dordrecht, thirty-eight miles southwest of Amsterdam.

Hundreds of troops were landed at Hoogezwaluwe, whose big bridge is the major communicating link between the northern and southern parts of the country. A large number of German troops landed by parachute at Leiden. Others landed at Waalhaven, major airport of Rotterdam, and at Rozenburg Island, near Rotterdam.

The lightning attack did not take the Netherlands completely by surprise as the country had been in intense fear of invasion for days and defense measures had been taken.

The Amsterdam radio announced that Netherland troops had captured a number of German parachute troops, wearing German uniforms, near The Hague.

Twenty-four planes appeared over Rotterdam, biggest port in the Netherlands, at 5:50 A.M.

Among towns throughout the country where foreign planes were sighted, including planes identified as German bombers in flights ranging from one to fifty, were Den Haag, Rotterdam, Hook of Holland, Haarlem, Tilburg, Zalt Bommel, Geldermalsen, Venloo, Alkmaar, Maastricht, Hengelo, Scheveningen, Arnhem, Leiden and Emmen.

The descent of swarms of foreign

war planes on the Netherlands came after a night of alarms and a week-long period of tension bred by fear the country would be invaded. All public communications between the Netherlands and the outside world were taken over by the government last night, canals were locked and extraordinary measures taken for national safety.

FIRST ACTIVITY AT AMSTERDAM

The first aerial activity began at 2:41 A.M., Netherland time, when Amsterdam anti-aircraft batteries first fired at foreign planes.

When the Amsterdam anti-aircraft batteries opened up they fired for four minutes at planes whose motors could be heard plainly over the residential section of South Amsterdam. Reports coming into Amsterdam from various points said numbers of planes crossed the northern half of the Netherlands and the Frisian Islands, flying from east to west.

Amsterdam's anti-aircraft guns blazed again at 4:05 A.M. Intense activity in the air was reported from points throughout the Netherlands, with huge squadrons of foreign planes crossing back and forth.

A squadron of foreign planes was reported circling over Helder, Netherland

---

MAY 10, 1940

ALLIED HELP SPED
Netherland and Belgian Appeals Answered by British and French

Special Cable to The New York Times.

LONDON, May 10—The British Government received appeals for help early today from both the Netherlands and Belgium.

The British and French reply to the Netherlands-Belgian appeals was prompt. Representatives of the respective governments here were told by 8:30 A.M. (3:30 A.M. New York time) they could expect all the help Britain could give them.

The Netherland Legation here received assurance that its country and Belgium were now regarded as Allies of Britain and France.

Within a few minutes after receipt of official news of the invasion of the

Low Countries, the British Cabinet was called to 10 Downing Street and was in session with Prime Minister Neville Chamberlain.

The German invasion of the Low Countries had been expected in London, and it must be presumed the Allies were ready for it to some extent.

ALLIES VISIBLE TO PLANES

The biggest handicap to the British and French was in the timing of the German thrust at dawn. This prevented the Allies moving troops under cover of darkness, and since hundreds of German planes already had flown over practically all of Netherland and Belgian territory for some hours, the disposition of Allied troops and their every movement must have been known to the German High Command.

While the Netherlanders and Belgians had taken every precaution against a surprise attack, the general belief had been that Adolf Hitler would try first to consolidate his position in Norway and make secure his new air bases at Trondheim, Bergen and Oslo before any fresh adventure. Now it is regarded here as probable that Herr Hitler sought to take advantage of the London political situa-

tion, when the minds of British leaders were engrossed with possible reconstruction of the government.

AIM AT BRITAIN IS SEEN

It now appears almost certain that the Germans decided to take a gamble to try to win the war this year while their superiority in men and machines was at its peak.

But unlike their strategy in the World War, it is generally believed in authoritative quarters here that the Germans have no intention of carrying out a great right wheel against France, but that their objective is to take the Netherlands and Belgium, solidify their positions there and then concentrate their entire attack against Britain.

Once in possession of the North Sea coast line all the way from Trondheim, Norway, to the English Channel, experts here believe Germany would then concentrate on trying by air and submarine attack to blockade Britain into starvation and submission.

While both Britain and France knew that, since last November the Germans had been in position to attack the Low Countries at a minute's notice and while French officials had expressed surprise yesterday that the Nazis had not then

naval base on the northwest coast at the entrance to Ysselmeer, and six German seaplanes were reported circling over Ijmuiden in Central Holland.

At 5:40 A.M. twelve Heinkel planes and five seaplanes were sighted over Sliedrecht flying westward.

It was said that the parachute troops who had floated down near Haagsche-schouw, between Leiden and The Hague, were dressed in Netherland military uniforms. At 5:50 A.M. informants said:

"A great number of parachute troops are landing at many places. All of them are clad in Netherland Army uniforms."

PLANE REPORTED DOWNED

It was reported that one German plane had been shot down near the Schiphol Airdrome.

A number of German parachute troops in German uniforms were captured by patrols on the outskirts of The Hague, it was reported.

It was reported without confirmation that German Messerschmitt planes had "landed" at the Schiphol Airdrome. It could not be ascertained immediately whether the planes had been shot down or whether they had landed of their own accord.

At 6 A,M. more parachute troops were dropped near Ravesteyn, close to Nijmegen.

Fifteen Heinkel bombers were sighted over Delft at 5:50 A.M. A few minutes later an additional twenty-one German planes passed over Rotterdam, apparently heading for the Ypenburg Airport.

At 6:20 A.M. the official radio for the first time said "foreign planes" were landing "enemy" parachute troops. The official announcer said a large formation of planes had just been sighted near The Hague.

At 6:30 A.M. the official radio said: "New and large formations of planes are arriving constantly from Germany."

At 6:40 A.M. twenty-two German planes were observed flying westward at Rhenen near Utrecht.

It was reported that at least two Netherland planes had been set on fire and destroyed on the ground during the bombing of the Schiphol Airdrome.

Roads leading out of Amsterdam were choked with automobiles soon after daylight. They were heaped with household goods as residents fled in fear of German aerial bombing of the city.

Parachutists began landing in increasing numbers after 7:30 A.M. in the southern part of the country, particularly in the Eindhoven area. ◊

---

made a new attack to take advantage of the British political crisis, there was very little evidence to indicate that the attack was coming this morning.

FRENCH TROOPS BELIEVED READY
Wireless to The New York Times.
PARIS, May 10—France today, in the midst of an air-raid alarm, learned of the double invasion of the Netherlands and Belgium by German forces. Appeals for help from the governments of both countries were transmitted by telephone, and a Cabinet Council was summoned immediately.

According to fragmentary reports received thus far, a memorandum from the German Government addressed to the Netherland and Belgian Governments announcing that German forces would enter their territories to prevent invasion by the Allies was covered by a mass arrival of airplanes.

The reaction here was immediate, and there is no doubt but that the divisions of French and British forces close to the Belgian frontier are ready. [At this point a few words were removed by the censor.]

Keen interest attaches here to the reaction of the United States, for it is felt that "this absolutely unjustified invasion

of strictly neutral countries" will arouse the highest indignation among Americans, as it does here.

It raises the question of international protection for Netherland and Belgian colonies and the assistance of the United States in watching over the Netherlands Indies, something that would be welcomed here with the warmest satisfaction.

The Allies doubtless will communicate directly to President Roosevelt their decisions on the Belgian and Netherland appeal. American condemnation, it is thought here, can hardly be withheld.

The case of the Netherlands and Belgium, which since the outbreak of the hostilities last September have scrupulously observed every possible rule to keep them from being involved, is held in French official circles to prove that there can no longer be any possibility for a nation within striking range of Germany to remain neutral. One by one, they must expect to meet the fate of Denmark, Norway, the Netherlands and Belgium, unless they call the Allies to their assistance in time.

Even outside Europe, it is argued, nations cannot now remain indifferent to the conflict in which it is obvious their interests will be utterly disregarded. ◊

MAY 11, 1940

CHAMBERLAIN RESIGNS, CHURCHILL PREMIER

COALITION ASSURED
Labor Decides to Allow Leaders to Join New National Cabinet

OLD MINISTERS STAY
Churchill Asks Them to Remain Until They Can Be Replaced

By RAYMOND DANIEL
Special Cable to The New York Times

LONDON, May 10—In the gravest crisis Great Britain has faced since the World War, Winston Churchill became Prime Minister tonight as Allied armies raced across Belgium again for a death grapple with invading German armies.

Neville Chamberlain, who had headed the government since just after King George VI ascended the throne, resigned early in the evening after convincing himself that it was impossible to remain and give the country the truly national government that the people want.

A genuine coalition Cabinet was assured when the executive committee of the Labor party declared that it would accept a share in a government headed by a new Prime Minister who had the nation's confidence. This is expected also to result in the entry of Liberals into the government.

INVASION FAILS TO SAVE CABINET
The German invasion of Belgium, the Netherlands and Luxembourg, which transformed the static conflict of the West into a total European if not yet World War, had been expected throughout the day to "freeze" Mr. Chamberlain in his job for a short time at least, despite the poor showing in Wednesday's division when the government's majority in the House of Commons was cut from 200 to eighty-one.

That Mr. Chamberlain would have to relinquish his high office became apparent last night when Clement R. Attlee and Arthur Greenwood, the ▶

❮ Opposition Labor leaders, informed him to his face that they would not consent to serve in a Cabinet that he headed. Thus they provided the cue for the undecided Liberals and Conservatives who were critical of the government.

Without these dissidents, it was felt it would be impossible for the man who brought back "peace in our time" from Munich to establish a government satisfactory to the disturbed Members of Parliament and their worried constituents. These were too angry at the let-down to their hopes of the Allied withdrawal from Norway after the optimistic buildup their press had given them about the success of operations across the North Sea.

DEMAND FOR COALITION

After the acrimonious debate that followed the Prime Minister's admission that the campaign in Central and Southern Norway was at an end, it was apparent that the country demanded a new administration in which the Opposition would share the responsibilities of leadership.

Early this evening Mr. Chamberlain drove to Buckingham Palace and told the King he thought the time had come for him to relinquish his seals of office. Soon afterward Mr. Churchill, who has been the nearest approach to a war leader this country has had since the conflict began went to the Palace also and accepted an invitation to form a government.

This came as something of a surprise, for it was known that as late as last night, Mr. Chamberlain favored Foreign Secretary Viscount Halifax as his successor. A small crowd was waiting at Whitehall when the following announcement was issued from there:

"The Right Hon. Neville Chamberlain, M. P., resigned the office of Prime Minister and First Lord of the Treasury this evening. And the Right Hon. Winston Churchill, M. P., accepted His Majesty's invitation to fill the position.

"The Prime Minister desires that all Ministers should remain at their posts and discharge their functions with full freedom and responsibility while the necessary arrangements for formation of a new administration are made."

Mr. Churchill, who will move from Admiralty House to No. 10 Downing Street as soon as Mr. Chamberlain can move out, is expected to announce selection of his colleagues tomorrow or next day.

The German invasion of the Low Countries made it urgently necessary that the confused political situation here should be resolved immediately and a government that would have the united support of all elements in Parliament be established to lead the nation. That this could be accomplished only after Mr. Chamberlain's resignation became clear this morning after the meeting of the executive committee of the Parliamentary Labor party. ◆

MAY 11, 1940

WARS CHIEF FACTOR IN CHURCHILL'S LIFE
New Prime Minister, Whether as Soldier or Civilian, Won Reputation In Battles

For Winston Churchill, the post of war Prime Minister of Great Britain brings to a peak a career inextricably bound with war, both as a soldier and as a governing official.

A grandson of the seventh Duke of Marborough, he was schooled at Harrow and at Sandhurst, British military academy. He served in four campaigns before he reached his twenty-fifth year, and when, in the First World War, he was forced from the post of First Lord of the Admiralty, he took a command in France as a major and was promoted later to lieutenant colonel.

Hardly had he been graduated from

MAY 11, 1940

ALLIES SEE VICTORY IN LOW COUNTRIES
Military Leaders Emphasize Strength Of the Defenses Of Netherlands And Belgium

By HAROLD DENNY
Special Cable to The New York Times.

LONDON, May 10—Though the scope and exact objectives of Germany's sudden invasion of the Low Countries cannot be defined this early, military leaders express complete confidence in

the ability of the British and French to defeat Germany if the new operation takes the nature of a wheel into Northern France, such as Britain's little army faced in 1914.

The German armies will meet far more effective opposition than they encountered in the last war. When the Kaiser's armies swept through the Netherlands and Belgium in 1914, the defenses, even forts such as the Germans reduced at Liege, were only embryonic compared with the deep, strong, elaborate fortifications of today.

The Netherlanders and Belgians have devised elaborate water and other obstacles the Germans must conquer if they are to arrive in Northern France. If the Germans manage to get through the Netherlands and Belgium and arrive at the French border it is believed here they would be a tired, battered force with much of their elaborate, costly equipment smashed.

The British and French have been confident of their ability to stop the Ger-

mans with terrible losses. The junior officers have been hoping Herr Hitler would attack the Low Countries because they believe that would end the war much more quickly.

Higher officers of the British Expeditionary Force in France have avoided overconfidence, never ruling out the possibility that Germany or some other combatant might devise some new means to overcome tank traps that now seem impregnable. But they remain confident that any right wheel through the Low Countries into France would do far less damage to the Allies and suffer far more itself than happened in 1914. Military opinion among the allies and neutral observers here tends to the belief that developments in defense since the last war have outstripped developments in offense.

If Herr Hitler's purpose turns out to be not to invade France, but merely to use the Netherlands and Belgium as bases for raids against England, then it will be a job for Britain's air force and navy as well as the army, and Britain

Sandhurst and joined his regiment, the Fourth Hussars, in 1895, than he began looking for a war, and the same year found him in Cuba as war correspondent for The Daily Graphic of London.

HERO IN BOER WAR

He returned to England and his regiment in 1896 and was sent to India, where he saw action in Malakand. He was in a campaign in Egypt under Lord Kitchener, and covered the Boer War for The Morning Post of London. He was made prisoner, escaped and eventually returned home to find all England hailing him as a hero.

He had written several books, and he entered politics for good now. He was elected to Parliament from Oldham, but switched from the Conservative to the Liberal party, and in 1907 became

Winston Churchill at his seat in the Cabinet Room at No 10 Downing Street, London, circa 1940.

president of the Board of Trade and a close friend of David Lloyd George. He served also as Home Secretary.

He became the First Lord of the Admiralty in 1911, and three years later he had the fleet in position when the declaration of war came. He was one of those responsible for the disastrous attempt to force the Dardanelles. Badly organized because coordination between the Army and the Navy was lacking, the campaign failed and Mr. Churchill was severely criticized. A reorganization of the Cabinet in 1915 left him out of the War Council, and he resigned a minor post as Chancellor of the Duchy of Lancaster to take a command in the Sixth Battalion of the Royal Scots Fusiliers.

RETURNS TO CABINET

Mr. Churchill returned to the Cabinet as Secretary of State for War and Minister for Air in the government formed by Mr. Lloyd George in December, 1918. His political influence waned in the middle twenties to the point where he was defeated for Parliament in Dundee, and it was a long time before he was called out of what amounted to a retirement. Then Prime Minister Stanley Baldwin made him Chancellor of the Exchequer, a post held by his father, Lord Randolph Churchill.

After the rise of Adolf Hitler Mr. Churchill was one of those who insisted that another war would be the result of the German rearmament program, and he kept on insisting until, in 1937, Great Britain took a step toward meeting the challenge by initi-

ating a naval building program.

On Sept. 4, 1939, the day after war between Great Britain and Germany was declared, all units of the British fleet received a code message which said, simply, "Winston is back." Prime Minister Chamberlain had made him once again the First Lord of the Admiralty. ◊

MAY 11, 1940

TIMES SQUARE THRONG IS SOMBER AND GRIM
Crowds Fill Area to Watch the Latest War Bulletins

The intense interest in the latest war developments was reflected again yesterday by the crowds that filled Times Square to read the bulletin boards about the base of the Times Building.

As night fell and the electric sign spun out the newer reports fifteen patrolmen and three mounted policemen were sent into the area to keep the crowds watching the bulletins on the move. The press became so great in the early evening that the roadway was partly filled by spectators and vehicular and pedestrian traffic was impeded.

During the daylight hours five patrolmen were needed to break up the groups that formed to debate the war after digesting the bulletin board notes and studying the detailed maps in the windows of the Times Building.

A month ago, when the Nazis invaded Scandinavia, the discussion of international affairs was of less interest to the cracker barrel forum than the airing of personal opinions about ideologies. The throngs yesterday were far more somber and tempers were more even. The orators seemed deeply concerned about the future attitude of the United States Government.

As homeward-bound throngs paused to read the bulletins their conversations indicated a growing fear that the war was getting close to home. Even the women, who during previous international crises had given the news reports scant attention, studied the bulletins carefully. ◊

---

also has confidence in these other arms. If Herr Hitler begins intensive air raids on London and other British centers, the air force and anti-aircraft defenses unquestionably will take a heavy toll of his planes and would present the question of how long he could keep on spending planes, pilots and gasoline.

FRENCH HELP IMMEDIATE
By G. H. ARCHAMBAULT
Wireless to The New York Times.

PARIS, May 10—The French military reaction to the invasion of the Low Countries was immediate. The German move had been threatened so long that there was little surprise. Defense plans had been perfected since the first alarm in mid-January.

It seems likely that the German intention is to cut off the Netherlands from Belgium and cut off Belgium from France by using swift, mechanized columns and large air forces. This process was applied in Poland and repeated in Norway.

But the Netherlands and Belgium are

prepared. Competent circles here believe the mechanized divisions will find their progress impeded soon after they cross the frontiers. In Belgium everything had been prepared east of the Meuse River to blow up highways, railroads and bridges in a few minutes. At other points roads have been obstructed by rock and felled trees for 100 yards or more.

Everywhere there are machine gun emplacements, sweeping all possible lines of advance. Similar precautions had been taken in the Netherlands. All the water defenses in both countries were ready to operate instantly.

It is no secret that the Allies have had a large mobile force constantly prepared at the Belgian border. It seems likely that once more Belgium will be the cockpit of Europe for a war of movement.

It must not be forgotten that the Maginot Line in the last eight months has been extended from the Luxembourg border to the North Sea, that everywhere it is very strong and that French morale is at its highest point. ◊

MAY 12, 1940

ARMY CORPS MOVES 600 MILES IN 6 DAYS
41,000 'Blue' Troops Travel From Georgia To Louisiana in a 'Lightning' War

Completing the largest and fastest mass movement of armed troops ever witnessed in this country during peacetime, 41,000 khaki-clad soldiers and officers of the Fourth Corps finished the first phase of the Third Army manoeuvres when they arrived in Louisiana yesterday after a forced overland march covering more than 600 miles in less than six days.

Airborne Infantry officer using a "walkie-talkie," a radio field telephone, during maneuvers of the Third Army, in 1940.

Long columns of army trucks, rumbling tanks, armored cars and official staff cars were still pouring westward along the nation's highways yesterday morning. The long route of march took them from Georgia across Alabama and Mississippi to converge at Alexandria, La., for a big ten-day "battle"—an unprecedented peacetime manoeuvre against the Ninth Corps, based on San Antonio, Texas.

Designated as the "Red" army, the Ninth Corps troops theoretically are invading the United States, pushing with mechanized and motorized units eastward through Texas to the Sabine River area in Louisiana, where the "Blues," or Fourth Corps troops, are converging to check the assault. Facing a superiority in numbers, plus sudden unexpected assaults by enemy planes, the advance guard of the "Blue" Fourth Corps lost in the first encounter with the invaders. But reinforced yesterday so as to reach its full strength of the some 41,000 soldiers, the "Blue" defending army will begin the second phase of the manoeuvres this week with a numerical superiority over the "Red" army, which numbers about 30,000 troops.

Along the route of last week's unprecedented military march, interrupted only by overnight bivouacs, the Fourth Corps, commanded by Major Gen. Walter C. Short, organized the services of about 9,000 civilians to warn the defending army of approaching enemy planes. Serving the "Blue" forces as they would in time of war, this watching group of citizenry, made up largely of American Legion members, reported to the staff of the defending army all enemy moves on land and in the air.

It was probably the most extensive aircraft warning system ever established in this country. In addition to the citizens' corps, fifty planes from the navy's training school at Pensacola, Fla., took part in the aircraft warning plan, but the navy planes will not participate in the actual field manoeuvres.

As the second phase of the fighting continues this week, practically every officer of the regular army and those reserve officers who have been invited to watch the manoeuvres are intently focusing their attention on the tactics of lightning war which the Third Army exercises, under Lieut. Gen. Stanley D. Embick, are expected to illustrate graphically.

With three of the army's new triangular, or "stream-lined," divisions, along with a provisional tank brigade, comprising the principal units of the Fourth Corps, and one triangular division, plus a horsed cavalry division which includes the army's only completely mechanized cavalry brigade, as principal units of the Ninth Corps, the manoeuvres are the first in the peace-time history of the country to involve two army corps of the regular army. The mechanized and motorized units of this highly mobile force are expected to provide military men with practical experience in handling powerful combat units, and to serve as excellent instruction in the military art of lightning war.

Product of the army's reorganization program, the new-type division has 11,000 men, about half as many as were mustered by the old "square" division which contained about 22,000 troops. Because it is fully organized with new and improved weapons, the "stream-lined" division has a fire power equal to that of the old unit, while in traveling speed the new division can make time considerably faster than the old.

About 400 tanks, some of them of experimental design, are participating in the Louisiana-Texas manoeuvres, while more than 340 scout and armored cars make up the combined mechanized reconnaissance forces.

In addition, there is an air armada of 128 planes, including bombers, pursuit, attack and observation ships, which will act to disorganize, if possible, the enemy infantry forces and to make air raids against communications and supply units. In all, more than 8,000 vehicles of all types are being used in the manoeuvres, and of this number some 3,500 are new, high-powered trucks, command cars or special vehicles. ◈

MAY 13, 1940

Adolf Hitler at his headquarters at Bruly-de-Peche, Ardennes, Belgium, with General Alfred Jodl to Hitler's left and Field Marshal Walter von Brauchitsc to his right during the campaign of May-June 1940.

GERMAN ARMY TACTICS

By HANSON W. BALDWIN

The attack upon the Low Countries, which was approaching its first climax yesterday, is apparently developing in accordance with the time-honored tactical system of the German Army.

The flank attack, or the "double envelopment," has long been the favorite German tactic; planes have now enabled the Germans to attempt the so-called "vertical envelopment" by means of parachute troops against the defenders of the Netherlands.

Where the front is continuous and no flank exists the Germans endeavor to make flanks by a break-through, and then enlarging the gap thus made. In Belgium the break-through of the first Belgian defensive line apparently has been made near Maastricht, north of Liège; and German mechanized and motorized forces, covered by air power, may now attempt to fan out over the Belgian plain to exploit the break and if possible to encircle the Belgian Army in much the same manner that Hannibal destroyed an army of Romans 2,000 years ago.

Throughout most of German military history the flanking or encircling attack has been a favorite manoeuvre, and it was the double envelopment—Cannae on the grand scale—that the Germans so successfully used in their Polish "Blitzkrieg."

Cannae in 216 B.C. (in itself a "conscious copy of the tactics of Marathon," 490 B.C.) was Hannibal's most brilliant victory against the Romans. With 50,000 troops he faced the Romans' 86,000. Hannibal made both his flanks extremely strong, the Carthaginians enveloped or outflanked the Romans on both wings, surrounded and annihilated them. Cannae has gone down in history as a classic of military perfection to be studied, and if possible emulated.

WORLD WAR TACTIC TRIED AGAIN

It was this same principle of the flank attack that the Germans, in their attack through Belgium, tried in the World War, and it is the same tactic of assault upon one, or preferably both, of the enemy's wings that dominates their military thought today.

But the steel and concrete fortifications of the Western Front and the more or less protected flanks of the French and British Armies may force—as was the case in the World War—an adaptation of the tactic of encirclement.

Captain Rohr, a young, brilliant German staff officer, was among the first to realize during the World War that the bloody battering against fortified lines and strong trench systems was getting nowhere. There developed the tactics of "infiltration," which are simply opportunistic tactics. In the offense a continuous pressure against the enemy's lines was developed; wherever a weak spot appeared it was immediately exploited; troops were poured into the breach, without regard to the strong points and citadels of resistance left unconquered on either side of them, and the local "break-through" was then exploited and widened by pushing on into the enemy's rear areas and by encircling the flanks thus created.

Tanks and mechanized forces are used to exploit the breaches made and to keep the battle moving; tank masses may be thrown against the weakened enemy lines after the main assault has cracked or split the defensive structure.

◀ The German offensive doctrine is methodical but not cautious. Careful and precise preparations for every attack are always made; secrecy and deception—to veil their intentions—and surprise—to give them maximum effect—are much valued.

FREE SCOPE IN ACTUAL BATTLE

But once the gage of battle is joined, much is left to the discretion of the field officers, particularly to battalion commanders; the battle is decentralized as much as possible; initiative is strongly stressed. For the German military mind—though popularly associated with rigidity and inelasticity—is prepared to accept risks, knowing that no battle can be fought, no war won without the assumption of risks, recognizing that "war, far from being an exact science, is a terrifying and passionate drama." And the German "Truppenfuehrung," or "Field Service Regulations," specifically state, that "in spite of technique, the worth of man is the decisive factor."

Initiative, flexibility and mobility are the keynote of German offensive tactics. The importance of fire effect is stressed. The artillery is handled somewhat like Pelham's famous battery of "Jeb" Stuart's cavalry; sometimes in the attack it trundles almost on the infantry's heels; indeed the German infantry regiment, to increase its fire effect and the power of its attack, is probably more heav-

---

MAY 14, 1940

ISOLATION HOPE FUTILE, SAYS HULL

He Tells International Lawyers We Cannot Close Our Eyes to 'Orgy of Destruction'

Special to The New York Times.

WASHINGTON, May 13—The world is threatened with "an orgy of destruction not only of life and property but of religion, of morality, of the very bases of civilized society," Secretary Hull declared tonight.

Americans cannot close their eyes to the menace abroad, strong though their nation is; nor can they delude themselves "with the mere hope that somehow all this will pass us by." Mr. Hull said before the annual meeting of the American Society of International Law, of which he is president.

"Our own nation, powerful as it is and determined as it is to remain at peace, to preserve its cherished institutions and to promote the welfare of its citizens," he warned, "is not secure against that menace. We cannot shut it out by attempting to isolate and insulate ourselves. We cannot be certain of safety and security when a large part of the world outside our borders is dominated by the forces of international lawlessness."

The United States is already feeling the repercussion of these lawless forces, he reminded his listeners, by being obliged to build up "immense" arma-

---

MAY 15, 1940

NETHERLANDS' FALL STUNS THE BRITISH

Raids on England Seen More Likely Now— Performance of Air Force Gives Hope

Special Cable to The New York Times.

LONDON, May 14—News of the virtual capitulation of the Netherlands to the German jackboot brought home to the British public today something for which the government has been preparing them since last week—serious reverses in the Low Countries.

Summarizing the situation in the Netherlands and Belgium, the British pinned swastika flags all over the map of the Netherlands and washed out that country as far as field operations are concerned. In Belgium the German advance has been less successful—but only slightly so. The Germans crashed through defenses along the Albert Canal. The Belgians were unable to hold them to the extent that had been expected. Now British and French troops are taking up another line of prepared positions to the southward and eastward. Preliminary contact probably has been made.

BIG BATTLE BELIEVED ON

British troops were rushed forward almost with the precision of a railroad timetable. There is reason to believe that a tremendous battle now is raging over Belgian territory northward from the east bank of the Meuse River at Sedan to the region of Liège—or even on the French side of that city.

If that battle is not actually in progress the British are being prepared for the news that it has started.

It is easy, here in London, to exaggerate the British difficulties without taking into full account the problems that must be harassing the Germans. Nevertheless, well informed persons here in this gloomiest moment are prepared to see the Germans crash through until once more the boom of German guns can be heard across the Channel.

There is a reverse side to this coin, but a no more cheerful one from the British point of view. The opinion of some here is that the Germans will not attack Paris and even will not move across the fortified Franco-Belgian frontier. Instead, it is argued, the Germans may dig in against counterattacks across this frontier, consolidate the Netherlands and Belgium and then use them as jumping-off places for a Blitzkrieg against Britain.

RAIDS ON ENGLAND LIKELY

By continuous air raids, coupled with the use of parachute troops, it is conjectured they might attempt to reduce this country to a jelly and then attack it.

ily equipped with howitzers and heavy machine guns than the regiment of any other army.

In the attack no rigid tactical objectives are set; modern German Army leaders believe, as Nelson did a generation before them, that no commander can do far wrong if he keeps in contact with the enemy. Schlieffen's Motto "Waegen und Wagen"—weigh the chances, then chance the risks—still expresses the spirit of German offensive tactics. ◊

ments at the cost of improvements in the standard of living.

CALLS FOR UNITED PUBLIC OPINION

The Secretary of State voiced a plea for "a wholly united public opinion" in support of this country's efforts to keep alive in the world the principle of order under law.

The "truly terrifying developments" of recent years have stunned millions of persons, who become "a prey to doubt, hopelessness and despair," Mr. Hull said.

He mentioned no nations by name and couched his speech in the language of an objective plea for the preservation and extension of international law as a basis for relations among sovereign countries. ◊

Meanwhile the Germans and the Italians might start trouble in the Balkans to draw off the Allied troops.

Against these gloomy prognostications must be set certain elements of cheer. First, there is a feeling that the British forces in France, which apparently are working on as close a schedule as an express train, are carrying out the campaign properly. Second, and more important, is the apparent success of the Royal Air Force. Detailed figures are not available, but it can be said definitely that the British are losing fewer men and planes than the Germans while taking on anything in the way of Heinkels, Dorniers, Junkers and Messerschmitts that the skies provide. It can be said also that the advance British force has not been hampered seriously by German bombing, as was the case in both Poland and Norway. The R.A.F. got its tail up taking on the Germans and keeping them off by using the air arm as a sort of superior artillery. Whether this equality in air can be maintained remains to be seen. ◊

MAY 16, 1940

GREAT BATTLE FLUCTUATES ON 60-MILE FRONT; NAZIS GAIN ON MEUSE, ALLIES COUNTER ATTACK; ROOSEVELT AGAIN CALLS ON ITALY TO KEEP OUT
The War in the West

The Battle of the Meuse, marking the first meeting of main bodies of the German and Allied Armies, started yesterday. The Germans, hoping for quick victory, struck with all their might. For the first time since the beginning of their offensive they encountered resistance commensurate with their blows. Their most spectacular feat was south of Sedan, where, according to the French, they advanced into the outer fortifications of the Maginot Line on a four-mile front. Reserves were rushed into the area and the French reported that a counter-attack had reduced the size of the pocket.

The apparent German strategy was (1) to cut the Allied line at Sedan and (2) to outflank Allied forces in Belgium by breaking through the Meuse defense line south of Namur. They succeeded in crossing the Meuse at several points between Namur and Mezieres, France.

The battle had not progressed far enough for the outcome to be indicated; that may take days. But the Germans, admitting that they were running into stiffening resistance, claimed to have pierced the Maginot Line at Sedan and to have forced the Meuse south of Namur "on a broad front." This latter action, if successfully pressed, would doom Brussels. Charging that Brussels was the scene of so many troop movements that it no longer could be regarded as an "open city," the Germans threatened to attack it with all the horrors of war. ◊

German army trucks passing through the ruins of a village near the river Meuse. France, May 13, 1940.

MAY 16, 1940

Editorial
A NATIONAL DEFENSE PROGRAM
The High Command

Any reconsideration of our program of defense must begin with the problem as a unified whole. We cannot first consider ships in isolation, then planes, then the army, then industrial organization, and let separate answers to these questions add themselves together as they will. Our defense must have the balance and integration of a single great machine, in which the numbers and kinds of planes, tanks, guns, ships, industrial plants, workers and fighting forces are recognized as being intimately dependent on each other, because they must work in practice in the closest coordination. At present we do not have any agency whose business it is to study this problem as a unified whole. We have merely the heads of separate branches of the services, each of whom makes his separate requests for appropriations solely from his special point of view.

The War Resources Board, headed by Mr. Stettinius of the United States Steel Corporation, though organized to study the special problem of industrial mobilization in case of war, was disbanded last Fall after only a few weeks of life. What is needed now is a much wider attack on the problem by a body of experts capable of seeing, as a related whole, problems of administration, the size and proper balance of our defense forces, the industrial organization necessary to support them, and the broader technical and economic questions involved. That can be done without loss of valuable time. Data are readily available. Some central agency is needed to shape them promptly into a definite program.

Such a board or commission, it is hardly necessary to add, should be composed of the ablest experts available in varied fields and should be strictly nonpartisan. The appointment of a board of this high type would be a gauge of good faith on the part of the Administration which would lift the defense issue above party or factional politics and would unite Congress on that issue under the leadership of the President. It would also do much to set at rest any further doubts of those who have been anxiously asking what we have got for the billions already spent on defense.

It is no less essential that we create a defense organization to assure far more coordination between our armed services than exists at present. The jealousies and frictions existing between our army and navy, and between air and ground officers, must be eradicated. We should do well to follow the example of France and create a war college at which officers of the army, navy and air corps, and related civilian officials, could study the problems of unified high command. Only by the cooperative effort of all arms unified under one directing head can our defense forces achieve their maximum efficiency in planning, in procurement, in strategy and in operations. Within the War and Navy Departments, further, there is still a clear need for reorganization in the interest of unity and the elimination of overlapping functions. There are still too many separate chiefs of equal rank working in watertight compartments.

These are not changes to be made in some vague future. Our peace and security gravely depend upon our ability to expand production of war supplies with sufficient promptness, not only for use by our own forces, but so that we can continue to sell immediately the vitally needed airplanes and other equipment to the democracies which still stand in the path of a nation seeking to dominate the world by intimidation, terror and mass murder. ◈

MAY 19, 1940

JAPAN SEES STAKE IN WAR'S OUTCOME
Visualizing a New World Order of Hegemonies, She Hopes to Rule East Asia

By HUGH BYAS
Wireless to The New York Times.

TOKYO, May 18—Stories of the battle in China go unread as the Japanese watch the battle in Europe moving toward its climax. They see that there is a death grapple going on between one world order and another and they feel very near to the ring. They may remain uninvolved in the war but they cannot remain uninvolved in its results. Not only the shape of the world they will live in but their own futures are going to be affected.

"If Germany wins, Japan will become like Germany," said a Japanese to this writer. If democracy proves stronger Nazi doctrines will be discredited and Japan will swing back from the extreme right to right center.

Public opinion here is neutral in form but pro-German in sympathy. The press commiserated with Finland when the Soviets invaded it, but has not had a word of sympathy for Norway, Holland and Belgium. Nationalist organs like the Hochi and Kokumin daily anticipate German victory and a new era opening on Nazi lines.

FRIENDS OF THE ALLIES
The few friends the Allies have are found among those Japanese who have lived abroad. About 80 cents out of every dollar of Japan's gainful foreign trade is done with America and the British Empire and business classes in general admire Anglo-America. Most senior educators and most Japanese Christians can be added.

At the other extreme are near-Nazis and Fascist sympathizers, also a minority but powerful because of the support they command among young officers and young bureaucrats. Among the masses the younger men, every one of whom is enrolled in some nationalistic youth organization, expect a German victory.

Amid the clash of empires Foreign Minister Arita confidently steers a course which this nation in its collective way understands and believes in. He sees the world of tomorrow falling into a new pattern no longer arranged as a liberal individualistic civilization with

MAY 21, 1940

CONFUSION MARKS BATTLE IN FRANCE
Reports of Commanders Fail To Go into Details and Lines Cannot Be Drawn

Wireless to The New York Times.

The devastation in Tours after a German bombing raid on the city during World War II, circa 1940.

PARIS, May 20—Few tactical accounts of the great battle in France have yet come to hand. No newspaper correspondents of any nationality have yet been permitted anywhere near the actual fighting line. Even reports from corps and divisional commanders do not go into details; obviously there is more pressing business.

Nevertheless one point stands out already—the great confusion on the battlefield and the virtual impossibility of defining the respective lines at any given hour. It was difficult enough at Verdun; this is Verdun plus.

The best description yet heard is this: Imagine the Place de la Concorde filled with a dense crowd. Then send into it from every adjoining street scores of motor street sweepers that begin zigzagging in every direction. Add to these several dozen airplanes spinning round the obelisk. Then multiply the Place de la Concorde 100-fold and let the street sweepers represent tanks and you may gather an idea of the scene. As for the noise it baffles all description.

In the region of Danain, north of Cambrai, yesterday authorized reports indicate that the milling mass included not only French and German troops but many peasants caught in the whirl. And through this mass tanks darted in all directions while planes dived and rose, dived and rose as they raked the ground with their machine guns. Near the Crozat Canal in the same region French, British and German tanks were so intermingled that the infantry troops could scarcely tell friend from foe.

The German tactical plan is manifestly to sow terror everywhere. Light motorized units make sudden dashes into towns and villages often without any thought of occupation but only to create panic. After this they fall back on their main body. In the air the policy seems to be the same—a few bombs in many places rather than many bombs in few places. But now that the first surprise is over the resistance is becoming more and more dogged and also more systematic. In the regions of Cambrai and St. Quentin, for instance, where small streams and canals abound, full use is made of them to retard enemy progress and at the same time permit the regrouping of units and the advance of supports. ◆

large and small nations living side by side in legal and political equality.

WORLD OF TOMORROW

The new world, as Japanese statesmen see it, will consist of vast regional aggregations, each grouped around a dominant power. The Americas, under United States hegemony, will form one such group; East Asia, under Japan, another, and Central Europe, under Germany, another; the Russians are big enough to constitute a unit and Britain and France are thought strong enough to survive, although their empires may be trimmed.

Japan's national policy is opportunist in method, clear and simple in principle. Its aim is to make Japan the overlord of East Asia, exercising that regional hegemony due it as a superior power. It means besides a new order in China a kind of Monroe Doctrine for the Western Pacific implying that there is to be no more foreign colonization in Japan's sphere. ◆

MAY 26, 1940

CRUCIAL STRUGGLE GOES ON FOR CHANNEL PORTS
German Success Has Been Notable but Invasion Of Britain Will Be Harder

By HANSON W. BALDWIN

Europe lived through one of the most crucial periods in its long and sanguinary history last week as the German legions moved to the Channel coast and threatened to annihilate vast Allied forces fighting with their backs to the sea.

In two weeks since the campaign in the West opened with the invasion of the Netherlands on May 10, the German forces have conquered the ❯

◀ Netherlands, overrun Belgium, won the titanic Battle of the Meuse, smashed a French army, broken through on a sixty-two-mile front in Northern France, swung to the sea and advanced to within seventy miles of Paris, placing both the French and British Empires in the gravest peril in their history.

The "Battle of the Channel Ports," or the "Battle of Flanders," as it has variously been called, was still raging yesterday. The issue was still in doubt as the week ended, but despite furious Allied attempts to break through the German pincers—forged last Tuesday when the Germans thrust to the sea at Abbeville—those pincers were slowly closing on 500,000 to 1,000,000 Allied troops caught in a wide net in Northwestern France and coastal Belgium.

DRIVE FOR ANNIHILATION

The German plan of conquest was neither von Schlieffen's nor Banse's, though indebted to both of them; it was Germanic in conception, Hitlerian in operation; it was total war ruthlessly applied—object annihilation of the enemy's fighting forces, destruction of the enemy's will to resist.

The German drive, in addition to imperiling some 500,000 to 1,000,000 troops, blazed a red trail of flaming ruins and broken bodies across Belgium and Northern France. It put villages far behind the fighting lines to the torch (with the aid of bombers and parachute troops). It was directed against the nerve center of a people—their morale.

The Allied counter-moves were quickly taken. Bridges were blown up leading to Switzerland; the Rhine valley was flooded on the French side; the Eastern frontier was stripped as much as possible of French soldiers, and troops from all over France were rushed to the Northwest to try to close the gap. On the home front extraordinary measures were taken by both nations not only to give greater power to the military effort but to meet the German thrust against morale.

WEYGAND THE DYNAMIC

General Maxime Weygand replaced General Maurice Gustave Gamelin—an exponent of dynamic action replaced a man dedicated to the concept of static strength. In Britain Parliament passed a bill bestowing broad powers upon the government and enlisting the entire strength of the nation in the war, thus definitely and finally abandoning the military policy with which Britain started the war—the policy of a war of limited effort, a defensive war.

The Allied counter-measures—the replacement of Gamelin by Weygand, the enlistment of all of Britain's powers in a totalitarian effort in the war against totalitarianism—may not have much effect upon the outcome of the crucial battle now raging. A substitution of the doctrine of "always the attack" for a doctrine of "always the defense" cannot win battles. The old military adage, "A good offensive is the best defensive," is just as much a shibboleth as the Liddell Hart aphorism, "Defense is the best attack." For a great leader, a great general, uses the offensive and the defensive; he knows when to attack and when to defend; generalship consists of knowing this and of seizing opportunity when it comes.

Now it is quite possible, in fact probable, that Weygand is a better general than Gamelin. Gamelin, however, has suffered for the sins of a system, and Weygand has inherited that system. Weygand may well manoeuvre that system better than Gamelin could have done, but he cannot change it overnight. Nor can the passage of an act of Parliament speed up the production of planes or war matériel.

FACTOR OF MORALE

It is, therefore, questionable whether the French shift to Weygand and the British shift to a totalitarian war machine can much affect, except in one way, the course of the Battle of the Channel Ports. And that way is morale. The measures of the Allied governments have undoubtedly restored much of the morale of the home fronts. The energetic measures taken by Premiere Paul Reynaud of France and Prime Minister Winston Churchill of Great Britain and by General Weygand have also excited the determination and restored the confidence of both the French and the British troops.

Morale is a vast but intangible factor, but in a tangible way the Allied counter—the drive to close the neck of the German corridor to the sea between Cambrai-Bapaume-Arras and Amiens-Peronne—is still possible of success.

But this gap must be closed quickly if it is to be closed at all; otherwise German forces pressing southward through Belgium and France and crowding into the corridor will so strengthen the German hold as to make the Allied efforts unlikely of success. Much depends upon this Allied counter. If it is successful the aspect of the battle can change overnight; if unsuccessful the Germans will almost inevitably win a second great victory—the victory of the Channel ports—and with it will accomplish their basic aim, the delivery of a terrific blow at the armies of the enemy.

At the week-end the prospects for the Allies were still grim, as both Paris and London recognized. The German corridor to the sea had been narrowed but not cut; German mechanized forces were operating in the rear of the Allied troops in the Channel port area, cutting up communications, perhaps destroying docks; the Channel ports and ships in the Channel itself were subjected to fierce bombardment from German planes. The Scheldt River line in the north had been lost, and the Allies were being pressed back upon the fortified city of Lille, where, perhaps, the isolated Allied armies of the North may have to make their last stand.

WHAT ARE THE PROSPECTS?

If the Allies win the battle and succeed in re-establishing a continuous and unbroken front, the Channel ports might yet be saved; a campaign of long duration would seem likely.

A considerable blow would have been dealt the German Army and the impetus of its rush into France would have been decisively checked in a battle which might ultimately have the same consequences as the Battle of the Marne. The war would not be over, for the Germans would not be "licked" after a single defeat, but the entire complexion of the war would have been changed overnight.

IF THE GERMANS WIN

If the Germans win the battle they have not won the war, although the staying power of France would depend to a great extent upon the character of the victory. Certainly a German victory, implying as it might, capture or destruction of large Allied forces, would be a smashing blow at France, perhaps a fatal one, if two or more French armies, reported yesterday from Berlin to be trapped in the net, should be destroyed. And even if a large number of Allied troops succeed in escaping the German net and were successfully evacuated by sea or sifted through the net to rejoin the main armies to the south, the Germans would be left in control of the Channel ports twenty-six miles from England.

What then? The answer would depend entirely upon the circumstances, upon the continuation of French resistance, upon the losses suffered by the Germans, almost certain to be heavy, in their attempt at a modern Cannae. But it would seem with the Channel ports in their possession, and hence direct communication between France and Britain severed and a round-about sea route enforced upon the Allies, that Germany, still utilizing, as she has done from the war's beginning, the advantage of her interior and central position, would turn her might first upon one, then upon the other of the Allies in an attempt to crush them. England is by far the most likely objective, although, with, or after the drive against England, might be a continuation of the drive against Paris if French resistance were not previously broken.

INVASION NOT EASY

Invasion of England would neither be simple nor certain of success; in fact the odds might be against the attackers. The British Navy still can make its might felt, even in the Narrow Seas; there are close to 1,000,000 armed men in various degrees of training in Britain today; she still has large metropolitan air squadrons, ready for defense.

Nevertheless German control of the Belgian and French Channel ports might be of such serious consequences to both France and Britain that the Allies may be expected to fight to the death to prevent it.

For it would mean across the Channel and the North Sea from the Orkneys to the Downs a coastline from which the Swastika flew from every inch of soil. It would mean another Napoleon, this one with a clipped mustache and a talent for forensics, dreaming on the heights above Boulogne of an invasion of England.

Perhaps this time the dreams might be possible of success (though not without a terrific struggle), for the dreaded wings of war can now leap the Narrow Seas, and England's insularity is no longer a sure security.

IF INVADERS COME

But even if an invading army—dropping from the skies, landing from fast ships, transported by planes—should successfully establish a foothold on English soil for the first time since Harold died at Hastings with an arrow through his eye in the Norman conquest in 1066 the war again would not necessarily be over. For certain it is that any invaders must fight for every inch of British soil; certain it is that their losses would be heavy. And were the tight little isles at last to be conquered—something that is still far from reality and is still only the substance of a dream, the dream that Napoleon dreamed and Hitler now dreams again—there is still the British Empire, immense, powerful with great potential strength.

That future outlook is something no man can foretell, but certain it is that the Battle of the Channel Ports, decisive in the history of the world, is rapidly approaching its climax this week-end twenty-two years after the war to end war. ◇

MAY 29, 1940

THE ALLIES LOSE A BATTLE

By HANSON W. BALDWIN

The surrender of the Belgian Army means that the Germans have won the battle of the Channel ports.

The Allies have lost the aid of 300,000 to 600,000 Belgians—perhaps eight to sixteen divisions—and an undetermined number of British, French and Polish troops, enclosed in the German pocket in coastal Belgium and Northwestern France are faced with extreme peril. Probably the only way these Allied forces can escape annihilation or surrender is an immediate attempt—in itself dangerous in the extreme—to evacuate them by sea from Dunkerque, possibly the only Channel port left open to Allied use.

The sudden surrender of King Leopold was obviously a shocking surprise to the Allies. But the surrender only hastened what had come to be regarded in recent days as the almost inevitable outcome of the battle of the Channel ports. For ever since the Germans smashed the French Ninth Army and broke through to the sea at Abbeville the scales of victory in this battle were heavily weighted in Germany's favor.

It was taken for granted, of course, that the 600,000 to more than 1,000,000 Allied troops hemmed in with their backs to the sea would fight terrifically—as they have done—but it was also realized that the situation could be rectified only if French forces south of the Somme were able to launch a successful counter-attack, smash across the neck of

the German corridor to the sea and re-establish communication with their beleaguered forces to the north. As an alternative, a French counter-attack from their positions south of the Aisne up the Meuse Valley might have relieved some of the German pressure. The other alternatives were a fight to the death by the trapped troops forcing the Germans to pay heavily for the price of victory and giving the French a chance to reorganize their Somme and Aisne lines, or voluntary evacuation by sea, thus abandoning defense of the Channel ports.

It seemed likely, as late as last Saturday, when the German communiqués spoke of increasing numbers of prisoners, that the disintegration of the Allied armies in the pocket had started and that it was probably too late for a successful French counter-attack.

Belgium had an ostensible maximum strength of eighteen to twenty-one divisions, plus 25,000 fortress troops. One of these divisions—the Ardennes Chasseurs, plus the fortress troops—were apparently destroyed or captured in Eastern Belgium and it is very doubtful if Belgium was able to mobilize her full strength or to equip more than eight to sixteen divisions, some of which must have been badly cut up in the fighting in Western Belgium. The German victory, so far, therefore, adds up to the capture or destruction of perhaps eight to sixteen Belgian divisions with their equipment. The rest of the Allied troops in the pocket are still fighting, but they cannot long maintain their position with most of the Channel ports behind them in German hands and with their left flank exposed because of the Belgian surrender. The Germans have won a victory of far-reaching consequence in the course of the war. ◇

German soldiers clear a Dutch bunker of weapons after taking control in Holland, May 1940.

JUNE 1, 1940

75% OF B.E.F. REPORTED SAFELY OUT OF FLANDERS

ROOSEVELT WARNS WAR IMPERILS WHOLE WORLD

BRITAIN HAILS MEN

By Harold Denny
Wireless to The New York Times.

LONDON, May 31—About three-quarters of the British Expeditionary Force thus far has been evacuated from Dunkerque and brought to England, it was estimated unofficially in well-informed quarters late tonight. Military authorities would not confirm or deny this estimate, the actual figures being kept secret.

[The United Press reported that it was estimated that 75 to 80 per cent of the British Expeditionary Force and some of its Allies trapped by the Germans in Flanders had been snatched from what had appeared to be the certain annihilation of more than 500,000 men. Original estimates of the strength of the B. E. F. ranged from 300,000 to 350,000.

"At least one Belgian army corps is still fighting side by side with the Allies," the British Broadcasting Corporation said early today in a news broadcast picked up in New York by the National Broadcasting Company. The corps was said to be under the command of the former commander of the Liége district

The evacuation of Dunkirk, June 1940.

who had refused to obey King Leopold's capitulation order.]

Ragged and battle-weary British and French soldiers who fought their way out of the shambles of Northern France and Belgium continued to stream into port during the day, still dazed but happy as they hurried inland for brief leaves at home.

They were greeted with almost delirious enthusiasm by the populace as they disembarked from the motley collection of large and small boats which had ferried them across the Channel and by cheering crowds all along the railway lines.

They were welcomed not sadly as a beaten army but proudly as the heroes in one of the bravest chapters in Great Britain's military annals.

Earlier this week high army officers had expressed the fear that almost the entire British Expeditionary Force would be lost. To date a far larger number has been returned safely to England than any one had dared to hope.

The primary reason for this result is said to have been the skillful coordination with the troops by the British Navy assisted by elements of the French Navy and by the Royal Air Force in conjunction with French aviators.

TROOPS' CONDUCT PRAISED

The behavior of the soldiers under a pounding by a vastly superior force such as no troops ever had had to withstand before is praised without measure by commanders returning with them, who have seen much of the war. These soldiers stood their ground and retired always in perfect order under admirable discipline. So these fine battalions, among them some of the best in the British Army, were not destroyed after all, but their survivors after a rest will be able to re-form with additions and take the field again better than they were before, because now they are used to the most terrible engines the Germans can hurl against them.

Part of the B. E. F. and a consider-

able force of French still are holding a narrow strip of coast behind Dunkerque covering the withdrawal. This strip now is being called the "Corunna line" in memory of Sir John Moore's classic withdrawal from Spain in 1809, when his army had been placed in a similarly hopeless situation by the defection of the Spanish. French troops are in this line with the British, while more are with General Rene Prioux among those who are fighting their way to the coast.

The part played by the British fleet is so brilliant that today's returning soldiers shouted to the crowds along the beach: "Thank God for the navy" and cheered sailors on shore whenever they sighted them. The French soldiers, also, wrung the sailors' hands and exclaimed: "Merci."

The navy has had two jobs in the evacuation. One has been to try to keep down the German fire on the British troops and to knock out tanks by fire from the warships lying out before Dunkerque. According to the returning soldiers, this strategy undoubtedly has done much to keep down the British and French casualties.

The warships have had to manoeuvre in shallow water against racing tides, in darkness and under a terrific German air bombardment, where the grounding of one ship, thus blocking the channel, might have spelled doom to many soldiers. One of three destroyers whose loss was announced last night was sunk by an aerial bomb which performed the incredible feat of dropping straight down the ship's smokestack without touching its sides.

Another destroyer, one of four, was attacked by German dive bombers as she approached the French coast. Her crew brought down one plane with anti-aircraft fire. Further in toward the coast the same vessel was attacked by high bombers, but took on a full load of soldiers and set out for England. A transport departing at the same time came under heavy air attack, but the destroyer crew put a blanket of fire on the German planes. These planes then turned their attention again to the destroyer and made twelve more attacks. The transport escaped unscathed, but a bomb struck the destroyer, breaking a steam pipe and causing some casualties, and forced the destroyer to halt. Another destroyer came to the assistance of the first and tried to tow her out, but as the German bombers again attacked the commander decided he was not justified in detaining the other ship and transferred his passengers to her.

It was an odd sight to see the fleet of transports, which, with destroyers, and other naval craft, came steaming into these waters today crowded to the gun-wales with cheering and smiling lads who a few days ago never had hoped to see the shores of England again. There were steamboats of all sizes, many of them had been pleasure boats in happier days, coastal tramp ships, dingy fishing boats and motor boats. A tug chugged in towing a string of five barges loaded with soldiers. One party of soldiers was brought by an officer—a yachtsman in civil life—in a sailboat he had "pinched" near Dunkerque when he could not find a transport.

The crews of these unorthodox transports were as varied as the coats—sturdy coastal seamen, fishermen and amateur yachtsman. They have not hesitated to take their little ships to that thundering beach to bring back the soldiers.

The soldiers who arrived here were dog-tired and ravenously hungry. Many said they had snatched only a few hours' sleep in seventeen days of fighting and had little to eat but biscuits. Townswomen heaped oranges, apples, sandwiches and cups of tea on the barricade separating them from the troops, and one family contributed wedding cake baked for a ceremony tomorrow.

The soldiers' torn and stained clothing gave a hint of what they had been through. Most of them had lost all their kit except their rifles and had only the clothes they stood in. One man was in pajamas with a blanket draped over his shoulders. However, almost all of them were smiling and many remarked after a meal and a night's sleep that they would be ready for "another go at Jerry."

Most of them were too tired to talk, however, and many fell asleep the moment they sat down in the troop trains. Those who could tell of their adventures added to the tale of rushing on German tanks, of the incessant bombing and machine-gunning from the air, of the slaughter of refugees by German airplanes and tank crews.

Several insisted that "Fifth Column" activities behind the British lines had been marked. Wherever they moved, they said, the Germans seemed to know it and greeted them in their new positions with bombs. Whenever a headquarters moved also the Germans seemed to get instant word of it and however obscure the house, even if it was one of a long row it was unerringly bombed.

JUNE 2, 1940

OUR ARMY WATCHES

General George C. Marshall, Army Chief of Staff, said yesterday it was "essential" that President Roosevelt receive authority to call out the National Guard, if needed, because of "the recognized possibility of dangerous developments in this hemisphere."

As one step in the defense program, the Army decided to assign 12,000 recruits to newly created tactical units of combat forces, increasing garrisons over the country.

Meanwhile, the German successes in Europe stirred fears in South America. Governments rushed rearmament programs, newspapers called for national unity, anti-fifth column groups were formed. The belief was general that, if they won the war, the Germans would physically invade South America; their present activity was described as boring from within, in an attempt to set up totalitarian regimes.

Experts of the Aeronautical Chamber of Commerce of America estimated that three to four years would be required to reach the production of 50,000 military planes a year.

Senator Taft said in a radio talk there was no evidence that the Administration had any defense plan or planners, and declared its principal activity was to get more powers for the Executive.

WARNING BY GENERAL

By FRANK L. KLUCKHOHN
Special to The New York Times.
WASHINGTON, June 1—General George C. Marshall, Army Chief of Staff, said today that, because of "the recognized possibility of dangerous developments in this hemisphere" which would require sending troops outside the United States for defense purposes, it was "essential" that Congress grant President Roosevelt authority to call the National Guard to active service at any time.

General Marshall pointed to the limited number of seasoned regular troops and emphasized the importance of the time element in the event of an emergency.

The General's statement followed criticism by some of the President's request to Congress for the authority to summon the Guard.

The statement caused considerable excitement in Congressional circles and gave weight to persistent reports that it may eventually be necessary to send American soldiers to South America to aid several countries in meeting the challenge of Nazi "fifth columns."

SITUATION UNDER STUDY

Reports that as many as 25,000 soldiers might be requested to aid in guarding airports and coastal harbors in such countries as Brazil and Uruguay have come from high circles in several countries, but have been formally denied.

Government officials have been giving serious consideration to the situation regarding Greenland, colony of Nazi-occupied Denmark, and other colonies in the New World.

General Marshall's statement was as follows:

"In view of the limited number of seasoned regular troops available in the continental United States—we have but five peace-strength triangular divisions with a sixth now in process of organization—and the recognized possibility of dangerous developments in this hemisphere, it is necessary that more troops be made available, trained and seasoned, to enable missions to be carried out without denuding this country of ground troops in a state of sufficient preparation to meet unexpected eventualities in some other direction.

"Time is the essential factor in such matters. In other words, this means that we should make the preliminary moves in time to be prepared against the unfortunate necessity of definite action.

"The War Department is opposed to ordering the National Guard out for active duty, and it is hopeful that by quickly building up, on the foundation of scattered organizations of the Regular Army still available, additional divisions and some special corps troops, we can avoid the necessity of utilizing the National Guard at this time.

NEED FOR TRAINING CITED

"Even if it were found necessary to bring the National Guard into service, it is believed that for the present only a portion of the Guard would be involved. However, it is essential in these days that the War Department, through the Commander in Chief, be in a position to act with rapidity to plan with the definite assurance that such plans can be made effective without uncertain delays. ◊

JUNE 2, 1940

IMPACT OF THE WAR ON THE NATION'S VIEWPOINT
Surveys Show Increasing Desire To Find Ways of Aiding the Allies

By HADLEY CANTRIL
Director, Princeton Public Opinion
Research Project

Since the war in Europe has become a grim reality challenging the attention of the American people, it has forced decision and the weighing of alternative courses of action. The crowded events of the past three weeks have jostled some opinions once held by the American people. Other opinions have been crystallized. People are not by any means as sure as they were that the Allies will win, and there is a growing feeling that this country will participate in the war and that we should do more than we are now doing to help the Allies. In short, the attitude of aloofness has nearly disappeared, even though the great bulk of the American people are still quite unwilling to go to war.

These conclusions are based on information obtained by the Princeton Public Opinion Research Project. This project, financed by a Rockefeller grant, has sampled nation-wide opinion over a period of time through the fact-finding machinery of the American Institute of Public Opinion (Gallup poll). The institute has, furthermore, given the project access to its own material. Carefully selected samples of the population in every geographical section have been questioned by the institute's interviewers. Men and women, old and young, rich and poor, Republican and Democrat, farmer and city dweller, are all represented in proportion to their numbers.

ACCURACY OF POLLS

According to statisticians, the size of the sample used in these surveys is sufficient to give results which probably would not depart more than 3 per cent from the figures that would be obtained if the whole population of the country were interviewed.

What, precisely, are the people thinking now, as revealed by the polls? First and foremost, the overwhelming majority of them do not want this country to declare war and send our army and navy to Europe. Only one American in fourteen is in favor of an immediate declaration of war against Germany.

But the percentage who believe that the United States will eventually get into the war is much higher. Although about one-fifth of the people have no opinion on this question, of those who do have an opinion five out of eight feel that we shall be drawn in if the war continues for any length of time, or if Germany appears to be winning. There is, apparently, a certain fatalism, a certain feeling of inevitability, of personal helplessness to avoid action which is not desired but which may be required under certain contingencies.

Even though only about 7 per cent want to declare war on Germany, when people are asked "Do you think the United States is giving too much help to England and France at this time, not enough help, or about the right amount of help?" nearly three-fourths of them answer, "not enough." In addition to those who would like to declare war now, 64 per cent of the American population believes that the United States should do everything possible to help England and France except go to war. Only 6 per cent think we should give less help than we are now; only 20 per cent think what we are doing is about right.

This general sentiment favoring more help to the Allies means that people are anxious to provide England and France with food supplies, munitions and planes. The public is more reluc-

---

JUNE 5, 1940

Excerpt from The Text Of Prime Minister Churchill's Address Before the House of Commons

By The United Press

LONDON, June 4—Following is the text of Prime Minister Winston Churchill's statement today in the House of Commons:

...We must never forget the solid assurances of sea power and those which belong to air power if they can be locally exercised. I have myself full confidence that if all do their duty and if the best arrangements are made, as they are being made, we shall prove ourselves once again able to defend our island home, ride out the storm of war and outlive the menace of tyranny, if necessary, for years, if necessary, alone.

At any rate, that is what we are go-

ing to try to do. That is the resolve of His Majesty's Government, every man of them.

That is the will of Parliament and the nation. The British Empire and the French Republic, linked together in their cause and their need, will defend to the death their native soils, aiding each other like good comrades to the utmost of their strength, even though a large tract of Europe and many old and famous States have fallen or may fall into the grip of the Gestapo and all the odious apparatus of Nazi rule.

We shall not flag or fail. We shall go on to the end. We shall fight in France

and on the seas and oceans; we shall fight with growing confidence and growing strength in the air...

We shall defend our island whatever the cost may be; we shall fight on beaches, landing grounds, in fields, in streets and on the hills. We shall never surrender and even if, for the moment I do not believe, this island or a large part of it were subjugated and starving then our empire beyond the seas, armed and guarded by the British Fleet, will carry on the struggle until in God's good time the New World, with all its power and might, sets for the liberation and rescue of the old. ◆

tant, however, to lend the Allies money which may sooner or later be needed to purchase war materials. For example, only half the population is willing to extend credit to England and France if they cannot pay cash for our airplanes. It is obvious in all poll results that the debts left from the World War still hang heavy over the heads of most Americans.

CHANGES DURING WAR

The war in Europe was for months regarded as a queer, quiescent war, distant and uncompelling to most Americans. It was something that they followed with interest through news reports, but something that they felt did not threaten the major social values of their culture. At the outbreak of the war 75 per cent of Americans thought that England and France would win the war and 10 per cent expected a German victory. After two months of war these percentages had not greatly changed. But German military successes following the invasion of Norway caused a rapid shift of opinion.

At the outbreak of the war 8 per cent thought we should declare war on Germany. This dropped to 3 per cent in October. Until the middle of May, despite important developments, this figure fluctuated only between 2 and 5 percent. It is only during recent weeks that it has crept up to 7 per cent.

When people were asked in March if they thought we were giving too much help, about the right help, or not enough help to the Allies, 50 per cent of them answered "About right" and only 15 per cent said "Not enough." Thirteen per cent said "Too much." Almost a fourth of the population then had no opinion on the matter. Now opinion is more crystallized. Only 4 per cent have not yet made up their minds. And what a close majority felt was "about right" in March is now regarded by a larger majority as "not enough." In April only a third of the people were willing to extend credit to the Allies, so they could buy our airplanes. By the end of May half of the population were willing to lend money.

THE OUTLOOK

The polls indicate opinions will undoubtedly continue to change. As the war proceeds, more and more people are reaching positive decisions; the trend suggests that what now appears as a "no opinion" response will decrease in favor of assistance to the Allies. In March, only 58 per cent of the total population believed they would be personally affected in any way if Germany won. Now 65 per cent believe they would be affected. As the possibility of a German victory comes to be regarded as more imminent there will probably be a uniform feeling of potential threat to American cultural values and a diminishing of what small differences now exist between various groups.

When people were asked early in the Spring whether or not they thought the Allies were fighting mainly to preserve democracy against the spread of dictatorship or mainly to keep their power and wealth, opinion was about evenly divided. Present results indicate the process of a shift of this opinion toward the side of preservation of democracy. This is due not so much to domestic or Allied propaganda as to a growing belief, brought about by events, that Hitlerism is a power which threatens whatever Americans hold dear, a set of conditions more generally accepted by people as democracy than as the preservation of national power and wealth.

AHEAD OF CONGRESS

Poll results indicate that at present there is a lag between the volume of desire of the people to help the Allies and Congressional action which would implement this desire. Almost all Americans want to keep out of war. Three-fourths of them want to give the Allies more help. Half of them are willing to extend credit. The majority seem to be groping for ways and means af assisting the Allies that would bring them no closer to the actual field of battle. When asked what such a policy might be the citizen is himself puzzled. The problem is too intricate and complex for him. ◊

The exodus of Paris in 1940.

JUNE 10, 1940

MANY FLEE PARIS, BUT HOPE PERSISTS
Gloom Grips Those Who Stay— Growing Refugee Throng Taxes Accommodations

By P. J. PHILIP
Wireless to The New York Times.

PARIS, June 9—Those who have lived through this day in Paris will never forget it. It is going to be remembered for all time as gloomy Sunday. The morning radio and the morning newspapers announced that the battle was nearing and was more furious than ever. [Here fifteen words were censored.]

The firing of the anti-aircraft barrage awakened those who were asleep. No one knew whether to hope or to fear, for the truth is that no one knew anything. The sugar-coated policy that has always characterized French comment on events left newspaper readers and radio listeners confused rather than enlightened.

Many of those who were left went to church, for there at least, they felt, they might find some quiet, some refuge from the anxiety that was gnawing in every heart. There were prayers to be said for those at the front in that fantastic battle that seems each day to rise from climax to climax of fury into which Chancellor Hitler keeps pouring more men and more machines with a frenzy of energy never before let loose on the world. There were prayers to be said for France and for the world, that it should be delivered from this nightmare.

The Cabinet met this evening at the Elysée Palace to consider the situation, and it was said that another meeting ❯

might be held tomorrow. A communication to the country may then be issued, stating the government's intentions in view of the military situation.

The city, greatly deserted in these last weeks and days, with only rare buses and taxicabs, was still and eerie. Neighbors gathered in little knots to talk, as people do in the waiting rooms of a hospital, caught between fear and hope and clutching at every human contact for comfort.

For most the great issue was whether to go or stay. Great gray trucks lined up outside public buildings showed that at least some of the public services were being evacuated. There were signs of packing everywhere. Private cars were being filled with the usual miscellaneous collection of oddments, from a bird cage to a bathtub, and usually with a mattress on the roof to do the double duty of protection in the day and a bed at night.

As the day advanced the evacuation fever seemed to spread. More and more loaded trucks and cars began to drift toward the outlets of the city. At the railroad stations from which any trains are still running the crowds of refugees, mostly incomers from the east and north waiting to go elsewhere, grew hour by hour and never seemed to lessen.

To the confusion of it all was added the uncertainty every one feels about where to go and how to go. The south and west are already packed with those who came from Belgium and the northeastern Provinces. Reports keep running that there is not a bed to be had and that food is beginning to present a problem for those already on the road. Foreigners are limited as to where they may go and there seems to be no way for most of them to find out just what they are expected to do.

Those who did not leave or try to leave spent most of the day packing, putting their most precious possessions in the cellars, organizing their money affairs—with all the banks closed—and preparing what must be taken if and when either an order or the evacuation infection might strike them.

It is not possible to describe in more detail what has been going on. However, it has been one of the most extraordinary things ever seen to watch how people cling to their habits, even despite bad examples and quite obvious preparations by those to whom they are accustomed to look for guidance and to whom they give respect as the authorities in their lives.

Thus, amid the confusion and bustle of packing in some places, one found the curious contrast of bourgeois people taking their walk in the Bois or sitting quietly in the shade of the trees all the length of the Avenue Foch, watching the spectacle of these trucks and automobiles leaving town. There was no rush, no panic among these people.

Every now and then the sound of the guns pushing back raiders who were attacking a district near the city would hit the ears and the little puffs of smoke from the exploding shells would dot the sky. They were matters for curiosity only. No one stirred from his or her seat under the trees.

Probably these people—and there are hundreds of thousands of them—have just quietly made up their minds to stay, whatever happens, most of them probably arguing that the discomfort and even danger of being a refugee is worse than staying at home. There is in most hearts, too, still a hope—though vague perhaps—that, whatever happens, the war itself will not reach and touch Paris, that the city will be saved.

And, of course, in it all there is comedy, the everlasting comedy of routine in the middle of an earthquake. One family cannot leave tomorrow because the son, 16 years old, is taking an examination. All day today he spent busily at his books. ◇

JUNE 11, 1940

DUCE GIVES SIGNAL
Announces War On the 'Plutocratic' Nations of the West

By HERBERT L. MATTHEWS
By Telephone to The New York Times.

ROME, June 11—Italy declared war on Great Britain and France yesterday afternoon, to take effect at one minute past midnight. The land, air and sea forces of the Italian Empire were already in motion.

It is a war, as Premier Benito Mussolini announced to the people from his balcony at the Palazzo Venezia at 6 in the evening, against the "plutocratic and reactionary democracies of the West." For the moment that does not include the United States, but few Italians believe that they will see the war to a finish without having the Americans against them.

Signor Mussolini expressly excluded Turkey, Switzerland, Yugoslavia, Greece and Egypt as enemies unless they attacked Italy or the Italian possessions.

Turkey provides the burning question of the day. Italians are absolutely convinced that the Turks will not move against them and will not honor their agreement with the Allies. It is hoped to confine Italian activity to France, Great Britain and the Mediterranean and to keep the Balkans tranquil. If that can be done, Italians think, the Turks will remain quiet.

SOVIET ACTION DISCOUNTED

Russia has washed her hands of the struggle. The Italians know that any disturbance in the Balkans will immediately bring her in; but as long as the struggle is confined to the west and south the Soviet will do nothing either to hinder or help. This was told to your correspondent a few hours ago by a very authoritative source.

It was emphasized there were no agreements about furnishing material or anything else, nor any threats or promises.

The Italian Ambassador, Augusto Rosso, left in the morning for Moscow and Ivan Gorelkin, Soviet Ambassador, is coming back to Rome, thus ending a long period without such representation. The Italians were anxious to restore full diplomatic relations in this critical period, according to this writer's informant, and the Russians agreed, but without compromising themselves.

It thus appears that Premier Mussolini has embarked on this dangerous venture without really knowing what Soviet Russia will do in the long run.

President Roosevelt's speech clearly has come too late. There was nothing that the United States could do to halt this conflict, the Italians say. Whatever brake Mr. Roosevelt may have exercised was overcome by the momentum of the whole Fascist policy. Once it was set in motion, nothing could stop it.

The Italians do not believe that the United States can affect the issue, whatever it does. They are sure American help cannot assume large proportions for many weeks, before which they believe the war will be over.

Ever since the beginning of the war Signor Mussolini had said that when he came out on the balcony of the Palazzo Venezia the people of Italy would be speaking. From that moment it was known that when he spoke Italy would already be at war. So when the word finally went around to gather in the Pi-

JUNE 15, 1940

REICH TANKS CLANK IN CHAMPS-ELYSEES
Berlin Recounts Parade into Paris—Third of Citizens Reported Remaining

By the United Press.

BERLIN, June 14—German tanks today clanked across the Seine bridges, past the Arc de Triomphe and down the tree-lined Champs-Elysées into the heart of Paris at the head of the first cavalcade of invaders to enter the French capital in nearly seventy years.

Flanked by armored cars, the dust-stained tanks swung triumphantly into Paris from the northwest at the head of Nazi units occupying the "City of Light," German accounts of the event said.

It was the ninth recorded invasion of Paris and the first since Bismarck's legions trod the broad boulevards in 1871. The jubilant German press proclaimed the fall of Paris to be the "symbol of decision" in Chancellor Adolf Hitler's Western offensive.

azza Venezia and all the squares of Italian cities and towns, no one could doubt what the announcement would be.

The first resolute words that were spoken ended the long and nerve-wracking period of suspense, with its dramatic ups and downs, its days of hope and pessimism, but its always rising tension.

Long ago your correspondent was able to say that Italy would be at war before June 20, probably between June 10 and 20. Sometimes it seemed that it was coming sooner, but never was there any hope that Italy would stay out of the war indefinitely.

Immediately after the great gathering in the Piazza Venezia, the crowd surged up the Quirinal Hill to the palace, where the King awaited them, wearing his field uniform. As he stood on the balcony and saluted, the crowd shouted, "Savoia!" again and again.

Already the Premier had spoken of Victor Emmanuel as "His Majesty the King and Emperor, who has always interpreted the soul of his Fatherland." With those words ended any doubts that might have been held about the King's feelings or actions. He has never thwarted any of the plans or desires of Signor Mussolini. ◇

[Berlin Nazis expected Adolf Hitler to visit Paris June 21, the twenty-first anniversary of Germany's acceptance of the Treaty of Versailles, an Associated Press dispatch said.]

ENTRY FROM NORTHWEST

The advance into Paris, through the suburbs of Argenteuil and Neuilly and into the aristocratic western part of the city began early in the morning, the Germans said. It was exactly five weeks after the massive western offensive began with the German drive into the Netherlands and Belgium.

The tanks rumbled between thin lines of tense and silent Parisians, the Germans said. Reports from the French capital estimated that probably a third of the city's normal population of 2,800,000 had remained in Paris.

Behind the tanks rolled anti-tank units, still dusty and laden with evidence of the furious fighting in which they had taken part to the north.

As the long shadows of the early morning retreated, more and more Nazi contingents streamed into the capital, evacuated by French Armies hoping to save their beloved Paris from the fate of Warsaw.

Motorized infantry, rising in steel-shielded trucks mounting machine guns to command the broad streets, converged from the Seine bridges to the Place de l'Etoile.

In that hub from which radiate eleven streets stands the Arc de Triomphe and its tomb of the Unknown World War Soldier, where flickers the Eternal Flame.

German reports indicated that the parade through Paris swung around the Arc de Triomphe to move down the Champs-Elysées. Speculation had suggested that the honor of being the first to march beneath that historic arch might be reserved for Germany's self-styled first soldier, Adolf Hitler.

The great arch, started in the course of the Napoleonic triumphs, is a 160-foot pile of stones, each bearing the name of a victory or a hero in French military history.

Nazi officers at the head of the procession set their course for the headquarters of French officials still in the city, it was said, and formally took it over.

The capital was like a city of the dead—shops closed, iron shutters in windows, those people who remained mourning in their homes and wondering what was coming.

Police and civil guards patrolled the streets slowly, almost alone. They had handed in their rifles and pistols. They were now a completely civilian force. ◇

The German parade on the Champs-Elysées, June 1940.

Editorial
HITLER'S WAY AND OURS

Why is Hitler winning such stupendous successes? Is there some black magic, some secret weapon or infallible prescription that enables this World War corporal to win Napoleonic triumphs? There are public men in this country, business men and ordinary men and women, who are sure they know the answer. They believe that Hitler is "competent" because he dispenses with faddists and theorists, because he is not shackled by red tape, because he knows what he wants and gets it. They are sure that this man "has something'" which the democracies lack and need and without which they will die.

But Hitler has no magic wand. The reasons for his colossal military conquests have been plain for years, and should have been plain long ago to the countries that have now been overwhelmed. For seven years, as Mr. Otto Tolischus writes in today's Magazine, Hitler has been mobilizing all the moral, military and economic resources of Germany "for the sole purpose of waging war with all means." For this terrible purpose he has destroyed Germany's economy, revolutionized Germany's moral concepts, subsidized his informers and used unwitting dupes in every country, and has infected the youth of Germany with a fanaticism that has now stormed the barricades of the bravest democracy on the European Continent.

It is no indictment of democracy to contrast Hitler's "total" mobilization of Germany with the slow halting, half-hearted mobilization of the democratic countries. The be-all and end all of democracy is not waging war. Free men will never share General Ludendorff's belief that "war is the highest expression of the racial life." The goal of democratic peoples has been life, liberty and the pursuit of happiness, in peace and freedom. Nor does it prove the failure of democracy to say that Hitler has been able to dispense with democracy's cumbersome procedure. The method of cooperation, which is the essence of true democracy, is more difficult than the giving of a dictatorial order. The crack of a Hitler whip could never have solved labor problems or achieved social security for millions as well as the British and French and Scandinavian democracies did in the past generation, nor could it ever have built a mighty republic out of a continental wilderness in the New World.

But the rights of democracy also demand the acceptance of democratic responsibilities. The real indictment of democracy, now being written in smoke and flame and destruction across half of Europe is that free peoples in our time cared too little for their privileges, too little for their democratic duties. The leaders thrown up by Britain and France in recent years did not lead but lulled and soothed. They saw the German threat rising, but shrank from facing it. They heard good advice, but shut their ears. They knew how to win elections, but not how to strengthen and safeguard their democratic birthright. And because these inadequate leaders were freely elected and kept in power by the votes of free men and women, the peoples of the Western democracies cannot be acquitted of blame. They, too, preferred to keep their comforts and shrink from inconvenient truths. They were not ready until too late to make sacrifices for keeping their way of life—sacrifices that would have meant universal training in England, or more efficient industrial production in France. If they knew their responsibilities, they chose to evade them, as we in the United States evaded ours when we washed our hands of Europe in 1920, and built tariff walls around ourselves in 1922 and 1930, and decided that courage and idealism in international affairs were counterfeit coin.

Democracy is now faced with frightful tests for which it never was intended. If it is to live it must marshal its strength with the same determination that its enemies have shown. The luxuries of indecision, of wishful thinking, of partisanship and petty bickering, have become deadly perils to the few free nations that still survive. This is no time for disbelieving in democracy but for proving a passionate faith in it by sacrifice, by clear vision and courage. ◊

Text of Prime Minister Churchill's Address Before House Of Commons

By The Associated Press.

LONDON, June 18—Following is the text of Prime Minister Churchill's war report today to the House of Commons:

WILL RESTORE FREEDOM TO ALL

If we are now called upon to endure what they have suffered, we shall emulate their courage, and if final victory rewards our toils they shall share the gain—aye, freedom shall be restored to all. We abate nothing of our just demands. Czechs, Poles, Norwegians, Dutch and Belgians, who have joined their causes with our own, all shall be restored.

What General Weygand called the Battle of France is over. The Battle of Britain is about to begin. On this battle depends the survival of Christian civilization.

Upon it depends our own British life and the long continuity of our institutions and our empire. The whole fury and might of the enemy must very soon be turned upon us. Hitler knows he will have to break us in this island or lose the war.

If we can stand up to him all Europe may be freed and the life of the world may move forward into broad sunlit uplands; but if we fail, the whole world, including the United States and all that we have known and cared for, will sink into the abyss of a new dark age made more sinister and perhaps more prolonged by the lights of a perverted science.

Let us therefore brace ourselves to our duty and so bear ourselves that if the British Commonwealth and Empire last for a thousand years, men will still say "This was their finest hour." ◊

EUROPE
Hitler at Compiègne Opens Third Act of War Drama

By ANNE O'HARE McCORMICK

On such a day as yesterday, sunlit and still, many a traveler has driven through the green aisles of the forest of Compiègne to see the wagon restaurant where the armistice of the first World War was signed. Compiègne is a very formal forest; unlike the deep woods of Germany, always a little wild and mysterious, the old trees stand in straight, neat rows. Planted long ago, they remind you that order is as innate in the Gallic mind as it is extraneous to the Teutonic, so that German history is a chronicle of forced marches and follow-the-leader episodes—of order invariably imposed from on top or from without.

Hitler could not resist this theatrical curtain for the second act of the Promethean drama he set in motion. He could not resist appearing in person to hand the terms of capitulation to the French delegates on the spot where the Germans made their surrender twenty-one years ago. He could not resist making the kind of curtain speech he thinks will read well in the history books. Hitler is increasingly conscious of his place in history; even before the heady victory over France and the Lowlands, he had begun to talk as if his mission was no longer merely to smash Versailles and extend German power, but to correct in one lifetime the mistakes of history. All the mistakes; he pants to impose order everywhere.

AT THE PEAK OF HIS POWER

Yesterday he was deeper in France than he had ever been before, and he could not have felt at home. The staid, level beauty of Compiègne is as different as possible from the romantic, savage scenery of his Magic Mountain. The defeated Frenchmen were too much at home. It must have rent their hearts to look out the car window at the bust of Foch and the sylvan allées where Louis Quatorze once hunted. But Hitler, too, was ill at ease; if the little Austrian inside the World Conqueror has any more qualms—and he can't have overcome all the agonies of doubt that unnerved him before every decision—he must have wondered if force, a force springing out of disorder and a primitive impulse to destroy, could long overcome the measured, indigenous, centuries-deep order of France.

Hitler at Compiègne, Hitler over France, must have been as incredible to Hitler as to the rest of the world. He has gone a long way since he stood on the balcony at Linz, scene of his first territorial conquest. He has gone a long way since he challenged France by a tentative expedition of ill-equipped troops into the Rhineland.

Far less clear at the moment is the answer to the questions that will follow the French surrender. We face a conflict of sympathy and of conscience that will hurt and divide us, and may have considerable influence on our attitude toward the war. The use of France as a weapon against England, the use of the blockade against France—here is an element of confusion and division that will make the third phase of the struggle the most terrible test of all. ◆

HALT AT 12:35 A.M.
Truce Goes into Effect Six Hours After Rome Notifies Hitler

DEMANDS NOT TOLD

By HERBERT L. MATTHEWS
By Telephone to The New York Times.

ROME, June 25—The Italo-French armistice was signed last evening at 7:15, Rome time. Twenty minutes later Foreign Minister Count Ciano, on behalf of the Italian Government, notified the Reich. Thus fighting ceased at 12:35 this morning, French time [7:35 P.M. yesterday in New York.]

[Italian troops began to march into the Savoy and Nice sectors of France this morning, according to The United Press. In London an authoritative source said the terms of the French-Italian armistice included occupation of the province of Savoy; withdrawal of all French troops from the Alpine passes; occupation of the Riviera, including Nice; occupation of Corsica; withdrawal of the French from Tunisia; surrender on the Tuniaisn-Libyan frontier; occupation of Jibuti, French Somaliland, and the railroad running from there to Addis Ababa, and extension to Italy of the same economic and financial agreements made with Germany.]

It was with the knowledge that for four days the French Army had been engaged in battle with the Italians in the Alps that the French plenipotentiaries studied the Italian terms, communicated with their government at Bordeaux and argued all afternoon with the Italian delegates. Finally they yielded and General Charles Huntziger put his signature to the armistice, which was signed for Italy by Marshal Pietro Badoglio, Chief of the General Staff.

The ceremony took place in the Villa Incisa, the same house in which the armistice terms were given to the French delegates Sunday.

The plenipotentiaries are scheduled to leave at 10 o'clock this morning on the same plane that brought them from Munich.

FRENCH OBJECTIONS INDICATED

Although nothing has been given out about the Italian terms, it has been obvious today that they contained some details to which the French were objecting. After all, it is a grave responsibility for the plenipotentiaries to keep their country at war and see more Frenchmen killed, more territory devastated and occupied while they are discussing a truce. One must suppose that only very grave demands could have caused hesitation.

Sunday evening it could hardly have taken General Mario Roatta, army corps commander, more than ten minutes or so to read the Italian terms to the French plenipotentiaries. That seemed to show the Italian demands were not as extensive or complicated as the German. It was therefore believed the armistice with Italy would be largely a formality. Yesterday's events showed that such an interpretation was incorrect.   ❯

◀ That became obvious as the hours passed and, instead of the plenipotentiaries leaving the Villa Incisa, high officers in small black Fiat automobiles drove in and out, evidently carrying messages back to Premier Mussolini in the Palazzo Venezia. Even after signing, the plenipotentiaries continued their discussions. An hour and a quarter later they had not left the villa.

QUIETEST SPOT TO BE FOUND

The Villa Incisa is as quiet and secluded as any spot could be only twelve miles from Rome. Like the Villa Manzoni, where the French delegates spent most of their time and from which they telephoned Bordeaux, it is on the Via Cassia, which goes to Viterbo.

The two correspondents of The New York Times were alone at the gate of the Villa Incisa when the French delegates arrived at 3:42 P.M. The Italian delegation had already been there for twenty minutes. A few carabinieri were standing about, but otherwise there was no sign to show that history was be-

ing made a few hundred yards up the side road. There were eight cars in the French group, escorted by two motorcycle carabinieri in front and in the rear.

MET BY CHIEF OF PROTOCOL

The scene inside the villa could only be guessed at from the official account of Sunday night's meeting issued yesterday morning. It related that the French plenipotentiaries were received at the entrance to the villa by Minister Celesia di Vegliasco, Chief of Protocol of the Ministry of Foreign Affairs, and other functionaries of that Ministry. After introductions they were taken to the hall, where the Italian delegation greeted them with the Fascist salute.

The two groups then sat down on opposite sides of the table. Count Ciano rose and announced that on Premier Mussolini's orders Marshal Badoglio would give the armistice conditions to the French plenipotentiaries. Marshal Badoglio then asked General Roatta to read the terms, which he did, presumably in Italian.

Afterward General Huntziger declared that the French delegates had taken note of the terms and asked to be allowed to convey them to the French Government, "giving the decision at the next meeting." That ended Sunday night's session.

The delegates went back to the Villa Manzoni, and there for the greater part of the night discussed the terms and kept in direct communication with the Bordeaux government.

All yesterday morning the exchange of conversations and discussions went on, showing how difficult the French were finding it to accept the terms the Italians were imposing. So the session at the Villa Incisa yesterday afternoon could hardly have had that same calm, quiet, formal character of the first meeting Sunday night. ◇

The French delegation escorted by the German victors about to enter Marshal Foch's railway carriage to sign the 1940 Armistice.

JUNE 30, 1940

Editorial
THE SUN ALSO SINKS

When we read the history of Napoleon Bonaparte we can say, on arriving at various pages, here he reached the summit of his glory, here he made a mistake, here a prophetic wind might have brought to his ears the sound of the surf at St. Helena. Naturally, we cannot read the day-by-day record of his Austrian understudy, Herr Hitler, with the same foreknowledge.

We do not know whether the recent battles have been Hitler's equivalent of the young Napoleon's Italian campaign, of Austerlitz and Jena, or of Eylau, Friedland or Borodino. We need not cherish the vain hope that it is Leipzig yet, or that Waterloo will be fought again tomorrow. But we can wonder at what stage of the great plot we have arrived.

In his own eyes the Nazi Chancellor is unmistakably a man of destiny. As such he plays a conscious part. He did so at Compiègne when he delivered terms to the French from the same chair occupied by Marshal Foch twenty-two years ago. He did so this week when, as an Associated Press dispatch from Paris states, he entered the city "incognito," "a light brown duster over his uniform," and stood, "apparently moved," before the tomb of Napoleon, whom he is known to admire.

We can guess his thoughts without bothering to put them into words. The former corporal, the struggling artist, the once despised fanatic, the former state prisoner, the man whose bluff was to be called, who had, as Mr. Chamberlain said, "missed the boat," had come into his own.

But those who live by theatricals must also die by them. The historical drama does not stand still. Anti-climax follows climax. The sun begins to sink at noon. Is it 10 o'clock or 12 for Adolf Hitler, the end of Act One or of Act Two? We do not know and had better not prophesy. But, soon or late, for each of the little band of conquerors with whom Herr Hitler not unreasonably classifies himself—for Caesar, for Alexander, for Napoleon—the curtain has fallen on tragedy. Each has had a part of a generation, not one a thousand years. ◆

Chapter 4

"BRITAIN IS DEFIANT"

July–September 1940

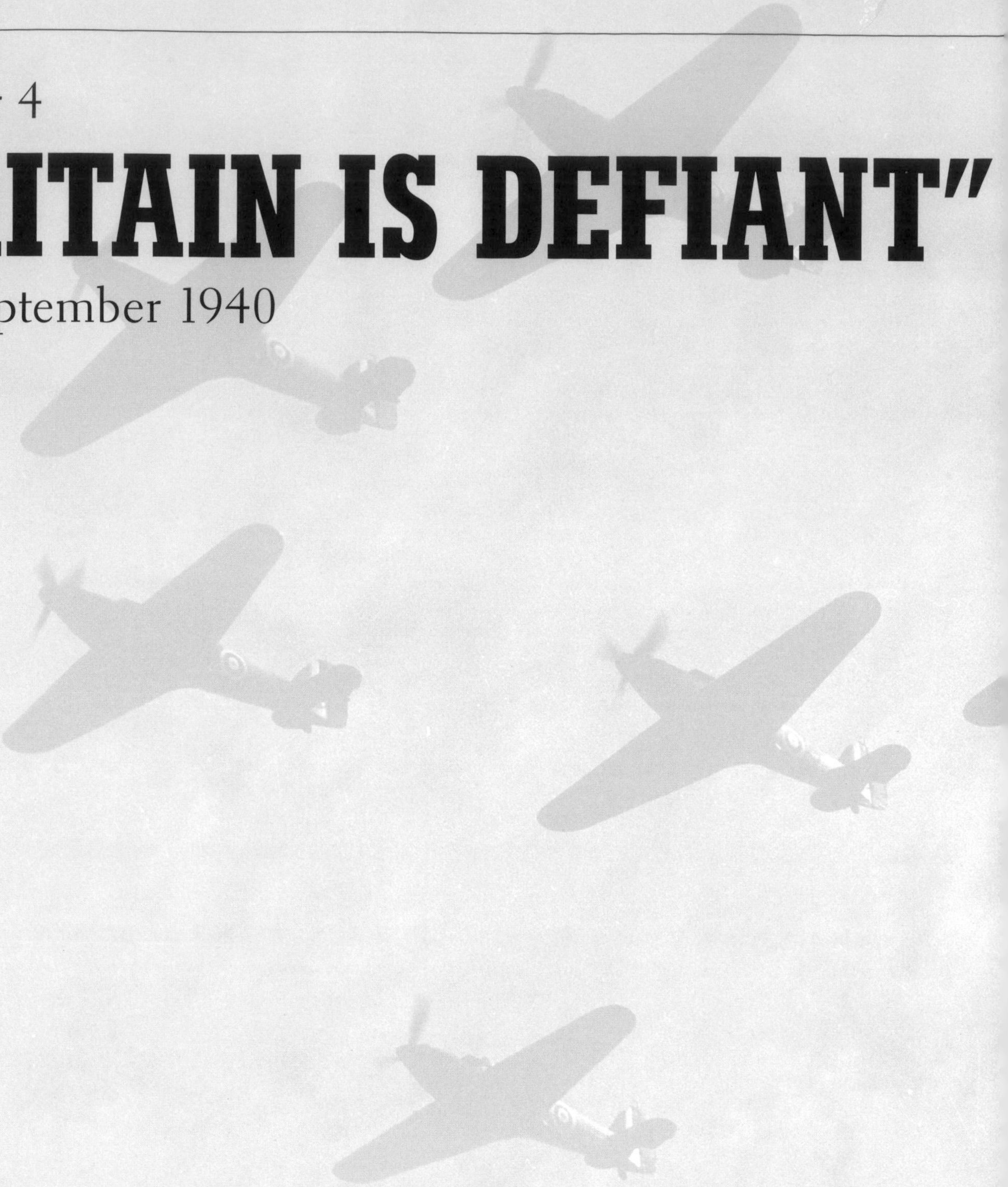

The weeks after the defeat of France and the evacuation from Dunkirk saw growing speculation about whether Britain would carry on fighting. In early July the Indian nationalist leader, Mahatma Gandhi, called on Britain to make peace. Anglo-French relations were soured by the British decision to sink units of the French fleet in the Algerian port of Mers-el-Kebir on July 3. American views of Britain were divided. Alongside popular support for Britain in the United States were those like the aviator Charles Lindbergh, as The Times reported in early August, who thought America should accept reality and cooperate with Hitler's Germany. On July 19 Hitler finally made a limp appeal for Britain to "see reason" and abandon the war. Without hesitation, the British government rejected the suggestion. On July 20 The Times carried a report from the head of its London Bureau, Raymond Daniell, that "Britain Is Defiant," unmoved by any appeal and committed to Churchill's promise of no surrender. The big question remained the possibility that Germany might invade Britain and it soon became clear that the Royal Air Force was likely to be the essential barrier between German invasion or safety.

The Battle of Britain that began in August took definite shape only after it was fought. The Times had other concerns closer to home. Black leaders demanded the right to participate in the American defense effort; on July 21 Roosevelt signed the Two-Ocean Navy Bill that laid the foundation for naval rearmament; a month later the Russian revolutionary, Leon Trotsky, was assassinated in Mexico City, attracting more attention from The Times than might have been expected. The course of the air battle over southern England that began seriously in the third week of August got less attention. Raymond Daniell decided to go on vacation to Cornwall for what turned out to be the first two weeks of the Battle of Britain. The big news before the onset of the more intensive air campaign in September was the announcement on September 4 of the "destroyers-for-bases" deal struck between the United States and Britain. The fifty old destroyers traded in return for U.S. bases on Britain's Caribbean island colonies had little immediate impact, since the destroyers were delivered only slowly, and needed modification before they could become operational, but it seemed to symbolize a greater American commitment to war. "British Jubilant," ran The Times headline.

The onset of heavy German bombing of London on September 7, the first day of what came to be known as the Blitz, brought the war home again to an American audience and prompted the fear that perhaps Britain might be invaded and defeated. "Can Britain Hold Out?," asked The Times on September 8. A few days later Churchill warned that invasion was near. A Gallup Poll taken in America found that 42 percent of respondents feared that if Britain were defeated, Hitler would invade the United States. But the same day, September 15, the heaviest defeat was inflicted on the attacking German air fleets, when sixty aircraft were shot down, and the invasion fear began to ebb. The day was later remembered as Battle of Britain Day, marking the end of a battle whose consequences, Drew Middleton of The Times would later write, were of enormous importance "to the war and to history."

While the future of Europe was being decided in the air battles, Japan took the opportunity to extend its influence in Asia, forcing French Indo-China to accept Japanese troops on French imperial territory. On September 27 German, Italian and Japanese representatives met in Berlin, where they formally signed the Tri-Partite Pact to divide the world into three new spheres of influence, including an Asian "new order" under Japanese domination, undeterred, as The Times observed, by the latest U.S. embargo imposed on exports to Japan. The Axis nations now seemed poised to fulfill their aspirations to dominate the world.

JULY 3, 1940

Gandhi Appeals To Britain to Seek Peace with Nazis

By The United Press.

NEW DELHI, India, July 2—Mohandas K. Gandhi tonight appealed to all Britons to cease hostilities with Germany and urged that they settle their differences with "non-violent methods."

The Indian Nationalist leader urged Britain not to enter "undignified competition with the Nazis in destructive power." He said he was placing his services at the command of the British Government to "advance the object" of his appeal. ◊

Mohandas K. Gandhi

JULY 7, 1940

THE ENTENTE CORDIALE ENDED AFTER 36 YEARS

JOHN BULL TOUGH OVER SHIPS

By EDWIN L. JAMES

In the Place Edouard VII, just off the Boulevards near the Opéra, there stands in Paris a monument to the British monarch who, with M. Delcassé, was the author of the Entente Cordiale. Edward VII loved France and he won a place in the hearts of Frenchmen which put him in an excellent position to swing his country into line with the French Republic. When, in 1904, London and Paris reached an agreement, which was largely immediately concerned with African matters, they actually ended a period of friction which stretched back for more than a century. It was not all love on Edward's part. He was building against Germany. As years passed the entente became closer and closer until, in 1911, as a result of the strength of the Triple Alliance, it became itself a virtual alliance. It was, of course, in the World War that the Entente Cordiale bore its great fruit when it aligned Britain with France against Germany.

Now the Entente Cordiale has been broken. It was broken on Friday when the Pétain government of France severed diplomatic relations with London. Its breaking will certainly form a page in the hectic history of our times. Formed as a bloc against Germany, it has fallen as an outcome of the victorious march of German armies into France. There may come reason and an opportunity for its rebirth or there may not. But for the present it is dead.

JOHN BULL GETS TOUGH

The reason for which the French Government broke with Britain was the British attack on French naval ships in the harbor of Oran. The purpose of the British was to prevent the French warships from passing into the control of the Germans and Italians. It was rough business. Prime Minister Churchill told the Commons it was rough business. But, so runs the British justification, when a country is fighting for its national existence there come moments when it had to be tough.

As yet the full story cannot be told. But there does stand out the fact that the British offered the French ships the

JULY 8, 1940

Editorial
CHURCHILL AS WAR LEADER

It has become commonplace by now to point to the Napoleonic aspect of Hitler's Europe; but is there not also a resemblance on the British as well as on the German side? If there is a Napoleonic quality in Hitler's military triumphs, in the fanatical drive of his armies and the frenzied acclaim of the Berliners as he returns from his conquests, is there not also some of the magic touch of William Pitt in the leadership of Hitler's enemies?

The leadership of Winston Churchill has now been tested in two months of desperate struggle. We have yet to learn its results on the home front in speeding up the production of tanks and some oth-

er war materials, but Lord Beaverbrook announced yesterday that home production of airplanes last month had set a new record, more than doubling the output of June, 1939. We have yet to know whether Mr. Churchill is able to smash all bottlenecks in production as effectively as Mr. Lloyd George did during the last war. But there is every evidence of a spurt in production all along the line in present-day England; and, what is more, there is every sign that galvanic leadership is having its reward. Unlike Premier Reynaud of France, who built his Cabinets on too narrow a foundation, Mr. Churchill has been wise enough to place labor leaders in the key positions of the war effort. Perhaps this is one of the many reasons why the British people are now united under his leadership, irrespective of politics, regardless of class, until, by now, they are truly a garrison of more than forty millions, grimly resolved that their fortress shall not surrender.

Winston Churchill has rallied his peo-

ple to face one disaster upon another without flinching. He has kept up their courage by keeping up his own, even in the face of the collapse of France, which must have been the bitterest blow of his lifetime. He has fired their spirits with imperishable words, and had given heart to his people and their friends throughout the world. Is it stretching parallels to feel that William Pitt is alive again? Now, as in Pitt's last days, every alliance built up by Britain has collapsed; the whole of the Continent is dominated by a ruthless enemy; the prospects of British survival look black. The disaster of Austerlitz came just before Pitt died, and final victory was withheld for more than nine years after he was in his grave; yet his example in organizing British resistance, in inspiring the British people, was felt until Waterloo and long afterward. Whatever the outcome of the present life-and-death struggle may be, future generations of Englishmen will have equal reason to honor the example which Winston Churchill has given them. ◊

option of going into the Western Hemisphere to be interned and the French admiralty refused, supposedly acting on the instructions of the Pétain government. Naturally, the Germans, in attacking the British action, took the position that, in the armistice terms with France, they had promised not to use the French ships against Britain. The answer to that, as Mr. Churchill said, was that one should not believe Hitler's promises. Look at a half dozen countries for proof, he said.

For Americans who saw the last war, when we fought with the British and French, it is sad to see our old friends and associates fall out. We do not know enough about what has been going on in recent weeks to assess accurately the responsibility for their coming to the parting of the ways. If they had been successful in Flanders it would not have happened—at least not yet. But even for the Flanders debacle it is too early to fix the blame. Who was responsible for the German break-through at Sedan? French? Belgians? Or was it plainly German superiority? Did the British quit the fight too soon? Did they fail to send the air forces they might have sent? Did France fail Britain or did Britain fail France?

We do not know the answers now.

All that can be said now is that the Entente Cordiale is one of the casualties of Hitler's war. ◊

JULY 12, 1940

NAZI DRIVE GROWS IN SOUTH AMERICA
Diplomatic and Trade Aides of Reich Intensify Pressure for Friendliness at Havana

By JOHN W WHITE
Wireless to The New York Times.

MONTEVIDEO, Uruguay, July 11—German diplomatic agents and commercial representatives throughout South America have combined to bring heavy diplomatic and commercial pressure on the South American counties on the eve of the Havana conference. This pressure is patently designed to keep them in line as friends of Germany despite any economic solutions which may be suggested at Havana.

The German propaganda machine throughout this continent has recently been conducting a particularly bitter campaign against the proposed economic union of the Americas, stating that this is a "blind" behind which the United States hopes to press its hegemony on the Latin-American countries. South American newspapers have given wide publicity to a recent warning appearing in the Berlin publication Berlin–Rome–Tokyo plainly telling Latin Americans that they are not to participate in the economic recovery which the publication says is to result from the new era in Europe unless they maintain a friendly attitude toward Germany during the rest of the war.

German diplomats and business agents are assuring South American governments and business men that the war will be over by the end of this year and that Germany and its occupied territories will immediately be in the market for huge purchases of South American products. German agents in Brazil are urging the government and the people not to be alarmed by the present crisis in the export trade, promising to empty the overloaded warehouses in the early months of next year, following termination of the war this year.

The strong diplomatic pressure which is being exerted on various South American governments is common gossip in diplomatic circles, but it is being done less brazenly than in Central America.

Nevertheless it has taken a form sufficiently effective to force the Uruguayan Government to release recently arrested Nazi leaders under fear of being subjected to a commercial boycott by Germany. Statements made by the chairman of the Argentine delegation to the Havana conference on his arrival in Rio de Janeiro yesterday, as well as those made by the Argentine Minister of Foreign Affairs, indicate that the Argentine delegation will not agree to any economic solutions which could tend to lead South American republics away from their former export customers in Europe of whom Germany is one of the best. ◊

JULY 16, 1940

ITALIANS ASK FRANCE TO GIVE UP 'MONA LISA'
Works of da Vinci and Titian Are Called 'Loot' of Napoleon

ROME, July 15 (UP)—The University of Rome through its official organ, Fascista, today demanded that France return all of the art works "looted" from Italy by Napoleon, including Leonardo da Vinci's priceless "Mona Lisa."

The university publication asked the return of all the allegedly stolen art treasures, which have been among the chief attractions of the Louvre museum in Paris, but particularly the works of da Vinci and Titian.

"Because these art works have been carefully packed by the French to protect them against wartime air raids and bombardments their return would be an exceedingly easy matter," it was stated.

"It would be necessary only to forward them from France to Italy in the packing cases in which they now rest."

The demand by the university publication revived demands made many times by various Italian quarters, particularly art experts, and if carried out would strip the Louvre of several of its biggest drawing cards. The "Mona Lisa," for instance, has been the greatest single attraction of the Louvre for years.

Other da Vinci works that have been in the Louvre include his "Annunciation" panel, his "St. Anne and the Virgin," the "Virgin of the Rocks" and his "La Belle Ferronière."

Among the Titians at the Louvre have been his "Portrait of Francis I," "Portrait of a Man with a Glove," "Laura Dianti" and his "Jupiter and Antiope." ◊

JULY 20, 1940

BRITAIN IS DEFIANT
Hitler's Peace Offer Not Worthy Of Comment, Officials State

By RAYMOND DANIELL
Special Cable to The New York Times.

LONDON, July 19—Chancellor Hitler's speech tonight left official Britain unmoved. The attitude of Whitehall officialdom, with ears glued to radios, was that "we have heard all this before."

To British ears there was discernible in Herr Hitler's speech the usual attitude of injured innocence and plausible expressions of peaceful intent, coupled with threats of dire consequences to follow the flouting of his will. It was this part of the speech in which Herr Hitler declared his recognition that the belligerents were engaged in a life or death struggle, which aroused the chief interest here, and this was taken as an indication that the long anticipated and long delayed Battle for Britain may not be far off.

The Nazi leader's words were interpreted here as designed for domestic consumption and indicative of a desire to get the struggle over with quickly before another Winter.

ALREADY "ANCIENT HISTORY"
The official reaction was that Herr Hitler's speech deserved no comment, inasmuch as it dealt with what is counted in these swift-moving days as ancient history and with threats that had been anticipated by Prime Minister Winston Churchill, who has said repeatedly that in the battle for this island there will be no surrender.

To officials here the most interesting passage in Herr Hitler's speech was his statement that he could see no reason why the war should go on and his assertion that this was his last appeal to the "common sense" of the one nation still on this side of the Atlantic and east of Russia that opposes his domination. That was interpreted as the ultimatum for which this country, armed to the teeth, has been waiting.

However, there was nothing in the speech of the Nazi dictator, who taunted Mr. Churchill for allegedly giving away his country's war secrets and thereby permitting Germany to steal the march in Norway, the Netherlands, Belgium and Denmark, to give a clue to his future plans. Therefore official circles were chary of comment lest even sarcastic remarks might provide direction for the Nazis, who, deprived of the French fleet's assistance, are believed to have had to recast their Blitzkrieg calendar.

British newspapers, however, were under no such restraint. With striking unanimity, from the Conservative Times of London to the Liberal Manchester Guardian, they snorted editorially at Herr Hitler's self-justification, his professed reasonableness and his veiled threats of terror to come. ◇

JULY 21, 1940

ROOSEVELT SIGNS 2-OCEAN NAVY BILL; START NOW SOUGHT
Knox to Ask House Tomorrow for $1,000,000,000 at Once to Get Program Under Way

ARMY TO STRESS INDUSTRY

By FRANK L. KLUCKHOHN
Special to THE NEW YORK TIMES

WASHINGTON, July 20—President Roosevelt signed today the $4,000,000,000 bill, authorizing construction of a giant two-ocean navy as Navy officials, including Secretary Knox, prepared to testify Monday before the House Appropriations Committee on a program for immediate expenditure of almost $1,000,000,000 under this authorization to get the six-year program rapidly under way.

On Tuesday Henry L. Stimson, Secretary of War, will lead Army officials to Capitol Hill to explain the Army's need for nearly $4,000,000,000 additional for thousands of tanks, airplanes, anti-aircraft guns and other modern equipment fully to supply an army of 1,200,000 men and to furnish 800,000 reserves with "critical" weapons. Of this sum about $1,500,000,000 will be requested for airplanes to bring this country's force to 26,000 planes.

PLANT EXPANSION AIDING BRITAIN
The stress in Army testimony, it is learned, will be upon plans for swiftly expanding facilities for production of all types of weapons for modern warfare, and, in addition to a long itemized list of weapons and supplies to be presented, about $400,000,000 will be requested as part of the $4,000,000,000 appropriation for the sole purpose of plant expansion.

In addition, officials revealed, the Reconstruction Finance Corporation will lend $72,000,000 for aircraft plant expansion and about $100,000,000 for general expansion. If Great Britain can withstand Nazi attempts at conquest in the coming weeks until uncertain weather begins, United States production of all types of materiel and munitions for modern warfare will be sufficiently increased by Spring to give the British tremendous, and perhaps decisive, supply aid, high Administration circles stated today.

In equipping a large American defensive army at top speed, American plant output will be stepped up to a point where, by May 10 of next year, it will be possible to sell the British enough to meet their needs without interfering with supplying needs at home, it was asserted.

DETAILS READY FOR CONGRESS
A rather astonishing picture of what War Department officials believe to be possible in rapidly utilizing American productive capacity and potential capacity is promised to Congress next week. Although the general objectives sought under the proposed expenditures and

JULY 24, 1940

DE GAULLE SAYS WAR ON NAZIS IS RESUMED

Special Cable to The New York Times.

LONDON, July 23—General Charles de Gaulle, head of the French forces in Great Britain, told France tonight through the British Broadcasting Corporation that the war with Germany was resumed on Sunday in the air above German territory and would soon be taken up on sea and land as well. He referred to bombing raids over Germany when French airmen cooperated with the R.A.F.

He exhorted those Frenchmen who are unable to join him but who might "in other circumstances" take up arms again to guard their weapons.

"This message," General de Gaulle said, "is meant in particular for French forces in North Africa. It is their duty to conceal from the so-called armistice del-

egations of the enemy all those arms that the enemy is trying to seize and which could be used against French troops who still carry on the fight."

To those who now had to work in German-occupied territory, General de Gaulle said it was their duty to offer

General Charles de Gaulle delivering his speech asking French people to fight Germany in spite of the truce signed by Marshal Pétain with Hitler.

passive resistance by all means in their power and never help to forge weapons that might kill other Frenchmen. ◇

the time limits set for the program will be outlined, a strong effort will be made to have Congress keep the detailed information secret to prevent its reaching

the hands of potential enemies. Whereas heretofore foreign attachés had been able to obtain information merely by reading the records of Congressional hearings, of-

ficials said that the time had come when detailed plans must be closely guarded.

With the Nazis threatening Great Britain, this country must spend every cent it can for defense as quickly as possible, it was stated in Administration quarters, where it was pointed out that the total of $4,848,000,000 requested by the President for additional Army-Navy development represented all that could be put into orders now.

It was regarded as likely, however, that the War Department would reveal to Congress the need somewhat later for what President Rooseevelt has termed "total defense."

The Two-Ocean Navy Bill signed by the President provides a 70 percent increase in currently authorized tonnage by 1946 and would permit the Navy to build its air force to 15,000 planes.

The completed program would bring the Navy's strength to 3,049, 480 tons, which would be divided as follows: Battleships, 1,045,000 tons; aircraft carriers, 454,500; cruisers, 899,024; destroyers, 478,000, and submarines 172,956. ◇

Battleship *Indiana* under construction in the shipyard in Newport, Rhode Island, 1940.

AUGUST 3, 1940

Where British Fliers Have Struck at Nazis

Reporting new raids on the Krupp works at Essen on the synthetic oil plants, supply depots and airdromes at various points, London asserted yesterday that military objectives in more than 100 German or German-held cities and towns had been badly damaged by its bombers since the war began. Points raided are indicated by heavy black dots. The British declared that the port of Hamburg was almost in ruins and that the docks, shipyards and plane factories of Bremen, the communications center of Cologne, the industrial cities of Ruhr and the naval bases of Kiel and Wilhelmshaven had also been hard hit. The raids have affected places 575 miles from England.

AUGUST 4, 1940

NEGROES REQUEST SHARE IN DEFENSE
Leaders Ask Training In Ratio to Population

LOG CABIN CENTER, Ga., Aug. 3 (AP)—Southern Negro leaders called today for racial opportunity "in proportion to population" to train for defense skills and combat service.

Dr. Benjamin F. Hubert of Savannah, chairman of the State Central Planning Commission, declared before that group that Negroes should be "more thoroughly coordinated" into the defense program.

Such coordination would materially assist in raising the economic level of the 14,000,000 Negroes in the country, he said.

Dr. Hubert asserted that the commission proposed to seek military training for all Negro high schools and land-grant colleges and to enlarge facilities of vocational training in metal work, mechanics and carpentry.

The commission outlined a proposal that Negroes be allowed to serve in all phases of combat service, such as Army, Navy and Air Corps, as well as "behind the lines in labor battalions." Commission members said pre-service training should be greatly increased for Negro youth.

Dr. L. A. Pinkston of Augusta, head of the State Baptist Convention, said that the commission should favor compulsory military training and insist that Negroes get a "fair share" in the selective drafts.

"If we are going to be drafted for service, we want to be trained for that service just as the white man is trained," he said.

Dr. Hubert pointed out that additional training should be provided for Negroes in agriculture so that they might get advanced scientific learning to produce foods efficiently.

More than 100 Negro leaders in college, fraternal, business and farm activities of several Southern States met for the commission session. ◊

Lindbergh Urges We 'Cooperate' With Germany if Reich Wins War

Special to The New York Times.

CHICAGO, Aug. 4—A move by the United States to bring about peace in Europe, to be undertaken without surrendering our traditional non-entanglement policy, was advocated today by Colonel Charles A Lindbergh. He called for "cooperation" with Germany if it wins the war, adding that an agreement could maintain peace and civilization throughout the world.

Delivering his plea in his third public statement of recent months concerning international policy, Colonel Lindbergh spoke before a rally in Soldier Field, attended by 40,000 persons and organized by the Citizens Committee to Keep America Out of War. His declarations were carried to other parts of the country by radio. The title of his address was "Keeping America Out of War, for American Reasons."

"If we want to keep America out of war, we must take the lead in offering a plan for peace," Colonel Lindbergh declared.

He did not offer any particular plan, but asserted that whatever suggestions might be put forward on the initiative of this country should be based on "the welfare of America," and supported by "an impregnable system of defense."

"It should incorporate terms of mutual advantage," he continued, "but it should not involve the internal affairs of Europe; they never were and never will be carried out to our desires.

"Let us offer Europe a plan for the progress and protection of Western civilization, of which they and we each form a part. But whatever their reply may be, let us carry on the American destiny of which our forefathers dreamed as they cut their farm lands from the virgin forest. What would they think of the claim that our frontiers lie in Europe?"

Colonel Lindbergh's stand in favor of cooperation with Germany, if necessary, found expression in the part of his address leading up to his advocacy of a peace proposal. Declaring that only by cooperation could the supremacy of Western civilization be maintained, he continued:

"In the past we have dealt with a Europe dominated by England and France. In the future we may have to deal with a Europe dominated by Germany. But whether England or Germany wins this war, Western civilization will still depend upon two great centers, one in each hemisphere.

"With all the aids of modern science, neither of these centers is in a position to attack the other as long as the defenses of both are reasonably strong. A war between us could easily last for generations and bring all civilization tumbling down, as has happened more than once before. An agreement between us could maintain civilization and peace throughout the world as far into the future as we can see." ◆

Charles Lindbergh arriving at the White House in 1939 for a meeting with President Roosevelt.

R.A.F. SEES MARGIN OF 4 TO 1 OVER FOE

British Fliers Claim Nazis Pay Dearly for Every Fighter They Down in Raids

By VINCENT SHEEAN
North American Newspaper Alliance.

LONDON, Aug. 12—A few American correspondents sat in the control center for the southeastern group of a fighter command while operations were directed against four important German attacks. We had gone there by appointment to hear the details of a previous large-scale air battle, but before we arrived and while we were there, the Germans were repeating their performance.

Fighter operations are centralized by a complex but smooth-running system of communications and warnings. Information comes from numerous sources in the navy, the Air Force and the Coastal Command, all of whom are centered at the Fighter Command. The Fighter Command has instantaneous communication with a separate group command.

Our group command was that which controls the most consistently attacked part of England, that in which both British and German fighters can operate best because each is operating within range of its airdromes. Our air vice marshal called it "the playground."

DEFENSE ACTION SWIFT

The central office where operations are directed is rather like the chart room of a big ship, with many maps, charts and scoreboards and a system of constant reporting. It runs so smoothly now that, within a very short time of warning that the Germans are coming, word had gone out to the waiting squadrons and British fighter planes are actually in the air.

The battle we saw started like the previous one with a big attack from the nearest coast—seventy to ninety airplanes. Hurricanes and Spitfires got into this cloud of Germans and did heavy execution. The next attack was in the same region, but a considerably heavier raid was started ten minutes later on another coast.

The fourth attack of the day, involving between thirty and forty Ger- ▸

◀ man planes, started shortly after noon on the east coast. In each of these four battles the group command that I observed was able to get squadrons into the air with record speed and important results.

A statement on gains and losses always must wait for an Air Ministry communiqué. When we left the control center eighteen German planes were "confirmed" as shot down, sixteen German casualties were "unconfirmed," three were "probable" and thirteen were "damaged." Pilots' claims are "unconfirmed" unless two or more witnesses report on them, although many "unconfirmed" kills are certainly true ones.

FOUR-TO-ONE SUPERIORITY CLAIMED

English fighters are keeping up a pretty steady average of a four-to-one superiority over German fighters—that is, they bring down four Germans for each fighter they lose. Hurricanes and Spitfires easily outclass Messerschmitts, both the 109 and 110, in performance. The new German fighter, the Heinkel 113, which first appeared over Dunkerque, is apparently now coming forward in greater numbers since last week.

In all recent attacks, the Germans have shown their healthy respect for British fighters by coming over with immense escorts. Nowadays they think it wise to provide fighter escorts in a proportion of five, six or even ten to each bomber. The British system of a dispersal of airdromes is so good and communications here are so rapid that they are able to give immediate combat wherever the attack appears. Many lessons have been learned from various failures in France.

To hear the reports coming in and the orders going out is to acquire renewed faith in the Fighter Command here. ◇

BERLIN IS EXULTANT OVER LONDON RAIDS
Devastation in Suburbs Is Said to Be Great— Fires Started

By C. BROOKS PETERS
Wireless to The New York Times.

BERLIN, Aug. 17—Masses of German bombers with their accompanying protectors yesterday raided the British Isles, including London. What has gone on heretofore, informed quarters in Berlin declared, has been but child's play, and real pressure is about to be felt for the first time by the British.

After six days of intensive air fighting, the Germans claim they have won air superiority over the British—with all that implies. To do this, they add, has required a number of days of furious fighting in which between Aug. 8 and Aug. 15 they claim to have shot down 505 British planes, mostly pursuit ships, with the loss of only 129 machines.

Yesterday, they add, because of indifferent weather conditions, their activities were confined, although they bombed a number of objectives successfully and brought down sixty-five British planes with the loss of fifteen of their machines.

British anti-aircraft batteries, the Germans declare, were unable to hold up the onslaughts of their bombers, and British captive balloons, traps or nets, as well as pursuit planes, were ineffectual in holding off the German raids. German pursuit planes and destroyers, it is said here, have demonstrated their superiority over British fighters, so that German reconnaissance machines can now fly over the scenes of the bombing and take pictures of the results achieved without fear of interference.

3,000 BRITISH PLANES FIGHT

BERLIN, Aug. 17 (AP)—Authorized German sources proclaimed last night that wave after wave of bombers had hurled destruction on the London environs late in the day, lining both banks of the Thames with fires, bomb craters and the wreckage of industrial plants.

The British fought back with 3,000 or more planes and with every weapon at their command.

But the mass-scale German attack, unprecedented in history, is designed to prove that "no power on earth can stop the Nazi air force," declared German sources. ◇

Hawker Hurricanes of Fighter Command, a first line of defense against the incoming German bombers attacking England, flying in formation during the Battle of Britain.

AUGUST 22, 1940

Trotsky Dies of His Wounds; Asks Revolution Go Forward

By ARNALDO CORTESI
Special Cable to The New York Times.

MEXICO CITY, Aug. 21—After twenty-six hours of an extraordinarily tenacious fight for life, Leon Trotsky died at 7:25 P.M. today of wounds inflicted upon his head with a pickaxe by an assailant in his home yesterday.

Mrs. Trotsky was with him to the last. Two of his secretaries also were present.

Almost his last words, whispered to his secretary, were:

"Please say to our friends I am sure of the victory of the Fourth International. Go forward!"

The 60-year-old exile's losing struggle for existence continued all last night and all day today with alternate ups and downs. He rallied somewhat at the middle of the day but by evening it was evident the end was near.

The assassin, Jacques Mornard van den Dreschd, for months an intimate of the Trotsky household, had a declaration written in French on his person when he was arrested yesterday. Police said today that in it he told of having quarreled with his leader when Mr. Trotsky tried to induce him to go to Russia to perform acts of sabotage.

The declaration adds that the writer decided to kill Mr. Trotsky because the latter did everything in his power to prevent van den Dreschd from marrying Sylvia Ageloff of Brooklyn, who had introduced the two men to each other.

Miss Ageloff, who is held as a witness, is said to have met van den Dreschd two years ago in Paris, and it was through her that he was able to win Mr. Trotsky's confidence, for her sister, Ruth, was Mr. Trotsky's secretary in 1937.

Questioned by police, she declared she introduced "Frank Jackson," as she knew him, to Mr. Trotsky in perfect good faith not knowing he had any designs on the former Soviet War Commissar's life.

She was so remorseful that she threatened to commit suicide if Mr. Trotsky died. She revealed that "Jackson" always seemed plentifully supplied with money and told police he once gave her $3,000 saying it was left him by his mother when she died.

The assassin, who entered Mexico posing as a Canadian, Frank Jackson, now is said to have been born in Teheran, Iran, son of a Belgian diplomat. Police say many letters in English, French and Russian were found in his hotel room.

With remarkable fortitude, Mr. Trotsky, despite his very severe wound,

Leon Trotsky

was able to grapple with his assailant and then run from the room in which he was attacked, shouting for help. He did not collapse until his wife and his guards had rushed to his aid. For some time he retained full lucidity of mind and was able to make a few statements.

Along the same corridor in the hospital, only two doors away, lay his assailant. Police guard the door of his room for fear that if there was an organized attempt on Mr. Trotsky's life, the organizers may murder "Jackson" to prevent his testifying. ◇

AUGUST 26, 1940

JAPANESE SEEKING INDIES OIL SUPPLY

U.S. INTERESTS INVOLVED

By HAROLD CALLENDER
By Telephone to The New York Times.

SURABAYA, Java, Aug, 27—The conference of the Japanese trade delegation, arriving in Batavia next week, with the Netherlands Indies Government and Netherland and American oil men may have a vital bearing upon the future of Eastern affairs, it is believed here.

The Japanese visitors, representing the Mitsui and other companies, are expected to seek increased exports of oil, tin and rubber to Japan, especially oil. Mr. Schultz of the Far Eastern Standard-Vacuum Company will fly to Batavia from Hong Kong, and Mr. Kany of the same company will fly from New York to consider the Japanese desires.

Hitherto the Japanese have obtained oil through the selling companies in Japan—Standard and Shell. But the Japanese contend that they are not getting enough oil through the normal channels. Hence, this visit to Batavia to confer with the Netherlands Indies Government as well as the oil producers in these islands.

It was said here tonight that the Japanese wanted increased oil in order to build up their reserves as Germany did up to a year ago.

EXPORTS TO BE DISCUSSED

Unlike tin and rubber, the oil exports are not controlled by agreed international limitation. But it is expected that the Japanese want to discuss all three commodities. Since exports are under government license under the "Crisis Decrees," this will bring the Netherland Government as well as the oil companies into the negotiations. The two producing oil companies here are American and a British-Netherland combine.

Hence, it is widely believed that the disposition of the East Indies oil is perhaps the main factor governing the immediate future in Asia. The importance of the issue, as viewed here, can hardly be overestimated.

The belief here is that the American embargo on aviation gasoline to Japan is one cause of the pressure from Japan for more oil from the East Indies. In the present circumstances, with Britain virtually out of Far Eastern affairs and American policy uncertain, the best informed observers think there is not much the Netherlanders can do but to try to appease Japan by meeting that country's ❯

desires. Hence, the Netherlanders in these islands say they intend to defend themselves if necessary, and they are making rapid preparations to that end.

An invader would not find the oil wells intact, and it would require months to repair them if they were destroyed. But in the defense preparations much depends upon the United States; it is the only source of war materials. ◊

AUGUST 30, 1940

Editorial
RAIDS ON EGYPT

So far, except in Somaliland and Libya, where marching columns and troop concentrations weave across the desert in a haphazard pattern that seems to have nothing to do with this war, the Italians have fought chiefly with their air force. This week they have bombed Port Said, at the head of the Suez, for the first time; at irregular intervals they drop a load of dynamite into the harbor of Alexandria, headquarters of the British Mediterranean fleet. The paradox of these raids on Egypt is that they are attacks on a country with which Italy is not at war; the Italians are fighting the British in Egypt but not the Egyptians, and the latter are in an equally paradoxical position; for while their land is an important military and naval base for Great Britain and is dependent for protection on British power, they are exceedingly reluctant to join in hostilities against Italy. This reluctance, fanned by a large and influential Italian colony in Cairo and by stubborn remnants of anti-British feeling left over from the fight for independence, explains the instability of the Egyptian Government since the Mediterranean became a battle front.

In sharp contrast with the methodical way the British use the air weapon, blasting night after night at the same objectives, the Italian squadrons appear to rush about at random. From Gibraltar to Malta they flit from port to port like a Mediterranean tripper, with no apparent aim except to harass the British as much as possible with as little cost as possible. In their operations there is much to support the theory that they expected the conflict to end with the fall of France; this is the best explanation of the gingerly and cautious fashion with which they keep up the appearances of warfare while husbanding their limited military resources. They strike wherever the British are exerting pressure.

The threat to Greece, the nervous haste of the effort to calm the Balkans, the dispatch of an Italian mission to Syria, can be taken as signs that the English are busier than they seem in the Balkans and the Near East. But Egypt is the key of their defenses and the core of the Mediterranean conflict. If the manoeuvres now in progress from the Black Sea to the Sudan foreshadow a shift of the battlefield to the south, as some observers believe, the place to watch is the bridgehead which straddles Asia and Africa at the Suez. ◊

SEPTEMBER 1, 1940

A YEAR OF WAR LEAVES BRITAIN FACING HITLER

PROSPECT OF INVASION FADING

By EDWIN L. JAMES

The end of the first year of the war finds Great Britain facing Germany in a conflict of bitterness which apparently has still some time to go. In that twelve months Hitler has conquered France and Poland and overrun Norway, Denmark, Belgium and Holland. The carving up of Rumania at his "advice" shows that he is very nearly master of the Continent of Europe. Italy came in with him after France was prostrate and is waging an indifferent war against the British in the Mediterranean and Africa.

As things stand now, Britain's fleet is maintaining a fairly effective blockade of the Continent to prevent food and supplies from reaching the Germans, while Germany is trying to maintain a blockade of the British Isles, using mostly her air force, her submarine warfare having slumped remarkably.

While these two efforts at attrition are in progress the German and British air forces are hammering away. Day and night the Nazi planes attack Britain. They have unquestionably done large damage but they have suffered heavy losses at the hands of the R.A.F. Britain, on the other hand, continues almost daily raids on German military objectives in France, Belgium and Holland and has taken the war to Germany. Against the bombing of London, there is the bombing of Berlin.

WARFARE IN THE AIR

The indications are that the Germans have given up, or are giving up, their plan for a military invasion of Britain, so loudly heralded by German propaganda. It is possible that the advice of German generals that it would be a very tough job indeed caused Hitler to think of the price a failure would cost him. In any event, the approach of bad weather in a few more weeks seems to make it evident that if the Germans have not forsaken their dream of capturing London with tanks and infantry, at least they have put it off until next year.

True enough, the current air attacks on Britain are intended to "soften" that country, to use Nazi terminology, to the point where an invasion could be attempted. It would not appear that the "softening" process has gone far enough to permit a military invasion to be imminent.

It looks, therefore, that the coming months will see the fight between Britain and Germany limited to air warfare. One may figure that the weather will have a hampering effect perhaps on both sides and also one may figure that neither side has as yet made its maximum effort.

There is so little definite public knowledge of so many important factors that it is difficult indeed to make any predictions as to what the Winter months will bring.

THE MONTHS TO COME

In the first place, there is little reliable information as to the relative air strengths. This is natural, inasmuch as such facts would constitute important military information for the enemy. The estimates of German plane production vary from 1,000 a month to 6,000 a month. This means simply that outside of Germany little is known of the Nazi plane production. Prime Minister Churchill stated in the House of Commons ten days ago that British production of planes had comfortably passed German production. The most commonly reported figure of British production is between 1,600 and 1,800 planes monthly, to which may be

SEPTEMBER 1, 1940

Fifteen Outstanding Events in the European War

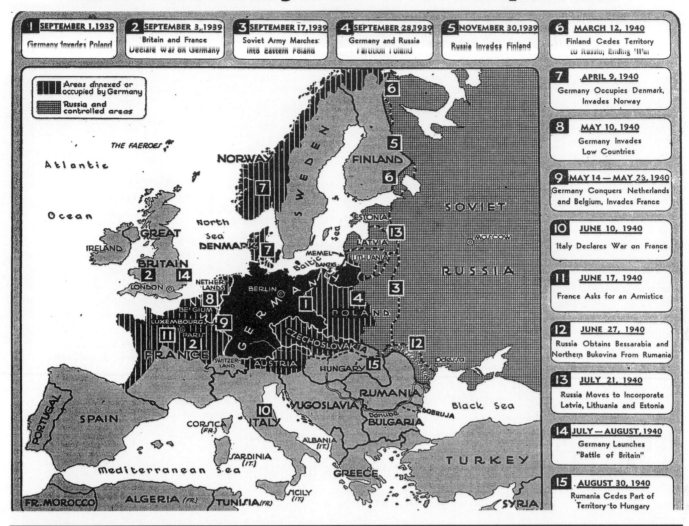

1 SEPTEMBER 1, 1939	2 SEPTEMBER 3, 1939	3 SEPTEMBER 17, 1939	4 SEPTEMBER 28, 1939	5 NOVEMBER 30, 1939	6 MARCH 12, 1940
Germany Invades Poland	Britain and France Declare War on Germany	Soviet Army Marches Into Eastern Poland	Germany and Russia Partition Poland	Russia Invades Finland	Finland Cedes Territory to Russia; Ending War

7 APRIL 9, 1940
Germany Occupies Denmark, Invades Norway

8 MAY 10, 1940
Germany Invades Low Countries

9 MAY 14 — MAY 28, 1940
Germany Conquers Netherlands and Belgium, Invades France

10 JUNE 10, 1940
Italy Declares War on France

11 JUNE 17, 1940
France Asks for an Armistice

12 JUNE 27, 1940
Russia Obtains Bessarabia and Northern Bukovina From Rumania

13 JULY 21, 1940
Russia Moves to Incorporate Latvia, Lithuania and Estonia

14 JULY — AUGUST, 1940
Germany Launches "Battle of Britain"

15 AUGUST 30, 1940
Rumania Cedes Part of Territory to Hungary

---

added a figure of 300 as representing roughly the number of planes received by Britain from the United States.

Of course, there is a possibility of error in figuring a blanket number of planes. A big bomber may cost ten times as much as a small chasse plane and yet in these popular classifications each is counted as one plane. There is also the element of aviators. Which country has the most aviators? One would suppose that Germany, with the larger population, could train more pilots. Over against that calculation could be placed the circumstance that when a British Spitfire brings down a German bomber, there are four or five men lost, whereas if the single-seater chasse plane is brought down one airman is lost.

It is therefore hard to guess what the effect of four or five months of the aerial warfare now going on will be on the two sides. Certainly there appears no good reason to think that either the British

resistance has been seriously weakened or that the Germans have seriously worn out their air force. The spirit and morale of Britain are excellent, from all accounts.

UNITED STATES PREPARES

In the meanwhile the United States, although somewhat lumberingly, is getting prepared. If the theory is correct that even if Hitler had designs on this country it would take him two or three years to get ready, then our situation is not so bad. The factor of Britain's so far successful resistance to Hitler has somewhat softened the fear which swept over much of this country after the defeat of France. However, the movement toward preparedness seems to have a solid popular backing.

There is much quotation here of the Germans' statement that they have no aspirations in this hemisphere. It would, therefore, be interesting if the United States were to propose to Denmark a ninety-nine-year lease on a slice

of Southern Greenland as an air and naval base. The Danish Government is under the thumb of the Germans and the advice Berlin might give on such a proposition would be significant. After all, Greenland is in the Western Hemisphere and once before we acquired bases from Denmark when we bought the Virgin Islands for $25,000,000 in 1917. If it be true that Greenland would be a convenient half-way point for bombers coming this way from Europe, it might be a strategic advantage to have a base there. And, of course, if the Nazis do not dream of ever sending any bombing planes across the Atlantic they ought not to have any objections to our building a base which might be an interference.

But there will not be any Nazi bombers, warships or transports coming this way until after Britain has been defeated. And Britain is not yet defeated. Mr. Churchill says the war will turn around in 1942. ◆

SEPTEMBER 4, 1940

BRITISH JUBILANT
Destroyers Strengthen Their Fleet At Point of Greatest Strain

By RAYMOND DANIELL
Special Cable to The New York Times.

LONDON, Sept. 3—It would be impossible to overstate the jubilation in official and unofficial circles caused today by President Roosevelt's announcement that fifty United States destroyers were coming to help Great Britain in her hour of peril. They will be manned by British crews and will fly the white ensign of the Royal Navy, it is true, but they are coming, nevertheless.

It was tangible proof that American talk of giving "all aid short of war" was more than idle chatter and that this country's friends across the Atlantic, despite German propaganda and the heavy bombardment of British cities and towns, had decided there was still lots of fight left in the British lion and that it was not too late to help turn the tide against totalitarian domination of Europe.

DESTROYER LOSSES OFFSET

Under the arrangement, it was pointed out by authoritative sources, the United States gained security against future aggression, while the British fleet at one stroke acquired fifty 1,200-ton destroyers as an offset to the thirty lost since the beginning of hostilities.

These destroyers are badly needed at this stage of the war with British sea power engaged in a death grapple with the German Empire. Since the French were knocked out as an ally, the whole job of protecting convoys and maintaining the lifelines of the Empire against the new enemy in the Mediterranean has fallen upon the British fleet, while the air force has concentrated chiefly on destroying the enemy's supplies and defending the homes of the people of this island, which is under repeated bombardment from the air throughout its length and breadth.

Added to this multiplication of the navy's duties has been the necessity of blockading the whole Continent of Europe while standing by to resist the very real threat of a German invasion which, as War Secretary Anthony Eden warned today, still hangs over this country.

As great as was Britain's need the material gain by today's transaction was matched in British minds by the intangible implications of the most open indication yet of Anglo-American cooperation for defense against the Nazi threats.

The Times, London, will point out editorially tomorrow that such cooperation between a belligerent and a neutral is "a new departure" but one that is dictated by the necessities of modern war. The editorial goes on to say:

"The tragic fate of some of the smaller peoples of Europe might have been averted if they had not been restrained from planning for their own safety by the punctilio of neutrality that has become an anachronism in a world containing Hitler and Mussolini."

President Roosevelt's announcement in Congress and the publication of a White Paper here containing the exchange of notes on the subject between Secretary of State Cordell Hull and the Marquess of Lothian, the British Ambassador, gave a fairly complete picture of what had taken place, but fuller details will be given in the House of Commons Thursday when Prime Minister Churchill reports on the progress of the war since the full force of Germany's air power was hurled against Britain, either as a prelude to an invasion, or, as some observers believe, to force a decision in the air.

THREE PURPOSES SERVED

Meanwhile it was pointed out here that the agreement served three principal purposes: First, it provides timely reinforcement of the British Navy in the task of maintaining control of the Atlantic. Second, it contributes to the security of the United States. Third, it strengthens the defenses of the entire Western Hemisphere.

While today's announcement dispels all doubt that the transfer of the destroyers

SEPTEMBER 6, 1940

INDO-CHINA GIVES IN TO TOKYO ON TROOPS
Basic Deal Between Vichy and Japan Is Said to Permit Landings at Haiphong

HONG KONG, Sept. 5 (AP)—A preliminary, basic agreement giving Japan right-of-way in French Indo-China for a back-door attack on China in an effort to wind up the three-year-old war was reported tonight by authoritative neutral quarters at Hanoi, Indo-China.

This concession of a "limited" right to land Japanese troops and supplies at Haiphong was said to have been reached between Tokyo and the Vichy Government of France. It was still subject to negotiation of details at Hanoi.

This was the latest and apparently best-informed version of the crisis in the most populous segment of defeated France's troubled empire.

INVASION THREAT FADES

The threat of a full-fledged, forcible invasion of Indo-China—the essence of a reported Japanese ultimatum of Monday—appeared to have passed. One explanation was that Maj. Gen. Issaku Nishihara, Japanese negotiator in chief, had overstepped himself.

Confronted with a French warning of armed resistance to any invasion and a declaration that acquiescence would be incompatible with Vichy's instructions, General Nishihara, under pressure from Tokyo, was said to have re-entered conversations with French colonial officials.

However won, the right to ship troops to the Yunnan border of Indo-China would open up for Japan a great new avenue of attack on the forces, resources and communications of Generalissimo Chiang Kai-shek's Central Chinese Government. Invasion of Yunnan Province would put a serious crimp in Chinese resistance because of the war industries centered there, and the Japanese would be able to cut the Burma road if Britain ever decided to reopen it.

Thus, a military foothold in Indo-China might serve the double purpose of bringing the "China incident"—as the Japanese call the war—to a close and carry Japan closer to her self-proclaimed destiny of dominance in "Greater East Asia." ◊

was connected with the British granting to the United States air and naval bases for hemisphere defense, it was said here that the negotiations started out as parallel talks that converged as they proceeded. The United States sent out feelers for naval bases at about the time the British sought to obtain over-age destroyers. Both bargainers were eager for what the other had to sell; but values and prices are matters over which experts might debate for years. Thus, it was said, it was decided to swap two valuable considerations as though equal in value, as perhaps they are.

However, before the deal was made, the governments of the members of the British Commonwealth of Nations affected were consulted and assured that no change in sovereignty was contemplated. A ninety-nine-year term for the leases was decided upon because twenty five years was regarded as too short for the scope of building and investment planned by the United States, while a 999-year lease might have implied surrender of sovereignty. ◇

SEPTEMBER 8, 1940

WAR'S KEY QUESTION: 'CAN BRITAIN HOLD OUT?' Men and Machines Are Meeting Test, and Morale of the People Is High

By JAMES B. RESTON
Wireless to The New York Times.

LONDON, Sept. 7—Can Britain hold out? For how long can she withstand this relentless battering from the air? Can these able and heroic people, outnumbered and outequipped, prevail against the mighty German air force and beat this air force at its own game?

These are the pre-eminent questions in the Western World today and the answers to them lie mainly with the men and the machines of the Royal Air Force.

There are in this country 2,000,000 men under arms. In an armed conflict, despite the loss of equipment that was made and the lack of equipment that was not made, they will give a good account of themselves. Similarly, the nation can count on its incomparable Navy, now standing at alert awaiting invasion, blockading the Continent of Europe and the protecting empire. But Britain will live or die with its men in the Air Force.

In the past month, during the greatest aerial battles in the history of warfare, the British have proved they have men and machines capable of meeting whatever planes and formations the Germans have sent over. What we know now is that Britain's "first team" is all right. Their training is excellent, their anticipation of the enemy has been a little uncanny and their fighting, particularly the Spitfires, superb.

QUESTION OF RESERVES

But the great question now is that of reserves. Rockne tactics work in this business, too. How good is Britain's second team, and third and fourth? Are the reserves coming up just as good and are they coming fast enough to meet the big push?

These are the questions which must be answered.

Look first at the question of machines. Since the mass raids started on Aug. 11 the Germans have lost, not counting today's score, 1,269 planes to the British loss of 376.

This admittedly is the official British figure and since these figures are the foundation for this argument a word should be said about them.

Because of the great discrepancy between British and German claims objective American reporters here have gone to the greatest difficulty to check and recheck British statements. They have observed individual squadrons for weeks at a time, watching them go out to meet the raiders, counting them coming back. They have checked them with records secured by the air attachés of neutral countries who have special facilities for gathering accurate information and they have talked with American pilots who are flying in these battles and who see the detailed secret reports of losses of each squadron each week.

The overwhelming impression created by this doublechecking is that the British figures are accurate.

In the first week of the mass raids the British lost 115 Spitfires and Hurricanes to Germany's 492 planes. In the second week of Aug. 17 to 24 they lost 51 to Germany's 243. In the third week they lost 104 to 291, and in the last six days they lost 106 to Germany's 243.

British Ministers have been maintaining for months now that their production of planes outnumbered their losses. There is no reason to doubt their statements. In fact, they are supported by evidence) gained elsewhere.

King George VI and Queen Elizabeth inspecting the bomb damage to Buckingham Palace after a heavy Nazi air raid during the Battle of Britain.

SUPPLY OF PILOTS

The question of supply of first-class pilots is another more complicated story. For weeks British officials have been telling neutral correspondents that British production of both well-trained pilots and planes is now greater than Germany's. This view is always a little puzzling when one sees a dozen Spitfires fighting 200 Germans. If the British didn't need fighter pilots they would not be appealing to the United States for them, but at the same time they do not seem to worry very much about fighting against great odds.

To Americans judging this gigantic air battle from headlines it must seem that every pilot of the R.A.F. must certainly be working night and day, and getting a little tired from the strain. Certainly there are individual cases of men who have had to take a rest, but pilots and officers of the R.A.F. appear almost casual about their jobs.

The other day this correspondent picked up a pilot who had made a forced landing near Dover. He had just come out of a battle in which he and the pilots of eleven other Spitfires had engaged sixty-three bombers and 200 fighters. These figures are almost unbelievable but it is a fact that this fellow who had been in the R.A.F. since 1929 acted like a substitute halfback straining to get back into the game. His only interest was being driven to the nearest town to catch a train back to his base.

It would be foolish to deny that the British would like to have a few thousand more pilots to throw into battle when it really gets hot but right now, as in the case of the planes, pilots seem to be coming along quicker than the Germans can shoot them down and the record of the substitutes is every bit as good.

SPIRIT OF PEOPLE

One simply cannot convey the spirit of these people. Adversity only angers and strengthens them. They are tough in a way we Americans seldom understand. That curious gentility among their men folk confuses us. We underestimate them.

Can Britain hold out? The British people can hold out to the end in this epic of human endurance. If the pace keeps as it is now, Britain will hold out in men, machines and morale, not for weeks, but for months. But if the pace is stepped up far beyond the present, it is, of course, impossible to predict what will happen. ◇

SEPTEMBER 9, 1940

LONDON'S EAST-END HEAVIEST SUFFERER
Raging Fires Make Thousands Homeless, But Spirit of the British Seems Unshaken

Special Cable to The New York Times.

LONDON, Sept. 8—Thousands of dwellers in London's East End—which looked today as if it had been struck simultaneously by a tornado and an earthquake—have been rendered homeless. They are being sheltered, under government auspices, in hotels, schools and other public buildings. Central London, which only a year ago was being evacuated, was tonight the reception area for refugees from one of its poorest and most congested areas.

Through the bar of one of this great city's big hotels tonight there passed a melancholy procession of old women and children, carrying pillows, bound for underground ballrooms to spend the night. Upon their faces was written tragedy, suffering and fear.

They look exactly like the people that this correspondent has seen fleeing from those inexorable floods that sometimes devastated the valleys of the Ohio and the Mississippi in the United States. And that is what this blitzkrieg of the air is like—some hideous upheaval of nature in which man is helpless to resist or protect himself from lightning or high water.

Perhaps that accounts for the calm fatalism that seems to pervade the people here. They are living through hell and behaving like angels.

Firemen played the most spectacular part in last night's garish show. All branches of the civilian defense units, however, did their bit with quiet efficiency in this war in which armies wait idly for a chance to strike at one another while old men, women and children suffer the major casualties.

That is what "total war" really means, and it is a pity that

some of those Americans who talked flippantly last Winter about the "phoney war" that the British were fighting could not see some of the scenes that this correspondent witnessed this afternoon, because they showed simultaneously what the Nazi bombers can give and what the little folk of Britain can take.

CHIEF AREAS OF ATTACK

For at least ten miles this correspondent drove through the area that the Germans had selected for their principal attack. Up one side of the Thames and down another were the grim and sometimes grisly marks of war. Here and there was a house of half a block in ruins, with rescue workers digging for bodies and survivors.

For miles there was hardly a window intact. Block after block, where delayed-action bombs lay buried beneath the pavement, was roped off and patrolled by the police who shooed off sight-seers. Children darted in and out of tenement house doorways at the edge of these abandoned residential sections, while cats and dogs foraged among garbage pails left unemptied.

The sorriest part of it is that for every military objective hit, grief and tragedy struck a score of humble homes. Churches, hospitals and old people's

Londoners with their furniture and belongings during the Blitz.

homes, it seemed to this correspondent touring London's stricken areas this afternoon, appeared to have a fatal attraction for German bombs. And this was a completely unescorted trip, undertaken—guided by the senses of smell and sound—without any guidance from official sources.

HOUSE FRONTS BLOWN AWAY

At edges of the sections that felt the fullest fury of the German attack broken windows indicated that somewhere near by a bomb had fallen. Demolished homes gaped like the spaces where teeth had been pulled out here and there. At other places there were great craters in the streets and the buildings there had the fronts torn off. There were exposed to gaping crowds of sightseers the bedrooms and living rooms of these humble homes, which are the castles of the still free men who dwell in them.

Nothing is more tragic than an "open house," which stands like a stage set after the curtain has been lifted by bombs, with its cherished household belongings and pictures hurled into topsy-turvy disarray, unless it be the sight of those helpless and homeless ones who poured into central London tonight, carrying babies and pillows, clutching prized belongings and unconsciously casting their eyes to the sky each time a bomb went off, as they went to the cellars of hotels and other buildings. They will try to sleep on boards or concrete, with the nightmare of what they have undergone still before their waking eyes. ◊

SEPTEMBER 12, 1940

CHURCHILL WARNS INVASION IS NEAR

Special Cable to The New York Times.

LONDON, Sept. 11—A crisis that ranks in Britain's history with the day of the Spanish armada's approach, or that on which Napoleon turned away from invasion by way of Boulogne is approaching. Prime Minister Winston Churchill, who is directing this last-ditch struggle, returned to his old role of reporter this afternoon to tell his people and the whole world so in plain and confident language.

From Hamburg, from German-occupied Brest and from conquered Norway's harbors the invading forces are gathering and ships and self-propelled barges are being concentrated for the assault upon the shores on this island on the heels of the murderous attack from the skies to which this capital has been subjected, the Prime Minister said.

He addressed his words to a people fighting mad and determined to carry on until the last bit of masonry in their proud city has been reduced to dust together with the kind of European civilization they are dying to defend.

It was with the threat of invasion that Mr. Churchill dealt chiefly in his broadcast. Not mincing words, he asked every Briton to do his duty and asserted that in the end Britain's cause would come out from the smoke of battle with the Union

Jack flying as the royal standard flew for a time this afternoon above Buckingham Palace, its walls shot away.

Not only was the Prime Minister sure that his people would not flinch, but he defiantly and bitterly assailed Adolf Hitler and Nazism as wicked, evil things that must be stamped out before free men could be at peace again. It was Mr. Churchill's voice, his words, his thoughts, his every word that echoed the inchoate hatred that the indiscriminate bombings of London's civilian population have instilled in British hearts.

"A VERY IMPORTANT WEEK"

The imminence of Britain's danger was emphasized by Mr. Churchill when he said that next week must be regarded as "a very important week." Then he told what he had learned of German plans for following up the air attack upon London with an invading force. Whether Herr Hitler would try an invasion in the few remaining days of good weather or, indeed, would attempt that hazardous task at all, the Prime Minister said, no man could guess, but that such an attempt was being prepared with typical German thoroughness and attention to detail was certain.

It might, he said, be undertaken at any time upon England, upon Scotland, or upon Ireland, or, for that matter, upon all three at once. Britain, he affirmed, was ready to repel any such seaborne attack as the people of London had withstood the cruelest, most trying bombardment from the air to which any people had yet been subjected. ◊

SEPTEMBER 15, 1940

MANY AMERICANS FEAR NAZI INVASION

Many Americans believe that Germany will attempt an invasion of the United States if England is defeated, and large numbers of citizens similarly are convinced that fifth-columnists are already active here, a survey of rank-and-file voters throughout the nation has disclosed, according to the American Institute of Public Opinion, directed by Dr. George Gallup.

"Even military experts are in disagreement," Dr. Gallup reports, "as to Adolf Hitler's most likely course in the event of a victory over England. But the

survey shows that more than four laymen in every ten now share the apprehension of United States Ambassador William E. Bullitt and others who have recently predicted a possible Nazi attack on this country.

"While some voters felt that such an attempt would not come for two years or more, nearly half of those who thought an invasion might come at all said they expected it 'immediately after an English defeat' or 'within a year's time.'

"The institute put the following question to a cross-section of men and women in each State: 'Mr. Bullitt, our Ambassador to France, says that if Great Britain is defeated the Germans will invade the United States. Do you think they will?'" The replies were:

Think they will 42%
Think not 45
Undecided or no opinion 13

"Whether Hitler plans an attack on

the United States or not, a popular belief that he is preparing such a blueprint would have a tremendous influence on United States policy.

"The survey also found that a majority of those who were able to define fifth column activities and who had definite opinions on the subject of fifth columns in the United States thought that such activities already were under way.

"The institute's question asked:

"Without mentioning names, do you think there are any fifth columnists in this community? The replies of those able to define fifth column activities were:

Yes 48%
No 26
Don't Know 26

"'We're not getting excited about it out here,' said a Midwestern voter, 'but we're not going to be caught napping.'" ◊

SEPTEMBER 18, 1940

R.A.F. 'POURS HELL' ON ITALIAN FORCES
Fascisti Pay Heavy Price For Rapid Thrust into Egypt as British Fall Back

By JAMES ALDRIDGE
North American Newspaper Alliance

CAIRO, Egypt, Sept. 17—There will not be any crystallization of the front in Egypt for some time yet. As the Italians make bigger stitches with their needle-point entry, British evacuation continues and Italy's crack armored units are quickly filling the vacuum.

For the first time in the war, Italy boasts that her navy is preparing to take combined action with the land forces, and shelling of British coastal positions is expected in the next few days. But as sure as Italy tries this, there will be a naval reception awaiting her that she has not dreamed of.

Today the real strength of the Italian thrust was manifested for the first time. Royal Air Force planes flying over Bagbag caught Italian armored concentrations in groups and poured hell on them. Through gaps made in the barbed-wire border defenses the Italians are cascading heavy equipment indiscriminately. They have pulled the barbed wire of the first few miles clean away to give them quicker transport.

BRITISH PATROLS DEADLY

As the sun lifted itself over the horizon this morning, a red haze covered the biggest field of dead on Egyptian soil in half a century as light spilled itself on the Britons' night's work. All night long British harassing patrols darted across the stony desert in the bright moonlight. Because you can't muffle the noise of motors, any Italian move in the still desert night is easily detected and the British, like picadors, struck Premier Mussolini's bull many times.

Italy's needle point so far is between Bagbag and Sidi Barrani, about fifty-five miles inside the Egyptian-Libyan border. Now the main British advance troops are trying to blunt the Italian

point. Superior by far in numbers and equipment, the Italians have up to now had the advantage of thrusting along a road that it is not strategic for the British to defend. With mechanized, armored vehicles, it is fairly easy to extend this thread along the coast.

The most advanced Italian vehicles seem to be tiny, flat tanks equipped to fire only frontward and built entirely for quick advance work. In long columns, like a black stream of ants, in small groups, they come along the seacoast. Based on what I have seen, approximately one mixed division seems to be making the attack.

At least ten infantry battalions, each of about 1,000 men, are in the thrusting division. The Italians allow to this one corps of tanks, medium, light and heavy, as well as armored cars. In the first line of vehicles they have placed heavy 75 mm, anti-aircraft guns on the cars and pompom quick firers.

As the armored vehicles make feelers ahead, the artillery is coming up behind and being established at the foot of the hills just off the sea. In the rear the Italians are establishing camps in positions that have been chosen for "stability" rather than a Blitzkrieg. ◆

SEPTEMBER 22, 1940

GERMANY STILL DELAYS INVASION OF ENGLAND

By CHARLES M. LINCOLN

"The people of England are very curious and ask, 'Why in the world don't you come?' We are coming. People should not always be so curious. When the British say, 'Why doesn't he come?' my answer is: Keep your shirts on. He is coming." Thus Der Fuehrer, Sept. 4. Perhaps he is coming, but England is beginning to doubt that Hitler is a man of his word. To record that another week has gone without an attempt by Germany to invade England is becoming monotonous. The navy waits; a million five hundred thousand soldiers wait. They would welcome a straightout fight. They believed they would have come to grips long before this. They now think that perhaps there will be no fight; that

Germany will delay or postpone the adventure. And they believe that, if it is further delayed or indefinitely postponed, the Royal Air Force will have been the explanation.

That Hitler has really abandoned his dearest dream cannot be safely assumed. He may make the attempt at any moment. He may never make it. What is going on right now between himself and the governmental and military groups which surround him we cannot know. But more and more, in Berlin, are heard the words "in the Spring," "Britain is vulnerable elsewhere," "the Mediterranean." Yesterday a highly placed German said, in Berlin: "Let's leave open for the moment whether the Britain of the future may be regarded as European." What do these, and similar expressions, coming from the German capital, signify? They certainly do not resemble the bombast of a few months ago. Whether Germany is to defer, or put aside, her attempt to invade England remains unanswered. But it would seem, from what has thus far transpired, that if the attempt is to wait upon mastery of the Royal Air Force and the breaking of the British people it will have to wait a long, long time. ◆

SEPTEMBER 27, 1940

MEETING IN BERLIN

By The United Press.

BERLIN, Sept. 27—Germany, Italy and Spain will sign a document of "historical importance" at noon in Chancellor Adolf Hitler's new chancellory, it was stated early today by a reliable Nazi source.

The document's contents were not disclosed, but it was hinted that it would have great bearing on the "final phase" of the war against Great Britain and future phases of the Axis's "new European order."

The document, it was said, will be executed by the German Foreign Minister, Joachim von Ribbentrop; the Spanish Minister of Government, Ramon Serrano Suñer, and the Italian Foreign Minister, Count Ciano.

[An important Japanese-German agreement will be announced today in Tokyo and Berlin, according to a message telephoned to Shanghai by The

SEPTEMBER 27, 1940

JAPAN UNDETERRED BY U.S. EMBARGO HELP TO REICH IS HINTED

By HUGH BYAS
Wireless to The New York Times.

TOKYO, Sept. 27—The embargo on scrap metal and the new loan to China are universally interpreted here as retaliation by the United States against Japan's policy in Indo-China. The press apparently is convinced that Japan has arrived at a point where increasing United States opposition will be encountered.

"It seems inevitable," says the newspaper Asahi, "that a collision should occur between Japan, determined to establish a sphere of self-sufficiency in East Asia, including the Southwest Pacific, and the United States, which is determined to meddle in affairs on the other side of a vast ocean by every means short of war."

Asahi declares that Japan has made full preparations to deal with the situation that the scrap embargo creates. Even more drastic economic reprisals by the United States are expected, and the newspaper Yomiuri reports that the government of Prince Fumimaro Konoye is preparing for the cessation of Japan's raw silk exports.

Arrangements are being made, according to the newspaper, to use all Japan's silk at home. Japan's sales of raw silk to the United States is this country's largest source of foreign currency and their suspension would be a staggering blow to Japanese economy.

It is noteworthy that no newspaper suggests that Japan's policy might be modified to reduce United States opposition. It is clearly understood that Premier Konoye's government is completely committed to its present policies and that while it remains in power nothing can be expected but a continuation along present lines.

Yomiuri finds a sinister design in the fact that the United States loan is being allocated to China's foreign exchange fund. This implies, according to the newspaper, that the United States is trying to control China economically, thus taking Britain's place in China's financial world and allowing United States capital to "eat China's heart." The newspaper adds that "this is a development that Japan cannot tolerate."

HELP TO REICH THREATENED

TOKYO, Sept. 26 (AP)—Japan, convinced finally that the United States stands unalterably opposed to her "legitimate" expansion in the Orient, can be expected to give Germany active support if America enters the European war, a highly qualified informant said today.

The United States, he said, has followed a strong policy of opposition to Japan even at times when Britain offered conciliation and Japanese hopes for an agreement with Washington seem futile.

The informant, a Japanese with close government connections, indicated that Japan, facing the possibility of conflict to the south and east, was ready to mend her long-strained relations with Soviet Russia to keep her northern and western flanks free from menace. A Japanese-Russian non-aggression pact is not unlikely, he said.

"Japan is and always will be opposed to communism," he went on, "but this does not mean that a working agreement cannot be effected.

"Japan has consistently sought only peaceful economic penetration in the Far East. Our sphere of action lies here and we prefer not to send troops and warships to various corners of the Far East to guarantee that penetration.

"The United States consistently has attempted to block Japan. Even during times when the British offered conciliation, American policy has increased in strength."

The Japanese leaders appear to have manoeuvred themselves into a perilous situation that they cannot handle. Their position is made more difficult by the fact that they have propagandized the home public into believing the empire to be invincible and that nothing can check its expansion and ultimate success. ◆

Associated Press bureau in Tokyo. The censor interrupted the conversation, but the Tokyo bureau was able to answer "no" to the question whether the agreement meant that Japan was becoming a belligerent in the European war.]

The representatives of the three nations, in addition to discussing the future course of the war in Europe, also are expected to take up its spreading ramifications in the Far East.

Count Ciano, now en route to Berlin, will return to Rome on Saturday after attaching Italy's signature to the new document, it was said.

SECRECY IS MAINTAINED

For days, since the arrival of Señor Serrano Suñer in Berlin and his talks with Chancellor Hitler and Herr von Ribbentrop, the Nazi press has been saying that Spain is "approaching the hour of great decision" with broad hints that Generalissimo Francisco Franco might be on the verge of entering the war.

Great secrecy was maintained as to the contents of the predicted "historical document," but it was emphasized that the tri-power talks in Berlin today would be of unquestioned far-reaching importance.

The newspaper Nachtausgabe jeered at London's comment on the continuation of the Italo-German talks in Rome last week, saying "it always has been the method of British politics to proclaim impending great actions by the enemy and then claim a victory when they didn't occur."

The general attack "against the entire way of living forced upon the world by the British Empire" is occurring at the same time that the Axis statesmen are working out "a new European and African order," the news paper continued.

"London knows very well that this new order does not involve a copy of British imperialistic methods of the past century, but a general plan reaching far into the future of European humanity in which we aim not only at the possession of some territories or gold and sources of supply, but at the securing of Germany's and Italy's positions of domination in a fully and newly ordered healthy Europe." ◆

Chapter 5

"HITLER WILL DECIDE LAW OF NEW EUROPE"

October–December 1940

The last months of 1940 saw the war opening out from the British-German aerial struggle that ended the threat of invasion. Unwilling to play second fiddle to Hitler in Europe, Benito Mussolini determined to take advantage of Britain's preoccupation with the bombing to launch his own campaigns in the Mediterranean theater. A large Italian army under Marshal Rodolfo Graziani crossed the Egyptian border and menaced the Suez Canal. Then on October 28 Italy launched an unprovoked invasion of Greece. The Times reported two days later that the Greeks had halted the offensive. By late November they had crossed into Albania and threatened the Italians with defeat. On November 14 British seaplanes attacked the Italian fleet at Taranto, inflicting serious damage. Then in December the British Commonwealth armies in Egypt launched a major operation codenamed "Compass" against the Italians, routing them completely and netting 130,000 prisoners. In this distant theater there was at last the whiff of an Allied victory.

The reality for Britain was nevertheless the Blitz, which continued night after night through the last months of the year. Most of the time London was the target, but in November and December the German bombers turned against provincial towns as well. In October The Times ran an article on life in wartime Europe reflected in a number of letters, including one from an Englishwoman on the "Bombing of a Family," who claimed that her household had become more optimistic about the war despite being bombed out twice. Raymond Daniell, in the Times's London Bureau, found that people really did get used to the bombing. He too was bombed out of his apartment and transferred The Times operation to the Savoy Hotel. After some weeks running to shelters, he experienced a "bomb-fright cure" and from then on slept in his bed regardless of the bombing all around him. In his wartime memoir of the Blitz, he recalled that ruthless bombing was not "as bad in reality as it is in anticipation." There was, he observed, no sign of panic among London's civilian population. The Times reporting on the bombing faded away during October and November to be overtaken by other news, except for the devastating attack on Coventry on November 14, which captured the popular imagination in Britain and the United States as much as the bombing of the capital.

At the top of the domestic agenda was Roosevelt's reelection on November 8 for an unprecedented third term, which The Times had not been enthusiastic about. Roosevelt was now pushing for large-scale American rearmament: "Vast Arms Output Seen for '41" was the headline a month before the election. Ten days after Roosevelt's return to the White House the first American draftees entered the Army and a few weeks later the redoubtable Admiral Ernest King was appointed commander of the U.S. Atlantic Fleet, a sure sign that greater American involvement in the Atlantic submarine war was now more than just a possibility. On December 29 Roosevelt broadcast his famous fireside chat in which he committed the United States to become "the arsenal of democracy," a prelude to the plan to introduce legislation for what was called "Lease-Lend," a program to supply the countries fighting the Axis powers with the goods and materials they needed. If Americans had to be reminded of the enemy they faced, news arrived in December about the creation of the Warsaw Ghetto, where the Jewish population of the city was walled up in an area in which they were forced to work and live with little contact with the outside world. The report was only a glimpse of the harsh reality now facing the large Jewish population living in the German-occupied area of Poland, most of whom would be killed over the following three years.

BRITAIN TO REOPEN BURMA-CHINA ROAD

LONDON, Oct. 3 (UP)—Prime Minister Winston Churchill received the Chinese Ambassador, Quo Tai-chi, tonight at 10 Downing Street and was believed to have informed him of Britain's intention to reopen the Burma road Oct. 17.

It was believed they also might have discussed the question of further British financial and economic assistance to China.

The decision to open the Burma road, following Japan's military alliance with Germany and Italy, was reported to have been made after a thorough exchange of views with Washington.

AGREEMENT EXPIRING

A three-month Anglo-Japanese agreement under which the Burma road was closed to all military supplies to China will expire on Oct. 17. The agreement was made on the understanding that during the three months Japan would seek a peace with China. Instead, Japan formed an alliance with Britain's enemies, and her armed forces penetrated French Indo-China to cut off supplies to the Chinese through Yunnan Province.

Now, as a gesture of friendship and to compensate China for the oil of which she was deprived while the Burma road has been closed, it was believed that the British Government intended to supply oil to China from Burma on credit.

Yesterday it was forecast here that as a consequence of the Axis-Japanese alliance, Britain henceforth would treat China more as an ally and provide Generalissimo Chiang Kai-shek with war supplies over the Burma road with much-needed credits. ◆

Editorial
REUNION ON THE BRENNER

The communiqué assures us that it was a "cordial reunion" between the dictators on the Brenner yesterday. But as Hitler and Mussolini examined their present position and looked into the future, they also confronted a stubborn fact which neither of them could have guessed when they last met in Munich in the early Summer. This is the fact of British survival, a fact that still compels them to meet in an armored train with anti-aircraft guns cocked on the roof against possible raiders. Great Britain still stands in their path, her naval power intact, her air force growing in strength and deadly skill, her people withstanding the most fiendish assaults that the Nazi mind has been able to contrive. The Axis time-table called for complete victory before Winter; the new time-table must be adjusted to the prospect of a long war.

This, in itself, is enough to have made the talk on the Brenner less pleasant than a mere Kaffeeklatsch between old friends. These dictators do not usually meet unless they have troublesome problems to solve. In this case it can be assumed that they tried to coordinate their future plans, but each possible move has its drawbacks for one partner or the other. A great German drive into the Balkans, with the Iraq oil fields as its glittering prize, would cut into an Italian sphere of influence in Europe, and it would risk complications with Turkey and perhaps with Russia. A combined Axis drive into Egypt, aimed at the Suez Canal, might expose men and supplies to the guns of the British fleet on the water crossing to Libya; it might also raise the delicate choice between German and Italian leadership in such an enterprise. An attack on Gibraltar through hungry and exhausted Spain would raise an infinity of supply problems, as Serrano Suñer seems to have made clear in Berlin and Rome. A possible attempt to bring France into the Axis might lead to the occupation of all France, but would also run the risk of bringing the French Empire back into the war.

Moreover, the dictators must have known, as they discussed their future plans, that every month of the Winter will throw the material power of the United States into the scales against them. They have already tried, by threats, to put a stop to American help to Great Britain; they may now attempt other tactics, perhaps another "peace" offer, perhaps more active courting of Soviet Russia, to confuse or frighten the American people. Their exact plan of campaign is a military secret; we are only told from Berlin that it will involve "cataclysmic" results for Great Britain. But whatever the Winter plan may be, it will be less important than the fact that the dictators have had to make a Winter plan at all. ◆

Benito Mussolini, Adolf Hitler and Italian Foreign Minister Count Galeazzo Ciano meet at the Brenner Pass.

HOW LONDON PRESS PLAYS WAR NEWS

AGITATION OVER SUBWAY
Tickets May Be Given for Its Use as Shelter, Says Paper Brought by Clipper

The big news in London on Thursday and Friday was the reshuffling of the Churchill Cabinet, which shared interest with a German bomber's raid on a Midlands playground and the machine-gunning of a London mainliner and with the parley of Hitler and Mussolini at the Brenner Pass, according to a batch of the British capital's newspapers that reached here yesterday aboard the British flying boat Clyde.

But Londoners were equally interested in the business of making their daily existence, harried by continual Nazi bombing attacks, more comfortable, the play of minor news items indicated. The Daily Mail featured a story that the police had orders not to open Central London subway stations as air-raid shelters until 7 P.M., except for women and children, to permit homeward-bound commuters to pass through with a minimum of discomfort.

TICKETS FOR SUBWAY SHELTER
The Daily Express gave a prominent page-one position to a story reporting that the Home Security Ministry was planning to issue tickets for shelter space in the subways to cope with overcrowding. The Daily Telegraph reported that the Ministry of Food was pushing plans for the opening of coffee stalls and milk bars in the subway stations so that "people sheltering in the Tube stations will soon be able to have hot drinks and snacks during the night and when they get up hungry in the morning."

All the papers made much of Herbert Morrison's appointment to the Home Secretaryship and the Home Security Ministry, and the belief was expressed that it indicated the government had decided on a policy of deep air-raid shelters—a project Mr. Morrison urged before the war—and that this would be Mr. Morrison's first task. The Daily Sketch said that "Mr. Ernest (Get-Things-Done) Bevin"—its identification of the Minister of Labor—was horrified by the darkness of shelters he inspected, and asked "Why on earth haven't they got lights?" and then or-

dered that lighting be provided at once.

The advertisements, too, indicated that Londoners were settling down for a long siege of air bombing, crowding into shelters for as much sleep as the dugouts afford, and then hurrying off to work, bleary-eyed but dogged. Chocolate bars are pushed as the best food "when you've only a minute for a stand-up meal." A petroleum jelly preparation is offered as a means of providing a sound-dimming coating for wads of cotton wool stuffed in the ears—"an air raid sounds much more dangerous than it really is," the ad-

vertiser assures his public.

THAT BLITZKRIEG INSOMNIA
Hot chocolate preparations are advertised for overcoming Blitzkrieg insomnia and digestive pills are suggested "to keep you fit in times like these." Even cologne manufacturers are doing their bit to keep business going as usual on the home front, for, while admitting that "zeal for the job may tend to fade after a long spell of duty," they make the claim that a touch of their products "brings back that feeling of freshness and alertness." ◆

Londoners seek shelter from German bombs in the Underground, 1940.

OCTOBER 6, 1940

EMPIRE AID TO BRITAIN NOW RISING TO A PEAK

From All Around the World Supplies Of Men, Food, Money Are Flowing In to Help Defeat The Dictators

By JAMES MacDONALD
Special Cable to The New York Times.

LONDON, Oct. 5—Behind Great Britain's front line of actual hostilities lies a vast support line that may well prove the final buffer on which John Bull's enemies will dash themselves to pieces.

This support line is not only a military one but, what is more important to Britain, also an economic one. It embraces such tiny colonial cogs as Bermuda and Cyprus and vast wealthy dominions like Canada and Australia. In other words, it is a strong line composed of the British Commonwealth of Nations, the subcontinent of India and colonial possessions all around the globe.

In steadily increasing volume this support line is furnishing men, money and materials with which Britain is keeping her foes at bay. The British family of nations and colonies, numbering millions of people and representing tremendous material resources, is in this war up to the hilt.

KEEPING SEA LANES OPEN

While the British Navy is keeping up the barrier to prevent any and all imports coming by sea to Italy or Germany, it is guarding the sea lanes through which butter, bacon, eggs, wheat, airplanes, soldiers, munitions and money from all parts of the world come streaming to Britain.

From Canada alone Britain is receiving huge quantities of bacon, wheat, flour, barley, salmon and apples. The Dominion Bureau of Statistics estimates, according to London officials, that the current wheat crop will total 561,000,000 bushels—only 5,000,000 below the record harvest of 1928. The oat crop is estimated at 405,000,000 bushels and the barley crop at 110,500,000 bushels. The linseed crop amounts to 3,500,000 bushels. Since early August bacon supplies have been averaging 9,000,000 pounds a week.

On the financial side, war expenditure in Canada during the first year of hostilities exceeded $550,000,000, which included some British but was mostly Canadian outlay for the war effort. During the fiscal year 1940-1941, Canada plans to spend $700,000,000 for war ends.

Total capital expenditure for new munitions plants and equipment planned in Canada by both Canadian and British Governments is $222,600,000. These plants are expected to yield an annual output of munitions valued at $800,000,000.

In Australia plans have been made to send 200,000,000 pounds of wool to the United States for storage under British ownership. Thus far Australia has sent the mother country her total surplus of copper, zinc and tungsten and 56,000,000 bushels of wheat.

WAR SAVINGS GROUPS

Sales of Australian war saving certificates exceed £13,000,000. In addition, Australia has war savings groups numbering 1,250,000 individuals, one-sixth of the population, and Commonwealth Treasury officials estimate the first year's savings all told will exceed £25,000,000.

At Whyalla, South Australia shipping port for iron ore, a great industrial center is being developed.

Seven Australian shipyards are building fifty patrol vessels, each to be

A queue for fish in London during the war.

manned by "Aussies."

New Zealand also is doing her bit. It is expected that by the end of this year she will have sent Britain 120,000 tons of butter and 107,000 tons of cheese compared to 115,000 and 84,000 tons respectively last year.

On Sept. 26 New Zealand authorities announced a war loan of £8,000,000. New Zealand also tightened her belt by forbidding imports of knitting yarn, bicycle tires and tubes and other commodities that her people formerly enjoyed.

South Africa is sending the motherland almost fabulous sums from her gold mines. The Transvaal gold output in August reached a new record, almost 1,200,000 fine ounces. Also Africa is supplying British householders with plenty of eggs. One recent shipment amounted to more than 10,000 cases containing almost 4,000,000 eggs. South Africa's war effort, it is estimated here, will cost at least £46,000,000 by the end of this year.

NEWFOUNDLAND'S EFFORT

The sturdy Newfoundlanders, too, do all they can to strengthen Britain's support trenches. Already they have subscribed a £300,000 war loan. Moreover, they have presented the R.A.F. with two Spitfire fighter planes that cost £5,000 each.

Despite her severe internal political and religious strife, India also is helping Britain in her economic warfare against Germany and Italy. Nearly £20,000,000 has been subscribed since the Indian defense savings movement was launched early in June to assist in strengthening Indian forces. At the same time wealthy Indian potentates have been contributing anywhere up to £75,000 for the purchase of planes for Britain.

So the story goes. Burma, East Africa, Borneo, Mauritius, the Seychelles, Malta, the Bahamas, Barbados, the Leeward and Windward Islands, the Falklands all are contributing to the best of their ability.

But that is not all. There is a purely military side. And since it was foreseen long ago that whether the German campaign would be successful would depend on aerial warfare, probably the most vital phase would be the Empire air training schools.

The more important seats of this grim university for teaching men how to pilot military planes, drop bombs and machine-gun an enemy—always at the risk of a fearsome death—are in Canada, but there are others in Australia, New Zealand and South Africa. At all of them there is reported to be no lack of recruits. ◇

VAST ARMS OUTPUT IN U.S. SEEN FOR '41
General Electric Heads Say Our Might Eventually Will Outstrip the World

While a huge crowd of General Electric employes, visiting the exposition in a body, gave the World's Fair its biggest Saturday and its fifth-best day of the season, the two ranking officials of the company announced yesterday plans for a $50,000,000 expansion program for national defense and predicted that the industrial might of democratic America, once in high gear, will far outstrip the armaments output of the totalitarian countries.

More than 47,000 men, women and children, comprising General Electric employees and members of their families from various plants throughout this section of the country, converged on New York in special trains, buses, autos—and even two chartered steamboats—and poured into the Fair grounds during the morning. Fair officials said it was the largest single exhibitor's group to visit the exposition this season.

With this "head start," the paid attendance at the Fair climbed steadily throughout the afternoon and evening. Shortly after 4 P.M. it passed the mark of 233,864, which had set the previous "best Saturday" record on Sept. 21. The total paid attendance for the day was 280,260.

General Electric's program for expanding its factories to keep up to schedule on its part of the country's national defense program was announced by Charles E. Wilson, president of the company, who said that the $50,000,000 will be spent during the next fifteen months in enlarging plants and purchasing new equipment.

Also present at the press conference at the General Electric exhibit was Philip D. Reed, the 40-year-old chairman of the board of the corporation, who was outspoken in his positiveness that nothing except Germany's defeat would cause the United States to slow down its defense program.

"NOT BUILDING FOR FUN"

Mr. Wilson had just remarked, in answer to a question, that he did not believe the Presidential election results would alter the defense program already under way, when Mr. Reed interjected:

"We aren't building armaments for fun, you know. We're building them to match conditions abroad, and the only thing that would stop it would be the collapse of Germany."

Then he declared that American industry could "enormously exceed" totalitarian output once orders were placed and manufacturers had "tooled up" for production.

"It's not a matter of days or weeks, but of months," he declared in reference to the "tooling up" process. "You won't see anything great this year, but after that the output will be enormous."

Asked to express an opinion on how long he thought it would take for the democracies to catch up with the dictatorships in arms manufactures, Mr. Reed said he thought the balance would begin to turn by the end of 1941.

"I don't mean that things aren't happening now," he said. "But, unfortunately, the last thing that happens is the first thing that the public sees."

Mr. Wilson agreed that "a year from now, it'll be rolling in tremendous magnitude." ◇

Berlin Starts Evacuation of Children Fleeing Raids

Wireless to The New York Times.

BERLIN, Oct. 8—Yesterday and today the first trainloads of children who are being voluntarily evacuated from Berlin left the capital. More than 1,000 are believed to have been shipped off in the first two days, and the movement to localities less frequently bombed will continue for the next few weeks.

More than 550,000 German children have been evacuated from cities within the Reich since the outbreak of the war, to get them out of reach of British bombers. More than 350,000 of them have been sent to private families in smaller communities, in the country or in cities like Dresden, that are rarely attacked. The 200,000 others have been sent to camps, hostels and similar refuges.

Children up to the age of 3 are sent with their mothers. Those from 3 to 10 go to private families. The Hitler Youth Organization cares for those between 10 and 14. ◇

OCTOBER 16, 1940

NEGRO AIR FORCE PLANNED

Special to The New York Times.

WASHINGTON, Oct. 15—Negro aviation units will be established, in the program of Army expansion, as soon as trained personnel can be obtained, it was said at the War Department today.

Training of flying personnel already is under way, with the assistance of the Civil Aeronautics Board, using government equipment. Negro pilots now are training at the Glenville Flying School in Chicago.

The National Youth Administration also is training mechanics and other ground crew personnel.

The decision is to establish Negro aviation units as part of a recently announced policy providing for Negro officers and enlisted men in proportion to their fraction of the country's population—about 9 per cent.

Negro reserve officers will be assigned to colored units officered by Negroes, and when officer candidate schools are opened Negroes will be admitted to them. Regular Army units now officered by whites will receive no Negro officers, however, except medical officers and chaplains. ◈

OCTOBER 28, 1940

DE GAULLE FORMING FREE 'GOVERNMENT'
Proclaims Authority over All Territory in Revolt, Calls Frenchmen to Arms

By JAMES B. RESTON
Special Cable to The New York Times.

LONDON, Oct. 27—In a broadcast proclamation from Leopoldville, in the Belgian Congo, General Charles de Gaulle announced his decision today to appoint a

---

OCTOBER 20, 1940

Life in Wartime Europe As Letters Reveal It

Great Britain

From a letter of a Briton engaged on work of military importance, to his wife in the United States:

Tell them [Americans] we in England are prepared to do all the fighting, but we want all the help they can give us. We are appreciative of what they are doing and what they have done, especially in the way of private collections, but it is more arrangements like the fifty destroyers they are exchanging for naval bases that we want.

Above all let them know that we can "take it" and will continue to "take it" until the time comes when we are strong enough to "give it" to the Nazi swine. Somehow I don't think they will like it a lot, and that this time next year the famous Dr. G. will not be half so cocky as he is now. Nor will the Nazi bunch be so popular after they have tried to invade us and have got it in the neck. I wish they would get on with it, we are all bursting to see them come over so that we can get to grips with them in real earnest. It will be a dreadful business, but we all feel that the sooner it is over the better. It will not be a walk-over for any one, but I think and feel that in the end we will wipe the lot out.

He [Hitler] seems to be spreading his favours fairly evenly, but mostly around London. Actually I don't think the damage he does is worth the trouble he takes, but he certainly makes himself a damned nuisance. It is singularly pathetic to see the damage he has done to the slum property in the East End. As far as the property is concerned, it does not matter a damn as it ought to come down anyway, but as far as the poor devils who are caught in it, it is pathetic.

As I got into London to see the Ministry and other officials the beastly air-raid warnings started and I found that most of my appointments were kept in air-raid shelters belonging to the various offices I had to be at. As I was going from one office to another I thought by the noise that the bombs were not very far away. I found afterward that they were the ones that were dropped on Buckingham Palace—the second lot. I was furious and so was every one. Actually in a way it was a good thing because the East End had most of it up to then and this sort of joined East and West. Now, rich and poor, high and low, men and women, we are all one and we are getting tougher every night.

On Sunday morning Harry and I set off for a game of golf. We were, of course, out of practice, but it was a nice day and we were enjoying ourselves—suddenly I said "Sounds like a hell of a lot of bombers" and sure enough a huge formation of Hun bombers could be seen in waves going over to London, guarded by fighters. We watched them coming toward us with hate in our hearts and hope in our breasts that our fighters would get them in time before they all got to London. Then—oh, joy of joys, came the boys in Hurricanes and Spitfires. How they came, bang into the lot of Germans. God knows how many they were to one, but our boys just crashed in and bust the lot up. It was marvelous. I thought I would go crazy—Harry nearly did.

Then crash, crash, crash, down came the Huns, some bursting in the air, some in flames, and some just flopping down. The Nazi pilots came down in parachutes and we hoped that they would break their necks in the process. Soon all the Huns were chasing back to the coast and we had given up our game. We were too excited to play any more. At the end of the day we heard on the radio that over 180 had been brought down that day. This was the last day the Hun sent over huge formations and I don't blame him. Our lads are too good for his men. What a sight!!!!!

BOMBING OF A HOME
From a cabled message on Sept. 29 by W. F. Leysmith, a London correspondent of The New York Times, whose home in a suburb had been hit by a bomb:

About midnight, when we were all upstairs and in bed, two heavy high-explosive bombs fell simultaneously fore and aft. They blasted away more than three-fourths of our house from front to back, and blew to the four winds our neighbor's house on the park side. Betty and I were precipitated with pieces of roof timbers, walls, fire grates and chimneys into a twenty-foot crater made by a bomb that burst under the cornerstone and blew out both walls.

Annie, our maid, who is 70, was suspended in mid-air on broken joists protruding from the tottering wall of her

Council of Defense for the French Empire.

With a declaration that "a few infamous politicians were delivering up the Empire of France," General de Gaulle, who is visiting in the Congo, issued an order stating:

"As long as the French Government and the representation of the French people do not exist normally and independently of the enemy, the powers formally performed by the Chief of State and by the Council of Ministers will be exercised by the leader of the Free French forces assisted by a Council of Defense."

These new powers, General de Gaulle said, would be enforced in accordance with the laws existing in France on June 23, 1940.

This declaration is of especial interest here because of its manifest assumption that Marshal Henri Philippe Pétain is ready to sell out to Chancellor Hitler. This is an assumption that is not yet accepted by the British Foreign Office.

It is pointed out in Whitehall that the official statement issued after Herr Hitler's meeting with Marshal Pétain merely stated that "an agreement in principle on collaboration was reached." On the basis of this vague declaration the British are not yet ready to believe, as General de Gaulle evidently is, that the Pétain government is ready to bow to Herr Hitler's terms.

British officials are carrying on tonight as if Herr Hitler were just another caller in Marshal Pétain's anteroom. For ex-

ample, they are even abiding by the strictest international etiquette by refusing to release the text of King George's message to Marshal Pétain on the score that since it concerns the head of the French State, Marshal Pétain's reply must be received before the King's message is released.

In other words, the British are not prepared to count their old ally out until France makes a much more specific deal with the Germans. Nobody would be surprised if Vice Premier Pierre Laval made a deal, but government here is still making a distinction between Marshal Pétain and M. Laval, and until M. Pétain signs up specific terms, Prime Minister Churchill is not going to assume that France is lost. ◊

---

bedroom. From this elevated position she coolly directed the rescue squad to where, in the white flashes of the anti-aircraft guns, she had seen Betty's head. Then fractured gas pipes set fire to the wreckage.

The promptness of the fire squad, working while another near-by house was being bombed, saved us from that, and soon they levered Betty out from the iron framework of her bedstead that providentially had been wound around her with the mattress inside.

I was equally fortunate farther down below. I was somersaulted from bed, and went down under a heavy tiled bedroom fire grate that, although it pinned my legs and shoulders, took the shock of the weight of the following cascade of materials.

I am sure that you'd like to know that your friend Peter [the dog] was unscratched. He was sleeping under my bed, but a night search revealed not even a whimper. I found him at dawn sitting on a high pile of wreckage demanding his morning walk.

The traveling clock you gave Betty was blown from her bedside to the bottom of the garden with the glass unbroken and still ticking. Otherwise, almost the only thing we salvaged was the old car. We dug it out of the garage in a drivable condition without a window broken, although the side wall had been lifted from its foundations and the doors at both ends of the garage were blown out.

The hospital reports favorably on Betty. Her body is badly bruised and her leg is crushed, but it isn't broken, as we first feared. I am temporarily hamstrung with about half the surface skin off my lower leg, foot, hand and shoulder, but otherwise I'm all right. ◊

Italian soldiers on the front line in Greece, 1940.

NOVEMBER 1, 1940

DRIVE INTO GREECE REPORTED HALTED
Italian Troops Said to Have Been Repulsed— Albanian Bases Attacked by Air

ATHENS, Oct. 31 (UP)—The Greek Air Force, attacking Italian troop columns and supply bases, tonight was reported to have aided in halting a strong Fascist land and air offensive aimed at the heart of invaded Greece.

The Greek radio announced that an Italian army corps had penetrated Greek territory but met strong resistance and immediately was repulsed. Two Italian companies were so completely routed, it was stated, that they threw away their guns and equipment and fled.

Military quarters said Greek bombers, striking for the first time on the northern mountain front, had dropped bombs on Italian forces trying to push southward on the Ionian coast and inland along the Kalamas Valley toward the fortified town of Yanina.

The outnumbered Greek defenders stiffened their resistance against the invaders.

Italian planes again bombed key Greek ports west of Athens today, including the port of Patras, where 110 ›

men, women and children were killed by bombs a few hours after the outbreak of hostilities on Monday and Naupaktos on the north shore of the Gulf of Corinth.

Frontier reports said the Greeks had halted and thrown back the Italian advance forces in battle at Melissopetra, on the main highway from the Albanian border to Yanina, with the Italians suffering 41 casualties. Other reports said the Italians were exerting strong pressure around the village of Kastanani, several miles south of Konispolis, which is just across the Albanian border.

ITALIANS REPORTED HALTED

The Greek High Command in a communiqué said that strong resistance had halted the Italian advance generally along the border and it was denied that the Italians had seized the Greek highway town of Breznica to open a route across Macedonia to Salonika, as reported in Belgrade.

The Greek defenders were said to be clinging tenaciously to their positions near the border after four days of sporadic fighting.

The High Command said guerrilla bands were operating with the enemy, apparently referring to Albanian and other mountain irregulars.

Unofficial frontier reports today said that an Italian detachment crossed the border early today from Konispolis in Albania and attacked Kastanani but was met by fierce fire that killed eleven Italians and wounded thirty others before the enemy force retreated.

In the push toward Yanina, Italian troops from the Albanian town of Mesarie were said to have advanced along the main road southward but to have been halted by Greek artillery fire when they attempted to cross the Viosa River. After an hour the Italians were reported to have withdrawn, leaving seventeen dead and forty wounded, while the Greeks suffered only four wounded. ◊

Nehru Seized in India for Pacifist Speech

Special Cable to The New York Times.

NEW DELHI, India, Oct. 31—Pandit Jawaharlal Nehru, former president of the Indian Congress party, was arrested near Allahabad this evening after a meeting with Mohandas K. Gandhi.

He was one of two men chosen by Mr. Gandhi to make anti-war speeches as a part of the plan of limited civil disobedience. Vinoba Bhave, the other nominee, was arrested a few days ago after making a series of pacifist speeches in defiance of the government's ban on anti-war activity.

Pandit Nehru was arrested under the Defense of India Rules, charged with delivering an objectionable speech at Gorakhpur recently. ◊

GREEKS THRUST ITALIANS BACK; NOW IN GUN RANGE OF KORITZA; BRITISH AGAIN BOMB NAPLES

By A. C. SEDGWICK
Wireless to The New York Times

ATHENS, Nov. 4—The news from the front is even more favorable today than it was yesterday. Information obtained from an authoritative source indicates that Greek troops not only have held the positions they took yesterday on the heights dominating the town of Koritza, but have advanced further and in diverse directions in this area, which is Albanian territory, occupying at least five more strategic positions in the surrounding mountains.

Koritza, which was bombed today by Greek bombing planes with damage claimed to troop concentrations, fuel depots and army storehouses, soon may be within range of Greek guns.

Throughout last night, working in total darkness lest enemy aircraft spot their activities, the Greeks succeeded in bringing up some heavier artillery—a feat that won the praise of British officers recently arrived.

Major Gen. M. Gambier Parry chief liaison officer, told the writer this evening that he was pleased with the Greek performance generally and spoke enthusiastically of the cooperation he was receiving from the Greek General Staff.

GREEKS' SKILL IN AIR CITED

Despite the tremendous superiority of the Italian air force the pilots of the Greek air force, made up of British, American, Netherland, Polish and Czech planes—some of them "decrepit" —have exhibited skill and daring that has proved fatal to the enemy on several occasions. Thus far, as far as it is possible to compute scores nine Italian planes have been shot down against four Greek planes.

This would appear to be a fictitious exaggeration, but the chances are that it is not, because Greek policy is directed against overoptimistic reports.

While the gains in the vicinity of Koritza might easily be pressed further, it is said here, it is unlikely that such an undertaking is planned in the immediate future, not because of the hazards involved but for the reason that it would be more expedient to continue to play a defensive game until mobilization— which is going on apace—is complete.

At the same time it should be pointed out that Koritza is important not only because the Italians have dressed it up as an important military center, but because of its position with regard to the Balkan peninsula as a whole. Once the Italians are driven out of Koritza their prospective drive on Salonika will suffer a setback. The capture of Koritza, moreover, would be bound to have an effect upon Yugoslav policy, because Italy's other alternative for her Salonika drive suggests the passage of troops through Bitlj [Monastir] Gap.

In the central sector—that is, in the vicinity of Koritza—the Greeks today were believed to have checked all Italian

A 5,000,000 MARGIN
President's Vote is Put at 27,000,000, but Rival's Gain Is Big

By ARTHUR KROCK

Almost complete returns from Tuesday's election in the United States reveal that, in general terms, the answer of about fifty millions of voters to President Roosevelt's request for a third term and a vote of confidence in his foreign policies was as follows:

They gave to the President the electoral votes of 39 States out of 48 over Republican Wendell L. Wilkie, with a total of 468 electoral votes when only 266 were required for his re-election, but a reduction of 55 from his total of 1936.

They retained the Democratic party and the Administration in control of the House of Representatives—the Senate is automatically Democratic until 1942 at the earliest—by adding eight Democratoc seats to increase the present majority of 88 to 96, with one seat still in doubt. ◆

CHAMBERLAIN DIES; BRITAIN MOURNING HER FORMER CHIEF
Death at 5:30 P.M., Saturday, Not Announced to Country Till Sunday Forenoon

By RAYMOND DANIELL
Special Cable to The New York Times.

LONDON, Nov. 10—In a low rambling farmhouse among tall larches in the heart of Hampshire Neville Chamberlain, for-mer Prime Minister, lies dead tonight. The man who thought by trade with the dictators at Munich he could assure "peace in our time" was not permitted to see even the outcome of the war to which he reluctantly committed his country after his efforts at appeasement failed.

The Birmingham business man who was one of the most controversial figures of his time died at 5:30 yesterday afternoon, but it was not until 10:20 this morning that the news of his passing was disclosed to the public. Many dwellers in the straggling cottages near the quiet house where Mr. Chamberlain passed his last days learned of his death through the official announcement in the noon news broadcast from London.

Adjoining the grounds of Heckfield House, within whose camouflaged walls Mr. Chamberlain sank into a coma yesterday with his wife and sisters at his bedside, is the fine old Norman Church of St. Michael. The Vicar, the Rev. H. R. P. Tringham, and the members of the congregation who attended the morning service were as ignorant of what had happened among them as the rest of the country.

PRAYER OFFERED AFTER DEATH

Just before the beginning of his sermon the Vicar suggested a prayer for Mr. Chamberlain, "who is very, very seriously ill."

It was Armistice Sunday and the church was fairly well filled with veterans of the war and soldiers and home guards serving in this one. At vespers, attended by a small number of countryfolk, the Vicar paid a tribute to the memory of the man for whom they had prayed earlier in the day. Mr. Tringham said:

"The first thought that comes to one referring to Mr. Chamberlain is, 'Blessed are the peacemakers, for they shall be called the children of God.' No one could have worked harder for our peace and although it seemed a failure it was a grand failure. The man, because of his ideals and unselfishness, was an inspiration not only to us but also to generations to come and probably what he has done was as great a work as that of people who had easy success."

It is expected the body will be brought to London for a state funeral.

Soon after the announcement of Mr. Chamberlain's death was received in his home city, Birmingham, where he had served as Lord Mayor and where his father and brothers had rendered distinguished civic service, flags on public buildings were lowered to half staff. Some followers in his constituency, Edgbaston, wore mourning brassards.

The Rev. Noel Hutchcroft, head of the Methodist Mission in Birmingham, expressed the feelings of his fellow-citizens when he said:

"His loyalty to his beliefs defied the material danger to which his ideals exposed him. Men of later generations will speak of him not as a man whose policy failed, but as one of invincible spiritual reality." ▶

advances. Reports from the West Epfrus sector, where it appears Italian attacks have had more force than elsewhere, enemy forces advanced until late last night accompanied by all the weapons of a Blitz-krieg—tanks, armored cars and planes.

Then just after midnight, it is asserted, they were checked by a ferocious counter-attack by Greek infantry. This attack, it was learned on the highest authority, was personally order by Premier John Metaxas. The result of this counter-attack was that the invaders' column was brought to a standstill and the infantry following the mechanized units was routed at bayonet's point.

The Italians have retaliated by again hurling death and destruction upon the towns and villages of the nation they meant to conquer within a day or so. Salonika again suffered tremendous losses in civilian life. Yesterday as many as fifty-eight were killed and many more were wounded. Destruction to the property was reported here as very great. How many were killed in today's raid is as yet unknown. Corfu also sustained considerable loss in life and property, but it is said that no military targets were hit. ◆

Mr. Chamberlain's illness began last August when he was Lord Privy Seal. At that time he underwent what his doctors described in a bulletin as "a successful operation for relief of intestinal symptoms of an obstructive nature." Whether the operation was "successful" or not, Mr. Chamberlain, who was 71, never really recovered and on Oct. 3 resigned as Lord Privy Seal. Last Friday his wife disclosed his illness had taken a grave turn.

When Parliament meets again tributes will be paid to the memory of Britain's leader in the early days of the war by men who served under him, including Winston Churchill, his successor as Prime Minister. It has not been decided whether Parliament will adjourn afterward until the following day, but it would not be surprising if the House of Commons decided the best way to respect Mr. Chamberlain's determination to win the war he entered so reluctantly would be to carry on business as usual. ◇

The British Prime Minister Neville Chamberlain leaves No. 10 Downing Street in 1939.

NOVEMBER 14, 1940

BRITAIN'S FLEET STRIKES

By HANSON W. BALDWIN

In the past few days the Italians have commenced to comprehend the meaning of war.

Prime Minister Winston Churchill's statement to the House of Commons yesterday that planes of the Fleet Air Arm—the Royal Navy's own air service—striking at the Italian naval base of Taranto, and light surface units of the Mediterranean fleet operating in the narrow waters of the Strait of Otranto, had dealt the Italian Navy severe blows, filled the Italian cup of woe to overflowing.

Coupled with the announcement that six more ships of the British convoy that was raided in mid-ocean last week by a German man-of-war had safely come to port and that now only eight were missing, yesterday's news was the best for many weeks for Britain, and the worst of the war for Italy.

Italy's part in the war to date, particularly her naval participation, has indeed been an inglorious one. She had lost, up until the most recent British attacks, one light cruiser—the Bartolo-meo Colleoni—six or seven destroyers and torpedo boats and from five to twenty-two submarines.

When Italy entered the war she had six battleships completed or almost completed, two of them powerful new vessels of the Littorio class (35,000 tons, nine 15-inch guns, twelve 6-inch; thirty-two knots speed), and four modernized ships of the 23,622-ton Conte di Cavour class. According to Mr. Churchill's announcement yesterday, one of the two new Littorios, and one of the Cavour class were apparently severely damaged. His announcement stated that it appeared probable a second ship of the Cavour class had been damaged, and two cruisers and two fleet auxiliaries were reported as listing or partially sunk.

The harbor of Taranto, like many European harbors, has a fairly restricted anchorage, which broadens out from a somewhat bottleneck entrance. The Italian fleet apparently was moored in the inner harbor; and torpedoes dropped in the entrance from British torpedo planes, perhaps of the Fairey Swordfish type, would almost certainly hit a ship.

It seems certain that the attack from the skies was aided by surprise and that the raiders put their main faith on torpedoes, rather than upon bombs, and struck at the most vulnerable part of a man-of-war, its underwater hull. Torpedo plane attacks can best be beaten off by defending planes. Anti-aircraft fire is sometimes effective, but ordinarily the torpedo planes come in too low, shielded by a smoke screen, fog, clouds, or in this case by the darkness of night, to permit accurate gunnery. The attacking torpedo planes skim over the water, perhaps twenty-five to fifty feet above the surface. Ships under way at sea can best protect themselves by manoeuvring to avoid the torpedoes dropped from the planes and by deliberately depressing their guns so that their shells will strike the ocean between the attacking planes and their target, thus creating shell splashes many feet high or a "water fence" that may bring down the attacking planes or cause them to veer off. But if the Italian ships were in port, moored bow and stern, as ships usually are in many Mediterranean harbors, they would not have been able to cast off in time to avoid the torpedoes and probably many of their guns could not be brought to bear.

If the measure of the British success is as great as the British claim, they have, indeed achieved a signal victory. The menace of the raider, the submarine, the plane and the mine has not yet been met. But in the Mediterranean the Italian reverses at sea and on land have lightened the load of British trouble. The Italians have not yet shot their bolt, but the British Empire's hour of darkness has been at least temporarily brightened. ◇

NOVEMBER 16, 1940

'REVENGE' BY NAZIS

Industrial City Bombed All Night in 'Reply' to R.A.F. Raid On Munich

By RAYMOND DANIELL
Special Cable to The New York Times.

LONDON, Nov. 15—Daybreak today unveiled scenes of devastation wrought in another night of widespread air raids, but there was nothing to match the bruised and battered face of Coventry, a little Midlands city that was the victim of one of the worst bombardments from the air since the Wright brothers presented wings to mankind.

There the Nazi bombers accomplished what they tried to do to this capital in the early days of the Battle of London, by using as big a force of sky marauders against that compact city of 250,000 as they used against London with its 8,000,000 inhabitants. The tons of bombs they dropped caused at least 1,000 casualties, wrecked countless homes and destroyed the lovely fourteenth-century St. Michael's Cathedral, one of the finest examples of perpendicular architecture left in these islands.

To accomplish the full purpose of the assault, which the Germans said was intended as revenge for the Royal Air Force bombing of Munich while Reichsfuehrer Hitler was speaking there last Friday, Nazi raiders made repeated feints against London to keep the defenders busy while the main body of attackers roared over Midlands industrial centers and concentrated the fury of their bombings on Coventry.

DEBRIS MARKS CATHEDRAL SITE

Visitors to Coventry today found a scene of devastation where the cathedral once stood. The blackened arches and window faces of fretted stone, for all their disfigurement, still retained traces of their stately grace. But blocks of masonry, heavy pieces of church furniture and plaques commemorating the lives of famous men merged in the common dust heaped up between the teetering walls.

Elsewhere in the city other buildings had been severely damaged. Throughout the day business men and shopkeepers salvaged what remained of their possessions by grubbing among shattered timber and piled-up bricks. Some shopkeepers were doing business on the sidewalks. On roads leading away from the city could be seen a pitiful parade of refugees who were trying to reach billets in the countryside before black-out time.

Coventry lies in the very heart of England, almost equidistant, about ninety miles, from four great ports—Liverpool, Bristol, London and Hull. An industrial center specializing in the manufacture of motor cars and cycles, Coventry is an important cog in Britain's war machine.

But it was not Coventry's factories that took the worst punishment from the raiders, but human life, little homes, churches and hospitals—as it has been everywhere in Britain since the Nazis, forced to fly high above barrage balloons and anti-aircraft guns, began their concentrated bombings.

SCENES OF DAMAGE EVERYWHERE

It was impossible today to stroll through many of the streets of the ancient city, where Lady Godiva is said to have made her famous ride, without seeing tragic evidence of the hell loosed from the skies through the night, when bombs crashed at intervals of one or two minutes.

Coventry is now like a city that has been wrecked by an earthquake and swept by fire. Its people looked dazed today as they poked about the ruins of their homes and surveyed the wreckage of the downtown business section, and they laughed bitterly at the chalked mottoes of defiance to Hitler scrawled on pavements and buildings.

Tonight this city was still at grips with the disaster, but the peak of horror had passed. At one place a pitiful group of small children with a small hand pump were squirting water on the flaming gable of their home.

A great corps of physicians and nurses worked throughout the night and day. Many were from near-by towns. At the changing of shifts in the local factories men from the work benches turned rescue workers, relieving the crews that had been on duty through last night and today. Many of the men dropped from exhaustion where their colleagues had fallen under explosions last night.

Firemen reeling with weariness played streams upon the smouldering fires consuming the last bits of timber in the rubble that remained of some of Britain's finest examples of Tudor architecture.

Men and women shuffled along the littered streets, their faces white and pinched, always looking for someone or, with dumb stares, looking for nothing at all.

Four persons, already set down officially as "missing," were found in an air-raid shelter. So shocked were they by the night of pounding concussion from bombs that they refused to come above ground.

They listened mutely to assurances that all was well, but they refused to budge. ◇

St. Michael's Cathedral in Coventry was reduced to rubble by attacking German bombers in 1940.

NOVEMBER 18, 1940

FIRST DRAFTED MEN ENTER ARMY TODAY
Trainees, Mostly Volunteers, Will Be Received in New England And West

WASHINGTON, Nov. 17 (AP)—The Army will get its first drafted men tomorrow, two months and two days after President Roosevelt signed the Selective Service and Training Bill.

War Department officials said that the first group, a small fraction of the 800,000 men to be called by June 30 for a year's military training, would be inducted in New England, at Chicago and at scattered points on the Pacific Coast. Some other corps areas will begin receiving men Tuesday, while in others the draftees will not be called until later.

Draftees will report to induction centers in all six of the New England States. Because of the time difference, they probably will be the first in the nation to enter the Army.

At Chicago, the Army said, its Sixth Corps Area would swear in an even 100 men, the only ones to be called in Illinois this year. On the West Coast the Ninth Corps Area will begin induction of 1,630 men, a task which officials said would take until Friday.

The men in the Ninth Corps Area will be sworn in at Army stations in Sacramento, Los Angeles, San Francisco, Fort Missoula, Mont.; Portland, Ore.; Tacoma and Spokane, Wash.; Boise, Idaho, and either Cheyenne, Wyo., or Salt Lake City.

The Army originally expected to call about 30,000 men by Dec. 1, but officials said that this number had been reduced, largely because of the number of volunteers who had been accepted in the interim.

Draft officials said that almost the entire number of men taken on the first call would be registrants who had volunteered.

71,000 VOLUNTEERS ARE LISTED
A poll of State selective service officials showed, they said, that some 71,000 of the men already classified and found eligible for immediate service had volunteered.

The men called tomorrow will get their first contact with the Army at the induction stations. There they will undergo a second physical examination, in which the Army doctors will check the findings of the examining physicians of the local draft boards.

Those accepted will be fingerprinted, start their service records, get an Army serial number and then swear this oath:

"That I will bear true faith and allegiance to the United States of America; that I will serve them honestly and faithfully against all enemies whomsoever; and that I will obey the orders of the President of the United States and the orders of the officers appointed over me, according to the rules and articles of war."

Then the draftees will be sent to an Army reception center, where they will receive uniforms, be vaccinated and get a short course of basic military training before being assigned to regular units. ◊

NOVEMBER 23, 1940

HITLER WILL DECREE LAW OF 'NEW EUROPE'

Wireless to The New York Times.

MUNICH, Germany, Nov. 22—Opening the Congress of the Academy for German Law in Munich today, the Justice Commissioner, Dr. Hans Frank, the head of this institution, dropped some significant hints as to the future legal structure of the "New Europe" that is being drafted under German leadership by the Axis powers.

He stated that while "the total authority of the Reich's leadership over all parts of the Reich" would be the basis for the "constitutional life of Germany," there would also be a "number" of "neighbor territories such as colonies, commissariats besides the protectorate [Bohemia and Moravia] and the Gouvernement General [Poland] which would belong to the Reich."

The legal relations of these territories to the Reich, he said, would be "clarified" in each case "by decree of the Fuehrer."

He said the war had not interrupted work on the civil code, which would recognize the replacement of individual rights by the rights of all, of class strife by comradeship of the national community, of exploitation of the poor by provision for their needs, of "capitalistic profit and greed by healthy personal development, guided systematically" by the State. ◊

NOVEMBER 26, 1940

GREEKS CLOSING IN
Fall of Second Vital Fascist Center in Albania Near

By A. C. SEDGWICK
By Telephone to The New York Times.

ATHENS, Nov. 25—Greek forces tonight are reported to have captured all important heights in the vicinity of Argyrokastron and to be within sight of the town itself. The fall of Argyrokastron—which is of strategic significance equal to that of Koritza—is expected from hour to hour. One of the few roads from Southern Albania into Greece passes through the city.

Another Greek success in this area will mean that this road may be blocked. All other roads leading into Greece from Albania already have been cut. The Greeks have only to destroy these thoroughfares to hamper seriously any repetition of invasion that the Italians may contemplate.

The Greeks appear to have advanced upon Argyrokastron not only from the west but over the Nemertska Mountains.

Italian troops, already having fled north from Argyrokastron, are reported to have reached Tepeleni. It was thought once—but only for a short while—that the Italians might try to make a stand

NOVEMBER 27, 1940

NOMURA HOLDS U.S., JAPAN NEED PEACE

HULL WELCOMES CHOICE

TOKYO, Nov. 26 (AP)—Admiral Kichisaburo Nomura, who expects to leave for Washington next month as Japan's new Ambassador to the United States, said today there was no issue between Japan and the United States that could not be solved without recourse to war.

"In many ways," the six-foot, 200-pound retired Admiral said in an interview, "the fate of the world hangs on American actions just now. If the United States becomes involved in con-

on a line passing through Tepeleni, Klisura and Frasheri. The Greeks, advancing from another quarter, seem tonight to be already in this vicinity and to have dispersed all possible opposition. British and Greek Air Forces are known to have bombed Tepeleni and troop concentrations near by.

GREEKS REACH TOMOR MOUNTAINS

From Moskopolis, which was taken yesterday, the Italians are in full retreat. They are reliably reported to have reached Protopapa, another town on the left bank of the Devol River, which is about half way between Koritza and Berat.

It was learned tonight that Greek advance guards had reached the foothills of the Tomor Mountain chain.

In the vicinity of Koritza, where mopping up operations continue, it is reliably stated that several thousand gallons of gasoline have been taken. Also, in addition to the enormous booty that fell into Greek hands yesterday, fourteen army trucks will henceforth be at the disposal of the Greek Army.

The Italians, apparently realizing the extent to which the Greeks would profit by the acquisition of war supplies, sent a detachment of soldiers back either to regain these stores or destroy them. But the Greeks shot them out and sent them fleeing.

Northeast of Koritza Greek soldiers, apparently with a minimum of effort, rounded up a large number of prisoners,

horses and mules, machine guns and a considerable number of trucks. This is only a part of the booty captured from the Italians during the last twenty-four hours. It happens to be only in this vicinity that the figures were published.

British Air Force Headquarters in Greece announced tonight that "a very heavy daylight raid was made by R.A.F. bombers yesterday on Durazzo, the only important port on the Albanian coast and which has been continuously damaged by bombardment since the opening of the war against Greece."

DIRECT HITS REPORTED

Direct hits are reported to have been made on shipping in the harbor. Two large bombs hit a 10,000-ton vessel and a smaller ship was set on fire. A large number of bombs, it was said officially, also fell on the quays. The Italians put up a vigorous anti-aircraft defense and also sent up fighter planes. Even so, all British aircraft were said to have returned safely to their bases.

At the same time, according to the R.A.F. announcement, British planes attacked military stores and motor transport columns in the region of Tepeleni, while north of Koritza three separate motor transport and mule columns were thrown into confusion by low flying aircraft.

The Italian columns were on their way to the rescue of the hard-pressed forces north of Koritza. Great havoc was caused, according to the communiqué, which adds that from these operations,

carried out in unfavorable weather, all British planes returned without damage.

At the same time Greek aviation wrought considerable damage on Elbasan and the airdrome at Argyrokastron.

In the Pogradec area Italians appear to be fleeing along the west shore of Lake Ochrida, while some detachments have chosen the mountains in this area as a safer means of retreat. These mountains were described to the writer today by a man familiar with them as being perhaps the wildest and roughest in Albania.

ALBANIANS GIVE GREEKS AID

ATHENS, Nov. 25 (UP)—The Greeks today were reported outflanking and outfighting the Italians in all sectors, but the rugged country of the Devol River canyons presents the toughest obstacles they have faced. It is in this sector that Albanian rebels are said to be giving the Greeks great aid.

The Albanians, comprising the famous Melisoros tribe, are said to be harrying constantly the Italian rear. This tribe, which inhabits the mountain range between the Devol and Shkumbi River valleys, is the largest and most warlike in Albania and never was entirely subdued by the Italians. The tribesmen were said to have brought arms out of hiding for attacks on the retreating Italians.

Athens newspapers reported that an Italian general in Albania had committed suicide. ◊

---

flict either in Europe or in the Pacific, civilization will go up in flames.... There are few—if any—Japanese who want war with the United States. What is important is how to prevent the situation from reaching its worst stage."

The Admiral, who speaks English well and with blunt directness, declared he was neither pessimistic nor optimistic about the possibilities of improving relations between his government and Washington, where he served in World War days as Japanese naval attaché. Those relations, he added, "apparently depend largely on Japan's continental and South Seas policies."

He said he viewed any possible United States embargo upon Japan as dangerous and asserted that "cutting ❯

Secretary of State Cordell Hull with Japanese diplomat Saburo Kurusu (right) and Japanese ambassador Kichisaburo Nomura upon their arrival in Washington for diplomatic talks a few days before the attack on Pearl Harbor.

such a large trade channel might result in abnormal actions here."

"If the United States refuses to sell us oil and other supplies," he said, "we must get them elsewhere."

A conflict between the United States and Japan probably would touch off a "chain of wars" stretching indefinitely into the future, he declared.

"Nations must live side by side," he said. "You can't exterminate a nation. I attended the Versailles conference [at the end of the World War] and saw the Germans apparently crushed to the ground. I never expected another European war—but today there is war.

"Similarly, conflict between the United States and Japan merely would begin a chain of wars. I, personally, know no issue between them impossible of peaceable solution."

Admiral Nomura said Japanese were more concerned with peace in China than any one else. He explained:

"For military reasons blockade and restrictions of business are necessary and business men of all nations suffer. That applies to Japanese traders along with the others. What we want is peace in China, then free and equal trade between China and all the rest of the world.

"When that comes—and it may come soon—the facts will speak for themselves, and this particular problem between Japan and the United States will disappear automatically."

He scoffed at the suggestion that Japan's program of expansion would mean exclusion of American business interests from the Orient.

"In the first place," he said, "it is impossible; and in the second, it is not being considered. Economic facts can't be overridden that way. Japan, China, the East Indies and all Oriental nations must continue free, unrestricted intercourse with other countries. Otherwise they would stagnate. Where would Japan be today had its historic policy of tight seclusion continued?" ◆

NOVEMBER 30, 1940

PESSIMISM ON BRITAIN IS DENIED BY KENNEDY

Envoy Brands as 'Nonsense' Reports On His Views

Joseph P. Kennedy, United States Ambassador to Great Britain, last night described as "nonsense" reports that "I do not expect Britain to win the war" and reiterated his stand against American entry into the conflict.

"What I am concerned with is keeping America out of the war," the Ambassador told The United Press in reply to a request for a restatement of his position. "Every one has known from the beginning that I have been against American entry into the war."

The Ambassador's statement follows:

"I am told that there is some gossip in London to the effect that I am making anti-British statements in this country and that I am even saying that I do not expect the British to win the war.

"This is nonsense.

"I have never made anti-British statements or said—on or off the record—that I do not expect Britain to win the war. I have never made in this country any statement which I did not make to four or five of the members of the British Cabinet before I left London.

"What I am concerned with is keeping America out of the war—but there has never been any secret about that. Everyone has known from the beginning that I have been against American entry into the war.

"I am constantly asked the question, 'Do you think England is going to win or lose the war?' But how can any one know that unless he knows what is the strength of Germany? I don't know what is the strength of Germany.

"I am personally very sorry that such an impression as appears to have been caused should have cropped up in England. If an interview, which was repudiated by me, and a story in a gossip column are going to be sufficient to wipe out the broadcast I made, coupled with my two years and nine months in London, then I begin to wonder if I ever had very much standing in London." ◆

DECEMBER 12, 1940

ADMIRAL KING GETS ATLANTIC COMMAND

Special to The New York Times.

WASHINGTON, Dec. 11—Appointment of Rear Admiral Ernest J. King to command the Atlantic Patrol Force of the Fleet was announced today by the Navy Department. Admiral King, who succeeds Rear Admiral Hayne Ellis, is a member of the General Board. He was formerly chief of the Bureau of Aeronautics and in 1938 and 1939 commanded the aircraft units of the Battle Force of the Fleet.

Admiral King is a native of Ohio and is 62 years of age. He was graduated from the Naval Academy in 1901. The command of the Atlantic Patrol Force is now one of the most important in the Navy, involving as it does the patrol of Atlantic and Gulf waters as well as the command of all aircraft units involved in Atlantic operations. With the establishment of naval air bases in the West Indies, Bermuda and Newfoundland, the command is now the main American defense force operating in the Western Atlantic. ◆

Rear Admiral Ernest J. King.

DECEMBER 12, 1940

ADVANCE ON LIBYA
10,000 of Fascist Force Reported Captured in Egyptian Fighting

By The United Press.

CAIRO, Egypt, Dec. 11—The British forces striking in the Western Desert have captured the Italian base of Sidi Barrani, the major advanced point of the Italian invasion of Egypt, and taken great numbers of prisoners, including three generals, it was announced officially tonight.

[It was reported in London that the British forces had captured at least 10,000 Italian and Libyan soldiers since the start of their desert offensive.]

The victory, after three days of heavy desert fighting and virtual encirclement of the town, which is on the Mediterranean coast, broke the spearhead of the Italians' drive seventy miles across Egyptian soil toward Alexandria and the Suez Canal.

The situation of Italy's divisions around Sidi Barrani is "perilous," because the British forces have drawn an arc of entrapment around the town for a distance of forty-five miles, it was stated.

It was admitted, however, that some of the 30,000 or more Italian troops reported to have been in the area might break through the encirclement, "owing to the extensive area of operations."

CAPTURE OF 6,000 CLAIMED

Before tonight's communiqué reporting the capture of Sidi Barrani—an ancient town where Marshal Rodolfo Graziani's Italian offensive had been stalled for three months—the British Middle East Command had reported the capture of more than 6,000 Italian prisoners.

Sidi Barrani was captured this afternoon, it was announced, and swift British mechanized forces immediately pushed on westward along the coast toward Bagbag, Solum and the Italian Libyan border with "considerable additional captures" of fleeing Italians.

The number of prisoners taken in the capture of Sidi Barrani was not disclosed in tonight's communiqué, but it had been reported earlier today that two divisions of Italian troops, or about 30,000 men, were holding the town and

that a great part of them had been encircled and cut off.

Planes of the Royal Air Force, blasting a path for the taking of the town, were said to have made heavy bombing attacks on Italian troops, camps, supply bases, airdromes and transport columns. Some of the heaviest fighting in the taking of the town was understood to have occurred around the important camp of Maktila, fifteen miles east of Sidi Barrani.

ITALIAN RESISTANCE STRONG

CAIRO, Egypt, Dec. 11 (AP)—The Italian forces put up a stubborn resistance before the British finally took Sidi Barrani today, and late tonight, on a 200-mile-square desert battleground, fighting still was going on between isolated groups, with the Italians holding out desperately.

It was generally believed, however, that with the capture of the base the present phase of operations had been concluded satisfactorily for the British.

South of the town the Fascist camps still holding out were areas of intense struggle. Each is protected by a deep outside trench and by anti-tank defenses behind which, around the whole camp, there is a low but deep wall built of rocks and boulders and mounted with anti-tank, anti-aircraft and machine guns.

These dangerous little nests were being attacked by British infantry under cover of heavy artillery bombardments, with the Royal Air Force supporting British armored columns and violently attacking the Italian rear. ◇

Italian soldiers, defenders of the fort at Bir Acheim, Libya, after their capture by the British.

DECEMBER 12, 1940

THE BATTLE OF THE NILE

In any long view of the war the surprise offensive of the British in Egypt surpasses in significance the continuing successes of the Greeks in Albania. The two battles are closely connected, for it was the valor of the Greeks that revealed the weakness of the Italians and supplied the impetus for the British attack, first on the naval base at Taranto and now on Marshal Graziani's forces, stalled for months at Sidi Barrani on an expedition aimed at the Suez Canal. The British have captured this important advance base and may have cut off two divisions holding a ring of outlying forts. The number of prisoners captured is variously estimated, but it would appear to be large if it includes three generals.

This victory is not in itself momentous. The British in Egypt, though they have been steadily increasing their forces while the Italians marked time, probably because of serious interference with the transport of supplies, are still inferior to the invaders in man power and air power. But in this drive, as in Greece, they are taking the measure of the enemy and discovering that superiority in numbers means little when fighting spirit is lacking and morale is low. All the signs indicate that something is wrong in Italy. Now that the feeble gestures have been countered and turned into defeats, it is clear that the half-hearted war the Italians have been waging reflects not merely the state of public opinion, which has been against the war from the beginning, but deep dissensions within the Government, exacerbated, it seems clear,

---

DECEMBER 13, 1940

Comanches Again Called For Army Code Service

By The Associated Press.

OKLAHOMA CITY, Dec. 12—Oklahoma's Comanche Indians, whose strange tongue not more than 30 white men in the world can fathom, will be ready again to defy decoders as they did in the World War.

A. C. Monahan, director of the Indian Service, had a War Department request to recommend 30 Indians, fluent in their language and able to understand each other, for enlistment to train in Signal Corps work. He chose Comanches, who have no written language.

Professor W. G. Becker of the English department at Cameron Agricultural College, Lawton, and an authority on the tribe, recalled that several Comanches from Southwestern Oklahoma were used for relaying secret messages in the last war, and added:

"One would be at a telephone at the front in communication with another back at headquarters. They would relay orders in their native language. The Germans had tapped the wires, and it must have driven them crazy."

The Army plans to send the Indians to Atlanta for training in Signal Corps work, including telephone and radio transmission. ◈

DECEMBER 15, 1940

NEW WARSAW GHETTO DESCRIBED IN BERLIN
Jews May Leave Walled Area Only with Nazi Permit

Wireless to The New York Times.

BERLIN, Dec. 14—The task of confining all Jewish residents of Warsaw within a ghetto, the boundaries of which have been newly walled for this purpose, now is reported to have been wholly completed. Entrance to and exit from

by strains in the Axis itself.

The British may be expected to take full advantage of this situation. The British people have long been insistent on an "all-out" campaign against the weaker member of the Axis, more irritating to them because Italy is friend turned foe. They have now taken the offensive, and this may turn out to be one of the crucial battles of the war. Italy seems marked out to bear the brunt of the Winter campaign, and reverses abroad and bombing at home may well have effects on the population as unexpected as the prodigious performance of the Greeks. ◇

the ghetto are controlled and allowed only upon presentation of a special permission card. The tram communication system has been changed to provide for complete separation of Jews from others.

The ghetto is administered by a Jew, who is a deputy of the district German chief and at whose disposal a Jewish "force for maintaining order" has been placed. The Jewish leader is responsible to the German chief for the maintenance of order in the ghetto. Public services, the Germans declare, such as hospitals and baths, are at the disposal of Jews within the ghetto.

The feeding of Jews, it is said here, also has been arranged for. Foodstuffs are delivered to the ghetto, where they are distributed to the inhabitants by Jewish retailers. Payment for these foodstuffs, the Germans declare, is made by the Jews through work—by which is probably meant manual labor on building or road projects—and by the manufacture of goods from raw materials delivered to them by the authorities. ◇

Jews in Warsaw were forced to wear identifying Star of David patches.

Chapter 6
"A CALL TO NATION"
January–May 1941

The New Year opened with the news that Winston Churchill had been selected as the "Man of the Year" by Time magazine in 1941. But it was President Roosevelt who dominated Times reporting in the early spring of 1941. On January 6 he told Congress that four freedoms had to be upheld in the world—freedom of speech, freedom of worship, freedom from want and freedom from fear. What Roosevelt sought was popular support for the introduction of Lend-Lease into Congress. There were powerful debates between isolationists and internationalists about how far the United States should go in helping any country at war, but in the end, on March 12, 1941, the House approved the legislation by 317 votes to 71. The Times ran long reports on the sweeping new powers that the president now enjoyed as a result of Lend-Lease, but rather than following the line from the 1930s against increased executive authority, Arthur Sulzberger, The Times publisher, continued to support American internationalism and the drive to rearm.

The course of the war abroad became even more confused as German bombers continued to pound British cities while the British Bomber Command dropped bombs whenever it could on German towns. But unlike coverage of the early Blitz bombing, news of the heavy raids between January and March 1941 faded away, to be replaced by keener interest in the Mediterranean and the Middle East. The British invasion of the Italian Empire in East Africa met scant resistance, while the Italian Army in Libya was pushed back across more than half the country. The crisis for the Italian troops in Greece and North Africa forced Mussolini to ask Hitler for help. On February 12 General Erwin Rommel was sent with the first units of a new German Afrika Korps to Libya and in March he began to push back the overstretched British Commonwealth forces. The German Army also prepared to invade Greece to keep the Italians from being defeated. Efforts were made to get Yugoslavia to join the Tri-Partite Pact as an ally, but no sooner had The Times reported "Belgrade in Axis" than a coup by the Yugoslav Air Force and Army overthrew the government and canceled Yugoslav agreement. Times reporter Ray Brock was in Belgrade and scooped the world in reporting the coup, which he watched from the street. He was at the forefront of the subsequent German invasion too, and by April 11 The Times headline was "Nazis at Belgrade."

The Yugoslav defeat opened the way for a series of disasters for Britain. In March Churchill dispatched an expeditionary force to Greece to help shore up Greek defenses, but by April 28 Greece was overrun by a combined German-Italian force and the British had to evacuate to Crete. On May 20, 1941, German paratroopers commanded by General Kurt Student dropped out of the sky onto British air bases on Crete. Despite heavy losses, the German troops consolidated their position and the British Commonwealth forces once again had to evacuate, leaving 10,000 in German hands. For the Allies at this point, the only bright spots in the war news were the sinking of the German battleship *Bismarck* on May 28, after the British *HMS Hood* had been blown up by a lucky hit from the *Bismarck*'s guns, and the successful suppression of an anti-British rebellion in Iraq. As more of the world succumbed to violence it was clear in the United States that a major crisis was approaching and 85 percent in a Gallup Poll expected to find America in the war at some point, though far fewer wanted it to happen. On May 28 Roosevelt proclaimed "an unlimited national emergency" so he could better assist the British in the Atlantic. "Germany must be defeated," he announced, "whatever effort, including war, might be involved." The Times headlined it "A Call to Nation."

BRITISH CENSOR EXPLAINS

Says Aim Is Simply To Bar Useful Data From Nation's Foes

Special Cable to The New York Times

LONDON, Jan. 1—The man who watches over British cables, telephones, mails and the radio stepped before the microphones last night and told why and how he did it.

He is C.J. Radcliffe, Acting Controller of the Press.

He described the censorship as "the rationing of news." Rationing is unpopular in this country where food is affected and even less popular as far as news is concerned.

Mr. Radcliffe's major point was that there was no intention of hiding ugly facts from the people.

He said the censorship's only aim was to bar information that might help the Nazis. He asserted that if the government permitted the announcement of town names after every bombing "it would enable the enemy to correct errors in navigation and be more accurate the next time." ◊

20-DAY SIEGE ENDS

Commander of Garrison Is Among The Italians Captured at Port

Special Cable to The New York Times.

CAIRO, Egypt, Jan. 5—Bardia, the first big Italian stronghold in Libya, has fallen after the greatest British onslaught of the war thus far—an onslaught in which Australian forces played a conspicuous part and in which the British Army, Navy and Air Force cooperated in simultaneous bombardment of Italian ports, batteries, ammunition depots and air bases.

Within thirty-six hours Australian infantry, fighting in perfect cooperation with the British mechanized units, warships and bombers, smashed the iron defense ring of the strategically important seaport base constructed by the Italians near the Libyan-Egyptian border. The port fell at 1:30 o'clock this afternoon after twenty days of siege.

Earlier in the day it was reported that more than 15,000 prisoners had been captured and that the northern sector of the Bardia defenses had been forced to surrender. The Italian defenders were pushed to a southeastern zone, where mopping-up operations went on. What remained of the Italian garrison of more than 25,000 men surrendered later in the day and the Italian flag was hauled down from the staff over Government House in Bardia. The British were unable to make a complete count of the number of prisoners, saying only that it exceeded 25,000.

BARDIA COMMANDER SEIZED

The British communiqué announcing the capture of Bardia said that the prisoners included General Annibale Bergonzoli, in command of the garrison; another corps commander and four senior generals. All the Italian stores and equipment were seized, it was stated. The British captured or destroyed forty-five light Fascist tanks and five medium tanks.

The Australians were in high spirits as they surged into Bardia, some of them shouting "Boy, what do you think of us now?" and "What time do the pubs shut in Bardia? We mean to get in this evening."

The full force of the British attack was launched against the Bardia garrison at dawn on Friday. A correspondent at the scene wrote that the "decisiveness of the British victory was due to the meticulous preparations made during the preceding weeks."

"Australian patrols had penetrated the defense perimeter night after night and obtained exact details of all anti-tank traps, pillboxes and other defense positions," the correspondent said. "At the zero hour on Friday Australian sappers advanced to cut barbed wire. The Australian infantry followed and kept the Italian first line busy while the sappers coolly blew up the sides of the tank traps, filled them in with earth and smashed a double apron of fencing.

RESISTANCE WAS DESPERATE

"In the initial stage of the offensive the Italians put up a desperate resistance and it was at this stage that the British casualties, slight throughout, occurred. By the end of the first evening the Australian brigades had penetrated the outer ring of defenses to a distance of 3,000 yards on a 12,000-yard front.

"Meanwhile, to the north British mechanized forces had infiltrated the positions for a considerable distance."

Before darkness fell yesterday the Italian troops occupying the northern sector of the Bardia defenses were forced to surrender. ◊

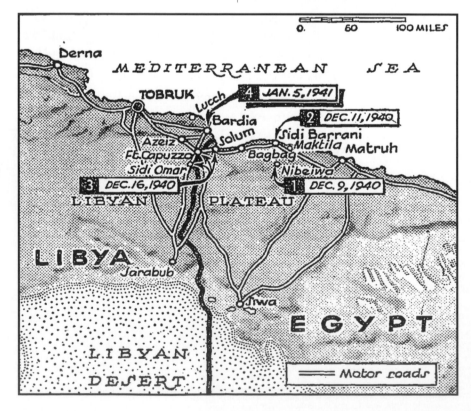

British take port in desert 'Blitzkrieg': Less than a month after the start of the Egyptian-Libyan offensive Australian troops have smashed into Bardia. Shown on the map are the successive stages in the campaign.

Text of Lease-Lend Bill

By The Associated Press.

WASHINGTON, Jan. 10—The text of the measure introduced in Congress today to effect President Roosevelt's plan of lending or leasing military equipment to "democracies" was as follows:

A BILL

To further promote the defense of the United States, and for other purposes.

Be it enacted by the Senate and House of Representatives of the United States of America in Congress assembled, that this act may be cited as "an act to promote the defense of the United States."

SECTION II

As used in this act:

The term "defense article" means:

Any weapon, munition, aircraft, vessel, or boat;

Any machinery, facility, tool, material, or supply necessary for the manufacture, production, processing, repair, servicing, or operation of any article described in this subsection:

Any component material or part of or equipment for any article described in this subsection:

DEFENSE ARTICLES DESCRIBED

Any other commodity or article for defense. Such term "defense article" includes any article described in this subsection: Manufactured or procured pursuant to Section 3 or to which the United States or any foreign government has or hereafter acquires title, possession or control.

The term "defense information" means any plan, specification, design, prototype, or information pertaining to any defense article.

SECTION III

Notwithstanding the provisions of any other law, the President may, from time to time, when he deems it in the interest of national defense, authorize the Secretary of War, the Secretary of the Navy, or the head of any other department or agency of the government:

To manufacture in arsenals, factories and shipyards under their jurisdiction, or otherwise procure, any defense article for the government of any country whose defense the President deems vital to the defense of the United States.

To sell, transfer, exchange, lease, lend, or otherwise dispose of, to any such government any defense article.

To test, inspect, prove, repair, outfit, recondition, or otherwise to place in good working order any defense article for any such government under Paragraph 2 of this subsection.

To communicate to any such government information pertaining to any defense article furnished to such government under the proposed bill.

To release for export any defense article to any such government.

The terms and conditions upon which any such foreign government receives any aid authorized under subsection (A) shall be those which the President deems satisfactory, and the benefit to the United States may be payment or repayment in kind or property, or any other direct or indirect benefit which the President deems satisfactory.

SECTION IV

All contracts or agreements made for the disposition of any defense article or defense information pursuant to Section III shall contain a clause by which the foreign government undertakes that it will not, without the consent of the President, transfer title to or possession of such defense article or defense information by gift, sale, or otherwise, or permit its use by anyone not an officer, employee, or agent of such foreign government.

SECTION V

The Secretary of War, the Secretary of the Navy, or the head of any other department or agency of the government involved shall, when any such defense article or defense information is exported, immediately inform the department or agency designated by the President to administer Section VI of the Act of July 2, 1940 (54 Stat. 714), of the quantities, character, value, terms of disposition and destination of the article and information so exported.

SECTION VI

There is hereby authorized to be appropriated from time to time, out of any money in the Treasury not otherwise appropriated, such amounts as may be necessary to carry out the provisions and accomplish the purpose of this act.

All money and all property which is converted into money received under Section III from any government shall, with the approval of the Director of the Budget, revert to the respective appropriation or appropriations out of which funds were expended with respect to the defense article or defense information for which such consideration is received, and shall be available for expenditure for the purpose for which such expend-ed funds were appropriated by law, during the fiscal year in which such funds are received and the ensuing fiscal year.

SECTION VII

The Secretary of War, the Secretary of the Navy, and the head of the department or agency shall in all contracts or agreements for the disposition of any defense article or defense information fully protect the rights of all citizens of the United States who shall have patent rights in and to any such article or information which is hereby authorized to be disposed of and the payments collected for royalties on such patents shall be paid to the owners and holders of such patents.

SECTION VIII

The Secretaries of War and of the Navy are hereby authorized to purchase or otherwise acquire arms, ammunition and implements of war produced within the jurisdiction of any country to which Section III is applicable, whenever the President deems such purchase or acquisition to be necessary in the interests of the defense of the United States.

SECTION IX

The President may, from time to time, promulgate such rules and regulations as may be necessary and proper to carry out any of the proposals of this act; and he may exercise any power or authority conferred on him by this act through such department, agency or officer as he shall direct. ◇

BEHIND THE SCENES IN EUROPE
William L. Shirer, Correspondent for Radio, Discloses the Obstacles Met in Following the History-Makers

By GEORGE A. MOONEY

"We take you now to Berlin. Come in, Berlin...." Until recently those words were the set patter by which WABC's announcer in New York introduced William L. Shirer, Columbia's correspondent in the German capital. Mr. Shirer, tall, scholarly and somewhat grayer than is usual for one of 30- ⟩

odd years, recently returned here after having "covered" Berlin and Eastern Europe since 1937. The job was not easy.

To listeners, relaxed comfortably in their easy chairs at home, his voice from a nation at war has been but another taken-for-granted bit of radio magic. For them the broadcasts from sources of world events involved only the snapping of a switch. For Mr. Shirer the programs meant working at all hours of the day and night under the combined hardships of censorship, blackouts, air-raids, limited rations and other wartime restrictions. Interviewed here soon after his arrival, he told how it was done.

A CORRESPONDENT'S SCHEDULE
While he was in Berlin his working "day" was patterned on the following schedule, he disclosed. The comments are his own.

10 A.M. Rise. ("Pretty tough if an air raid has kept you up to 6 or 7.")

10:20 A.M. Breakfast.

11 A.M. Read papers, magazines, etc.

12 P.M. Visit persons passing through, from occupied areas and elsewhere; diplomats and government officials.

1 P.M. Attend Foreign Office press conference. ("The information is read out and questions are permitted.")

1:30 P.M. Go to short-wave station about five miles from the center of Berlin. Read German news agency [D. N. B.'s] ticker radio reports. Write script. ("The censors, most of whom learned their English in England or America as professors or business men, are right there in the station and usually I submitted my script page by page. After it was found acceptable an English-speaking checker stood next to me in the studio during the broadcast. Until the occupation of Scandinavia the censors were fairly liberal. It's funny: some days an item would get by, other times it was

killed. You had to keep trying.")

3 P.M. Broadcast. ("On German Summer time that was 8 A.M. in New York. When the broadcast was finished it was too late to get lunch. Berlin restaurants are required to close at 3 on account of limited help and fuel. I would go back to my hotel, where I had a supply of cheese I got from Denmark each week. Then I'd send out for hot water and have tea and a cheese sandwich.")

5 P.M. Attend Propaganda Ministry's press conference in the Theater Salle; prepare for late broadcast, etc.

The Theater Salle, an auditorium decorated in the modernistic manner, was constructed especially for the accommodation of such conferences, Mr. Shirer explained.

VISITS BY GOEBBELS
"It seats about 200 people in very comfortable upholstered chairs, facing the stage where the officials sit. On the stage, as a sort of backdrop, there is a huge illuminated map where the High Command boys used to try to tell us what it was all about. Goebbels himself occasionally dropped in."

Other, lesser officials and military men figuring in the news, Mr. Shirer said, would occupy the stage from time to time, and interviews were often conducted more or less "over the footlights." Occasionally, uncensored newsreels and "nonpolitical" American movies were shown for the enjoyment of the correspondents, he said, for "the Germans did everything possible to keep the correspondents in the best possible humor."

Foreign correspondents in Berlin are classified as "heavy laborers," a device which doubles their food allotment, he continued. At the time he left, he said, the double ration consisted of two pounds of meat each week, a half pound of butter

and four pounds of bread. In addition the Germans established a club for the correspondents where they could get "better food and real, honest-to-goodness coffee."

"The chance to get a cup of real coffee and a juicy steak there WAS a temptation," he added.

For all the official "cooperation," however, Berlin life was scarcely pleasant in any normal sense, and in general the correspondents were required to observe the regulations. During November, December and January it is dark in Berlin by 6 P.M., Mr. Shirer recalled, "and the raiders could be over by 8, which meant you had to stay where you were caught by the sirens."

"It was strictly verboten to circulate in the city during an alarm," he said. "All transportation stopped and if you were in a car you had to leave it at the curb and take shelter. So, although my second broadcast was not until 1:45 A.M.—6:45 P.M. here—I had to be at the station by 8 in the evening and then just sit."

Greater than the inconvenience of time differences were the difficulties encountered in "filing a story" from battle areas. In covering the Battle of Gdynia, in the Polish campaign, Mr. Shirer had his observation post on a hill about two miles from the front.

"But to get on the air," he explained, "I had to go to Danzig, twelve miles away. There a time had to be arranged with New York. I telephoned the people in our office in Berlin and got from them the list of times available. After I'd picked one they reported it to New York over the two-way hook-up. At the appointed minute Berlin got its cue from New York and I started talking when I got the signal from Berlin by phone."

COVERING THE WESTERN FRONT
Covering the campaign in the west was even more difficult, Mr. Shirer said. The only outlet then was a station in Cologne, nearly 200 miles from the front; so "it meant plenty of night driving to make a 4:30 A.M. broadcast."

About the war in general and its effect on the German public Mr. Shirer said the chief effect of the Royal Air Force raids so far has been to cut down the number of hours Berliners may sleep.

"They seem convinced that they will win the war," he said, "and food restrictions have not been severe enough yet to affect morale seriously."

Mr. Shirer said that while it was impossible to know how many Germans listened to foreign radio broadcasts, "certainly some do." ◆

American foreign correspondent William L. Shirer (center) with other reporters in France, June 1940.

NO DOLLARS LEFT
Secretary Says Fate of Democracies Is Now Up to Congress

By HAROLD B. HINTON
Special to The New York Times.

WASHINGTON, Jan. 28—Secretary Morgenthau told the Senate Foreign Relations Committee today that Great Britain, Greece and China could not continue to fight unless Congress passed the pending lease-lend bill. The Secretary made the statement at the morning hearing and amplified it when the committee reconvened after luncheon.

"Lacking a formula by which Great Britain can buy supplies here," Mr. Morgenthau said in a colloquy with Senator Nye, "I think Britain will just have to stop fighting, that's all. I am convinced after having lived with this for several years, wanting to satisfy myself as to the financial necessity.

"I have come to the conclusion they haven't any dollars left and I am convinced, if Congress does not make it possible for them to buy more supplies, they will have to stop fighting."

The reply was given in answer to Senator Nye when he asked why the situation has suddenly become "so urgent as to necessitate this all-out effort on our part." Just before the committee recessed for luncheon, Mr. Nye asked the Secretary of the Treasury if he considered Great Britain a good loan risk.

At that time, Mr. Morgenthau replied that he did consider Great Britain a good risk, not thinking in terms of dollars, but with a view to gaining time for the rearmament program of the United States. For many reasons, which he out-lined at various points, he had asked the British Government to make known its financial position.

SAYS IT IS UP TO CONGRESS
"They are not hysterical about it," he said. "They simply placed the facts before us. If this bill doesn't pass they cannot continue to fight. Congress must weigh very seriously the question whether it wants Great Britain, Greece and China to continue to fight."

Asked by Senator Nye whether the British Government had expressed this view, Mr. Morgenthau replied:

"Not in so many words, but that is the situation."

Mr. Morgenthau said that an expert from the British Treasury was waiting in Lisbon to come here and sell to American investment trusts all American securities held by British subjects.

"England being willing to sell every dollar of properties in the United States, and the American investor being willing to buy, will only enable her to get dollars to pay for what is already ordered," he said. "We have searched every possible corner to see if there are any hidden assets, and we don't know of any." ◊

BRITISH FAST WRECKING ITALY'S AFRICAN EMPIRE

By EDWIN L. JAMES

When Winston Churchill some weeks ago in making an appeal to the Italian people told them the British would chew their African empire to pieces, Rome retorted that it was just a bit of braggadocio propaganda. Now Rome knows more about it.

Soon after Mussolini took what he thought was a cheap ride on Hitler's bandwagon he started Graziani toward the Suez Canal from Libya. The orders were to take over Egypt as a part of the movement to make the Mediterranean really "Mare Nostrum." Now, in a few weeks, the Italians have been driven out of Egypt and back and back until with the capture of Bengazi the British are in control of most of Eastern Libya. Graziani has lost about 120,000 men, most of them prisoners, which is to say about half of his army.

In the British drive which took them from Sidi Barrani the first part of December, and then to Bardia, to Tobruk and to Derna at the end of January and thence on to Bengazi, the Italians were nowhere able to hold even with superior forces. The only real fight put up was at Bardia, where the garrison resisted in order to give the main Italian forces time to retreat westward. Now the British have reached the coast south of Bengazi, cutting off an Italian force of several divisions. It is a major defeat for Mussolini.

THE DRIVE IN ERITREA
In the meanwhile the British have been chewing on the Italian territory to the south of Egypt. A drive has taken them halfway across Eritrea and they are after Massawa and Asmara, supply headquarters for the Italian Army holding Eritrea and what was Ethiopia, which Mussolini conquered in 1936. Haile Sellassie, former Emperor of Ethiopia, has again been recognized by London as the ruler of Ethiopia and his men are harassing the Italians in a savage form of guerrilla warfare.

The Italian forces in Eritrea and Ethiopia are in a peculiarly difficult position. Every bullet they shoot can not be replaced and the same is true for every gallon of gasoline they use. They have no communication with the homeland, since the British control the Suez Canal and the southern approach to the Red Sea, even if Rome could get ships around Africa past the British blockade.

Naturally, the Italians have large supplies in the region, but these supplies have been kept around Asmara, which is now the target of the British push eastward from the Sudan. If the British can reach the supply bases, the Italian forces in Ethiopia will be in a perilous position, with troops advancing north from Kenya and east and south from the Sudan regions, not to mention the activities of Haile Sellassie's men.

IMPORTANCE OF CAMPAIGN
It is frequently said that the British success in Libya is all right but that it does not beat Hitler. In one way that is, of course, quite true. On the other hand if the Italians had succeeded in reaching the Suez Canal, which was their hope, it would have seriously crippled British lines of communication and would have made it much easier for the Axis powers to try to wrest control of the Mediterranean from the British Navy.

The defeat of the Italians in Africa, following their defeat by the Greeks, certainly puts Hitler's Axis partner ❯

on the spot. There must be a difference between an Italy victorious and an Italy defeated, so far as Mussolini's value to Hitler is concerned.

An interesting aspect of the campaign in Libya is the failure of Germany to give efficacious aid to Italy. It is true that German planes bombed British ships one day and made several minor raids from Sicily against Malta. But that is a long way from what may have been imagined possible. Indeed, so far, Hitler's aid to his partner in Africa has been as weak as his aid in Albania. And now it is to be noted that the coming of hot weather in some five weeks casts doubts upon the practicability of the Germans sending a force into Libya or Tripoli capable of aiding successfully the retreating forces of Graziani, even if troop ships could make the trip in the face of the British Navy. While planes could be sent even now, there is room for doubting that a German army could be sent. ◆

FEBRUARY 16, 1941

LEASE-LEND BILL EXTENDS WIDE POWERS OF PRESIDENT

Under the Constitution He Has Control of All Executive Functions Of Government, But More Authority Would Be Added

By DEAN DINWOODEY

WASHINGTON, Feb. 15—Debate in Congress on the bill to aid Britain is revolving about the issue primarily, not of aid to Britain, but of the powers of the President. Upon this issue the Senate

this coming week will continue the debate. The question before the Congress and the country which has evolved relates not so much to the objective of aiding Britain as it does to the means for attaining that objective.

The question is one, like other fundamental issues at various times confronting the nation, that involves the so-called doctrine of separation of powers embodied in the Federal constitution. This time, the discussion pertains to the respective powers of the President and Congress.

TWO MAJOR POWERS

Under the Constitution, the President has two great powers legislation cannot affect, which have a direct relation to the present situation:

To conduct the foreign relations of the United States;

To act as Commander in Chief of the Army and Navy of the United States.

The latter power places in the President the supreme command over all the country's military forces and the sole authority to direct and employ these forces in time of peace and war. This authority of the President, however, is depen-

MARCH 12, 1941

THAI BORDER DEAL CLOSED FORMALLY

Japanese See Victory for 'New Order in Asia'—Vichy Explains Surrender

Wireless to The New York Times.

TOKYO, March 11—Foreign Minister Yosuke Matsuoka today registered what the Japanese call his first diplomatic victory for the "New Order in Greater East Asia" as France and Thailand accepted his adjudication of their frontier quarrel. Simultaneously Mr. Matsuoka announced his immediate departure for Berlin and Rome.

In the background of both events was the passage, seventy-two hours earlier, of the American lease-lend bill. According to Japanese press comments,

this heralds America's appearance on the Pacific stage in the role of a formidable naval, air and military power, collaborating with Britain to obstruct Axis plans for new world orders.

Amid the whirr of movie cameras and the glare of calcium lights, in the presence of press representatives from all parts of the world Japan formally assumed what is called her role as the leader in East Asia when Mr. Matsuoka presided at the final session of the Franco-Thai conference. The affair had been speeded up to allow Mr. Matsuoka to start his European trip, and the document that the delegates initialed was a preliminary protocol, the terms of which will be embodied in a formal treaty drawn up by the three Foreign Offices later.

CEREMONY IN KONOYE'S HOUSE

The ceremony took place in the main hall of the official residence of Premier Prince Fumimaro Konoye, in the presence of the full Japanese, French and Thai delegations. They were grouped

around a horseshoe table, while the heads of the delegations sat at a smaller table in the center.

After being briefly welcomed by Mr. Matsuoka the heads of the delegations affixed their initials. French Ambassador Charles Arsene-Henry and René Robin, head of Indo-China's delegation, signed with pens from France. Mr. Matsuoka and Hajime Matsumiya, Japan's plenipotentiaries, stressed the Oriental note by painting their names with brushes. Prince Varvarn and Thai Minister Phya Aria Sena signed for Thailand with pens.

Besides initialing the boundary agreement the French and Thai delegates exchanged letters with Japan in which Japan guaranteed the settlement now reached, and all the signatories undertook subsequently to enter into an agreement "with respect to the maintenance of peace in Greater East Asia and the establishment and promoting of specially close relations between Japan and Thailand and Japan and Indo-China. Nothing was disclosed today regarding the nature of those prospective agreements. ◆

Edward R. Stettinius, Jr., chairman of the War Resources Board and administrator of the Lease-Lend Bill.

dent upon the exercise by Congress of its complementary constitutional powers "to raise and support armies," and "to provide and maintain a navy."

These powers of the President and the Congress are stated, but not defined by the Constitution. It seems to be gen-erally recognized though, for instance, that his constitutional authority to com-mand the military forces empowers the President, if he sees fit, to provide convoy by the Navy of merchant shipping.

EXCLUSIVE AUTHORITY

The constitutional power of the Presi-dent to conduct foreign relations also is an exclusive power. The Supreme Court has said that the President alone is the constitutional representative of the Unit-ed States with regard to foreign nations. In 1936, in an opinion written by Justice Sutherland, which the administration is utilizing in support of its lease-lend bill, the Supreme Court described this power as a "very delicate, plenary, and exclusive power of the President as the sole organ of the Federal Government in the field of international relations—a power which does not require as a basis for its exercise an act of Congress."

To these primary constitutional pow-ers of the President, the Congress has add-ed many other statutory powers having to do with national defense in an emergency period. Some of these enactments are of long standing; others, the more important ones, are of recent origin. They include, among others, the power to:

Prohibit or curtail exports.

Requisition materials denied export.

Regulate foreign exchange.

Control shipping.

Restrict the business of banks.

Regulate or close broadcasting stations.

Place mandatory orders for materials with any business.

Commandeer any plant refusing to comply with mandatory orders.

Establish priorities for essential ma-terials.

Suspend labor conditions relating to government contracts.

PURPOSE OF AID BILL

These statutory powers which Congress already has enacted that the President may exercise are operative within the United States; they relate to internal, not to external, affairs. Congress, by its enactments has not intruded upon the Constitutional powers of the President to conduct foreign relations and com-mand the military forces; rather, Con-gress has implemented the President's constitutional powers. ◆

MARCH 22, 1941

'JEEP WAGONS' GET TESTS AT FORT DIX
Powell Passes 'Drivers' Clinic' And Finds New Vehicle Does All but 'Climb a Tree'

Special to The New York Times.

Jeeps for use during WWII waiting for shipment at dock in San Francisco, 1941.

FORT DIX, N.J., March 21—Driving one of the Army's new "jeep wagons," Major Gen. Clifford R. Powell, Forty-fourth Di-vision commander, passed the division's "driver's clinic" today with flying colors.

The tests comprise indoor and out-door examinations and are conducted by enlisted personnel of the 119th Quarter-master Regiment, under the supervision of the New Jersey Motor Vehicle Depart-ment and the Pennsylvania State Police.

After driving the "jeep wagon," of-ficially known as a command car, cross-country through muddy fields and up and down steep slopes in gravel pits on the west side of the camp. General Pow-ell said he was convinced that the new vehicles could do everything "except swim or climb a tree."

Considered far more rigid than the examinations for State drivers' licenses, the Army test includes, besides cross-country driving, indoor tests for color blindness, steering with an artificial horizon, headlight glare and coordina-tion. About 30 per cent of the nearly 5,000 auto and truck drivers of the divi-sion have failed to pass the tests. Those with poor coordination or those suffer-ing night blindness are permanently re-jected, but those who fail the road tests receive further training.

More than 3,000 divisional licenses have been issued by Colonel David S. Hill, division quartermaster, to drive any government vehicle. General Powell will also receive one of the cards. ◆

BELGRADE IN AXIS
Joins Three-Power Pact on Pledge No Troops Will Cross Nation

By C. BROOKS PETERS
By Telephone to The New York Times.

BERLIN, March 25—The role Yugoslavia will play in world political and military developments received some clarification today when that country became the fifth European nation, exclusive of the original signatories, formally to adhere to the Tripartite Pact and therewith recognize the validity of the principles of the "new order" for Europe and the world.

In the presence of Reichsfuehrer Hitler in Belvedere Castle in Vienna—where less than four weeks ago Bulgaria also formally joined the Axis powers—Premier Dragisha Cvetkovitch and Foreign Minister Alexander Cincar-Markovitch, as representatives of the Belgrade government, early this afternoon signed a protocol of adherence to the Tripartite Pact. This protocol is identical in content with those signed previously by Hungary, Rumania, Slovakia and Bulgaria.

At the same time, however, the governments of Germany and Italy delivered notes of identical text to the Yugoslav Government informing the latter, first, that the Reich and Italy were determined at all times to respect the sovereignty and territorial integrity of Yugoslavia, and, second, that the Axis powers had agreed not to request from the Yugoslav Government during the war the right to march through or transport troops over Yugoslav territory.

CVETKOVITCH VOICES PEACE AIM

Yugoslavia thus enters the Axis orbit, leaving Greece as the only Southeastern European State that is not an active collaborator of Berlin and Rome, for by signing the pact Yugoslavia obligates herself to "assist with all political, economic and military means" the other signatories in case any one of them is "attacked" by any power not now engaged in the present European war or the Sino-Japanese conflict.

In his speech following the formal signing ceremonies M. Cvetkovitch declared that "the main objective and practically the only objective of Yugoslav foreign policy was and remains: To preserve peace for the Yugoslav people and to strengthen their security."

With this end in view, he continued, Belgrade's efforts had always been directed toward intensifying Yugoslavia's relations with her neighbors. Yugoslavia, he remarked, had always enjoyed the best possible relations with Germany, which had found expression in a number of important events from 1934 to the present.

Whereas Yugoslavia has no demands on others, M. Cvetkovitch continued, interests vital to her existence and progress require that Southeastern Europe be preserved from a new extension of the war and that European economic "cooperation, which prepared the way for European pacification—the only salvation for our European continent and its thousand-year civilization"—be strengthened.

It is only on the basis of "sincere and positive cooperation," the Yugoslav Premier continued, "that Europe will be able to find the basis for its new order, which will be in position to eliminate the old prejudices and artificial moral and material obstacles from which all of us in Europe today are suffering."

In closing his brief address, M. Cvetkovitch declared:

"On this day on which Yugoslavia joins the tripartite pact she is doing so with the intention of assuring her peaceful future in cooperation with Germany, Italy and Japan. In so far as she is contributing her part to the organization of the new Europe, she is fulfilling the highest duty as much to herself as to the European community." ◆

BRITISH GIRLS HERE EXCITED BY BUTTER

SILK IS ALSO THRILLING

New York received an enthusiastic vote of approval yesterday from twenty "convoy-weary" British models, who arrived by ship and by train.

But mystery as ironclad as that which surrounds the next move of the R.A.F. cloaked twenty-four cases of clothing that arrived with three models and three representatives of the British Department of Overseas Trade on the Dutch freight and passenger ship Bodegraven, and represent the latest fashion creations from London.

But for a private preview showing given before the King and Queen in February, the costumes by nine French and English houses in London are not to be exhibited until they arrive in a few weeks in Rio de Janeiro and Buenos Aires. According to William Young and C. J. Roberts of the D.O.T., "this is the first official trade mission to cross the ocean in an attempt to establish London as the heart of the fashion world and this showing is especially for South America."

Vollying light-hearted banter from the moment of their arrival until it was muffled under dryers in a mass recoiffing, hair-do expedition, the young models dismissed the subject of fashions. From brief murmurings of Empire styles and bouffant skirts they turned to talk of buying all the fresh vegetables and silk stockings in sight.

Seventeen who arrived in Grand Central Terminal at 12:45 P.M. came from Halifax, where they landed Monday, were excited over the "grandeur" of the train and terminal and the large portions of butter obtainable in restaurants. "Just about a whole week's ration in one serving," they marveled.

Met soon after their arrival at the station by the three others, the models joked about the long woolen socks many were wearing. The ships were very cold, and besides, silk stockings are not for sale now in England, they explained. They chided each other over "pre-war" dresses they were wearing.

"We're not spending our time buying dresses," several declared.

Asked if modeling was a glamorous and gift-receiving career in London, they replied: "Definitely and unfortunately not." "Anyway, at this point, we'd prefer a string of onions to one of pearls," one of them said.

In their eleven days here they want to see "everything." Skyscrapers were a first "must" for Miss Cynthia A. Maughan, niece of Somerset Maughan. Others said they intended to make a short visit to Washington to see the Lincoln Memorial and the capital. After their trip to South America they will return to England, probably in June. A recent bill in England calls for the conscription of all women over 18, it was explained. ◆

APRIL 4, 1941

BRITISH PUSHING ON FOR ADDIS ABABA

ITALIANS RETREAT RAPIDLY

Morale Is Held Deteriorating Under Air Bombing

Special Cable to The New York Times.

CAIRO, Egypt, April 3—British and Indian forces, rolling rapidly southward from Asmara in Eritrea toward Adowa in Ethiopia today, found many groups of Italians along the road waiting to surrender, and the total of prisoners was increased over the already large figure.

The Italians were badly disorganized and were retreating with little regard for precautions of defense, abandoning quantities of guns and other war materiel to the British.

The state of Italian morale was illustrated by the situation at Asmara after the main Italian force had moved south. Native troops, probably Ethiopians, left the city and began a desert riot that became so dangerous that the police chief and a priest went out to ask the British to enter to protect the white citizens of that city of 100,000, which is the administrative capital of Eritrea.

Some British forces were investigating the situation around Massawa today, but that port and Assab, farther south, were believed here to have been evacuated. An indication of this came from a Royal Air Force report that British planes had bombed and strafed trucks along the road from Assab to Dessye in Ethiopia.

[British troops have already taken 6,000 Italian prisoners in the vicinity of Massawa and the occupation of that city is imminent, the British Broadcasting Corporation said last night in a statement recorded here by the National Broadcasting Company.]

The morale of the Italians retreating south from Asmara was being pushed nearer and nearer to the breaking point by constant British bombing and strafing. "Free French" forces, meanwhile, bombed an Italian encampment on the road between Aksum and Adowa.

RAILROAD TOWN CAPTURED

African advance troops captured the fire and bomb-razed town of Miesso, 180 miles east of Addis Ababa along the Jibuti railroad. The South African Air Force made the place a shambles during the process of blasting Italian trains, and the station was ablaze for days.

The Italians were retreating rapidly. There was some skirmishing, but the Awash River, ninety miles farther west, appears to be the first place where a stand is likely to be made.

Although it is possible that Italian morale will crack and the Fascist forces will disintegrate before Addis Ababa falls, the British are already considering the possibility that the Italians may retreat toward Dessye or Gondar. The latter place, north of Lake Tana, is easy to isolate and difficult to capture because the country is rough and has positions guarded by pillboxes, hidden gun emplacements and other modern defenses.

The British may, however, cut off and surround the Italians before any such move can be completed, and it seems probable that the Italians will fight somewhere in the Addis Ababa region because of the tremendous damage to the vestiges of Italian prestige that the fall of the Ethiopian capital would entail. ◇

The rising tide of British occupation edged farther into East Africa: In the north retreating Fascisti were bombed and strafed south of Asmara (1). British troops marching on Addis Ababa captured Miesso, west of Diredawa (2) and 180 miles from the capital. In Southern Ethiopia another column took Soroppa (3). Shading indicated approximate area held by British.

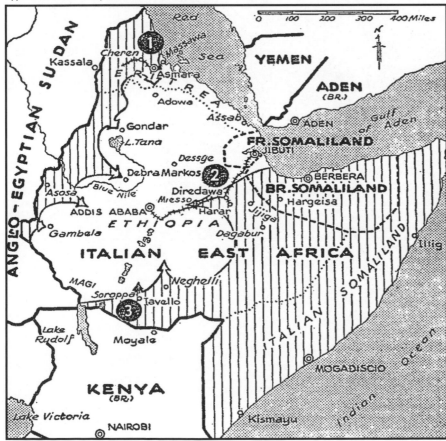

APRIL 6, 1941

YUGOSLAVIA FIGHTS

Belgrade Has Air Raid as Armies Resist

DRIVE FROM BULGARIA

By RAY BROCK
Wireless to The New York Times.

BELGRADE, Yugoslavia, April 6—At 3:25 o'clock this morning the air-raid sirens in Belgrade sounded an alarm. For the Yugoslavs it was the first indication that the nation was at war.

An hour later, at 4:32, two Yugoslav fighter planes appeared over the city, flying in an easterly direction. They came from the Zemun airdrome. Two more fighter planes appeared a short time later.

[At this point wireless connections with Belgrade were cut.] ◇

APRIL 12, 1941

NAZIS AT BELGRADE!
Another Force Occupies Zagreb and Ljubljana— Battle in the South
ITALIANS STOPPED

By DANIEL T. BRIGHAM
By Telephone to The New York Times

BERNE, Switzerland, April 11—Two heavy German columns pushing down the Sava and Drava valleys in Yugoslavia, from the Austro-Italian frontier and down the valley of the Mur from Graz during the last twenty-four hours have succeeded in occupying a line running roughly southeast by east through Ljubljana and Zagreb eastward.

Another column, moving westward, presumably from Virset, at the Rumanian border, have arrived on the outskirts of the devastated city of Belgrade. That this column had effected a junction with the Ljubljana-Zagreb column was denied in reports reaching Berne last night.

In the southeast the situation was reported to be "stationary," with Germans vainly trying to force the Kachanik Pass, where the Bulgarians were held in 1915. In many respects today's lines recall those of that campaign. If the Yugoslavs hold they threaten the German bases for the Tetovo action at Skolpje; if they are trapped the possibilities of resistance in the Kosovopolj Valley toward the flat plains in the north are restricted, to say the least.

ITALIANS DRIVEN BACK

Four attempts by the Italians in Albania to effect a sortie through the Rara Orman heights in an attempt to join the Germans pushing down the Tetovo were driven back with "heavy losses to the attackers."

With the occupation or Zagreb and Belgrade it was understood here the Yugoslav Fourth Army on the west, based at Zagreb, and the First Army on the east, based at Novi Sad, had withdrawn according to plans, moving southward and toward the center from their original position toward a fixed point probably south of Brad and the Sava River. It was reported that those armies withdrew fighting only small rear-guard actions.

The Yugoslav High Command communiqué covering operations up to noon yesterday and dated "Somewhere in Yugoslavia" said "the enemy continued his advances in the valley of the Morava, occupying Paracin and Cuprija.

On the northern front," It said, "the enemy had little success on the Virovltitza sector, where he was halted by the vigilant action of our troops."

"Some activity" on the Italian front in the northwest was reported. "Parachute troops, dropped in different places, were all surrounded and captured," the communiqué said.

After remarking, "No change in the situation in Albania," the communiqué added that "owing to poor weather conditions aerial activity was restricted."

The drive down Morava Valley was being made from Nish, captured yesterday by motorized forces under General Paul von Kleist. Yugoslav military circles pointed out, however, that the Morava Valley was still east of the main defensive positions and that, although the situation was serious, it was not disastrous.

Contact with the Hungarian border was still maintained, as proved by the reports of frequent clashes between frontier guards on both sides of the line yesterday. These actions, it was reported here, were brought about by Hungarian units attempting to advance into Yugoslav territory and, on encountering Yugoslav units, opening fire.

The Yugoslavs reported they returned this fire with heavy machine-guns and "other automatic arms." There were casualties on both sides.

Despite the terrific destruction inflicted upon Belgrade during five German air raids, order was rapidly being restored there yesterday. Communications were being re-established and food and health services restored. By order of General Krsisch, civilian evacuation ceased and refugees, after having spent four days and three nights in fields to avoid aerial bombardment, were returning.

It is reported that neutral diplomatic intervention succeeded in extracting a promise from the Germans that Belgrade would be spared further bombardment. There was no confirmation of this. ◆

Civilians remove rubble after a German armed forces attack on Belgrade, Yugoslavia, 1941.

APRIL 27, 1941

Letters to the Editor
IRAQ DANGER SPOT

MANY FACTORS INDICATE NEED FOR WATCHFULNESS

To the Editor of The New York Times:

While events in Iraq and other Arab States are temporarily overshadowed by the war in the Balkans, there is little doubt that they will assume crucial importance in the next phase of the world struggle between the British Empire and the Axis powers.

The recent coup d'état in Iraq deposed the pro-British government of General Taha al Hashimi and the regency of Prince Abdul Ilah and set up an ultra-nationalist government under the Premiership of Rashid Ali al Gailani, Sunni Moslem religious leader, revered by millions of Sunnis in Iraq, Persia and India. He has been in and out of the Iraqi Cabinet several times in the past, and while dispatches describe him as a friend of the Axis powers the truth of the matter is that he is pro-nationalist and anti-foreign.

German emissaries headed by the astute Franz von Papen, in Ankara, with the active collaboration of the shrewd Grubba, German Consul General in Baghdad, are undoubtedly leaving no stone unturned to win the Iraqis, but there are deeper rooted factors than a mere tug-of-war for Arab friendship. It is absurd to assume that the warrior-like Iraqis would willingly and voluntarily give up their hard-won independence and exchange the satisfactory Anglo-Iraq treaty for Axis domination.

OIL THE BIG ISSUE

First among these factors is the battle for oil and the long cherished German ambition of a Berlin-to-Baghdad route first promulgated by the ex-Kaiser upon his visit to the tomb of Saladin in Damascus at the turn of the century. The Mosul fields supply about four million tons of crude oil annually. The concession for this coveted prize is held by an Anglo-Dutch American company which pays a royalty to the Iraq Government, but it is possible, though purely conjectural, that a more liberal partnership may have been offered by Nazi agents in the event of a British defeat. Other oil wells are located in Bahrein along the Persian Gulf, and control of the Persian Gulf opens the pathway to India.

It may be a mere coincidence that the coup in Iraq took place soon after the Arab conference convoked by Ibn Saud at Ryadh last March. But shortly after this conference the nationalist agitation in Syria was resumed, and it is possible that both these events are parts of the Arab program for the complete independence of all Arab States and the creation of a United States of Arabia.

F. I. Shatara.
Brooklyn, April 23, 1941. ◊

APRIL 28, 1941

GREECE 14th STATE FALLING TO REICH
Nazis' Occupation Of Athens Brings 152,000,000 Of Other Peoples Under Germany

With the occupation of Athens yesterday the fourteenth nation to come under the domination of Germany in a little more than three years fell to Adolf Hitler. He has now become master of 767,305 square miles of "Lebensraum," or more than three times the 182,471 square miles that compose the German Reich. The lands under German domination contain a population of 152,028,036, or nearly twice the 79,375,281 population of Germany.

All but three of the nations were conquered by armed invasions and the three, Hungary, Rumania and Bulgaria, capitulated to "diplomatic control," as German armed forces massed at their borders.

The following is a timetable of the German military and diplomatic conquests:

1938

Austria—34,064 square miles, population 8,009,014. Absorbed into Germany by invasion in March.

Sudentenland of Czecho-Slovakia—Occupied by Germany after the Munich Pact, October.

1939

Czecho-Slovakia—44,500 square miles, population 13,000,000, including the Sudetenland. Occupied in March, with Bohemia and Moravia organized as a Protectorate of Germany.

Poland—74,254 square miles, population 22,400,000. Invaded and conquered, September, as Britain and France declared war on Germany. Eastern Poland, about 78,000 square miles with a population of 12,775,000, was occupied by Soviet Russia.

1940

Denmark—16,575 square miles, population 3,800,000. Occupied in April.

Norway—124,556 square miles, population 3,000,000. Invaded in April, conquest completed in June.

Luxembourg—999 square miles, population 300,000. Occupied in May.

The Netherlands—12,000 square miles, population 8,728,569. Occupied in May.

Belgium—11,775 square miles, population 8,386,553. Invaded and conquered in May.

France—127,000 square miles, population 27,900,000. Invaded in May, conquered in June. (The figures are for the area occupied by German forces.)

Hungary—59,830 square miles, population 13,507,000. German troops sent to the country under an arrangement for diplomatic control, November.

Rumania—72,425 square miles, population 14,100,000. Occupied by troops for diplomatic control, November.

1941

Bulgaria—42,808 square miles, population 6,500,000. Occupied by troops for diplomatic and military control, March.

Yugoslavia—95,558 square miles, population 16,200,000. Invaded and conquered, April.

Greece—50,257 square miles, population 7,196,900. Invaded and conquered, April. ◊

MAY 1, 1941

RUSSIA REPORTED BOLSTERING LINES

Said to Be Increasing Forces in Ukraine, Poland and Estonia Against Reich

By DANIEL T. BRIGHAM
By Telephone to The New York Times.

BERNE, Switzerland, April 30—Threatened in the south with the closing of the Dardanelles, because of a vacillating Turkey, and in the north by the reported recent arrival of a German armored division at Abo, in Finland, Russia was reported here today to be taking extensive steps for the immediate bolstering of already strong Soviet forces in the Ukraine, Poland and Estonia in preparation for a worsening of Russian-German relations in the near future, which, it is said, might even lead to war.

These measures are understood to include the rushing of another twenty-five Russian divisions to join the reported forty already strung along the Dniester and Pruth Rivers from Lwow to Odessa. In the same region the Russians recently amassed so much aviation material that it was reported a

German inquiry was made in Moscow to ascertain the reason. The inquirer was informed that between 600 and 700 first-line bombers and a considerable number of pursuit ships were there for the purpose of "spraying the wheat crops this Spring."

In Estonia it is understood no attempts are being made to conceal the defensive preparations of Russian long-range artillery on the southern shores of the Gulf of Finland. With approximately twenty divisions in the neighborhood, the Russian High Command is understood to be moving another fifteen to twenty to protect its newly acquired territories of Latvia, Estonia and Lithuania.

REPORTED JOINING RUSSIANS

Meanwhile in the seized Polish territory the Russians are understood to have won over "a considerable number" of the conquered Poles in Russian-occupied territory, who are reported to have joined Russian ranks in the hopes of getting revenge for the German assault on their territory—freely promised by local Russian commanders.

The fact that most of these Russian reinforcements consist of strong regiments drawn from the Far East has led to speculation in diplomatic quarters here as to the exact extent of the "published" Russo-Japanese pact of mutual friendship and non-aggression. Most quarters here feel that it provided a welcome escape for the Japanese Government, whose Foreign Minister, during his stay in Europe, witnessed several Axis rebuffs.

The Russian concentration of the main reinforcements in the south, however, is interpreted here as a measure of

the gravity with which Russia regards the German occupation of the islands of Lemnos and Samothrace following the collapse of Greek resistance. From these positions German forces not only could threaten an intransigent Turkey with aerial attacks but could bottle up any Russian fleet bent on operating in the Mediterranean from the Black Sea.

It further shows the importance that the Russian High Command attaches to the possibility of Germany's re-employing the famous "Hoffman Plan" used so successfully by Generals Hoffman and von Mackensen in 1917 against the Russians. That plan envisaged an enveloping operation of the Russian armies in the Ukraine by simultaneous pushes from the north and south and, only if these operations progressed, a direct frontal attack from the west. The success of these operations resulted in the Treaty of Brest-Litovsk in March, 1918.

Russian apprehension is further heightened by an increasingly acrimonious tone in the Axis press in its references to the Soviet Union. According to one report reaching this capital tonight, several German newspapers and one Italian paper this afternoon, after sarcastically referring to Russia's repeated statements she "wished to preserve Europe from a further extension of the conflict," listed the following five actions on the part of the Moscow government, qualifying each as a deliberate attempt to disturb the "construction of a new order in Europe."

1. Repeated conversations in London between Ivan Maisky, Soviet Ambassador, and Anthony Eden, British Foreign Secretary, which the Axis interprets as indicating a hostile attitude on the part

---

MAY 4, 1941

OUR ARMY TRAINS FOR NEW WARFARE

Military Experts Say Germans Have Made First Change in Basic Methods Since Crecy

By CHARLES HURD

WASHINGTON, May 3—Behind the drilling and marching of the new American Army and the record production of war material, military experts in this country are shaping a force based on the conviction that the German staff has invented the third basic change in

military science to occur since masses of men waded into each other armed with clubs, swords and spears.

The first vital change in warfare occurred in the fourth century A.D., when a horde of wild horsemen rode down the formerly invincible Roman legions.

Their victories, which destroyed the old Roman Empire, started the career of the mounted soldier and laid the foundations for the age of chivalry.

That age lasted for about 1,000 years, until the Battle of Crécy, when an English army of men appeared with powerful longbows and fired arrows that penetrated the armor of the knights and their horses, and thus restored the basic power of war to the man on foot. From the longbow came the development of missiles, ranging from bullets to 2,000-pound shells.

NEW TACTICS

The European conquests of 1940 again took basic striking force from the man on foot, the infantry, and put it in the hands of two types of "mounted" men, acting in unison.

of Moscow, which is held to be desirous of entering into "a closer alliance with Britain."

2. The Russian assurances to Turkey on the eve of the Vienna visit of Dragisha Cvetkovitch and Dr. Alexander Cincar-Markovitch, former Yugoslav Premier and Foreign Minister, respectively, to adhere to the Axis pact. The reported extension of Russian-Turkish exchanges, which Berlin allegedly interprets as directed against herself, further irritates the Axis Powers.

3. The Russian-Yugoslav agreement on non-aggression and mutual friendship, signed in Moscow a bare three hours before the German onslaught against Yugoslavia, was entered into, according to these papers, despite Russian knowledge of the impending German action. It was interpreted as a deliberate and calculated act of "passive hostility."

4. Russia's sharp accusation that Budapest should "be ashamed of itself" for attacking a country with which it had just concluded a non-aggression pact and the subsequent polemics in the world press were, according to the Axis charges, "deliberately engineered to put the worst possible interpretation on a delicate situation."

5. Russia's repeated attempts to keep Bulgaria in line and prevent her from gravitating to "her natural allies, the Axis powers," are not interpreted as the outcome of normal Russian apprehension at German expansion in the Balkans and the Middle East, but as an unwarranted interference in "Germany's sphere of influence." ◊

Careful studies of the German campaigns in the Low Countries and in France last year, and more recently in Cyrenacia and in the Balkans, have revealed the union of tanks and airplanes.

Tanks themselves needed artillery preparation to lay a path of destruction ahead of them. Airplanes can bomb and machine-gun objectives, but these air raids have little value unless places attacked by airplanes can be raided and "mopped up" immediately by forces strong enough to hold them. And infantry cannot keep up with the pace of modern lightning thrusts.

Accordingly, the Germans "married" their aircraft and tanks, relegating infantry to the job of occupation. ◊

MAY 7, 1941

WASHINGTON WARY ON STALIN'S MOVE
Diplomatic Observers Believe It May Mean Opposing Axis or Joining It

Special to The New York Times.

WASHINGTON, May 6—The replacing of Vyacheslaff M. Molotoff as Soviet Premier by Joseph Stalin aroused great interest here. It was considered to be significant, although official experts recognized that in the light of experience the full import might not become known to the outside world for some time.

The State Department had no official confirmation of the change, but the Moscow radio announcement was accepted at its face value. However, the fact that Mr. Molotoff will remain as Foreign

Joseph Stalin in the 1940s.

Commissar, it was believed, robbed the announcement of overshadowing importance, even though that office is subject at all times to the orders of Mr. Stalin.

Diplomatic experts thought the change might mean one of three things:

The merging of the Communist party and the State so that Mr. Stalin can deal with problems as head of the State in a critical time.

The taking over of power by Mr. Stalin in the face of a threatened German attack on the Soviet Union.

The discarding of old policy for a new one of doing what Germany wishes. This presumably could mean joining the Axis.

At least officials were satisfied that the announcement meant the merging of the party with the State for the present. In their opinion that obviously must inevitably weaken the party.

Although there have been rumors of a German attack on the Ukraine, diplomats were inclined to doubt that Reichsfuehrer Hitler intended to launch such an attack.

On the other hand, they weighed more carefully the question as to whether it meant a new policy of more complete friendship between the Soviet Union and Germany, even to the point of Moscow joining the Axis.

Had Mr. Molotoff gone as Foreign Commissar also, this possibility would have been treated very seriously. It was recalled in this connection that when Maxim Litvinoff was ousted as Foreign Commissar there followed the Russo-German pact that precipitated the present war.

While this condition, according to the reports, does not now exist, there have been rumors recently that Russian generals were exerting pressure on Mr. Stalin to adopt a more conciliatory policy toward the Axis. These reports have been without official confirmation. ◊

MAY 7, 1941

INDO-CHINA SIGNS PACT WITH JAPAN

Wireless to The New York Times.

TOKYO, May 6—After four months of negotiations Japan and France today signed two agreements for economic collaboration between Japan and French Indo-China. They are hailed here as another concrete step in the establishment

of a "Greater East Asia Co-Prosperity Sphere" under Japanese leadership.

Signatures were affixed this afternoon in a ceremonious setting by Foreign Minister Yosuke Matsuoka and Hajime Matsumiya, Special Ambassador to Indo-China, for Japan, and by French Ambassador Charles Arsene-Henry and former Governor General René Robin for France and French Indo-China.

The first agreement is a convention regarding residence and navigation, providing reciprocal treatment of nationals as the basis, and most-favored nation

‹ treatment, as the occasion demands, for entry, establishment, acquisition and possession of movable and immovable property, conduct of commerce, manufacture, imposition of taxes and treatment of companies.

In particular, French Indo-China agrees to admit Japanese capital in the development of agriculture, mining and hydraulic concessions. Ships of the two countries are to be treated on an equal footing in principle.

The second agreement, a bulky document that will require months of study before ratification, concerns trade, tariffs and payments.

TARIFF CUTS FOR JAPAN

It provides reciprocal most-favored nation treatment in respect to customs and tariffs, but French Indo-China agrees to admit Japan's principal products either duty free or at reduced minimum duties and to impose only minimum duties on all other Japanese products. In return Japan agrees to give favorable customs treatment to the principal products of Indo-China.

The trade provisions envisage increased mutual trade. French Indo-China will export rice, maize, minerals and other principal products to Japan and will import Japanese textiles, other manufactured articles and miscellaneous products.

Payments are to be made in Japanese yen and Indo-Chinese piastres and will be cleared on a basis of compensation through Japanese and Indo-Chinese banks without the intermediary of foreign currency. French Indo-China agrees to afford a "special favor regarding the payment for Indo-China rice purchased by Japan."

Furthermore, French Indo-China agrees to the admission of Japanese commercial firms into the Federation of Importers and Exporters, which has been one of the principal issues until recently. Indi-China agrees also to the establishment of Japanese schools and the institution of periodic economic conferences to examine general economic questions between the two countries. ◊

MAY 13, 1941

BRITISH ASTOUNDED

Hitler's Deputy Is in Hospital After Bailing Out Of War Plane

By ROBERT P. POST
Special Cable to The New York Times.

LONDON, May 13—Rudolf Hess, deputy leader of the German Nazi party and the third-ranking personage in the German State, parachuted to earth in Scotland on Saturday night and is now a prisoner of war.

That may sound like something from a mystery thriller by Oppenheim. But in sober truth, 10 Downing Street issued a communiqué last night that is prob-

---

MAY 8, 1941

IRAQI SIEGE BROKEN BY BRITISH ASSAULT

By DAVID ANDERSON
Special Cable to The New York Times.

LONDON, May 7—Iraqi troops threatening the British garrison at the airport between Lake Habbania and the Euphrates River were blasted from their strong position in the sandhills yesterday by a sustained Royal Air Force attack with bombs and machine guns, supported by infantry.

The insurgent Iraqi force withdrew in the direction of Feluja on the Baghdad road after suffering heavy losses—estimated by Prime Minister Winston Churchill today at 1,000, including twenty-six officers and 408 men taken prisoner. The Air Ministry disclosed that howitzers were transported by plane from Basra to enable the British force at Habbania to return some of the shelling to which they had been subjected for more than four days.

[Germany is reported to have demanded that Syria permit her troops to pass through in their push toward the Suez Canal. She is also reported to have threatened that they would enter by parachutes if barred at the frontier. The British Press Service in New York said reports from abroad showed that Palestine had "never been so quiet" and branded Axis reports as "fantastic."]

Headquarters of the British Middle East Command at Cairo reported that Imperial troops, bolstered by Iraqi levies, had advanced up a slope of the Habbania escarpment after R.A.F. night patrols had told of finding Iraqi trenches and gun emplacements empty. Aircraft then located Iraqi detachments clustered around the oil pipeline to the East. They were waving white flags.

The motley garrison of Habbania, consisting of regular soldiers, Arabs and airmen, occupied the site from which the forces of Premier Rashid Ali Beg Gailani had menaced them since Friday. The communiqué said it was the Iraqi levies who faced their fellow countrymen remaining on the hilltop and drove them toward the flood waters of the Euphrates.

While this was going on, the Royal Air Force harried the retreating foe by skimming over the disorganized columns and showering high explosives and bullets on them. They were in no mood to offer resistance, for the British planes had kept up a relentless attack the previous night.

BAGHDAD AIRPORT DAMAGED

Moascar Rashid, the airport of Baghdad, was bombed again. One hangar was completely destroyed by fire, a twin-engined aircraft standing on the apron was blown up and others were damaged.

Basra, where the British troops landed from the Persian Gulf, remained quiet throughout the day. Action was reported at Rutbah Wells, a desert air station on the pipeline to Haifa, where the hostile Iraqis surrendered when an R.A.F. patrol appeared at the same time as a small group of British soldiers. The communiqué said "the gate was opened and the troops were allowed to enter. A number of families were rescued and removed to safety."

The Prime Minister left the door open for news of German intervention in Iraq, saying it might happen before the revolt was crushed—"in which case our task will become more difficult." He explained that Britain was not at war with Iraq, being intent rather on speeding the restoration of a "constitutional government and assisting the Iraqis to get rid of their military dictatorship at the earliest possible moment." ◊

ably the strangest and most dramatic document ever to come from the official home of a British Prime Minister.

THE BRITISH STATEMENT

This statement said:

Rudolf Hess, the Deputy Fuehrer of Germany and party leader of the National Socialist party, has landed in Scotland in the following circumstances:

On the night of Saturday, the tenth, a Messerschmitt 110 was reported by our patrols to have crossed the coast of Scotland and to be flying in the direction of Glasgow. Since a Messerschmitt 110 would not have fuel to return to Germany, this report was at first disbelieved.

Later on a Messerschmitt 110 crashed near Glasgow with its guns unloaded. Shortly afterward a German officer who had bailed out was found with his parachute in the neighborhood, suffering from a broken ankle.

He was taken to a hospital in Glasgow, where he at first gave his name as Horn, but later on he declared that he was Rudolf Hess.

He brought with him various photographs of himself at different ages, apparently in order to establish his identity.

These photographs were deemed to be photographs of Hess by several people who knew him personally. Accordingly, an officer of the Foreign Office closely acquainted with Hess before the war has been sent up by airplane to see him in the hospital.

IDENTIFIED BY OFFICIAL

Ivone A. Kirkpatrick, who used to be first secretary in the British Embassy in Berlin, was the official sent to Scotland, and the Ministry of Information an-

nounced early this morning that Herr Hess's identification had been definitely established.

Earlier the Germans had announced that Herr Hess, who was outranked only by Reichsfuehrer Hitler and Reich Marshal Hermann Goering in the Nazi hierarchy, had been suffering from hallucinations and had violated Herr Hitler's orders in taking the plane.

It was just before nightfall Saturday that Herr Hess was found by a Scottish farm worker; he was groaning in agony, with his parachute wrapped around him. He was taken first to a little two-roomed cottage and then was turned over to the military authorities. This morning he was in a military hospital somewhere near Glasgow.

That is the bare outline of the facts as they are known so far. What do they mean? The Germans have already announced that Herr Hess's "adjutants" have been arrested. The British are inclined to believe that there may be another purge in Germany—a purge similar to the one following the arrest of Captain Ernst Roehm, who was also one of Herr Hitler's closest collaborators, on June 30, 1934.

But from this distance it is almost impossible to say what this development means as far as Germany is concerned. One can record only what the British believe it means. One Briton told the writer that "this is the first 'break' we have had since the war started."

The British are not inclined to believe the German contention that Herr Hess was unbalanced. They assert that it is impossible to fly a Messerschmitt fighter adequately if one is suffering

from "mental disorder." Furthermore, the British emphasize, there is the fact that Herr Hess had with him photographs to establish his identity. That, it is insisted here, is clear proof that Herr Hess was in his right mind.

POSSIBILITY OF ROW

It is possible, of course, that Herr Hess had been in some sort of row with other leaders of the Nazi party and got out while the getting-out was good. It is also possible that Herr Hess, a fanatical Nazi, found that there was some sort of "monkey business" going on that he could not stomach.

In either case, the British would appear to have caught a prize of untold worth. If Herr Hess is sane and really fled from Germany, he can be an intelligence officer's dream. The information he could give, if he were willing to give it, would be invaluable. Since he apparently set a course straight for Britain it would not appear that he is unwilling to help the British.

There is one other consideration that the British are thinking about. For months—indeed, ever since the war started—many British officials have been basing hopes for a final victory on a crack-up in Germany. Others have believed that a crack-up would not come until Germany had been hit so hard that the Reich would crack under the force of the blow.

In view of the Hess development, one British problem will be to choke off those persons who will interpret this dime-novel occurrence as indicating that Germany is cracking. Of course, these persons may be right. But British leaders know that they must not make any such assumption.

From the British point of view it is still a long, hard war. It is not likely that Prime Minister Winston Churchill or anybody else will succumb to an overoptimistic interpretation of this development. ◇

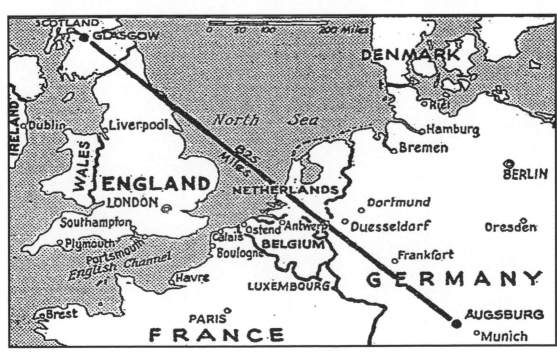

Rudolf Hess's starting point—Augsburg—was disclosed by Berlin; his point of arrival—Glasgow—was disclosed by London. The flying distance between the two places is 825 miles.

MAY 13, 1941

HESS ACTED SANELY, PSYCHIATRIST NOTES
Flight Called for Calm Plan, Dr. Overholser Remarks

WASHINGTON, May 12 (AP)—One of the country's leading psychiatrists said today that Rudolf Hess, Adolf Hitler's second lieutenant who landed from a Messerschmitt plane in Scotland on Saturday, was probably "much more sane than crazy."

Dr. Winfred Overholser, head of St. Elizabeth's Hospital, the Federal Government's principal institution for the insane, said that while it was possible that Herr Hess "got the jitters and thought the world was coming to an end," he probably did a cool, sane job of calculation and estimated his chances were better in being interned in Britain than they were in staying in Germany.

Even if the man were insane he still could pilot an airplane, the psychiatrist said, "but it is much more reasonable to think that he was in full possession to his faculties and merely wished to escape" from some situation that he considered no longer tenable for him.

Such an escape by a man who had been discouraged from flying by Herr Hitler himself would indicate calm deliberation and planning well in advance, which a man with a very unbalanced mind would be hardly capable of carrying out, Dr. Overholser said. ◇

MAY 16, 1941

5,000 PARIS JEWS GO TO LABOR CAMPS
Refugees Routed from Beds And Interned— Vichy Denies Order Originated There

Wireless to The New York Times.

VICHY, France, May 15—Reports from Paris tell of the rounding up there of 5,000 Jews between the ages of 18 and 40, mostly from Central and Southeastern Europe, and their transfer to labor camps near Orleans.

The reports indicate that this action has been taken "under the law of Oct. 4, 1940," which must be an error. The law affecting Jews is dated Oct. 3 and contains no reference to their conscription for labor. However, there is a law that enables the authorities to enroll destitute and unemployed aliens in labor companies without distinction as to race or origin.

In government circles here it was declared that the measures of internment in the occupied zone were not ordered by this government.

[The British radio quoted German controlled sources as saying that Vichy authorities had arrested 20,000 foreign Jews in unoccupied France. The British report, attributed to the Hilversum radio in the Netherlands, was heard here by the Columbia Broadcasting System.]

FURTHER LAWS EXPECTED

Further measures relative to the status of Jews in France are expected in the near future. If it had not been for the importance of the present phase of French-German relations, it is probable that the Cabinet would already have approved a draft that came under the consideration of several Ministers last week when both Marshal Henri Phillipe Pétain and the Vice Premier, Admiral François Darlan, were absent from Vichy.

It is understood the new measures are intended to complete the law of Oct. 3, which excluded Jews from high government posts, including the armed forces, as well as from journalism and the cinema.

It is declared in authorized circles that the intention now is to complete, enlarge and codify all the steps already taken concerning Jews, not because of ideological or religious considerations but because of "necessities of national protection." Present indications are that most of the Jews in France will be subjected to the laws regulating the presence of aliens on national soil.

Several exemptions are likely to be included in the new law in favor of Jews who fought for France in the last two wars, those converted to a Christian faith before June 20, 1940, and those who have rendered signal service to the country or whose forebears have long lived here.

It may be recalled that at present the treatment of Jews differs in the occupied and unoccupied zones. In the former the German authority has issued ordinances on the lines of the Nuremberg "ghetto laws." The latest of these comes into application on May 20; in brief, it excludes Jews from all commercial activities without compensation. ◇

Jews at the Austerlitz station in Paris departing for an internment camp in Orleans, France, May 1941.

BRITISH PUSH RAIDS ON NAZIS IN SYRIA
Report German Planes Ruined— Iraqis Claim Gains in Clashes with Foe

Special Cable to The New York Times.

CAIRO, Egypt, May 19—While General Henri Fernand Dentz, French High Commissioner for Syria and Lebanon, talked belligerently over the radio last night about British intervention in Syria, Royal Air Force planes again were bombing German aircraft on Syrian airdromes.

[French chaser planes shot down their first British bomber over Syria yesterday, according to a German broadcast heard here by the Columbia Broadcasting System.]

A Heinkel-111 and another large plane were burned out as a result of a new raid on the airfield at Tadmur [Palmyra] and German machines at both Damascus and Rayak were damaged by bombing and strafing, according to a British communiqué issued here today. The Iraqi airdrome at Rashid, near Baghdad, also was bombed again.

R.A.F. raids Saturday night started several fires on the Axis airdrome at Calato, on the Island of Rhodes, believed to be used as a stopping place in the transport of planes, men and materiel to Syria and Iraq. ◇

The German battleship *Bismarck* firing on the Royal Navy ship HMS Hood which sank almost immediately.

[In Berlin it was reported that the Hood had been sunk off Iceland during a five-minute engagement between a German flotilla and "heavy English naval forces." The German units suffered no damages "worthy of mention," it was said, and continued their operations.]

SYMBOL OF BRITISH POWER

The news of the Hood's sinking is bound to cast a spell of gloom over the British people, because she was a symbol of British naval power. She was the show ship of the Royal Navy, and the British liked to think that they had the biggest warship afloat.

The Hood was of the same general type as the battle cruisers Queen Mary, Indefatigable and Invincible, which were blown up in the Battle of Jutland, supposedly as a result of insufficient armor over their turret magazines. The Hood, laid down in 1916, was redesigned to meet the lessons of Jutland, but apparently this was not enough.

At any rate, the greatest naval victory of the war since British cruisers bottled up the German pocket battleship Admiral Graf Spee, which was scuttled at Montevideo, Uruguay, must be chalked up for the German Navy.

This is the first time the world has known that the Bismarck, a ship of 35,000 or more tons, is loose on the seas. She was launched on Feb. 14, 1939, with Reichsfuehrer Hitler present. The Bismarck is supposed to have three sister ships, the Tirpitz, launched April 1, 1939, and two others believed to be still under construction. ◇

HOOD IS BLOWN UP
World's Biggest Warship Sunk Between Iceland And Greenland

1,300 FEARED KILLED

By ROBERT P. POST
Special Cable to The New York Times.

LONDON, May 24—The 42,100-ton battle cruiser Hood, pride of the British Fleet and the world's biggest fighting vessel, was blown up today by an "unlucky hit" scored on a munitions magazine by the new German battleship Bismarck in an engagement off Greenland, the Admiralty announced. The Bismarck was damaged.

Apparently the British had had word that the Bismarck, accompanied by other German naval units, was trying to slip into the North Atlantic by the Germans' favorite route—the northern route via Norway, Iceland and Greenland. The British sent a strong force, including the Hood, to intercept the German ships. The two forces clashed and the Hood was sunk.

The Hood carried a normal complement of more than 1,300 men, and the Admiralty said it was feared that there would be few survivors.

"The pursuit of the enemy continues," the Admiralty reported. This statement probably means that the British ships are attempting to intercept and finish off the Bismarck if she is really crippled. Undoubtedly they are maintaining wireless silence, and therefore it remains to be seen whether the Hood will be avenged.

THE HOOD AVENGED

U.S.-MADE PLANE AIDS

Sights Quarry and Puts Big Fleet on Trail— Reich Cruiser Flees

By ROBERT P. POST
Special Cable to The New York Times.

LONDON, May 27—The Bismarck, Germany's newest and finest capital ship, was sunk at 11:01 o'clock this morning [5:01 A.M. New York time] about 400 miles due west of Brest after naval action that had lasted for three and a half days and covered 1,750 miles from Denmark Strait. The British battle cruiser Hood, blown up by an "unlucky" hit from the Bismarck, was thus avenged.

The full account of the action, released by the Admiralty tonight, is a tale not only of gallantry and courage at sea but also of excellent staff work and quick, effective action into which the British threw all the might of their sea and air power, even leaving convoys unprotected and pulling the Western Mediterranean Fleet away from Gibraltar.

The far-ranging British aircraft that worked with the navy really deserve most of the credit for the most successful naval search in history. The plane that found the Bismarck after the pursuing forces had lost contact with her was a United States-built Consolidated flying boat. In the British service this plane is known as a Catalina; it is known as a PBY-5 when it patrols for the United States Navy.

WARSHIPS SEEN AT BERGEN

The story begins with the little-sung Coastal Command of the Royal Air Force. Its patrols, endlessly winging over Norway, discovered the battleship Bismarck and the Prinz Eugen, a new 8-inch-gun cruiser, lying in Bergen harbor some time last week. The Admiralty began at once to throw its net around the North Sea.

The 8-inch-gun British cruisers, Norfolk and Suffolk, the former wearing the flag of Rear Admiral W. F. Wake-Walker, dug out for Denmark Strait, between Iceland and Greenland. The British apparently guessed that the two German ships might go north around Iceland and try to slip down into the Atlantic. Prime Minister Winston Churchill suggested today that their mission was commerce raiding, but another suggestion was that they might have been trying to slip into the Mediterranean to turn the balance of power there.

At any rate the guess as to their immediate move was a good one. Last Friday evening Admiral Wake-Walker flashed to the Admiralty the signal that he had sighted the Bismarck and the Prinz Eugen steaming under forced draft to the southwest. The range was only six miles when the ships were first sighted, but storms, snow, sleet and patches of mist sometimes reduced the visibility to one mile. Nevertheless the two British cruisers swung around and began to shadow the enemy. They successfully kept touch throughout the night.

HOOD GOES TO INTERCEPT

Meanwhile a signal had gone out and the British Fleet began to move. The Hood, largest fighting ship in the world, went steaming to intercept. She was accompanied by the Prince of Wales, one of Britain's newest battleships and a sister ship of the King George V, which took Ambassador Viscount Halifax to his post in the United States.

Early Saturday morning lookouts on the Hood sighted the German squadron. The action began across miles of wallowing water, with big guns blasting at each other. Then German gunnery found one of the Hood's turret magazines and she blew up with heavy casualties. The Prince of Wales, in action for the first time, was damaged slightly. But the Bismarck did not go unscathed. She also was hit, and at one point was seen to be on fire.

But the first round went to the Germans. The Bismarck and Prinz Eugen sped away, still steering to the southwest, and the two British cruisers continued to trail them. The Bismarck apparently had been damaged in the engines, for her speed was reduced. Coastal Command aircraft—they also formed a part of the net that was being flung around the Bismarck—reported that she was spewing oil.

Throughout Saturday the chase continued. By Saturday night the Prince of Wales had made good her damage and caught up with the fleeing Germans again. There was a short action, entirely inconclusive. The German ships turned westward, and the Prince of Wales and the British cruisers swung around to conform. Then the Germans turned southward again. Night fell and the pursued ships drew away.

NEW CARRIER IS SENT OUT

But British forces were converging on the scene, and Fleet Admiral Guenther Luetjens, aboard the Bismarck, must have known that he was trapped and could escape only with exceptional luck. Among the British ships speeding to the battle area was the new aircraft carrier Victorious. Miles away from the Germans she threw her torpedo bombers into the air. One of them hit the Bismarck with an aerial torpedo.

All through Saturday night and early Sunday morning the Norfolk, Suffolk and Prince of Wales continued the pursuit. Their lookouts strained their eyes, but the weather grew worse and the visibility poorer and at 3 o'clock Sunday morning contact was lost. The German ships were then about 350 miles south-southeast of the southern point of Greenland—not so very far from Canadian shores.

It was a bitter moment, both on the bridges of the pursuing ships and in the Admiralty operations room, when it was realized that contact had been lost and that from then on it would be a question of searching the wide seas. Naval officers knew that it might be a long and hard search, with the odds favoring the enemy. But it had to be faced, and the order to take up searching dispositions was flashed out to the fleet.

At the time contact was lost the Bismarck was heading southward. Already the Home Fleet had sailed from the north—probably Scapa Flow—with the commander's flag of Admiral John C. Tovey on the King George V. The Western Mediterranean Fleet—or part of it—with Vice Admiral Sir James F. Somerville's flag on the Renown, a battle cruiser of the Hood class, had weighed anchor and left Gibraltar, steaming northeastward to intercept. Both fleets doubtless were trying to keep between the probable course of the Bismarck and the French and Spanish coasts, where there might be ports to receive her.

BATTLESHIPS LEAVE CONVOYS

Out in the Atlantic the battleships Rodney and Ramillies, which were escorting convoys, turned and raced for the enemy from east and west. So from four directions British ships were closing in on the Bismarck.

British submarines were moving to cover German ports and ports on the French coast, especially Brest, where the damaged Bismarck might possibly take refuge.

But the most important search of all was the one in the air. At the Coastal Command airports rimming Britain's shores all pilots were at action stations. Patrols were doubled and tripled and Sunderlands, Lockheeds and Catalinas thundered over the sea in a wide hunt.

Newfoundland, far away across the Atlantic, felt the excitement. From bases there the Royal Canadian Air Force flew away eastward and took up the patrol of its waters. To these patrols was added a ceaseless search by the Fleet Air Arm planes launched from carriers.

For a while these searches were in vain. Contact with the German ships had been lost at 3 A.M. Sunday, 350 miles south-southeast of Greenland. It was not established again until 10:30 A.M. yesterday, when a Catalina of the Coastal Command, patrolling the waters off England, spotted the Bismarck 550 miles west of Lands End.

The Catalina was immediately attacked, probably by a plane launched by the Bismarck's catapult. The Bismarck, by now, was alone. As a result of the attack, the Catalina, big and clumsy, lost contact again, but not before she had given tongue by wireless to the rest of the pack.

PLANES FROM ARK ROYAL

Luckily the aircraft carrier Ark Royal, apparently with Vice Admiral Somerville's squadron, was somewhere near by. At 11:15 A.M. one of the Ark Royal's flights sighted the Bismarck, which was still alone and steering eastward. It is interesting to note that this contact was made by planes from a carrier that the Germans have reported as sunk many times.

From then on contact was never lost. As soon as he had received the Ark Royal's report, Vice Admiral Somerville

threw the cruiser Sheffield out ahead to shadow the Bismarck. During that afternoon, while the chase continued, the Ark Royal launched an aerial-torpedo attack, but it was unsuccessful.

How the use of air power widens the extent of a modern naval battle is shown by the fact that, while the Ark Royal's planes made contact at 11:15 A.M. yesterday and the Sheffield, which probably was steaming far ahead of the Ark Royal at the time, started her shadowing mission almost at once, it was not until 5:30 in the afternoon that she sighted the Bismarck.

Within twenty minutes after word had been received that the Sheffield was in touch, the Ark Royal launched another squadron of planes. They torpedoed the Bismarck amidships and also on the starboard quarter. It was reported that after this attack the Bismarck made two complete circles and her speed was reduced. The Germans said that one of these torpedoes had smashed the rudder and screws.

All the British forces were now converging on the doomed ship. British destroyers in the pursuit were determined not to let the big ships and the air forces have all the glory, and last night it was their turn.

DESTROYERS SCORE HITS

A squadron of Tribal-class destroyers made contact about 11 o'clock last night. Between 1:20 A.M. and 1:50 A.M. this morning they went in to attack. First the Zulu and then the Cossack and the Maori drove in on the Bismarck. The latter two destroyers scored hits with torpedoes.

After the Maori's attack the Bismarck's forecastle was seen to be afire.

One hour after the attack the shadowers reported that the Bismarck had halted. She then was about 400 miles due west of Brest. Subsequently she started out again, but the trap had clamped shut and she could only crawl away, making only eight miles in one hour. Her armament apparently was not damaged.

A cloudy dawn broke over the Atlantic this morning as the last phase of action developed. The Bismarck could not get away. It only remained to be seen what damage she could do before she ended the briefest and most adventurous career of almost any ship in naval history, with the possible exception of the Merrimac.

At dawn the Ark Royal tried again with another squadron of torpedo planes, but visibility was so poor that the attack had to be broken off. The trapped ship then struck back at the hovering destroyers with gunfire. But by now the main British battle line was pounding up to the scene and by poetic justice it was the Norfolk, which had borne the brunt of the chase, that first opened fire. Soon afterward 16 and 15-inch salvos from the biggest British ships were pounding the Bismarck.

Details of the kill are not known here, but it is known that the cruiser Dorsetshire was ordered to sink the Bismarck with torpedoes. By then she must have been a helpless, blazing wreck. The long battle was over at 11:01 o'clock this morning. ◊

MAY 28, 1941

A CALL TO NATION
President Takes Step Permitted Only When War Threatens

STRIKES MUST END

By FRANK L. KLUCKHOHN
Special to The New York Times.

WASHINGTON, May 27—President Roosevelt tonight proclaimed that "an

President Roosevelt declares an 'unlimited' national state of emergency over the radio in response to German aggression on May 27, 1941.

unlimited national emergency exists," a step which, under the law, the Chief Executive can take only when he believes war to be "imminent."

The President himself made the announcement in a radio address to the nation.

The United States, he declared, will not permit Germany to dominate the high seas and thus make ready for an attack on the Western Hemisphere.

The United States was prepared to take any steps necessary to assure the ❯

❬ delivery of war materials and supplies to Great Britain and the eventual defeat of the Axis powers.

Declaring in so many words that the aim of the Nazis and their leader, Adolf Hitler, was world dominance, the President called upon all Americans to join in the defense effort and warned management and labor that the government is prepared to use all of its power to assure the production of armaments.

TO TAKE A HAND ON BASES

The President made it clear that the United States would not permit Germany and her allies to get bases, such as Dakar, the Azores, the Cape Verdes, Iceland and Greenland for a possible attack on the New World, and stated that, with further American naval units

transferred, and to be transferred, to the Atlantic, this government intended to assure war supplies reaching Britain.

"The delivery of needed supplies to Britain is imperative," he declared. "This can be done; it must be done; it will be done."

At another point he said the nation was placing its armed forces in strategic military positions, and added:

"We will not hesitate to use our armed forces to repel attack."

With this he warned the nation that because of the development of modern instruments of war attacks may be started from farther away than heretofore.

"With profound consciousness of my responsibilities to my countrymen and my country's cause, I have tonight issued a proclamation that an unlimited

national emergency exists and requires the strengthening of our defense to the extreme limit of our national power and authority," the President said.

In his proclamation of the national emergency, made under the law of 1917, the President gave as his formal reasons:

1. That a succession of events made it clear that the Axis belligerents plan "overthrow throughout the world of existing democratic order," accomplished by the destruction of all resistance on land, sea and in the air.

2. That indifference to this on the part of the United States would place the nation in peril, so that common prudence dictates a policy of passing beyond peacetime military measures to a basis which will permit instant repulse of aggression "as well as to repel the threat

---

MAY 30, 1941

85% SEE US IN THE WAR, GALLUP SURVEY FINDS

Number Holding That Opinion Doubled Since Conflict Began

By GEORGE GALLUP
Director, American Institute of Public Opinion

These surveys are made by a system of highly selective samplings in each of the forty-eight States in proportion to voting populations; thereby, the American Institute of Public Opinion holds, is obtained a result which would not vary from that of a

numerically much larger canvass.

PRINCETON, N.J., May 29—The number of American voters who think the United States will likely get into the European was some time before it is over has nearly doubled since the war began twenty months ago.

Although public opinion surveys by the American Institute of Public Opinion have repeatedly shown that the majority oppose entering the war at this time, a survey just completed indicates that more than eight voters in every ten hold the fatalistic belief that the United States will be drawn into the conflict.

This sentiment began to rise sharply at the beginning of the year—during the period of debate over the lease-lend bill and the period when British ship losses were mounting rapidly—and was accelerated by Hitler's invasion of the Balkans in April.

The trend on the question whether the United States will go to war, as measured in twelve successive surveys since October, 1939, follows:

"Do you think the United States will go into the war in Europe sometime before it is over, or do you think we will stay out of the war?"

	Think U.S. Will Go In	Think U.S. Will Stay Out
October, 1939 (outbreak of war)	46%	54%
February, 1940 (war's quiet phase)	32	68
May, 1940 (invasion of France)	62	38
June, 1940	65	35
September, 1940	67	33
December, 1940 (Greek-British successes)	59	41
January, 1941	72	28
February, 1941	74	26
March, 1941	80	20
April, 1941 (Balkan invasion)	82	18
Today	85	15 ◆

MAY 30, 1941

NAZI TROOPS POURING TO RUSSIAN BORDERS

Forces Returning From Balkans Said to Be Sent to Frontier

Special Broadcast to The New York Times.

ANKARA, Turkey, May 29—Further confirmation was received from diplomatic sources today that the German High Command is withdrawing German troops from the Balkans and concentrating a formidable army on the Russian frontiers in Rumania and Poland.

The motorized assault divisions hurled against Yugoslavia and Greece and the vast reserves concentrated in Western Rumania and Bulgaria are being transported into Rumania's Siret Valley and back through Budapest and across Slovakia to the Russo-German frontier in Poland, these reports said.

Though there is no accurate estimate of the German strength in Poland, this correspondent was reliably informed in Bucharest only recently that the concentrations in Rumania numbered upward of forty-one divisions. These are said to include two armored divisions and one parachute division. ◆

of predatory incursion by foreign agents into our territory and society."

"Now therefore," said the proclamation, "I, Franklin D. Roosevelt, President of the United States of America, do proclaim that an unlimited national emergency confronts this country, which requires the use of its military, naval, air and civilian defenses to be put on the basis of readiness to repel any and all acts or threats of aggression directed toward any part of the Western Hemisphere."

Paraphrasing Hitler's own statement that there are today "two worlds," the President declared that today the entire world is divided "between human slavery and human freedom." He said that the United States chooses human freedom. ◇

JUNE 1, 1941

BRITISH IN BAGHDAD
German Fliers Reported Fleeing— Civil Group Rules The Capital

By DAVID ANDERSON

LONDON. May 31—An armistice signed in Baghdad late this afternoon brought to an end the rebellion in Iraq against Britain, London learned tonight. Indian fighters of the British forces took up positions in the outskirts of the capital city from which Premier Rashid Ali el Galiani, leader of the revolt and all his followers able to do so had fled.

The Emir Abdul Illah, the Regent deposed by Rashid Ali, will form a new government without delay. Apparently the sole damper on celebrations at these developments is the absence of 6-year-old King Feisal II who is said to have been kidnapped by Rashid Ali.

[An Associated Press dispatch from London said that a British motorized force had driven into Baghdad. The same dispatch contained a report that German airmen were fleeing from Iraq.]

A British armored car waits outside Baghdad, while negotiations for an armistice take place between British officials and the rebel government during the Iraqi Revolt, May 30, 1941.

MAYOR ASKS ARMISTICE

A request for armistice terms was made to the British by the Mayor of Baghdad after Rashid Ali had crossed the Iranian frontier at the town of Kasr-i-Shirin yesterday and British troops had closed in on Baghdad. A committee of four citizens, headed by the Mayor, took charge of Baghdad's affairs first ordering all irregular military organizations to disband according to reports that reached London by way of Cairo.

An Iraqi officer carrying a white flag presented himself at the British headquarters before Baghdad as the first step in the armistice negotiations. Earlier the Mayor had seen Sir Kinahan Cornwallis, the British Ambassador to Iraq, who recommended parleys with British military commanders.

The terms of the armistice guarantee Iraq's unity and independence. The people are asked to return to work at once. The blackout has been lifted in Baghdad but no traffic is permitted on the streets after nightfall. Without question the British will receive the right to use all highways, railroads, airports and other communication facilities in Iraq which figured in the treaty over which Rashid Ali started the dispute.

Archad el Omari Mohafez, president of the Iraqi Commission of Internal Security, said in a statement today:

"The hostilities for which there is no longer any reason, will be ended as soon as the commission has received assurances that the complete independence of the country and the honor of the army will be guaranteed."

ITALIAN MINISTER HAS FLED

Significantly, among the reports received after the armistice was one that the Italian Minister at Baghdad and the legation staff had departed in haste. They are believed to have gone to Iran with Rashid Ali. It was through an Italian diplomatic outlet that Germany conducted a long and patient drive, utilizing propaganda and intrigue, against Britain In Iraq.

It is thought here that this German effort was supposed to blossom into revolt when Reichsfuehrer Hitler was ready to strike for the oil fields. However, fighting broke out in Iraq soon after Rashid Ali had seized the government on April 3. It probably would have suited Berlin better if this had occurred June 3 or even later, thus giving the Luftwaffe time to complete the Crete offensive first.

Authorized statements clarifying the situation in Iraq have been given out in London. They say that the trouble has been cleared up and that it now is plainly evident that the dispute was not between the British Government and the Arab peoples but between Britain and Germany. It is thought that the Nazi failure to go to the aid of Rashid Ali in force was due in large measure to the way the British troops fought tooth and nail in Crete, thereby tying up the German schedule.

Stress is laid in the fact that Rashid Ali fled to Iran instead of going to Mosul, where Germans still are to be found. The campaign against these German forces, mostly air units, will continue; the struggle in Iraq is over only as far as the Arabs are concerned. ❯

❧ FIELDS BOMBED BY R.A.F.

The British forces now operating at Baghdad advanced from Feluja, according to a communiqué issued in Cairo today. The Royal Air Force had bombed the Washwash and Rashid airports near the capital and raided Kazimain in support of the ground troops. If, as many observers in London assume, Syria is the next battleground, it will mean a race between the British and the Germans to determine who consolidates the position first. The British have gained an advantage by settling the Iraqi conflict before the Germans got control of Crete. Should the British sweep northward along the banks of the Tigris to Mosul and westward across the desert in the direction of Syria in sufficient force in the next few weeks, they may be able to forestall a German thrust.

Britain conducted the operations in Iraq with a small number of men, drawn mainly from India. She practiced economy there much as she did last Winter in the sensational exploits in Libya that culminated in the capture of Benghazi. This is one reason why it has taken so long to defeat the Iraqis, who at only one place—Habbania airport—threatened to score a telling blow.

Looking over the field from the viewpoint of General Sir Archibald P. Wavell, the British Commander in Chief in the Middle East, The Times of London will say tomorrow:

"One may distinguish two forward areas, Crete and the Western Desert and two rearward areas, Iraq and Abyssinia. In both of the former we are heavily pressed by the Germans. In both of the latter we have made a timely clearance of weaker but dangerously placed opponents. The news from Iraq is particularly gratifying. The success should confirm the faith placed in the US by the Arab world generally." ◆

JUNE 2, 1941

WAR IN IRAQ ENDS

Vital Oil Fields of Mosul Are Under Control of London's Friends

ARMISTICE TERMS GIVEN

By DAVID ANDERSON
Special Cable to The New York Times.

LONDON, June 1—Hostilities ceased throughout Iraq today as Emir Abdul Illah, the Regent, entered Baghdad. Six-year-old King Feisal II, who had been reported kidnapped by Premier Rashid Ali el Gailani, who fled to Iran, is said unofficially to be safe.

A brief outline of the terms of the settlement of the Iraqi-British war reached here tonight. The British, it is stated, are certain to gain access to all highways, railroads, airports and all other communication facilities, as provided in the original Anglo-Iraqi treaty, which Rashid Ali broke two months ago. The Premier's action brought about the war.

Iraqi troops are to be returned to their peacetime stations—including the Ramadi garrison, which threatened the Royal Air Force station at Habbania. British prisoners are to be released and Germans and Italians are to be interned. Iraqis who were captured will be handed over to Abdul Illah, who will deal with them.

UNITED STATES ENVOY PRESENT

A large gathering of Baghdad's prominent citizens joined Sir Kinahan Cornwallis, the British Ambassador to Iraq, in greeting Abdul Illah at the gates of the capital this morning. He received them a short time later at a reception. Among those present was Paul Knabenshue, the United States Minister.

Word has reached London from Cairo that the important Mosul oil fields in Northern Iraq are controlled by authorities friendly to Britain. This tempers anxiety over German activity there, as it is known that German agents have been entrenched there for months and have established air bases. The Iraqi

---

JUNE 2, 1941

NAZIS LIST CAPTIVES IN CRETE AT 10,000
Berlin Says That Invasion Has Been Completed as Port on South Coast Is Taken

By C. BROOKS PETERS
By Telephone to The New York Times.

BERLIN, June 1—It was said in Berlin tonight that the invasion of Crete had now successfully been completed. With the joining of hands between Italian and German forces at Ierapetra, which occurred yesterday, the single harbor at all navigable on the otherwise precipitous southern Cretan coast is in Axis hands.

Therewith the only possible avenue of escape for any sizable contingent of the remaining British and Greek troops is said to have been closed. It was announced here tonight that around 10,000 of them had already been captured. At Ierapetra there is a sandy beach from which small groups of soldiers might

Governor in Mosul is said to have long opposed Rashid Ali, so it is expected that he will take steps to counteract the German influence.

The British, taking stock of their month-long campaign in Iraq, have come to the conclusion that close cooperation between the ground and air forces played a decisive part. Air Vice Marshal John H. d'Albiac, who commanded the Royal Air Force in Iraq, was in hourly consultation with the General Staff of the Imperial troops from 6 o'clock each morning until midnight, working out a system for mutual support.

HABBANIA FORCE PRAISED

"The flying training school at Habbania did a fine job in handling the Iraqi revolt by taking on an operational task with the greatest success," an R.A.F. spokesman said. He added that reinforcements of aircraft were pouring into the Middle East steadily.

The first account of events in Baghdad during the last few weeks was received today. As far as the stranded colony of several hundred Britons was concerned, Mr. Knabenshue, the United States Minister, played a leading role. Altogether 500 persons were sheltered at the British Embassy and the United States Legation for more than a month. British women and children had been evacuated from the capital on April 29. The men were placed under the orders of Sir Kinahan and Mr. Knabenshue.

Police guards and then Iraqi soldiers took up posts outside the legation on May 2, but two days later they were withdrawn. Excitement was greatest when the Iraqi Foreign Minister telephoned to say that Iraqi subjects must leave the building, as it might be bombed within the hour. It was explained that the British had threatened to destroy Baghdad's public buildings unless the Iraqi troops menacing the R.A.F. garrison at Habbania were withdrawn. Rashid Ali, it is stated, sent a counter-ultimatum saying that all British subjects within the capital would be bombed in retaliation.

Mr. Knabenshue refused to listen to his guests' offers to surrender to the Iraqis to save the United States Legation. He helped them to toss out all inflammable material, including old records, from the basement. Any kind of bomb would have flattened either the British Embassy or the legation, but the crisis passed without an attack. From then on Mr. Knabenshue remained close to his British charges, sharing hardships with them. ◊

have escaped in light craft from the pursuing Axis forces.

The harbor at Ierapetra itself, Germans declare, however, is so badly in need of dredging that the entrance of any sizable vessel into it is impossible. Small groups of British and Greek troops have attempted to flee and gain the open sea in light boats, it is reported here. Not many of them, however, it is added, have been successful.

EXPECT MORE PRISONERS

The Germans apparently count upon either capturing or destroying whatever Allied forces are still operating on Crete. Even those forces that succeeded in reaching open water are not necessarily safe. Yesterday the German Air Force is reported to have attacked British naval units endeavoring to cover the escape of as many troops as possible in the waters between North Africa and the southern coast of Crete. They are reported to have hit directly and badly damaged a destroyer, sunk a merchant vessel of 3,000 tons, destroyed a schooner loaded with ammunition and damaged a small troop transport—which was already within seventy-five miles of the Egyptian coast.

The cleaning up of the dispersed remnants of the Allied forces in the southern portion of Crete is making good progress, according to the German High Command. Authoritative quarters declare, moreover, that although some of the dispersed Allied units have taken to the mountains, the breaking of all resistance and therewith the total occupation of Crete will be completed in a very few days. ◊

Chapter 7

"NAZIS TRY THE BLITZ ON RUSSIANS"

June–July 1941

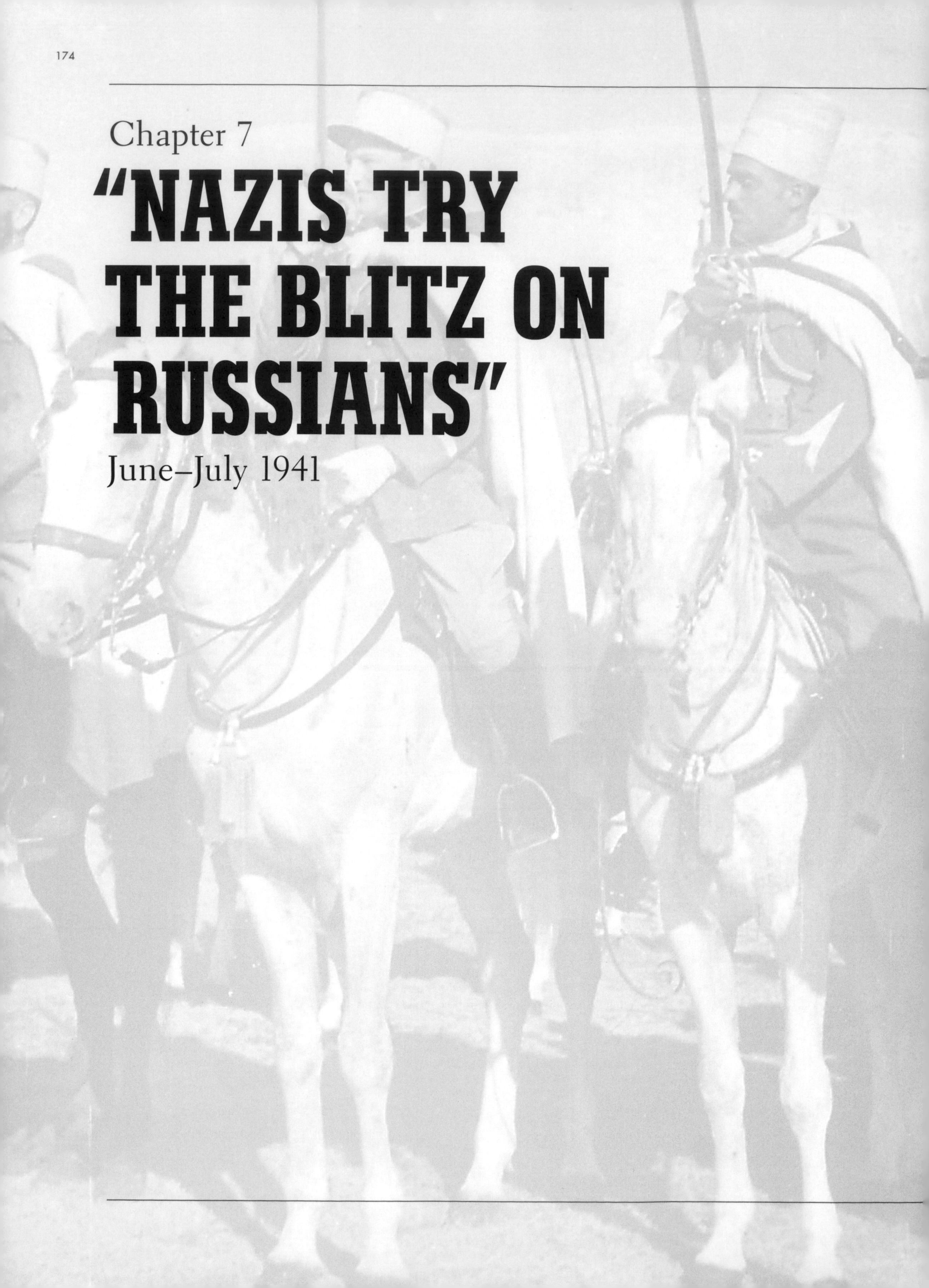

There was no secret by June that something major was poised to happen on the long border between Germany, its Axis partners and the Soviet Union. However, not everyone thought it would happen. The veteran newsman Walter Duranty wrote a piece for The Times on June 17 in which he argued that the two dictatorships were more likely to make a deal than go to war. Joseph Stalin, the Soviet dictator, refused to believe any of the intelligence evidence he was given because he thought the British were trying to deliberately foment a Soviet-German war. But if Stalin had read The Times, the prospect of war was hard to avoid: "Nazi Troops Pouring to Russian Border" on May 30; "Clash Is Expected Soon" ran on June 10 and, on the very day of the invasion, "Big Armies Mass on Eastern Front." The invasion was the biggest news since the campaign in the West more than a year before and the Times office in Berlin had the news out to America the same morning, while Ralph Parker in Moscow confirmed it. The invasion, code-named "Operation Barbarossa" by the Germans, was the largest invasion in history, with four million German, Hungarian, Romanian and Slovakian soldiers, joined by the co-belligerent Finns a few days later. It had been planned since the previous year for May 1941 but had to be postponed not just because of the Mediterranean campaign, but primarily because of a late-winter thaw and the muddy roads that followed. Hanson Baldwin, Times military correspondent and something of an expert on German tactics, wrote a story under the title "Nazis Try the Blitz on Russia," arguing that this colossal campaign marked for Hitler "the fork in the road toward smashing conquest or ultimate defeat." The invasion focused everyone's attention on the Eastern Front. "Reds Here Urge Lend-Lease," reported The Times, and although

Lend-Lease could not formally be extended to Russia, a way was found to promise material aid. The anti-Bolshevik Churchill pledged assistance the very day of the invasion, insisting that he was supporting the ordinary patriotic Russian against the Axis aggressor rather than supporting Communism.

The main problem for reporters was the paucity of solid news material. The German High Command was unusually silent, though the German press hinted at great victories. Soviet news was unreliable but was relayed to New York nonetheless. In truth the Soviet defenders in the first two months of the campaign suffered terrible losses and within weeks German armies had swept across eastern Poland into the Baltic states and toward Leningrad in the north, Minsk and Kiev farther south. On July 30 Brooks Peters from Berlin reported "Berlin Confident of Soviet Defeat," though the German communiqués continued to lack detail and conviction, while on the same day from Moscow came the news of "New Soviet Blows." This was one of the few areas of the war where the press had to rely on secondhand information.

While the invasion went on, America also had to watch the Pacific. On July 26 Roosevelt approved a further embargo on oil supplies for Japan and a freezing of Japanese assets in the United States. A day later The Times reported that Japanese troops had occupied Saigon in southern Indo-China (this later became Vietnam). General Douglas MacArthur was appointed overall commander-in-chief in the South Pacific area, with a brief to reinforce the American military presence in the Philippines. Japan now directly threatened the European empires in Southeast Asia where there was oil and raw materials to compensate for the American embargo. The United States was edging closer not just to war, but to war across two different oceans.

JUNE 1, 1941

BRITISH IN BAGHDAD
German Fliers Reported Fleeing— Civil Group Rules the Capital

By DAVID ANDERSON

LONDON, May 31—An armistice signed in Baghdad late this afternoon brought to an end the rebellion in Iraq against Britain, London learned tonight. Indian fighters of the British forces took up positions in the outskirts of the capital city, from which Premier Rashid Ali el Gailani, leader of the revolt, and all his followers were able to do so had fled.

The Emir Abdul Illah, the Regent deposed by Rashid Ali, will form a new government without delay. Apparently the sole damper on celebrations of these developments is the absence of 6-year-old King Feisal, who is said to have been kidnapped by Rashid Ali.

MAYOR ASKS ARMISTICE

A request for armistice terms was made to the British by the Mayor of Baghdad after Rashid Ali had crossed the Iranian frontier at the town of Kasr-i-Shlrin yesterday and British troops had closed in on Baghdad. A committee of four citizens, headed by the Mayor, took charge of Baghdad's affairs, first ordering all irregular military organizations to disband, according to reports that reached London by way of Cairo.

An Iraqi officer carrying a white flag presented himself at the British head-quarters before Baghdad as the first step in the armistice negotiations. Earlier the Mayor had seen Sir Kinahan Cornwallis, the British Ambassador to Iraq, who recommended parleys with British military commanders.

The terms of the armistice guarantee Iraq's unity and independence. The people are asked to return to work at once. The blackout has been lifted in Baghdad but no traffic is permitted on the streets after nightfall. Without question the British will receive the right to use all highways, railroads, airports and other communication facilities In Iraq, which figured in the treaty over which Rashid Ali started the dispute.

Archad el Omari Mohafez, president of the Iraqi Commission of Internal Security, said in a statement today:

"The hostilities, for which there is no longer any reason, will be ended as soon as the commission has received assurances that the complete independence of the country and the honor of the army will be guaranteed."

Authorized statements clarifying the situation in Iraq have been given out in London. They say that the trouble has been cleared up and that it now is plainly evident that the dispute was not between the British Government and the Arab peoples, but between Britain and Germany. It is thought that the Nazi failure to go to the aid of Rashid Ali in force was due in large measure to the way the British troops fought tooth and nail in Crete, thereby tying up the German schedule.

Stress is laid on the fact that Rashid Ali fled to Iran instead of going to Mosul, where Germans still are to be found. The campaign against these German forces, mostly air units, will continue; the struggle in Iraq is over only as far as the Arabs are concerned. ◇

JUNE 15, 1941

CLASH IS EXPECTED SOON
Germans Are Expected to Attack

By DANIEL T. BRIGHAM
By Telephone to The New York Times.

BERNE, Switzerland, June 14—The latent rivalry between Russia and Germany is believed in diplomatic circles here to have reached a point where political-military developments are expected at any moment.

Indications point to military action, probably along the Russian-German dividing line in Poland. within the next ten days. But some observers hold that Adolf Hitler will make at least one more political move to bring Russia into line before he launches his forces on a campaign directed at taking the Ukraine.

Recurrent reports of steadily reinforced garrisons on both sides of the demarcation line in Poland have long given indications of which way Russian-German negotiations have been turning. Each time at the last minute the Kremlin, apparently, has acceded to one more request.

Now, however, the latest German demands, as reported to neutral foreign diplomatic quarters here, include the withdrawal of at least half of the Russian forces east of the demarcation line; withdrawal of aerial garrisons at Brest-Litovsk and Lwow increased deliveries of Russian gasoline, oil and wheat and the acceptance of German control commissions to supervise the withdrawals of the

JUNE 7, 1941

ONE-THIRD OF JEWS FOUND IN NAZIS' GRIP
Joint Distribution Official Puts Figure at 5,000,000

Special to The New York Times.

ATLANTIC CITY, N.J., June 6—More than one-third of the 15,000,000 Jews in the world are now in countries under German domination, subject to discriminatory anti-Jewish regulations that make sound economic and social existence impossible, Joseph A. Schwartz, vice chairman of the European field of the Joint Distribution Committee, reported in an address before the national conference of Jewish Social Welfare here today.

Another third of the world's Jewish population is now in Russian territory or in countries recently acquired by Russia, he said, with the remaining one-third in the Western Hemisphere, mostly in the United States. It is to the Jewish population of the United States that European Jews, subject to persecution and discrimination, look for support, Mr. Schwartz stressed.

"Despite all the obstacles and difficulties arising out of the war situation, the Joint Distribution Committee is today functioning throughout Europe," Mr. Schwartz said. "Help is being extended in Poland, Hungary, Yugoslavia, France and Holland, and possibilities of immigration are being made available to the Jews still remaining in Germany, Austria, Bohemia and Slovakia."

Mr. Schwartz estimated that through the activities of the Joint Distribution Committee 1,000,000 persons were receiving help or service of some kind. ◇

Russian forces and speed up production.

Russia's answer to this, according to these circles, was to increase her military forces along a line running from the corner of former East Prussia and Lithuania to the Bessarabian northern frontier, from 105 divisions to about 160. On the other side of the line the Germans are reported to have just completed the concentration of 143 divisions plus several aerial detachments.

In the North Baltic States, the Russians are reported to have massed twenty-five divisions equipped with new material, while in the South, in Bessarabia, Russian forces have been reduced in the ceded territory but withdrawn behind newly constructed fortifications on the eastern bank of the Dniester Rover. The Dniester forces have been greatly strengthened during the last ten days, presumably in preparation for a counter-move to a potential "political move" by Herr Hitler.

This "political" move directly concerns Rumania in that, in exchange for the use of Rumanian bases and the wholehearted "collaboration" of the Rumanian Army, Herr Hitler is reported to have offered General Ion Antonescu, Premier of Rumania, two days ago the return of the Bessarabian Province seized by Russia early last year.

Reports arriving from neutral military observers in Bucharest tell of a total of twenty-seven new German divisions just arrived there and being deployed to the East. Another "political" move also apparently on the books is the rumored forthcoming adherence of Finland to the Axis pact. This Helsinki denies, pointing to her fundamentally neutral stand so far in the Russian-German "negotiations." ◆

JUNE 17, 1941

Soviet-Nazi Deal Held More Likely Than Clash Despite All Rumors
Lack of Scruples on Part Of Stalin and Hitler, Cited As Opening Way— Negotiations Are Declared to be Going on

By WALTER DURANTY

It is not wholly an accident that reports of an impending clash between Russia and Germany coincide with the arrival in London of Sir Stafford Cripps, Britain's Ambassador to Moscow. As early as last February Sir Stafford made no secret of his belief that Germany would attack Russia this Summer, probably before the end of July.

The Ambassador argued that Adolf Hitler already realized he would be unable to reach a quick decision against "Britain and that he must therefore," seek "a solid" foundation" for subsequent peace proposals by occupying the Ukraine and perhaps part of the North Caucasus. That sounded reasonable enough, but few persons in Moscow thought anything of the kind would occur this year.

However, Sir Stafford maintained that Herr Hitler knew better than any-

one the degree, speed and "volume of the current upswing in Soviet " industrial-especially military-production, in labor discipline "generally and in the reorganization and the reinforcement of the Red Army and Air Force.

UNCENSORED LETTER CITED

The British Ambassador's views were not shared by well-informed foreign circles in Moscow, who thought he was over-ready to accept Soviet figures and assertions at their face value; but it is worth noting that I have just received an uncensored letter from a competent friend in Moscow, dated April 27, stating:

"Various indications are that the Germans intend eastward action in June. Many folks here now take it very seriously."

The recent Tass (Soviet news agency) denial of friction between the U. S. S. R. and Germany alleged to have resulted from the failure of negotiations that Tass rather ambiguously disavows contains a definite Soviet recognition of heavy German troop concentrations along Russia's western frontier.

Nothing, of course, was said about corresponding Soviet measure but I learned in Siberia that the protection of the eastern maritime provinces had been entrusted to the long-term-service frontier guard (say a quarter of a million strong) and local territorial units, while the rest of the former Special Far Eastern Army had been moved westward. The neutrality pact with Japan would give further reassurance to Soviet eastern security.

There are other items that appear to herald a speedy Russian-German clash, improbable as it still appears to me. The Soviet Ambassador to Rumania, Arkady Lavrentieff, has just been recalled to Moscow. The Finns announce restrictive :measures on frontier travel, and the presence of German troops jn Finland is admitted, although their number is disputed.

From Istanbul and Ankara we hear that tension between Turkey and Germany is less acute and that Turkish anxiety has diminished. Finally, there is the fact, neglected by war prophets and pundits, that climatic conditions at this time of the year in the South Palestine North Arabian desert and the Libyan desert, the two land approaches to Egypt, are more like hell than anything on earth save the crater of a volcano. ◆

Russian civilians digging an anti-tank ditch outside of Moscow for defense in preparation for the attack of advancing German troops in June 1941.

JUNE 20, 1941

INVASION OF RUSSIA IS DENIED BY REICH

Berlin Spokesman Admits 'Flood Of Rumors'— No Border Clashes

BERLIN, June 19 (UP)—Authorized Nazi spokesmen denied flatly today that a German invasion of Russia had started or that border clashes had occurred, although they admitted that a "tremendous flood of rumors" had burst out concerning Nazi-Soviet relations.

Although jubilantly acclaiming the new German-Turkish friendship pact as one of the diplomatic sensations of the war, the Germans refused to discuss its obvious bearing on German-Russian relations—the topic of sensational rumors all over Europe. Rumors circulated in Berlin that actual border clashes had occurred between German and Russian troops. A spokesman said, however, that he had no knowledge of any such occurrences.

RUMORS OF FOREIGN ORIGIN

He said that "most of the rumors" of German-Soviet tension were of foreign origin and that "that is the best indication of their unreliability."

[The British charged, according to a British broadcast, that the rumors were of German origin and were a new phase of a "war of nerves" to force Russia to agree to German demands for fuller cooperation.]

An indication that German-Soviet relations had not reached the state of open hostilities was the fact that Russian residents of Berlin went about their business as usual today.

A German spokesman, although declining to discuss relations in general between Germany and Russia, denied reports that a new German-Russian economic agreement was signed here yesterday. Russian quarters in Berlin also said they had no knowledge of any such agreement.

NO COMMENT ON BESSARABIA

German authorized quarters declined comment of any kind on reports that Germany had confronted Russia with positive demands. They said they had no knowledge of reports that Rumania, with German support, was demanding the return of Bessarabia from the Soviets.

It is known that talks on the technicalities of carrying out existing German-Russian trade agreements, particularly in connection with deliveries by individual industries and firms, are being carried on here regularly by a permanent Soviet trade commission and German economic authorities. Russian sources said that these technical talks had not led to any new economic agreements.

It was believed generally in political quarters that any new economic agreements that might be reached would be only a part of some new broad German-Soviet agreement. ◊

JUNE 22, 1941

BIG ARMIES MASS ON 'EASTERN FRONT'
All Along Russian Frontiers Troop Movements Suggest Clash May Be Near

By C. L. SULZBERGER
Wireless to The New York Times.

ANKARA, Turkey, June 21—The strange marriage of convenience between Soviet Russia and Nazi Germany, even if reaffirmed by some startling but now unforeseen development, seemed as close to the breaking point this week as at any time since it was cemented in August, 1939.

Despite occasional pronouncements of Berlin and Moscow that all continued well between the partners, everything pointed to the contrary, and it was the general belief in diplomatic circles that either Russia would have to fork over a larger dowry or forfeit her rights to nonviolence from the Reich.

From Finland to Rumania a martial atmosphere prevailed on both sides of the frequently changed frontiers of these two revolutionary powers. Nazi troops shuttled back and forth on the Finnish railway system on the pretext of returning to East Prussia from Norway. However, it must have appeared strange to Moscow that more Germans were entering Finland than leaving.

In Rumania, whence originated the most sensational rumors of impending Russo-German hostilities—obviously because of a devout national wish that war would break out and bring about a return of territories grabbed by the Soviet—mobilization was completed, and last-minute preparations were effected.

HUGE ARMIES FACING

Between these two extremes rested the largest army Germany had assembled on one front since the Battle of France, and it would be a safe assumption that it was not there merely to admire the scenery. Across the way was concentrated a vast Soviet force, which, according to Tass, Soviet news agency, was merely completing the usual manoeuvres, although when the Russians here were asked why it was necessary to exercise 155 divisions in one area the subject was nervously changed.

It was clear that the recent Turkish-German friendship pact was connected with the diplomatic background of this situation. Stated in a broad fashion, it meant that Germany's flank in the entire region from the Balkans across the Black Sea to the Caucasus was protected against British interference in case of a war with Russia, just as Britain's position in Syria was safeguarded against German intervention through Turkey.

This protection on the Black Sea was of extreme importance to the Reich in the event of action against Russia. The Nazis have concentrated large quantities of seagoing barges along the Lower Danube, which could be useful for an attack on the Crimea—one of the moves considered likely by strategists. Six German-controlled submarines are now operating in the Black Sea, and, while the Soviet has a considerable portion of its navy there, the Germans are confident this could be dealt with by the Luftwaffe. Since the Reich is not among the signatories of the Montreux Convention a de-

JUNE 23, 1941

HITLER SAYS ARMY HOLDS REICH'S FATE
Order of Day Tells Troops of 'Hard and Momentous' Struggle Now Begun

By Telephone to The New York Times.

BERLIN, June 22—With the advance into Russia by the Reich's armed forces at the sunrise hour today, the political, military and economic liaison between Berlin and Moscow came to a spectacular end.

That liaison had sprung from considerations of war expediency less than two years ago, but, despite all outward appearances, it had impressed numerous neutral observers as a highly fragile alliance, despite the force of its impact on the international situation then existing.

Among the official pronouncements droned out by the German broadcasts since early morning was the proclamation of Reichsfuehrer Adolf Hitler.

"Weighted down with heavy cares, condemned to months-long silence, the hour has now come when at last I can speak frankly," were Herr Hitler's introductory words to his recital of what he termed "Russian treachery."

ORDER TO HIS ARMIES
Considerations of a grave and fateful nature, he stated, made that silence imperative, as, he said, he had hoped against terrific odds that the tension obtaining between the two countries might yet find an amicable solution.

The Commander in Chief's order of the day to his soldiers was:

"German soldiers! You are entering on a hard and momentous struggle. The fate of Europe, the future of the German Reich and the very existence of our German people now is committed into your hands. May Providence help us in this struggle."

German-Russian relations first came into the spotlight of critical scrutiny about six months ago, when it was asserted that the Soviets had assumed a lukewarm attitude toward further hard and fast collaboration with National Socialist Germany. It is stated in neutral diplomatic quarters that Germany, Italy and Japan, for the last six months, have individually sought, through diplomatic pressure, to win over Soviet Russia to an unequivocal adhesion to the Tripartite Pact and all that it implies.

The visit of the Japanese Foreign Minister, Yosuke Matsuoka, to Moscow a few months ago was held to give some assurance that Moscow was in accord with such a union, but today's statement by Foreign Minister Joachim von Ribbentrop would seem intended to suggest that the visit of the Soviet Foreign Commissar, Vyacheslaff Molotoff, to Berlin last November had already given rise to suspicions that the Soviet Union was not yet appeased. It is asserted that, if the Reich willingly paid the price demanded by Moscow, it was only because of pressing military and economic considerations.

LONG A FORBIDDEN TOPIC
For the last three months Russo-German relations have become the "great taboo" for foreign correspondents. Mention of them, no matter how skillfully veiled, was the first item on the prohibitory news index, and up until today these relations were only privately discussed in hushed whispers and out of general earshot.

DIPLOMATS HEAR NEWS
Foreign correspondents were summoned to the Foreign Office press conference at 7 o'clock this morning. Herr von Ribbentrop and his personal staff appeared soon after that hour, and the German Foreign Minister then began his recital of the events that led to the scrapping of the Russo-German pact.

Previously, Propaganda Minister Joseph Goebbels had broadcast Herr Hitler's proclamation to the German people.

Berlin's streets were completely deserted at the hour when the German people were apprised of the shift of scene in the theatre of war. The windows of the Soviet Embassy on Unter den Linden were still curtained, and it could not be learned whether Ambassador V. G. Dekanozoff and his personal staff had already entrained for Moscow. ◇

mand might be made for free passage of Axis warships through the Dardanelles.

UKRAINE AN OBJECTIVE
The main German drive in case of war would probably be aimed at the heart of the Ukraine and would persevere eastward in an attempt to cut off the Caucasian oil resources of the Red Army, whose mechanical arms would be befuddled through the lack of fuel. It is then thought likely the Germans might seek to continue to the Iranian frontier and beyond as far as the Persian Gulf, thus outflanking the British position in the Middle East by a wide sweeping manoeuvre.

For some time rumors have circulated setting the actual date for war's outbreak. The denials from Moscow concerning such reports are becoming notably less sure themselves and less heated, and the Red Army organ, Red Star, has admitted that heavy artillery practice has been taking place in the Western Soviet and that debarkation manoeuvres have been tried at Odessa.

German troops have been filing through Slovakia from the west, and that puppet State has itself mobilized ten classes. Sano Mach, the Minister of the Interior, announced at Bratislava that a "German liberation" of the Ukraine was imminent. ◇

JUNE 23, 1941

Prime Minister Churchill's Broadcast on New War

The following is the text of Prime Minister Winston Churchill's address, broadcast yesterday from London, as transcribed by

The New York Times:

I have taken occasion to speak to you tonight because we have reached one of the climacterics of the war. In the first of these intense turning points, a year ago, France fell prostrate under the German hammer and we had to face the storm alone.

The second was when the Royal Air Force beat the Hun raiders out of the daylight air and thus warded off the Nazi invasion of our islands while we were still ill-armed and ill-prepared.

The third turning point was when ❯

the President and Congress of the United States passed the lease and lend enactment, devoting nearly 2,000,000,000 sterling of the wealth of the New World to help us defend our liberties and their own.

Those were the three climacterics.

The fourth is now upon us.

At 4 o'clock this morning Hitler attacked and invaded Russia. All his usual formalities of perfidy were observed with scrupulous technique. A nonaggression treaty had been solemnly signed and was in force between the two countries. No complaint had been made by Germany of its non-fulfillment. Under its cloak of false confidence the German armies drew up in immense strength along a line which stretched from the White Sea to the Black Sea and their air fleets and armored divisions slowly and methodically took up their stations.

STALIN HAD WARNING

Then, suddenly, without declaration of war, without even an ultimatum, the German bombs rained down from the sky upon the Russian cities; the German troops violated the Russian frontiers and an hour later the German Ambassador, who till the night before was lavishing his assurances of friendship, almost of alliance, upon the Russians, called upon the Russian Foreign Minister to tell him that a state of war existed between Germany and Russia.

Thus was repeated on a far larger scale the same kind of outrage against every form of signed compact and international faith which we have witnessed in Norway, in Denmark, in Holland, in Belgium and which Hitler's accomplice and jackal, Mussolini, so faithfully imitated in the case of Greece.

All this was no surprise to me. In fact I gave clear and precise warnings to Stalin of what was coming. I gave him warnings as I have given warnings to others before. I can only hope that these warnings did not fall unheeded.

All we know at present is that the Russian people are defending their native soil and that their leaders have called upon them to resist to the utmost.

Hitler is a monster of wickedness, insatiable in his lust for blood and plunder. Not content with having all Europe under his heel or else terrorized into various forms of abject submission, he must now carry his work of butchery and desolation among the vast multitudes of Russia and of Asia. The terrible military machine which we and the rest of the civilized world so foolishly, so supinely, so insensately allowed the Nazi gangsters to build up year by year from almost nothing; this machine cannot stand idle, lest it rust or fall to pieces. It must be in continual motion, grinding up human lives and trampling down the homes and the rights of hundreds of millions of men.

THIS BLOODTHIRSTY GUTTERSNIPE

Moreover, it must be fed not only with flesh but with oil. So now this bloodthirsty guttersnipe must launch his mechanized armies upon new fields of slaughter, pillage and devastation. Poor as are the Russian peasants, workmen and soldiers, he must steal from them their daily bread. He must rob them of the oil which drives their plows and thus produce a famine without example in human history.

And even the carnage and ruin which his victory, should he gain it—though he's not gained it yet—will bring upon the Russian people, will itself be only a stepping stone to the attempt to plunge the four or five hundred millions who live in China and the 350,000,000 who live in India into that bottomless pit of human degradation over which the diabolic emblem of the swastika flaunts itself.

It is not too much to say here this pleasant Summer evening that the lives and happiness of a thousand million additional human beings are now menaced with brutal Nazi violence. That is enough to make us hold our breath.

But presently I shall show you something else that lies behind and something that touches very nearly the life of Britain and of the United States.

The Nazi regime is indistinguishable from the worst features of Communism. It is devoid of all theme and principle except appetite and racial domination. It excels in all forms of human wickedness, in the efficiency of its cruelty and ferocious aggression. No one has been a more consistent opponent of Communism than I have for the last twenty-five years. I will unsay no words that I've spoken about it. But all this fades away before the spectacle which is now unfolding.

The past, with its crimes, its follies and its tragedies, flashes away. I see the Russian soldiers standing on the threshold of their native land, guarding the fields which their fathers have tilled from time immemorial. I see them guarding their homes, their mothers and wives pray, ah, yes, for there are times when all pray for the safety of their loved ones, for the return of the breadwinner, of the champion, of their protectors.

NAZI 'CATARACT OF HORRORS'

I see the 10,000 villages of Russia, where the means of existence was wrung so hardly from the soil, but where there are still primordial human joys, where maidens laugh and children play. I see advancing upon all this, in hideous onslaught, the Nazi war machine, with its clanking, heel-clicking, dandified Prussian officers, its crafty expert agents, fresh from the cowing and tying down of a dozen countries. I see also the dull, drilled, docile, brutish masses of the Hun soldiery, plodding on like a swarm of crawling locusts. I see the German bombers and fighters in the sky, still smarting from many a British whipping, so delightful to find what they believe is an easier and a safer prey. And behind all this glare, behind all this storm, I see that small group of villainous men who planned, organized and launched this cataract of horrors upon mankind.

And then my mind goes back across the years to the days when the Russian armies were our Allies against the same deadly foe, when they fought with so much valor and constancy and helped to gain a victory, from all share in which, alas, they were, through no fault of ours, utterly cut off.

I have lived through all this and you will pardon me if I express my feelings and the stir of old memories. But now I have to declare the decision of His Majesty's Government, and I feel sure it is a decision in which the great Dominions will, in due course, concur. And that we must speak of now, at once, without a day's delay. I have to make that declaration but, can you doubt what our policy will be?

We have but one aim and one single irrevocable purpose. We are resolved to destroy Hitler and every vestige of the Nazi regime. From this nothing will turn us. Nothing. We will never parley; we will never negotiate with Hitler or any of his gang. We shall fight him by land; we shall fight him by sea; we shall fight him in the air, until, with God's help we have rid the earth of his shadow and liberated its people from his yoke.

WILL ASSIST RUSSIANS

Any man or State who fights against Nazism will have our aid. Any man or State who marches with Hitler is our foe. This applies not only to organized States but to all representatives of that vile race of Quislings who make themselves the tools and agents of the Nazi regime against their fellow countrymen and against the lands of their births. These Quislings, like the Nazi leaders themselves, if not disposed of by their fellow-countrymen, which would save trouble, will be delivered by us on the morrow of victory to the justice of the Allied tribunals. That is our policy and that is our declaration.

It follows, therefore, that we shall give whatever help we can to Russia and to the Russian people. We shall appeal to all our friends and Allies in every part of the world to take the same course and pursue it as we shall, faithfully and steadfastly to the end. ◆

1938 to 1942

▲ German soldiers at the Austrian border after the Anschluss, the occupation and annexation of Austria by Nazi Germany, on March 12 1938.

Adolf Hitler at a victory ▶ parade in Warsaw after the German invasion of Poland, October 1939.

▲ The march in remembrance of 1923 Beer Hall Putsch, Munich, Germany, November 9, 1938. Top Nazi Party members include, from left, Friedrich Weber, Hermann Goering, Adolf Hitler and Ulrich Graf, The ceremony was a precursor to Kristallnacht, a series of coordinated attacks on Jews, which began that night.

▲ Jewish residents of Warsaw, Poland, lining up for water near a sign stating "Infected Area" in January, 1940. The occupying German army used these signs as one of their steps to establishing the Warsaw Ghetto.

▲ Adolf Hitler delivers an address at the Haus der deutschen Kunst (House of German Art), Munich, Berlin, 1939

▲ Jewish inhabitants of the ghetto in Kutno, Poland, which was established shortly after the German invasion. The majority of its inhabitants were sent to the Chelmno extermination camp in early 1942.

▲ Rotterdam, the Netherlands, after heavy German bombardments, which killed 850 people, during the Nazi blitzkrieg (lightning war) across the Low Countries, 1940.

▲ Belgian citizens erected makeshift roadblocks in an effort to slow the progress of German troops during the Nazi invasion, May 1940.

▲ Belgian soldiers captured by German troops after the Nazi invasion of the Low Countries, 1940.

▼ Ruins of a French city, 1940.

▲ German troops passing though Belgium on their way to France, May 1940.

▲ German soldiers during the invasion of France in Yonne, 1940.

▲ Vehicles near Dunkirk after the British retreat, June 1940.

▼ Place de le Concorde during the announcement of the French government's willingness for armistice, 1940.

▲ General Field Marshal von Bock (center) and German soldiers in Place de la Concorde, 1940.

▲ German forces advance on Paris, 1940.

English soldiers ▶ taken prisoner by the German army at Dunkirk, June, 1940.

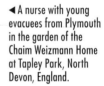

▲ A group of U.S. B-17 Flying Fortress bombers practicing above England, ca 1942.

▼ A London street during the Battle of Britain.

▲ Poster with a quote from newly elected British Prime Minister Winston Churchill's first speech to the House of Commons, May 1940.

◄ A nurse with young evacuees from Plymouth in the garden of the Chaim Weizmann Home at Tapley Park, North Devon, England.

▲ Auxiliary Territorial Service women recovering shells from the mud flats at the Royal Artillery Experimental Unit, Shoeburyness, Essex, 1942.

Rubble in London after ▶ the Blitz in the winter of 1940-1941.

◄ German soldiers attack a bunker on the Eastern Front in Russia, 1941, during Operation Barbarossa.

▲ London fireboats battle flames on the Thames after a German air raid during the Battle of Britain, September 1940.

▲ The Hungarian army guarding the Danube, March 1941.

▼ German soldiers during the battle of Stalingrad (now Volgograd), July 1942.

▲ SA (or Sturmabteilungen) officers at a Christmas party given by Adolf Hitler at the Lowenbraukeller, Munich, Germany, December 18, 1941.

▲ General Sikorski of Poland, pointing to the map, with his staff in Britain, November 1942.

▲ A military airfield near Pearl Harbor after the Japanese attack on December 7, 1941.

▲ U.S. Marines in basic training, Parris Island, South Carolina, 1941.

"I've found the job where I fit best!"

FIND YOUR WAR JOB In Industry – Agriculture – Business

EVERYTIME YOU TWIST A **NUT**

THINK OF **HITLER**

◄ World War II poster.

▲ American propaganda poster by Office for Emergency Management, War Production Board, 1942.

▲ Crew of a Japanese aircraft-carrier send off a plane to bomb Pearl Harbor, December, 1941.

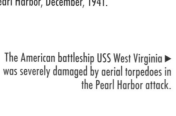

The American battleship USS West Virginia ▶ was severely damaged by aerial torpedoes in the Pearl Harbor attack.

◀ President Roosevelt with cavalry officers on a tour of an Army Camp in 1942.

▼ Soldiers training in M-3 tanks, Fort Knox, Kentucky, 1942.

▲ An M-4 tank line, Fort Knox, Kentucky, 1942.

Millions of troops are on the move...

Is **YOUR** trip necessary?

OFFICE OF DEFENSE TRANSPORTATION

▲ American propaganda poster put out by the Office of Defense Transportation, 1943.

Women assembling bomber at ▶ the Douglas Aircraft Company factory, Long Beach, California, 1942.

▲ US troops landing during the Aleutian Islands Campaign, early 1940s.

▲ Chinese soldiers in combat training at a military academy near the Yellow River, Tungkwan, China, 1941.

▼ Troops aboard ship arriving in North Africa, 1942.

▲ Benito Mussolini, Italian dictator, 1940.

American soldiers check for ▶ breaks in field telephone wires after a battle against Axis forces in the El Guettar Valley, Tunisia.

JUNE 25, 1941

REDS HERE URGE LEASE-LEND AID

Full aid under the lease-lend act to the Soviets in their attempt to stem the Nazi invasion was urged yesterday by The Daily Worker, Communist newspaper, in a front-page editorial.

While the editorial termed Under-Secretary of State Sumner Welles's condemnation of the Nazi attack as inadequate because it "proposed no plans of action," various groups, while rejecting Communist aims and tactics, released appeals for aid to the Soviet Government. The groups included the Legion for American Unity, Union for Democratic Action, Non-Sectarian Anti-Nazi League and the Socialist Courier, organ of the Central Committee of the Russian Social-Democratic Labor Party.

The one organization that counseled against aid to Russia was the Keep America Out of War Congress. Through its executive director, Mary W. Hillyer, this group said: "We oppose giving military aid to the Soviet Union. The predatory struggle between the two bloodiest dictators can result in the domination of either equally abhorrent despotism or in unimaginable chaos and disintegration."

The Daily Worker editorial declared: The sentiment of the American people requires that there be full aid and support to the Soviet Union in its fight against Hitler's attack; that there shall be, for example, application of the lend-lease provisions for such aid; that all restrictions and obstacles to United States–Soviet trade, such as have recently blocked machine shipments, for example, shall be immediately lifted; that Soviet credits be freed from restrictions, and that the government take all other necessary measures to implement a policy of aid and cooperation to the Soviet Union in its just defense against Hitlerism.

"The American people will ask why it is that Secretary Welles, speaking in the name of the government, proposed no plans of action, offered no concrete measures of aid with which to implement his characterization of the Nazi attack on the Soviet Union."

The Legion for American Unity, 103 Park Avenue, of which Supreme Court Justice Ferdinand Pecora is the head, warned America's 30,000,000 citizens of foreign birth and ancestry to be "on guard against fifth columnists and Quislings."

Warning against the "Communist party line which may shift again," the Non-Sectarian Anti-Nazi League added: "We must not make the mistake of blindly clasping the Communists to our bosoms now that they have become anti-Nazi since Sunday. Let us by all means aid the Soviet in its fight, however, because the greatest danger which must be fought by every means, with every ally, is the threat of Nazi world domination." ◆

JUNE 29, 1941

NAZIS TRY THE BLITZ ON RUSSIANS
Their Old Strategy Is Being Applied On a Huge Scale

By HANSON W. BALDWIN

Germany's invasion of Russia a week ago today brought to a sudden climax the struggle that is now twenty-two months old. The new campaign—measured by area and number of troops engaged, the greatest campaign of this or probably any other war—may shape Europe for generations to come. The German-Russian fighting marks a turning point; for Britain it provides a military opportunity which probably will not come again; for Hitler's Reich it marks the fork of the road toward smashing conquest or perhaps ultimate defeat. Hitler knows, and the Germans know, that if their plans miscarry and their campaign bogs down into Napoleonic futility, they have not only lost the Russian campaign, but quite probably the war.

It cannot be too much emphasized that the start of this new struggle means a breathing spell for Britain—one ▶

Heavy Russian bombers shortly before the German invasion of Russia, June 1941.

{ that was desperately needed; it means intensified British bombing raids in the West; it means a new ally—though one of uncertain strength and faith—for Britain; it means the main military strength of the Germans must now for at least a period of weeks, perhaps of months, be extended to the East; it means a further extension of that strength over vast area.

THE STRENGTH ENGAGED

Not all of the strength of either side, of course, can be utilized in the fighting, since Russia must maintain large forces in the Far East and Germany throughout Europe and in North Africa. The forces believed to be involved and the strengths and weaknesses of each side follow:

GERMANY

Planes—4,500 to 6,000. Many dive-bombers and other types designed for land cooperation work. Fliers thoroughly trained and with great combat experience. The best of Germany's new types, including a new Heinkel fighter, in action in the East.

Army—About 151 divisions, plus ten Finnish and twenty Rumanian divisions, plus twelve German divisions in Norway, one or more of which might be used. These were disposed about as follows at the start of hostilities: Four German divisions in Northern Finland; ten Finnish divisions in south and central Finland; twenty-five German divisions in the East Prussia-Lithuania area, with fifteen more farther south in the Lodz-Warsaw area. These were backed up by fifty more divisions in reserve. Approximately twenty-five more German divisions were based on South Poland; twenty on the horseshoe of the Carpathians; twelve German plus twenty Rumanian in Rumania. The strength of the German infantry division is almost 16,000 men; the armored division is about 12,000. Probably twenty armored divisions plus motorized divisions are being used on the whole front. Total strength of Axis forces probably between 2,800,000 and 3,600,000 men.

Navy—The new battleship Tirpitz, sister ship of the Bismarck and the new German aircraft carrier Graf Zeppelin, plus possibly two pocket battleships, two obsolete training battleships, seven cruisers, twelve destroyers and numerous torpedo boats and submarines are in the Baltic. A number of submarines, motor torpedo boats, reinforced by light craft of the Rumanian Navy, are in the Black Sea.

RUSSIA

Planes—Between 2,500 and 4,000. Few dive-bombers and relatively few types designed for land cooperation work. Many long-range but slow bombers. Plane types generally not on a par with German designs and represent essentially copies of other nations' designs. Fliers good and brave but air staff work spotty and coordinated training as a combat air force of dubious quality.

Army—About 170 to 215 Russian divisions (thirty to fifty-odd in the Far East, ranged against Japan's eleven in Manchukuo), a total of about 2,000,000 men, were mobilized when hostilities started. About 2,000,000 of these were available in the West. Mobilization of other classes may almost double this number, though it is doubtful if full equipment is available for all, and Russian mobilization is very slow. Troop dispositions in West were approximately as follows: Twenty-three plus divisions in the Leningrad area opposite Finland; twenty-four plus in the Minsk-Smolensk-Gomel-Pinsk area; forty-two in the Baltic States area, plus twelve in reserve; forty-eight in the Kiev military district and from Southern Poland to the Black Sea; eighteen in reserve around to the southeast of Moscow. The Russian Army has a large proportion of horsed cavalry—more than any other army in the world; probably one-eighth the number of divisions in the West are cavalry. The Russian infantry division varies in size between 10,000 and 20,000 men; the standard is 18,000 but the average size is not much larger than the German. Tanks are generally organized in brigades, roughly about half the size of the German armored division, of which the Russians have about forty available for the West. There are probably 25,000 to 50,000 parachute troops and some airborne infantry divisions.

Navy—One obsolete battleship; seven cruisers; twenty-odd destroyers; fifty to sixty submarines in the Baltic; perhaps a few submarines, torpedo boats, etc., in the Arctic. Two obsolete battleships; one aircraft carrier; sixteen destroyers; fifty to ninety submarines in the Black Sea; a few light vessels and patrol craft in the Caspian.

TANKS NOT MATCHED

Only in numerical size, therefore, do the Russian armies approximately match the German. Russian tanks are numerous; some are technically good but on the whole they are not as modern or effective as German tanks, and there is little evidence that the Russians have developed the plane-tank team which has spearheaded the German conquests.

The Russians are stubborn and good defensive fighters; their best troops unquestionably have a high morale. But in staff work and leadership, in training and equipment they are no match for the Germans; Timoshenko and Budyenny and Stern are not of the same caliber as Keitel and Brauchitsch. Purges and politics have hurt the Red Army.

The German Army has proved itself in its twenty-two months of unparalleled victories; the Russians revealed major weaknesses in the campaign against Finland. Yet the concluding Russian offensive across the Karelian Isthmus was conducted with skill and Russian artillery fire was particularly effective. The Russians are impressive in the type of "glacial offensive" which depends upon mass; they are determined, defensive fighters, though sluggish in manoeuvre, and the transportation, communication and industrial system which backs up the Red Army is liable to failure under stress.

THE GERMAN OFFENSIVE

Operations last week indicated that they would, indeed, have to fight desperately if the German thrust was to be parried at all. Using the same type of tactics which had won them their previous victories, the Germans launched an offensive along 2,000 miles of front. Thousands of German planes struck at Russian air fields and communication and transportation centers without warning, and, by mid-week, the Germans had claimed—probably truthfully—clear-cut air superiority.

Panzer divisions, cooperating with Stuka dive-bombers and motorized infantry, drove through the Russian lines and fanned out in the rear areas to cut communications and disrupt the Red Army.

Troop dispositions and early operations gave some indications of the German strategy. As expected, the heaviest blows were delivered from Poland as a base. Two offensives—the one north of the Pripet Marshes, the other south of them—were in the direction of Minsk-Smolensk-Moscow, and in the direction of Kiev. Another drive spearheaded north from East Prussia along the Baltic Coast littoral toward Leningrad. Still another was expected to develop from Finland across the Karelian Isthmus toward Leningrad, accompanied perhaps by land and sea operations against Murmansk.

In the south two drives across Northern Bessarabia toward Kiev, across Southern Bessarabia toward Odessa were apparently developing.

It was evident, however, that territory occupied and cities taken meant little in the fighting, except when these cities were important in the mobilization, transportation and communication scheme of the Red Army, as Minsk and Kiev are. The primary objective of the Germans is annihilation of the Red Army; they hope to accomplish it by the same tactics of mechanized infiltration, disruption of the enemy into segments and encirclement and destruction which they have used previously.

Thus began the greatest battle in history, of which the outcome, despite early German successes, is still uncertain. Most military observers believe that the only adequate strategy the Russians can follow is to fight delaying actions and to withdraw gradually—careful to keep their army as nearly intact as possible—deeper and deeper into the interior. If they can do this, keeping their army in being and mobilizing more men, and still retain part of the industrial area upon which they must depend for military supply (most of which, except for the Ural Mountain development, is roughly south and west of the Volga), the German attempt to win a quick victory has failed; Britain has gained much time, and perhaps eventually with United States help will win the war. On the other hand, if the Germans destroy the bulk of the Russian Army quickly and completely—say before Sept. 1—it seems quite probable that the Third Reich of Adolf Hitler will be in an even more powerful strategic position than it was before the two great totalitarian ideologies came to clash of arms. ◆

JULY 3, 1941

TEXT OF STALIN BROADCAST

By The Associated Press.

MOSCOW, July 3—The text of the broadcast address by Joseph Stalin, Premier and chairman of the State Committee of Defense, as translated by Tass, the official Russian news agency, follows:

Comrades! Citizens! Brothers and Sisters! Men of our Army and Navy!

I am addressing you, my friends!

The perfidious military attack on our fatherland, begun on June 22 by Hitler's Germany, is continuing.

In spite of heroic resistance of the Red Army, and although the enemy's finest divisions and finest air force units have already been smashed and have met their doom on the field of battle, the enemy continues to push forward, hurling fresh forces into the attack.

Hitler's troops have succeeded in capturing Lithuania, a considerable part of Latvia, the western part of Byelo-Russia [White Russia] and a part of the Western Ukraine.

The Fascist air force is extending the range of operations of its bombers and is bombing Murmansk, Orsha, Mogilev, Smolensk, Kiev, Odessa and Sevastopol.

A grave danger hangs over our country.

How could it have happened that our glorious Red Army surrendered a number of our cities and districts to the Fascist armies?

Is it really true that German Fascist troops are invincible, as is ceaselessly trumpeted by boastful Fascist propagandists? Of course not!

'NO INVINCIBLE ARMIES'

History shows that there are no invincible armies, and never have been. Napoleon's army was considered invincible, but it was beaten successively by Russian, English and German Armies. Kaiser Wilhelm's German Army in the period of the first imperialist war was also considered invincible, but it was beaten several times by Russian and Anglo-French forces, and was finally smashed by Anglo-French forces.

The same must be said of Hitler's German Fascist Army today. This army has not yet met with serious resistance on the Continent of Europe. Only on our territory has it met serious resistance, and if as a result of this resistance the finest divisions of Hitler's German Fascist Army have been defeated by our Red Army, it means that this army, too, can be smashed and will be smashed as were the armies of Napoleon and Wilhelm.

ENEMY 'ARMED TO THE TEETH'

Our troops are fighting heroically against an enemy armed to the teeth with tanks and aircraft. Overcoming innumerable difficulties the Red Army and Navy are self-sacrificingly disputing every inch of Soviet soil.

The main forces of the Red Army are coming into action armed with thousands of tanks and airplanes. Men of the Red Army are displaying unexampled valor. Our resistance to the enemy is growing in strength and power. Side by side with the Red Army the entire Soviet people is rising in defense of our native land.

What is required to put an end to the danger hovering over our country, and what measures must be taken to smash the enemy?

Above all, it is essential that our people, the Soviet people, should understand the full immensity of the danger that threatens out country and abandon all complacency, all heedlessness, all those moods of peaceful, constructive work which were so natural before the war but which are fatal today when war has fundamentally changed everything.

The enemy is cruel and implacable. He is out to seize our lands watered with our sweat, to seize our grain and soil secured by our labor.

ISSUE OF 'LIFE OR DEATH'

Thus the issue is one of life or death for the Soviet State, for the peoples of the U.S.S.R.: the issue is whether peoples of the Soviet Union shall remain free or fall into slavery.

The Soviet people must realize this and abandon all heedlessness, they must mobilize themselves and reorganize all their work on new, wartime lines, when there can be no mercy to the enemy.

Further, there must be no room in our ranks for whimperers and cowards, for panic-mongers and deserters; our people must know no fear in the fight and must selflessly join our patriotic was of liberation, our war against the Fascist enslavers.

Lenin, the great founder of our State, used to say that the chief virtue of the Soviet people must be courage, valor, fearlessness in struggle, readiness to fight together with the people against the enemies of our country.

This splendid virtue of the Bolshevik must become the virtue of millions and millions of the Red Army, of the Red Navy, of all peoples of the Soviet Union.

All our work must be immediately reconstructed on a war footing, everything must be subordinated to the interests of the front and the task of organizing demolition of the enemy.

The peoples of the Soviet Union now see that there is no taming of German Fascism in its savage fury and hatred of our country which has insured all working people labor in freedom and prosperity.

The peoples of the Soviet Union must rise against the enemy and defend their rights and their land. The Red Army, Red Navy and all citizens of the Soviet ▸

Union must defend every inch of Soviet soil, must fight to the last drop of blood for our towns and villages, must display the daring initiative and intelligence that are inherent in our people.

FIGHT ON SPIES AND SABOTEURS

We must wage a ruthless fight against all disorganizers of the rear, deserters, panic-mongers, rumor-mongers, exterminate spies, diversionists, enemy parachutists, rendering rapid aid in all this to our destroyer battalions. We must bear in mind that the enemy is crafty, unscrupulous, experienced in deception and dissemination of false rumors.

We must reckon with all this and not fall victim to provocation. All who by their panic-mongering and cowardice hinder the work of defense, no matter who they are, must be immediately hauled before a military tribunal.

AIM OF THE WAR

The aim of this national war in defense of our country against the Fascist oppressors is not only elimination of the danger hanging over our country, but also aid to all European peoples groaning under the yoke of German Fascism.

In this war of liberation we shall not be alone.

In this great war we shall have loyal allies in the peoples of Europe and America, including German people who are enslaved by Hitlerite despots.

Our war for the freedom of our country will merge with the struggle of the peoples of Europe and America for their independence, for democratic liberties. It will be a united front of peoples standing for freedom and against enslavement and threats of enslavement by Hitler's Fascist Armies.

In this connection the historic utterance of British Prime Minister Churchill regarding aid to the Soviet Union and the declaration of the U.S.A. Government signifying readiness to render aid to our country, which can only evoke a feeling of gratitude in the hearts of the peoples of the Soviet Union, are fully comprehensible and symptomatic.

Comrades, our forces are numberless. The overwhelming enemy will soon learn this to his cost. Side by side with the Red Army and Navy thousands of workers, collective farmers and intellectuals are rising to fight the enemy aggressor. The masses of our people will rise up in their millions.

In order to insure a rapid mobilization of all forces of the peoples of the U.S.S.R., and to repulse the enemy who treacherously attacked our country, a State Committee of Defense has been formed in whose hands the entire power of the State has been vested.

The State Committee of Defense has entered into its functions and calls upon all our people to rally around the party of Lenin-Stalin and around the Soviet Government so as self-denyingly to support the Red Army and Navy, demolish the enemy and secure victory.

All our forces for the support of our heroic Red Army and our glorious Red Navy!

All the forces of the people—for the demolition of the enemy!

Forward, to our victory! ◆

ETHIOPIAN MOP-UP NETS TEN GENERALS

Special Cable to The New York Times.

CAIRO, Egypt, July 6—General Pietro Gazzera, General de Simone, who commanded the Italian forces that took British Somaliland last August, and eight other Italian generals have surrendered in accordance with the agreement for the capitulation of the Galla Sidamo area of Ethiopia, the British announced today. This raises the number of Italian generals captured by the British to forty-one, not including brigadiers. ◆

LITVINOFF EXHORTS BRITAIN TO INVADE

Former Commissar In a Radio Plea from Moscow Advises Quick Drive on Reich

By The United Press.

LONDON, July 8—In a radio appeal by Maxim Litvinoff, Russia tonight urged Great Britain to hurl her full weight against Germany in the West while the Red Army withstood the shock of the Nazi war machine in the East and thus force Adolf Hitler to wage war on two fronts.

The former Soviet Foreign Commissar and longtime foe of the fascist dictators, implying that the moment was ripe for a British invasion of the Continent, said that the battle of Russia was forcing Herr Hitler to "withdraw more and more forces from the West to the East."

Broadcasting in English over the Moscow radio, Mr. Litvinoff promised that, whatever the sacrifices, Russia would "fight to the bitter end."

"Firm in our determination, we will fight until the Fascist barbarity is erased from the earth," Mr. Litvinoff said in concluding his speech.

HOLDS TIME OF ESSENCE

He told Britain that there was no time to be lost in striking mighty blows at Germany in the West, even though the British themselves had gained "some respite" from Herr Hitler's mammoth undertaking against Russia.

"It is important that Hitler should have no moment's rest," he said. "While his strategy was to strike at each of his adversaries at different times, ours is to strike simultaneously. Each blow now is ten times more effective and less costly than later, when each of us might be weaker."

Mr. Litvinoff, who was removed as Russian Foreign Commissar in May of 1939, about three months before the signing of the Russian-German pact of non-aggression, appealed to all countries to support Russia and Britain against "Hitler and his clique of murderers." No country, no matter how small, is secure so long as Hitlerism—he called it "the most shameful phenomenon of our age"—exists, Mr. Litvinoff warned.

He made no statement as to the course of the titanic battle of Russia but asserted bluntly that "there is no doubt that we will strain in our effort to fulfill our historic mission" alongside Britain, whatever the privations. His whole speech carried a note of caution that the war to crush Germany would be long and difficult. ◆

JULY 12, 1941

DONOVAN IS NAMED INFORMATION HEAD
Roosevelt Puts Him in Charge Of New Agency to Digest Intelligence Reports

Special to The New York Times.

WASHINGTON, July 11—William J. Donovan, commander of the Sixty-ninth Division in the World War, was appointed today by President Roosevelt to head a new intelligence agency with the title of Coordinator of Defense Information.

He will act in a civilian status, supervising reports received by the agencies of the government and digesting them for the information of President Roosevelt

Commander William J. Donovan

and the departments concerned.

The White House described Mr. Donovan's duties in a brief statement, thus:

"The President today, as Commander in Chief of the armed forces, appointed William J. Donovan Coordinator of Information.

"In his capacity as coordinator, Mr. Donovan will collect and assemble information and data bearing on national security from the various departments and agencies of the government and will analyze and collate such materials for the use of the President and such other officials as the President may designate.

"Mr. Donovan's task will be to coordinate and correlate defense information, but his work is not intended to supersede or to duplicate, or to involve any direction of or interference with the activities of the General Staff, the regular intelligence services, the Federal Bureau of Investigation or of other existing departments and agencies."

Assisting Mr. Donovan will be a relatively small staff, of whatever size is found to be necessary to carry out his assignment.

Heretofore, each department has handled its own intelligence service, in the usual manner of government bureaus, with relatively little interchange of information.

The President has told associates that the scattered reports which came to his desk often were hopelessly confusing.

Mr. Donovan's salary is not specified and there is no indication when his bureau will be ready to function. ◊

JULY 13, 1941

NAZIS DRIVE AHEAD
High Command Declares Troops Made Big Gain On Moscow Road

By C. BROOKS PETERS
By Telephone to The New York Times.

BERLIN, July 12—The German High Command announced in a special communiqué late tonight that the Stalin Line had been broken at "all decisive points." The bulletin came after days in which the High Command had maintained complete reticence about operations on the Eastern Front, and just three weeks after the invasion of Russia began.

In the northern sector, it was reported, German tank units operating in the region east of Lake Peipus, which is near the Estonian border, are advancing toward Leningrad. [According to The United Press, German forces were reported to be about 125 miles from Leningrad.]

The High Command said that strongly fortified Russian positions on the Dnieper River, in the central sector north of the Pripet Marshes, had been captured and that German troops now stood approximately 125 miles east of Minsk, on the route to Moscow. Vitebsk, in this zone, has been in German hands since yesterday, it was stated.

Farther south, the special bulletin declared, the German forces that took Lwow and advanced eastward are now "close before" Kiev, the capital of the Ukraine.

PUSH TO DNIESTER CLAIMED

The allied German and Rumanian forces, operating from Moldavia, were said to have thrown the Russians back to and across the Dniester River on a wide front. Slovak, Hungarian and German forces, according to the communiqué, are pursuing the Russians out of Galicia.

The Germans asserted that along the entire front numerous Russian formations already showed signs of disintegrating. Any hopes the Russians may have entertained of engaging in counter-operations on a large scale, it was stated, have already been destroyed by the actions of the German Air Force, which

reportedly has ruined the Russian railway system.

On the other hand, the reinforcements and supplies necessary for the continued advance of the vanguard of German motorized and tank units have been assured, the Germans declared. According to tonight's communiqué, supply bases already have been advanced and established "close to the former Stalin Line."

Yesterday German infantry units fought their way into the "wet zone" of the Stalin Line in the northern sector, according to reports received before the special bulletin was issued. An attack was launched on the Russian positions in the swampy terrain south of Lake Peipus, somewhere between Pskov and Ostrov.

RUSSIAN POSITIONS STORMED

Since dawn today German shock troop formations had been reported storming the Russian fortifications that lie behind the "wet zone." There were few details, however—today's regular High Command communiqué said merely that "operations of the allies forces on the Eastern Front are proceeding according to plan."

The German forces engaged in ❱

Dispersed remnants of the Russian forces that had been caught in a pocket between Bialystok and Minsk were reported today to have been completely wiped out. All lines of retreat had been cut off, the Germans declared, and the Russians' position was hopeless.

In the middle of the extensive front, in the territory around Vitebsk, Russian units attempted to counter-attack the German vanguard on Thursday, according to the Germans. Before the attack could be set in motion, it was asserted, German motorized units slashed into the center of the Russian concentrations and dispersed them, destroying 109 Russian tanks.

According to information received in Berlin tonight, a new pocket has been closed about Russian forces in the Vitebsk sector. The Germans declared that trapped Russian units had endeavored to escape yesterday. Twenty-one Russian tanks, eight of them fifty-two-ton machines, were reported to have been destroyed in twenty minutes by German units with anti-aircraft guns.

It was said that in the southern sector heavy rains had made the German advance more difficult. Nonetheless, according to the official news agency, the Reich forces were able yesterday to throw back Russian tank and infantry units that endeavored to halt their drive. ◇

355 miles in the last sixteen days. These marches, it was asserted, were particularly difficult because the Russians had placed all sorts of obstacles along the line of advance and these had to be removed by sappers. Roads were destroyed, bridges permitted to fall into disrepair and wells destroyed or poisoned, the Germans said.

◀ this new offensive in the northern sector were reported to have marched

---

SYRIA AND LEBANON OCCUPIED BY ALLIES
British and Free French Get Use of Airports and Harbors, Heading Off Germans

By HAROLD DENNY
Special Cable to The New York Times.

CAIRO, Egypt, July 15—British troops at noon today began full occupation of Syria and Lebanon under the terms of the agreement signed yesterday at Acre, Palestine, by General Sir Henry Maitland Wilson for the British and General Joseph de Verdillac for the Vichy military authorities. Thus Great Britain has at last forestalled the Germans in one important theatre of the war.

The terms of the truce, as announced by the British Embassy in Cairo, follow faithfully those offered to General Henri Fernand Dentz, Vichy's High Commissioner, last Thursday, by General Wilson and General Georges Catroux on behalf of the Free French through the United States Consul General in Beirut.

General Dentz then demurred at having any dealings with the Free French. The British insisted, however, and General Dentz assented to General Catroux's participating in all the negotiations.

PRINCIPAL TERMS OF TRUCE

In addition to full occupation of the mandated areas, the agreement called for the surrender of all except personal weapons and of planes and aeronautical equipment, ships and port installations, other materiel, munitions and fuel stocks. The British are to have the use of all air fields in Syria and Lebanon.

Prisoners on both sides are to be freed and the British agree not to impose sanctions on Vichy soldiers or officials. The British reserve the right to enlist in their forces "special troops" (native levies) as these are released from Vichy's military service. French soldiers and civilians are to have the choice of repatriation, joining the British and Free French forces or remaining in the mandated regions as civilians.

A commission of three persons to be named by the British and two by the Vichy authorities will supervise execution of the truce terms.

The convention, which is purely military, does not mention independence for Syria and Lebanon. However, this was an essential point in original terms and is implicit in the new accord. The

JULY 22, 1941

'V' CREDITED TO BELGIAN
Key-Sign in Flemish and French to Worry Nazis In His Country

LONDON, July 21 (UP)—The V symbol was revealed today as the conception of Victor de Laveleye, 46-year-old Belgian broadcaster with the BBC. He said the idea came to him last January as he sat with a Flemish refugee in the lobby of a London hotel. They were discussing means of uniting their compatriots.

"We were searching for a sign the Belgians could put up everywhere to worry the Nazis," he said. "Finally we agreed it had to be one with the same meaning in French, Flemish and English. We went through the alphabet.

"I hit on the letter V because it is the key in the French 'victoire,' the Flemish 'vrijheid' and the English 'victory.' I first mentioned it in my Belgian broadcast on Jan. 14, saying it was the perfect symbol for the Anglo-Belgian entente." ◆

next step is expected to be a meeting of General Catroux with Syrian leaders to work out arrangements.

TERMS DEEMED GENEROUS
Satisfaction is expressed here at the outcome of the negotiations, and it is made clear they are considered generous.

As a result of the signing of the agreement, the use of bases in Syria is now denied to the Germans and direct land communication is established between the British–Free French allies and Turkey.

It is stated that the British sought not to humiliate their former allies and showed only respect for men who conceived it their duty to obey orders. A heavy responsibility, however, is held to rest on those who gave the orders. Vichy's resistance is described here as a hopeless struggle that could only help Germany and Frenchmen fight for Reichsfuehrer Hitler without spending a drop of German blood. ◆

JULY 27, 1941

TOKYO IS SHOCKED BY ECONOMIC WAR
Silk Exchange Closes—Stocks Fall To 10-Year Low In Excited Trading

By OTTO D. TOLISCHUS
Wireless to The New York Times.

TOKYO, July 26—Within a few hours after President Roosevelt's order freezing Japanese assets and credits in the United States was announced, the Japanese Government retaliated by freezing the assets and credits of American and Philippine nationals and corporations within the Japanese Empire. The government was in consultation with the Manchukuoan and Nanking regimes to extend the freezing operations in their territories as well.

The freezing order, which takes the form of putting transactions of the affected nationals under the foreign exchange control law, will be promulgated on Monday and become effective immediately. Inasmuch as the British Government has likewise frozen Japanese funds throughout the British Empire and in addition has abrogated all commercial treaties with Japan, the same regulations will be applied to British Empire subjects as soon as official notification of the British action has been received.

Therewith, in the view of Japanese official quarters, business circles and the press, has begun an open economic war between the United States and the British

Empire on the one hand and the Japanese Empire and the areas it controls on the other hand. It is expected to wither whatever international trade remains and in the words of the ultranationalist Nichi Nichi is but "one step from armed warfare." The announcement of Mr. Roosevelt's action and Japan's counter action came simultaneously with the announcement here of Japan's agreement with Vichy for the "joint defense of French Indo-China." It trailed Vichy's announcement of the agreement by some forty-eight hours, but that made the inter-relation between the various actions all the more impressive.

It was obvious that not only to the uninformed Japanese public but even to otherwise well-informed business quarters the various developments of the day came as a profound shock. The Stock Exchange average, which had ranged between 150 and 170 during the last two years, dropped more than six points touching 94.8 or the lowest point since 1931.

In point of fact there were indications that President Roosevelt's swift action had surprised even the government, which, though it had taken some precautionary measures to meet the consequences of its move on French Indo-China, had been rather hopefully relying on former Foreign Minister Yosuke Matsuoka's past assurances of America's passivity and on the influence of American isolationists. These latter have been commanding considerable attention in the Japanese press.

NO FURTHER AGGRAVATION
At the same time perhaps the most notable feature of the situation is that, except for some alarming newspaper statements, there is no desire in any Japanese quarters to aggravate the situation any further. Business circles even express the hope that the American decrees may ❯

Japanese Foreign Minister Yosuke Matsuoka circa 1940.

leave some loopholes for a modicum of trade on a cash basis.

In respect to its advance into French Indo-China, the government, both in its official announcement and in a radio broadcast by Dr. Nobufumi Ito, president of the Information Board, who is sometimes referred to as the "Japanese Goebbels," has emphasized that Japan was acting in "self-defense" and in perfect agreement with the Vichy government.

The official announcement stressed France's consistent friendly cooperation with Japan and the long-standing friendly relations between Japan and French Indo-China, antedating Japan's century-long self-isolation. It asserted, however, that new developments in Europe and East Asia were threatening the security of French Indo-China, which in self-defense neither Japan nor France could overlook.

NEGOTIATIONS CALLED FRIENDLY

For that reason, the announcement continued, Japan opened up negotiations with Vichy, which, it said progressed smoothly in a friendly atmosphere and led to the conclusion on July 21 of a joint defense agreement for Indo-China, the exact nature of which was not specified.

"Japan and France," the announcement says, "thus have been ushered into more intimate relations with each other, with French Indo-China serving as their connecting link." Needless to say, it will greatly contribute toward the stabilization of co-existence and co-prosperity in Greater East Asia.

In line with this announcement Dr. Ito repeated the constant complaint of all Japanese quarters, that "the United States Government fails to understand Japan's real intentions."

Government quarters have been careful to refrain from any direct charges against either the United States or Britain. The press, however, asserts that French Indo-China was threatened with the fate of Syria because of British measures, and a large de Gaullist element in Saigon as well as concentrations of Chungking troops on the north.

Domei, the official news agency, says that the Japanese step involves "neither territorial aggression nor a prerequisite for Japan's armed southward advance, but merely a peaceful economic policy."

In the view of some seasoned observers here the Japanese advance into French Indo-China might in fact be more a flanking move to cut off the last communications of Generalissimo Chiang Kai-shek for the "last big push" advocated by Major Gen. Shunroku Hata, Japanese Commander in Chief in China, to "settle the China incident," which is still Japan's primary concern rather than another step in Japan's southward advance.

THREAT TO THAILAND

But the government radio suggested today that Britain might undertake the "military oppression" of Thailand as a countermeasure to the Japanese step. This suggestion holds ominous possibilities.

As regards the American and British freezing order, it is generally admitted here that it is bound to have a crippling effect on Japan's trade, not only with the United States and the British Empire but also with South America. It will necessitate a drastic readjustment and more cash payments, even within the "Greater East Asia Co-prosperity Sphere," where balances still have been settled in New York in dollars.

But Finance Minister Masatsune Ogura, in a reassuring statement to the press, declared that Japan's American balances were small and that American-Japanese trade had been diminishing, so the effect of President Roosevelt's measure would be "comparatively slight." ◊

JULY 27, 1941

MacARTHUR MADE CHIEF IN FAR EAST
Former U.S. Army Head To Lead Combined Force with Rank Of Lieutenant General

Special to The New York Times.

WASHINGTON, July 26—General Douglas A. MacArthur, who retired in 1937 at the age of 57 years, was today recalled to active service in the United States Army, and supplementing President Roosevelt's order creating a new Army component to be known as "The United States Army Forces in the Far East," received the rank of lieutenant general and command of the combined United States Army in the Philippines and the entire Filipino forces.

Under his new appointment General MacArthur, who has been military adviser to the Philippine Commonwealth since 1935, and has ranked as a field marshal of the Philippine Army in the islands since 1937, will now outrank Major Gen. George Grunert, commander of the Army's Philippine Department. He will have the task of welding into a single efficient military unit the United States troops now in the islands and the partially trained Filipino reserves. His new appointment created a stir in military and political circles here today because of the divisions of expert opinion on his plans for defending the islands.

WAS ADVISER IN PHILIPPINES

General MacArthur, who was the youngest Chief of Staff the United States Army has ever had, was assigned as military adviser to the Philippine Commonwealth in 1935, two years before he retired, and just after he completed five years as Chief of Staff in Washington.

His plans for raising and training a defense force for the Philippines were at first received with acclaim by President Manuel L. Quezon and many other Filipino leaders, but a year ago continuing criticism of the feasibility and effectiveness of his scheme evidently cooled Mr. Quezon's enthusiasm for the project, for the Commonwealth President then stated publicly that he did not believe an invader could be repelled even if every citizen were to be well equipped militarily and perfectly trained.

A month before President Quezon's statement the American High Commissioner to the Philippines, Francis B. Sayre, had criticized the MacArthur plan, stating that he did not believe that even the then whole military strength of the United States Army could successfully defend the islands.

STATEMENT OF CONFIDENCE

In 1939, envisaging a possible Japanese attempt at an invasion, General MacArthur issued a statement at Manila saying:

"The battle would have to be brought to these shores, so that the full strength of the enemy would be relatively vitiated by the vicissitudes of an overseas expedition. ... In any event, it would cost the enemy, in my opinion, at least a half million men and upward of five billions of dollars in money to pursue such an adventure with any hope of success."

This led to a series of sharp disputes with other military men, who cited Japan's overseas expeditions to China, their successes against Chinese armies infinitely better drilled and equipped than the Filipino forces, and the fact that long before the Japanese suffered 500,000 casualties in China they had conquered an area more than five times as large as the area of the whole Philippine Archipelago.

The MacArthur plan, adopted by the Commonwealth in 1936, envisaged a Filipino defense force of 400,000 men by 1947, each of whom would have had roughly half a year of training. The plan was to train 40,000 youths of 20 years of age every year. When the plan first went into effect it was received with enthusiasm by the Filipinos, and in the first two years there were many more than the 40,000 desired applicants, but only 40,000 were accepted each year.

Early in 1939 General MacArthur declared that the Commonwealth then had a well-trained army of 80,000 men. In view of this statement, more than two years ago, today's estimate issued here by the War Department, that the force now consists of only 75,000 men, occasioned considerable surprise. ◆

Philippine President Manuel Quezon, left, congratulating General Douglas MacArthur on his return to active duty.

JULY 27, 1941

JAPANESE OCCUPY BASES AT SAIGON
Observers in Indo-China Think Japan Will Move Toward Russia as Next Step

SAIGON, Indo-China, July 26 (AP)—A Japanese military outpost far down the coast of French Indo-China toward Singapore and the Netherlands Indies began sprouting in Saigon today with the arrival of the first Japanese equipment and high army and navy officers.

Japan apparently was losing no time transforming her newly acquired site into a base for her own uses. The French already have begun vacating Saigon's modern air field and the half-mile of warehouses at the waterfront.

With Japanese here out for a flag-waving reception, Maj. Gen. Raishiro Sumita, chief of the Japanese military mission in Indo-China, landed with three army and navy aides in a French civilian air transport from the north and the first column of Japanese military trucks rolled in.

Naval and transport ships are expected here within the next three days, possibly tomorrow, and trains were understood already to be en route from Hanoi with more Japanese Army and Navy officers and business men.

It is believed here, however, that the accomplishment of this new advance completes Japan's plans for the present in Southern Asia. Observers here contend that the Japanese now will turn their attention toward Russia before undertaking any new venture in this direction. ◆

JULY 27, 1941

RUSSIANS SKILLED IN GUERRILLA WAR
Army and Civilians Trained to Fight Behind Lines

By BERTHOLD C. FRIEDL

Five weeks of the Battle of Russia have thrown into clear relief the chief difference between German and Russian military education. German shock troops are drilled in isolated offensives in enemy territory, in destruction of the enemy's communications and opening the way for the advance of their own infantry columns. The psychological basis of German initiative is an offensive war.

The Red Army is quite different. One of its outstanding activities has been the training of soldiers and officers for guerrilla war, and the providing of technical bases for this type of fighting. Emphasis has been laid on making small army units independent of the center, through the development of initiative even among the lowest-rank commanding officers. All its units are capable, if cut off from the main body, of continuing the battle. When the army is forced to fall back, predetermined groups remain behind the enemy lines and form the kernel of future guerrilla units. Not only do these groups have at their disposal specially made small, speedy tanks and sometimes even artillery (an entirely new feature in this type of fighting), but there are also previously located bases to which they can retreat and where they find supplies, arms and munitions.

GUERRILLA STRONGHOLDS
Because of these preparations the German Army has not been able to clean up the Pripet marshes, in which there is an enormous network of guerrilla bases. The widespread forests of the Ukraine and White Russia are also strongholds of the "irregulars." In cases where Red Army divisions, or even whole armies, have been encircled, these large units divided up into prearranged small groups.

In such a guerrilla war, ordinary methods of assessing victory and defeat and old conceptions of what positions are militarily defensible or indefensible become worthless. While in past Nazi campaigns the conquest of a key position was the end of a battle, in this one it is only the beginning.

The new development in warfare is one of the reasons for the reintroduction of political commissars in the ❭

Red Army. While it may be that to a certain extent the task of the commissars is the supervision of unreliable military commanders, their main purpose today is coordination of the general political interest with the military one. Continuation of a battle may thus be possible long after the position has become untenable from the military specialist's point of view.

How have the people been prepared for this type of fighting?

To begin with, the whole Russian nation has had a certain amount of military training. Factories and collectives are armed. At least a quarter of the population knows how to handle firearms. Throughout the last twenty years all life has been organized around the central idea of meeting the threat of war and of planning the role of each individual in the common task of national defense.

Even the education of youth is conducted along lines of national defense. Care of physical health, strengthening of emotional stability, early socialization, organization of sports, have been bound up with this motif of raising a race of strong, courageous fighters. Contemporary Soviet dramas are often based on the deeds of heroes in the civil war. Children practice parachute jumping, and do exercises of defense against enemy parachutists. The pupils of every Soviet school receive physical training. If they can pass a rigorous examination they are entitled to wear the GTO (Ready for Work and Defense) button, a great honor. Eighty-four per cent of Red Army men of 1940 wore this button.

Russian guerrillas discuss a plan to attack German positions in 1941.

EVERY FACTORY A FORT

When young people come out of school into the factory or kolkhoz they are enrolled in the armed workers' and peasants' groups, which are a continuation of the old partisan troops of civil war days. Every industrial plant has an armed defense force. Wrecking of factories, roads and bridges in consonance with Stalin's "scorched earth" policy is an easy matter, since every plant has its secret munitions depot, where is stored sufficient dynamite for use in case of need. Furthermore, the psychological handicap of private ownership—reluctance to damage one's personal property—is not a factor. In regions overrun by German troops those Soviet citizens organized in collective farms and workshops remain together as guerrilla groups.

The attitude of the ordinary worker in Russia, an attitude traditional in Russia, is that the welfare of the Fatherland depends on him and him alone. War has, if anything, strengthened this attitude, so that any given Russian may be counted upon at the proper moment to risk all he has, even his life. This may be noted in contrast with the psychology of the French, who for years were told that the Maginot Line would defend them and that they might go about their business even in case of an enemy invasion. Just as this teaching tended to stifle in the French people all initiative and desire to fight, so, on the contrary, Russian psychological preparation has not only built the resistance of the Red Army, but created the basis for its support by the entire population. ◊

JULY 30, 1941

BERLIN CONFIDENT OF SOVIET DEFEAT

By C. BROOKS PETERS
By Telephone to The New York Times.

BERLIN, July 29—In its communiqué today, the German High Command revealed little of importance of its operations on the Eastern Front. Other reports from the Russian theatre also gave slight indication as to how quickly or slowly the German forces are advancing against the tenacious resistance of the Red Army.

The vital battle of Smolensk continues. According to an editorial in tomorrow's Voelkischer Beobachter, it is being fought in the zone between Vitebsk and Mogilev, where the Germans reportedly cracked the Stalin Line at Vyazma, some sixty miles east of Smolensk.

After the gigantic hole in the Stalin Line between Vitebsk and Mogilev had been made, it is said here, tanks and motorized infantry were to push through it and resume the tactics of a war of movement.

To close this hole, however, the Russians are reported to have hurled wave after wave of men into the opening. The attempt, the Germans report, "can now be viewed as having failed." The war of movement, they add, is in full progress between the Dvina and Dnieper Rivers in a zone at least 100 miles deep.

Most of the Soviet units reported pocketed by German pincer movements between the Stalin Line and Smolensk were said officially today to have been wiped out. The "last pocket east of Smolensk," the High Command asserted, was in the process of being destroyed.

This pocket evidently is between Smolensk and Vyazma. Whether other Russian forces in this same sector broke through the German pockets has not been revealed here.

In a few days, the German command promised, the results of the Smolensk battle would be disclosed to the world. For the present the Germans asserted only that large numbers of prisoners and sizable quantities of materiel had been taken.

From the southern wing of the invasion, the Germans announced that Rumanian troops had occupied Akkerman, at the mouth of the Dniester River and on the Black Sea. Therewith, they asserted, German and Rumanian forces under General Ion Antonescu, Premier of Rumania, had freed Bessarabia from the

Spires of the Kremlin are silhouetted by a Luftwaffe flair during a German air attack on Moscow in 1941.

Soviet. Odessa, the Germans pointed out, is only thirty air miles from Akkerman.

In the southern Ukraine, allied German, Rumanian, Hungarian and Slovak forces were reported to have the Russians in retreat, to be meeting only local resistance and to be approaching the Black Sea on a broad front, although the weather remained inclement. Kiev, the capital of the Ukraine, appears still to be in Russian hands, and there is no reason to believe that German troops succeeded in crossing the Dnieper River in this sector.

In the north the Finns and Germans were reported to be making progress. Between Lake Ladoga and Lake Onega, units under Field Marshal Carl Gustav Mannerheim were said to have crossed the old Russian-Finnish border at three points.

West of Lake Peipus, the Germans officially reported that Soviet forces had been trapped and were about to be destroyed by the Nazi forces charged with cleaning up Estonia.

MOSCOW BOMBED AGAIN

Moscow was attacked for the seventh time last night by the German Air Force. Continued air raids on the Russian capital, which is at the same time the Russians' major communications and industrial center, must "in time" reduce the Soviet power of resistance, authoritative military quarters here asserted.

The present war, declares the Nazi party organ, the Voelkischer Beobachter, finds "the two strongest military powers in the world" opposing each other. Time, therefore, in the present opinion of German editors, is an element that can well be considerable in a campaign being fought over so extensive an area as the Russian theatre. ◆

Chapter 8

"AIM OF PRESIDENT IS WAR"

August–November 1941

As the crisis in Russia and in the Atlantic deepened, the chances of keeping the United States out of the conflict seemed slim. American public opinion on the issue, however, remained divided. When a survey of all the nation's newspaper publishers and editors was conducted to find out their views on immediate war, the 871 replies were two to one against U.S. entry.

Roosevelt edged closer to belligerency when on August 9, at Placentia Bay in Newfoundland, aboard the American cruiser *Augusta,* he met Churchill face-to-face to discuss the future of the war. The press were held at bay until the public announcement on August 14 of a communiqué from the historic meeting, which has been known ever since as the Atlantic Charter. The two leaders pledged their countries to reestablish democracy and national self-determination throughout the war zones. No formal military commitment was made by the United States, but it was plain for all the world to see that Roosevelt had thrown his political and moral weight behind the efforts of the Allied powers. Hitler reacted angrily to the announcement and assumed that American intervention was only a matter of time. The Japanese poured scorn on a statement that challenged their right to an Asian empire. Churchill was glad they had forged the joint agreement but he doubted whether it would mean immediate American entry into the war.

On the other side of the world, the vast contest in the Soviet Union, along a front of a thousand miles, grew fiercer as the Red Army battled to keep the enemy away from the Russian heartland. By September, Leningrad was surrounded, but not captured. A siege began that was to see the death of up to a million people over the following two years. The war news from both sides presented as rosy a picture as possible, but there was no disguising the slow Soviet retreat. On September 19 Kiev surrendered to the Germans and Soviet forces suffered 527,000 casualties. On September 30 Hitler launched Operation Typhoon, aimed at capturing Moscow, the Soviet capital. The Soviet government left the city to go to Kuibyshev, farther east, to safety. Hitler flew to Berlin where he boasted before an ecstatic crowd that the Soviet dragon was slain and would never rise again.

The Nazi regime was already planning to ship German Jews to the East, where, unbeknownst to most people in the West, hundreds of thousands of Soviet Jewish men, women and children had already been killed by SS murder squads. The German high command thought there were few Soviet reserves left and expected Stalin to sue for peace, as the French had done in 1940, so that the harsh racial empire could be built. But the winter was approaching and time, as Hanson Baldwin wrote in The Times, was a key factor in war.

For the United States the greater crisis remained in the Pacific. The Times reported on September 21 that negotiations between the Americans and the Japanese were at "a virtual standstill." The British continued to express confidence in their major base at Singapore as a barrier to sudden Japanese expansion, but the news from Asia had a new edge of menace to it. The isolationists remained committed to American neutrality and continued to condemn Roosevelt's foreign policy, though with Japan there was little hope of rational compromise.

In late September Senator Gerald Nye announced at a dinner of the Steuben Society, a group of American citizens of German heritage, that the "aim of the President is war." Outside, protesters gathered bearing placards that read, "Der Fuehrer thanks you for your many services!" The news of German success continued to pour in from the Russian steppes to the gray seas of the Atlantic. The Times's tone was unmistakable: "U-Boats Roam Sea with a New Fury"; "Germans Smash On." But the crisis was to come not from Europe but thousands of miles away in the central Pacific.

AUGUST 1, 1941

NEWSPAPERS OPPOSE OUR ENTRY INTO WAR
2 to 1 Against It,
A Survey by Editor and Publisher Shows

The daily newspapers of the country in a proportion of more than two to one oppose immediate participation by the United States in the war, it was announced yesterday by Editor and Publisher as a result of a survey made by the magazine that will be published in its issue tomorrow.

A questionnaire was sent to the 1,878 dailies listed in the magazine's international year book, and 871 replies were received. Of these, 615 opposed active military and naval participation, 250 favored such action and the rest failed to reply. The magazine commented that the survey demonstrated that "the majority of

editors are opposed to United States participation in a European war, now or in the future, assuming the continuance of the present situation of the United States in relation to the warring nations."

"However, there is no doubt but that this opinion would change overnight following an overt act on the part of any of the Axis powers," it continued.

A majority of editors also held, the survey showed, that the United States, in its own strategic interests, should seize bases owned by foreign powers. Majorities also favored Federal laws regulating commodity prices and compelling arbitration in labor disputes. ◇

AUGUST 7, 1941

NAZIS DEPICT HAVOC
Claim 895,000 Prisoners and Vast Materiel in 'Destructive' Feats

By C. BROOKS PETERS
By Telephone to The New York Times.

BERLIN, Aug. 6—After weeks of almost absolute silence on the course of the invasion of Russia, the Supreme Command of the German armed forces released at noon today a series of special communiqués, partly recapitulating the results of the operations on the Eastern Front from the break through the Stalin Line announced on July 12 up to the present.

Aside from reporting on the total losses in men and equipment suffered by the Soviet since the invasion began on June 22, however, today's series of

Russian prisoners in one of the first German concentration camps in Soviet territory, July 1941.

The German Claims and Russian Counter-Claims: In a series of special communiques yesterday the Nazi High Command reported in the progress of its drives for Leningrad, Moscow and Kiev. Arrows indicate the extent of the advances credited to the German spearheads; numbered squares show where the Russians claim to be fighting. In their drives for Leningrad (1) the Nazis say they have pierced the Stalin Line, captured Pskov, Porkhov and Kholm and pushed north up both sides of Lake Peipus; the Russians report they are standing firm in Northern Estonia (5), counter-attacking near Porkhov (6) and beating off Nazi assaults around Kholm (7). The Germans say the battle of Smolensk (2) has been victoriously concluded; the Russians assert they still hold Smolensk and are counter-attacking from Orsha to Dorogobuzh (8). On the Kiev front (3), according to the Nazis, they are successfully continuing a battle of encirclement; Moscow, however, says Nazi spearheads at Korosten and Byelaya Tserkov (9) have been smashed. In the far south (4), Berlin declares, German and Rumanian troops have reconquered all Bessarabia and pushed northeast across the central Dniester to join the forces from the north.

announcements added little to the information previously revealed about the present positions of the opposing armies. Moreover, they neither asserted, as did the special announcement released on July 2, that another "decision of world political import" had been forced, nor implied that the definite defeat of the Russian Army was imminent.

Since June 22, the Germans declared, the Russians have suffered the following losses in man power and materiel captured or destroyed: 895,000 prisoners, 13,145 tanks, 10,388 pieces of artillery and 9,082 planes. The number of Soviet killed or wounded is officially

said to be "many times" the number captured, but authoritative military quarters refused to explain whether that meant more than twice the number captured.

Informed German quarters, however, estimated that between 2,500,000 and 3,00,000 Russians have been killed or wounded. Thus the total loss in effectives is estimated here to be between 3,500,000 and 4,000,000.

The Russian census figure of 1939 gives the total population of the U.S.S.R.—without the annexed Finnish, Baltic and southeastern territories—at around 170,000,000. Allowing three divisions for each million of the population, the Russians may have some 510 divisions. If each division totals 25,000 men, the total Soviet force would be 12,750,000. Other neutral sources have estimated the Russian military potential at 17,500,000 men.

Therefore, if the Red Army losses are already between 3,500,000 and 4,000,000, this would be between one-fifth and one-third of the total strength in manpower. Conservative informed German quarters, however, declare merely that most of the Russian forces

that had been deployed at the outbreak of hostilities have been defeated. Step by step, they add, the Russians are approaching destruction.

SILENT ON GERMAN LOSSES
The Germans did not make a single reference to their own losses on the Eastern Front. In recapitulating the double battle of Bialystok and Minsk they asserted that their losses were "happily small." Informed quarters declared that, "relative to enemy casualties, Reich losses were small."

The last of today's series of announcements asserted that several factors had made it possible that the "tremendously armed Soviet forces could be beaten." This is interpreted to refer to the forces already defeated and not to the entire Russian armed forces. The Supreme Command declared that a new phase of the operations had begun.

Particularly interesting is the statement that it has been possible for the Germans to restore rail connections in the territory occupied. They declare the rail system is functioning to its full extent almost as far as the fighting zones.

The five communiqués were read in unbroken succession over a national hook-up. The introduction admitted that the German population had misinterpreted the long silence of the Supreme Command. But, it added, this had been necessary because the Russians' communications did not give them an accurate picture of the fighting front. Now, however, the "just" wish of the German people to be informed daily of the newest developments could be fulfilled. ◇

AUGUST 14, 1941

NEW 'DUNKERQUE' IS SEEN AT ODESSA ALL FRONTS UNDER STTACK

By C. BROOKS PETERS
By Telephone to The New York Times.

BERLIN, Aug. 13—According to official German reports, the German armed forces are successfully attacking on all fronts in the Russian theatre of war, including the sector east of Kiev, and are making particularly rapid headway in the Southern Ukraine.

There German and allied motorized units and infantry divisions are said to be still pursuing Soviet forces that are retreating southward. The Russians are being pushed into their Black Sea ports, the Germans declare, and thus may be trapped with that body of water at their backs and no possibility of escape eastward across the Dnieper River.

According to German reports, it begins to appear probable that sizable Soviet forces may face a new Dunkerque between Odessa and Ochakov—that is, be barred from all save sea lines of escape. To what extent the Russian Black Sea Fleet and air force will be able to evacuate troops from harbors in the Southern Ukraine may be seen within the next few days, it is remarked here.

TOLL ON SHIPPING CLAIMED
In fact, informed Berlin quarters de- ▶

clare the pressure on the Russians in this sector already is so great that the Soviet command is trying to evacuate forces trapped in Odessa and ship them to the Crimea. According to these quarters, the German Air Force has taken measures to hinder this evacuation and has sunk 22,100 tons of transport shipping and two destroyers in this region, in addition to damaging a vessel of 4,000 tons.

The Russians, it is said, have begun to use lighters to evacuate their forces. This, informed quarters add, suggests another Dunkerque, but they express doubt that the Russians are able to effect as successful a retreat as the British did across the English Channel last year.

The retreat southward in the Ukraine appears to be general, according to German reports. The only engagements mentioned are with rearguard units that are trying to slow down the German pursuit sufficiently to enable the Soviet units to retire in order. In these encounters, the Germans officially declare, the Russians are suffering heavy losses in men and equipment.

Today, according to the official news agency D.N.B., the attacks of the German air arm were directed chiefly and with particular intensity against "crossings" over the southern reaches of the Dnieper. These "crossings" are said to be jammed because of the size of the forces trying to escape.

GERMAN BOMBERS ACTIVE

In the southern sector German bombers are credited with having destroyed yesterday 240 motor vehicles, eight tanks, two armored trains and stretches of railway. Along the entire front the Germans claim to have destroyed 184 planes, 121 in dogfights and sixty-three on the ground, with the loss of only three of their own planes.

In the center of the Eastern Front the Germans report that encircled Soviet units frantically attempted yesterday to escape from the pocket in which they are held. No indication is given of the present geographical stand in this sector, but the Germans declare the Russians suffered heavy losses there yesterday.

In the north, the Germans assert, bombs from their planes destroyed various stretches of the Leningrad-Moscow railway. In the same sector attacks are said to have been repulsed with the loss of eighteen Russian tanks. Counterattacks by the Germans are reported to have been successful and ten additional tanks and thirty-two pieces of artillery are said to have been destroyed.

South of Lake Ilmen the 103d Russian Infantry Regiment is said to have been encircled and, except for a few prisoners, annihilated. ◆

The Official Statement

By The United Press.

WASHINGTON, Aug. 14—The text of the official statement on the Roosevelt-Churchill meeting follows:

The President of the United States and the Prime Minister, Mr. Churchill, representing His Majesty's Government in the United Kingdom, have met at sea.

They have been accompanied by officials of their two governments, including high-ranking officers of their military, naval and air services.

The whole problem of the supply of munitions of war, as provided by the Lease-Lend Act, for the armed forces of the United States and for those countries actively engaged in resisting aggression has been further examined.

Lord Beaverbrook, the Minister of Supply of the British Government, has joined in these conferences. He is going to proceed to Washington to discuss further details with appropriate officials of the United States Government. These conferences will also cover the supply problems of the Soviet Union.

JAPANESE SCORN THE EIGHT POINTS
Roosevelt-Churchill Plan Is 'Nothing New' And Besides It Is 'Too Late,' They Hold

TOKYO, Aug. 15 (UP)—The joint declaration yesterday by President Roosevelt and Prime Minister Winston Churchill "contains nothing new," and even if their eight points for a new world order could be enforced they are "now too late," authorized quarters said today.

Tokyo was most interested in the fourth point of the "Anglo-American bloc"—the one concerning trade and equality of access to world supplies of raw materials—but its language was denounced as "vague" and "noncommittal." In this point, it was said, lies the "whole cause of the present world struggle."

Japan, it was added, has reason to know that London and Washington never have been able to envisage economic equality on the part of any "have-not nation," and Japan will be unwilling to believe that President Roosevelt and Prime Minister Churchill intend, or will be able in the future, to give this country "an equal chance in world markets."

REVERSAL IS SEEN

It is strange, an informed source said, to hear two nations that for years jealously have guarded the bulk of the world's wealth both in raw materials and consuming markets now talking of a new era of economic equality.

Newspapers considered the Roosevelt-Churchill declaration of less importance than German reports of victories on the Ukraine front in the war against Russia.

The Russo-German conflict remains the key to the international situation, Nichi Nichi said, and Japan must not "relax her watchfulness for a single moment."

The small ultra-Nationalist newspaper Kokumin, commenting on the Roosevelt-Churchill declaration, asserted that Britain was in her last struggle to preserve the status quo in the Far East, but would fail because of Japan's "immutable determination to establish a new order in East Asia regardless of British-American plots and manoeuvres." A reckless attitude on the part of London and Washington, this newspaper said, will "only push the Far Eastern situation into a more dangerous stage."

"Americans should realize their laughable folly in playing into British hands," it added.

If the Roosevelt-Churchill declaration serves any purpose at all, Kokumin declared, it will be to "mark a turning point for an intensified Axis offensive." ◆

The President and the Prime Minister have had several conferences. They have considered the dangers to world civilization arising from the policies of military domination by conquest upon which the Hitlerite government of Germany and other governments associated therewith have embarked, and have made clear the steps which their countries are respectively taking for their safety in the face of these dangers.

They have agreed upon the following joint declaration:

The President of the United States of America and the Prime Minister, Mr. Churchill, representing His Majesty's Government in the United Kingdom, being met together, deem it right to

President Roosevelt, left, with British Prime Minister Winston Churchill aboard the HMS Prince of Wales, during their Atlantic Meeting in August 1941.

make known certain common principles in the national policies of their respective countries on which they base their hopes for a better future for the world.

FIRST, their countries seek no aggrandizement, territorial or other;

SECOND, they desire to see no territorial changes that do not accord with the freely expressed wishes of the peoples concerned;

THIRD, they respect the right of all peoples to choose the form of government under which they will live; and they wish to see sovereign rights and

self-government restored to those who have been forcibly deprived of them;

FOURTH, they will endeavor, with due respect for their existing obligations, to further the enjoyment by all States, great or small, victor or vanquished, of access, on equal terms, to the trade and to the raw materials of the world which are needed for their economic prosperity;

FIFTH, they desire to bring about the fullest collaboration between all nations in the economic field with the object of securing, for all, improved labor standards, economic adjustment and social security;

SIXTH, after the final destruction of the Nazi tyranny, they hope to see established a peace which will afford to all nations the means of dwelling in safety within their own boundaries, and which will afford assurance that all the men in all the lands may live out their lives in freedom from fear and want;

SEVENTH, such a peace should enable all men to traverse the high seas and oceans without hindrance;

EIGHTH, they believe that all of the nations of the world, for realistic as well as spiritual reasons, must come to the abandonment of the use of force. Since no future peace can be maintained if land, sea or air armaments continue to be employed by nations which threaten, or may threaten, aggression outside of their frontiers, they believe, pending the establishment of a wider and permanent system of general security, that the disarmament of such nations is essential. They will likewise aid and encourage all other practicable measures which will lighten for peace-loving peoples the crushing burden of armaments.

Franklin D. Roosevelt.

Winston S. Churchill. ◇

AUGUST 15, 1941

WIDE ACCLAIM HERE FOR 'EIGHT POINTS'
Hailed as the 'Mein Kampf' of Democracy and Blueprint for a New Order

The Roosevelt-Churchill declaration was generally hailed by organizations and individuals here yesterday as a blueprint for a democratic "new order," as a "victory code" and as "the 'Mein Kampf' of democracy."

A dissenting opinion was expressed, however, by John T. Flynn, chairman of the New York Chapter of the America First Committee. He characterized the declaration as "a lot of words—a cover-up statement."

Clark M. Eichelberger, acting chairman of the Committee to Defend America, said the President of the United States and the Prime Minister of Great Britain "have raised the curtain of the future and have given the world the general principles of the world order which a democratic victory will make possible."

Speaking for Fight for Freedom, Inc., the Right Rev. Henry W. Hobson, Protestant Episcopal Bishop of the Southern Ohio Diocese and national chairman of

the organization, said the eight points of the joint declaration were "our victory code," but that it could be put into effect only "after we start shooting at the enemy of all mankind."

FLYNN VOICES SKEPTICISM

Mr. Flynn, in a statement issued from the offices of the America First Committee here, asserted that President Roosevelt and Mr. Churchill "didn't meet to draw up a statement such as they issued."

"They should be frank and tell the American people why they did meet and what they actually decided to do," he said. "What the American people would like to know is what Churchill demanded and what Roosevelt promised.   ▶

"All of their words about all the peoples in the world naming their own kind of government is meaningless unless it applies to such countries as India, Indo-China, the Dutch Indies, British Malaya, Lithuania, Latvia, Estonia and Finland."

Speaking as an individual, Bishop William T. Manning said the declaration "cements the fellowship between our country and other English-speaking nations," and that it "unites us irrevocably with them for the overthrow of tyranny and aggression and for the maintenance of justice and human liberty."

ANTI-NAZI LEADERS' VIEWS

James H. Sheldon, chairman of the board of directors of the Anti-Nazi League, who called the declaration the 'Mein Kampf' of democracy, said it would go down in history as "a 1941 Declaration of Independence, written on behalf of the oppressed peoples of the world." He said the eight points comprised "a strategy of democracy against the Nazi strategy of terror."

The Rev. A. J. Muste, secretary of the Fellowship of Reconciliation, said the declaration was not reassuring to those who "recall how completely the Idealistic Wilson–Lloyd George statements of the last war failed to justify the hopes which they aroused." Asserting that the declaration would lead to "another Versailles," he said that "World War III will spring as surely out of World War II as it did out of World War I." ◆

NAZIS IN KEY CITIES

RUSSIANS GIVE UP GOMEL

By C. BROOKS PETERS
By Telephone to The New York Times.

BERLIN, Aug. 21—Considerable gains in all sectors of the Russian front are claimed by the German High Command today.

In the Southern Ukraine, Kherson, Dnieper River port southeast of Nikolaev, was captured by Elite Guard troops, according to the communiqué.

In the Gomel sector, about midway between Smolensk and Kiev, the advance continues beyond the city, probably southward along the Dnieper in a drive to flank Kiev, the capital of the Ukraine.

On the northern wing Novgorod, Kingisepp and Narwa have been taken, and therewith the drive to cut the vital Leningrad-Moscow railroad has been brought within forty miles of its goal, it is asserted.

TWO-MONTH GAINS TALLIED

Units of the German Air Force rained bombs on Odessa and Ochakov, from which Black Sea ports Russian soldiers

are being evacuated on ships. One transport of 6,000 tons is reported to have been sunk in this "super-Dunkerque." Three other large vessels, one of which was a 15,000-ton passenger ship, were damaged, according to the official news agency D.N.B.

Two months ago tomorrow, on June 22, the Germans began their invasion of Russia. In this period, authoritative military quarters here report, about 5,000,000 Russians have been killed, wounded or captured. The number of prisoners is said to total more than 1,200,000, so that, according to German casualty estimates, the Soviet has lost nearly 3,800,000 dead and wounded.

[A Russian communiqué this morning admitted the abandonment of Gomel, and an earlier Soviet statement told of a "direct threat" to Leningrad. A Soviet spokesman said, however, that in the eight weeks of the conflict the Germans had lost nearly 2,000,000 men in dead and wounded, and that the Russians would win eventually whether the war lasted for "months or years."]

In addition, 14,000 pieces of artillery of all calibers, 14,000 tanks and more than 11,000 planes are said to have been captured or destroyed.

SPRING FIGHTING WEIGHED

The Germans definitely have the upper hand in the fighting, informed quarters assert, although it cannot yet be said that a decision in the war has been reached. The Soviet officers' corps has suffered heavily, these circles add, which increases the Russians' problem for future resistance.

Since the single important strategic consideration of the present stage of the invasion is to cripple the Russians' powers of resistance so badly that they cannot revive it by next Spring, the capturing of cities is a minor consideration, informed circles say.

Moscow, for example, probably will "remain in the rear of our troops for some time," they declare. Leningrad, moreover, is a fortress, they add, and may not be stormed, but merely surrounded.

To Marshal Klementy Voroshiloff's appeal to the residents of Leningrad to arm and prepare to resist the threat to their city, the Germans reply that should they attack the city and the Russians employ the franc tireur method, they should recall Warsaw and compare the latter city with unscathed Paris and Brussels. ◆

German troops are ferried across the Dnieper River after having set fire to Mogilev, Belarus, July 1941.

AUGUST 28, 1941

NEW IRAN REGIME ENDS RESISTANCE
British and Russian Forces Continue Advance—Offers by Teheran Awaited

By JAMES MacDONALD
Special Cable to The New York Times.

LONDON, Aug. 28—An announcement that the new Iranian Government, formed yesterday, had issued orders to its forces to "cease fire" was received simultaneously in London and other European capitals today via the Teheran radio, and was regarded here as most welcome.

At the same time it was emphasized in London circles that British and Russian troops would continue to advance through the country. Officials of both countries are waiting to see what offers will be made by the new Iranian Government, headed by Ali Furanghi, with regard to various aspects of the general situation, including expulsion of Nazis still in Iran and safeguards against any creeping back into the country. Although the expulsion of Nazi technicians and others from Iran was one avowed cause of the Russo-British entry into the country, one of the underlying aims of both invaders was to establish direct land communication with each other, as well as to keep the rich oil fields from falling into German hands.

EXPECT FORCES TO MEET

In welcoming the Iranian order to "cease fire," some persons in London pointed out that further opposition on the part of the Iranian forces in the large and mountainous country would not only have caused serious bloodshed but would have been useless from a practical point of view.

The British and the Russian forces will now be enabled to extend their control of communication lines speedily toward vital objectives via the trans-Iranian railroad and the Teheran-Tabriz road. It is assumed in unofficial quarters that the British and the Russian forces will continue to advance until they have met and thereby solidified communication lines and established protection for the oil lines.

Before the Teheran radio's announcement, news reached London that there had been an order for general mobilization. This made it appear that ultimate Anglo-Russian occupation would not be readily accepted. In the light of later developments, this order was interpreted merely as meaning that Iranian men of military age were to be brought under control at a moment of crisis.

As an example of the futility of Iranian resistance it was pointed out that in less than twenty-four hours British forces had taken control of the world's largest oil refinery plant at Abadan, had captured the entire Iranian Navy, had seized the strategic wireless station at Muhammereh and had trapped several Axis merchant ships in the harbor at Bandar Shahpur. Moreover, a column of troops had advanced from Khaniqin, Iraq, to Shahabad, Iran—a distance of about 100 miles—in less than three days.

STATEMENT BY PREMIER

The Teheran radio's announcement, as picked up in London, quoted the new Premier as saying that the government would do its utmost to maintain good relations with foreign powers, "and especially our neighbors," and continue to have peace with the rest of the world.

"In order that these intentions should be made clear to the world at large," the Premier said, "we declare at this moment, when the governments of Soviet Russia and Britain have ordered certain actions to be taken, that the Government of Iran, in pursuance of the peace-loving policy of His Majesty, is issuing orders to all armed forces of the country to refrain from any resistance so that the causes for bloodshed and disturbance of security shall be removed and public peace and security assured." ◆

AUGUST 31, 1941

BOOM IN STRAW SHOES
Nazi Industry Is Unable to Fill Orders for Footwear

By Telephone to The New York Times.

BERLIN, Aug. 30—Shoes of straw, last year a novelty for children, are now being demanded in such quantities that the new "industry" is unable to fill all orders.

Made of a very close weave of straw, the shoes are said to be waterproof. They are lined with cloth and thin leather and their arches are braced with light metal spans. They last about a year but must be resoled every four to six weeks. A pair costs 16.50 marks.

Experiments for the manufacture of shoes from the bark of trees are also being made, but thus far have met with little success. The sale of leather shoes to the public was drastically limited at the beginning of this Summer. ◆

SEPTEMBER 21, 1941

TOKYO STILL FIRM
Japanese Are Insisting on Special Status in the Far East

By FRANK L. KLUCKHORN
Special to The New York Times.

HYDE PARK, N.Y., Sept. 20—Negotiations with Japan looking toward a settlement of Japanese-American relations have reached a virtual standstill, although they are being kept open in the hope of effecting an eventual settlement, it was reported on good authority today.

Japan's insistence upon terms that would give the Japanese considerable control in China and the unwillingness of Secretary of State Cordell Hull to depart from his insistence that Japan should have no special status in East Asia are understood to have caused negotiations to bog down for the moment at least.

Meanwhile, more than half of the United States Navy is forced to remain in the Pacific at a time when it is operat- ›

ing against German and Italian submarine, surface and air raiders in the Atlantic. It is feared the reverses suffered by Russia in the Ukraine and around Leningrad will encourage Japan and increase the difficulties in the way of a settlement of the Far Eastern situation.

According to reliable diplomatic sources, Secretary Hull's insistence that Japan drop her plans to obtain a privileged status in China, and his refusal to talk detailed terms until the Japanese altered their present attitude, led to the decision of Prince Fumimaro Konoye, Japanese Premier, to attempt to negotiate directly with President Roosevelt.

The President, however, has consulted constantly with the Secretary of State on the matter and, according to the information available, neither this government nor the Japanese has to this point softened its position. The President told reporters yesterday that he was in constant touch with Mr. Hull even when he was at Hyde Park.

Mr. Roosevelt has not made public any reply to the letter received from Prince Konoye, and in his press conference yesterday hinted strongly that there had been no recent developments regarding Japan. The Japanese Embassy in Washington revealed last week, however, that one of its staff was on the way from Tokyo to the United States by way of Peru because Japanese ships do not now travel to American ports. It was thought likely that he was bringing new instructions from his government.

Prince Fumimaro Konoye of Japan. Rebuffed by Secretary of State Cordell Hull, he sought direct contact with President Roosevelt.

At the moment, however, American trade with Japan is virtually at a standstill and American embargoes on shipments to Japan have increased sharply the economic pressure under which the Japanese are laboring.

THREAT IN PACIFIC IS FEARED

Should the German Army continue to be victorious against the Soviet armies, and Tokyo come to believe a Nazi victory over the Russians is inevitable, it is widely feared that Japan will tighten her Axis bonds and move north or south, thus threatening the United States with simultaneous naval struggles in the Atlantic and Pacific.

There is every reason to believe that President Roosevelt is still giving considerable personal attention to this two-ocean threat, which may become more acute at any moment. No doubt exists, however, that this government was encouraged to believe that the recent Japanese governmental shake-up, with the Emperor taking personal control of a large part of the military establishment, was forced by economic pressure on the part of this country. But the best information available here is that a solution of difficulties is unlikely unless Japan softens her attitude.

While no specific proposed terms for a settlement have been made public, it is reported that Japan seeks to maintain control of the Chinese treaty ports and the four Northern Provinces of China and to maintain "token" military garrisons in some other parts of China. In exchange, it is reported, Japan is willing to withdraw from French Indo-China and give up any idea of southward conquest. Although these terms may not be exactly correct, in a general way, diplomatic sources believe, they give a reliable idea of the Japanese position.

Equally reliable sources report this government is unwilling to come to terms with Japan at the expense of China, but will go so far as to give Japan economic aid and restore trade to a normal basis if Japan is prepared to eschew conquest by force. ◆

SEPTEMBER 21, 1941

AIM OF PRESIDENT IS WAR, NYE SAYS
Urges 'All Loyal Americans' to Oppose Foreign Policy

Senator Gerald P. Nye appealed last night to "all loyal Americans" to oppose President Roosevelt's foreign policy program of all-out aid to nations fighting against Nazi Germany on the ground that it represented a deliberate attempt by the President and British leaders to involve this country against its will in the war.

Speaking at the annual dinner of the Steuben Society of America, held at the Hotel Biltmore, Senator Nye, a leading member of the Congressional isolationist bloc, contended that the United States was "still at peace with the world" and that national unity here was impossible of achievement as long as the President and his supporters continued to uphold their foreign policy.

One thousand members of the society attended the dinner and applauded Senator Nye's speech. Although a heavy police guard was on duty within and outside the hotel, no disorders occurred during the evening.

"Americans, when America is at stake, will give every ounce and every measure of unity that an intelligent people can and will afford," Senator Nye asserted. "But that unity can be invited only by frankness; that unity can never be won on the issue of hunting and building a war for America."

"I insist that the manner in which the President has brought our country to the peril of involvement in war is not a thing inviting of 'unity' however great may be the desire to afford loyalty to one's government. There is a thing to which none can shut their eyes; namely, that so long as the present situation in the world remains only what it is today, never, never, never can there be unity in America on the issue of asking ourselves into these foreign wars."

As Senator Nye spoke in the grand ballroom to the members of the society, which is composed of Americans of German descent, the outside of the hotel was picketed by representatives of the Fight for Freedom Committee, the American Youth Congress and several other organizations in protest against the Senator's isolationist stand.

Senator Gerald P. Nye

These pickets carried placards which read: "'Der Fuehrer thanks you for your many services,' Senator Nye." The Fight for Freedom Committee and other organizations had urged Theodore Hoffman, society president, to permit a speaker expressing an opposite viewpoint to Senator Nye to be heard at the dinner "in fairness to loyal Americans of German descent." But the request was declined.

Throughout the night a heavy detail of police was on hand at the hotel to prevent any possible disorder. Commanded by Deputy Chief Inspector John J. De Martino, the police, 175 strong, permitted the pickets to parade before the hotel, but chased away curious passersby who sought to congregate in front of the building.

Theodore H. Hoffman, president of the Steuben Society, in a message printed in the dinner program, declared that the members of his organization resented the attempt of "professional agitators, certain newspapers and certain commentators to brand the American of German ancestry as being un-American or fifth columnist."

"Americans of Germanic extraction do not want communism, fascism, nazism or British imperialism," he said. "They believe in only one ism and that is Americanism. The aims and principles of our society teach us to have faith in our country, faith in our form of government and faith in the principles on which our government was founded." ◆

SEPTEMBER 21, 1941

KIEV MOPPED UP, NAZIS ANNOUNCE

By C. BROOKS PETERS
By Telephone to The New York Times.

BERLIN, Sept. 20—Surrender of the Kiev garrison, mopping up operations in the Ukrainian capital and progress in liquidation of 200,000 Russians trapped in the triangle between Kiev, Priluki and Kremenchug to the east were featured in today's German Supreme Command communiqué. Desperate Russian attempts to break out of the trap were declared thwarted in every instance.

Kiev's conquerors were said to be pushing east past Poltava, while attention shifted to the Baltic front, where two islands were reported taken in a drive to clear the sea approaches to Leningrad.

[The Associated Press transmitted a D.N.B. report that a "very heavy" air attack was carried out yesterday against Leningrad and Soviet troops encircled in the city's defense zone.

A number of fires were started in the city and anti-aircraft positions, supply centers and barracks were hard hit, the dispatch said. The main force of the Luftwaffe's attacks, however, was said to have been directed against Russian artillery positions and bunkers.]

AIMS HELD ACHIEVED

Tomorrow the German invasion of Russia enters its fifteenth week. In the opinion of informed Berlin quarters, the major portions of the German plan of operations in the East have already been fulfilled. The objective of the German leadership is said here to encompass explicitly the destruction of Russian resources for resistance in five ways:

By continuing to attack the Russian reservoir of men, which in former wars was regarded as inexhaustible, until all trained soldiers had been captured or killed.

By destroying or capturing as much of the Soviet's available war materiel as possible.

By so weakening Soviet industrial potential that the Russians are no longer competent to carry on effective large-scale operations.

By destroying Russian lines of communication, particularly through the use of the German Air Force, making cooperation between the war industry and fighting units at the front difficult, when not impossible.

By Luftwaffe air raids on political centers, making it extremely difficult for the Russians effectively to administer their country, thus placing a tremendous strain upon attempts to continue a centralized direction for the war.

The concentrated attack on Kiev, it is stated, began last Wednesday. Yesterday morning the citadel with its arsenal and barracks was taken by storm. Throughout the remainder of the day one portion of the city after another was cleaned up and occupied, says today's communiqué.

The Russians are reported to have made elaborate preparations for defending Kiev in street fighting. Civilian formations and N.K.V.D. [Soviet secret police] regiments, according to D.N.B., erected barricades, tank traps and other obstacles in the streets. All these measures, however, are said to have been rendered fruitless by the suddenness and speed of the German attack from the north and south.

DONETS DRIVE WELL STARTED

Following the successful German operations in the Kiev sector, all of the Northern Ukraine appears already lost to the Russians. In the drive on Kharkov and the Donets Basin the Nazi legions are already beyond Poltava, which they captured Thursday.

German vanguard units are thus already less than seventy-five miles from Kharkov. Therewith the threat to the entire Eastern Ukraine has become acute, it is emphasized.

Crimea is believed entirely to be cut off from land connections with the north by the Nazi thrust on Perekop. How deeply the German forces have already penetrated into this peninsula on their drive to Sevastopol is not revealed. The attack is believed to be in constant motion, however, and official information from this sector may be expected in the near future. ◆

SEPTEMBER 24, 1941

NAZIS TO BANISH JEWS FAILING TO WEAR STAR
Prison Camp To Be Punishment Even for Children's Laxity

BERLIN, Sept. 22 (AP)—Thirty-five provisions on the required wearing of the Star of David by Jews have been communicated to the Jewish Central Council to clear up uncertainties as to when and how the star, first required last Friday, must be displayed.

The Jews were informed it must be worn where it may be seen every moment a Jew is outside his own home. It is not sufficient to have a star affixed to a coat or topcoat. If a Jew steps into his yard in his shirtsleeves, he must have a star on his shirt.

By Nazi edict, German Jews were forced to wear the Star of David.

If a Gentile rings his doorbell, the Jew must wear the star when he opens the door. Jews who hide the star by covering it with a briefcase or shopping bag in the streets may be sent to concentration camps.

[Usually reliable sources said a sentence to a concentration camp was the standard punishment for violation of these regulations, The United Press reported. Parents and guardians were said to be liable to punishment for violations by children.]

Jews are barred from railway waiting rooms or station restaurants unless they have written permission to leave the city and have purchased tickets. Jews without written permission may not use taxicabs, hospital cars or first-aid trucks.

Two "non-Aryan" Catholic priests in Cologne are wearing Stars of David on their cassocks. ◈

SEPTEMBER 28, 1941

RUSSIANS MAKE READY FOR WINTER CAMPAIGN
They Believe Their Chances Then Will Be Much Better Than The Germans'

By CYRUS L. SULZBERGER
Wireless to The New York Times.

WITH THE RED ARMY ON THE CENTRAL FRONT, Sept. 27—"This is a war of blitz grinding. On a large part of the front the German troops already are digging in. What lies ahead of them is trench warfare, the mud of Russian roads and Winter." Such is the opinion of Lieut. Gen. Vassily Sokolovsky, one of the Red Army's ablest generals on the central sector. It is his belief that, as has already occurred along most of the length of that front where Marshal Timoshenko is operating, stabilization of the fighting lines will soon come about in both north and south.

According to General Sokolovsky, the Russian soldier will have a tremendous advantage as soon as this situation is established. The German Army will have lost its hitting power when its manoeuvrability is obviated by terrible road conditions. German morale, he believes, will be cracked with the shattering of the Blitzkrieg tradition.

WEATHER AS ALLY
How accurate these predictions will prove the next few months can demonstrate. The Nazis already are sending sheepskin-lined coats to the front, as shown by tattered garments in reconquered central trenches. The Russians, however, are confident the invaders won't be able to face the climatic rigors for long.

Whatever should prove to be the case—and in this respect it may be recalled that difficulties of climate or terrain facing the Germans in other campaigns of this war have been habitually exaggerated—the Red Army is making ready for Winter and organizing thoroughly for a long struggle in which it is hoped Hitler's war machine will not only be ground to a stop but entirely disintegrated.

These preparations may be divided into three categories—those of the rear, those behind the front area and those of the front itself. The first include such essential steps as opening new trade routes to Iran whence Allied matériel may arrive, the continued moving eastward of important quantities of machinery from threatened areas in order to maintain sufficient internal manufacturing power, the training of new groups of soldiers including a hundred thousand Poles encamped in the Urals region and the institution of military science courses in all high schools.

FACTORIES REORGANIZE
Factories in the rear are reorganizing production schedules—and the success of this phase already is signalized, according to General Sokolovsky, by the fact that twice as many aircraft as a month ago are now functioning with the Red Air Force in the central sector. One of the great staff problems is to keep transport routes clear to the front during the Autumnal spells of bad weather which naturally hamper both sides.

With the exception of the few highways which are paved, most of the roads can be used only with the greatest difficulties except during the short period between the evaporation of the Spring meltings and the commencement of the Autumnal rains. Even in Winter when the mud is frozen the passage is not easy because of vast drifts of snow.

This at best slows up, at worst enormously impedes, the transport of the mobile invading forces at the same time that a lesser if still difficult problem is presented to the Red Army's supplying lines. Therefore as the cold comes up and the rains continue one can notice more and more attention devoted to maintenance of communications.

LABOR ON THE ROADS
Quoting from this correspondent's own notebook jottings:

"After the macadam road ends squads of workers keeping up the dirt highway; men and woman peasant laborers; steamrollers; piles of earth interspersed along sides for surfacing; intermittent sentries and patrols; helmeted soldier driving a procession of tractors down the road; truck stations hidden in the trees off the road; squads of workers by the roadside in charge of armed guards; a blazed trail in the woods avoids the regular road which is a terrible soup of mud; a squad of peasants with spades working on a bad patch; soldiers laying a corduroy road over a marsh; gangs of soldiers stationed at bad places to help shove traffic across."

In order to maintain the army during the Winter it is essential to keep up a high standard of health, which in itself necessitates ample food and warm clothing. Russians are proud of their ability to withstand cold. As General Sokolovsky says:

"Winter will create even greater difficulties for the Germans. Every Russian has his sheepskin coat. He is also used to hard weather and he has his felt boots. As the Finnish campaign showed, we can stand 50 degrees of frost. The Red Army man can remain in the open day and night when necessary, but the German will freeze. In this very part of the country we have 35 to 40 degrees of frost Centigrade—about the same as Siberia. Although the Germans are buying up skis in large numbers in Norway I doubt whether many of their soldiers know how to use them. They are no good for transporting tanks and heavy equipment. As a result there will be further stabilization of the war and gradual exhaustion,"

This Winter will scarcely be a pleasant one for either party, but the Red Command is determined to do its utmost to make it physically bearable for its soldiers. The motto is, "A Russian's meat's a German's poison." ◆

SEPTEMBER 29, 1941

WAR GAMES OVER; BLUES NEAR GOAL

MARSHALL PRAISES MEN
New Army Fast Becoming a 'Powerful Machine'—350,000 Troops Ready for Rest

By HANSON W. BALDWIN
Special to The New York Times.

FIELD HEADQUARTERS, Second Army, Shreveport, La., Sept. 28—As the hot Southern sun sank in a red blaze above the Texas plains tonight, the concluding phase of the greatest manoeuvres in the country's history ended with Shreveport almost ringed by "enemy" forces.

Tired, sweat-soaked, mud-covered and dusty after the hardest two weeks of mimic war in which any American troops have ever engaged, the 250,000 soldiers of the Second and Third Armies were moving to bivouacs all over this 30,000-square-mile manoeuvre area tonight, happy over the prospect of a fifteen-day furlough which awaits them on their return to home stations.

They were cheered, too, by the knowledge of a job well done and a pat on the back from the Army's Chief of Staff.

MARSHALL PRAISES SPIRIT
General George C. Marshall, in a telegram addressed to "all commanders and their officers and non-commissioned officers and to the men in the ranks," said:

"The manoeuvres just completed have been a great success on the ground, in the air and for the supply and maintenance services. The zeal and energy, the endurance and the spirit of the troops have been a model of excellence. There is much more to learn, but the mistakes of the past two weeks will be corrected, the deficiencies in material will be made good.

"The armored units and the air squadrons are now a part of the military team supported by dive bombers of the Navy and Marine Corps. The supply services have proved they know their business. The new citizen army is rapidly on its way to becoming a powerful machine with all its parts in close cooperation.

"To all of you, and especially to those older men soon to be released from active service, my thanks and those of the entire War Department for having done a grand job."

The "cease firing" order came at 4:45 P.M. after a grueling day in the sun for the armies of both sides.

When the umpires waved their flags for the last time small units of the attacking Blue Third Army had seized Shreveport's water works, pushed into the city's northern suburbs and were fighting units of the defending Red Second Army at the end of the Cross Bayou Bridge in the city's outskirts.

MAIN FORCES TWENTY MILES AWAY
The center of Shreveport was clearly within artillery range from the north, but the Blue forces to the north were described by the Red defenders as light harassing forces only; the main Blue forces were still eighteen to twenty-five miles distant, and Lieut. Gen. Ben Lear, commanding the Second Army, still had used only part of his powerful Army reserve—the First Armored Division and the Sixth Infantry Division.

Tonight General Lear particularly praised three aspects of the Second Army's work in the manoeuvres. He put first, as the finest thing about the Louisiana exercises, "the thorough willingness of the men to do their job." He described the functioning of his intelligence services, including his reconnaissance and security elements, as outstanding, and declared that "I got everything I asked for from the aviation."

The "cease firing" order, although issued from Lieut. Gen. Lesley J. McNair's director headquarters in late afternoon, did not reach all elements in the field until almost sunset. At that time armored elements of the Blue First Armored Division, supported by infantry, were battling in the thick woods along the Sabine River in East Texas with units of the Second (horsed) Cavalry Division, supported by a corps reconnaissance regiment of cavalry, a regiment of infantry and an anti-tank group.

DEADWOOD, TEXAS, BUZZES
At and around the little town of Deadwood, Texas, which has never known such excitement since the frontier days, there were gathered several regiments of the old "hell-for-leather" cavalry of tradition, their horseflesh plainly showing the grueling tests that the men have been through in the last two weeks. And near by were parked captured thirteen-ton light tanks, their steel sides splashed with mud and dust.   ❯

The two horsed cavalry divisions and the horsed cavalry brigade participating in the war games have done outstanding service. The horsed cavalry available at these manoeuvres probably outnumbered the horsed cavalry which the German Army possessed at the outbreak of war, for the German Army then mustered only one division, besides numerous regiments, although this number may have been increased since.

There has been, and still is, considerable difference of opinion as to the tactical value of horse cavalry in modern war. But in this manoeuvre, the two divisions, the First under Major Gen. Innis P. Swift and the Second under Major Gen. John Millikin, acquitted themselves with pride. They were operating in tangled terrain, extremely difficult for tanks, in fact, in places too difficult for horses.

Both divisions, in addition to the Fifty-sixth National Guard Cavalry Brigade from Texas, now commanded by a regular officer, earned commendations for their work.

WEATHER AND TERRAIN BAD

The two brigades of the Second Division—the Third, led by Brig. Gen. Terry de la M. Allen, and the Fourth, by Colonel Duncan G. Richart—were in the thick of most of the fights and traveled hundreds of miles through some of the worst weather and over some of the most difficult terrain these States can muster.

On one occasion the Second Division marched seventy miles and fought an action in a thirty-hour period; the Fourth Brigade covered forty-five miles in one day, and the night of this week's hurricane, when a twenty-five to forty-five-mile-an-hour wind was blowing, the rain was pouring in torrents, the back woods roads were fetlock deep in mud and many motorized vehicles were bogged down, the horsed cavalry marched twenty-five to thirty miles.

The horses, thin but still strong, and the men, sun-baked, wind-burned and drawn-looking, show the results of this sort of grind, but they are proud of their record and their endurance and they are heading back to home stations in Texas and Kansas singing the old songs of the cavalry with a new lilt.

The Fourth Brigade's songs are generally a little off the Army line, however, for the Fourth is a Negro outfit, and tonight as they marched to their bivouacs, the strains of "Flat Foot Floogi" echoed over the cactus and through the pines, supplanted often by the mournful notes of the Negro spirituals, such as "All Gods Chillun Got Shoes." ◊

SEPTEMBER 30, 1941

BRITISH CONFIDENT AT SINGAPORE BASE
Steady Improvement Has Made Far Eastern Bastion Even More Formidable

By F. TILLMAN DURDIN
Wireless to The New York Times.

SINGAPORE, Sept. 29—The British now face the possibility of war in the Pacific "without anxiety," Vice Admiral Sir Geoffrey Layton, Commander in Chief of the British fleet based on Singapore, told this correspondent today in an interview at his shore headquarters at the famous Singapore naval base.

Asked to give an indication of the increase in British strength at Singapore, Sir Geoffrey said that had Singapore been attacked a year ago the defenders would have had "definite cause for anxiety." "Now," he said, "we view the possibility of attack without anxiety."

Britain, he said, "obviously does not want a war in the Pacific now," but he declared that "if any of our territories are attacked we shall certainly fight."

He made it clear that the British in the Far East now felt their strength sufficient successfully to resist attack from any quarter. Based on Singapore, Admiral Layton commands the British ships in the vast expanse of ocean that includes not only the Malay archipelago but also the seas from mid-Pacific westward to the Bay of Bengal.

SILENT ON INDIES DEFENSE

Asked about arrangements for mutual defense with the Netherlands Indies, Admiral Layton declined to comment saying that a statement on such a matter would have to come from the Brit-

ish Government. But, he asserted, "obviously an attack on any part of the Netherlands Indies would be a matter of immediate concern to us as it would jeopardize our life line to Australia."

He emphasized the importance of Malaysia to the United States.

"I hope Americans are coming to realize," he said, "that if this area ever comes under Japanese control the United States will have to go to Japan to beg for the rubber, tin and oil here, which are indispensable to American defense and industry."

Explaining how the British position is becoming stronger day by day, Admiral Layton from the window of his office surveyed the enormous expanse of the naval base, pointing out the sites where thousands of men are working on projects designed to improve the facilities and defenses of the base.

NEW BUILDING IN PROGRESS

"Over there," he said, "we are building a new torpedo depot; there work is starting on a new dock; yonder we are constructing new facilities for the Fleer Air Arm. The base is completely ready for any use to which we might want to put it now, but we shall always be improving its facilities and protection."

The correspondent toured the base following the interview. Two ships being repaired in the huge graving dock—one of the world's largest—looked like midgets. One construction crew was rushing the erection of quarters for additional forces which Admiral Layton had said "keep coming in so fast we hardly know where to put them."

Everywhere, from the sites where more anti-aircraft guns are being erected to the big kitchens in the comfortable quarters for fleet crews come ashore, were scenes of efficient and well-ordered activity. They added up to that impression of impregnable power that the base has come to signalize for Britain in the Far East. ◊

Air Force Marshall Conway Pullford, Major Gen. Arthur E. Percival, Air Chief Marshall Sir Robert Brooke-Popham and Vice Admiral Sir Geoffrey Layton discussing maneuvers in 1941.

OCTOBER 2, 1941

MOSCOW PARLEY PLEDGES HUGE AID
Talks Ended Speedily as U.S. And Britain Agree To Supply Almost All Soviet Asks

By The Associated Press.

MOSCOW, Oct. 2—The United States and Great Britain agreed to fill virtually every Soviet need for war supplies in exchange for "large quantities" of Russian raw materials at the concluding session last night of the three-power conference.

The conference closed two days ahead of schedule after only three days of sessions—probably the shortest international council of such dimensions ever held. A communiqué issued by the British and United States delegations and one by the Russians announced its results.

For the United States and Great Britain, W. Averell Harriman and Lord Beaverbrook, heads of their delegations, promised "to place at the disposal of the Soviet Government practically every requirement for which the Soviet military and civil authorities have asked."

In return, said the communiqué issued by Mr. Harriman and Lord Beaverbrook, "the Soviet Government has supplied Great Britain and the United States with large quantities of raw materials urgently required in those countries."

Arrangements were said to have been made to "increase the volume of traffic in all directions."

The Soviet communiqué stressed the "atmosphere of perfect mutual understanding, confidence and good-will," and said that the delegates had been "inspired by the eminence of the cause of delivering other nations from the Nazi threat of enslavement."

In a speech to the closing session Foreign Commissar Vyacheslaff M. Molotoff said that the conference had shown that "deliveries of arms and most important materials for the defense of the U.S.S.R., which were commenced previously, must and will become extensive and regular."

Mr. Molotoff added that "these deliveries of airplanes, tanks and other armaments and equipment and raw materials will be increased and will acquire growing importance in the future."

U.S.-BRITISH STATEMENT

Mr. Harriman and Lord Beaverbrook issued the following joint statement:

The Moscow conference of representatives of the Soviet, American and British Governments has been brought to conclusion.

Members of the conference were directed to examine the requirements from the United States and Great Britain necessary to supply the Soviet Union, fighting to defeat the Axis powers.

The conference, which assembled under the chairmanship of Vyacheslaff Molotoff, Commissar of Foreign Affairs, has been in continuous session since Monday. It examined available resources of the Soviet Government in conjunction with the productive capacity of the United States and Great Britain.

It now has been decided to place at the disposal of the Soviet Government prac-

tically every requirement for which the Soviet military and civil authorities have asked. The Soviet Government has supplied Great Britain and the United States with large quantities of raw materials urgently required in those countries.

Transportation facilities have been fully examined and plans made to increase the volume of traffic in all directions.

Mr. Stalin has authorized Mr. Harriman and Lord Beaverbrook to say he expressed his thanks to the United States and Great Britain for their bountiful supplies of raw materials, machine tools and munitions of war.

The assistance has been generous and the Soviet forces will be enabled forthwith to strengthen their relentless defense and develop vigorous attacks upon the invading armies.

Mr. Harriman and Lord Beaverbrook, speaking on behalf of the United States and Great Britain, acknowledged the ample supplies of Russian raw materials from the Soviet Government which will greatly add to the output of their own weapons of war.

Mr. Harriman and Lord Beaverbrooks emphasized the cordial spirit of the conference which made the agreement possible in record time. In particular they made it plain that M. Stalin was always ready with sympathetic cooperation and understanding. They thanked Mr. Molotoff for efficient chairmanship of the conference and all Soviet representatives for their help.

In concluding its session the conference adheres to the resolution of the three governments that after the final annihilation of Nazi tyranny a peace will be established which will enable the whole world to live in security in its own territory in conditions free from fear or need. ◊

OCTOBER 3, 1941

NAZIS SAID TO BID FOR SOVIET PEACE
Washington Foreign Circles Hear Stalin Has Not Yet Rejected Offer by Hitler

By BERTRAM D. HULEN
Special to The New York Times.

WASHINGTON, Oct. 2—Reports received in some foreign diplomatic circles

from Moscow today were to the effect that Reichsfuehrer Hitler had made what was described as a liberal peace offer to Premier Stalin and that it had not yet been definitely rejected. The circles are not closely identified with any of the belligerents. Details were not available.

No such reports have been received by the United States, as far as could be ascertained. There was a disposition in this quarter to question the accuracy of the information. On the other hand, the reports were not considered beyond the realm of possibility.

HALIFAX DOES NOT SHARE VIEWS

Viscount Halifax, the British Ambas-

sador, just back from London, however, did not share even these qualified views. As he left the White House after a conference with President Roosevelt, he was asked about rumors that Russia might enter peace negotiations with Herr Hitler.

"I did not see anything of that at all [in England]," he replied. "Indeed, I would put it stronger. Those sorts of rumors received flat contradictions from the communiqué issued [yesterday] in Moscow by Mr. [W. Averell] Harriman and by Lord Beaverbrook and by the Russian Government. Their conference seems to have been successful."

Nevertheless, the neutral reports received here are said to hint that Mr. ›

Stalin impressed the Americans and British at the tripartite conference so deeply with the urgency of his position that promises to give all the aid requested were speedily forthcoming. Provided the reports have substance, diplomatic observers comment, the offset to these pledges could be the ability of Herr Hitler to make concessions to Russia in the Near East, as well as in reference to territory in European Russia.

The determining factor, it was suggested, might turn out to be the disposition to be made of the Soviet Army, rather than territory. If the reports were true, it was commented, Mr. Stalin still could be weighing one side against the other before reaching a final decision. ◇

OCTOBER 13, 1941

GERMANS SMASH ON

One Spearhead Is Said to Be Only 90 Miles from Capital

By Telephone to The New York Times.

BERLIN, Oct. 12—Military observers here are of the opinion that a spearhead of the German invasion forces is less than ninety miles from the gates of Moscow. The progress achieved in the

last forty-eight hours, German sources said tonight, has been possible because the Red Army is able to offer only desultory opposition.

A special war bulletin announced that the German forces pressing toward Moscow had left the Vyazma and Bryansk battlefields far behind them, and the Berlin press stated flatly that Marshal Semyon Budenny's armies defending the Donets Basin had been "completely dissolved."

200,000 CAPTIVES CLAIMED

The German communiqué reported that 200,000 Russian soldiers had been captured thus far in the Vyazma and Bryansk battles of encirclement. It added that despite desperate Soviet resis-

---

OCTOBER 7, 1941

U-BOATS ROAM SEA WITH A NEW FURY
Battle of Atlantic Held More Critical In Iceland Than London Had Believed

By The Associated Press.

REYKJAVIK, Iceland, Sept. 28 (Delayed)—The Battle of the Atlantic is entering a crucial period.

A great onslaught of German submarines against the North Atlantic supply line

Crew of an English cargo liner ship leaves it to the Germans, June 1941.

equal in scope to that of March and April is well under way, informed persons say.

A vast amount of war material, much of it the product of American industry, is the objective of a campaign designed to cripple the British war effort.

There was some complacency in high political circles in London this

Summer over the Battle of the Atlantic, but this is not reflected in the minds of British and United States naval officers or merchant captains here. They regard the situation as critical.

The actual figures of tonnage losses are secret.

STRENGTH PUT AT 600 U-BOATS

The popular estimate in London of the German U-boat strength last Spring was 600 submarines of all types operating in the Atlantic, plus a third as many Focke-Wulf Kuriers and Condors for observation and bombing.

Despite German losses of last Summer, in which an increased number of destroyers and aircraft dealt severe blows to U-boats, the German submarine strength is believed in informed quarters to remain at 600.

Considering the required rest in port for crews, periods of refit for the submarines themselves and the time spent in reaching the hunting grounds, it appears probable that always 200 German submarines are operating in the Atlantic north of the Azores, and that these are replaced by another 200 at the end of each two weeks.

Guenther Prien and other U-boat commanders who were the most accomplished and boldest of the German undersea fighters in the first months of the war are now dead or missing. However, the fall of France gave the German Navy unequaled facilities for submarine warfare, and newly trained commanders and crews have gained in audacity with each voyage.

Now submarines are again hunting in packs. They are directed to the quarry by Kurriers and Condors, which can sight the prey without being seen, then

tance and continued attempts to break out, the Russians "have no prospect of escaping their fate." The number of captives is rising steadily, the High Command said.

The communiqué also declared that a "new phase" in the operations begun on Oct. 2 had opened with the approach to Moscow, but it did not make clear just what that new phase was. It was said that from the Sea of Azov to the Valdai Hills south of Lake Ilmen, a front 750 miles long, the troops of Germany and her allies were in offensive movement eastward.

A statement in the communiqué relating to the closing of a trap on Soviet forces north of the Sea of Azov led the press to declare almost unconditionally that Soviet resistance in the south had

ceased. An official military spokesman was slightly more cautious, declaring that Marshal Budenny possibly could "throw against the German forces a few quickly assembled reserve troops."

"However," the spokesman continued, "it must be said that a regular army, or army group, no longer exists there. With the prospect of an early loss of the Donets Basin, the Russians are robbed of the possibility of ever making good, even in part, the war materials they have lost."

NAVAL ACTIVITY REPORTED

D.N.B., the official news agency, reported that units of the German Navy were operating in the Black Sea. A number of captured Soviet bases on the Black Sea coast have been rebuilt and, with captured Soviet merchant ships, are being used to supply German land forces, D.N.B. said.

In the Leningrad area the Red Army forces of Marshal Klementy E. Voroshiloff continued their bitter counter-attacks, according to other German dispatches, but these attacks were said to have been crushed by German fire. There are, however, no reports of further German advances in that region. An eyewitness account published in the German press gave one reason for this. The report came from an observer who made a flight over the Soviet defenses around Leningrad.

"Below us we saw nothing but one single enormous field of forts," the observer said. "One could try for half an hour and longer and the picture remained the same: anti-tank guns, trenches, innumerable little machine-gun nests and other trenches. The land southwest of Leningrad is like this for a depth of about thirty miles." ◇

transmit the speed of the sighted convoy to U-boat commanders. The hour before dawn is still most favored by the Germans for the attack.

The announcement by Secretary Knox that the American navy would convoy lease-lend material was said to have taken some weight off the British fleet, however.

Destroyers, not in scores but in hundreds, appear to some observers to be the ultimate answer to the U-boat. Well does the British Navy remember Admiral Lord Beatty's statement on the eve of his death: "We must have 300 destroyers."

This island is one of the centers of the counter-offensive to the German U-boat campaign. British and American destroyers, equipped with the most modern detection devices and powerfully armed, are shepherding convoys.

The most heroic part of the story comes from the merchant sailors who emerge alive from attacks at sea. Among them it is common to meet seamen who have been torpedoed twice and even three times. Without exception they are eager to "get another ship."

Thousands of their fellows are dead. Others are in hospital, permanently crippled. Gangrene is the deadly enemy of the man in lifeboats.

Theirs are terrible stories: of men who went insane and leaped into the sea from lifeboats; of tongues that swell for lack of water; of nights when waves break over the frail lifeboats and half of the crew bails while the other half rows; of horrible minutes when the smoke of a far-off convoy dies on the horizon; of hours in biting cold water that numbs the body and senses before it drags men to the bottom. ◇

Danger to the Soviet Capital Increases: Of the several German drives on the central front, indicated by black arrows, the most menacing ones seemed to be those stemming from the Vyazma region (1) and the Bryansk region (2). The eastward thrust above Vyazms was the one that had reached closest to the capital. Moscow acknowledged that its forces had evacuated Bryansk and Berlin said that a German column sweeping around that place had reached Kaluga (3). The solid line shows the front at the beginning of the offensive; the broken line shows delineation of the present forces as issued in Berlin.

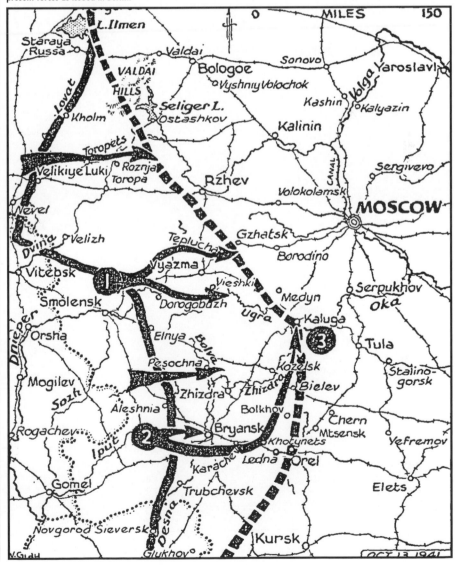

Chapter 9

"JAPANESE ATTACK UNITES AMERICA"

November–December 1941

No one reading the daily headlines in The Times through November should have been surprised by the sudden Japanese assault on the U.S. Pacific Fleet at anchor in the Hawaiian base at Pearl Harbor on December 7. Yet the attack, when it came, achieved complete surprise. The news from Russia showed Moscow girding for its ordeal as German armies edged ever closer through the tightening grip of a Russian winter, but the focus of all the news was on Japan. The Times's correspondent in Tokyo, Otto Tolischus, sent what information he could get through the censor, but the news was all bad. On November 5 the Japanese asked the United States to reverse its policy or "face conflict." On November 17 the Japanese premier, Hideki Tojo, in a speech to the Japanese Diet, gave the United States a virtual ultimatum to cancel the economic blockade and abandon interference in Asia. Privately the Japanese cabinet decided to wait until November 30 and if America had not backed down, to go to war to create a southern empire in Southeast Asia and the Pacific from which Japan could get oil and other raw materials that she could no longer obtain on world markets. On December 1 The Times announced that American aims were "Rejected by Japan as Fantastic." That same day Tojo had asked Emperor Hirohito at a formal Imperial Conference to authorize the decision for war a week later. To mask the decision another negotiator had been sent to Washington to keep up the pretense of discussion. The Times reported on December 6 "Japan Confident Talks Will Go On." News from Singapore again showed that the British doubted the threat from Japan, but in Australia preparations began for the possible onset of hostilities.

On December 7 The Times reported the Japanese view that a supreme crisis loomed, little knowing what was actually happening. It was a Sunday in New York and the Times office was quiet. Suddenly the news came through that the Japanese naval air arm had launched a major attack on Pearl Harbor, on what for Japan was December 8. There were few details, but the news was electrifying. Arthur Sulzberger, The Times' publisher, was away from New York but traveled back as quickly as he could to be in the thick of the crisis, sleeping in the office all that night. The full news could only be published the following day, on Monday morning. The effect all over America was profound, but the news was difficult to piece together since Japanese air and naval forces attacked in a wide arc from Malaya to Guam. All hint of isolationism or pacifism melted away. Arthur Krock, chief of the Times's Washington bureau, reported immediate national unity: "You could almost hear it click into place in Washington today." On December 9 Roosevelt signed the declaration of war against Japan, announcing to Congress the grim consequences of "a date that will live in infamy."

The news over the following three weeks was to become grimmer still. On December 10 the British battleships Prince of Wales and Renown were sunk off the coast of Malaya by Japanese naval aircraft; the same day the invasion of the Philippines was reported. The British Commonwealth garrison at Hong Kong surrendered two weeks later. Japanese soldiers advanced down the Malay Peninsula in the direction of Singapore, and through the island of Luzon toward Manila. For Tolischus in Tokyo the coming of war was a personal tragedy. He was arrested by the Japanese secret police for allegedly sending secret information to America, and tortured for weeks to confess that he was a spy. Beaten regularly, his legs and feet became swollen and bloody, reaching a point where he thought death might be preferable. But he refused to give way and eventually he was summoned before a court and given a suspended prison sentence. He was exchanged along with other newsmen for Japanese personnel and arrived back in New York amid tears of relief in August 1942.

REUBEN JAMES HIT

First American Warship Lost in War Torpedoed West of Iceland

By CHARLES HURD
Special to The New York Times.

WASHINGTON, Oct. 31—The United States lost its first warship in the Battle of the Atlantic when the destroyer Reuben James was torpedoed and sunk last night west of Iceland while on convoy duty, the Navy Department announced today.

The Navy later announced that forty-four members of the crew had been rescued. It was without word, however, as to the fate of the other members of the crew of 120 officers and men which made up her complement.

The meager reports on the sinking were believed to be due to the fact that radio silence for all but the most urgent messages is an inviolate rule of ships serving on the Atlantic patrol. The flashing of detailed messages by wireless serves in effect as a beacon to notify other enemy vessels where to find the ships which sent them out.

News of the sinking of the Reuben James created an immediate stir in Washington, on Capitol Hill particularly, but President Roosevelt sounded a conservative note in a press conference when he stated that the sinking did not change any aspect of the international position of the United States.

THIRD ATTACK ON U.S. WARSHIPS

The sinking of the Reuben James represented only the result which might have attended torpedo attacks on two other destroyers which recently have engaged German submarines. The destroyer Greek, first to figure in such an incident, escaped without being hit. The destroyer Kearny was hit by one of three torpedoes launched simultaneously and survived, but with the loss of eleven members of her crew.

The Kearny was a new destroyer, which proved the strength of its type in surviving a torpedo hit. The Reuben James, twenty-one-year-old member of the "tin-can" fleet, met the fate that all sailors long have agreed a destroyer faced if hit by a torpedo.

The Reuben James is believed to have gone down in the area where the other American destroyers were attacked.

If the engagement which cost the Reuben James occurred in the place where the previous attacks were made the vessel or vessels which witnessed and reported its sinking presumably would be some hundreds of miles from land, whether Iceland or Newfoundland, and perhaps a day or more would elapse before they could fully determine who survived and reach a safe place from which to relay further news.

It seemed probable to informed persons here acquainted with fleet operations and with the destroyer itself (in the absence of official comment) that the Reuben James probably was sunk in a general engagement rather than in single combat with a submarine.

American destroyers, like the British ones, are equipped with various devices which make it virtually impossible for a single submarine to catch a destroyer unawares and approach within torpedoing distance. It appeared probable, therefore, that a "pack" of submarines was involved in this attack. By the same token, in view of the system of naval operation, it is probable that other destroyers were on the scene in addition to the Reuben James and there is at least an even chance that the submarine which won this victory did not long survive it. ◊

OUR 'ARSENAL OF DEMOCRACY' BEGINS TO FUNCTION

Arms Output for Ourselves and Others Has Now Assumed Impressive Size

By HANSON W. BALDWIN

The "Battle of Production" entered a new phase last week as an additional lease-lend appropriation was made available and the President and his industrial advisers put the finishing touches to a new "victory program" designed to double the present plan with its enormous output of munitions.

For the first time since the passage of the Lease-Lend Act the "Arsenal of Democracy" has commenced to bristle with arms. The first twenty-four of the Army's new 90-mm. anti-aircraft guns reached the hands of troops at Camp Davis, N.C., in September; medium tanks are beginning to roll off the lines in considerable number; aircraft production stands at about 2,000 a month; ships are being launched almost daily.

In many items we are still in what William S. Knudsen calls the "make-ready" stage. In others we are still designing and blueprinting. Some weapons are already "flops"; others have encountered major delays of one sort or another—some of them technical difficulties, others difficulties of labor, matériel or management. There are shortages and bottlenecks in nearly every line. Many items have been delayed beyond anticipation. Lipstick and compact manufacturers are still using brass when there is a shortage of it for cartridge cases. Strike after strike—many of them jurisdictional—still plague, delay and seriously hurt output. Yet, despite all this, the wheels of America are beginning to turn.

START OF PRODUCTION

The production program was started two and a half years ago as an attempt to strengthen the defenses of this country. Before and after the war began in Europe orders for munitions were placed in this country by Britain and France, and these orders immediately caused a limited expansion of the aircraft industry. With the fall of France the entire American program underwent a tremendous expansion and was redrafted to meet the needs of a two-ocean Navy, a great air strength and a large Army, plus some supplies for Britain. But there was little attempt to key the program to actual war strategy needs and there was no detailed specific information in this country as to British production or British productive capacity.

It was not until last Summer, after Stacy May of the OPM went to England, that our production planners gleaned the

Under the Lease-Lend Act American lathes were used for turning out gun parts.

full facts about British production and it was not until then that we were able to lay a sound groundwork, in terms of industrial planning, for a program which would supply our own needs, Britain's and half the rest of the world.

The requests of Russian, Chinese, Greek and Latin-American requirements and the necessities of scores of other nations all had to be thrown into the hopper, to come out in the form of arms. So new and additional requirements have constantly been superimposed upon preceding ones.

The result is a $60,000,000,000 armament program, authorized or appropriated for the new "Victory Program," of which none of the details is known except that tank production is to be doubled, which is expected to at least double this cost.

THE NEW PROGRAM

This new program is supposed to be conceived in terms of "what it takes to beat Hitler" and is intended to be geared to strategic plans. Yet there are still many loose ends and the bottleneck of all plans—merchant tonnage to carry the munitions produced—has not been solved.

The present program—not the greatly increased "Victory Program"—is based upon the construction of a two-ocean Navy, the production of complete equipment for an Army of 1,725,000 men, with critical items for an Army of 3,000,000 and with factories capable of filling the battle needs of 4,000,000 troops and an annual production rate of almost 42,000 planes. The new program is expected to skyrocket this to what once would have been considered almost fantastic proportions. Under the terms of the "Victory" plans, for instance, total planes to be produced in the factories of America, from the beginning of the wartime boom until the end of the program, would be well over 100,000.

New munitions factories for the Army alone have already cost $1,750,000,000. In addition, $460,000,000 has been spent by the Navy on the expansion of shipbuilding facilities: the steel industry has added facilities for 6,000,000 net tons to boost its capacity to 88,000,000 tons a year; the aircraft industry has increased its floor space from 9,454,550 productive square feet on Jan. 1, 1939, to almost 54,000,000 square feet today. The monthly expenditures for defense in September, 1940, was $200,000,000; this year it was $1,360,000,000; next year it may be $2,000,000,000 or much higher, for the goal of many of the statisticians and industrialists in OPM is a $40,000,000,000 armament program annually.

The total picture presented is not an uncheerful one. Chief problems now and in the future will be those of controlling the vast machine that has been started, supplying it with sufficient raw materials without wrecking the rest of our industry, and controlling prices and wages. It is the greatest task this nation has ever undertaken. ◇

NOVEMBER 4, 1941

MOSCOW A CITADEL CLEARED FOR BATTLE
Reports to Kuibyshev Tell of the Spirit Of Its Defenders

Wireless to The New York Times.

KUIBYSHEV, Russia, Nov. 2 (Delayed)—The city of Moscow, which represents an architectural bridge between Europe and Asia has now been transformed into a fortified citadel—probably the largest defended city in the history of modern warfare. It is a city stripped to the essential, its supernumery population evacuated and diplomats and other foreigners cleared out.

Hundreds of thousands of workers, men and women—builders, forgers, weavers, railwaymen, locksmiths, subway conductors, architects, housewives, engineers—are busily completing concentric rings of fortifications about the Soviet capital that never for a moment has thought of avoiding the struggle by declaring itself an open town.

Ravines, fields and forests around the city are now cut by deep rings of anti-tank ditches, lined with bunkers and pillboxes and interspersed with riflemen's trenches. Day and night streams of mobilized automobiles carry new shifts of workers to the outskirts to maintain twenty-four-hour labor on the defenses.

A competitive spirit is encouraged among volunteers from each district constantly to speed up the construction.

Reports here today said men and women from the Timiriazev district held the title of "Stakhanovites" of the capital because of their speed in fortifying an allotted strip, and one man of that group was said to be excavating seven cubic meters of earth daily.

The Muscovites are adopting all sorts of slogans expressing their determination to prevent a Nazi entry of their city, the "heart of Russia." ◇

NOVEMBER 5, 1941

JAPANESE ASK U.S. TO REVERSE STAND OR FACE CONFLICT
Foreign Office Organ Demands Complete About-Face on Pain of 'Alternatives'

By OTTO D. TOLISCHUS
Wireless to The New York Times.

TOKYO, Nov. 5—The Japanese press is continuing its campaign to bring the United States to "self-reflection" about its Far Eastern policy. There is a growing crescendo, though with some confusion and contradiction in arguments.

The Japan Times Advertiser, organ of the Foreign Office, today made up its own list of what the United States must do "or face the alternatives"—as follows:

Japanese General and Prime Minister Hideki Tojo in 1941.

1. All military and economic aid to Chungking must cease.

2. China must be left "free to deal with Japan," and Chungking must be advised to make peace with Japan.

3. Military and economic encirclement of Japan must end.

4. Japan's "co-prosperity sphere" must be acknowledged, and Manchukuo, China, Indo-China, Thailand, the Netherlands Indies and other States and protectorates must be allowed to establish their own political and economic relations with Japan without interference of any kind.

5. Manchukuo must be recognized; "nobody will undo what has been done there."

6. The freezing of Japanese and Chinese assets must be ended unconditionally.

7. Trade treaties must be restored and all restrictions on shipping and commerce ended.

The National General Mobilization Council of the new Cabinet is scheduled to hold its first meeting Friday.

The Cabinet decided to call an extraordinary conference of prefectural Governors on Nov. 24 (following the extraordinary Diet session) at which special instructions are to be issued to the local authorities for the maintenance of domestic peace and order. At this conference Premier Hideki Tojo is expected to impress on the local Governors that the instructions designed to prepare Japan for war must be carried out with unflinching determination, while individual Ministers are expected to issue specific instructions in their respective fields, especially in the line of distribution of food and materials and an increase in production. The conference will last only one day.

All papers predict that in his Diet speech Premier Tojo will reiterate what the Japan Times Advertiser calls Japan's "standpat aims"—namely, the successful conclusion of the China "incident" and the establishment of the "East Asia co-prosperity sphere"—and at the same time reveal the truth about the American-Japanese conversations. But a "standpat" attitude on the part of the United States is denounced as "outrageous."

All the papers also insist that Japan has tried to conduct these conversations with patience and sincerity, and Soho Tokutomi declares in Nichi Nichi:

"Japan's friendship for the United States has been complete. Japan has done everything in her power to seek a compromise with the United States. The Konoye message [to President Roosevelt] represented the maximum limit of Japanese concessions."

The author of that assertion admits that he does not know the details of former Premier Prince Konoye's message and, therefore, is unable to suggest just what concessions Japan made. The only concession suggested in the press is an increasing reference to the "East Asia co-prosperity sphere," instead of a "greater East Asia co-prosperity sphere," though the significance of the difference remains obscure.

U.S. AS ENCIRCLER

Nichi Nichi further proclaims in a banner headline, "U.S.A. inspired encirclement designed to destroy Nippon empire in East Asia at sacrifice of Chungking and Netherlands East Indies." But Hochi reiterates: "Japan's objective is to eradicate unjust rights and interests in East Asia of various countries of the world which are intent upon treating East Asian peoples as slaves."

Or, as Teiichi Muto, a Hochi writer, declared recently, "Drive out the foreign barbarian."

In Nichi Nichi Generalissimo Chiang Kai-shek is represented as merely a tool of the United States, which is gradually taking the place of Britain in attempting to dominate Asia.

Whatever their arguments, however, all the papers constantly emphasize Japan's determination to cope with the situation and warn that the time limit of Japan's patience is about up. Nichi Nichi says it is a mistake to expect much from American and Japanese negotiations alone because all problems are now international in scale and peace can be constructed only on an international conception, but it also warns against the idea that Japan will remain motionless while being strangled economically.

"That is a completely Jewish theory," says this champion of the Axis alliance. ◆

NOVEMBER 7, 1941

GERMANS REPORT CAPTURE OF TULA

SEVASTOPOL SIEGE LOOMS

By GEORGE AXELSSON
By Telephone to The New York Times.

BERLIN, Nov. 6—The city of Tula, to which the southern end of the Moscow defenses has been anchored for almost a month, is in German hands, according to what are considered reliable reports from the front received in private quarters here today.

Bitter fighting continues in Crimea, according to the High Command, with the Germans claiming to have widened the breach on the Yaila Mountain front, pouring troops down to the shallow Black Sea coast between Theodosia and Yalta. If this is true, Yalta may already have been captured.

If the Germans have captured Tula, which lies in the low and marshy Upa Valley, some 100 airline miles south of Moscow, it is the result of some major action about which the German High Command has chosen to be silent.

ENCIRCLEMENT PLAN INDICATED

Indeed, military spokesmen in Berlin say even tonight that they do not know anything about the capture of Tula and refer to the communiqués, which have refrained from mentioning any actions of consequence along the Moscow front for many days.

The taking of Tula, where Czar Boris Godunoff built the first Russian gun factory in 1595 and whose main industry is rifle-making, might mean that the Germans are in the process of throwing a ring around Moscow similar to that around Leningrad.

If the Germans need not halt to consolidate their gains, as they are interpreted by neutral military experts here, they may be pushing straight on to Zaraisk and Ryazan Province and the Oka River, whence they would try to strike north and west to join the German units in the Kalinin sector, northwest of Moscow.

The passage through the Yaila Mountains is reported to have been forced at the Alushta Pass on the road from Simferopol to the town of Alushta. This road is at the bottom of a fairly broad valley, suitable for main traffic, and is the best if not the only road by which mechanized units could have reached the Black Sea coast.

SEVASTOPOL SIEGE EXPECTED

The Russians, however, are not abandoning Crimea without further fighting, for the Germans admit serious attempts by Soviet units to break out of their trap and fight their way through the German lines. These attempts, of course, are said to have failed.

The Germans expect that they must lay siege to Sevastopol before they can hope to capture this important Soviet naval base. But they are confident that they can rid the rest of Crimea of Soviet troops in short order.

Leningrad, which rounds out its second month of siege tomorrow on the twenty-fourth anniversary of the October revolution, has been particularly tried in the last few days by aerial and artillery bombardment, according to German reports, but these attacks evidently register no progress in the long-drawn-out effort to induce the city to surrender.

As the front line before Leningrad remains largely where it has been since the Germans marched into Schluesselburg on Sept. 8, and in view of German reports of local activity and repeated attempts of the beleaguered defenders to break the iron ring around the city, it does not appear that the Germans are much nearer their objectives than they were two months ago. ◇

NOVEMBER 9, 1941

FABLED RUSSIAN WINTER CLOSING IN ON INVADERS

Months of Bitter Cold and Deep Snow Will Test German Fighting Spirit

By C. L. SULZBERGER
Wireless to The New York Times.

KUIBISHEV, Nov. 8—Russia's traditional ally, General Winter, is slowly moving into action. The Russian Winter is one of the favorite subjects of this country's songs, poetry and painting—and well it might be. For at least five months every year the major part of the country is blanketed in snow and the peasants' activity is limited to feeding the livestock, talking, singing, drinking, hunting and protecting their cattle from foraging wolves. The women and children sit about the samovar brewing endless cups of tea, while the menfolk sit smoking long, half-filled cigarettes, exchanging yarns or singing mournful folksongs to the accompaniment of the triangular balalaika or the accordion.

Traditional are the peasant legends of the cold. Tales of the ravages of wolves are manifold. There are countless versions of the story Willa Cather tells of a peasant's bridal party drunkenly swinging home across snow-filled roads in troikas and being chased by voracious wolf packs. First one sled overturned and occupants and horses were eaten. Then another and another piled into the drifts as the lead wolves slashed at the terrified steeds. Eventually only one sled was left and the driver of it hurled out bride and groom to lighten the load and escape.

FOUNDED IN TRUTH

How many of these tales have a foundation in truth is hard to know. But wolves are plentiful and when the Winter blanket covers everything they frequently are driven to the outskirts of villages, hunting anything in order to exist.

A wolf, a belled horse-drawn troika, and a forest loaded with snow are traditional subjects in Russian art. Two hundred miles from Moscow, in little villages, peasant craftsmen still paint lacquered boxes that are famous the ❯

German infantry unit advances toward Rostov, November, 1941.

world over, laboring with squirrel's-tail brushes, egg-yolk kvas and colored pictures, depicting these scenes on small surfaces which have been transported by tourists throughout the world. Ancient folksongs, legends of Prince Igor and peasant fairy tales are all steeped in the lore of Winter.

The stamp of Winter has always marked the traditional picture of Russia since traders from Moscow first began to circulate among the capitals of Europe in medieval times. Muscovites are thought of as bearded, befurred and dressed in heavy coats. The earliest international commerce with Russia was for the purpose of securing products from its cold clime—furs, timber, pitch and gum.

A COLD WORLD

An old peasant used to say: "Russia is not a country; it is a world." To this peasant it is a cold world. Living in his wooden house, over which sweeps the Winter wind, he has learned how to protect himself by warm clothes and strong drinks against his greatest natural enemy—Winter. It is only in times of war that this enemy becomes an ally. How effective this aid has been can be realized by anyone who has seen some of Meissonier's paintings of Napoleon's catastrophic retreat.

To strangers unaccustomed to this climate and unaided by the local population, desolation can prove disastrous. The Russian says about his enemy: "A German will thrash wheat out of the head of an axe." That's about what he will have to do this Winter. Major crop stores have been removed or burned in the evacuated territories. Village after village and town after town have been destroyed in battle or by rear-guard units.

As cold sets in, salient after salient on the vast front becomes inactive. All along the Karelian and Kola peninsulas, it is reported that the Germans are digging in, not against the Russians but against the cold.

What actual effect Winter can have on military operations is hard to predict. There is no doubt that armies can fight in Winter and fight hard, discomfort or not. That was proved in the last war. It was proved in Finland more recently.

PAST EXPERIENCE

But, undoubtedly, continued fighting under Russian Winter conditions will not improve the morale of the invader. During the period of Allied intervention after the last war, General Sokolovsky told the writer, the Japanese could not stand the Siberian climate, despite the fact that they brought electric heating pads with them. If the Russians can continue to hold Leningrad and Moscow the Germans will not have any bases where warm housing can be afforded behind the lines on two fronts.

Up around Murmansk it is reported that Col. Gen. Dittel, the German commander, is calling for Finnish reinforcements who are better able to stand the Winter cold. One of the chief reasons that the Germans are trying so hard now to take the Crimea is that they may acquire warm hospitals and sanitaria on the Soviet Riviera to house their wounded.

Hitler is making desperate efforts to attain the major goals of his latest offensive before Winter sets in. Speed is essential to his task. Every day now that the Red Army holds its lines can be counted as a day's gain.

Russia has been invaded many times and many times these invasions have been finally checked by resistance aided by cold. Who knows whether this will make a great difference against modern mechanized tactics. Can the Luftwaffe continue to operate effectively in an icy sky? Will Hitler's troops easily face another Winter—the third of a slowed down Blitzkrieg? These things are imponderables at present. But there is one certainty—Winter comes early here; and it stays long. ◇

NOVEMBER 12, 1941

PRESIDENT WARNS NATION IS FACING WORLD WAR AGAIN

FOR LIBERTY AND DECENCY

By FRANK L. KLUCKHORN
Special to The New York Times.

WASHINGTON, Nov. 11—As the United States celebrated today the signing of the World War armistice, President Roosevelt declared in his address that this country may be forced by Germany into another war. Other speakers emphasized the same theme of the Nazi peril.

Standing bare-headed on a windswept hill in Arlington National Cemetery, near the tomb of the Unknown Soldier, where solemn and impressive rites had just taken place, the President told a nationwide radio audience and a large crowd gathered in the amphitheatre, that the United States fought in the World War to protect liberty and democracy. The people of America, he remarked, believe liberty to be worth fighting for. And of liberty, he said:

"If they are obliged to fight they will fight eternally to hold it. This is the duty we owe, not to ourselves alone, but to the many dead who died to gain freedom for us—to make the world a place where freedom can live and grow into the ages."

SOLEMN SCENE AT ARLINGTON

It was with solemn mien that the President heard the ceremony at Arlington, the playing of the national anthem, the bugle's Taps and the two twenty-one-gun salutes. The hour was 11, just twenty-three years after the end of the World War. He spoke to the distinguished gathering assembled under the banners of the American Legion. He spoke with a calm determination.

Those who died in 1917–18, he said, had indeed died to make the world safe for decency and self-respect.

"We know," he went on, "that these men died to save their country from a terrible danger of the day. We know, because we face that danger once again on this day."

Recalling that those who gave their lives on the battlefields of Europe had sacrificed themselves for democracy, "to prevent then the very thing that now, a quarter of a century later, has happened from one end of Europe to another," the President of the United States declared that now, in their memory and so that they may not have perished in vain, the obligation and the duty are ours.

"Whatever we knew or thought we knew a few years or months ago, we know now that the danger of brutality, the danger of tyranny and slavery to freedom-loving people can be real and terrible."

The President stood at attention as the band played The Star-Spangled Banner. Then flanked by his military and naval aides, Maj. Gen. Edwin M. Watson and Captain John Beardall, he moved forward. There was a minute of silence, and Captain Beardall took a wreath of white chrysanthemums from an Army sergeant in full-dress blue and, acting for the President, placed it at the foot of the Tomb. ◊

NOVEMBER 15, 1941

ARK ROYAL SUNK NEAR GIBRALTAR BY AXIS TORPEDO

By CRAIG THOMPSON
Special Cable to The New York Times.

LONDON, Nov. 14—The airplane carrier Ark Royal—so often reported sunk by the Germans and Italians that she became a sort of phantom ship ranging the seas from the Arctic Circle to the Equator and in the Mediterranean—has finally gone to the bottom. Torpedoed by an Italian submarine yesterday she sank today about twenty-five miles east of Gibraltar while being towed to that port.

A. V. Alexander, First Lord of the Admiralty, announced that the casualties were "very light." It appears at present that it was impossible to get off her aircraft, which means that about seventy planes, mostly Swordfish torpedo-carriers, Skua dive-bombers and reconnaissance craft, went down with her. The Ark Royal is the third British carrier lost in this war, the others being the Courageous and the Glorious.

The Ark Royal, the 'phantom' British carrier.

OFTEN REPORTED SUNK

From the time only a few days after the war began, when the German radio inquired nightly "Where is the Ark Royal?" and coupled this question with the assertion that she was sunk on Sept. 26, 1939, until recent months there have been repeated claims that the carrier, the third bearer of its illustrious naval name, had been destroyed. All during that time she was actively in service, searching the Atlantic for the pocket battleship Admiral Graf Spee, participating in naval action off Norway, fighting Italians in the Mediterranean, playing a major role in the destruction of the battleship Bismarck and finally performing invaluable service spotting Axis convoys in the Mediterranean.

In the whole term of her service, which began in midsummer 1938, the planes of the Ark Royal brought down more than 100 German or Italian aircraft, sixty-nine of these within recent months in Mediterranean operations. Her loss will be a serious blow to British naval forces there and at a critical time, when the Germans and Italians are making a determined effort to add men and supplies to the garrison in Libya. ▸

◀ **ACTION IN "MARE NOSTRUM"**

In patrolling Premier Mussolini's "Mare Nostrum" the Ark Royal performed a major service. Her normal complement of seventy planes flew off her 800-foot deck for several purposes. There were some that ranged over a long stretch of water locating Africa-bound Axis convoys and bringing to them ships of the British Fleet, which has been busy cutting off Italy and Germany from Africa.

Then there were the Swordfish planes, which flashed low on the water and loosed torpedoes. A year ago while taking part in the pursuit of the Italian Fleet southwest of Sardinia a Swordfish torpedoed a Littorio-class battleship and hit cruisers and destroyers, while Skua bombers, also from the Ark Royal, attacked them from above.

This was only one of her performances during the time when the German radio claimed she was on the ocean's bottom. After having sunk her numbers of times in the past, radio stations and official pronouncements from Axis capitals were strangely silent today. It was assumed here that their claimed performance was awkwardly late. ◆

DECEMBER 1, 1941

U.S. Principles Rejected By Japanese as 'Fantastic'

Foreign Minister Togo Makes First Official Comment on Washington Note— General Threatens Fresh Aggression

By OTTO D. TOLISCHUS
Wireless to The New York Times.

TOKYO, Dec. 1—In the first official statement on the American proposals for a settlement of the issues in the Pacific submitted to Japan, Foreign Minister Shigenori Togo today rejected the principles underlying them as "fantastic," and characterized the American attitude as unrealistic and regrettable. He reiterated Japan's determination to proceed with the construction of a "New Order in East Asia."

Following the lines of a strong message from Premier General Hideki Tojo, the reading of which was the highlight of yesterday's mass meetings, the Foreign Minister declared:

"The world is confronted with unprecedented disturbances. In Greater East Asia, however, close relations of Japan, Manchukuo and China must be further cemented. Japan, Manchukuo and China must go forward toward the construction of a new order in East Asia on the basis of their coexistence and coprosperity.

"In our negotiations with the United States we have consistently upheld this principle. However, the United States does not understand the real situation in East Asia. It is trying forcibly to apply to East Asiatic countries fantastic principles and rules not adapted to the actual situation in the world and thereby tending to obstruct the construction of the New Order. This is extremely regrettable."

Opposing the slogan of "Asia for the Asiatics under Japan's leadership" to the American principle of the Open Door, Japan, Manchukuo and the Nanking puppet regime yesterday celebrated the first anniversary of their joint declaration of cooperation with mass meetings in their principal cities organized by their governments. Semi-official organs reiterated the firm determination of the three countries to "liberate" the one thousand million people of East Asia from the "exploitation" of Europe and America by the construction of the "Greater East Asia Co-Prosperity Sphere," as a guiding torch for mankind and to crush all outside powers' obstruction of this "holy and historic mission."

The press echoes sentiments expressed at the meetings. Yomiuri declared that there was special meaning in the fact that this anniversary came in the midst of tension in Japanese-American negotiations, "for the complete independence of East Asia must be strengthened and western imperialism must be wiped from this part of the globe." ◆

DECEMBER 4, 1941

SINGAPORE DOUBTS JAPANESE THREATS

Arrival of the British Fleet Is Expected To Cause Tokyo To Order General Retreat

By F. TILLMAN DURDIN
Wireless to The New York Times.

SINGAPORE, Dec. 3—Authorities here agree that the arrival of powerful British naval units, headed by the new battleship, Prince of Wales, yesterday raises the odds against Japan more than ever before.

DECEMBER 5, 1941

AUSTRALIA GIRDS FOR PACIFIC WAR

TOKYO WATCHES BRITISH

Wireless to The New York Times.

MELBOURNE, Australia, Dec. 4—A War Cabinet meeting in which service chiefs participated has completed comprehensive plans to put Australia on a new

---

DECEMBER 6, 1941

JAPAN CONFIDENT TALKS WILL GO ON

Spokesman Says Both Sides Are 'Sincere'

By OTTO D. TOLISCHUS
Wireless to The New York Times.

TOKYO, Dec. 6—Tomokazu Hori, spokesman of the Cabinet Information Board, announced at a press conference

It is pointed out that an advance against British or Netherland territories in Southeast Asia, which a year ago might have been easy for the Japanese, now would be a desperate effort with remote chances of success.

The capital ships and auxiliaries that make up Britain's new Far Eastern fleet constitute a formidable force, especially when considered in conjunction with Netherland naval power in the East. The Netherland Navy of cruisers, destroyers, submarines and scores of fast small torpedo boats complements the naval units the British have sent to the Orient in a way that could not have been a coincidence and makes the combined strength of the two navies considerably more than is indicated by tonnages or the number of ships.

Political observers here say the arrival of the British fleet brought powerful new pressure on the Japanese in connection with the Washington negotiations and believe it may be decisive in forcing Japan to drop her plans for new aggressions and to begin a general retreat. ◊

emergency footing if war spreads to the Pacific. The Cabinet resumes tomorrow.

Prime Minister John Curtin said the Cabinet reviewed the services and the state of preparedness, examined precautionary measures to meet any contingency and authorized further precautions when necessary.

News of the arrival of a battle fleet in Singapore gave the government special satisfaction, for the Ministers when in opposition consistently urged the dispatch of capital ships to Malaya as a bulwark against a southward move by an Asiatic aggressor. Thus, Australia's northern defenses are now regarded as more secure. ◊

yesterday that the Washington negotiations would continue. He repudiated charges by the Japanese press that America lacked sincerity and was protracting the negotiations purposely.

"Both sides," Mr. Hori said, "will continue to negotiate with sincerity to find a common formula to ease the situation in the Pacific. If there were no sincerity there would be no need to continue the negotiations."

Spokesman Hori said the Japanese Government was amazed at the continued existence of great American misunderstanding regarding Japan's policy in the Far East. United States Secretary of State Cordell Hull, he said, charged that Japan was following a policy of force, conquest and military despotism.

CITES PUPPET REGIME

Naturally, Mr. Hori said, conditions in China are not normal on account of hostilities, but he maintained that the ultimate objective of the "China incident" had been fixed in the statement of former Premier Prince Fumimaro Konoye, which disclaimed territorial ambitions and indemnities. This principle, Mr. Hori asserted, was incorporated in the basic treaty with Nanking [puppet regime in China].

The Washington negotiations, he continued, have the purpose of removing this misunderstanding. Although he did not subscribe to Mr. Hull's statement that the negotiations were virtually back at their starting point, he made it clear that there was still a wide difference of opinion on the two sides.

As for the occupation of French Indo-China he declared that there were many examples of sending troops to a foreign domain with the consent of its government. Mr. Hori declared, in regard to American inquiries, that the number of Japanese troops in French Indo-China was within the agreed limit as reported in news dispatches from Vichy.

"If Vichy says so," he said, "there cannot be any complaint from any other side."

EPITHETS FOR AMERICA

Meanwhile, in contrast with the vernacular press, which confines itself in the main to scouring the dictionary for epithets to hurl against Mr. Hull and the United States, the Japan Times Advertiser, the Foreign Office organ, attempts to present a reasoned argument in contravention to Mr. Hull's fundamental thesis. Mr. Hull's revelations, it says, appear to be a scarcely statesmanlike attempt to seize the propagandistic initiative and put the responsibility for a breakdown in the negotiations on Japan. The Japan Times Advertiser raises the following points, which may be summarized as follows:

1. America maintains the Monroe Doctrine and President Roosevelt himself has declared that other regions have the right to a similar doctrine. Japan, therefore, feels itself entitled to establish one for the Far East to prevent distant powers from encroaching on the territories of the Western Pacific. But while a statement about non-interference with existing colonies and dependencies of distant powers is left in the quotation of the Monroe Doctrine, that point is not further discussed.

2. President Roosevelt declared nations must be free to choose their own forms of government free from interference by outside nations. Therefore Far Eastern States should be free to determine their own destiny free of interposition by the United States—not, however, of Japan, which is promoting a co-prosperity sphere.

3. Mr. Hull charges Japan's policy is based on force. The very core of Oriental business is compromise and adjustment, but Japan will apply force when it finds itself confronted with a hostile disposition.

4. Mr. Hull says he put the negotiations back on a basis of fundamental principles. These principles are obscurantist.

5. Japan put forward a practical principle of the highest human order, including non-intervention in Far Eastern affairs. The United States, Chungking, the Netherlands and the Soviet oppose Japan.

The paper concludes:

"The American and British people will now use their influence on Mr. Hull to make some practical efforts at agreement with Japan on pacific principles, instead of appealing to publicity for the purpose of discrediting one nation that is seriously trying to avoid war." ◊

DECEMBER 7, 1941

JAPANESE HERALD 'SUPREME CRISIS'

U.S. IS HELD AGGRESSIVE
Press Intimates Efforts for Negotiated Settlement May Soon Be Abandoned

TOKYO, Dec. 7 (UP)—Japan indicated early today that she was on the verge of abandoning efforts to achieve a settlement of Pacific issues by diplomatic negotiation at Washington.

At the same time warnings circulated that Soviet Russia—with an estimated Far Eastern army of 840,000—had joined the United States, Britain, China, the Netherlands Indies and the British Dominions in a united front against Japan. ▸

‹ The press, bellwether of Japanese opinion, thundered that the moment of supreme crisis was at hand. A government spokesman said Japan's "patience" may be tried only a little longer.

Japanese economic preparations against what is called the "open strengthening of anti-Japanese encirclement" were believed completed with adjournment of a highly significant meeting of 300 Japanese industrial and business leaders who comprise the East Asia Economic Council.

The report that Russia was casting her lot with the so-called ABCD powers appeared in the newspaper Hochi, which attributed it to "undisclosed Tokyo quarters."

LITVINOFF VIEWED OMINOUSLY

The imminent arrival of Maxim Litvinoff, new Soviet Ambassador to the United States, in Washington was said to increase the prospect of Russia's participation in moves against Japan.

The newspaper estimated the strength of the Russian Red Banner Far Eastern armies at 840,000 men despite reported transfers of some troops from the eastern theatre to the western front.

The statement that Japan's "patience" is drawing to an end was made by Lieut. Gen. Teiichi Suzuki, president of the Cabinet Planning Board, in an address to the East Asia Economic Council.

"Japan's patience," he said, "will no longer be necessary in the event the countries hostile to peace in East Asia—countries whose identity now is becoming absolutely clear—attempt to continue and increase Far Eastern disturbances.

"We Japanese are tensely watching whether or not President Roosevelt will commit the epoch-making crime of further extending the world upheaval." ◊

DECEMBER 8, 1941

TOKYO ACTS FIRST

Declaration Follows Air and Sea Attacks On U.S. and Britain

TOGO CALLS ENVOYS

By The Associated Press.

TOKYO, Dec. 8—Japan went to war against the United States and Britain today with air and sea attacks against Hawaii, followed by a formal declaration of hostilities.

Japanese Imperial headquarters announced at 6 A.M. [4 P.M. Sunday, Eastern standard time] that a state of war existed among these nations in the Western Pacific, as of dawn.

Soon afterward, Domei, the Japanese official news agency, announced that "naval operations are progressing off Hawaii, with at least one Japanese aircraft carrier in action against Pearl Harbor," the American naval base in the islands.

Japanese bombers were declared to have raided Honolulu at 7:35 A.M., Hawaii time [1:05 Sunday, Eastern standard time].

Premier-War Minister General Hideki Tojo held a twenty-minute Cabinet session at his official residence at 7 A.M.

Soon afterward it was announced that both the United States Ambassador, Joseph C. Grew, and the British Ambassador, Sir Robert Leslie Craigie, had been summoned by Foreign Minister Shigenori Togo.

The Foreign Minister, Domei said, handed to Mr. Grew the Japanese Government's formal reply to the note sent to Japan by United States Secretary of State Cordell Hull on Nov. 26.

[In the course of the diplomatic negotiations leading up to yesterday's events, the Domei agency had stated that Japan could not accept the premises of Mr. Hull's note.]

Sir Robert was summoned by Foreign Minister Togo fifteen minutes after Mr. Grew was called.

At the brief Cabinet session Premier Tojo reported on the progress of war plans against the British and American forces, according to Domei, and outlined the Japanese Government's policy. ◊

Smoke pouring from sinking battleship USS California, which was attacked during the surprise Japanese raid on Pearl Harbor.

DECEMBER 8, 1941

Japan Wars on U.S. and Britain
Makes Sudden Attack on Hawaii

By FRANK L. KLUCKHOHN
Special to The New York Times.

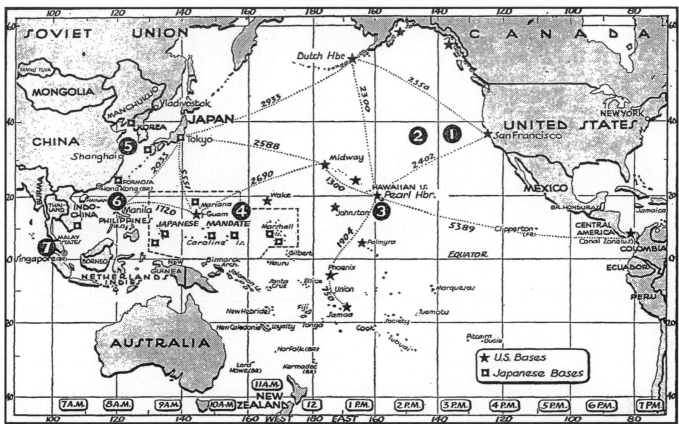

WASHINGTON, Dec. 8—Sudden and unexpected attacks on Pearl Harbor, Honolulu, and other United States possessions in the Pacific early yesterday by the Japanese air force and navy plunged the United States and Japan into active war.

The initial attack in Hawaii, apparently launched by torpedo-carrying bombers and submarines, caused widespread damage and death. It was quickly followed by others. There were unconfirmed reports that German raiders participated in the attacks.

Guam also was assaulted from the air, as were Davao, on the island of Mindanao, and Camp John Hay, in Northern Luzon, both in the Philippines. Lieut. Gen. Douglas MacArthur, commanding the United States Army of the Far East, reported there was little damage, however.

Japanese submarines, ranging out over the Pacific, sank an American transport carrying lumber 1,300 miles from San Francisco, and distress signals were heard from a freighter 700 miles from that city.

The War Department reported that 104 soldiers died and 300 were wounded as a result of the attack on Hickam Field, Hawaii. The National Broadcasting Company reported from Honolulu that the battleship Oklahoma was afire. [Domei, Japanese news agency, reported the Oklahoma sunk.]

NATION PLACED ON FULL WAR BASIS

The news of these surprise attacks fell like a bombshell on Washington. President Roosevelt immediately ordered the country and the Army and Navy onto a full war footing. He arranged at a White House conference last night to address a joint session of Congress at noon today, presumably to ask for declaration of a formal state of war.

This was disclosed after a long special Cabinet meeting, which was joined later by Congressional leaders. These leaders predicted "action" within a day.

After leaving the White House conference Attorney General Francis Biddle said that "a resolution" would be introduced in Congress tomorrow. He would not amplify or affirm that it would be

Shortly after the outbreak of hostilities an American ship sent a distress call from (1) and a United States Army transport carrying lumber was torpedoed at (2). The most important action was at Hawaii (3), where Japanese planes bombed the great Pearl Harbor base. Also attacked was Guam (4). From Manila (6) United States bombers roared northward, while some parts of the Philippines were raided, as was Hong Kong, to the northwest. At Shanghai (5) a British gunboat was sunk and an American gunboat seized. To the south, in the Malaya area (7), the British bombed Japanese ships, Tokyo forces attempted landings on British territory and Singapore underwent an air raid. Distances between key Pacific points are shown on the map in statute miles.

for a declaration of war.

Congress probably will "act" within the day, and he will call the Senate Foreign Relations Committee for this purpose, Chairman Tom Connally announced.

[A United Press dispatch from London this morning said that Prime Minister Churchill had notified Japan that a state of war existed.]

As the reports of heavy fighting flashed into the White House, London reported semi-officially that the British Empire would carry out Prime ▶

❨ Minister Winston Churchill's pledge to give the United States full support in case of hostilities with Japan. The President and Mr. Churchill talked by transatlantic telephone.

This was followed by a statement in London from the Netherland Government in Exile that it considered a state of war to exist between the Netherlands and Japan. Canada, Australia and Costa Rica took similar action.

LANDING MADE IN MALAYA

A Singapore communiqué disclosed that Japanese troops had landed in Northern Malaya and that Singapore had been bombed.

The President told those at last night's White House meeting that "doubtless very heavy losses" were sustained by the Navy and also by the Army on the island of Oahu [Honolulu]. It was impossible to obtain confirmation or denial of reports that the battleships Oklahoma and West Virginia had been damaged or sunk at Pearl Harbor, together with six or seven destroyers, and that 350 United States airplanes had been caught on the ground.

The White House took over control of the bulletins, and the Navy Department, therefore, said it could not discuss the matter or answer any questions how the Japanese were able to penetrate the Hawaiian defenses or appear without previous knowledge of their presence in those waters.

Administration circles forecast that the United States soon might be involved in a world-wide war, with Germany supporting Japan, an Axis partner. The German official radio tonight attacked the United States and supported Japan.

A nation-wide round-up of Japanese nationals was ordered by Attorney General Biddle through cooperation by the FBI and local police forces.

Action was taken to protect defense plants, especially in California, where Japanese are particularly numerous. Orders were issued by the Civil Aeronautics Authority to ground most private aircraft except those on scheduled lines.

FLEET PUTS OUT TO SEA FROM HAWAII

The Navy last night swept out to sea from its bombed base at Pearl Harbor after Secretary of State Cordell Hull, following a final conference with Japanese "peace envoys" here, asserted that Japan's had been a "treacherous" attack. Neither the War nor the Navy Department had been able to communicate with its commanders in Manila.

Secretary of War Henry L. Stimson

A San Francisco corner on December 8, 1941.

ordered the entire United States Army to be in uniform by today. Secretary Frank Knox followed suit for the Navy. They did so after President Roosevelt had instructed the Navy and Army to expect all previously prepared orders for defense immediately.

United States naval craft are expected to operate out of Singapore as soon as possible in protecting the vital rubber and tin shipments necessary to our national defense program.

Despite these preliminary defense moves, however, it was clear that further detailed discussions would soon take place between officials of the United States, Great Britain, China, the Netherlands and Australia to devise a total scheme of limiting the activities of the Japanese Fleet.

Immediate steps will be taken also to meet the increased menace to China's lifeline, the Burma Road. Reliable information indicates that the Japanese are preparing a large-scale assault on the road in the hope of cutting off American supplies before the Allies can transport sufficient forces into defensive positions.

Censorship was established on all messages leaving the United States by cable and radio.

In Tokyo United States Ambassador Joseph C. Grew obtained a reply to Secretary Hull's early message, according to dispatches from the Japanese capital.

The attack on Pearl Harbor and Honolulu began "at dawn," according to Stephen Early, Presidential secretary. Because of the time difference, the first news of the bombing was released in Washington at 2:22 P.M. Subsequently it was announced at the White House that another wave of bombers and dive bombers had come over Oahu Island, on which Honolulu is situated, to be met by anti-aircraft fire again.

An attack on Guam, tiny island outpost, subsequently was announced. The White House at first said that Manila also had been attacked but, after failure to reach Army and Navy commanders there, President Roosevelt expressed the "hope" that no such attack had occurred. Broadcasts from Manila bore out this hope.

HAWAII ATTACKED WITHOUT WARNING

Reports from Hawaii indicated that Honolulu had no warning of the attack. Japanese bombers, with the red circle of the Rising Sun of Japan on their wings, suddenly appeared, escorted by fighters. Flying high, they suddenly dive-bombed, attacking Pearl Harbor, the great Navy base, the Army's Hickam Field and Ford Island. At least one torpedo plane was seen to launch a torpedo at warships in Pearl Harbor.

A report from Admiral C. C. Bloch, commander of the naval district at Hawaii, expressed the belief that "there has been heavy damage done in Hawaii and there has been heavy loss of life."

This was subsequently confirmed by Governor Joseph B. Poindexter of Hawaii in a telephone conversation with President Roosevelt. The Governor also said that there were heavy casualties in the city of Honolulu.

Many Japanese and former Japanese who are now American citizens are in residence in Hawaii.

Saburo Jurusu, special Japanese envoy who has been conducting "peace" negotiations while Japan was preparing for this attack, and Ambassador Kichisaburo Nomura called at the State Department at 2:05 P.M. after asking for the appointment at 1 P.M. They arrived shortly before Secretary Hull had received news Japan had started a war without warning. Mrs. Roosevelt revealed in her broadcast last night that the Japanese Ambassador was with the President when word of the attacks was received.

The two envoys handed a document to Mr. Hull, who kept them waiting about fifteen minutes. Upon reading it, he turned to his visitors to exclaim that it was "crowded with infamous falsehoods and distortions."

President Roosevelt ordered war bulletins released at the White House as rapidly as they were received. A sentence or two was added to the story of the surprise attack every few minutes for several hours.

Cabinet members arrived promptly at 8:30 last evening for their meeting in the White House Oval Room. President Roosevelt had been closeted with Harry L. Hopkins in the Oval Room since receiving the first news. He had conferred with Secretaries Stimson and Knox by telephone and also with General George C. Marshall, Chief of Staff. Admiral Harold R. Stark, Chief of Naval Operations, was too busy to talk to the President even by telephone.

PRESIDENT VOICED HOPE FOR PEACE

The President's message expressed a "fervent hope for peace" and outlined the dangers of the situation.

"We have hoped that a peace of the Pacific could be consummated in such a way that the nationalities of many diverse peoples may exist side by side without fear of invasion," the President told the Emperor.

The President, recalling that the United States had been directly responsible for bringing Japan into contact with the outside world, said that in seeking peace in the Pacific "I am certain that it will be clear to Your Majesty, as it is to me, that ... both Japan and the United States should agree to eliminate any form of military threat."

The Japanese document, despite the obviously carefully prepared attack on American bases, insisted that:

"On the other hand, the American Government, always holding fast to theories in disregard of realities and refusing to yield an inch on its impractical principles, caused undue delay in the [peace] negotiations." ◆

DECEMBER 8, 1941

HULL DENOUNCES TOKYO 'INFAMY'
Brands Japan 'Fraudulent' in Preparing Attack While Carrying On Parleys

By BERTRAM D. HULEN
Special to The New York Times.

WASHINGTON, Dec. 7—Japan was accused by Secretary of State Cordell Hull today of making a "treacherous and utterly unprovoked attack" upon the United States and of having been "infamously false and fraudulent" by preparing for the attack while conducting diplomatic negotiations with the professed desire of maintaining peace.

But even before he knew of that attack, Mr. Hull had vehemently brought the diplomatic negotiations to a virtual end with an outburst against Admiral Kichisaburo Nomura, the Japanese Ambassador, and Saburo Kurusu, special envoy, because of the insulting character of the reply they delivered to his document of Nov. 26 setting forth the basic principles of the United States.

This proposed a multilateral non-aggression pact in the Pacific, taking in all the interested powers in that area except France.

REJECTION BY JAPANESE

The Japanese reply was a flat rejection in stiff language and a termination of the negotiations. Japan charged that the United States was "conspiring" with Great Britain in the Far East, was trying to detach Japan from the Axis, and was ignoring Japan's position.

The American position, it charged, was utopian and not in accordance with realities. All the good it could see in Mr. Hull's proposals had to do with possible relaxation by the United States of some economic pressure.

The document revealed definitely that the Japanese Premier had sought to meet President Roosevelt last August for a conference, but that this was refused until an agreement had been reached. It also said that Mr. Roosevelt had offered to act as "introducer" of peace between Japan and China.

Secretary Hull considered the reply so filled with false statements and distortions that in an outburst that recalled the vigor of speech of his youth in Tennessee, he declared to Admiral Nomura "with the greatest indignation," as the State Department's announcement described it:

Secretary of State Cordell Hull in 1941.

"I must say that in all my conversations with you [the Japanese Ambassador] during the last nine months I have never uttered one word of untruth. This is borne out absolutely by the record. In all my fifty years of public service I have never seen a document that was more crowded with ❯

infamous falsehoods and distortions on a scale so huge that I never imagined until today that any government on this planet was capable of uttering them."

UNAWARE OF ATTACK

When this meeting took place at 2:20 P.M. word was being received at the White House of the attack on Hawaii. Mr. Hull was unaware of it, and apparently so were the Japanese envoys. Several hours later, Mr. Hull issued his general statement of condemnation of Japan.

"Japan has made a treacherous and utterly unprovoked attack upon the United States," Secretary Hull said.

"At the very moment when representatives of the Japanese Government were discussing with representatives of this government, at the request of the former, principles and courses of peace, the armed forces of Japan were preparing and assembling at various strategic points to launch new attacks and new aggressions upon nations and peoples with which Japan was professedly at peace, including the United States.

"This government has stood for all the principles that underlie fair dealing, peace, law and order, and justice between nations and has steadfastly striven to promote and maintain that state of relationship between itself and all other nations.

"It is now apparent to the whole world that Japan in its recent professions of a desire for peace has been infamously false and fraudulent."

Mr. Hull's conference with the Japanese envoys lasted ten minutes.

When they emerged they were glum and downcast. ◇

DECEMBER 8, 1941

NEGROES PLEDGE LOYALTY
Leader Wires Roosevelt 12,000,000 Are Ready to Serve

Special to The New York Times.

WASHINGTON, Dec. 7—Assurances of the loyalty and support of the Negroes of the United States in the hostilities with Japan were sent to President Roosevelt tonight in a telegram by Edgar G. Brown, director of the National Negro Council and president of the United Government Employes. His telegram said:

"Twelve million American Negro citizens renewed today their pledge of 100 per cent loyalty to their country and our Commander-in-Chief against Japan and all other invaders. Negro youth awaits your call for an unrestricted and full opportunity to serve their country at this critical hour in all capacities of the Army and Navy, the Marines, the Coast Guard and the Air Corps and national defense." ◇

DECEMBER 8, 1941

NETHERLANDS JOIN IN WAR ON JAPAN
Exiled Government in London and Indies' Governor General Issue Declarations

LONDON, Dec. 8 (AP)—The Netherland Government in exile considers itself in a state of war with Japan, said an authorized statement issued early today.

The statement said:

"In view of Japan's aggression against two powers with whom the Netherlands maintain particularly close relations, aggression directly threatening vital Netherlands interests, the Government of the Kingdom considers a state of war exists between the Netherlands and the Japanese Empire."

It was learned that instructions to this effect have been sent to the Governor-General of the Netherlands Indies and the Governors of two Western Hemisphere possessions, Surinam and Curacao. ◇

DECEMBER 9, 1941

UNITY IN CONGRESS
Only One Negative Vote as President Calls to War And Victory

ROUNDS OF CHEERS

By FRANK L. KLUCKHOHN
Special to The New York Times.

WASHINGTON, Dec. 8—The United States today formally declared war on Japan. Congress, with only one dissenting vote, approved the resolution in the record time of 33 minutes after President Roosevelt denounced Japanese aggression in ringing tones. He personally delivered his message to a joint session of the Senate and House. At 4:10 P.M. he affixed his signature to the resolution.

There was no debate like that between April 2, 1917, when President Wilson requested war against Germany, and April 6, when a declaration of war was approved by Congress.

President Roosevelt spoke only 6 minutes and 30 seconds today compared with Woodrow Wilson's 29 minutes and 34 seconds.

The vote today against Japan was 82 to 0 in the Senate and 388 to 1 in the House. The lone vote against the resolution in the House was that of Miss Jeanette Rankin, Republican, of Montana. Her "no" was greeted with boos and hisses. In 1917 she voted against the resolution for war against Germany.

The President did not mention either Germany or Italy in his request. Early this evening a statement was issued at the White House, however, accusing Germany of doing everything possible to push Japan into the war. The objective, the official statement proclaimed, was to cut off American lend-lease aid to Germany's European enemies, and a pledge was made that this aid would continue "100 per cent."

A SUDDEN AND DELIBERATE ATTACK

President Roosevelt's brief and decisive

President Roosevelt delivers his 'Date which will live in infamy' address on December 8, 1941.

words were addressed to the assembled representatives of the basic organizations of American democracy—the Senate, the House, the Cabinet and the Supreme Court.

"America was suddenly and deliberately attacked by naval and air forces of the Empire of Japan," he said. "We will gain the inevitable triumph, so help us God."

Thunderous cheers greeted the Chief Executive and Commander in Chief throughout the address. This was particularly pronounced when he declared that Americans "will remember the character of the onslaught against us," a day, he remarked, which will live in infamy.

"This form of treachery shall never endanger us again," he declared amid cheers. "The American people in their righteous might will win through to absolute victory."

Then, to the accompaniment of a great roar of cheering, he asked for war against Japan.

The President officially informed Congress that in the dastardly attack by Japan, delivered while the Imperial Japanese Government was expressing hope for continued peace, "very many American lives have been lost" and American ships reportedly have been "torpedoed on the high seas between San Francisco and Honolulu."

Mentioning one by one in staccato phrases the Japanese attacks on the Philippines, American Midway, Wake and Guam Islands, British Hong Kong and Malaya, he bluntly informed the people by radio and their representatives directly:

"Hostilities exist. There is no blinking the fact that our people, our territory and our interests are in grave danger. The people of the United States have already formed their opinions and well understand the implications to the very life and safety of our nation."

VICTORY MAY TAKE TIME, HE WARNS

It may take a long time, Mr. Roosevelt warned, "to overcome this premeditated invasion," but of the unbounding determination of the American people and confidence in our armed forces neither he nor they had any doubt. Then he said:

"I ask that the Congress declare that since the unprovoked and dastardly attack by Japan on Sunday, Dec. 7, a state of war has existed between the United States and the Japanese Empire."

It was to a solemn Congress and to grim galleries that the President mentioned the casualties in Hawaii—officially estimated at 1,500 dead and 1,500 wounded.

Before him, on his left was the Supreme Court, its members clad in black robes. On the right in the front row sat the Cabinet, with Secretary Hull in the ranking position on the aisle. Behind the Cabinet were the Senators and then the members of the House.

Mr. Roosevelt spoke concisely, clearly and to the point to an already convinced audience already stirred to belligerency by the wantonness of the Japanese attack.

Extraordinary precautions were taken by the Secret Service to guard the President during his short trip over the indirect mile and a quarter route from the Executive Mansion to the Capitol and back to the White House.

Crowds, solemn but determined, greeted the Chief Executive with cheers from the time he was driven out of the East Gate of the White House until he reached the rear entrance of the House after passing through crowded Capitol Plaza. The same crowds stood silently by as he returned.

JOINT SESSION IS ENDED

The two houses split up immediately after the address and passed the war resolution separately without debate, the time consumed being accountable to having the resolution officially introduced and in the physical problem involved.

Stephen T. Early, Presidential secretary, said that nothing official had been received by this government tonight on European reports that Germany and Italy were contemplating declaration of war against the United States. Germany, however, was widely expected to carry out its treaty commitments arranged by Hitler with Japan and to declare war on the United States with her Italian satellite following suit.

Since the Constitution provides that Congress alone can declare war, there was some doubt here as to whether the United States was officially at war with Japan from the time the House adopted the war resolution at 1:10 P.M., ten minutes after the Senate, or from the time the President signed the resolution at 4:10 P.M. Most attorneys consulted inclined to the belief the latter time marked the historic step. ◊

DECEMBER 9, 1941

The President's Message

Following is the text of President Roosevelt's war message to Congress, as recorded by The New York Times from a broadcast:

Mr. Vice President, Mr. Speaker, members of the Senate and the House of Representatives:

Yesterday, Dec. 7, 1941—a date which will live in infamy—the United States of America was suddenly and deliberately attacked by naval and air forces of the empire of Japan.

The United States was at peace with that nation, and, at the solicitation of Japan, was still in conversation with its government and its Emperor looking toward the maintenance of peace in the Pacific.

Indeed, one hour after Japanese air squadrons had commenced bombing in the American island of Oahu the Japanese Ambassador to the United States and his colleague delivered to our Secretary of State a formal reply to a recent American message. And, while this reply stated that it seemed useless to continue the existing diplomatic negotiations, it contained no threat or hint of war or of armed attack.

ATTACK DELIBERATELY PLANNED

It will be recorded that the distance of Hawaii from Japan makes it obvious that the attack was deliberately planned many days or even weeks ago. During the intervening time the Japanese Government has deliberately sought to deceive the United States by false statements and expressions of hope for continued peace.

The attack yesterday on the Hawaiian Islands has caused severe damage to American naval and military forces. I regret to tell you that very many American lives have been lost. In addition, American ships have been reported torpedoed on the high seas between San Francisco and Honolulu.

Yesterday the Japanese Government also launched an attack against Malaya.

Last night Japanese forces attacked Hong Kong.

Last night Japanese forces attacked Guam.

Last night Japanese forces attacked the Philippine Islands.

Last night the Japanese attacked Wake Island.

And this morning the Japanese attacked Midway Island.

Japan has therefore undertaken a surprise offensive extending throughout the Pacific area. The facts of yesterday and today speak for themselves. The people of the United States have already formed their opinions and well understand the implications to the very life and safety of our nation.

As Commander in Chief of the Army and Navy I have directed that all measures be taken for our defense, that always will our whole nation remember the character of the onslaught against us.

VICTORY WILL BE ABSOLUTE

No matter how long it may take us to overcome this premeditated invasion, the American people, in their righteous might, will win through to absolute victory.

I believe that I interpret the will of the Congress and of the people when I assert that we will not only defend ourselves to the uttermost but will make it very certain that this form of treachery shall never again endanger us.

Hostilities exist. There is no blinking at the fact that our people, our territory and our interests are in grave danger. With confidence in our armed forces, with the inbounding determination of our people, we will gain the inevitable triumph. So help us God.

I ask that the Congress declare that since the unprovoked and dastardly attack by Japan on Sunday, Dec. 7, 1941, a state of war has existed between the United States and the Japanese Empire. ◊

DECEMBER 9, 1941

PRESIDENT'S POWER GREATLY ENLARGED
State of War 'All But Lifts The Limit,' Legal Advisers In the Capital Say

WASHINGTON, Dec. 8 (AP)—A state of war all but lifts the limit from Presidential powers.

Statutes which operate in such periods authorize the President to take over transportation systems, industrial plants, radio stations, power facilities and ships, and place some controls on communication systems.

Many of these powers have been available to the President under his emergency proclamations and as Commander in Chief of the armed forces.

One highly placed Administration legal adviser says that in wartime the government has the power "to take what it needs to meet the emergency."

The same thought was expressed by Alexander Hamilton more than a century ago when he wrote:

"The direction of war implies the direction of common strength; and the power of directing and employing the common strength forms a usual and essential part in the definition of the executive authority."

Here, in brief, are some of the other powers given to the President in times of war or great emergency:

Temporary connections of power lines may be required.

Parts of the 1930 Tariff Act may be suspended to permit free entry of needed commodities.

Additional Army officers may be commissioned and their rank may be raised. Retired officers and nurses may be recalled to active service.

The Coast Guard operates as part of the Navy (already ordered).

The Army may take over lands for certain purposes.

The Secretary of War may rent any building in the District of Columbia.

Use may be made of strategic materials purchased for stock piles.

Securities Exchanges (there are nineteen in eighteen cities) may be closed, or trading in any selected securities may be suspended.

Restrictions may be placed against imports from countries found to be discriminating against United States products.

Labor laws providing for an eight-hour working day may be suspended in connection with work on government contracts.

Some of the formalities in making purchases, such as advertising for bids, may be omitted.

The monthly apportionments of funds for governmental departments and agencies may be disregarded. ◊

DECEMBER 10, 1941

ISLANDS INVADED
Landings at 2 Places in Philippines Reported in 'Heavy' Attack

By The Associated Press.

MANILA, Dec. 10—Two Japanese landings on the Philippine island of Luzon were reported today by the Filipino Constabulary, and an Army spokesman announced that "all indications point to a heavy enemy attack with land troops supported by naval contingents and aircraft."

A communiqué issued a short time later from the headquarters of Lieut. Gen. Douglas MacArthur, United States commander in the Philippines, declared that "the enemy is in heavy force off the northern coast of Luzon, extending from Vigan to Aparri. [Vigan is on the coast of Luzon, about 200 miles north of Manila; Aparri, 200 miles farther north, is the northernmost port of Luzon.]

The communiqué reported that United States bombers had done heavy damage to Japanese naval units, scoring direct hits on three transports, one of which capsized.

[Six transports, believed to have been under heavy naval protection, were in the fleet that the United States bombers attacked, The United Press reported. Bomb hits were scored close to the three ships remaining after one had capsized and two had been hit.]

The announcement came soon after officials had uncovered a fifth-columnist plot that set off two false air-raid alarms and pointed the way to military targets with lights on the ground while Japanese planes were first attacking the Philippines.

Before last midnight this blacked-out capital had two alarms declared officially to have been fraudulently turned on. Alfredo Eugenio, Philippine national air-raid precautions head, announced the arrest of two workers, and he said two others were under surveillance. Their nationality was not disclosed.

Earlier a United States Army spokesman had announced that "certain areas were marked out by light signals"—both flares and fireworks—during the raids on Nichols Field, outside Manila, early yesterday.

Last night, he said, the persons in charge of the sirens sounded the two false alarms after having received telephone calls from unidentified persons. He expressed the belief that fifth columnists hoped to cause panic among the uneducated masses by a multiplicity of alarms and to lull others into a feeling that the alarms were not worth heeding.

The first alarm last night sounded at 7:41 o'clock and the second at 9:50. Each lasted about an hour.

United States pilots and anti-aircraft crews were said to have stood up well under their first bombings and ground-strafing at Clark Field, sixty miles north of Manila.

Despite a bright moon, no Japanese air attacks on the Philippines were reported overnight. A few anti-aircraft shots were heard, and United States planes droned steadily overhead on patrol, but there were no bombs. Army authorities had expected the Japanese to take advantage of the favorable attacking weather.

Newspapers reported that a single Japanese plane had appeared over Davao but dropped no bombs, and residents of Lucena, Tayabas, reported that Unit- ▸

The Cavite Naval Yard aflame following a Japanese bombing raid, Luzon, Philippines, December 10, 1941.

‹ ed States planes had driven off three Japanese planes.

"It was tough enough and we were glad when it ended," one gunner said, "but the next time we'll do better. Even when the bombs were raining down we kept noticing little things we were not doing right. These kinks are ironed our now. The next time we'll give 'em hell."

An American pilot expressed confidence that the United States fliers could take care of the Japanese fighter planes, which he said were heavily armed with 20-millimeter hub-firing cannon and numerous machine-guns. The Japanese ground-strafing tactics, he said, indicated German tutelage if not actual German participation. Reports that a German flier had been captured after having parachuted out of a burning plane could not be confirmed.

The Japanese Air Force is using German equipment in its attacks, informed sources said. Participants in yesterday's air clash at Clark Field said they had picked up and identified beyond question empty German-marked 20-millimeter shells fired by the cannon-carrying Japanese pursuit planes. American

machine-gunners also shot a small spare gasoline tank bearing the name of a German manufacturer from the underside of a Japanese fighter.

An American aircraft gunner said rumors were afloat that some Germans had been shot down in Japanese planes, but, he asserted:

"The Japs we shot down were Japs."

Thus far the Japanese pilots were reported to have got decidedly the worst of it in individual dogfights over the islands.

Still unverified was the report that Japanese troops now were in full control of Lubang Island, southwest of Manila Bay, with the help of fifth columnists.

An official Army announcement yesterday said material losses in planes as a result of Monday's air fighting over the Philippines had been "heavy on both sides." No figures were given.

United States naval sources denied reports that the seaplane tender Langley had been bombed during a Japanese attack on Davao. They said the vessel was safe and carrying out routine duties. ◆

Blackout Rules Listed

Orders by the Police Department of New York City to be followed by all residents in a total blackout were issued to thousands of air-raid wardens last night at special meetings. The principal orders and instructions follow:

LARGE BUILDINGS

Extinguish all exterior lights, illuminating signs, etc.

Extinguish or effectively screen off all interior lights.

Superintendents and managers of all apartment buildings will be responsible for shutting off all lights or drawing window shades if the main switches in buildings are not pulled.

Managers and superintendents are responsible for the instruction and training of protection personnel of building premises.

CENSORSHIP RULES SET BY PRESIDENT

FIRST, IT MUST BE TRUE

Special to The New York Times.

WASHINGTON, Dec. 9—President Roosevelt laid down two primary rules of censorship of war news today, reserving to himself and high-ranking officials the right of decision over material released. News to be released, he said, first must be true, and then it must pass a test whether it conforms with a rule that it must "not give aid and comfort to the enemy."

These basic stipulations were described at the first press conference held by the President since the outbreak of the war with Japan. After reporters had protested that officials at the War and Navy Departments had given inquirers the "run-around," even on matters of record, Mr. Roosevelt said that discretion

for giving out news could not be left to captains or majors, to lieutenant commanders or commanders.

Reporters would get news as soon as information is available, if it conforms to the rule, Mr. Roosevelt said. The mere fact that one bureau in a government department gets a flash, he went on, is not sufficient authority for its release. He told reporters that they were in no position to determine whether it conformed to the rule and neither were heads of these bureaus.

CITES BRITISH COMMUNIQUÉS

The decision is up to the heads of the War and Navy Departments, said the President,

and news has to be accurate and has to be approved. He cited the current London communiqué system as a model which might be followed by this government in its eventual handling of war reports.

In reply to a question, the President said that officers in the services were being checked for leaks.

"Can you make any comment," a reporter asked, "on domestic responsibility for the surprise of the command at Hawaii by the Japanese?"

Mr. Roosevelt replied that he did not know and neither did any member of Congress.

The President's mention and support of the British system aroused some apprehension here among reporters who have worked in London during the war. There, too, the rule was that stories must be accurate and must not give aid and comfort to the enemy. There, also, the final decision was left to military and naval officials, and the chief criticism of the American reporters in London was that the military mind often tended to rule that almost any news that was bad for the British gave aid and comfort to Germany and Italy. ◆

HOUSEHOLDERS

Remain in the house if possible.

Turn out or effectively screen off all lights at the blackout signal or on orders from responsible person.

Use no matches or lights outside the home.

Keep pets under control.

Keep off the streets or highways.

MOTORISTS

Pull over to the side of the highway, extinguish lights, close car and seek shelter.

Do not park at intersections, hydrants, police stations, hospitals or fire houses.

Avoid all congested areas.

PEDESTRIANS

Remain away from all congested areas.

Do not attempt to cross streets or highways.

Proceed to and remain at some place of safety.

Use no flashlights or matches; light no cigarettes on the street.

The orders requested that wherever possible the main electric switches and main gas cocks in large buildings should not be pulled. They closed with the request that all lawful instructions be obeyed. ◆

A switch for an air raid blackout.

The British battleship HMS Prince of Wales in 1941.

DECEMBER 11, 1941

Blow Staggers London

By JAMES MacDONALD
Special Cable to The New York Times

LONDON, Dec. 10—Great Britain was plunged into sadness today by the staggering blow suffered by the Navy in the loss of two of its most powerful vessels, the 35,000-ton battleship Prince of Wales, flagship of the newly constituted British Far Eastern Fleet, and the 32,000-ton battle cruiser Repulse.

Both apparently were sunk by Japanese planes off Malaya. Some reports indicated they might have fallen victims to "suicide" fliers who dived on them with full bomb loads.

These are the first British capital ships sunk by the Japanese. Their destruction has given Japan a tremendous initial advantage in Malayan waters. Far from minimizing the loss of these vessels, some British observers foresee that their sinking will have a direct bearing on the course of the war all around the globe.

Prime Minister Winston Churchill made a brief solemn announcement in the House of Commons, confirming the Japanese announcement that the Prince of Wales and Repulse had been sent to the bottom.

The Prince of Wales, a sister ship of the King George V, was one of this country's newest men-of-war and carried among her complement of at least 1,500 officers and men, Admiral Sir Tom S. V. Phillips, whose appointment as commander in chief of the newly established Far Eastern Fleet was announced Dec. 1. [Alfred Duff Cooper, British Minister in the Far East, confirmed that Admiral Phillips was aboard and said patrol boats were searching for survivors.

The Repulse, although built in 1916, was a hard-hitting modernized battle cruiser and normally carried a complement of about 1,200 officers and men.

The wife of Captain W. G. Tennant of the Repulse said she received word her husband had been saved by a destroyer. The fate of Admiral Phillips and of Captain J. C. Leach of the Prince of Wales was not determined.

The sinking of these vessels, combined with losses suffered by the United States Navy since Japan began the war, has taken on the aspect of a catastrophe. Virtually every one in this country is watching the Far Eastern theatre of hostilities with anxious eyes.

Britain's grim determination to win through to a victorious finish, which was strengthened when the United States declared war on Japan, remains unswerving, however. ◆

DECEMBER 12, 1941

SILENT GALLERIES WATCH WAR VOTE
Hear President's Message And the Roll-Call On Germany, but Refuse To Stay for Italy

Special to The New York Times.

WASHINGTON, Dec. 11—Without hesitation and without debate, and as rapidly as parliamentary procedure would permit, the Congress cast two more war votes today to carry the United States formally and constitutionally into battle to the finish with the Axis on all fronts.

No member of either house voted "no" on going to war against Germany and Italy.

One, Representative Jeannette Rankin of Montana, who voted against the 1917 declaration of war against Germany and who voted on Monday against accepting the Japanese challenge in the Pacific voted "present."

Substitution, by unanimous House consent, of Senate texts to prevent procedural delays removed even this reservation.

Formally the Senate voted war against Germany by 88 to 0. When the resolution accepting Italy's declaration followed, the vote was 90-0, two Senators having reached the floor after missing the first speedy vote.

In the House the roll call on the resolution against the German Government showed a vote of 393 to 0. Six additional members appeared for the tally on the resolution on Italy, making the vote 399 to 0.

GALLERIES ARE CROWDED

Viscount Halifax, the British Ambassador, and Lady Halifax leaned tensely over the rail of the diplomatic [words missing] Roosevelt's brief message was read. They departed before any votes were taken.

Visitors' galleries of Senate and House were crowded and silent, through the reading of the message and throughout the slow, methodical roll calling on the declaration against Germany. When the voting started on the resolution against Italy the spectators lost interest. In the House chamber the leave-taking was so general and so noisy that Speaker Rayburn halted the balloting to restore order. The exodus continued. ◊

President Roosevelt signing the declaration of war against Germany, Dec. 11, 1941.

DECEMBER 21, 1941

Admiral King Heads Navy, Rules All Sea And Air Fleets

Special to The New York Times.

WASHINGTON, Dec. 20—Admiral Ernest J. King, in command of the Atlantic Fleet since February, was designated today Commander-in-Chief of the United States Fleet, directly responsible to the President under general direction of the Secretary of the Navy and in supreme command of all naval operating forces in Atlantic, Pacific and Asiatic waters.

Rear Admiral Royal E. Ingersoll was named to succeed Admiral King as commander of the Atlantic Fleet.

These actions were taken by Secretary Knox in accordance with an Executive Order signed by President Roosevelt on Thursday, a day after Rear Admiral Chester W. Nimitz, Chief of the Bureau of Navigation, was ordered to relieve Admiral Husband E. Kimmel as Commander-in-Chief of the Pacific Fleet at Hawaii.

Admiral King, an aviation expert who has served also as chief of the Bureau of Aeronautics, is put in entire charge of the Navy's surface, air and coastal frontier operating forces.

His staff will be composed of a chief of staff and such other officers and agencies as appropriate and necessary, the Presidential order specified, to perform duties in general as follows:

Make available for evaluation all pertinent information and naval intelligence.

Prepare and execute plans for current war operations.

Conduct operational duties.

Effect all essential communications.

Direct training essential to carrying out operations.

Serve as personal aides.

DECEMBER 14, 1941

JAPANESE ATTACK UNITES AMERICAS
In the Southern Continent Popular Sentiment Is Aroused and Angry

By ARNALDO CORTESI
Special Cable to The New York Times.

BUENOS AIRES, Dec. 13—The popular South American reaction to the Japanese aggression against the United States, after a moment of shocked and incredulous surprise, has been one of anger—blazing, red-hot anger—that any power foreign to this continent should have dared to attack one of the American republics.

The people who feel the most outraged by what Japan has done include many who up to the present had no particular sympathy for the United States, for the fact that the victim of Japanese aggression happened to be the United States is of secondary importance, and the reaction would undoubtedly have been the same if the least instead of the greatest of American republics had been attacked. The point is that violent hands have been laid upon an America

regarded as a single unit stretching from the Arctic to the Antarctic, and this has caused the blood of all of the citizens of the continent to boil, regardless of nationality or political opinions.

The people of South America have suddenly discovered—and have not been a little surprised by the discovery—that there are certain things about which they all feel alike.

SAME FAMILY

The first and most important of these is the intangibility of this continent. When it is a matter of an American country versus a non-American power—any non-American power—Argentine and Brazilian, Chilean and Venezuelan, Uruguayan and Colombian all feel that in very truth they are members of the same family. Japan has contributed more in

five minutes than all of the statesmen of the Americas in a century toward bringing such a feeling of brotherhood about.

How large a part of the popular reaction in South America has been determined by the fact that the United States was the victim of a treacherous attack is shown by the comparatively slighter impression made by the German and Italian declarations of war. These were taken almost as a matter of course, as a necessary consequence of the irresistible development of events. They have caused interest, speculation and excitement, but nothing even faintly comparable to the spontaneous emotion produced by the first news that Japanese aircraft had bombed the United States possessions in the Pacific. ◆

Although Admiral King's principal offices will be in the department, the Navy emphasized that the orders did not relieve him from duty at sea.

"He is free to exercise personal command at sea as in his judgment circumstances make advisable," it stated.

KING'S SERVICE IN ALL BRANCHES
Admiral King was born in Lorain, Ohio, on Nov. 23, 1878, and was appointed to the Naval Academy from Ohio in 1897. His subsequent career brought him experience and distinction in all branches of naval service, on the sea, in the air, on submarines and in administrative posts.

During the Spanish-American War he served on the U.S.S. San Francisco engaged in patrol duty off the Atlantic coast. From 1916 to 1919 he was Assistant Chief of the Staff of Admiral Henry T. Mayo, Commander in Chief of the United States Fleet, and for that service he received the Navy Cross.

In 1923 he took command of the submarine base at New London, Conn., and

was in charge of the salvage operations of Submarine S-51, which sank off Block Island in September, 1925. For that service he received the Distinguished Service Medal.

After the sinking of the Submarine S-4 off Provincetown, Mass., in December, 1927, he directed the salvage force and the Distinguished Service Medal, Gold Star, was awarded to him for that task.

In 1927 Admiral King qualified as a naval aviator at Pensacola, Fla., and in 1928 was appointed commander, Aircraft Squadrons, Scouting Fleet.

He served as assistant chief of the Bureau of Aeronautics, 1928–29, and was in command of the aircraft carrier Lexington until 1932, when he attended the senior course at the Naval War College. He was appointed chief of the Bureau of Aeronautics in May, 1933.

His decorations also include the Sampson Medal, U.S.S. San Francisco, 1898; Spanish Campaign Medal; Mexican Service Medal, U.S.S. Terry; and Victory Medal, Atlantic Fleet Clasp,

Admiral Ernest J. King in 1941.

U.S.S. Pennsylvania.
His home is at Annapolis. ◆

DECEMBER 23, 1941

Editorial
HITLER PROMOTES HITLER

Though the German armies in Russia have not been destroyed, they have failed in their primary objective. This was to destroy the armed forces of the Soviets. They have also failed in their secondary objectives, which were to reach the southern oil fields and to take Moscow before the coming of cold weather. The attempt has cost them dearly. And with this failure added to the entrance of the United States into the war, it must be a dull German who does not wonder whether something has gone wrong.

Is this the explanation of the sudden mysterious removal of Field Marshal von Brauchitsch as Commander in Chief of the German Army and the assumption of superior command by the man who describes himself as "the statesman Adolf Hitler"? Certainly it is possible that Hitler, relying on German confidence in the infallibility of his "inner call" and his "intuition" and the dynamics of his "fanatical will power," has sought to allay anxiety among his people by taking command himself and at least by implication charging responsibility for the failure in Russia against the soldier whose task it was to execute his orders. It is also possible that the suspected rift between the Nazi party and the Army

has been widened by the Russian failure and that Hitler does not wholly trust his high command. A third possibility is that Hitler is dreaming dreams of new campaigns which the hardheaded army men are reluctant to attempt to carry out.

In any case Hitler has strained the legend of his infallibility pretty far, even for the German people. The year is almost gone, and the Nazi leaders themselves have stopped promising that the war is nearly over. Yet when 1941 began Hitler pledged his countrymen that it would bring victory and an end to all their hardships and privations. In his New Year's Day proclamation he made the unequivocal statement: "The year 1941 will bring consummation of the greatest victory in our history." At the end of January, on the anniversary of his assumption of power, he boasted: "The year 1941 will be the historical year of the great new order for Europe." In mid-March, at the annual German Memorial Day services, he promised that the year 1941 would "end what started the year before." And in mid-April, celebrating his own birthday, he echoed the confidence of Dr. Goebbels that victory was "already as good as assured." Again, at the outset of the Russian campaign, he promised his people that this would be the decisive battle for the establishment of the "New Order," and still more recently he assured them that the resistance of Russia "is already broken and will never rise again."

Even the regimented people of Germany must be aware of the obvious inconsistencies between these statements and the recent semi-hysterical

Adolf Hitler saluting from a train window, April 1941.

wheedling pleas for greater sacrifices on their part, in order to overcome an enemy superior in numbers to, and better equipped than, the hitherto invincible German Army. How long will it be before the German people isolate and identify and destroy Hitler himself as the root-cause of all their suffering? ◆

DECEMBER 25, 1941

Heroic Defense of Wake Isle an Epic In Marines' Annals

By CHARLES HURD
Special to The New York Times.

WASHINGTON, Dec. 24—The Navy reluctantly closed today its chapter of exploits at Wake Island, which is now assumed lost to the Japanese, by revealing that 378 Marines, assisted by seven members of naval medical personnel, held off Japanese attacks by sea, air and land for fourteen days before radio silence signaled the end of their vigil.

This little group of fighting men, armed only with light weapons and

twelve fighter planes—without bombers—took a toll of one Japanese cruiser and three destroyers in the course of their defense of the tiny island, which lies about 2,000 miles west of Honolulu.

In the fighting, which lasted from Dec. 9 through Dec. 23, no aid reached the defenders of Wake and there apparently was no chance to try to evacuate them. This they knew, but they continued fighting for a length of time and against odds that made their work without parallel in the service records.

The fall of Wake removed another link between Honolulu and Manila; Guam was captured by the Japanese about two weeks ago. So far as is known, Midway Island still is holding out and has not been attacked for some days.

THE HEROISM OF WAKE
A collection of facts marshaled by the

Navy Department here, on the basis of radio reports from Wake Island, pictured a fight in which the Marines, outnumbered from the start, sustained wave after wave of smashing attacks, even after the loss of most of their fighting equipment.

The report that they had sunk two more destroyers on the last day of the defense, when most of their weapons had been smashed, was confirmed by the Tokyo radio last night.

In addition to the planes based on Wake Island the Marines had only weapons classed as "light." The garrison had no heavy artillery and there was no protective fort—only the garrison buildings, hangars and the usual buildings that would be erected on a watch post. The Navy listed the weapons at Wake at the start of the fighting as six 5-inch guns, two 3-inch anti-aircraft guns,

DECEMBER 25, 1941

Roosevelt, Churchill Voice Faith To War-Weary World

Special to The New York Times.

WASHINGTON, Dec. 24—Speaking from the high south portico of the White House, in the twinkling lights of the community Christmas tree on the lawn below them, President Roosevelt and Prime Minister Winston Churchill this evening called on the people of their two nations to rededicate themselves in a righteous cause and to "arm their hearts" for labor, suffering and for the ultimate victory ahead.

Thousands of men and women, banked on the south lawn in the clear, mild twilight, heard the two leaders speak, while the radio carried their voices throughout the world, with the hymns and carols of the traditional Christmas ceremony.

Standing between the central columns of the porch, at the President's left hand, Mr. Churchill spoke publicly for the first time since he arrived to start the historic discussions of the joint conduct of the war.

It was the first time, too, that a President of the United States and a Prime Minister of Britain had ever met on Christmas Eve, with what at least approximated a joint message to their peoples.

CHURCHILL IS HAILED AS FRIEND

Hailed by the President as "my associate, my old and good friend," Mr. Churchill spoke to his American audience as "fellow-workers, fellows, soldiers in this common cause." He had "a right to sit at your fireside and share your Christmas joys," through ties of unity and association, he said, and he urged them, at this season, not to overlook the character of their cause.

"Ill would it be for us this Christmastide if we were not sure that no greed for the lands or wealth of any other people has led us to the field, that no vulgar ambition, no sordid lust for material gain at the expense of others has led us to the field," he said.

"Here in the midst of war, raging and roaring about us over all the lands and seas, creeping nearer to our hearts and homes, here, amidst all these tumults, we have the spirit of peace in each cottage home and in every heart."

Armed soldiers surrounded the White House grounds, ropes held the crowd 100 yards from the portico and policemen and members of the Federal Bureau of Investigation patrolled the interval, but the grim wartime precautions did not dampen the enthusiasm of the audience as the President spoke and Mr. Churchill followed.

APPLAUSE INTERRUPTS SPEAKER

The vibrant voice, the strong Victorian phrases, the quick, descriptive lift of the left hand, the set of chin and mouth marked an expressive and defiant Churchill, and the audience, again and again as he spoke, interrupted him with applause.

But not all his message was of determination and defiance. Seasonably, he wished his hearers, "In God's mercy, a happy Christmas to you all." And he asked, "for one night only," a revival of the season's cheer. ◊

Winston Churchill demonstrates the easy zipper on his famous siren suit on the White House lawn at dusk, December 1941. Next to him, Diana Hopkins, the daughter of White House aide Harry Hopkins, struggles to keep President Roosevelt's dog, Fala, next to the chair.

eighteen 50-calibre machine guns, "plus the usual light weapons." There also were six searchlights.

The official report of action in the last fortnight read as follows:

"Early as Dec. 9 Wake was under enemy attack by sea and air. Four separate attacks in forty-eight hours were beaten off, and most of the fighter planes were lost in these actions. The marines, however, succeeded in sinking one enemy light cruiser and one destroyer by air action.

LANDING FIELD ATTACKED

"They reported to the Navy Department that they expected these attacks would be resumed and a landing attempted by the enemy. They were prepared to resist to the best of their ability. President Roosevelt reported on Dec. 12 that Wake was still holding out. On Dec. 14 the marines suffered a moonlight raid by enemy bombers, which attacked their landing field. They reported no damage had been suffered, but by the following morning forty-one bombers were over Wake. In this raid one of their fast-diminishing number of fighting planes was destroyed on the ground.

"The defenders reported two of their men had been killed, but that they had succeeded in bringing down two enemy bombers and damaging several others by anti-aircraft fire. They would continue to resist.

"Two additional bombing attacks were sustained on 15 December, and an enemy submarine was reported hovering around Wake. These were to be followed by still two more attacks in force on the 17th and 18th.

"By 21 December the little garrison was in serious trouble. Seventeen heavy Japanese bombers attacked the island and were beaten off after heavy damage. The 3-inch batteries were struck, the power plant was damaged and the Diesel oil building and its equipment were destroyed. Only one 3-inch battery of four guns was now effective.

"The following day, Dec. 22, the Wake defenders reported that they had sustained still another heavy attack by air, but that several enemy ships and a transport were moving in. This landing attempt was in great force, but two enemy destroyers were put out of action by the Marines before the invaders could effect a landing on the island.

"For many hours the issue was in doubt. On Dec. 23 Tokyo claimed that Wake Island was completely occupied by Japanese forces, and the Navy Department was forced to admit that all communications with Wake had ceased." ◊

DECEMBER 26, 1941

BRITISH GARRISON ENDS 16-DAY SIEGE
Water Supply Exhausted, Hong Kong Defenders Bow to Crushing Odds

By CRAIG THOMPSON
Special Cable to The New York Times.

LONDON, Dec. 25—Even while long-delayed communiqués from Hong Kong reached here today, the Colonial Office announced the colony's fall after a sixteen-day siege. It appeared that Governor Sir Mark Young had been instructed to seek a negotiated surrender rather than attempt to stand off the Japanese to the last defender.

Early this evening the Colonial Office revealed that Sir Mark had been advised by the naval and military commanders at Hong Kong that further effective resistance was impossible and that he was taking action accordingly.

This pieced neatly into a Japanese report that the Governor was participating in a conference at Kowloon with Japanese military leaders. It was only in Japanese broadcasts that any direct statement was made that Hong Kong had surrendered.

END SEEN AS AT HAND

Even as Sir Mark talked with the Japanese in Kowloon, there were reports that Chinese troops pressing toward Hong Kong were meeting with successes.

To many here, however, it seemed that the end must be near. For seven days under relentless observed artillery fire not only from the mainland but on the heights of Hong Kong Island, the British garrison fought on, rejecting two demands to surrender.

The water supply gave cause for anxiety, as three reservoirs had fallen into Japanese hands. Water mains destroyed by bombardment were repaired, but the invaders destroyed them again and again. On Tuesday there remained but one day's supply of water.

Military and civilian casualties in Hong Kong were heavy, but under the Governor's inspiring leadership morale was admirable.

"So ends a valiant fight against overwhelming odds," said the official statement. "The courage and determination of the Royal Navy and troops from the United Kingdom, Canada and India, as well as local levies, including many Chinese, will long be remembered."

In eight days Hong Kong had forty-five air raids. Heavy shelling was maintained by the Japanese. They sent two peace offers, which were rejected out of hand.

"We are going to hold on," the Governor cabled Lord Moyne, the Colonial Secretary.

Tokyo reported the capture of Hong Kong last Friday, but this claim was refuted by a British communiqué telling of heavy losses being inflicted on the invaders. ◊

DECEMBER 27, 1941

CHURCHILL MASTER OF TELLING PHRASES
His War Addresses Have Contained a Succession of Striking Passages

By The United Press.

WASHINGTON, Dec. 26—Winston Churchill is a master phrasemaker and passages from his addresses have a majestic cadence. Highest honors for a single sentence probably go to eleven words Churchill uttered on May 13, 1940, after Great Britain had dropped the Chamberlain government and was adjusting itself to the prospect of total war. Then Mr. Churchill told his countrymen:

"I have nothing to offer but blood, toil, tears and sweat."

And with the hard going in June, 1940, and the Germans in possession of beaches a few miles across the English Channel, Mr. Churchill made this promise:

"We shall defend our island whatever the cost may be. We shall fight on the beaches, we shall fight on the landing grounds, we shall fight in the fields and in the streets, we shall fight in the hills, we shall never surrender."

In that same June, when the British Army in Europe was beaten and disorganized, he said:

"Let us therefore brace ourselves to our duties and so bear ourselves that if the British Empire and its commonwealth last for a thousand years men will still say: 'This was their finest hour.'"

In August, 1940, after Germany had begun all-out efforts to bomb Britain into submission, Mr. Churchill said of the British airmen: "Never in the field of human conflict was so much owed by so many to so few."

On Sept. 11, 1940, Mr. Churchill said of Adolf Hitler:

"This wicked man, the repository and embodiment of many forms of soul-destroying hatred; this monstrous product of former wrongs and shame, has now resolved to try and break our famous island race by a process of indiscriminate slaughter and destruction. What he has done is to kindle a fire in British hearts, here and all over the world, which will glow long after all traces of the conflagration he has caused in London have been removed."

"Do not suppose," he warned again in January, 1941, "that we are at the end of the road. Yet, though long and hard it may be, I have absolutely no doubt that we shall win a complete and decisive victory over the forces of evil, and that victory itself will only be a stimulus to further efforts to conquer ourselves and to make our country as worthy in the days of peace as it is proving itself in the hours of war."

To Americans in February, 1941, he directed this message: "Give us the tools and we will finish the job." ◊

DECEMBER 28, 1941

JAPANESE ADVANCE SLOWLY ON MANILA

By The United Press.

FIELD HEADQUARTERS, United States Forces on Northern Luzon Front, Dec. 27—Japanese forces tonight advanced slowly against stubbornly resisting American and Philippine troops in a huge north-and-south pincers upon Manila. On this Northern Front the Japanese spearheads have debouched from narrow, mountainous defiles of the north onto the broad Pampanga plains. Their advance guard was reported at Urdaneta, eight miles south of Binalonan and about ninety-seven miles from Manila.

Reports from the Southern Front placed the Japanese advance at Lucena, sixty-four airline miles from Manila, but separated from the capital by several mountain ranges, lakes, swamps and difficult terrain. At this point the Japanese had driven forward about twenty-six miles from their landing stage on Lamon Bay, a twenty-mile strip of beach from Atimonan to Mauban.

Both the Japanese thrusts were regarded as dangerous. They were backed by increasing numbers of mobile Japanese troops, landed with light arms and equipment from transports standing off Lingayen Gulf in the northwest and Lamon Bay to the southeast.

However, neither in north nor south had the main battle yet been joined as General Douglas MacArthur, Commander in Chief of United States forces in the Far East, carefully deployed his inferior numbers against the invaders.

Despite the Japanese advances there was an air of confidence here at Major Gen. J. M. Wainwright's field headquarters. General Wainwright reported in a communiqué that he was slowly moving his troops back to strong battle lines carefully selected long in advance. There was no indication where the main defense line had been erected, but several water courses bisect this long, easy valley that provides a broad highway to Manila.

The Japanese northern thrust is being made in two main columns. One column is trying to force its way toward Lingayen at the head of Lingayen Gulf, along whose shores the Japanese landings were made. This column is circling along the coast, following the coastal plain highway. The second column has struck down through Rosales and Urdaneta, ninety-seven miles due north of Manila in Pangasinan Province.

General Wainwright reported that the Japanese were "now making slow progress on the Northern Luzon Front as the withdrawal of our troops to a stronger line is proceeding in accordance with plans." He said that "the resistance of our troops continues undiminished."

A communiqué from General MacArthur gave no details of the fighting except to say that it was "desultory" in the North and "very heavy" in the Southeast.

"The enemy is steadily bringing reinforcements from his fleet of transports off Lingayen and Atimonan," the communiqué reported. "Enemy air activity is heavy."

Reports from the South said that the Japanese flag now was flying over Lucena, capital of Tayabas Province on the Southern Luzon Coast.

Capture of Lucena plants the Japanese squarely across Tayabas Isthmus, a narrow neck of land that links the central portion of Luzon with the long narrow southern extension stretching 175 miles to the southeast. Japanese control of the Tayabas Isthmus appeared to cut off any United States forces in the south combating the Japanese landing forces at Legaspi, except by sea.

The strength of the Japanese forces now ashore in the Atimonan-Mauban sector was estimated as between 10,000 and 15,000—possibly more. The northern force was placed between 80,000 and 100,000. In all, the Japanese may have between 150,000 and 200,000 troops ashore on Luzon or awaiting landing from transports.

The American-Philippines forces in the South are believed strong enough to cope with the Japanese, at least for the time being. ◇

Japanese soldiers in the Philippines, late 1941.

Chapter 10

"MILLION WOMEN ARE NEEDED FOR WAR"

January–February 1942

The coming of war prompted many and far-reaching changes in the United States. Presidential powers were immediately strengthened. Production was organized under a War Production Board that cut back on all civilian production, but particularly the manufacture of tires and automobiles. Civil defense measures were slowly introduced; a blackout (or "dimout" as it came to be called) was enforced, though not soon enough to prevent German submarines from cruising off the Eastern Seaboard at night to torpedo merchantmen sailing against the lit-up coast in full silhouette. The Times's own electric bulletin was a victim of the lighting restrictions and Times Square was sunk in unaccustomed gloom. From a situation of high unemployment, the war economy now needed all the labor it could get. In late January the labor director of the War Production Board, Stanley Hillman, called for a million women to join the war industry. "Women can build airplanes," he said, and millions of American women responded to the call over the three years that followed.

The black community lobbied to be allowed to join the war effort, prompting the formation in January of the first all-black Army division, though prejudice did not disappear. The American Red Cross refused to use the blood of black Americans for transfusions until pressured to do so by the government.

Roosevelt was feeling his way for the first weeks of war. In February The Times complained in its editorial, "Washington Paints a Confused Picture," that the people had not yet been told the whole truth about the war crisis. The truth was bad enough. On February 15, the day the Japanese captured Singapore and more than 100,000 Allied prisoners, The Times's military correspondent, Hanson Baldwin, warned that worse was to come from the "fanatical little fighters" of Japan. The early weeks of war were, he continued, "perhaps the blackest period in our history." On January 2 the capital of the Philippines, Manila, fell to the Japanese Army and American and Filipino forces were pushed back onto the Bataan Peninsula and eventually into the fortress of Corregidor. Japanese troops swept all before them, capturing the Dutch East Indies in a lightning campaign and smashing an Allied naval force on February 27 in the Battle of the Java Sea. On February 22 General MacArthur was advised to leave the Philippines and to go to Australia. Earlier that month the popular Times journalist Byron (Barney) Darnton was sent to Australia to report on the Pacific crisis, only to lose his life nine months later when an Allied aircraft mistakenly attacked the landing craft Darnton was in on the way to the coast of New Guinea.

There was little news that was good. Benghazi in Libya fell to Rommel's Afrika Korps; submarine sinkings reached new heights. The one ray of hope lay on the Eastern Front where the German armies were stuck in the snow and bitter weather, though far from defeated. Ilya Ehrenburg, the famous Soviet war correspondent, wrote for The Times from the front line where General Zhukov, Stalin's military troubleshooter, claimed that the Germans had at last tasted "real war," having grown too "used to easy victories." The Times reported how well-equipped Soviet soldiers were, with their high felt boots (valenki) and sheepskin jackets, while the German Army was forced to appeal to countrymen back home to send their fur coats and sweaters to clothe German soldiers. Although the Pacific took pride of place in news reports, Roosevelt was clear when he met Churchill in Washington for the Arcadia conference in December 1941 that the priority was to destroy the German threat. On January 26 the first units of an American Expeditionary Force landed in Northern Ireland, the early contingents of what was to become the largest overseas army ever raised by the United States.

WAR PACT IS SIGNED
U.S., Britain, Russia, China and 22 Others Join in Declaration

By FRANK L. KLUCKHOHN
Special to The New York Times.

WASHINGTON, Jan. 2—All twenty-six countries at war with one or more of the Axis powers have pledged themselves in a "Declaration by United Nations" not to make a separate armistice or peace and to employ full military or economic resources against the enemy each is fighting. The agreement was signed in Washington and made public today at the White House.

The declaration, which is an outcome of the recent conferences between President Roosevelt and Prime Minister Churchill of Great Britain, is not in treaty form, and therefore does not require ratification.

President Roosevelt signed for the United States; Prime Minister Churchill for the United Kingdom; Maxim M. Litvinoff, the Soviet Ambassador, for Russia, and T. V. Soong, Foreign Minister, for China. Representatives here affixed their signatures on behalf of the Dominion and India governments and for the exiled and Central American governments. The Free French did not sign and neither did any South American government, but other nations "rendering material assistance" may adhere for "victory over Hitlerism."

ALL IN 'A COMMON STRUGGLE'
The declaration, carefully phrased to make it unnecessary for Russia to go to war against Japan, was made public at 3 P.M., only a few hours after announcement that Japanese forces had occupied Manila.

The adherents expressed conviction that "complete victory over their enemies" is essential for defense of "life, liberty, independence and religious freedom," not only in their own but in other lands. Each declared itself engaged in "a common struggle" against evil forces seeking world dominance.

Therefore each signatory, on behalf of his government, pledged cooperation with the other governments involved and "not to make a separate armistice or peace with the enemies." Some Latin-American nations at war have small armies, which may explain why each government pledged employment of full military "or" economic resources "against those members of the Tripartite Pact and its adherents with which such government is at war."

The declaration was on a common war policy, but it pledged all nations involved to accept, after "final destruction of the Nazi tyranny," the eight bases for establishment of peace contained in the Atlantic Charter signed by President Roosevelt and Mr. Churchill at their sea conference on Aug. 14, 1941. ◆

Editorial
CIVIL LIBERTIES IN WAR

"Total war" is a crucial test of our ordinary theories and practices of government and of the democratic and libertarian principles by which we strive to live. The fearful exigencies of war force us to re-examine many of our political premises. Among those are the premises concerning our civil liberties. One set of extremists is apt to take the position that all civil liberties have to be suspended during the period of the war. Those at the opposite extreme are apt to contend that there should be no abridgment whatever of any peacetime civil liberty.

Obviously the truth is somewhere between these extremes. But to find precisely where it lies in particular cases is not easy. Dr. Stuart A. Queen, retiring president of the American Sociological Society, in an address posed a few questions designed to show the nature of the dilemmas which the present war raises: "Shall freedom of communication," he asks, "be maintained for all, thus aiding enemies in our midst, or shall it be restricted, thus threatening the very democracy for which we fight?" Such a question may overstate the problem, but it does serve to emphasize the truth of Dr. Queen's conclusion that civil liberty is "one of the most difficult problems for a democratic people in time of emergency."

In normal times we are apt to say that the various civil liberties we enjoy are "absolute" and "inalienable rights." Yet our actual practice has never corresponded with these phrases. It would be difficult to name a civil liberty that has not in practice been subject to some qualification. Thus the right of free speech has never been absolute. It has been curbed by the laws against libel, against obscenity, against direct incitement to riot or violence. Different ages and different communities have varied widely in where they draw the line in all these cases, but it is extremely seldom that they have failed to draw a line at all. In war-time these qualifications are necessarily greater. The press is not allowed to print military secrets. Individuals are not allowed to make treasonable utterances, and the definition of what is likely to cause internal dissension is in practice greatly broadened.

Liberty should never be conceived in a purely negative sense, as the mere absence of restraint. Such a conception would lead only to anarchy. To determine what are desirable liberties, we must refer to some end beyond mere absence of restraint itself. This end is the national welfare, considered in the broadest sense. Obviously the national security demands more qualifications to individual liberty in wartime than in peacetime. But all this does not mean that individual liberties should be reduced to such a point that the future of liberal and democratic institutions is endangered. It does not mean that any one Government authority or small group is to have unrestricted power to dictate what liberties are to be abridged. It does not mean that individuals are to be restricted in their right freely to criticize the Government's diplomatic policies or its conduct of the war. Long established legal safeguards designed to protect individual rights are not lightly to be put aside.

We cannot surrender at home the very liberties and democratic principles for which we are fighting. But we must recognize that in particular cases decisions concerning the qualifications to civil liberties will often be much more difficult to make now than in times of peace. ◆

JANUARY 4 1942

DETROIT RESIGNED TO AUTO-BAN EDICT
Gradual Slashing of Production Schedules Had Prepared Area for Shift to Arming

By FRANK B. WOODFORD

DETROIT, Jan. 3—The virtual wiping out of Detroit's chief industry through Federal Price Administrator Leon Henderson's order banning the production of new passenger cars and trucks has been accepted here with resignation which is tinged, in some quarters, with resentment.

For several months now the automobile industry has watched its production schedules being slashed. Throughout most of the industry it was accepted as inevitable that some such order as Mr. Henderson's would eventually come through. Particularly has this been the feeling since the entry of the United States into the war with the attack on Pearl Harbor on Dec. 7.

HOPED-FOR DELAY

But while it was preparing to accept the inevitable, Detroit and that part of the industry which is located in and adjacent to the city had hoped that the total end to the sale and production of civilian cars would be delayed until the automobile factories could reabsorb their entire employment and shift their manufacturing facilities to war production.

The immediate effect of Mr. Henderson's order stopping all production on or about Feb. 1 will be large and accelerated lay-offs which will bring almost total unemployment to about 250,000 persons in this area.

This, in turn, creates other problems. Governmental agencies have already begun a frantic search for revenues to carry the welfare loads and to handle the demand for unemployment compensation. War employment in the factories where the automobiles have been produced is gaining steadily, but it will be months before all the unemployment slack can be taken up in the production of war materials.

THE JOBLESS WORKER

To the jobless worker now or about to be on the streets there is small comfort in the statement at this time from some of the industry heads that a few months will not only find them all back at work but will see an acute labor shortage in the automobile plants at the same time.

The new order has been accepted cheerfully and willingly by the industry. Alvan Macauley, chairman of the Packard Motor Car Company and president of the Automobile Manufacturers Association, spoke for the industry when he pledged its complete cooperation under the edict of the Office of Production Management which ended the manufacture of automobiles and trucks.

"If that's what the government wants, we're going to be with it all the way," Mr. Macauley said concerning the stop-production order.

"But manufacturers must have more defense contracts which they can put into production on a mass scale," he added.

On the other hand, the United Automobile Workers (C.I.O.), while accepting the situation with patriotic good grace, criticized the fact that adjustment had not been made earlier in order to avert the mass layoffs which will come with the changeover from peace to war production.

THOMAS'S STATEMENT

"The automobile workers are ready to endure any hardship which will contribute to the victory of our nation," said R. J. Thomas, president of the union. "However, we can't see the sense in blacking out the country's greatest reservoir of machinery and trained labor.

"Most of the automobile industry machinery can be converted to production of armaments. We proposed that a year ago. We did not get far. Now that the industry knows it cannot make cars any longer, it is freely granting that its facilities can be changed over to make the materials of modern warfare.

"The most important single task before the nation is the rapid conversion of the automobile industry to war production. It can and should be made the major production arm of the arsenal of democracy. Meanwhile, hundreds of thousands of unemployed automobile workers must have their needs and those of their families taken care of by adequate unemployment compensation allowances and WPA appropriations."

One very real fear, affecting both management and labor, is what effect the ❯

The factory floor of a former Chrysler automobile assembly plant after its wartime conversion to manufacturing tanks for the military, Detroit, 1942.

(possible shortage of private cars, coupled with the strict rationing of tires, will have on needed transportation in connection with war production in this area. A large part of the production facilities, notably the Chrysler tank arsenal, the Hudson arsenal and the Ford bomber plant, are on the outskirts of the city, unserved by existing bus or street car facilities.

Private transportation is relied on in each instance to get the men to and from work.

Although dealers report an adequate stock of used cars in this area, there has been the expression of belief that these may be commandeered to relieve shortages in other sections of the country, leaving Detroit with a serious new and used car shortage.

The Willow Run bomber plant of the Ford Motor Company is located nearly twenty miles from Detroit. By early Summer the company contemplates employing 60,000 workers there. Nearly all of these will be drawn from Detroit and will be forced to use private transportation. Not only are there no present bus lines to the plant, but transportation officials here doubt that there will be sufficient equipment available to establish new lines. ◇

JANUARY 12, 1942

NAZIS LIST CLOTHING GIFTS

BERLIN, Jan. 11 (From German broadcast recorded by The United Press in New York)—D.N.B., official news agency, reported today that in the sixteen-day collection of clothing for German soldiers 56,325,930 items had been donated.

The donations included 2,958,155 fur garments, 4,948,766 sweaters and other wool clothing, 7,781,711 pairs of hose, 104,841 pairs of fur-lined boots, 170,214 pairs of plain boots, 1,174,748 pairs of skis, 3,138,405 wool hoods, 3,854,064 pairs of gloves and 1,485,115 wool and fur blankets.

The Prague radio was quoted by the London radio in a broadcast heard by the Columbia Broadcasting System as announcing that today was the forty-ninth birthday of Reichsmarshal Hermann Goering and that "the people of Czecho-Slovakia are expected to celebrate the occasion by contributing old clothes to the national rag bag now being assembled for troops on the Russian front." ◇

JANUARY 13, 1942

WAR INCREASES BICYCLE'S POPULARITY AMONG WOMEN

Speculation on the influence on transportation of the recent tire rationing order has brought the bicycle industry into the forefront of discussion, especially among housewives in suburban areas, many of whom took up cycling some time ago. Investigation indicates that travel to market by bicycle will increase rather than diminish.

Mrs. Franklin D. Roosevelt is among those who have acquired bicycles in the last few months. Her activities at Civilian Defense headquarters in Washington, however, have prevented her usual visits to Hyde Park, where the bicycle awaits her leisure. She has not yet had time to learn to ride.

Although production of bicycle tires will remain under curtailment, those already manufactured may be sold. Additional reassurance may be forthcoming in the expected final approval of the industry's scheduled program of production for 1942. A clearance signal is now awaited on the general lines of a tentative program drawn up at a meeting late in December of industry representatives and officials of the OPM. The plan calls for the manufacture of 1,000,000 bicycles this year, stipulating that a universal, simplified design of light-weight will be used.

The return of the bicycle as a means of recreation has not yet given rise to a definite trend in feminine sports wear. Unlike the Gibson Girl bicyclists of another day, today's women riders have been content with makeshift ensembles, often unsuitable. The most practical and becoming outfit yet evolved is the jupe-culotte, worn with a pullover, and a leather jacket or wind-breaker. A hood that ties securely under the chin, fleece-lined mittens and sturdy shoes complete a well-planned cycling costume for current months. ◇

Two-wheeled transport in upstate New York, 1942.

JANUARY 13, 1942

THE NAVY IN TWO SEAS

One answer to the question of what the American Navy is doing in this war was given yesterday by Secretary Knox in a speech prepared for delivery at the annual Conference of Mayors in Washington. The Navy is achieving notable success in keeping open the most important highway in the world—the sea-lanes between the United States and the British Islands.

It is because so large a force is engaged in this essential task that Mr. Knox warned his audience not to expect "full-scale naval engagements in the Pacific in the near future." He asked for popular understanding and approval of the strategy that keeps so large a part of the Navy occupied in the Atlantic: "We know who our great enemy is—the enemy who, before all others, must be defeated first. It is not Japan; it is not Italy; it is Hitler and Hitler's Nazis, Hitler's Germany."

Fortunately Mr. Knox does not need to argue his point. The country accepted it from the moment we went to war. It is proof of the level-headedness

ROOSEVELT SIGNS DAYLIGHT TIME ACT
Clocks Are to Be Moved Ahead by One Hour At 2 o'Clock on Morning of Feb. 9

LARGE SAVING OF POWER

By The Associated Press.

WASHINGTON, Jan. 20—President Roosevelt signed the Daylight-Saving Bill today and it becomes effective at 2 o'clock in the morning of Feb. 9 for all interstate commerce and Federal Government activities.

During Congressional debate it was assumed that the new time, by which clocks are moved ahead one hour, would become general throughout the country.

The measure will become inoperative six months after the war ends, unless Congress votes to terminate it before then.

Stephen Early, Presidential secretary, said that the measure had the same objectives as the Daylight-Saving Act of the first World War, that is, "greater efficiency in our industrial war effort."

The Federal Power Commission estimated there would be a saving of 736,282,000 kilowatt-hours of electricity annually. It said the nation used 144,984,565,000 kilowatt-hours in 1940. The real benefit from the change, the F.P.C. said, would come from relieving the present peak demand for power between dark and bedtime. The commission estimated that the change would provide relief to the extent of 741,160 kilowatts of production capacity.

Congressional action was necessary, Mr. Early pointed out, so that there would be a uniform system in all the States.

President Roosevelt directed that the pen which he used in signing the bill should be sent to Robert Garland of Pittsburgh, who headed a national committee that appeared at hearings on the legislation and urged its enactment.

Mr. Early said Mr. Garland also was active in advocating daylight saving for the first World War and had asked for no greater return than the pen used by President Woodrow Wilson in signing the act at that time. ◊

Foe Hurled Back in Bataan; Guerrillas Kill 110 at Base

Special to The New York Times.

WASHINGTON, Jan 21—The small force holding the Bataan Peninsula on Luzon Island, in the Philippines, scored a new victory in "savage" fighting by throwing back with heavy losses Japanese attackers who had penetrated their lines, the War Department announced today. In addition to taking the initiative and sustaining it with "relatively moderate" losses to the United States–Philippine Army, General Douglas MacArthur reported to the War Department that one of the guerrilla bands cooperating with the defending army raided a hostile airdrome at Tuguegarao to the north, killed 110 Japanese and routed 300 others.

ENDS DRAMATIC CHAPTER

Today's communiqué on fighting in the Philippines closed a chapter of operations made more dramatic by the fact that the communiqué of yesterday was issued while the end of the battle was a matter of grave doubt.

For two days the augmented Japanese forces, supported by air bombers and strafing planes, had lunged at the center of the fifteen-mile line across the neck of the Bataan peninsula in an effort to force a break in the lines and open up the hilly country to raiding.

"In particularly savage fighting," the communiqué today said, "on the Bataan peninsula, American and Philippine troops drove back the enemy and re-established lines which previously had been penetrated. The Japanese, by infiltrations and frontal attacks near the center of the lines, had gained some initial successes. Our troops then counter-attacked and all positions were retaken. Enemy losses were very heavy. Our casualties were relatively moderate."

To military observers here, this report indicated a picture of fighting by which General MacArthur adapted frontier methods to his defense against an army which is overwhelming in size and which apparently has attempted to adapt German blitz methods to its campaign in mountains and swamps.

When the Japanese have advanced, with tanks crashing through ground defenses and airplanes raining explosives from the sky, the MacArthur lines apparently have dissolved into nothing, while the defenders have fallen back into shelters prepared for this eventuality. Then, when the attack has spent itself, they fall on the advancing units in groups, catching them completely disorganized.

These tactics have been indicated repeatedly by statements that the defending line is hardly a "line" at all but)

---

of the American people that even in the first days after the infuriating attack at Pearl Harbor—in the days before Mr. Churchill came to this country and before the importance of the front against Hitler was emphasized by the organization of the grand alliance of twenty-six United Nations—the American public never lost sight of the real objective. On this point the evidence of the Gallup survey is convincing. During the period of Dec. 11–19, a period beginning immediately after Pearl Harbor, Dr. Gallup's organization found that more than four times as many Americans regard Germany as a greater threat than Japan. Moreover, there was no sectional disagreement on this fundamental point. The opinion of the Far West coincided almost exactly with the opinion of the rest of the country.

The average American knows that a victory over Japan would bring us no security whatever so long as Hitler remained unconquered, whereas the defeat of Hitler would enormously hasten, if it did not almost automatically accomplish, the defeat of his Eastern ally. But to beat Hitler we need production and still more production, and the sacrifice of every group interest to the national purpose. ◊

rather a series of prepared positions. In the heart of the small Bataan peninsula itself, the defenders have prepared countless positions carved out of stone mountains, which serve as bombproof shelters in air attacks and in which they have cached sufficient supplies to give them a long period of waiting.

The guerrilla raid, the communiqué reported, occurred in the Cagayan Valley in Northern Luzon, which is far removed from the scene of the principal fighting. The mere fact that it occurred gave increasing evidence that the Filipinos had not been completely defeated by any means. Only yesterday, another report told how another band 500 miles southward on the island of Mindanao was engaging Japanese forces that hold the port of Davao.

The guerrillas in Northern Luzon were said to have taken the Japanese "completely by surprise" and to have "scored a brilliant local success." ◆

Members of the first class of black pilots in the history of the U.S. Army Air Corps who were graduated at the advanced flying school at Tuskeegee, Ala., as second lieutenants by Major General George E. Stratemeyer.

JANUARY 23, 1942

ALL-NEGRO DIVISION FORMING FOR ARMY MANY IN OFFICER COURSES

Special to The New York Times.

WASHINGTON, Jan. 22—A Sixth Armored Division will be added to the Army's battle force of tank troops Feb. 15, Secretary Stimson said today at a press conference in which he described plans for expediting the work of expanding the Army this year to a force of 3,600,000 men.

The Secretary said that four-week training programs in special operations would be given to all officers to be assigned to the thirty-two new "triangular" divisions and a new Negro division and a second Negro aviation squadron would be set up.

The Army expects to have its new Negro division in final shape by May, on station at Fort Huachuca, Ariz. This division, a triangular one, will be built up around various Negro units already in existence.

The squadron, to be known as the 100th Pursuit Squadron, will be trained at Tuskegee, Ala., site of the Negro institute, where the first organized Negro pursuit squadron, known as the Ninety-ninth, is completing its training.

NEGROES TRAINING TO BE OFFICERS

Coincident with this announcement of new Negro organizations, Secretary Stimson stated that Negroes were attending officer candidate schools for men selected from among draftees. In addition he noted that the main parade ground at Fort Knox recently was named Brooks Field, in honor of Private Robert H. Brooks, a Negro who was the first casualty in the armored force in the Philippines.

The new armored division will undertake training at a time when part of the armored force has already matured in training and achieved the goal of 100 per cent equipment, fitting it for duty anywhere in the world, Secretary Stimson said. Some units are less than fully equipped, but he asserted that they had sufficient arms for thorough training of the officers and men.

Each armored division consists of more than 10,000 officers and men, is composed of two tank regiments, three separate field artillery battalions, an infantry regiment, a reconnaissance battalion, an anti-tank battalion of motorized artillery, an engineer battalion, observation aircraft and the usual units to provide for the men and service the vehicles.

DIVISIONS ARE MINIATURE ARMIES

Each division, therefore, is a miniature army of extraordinary striking force, so composed that it may be divided into two or more independent arms. The new division, like those already formed, will be trained at Fort Knox, Ky.

The new training programs for officers are designed to send these men into their new commands completely equipped to teach their units the specialties of modern warfare required of each type of fighting unit. The first group to take the course will include 500 officers assigned to the three new triangular divisions to be formed within the next few weeks in the start toward a goal of thirty-two new divisions. ◆

JANUARY 26, 1942

RUSSIAN UNIFORMS KEEP OUT THE COLD
High Boot of Felt Is Regarded as Important Factor In Red Army's Winter Gains

Special Cable to The New York Times.

MOSCOW, Jan. 25—The battle dress that is serving the Russian Army so well this winter provides a maximum of warmth with a minimum of handicap to freedom of movement.

Most important from the viewpoint of warmth are the Russians' knee-high boots of thick felt—"valenki"—which many foreign military observers regard as a prime factor in the present Russian victories. These boots, which appear to be clumsy and shapeless, are made of a single piece of quarter-inch-thick felt and nothing more. One weighs about a pound and a half. Soldiers wear no socks beneath the boots, but bind their feet in cloth. The valenki give excellent protection when soldiers are standing or sitting. The snow is dry during most of the Winter, so the boots do not get wet.

Soldiers on the move sling their felt boots around their neck and wear high boots that are slightly higher in front than in back and are relatively light, weighing a little more than a pound apiece. They are very broad in the toe and give the Russian soldier on the march a somewhat ungainly pace, but they undoubtedly are highly practical. Many men wear an extra sole inside the leather boots, which are called "sapogi."

Red Army breeches are of quilted kapok or padded with down, and they vary in weight according to the passing. They keep warm the vital part of the leg just above the knee, which, if chilled, seems to affect the whole body. Underneath the breeches are worn coarse trousers of no particular standard quality or weight.

Over his vest and tunic the Red Army man wears a sheepskin jacket—"shuba." The jacket used in action is about knee length, but longer ones are issued for other activities. The jacket, with the wool inside, weighs about nine pounds and is a comfortable garment. It is rather tight at the waist, but loose in the shoulders.

The Red Army fur hat varies in weight, the average being twenty ounces, but the design is standard. The hat is basin-shaped and it is thickly padded. There are broad flaps that may be worn turned up and tied over the top of the head, or turned down to cover the ears and cheeks and tied under the chin. Most of the hats are lined with lamb's wool, but some are lined with thick woolen cloth. Officers' hats, while no warmer than those worn by the men, are more smartly finished.

Gloves are not standardized. They are made of cloth or leather and have wool lining. The soldiers sometimes wear their own woolen gloves or mittens underneath the Army gloves, just as they often wear their own pullover sweaters. ◊

JANUARY 27, 1942

ASSAILS NEGRO BLOOD BAN

Special to The New York Times.

ALBANY, Jan. 26—Assemblyman William T. Andrews, a Negro, read on the floor of the Assembly tonight a letter signed by E. Sloan Colt, from the Red Cross national headquarters in Washington, explaining why the Red Cross was refusing to accept blood from Negro donors for war purposes.

The letter stated that sufficient blood was being obtained from white donors and in view of the prejudices held by some against Negro blood, the Red Cross had adopted this policy, even though "there is no known difference in the physical properties of white and Negro blood."

Mr. Andrews assailed the policy as a violation of the spirit of democracy.

The Assembly passed and sent to the Governor the Hanley bill permitting corporations to make contributions to the Red Cross. ◊

Red Army troops in 1942.

JANUARY 28, 1942

SAYS MILLION WOMEN ARE NEEDED FOR WAR

WASHINGTON, Jan. 27 (AP)—More than 1,000,000 women will be needed as skilled workers in America's arms and munitions plants this year, Sidney Hillman, labor director of the War Production Board, estimated today.

"Airplanes can sink battleships," Mr. Hillman said in a statement. "Women can build airplanes. War is calling on the women of America for production skills. The President has stated it is the policy of this government to speed up existing production by operating all war industries on a seven-day-a-week basis.

"Women will be called to work on the production of war materials in greater numbers than ever before.

"Women can do almost anything in wartime production. Here, as in England, they are already employed in airplane plants, ammunition plants, ordnance, fuse and powder plants."

Mr. Hillman's office has estimated that war industries will have to take on some 10,000,000 more workers this year, in addition to the 5,000,000 already employed, if war production goals are to be met.

Women were urged by Mr. Hillman to prepare themselves immediately for the jobs they may have to take over. He called attention to the government's defense training programs and State employment services and urged women with factory experience to register with the latter as soon as possible. ◇

Twenty-year-old Annie Tabor working a lathe at a large Midwest supercharger plant, making parts for aircraft engines in 1942.

JANUARY 31, 1942

BRITISH CONCEDE FALL OF BENGAZI

Report Evacuation In Face of Superior Axis Force, Which Has Seized Many Supplies

By JOSEPH M. LEVY
Special Cable to The New York Times.

CAIRO, Egypt, Jan. 30—Despite courageous fighting by Indian troops, the jaws of a German pincers operation closed on Bengazi yesterday. Apparently greatly reinforced within the last few days, the Germans threw such numbers of tanks and mechanized infantry into the fray that British Imperial units in the immediate vicinity found themselves heavily outnumbered.

It is believed that before Bengazi was evacuated the Indians destroyed most of the supplies kept there. However, some anxiety is felt for the Seventh Indian Brigade, which was fighting south of the city, and part of it may have been caught in a German trap.

Using considerable numbers of tanks, two heavy Nazi columns had attacked the Seventh Indian Brigade well south of Bengazi. The strength of the attackers was so greatly superior that by Wednesday the Indians had to give ground. They fought bravely and clung to each position, but eventually they were driven back into the vicinity of the city itself.

JANUARY 29, 1942

U-BOATS CAUSE TEXAS BLACKOUT
Shipping Warned to Remain in Ports— Enemy Craft Signal in Gulf of Mexico

CORPUS CHRISTI, Texas, Jan. 28 (UP)—A complete blackout of a 100-mile strip of the Texas coast was ordered for tonight following an announcement by Captain Alva D. Bernhard, commander of the naval air station here, that two Axis submarines were reported operating off the South Texas coast.

One submarine was seen lying on the surface of the Gulf of Mexico fifteen miles south of Port Aransas by United States patrol craft. It submerged within ten minutes

after another submarine, about four miles to the east, had released a smoke bomb to warn the first U-boat. The second vessel submerged almost immediately, it was said.

A patrol of twenty-one naval planes was established at once from the Corpus Christi base and Army planes from interior Texas points were ordered to the area.

The blackout was ordered from Rockport to a point thirty miles south of Corpus Christi.

Captain Bernhard said he was authorized by the Navy Department to release the information but that any

DRIVE TO COAST ROAD

Meanwhile an even stronger Axis force reached Er Regima, sixteen miles east of Bengazi, and by nightfall Wednesday held the coast road north of the city. The Fourth Indian Division, which remained in Bengazi, was thus put into a dangerous position and it withdrew in a northeasterly direction, escaping the Nazi pincers but leaving Bengazi open for Axis occupation.

The Germans have yet to meet the large British forces operating outside the immediate region of the captured city, but considering Field Marshal Erwin Rommel's tendencies toward optimism, it is held likely that he will attempt to move farther eastward, even at the expense of another battle.

The British lost considerable amounts of material and supplies, and the Germans picked up enough British gasoline to free them temporarily from pressing supply difficulties.

Yet Marshal Rommel's achievement in capturing Bengazi is regarded as being of scant use except to help protect his northern flank if he chooses to attempt to fight his way eastward across the desert. The ease with which Bengazi itself may be outflanked by desert operations makes its value doubtful.

MEKILI MORE VALUABLE

The British will not give up Mekili, which, much more than Bengazi, controls the Jebel el-Achdar range, without a fierce struggle, and Marshal Rommel

will have a considerable communications problem if he risks an assault. Whether he will try an immediate advance depends on the extent of his reinforcements, which, though quite enough to have overwhelmed the Bengazi defenders, may be insufficient to cope with the tremendous obstacles of a long desert advance.

A substantial German force still remains in the Msus area, between Bengazi and Mekili, but activity there yesterday was confined to patrol fighting. German detachments patrolling northeastward from Msus met British patrols and withdrew. The German units in this area probably will form the spearhead of the Nazi drive if Marshal Rommel has not given up the idea of reaching the Egyptian frontier area. ◇

FEBRUARY 2, 1942

QUISLING RECEIVES TITLE OF PREMIER

German Commissar Terboven Installs Head Of the Puppet Government of Norway

By BERNARD VALERY
By Telephone to The New York Times.

STOCKHOLM, Sweden, Feb. 1—Major Vidkun Quisling was today proclaimed Premier of Norway by Reich Commissar Joseph Terboven. The new title did not change anything in Major Quisling's status as puppet.

Symbolically, the ceremony took place in the sixteenth-century Aker fort of Oslo, which the Germans are using as a military headquarters and on the ramparts of which they execute Norwegians sentenced by their courts-martial.

The Norwegian capital was thronged with subordinate Quislings who came from every part of the country. All the larger hotels and houses were requisitioned for their use. There was but one exception. The building of the Royal Norwegian Automobile Club is occupied by the commander of the German troops in Norway, Col. Gen. Nikolaus von Falkenhorst, who, it is rumored, refused to allow one Quislingist in his residence.

OFFERS SUPPORT FOR ACTION

According to the summary of Commissioner Terboven's speech issued by the Norwegian Telegraph Agency, he "produced hitherto documentary proof that Bishop Einar Berggrav of Oslo declared before the war that Britain was the enemy of Norwegian neutrality, while Germany was its friend." Thereby, said Herr Terboven, the Bishop proved himself "a typical classical Crown witness in the question of the absolute righteousness of the policy of the Nasjonal Samling [Nazi party].

Apart from the fact that Bishop Berggrav is in no position today to confirm or deny the authenticity of this "documentary proof," observers here point out that he led the joint protest of all Norwegian Bishops against the policies of the Samling, that courageously he has continued the struggle and that Quislingists make no secret of their intention to have his head at the first opportunity.

The German commissioner further compared the struggle for power of the German National Socialists with the attitude of Major Quisling's party. He ended by declaring that "today this movement—the Nasjonal Samling—even from a purely numerical point of view is the strongest Norway has ever had."

It is asserted here that the Quisling party membership does not exceed 30,000 while the old Social Democratic party in Norway had a minimum of 125,000 members.

QUISLING THANKS HITLER

Speaking in German, Major Quisling thanked "on behalf of the entire Norwegian people" Reichsfuehrer Hitler and Herr Terboven "for the under- ⟩

---

further details would have to come from Washington. He said the submarines were "probably German."

The first announcement of the presence of a submarine was issued at Port Arthur by Commander R. R. Ferguson, naval port director there, who warned shipping that a U-boat had been sighted fifteen miles off Aransas Pass. The pass leads between two shoals into Aransas Bay, fifty miles from here, and is 130 miles north of the southernmost tip of Texas.

Commander Ferguson said it had not been determined that the submarine

was an "enemy" ship, "but it may be presumed it was."

Shipping in this area alongshore is generally quite heavy and prior to the United States' entry into the war hundreds of tankers put out from Texas seaports. ◇

standing they have shown for the deepest desire of the Norwegian people." Then, in Norwegian, he turned toward his countrymen and said among other things that "our movement is the only lawful Norwegian authority" and that "the foremost aim of the national government is to make peace with Germany."

As for Sweden, Major Quisling declared that as soon as possible a change would be made in the abnormal relations by which Sweden represents the "emigre government" in protecting Norwegian interests in foreign countries. But he promised to follow an "honest and sober policy" toward Sweden.

Observers here say that the whole ceremony was entirely unconstitutional. Major Quisling was not appointed Prime Minister by the King nor did he receive a vote of confidence from the legal parliament.

Herr Terboven, who apparently will remain in Norway as chief of the German civilian administration and Major Quisling's adviser, will continue to rule the country from the background. It is

Vidkun Quisling, Premier of Norway's puppet government.

presumed that, realizing that the struggle against Norwegian opposition will become more bitter, the Germans have decided to have Major Quisling ready as an eventual scapegoat. ◊

FEBRUARY 15, 1942

10 WEEKS OF PACIFIC WAR SHOW JAPAN UNCHECKED
Tottering Singapore Gives Foe Access to Rich Indies And Indian Ocean

By HANSON W. BALDWIN

WASHINGTON, Feb. 14—Ten weeks ago today at Pearl Harbor the Japanese won their first major victory of the war. Last week, as thousands of fanatical little fighters swarmed across the Johore Strait on to Singapore Island they had won their second great victory—one with unpredictable implications—and the second phase of the Pacific war was ending with the Malay barrier breached

---

FEBRUARY 9, 1942

EDITORIAL
This is an Air War

The American Army alone, it is announced, plans to create a 2,000,000-man air force. Such an Army air force would compare with a reported strength of 1,000,000 to 1,250,000 in the Nazi Luftwaffe and of about 1,000,000 in the British R.A.F. In addition to the Army's plans. the Navy is preparing an immense air arm of its own.

These plans reveal that the Administration recognizes the tremendous and determining role that air power is going to play in this war. Even more than any other nation, the United States must concentrate on air power. The great ocean distances that have so far kept our mainland free of air attack are also the chief barriers that stand in the way of our own offensive action against the Axis. There are only two ways in which we can bring that offensive action to breakthrough long-range bombers and through ships.

We need the ships to transport men and tanks and guns and pursuit planes.

But our ships are limited in number; compared with planes, they move with painful slowness, and cargo space must be rigorously economized. This means that they must only to a small extent be used to ship mere manpower; they are needed mainly to transport short-range planes, air personnel and fully mechanized divisions. If we can get these air forces and mechanized forces to Russia and China they can act as spearheads to turn the almost unlimited manpower already in these nations, particularly China, from defensive to vigorous offensive action. The merchant ship and the plane, with the protection of warships and of airplane carriers, are the two chief weapons with which America must win this war.

An air force of the huge dimensions that we now contemplate raises once more important questions in war organization. When it has grown to this size, an air force can no longer be thought of as a mere "supporting arm" to the older services. The question may be seriously raised whether in our own case the relationship will not be the reverse of this, and whether this should not be reflected in a new form of organization.

It is at least clear that at any given point the Army, Navy and air force must

all be under a single unified command. And those in command of the air forces must have a thorough training in and understanding of air tactics and strategy. This training and understanding certainly did not exist at Pearl Harbor. It they had, our planes there would not have been concentrated and exposed in such a way that the Japanese were able to inflict the maximum rather than the minimum damage upon them on the ground. Our apparent lack either of sufficient airplanes or of proper protection for airplanes at Guam, Wake, and the Philippines also raises a serious question whether those in charge of strategy in Washington before Dec. 7 really understood the role of the air force and were alive to the needs of the situation.

Not less important than having a huge air force is to have men in command who know how to use it. And this must raise one more question: whether men whose whole training has been in the older services with the older weapons can be relied upon to assign air power its proper share in their plans. There has been an increasing tendency since Pearl Harbor to put in command men with a better understanding of air power. This reform must be thoroughgoing. ◊

and the strategic picture for the United Nations somber with defeat.

Within ten weeks the Japanese have swept to astounding triumphs. The bitter cup of the United Nations is almost full. But not to overflowing. For, to put it baldly—and that is what the people of the United Nations need, bald, frank, pitiless truth—the worst is yet to come.

There can now be no doubt that we are facing perhaps the blackest period in our history. The escape of the Scharnhorst and Gneisenau, the success of the German drive in Libya, which is developing into a determined and ruthless offensive, the impending Nazi offensive in Russia, and the increase in ship sinkings in the Atlantic add to the gloom of the Pacific picture. But the threats in Europe are still largely potential; in the Pacific the headlines of the newspapers have recorded their actuality.

ORIENT PICTURE IS BLACK

Singapore was the keystone of the Malay barrier. Amboina, advanced naval and air station for Surabaya in Netherland Java, has gone. Most of the ports of Borneo, with their oil fields, are in enemy hands. The Celebes have gone. The Japanese have forced a crossing of the Salween River line in Burma and are on the road to Rangoon. The picture in the Orient is black.

Singapore's chief importance was not only as a key bastion in the Malay barrier. It was the only major naval and air base available to the United Nations in the entire Far East. Its value in this respect had been largely nullified ever

since the Japanese offensive down the Malay Peninsula drove within fighter-plane range of the $400,000,000 base.

But not only was it thought to be a strong point defensively in the Malay barrier line, but as long as it remained in the hands of the United Nations it was a potential springboard for offensive operations against Japan, the kind of operations that alone bring victory. It was the only port between Calcutta, India, and Sydney, Australia, that had drydocks large enough to accommodate large men-of-war—battleships and carriers—and it possessed at least four air fields.

DRYDOCK MAY BE SAVED

The British may have been able to save something from the wreckage of disaster. The drydocks may have been towed to safety rather than destroyed. But the possibility is unlikely.

As it is, Surabaya, a second-class naval and air base on the island of Java, is now the only principal base available in the theatre of operations, and it has already been bombed several times. And Java is now the final citadel of Dutch resistance in the Netherlands Indies.

It is the most heavily defended of the Indies; there are probably the equivalent of two to four divisions, plus supporting troops (Netherland and native) on the island, and the principal Netherlands Indies air bases and air forces are there. The small forces of the Netherlands Indies Navy and of our Far Eastern naval forces are available for its defense, and behind it lies Port Darwin and the great subcontinent of Australia, now becoming a base of supplies for our Far Eastern operations. ◇

British soldiers taken prisoner by the Japanese in Singapore, 1942.

FEBRUARY 16, 1942

BRITISH CAPITULATE
Tokyo Claims Toll of 32 Allied Vessels South of Singapore

By JAMES MacDONALD
Special Cable to The New York Times.

LONDON, Feb. 15—Singapore has fallen.

The long dreaded news that the key British base of the Pacific and Indian Oceans would be captured by the Japanese—a major reverse clearly foreseen many days ago—was announced tonight by Winston Churchill, a few hours after dispatches from Vichy and Tokyo reported that Lieut. Gen. Arthur E. Percival's forces had surrendered unconditionally at 3:30 P. M. today British daylight saving time [9:50 P.M. Sunday Singapore time and 10:30 A.M. Eastern war time].

London officials naturally declined to disclose what plans had been made or were perhaps in the making for establishing a naval base elsewhere to meet the grave emergency arising from the loss of Singapore. They could not or would not divulge how many Imperial troops were taken prisoner or how many got away.

COMMANDERS MEET

According to the official Tokyo announcement, fighting ceased along the entire front three hours after a meeting between General Percival and the Japanese Commander in Chief, Lieut. Gen. Tomoyuki Yamashita, in the Ford motor plant at the foot of Timah Hill, where the documents of surrender were signed. The terms were not disclosed here, but a Japanese Domei Agency dispatch late tonight said that under the capitulation up to 1,000 armed British soldiers would remain in Singapore City to maintain order until the Japanese Army completed occupation.

Similar terms, it is recalled, were contained in the surrender of Hong Kong on Christmas Day.

The Tokyo radio said the Japanese had constantly kept pouring in fresh troops to make up for losses from the fierce resistance of British Imperial troops.

In the final battle, three Japanese columns were said to have advanced on the city. Yesterday the central column completed occupation of the water reservoirs and a part of this column reached the northern outskirts of the city on a six-mile front. Another column bypassed the ▸

◀ reservoirs, crossed the Kalang River and cut the road from Singapore to the civil airport. The third column reached Alexandris Road in the western part of the city.

SOME RESISTING, TOKYO SAYS

[Japanese units left the main island in barges and seized Blakang Mati, the island opposite Keppel Harbor, thereby gaining control of the sea approach to Singapore from the south, according to a Tokyo broadcast recorded by The United Press.

[Japanese troops entered Singapore City today under the terms of the surrender by the British, but a Domei dispatch said some of the defending forces and "other hostile elements" still were resisting, another Tokyo broadcast heard by The United Press stated.]

The Berlin radio, quoting the Japanese newspaper Asahi, said the largest part of the British and Australian forces "obviously" left Singapore Friday for Sumatra.

Unofficial reports reached London late tonight that 2,000 persons evacuated from Singapore had arrived in Bombay.

Just about the time "cease fire" was ordered in Singapore, the city's radio station was broadcasting as usual, giving a news bulletin and announcing in conclusion:

"This is the Malayan Broadcasting Corporation closing down its news program. We'll be broadcasting again tomorrow evening. Good night, everybody, good night."

Earlier in the day a Singapore broadcast had been heard in New Delhi, India, announcing, "We're still offering stiff resistance to the enemy's attacks." Listeners in India had vital reason for watching the battle of Singapore because its loss involved possible domination of the Indian Ocean by Japanese naval forces. Immediate attacks in great strength on Sumatra, and other Netherlands Indies points, were also anticipated.

News of the capture of Singapore was greeted jubilantly in Japan. A Tokyo dispatch said Emperor Hirohito "heard with great satisfaction" the Japanese Imperial Headquarters announcement about the fall of the historic base that the British had held for 123 years. Both Houses of the Japanese Parliament are scheduled to meet tomorrow in a special session at which Premier Hideki Tojo and Admiral Shigetaro Shimada, Minister of the Navy, will make their official reports. ◆

DARWIN IS BOMBED FOR SECOND TIME
Port Machine-Gunned in New Raid—
Tokyo Reports Landing on Island of Timor

By The Associated Press.

SYDNEY, Australia, Feb. 20—Air raid alarms sounded in Darwin today for the second successive day, but Japanese planes did not appear to follow up the two blows struck yesterday, in which fifteen persons were killed and twenty-four wounded at the vital Allied naval base on Australia's north coast.

Air Minister Arthur S. Drakeford announced that a third raid had occurred, but later information said no enemy planes appeared although the "alert" was sounded.

[A Tokyo broadcast recorded by The United Press this morning said Japanese troops had landed on both the Netherland and the Portuguese portions of Timor, north of Australia.] ◆

GUN DUEL IS HEAVY IN BATAAN BATTLE

By C. BROOKS PETERS
Special to The New York Times.

WASHINGTON, Feb. 21—The Battle of Bataan was marked today by the growing extent of Japanese assaults upon General Douglas MacArthur's positions in the Philippine area, the War Department reported.

During the past twenty-four hours the Japanese and the American-Filipino forces poured shells into each other's positions in what the War Department called "heavy artillery firing."

All along the front on the Bataan Peninsula infantry patrols were reported active and skirmishes were frequent.

Increasing and effective resistance by Filipino civilians to the Japanese invaders, and the extent to which General MacArthur's fight is bolstered by naval men and guns and other equipment evacuated from the United States base at Cavite, near Manila, were emphasized in other communiqués.

The Japanese air force was again reported dropping incendiary bombs on objectives over and behind the United States lines. The enemy was said to have made frequent flights over General MacArthur's lines for this purpose.

The Japanese resumed firing with long-range batteries on all of General MacArthur's defense fortifications. Fort Frank, one of the auxiliary fortresses to the bastion of Corregidor that holds the entrance to Manila Bay against the enemy bore the brunt of this artillery attack.

The Japanese have emplacements across Manila Bay at Cavite from which they have intermittently bombarded the Americans' island fortifications. There was no indication as to the effectiveness of the Japanese shellings. The War Department reported that the harbor defense batteries returned the fire.

MacARTHUR HAS 'NAVAL SUPPLY'

The Navy Department reported that the battalion of bluejackets and Marines, under the command of Rear Admiral Francis W. Rockwell, commandant of the Sixteenth Naval District, which has been fighting with General MacArthur, had succeeded in taking "considerable equipment" from the Cavite naval base before it fell to the enemy. It said also that materiel from "other sources of naval supply" has been used to good advantage in the defense of the Bataan Peninsula.

The naval equipment that is helping General MacArthur's forces in their defense includes three-inch and four-inch artillery, as well as boats, guns and machine guns of several types, with ammunition, the Navy Department said.

In addition the Navy reported that a large number of hand grenades, aircraft bombs and depth charges, stores of gasoline, Diesel oil and lubricating oil were saved and were being used effectively in the Americas in field operations.

Motor launches and tugs were provided for General MacArthur by Admiral Rockwell's force.

The Navy said also that the battalion had salvaged facilities for repair of

FEBRUARY 22, 1942

INDIA'S ROLE IN WAR BECOMES VITAL
British Seek Ways To Unite People in Great Effort

By CRAIG THOMPSON
Wireless to The New York Times.

LONDON, Feb. 21—In steady thrusts the Japanese have been pushing their way through British and Netherland Far Eastern barriers toward India and the Indian Ocean. Adolf Hitler meanwhile has been piling up ever greater artillery, tanks, and trucks, in addition to electrical and ordnance supplies.

Furthermore, the Navy reported, personnel of the naval air base organization, who were formerly employed on government contracts, has constructed and repaired airfields and roads in the fighting area. Steam shovels, tractors, cranes, trucks and graders, the Navy revealed, have been operated by this organization to useful advantage on Bataan and Corregidor.

FILIPINO CIVILIANS' RESISTANCE
The War Department announced that General MacArthur has sent reports relative to the loyalty and morale of the Filipinos in the areas occupied by the enemy.

"Despite the harshness and severity of the military rule imposed by the invaders," the War Department said, "the spirit of the liberty-loving Filipinos remains undaunted."

Filipino civilian resistance to the Japanese was becoming "increasingly effective," the report said. A secret society had been formed, the "F.F.F." or "Fighters for Freedom," which fostered civilian resistance to the invaders.

Informers to whom the Japanese in the Philippines have been reported as offering rewards, have been done away with by patriotic Filipinos.

Several days ago an enemy proclamation posted in Manila and throughout the countryside, enumerating offenses against the Japanese that were punishable by death and declaring that ten Filipinos would be shot for every Japanese killed, was altered overnight, the report said.

It had been changed to read that "for every Filipino killed, ten Japanese soldiers would lose their lives." ◊

quantities of guns, tanks and war chariots, which may head eastward through Turkey and Iran toward India. Since the fall of Singapore Britain has discovered, with a sharpness that has left many persons stunned, the possibility that some of this war's most important actions may be fought out among the cool hills and hot valleys of that fabulous land of princes and Untouchables.

A junction of the Axis forces anywhere in the Middle East or Far East automatically means that the wealth of the Indies will be available to both. In this world-girdling struggle between two philosophies, Britain's foes could hardly choose a spot where dissension and Imperial antipathy would be more likely to play into their hands. India is a place where people are torn into almost implacable groups opposed to unity on anything except a common desire to be rid of British dominance.

PRESSURE FOR UNITY
Politically, everything now is staked on the possibility that the peril of all may bring about a degree of unity in which the war effort may approach something that is closer to the potential power of the naturally rich country, with 388,000,000 people, than has heretofore been possible. There have been signs of a tendency in this direction, although India has been host to many political prophets with imported views, whose general endeavors might be classed as fifth-column work.

EXPANDING INDUSTRY
The development of war power means industrial advancement, and in this direction India has been growing by bounds since the war began, although many Indians insist that British policy has had a stunting effect.

The visit of Generalissimo Chiang Kai-shek of China—inspired in London—was a step in the direction of unity. It was hoped that he and Madame Chiang would impress on the Indians the resilient strength of a united people, who, far from being crushed after nearly five years of warfare, have become actually stronger.

Underlying this was still another motive, seldom expressed but causing genuine concern among the British and Netherlands government; that is the power of the Japanese slogan, "Asia for the Asiatics."

General Chiang's visit seems to have left the situation about where it was. The Indians have given certain indications that they will drop—temporarily—some of their differences, but only on condition that the British Government lay down guarantees of post-war independence on such unqualified and specific terms that there can be no misunderstanding or recall when and if the present crisis is passed.

If the Britain Government is now prepared to make such concessions no sign of it has yet been seen in London, but there is growing anxiety about India in view of the Far Eastern developments, and it may be easily forced by the circumstances of war to make concessions. The concession, however, would be no greater than the concessions from the Indian parties in willingness to buckle down in a cooperative manner behind the war effort.

POLITICAL DIVISIONS
India has two main parties—the Moslem League, led by Mohammed Ali Jinnah, and the Congress party, which Mohandas K. Gandhi so long led and which has now been lined up behind Pandit Jawaharlal Nehru, who has only been out of jail for a few months. He served nearly a year of a four-year sentence for a political speech that was deemed to be in violation of the Defense of India Rules. He was only one of thousands jailed for the same reason in the months that followed the war's outbreak.

Nearly two years ago, when it was first proposed to establish a broad executive council under Viceroy Linlithgow, Mr. Gandhi countered with a proposal that his following insisted on guarantees of complete independence. Since these were not forthcoming he spread the doctrine of nonresistance to cover everything, including war, and even advised that Britain should lay down her arms and let Germany trample over her, and, suffering every possible indignity, refuse nothing except allegiance. The British politely replied that they appreciated the spirit in which his advice was offered but that they could not accept it.

Pandit Nehru then led a group within the Congress party who modified the nonresistance application to the essential degree that made it inapplicable to wars or national defense. But the party would have nothing less in return than guarantees of independence. ◊

Chapter 11
"LIDICE, ILLINOIS"
March–June 1942

The spring and summer of 1942 saw the Axis powers reach their fullest territorial extent. German forces rallied in the spring and recaptured the city of Kharkov, while Hitler ordered a new major operation, code-named "Blue," to capture the oil and wheat areas of southern Russia and the Caucasus. Operation Blue was launched by the Germans on June 28 after they first destroyed the Russian port of Sevastopol. In North Africa, Rommel's German and Italian armies proved unstoppable as they swept through Libya to seize the port of Tobruk on June 21 with the capture of 32,000 British Empire and Allied forces.

The unpredictable story was just how far the victorious Japanese armed forces would go. From Tokyo there was talk of complete victory over the United States and the European colonial powers. On April 6 the capital of Ceylon (now Sri Lanka) was shelled by Japanese warships, and it seemed likely that Japan would sweep on into India following its brief but effective campaign to capture Burma (Myanmar) by late April. American eyes were turned to the final death throes of the large American force holed up on the Bataan Peninsula on the island of Luzon in the Philippines. On March 9 General MacArthur left to go to Australia, placing his garrison under the command of Lt. General Jonathan Wainwright. Under constant pressure from General Masaharu Homma's Fourteenth Army, American and Filipino troops retreated farther toward the fortress of Corregidor. But on April 9, short of ammunition and supplies, 78,000 of them were forced to surrender. Some 2,000 escaped to Corregidor, where Wainwright and around 11,000 men defied the Japanese invaders for another month, finally surrendering on May 6. Thousands of tired and hungry soldiers were forced on what became known as the Bataan death march to POW camps, mistreated by Japanese soldiers whose military culture of death to the end left little sympathy for an enemy who surrendered.

The universal bad news put pressure on Churchill's leadership in Britain. The failure in North Africa, the relentless bombing of the island base of Malta, and the rising losses in the Atlantic war all raised a chorus of criticism of Britain's strategic leadership. "Churchill Weathers Storm," reported The Times, but it was evident that the British public, after more than two years of war, was tired of failure. Amid the gloom, there was sudden evidence that the Japanese onslaught might finally have reached its limit. Between May 5 and 7 an inconclusive naval engagement was fought in the Coral Sea between American and Japanese aircraft carriers as the Japanese Navy sought to capture the southern area of New Guinea and the Solomon Islands. The air battle resulted in the loss of the U.S. carrier *Lexington,* and the loss of the small carrier *Shoho* plus heavy damage to the Japanese carrier *Shokaku.* The Japanese captured the Solomons, but were driven back from southern New Guinea. The real turning point came with a second major engagement a few weeks later when the Japanese naval commander, Admiral Isoroku Yamamoto, led a huge Japanese task force to capture the island of Midway in hopes of destroying the remains of the U.S. Pacific Fleet. The Times reported Admiral Ernest King's communiqué on June 8 about what came to be called the Battle of Midway. The details were uncertain and the Times's reporting hardly reflects just how important this battle proved to be . All four major Japanese fleet carriers were sunk and one-third of the naval pilots killed, while the Allies only lost the carrier *Yorktown.* The Battle of Midway would prove to be a turning point in the Pacific war, but its significance was only fully understood later in the year.

While Midway was being fought, the popular mood in America was absorbed by the assassination of the cruel head of the Reich Security Office, Reinhard Heydrich, who on June 4 died of wounds suffered in an assassination attempt by Czech partisans. The German authorities chose to single out the Czech village of Lidice as an example: all the men were murdered, the women sent to camps and the children forced into foster homes. The outrage was soon world news. The Times asked how the atrocity should be remembered, and a few days later on June 30 it was reported that the Stern Park suburb of Crest Hill, Illinois had renamed itself Lidice in honor of the vanished village.

MARCH 1, 1942

MacARTHUR HOLDS NEW BATAAN LINE

Special to The New York Times.

WASHINGTON, Feb. 28—Having pushed back the Japanese lines on Bataan Peninsula this week, General Douglas MacArthur's American and Filipino forces were today holding positions along their farthest front of advance, the War Department reported.

Fighting had lessened, the day's communiqué said, and operations were "limited to relatively minor patrol skirmishes."

General MacArthur's troops, after their surprise penetrations of the Japanese positions, the communiqué said, held a line that "extends from slightly north of Abucay on Manila Bay across the Bataan Peninsula to a point on the China Sea, midway between Bagac and Moron."

The Japanese retain their main battle positions and the most recent fighting has been confined to skirmishing. ◇

MARCH 8, 1942

MAKING OF RADIOS AND PHONOGRAPHS TO END APRIL 22
Nelson Orders That Plants Then Devote Entire Time to War Production

Special to The New York Times.

WASHINGTON, March 7—The War Production Board, headed by Donald M. Nelson, gave orders today that the manufacture of radios and phonographs for civilian use be discontinued after April 22 so that the fifty-five manufacturers in the industry could devote their plants to war production, chiefly radio sending and receiving sets and airplane detection apparatus for the Army and Navy.

In an earlier order civilian production by large manufacturers was limited between Jan. 23 and April 23 to 55 per cent of their production rate in the first nine months of 1941 and that of small producers to 65 per cent.

Today's order permits each manufacturer to complete sets begun before April 22 if he does not use more than $500 worth of materials, not including the cost of wooden cabinets. Continued manufacture of replacement parts is permitted and this, the WPB said, will make it possible to keep the bulk of existing home radios in efficient operating condition during the war.

1941 EMPLOYMENT 30,000
The order affects companies which in 1941 employed about 30,000 persons, produced more than 13,000,000 sets, and did a business of about $240,000,000, using 2,100 tons of aluminum, 10,500 tons of copper, 280 tons of nickel and 70,000 tons of steel, all critical materials.

Robert Berner, chief of the WPB radio section, said the order would not result in unemployment for any appreciable period, but that employment would be greatly increased by the switch to military production, with 95 per cent of the switch expected to be completed before June 30.

The fifty-five companies already have military orders aggregating $500,000,000, it was said, while an equal amount of such contracts is held by other radio companies not normally engaged in civilian production. All except thirteen of the fifty-five companies affected by today's order have begun participating in the military business.

SUBCONTRACTING PLAN READY
The ordnance branch and the radio section of the consumers durable goods branch of the WPB, to facilitate the conversion of the smaller companies, have worked out a subcontracting plan whereby each affected company which is not a prime contractor will be assigned to a prime contract holder, thus forming a series of "family production groups."

The load of war production, it was stated, would be so evenly distributed that there would be work for every company which is capable of performing the precise operations demanded by the Army and Navy.

The WPB estimated that production of home radios this year will be 3,000,000 before production stops, increasing to about 50,000,000 the number of home radios in the nation. ◇

APRIL 2, 1942

BLONDES MAY AID IN WAR
Undyed, Unwaved Hair Needed For Airplane Instruments

Blonde glamour girls who plan to get the short Victory haircut may make a substantial contribution to the war under the terms of an announcement made yesterday by the Office of Emergency Management. However, there are two big "ifs" to the bargain.

War plants making flight instruments, including Julien P. Friez & Sons, a division of the Bendix Aircraft Corporation of Baltimore, need straight blond hair measuring fourteen or more inches in length, but the hair must have been untouched by any dye or chemical, and it must never have been subjected to a permanent wave.

If a girl's "crowning glory" meets these qualifications, she may sell it, or the factory will give her pay to the American Red Cross or the U.S.O. In the latter case, she will receive a certificate as a donor of strategic material to war production. ◇

APRIL 6, 1942

COLOMBO ATTACKED
First Assault on Base at Tip of India Causes Little Damage

Special Cable to The New York Times.

LONDON, April 5—In the first attack on Ceylon, British base off the southern tip of India, seventy-five Japanese planes today raided the harbor, airdrome and Ratmalana railway at Colombo and were repulsed with the certain loss of twenty-seven craft shot down.

The heavy loss suffered by the Japanese was cited here as an indication of what happens when their aircraft encounter real opposition.

Little damage was done to the Ceylon capital in the Easter Sunday assault, it was reported here.

Vice Admiral Sir Geoffrey Layton, Commander in Chief of the armed forces on Ceylon, said that besides the twenty-seven raiders definitely shot down, five were believed to have been damaged so badly that they crashed at sea and twenty-five other planes were hit. The raiders operated from an aircraft carrier, he said.

RAID STARTS AT 8 A.M.

The attacking planes swept in from the Bay of Bengal about 8 o'clock in the morning, heralded by the shriek of sirens, the crash of bombs and the bark of anti-aircraft guns.

Since Japanese occupation of the Andaman Islands, 900 miles from Ceylon and an excellent base for aircraft carriers, Colombo has been strengthening its defenses. Recently fire lanes were cut through the city by the demolition of tenements in the slum areas, and today the Air Raid Precaution services functioned smoothly while the bulk of the population took shelter in open slit trenches.

Some civilians were killed and wounded. Information here was that aside from some excitement caused by the separation of families, there was no trace of anything approaching panic or disorder.

Powerful forces of defending fighters went up to attack and shot down twenty-five enemy planes. Two other planes were shot down by anti-aircraft fire.

The raid on Colombo was the closest approach the Japanese have yet made to the mainland of India, and the attack was viewed in many quarters here as the beginning of Japanese concentration on the Asiatic subcontinent.

As long as Singapore and Java remained in the hands of the United Nations, Ceylon was of secondary importance in the war with Japan. Now the Trincomalee naval base and air bases in Ceylon have assumed tremendous importance. Ceylon, a Crown colony, is a little larger than West Virginia, and is in a position not only of a strategic guardian of India from sea attack, but also is on the supply routes through the Persian Gulf and the Indian Ocean. ◆

Foes Attempt at Surprise Raid Backfires: A Japanese force of seventy-five planes attacked Colombo (1), on Ceylon, perhaps as an intended prelude to an effort to knock out the naval base at Trincomalee (2), but at least twenty-seven of the planes were shot down. The attackers were said to have come from an aircraft carrier, which may have been based on the recently captured Andaman Islands (A on inset). American planes heavily raided the port of Rangoon (B), setting three large fires.

APRIL 7, 1942

Editorial
FOUR MONTHS OF WAR

Four months ago today Japan struck the blow at Pearl Harbor that brought this country into the war. Since then Japan has been moving forward with uninterrupted success over the longest front in the history of modern warfare. With our allies, we have suffered enormous losses in the East. What can we match against those losses, on the credit side of the ledger? What beginning have we made, against Japan and Hitler? What has this third of a year of war to offer, by way of assurance for the future?

Without minimizing either the losses we have suffered or the task that lies ahead, at least we can say this much:

We can say that the American people have kept their heads, their courage, and their faith. They have taken in their stride the abrupt change from peace to war. They are prepared for a long war and a hard one. Bad news has neither discouraged nor divided them. They have accepted with their heads up the worst defeats that the United States has ever suffered. They have responded ❱

willingly and eagerly to every call that has been made upon them. Every test of public opinion shows that they are out in front of their leaders in their readiness to pay any price and make any sacrifice that is needed to win the war.

We say this much; and we can also say that good use has been made of these four months toward solving some of the most important material and tactical problems of the war. The High Command has been overhauled. It is unfortunate that it took Pearl Harbor to give us a unified command at outposts like Hawaii, a reorganization of the War Department, a single responsible head for the machinery of war production. But at least these steps have now been taken, and the results are coming into evidence. The output of weapons of every kind is increasing. Great industries which were encouraged too long to busy themselves with peacetime goods are coming into war production. American troops are taking their places on distant battlefronts. American planes and guns and tanks are counting with increasing force on the side of the United Nations.

All this is gain. But not until every machine in America that can make a weapon has been harnessed for that purpose; not until every able-bodied man is working longer hours than he works today; not until every lesser interest has been subordinated to the national need—then, and not until then, will we be prepared to fight our hardest. ◊

60,000 CAPTURED BY FOE ON BATAAN
35,000 Combat Troops and 16 Generals Taken with 25,000 Civilians, Stimson Reports

By CHARLES HURD
Special to The New York Times.

WASHINGTON, April 17—While beleaguered Corregidor continued today to nick the edges of sustained Japanese aerial attacks, the War Department announced that approximately 35,000 United States and Filipino "combatant troops" on Bataan Peninsula were presumably in the hands of the enemy.

Included among these forces, unreported since April 9 and believed to be prisoners, were three major generals and seven brigadier generals of the United States forces and one major general and five brigadier generals of the Philippine Army.

In addition, it was stated, the Japanese captured "several thousand noncombatant and supply troops and about 25,000 civilians." The civilians were refugees who had followed the armies into Bataan from cities and villages of Luzon Island.

The losses were detailed in a communiqué distributed this morning at a press conference held by Secretary of War Henry L. Stimson. The report of the latest military action was released this afternoon.

RESISTANCE ON PANAY

No details were given of the fighting on Panay Island, but an official report of "fierce fighting" in the vicinity of Iloilo and Capiz, where the Japanese made landings yesterday, indicated that the invaders were being forced to buy occupation of this island at a heavy price. Panay, in the middle of the Philippines, is about as large as Connecticut and is a wealthy sugar-producing center.

In its summary of the losses on Bataan the War Department said that sixty-eight Army nurses had been removed safely to Corregidor, but 5,536 patients in hospitals were left behind. A "relatively small number of troops" also were transported to Corregidor, but these apparently were few, compared with the 1,500 Marines and about 2,000 sailors sent to the fortified island by specific order of Lieut. Gen. Jonathan M. Wainwright.

NO CONTACT SINCE APRIL 9

Corregidor has had no communication with Bataan since April 9, the War Department reported, and accordingly there is no way of knowing how many of the missing persons were killed and how many are prisoners.

The War Department stated that "no reports of casualties for the last few days of fighting have been received, but it is probable that they were heavy on both sides."

Heading the list of units lost in Bataan was the famous Thirty-first Infantry, which had been on permanent Philippine station for many years. ◊

Japanese soldiers march prisoners of war across the Bataan peninsula in what became known as the Bataan Death March, Luzon, Philippines, April 1942.

Four members of the U.S. army on leave in Manchester, England watch a soccer game.

APRIL 19, 1942

Letters to The Times NEGROES SEEK EQUALITY War, to Them, Is National and Not Racial Matter

To the Editor of The New York Times:

Let us understand each other. Here we are black and white living in America, a land dedicated to the proposition that all men are created equal and are endowed by their Creator with certain unalienable rights, among which are life, liberty and the pursuit of happiness. For more than a century and a half now we have been struggling to realize this goal for our nation.

Yesterday we had not arrived, we shall not arrive tomorrow. Let all Americans admit that we have not yet attained a society or government in which these unalienable rights are guaranteed to all individuals. It will be best for all of us to face this fact frankly and honestly, and make a sincere effort to correct all political and economic practices which undermine the pillars upon which our democracy rests.

At the present time democracy, as never before, is being subjected to the scrutiny of friend and foe. Our American way of life is being challenged by forces within and without. These enemies of our system would substitute for our liberties and freedom tyranny and regimentation.

FULL SHARE DESIRED

Most Americans, black and white, are against these common enemies. When Negroes insist upon full participation in the war effort of their country they do so because they believe that it will require the full use of all available manpower and material resources to win this war. They further believe that individuals or groups who use the present emergency to realize purely selfish ends are just as much enemies of democracy as the totalitarian powers.

Each day brings new evidence of the need for an all-out effort on the part of everyone, and Negroes feel that those who deny every loyal American citizen the chance to do his part, whether in the armed forces of the nation, the training center or the industrial plant, are a menace to our successful prosecution of the war.

On the other hand, citizens who permit themselves to be denied the chance to help win the war without protest and without exposing to public opinion those individuals or groups who engage in these un-American and subversive activities are also aiding and giving comfort to the enemies of democracy.

WILLING TO FIGHT

Negroes want to win the war. They are willing to fight and work to win the war, and they do not propose to stand silently by and see democracy crucified on a cross of gold, greed, prejudice or self-centered selfishness.

To Negroes this is not a racial war. It is a war between conflicting and diametrically opposed philosophies. On one side are those who despise any semblance of individual liberty and freedom. Against these are those peoples of every race who have been struggling toward democratic government and increasing liberty, opportunity and freedom for the individual. Is it inconceivable that Negroes, having desired liberty, opportunity and freedom all these years, should about-face and cast their lot with those who seek to destroy the very things they prize most?

As American citizens they will continue to strive for a full measure of the rights, opportunities and obligations which the Declaration of Independence and the Constitution guarantee to all Americans. At the same time they are irrevocably opposed to any nation that makes war upon our country.

James T. Taylor,

Dean of Men, North Carolina College for Negroes.

Durham, N.C., April 15, 1942. ◊

MAY 10, 1942

The Coral Sea Battle

Engagement Is Viewed as the Opening Clash in Decisive Phase Of the War

By HANSON W. BALDWIN

The great Battle of the Coral Sea is the opening engagement in the decisive phase of the Battle for the World.

Prime Minister John Curtin of Australia correctly interpreted that action as the beginning of the days that will shake the world. The belligerents are commencing the operations that during the Summer will probably preface the ▸

way to victory or defeat.

In the exotic and island-studded waters off Northeastern Australia the initial success in the great campaigns that have now been joined has probably gone to the United Nations. We appear to have had the advantage in the sea-air clash that late yesterday was reported in some dispatches to be continuing.

The Japanese almost certainly have lost a considerable number of naval units and of planes, and it seems certain that their losses in this engagement are more important than those they have suffered in any previous action.

Our own losses are not yet given, though they are described by a communiqué from General Douglas MacArthur's headquarters in Australia as "relatively light" compared with those of the Japanese. We must be prepared, however, for losses; perhaps for heavier ones than this phrase seems to mean, though the Navy Department's communiqué last night, saying no reports yet received substantiated the loss of any American carriers or battleships, was an encouraging one.

MAIN FLEETS NOT ENGAGED

There is no clear picture of the Battle of the Coral Sea, and none may be available for some days. But, judging from the fragmentary reports, the action was not fought between the main bodies of the opposing fleets, but between large task forces.

The fact that the communiqués about the battle have been issued by General Douglas MacArthur's headquarters in Australia indicates that the United States naval forces participating were under his command. Most of our Pacific Fleet is under command of Admiral Chester W. Nimitz, with headquarters in Hawaii. It is, however, possible that forces of our main fleet might have been temporarily attached to General MacArthur's Southwest Pacific command. If the operations in the Southwest Pacific should be intensified it is probable that a large part of our main Pacific Fleet might have to be concentrated there.

The Battle of the Coral Sea seems to have been a prelude to greater actions. Official and unofficial comment still stresses that even our most optimistic claims yield no ground for hope that the strength of the Japanese Fleet has been broken.

Large parts of that fleet, including capital ships and carriers as well as light forces, have been concentrated in the mandated islands in the vicinity of Truk since the war started, and from the ap-proximate vicinity of the battle in the Coral Sea to Truk is only 1,200 to 1,500 nautical miles. Japan probably will—if her mind is set upon Australia or New Caledonia or the islands in the vicin-ity—readily reinforce her naval units in the Coral Sea.

One characteristic of the Japanese is tenacity; they will keep trying until they win or are dead. For them there is no middle ground. Nevertheless, if Japan has lost two carriers and the other units claimed, she has suffered her most se-vere setback of the war.

JAPANESE MASK INTENTIONS

The sparse information from the scene of action makes impossible any logi-cal deduction as to whether or not the Japanese task force was really attempt-ing invasion of the New Hebrides, New Caledonia or Australia. The Japanese intentions in the Battle of the World are not yet clear.

Vice President Wallace has warned of a Japanese attempt against Alaska and the Aleutians and even our West Coast—a step that is possible, but until other things are accomplished by the en-emy, improbable. Reports from London and China indicate the enemy is mass-ing troops in Manchukuo opposite the Russian frontier for the "inevitable war" for the Maritime Provinces.

Meantime, the Japanese are still fight-ing along the Burma Road in Southern China, and from Akyab airport they have raided the railhead and port of Chittagong in India, a step that might be a possible precursor to full-fledged inva-sion. With typical Hitlerian technique they are threatening everywhere, thus masking their real intentions.

But the naval battle in the Coral Sea may soon force the showing of their hand.

In Europe, Adolf Hitler still marks time as the ground dries on the Eastern Front. His armies might have marched against the Russian guns in the south at nearly any time after April 20, but if the German intention is to strike for Moscow and also in the north, it will be some days or weeks before the terrain is dry enough after the Spring thaws to permit extensive operations. Any time between now and June 15 may be the deadline in Russia.

But this is an indivisible war and what happens in Russia is closely linked to what has happened in the Southwest-ern Pacific. For the wrecks of ships lit-tering the waters of the Coral Sea may typify—if they are Japanese ships—the wreckage also of Herr Hitler's hopes. ◆

CHURCHILL WEATHERS STORMS
Less Popular, He Holds His Leadership Because No Man Has Arisen to Challenge It

By RAYMOND DANIELL
Wireless to The New York Times.

LONDON, May 9—Two years ago to-day, as dawn broke over Europe, the Nazi Wehrmacht opened the attack that was to crush the Netherlands, Belgium and Luxembourg and even the might of France in a few short weeks. Before sun-set that night Neville Chamberlain had resigned as Prime Minister and Winston Churchill succeeded him.

Two full years have elapsed since that historic date—two years of blood, toil, sweat and tears, two years of al-most unbroken British defeats. Yet Mr. Churchill still stands almost unchal-lenged as the leader of his country. The chain of disasters set in motion that May morning in 1940 when Adolf Hitler gave the order to advance came with breath-taking rapidity. First the Netherlands fell, Belgium capitulated, leaving the stranded British Expeditionary Force to be rescued by the miracle of Dunkerque. In a short time France sued for peace, leaving Britain almost defenseless and alone against the Nazis across the nar-row moat of the English Channel.

CHURCHILL'S SPIRIT PREVAILED

By his unflinching courage and deter-mination and the power of his oratory, Mr. Churchill was able to galvanize the spirit of his people, to lead them in passive defense against the Nazi effort to terrorize them into surrender by al-most incessant air raids on their towns and cities. He called on them to behave so that after 1,000 years men thumbing through the pages of history would say, "This was their finest hour."

And the people have fulfilled his ex-pectations.

In those days there was no thought of the possibility of defeat, but neither was there any definite plan of victory. Mr. Churchill, who promised so confi-dently that if the United States would "give us the tools we will finish the job," has admitted recently that in those days he himself could not see or clearly define the road to victory. But the writer is in a position to say that he never doubted that the day would dawn when "the New World with all its majesty and might will come to the rescue of the Old."

That may be history's verdict of his leadership. That he inspired and led his people, carrying on an almost hopeless fight against awful odds because of his conviction that the English-speaking, freedom-loving peoples on both sides of the Atlantic must surrender or die.

SHUNNED DICTATOR RULE

In those first weeks and months of his leadership he was a man of destiny. There was nothing he could have demanded of his people that they would not have given freely and gladly. President Roosevelt's first 100 days after his inauguration on that drear day in March, 1933, are the only American parallel.

Mr. Churchill could have made himself a dictator, but he did not. Instead he gathered to himself and his Cabinet absolute powers over the life and property of these islands and then shrank from using them.

One criticism of his government frequently heard in Leftist circles is that it has been more sparing in the use of the powers over property than over life, but that is a rather doctrinate view. It is true that under Mr. Churchill British men and women can be conscripted for military service or work in essential industries. It is also true that private enterprises have sometimes placed the interests of their stockholders ahead of national interests, but it is also true that, along with free enterprise there have been maintained free speech, a free press and the essentials of civil liberties.

There has been considerable grumbling about the inequalities of sacrifice among the British people and to a large degree it is justified. But it is no unique peculiarity of this country that great wealth brings special privileges. Thus it is true that, even under rigid rationing of foodstuffs, clothing and gasoline, the rich come off a little better than the poor.

ATTACKED ON HOME FRONT

A balder criticism of Mr. Churchill is that he is so preoccupied with problems of grand strategy that he has not the time to give the attention they deserve to the home front or to matters of domestic policy. The truth is that Britain today has no Prime Minister in the peacetime sense. She has a Minister of Defense who holds the title of Prime Minister and she has a supreme war lord in the same person. But there is no one with the responsibility and authority to look after things at home, for it is one of Mr. Churchill's greatest weaknesses that he cannot delegate power or jettison friends and associates who have become burdens to him.

Today Mr. Churchill is less popular and holds a less powerful grip on the loyalty of the people than he did even a year ago. It is likely that if the same situation existed as in World War I when Minister David Lloyd George challenged Prime Minister Asquith's leadership there would be substance to the rumors that Mr. Churchill's term is about up. The fact is that there is no outstanding leader to whom the people could turn, except perhaps Sir Stafford Cripps, who seems content for the moment to serve under Mr. Churchill's leadership.

This country is suffering from a dearth of victories. It is tired of retreats, of Dunkerques. It is disillusioned with defensive psychology, and it is beginning to be fed up with oratorical eloquence, unmatched by successes on the field of battle. In short, the people here who were willing to accept the will for the deed during the period from Dunkerque to the German retreat from Moscow are now demanding action.

Victories would restore that confidence. More defeats will destroy what is left of it. It is beginning to be whispered about that Mr. Churchill is too much under the influence of such members of his kitchen cabinet as Professor Frederick A. Lindemann, his economic adviser, and Major Gen. Hastings Ismay, his personal chief of staff.

Mr. Churchill is caught between two political fires now. His Tory associates have begun to say that perhaps Britain has "had the best of him." They complain that he is too friendly with the Left. The Laborites, on the other hand, hold that he is not enough so.

But he has guided the country safely through the darkest period of its history, and the British people will not turn to another for leadership until they are satisfied that they are getting something more than they have already. Britain, which fought so long alone, now has powerful allies in Russia and the United States, both brought into the war not through their choosing but by Axis aggression. ◊

Prime Minister Churchill in a familiar pose, 1942.

TOKYO DESCRIBES CORREGIDOR'S END

Wainwright Called 'Haggard' as He Advanced to Foe's Lines With White Flag

TOYKO, May 10 (From Japanese broadcasts recorded by The Associated Press)— Nichi Nichi's correspondent today gave the following "eye-witness account" of the surrender of United States Lieut. Gen. Jonathan M. Wainwright at Corregidor:

"The surrender of the American commander was one of the most pathetic scenes witnessed by Japanese expeditionary forces in the Philippines.

"The initial step in the surrender of the American forces came when the six-foot-high American commander, haggard from lack of sleep and from worry, advanced toward the Japanese lines, carrying a white flag and accompanied by his aides.

"Ushered into the room of the Japanese commander, General Wainwright slumped into a chair offered him by one of the Japanese officers.

General Douglas MacArthur (right) with Lieut. Gen. Jonathan M. Wainwright, 1942.

"The defeated American commander presented a pitiful sight, as he sat in the faint glimmer of a candle light, his head held in both hands, his eyes staring at the ground. In the barren room the candle light played on the three stars on Wainwright's lapels as he awaited the entrance of the Japanese commander.

FOE'S CHIEF GRIPS SWORD

"When the Japanese commander entered the room with his hands gripping the handle of a sword, Wainwright and his aides stood up at rigid attention and saluted. The look of fatigue vanished from the faces of the American soldiers and they showed they were soldiers above all.

"After a few minutes of impressive silence the Japanese commander asked Wainwright if all the Filipino-Ameri-

---

Editorial
MIRACLE OF MALTA

When Hitler said, "There are no islands any more," he overlooked Malta. As an island Malta is insignificant and, except for its strategic position in the Mediterranean, might easily be overlooked. With its smaller neighbor Gozo it covers only 122 square miles. But this rock in the sea has had more bombs dropped on it than any comparable area in the world. For almost two years the hail of explosives from more than 2,200 air raids has never ceased. Three-quarters of its buildings are in ruins. Thousands of its people have been killed. Yet Malta is still an unconquered fortress.

Napoleon called Malta "the strongest island in all Europe." That was when he thought he could conquer England, but before Helgoland had been fortified. But Malta has withstood the most continuous assault ever launched against so small a place. It was attacked within twenty-four hours of Italy's declaration of war. Mussolini thought he could occupy it in three weeks. A year ago the Germans took over his unfinished task. No one can say they have not been efficient and persistent. So far they have lost more than 1,500 planes trying. But British and now American planes still rise in the air to meet them, plane for plane, and they must chance the most concen-

trated anti-aircraft fire on earth.

The British mean to hold Malta to the death. They have just sent Lord Gort, one of their most dogged fighters, to direct its defense. Bombs fell on the court where he was being sworn in. They fall almost every day, sometimes every hour. But the Maltese are as hard to terrorize as the British. For supreme courage under fire the King last month awarded the civilians of Malta the George Cross, now treasured in their cathedral. No other portion of the British Commonwealth has ever received such a distinction. None has better earned it. ◆

can forces were ready to surrender. On failing to receive a prompt reply, the Japanese commander told Wainwright he did not want to waste any time in mere talk if his terms for unconditional surrender were not accepted. He made it clear to Wainwright that the Japanese were prepared to wipe out the American troops if they wished to continue resistance and told Wainwright frankly that he could go back and prolong the struggle if he so desired.

"Wainwright replied frankly that he had come to talk surrender, whereupon the Japanese commander asked him to issue an order for all American-Filipino troops in the Philippines to lay down their arms.

"Wainwright informed the Japanese commander that this was rather hard for him to carry out, as the Filipino-American forces, though technically under his supreme command, were "scattered throughout the islands and there was a possibility that they would not obey his orders to the letter.

"Wainwright, however, promised that the entire Filipino-American forces on Corregidor as well as on the islands in Manila Bay would surrender according to his orders.

"The Japanese commander finally consented to accept Wainwright's offer, as a result of which fighting was brought to an end on Corregidor Island." ◆

MAY 22, 1942

WILLOW RUN PLANT A WONDER OF WAR
Seemingly Large Enough To Hold a City, It Is About Ready for Giant Output Of Bombers

By SIDNEY M. SHALETT
Special to The New York Times.

DETROIT, May 21—There she stood—one of the seven wonders of the world of war; vast enough to swallow up an entire city; awesome enough to reduce man, her creator, to a lost speck in a jungle of giant machines.

The name is Willow Run. Mark it. If America's coming offensive depends on her power to blast, and blast hard, from the air, the news learned here yesterday may presage one of the turning points of the battle of production. For Willow Run, the big bomber factory which "Charlie" Sorensen described as "the invitation for Hitler to commit suicide," is "just about on the edge of turning over and becoming a real plant."

Newspaper correspondents on the "Production for Victory" tour arranged by the National Association of Manufacturers yesterday visited the Willow Run plant in the Detroit area and saw the first bomber that has made a test run of an assembly line unparalleled in the history of airplane manufacture. It was a monster Consolidated B-24-E, a bomber in the size-class of the Boeing Flying Fortress.

They also heard Edsel Ford, president, and Charles E. Sorensen, vice president, of the Ford Motor Company, which will operate the plant for the government, explain how their stupendous dies and presses will stamp out the big bombers almost as easily as Model T's once were produced.

Bombers are not the only things on the crowded schedule in Henry Ford's industrial empire. There are at least fourteen major jobs, including the Army's new model medium tanks which Mr. Sorensen considers much better powered than the German tanks; a Pratt & Whitney airplane engine (the 2,000th of which was completed recently); another aviation engine; various types of armored cars, precision aircraft parts and high precision fire-control instruments. Then there is a new tank engine of the liquid-cooled V-8 type.

As Mr. Sorensen put it, "Ford is ninety-nine and nine-tenths converted to war industry," and, as Edsel Ford announced, its employment today is as large as it was in peacetime and probably will be doubled by the end of the year.

But it was the Willow Run plant that made the executives leave their desks and ride a bus across the Michigan countryside to show it off. Financed by the government and operated by Mr. Ford, the huge factory stands on a site that was a farm field covered with soy-bean stubble only thirteen months ago. Mr. Sorensen—his colleagues call him Charlie—pointed out pridefully that even now the machine-installation crews were pushing the still-working contractors out of the last incompleted stretch. Edsel Ford, a quiet son of a famous father, fiddled in his pocket as the bus neared the war plant and said: "I guess I'd better get out my badge."

ELDER FORD GREETS VISITORS
Henry Ford, too, walking with a springy step despite his nearly eighty years, was waiting to greet the visitors. The elder Ford smiled warmly as he shook hands, and the son, looking at his father affectionately, said: "He put a lot of his own ideas into this place. He's quite proud of it."

It loomed there, an unbelievable symbol of the machine and bomb age. Great doors, which one day will spit ▶

View of the former Ford Willow Run plant after its wartime conversion where workers lay out and construct parts for military airplane wings, near Ypsilanti, Michigan, 1942.

◀ out the big bombers, yawned open. A mammoth air field and concrete apron made a crisscrossed lap for the giant.

The newspaper men on the "Production for Victory" tour have been cooperating with Army and Navy censors in observing regulations against printing anything that would give aid and comfort to the enemy. Mr. Sorensen, the Danish-born mechanic who teamed up with Henry Ford at the beginning of the Dearborn days and rose through the years to the vice presidency of the company, felt "cramped" by some of the rulings. Making a sweeping gesture within the incredible confines of the factory, he said in a voice that had a bite in it:

"Bring the Germans and Japs in to see it—hell, they'd blow their brains out."

ENTHUSIASM AMONG OFFICIALS

This is only the sketchiest description of the way the planes will come off at Willow Run, but it may be said that the system looked convincing, and the parts being run through sections of the line yesterday seemed extremely well-fashioned. The place suggested tremendously exciting possibilities in the turning out of sky-commanding bombers along automobile mass-production lines, and it was easy to catch the enthusiasm that Mr. Sorensen, Mr. Ford and the other officials displayed. Once it gets moving, it should be the most amazing sight in plane manufacture anywhere in the world. ◆

MAY 24, 1942

GERMAN DRIVE AND 'SECOND FRONT' LOOM LARGER
Next Developments in Europe Hang on Outcome of Russian Fighting

By HANSON W. BALDWIN

The gradual increase in the tempo of the Russian fighting and the arrival of more American troops in Northern Ireland focused attention last week on probable Nazi moves in Europe and possible counter-operations of the United Nations.

One week of May remains and the Nazis have not yet opened the gigantic offensive against the Red armies which has so long been expected. Last year the Nazis did not move against the Russians until June 22, but the prior Balkan campaign unquestionably delayed their attack. This year there is no second land front in Europe, and the warm sun of late Spring is drying the vast plains of Western Russia. In the south the ground for some weeks has been fit for the passage of land armies, yet the Nazis have launched only a preliminary and localized but significant offensive, which has resulted in the taking of the Kerch Peninsula in the Crimea and a localized counter-drive south of Kharkov.

GERMAN PRESSURE

However, yesterday's news showed that German pressure was gradually building up from Taganrog to Kharkov and that the initiative in the Kharkov sector was passing, as expected, to the Nazis. The "big push" may come at any time.

There is as yet not much reason for surprise at what some observers believe to be Hitler's new Fabian tactics. For actually it is premature to say that the German Spring offensive has been delayed. The ground in the central and northern fronts in many places is still covered with melting snow patches and vast acreage of mud. In Karelia and in the northern tundra, dispatches from Russia last week reported, lakes and swamps are still frozen, though not sufficiently to bear the weight of man and his war machines.

In parts of the central and most of the northern fronts, therefore, this is still a period of thaw—the period when land armies are chained and bogged down by water and mud. This period is rapidly passing, and if Hitler does not move against Russia, or elsewhere, in great force within the next three weeks, there will then be sufficient reason for surprise and perhaps new evaluation of Nazi plans, strength and weakness.

There is as yet no certainty that Hitler's first great blow of 1942 will be against Russia, though the blow there is most probable. Hitler might strike against Britain. Some observers believe that he could land several hundred thousand troops by transports and gliders in Britain during the course of three or four nights and that these troops might seize and establish village strong points and perhaps eventually several beach-heads by which they would be reinforced by sea-borne troops—if necessary at the cost of sacrificing the entire Germany Navy in the action.

Such a blow against Britain is possible at any time. So, too, is an air-borne and amphibious expedition against Cyprus, Syria and the coast of the Levant from bases in the Dodecanese and the Greek islands, or (less likely) a land push through Turkey. Either of these moves would probably be accompanied by one toward Suez by General Erwin Rommel, commanding the North Africa Corps in Libya, and the Summer heat of the desert can be expected to hamper but not to prevent altogether such a drive.

OFFENSIVE IN RUSSIA

Though these possibilities exist, a German offensive in Russia still seems far more probable, and it is likely that the battles that are now joined are actually the start of a fierce Summer of conflict between the armies of Stalin and Hitler. The limited operations now under way may gradually be enlarged until the whole 2,000 miles of Russian "front" are aflame once again, as it was last Summer and Autumn.

And it is quite possible, indeed probable, that the German drive may have considerable successes—successes so large that the establishment of a "second front" becomes imperative as a diversionary measure. It is also possible that the Germans will sustain major reverses—reverses so considerable that a "second front" will become feasible and desirable urgency but as a step toward exploitation of the enemy's weakness and victory quicker than it could be achieved without that step.

In any case, an attempt to establish a foothold upon the Continent of Europe may be one of the moves the United Nations will make this year, though the shipping shortage, our long lines of communication and our lack of readiness for a major strategic offensive would handicap any such operation. The arrival of more American troops in Northern Ireland last week concentrated attention upon this possibility, but the successful transport of troops across the Atlantic certainly does not imply that the United

MAY 31, 1942

HEYDRICH ATTACK LAID TO 'CHUTISTS
Germans Execute 44 More in Hunt for Men Who Bombed Nazi in Czechoslovakia

LONDON, May 30 (AP)—The Germans were reported tonight working on the theory that parachutists dropped from foreign planes had a hand in the attempted assassination of Reinhard Heydrich, Protector of Bohemia and Moravia, as the Gestapo speeded its executions of Czechs to a total of sixty-two, putting to death forty-four during the day.

The German-controlled radio in Prague stated flatly that foreign saboteurs had landed by parachute in Bohemia and Moravia. It said some of those executed "had been convicted of having sheltered agents who had landed in the protectorate from airplanes by parachute in order to perpetrate acts of sabotage."

Ten women were among the forty-four executed today by the Germans in ruthless reprisal for the attack upon Herr Heydrich, the Gestapo's second in command, who was critically wounded.

The Prague radio announced the latest victims died before firing squads immediately after they were sentenced by a quick-action Nazi court-martial. Up to today eighteen Czechs had been shot following the attack Wednesday upon Herr Heydrich, Adolf Hitler's Protector for Bohemia and Moravia, the German-ruled remnants of dismembered Czechoslovakia.

All of those executed were accused of failing to register with the police or harboring or aiding unregistered persons accused of anti-German activities.

The executions today were carried out at Prague and Bruenn, said the announcement from Prague. The youngest victim was 18 years old. The others included two former officers of the Czech Army and a former public prosecutor. The State confiscated the victims' property.

Nations are immediately ready for any attempt to invade Europe. The troops that arrived in Northern Ireland included units plainly identifiable as armored forces, and the convoy was said to be the largest yet, including "thousands upon thousands" of American "dog-faces" (the 1942 slang for "doughboys"). But it takes many thousands (about 16,000) to make one division, and our forces in the British Isles certainly cannot yet be large—measured in divisions—beside the forty to 100 divisions the Germans and their allies may be able to concentrate in Western Europe.

Moreover, the British air offensive—in itself a "second front" of the air—has not yet reached its peak; American planes piloted by Americans have not yet augmented the weight of the British raids and British air superiority is not yet decisive enough to permit much hope of immediate invasion. And there is always the problem of shipping; it takes about 100,000 ship tons to move one division.

COMMANDO RAIDS
Despite these difficulties the "second front" on land in Europe remains a possibility. It may take many forms. It will certainly take the form of Commando raids, intensified, enlarged, striking at German submarine bases and military objectives of all sorts—harassing, worrying and chivvying the enemy.

If we should attempt more than an intensive bombardment of the Reich, more than intensified and repeated commando raids, the land offensives of the United Nations might take shape: (1) in Russia by the Red armies; (2) in North Africa by the British supported by their allies; (3) against Sardinia or other Italian points; (4) on the coast of Western Europe.

Either of the first two offensives is quite possible—though probably for the time being on a limited scale. An invasion of Sardinia, Italy and Sicily or other Mediterranean points is probably impractical until such time as the enemy is driven out of his position in North Africa.

An attempt to establish a foothold in Western Europe would be fraught with hazard, but so is all war. Any landing on the coast of France or in the Low Countries might be covered by air power based on Britain and it is quite probable that the British—so long as the Russian armies remain in being—could establish a local air superiority sufficient to permit a landing.

CHIEF INVASION PROBLEM
The communications network of France and the Low Countries and the large numbers of airfields in this area would permit a very rapid concentration by the enemy against any United Nations beach-head. The problem clearly is not so much in making a landing—that probably could be done at a number of points—but in maintaining a foothold once the landing was made, against ground forces that are almost certain to be superior in numbers to our own. Our numerical inferiority might be compensated in part by air superiority (established from near-by British bases) and mechanized superiority; yet we might have to face the possibility of eventually being pushed back into the sea.

The establishment of a "second front," therefore, would require the frank facing of grave risks. For the immediate months to come—unless Germany is defeated in Russia—the odds against success would be large.

But the power of the United Nations is slowly growing, and the "second front" in the air above Western Europe is becoming a tangible and effective instrument in the strategy of victory. A "second front" on land may well have to be the product of opportunistic strategy, but the "second front" in the air plus strong Russian resistance may in time help to provide that opportunity. Much, indeed most, depends on the Russian armies. ◊

COMPLETE RECOVERY DOUBTED
Herr Heydrich, whose orders have resulted in the deaths of several hundred recalcitrants and innocent hostages in occupied France, was reported in a serious condition and injured so severely that should he live he probably would be forever a crippled invalid.

The car in which he was riding from Prague to Munich was said to have been waylaid by assailants who tossed a bomb and followed up with a burst of gunfire. Herr Heydrich was reported to have been wounded in the back and spine.

Czech circles here said the firing squad victims all died proudly with their lips sealed.

Heinrich Himmler was reported directing the manhunt for his assistant's assailants, and the Prague radio broadcast purported descriptions of the men, one of whom was declared wounded. Rewards of the equivalent of $250,000 were first offered for information leading to arrests. A Prague broadcast later announced that the reward had been doubled. ◊

JUNE 1, 1942

COLOGNE 'INFERNO' ASTONISHES PILOTS
Defenses Overwhelmed, British Fliers Say— Germans on Air Describe Horrors

By The United Press.

LONDON, May 31—Seven-eighths of Cologne, a city the size of Boston, was in flames, an inferno "almost too gigantic to be real," when the history-making raid was over last night, pilots who took part in it said tonight.

"When we got there, I almost felt like leaving and trying to find another target. It didn't seem possible to do more damage than had already been done," Wing Commander Johnny Fauquier, Canadian pilot officer, related.

"Cologne was just a sea of flames," said Squadron Leader Len Frazer of Winnipeg, one of the more than 1,000 Canadian airmen who had a hand in the epic raid.

"I saw London burning during the Battle of Britain, and it was nothing compared with Cologne," Pilot Officer H. J. M. Lacelle of Toronto, gunner in the tail of a Canadian bomber, contributed.

Members of the Royal Air Force who helped to make history over Cologne in the early hours of May 31, 1942

Their reports were typical of the thousands being sifted tonight and compiled into a record of the mightiest piece of destruction ever devised by man.

DEFENSES OVERWHELMED

The lurid sky over Cologne for ninety minutes was as busy as Piccadilly Circus as the great Lancasters and Halifaxes, Stirlings and Manchesters, streaked in at the rate of one every six seconds to unload their total cargo of steel-cased death.

Before the overwhelmed and bewildered German defenses could focus on one plane, it was zooming away and another was on its tail. The Royal Air Force plan of super-saturating the enemy's target field was described as an absolute success. German fighter planes were there, but not enough to interfere seriously with the attack.

"It was almost too gigantic to be real," said the pilot of one Halifax. "But it was real enough when we got there. Below us in every part of the city buildings were ablaze. Here and there you could see their outlines, but mostly it was just one big stretch of fire.

"It was strange to see the flames reflected on our aircraft. It looked at times as if we were on fire ourselves, with the red glow dancing up and down our wings."

"I could identify every type of bomber in our force by the light of the moon and fires," another said.

Many of the airmen had been in the bombings of Rostock and Luebeck, and they said Cologne made those places look like a warm-up. ◊

JUNE 4, 1942

All Alaska Put On Alert

JUNEAU, Alaska, June 3 (AP)—Governor Ernest Gruening called today for all civilian defense units in Alaska to be on the alert following the first Japanese raid against the northern territory at Dutch Harbor. His statement said:

"To the people of Alaska:

"An anticipated air raid on Alaska began this morning with an attack by Japanese planes on Dutch Harbor.

"Our Army and Navy are rendering an excellent account of themselves. All civilian defense units should remain on the alert. Details, as deemed advisable, will be released in time by the military authorities."

A report was received from Ketchikan, 1,200 miles to the south, that it underwent a 20-minute alert at 9:50 A. M., approximately one hour after the raid on Dutch Harbor. [There is a three-hour time difference between Dutch Harbor and Southeastern Alaska.] ◊

JUNE 7, 1942

'What Can I Do To Help Win the War?'

By Anita Brenner

"I am a civilian. What is my place in the war?" This question, underscored by news of America formidably on the move, by the beginning of rationing and by appeals from many different kinds of organizations, is foremost in the mind of a host of Americans. It is a question just beginning to be fully grasped, even by those who went through the last war as adults, for now it is realized that the line between fighter and civilian has been erased and the war job of each is only a matter of circumstance and degree. There are some who put the question the old way, "How will the war affect me?" But the majority turn it actively into this: "What is my job? What can I do that will count most toward winning, and winning faster?"

How is it answered? To this reporter, who made inquiries among New Yorkers of every degree, has come a wide variety of answers and from all of them one important fact emerges: If the mood of New York is any clue to the nation's state of mind, there is no apathy or complacence among us. Nor is there fear; there is a complete sense of certainty as to the outcome of the war. Our strength and capacity are taken as a matter of fact. But when we shall win depends, every citizen seems to feel, on how quickly and efficiently every American gets in on the job.

"We're on the spot; this is no time for politics," they say. "We've got what it takes—men, materials, plants. We've got started at last. Now let's clean out all the business-as-usual and the politics-as-usual and get a hump on."

Along with this forthrightness there is another attitude, a feeling rather than a clear idea, which can be summarized more or less thus: "Why do we have to wait for the government to organize everything? The government has enough on its hands in getting war stuff out and troops going. Let the government tell us what is needed; we don't have to sit around until somebody behind a desk gets it all set up on paper. Give us the facts. We'll do the job. Washington hasn't even begun to tap our skills and resources. What are they waiting for?"

But most people do not feel that they can find, by themselves, the place where what they can do will count heavily. Some are satisfied with what they have found to do, but many are not, and are asking for more information, organization and direction. Right now they are first of all trying to decide this question: "Shall I continue with my job as usual, and give all left-over time to some volunteer work, or shall I try to shift my work to something directly essential for war and protection?" The answers that many New Yorkers have found depend, of course, on individual circumstances, but here are representative stories of how the question looks to some people and what they are doing about it.

"I'm Joe Smith. I work in a lunch counter. I've got dependents, so I can't enlist, but it's plain to me that what I'm doing is entirely superfluous. Sure, people have to eat, but any girl can do what I'm doing. So I've been scouting around and I'm lined up now for heavy work in a war industry plant. Pay is about the same, and the job is harder to get to from where I live, but I'm sick of hearing the news and then listening to some customer or other complaining about sugar. Say, some people don't seem to know how lucky we've been, or have any idea of what's coming. We'd better all pitch in and help keep what we've got, or else! Those Japs ain't doll babies. Sure we can lick 'em, if—if. So I'm shifting."

"I'm May Green, I'm an insurance clerk. I work from 9 to 5, been there for some time. I don't have any family to look after so I have plenty of time, but it didn't seem to fit in with the hours for most women's volunteer work. I'd read that in England women were used in plane-detector stations and I thought that's work I can do at night. I had a hard time finding where to go and how to enroll for training, and finally I wrote a letter to a newspaper and they told me. They were swell. So I'm in now. It's grand. I work three or four times a week from 4 A.M. to 8 A.M. It's exciting, and I know I'm doing something useful, so the news doesn't get me down the way it did."

"My name's Cohen. I'm a manufacturer of children's clothing. My family's all grown up, my boy's in the Army. I've been an air raid warden from the start. I'm running the plant. I've been looking around to find out how to turn it into war work, but they don't seem to have got around yet to the little factories, even though I hear we amount to about 50 per cent of the manufacturing in the country. Don't know how true it is. Anyway, I've been thinking of closing up and enlisting in any service that will have me. This is an emergency, there's an increasing shortage of materials, and I sure don't feel like sitting around and trying to do business as usual."

"I don't work—I just take care of my mother. We live in a slum section and there are a lot of children in the apartment house. For a long time I've felt that those children don't get much sympathy or attention, so I got into the habit of taking them to the playground, or reading to them, just being with them. I thought I might as well enroll in some courses and learn more about it; I can at least help look after the ones in my neighborhood. I heard that many day-nursery workers now—and I hear the day nurseries are getting crowded and new ones are going to be opened up. I could volunteer there. I heard that many day-nursery workers are rushing off to do war work, but it seems to me taking care of children is just as essential as anything, and it's certainly something I can do. So I'm training for that."

"I'm a school teacher. My husband's a fire warden and I enrolled in first-aid courses. When I got through, I felt better because I knew something, but in another way I realized that people like me really couldn't do much for the injured except see that they aren't moved around, and maybe stop flowing blood. In my apartment house there are twenty tenants. We got together and divided up the work; a chemist took charge of learning about bombs and fires and what to do, and one woman took charge of tracking down rumors and checking them against the news, to help fight fears and panics. I found a nurse on the floor above, and we located a couple of doctors, and we have a real first-aid unit now. Then we set up, in the safest part of the building, a child-care station. I'm the child warden."

These and many other stories of civilian defense at the grass—or macadam—roots may not all contain the efficient and desirable answers to the questions that have been raised, but they do reveal that the human essentials for waging and winning a total war, and not losing democracy in the process, are with us. One is told, over and over, in many ways: "We are not children. Morale for us is not something that must be created by propaganda. We don't need speeches to tell us we are in danger, nor soothing news to make us work, nor Mickey Mouse to sell us bonds and stamps. We'd rather have the facts, know where we are, know what to do, get a chance to do it."

One is thus told, by civilians, specifically what civilians think is needed for working together fast and efficiently: (1) organization, with neighborhood bureaus if possible; (2) information, published daily, of what or who is needed where; (3) placement for action. This way of talking and acting reveals, too, what a gulf there is between ourselves and fear-ridden, official-driven peoples. And it discloses again the ultimate sources of American strength—the energy, initiative, common sense and social responsibility of the American people. ◊

JUNE 8, 1942

WEST COAST FINISHES REMOVING JAPANESE
100,000 Sent Inland, Leaving Only the Incapacitated

SAN FRANCISCO, June 7 (AP)—Evacuation of the Western seaboard's entire Japanese population, a mass movement described officially as without precedent in American history, has been completed.

Except for a handful of ill or otherwise incapacitated persons and a ⟩

(still smaller number considered irreplaceable in their work, not one of about 100,000 Japanese remained at liberty today in that roughly 150-mile-wide strip of the three Coast States and Arizona which was their home when war began.

Most of the 99,770 actually removed were congregated in the seventeen assembly centers, the receiving points established by the Army to make quick control possible pending the slower arrangements for permanent resettlement.

Some thousands already have gone to inland relocation centers, of which three are ready now. Others are being built and sites for still more are being acquired. A considerable number have volunteered for farm work on private lands well in the interior.

This is the second phase of the evacuation program, but the first and militarily important step, the actual removal of the Japanese from their homes in the zone where the Army believes their presence might be dangerous, has been achieved.

Furthermore, said the Wartime Civil Control Administration, the transfer was made "within the time designated, without mischance, with minimum hardship and almost without incident." ◆

JUNE 8, 1942

Report by Admiral King

By C. BROOKS PETERS
Special to The New York Times.

WASHINGTON, June 7—Two battles between American and Japanese naval and air forces are in progress in the Pacific and their final outcome may well decide the course of the war in that ocean, Admiral Ernest J. King, Commander in Chief of the United States Fleet, told reporters this afternoon.

One of the battles is being fought west of Midway Island, and the other in the vicinity of Dutch Harbor, in the Aleutian Islands.

The Japanese forces that attempted to assault Midway represented the bulk of the enemy's naval strength, Admiral King declared, and their objective was to capture that vital outpost of the Hawaiian Islands. The islands, he added, "must be held at all costs" because they are the key to our entire Pacific defense system.

A communiqué received yesterday from the headquarters of Admiral Chester W. Nimitz, Commander in Chief of the United States Pacific Fleet, said that two or three enemy aircraft carriers had been sunk in the Midway engagement and that eleven or twelve other vessels, including three battleships, had been damaged.

"In comparison with the losses of the enemy," Admiral King declared today, "United States losses are inconsiderable."

Naval operations are still in progress from the Hawaiian Islands to the Aleutians, Admiral King said. Although the enemy's forces have taken some hard knocks, he added, "I would not say they have been defeated yet; they have 'withdrawn.'"

The situation in the Dutch Harbor area, where the Japanese made an aerial assault last Wednesday, remains obscure, the admiral declared. This was the first official indication that action in that region had continued after Wednesday's raid.

The reason for this obscurity, the admiral explained, is that the weather in the Dutch Harbor area has been bad for the last several days and, therefore, contact with the enemy has been intermittent. Also, Admiral King depends on the ability of the local commanders to master situations, along a line set down by general orders issued in Washington, and does not require the relaying to the capital of more than a minimum of information.

"We have none too clear a picture about what is going on up there," Admiral King stated, "but it is going on."

Most of the admiral's observations, given in replies to reporters' questions and in a prepared statement, were devoted to the Midway Island engagement and the events leading up to it. This battle in particular, he declared, may decide the course of the war in the Pacific, but to what extent will depend on the damage inflicted on the Japanese forces engaged.

Asked whether the Japanese had thrown everything into their endeavor to assault Midway, Admiral King replied: "Perhaps not everything, but the bulk of it. One of their methods of doing things is not to send a boy to do a man's job."

The Commander in Chief said that it was obvious that the losses suffered by the Japanese had weakened them for future offensive action. Both the Midway and Coral Sea battles have reduced the naval strength of the Japanese, he continued, and "their capacity to replace their losses is all too obviously not equal to our capacity."

Admiral King indicated, however, that although the Japanese had suffered telling losses in the Midway battle, it was unlikely that our forces would endeavor

JUNE 11, 1942

Nazis Blot Out Czech Village; Kill All Men, Disperse Others

By The Associated Press.

BERLIN, June 10 (From German broadcasts recorded in New York)—All men in the Czechoslovak town of Lidice have been shot, the women sent to concentration camps, the children placed in "educational institutions" and the town itself "leveled to the ground" on the charge that the population gave shelter and assistance to the slayers of the Nazi leader Reinhard Heydrich, the Berlin radio announced tonight.

The announcement, quoting an official statement issued in Prague, gave the population of Lidice as 483. [Czechoslovak sources in London said the population was 1,200.] The town was utterly wiped off the map, the statement made clear, by noting that "the name of the community was extinguished."

The German radio said:

to pursue them and to assault them in their home waters.

MOPPING UP IS PERILOUS

"They still have a great deal of shore-based air power, as they found we had in the Coral Sea victory and at Midway," the admiral declared. "For us to rush in in a mop-up action might not be well-advised."

This point, Admiral King emphasized, is important because, "with 130,000,000 amateur strategists in this country, many would undoubtedly advocate some such follow-up action."

Today's press conference, the first held by Admiral King since he took over command of our Navy, came six months to the day after the Japanese assault on Pearl Harbor.

Following the successful bombing of Tokyo and other Japanese cities in April, the admiral said, American military leaders anticipated assaults on Midway and Alaska.

"The force they [the Japanese] had at hand and the general military situation could mean nothing but that they would try to break out somewhere because they could not afford to sit idle while Australia and other bastions threatened their existence and grew steadily stronger," Admiral King explained. ◆

"The following official announcement was made Wednesday evening concerning the extermination of the township of Lidice near Kladno in the Protectorate:

"'The investigation of the murder committed on Deputy Reich Protector for Bohemia and Moravia, S. S. [Elite Guard] Upper Group Leader Reinhard Heydrich, revealed beyond doubt that the population of the township of Lidice, near Kladno, gave shelter and assisted the murderers.

"'In addition evidence was found of hostile actions committed against the Reich. Subversive printed matter as well as arms and ammunition dumps, an illegal radio transmitting station and huge supplies of rationed commodities were discovered.

"'In addition, the fact was ascertained that inhabitants of this township were in active service of the enemy abroad.

"'After these facts had been ascertained all male grownups of the town were shot, while the women were placed in a concentration camp, and the children were entrusted to appropriate educational institutions.

"'The township was leveled to the ground and the name of the community extinguished. The inhabitants of Lidice near Kladno numbered 483.'" ◆

JUNE 13, 1942

Gandhi Seeks to Oust U.S.-British Forces

NEW DELHI, India, June 12 (UP)—Mohandas K. Gandhi is about to unleash a large-scale "quit India" campaign in which American as well as British forces will be urged to get out of India immediately.

Reports from his headquarters at Wardha indicated today that he had won for such a movement the unqualified support of Maulana Abul Kalam Azad, President of the All-India Congress party. Pandit Jawaharlal Nehru, most influential party member, a few days ago endorsed the campaign.

Before launching the campaign Mr. Gandhi wants the formal approval of the party's working committee, which is expected to meet at the end of this month or early in July. ◆

JUNE 21, 1942

The Leaders Meet Grand Strategy Studied

The advance guard of America's armed might was spread around the world last week. Strong ground units were in Ireland in the Atlantic, Australia in the Pacific. United States airmen were guarding the nation's coasts and the coasts of the nations to the south, they were fighting in the Aleutian Islands, China, the Southwestern Pacific, the Black Sea and the Mediterranean. In some places they were few, in others many; but they seemed to be everywhere.

Against this world-wide background President Roosevelt and Prime Minister Churchill met unexpectedly to talk, according to an official announcement, "of the war, the conduct of the war and the winning of the war." The British leader had arrived suddenly, his time of arrival, the way of his coming, closely guarded secrets. The two statesmen, flanked by their highest generals, opened a series of conferences. The most important question before them was where the full strength of their two nations was to be employed.

The question was not easy to answer. Russia, hard pressed at Sevastopol, wanted a second front in Europe to help ease the strain. The British Eighth Army, fighting to stave off disaster in Libya, required reinforcements. From China came calls for help, for Japanese columns were crawling closer to her vital communication points, cities. The great danger was that in attempting to answer all these calls, Britain and America might disperse their strength, dissipate their striking power.

The meeting between the executive chieftains of the two great English-speaking democracies was their third in ten months. From the first, the dramatic meeting at sea last August, came the Atlantic Charter.

SECOND CONCLAVE

The second Churchill-Roosevelt meeting was held in the White House last December and January. It sought to tighten the cooperation between England and her new ally, America. From it came a combined chiefs of staff group to plan joint military operations, committees for joint control of raw materials, munitions and shipping. On the groundwork it laid, combined boards for war production and food have since been erected.

Decisions on the problems of grand strategy reached at the third meeting are not likely to become known through joint statements from the two statesmen; they will be revealed in battle communiqués weeks, months from now.

BATTLE FOR EGYPT

The Nazis hammered at the gates of Egypt last week. Squat German tanks, guns firing, were roaring over the coastal plain. Part of the British Eighth Army was retiring eastward from Tobruk toward the border, eighty miles away. Behind, in battered Tobruk, General Neil Metheun Ritchie had left a garrison which may have to hold out, as another garrison did in the Summer months of last year, against protracted Axis siege.

Tobruk, many observers thought, was the key. If it were stormed and lost the road would be open for a Nazi attempt to drive eastward toward Suez, possibly beyond. Such a campaign, it has been believed, might coincide with an invasion by the Wehrmacht of the Caucasus, thus forming a giant pincers move which would envelop the Mediterranean, the entire Near East.

A THORN TO ROMMEL

Seven months have passed since British forces last November relieved the first siege of Tobruk. For seven months before that they had held the town, reduced to rubble, against repeated onslaughts. Tobruk last Summer became an Allied symbol of resistance. To Marshal Erwin Rommel, Axis commander, it was a thorn in his flank; it hindered a drive across the Egyptian frontier toward Suez.

The events leading up to the second encirclement of Tobruk followed the now familiar pattern of desert war. In the first move of Libya's sixth campaign Marshal Rommel struck out three weeks ago to pierce a British defensive system strung southward through the desert from the coast forty miles west of Tobruk. The British met the onslaught with new tank units, including American-built "General Grants," "General Lees" and the light "Honeys." For nearly a week, the struggle swirled back and forth until the initial energies of both sides were exhausted. But the equipment of the Africa Corps of Marshal Rommel came through better than that of the desert armies of the British. The Germans renewed the fight.

Through a breach in the defense line, the Axis commanders manoeuvred their tanks in a series of encircling thrusts. One cleaned out, after a fiercely pressed siege, the Free French garrison of Bir Hacheim, southernmost anchor of the line. Others swept northward and eastward, curved toward the coast. British tank units south and east of ❯

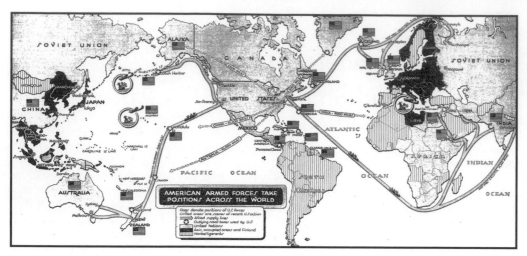

AMERICAN ARMED FORCES TAKE POSITIONS ACROSS THE WORLD

❬ Tobruk faced a trap. The Axis vanguard reached the coastal plain around the port just after most of the weakened British armies had withdrawn.

Realization of the crucial importance of holding her Mediterranean outposts prompted desperate actions by Britain's Navy. Two convoys were sent out; one to Tobruk, the other to beleaguered Malta, one from Alexandria, the other from Gibraltar. Their coming roused the greatest sea-and-air action ever fought in the area. Germany and Italy sent waves of planes, scores of U-boats and strong squadrons of Italian battleships, cruisers and destroyers to intercept the ships. American Army planes participated in the action, were credited with badly mauling Italy's sea strength. The convoys, London said, got through.

RUSSIA'S BLOODY YEAR

Today, on the last day of the first year of their campaign in Russia, the German armies are still fighting far short of the goal they set out to reach at dawn on June 22, 1941. Behind them lie the greatest victories and the severest setbacks ever to come to Hitler's Wehrmacht. The Russians have estimated upward of 5,600,000 Germans killed, wounded and captured; Berlin four months ago admitted 1,500,000 casualties. In the initial five months of the year the German soldiers overran 500,000 square miles of territory with 42,500,000 people. In five months of Winter war they lost one-fifth of the conquered area to Russian counter-attacks. The coming of Spring brought local battles on the southern front; a Russian offensive in the Ukraine, launched five weeks ago while the Wehrmacht was taking Kerch in the Crimea, forestalled, it was believed, the German plan for resumption of a major drive eastward toward the Caucasus and oil.

TERRIFIC TOLL

Soviet losses, in the first year of war, were likewise enormous. Six months ago, in an official estimate, Berlin claimed between 8,000,000 and 10,000,000 Red Army casualties; Moscow, more recently, has admitted close to 3,000,000 lost. Yet in those months of fighting Russian soldiers found a technique of resistance which, it appeared, blunted the Blitzkrieg and forced on the German Fuehrer an ever-lengthening war.

Last week the Soviet soldier's power of resistance was again evident in two battles raging in South Russia. Sevastopol, the citadel on the southwestern coast of the Crimea, was still in Russian hands after more than seven months of siege. For more than two weeks the Germans had pitted tanks and guns and planes in an all-out attack against the city's defenders ensconced in the limestone hills. Siege guns believed larger than the "Big Berthas" of the first World War had shelled Sevastopol's defenses, which then had been attacked repeatedly by tanks and foot soldiers. The city's people had lived out countless air raids in deep caves carved in the cliffs. "To the last soul" they had sworn "to die before surrendering."

Before Kharkov a second German offensive launched eleven days ago appeared to have been halted along the Donets River. The Wehrmacht's newest drive had been launched, so observers held, to eliminate Russian pressure on the Nazi flank and to prepare the ground for an all-out campaign across the Donets Basin, with its teeming industries, toward Rostov, gateway to the Caucasus. From there the Germans might swing south onto the oil-rich isthmus to meet Wehrmacht forces ferried across the narrow straits from Kerch, easternmost point of the Crimea.

AID FROM AMERICA

This was the threat faced by the Russian nation as the Red Army battled at Sevastopol and Kharkov. To help in staving off the danger direct aid was coming from the United States. American-made tanks and planes were on the Russian front; to these were added—the report came from Turkey, remains unconfirmed—bombers of the American Army Air Corps with American crews which had flown to participate in the defense of the Crimean bastion. From bases in the Middle East, moreover, four-motored United States "Liberators" had taken off for damaging raids on Nazi oil fields and supply dumps in Rumania. Yesterday Berlin reported that the Red Army, in a move to relieve German pressure in the south, had launched a counter-attack near Smolensk, on the central front.

JAPAN PRESSES ON

Over the far reaches of the Pacific and on the lands lapped by its northern and southwestern waters, Japan's drive for conquest ground relentlessly onward last week. Her troops fought their way over the dusty hills and valleys of China's Kiangsi Province. Her ships defied the shipwrecking williwaw of Alaska's Aleutian Islands and poked their noses into fog-shrouded inlets. Southwestward over the sea there were indications that little naval skirmishes growing out of the great Midway Island battle that had set back Japan's eastward drive were continuing here and there. Australia's Darwin and Southeastern New Guinea's Port Moresby were pounded relentlessly. At every point Japanese objectives were the same: to capture bases from which Japan could be attacked, to obtain bases from which Japan can extend her conquests, to consolidate gains.

The heaviest Japanese thrust was made in China. There are Hangchow-Nanchang railroad which might help link occupied Malaya to Japan by a safe route going most of the way over land was the objective. At the beginning of last week the Chinese still held eighty of the 450 miles of the line. Powerful Japanese columns moving from the northeast and west closed on those eighty miles in a nutcracker movement that, after bloody street fighting, forced the Chinese out of towns, narrowed the Chinese-held area. The Chinese fought back grimly, struck at the rear and flanks of the advancing Japanese columns. From Chungking came grave warnings of the danger to China in the fighting, the value of the contested area to the Japanese; suggestions that America and Britain help the hard-pressed Chinese troops with an attack from the Pacific were made. ◈

Editorial
THE FALL OF TOBRUK

In the seven months that it stood last year, surrounded by Axis forces, and hurled back every assault, Tobruk became a symbol of courage and resistance. Its sudden fall, coupled with the almost simultaneous loss of Bardia and Bir el-Gobi, is a hard blow. The explanation of Field Marshal Erwin Rommel's success repeats the weaknesses which have beset the British forces in Libya from the start. In tanks and guns Germany had both numerical and qualitative superiority. Her forces excelled in the rapid repair and servicing of mechanical equipment, in the blitzkrieg technique of using tanks, planes, and guns as an integrated assault team, and in resourcefulness of staff work and generalship. Above all, the British again suffered from the great handicap of the United Nations in having to spread their forces too thinly over too many places at the ends of long and perilous supply routes in order to meet an enemy free to strike outward from the center of the circle.

Presumably the Nazi campaign in Libya is a prelude to a full-scale assault upon Egypt in an effort to drive the British from the Mediterranean and conquer the entire Middle East. The drive may be viewed as one arm of an enormous pincer reaching toward the prize of Middle Eastern oil, the other arm being the German drive in Russia which has driven a wedge in the defenses of Sevastopol. This is a dangerous threat which must be occupying a major place in the discussions now going on between Prime Minister Churchill and President Roosevelt.

The loss of Tobruk itself is not so important as the circumstances surrounding that loss. The Nazis claim to have captured 25,000 men and large stores of material, including supplies freshly brought in by the convoy which came through the battle in the Mediterranean. If this is true it must mean that Lieut. Gen. Neil M. Ritchie's Eighth Army has been seriously weakened and that Marshal Rommel has been strengthened. He has helped to solve his own supply problem by capturing food and munitions transported at the cost of Allied ships and lives. Tobruk is not vital to the defense of Egypt, but Egypt is vital to the defense of the Middle East. The battle which now impends will be crucial. It must be won at all costs. ◊

Gen. Eisenhower Takes Up Headquarters in London

By CHARLES HURD
Special to The New York Times.

WASHINGTON, June 25—The United States today created in London the headquarters for a European theatre of operations for United States forces under command of Major Gen. Dwight D. Eisenhower, 51-year-old veteran of armored warfare. Announcement of his new post was made without elaboration, but among informed observers there was a unanimous feeling that the new office and its incumbent foreshadowed definite plans for the opening of a second front, based upon the British Isles, when circumstances and accumulation of men and arms gave promise of success in this venture.

It was understood on usually reliable authority that General Eisenhower, who arrived in London shortly before announcement of his new command, had left the United States after Prime Minister Winston Churchill had reached an agreement with President Roosevelt on the feasibility of planning for a second front, despite current setbacks in Libya and Egypt.

The second front, it is known, found receptive response in Mr. Roosevelt and was particularly urged by Maxim Litvinoff, Soviet Ambassador, as the surest means of relieving German pressure on the Soviet armies.

Additional significance was seen in the fact that the appointment was made public within a few days after the first official announcement that American troops were now in East Anglia, England, as well as on Irish soil, and encamped probably within thirty miles of the East Coast of the English Channel, now occupied by German soldiers.

General Eisenhower is considered generally to be one of the most brilliant among the younger crop of distinguished Army officers. ◊

Editorial
LIDICE, ILLINOIS

The suggestion was made in these columns on June 13 that some American town honor itself by taking the name of the Bohemian village which the Nazis announced on June 10 that they had "extinguished." They had, indeed, done all that Nazis can do. They had murdered all the men, placed all the women in internment camps, sent all the children to Nazi "schools," burned all the houses. They had done this because, as they charged, the men who eliminated Reinhard Heydrich had been sheltered in Lidice. They forgot that while a town may be physically destroyed and its people murdered, jailed or scattered it is utterly impossible to "extinguish" an idea by such methods. In its physical obliteration Lidice became immortal because it stood for three ideas that no free man can forget: first, for hospitality to fugitives who had cleansed the earth of a monster; second, for an unwavering courage and loyalty that permitted no person in the village to denounce another; third, for resistance to tyranny. Lidice, the little village, did more to keep alive the Freedom of Europe by being wiped out than the great city of Paris did, in 1940, by a surrender that kept its buildings intact.

It is, therefore, good to learn that the unincorporated Illinois town of Stern Park Gardens, near Joliet, has decided to adopt the honorable name of Lidice, in a ceremony to take place on July 12; and that funds are being collected to erect there a monument, with a flame burning perpetually "to symbolize the light of liberty which America is determined to preserve." We need tanks, planes and guns. We need symbols, too. ◊

Chapter 12
"RED VERDUN HOLDS"

July–September 1942

Two campaigns thousands of miles apart dominated the news in the summer and autumn of 1942. In the Pacific the U.S. Marine Corps opened the long campaign to wrest control of the string of Japanese-occupied islands with the landing on Guadalcanal in the Solomons on August 7. Deep in Russia, the German armed forces drove south and east toward the rich oil supplies of the Caucasus region and the city of Stalingrad on the Volga. While the German campaign was understood to be a critical one, its outcome was anything but certain. By late August the German Army had broken through to the Volga and in mid-September began a major offensive to take the city. "Red Verdun Holds" ran The Times headline, recalling the heroic defense in World War I of the French fortress. "If the Russians accomplish a miracle," noted an editorial, "the event could mark the turning of the tide."

The Soviet leaders were desperate for assistance and expected the Western Allies to open a second front somewhere in Western Europe to relieve the pressure on them. In July a Gallup Poll in America found that 48 percent of respondents wanted a second front at once, while 34 percent wanted to wait. In July Churchill and Roosevelt agreed that the best they could do was to plan a major operation in North Africa, postponing until at least 1943 any prospect of a major campaign. On August 19 a major raid was mounted on the French port of Dieppe, but the results were disastrous. It was evident that the Allies could not yet cross the Channel in force. Not surprisingly, The Times reported, "Moscow Is Bitter." What the West could do was to bomb Germany to increase pressure on the German home front. In the summer of 1942 the first units of the U.S. Eighth Air Force arrived in Britain and on August 17 conducted the first American operation against Rouen, in France. Throughout the year RAF Bomber Command conducted "area" bombing raids against the city centers of German industrial regions; these were designed to destroy civilian housing and kill civilian workers. The only ground fighting in Europe came from the Yugoslav resistance, divided between a national liberation army and Communist partisans, holding down valuable Axis divisions away from the Eastern Front.

The Times sent extra correspondents to the South Pacific to cover the start of the campaign to reverse the Japanese tide. The onset of what became the five-month Battle of Guadalcanal was a bloody engagement between the First Marine Division under Brig. General Alexander Vandegrift and the Japanese Seventeenth Army. The Marine Corps Raiders formed a tough, elite force to infiltrate Japanese lines. Troops were taught, The Times reported, "to gouge, strangle and knife." Despite repeated suicidal frontal attacks by Japanese infantry, the Marine Division captured the airfield on Guadalcanal at Lunga and the Japanese-held port at Tulagi. "It's Never Dull on Guadalcanal" ran The Times's headline in September. "If the enemy is not attacking," noted the report, "the Marines are."

Elsewhere the Japanese enjoyed greater success. In China Japanese forces continued to consolidate their grip on the central and southern regions. The Japanese Army stopped short of invading India, but cut off the long supply route along the Burma Road, originally opened up to help the Chinese Army.

In India, a political crisis loomed as Gandhi and the Indian nationalists urged Britain to promise Indian independence, while Indian Muslims looked for a solution that would protect their religious interests. On August 8 the Indian government arrested twenty-one nationalist leaders. The Times devoted significant column space to the Indian question. British imperialism was regarded as an issue in the war alongside the military struggle for survival.

JULY 1, 1942

ROMMEL IS GAINING
Reinforced U.S. Air Units Help R.A.F. Hammer Axis Army and Assault Tobruk

By RAYMOND DANIELL
Special Cable to The New York Times.

LONDON, June 30—The German tide in Egypt continued today to sweep eastward toward Alexandria. News reaching here from various sources indicated that the enemy had been slowed down but not halted. It was obvious that the fate of the great naval base and perhaps the Nile and Suez depended on the outcome of the race between General Field Marshal Erwin Rommel's advancing troops and the British reinforcements being rushed up from the east.

A report received here tonight said that advance units of Marshal Rommel's forces had passed the coastal point of El Daba, about seventy-five miles east of Matruh and 100 miles from Alexandria. It had been hoped that General Sir Claude J. E. Auchinleck, now in command of the Eighth Army, would be able to anchor one end of his line on El Daba, with the other on the Qattara Depression.

ALEXANDRIA THREATENED
The Axis drive eastward seriously threatens the most important British naval base in the Eastern Mediterranean. The possibility that the British Navy may have to leave its base at Alexandria, where it has in its custody important demilitarized warships of the French Navy, should not be overlooked.

The best and safest way for the British ships to leave would be through the Suez Canal, which is wide enough and deep enough for the biggest battleships and aircraft carriers. But even if Alexandria is lost, some warships might be based on Haifa, Palestine.

[Sir Andrew Browne Cunningham, commander of Britain's Mediterranean Fleet until recently, said in Washington that the loss of Alexandria would be "awkward," but that Haifa, Port Said and Beirut could be used as bases for many British warships.]

Any weakening of British naval strength in the Mediterranean not only would threaten Malta, but also would increase the danger of an Axis push toward the oil of the Middle East.

NEW TANKS ENTER BATTLE
New tanks were thrown into the battle in Egypt this afternoon by General Auchinleck. The battle now covers several hundred square miles of desert and British mobile units seem to be having some success in breaking up Marshal Rommel's massed forces. Indeed, there is some reason to believe that a few scattered British units still are snapping at Marshal Rommel's heels as far westward as a point south of Matruh. All this may be taken as an indication that reinforcements in men as well as material have improved the British position, although there certainly is no ground for optimism.

General Auchinleck seemingly has called on all available reserves in an attempt to halt the enemy somewhere west of the Nile. Among these are fresh troops from Syria and Palestine, Free French units of Foreign Legionnaires, motorized Spahi units and Senegalese. British, Australian, South African, United States, Free French and Greek planes are being used to blast the enemy's supply depots and drawn-out communication lines.

It appears that General Auchinleck is awaiting further tank reinforcements and is trying to avoid a decisive combat now and keep the fighting open and fluid. He may attempt to form a line from El Alamein to the Qattara Depression, using the Eighth Army to cork the coastal bottleneck and block Marshal Rommel's advance. ◆

Field Marshall Erwin Rommel with the 15th Panzer Division in North Africa, 1942.

NAZIS CLAIM PORT
Crimean Base Captured after 25-Day Assault, Berlin Asserts

By DANIEL T. BRIGHAM
By Telephone to The New York Times.

BERNE, Switzerland, July 2—After four days' incessant bombing and shelling, German and Rumanian forces shortly before noon yesterday, in an action that for sheer bloody horror must have surpassed anything seen at Verdun in the last war, stormed the last line of Sevastopol's defenses and, according to a special announcement in Berlin late last evening, captured Russia's great Black Sea naval base.

"Sevastopol has fallen," the announcement said. "Over the bastion, city and harbor the German and Rumanian war flags are flying."

The bulletin added that "the remnants of the beaten Soviet Sevastopol army have fled to the Chersonese Peninsula," which juts into the Black Sea west of the city, where, "pressed closely together within the narrowest space, they are facing destruction."

MOSCOW LACKS CONFIRMATION
The midnight Soviet communiqué admitted German advances in the Sevastopol lines and mentioned fierce hand-to-hand fighting. The lack of information in the Russian military commentator's broadcast indicated that wireless communication with the beleaguered city was cut off early yesterday.

Pounded to rubble by merciless bombing attacks that tore blocks the size of buildings from the rock east and south of Sevastopol, which formed an important part of the city's defenses and its main hope that the defenders could hold out, the fortress fell after twenty-five days of hammering by constantly reinforced formations. The city and naval base had been under intermittent siege since last November.

With the fall of Sevastopol, the last strong point in the Crimea has gone into German hands, theoretically opening the way for a violent drive on the Caucasus, which was predicted by German commentators two days ago.

Lieut. Gen. D. T. Kozloff's marines, which made a heroic bid from Yalta to divert some of the Axis pressure against Sevastopol by breaking through the Inkerman pass, apparently are fighting rearguard actions back toward their bases, inflicting still further losses on the Germans. ◈

NAVAJOS COMPLETE TRAINING AS MARINES
Group of 29 Indians Is Ready for War Assignment

SAN DIEGO, Calif., July 4 (AP)—Twenty-nine Navajo Indian warriors have ended Marine Corps training and are ready for assignment.

The descendants of braves who roamed the Arizona and New Mexico plains enlisted in a body at Fort Defiance, Ariz., several weeks ago and were sworn in at Fort Wingate, N.M. All are from the Navajo Reservation, which covers Northeast Arizona and Northwest New Mexico.

Marine platoons number sixty-three men, but provisions were made for this one of twenty-nine.

It set an aggregate rifle range record of 93.1, outshooting any platoon which fired on the range in that particular week. One Navajo emerged as an expert, fourteen as sharpshooters and twelve as marksmen.

In the platoon is Private Johnny Manuliete, who bears the name of the last war chief of his tribe. ◈

SOVIET OIL SUPPLY HELD NAZI TARGET
Hitler Said to Stake All on Cutting Off Army of Caucasus From Rest of Russia

The writer of this article is a veteran foreign correspondent who has just returned to England after several months in Russia.

By NEGLEY FARSON
North American Newspaper Alliance.

LONDON, July 6—It is perfectly plain now that the Germans are staking everything on their ability to cut off the bulk of Marshal Semyon Timoshenko's army and the army of the Caucasus from the rest of Russia. Once they do this—and they have not done it yet despite their swift success in reaching the main railway line—they must carry on to demolish Marshal Timoshenko's forces before they enter the Caucasus.

If they can do that the Caucasus lies wide open to them. They can ship troops from Odessa to Sevastopol and across the Crimean Peninsula to land across the five-mile-wide Strait of Kerch on the Caucasian mainland. They can march from Taganrog, where they are heavily engaged with the left flank of Marshal Timoshenko's army now, around the eastern corner of the Sea of Azov, and go down main roads and railway lines that lead from Rostov-on-Don into the Caucasus to Makhach Kala, then down along the railway line and the coast of the Caspian Sea to the one prize of all prizes they have been trying to grasp in this war—the oil fields of Baku, which supply 82 per cent of all Russia's oil.

But the army of the Caucasus is well supplied and has big reserves and the Russians have a strong base, though not nearly as strong as Sevastopol, at Rostov-on-Don.

NAZIS FORTY MILES FROM ROSTOV
Mark these facts: The Germans today at Taganrog are only forty miles from Rostov, but they have demonstrated that they know they could not swing around the corner of the Sea of Azov from there, leaving Marshal Timoshenko's fighting army still intact on their left flank. ❯

They must shatter Marshal Timoshenko's army before they enter the Caucasus themselves. That is hopeful, for it shows that they seem to have abandoned the idea of any straight attack across the Black Sea or even of using badly weakened Turkey as a base for an attack on Baku across the southern Caucasus.

Rostov is the gateway not only to the Caucasus but also to Astrakhan, at the head of the Volga delta, to which all oil tankers from Baku must eventually come. It is also the southern land gateway to the Urals, and unfortunately Rostov is only 250 miles from Stalingrad, on the Volga, at which point German shore batteries could sink any oil barges that tried to come up.

There is always the possibility that the Germans, with a quick change of tactics, might suddenly cut across this 250 miles of country to the Volga itself. But as a main German objective is to keep this oil from the Russians, there is another alternative that they might use. That is to destroy the refineries.

There are seven big Russian oil refineries. Two of these are already in German hands—at Odessa and Kherson. The five others are all in the Caucasus, at Krasnodar, Tuapse, Grozny, Batum and Baku. Both Krasnodar and Tuapse are about 150 miles from the present German flying fields on the Kerch Peninsula. The big oil refinery at Batum could function to refine and ship by rail back again to Baku to compensate for the loss of refinery capacity, but there would be no use in trying to ship from Batum up the Black Sea with the Germans less than eighty miles from the railhead at Novorossisk.

So there remain Grozny and Baku. Grozny is 500 miles from German air attack and Baku is 850—that is, unless Turkey permitted the Germans to use the Black Sea Anatolian coast as an air base. Then the rich fields and refineries of Baku might be brought within 450 miles of German flying fields and Batum would be right next door.

This is the blackest, perhaps the very blackest side of the picture that one could paint. The bright side is that the Germans have not got Rostov yet.

EVERY GALLON A NECESSITY

If Alexandria falls and the British fleet has to evacuate the eastern end of the Mediterranean, then the oil of Iraq is lost anyway. Only the Iranian oil would remain. But you must be hard-boiled about the realities of oil. The Iraq fields produce only 1.5 per cent of world production, the Iranian fields only 3.7 per cent and the Netherlands Indies only 2.8 percent.

The United States still produces more than 60 per cent of the world's oil, although in normal times the Americans themselves consumed more than 90 per cent of that.

But for the Russians—the world's third largest oil producers with 10.2 per cent of the global total, every gallon of which was used in Russia—the situation is desperate. If they lose the Caucasian oil they have no alternative supply. It will be only a question of time before their highly mechanized Red Army is paralyzed and famine must come because of idle tractors on the vast collective farms.

This is Reichsfuehrer Hitler's main blow of this war and we see now why he is willing to murder the flower of German manhood to put it over. ◆

German infantrymen carrying work tools in the Caucasus area of Russia, 1942.

JULY 8, 1942

GEN. SPAATZ NAMED AIR CHIEF IN EUROPE
U.S. World War I Veteran, Who Set Endurance Record, Takes London Post

By CHARLES HURD
Special to The New York Times.

WASHINGTON, July 7—Further indication of the growth of American air power in the British Isles developed here today with the appointment of Major Gen. Carl A. Spaatz as commander of United States Air Force in Europe.

General Spaatz already has assumed his command in London, under the direc-

JULY 15, 1942

'DOOR-KEY' CHILDREN OFFER BIG PROBLEM
WPA Nursery School Director Tells of 'War' Mothers

WASHINGTON, July 14—Dr. Grace Langdon, director of the nursery school program of the Work Projects Administration, reported today a great increase in "locked-up" or "door-key" children as more mothers go into war industry.

In Memphis, Tenn., she said, some children brought younger brothers and sisters to school because there was no one at home to look after them.

In Washington, a government worker locked her child in a car outside the

tion of Major Gen. Dwight D. Eisenhower, commander of American forces in the European theatre. The latter was nominated today by President Roosevelt for promotion to the rank of lieutenant general.

The new Army Air Force commander in Europe is a veteran pilot who shot down three German planes over the Western Front in World War I and won the Distinguished Service Cross for heroism in action. He won the Distinguished Flying Cross in 1929 for establishing an endurance record of 150 hours 40 minutes 15 seconds.

Among other announcements of changes in military personnel today by the War Department was that Major General George E. Stratemeyer had taken over the duties of Chief of Staff of the Army Air Force, relieving Major General Millard F. Harmon. General Harmon was assigned "to another very important post, which has not been announced." ◆

office and peered out of the window from time to time to see if she was asleep, Dr. Langdon added.

Dr. Langdon ascribed the condition to the difficulty in obtaining servants in war production areas and the increasing employment of mothers in cities where no adequate nursery system exists. The result, she said, is often that small children are locked out of the house with keys around their necks.

Mrs. Florence Kerr, Assistant Commissioner of WPA, said that many school-age children are tardy because they have to clean house after their parents go to work in the morning. She said that the problem is worse in summer when women in low-income groups take jobs while children are on vacation.

Congress has appropriated $6,000,000 for nursery schools and Mrs. Kerr's office has set up 1,250 free or nominal-fee schools to care for 55,000 children in defense areas where women are employed. At Long Beach, Calif., twenty-two children whose fathers were killed at Pearl Harbor are cared for in a nursery school while their mothers work in aircraft factories. ◆

ALLIED INVASION OF EUROPE IS URGED

48% of Nation's Voters Favor 2d Front Abroad Now, Gallup Poll Finds

DELAY SEEN AIDING HITLER

These surveys are made by a system of highly selective samplings in each of the forty-eight States in proportion to voting populations; thereby, the American Institute of Public Opinion holds, is obtained a result which would not vary from that of a much larger canvass.

By GEORGE GALLUP
Director American Institute
of Public Opinion

PRINCETON, N.J., July 16—Nazi military successes in Russia have given rise to renewed demands both here and in England for a second front against Hitler in Europe.

The decision rests, of course, with military leaders, but when and if they make such a move it will be closely in line with the ideas of the nation's armchair strategists, barber shop generals and country-store tacticians whose military judgment on such matters as air power has, incidentally, proved better than that of many military experts.

At any rate, the consensus of amateurs in the United States, as well as in Canada and Britain, is that the Allies should undertake a large-scale invasion of Europe with what equipment they now have rather than wait until they are stronger.

This is by no means a unanimous opinion. About one-third of the country counsels a waiting policy to accumulate greater military strength and reserves for the blow.

As measured by an institute survey, the attitude of the country shapes up as follows on the second-front issue:

	%
Attempt attack now	48
Wait till we are stronger	34
Undecided	18

A recent poll by the Canadian Institute of Public Opinion showed that approximately half (46 per cent) of all Canadians interviewed were in favor of the opening of a second front now, while 18 per cent wanted to wait, 6 per cent were against a second front, and the rest were undecided.

A similar survey in Britain conducted last month found 49 per cent believing that an invasion of the continent this Summer would be worth the cost, while 17 per cent disagreed and the rest were without opinion.

In the United States the chief argument put up by those who favor a second front this year is that every hour of delay works in Hitler's favor. ◆

Portrait of a Chiupa

A chiupa is a Chinese doughboy, far different from the mercenary of the old war lords. He has courage, stamina, and knows what he is fighting for. His pay is only 30 cents a month.

By Harrison Forman

Li Pao-shan (pronounced Lee Bow-shan) is a typical chiupa (pronounced jooba)—a Chinese doughboy or Tommy. He is a bright, eager farm lad: diligent, inherently honest, possessed of amazing stamina and ability to undergo extreme hardships uncomplainingly, with courage to challenge the hated Japanese despite their overwhelming arms, and beating them every time he has met them on anything like equal terms.

Above all, LiPao-shan has a revolutionary sense of nationalism and appreciation of what he is fighting for.

This is perhaps the most significant feature of Li Pao-shan's psychological make-up, especially to those of us who knew the chiupa of old—the Liangtze mercenary in the service of some grasping, greedy, selfish war lord. Liangtze means "nothingness," implying that a soldier is an unproductive person ❯

who is, moreover, a parasitic, wasteful food eater. Hence the old saying, "A good son does not become a Liangtze," for the soldier for centuries right up to recent decades has been considered at the very bottom of the social scale.

But LiPao-shan, the chiupa of today, upon whose shoulders will devolve the burden of land operations when the Allied counter-offensive comes in the Pacific, is a different individual from the Liangtze of old. No longer outcasts and dregs of society, Li Pao-chan and his chiupa conscript companions are now mostly farmers, workers or students from respectable lao pai shing (peasant masses), who themselves, coming from the soil, fully appreciate the urgent necessity to keep the ruthless, pillaging, exploiting aggressor from invading the good earth, which to the lao pai shing is a most precious heritage from venerated ancestors.

What a far cry from the Liangtze of old, who never fought when it rained or was too hot, are the inspired volunteers of today! Li Pao-shan's three Yunnan friends, calling themselves "three going to front youths," began a recruiting service with pleas through advertisements in the local press: "We lose our homes, our work, our studies. We are driven by thirst and hunger. Pain and distress afflict our daily lives. For all this none other than our race's enemy the Japanese are responsible. Unitedly should we marshal our resolute will to weather adversities, and we should with our brain and blood fight for final victory on the battlefield."

Coming of law-abiding peasantry, Li Pao-shan is much more amenable to discipline and the people no longer fear his coming as they did the predatory Liangtze of old. From the lao pai shing himself, he is sympathetically cooperative to native farmers in districts where he is stationed. The common bond contributes to closer relations wherein Li Pao-shan exchanges helpful farm hints, suggestions and advice. Oftentimes he joins the farmer in putting these ideas to practical use, such as helping to install an improvement which results in betterment of the irrigation system or illustrating a different method of planting or of crop care. At harvest time Li Pao-shan and his comrades will frequently pitch in and help the farmers gather their crops, which service the grateful farmers repay with feasts and information of military value, all of which is knitting the country and its peoples closer together through a wide exchange of ideas and confidence.

Li Pao-shan's camp life is simple and Spartan yet progressively constructive. His camp is usually made of mat sheds wherein scores sleep together on one huge earthen platform called "the kang," which is heated from below through openings from the outside. His regular rations are two meals of rice or noodles daily, with two dishes of vegetables per meal apportioned to each table of eight. On garrison duty he supplements his fare by raising vegetables, pigs, chickens, rabbits and goats. Dur-

ing hand-grenade practice, when grenades are hurled into a river or a lake, a squad is detailed to pick up the stunned or killed fish. His pay is only six Chinese dollars (the Chinese dollar is equal to about five cents in American money) monthly, but since he is unused to luxuries he does not require much more than the simple food and keep which the army supplies. He rises before dawn to the sound of bugles, then has an hour of exercise, which sometimes involves shadow boxing or, more often, merely trotting in a circle while shouting "Ee, er, san, shu" (One, two, three, four). After exercise, all assemble for the flag-raising ceremony, which is followed by the singing of the national anthem.

Li Pao-shan's battle experience began almost from the first day he arrived at the front. There is an old Chinese saying that "Newborn calves do not fear tigers"; hence eager fresh recruits are found most useful in attacks, though through recklessness they usually have proved easier targets than veterans, whose experience has taught them better use of cover from the enemy's fire.

Soon, indeed, Li Pao-shan saw Japanese at their very worst. He saw towns and villages ruthlessly destroyed, saw the tortured and mutilated bodies of luckless captives, the haggard, terrified faces of survivors, clearly bespeaking the awful ordeals to which they had been witness, while the blackened ruins of peasant homes where lay charred bodies and tatters of women's clothing offered the lie to a Japanese poster on the tottering wall near by which read, "The Japanese Imperial Army will not disturb the Chinese peasantry."

All this aged and hardened him and steeled him in the determination to fight the enemy to the bitter end at whatever cost.

Once Li Pao-shan's unit found itself cut off during an engagement. Unperturbed, his commander ordered the unit "to retreat" by advancing, for he knew the Japanese rear was always empty. Whereupon Li Pao-shan and his chiupa comrades became members of a ghost army of guerrillas, legions of whom are operating freely behind the Japanese lines, which actually run only along railways and highways with garrisons at strategic towns and bridges.

Li Pao-shan quickly learned that guerrillas don't try to oust Japanese from railways or highways, for they look upon these lines of communications as their principal sources of food supply, clothing, money and, even more important, of arms. Example, a Japanese detachment

A Chinese Army unit during troop drills, China, 1942.

of three or four thousand has upward of a hundred trucks shuttling between its base and its garrison outposts carrying ammunition, food and gasoline. Glass spikes scattered along the road will halt a transport convoy and while the tires are being changed guerrillas waiting in ambush pour a withering machine-gun fire into the bewildered Japanese guards, finishing them off with grenades.

At other times Li Pao-shan and his band of fellow-guerrillas planted mines under the rail bed, then patiently sat down and waited until a Japanese supply train came along. When the train had been derailed they swooped down and looted the twisted cars.

A favorite sport of Li Pao-shan and his buddies was to bait garrisons of Japanese who did not dare to leave their fortified shelters after dark. Night after night sham attacks were made, to which the terrified Japanese replied with furious fusillades until they were near collapse from tension and sleepless nights. They learned the guerrilla ghost army creed, which may be summarized as: "Withdraw when the enemy advances; harass him when he settles down; attack him when he is exhausted; give chase when he flees."

Li Pao-shan and his guerrilla companions enjoyed the complete confidence of the people. They traveled light and were fed, clothed and protected by the lao pai shing. When the Japanese took the town of Shichiachwang, on the Peiping-Hankow railway where a narrow gauge branches off to Taiyuan, farmers were highly incensed at the Japanese, who attacked almost every woman, young or old. The vengeful farmers made contact with the guerrillas and formed a plan. Slim farmers dressed as attractive girls inveigled the Japanese to pursue them into an ambush, where Li Pao-shan and his buddies quietly dispatched them.

The time Li Pao-shan spent with the ghost army until his unit once again was able to rejoin the ranks of the regulars gave him increased confidence in himself and in the ultimate victory of his country. For on the battlefields he had seen few live Japanese, and they were usually at rifle-shot distance. But serving with the ghost army he saw the hated despoiler when he was shorn of his awesome armor of tanks, planes and artillery and found him then far from invincible.

Best of all, he has learned that newfound Allies are bringing him arms even better than those possessed by the Japanese—which just about settles the question of ultimate victory in his mind. ◆

AUGUST 1, 1942

AIRCRAFT CARRIER LAUNCHED BY NAVY
Essex Is First Such Vessel to Take To Water Since the Attack on Pearl Harbor

By C. BROOKS PETERS
Special to The New York Times.

NEWPORT NEWS, Va., July 31—The first aircraft carrier of the Navy to be launched since Pearl Harbor and since the recent decision of our naval experts to concentrate on building carriers at the expense of battleships slid down the ways this afternoon at 2:49 P. M.

Named by her sponsor, Mrs. Artemus L. Gates, wife of the Assistant Secretary of the Navy for Air, the 25,000-ton Essex, first of a scheduled class of eleven similar carriers, slid into the James River as the working men who built her and about a hundred guests cheered. There were ten newspaper men, brought in a plane from Washington by the Navy, and almost all the rest were military men and their wives.

As soon as she took to the water, however, a crew of workmen began preparations to lay the keel of another warship.

The ceremony at the Newport News Ship Building and Dry Dock Company's yard was simple. Almost all the peacetime ceremony was missing. There was not even a band and workers in the yard continued at their tasks without interruption during the two minutes while the Essex slid into the James River and was tended by a fleet of tugs. The public, because of war restrictions, was not admitted.

KEEL OF ESSEX LAID 15 MONTHS AGO

The Essex, launched fifteen months and three days after her keel was laid, was almost bare of decoration. The elevated wooden stand for the sponsor and guests and the scaffolding about the prow, however, were adorned with red, white, and blue bunting.

Rear Admiral K. H. Van Kuren, chief of the Bureau of Ships, presented bouquets, two of yellow roses, one of red roses and one of pink roses, to Mrs. Gates, her daughter, Miss Diana Gates, and her two nieces, the Misses Alessandra and Anne Cheney, who served as maids of honor.

There was no formal speaker. Soon after 2:30 Admiral Van Kuren issued the order, "Uncover." All men present removed their caps or hats while a Navy chaplain, Commander Albert E. Stone, blessed the warship. His words, although spoken through a microphone, were drowned out by the noise of the riveters and fitters building other naval vessels in the yard.

The Essex was scheduled to leave her drydock at 2:45 P. M. She did not get started, however, until 2:47 P. M. Fifteen seconds before the Essex slid down the ways a warning siren sounded.

A second siren was set off as the carrier started down the ways. At the same instant, Mrs. Gates smashed the bottle of champagne against the ship's side.

TUG BOATS SURROUND VESSEL

Sailors, naval officers and civilian workmen were on the new carrier as she slipped into the water. A few minutes after the Essex cleared her dock a fleet of tug boats led her off to be fitted out and commissioned.

The keel of the fourth Essex, named after three earlier vessels famous in the history of the United States, was laid on April 28, 1941. She is, the Navy said today, "the first of several new carriers authorized by Congress to make the United States superior to all other nations combined in this category."

Navy officers said that they could not mention specifications of the new vessel, such as speed, tonnage, design, ordnance or armor. Jane's Fighting Ships and other publications devoted to fighting vessels which can be purchased at any bookseller's, however, give the tonnage of the Essex as 25,000 and point out that she is the first of a class of eleven carriers. ◆

NAZIS SWEEP ON IN CAUCASUS AND ADVANCE IN DON ELBOW

STALINGRAD LINE DENTED

By The Associated Press.

MOSCOW, Aug. 5—German troops have made another fifty-mile advance in the Caucasus to threaten Tikhoretsk, an important junction on the Soviet railway system, and also have gained in the Don River elbow northwest of Stalingrad, the Russians announced early today.

Driving southwest of Salsk along the severed Stalingrad-Krasnodar railway, the Nazis have reached Byeloglina, and their apparent goal is Tikhoretsk, another fifty miles away. Seizure of Tikhoretsk would outflank the Russian Army still fighting the Nazis at Kushchevka, fifty miles to the north, and enable the Germans to control large segments of Russian railways in the Western Caucasus.

German reserves succeeded in punching a hole in Soviet positions in the Don River elbow some eighty miles northwest of Stalingrad.

NAZIS' RESERVES TURN TIDE

"In the Kletskaya area and south of it," the midnight communiqué said, "our troops repulsed many enemy attacks and inflicted many blows on the enemy. Fighting in a large populated place has been in progress for several days. In one sector the tankists of our unit attacking enemy infantry crushed with their caterpillars 270 German officers and men.

"The Germans threw in many reserves, and only at the cost of heavy losses pressed back our troops somewhat."

[The Germans reported the capture of Voroshilovsk, 180 miles southeast of Rostov, and said other forces had reached the Kuban River at several points. Soviet counter-attacks in the Don elbow were described as unsuccessful, and a further advance eastward between the Don and Sal Rivers also was claimed.]

The push to Byeloglina represents a 125-mile thrust into the Caucasus by the Nazi salient that, after crossing the Don, bridged the Manych River to reach Salsk, then turned southwestward toward Tikhoretsk.

KUSHCHEVKA RING THREATENED

"In the area of Byeloglina," the communiqué related, "our troops fought heavy defensive engagements against superior numbers of enemy talks and motorized infantry. The Germans are sustaining heavy losses."

Already threatened with encirclement, the Russians in the Kushchevka area were falling back slightly under a German drive southward along the Rostov-Tikhoretsk-Baku railway.

"In the Kushchevka area," the bulletin said, "the German Fascist troops continuously attack our defense lines. Most of the attacks are repulsed. In one sector only the enemy succeeded in pushing forward. Fierce fighting with varying success continues in the area of a populated place."

Cossack cavalrymen equipped with modern weapons were in the thick of the Caucasian fight, but the tone of the Russian communiqué made it only too evident that the German mechanized might was telling in most sectors, except perhaps at Tsimlyansk.

Earlier Russian reports had said that all Nazi attempts to cross the stream in the Kletskaya region were repulsed and on the Lower Don near Tsimlyansk German forces that poured across bridgeheads apparently were contained in a pocket on the south bank.

The Caucasus was the most critical zone along the 2,000-mile battlefront, because German troops were nearing the Maikop oil fields, which produce 7 per cent of Russian petroleum, and were striking hard for the derricks of Grozny, which yield another 3 per cent or more. The vast Baku pools near the Caspian were more than 600 miles away. These producers of 75 to 80 per cent of Russian oil were protected by the towering Caucasus Mountains. ◇

The Russians acknowledged that they had given ground in the Kushchevka sector (1) and that the enemy had swept down from Salsk to the Byeloglina area (2). The Germans claimed that their forces on the latter front had driven 180 miles south of the Don to take Voroshilovsk (3) and that mechanized spearheads had reached the Kuban River to the west at several points (broken arrows). The Soviet armies south of Tsimlyansk (4) were still standing firm, but in the Kletskaya region (5) west of Stalingrad reinforced Nazi attackers pressed the defenders back. The Russians enlarged their bridgehead south of Voronezh (6).

AUGUST 9, 1942

21 SEIZED IN INDIA
India Government Announces It Will Meet Challenge With Firm Curbs on Rebels

BOMBAY, India, Aug. 9—Mohandas K. Gandhi and other Indian Nationalist leaders were arrested today within a few hours after the All-India Congress party had approved a resolution authorizing a mass campaign of civil disobedience to support its demands for immediate Indian independence.

Among those taken into custody were Maulana Abdul Kalam Azad, president of the Congress party; Pandit Jawaharlal Nehru and Mr. Gandhi's secretary, Miss Madeline Slade.

No warrant was issued for Mr. Gandhi's wife, who was told by police that she could accompany her husband, but who elected to remain behind.

[Reuters, British news agency, said those arrested were taken by special train to Poona.]

ROUND-UP FOLLOWS CONGRESS VOTE

Seventeen arrests were reported to have been made in the city of Ahmedabad, where the round-up started soon after the Congress party session adjourned. The Congress resolution gave complete authority to Mr. Gandhi, 72-year-old leader of the Indian nationalist movement, for a drive aimed at forcing an end to British rule in India.

The government has placed a ban on gatherings of more than five persons, issuing the order under the Criminal Procedure Code.

In a statement at New Delhi, the government reply to the Congress party's resolution said:

"There is nothing the government of India regret more than this challenge at so critical a juncture but on them lies the task of defending India ... that task the government of India will discharge in the face of the challenge now thrown down by the Congress party with clear determination."

"I am pledged to the Congress and the Congress is pledged to do or die," Mr. Gandhi declared in concluding a two-hour address that wound up the meeting of the party's general committee.

He said, "We shall make every effort to see the Viceroy before starting the movement," but advices from New Delhi tonight said the government of India declined to negotiate with the Congress on its demands.

The New Delhi statement said the government "would regard as wholly incompatible with their responsibilities to the people of India and their obligations to the Allies discussions about a demand, the acceptance of which would plunge India into confusion and anarchy and paralyze her effort in the common cause of freedom."

The New Delhi government statement noted that "the Congress working committee admit 'there may be risks involved.'" It then continued:

"They are right. Acceptance of the resolution must mean the exposure of India to an Axis attack from without.

"Internally, withdrawal of British rule invites civil war, the collapse of law and order, the outbreak of communal feuds and the dislocation of economic life with its inevitable hardships."

It accused the Congress party leaders of having worked "in the interests of securing their own dominance and in pursuit of a totalitarian policy," and added that they have "consistently impeded the efforts made to bring India to full nationhood."

"But for the resistance of the Congress party to constructive efforts, India might even now be enjoying self-government," the statement added.

"It is not too much to say that acceptance of the demand must mean the betrayal of the Allies, whether in or outside India, the betrayal in particular of Russia and China."

It urged the people of India to unite with the government "in resistance to the present challenge of a party."

Britain's own previous offers of post-war independence have been rejected by the Congress party, which is primarily Hindu, and by the Moslem League and other major and minor elements of the mutually distrustful and complex elements of India's racial, religious and political life.

TIME FOR ACTION NOT SET

As provided in the resolution, Mr. Gandhi was in full control of the campaign, but there was no indication of the exact moment he intended to get it started.

In his concluding Congress address he called on all Indians to "begin to feel that they are free men," asked all Indian newspapers to stop publication until independence was granted, and told teachers and students to be ready to cease work.

He urged Indian princes to "act as trustees for their people" and stop being autocrats. He already has said his campaign this time would include the princes' States as well as the areas known as "British India."

In the morning, before the civil disobedience resolution was taken up, Mr. Gandhi announced he was appealing to the United States, in a letter "to American friends," to act "while there is yet time" to bring about independence and ally Indians wholeheartedly on the ❯

An injured man being taken during the Bombay riots, India, 1942.

Allied side. He predicted a repetition of the disasters of Malaya, Singapore and Burma "unless Britain trusts the people of India to use their liberty in favor of the Allied cause."

Mr. Gandhi also complained that he had been "painted as a hypocrite and an enemy of Britain under disguise," and said nothing he could say would offset "the false propaganda that has poisoned American ears." He said the United States, having made common cause with Britain, "cannot therefore disown responsibility for anything that her representatives do in India."

In a concluding speech Jawaharial Nehru, the No. 2 man of the Nationalist movement, declared that the "Quit India" resolution was not a threat but an "offer of cooperation." Nevertheless, he warned that "behind it is the certainty that consequences will follow if certain events do not happen."

"We are on the verge of a precipice and we are in deadly earnest about it," he asserted. "The very act of freeing India will make the Allied cause a completely right cause. It is only negatively right just now because Germany is worse and Japan is worse.

"If Japan comes to this country you and I will suffer or die, not the people sitting in London, New York or Washington. They say we do not know what Japan is. We know what Japan is. We know what subjugation is better than any people in the world. We have had 200 years of it. We prefer to throw ourselves into the fire and come out a new nation or be reduced to ashes." ◊

AUGUST 19, 1942

COMMANDOS RAID NAZI-HELD DIEPPE
French Advised Blow Is Not 'Invasion'

By The Associated Press.

LONDON, Aug. 19—The Commandos raided the Dieppe area of occupied France early today, British Combined Operations Headquarters announced. A bulletin said that the operation was still in progress.

The French people were being advised by radio that the raid was not a

---

AUGUST 11, 1942

MARINES ON SHORE
Fighting Is Heavy After Surprise of Japanese in Tulagi Region

By CHARLES HURD
Special to The New York Times.

WASHINGTON, Aug. 10—American forces have landed in the Tulagi area of the Solomon Islands in the course of an engagement that has been in progress for about three days and is continuing, according to a Navy announcement issued today over the signature of Admiral Ernest J. King, Commander in Chief of the United States Fleet.

[According to The Associated Press, a naval spokesman in Washington identified the landing groups as parties of Marines. The spokesman was not clear at first as to whether troops other than Marines were engaged, but he said later that the best information available was that Marines alone were making the landings.]

Heavy fighting has developed, the announcement stated. After "an initial surprise was effected and planned landings accomplished," Japanese forces "counter-attacked with rapidity and vigor," the admiral declared.

ENEMY PLANES DESTROYED

Incomplete information from the scene of operations, Admiral King said, indicates that the Navy has lost one cruiser and suffered damage to two cruisers, two destroyers and one transport. Japanese losses include "a large number" of planes destroyed and "surface units put out of action."

"This operation in the Tulagi area is significant," said Admiral King's statement, "in that it marks our first assumption of the initiative and of the offensive. All of the previous operations in the Pacific, however successful, have been essentially defensive in character.

"It should be understood that the operation now under way is one of the most complicated and difficult in warfare. Considerable losses, such as are inherent in any offensive operation, must be expected as the price to be paid for the hard-won experience which is essential to the attainment of far-reaching results."

"Far-reaching results" involve a series of prospective actions by which United States and other United Nations forces eventually must roll back the Japanese from the string of fortified bases and outposts that run from Japan on the north to the Solomons and New Guinea on the south.

THE OBJECTIVE IS GIVEN

The present operations, Admiral King explained, are designed essentially to take away an important base from the Japanese so that it can be used for our own purposes. Because of Tulagi's position, 600 miles east of the southern tip of New Guinea, enemy forces there can threaten the supply line from the United States to Australia. On the other hand, Tulagi is a stepping stone from which United Nations offensive operations could be conducted toward the Japanese defenses that dot the islands to the north.

The fleet and air units that are making the attack in the Tulagi area are commanded by Vice Admiral Robert L. Ghormley, former naval observer at London and now Supreme Commander of United Nations Naval Forces in the South Pacific. The attacking force—obviously formidable—is under the general direction of Admiral Chester W. Nimitz, Commander in Chief of the Pacific Fleet.

Admiral King's report was considered by observers to mark an important step in giving the public a type of explanation generally lacking heretofore in news released in the form of communiqués. It differentiated between offensive action, like that now undertaken, and defensive operations, like those in the battles of the Coral Sea and Midway Island, in which American forces—principally planes—fought off invasion fleets sent out by the Japanese.

It has been demonstrated that an attack based on surprise, as were the Japanese attacks on Pearl Harbor and Dutch Harbor, can cause extreme damage to the offender. This, it appeared, was the initial result of the attack on the Solomon Islands.

In this new engagement, however, the American forces are attempting something that the Japanese did not attempt at Pearl Harbor—permanent

full-fledged invasion, headquarters said.

Dieppe is on the French shore of the English Channel, a short distance west of Dover Strait.

A raid on that section of the coast might be aimed at silencing Nazi long-range coastal batteries, a constant menace to shipping through the Channel. These recently have been unusually active and their volume of fire has indicated that they have been reinforced.

Another possibility was that such a raid was a feeler of German coastal defenses as a forerunner of the actual opening of a second land front in Continental Europe, or that it sought—as Commando raids on the French Channel coast have in the past—to knock out anti-aircraft emplacements or radio location stations.

Now that United States Army Air Forces and the Royal Air Force have launched attacks in greater weight on Northern France, a break in the Nazi air raid alarm network would be helpful to the Allied airmen roaring in from the Channel coast.

Dieppe is only thirty-three miles north of Rouen, target of the first big United States Flying Fortress raid on Nazi-held France, and is, itself, a Channel port and junction of two railroads to Paris. In past centuries it was France's chief seaport. ◆

landings as a follow-up to the surprise attack. This necessarily involves changing over from the operations that mark a raid or foray to a determined fight to take and maintain a foothold despite the reserves that the enemy will bring to bear.

RAIDS ON OTHER BASES

Admiral King's statement of known American losses indicated that the invading forces had found formidable opposition waiting for them, despite repeated aerial attacks against Tulagi and three supporting bases lying to the north and west—the Japanese-held port of Rabaul, on New Britain, and the bases at Salamaua and Buna, on New Guinea.

Tulagi was used in May as the embarkation port for a Japanese invasion force aimed at Australia. That force was "all but annihilated" by air attacks. The island has been a base for sea raiders that have threatened the most direct line of communications between the United States and Australia, a route that is so long as to require a disproportionate amount of shipping to maintain the forces in Australia.

More recently the Japanese were reported to be constructing an air base on the island of Guadalcanal, near Tulagi. This base would extend by several hundred miles the radius of operation for Japanese bombing planes sent out to intercept supply convoys. By the same token, its capture would give American land-based planes a great advantage in their operations to disrupt Japanese concentrations in New Guinea and the Bismarck Archipelago, where Rabaul is situated. ◆

AUGUST 23, 1942

Text of Nelson Statement on War Production

By The Associated Press

WASHINGTON, Aug. 22—The text of the statement by the Office of War Information on the second war production report by Donald M. Nelson, chairman of the War Production Board, was as follows:

Munitions production increased 16 per cent last month, continuing recent months' expansion in the output of planes, guns, tanks, ships and other war equipment, WPB Chairman Donald M. Nelson announced today in his second war production report.

Although progress was uneven, and efforts are being directed toward bringing about balance between production items, the WPB index of munitions production advanced in July to 350 (preliminary)—three-and-a-half times as great as in November 1941, the month before Pearl Harbor, upon which the index is based. The June index (revised) was 303.

But July output was 7 per cent short of the production forecasts made on the first of the month. It was, nevertheless, an improvement over June performance, indicating that progress is being made in working up toward scheduled objectives.

In brief, the score on war production for July (measured by the index) was as follows:

Aircraft production: Up 11 per cent over June.

Ordnance production: Up 26 per cent over June.

Naval ship production: Up 22 per cent over June.

Merchant ship tonnage: Up 6 per cent over June.

Based on figures before the month of the Pearl Harbor attack, this index was used by Mr. Nelson in arriving at his conclusions.

PRODUCTION REPORTED UNEVEN

Study of the results reveals that production is uneven in relation to schedules. In some cases July production outstripped the forecasts; in others the forecasts were not approached. Even within certain categories, such as ordnance, we find unequal progress as between various types of equipment. Particularly is it important to keep the production of finished weapons and their component parts in step.

Analysis of these factors suggests that the war production effort has entered a new phase—one in which more careful balancing of requirements will become increasingly important. For a long-range solution there must be a close, effective control of the flow of materials and a comprehensive system of production control, to make certain that the right materials get to the right places at the right time.

EXPANSION PROGRAM PUSHED

This does not involve a reduction of our major programs. It will mean that while we expand the production of raw materials we shall have to limit the production of some items which are easy to make. At the same time, we shall have to exercise care that production of vital weapons needed right now continues to increase.

The real test of what our industrial machine is doing is how much are we turning out—what are we producing. So far, we are running at a rate three-and- one-half times as great as during the month before Pearl Harbor; the rest of the year will tell the story. ◆

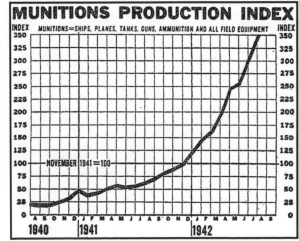

MUNITIONS PRODUCTION INDEX

INDEX   MUNITIONS=SHIPS, PLANES, TANKS, GUNS, AMMUNITION AND ALL FIELD EQUIPMENT   INDEX

NOVEMBER 1941=100

1940   1941   1942

SEPTEMBER 5, 1942

'RED VERDUN' HOLDS
Greatest Nazi Onslaught Kept from Advancing by Volga Defenders

By RALPH PARKER
Wireless to The New York Times.

MOSCOW, Sept. 5—The defenders of Stalingrad held their ground today as the gigantic struggle for the city—the greatest battle of the war—moved inexorably toward its climax.

The midnight Soviet communiqué reported that the Germans kept up their attacks in the critical sector southwest of the city, but were beaten off with heavy losses. New German reserves were thrown into the battle in an attempt to follow up an assault by 100 tanks on the Russian defenses. No further advance was made and counter-attacking Soviet tanks did heavy damage, it was reported.

Northwest of Stalingrad the Russians struck powerful counter-blows and withstood the attacks of enemy tanks thrown into the assault without respite. Across the Don the Russians deepened their dent in the top of the German salient.

FLEET JOINS COAST DEFENSE
Furious fighting was reported in the region of Rzhev, while operations continued without significant change northwest of Novorossiisk, where units of the Black Sea Fleet used their guns in coordination with land forces against German and Rumanian forces striving to reach the Caucasian port and naval base. The battle with the Germans, who breached the water line at Mozdok, in the mid-Caucasus, also continued.

[The Germans reported that their forces were in the suburbs of Stalingrad and claimed a virtual blockade of Volga River traffic. Other troops were said to have crossed the Kerch Strait from the Crimea to join in the advance down the Black Sea coast on Novorossisk. Defensive Axis operations continued west of Moscow and south of Leningrad.]

The Red Army defending Stalingrad is withstanding the greatest land and air assault that Germany has ever launched against a single objective. It is doubtful whether less than forty German divisions—about 500,000 men—are involved, and the strength of the German air force there is computed at 1,000 front-line planes. As many as 150 planes have appeared over Stalingrad at once recently.

Yet despite the terrible weight of the attackers, some of whose troops are comparatively fresh, and the numerical superiority they have established in some sectors—as much as three to one in parts of the northwestern salient—the defenders yield ground very slowly and only after taking a great toll of the enemy.

'RED VERDUN' IS RECALLED
The Stalingrad battle was described in Red Star as unprecedented in the present war in the number of men involved and the violence of the fighting. The army newspaper reminded the Red Army that the city, then Tsaritsyn, was known during the civil war as "Red Verdun" and exhorted the troops to show the same resolute devotion in defense of this gateway of the Caspian and heart of the Volga basin as did their fathers.

Stalingrad can be held, Red Star asserted, and no superiority of tanks and planes can prevail over a resolute, well-organized defense.

Earlier reports indicated that the Germans were continuing to edge the defenders back in individual sectors of the two fronts northwest and southwest of the city, though nowhere had the main enemy forces been able to advance their lines generally.

The most serious threat from the south comes from a force of about 100 tanks, the remnants of a full panzer division that entered the attack forty-eight hours ago and forced its way through village "K" and strongly defended high land. This break-through had the support of 250 planes, which concentrated on Soviet gun positions, and a considerable force of self-propelled artillery.

Lodged in the city's defenses, the foe's mechanized vanguards now are attempting to worry their way into Stalingrad's approaches from the southwest, rip open the Russian lines and win passage for large infantry forces lying before Kotelnikov and along the railroad to Stalingrad.

In the other sectors of General Field Marshal Fedor von Bock's lower thrust the Germans are attacking relentlessly, varying their direction and power in an attempt to bewilder the defense. Though their tank strength is being whittled down by Russian artillerymen, whose heroism defies description, reserves continue to reach the enemy and the pressure is maintained day and night.

MANY ATTACKS REPULSED
One Russian unit defending direct approaches to Stalingrad repulsed several tank attacks Wednesday, in each of which the Germans used about forty machines, with powerful infantry and artillery support. A series of violent attacks failed to dislodge the defense and twenty-six tanks were destroyed and three battalions of infantry are believed to have perished in the anti-tank zone before the Russian positions.

Abandoning their frontal assault, the Germans wheeled to the northwest with

Key Soviet City's Defenders Hold Firm: Northwest of Stalingrad (1) the Russians repulsed all attacks and launched powerful counter-blows; southwest of the city, too, they reported, they stopped the German advance and inflicted huge losses. In the Caucasus, however, the Nazis fought their way across a river in the Mozdok area (2) and dislodged the Soviet forces from a height northwest of Novorossiisk (3). The German High Command announced that other Axis troops had crossed Kerch Strait, were fighting on the Taman Peninsula (4) and had made contact with Rumanians advancing from the east.

a great force of tanks and motor-borne infantry, broke through to a railway, cut a highway, advanced north, then swung sharply eastward. On this new battle-field Soviet heavy mortars were awaiting the Germans and twenty-five of their tanks were burned out in a barrage. As the German attack faltered, Soviet tanks drove the remaining enemy machines from the field and suppressed their accompanying guns and mortars.

Northwest of Stalingrad, after having been checked for several days, the Germans resumed their advance in isolated sectors Thursday. Farther west six German attacks were reported repulsed on Wednesday, when the Germans

were driven from a tactically important height. In another sector the Russians, forced to retreat, restored the situation by counter-attacking. The chief threat still comes from the south.

Reports show that when advance forces of the twenty-five divisions used by Marshal von Bock in the Don bend crossed the river west of Stalingrad they advanced northeastward before wheeling to attack the city from the northwest. This move apparently was designed to seize a long stretch of the Don and perhaps trap Russian forces still west of the river before advancing on Stalingrad.

At Voronezh the Germans made the mistake of holding only short stretches

of the river, across which the counter-attacking Russians were able to move and attack enemy bridgeheads from the rear. Marshal von Bock, on the other hand, prudently consolidated a long river-line belt and thus was able to transport a great number of tanks across.

The German Air Force is playing a more important part in the Stalingrad battle than at any other time on the Eastern Front. Red Star estimates that about 1,000 planes are operating against the city and its defenses. They are being used in three principal ways—to blockade Russian airfields, bomb outlying communications and give close support to the field forces. ◆

SEPTEMBER 6, 1942

PLAN OF SECOND FRONT UNDER CAREFUL STUDY
United States and British Military And Air Chiefs Busy on the Manifold Problems of an Invasion

By EDWIN L. JAMES

Public clamor about a second front seems to have died down a bit, which is all to the good in that it leaves the military experts a better opportunity to make their plans, free from political pressure. Especially noticeable is Moscow's silence on the subject for the past two weeks. Of course that does not mean that Russia still does not hope for a second front on the Continent to relieve German pressure on Stalin's army. But it may mean that the disadvantages of propaganda on the subject have been brought home to Moscow. It is noted that the lessening of the Red cry for a second front, somehow or other, coincided somewhat with the visit of Prime Minister Churchill to the Red Capital.

Now it stands to reason that the raid on Dieppe was not made for fun. It also stands to reason that increasing thousands of United States and Canadian troops are not being sent to England just to make the trip. In other words, it may be taken for granted that plans for military action against Germany are under way and are being studied from every useful point of view. The lessening of public demands that the second front be launched this week or next month leaves

the military experts in a much better atmosphere to make their plans. And many plans need to be made.

THE EXPERTS ARE AT WORK
There is no good reason to believe that President Roosevelt or Prime Minister Churchill is bringing pressure to bear on their generals of a nature to warp expert opinion. There is every reason to believe they are doing nothing of the sort. Both leaders have made it plain that they favor a second front. They have said so publicly. But neither of them wishes a second front unless it is a success. For that reason they are undoubtedly giving their military men time to work it out.

Many minds bring many plans, and so it is not surprising that the United States and British generals have plans which need adjustment and accommodation. Each party to the undertaking is to make its contribution. Both British and Americans are to contribute land and air power. By the nature of things one must look to the British for a major part of the shipping needed for operations between England and the Continent. On the other hand, for the supplies for an invasion of the Continent

the United States would be expected to furnish a large part of these.

There is nothing strange about it taking time to work out the enormous problems involved. One hears from London and other quarters that a really serious second front is not expected before next Spring. Such a conclusion might readily be assumed from the complexity and number of the plans to be made. However, that conclusion is by no means a sure one. There may be more than one invasion point and there may be different times fixed for each.

MANY PLANS UNDER STUDY
A review of news dispatches passed by censors and published reveals the number of suggestions which have been brought forward. There has been talk of an invasion of Norway, one has heard of plans for using the shortest water route to the French coast opposite the south coast of England, one has heard of the advantages offered by the Finisterre Peninsula. It has been argued that the coast around Bordeaux is not so strongly held by the Germans as the coastline farther north. There has been talk of a project for the invasion of the Continent through Spain. The Germans have informed us that the United States has plans for landing on the Atlantic Coast of French North Africa. It may be guessed that fully a dozen or more, plans have been brought forward for consideration.

Since both President Roosevelt and Prime Minister Churchill approve the principle of a second front, it may be surmised that they are waiting for their experts to agree on a plan. No layman would wish to hazard a guess as to what they will agree upon. When the experts have decided upon the best technical plans and the probabilities ❯

of success or failure, it will then be the role of the two leaders to consider the political aspects of the situation, for they are very real.

It is perfectly plain that any large landing of United Nations troops anywhere in Western Europe will draw German attention and thus perhaps help relieve pressure on Russia. From that viewpoint there would always be a gain for Russia in any attempted second-front project, whether it succeeded or not.

WANT SUCCESS ASSURED

But surely the President and the Prime Minister will have in their minds the dire results of failure to such an extent that they will wish every possible assurance of success. Each of them has shown the importance he attaches to the resentment of millions of Europeans in conquered countries toward the German invaders. They know that there are millions of Europeans waiting for a chance to help beat the Germans. They know that and attach great importance to that factor. By the same token they have a full realization of the unhappy results of an invasion of the Continent which would not succeed. ◊

SEPTEMBER 10, 1942

MOSCOW IS BITTER; SEES ALLIED DELAY
Views Churchill's Speech as Indicating Little Prospect of Early Second Front

By The United Press.

MOSCOW, Sept. 9—British Prime Minister Winston Churchill's statement in Parliament indicating a disagreement between himself and Premier Joseph Stalin during their conversations here was published in Moscow newspapers without comment today, but it strengthened the Russian belief—correctly or incorrectly—that there was little prospect of an early second front.

Consequently there appeared to be an intensified bitterness among those Russian leaders who believe the Soviet Union is not being treated as a full-fledged Ally in the grand strategy of the British and Americans.

This feeling was strengthened by the fact that the Russians presumably were not invited, or at any rate did not attend, the Allied conferences in London at which Britain and the United States "reached complete agreement on all fields of military operations." The belief is strong that the Allies are not taking Russia's necessities into proper consideration.

The published summary of Mr. Churchill's address omitted some portions of the Prime Minister's speech but included those in which Mr. Churchill noted differences of opinion between the British and the Russians. The summary omitted Mr. Churchill's disclosure that he found difficulty in getting the Russians to understand the nature of the war at sea. It also omitted Mr. Churchill's personal appreciation of Mr. Stalin's character.

The Soviet Government had never previously gone beyond the formal communiqués to tell the public what happened at the Churchill-Stalin meetings. However, informed persons here were well aware that a sharp divergence of views over the war arose in the course of the discussions. Aside from this small group of persons, the Russian populace as a whole assumed that the results of the conference were far from satisfactory but still hoped vaguely that the much-desired second front would be opened.

Mr. Churchill's announcement that Britain and the United States reached a complete agreement in all fields of military operation in London in July was the first inkling to Russians outside of the government that such an accord had been achieved. There was also a feeling here that Britain and the United States were making their war plans without taking the necessities of Russia's situation into consideration and there was a suspicion here that Russian resistance only played a part in the Allied grand strategy. ◊

Nazi tanks and soldiers attacking a Moscow sector, 1942.

SEPTEMBER 13, 1942

INDIA IS PULLED THREE WAYS
No Middle Ground Appears in the Dispute Which Is Vital to United Nations

By HERBERT L. MATTHEWS
Wireless to The New York Times.

NEW DELHI, India, Sept. 12—The first impression of anyone arriving fresh in India with an honest desire to find out what it's all about is sheer, overwhelming bewilderment. It is not so much the magnitude of the problems involved as the absence of a middle ground upon which one can take one's stand and calmly survey the countryside.

It is customary for foreigners to come here and discover that India is not a country, that it is a continent and that it has got ever so many races, religions and languages, and that one might as well write about Europe as one nation. Actually that is a superficial difficulty which can be overcome with enough time, patience and energy.

CONFUSION OF VIEW

The real trouble is the all too human one of different people looking at the same things and drawing opposite conclusions. It is a case of distrust and misunderstanding, of sordid interests being rationalized into pious convictions, of struggles for political power and patronage being disguised as patriotism. Shot through it all is a lot of honesty, sincerity, courage and patience under desperately trying conditions. What is most lacking is the spirit of compromise and good-will.

It would certainly simplify matters if one could take a particular point of view and interpret everything in India along that line. That is what a British official would do, or a follower of the Indian Congress, or a Moslem Leaguer. To them it is all as clear as crystal—granting their premises.

The British say: "We came here at a period when conquest was the natural order of things. We put our genius, our soldiery, our commercial and administrative experience to the service of India and Britain. We brought peace and the benefits of Western civilization to India, and it is we who taught the Indians what democracy and freedom mean. We are willing to go now, and we have promised to do so, but first we have got to win this war, and be assured that our vast interests are protected, and that India herself will not be torn by internal strife."

THE CONGRESS VIEW

Congress followers say: "The British are conquerors, usurpers, tyrants. They have exploited India for their own selfish ends and deliberately kept the people in ignorance and poverty. India is a potentially rich country and yet her masses are just about the wretchedest in the world because the British will not let us develop our own industries or intensify our agriculture. The world has gone beyond the age of imperialism, as your Sumner Welles has said, and each nation has the right to independence and self-government. Let the British stay here to win this war. If they give us our own civil government we will help them win the war. But why should we fight for one tyrant against another?"

The Moslem Leaguer is not so sure of that. He too says "We want the British to go," but he adds that he sees little advantage in exchanging the British Raj for the Hindu Raj. "Your two years and seven months rule in the Provinces," he tells the followers of Congress, "has taught us that you intend to keep us in subjection. Therefore, the only solution is for you to give us the same self-determination that you are demanding, and permit us to set up our own nation of Pakistan. Then Hindus and Moslems will live side by side in complete understanding and friendliness, and we will get rid of the British quickly."

CONTRARY APPEALS

It will be noted that the Britisher addresses himself to the world, the Congress follower to the British and the Moslem Leaguer to the Congress follower, and nothing seems so beyond the realm of possibility now than that the three should get together and talk to one another. The Britisher is determined that he will pacify India by force and carry on as he always did. The Congress follower is determined on what Gandhi has called "open rebellion" to drive out the British. The Moslem Leaguer sits on the sidelines and tells his fellow-Indians, "If you want my help, give me Pakistan first."

Those are the main points of view in India and as things are going on now they are irreconcilable. True, complications of the situation lie in such questions as why a handful of British can dominate India, why so many Indians distrust the British, why Hindus and Moslems cannot solve the communal problem. There is much that cannot be settled by logic and reason, much that is emotional, many problems that will work hardship to one side or the other, whatever the solution may be.

The more one studies it the more confused and hopeless the situation seems to get, yet if there is one sure thing about it all it is that, willy-nilly, some solution has got to be found. In the long run there is no question that the British must lose in the sense that they can win this particular battle and they are putting everything they have into it. ◇

SEPTEMBER 14, 1942

Editorial
STALINGRAD

Whether Stalingrad stands or falls, its desperate defense must have a profound effect on the development of the war. If the Russians accomplish a miracle and hold out, the event could mark the turning of the tide not only in Russia but all over the world. If the city falls, the war will certainly be prolonged, though the cost of a delayed victory will be felt by Germany in all her future campaigns. She cannot revive the heaps of dead sacrifices in the gigantic assault or restore the vital weeks lost on the Volga.

The defense of Stalingrad has been compared to that of Verdun in the World War. The city itself is not a natural stronghold, as Verdun was, but control of the banks of the Volga is as important to Russia as domination of the Meuse heights was to France. In February, 1916, the Germans launched their attack on Verdun and maintained a relentless pressure for four months. They battered their way to within three miles of Verdun before the campaign collapsed. On this battlefield the Crown Prince used up forty-three divisions of elite troops, and the German army never quite recovered. But it was not alone the stubborn defense of Verdun which saved the city. The Germans were compelled to meet almost simultaneous counter-offensives by Earl Haig on the Somme and by General Brusilov in Russia. No comparable relief seems in sight for Stalingrad, with the Nazis even now in its southern suburbs.

▸

The fall of Stalingrad would be a disaster not only for Russia but for all the United Nations. Whatever cripples the Russian giant cripples us. In the words of the Soviet army newspaper, Red Star, "Stalingrad is Grozny, Baku and Transcaucasia." This means that its loss would cost Russia her main oil supply and all the riches that lie between the Caspian and Black Seas. It would dislocate the Russian armies, reduce their striking power and permit Hitler to face the West again. It may bring Japan into Siberia. It might result in the conquest of Egypt. Yet for Hitler even such a victory would not be decisive. Russia will fight on. The cruel Russian Winter is approaching. Hitler can hardly launch another major offensive there this year. But if the Russians fail now on the Volga, next year's burden on Britain and the United States will be immeasurably increased. ◆

SEPTEMBER 18, 1942

IT'S NEVER DULL ON GUADALCANAL
Snipers, Air Attacks, Shelling from Sea, Mud, Mosquitos All in a Marine's Day

By F. TILLMAN DURDIN
Special to The New York Times.

GUADALCANAL, Solomon Islands, Sept. 7 (Delayed)—Life has never a dull moment for the Marines on Guadalcanal, site of the important Solomons air base that was wrested from the Japanese a month ago. There are Japanese air attacks one day, followed by raids from the sea the next day, and there are nighttime forays by Japanese jungle snipers; such action is interspersed with duels off shore between United States dive-bombers and enemy cruisers. If the enemy is not attacking, the Marines are.

Existence is an incessant struggle for survival and a continuous series of alarms and surprises and battles and excursions. Marines here say it isn't so bad now as it was a week or two ago, but there is still plenty of excitement—enough to make "never a dull moment" almost the universal phrase for passing the time of day out here.

My diary records that on the night of my arrival on Guadalcanal a week ago the Marine positions were bombed twice by large flights of Japanese aircraft. Shortly after midnight three enemy warships, either cruisers or destroyers, slipped in to shore some fifteen miles to the east of our bivouac and were landing troops and supplies to reinforce a contingent of troops that the Japanese evidently hoped some day might be large enough and strong enough to attempt to eject the Marines from Guadalcanal.

The night vibrated with the whirl of wings as our planes took to the skies to attack the Japanese air and sea raiders. Enemy bombs bracketed our encampment and a few were killed and several injured. The Marines, cursing "tojo"—generic term here for the Japanese—tumbled from their bed rolls to their foxholes and then back to bed again. The moon broke hazily through the scudding clouds and made splotches of pale light beneath the palm and ironwood trees. It was a typical night on Guadalcanal.

The Japanese bombed us again about noon the next day and our fighters got four Zeros and two bombers in an air battle.

The following night "Oscar"—the Japanese submarine that seems to lurk continuously offshore—surfaced at midnight and indulged in some ten minutes of scattered shelling of Marines. There were no casualties and no great harm was done.

"Never a dull moment," said the Marines the following morning as they broke out their shaving kits and wash basins. "Did you ever read 'The Forty Days of Musa Dagh'? asked one officer reflectively as he sorted out his mess gear at breakfast table. Life is like that on Guadalcanal.

Two nights later two Japanese destroyers and a light cruiser crept into the bay off Guadalcanal and shelled the shore positions. The destroyers the day before had taken a Marine raiding party to little Savo Island off Guadalcanal to clean up the remnant of Japanese forces there. Life is like that on Guadalcanal. If trouble does not come to the Marines, they go out looking for it.

Meanwhile, the routine camp life goes on. The Marines bivouacked in encampments over an area of jungles and palm trees. The palm trees here are part of the world's largest coconut plantation, owned by Lever Brothers, and are the source of copra for soaps that are sold all over the globe.

Most of the Marines live on the ground under tiny pup tents. The others, who are without tents, have rigged up makeshift caves in the sides of the hills. Some have strung hammocks be-

Army landing troops and supplies on Guadalcanal in 1942.

tween trees and some have found haven in a few shamble tin-roofed houses that escaped the complete destruction in the bombardments by United States ships that preceded Marine landings.

Men sleep with their jobs—gunners with their guns, drivers with their trucks and jeeps. Mosquito nets are a necessity against anopheles. It rains almost every night—weepy tropical rain soaks into the bed rolls and seeps through tarpaulin. The nights are passed in wet chill and discomfort and the days in mud and filth that the Marines, who have been too busy fighting, have not had time to clean up.

Japanese materials—great dumps of gasoline, trucks (many broken down), food, clothing, piping, steel, cement, one-cylinder engines, bicycles, ammunition, boxes, lumber and sand bags—are still strewn throughout the Marine area. They are interspersed with supplies that the Marines themselves have brought in. The Marines deal with filth on their clothes and bodies in the Unga River, which runs miraculously swift and clear through the occupied area.

The swim in the Unga is one of the daily necessities on Guadalcanal. Many of the men drive mud-covered jeeps and trucks into the shallow, pebbly stream and wash themselves, vehicles and clothes all at one session.

The Marines were on pretty poor rations for a short time after landing and had to eat lots of captured Japanese rice and canned goods, but now the supply situation is well ahead.

Nevertheless, there are still only two meals daily. They are generous meals, however, and a typical menu, includes steak, beans, bread and butter with jam, canned peaches and coffee. The men supplement regular meals with coconuts and occasional local tangerines. There are no natives around to climb trees and get them coconuts, but high winds have solved this problem by breaking off tops of trees and bringing down a bonanza of nuts.

Many of the men still are smoking captured Japanese cigarettes and eating captured Japanese peppermint candy, which is not so bad as wearing Japanese underwear. There is a thriving black market in Japanese souvenirs, which range all the way from fencing shields to occupation bank notes.

Life is reduced to essentials and Guadalcanal's greatest pleasure is just in still being alive, in mail from home, in nighttime camaraderie around radio programs from home, in group singing of all songs that have become American folk music. ◊

43 BIG R.A.F. RAIDS SMASH NAZI CITIES
More Than a Dozen Industrial And Maritime Centers Feel Weight of 110-Day Havoc

By GEORGE GARROTT

Since the 1,000-plane British raid on the German industrial city of Cologne on May 30, constituting until that time the largest concentration of bombers over a city in the history of warfare, the Royal Air Force has carried out forty-three large-scale raids on more than a dozen German industrial cities.

In London the Air Ministry disclosed early today that new 8,000-pound bombs had caused vast destruction in the raid on Duesseldorf Sept. 10 and that against Karlsruhe Sept. 2. Reconnaissance photographs taken after the raids showed that 270 acres of Karlsruhe and 370 acres of Duesseldorf had been devastated.

The tonnage of British bombs dropped on German rail, industrial, munition and shipping centers far exceeds the weight of German bombs dropped on London in the Blitz two years ago. During the 110-day period the British Air Ministry has acknowledged the loss of 639 bombers in its daily communiqués, but observers estimate the losses at materially less than the 10 per cent considered the limit in successful aerial warfare.

At the time of the Cologne raid, British spokesmen heralded the beginning of a prolonged aerial offensive of 1,000-plane-a-night raids with the object of devastating German industrial centers one by one. While the 1,000-plane schedule has not been maintained, according to figures from British communiqués of the last two months, the announced purpose of destroying German industry has been followed with raids in smaller force every few days.

FIGHTERS IN DAILY SWEEPS
In addition to the large-scale bombing raids over industrial objectives, R.A.F. fighters by the hundred have been making almost daily sweeps along the Channel coast to blast German airfields, troop concentrations and isolated factories in occupied France and along the Belgian and Netherland coasts. Some of these raids have included more than 500 planes in sorties against objectives spread hundreds of miles along the "invasion coast."

Bremen, an important German port with shipyards for building submarines and factories producing dive-bombers and the long-range Focke-Wulf and Kondor planes, has been bombed seven times since May 30 by aerial armadas ranging in force from 200 to more than 1,000 planes. Hamburg, the largest German port and the center of submarine building, has been bombed twice with forces of 600 planes. Emden, a North Sea naval and industrial center, has been raided four times with large forces.

Other frequent objectives of large-scale British raids have been Essen, home of the Krupp munition works, bombed twice, once with a force of more than 1,000 planes, and Duisburg, industrial center of the Ruhr Valley, which has been attacked five times.

Osnabrueck, Prussian rail and war factory hub, and Saarbruecken, large steel-producing center, have been heavily bombed three times. The naval base and shipbuilding yards at Wilhelmshaven, a constant target since the beginning of the war, have been bombed twice in large force since the Cologne raid, and Duesseldorf, an important Rhenish steel-producing center, also has been visited twice. Two raids each also have been made on the war factories of Mainz, Frankfort on the Main and Wiesbaden.

The pattern of successive raids shows almost equal alternation between coastal shipbuilding centers, devoted principally to making submarines, and inland industrial points manufacturing munitions for the Nazi land war machine. ◊

Chapter 13

"HIMMLER PROGRAM KILLS POLISH JEWS"

October 1942–January 1943

Through most of 1942, while the battles were going on in the Pacific and Europe, the German authorities were carrying out the genocide of the Jews of Europe. The details remained obscure, but in November The Times published a full account supplied by Polish witnesses of what was later to become known as the Holocaust, or Shoah. The article described the whole process—the rounding up of Jews; the cattle-truck transport in which half the victims died; the extermination camps in occupied Poland at Treblinka, Sobibor and Belzec; the selection of a fraction of fit Jews for forced labor; and the arrival of Jews from Germany and Western Europe, slated for liquidation. On December 18 The Times reported that the "War on Jews" had been formally condemned by the Allied nations as a manifestation of Hitler's "oft-repeated intention to exterminate the Jewish people in Europe." Despite German efforts to conceal the crime, the details of the genocide were there for people to read years before the end of the war.

At last the military conflict between October 1942 and January 1943 swung decisively in the Allies' favor. News gradually emerged in early November about a major battle being fought in North Africa between Rommel's Axis armies and the British Commonwealth Eighth Army under the command of General Bernard Montgomery. The Battle of El Alamein swung first one way then the other, but overwhelming Commonwealth air and sea power turned the tide; by November 4 it was clear that Rommel had been beaten. He escaped encirclement and capture and retreated back to Tunisia, but Axis days were numbered.

On November 8 Roosevelt announced "the first great American blow at the Axis" when he revealed the landings in Northwest Africa in French colonial territory, called Operation Torch. Correspondents in London had been, in Raymond Daniell's words, "custodians of one of the war's biggest secrets." Nothing leaked out from the press and complete surprise was achieved in the invasion. The landing provoked an immediate move by German forces into the unoccupied area of Vichy France, and it also prompted a political crisis in Africa. The leader of the Free French, Charles de Gaulle, wanted to take the lead in reestablishing French rule in North Africa, but the Americans preferred Admiral François Darlan as their local collaborator and General Henri Giraud as commander-in-chief of French forces. Darlan was assassinated on December 24, prompting a long struggle between de Gaulle and Giraud for leadership of the French forces and territory now on the side of the Allies. The conflict surfaced sharply in January 1943 when Roosevelt and Churchill traveled by airplane to a summit meeting in the Moroccan city of Casablanca on January 14. Here they worked out their strategy for 1943, deciding to invade Sicily and Italy, maintain a combined bomber offensive to weaken Germany, but to postpone a full second front. An uneasy truce was established between de Gaulle and Giraud, whose arguments took up a significant part of the whole conference.

North Africa took away news from the other major battles. On Guadalcanal the Americans continued to build up their ground and air forces and to hammer away at the Japanese forces and supply lines. By late January the Japanese began to pull out and on February 8 the island was in American hands. The Japanese lost 20,000 men, the Americans 1,752 dead, a disparity that was to repeat itself across the Pacific campaign. In Russia the Red Army sprang the greatest surprise of the war. Unbeknownst to the Germans, a huge reserve army was moved into place to cut off the German Sixth Army under General Friedrich Paulus in Stalingrad. Operation Uranus was launched on November 19 and 20, 1942 and was an immediate success. German and Axis forces were smashed and Paulus encircled. The battle in Stalingrad became a terrible struggle of attrition. Each soldier, Hanson Baldwin later wrote, "endured the unendurable" in his own way. On January 31, Paulus surrendered. Over 300,000 soldiers died in the final struggle to capture the city.

OCTOBER 2, 1942

Editorial
HITLER AND THE EAST

Lost in the verbiage of Hitler's latest speech is a remarkable passage which has received less attention than it deserves. The program he announced for this year—"to hold everything that must be held and let the others attack"—has been generally interpreted as a turn from the offensive to the defensive. There is not the slightest doubt that Hitler would stop if he could. For some reason he is already saving his air power. The "reprisal" bombings he promises England are not taking place. The activity of the Luftwaffe is almost negligible in Egypt and even at Malta is reduced to a minimum. The losses of men and machines sustained in Russia, plus the dangerous strains that have developed in the whole structure of production and supply, are compelling reasons for a shift to a conservative strategy. Supposing Hitler were still free to choose his course, supposing further that he could control the forces he has set in motion, he would naturally want to halt where he is.

Concretely and immediately, he proposes to take over and develop the territory he has occupied in Russia. He does not say merely that Stalingrad will be taken. He declares that "no human being will ever push us away from that spot." He goes on to assert that his aim is to organize the vast space he has conquered, not simply for the purpose of rendering it usable in war but "to link it with the nutrition of our people and the obtaining of raw materials for the maintenance of all Europe." He speaks of "freeing the population from Bolshevist power" and refers

---

OCTOBER 7, 1942

CHURCHILL BLOCKS 2D FRONT DEBATE
Asks Commons Not to Press Issue at 'A Period Which Is Certainly Significant'

STALIN'S LETTER IS CITED
British Premier Indicates He Regrets Timing of Soviet Leader's Statement

By RAYMOND DANIELL Wireless to The New York Times.

LONDON, Oct. 6—Soviet Premier Joseph Stalin's letter to an American newspaper man declaring a second front in the West the best way the Allies could aid Russia had its repercussions in the House of Commons this afternoon. Prime Minister Churchill refused, however, to be lured into debate about whose move it was "at this period, which is certainly significant."

Nevertheless, parliamentarian that he is, the Prime Minister could scarcely hide the inference that Mr. Stalin's sense of timing was almost as unfortunate as his choice of words in the present circumstances.

Neither the Prime Minister nor anyone else enjoying the privileges of the Commons has made any direct reference to Wendell L. Willkie's suggestion that it would take prodding to get the United Nations' military leaders to act. The British press hitherto has been somewhat divided on Mr. Willkie's Moscow statement

DEBATE HAS BEEN REVIVED
Premier Stalin's letter, coming atop Mr. Willkie's statement, has tended to revive a debate that cannot be openly conducted without revealing secrets to the enemy. The Times, London, editorially puts the problem thus:

"Stalin's recent letter to an American journalist is a disturbing document, obviously intended to disturb. It closely follows utterances in which Mr. Willkie has declared the need for 'publicly prodding' the strategic authorities who alone, it is acknowledged, can determine the time and place for Allied offensive action.

"Echoes of these utterances were heard in Parliament yesterday. Whether criticism is justified is a question which none can judge who is not technically expert and fully informed.

"But the fact that such a debate should be carried on in the enemy's hearing among allies in a life and death struggle implies that something is wrong with the organization of the United Nations for war. It is evidence, if not of divided, at least of undefined purpose. It limits mutual confidence, and without a clear purpose absolute confidence in the enemy's dominion is not to be overthrown."

The Times declares that while Germany has isolated Russia from her friends and Japan has cut off China from Allied aid, this is no reason why the Allies should acquiesce in "fighting separate wars." Continuing, the newspaper says:

"There must be a common plan for all the United Nations, so unified and so completely worked out by a joint organ of supreme policy and command that each can feel unquestioningly confident that the actions of all the others are being completely coordinated toward achievement of the same ultimate goal—the immediately necessary means to bring in all latent power for effective action at the earliest possible time.

"Recent utterances of Allied leaders have encouraged doubt whether in this fourth year of the war any such complete plan yet exists."

CHURCHILL PARRIES QUESTION
This last is a doubt that is plaguing most Britons. It found expression today in a question put to Mr. Churchill, which evoked the following response:

"I have, of course, read and considered the statement referred to, and we are quite clear that no statement by His Majesty's Government is called for at present beyond those that have been already given on this subject." The only government statement on this matter was that made by Mr. Churchill Sept. 8. when he noted Russia's continued resistance. He said then that, while the Soviet Government felt that the Allied nations were not doing enough to relieve Nazi pressure, it was the determination of the United Nations to go to the aid of the Russians as soon as possible.

Today's statement, however, was not enough to satisfy Aneurin Bevan, one of Mr. Churchill's severest critics. Mr. Bevan asked:

to detailed and gigantic plans to build up and exploit the region. When he describes how roads and factories, mills and mines are being opened up, he states flatly that what is being done is being done "forever." Instead of bringing coal from Germany to the East, "we shall build our own industry there," he says, with the object of supplying a great part of Europe with Russian coal.

This is a pronouncement of striking, almost sensational, importance. If it means anything, it means the annexation of the Ukraine and the Black Sea and the intention to annex the Caucasus. Hitler is not occupying this region as a

military measure; he is taking possession. In affirming that Germany is on the defensive in the north and in the west in order to gain the necessary conditions for the organization of the rest of Europe, he proclaims that his purpose is to stay in Russia and rule Russian territory. This is a reversion to "Mein Kampf." It is an attempt to realize "the German mission in the East" and to place the frontier of Europe where the Nazis claim it should be—on the Volga. More clearly than any previous war utterance, it stakes the bounds of the German "lebensraum" and gives substance to Hitler's concept of the Third Reich's

"colonial space."

There may be method in this madness. In telling the world that his ambitions lie in the East and he will move in the West only if attacked, Hitler may be launching the peace offensive we have all been expecting as soon as he is able to establish his Winter line in Russia. But it is no use. Although he scorns the strategy of his opponents, he should know by now that its central aim is to keep him from ending the war on any front until they develop enough power to smash him and all his works and plans. Wherever he turns, he will never be allowed to rest. ◇

"Does the Prime Minister realize the serious effect on war production that may follow if the feeling grows that there is any misunderstanding between the Soviet Union and ourselves? Will there not be an early opportunity of clearing the public mind in this matter?"

PERSISTS IN REFUSAL TO REPLY
It has been argued, with documentary proof, that production in British mines and factories went up the day of the Dieppe raid. Some advocates of a second front have undertaken to argue the converse of the proposition that workers will work harder if they are satisfied that their labor is contributing directly to the defeat of the Axis. However, Mr. Churchill drew cheers today when he declined again to add to his earlier statement.

Oliver Stanley, former War Secretary, interposed a friendly question suggesting that whatever else the people of this country might suspect they knew their Prime Minister was "the last man in the world who needs prodding."

F. J. Bellenger, Laborite, then asked the Prime Minister for assurance "that there is the closest integration of staff matters between Russia and this country."

"I have really nothing to add, certainly not on the spur of the moment, to the carefully weighed statement I have made on this subject," Mr. Churchill replied, "and I would strongly advise the House not to press these matters unduly at a period which is certainly significant."

To demands that, in view of the discussion Premier Stalin's letter had aroused, the British Government make an early statement of its attitude on a second front, Mr. Churchill appealed to the Commons to support the position his government had taken. After that the Speaker intervened to prevent further interrogation. A majority of the members seemed to welcome that intervention. ◇

NOVEMBER 1, 1942

AFRICA BATTLE ON
British Advance Under Cover of Artillery Fire and Air Bombings

FLIERS INCREASE BLOWS
Germans Say Sandstorm Was Used to Hide Preparations for Allies' Big Thrust

By The United Press.

CAIRO, Egypt, Oct. 31—The Imperial Eighth Army was reported driving home a major attack against General Field Marshal Erwin Rommel's anchor positions near the Mediterranean coast tonight under cover of a rolling artillery barrage and sweeping air assaults in which American and British planes ranged from the desert battleground to Axis reinforcement bases on Crete.

[A German radio report heard in London said the Eighth Army opened a powerful attack at dawn yesterday after massing reinforcements drawn from the center and southern sectors of the Alamein line under cover of a sandstorm. Heavy tanks and artillery, the report said, were pacing the attack and the progress of the fighting was not yet certain. The Germans said their dive-bombers and fighters were attacking the British during lulls in a sandstorm and claimed five Curtiss P-40's had been shot down.]

The Allied air attack appeared to be growing in intensity. American bombers ranged over Crete, attacking the Maleme airdrome and Canea and leaving fires that were visible thirty miles away.

AXIS REINFORCED FROM MALEME
The Maleme airdrome is the chief landing point for German troop-carrying Junkers-52's and glider trains that bring reinforcements from Europe to the North African battleground.

The American pilots reported that their bombs landed in the target area and, together with persistent submarine attacks on Axis surface transport on the Mediterranean, were believed to have complicated the Axis supply and reinforcement problem.

The fighting along the Alamein line was reported to be a dogged, hard struggle with the Germans repeatedly launching counter-attacks despite huge losses from British artillery and machine-gun fire. Each time the Germans brought up tanks, it was reported, the armored forces were driven back, leaving the battleground strewn with wrecked and damaged machines.

The Germans were said to show particular anxiety over night attacks by the Imperials, in which two valuable positions have been seized.

British pressure reportedly was concentrated along the Mediterranean end of the front in an effort to straighten ❭

A large convoy of military trucks traveling along a road near Alamein, Egypt.

the Imperial right flank. However, progress was not easy, it was said, despite bombardments in which the Imperial artillery in the past seven days has fired more shells than were employed in the entire preceding three months.

In the air attacks over the battlefield American planes attacked the Axis landing ground at El Daba, where they smashed German planes on the ground. Other attacks were directed at El Adem, where at least four Junkers-52 troop transports were smashed; at Ba-

gush, where two or more fighters were wrecked; at Fuka, where more planes were hit, and at Sidi Abd El-Rahman, where Axis guns were hit.

The Imperial communiqué credited the Allied air force with nine victories in the air, with a loss of three machines. The bag included two 109's, a Junkers-52, a dive-bomber and several Italian Macchi-202's. ◆

NOVEMBER 3, 1942

OFFICER DEPICTS SINKING OF WASP

Tells Here How Carrier's Fate Was Decided 30 Seconds after First Torpedo Hit

MANY FIRES SET ON SHIP

Lieutenant A. J. Tucker Says Marines Piled Up 22,000 Tons Of Japanese Scrap

The marines at Tulagi Harbor and Henderson Field have piled up 22,000 tons of Japanese scrap, it was estimated here yesterday by Lieutenant A. J. Tucker, U.S.N.R., who was in command of underwater stabilization aboard the aircraft carrier Wasp when she was sunk in the battle for the Solomon Islands.

Lieutenant Tucker described the loss of the Wasp at a meeting of 200 salesmen

NOVEMBER 4, 1942

War Election History Is Repeated; Times Sq., as in 1918, Is Subdued

By MEYER BERGER

History repeated itself in Times Square last night. Sober soldiers, sailors and civilians eddied northward, southward and flowed across the intersections in the enshadowed canyon under a sharpening November wind just as they had on election night in 1918, when the world was at war.

Reporters who were out that night,

twenty-four years ago, came back to the office to write: "The city took the election news soberly last night. It was a new experience for the city to have its Great White Way turned into darkness and gloom. There was an utter absence of jollification and scarcity of noise."

Last night Times Square wore its melancholy cloak of darkness to keep down skyglow that might betray Allied ships to German submarines off the coast. Twenty-four years ago last night the Square was darkened for coal conservation. No street signs burned and shop and restaurant windows wore the same gloomy habit as the shops wore last night.

After the early crowds vanished into the theatres and motion picture houses, the Square seemed almost desolate. Open pavement glistened in the feeble light. No traffic moved on it to break

wide sweeps of open space. Mounted men lined at the curbs were silhouetted against the faint marquee glow with no surging thousands to handle. The foot patrol walked the windy beat with hands clasped behind their backs. Times Square looked almost like a semi-rural main street.

There were two major differences between this morning's headlines and the headlines of the election night of the first World War. On Nov. 6, 1918, Alfred E. Smith, the Democratic candidate, was ahead of Charles Whitman, the Republican candidate. Sharing the banner space at the top of the morning newspapers was the news in large black type: "Allies Fix Terms That Germany Must Take."

Below this another headline told of the Austrian Army's surrender to the

representing steel warehouses in the New York area who were opening a campaign to search for scrap metal in 5,000 industrial plants as part of a national movement of the American Steel Warehouse Association to collect 2,000,000 tons of scrap by Dec. 31. The meeting was held at the Hotel New Yorker.

"I don't know how long it takes to collect 22,000 tons of scrap metal," said Lieutenant Tucker. "I do know how long it takes to assemble that amount of steel into a big fighting ship, with an air group unexcelled, an internal organization which has been cohered by the rigors of thousands of miles of steaming, months of gunnery practice, hundreds of drills of all sorts, and the whole possessing a degree of keenness available only to those who have sailed through a large part of the ocean war zones. And, to my sorrow, I know how long it takes to reduce that living organism to junk.

FIGHT DECIDED IN THIRTY SECONDS
"Thirty seconds after the first torpedo struck we were licked. We fought a rear-guard action for over an hour and a half, but no power on earth could have stemmed the tide of fire, flame, concussion, smoke and flying fragments that resulted from the number of hits, the type of explosion, the internal fires, the tons of ready ammunition at the guns and on the planes, and the devastation of a gasoline system on the rampage.

"The under-water damage was not severe and we were able to control the sickening list that resulted from the opening up of the hull, so that we were not faced with the immediate foundering of the ship. Also, the engineering

plant was in good enough shape to answer almost any demand for speed or steam. So far as the down-below personnel were concerned, we were not faced with immediate destruction.

"This, however, was not the determining factor. I could not possibly do justice to the hideous devastation that existed in the hangar when I went over the side amidships. Every plane forward of that point was attired with flaming pools of gasoline, exploding bombs, ammunition in the machine-gun belts pattering in a steady chatter—all making the sound effects for a Disney color scheme and the whole serving as the unchallengeable reason for abandoning ship.

TELLS OF JAPANESE TOUGHNESS
"How did it happen that the heathen had more guts than brains to throw himself into the face of sure destruction to pick off the ripe plum in the middle of the force? It was because we are up against the toughest proposition that the world has seen, despite the observations before the war that he was a mimic, he was too myopic to fly, he didn't have financial stamina for a sustained war, and that inbreeding and syphilis had made him unfit for any class of combat work.

"We have had almost eleven months of war. I hope by now we have dispelled this illusion. He has displayed resourcefulness and initiative and military intelligence and a full understanding of the offensive spirit. He wages no war of limited liability and recognizes the expendability of both men and machines in the balance of the goal to be attained. His every soldier and sailor has an awe-

inspiring attitude of courage that makes all men pause. And very evidently he doesn't have any controversial Russian geniuses to upset his employment of every weapon and force at his disposal in order to attain his ends.

PAYS TRIBUTE TO MARINES
"If I wasn't sure of all these things before, I am now. And if the Marines in the Solomons weren't sure of it, they are now. And it is a tribute to them that they were either prepared to meet him on equal terms or else they learned damn fast; at any rate, they still hold this little theatre of war in spite of all his efforts and have displayed courage and resourcefulness enough to make Henderson Field and Tulagi Harbor a scrap pile of approximately 22,000 tons. This is no satisfaction to me; but it is comforting to think about."

The American Industries Salvage Committee announced that the honor of naming a Liberty ship, as a reward, for their collections of scrap metal in a nation-wide competition, had been won by school children of Oklahoma. They will name the ship the Will Rogers, and the widow of the cowboy humorist has been invited to accompany the youngsters to the launching of the 10,000-ton ship in an Eastern shipyard this month.

The winners are H. J. Terry, 10 years old, Oscar School in Jefferson County, whose twenty-three pupils gathered an average of 5,500 pounds, either Dorothy Lipsey, 10, or Margaret May Snell, 8, Gyp Valley School, Harper County, after a deadlock in the race for second place is broken, and Bobby Lee Walker, 10, Walco School, near Tulsa. ◊

Italian forces. "End of War in Sight," the newspapers said and so it was. Five days later blacker headlines proclaimed "Armistice Signed, End of War! Berlin Seized by Revolutionists; New Chancellor Begs for Order."

Last night, with the war's end apparently nowhere in sight, the Square carried comparatively light pedestrian and motor traffic. Service men and civilians took up most of the sidewalk space, but there were frequent empty patches in every block. No returns were flashed on The Times's bulletin board, as in peaceful years, because of the dimout. No giant spectacular signs glowed in the Square. There seemed to be more light in the clear sky than in the streets.

LONGS FOR 'OLD DAYS'
The police detail was the smallest in

more than a score of years. Only 300 men patrolled the Square, 150 on foot, the rest on horses, motor-cycles or in squad cars. Looking northward from the police information booth at Forty-third Street, down the lanes of crisply glowing red and green traffic lights, one policeman wistfully recalled when elections WERE elections.

"I've seen election nights in this Square," he mused aloud, "when the foot detail alone came to 600–700 and when the whole detail came to around 1,500. There aren't enough cops out here tonight to handle the fag end of a lively weddin'."

With no cheering, shoving thousands clustered around the projection booth damming up hundreds of thousands behind them, as in other years, last night's tides flowed smoothly. The general pace was quick because of the increasing wind. There seemed to be no interest in the election outcome, certainly no talk about it. Even at the bars the talk was mostly of war in the Pacific and in Egypt and Russia, not of Dewey and Bennett.

The temperature by The Times Tower thermometer, oddly enough, was exactly as it was that election night twenty-four years ago. It stayed in the lower forties. The air was sharp enough to keep the police mounts curveting, restlessly pawing the pavement. These hoof clashes carried far in the comparative quiet. What with gasoline rationing and other restrictions, motor traffic was thinned to a trickle.

There was no sound but the subdued murmur of conversation from the eddying throngs. Stern priority had stripped the Square of the peacetime venders ►

of tin horns and Bronx blubber blowers. Mood, of course, had something to do with the quiet.

In the lower Square, though, one bell tinkled and jangled in a tired sort of way. Pushing through the crowd toward this sound you discovered it wasn't an election reveller stubbornly clinging to tradition in the face of war. It was a woman in a fur coat, haloed by the Paramount Theatre lobby lights, seated at a War Bonds sales booth.

If last night's Times Square crowd was not the smallest in city history, it made a bid for the distinction.

THEATRE CROWD MELTS QUICKLY

The theatre break around 11 o'clock brought a brief gush of traffic, a sudden surge of pedestrians, but the crowds moved silently toward subways and buses. In the weak light under the Paramount marquee a newsdealer cried the election results, "Dewey Wins." The home-bound passed the stand unheeding. The crowds drained off quickly, whipped by the cold wind.

The City Hospital intern, his coat blowing as he stood beside the ambulance on call at the police booth, watched the departing thousands. "What an election," he said. "Not a turned ankle, not even a single belly ache." He lapsed into gloomy silence. Pretty soon the shrill traffic whistles died away. The Square was a huddle of scattered soft lights. The wind swept down deserted side streets. The mounted men swung into the saddle, clattered westward in Forty-third Street in the darkness. ◆

NOVEMBER 6, 1942

London Elated by Triumph; Axis Tasting Punishment

Wireless to The New York Times.

LONDON, Nov. 5—Confidence that General Field Marshal Erwin Rommel's forces would be crushed was voiced today in authoritative British quarters. It was asserted that General Sir Harold R.L.G. Alexander was not only rocking back the enemy on their heels, but at the same time was inflicting deliberate punishment of the kind the Nazis had meted out to helpless civilians in France, Belgium and the Netherlands.

The Axis forces were described as being subjected to the worst sort of beating any army could suffer. They are being bombed and machine-gunned from the air as they struggle westward, a confused mass, on the desert tracks. They are harried over dusty ground by relentless ground attacks on their rear and flanks and pounded from the sea by the Royal Navy's gunners following the course of the retreat.

All this is not just something that is happening accidentally. It was carefully planned months ago.

"We are not interested in towns or provinces—in Matruh, Derna, Tobruk or Bengazi," said British officials. "Libya and Cyrenaica don't mean much to us, but it is Rommel and his army we are after, and to smash him we will do our utmost.

"This is their kind of war. We wouldn't do it to civilians the way they did in France and the Low Countries, but we are punishing them now, no doubt about it. We have waited two long years for this chance."

When it was suggested that it might be premature to claim too much so early, the retort was that there was good reason to accept General Alexander's accomplishment as a great victory.

True, Marshal Rommel might extract some of his forces, and the chances are that he will live to fight another day, it was acknowledged, but the Axis Army of El Alamein no longer exists. Its remnants are "getting the works."

Emphasis is placed here on the part General Alexander has played. It is deemed a personal triumph for him, as it was he who planned the campaign, and since it opened he has been close to the scene of action. General B. L. Montgomery, commander of the Eighth Army, has received due credit, as General Alexander recognized his skill and personally wrote the communiqués.

VICTORY GOOD PROPAGANDA

Valuable material for propaganda is coming out of the sudden collapse of Marshal Rommel's armies. The British explain their willingness to talk today on the ground that what they say is true and that it will have a tonic effect throughout the free world.

Adolf Hitler has played into their hands, it is felt, by building up Marshal Rommel as a superman. He and General Alexander commanded forces of about equal strength. The former's was composed of some 60 percent Germans and the remainder Italians, it is disclosed here.

Of the British Eighth Army the outstanding fact is that its morale is higher than that of any other army to leave these islands since the war began. The men in it, who have known discouragement time and again, longing for a crack at the Germans, now are getting their heart's desire.

A flood of congratulations started by the news of last night with King George's message to General Alexander continued today with a message to the King from Mrs. Franklin D. Roosevelt The commander and army in Egypt received others from Premier Jan Christiaan Smuts of the Union of South Africa and General Charles de Gaulle.

Mitchell B026 bombers of the United States Army Air Forces and Baltimore bombers of the South African air forces on their way to attack Rommel's position in North Africa, 1942.

Field Marshal Smuts sent messages to General Alexander, Air Marshal Sir Arthur William Tedder and General Dan Pienaar of the South African Division. In the first he noted the relief of the world at "this magnificent victory, the final dimensions of which will, I hope, make it the turning point of this war."

General de Gaulle cabled that "the French Army will never forget that General Alexander led to victory some of its forces beside the British."

Prime Minister Winston Churchill congratulated the Union of South Africa on its part in the successful operation.

Throughout the past twenty-four hours the British Broadcasting Corporation has been plugging reports from the Egyptian front in forty-six languages and dialects. Four-fifths of all its news bulletins to Europe have been devoted to accounts of events in the desert.

The Italians have been told their "German masters" have led them into grave trouble.

ALL BRITAIN IS HEARTENED

The effect of the Eighth Army's cracking of Marshal Rommel's defenses has been deep and wide among the British people. A majority are keeping their fingers crossed, for every one remembers earlier hopes that died away and almost turned to despair in North Africa. Yet many persons, high and humble alike, hungry for good news, gladly accept what they know for a fact to be true.

There are millions who have some stake in the battle now being fought out, millions with sons and husbands serving under General Alexander or who have helped make the weapons being used to beat the enemy for the first time in this war. Barring some unforeseen disaster, the spirit of Britain will pick up this week as it has not for many a long month.

Pointing to the Egyptian campaign and Malta's resistance as reasons for increasing production at home still further, Sir Stafford Cripps, Lord Privy Seal, told war workers in a London factory that as United States and British strength increased, "other offensives will be started in other areas, for we are determined to do our utmost to hasten victory."

"You will help this launching of offensives much more," he added, "by speeding up war production than by talking about a second front, which the government is only too anxious to launch."

Sir Stafford hailed the Egyptian campaign as "a glorious victory for our arms," adding that the Allies were destroying German and Italian land and air forces that might otherwise attack the Soviet armies. ◊

NOVEMBER 8, 1942

President's Statement

Special to The New York Times.

WASHINGTON, Nov. 7—President Roosevelt's statement announcing the opening of a second front in French North and West Africa follows:

In order to forestall an invasion of Africa by Germany and Italy, which, if successful, would constitute a direct threat to America across the comparatively narrow sea from Western Africa, a powerful American force equipped with adequate weapons of modern warfare and under American command is today landing on the Mediterranean and Atlantic coasts of the French colonies in Africa.

The landing of this American Army is being assisted by the British Navy and air forces, and it will, in the immediate future, be reinforced by a considerable number of divisions of the British Army.

This combined Allied force, under American command, in conjunction with the British campaign in Egypt. is designed to prevent an occupation by the Axis armies of any part of Northern or Western Africa and to deny to the aggressor nations a starting point from which to launch an attack against the Atlantic coast of the Americas.

In addition, it provides an effective second-front assistance to our heroic allies in Russia.

The French Government and the French people have been informed of the purpose of this expedition and have been assured that the Allies seek no territory and have no intention of interfering with friendly French authorities in Africa.

The government of France and the people of France and the French possessions have been requested to cooperate with and assist the American expedition in its effort to repel the German and Italian international criminals, and by so doing to liberate France and the French Empire from the Axis yoke.

This expedition will develop into a major effort by the Allied Nations and there is every expectation that it will be successful in repelling the planned German and Italian invasion of Africa and prove the first historic step to the liberation and restoration of France. ◊

NOVEMBER 12, 1942

FRANCE IS OVERRUN
Nazis Reach Marseille After Hitler Scraps Armistice Pact

ITALIANS IN CORSICA
Resistance Is Reported in Their Invasion of Riviera and Savoy

By DANIEL T. BRIGHAM
By Telephone to The New York Times.

BERNE, Switzerland, Nov. 11—Twenty-four years, less six hours, after the signing of the armistice in World War I, the last vestiges of a "free" France disappeared from the map of Europe today when, preceded by two notes from Adolf Hitler—one to Marshal Henri Philippe Pétain and the other to the nation—German troops once again marched into territory that the Reichsfuehrer had promised to respect.

Simultaneously with this invasion from the north, Italian troops pushed westward from the French-Italian border into regions long coveted as "legitimate Italian aspirations," including the "thousand-year-old Italian possession," Nice. The Italians' advance was reported late tonight not to have passed without incident; several battalions of Chasseurs Alpins—the same who held back the Italians in June, 1940—were said to have "misunderstood" Italian motives.

As was the case in certain larger cities for the Germans, the Italians were escorted into some of their "objectives" by detachments of local police.

NAZIS SEND TWO COLUMNS

The German invasion began simultaneously from two points—Chalons-sur-Saone, north of Lyon, when columns of German infantry massed along the Doubs River moved southwestward, and Moulins, north of Vichy, from where an armored train was dispatched to St. Germain-des-Fosses, ten miles from the provisional capital. By noon the Germans had passed Lyon in considerable numbers without meeting resistance.

In Vichy just before 11 A.M. an outrider detachment accompanied General Field Marshal Karl von Rundstedt to his meeting with Marshal Pétain, who informed the German commander that he protested this latest German violation of the armistice convention.

[The German radio announced early this morning that Marseille, Montpelier, Pau and Toulouse had been occupied. There was no indication that the Germans had reached Toulon, where a large part of the French fleet is believed to be based.] The progress of the German motorized forces throughout the day proceeded almost without a hitch, except for some incidents in Toulouse and Marseille, where the regional prefects have imposed a state of siege with 7 o'clock curfews. The Toulouse radio at intervals this evening broadcast appeals to the population to remain calm, as the national networks had done all morning.

Private reports from many sources inside the country throughout the day stressed the apathy with which the French "greeted" the new invasion. There was no sign of panic or even of interest. Indeed, compared with June 26, 1940, today's spectators gave the Germans a dismal reception. One eyewitness in Lyon declared an entire street had emptied so no German would feel he had been "welcomed."

Just before midnight the advance guards of the Germans reached the outskirts of Marseille. They apparently did not intend to enter the blacked-out city tonight with the population in scarcely a welcoming mood.

On the western border regions other German units pushed into the interior and by noon had occupied Canfranc in the Basses Pyrenees, controlling the last railhead of French communication with Spain. Up to a late hour, except for rearguards left at strategic points along their communications, the Germans did not appear to have made any gesture toward complete occupation.

The Italians, after crossing the frontier at Ventimiglia-Menton at 5 A.M. reached the outskirts of Nice, some twenty-five miles away, at 3 P.M., reportedly having encountered some resistance along the Grande Corniche Road. Other "engagements" were said to have occurred at Villefranche and Montauban.

Northward from the coast the first practicable road runs parallel with the sea some twenty-eight miles away. Along this road, too, advance could not have been hasty, for the infantry reached Puget Theniers, near the head of the Var Valley, about 3 P.M. Official Italian reports said that, after reaching Nice, "strong formations of Italian mechanized troops rushed through the town, continuing their unhampered advance to the west." There was no report from any quarter of the occupation of Cannes or Toulon.

ITALIANS REACH CORSICA

Another Italian bulletin late tonight reported that "Italian troops have reached the shores of Corsica and occupied the island without incident."

Advancing into Savoy, long coveted by the Fascisti, other Italian formations were reported to have reached the Pont des Chevres, about midway between Modane and St. Michel de Maurienne. Tomorrow, it was added, the Italians are expected to push on to Pont Royal, thirty miles from Chambery, the limit of the demilitarized zone.

Shortly after 2 P.M. the Germans assumed control of the French side of the frontier post at Moillesullaz, near Geneva. The "ceremony" was carried out with the arrival of an Elite Guard captain, assisted by a few soldiers, who closed the French barrier. After remaining closed for more than an hour, the barricade was reopened to permit access to France, but everyone passing over was warned there would be no exit except with special permission. ◆

German soldiers in front of the Rex movie theater, which was used to house them, Paris, 1942.

RUSSIA ACCLAIMS 'FIGHTING ALLIES'
Press and Radio Extol
Effects of African
Campaign to All Soldiers and Workers

PRAVDA SOUNDS KEYNOTE
30,000,000 Copies of Paper Broadcast That Burden Is Not Being Carried Alone

MOSCOW, Nov. 15 (AP)—Russian soldiers and workers received by every available channel today the glad news that they had fighting Allies, and that powerful British and American forces in Africa were striking effective blows at the Axis.

The news had been told before, in newspaper accounts and by radio announcements. But today all agencies imparting information—press, radio, factory announcing systems and club gazettes—combined to tell fully and in elaborate detail the story of the arrival of the Americans and the smashing of the Axis African Corps.

More than 30,000,000 copies of Pravda alone went out to the people of Russia on all fronts, its headlines proclaiming the effectiveness of the Anglo-American-Soviet alliance.

Army newspapers, which go out to the men in the most advanced fighting fronts, carried enthusiastic accounts, and it was safe to assume that not a Russian soldier was unaware of the second front being created in the Mediterranean.

The impression prevailed that for days Russia had been holding back, waiting to see whether the African operations were a large-scale campaign that would have a decisive influence on the course of the war. Today that reserve was cast aside and Russia's 200,000,000 citizens were informed fully of the Allied success in Africa and its far-reaching implications.

Americans felt a new warmth in conversations with Russian people, on the subways, in streets, on buses.

"We are leading in a great war of liberation," said Pravda. "We don't carry the burden alone, but together with our Allies. Our fight is bringing victory over the enemies of humanity, over German, Fascist imperialism. On its banners are written 'Long live victory, and the Anglo-American battle alliance.'" ◊

ENEMY 'COMPLETELY FRUSTRATED' IN SOLOMON ISLANDS
Our Losses Are Only 2 Light Cruisers and 6 Destroyers Sunk

WE SINK BATTLESHIP
5 Cruisers Also in Toll—Japanese, Confused, Fire on Each Other

By CHARLES HURD
Special to The New York Times.

WASHINGTON, Nov. 16—United States naval forces in the Solomons overwhelmingly defeated a formidable Japanese force, destroying twenty-three warships and transports, including one battleship and five cruisers, in a three-day series of actions that ended yesterday (Solomons date), the Navy Department reported today.

Our losses in this fighting—the Navy stated without reservation that all known ones had been included—were listed as two light cruisers and six destroyers sunk.

The Navy announcement further stated that a Japanese battleship and six destroyers had been damaged. There was no announcement of damage suffered by American warships because this is information that would be of great value to the enemy.

PLANES NOT DOMINANT

Air power played an important role in the victory, the Navy stated, but it was not the dominant factor as in the battles of the Coral Sea and Midway Island. The bulk of the destruction was accomplished by gun crews of American warships who outfought the enemy in slashing engagements of the traditional sort.

Navy spokesmen who supplemented the factual announcement contained in the communiqué said that this action should not be considered a decisive and conclusive victory, assuring our domination of the Pacific. It was apparent, however, that the naval victory had cleared away one critical threat hanging over our land forces on New Guinea and in the Solomons.

This was the largest surface engagement yet fought in the Pacific and possibly set a record for the war.

The running battle occurred after victories by our ground and air forces in the battle area of the southwestern Pacific had forced the Japanese to attempt to counterattack in force to relieve their own soldiers. For that reason, the American command, operating through Admiral Halsey and General Douglas MacArthur, whose army bombers have collaborated in every sea engagement for months past, could lay their plans to meet the enemy at some distance from his own bases rather than undertake an expedition into the heart of Japanese waters.

The reasoning behind that plan proved to be correct, with the following results:

One Japanese battleship sunk, three heavy cruisers sunk, two light cruisers sunk, five destroyers sunk, eight transports sunk, four cargo transports de- ❯

⟨ stroyed where they were beached on Guadalcanal, one battleship damaged and six destroyers damaged.

"Two light cruisers and six destroyers are the only United States naval vessels reported sunk in the actions which were fought on Nov. 13, 14 and 15," the communiqué added. "The next of kin of casualties will be notified by telegram immediately upon receipt of information."

A high-ranking naval spokesman who was present when the communiqué was handed to newspaper reporters said that this information "is absolutely up to date."

The communiqué pointed out that during the night of Saturday–Sunday (Solomons date) some naval forces engaged Japanese surface units "in the Guadalcanal area," and details of this engagement have not been received. It was stated officially, however, that this action represented "sniping around by light stuff," and that any reports of that engagement yet to be received should not appreciably change the results as reported.

A "necessarily incomplete resume" of the battle was issued by the Navy, which traced the action from air reconnaissance reports early in November. These revealed a "heavy concentration" of warships, transports and cargo ships

by the Japanese in the vicinity of New Britain, site of the Japanese base at Rabaul and the Northwestern Solomons.

This force began to move toward Guadalcanal and Tulagi Islands, our important strongholds in the Solomons, on Nov. 10. Some naval forces steamed down from the north, while escorted transports moved southeastward from Rabaul and Buin, the advance Japanese base on the island of Bougainville.

General MacArthur's bombers, which had made almost daily attacks on the concentrations at Rabaul and Buin, attacked the moving columns of transports with considerable success, as was reported from Australian headquarters last week. Our own naval forces, generally described in informed quarters as being inferior in size to the Japanese, apparently lay in wait for the enemy.

Two Japanese battleships of the Kongo class, accompanied a force of vessels believed to include two heavy cruisers, four light cruisers and ten destroyers, reached the Guadalcanal area shortly after midnight Friday morning (Solomons date). They intended, the Navy announcement stated, "to bombard our shore positions prior to a large-scale landing from a large group of transports which had been observed in the Buin-Shortland area."

This Japanese force was formed in

three groups, each in line. Our own ships steamed between these lines at what must have been point-blank range for the heavy guns and opened fire.

"During this furious night engagement," the communiqué stated, "the Japanese seemed confused and during the latter part of the battle two of the three Japanese groups were firing at each other. Shortly thereafter the enemy fire ceased and the Japanese withdrew from the battle and retired to the northward."

Our aircraft swung into action as soon as light permitted Friday morning and found twelve transports, "under heavy naval escort," running from the Bougainville area toward Guadalcanal, where the planned bombardment should have prepared the way for their landing. Other aircraft were bombing the Japanese vessels still in the Guadalcanal area.

Shortly after midnight Friday a Japanese surface force bombarded Guadalcanal, but when the Japanese transports arrived near our beaches later in the morning they were met by American bombers that sank "at least eight of the transports." The four others continued toward Guadalcanal.

By Sunday morning American patrol aircraft reported that the Japanese forces were withdrawing northward, "and no reports of any further action have been received."

Other scouts discovered four Japanese cargo transports beached at Tassafaronga, about seven and one-half miles from our Guadalcanal positions. They were destroyed by combined air, artillery and naval gunfire.

Estimates here of the Japanese loss of life in the battle are based on the known number of men carried in various enemy ships and the fact that night actions make rescue difficult. The sunken transports carried an estimated 25,000 men. The battleship sunk would have had a crew of about 1,600 men. Aboard the three heavy cruisers sunk were probably 2,100 to 2,400 men, while the two light cruisers were manned by about 1,000 or 1,200 men. The five destroyers were manned by crews totaling about 1,000. ◈

Wounded American soldiers on the overcrowded hospital ship USS Solace during the Solomon Island campaign, 1942.

NOVEMBER 22, 1942

CEMETERY STEEL DIGS GRAVE FOR THE AXIS
Thousand Tons of Enclosures And Urns Salvaged for Scrap

A thousand tons of iron and steel urns, plot enclosures and other graveyard accessories have been salvaged by seventy cemeteries in the metropolitan area for conversion into implements to deal death among the Axis, the regional office of the War Production Board's general salvage section disclosed yesterday.

The WPB made public a report from Harry C. Vail, salvage chairman of the Association of Cemetery Officials of the Metropolitan District, which said that all religious faiths were cooperating in the cemetery scrap project.

Mr. Vail said the project was slow in getting started because of the necessity of obtaining written permission from the plot owners, many of whom were hard to locate. Authorizations were coming in faster now that the preliminary work has been done, he said. One plot owner, located in Mexico, wrote back, authorizing removal of iron gateposts, markers and "anything to beat the Axis."

The 1,000 tons of metal already started toward the steel mills will furnish enough scrap for 200 3-inch anti-aircraft guns or 40,000 machine guns of .50 caliber, according to the WPB.

Mr. Vail said the cemetery officials' salvage committee had outlined its program to all cemeteries in the State and hoped to extend the salvage campaign beyond the metropolitan district. He suggested that plot owners who wished to contribute the metal on their plots inform their cemetery managers of their wishes. ◆

NOVEMBER 19, 1942

NAZI ARMY IN PERIL
Two Russian Forces Are Advancing North and South to Trap Foe

MUCH BOOTY IS CAPTURED
Soviet Also Reports Victories over Germans in 2 Regions of the Caucasus

By The United Press.

MOSCOW, Nov. 23—Germany's Stalingrad salient is in grave peril under a pulverizing Russian onslaught that has killed more than 15,000 Nazi troops, recaptured the Don River stronghold of Kalach and rolled up Soviet advances of forty to fifty miles, the Red Army reported today.

Shortly after the announcement of a tremendous offensive against both flanks of the German salient tipped by Stalingrad, the midnight communiqué said the Russians were forging rapidly ahead south and northwest of the city.

A special communiqué last night said the Red Army, smashing through the German lines, had slain 14,000 enemy troops and captured 13,000 prisoners in the opening phase of the greatest offensive it has started since last Winter.

GERMANS' RAILWAYS CUT
The capture of Kalach, on the east bank of the Don forty miles west of Stalingrad, and with it the railroad towns of Krivo Muzginskaya, on the line ten miles southeastward, and Abganerovo, thirty-two miles southwest of Stalingrad on the main Caucasus railway, had cut Nazi rail communications with their forces east of the Don bend.

The midnight communiqué listing more Russian victories on both German flanks, said another 1,000 Nazis were killed northwest of Stalingrad and 5,000 more captured south of the city.

The initial impact of the Soviet offensive, a huge nutcracker clamped on the tottering German positions in and behind Stalingrad, blasted a twenty-mile breach in the Nazi lines northwest of the city and a thirteen-mile gap in those on the southern flank, the High Command revealed.

Six Axis infantry divisions and one tank division were "completely routed," and heavy losses were inflicted on seven infantry, two tank and two motorized divisions, the first announcement said.

REDS ATTACK IN STALINGRAD
In Stalingrad itself the Russians repulsed attacks by German infantry and tanks, killing "several hundred" assault troops. In one sector the Russians swung over to the attack and, after breaking German resistance, occupied a height dominating a broad sweep of the city.

The successful advance continued northwest of Stalingrad, the midnight communiqué said. In one sector about two regiments of 6,000 German infantry were routed, eighteen tanks destroyed, twelve guns and thirty dugouts wrecked, and large Nazi stores captured.

In another sector the Russians dislodged the Germans from a fortified stronghold, killing more than 1,000 enemy troops and destroying twenty-three machine guns, fourteen mortars, two munition dumps and one food base.

South of Stalingrad, Soviet troops, overcoming resistance, are forging determinedly ahead, the late report said. Several dozen inhabited localities have been captured, it asserted.

There one Soviet unit routed a full Axis infantry division, taking more ❱

than 5,000 prisoners. A whole artillery regiment of the division, together with the commander, surrendered.

In a single day of fighting south of Stalingrad, the Russians were reported to have captured three German tanks, thirty-six cannon, twenty-two mortars, 100 anti-tank guns, 2,000,000 rifle cartridges and other materiel.

In the Central Caucasus the Russians disabled two tanks. A factory was occupied in another sector.

Across the Caucasus in the Tuapse area a German battalion attacked a height and was repulsed with 100 men killed, the high command said.

The recapture of Kalach was the first big victory in the Red Army's Winter offensive against the German invaders. After Kalach fell, the Russians pressed ten miles southeastward and seized the railroad town of Krivo Muzginskaya on the line to Stalingrad, indicating that they were driving eastward to attack the Stalingrad siege army from the rear.

At the same time Red Army forces pushing up from the south took Abganerovo, thirty-two miles southwest of Stalingrad on the main railway running down into the Caucasus. Thus the Germans lost both of their rail connections with the advanced forces at Stalingrad.

The massive Russian drive was reminiscent of Marshal Semyon Timoshenko's counter-offensive a year ago which recaptured Rostov, gateway to the Caucasus, and set in motion the Winter campaign of the Red Army. Rostov fell to the Germans a year ago today and exactly a week later Marshal Timoshenko threw them out and began chasing them back along the Sea of Azov coast and into the Ukraine.

The Russian Armies deployed along the outer approaches to Stalingrad struck with deadly effect several days ago, according to the special communiqué the second in a week revealing a great Soviet success in South Russia. They converged from two directions on both the exposed flanks of the German Army, which had spearheaded across the Don to Stalingrad and besieged the defiant city for nearly three months.

The initial breakthrough northwest of Stalingrad was in the region of Serafimovich, on the Don 100 miles above the Volga city.

MUCH BOOTY IS TAKEN

The booty in three days of fighting

Soviet Offensive Imperils the Germans: Breaking broad gaps in the enemy positions, the Russians captured Kalach and Krivo Muzginskaya (1), west of Stalingrad; and Abganerovo (2), to the south. They thus severed two of the rail lines supplying the Nazi forces assaulting the Volga city. A Red Army offensive was also progressing to the northwest in the neighborhood of Serafimovich (3) on the Don River.

included 360 field guns, great lots of smaller arms and trucks, and mountainous stores of various war supplies, ammunition and fuel, the High Command said. The enemy left on the battlefield more than 14,000 corpses of officers and men, the communiqué said.

The government newspaper Izvestia said the German command still was moving reserves "into the mouth of the furnace" at Stalingrad, which it described as the crematorium" of the Nazi Army.

"There are more German corpses amid the ruins of Stalingrad than there are stones," Izvestia said.

It was three months ago, on Aug. 23, that the Germans began the battle for Stalingrad with the first mass air attack on the city. The latest German offensive was begun Nov. 12.

The German attacks in the northern factory area recently had been limited to platoons supported by individual tanks. The Russians have been slicing off the tips of Nazi salients and wiping out encircled detachments, front reports said.

After Germany's disastrous defeat before Orjonokidze, the Central Caucasus, the invasion forces fell back beyond a water barrier and tried to dig in among the hills southeast of Nalchik. Soviet sappers cleared a path through the mine fields and anti-tank obstacles, enabling Red Army infantry to go forward and overwhelm a fortified hill.

Rains were said to have transformed the roads southeast of Nalchik into bogs in which German transport and armored units wallowed helplessly. The Nazis no longer are using their tanks to spearhead attacks but as roving gun posts supporting their infantry, front reports said. ◆

NOVEMBER 25, 1942

HIMMLER PROGRAM KILLS POLISH JEWS
Slaughter of 250,000 in Plan To Wipe Out Half in Country This Year Is Reported

REGIME IN LONDON ACTS
Officials of Poland Publish Data— Dr. Wise Gets Check Here by State Department

By JAMES MacDONALD
Special Cable to THE NEW YORK TIMES

LONDON, Nov. 24—Old persons, children, infants and cripples among the Jewish population of Poland are being shot, killed by various other methods or forced to undergo hardships that inevitably cause death as a means of carrying out an order by Heinrich Himmler, Nazi Gestapo chief, that half the remaining Polish Jews must be exterminated by the end of this year, according to a report issued today by the Polish Government in London.

The report, some details of which have been printed recently in Palestine newspapers, said the only Jews being spared in Poland were the able-bodied who could provide "slave labor" for the German war effort.

The Polish authorities gave out statistics showing that up to Oct. 1 about 250,000 Polish Jews had been killed under the Himmler program, put into effect this year.

As an instance of the rapidity with which the Jewish population had been cut down, either by evacuation to Nazi war factories, deaths from disease or by liquidation, the Polish officials said only 40,000 October ration cards had been printed for the Jews in the Warsaw ghetto, where the population last March was 433,000. This had been a reduction from 130,000 ration cards in September for the Warsaw Jews.

MASS KILLINGS IN FREIGHT CARS

Declaring that the Nazi program to reduce the number of Jews in Poland by 50 per cent this year was a "first step toward complete liquidation," the report said:

"The most ruthless methods are being applied. The victims are either dragged out of their homes or simply seized in the streets.

"The Germans have mobilized a special battalion under the command of S. S. men and these are characterized by their utter ruthlessness and inhumanity. The victims when caught are driven to a square where old people and cripples are selected, taken to a cemetery and shot there.

"The remainder are loaded into goods trucks [freight cars] at a rate of 150 to a truck that normally holds forty. The floors of the trucks are covered with a thick layer of lime or chlorine sprinkled with water. The doors are sealed.

"Sometimes the train starts im- ⟩

A Nazi roundup of Jews in Warsaw, 1942.

⟨ mediately on being loaded. Sometimes it remains on a siding for two days or even longer.

"The people are packed so tightly that those who die of suffocation remain in the crowd side by side with those still living and with those slowly dying from the fumes of the lime and chloride and from lack of air, water and food.

"Wherever the trains arrive half the people are dead. Those surviving are sent to special camps at Treblinka, Belzec and Sobibor [in Southeastern Poland]. Once there the so-called settlers are mass-murdered.

FEW SURVIVE
FOR LABOR BATTALIONS

"Only the young and relatively strong people are left alive for they provide valuable slave labor for the Germans. However, the percentage of these is extremely small, for out of a total of about 250,000 resettled, only about 4,000 have been sent to do auxiliary work on the battle fronts.

"Neither children nor babies are spared. Orphans from asylums and day nurseries are evacuated as well. The director of the biggest Jewish orphanage in Warsaw and well-known Polish writer Janusz Korczak, to whom the Germans had given permission to remain in the ghetto,

preferred to follow his charges to death.

"Thus under the guise of resettlement in the east, the mass murder of the Jewish population is taking place."

The report remarked in connection with the data showing the population of the Warsaw ghetto as 433,000 in March that, although there was extremely high mortality there because of bad hygienic conditions, starvation, executions and the like, the number in the ghetto had remained more or less stable because Jews from other parts of Poland and from Germany, Austria and the Netherlands had been taken there. ◊

DECEMBER 5, 1942

AXIS FIGHTS HARD TO HOLD VITAL NORTHEAST TUNISIA

ALLIES LOSE TOWNS
Nazis Retake Tebourba, Hold Mateur and Part of Djedeida

DECISIVE PHASE IS NEAR
Both Sides Recouping Strength— U. S. Troops Drive Foe East from Tebessa

By JAMES MacDONALD
Special Cable to THE NEW YORK TIMES.

LONDON, Dec. 4—A fierce tank battle raged today in the vital railroad and highway triangle between Bizerte and Tunis, the immediate objectives of the Allied drive in Tunisia, according to reports reaching London tonight from both Allied and enemy sources. Both sides were said to be using parachute troops on a large scale.

Apparently the Axis forces have recaptured the town of Tebourba, which is about twenty miles west of Tunis. Also, they again hold the eastern half of Djedeida, twelve miles west of Tunis—Djedeida having changed hands several times.

Meanwhile Mateur, twenty-two miles southwest of Bizerte, is still in the possession of the enemy despite intense pressure by Allied forces. The Morocco radio reported tonight that violent fighting was going on in the Mateur sector as the Allies strove to retain their grip on the railroad linking Mateur and Djedeida.

DECISIVE STAGE STILL AHEAD
How the battle was progressing was not disclosed in the Allied headquarters communiqué but unofficial reports indicated that thus far the struggle had not reached a decisive stage. It marked the climax of the recent fighting, in which both sides suffered big losses in armor, and the Allied forces were temporarily, but not seriously, checked, chiefly through enemy superiority in the air.

[American combat troops, striking southeast of Tebessa, near the Algerian border, drove a Nazi armored column

back toward the coast yesterday in disorderly retreat, capturing more than 100 prisoners and taking a town, it was reported from Allied headquarters in North Africa by The Associated Press. The Americans, fighting with French allies, were commanded by Colonel Edson Raff, United States parachute leader, and included infantry, mechanized and parachute troops. Apparently the same action was reported in a French communiqué, which placed it at Sidi bou Zid, about eighty miles from Tebessa.

[British warships, still so new that they are on the "secret list," were reported from London to have joined the Mediterranean Fleet in the struggle to keep Axis reinforcements from reaching Tunisia. At the same time London

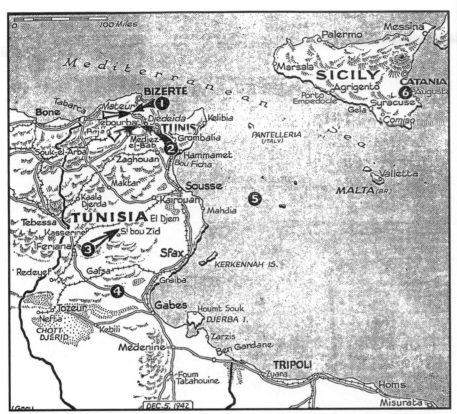

Axis Fights Hard to Hold Vital Northeast Tunisia: Another fierce tank battle raged in the mountainous region southwest of Bizerte and west of Tunis, with the Germans reported to be clinging to Mateur (1), and to have definitely retaken Tebourba (2), near which the Allies were consolidating their positions. The docks at Bizerte and an airdrome at Tunis were heavily bombed. United States and French troops routed a Nazi armored column in the region of Sidibou Zid (3) and Axis patrols were routed between Gafsa and Gabes (4). Allied airmen struck hard at positions around Gabes. Off the eastern coast of Tunisia (5) at least two Axis merchantmen and an Italian torpedo boat were sunk. Several places in Sicily were raided, one British plane crashing near Augusta (6).

announced that Allied aircraft had sunk two more Axis merchantmen off the eastern coast of Tunisia and that naval craft had sunk an Italian torpedo boat.]

A spokesman at Allied headquarters said the battlefield was strewn with wrecked Allied and Axis tanks after forty-eight hours of fierce combat.

Tonight's Allied communiqué said the attacking forces in the neighborhood of Tebourba were consolidating their positions. In the southern sector French and Allied troops, who are seeking to wrest the port of Gabés from the enemy, captured an undetermined number of prisoners.

Allied planes kept up constant attacks on Bizerte, Gabès and Tunis. The communiqué issued in London tonight said the Bizerte docks were bombed in daylight yesterday and that both day and night raids were carried out against the Tunis air base, the landing point for enemy air-borne reinforcements of men and supplies. Allied fighter pilots made sweeps throughout the forward areas and along the coast between Tunis and Gabès.

The Berlin radio boasted that heavy German tanks and long-range guns had knocked out so many Allied tanks in the Tebourba area that activity there had "slackened considerably." The Na-

zi claimed that forty United States tanks were destroyed or captured by Axis troops near Tebourba and upward of 800 prisoners taken. On the other hand, reports from British sources said 25-pounder guns were taking a heavy toll of the Germans.

An Allied headquarters spokesman cautioned against overoptimism at the present stage of the fighting.

He pointed out that the German and Italian forces were as large as those of the Allies and had the advantage of shorter lines of communication from Sicily. He estimated that the Germans numbered 10,000 and the Italians 8,000 in the Tunis-Bizerte area. ◆

DECEMBER 29, 1942

The Battle of Buna

By F. TILLMAN DURDIN
Wireless to THE NEW YORK TIMES.

WITH ADVANCE UNITED STATES FORCES, in New Guinea, Dec. 5 (Delayed)—The commanding officer in the first of two peeps waved and boomed in broad American, "Good morning, boys," as we passed between long lines of native carriers toting supplies to this front. The natives, some dressed only in breechclouts and others in shorts or laplaps, smiled and waved back, some shouting:

"Good morning, Toboda. Good morning, sir."

The sun warmed the verdant jungle, made fresh by a night of rain. The narrow peep track wound between walls of green and occasionally crossed creeks and swamps made passable by layers of fresh-cut logs.

Hearty and confident, the commanding officer stopped before each group of American soldiers along the route— engineers and service troops mostly— asked about their works, and said:

"Keep the stuff coming up, boys. I am proud of you. You are doing a wonderful job. This is a big day, you know."

The grimy and bearded men grinned, "Thank you, sir; we'll do our best, sir."

BEGIN WALKING TO FRONT

The commander, his staff of unit commanders and two newspaper men dismounted from peeps as the ground petered out two miles from the front. We slogged on over the tortuous trail ankle deep in mud, pushing dangling vines and ducking under the spiny fronds of pandanus trees. Jungle birds uttered low, ironic notes in the dense canopy above us. They seemed to be saying:

"Oh, no. Oh, no—no, no, no."

We passed a little group of men sitting in the mud putting on new pairs of shoes that had just been brought up. At advance headquarters—two tents, flanked with foxholes at the roots of two giant trees—the commanding officer conferred briefly. The American troops were to attack toward Buna village at 10 o'clock in one of the biggest assaults of the Buna front.

There was to be an intensive artillery and air bombardment preparation.

The air show started first. Through the trees we caught fleeting glimpses of B-25 bombers in threes, roaring overhead. Their bombs rustled down and shook the ground as they exploded ▶

(200 yards away in Buna village and in Buna mission a few hundred yards farther east along the coast. A Japanese anti-aircraft gun pounded away at them, its detonations making the swamplands quiver beneath us in a curious likeness to an earthquake.

Then the artillery joined in the bombardment, their shells whistling overhead in steady succession. The telephone rang. An advance observation post reported some artillery shells were falling too short and that one had just hit within thirty feet of the post. A unit commander called the artillery post and told them to open the range a hundred yards.

"I'll go up and see for myself," the commanding officer said. "I want those shells to be pretty close in there."

Al Noderer of The Chicago Tribune and I followed along with several staff officers and unit commanders. The artillery had ceased hitting the Buna village sector when we reached the observation post, but it continued pounding the Mission area. The land attack had just started from the vicinity of the observation post.

BULLETS FLY IN THE JUNGLE

It was 10:30. The jungle flamed with machine-gun, rifle and tommy-gun fire. Bullets seemed to be flying from all directions through the trees around the observation post. Leaves fluttered to the ground as lead spat against the branches and whined in ricochet off into the distance. We crawled into foxholes.

Our troops had advanced only a few yards through the jungle on both sides of the trail leading to Buna village, but were already out of sight in the thick foliage. Between them and the village on the east bank were 150 yards of jungle palm trees in which the Japanese were strongly ensconced in elaborate concealed dugouts, entrenchments and foxholes.

Snipers seemed everywhere in the trees, their little explosive bullets bursting with loud cracks at the slightest impact with limbs or twigs. Their fire seemed aimless, merely designed to confuse or harass. Our bombers continued to come over and drop 500-pounders into the Buna Mission and Cape Endaiadere, farther east.

Around the observation post telephone, officers had to shout to be heard above the racket of the battle. Our troops made slow progress against the 150-yard barrier that separated them from Buna village. Hollow-eyed and unshaven, their splotchy green uniforms caked with filth from two weeks in the slime around Buna, they stalked invisible Japanese machine-gun nests, routed out snipers they couldn't see, hurled grenades and sprayed the jungles with tommy-gun fire.

WOUNDED CARRIED BACK

The wounded started coming back, some on litters, some afoot. Those on litters lay quietly, their lips compressed as stretcher-bearers hurried them off to dressing stations. One man's shattered arm kept wabbling limply over the side of the stretcher, and the rear bearer would reach over and lay it back in place.

The commanding officer and three staff officers went off down the trail seeking a sniper that was harassing the observation post. The sniper threw grenades at them, but they ducked, escaped and raked his tree with tommy guns. A bullet from somewhere grazed a unit com-

---

DECEMBER 11, 1942

General Chennault Is Optimistic on China's Prospects Of Victory

By BROOKS ATKINSON
Wireless to The New York Times.

A UNITED STATES ARMY AIR BASE in Central China, Dec. 9 (Delayed)— Although China lies at the dim end of our long lines of communication, Brig. Gen. Claire L. Chennault, commander of our China Air Task Force, retains his enthusiasm and confidence. Free China may be pinched and poor behind the Japanese blockade, but General Chennault is rich in ideas and energy.

He and his staff inhabit a headquarters building that vividly symbolizes our investment in the Chinese theatre of war. It is part of the Chinese compound, and its yellowish loft buildings are of plastered mud construction with a mud-tile roof.

Officers and enlisted men sit at unpainted pine desks, wrapped in field jackets or sheep-lined coats, while a Chinese orderly in a bulgy padded uniform keeps making the round of stoves with fresh fuel.

Major General Claire Chennault in 1942.

Clogged with visitors who stand because there is no place to sit, this headquarters gives an impromptu impression of making the most of the least without grumbling.

In a small room at the end of the building General Chennault offers visitors the incomparable luxury of a striped porch chair that looks more hospitable than it is. But the general, who has had five and one-half years' experience in fighting the Japanese with next to nothing, radiates hospitality and is the graveyard of all doubts about the war in China.

As an airman who organized and led the fighting American Volunteer Group before he took over his present command, he believes he is fighting the weakest arm of the Japanese war machine and that destroying Japanese aviation is the first step toward defeating Japan. By frugally husbanding his resources and planning every action with exactitude, he has led an air force that has made an astonishing record, destroying ten or more Japanese planes for every one lost by an American. It has established air superiority wherever it has been able to operate.

Although General Chennault does not indulge personally in mathematical rationalization, he has no objection to a visitor's estimate that, if the same ratio of success could be maintained, 500 American planes in this theater could destroy the effective Japanese air force. In his opinion, the Japanese air force is deteriorating. He does not think it now includes many pilots of more than four to six months' experience, and, while new Japanese planes have excellent performance, the quality of the engines is deteriorating noticeably.

He estimates Japan's ability to replace combat planes at not more than 250 a month, "which is a high estimate" he says. To his way of thinking, these facts bear directly on the job of defeating Japan.

"As everyone knows," he said in an interview yesterday afternoon, "no army or navy can operate without an air force. China is the logical place for the Japanese air force because the Japanese must have some place from which to get at

mander's neck, causing a bright red burn.

Japanese mortar fire started falling about, but it seemed to do little damage. The time went fast. At 11:30 a runner came back from a forward unit.

"We have reached the sea, sir," he told the commanding officer.

Some of our troops had worked through the Japanese and reached the beach east of Buna village. The commanding officer was pleased.

"Tell the captain to hold if he possibly can," he directed the runner. "That cuts them off from reinforcements from Buna mission."

There was a slight lull. Young Major C. M. Beaver, whose home is in Yanktown, S. D., led Noderer and me forward to see a Japanese bivouac and defense position that we had just occupied. There was a surface dugout strongly reinforced with logs up against a wooden-floored tent. In the dugout were two dead Japanese.

The floor of the tent was littered with packs, canvas bags, medicines and canteens. We sorted through the stuff. I ran across Australian soap, pictures, and several big slabs of bomb casing with American lettering, evidently parts of one of our bombs being kept as a souvenir.

There were lots of canned meat, rice and boxes of matches made in the Philippines. Each pack had lots of fresh, clean underwear. The area around the tent was a network of foxholes. We got a few souvenirs, returned to the observation post and half a "ration bar" for lunch.

At 1:10 the commanding officer ordered mortar fire on the palm-grove just outside Buna village preparatory to an attack through it. A sergeant was sent up a tall tree to act as an observer. He stuck to it through several explosions, but ants got in his ears, nose, pants and eyes, and he finally had to come down.

The American attack had reached a critical stage. Our men had cleaned out about half the distance to the village and seemed to be bogging down. After a conference, the commanding officer sent in a unit that he had held in reserve, to make a running attack and final bayonet charge toward the village. The men hustled up past the observation post, and the commanding officer encouraged them by slapping them on the arm as they passed.

A group ran ahead spiritedly. We could hear their cries ten minutes later as they swept toward the village, bypassing some Japanese positions and taking others out with grenades and tommyguns as they went. A high officer, the second in command, came by on a stretcher with a wound in his shoulder.

The commanding officer went forward with an aide to watch the attack. Only twenty yards ahead a sniper who had been lying doggo, probably for hours, fired, and the aide crumpled with a wound in his body. He was hurried to the rear on a stretcher. The attack carried through to the very edge of Buna village. There was savage bayonet fighting, and then the lines parted and our men dug in.

The commanding officer sent another contingent through to the village on the left. They reached a little collection of huts almost without opposition. It was now 4:30 P. M. By and large the attack had succeeded, and a big area had been cleared except for a few isolated Japanese positions, We had virtually surrounded the village and were set for the final kill. ◇

---

and protect the China posts they have occupied. Look at the map for yourself and you will see what I mean."

By now General Chennault is an old China hand. He not only likes the Chinese, who naturally regard him as something of a miracle man, but believes in them as soldiers.

"So far," he points out, "they are the only soldiers who have defeated the Japanese in open battle, man for man. They have done it many times.

"Since one thing they do not lack is manpower, our function is to supply them with equipment so they can fight."

General Chennault points out that the Chinese fought the Japanese alone for four and one-half years, while Americans were still selling war materials to the Japanese.

He has also found the Chinese wonderfully cooperative, from the common soldier to the commanding officer, and generous with whatever material they have had.

As for the assumption that the Americans came to the rescue of China, General Chennault reports the Japanese had been preparing for twenty years to attack us.

"Do you suppose that the attack on Pearl Harbor was on the spur of the moment?" he inquired. "Do you suppose the attack on the Philippines was extemporaneous?

"It took years of intelligence, work and planning to carry out those attacks with so much exact knowledge of our airdromes, equipment, installations and forces. We are in this war because the Japanese attacked us, as they had been planning to do deliberately for many years."

Apart from the war, General Chennault is interested in the future of China as a market for American goods and a source of raw products. We are the only nation, he says, that is not at this moment studying China and paving the way for post-war trade.

According to General Chennault, Wendell L. Willkie got a better grasp on China in a few days than most Americans do in months and understood the fact that after the war millions of Chinese who have been seeing America's products for the first time will want to use them and that China will be able to exchange for them silk, tungsten, certain grades of tea, tin, hog bristles and many other materials we need or can use.

Since the Chinese have high regard for Americans generally, he does not understand why the Americans are not getting organized on a large scale for a huge market that will keep our factories working.

In fact, General Chennault is a stimulating man to listen to on one's first day in China and much warmer of heart than the feeble little charcoal stoves in his draughty headquarters. ◇

DECEMBER 12, 1942

GUADALCANAL JOB NOW HELD MOP-UP
Vandegrift, Reviewing 4-Month Work, Says Remaining Task Is One of Consolidation

TAKES PRIDE IN HIS MEN
Points to Their 10-to-1 Killing of Enemy— A Guerrilla Saga of Marines Is Unfolded

GUADALCANAL, Dec. 7 (Delayed) (UP)—Japanese troop losses in killed have exceeded ours by more than ten to one and more than 450 enemy planes have been destroyed in the four months' campaign on Guadalcanal, and our positions now are stronger than ever before, Major Gen. Alexander A. Vande- ❯

grift, Marine commander, said today.

About 6,640 enemy troops have been slain. On that basis American casualties would be fewer than 700 killed.

Japanese fatalities, General Vandegrift emphasized, do not include the many thousand slain in sea and air battles or those killed in unsuccessful landing attempts.

Air losses are running about seven to one in our favor, he said, with American fighters alone bagging more than 450 Japanese planes.

These heavy enemy losses and our growing air and sea power have sharply reduced the threat to American positions, which are being strongly consolidated, the general declared.

It is still possible, he said, for the Japanese to take advantage of bad weather and land reinforcements and supplies, "but with our augmented air power and the work of our Navy, such a development is no more than a possibility."

OUR SUPPLY LINES SAFEGUARDED

"Our seizure of key bases has blocked the Japs from preying on American supply lines to Australia," he said, "and their futile counter-assaults on Guadalcanal have cost them dearly."

General Vandegrift listed the following highlights of the Solomons campaign:
1. The American landing on Aug. 7 and mopping-up of Japanese occupation forces in the vicinity of Henderson Field, which took about two weeks.
2. Landing of about 1,000 crack Japanese troops and their attempt to capture our positions to the southeast which resulted in wiping out 926 of them on Aug. 21 in the battle of the Tenaru River.
3. The Sept. 13–14 "battle of the ridge" west of Henderson Field. In this battle, which followed heavy enemy artillery bombardment, about 1,500 out of 3,000 Japanese attackers were killed and the others caught by our subsequent offensive.
4. The Nov. 13–15 action, when American sea and air power smashed a big landing attempt, sinking 28 Japanese ships and damaging 10 others. General Vandegrift said that the Japanese managed to get about 1,000 troops ashore and a few supplies from the transport and three cargo ships which were beached on Guadalcanal in the action.

"Thus in four months," he said, "our forces have completed the occupation and initial maintenance of Henderson Field and the surrounding area. Our operations now consist of mopping up the remnants of the enemy and strongly consolidating our base and garrison here."

EACH MAN COOKS OWN MEAL

General Vandegrift's interview was granted as the base welcomed a rugged band of Marine raiders who arrived yesterday, bearded and footsore, after killing 400 Japanese and seizing three enemy artillery positions in a month's guerrilla operations in the sniper-infested jungle.

The guerrillas were led by tough, sun-tanned Lieut. Col. Evans F. Carlson, 47, of Plymouth, Conn.

He and his men waded streams, hacked their way through dense undergrowth and lived on rice, bacon, raisins and tea during one of the longest sustained guerrilla treks on record.

"We started on a forty-eight-hour mission and remained a month," Colonel Carlson said. "The men proved self-reliant and resourceful, traveling light and fast."

Each man cooked his own meal and at night in the absence of blankets they cut boughs from trees and gathered leaves to make beds.

Colonel Carlson, who led American forces in a commando-type raid on Makin Island on Aug. 17, said they penetrated miles beyond the American lines "in danger of snipers at every step."

"The Japs are capable fighters, and they fight to the last man," he said, "but our men can play that way, too."

On armistice day, Colonel Carlson said, the guerrillas met their first large enemy force.

"We caught them crossing a river and wiped out twenty or thirty," he related. "That was only the beginning. The next two days we got forty to fifty more."

One of Colonel Carlson's force, Captain Richard Washburn of West Haven, Conn., told how his patrol group attacked a Japanese unit.

"We caught a party of about thirty having a holiday, laughing and shouting," he said. "We slipped up close and let them have it with machine guns and automatics. We killed most of them before they recovered from surprise and returned the fire." ◆

DECEMBER 16, 1942

HOLLYWOOD GROUP SHOWS WAR WORK
Victory Committee Tells Of Entertainment Provided by Artists During the Year

SERVICES GIVEN BY 1,141
6,828 Individual Appearances Made— Government, Charity Agencies Were Aided

The Hollywood Victory Committee, organized three days after the Pearl Harbor attack to coordinate the efforts of film, stage and radio personalities in the entertainment of the armed forces and in otherwise assisting the national war effort, released yesterday its first annual report through the Industry Service Bureau of Motion Pictures in Hollywood.

The Victory Committee organized a talent pool of 1,141 artists who not only provided entertainment for men in service, according to the report, but also rendered service to the Treasury Department in bond-selling campaigns, Office of War Information, War Production Board, Office of Emergency Management, Office of the Coordinator of Inter-American Affairs and other governmental agencies. Also to the USO, Red Cross, Russian War Relief, China War Relief, Army and Navy Relief, Community Chest and other charitable organizations.

USO CAMP SHOWS GIVEN

Highlights of the twelve months' report include the presentation of 352 USO shows at Army, Navy, air forces

DECEMBER 18, 1942

11 ALLIES CONDEMN NAZI WAR ON JEWS
United Nations Issue Joint Declaration Of Protest on 'Cold-Blooded Extermination'

Special to The New York Times.

WASHINGTON, Dec. 17—A joint declaration by members of the United Nations was issued today condemning Germany's "bestial policy of cold-blooded extermination" of Jews and declaring that "such events can only strengthen the resolve of all freedom-loving peoples to overthrow the barbarous Hitlerite tyranny."

The nations reaffirmed "their solemn resolution to insure that those responsible for these crimes shall not escape retribution and to press on with the necessary practical measures to this end."

The declaration was issued simultaneously through the State Department here and in London. It was subscribed to by eleven nations, including the United States, Britain and Russia, and also by the French National Committee in London.

The declaration referred particularly to the program as conducted in Poland and to the barbarous forms it is taking.

The attention of the Belgian, Czechoslovak, Greek, Luxembourg, Netherlands, Norwegian, Polish, Soviet, United Kingdom, United States and Yugoslav Governments and also of the French National Committee has been drawn to numerous reports from Europe that the German authorities, not content with denying to persons of Jewish race in all the territories over which their barbarous rule has been extended, the most elementary human rights, are now carrying into effect Hitler's oftrepeated intention to exterminate the Jewish people in Europe.

From all the occupied countries Jews are being transported in conditions of appalling horror and brutality to Eastern Europe. In Poland, which has been made the principal Nazi slaughterhouse, the ghettos established by the German invader are being systematically emptied of all Jews except a few highly skilled workers required for war industries. None of those taken away are ever heard of again. The able-bodied are slowly worked to death in labor camps. The infirm are left to die of exposure and starvation or are deliberately massacred in mass executions. The number of victims of these bloody cruelties is reckoned in many hundreds of thousands of entirely innocent men, women and children.

The above-mentioned governments and the French National Committee condemn in the strongest possible terms this bestial policy of cold-blooded extermination. They declare that such events can only strengthen the resolve of all freedom loving peoples to overthrow the barbarous Hitlerite tyranny. They reaffirm their solemn resolution to insure that those responsible for these crimes shall not escape retribution, and to press on with the necessary practical measures to this end.

PRELIMINARY STEPS TAKEN

The declaration had been forecast through diplomatic conversations that had been conducted in recent days looking to a joint denunciation of the persecution. The nations for some time have been assembling evidence, sifting it, and exchanging it among one another.

Secretary of State Cordell Hull was asked today what practical steps could be taken to reinforce the protest.

Statements have been made by President Roosevelt and heads of other governments during recent months, he replied, in regard to the development of plans, and concrete progress to discover and assemble all possible facts relating to these inhuman acts together with the names of the guilty persons, to the end that they may be apprehended at the earliest possible opportunity, not later than the end of the war, and properly dealt with. These undertakings, he added, are being carried forward now.

The matter has been active for months, not only with reference to Jews but also to other innocent civilians who have been the victims of reprisals and persecution.

President Roosevelt, in a statement on Oct. 25, 1941, denounced the execution of innocent hostages. On Jan. 13, 1942, the representatives of nine governments whose countries are under occupation issued a protest in London and declared that those responsible would be "handed over to justice and tried."

Subsequently the attention of Secretary Hull was formally called to "the barbaric crimes against civilian populations" in occupied countries through a communication from the governments of Belgium, Greece, Luxembourg, Norway, The Netherlands, Poland, Czechoslovakia, Yugoslavia and the French National Committee.

ROOSEVELT STATEMENTS RECALLED

President Roosevelt on Aug. 21, 1942, issued a statement denouncing the persecutions and warning those respon- ❱

and Coast Guard camps along the Pacific Coast and in the desert regions of California, Arizona and New Mexico; participation in 273 USO-Camp Show Tours throughout the country, and the 2,773 personal appearances made throughout the country by 270 players in War Bond drives for the Treasury Department.

To entertain American troops abroad, nine players journeyed to England and North Ireland, and fourteen visited such other offshore bases as Alaska, the Aleutians, Newfoundland, Panama Canal Zone and the Caribbeans. Moreover, 474 players participated in 222 "live" radio broadcasts and 507 gave their services in the recording of 111 radio transcriptions, of which fifty-six were for the War Department.

CARAVAN VISITED THIRTEEN CITIES

Assisting various charity drives were 338 performers who appeared at 150 different events, including the Victory Caravan in which forty-one stars visited thirteen cities on behalf of Army and Navy Relief. The total of individual appearances for the year was 6,828, the report states. It estimates that the mileage traversed by the stars in the various personal appearances in the twelve-month period came to approximately 1,000,000 miles.

The report states that plans for 1943 call for an expansion of the activities of the Victory Committee's talent pool. In conferences with Lieut. Col. Marvin Young of the Special Services Division of the War Department, the committee says arrangements have been made for performers to entertain at 700 Army camps throughout the country, and that 100 players will be sent overseas to entertain wherever American troops are stationed. ◆

(sible that "the time will come when they shall have to stand in courts of law in the very countries which they are now oppressing and answer for their acts."

In another statement, on Oct. 7, 1942, President Roosevelt advocated a United Nations Commission for the Investigation of War Crimes for meting out "just and sure punishment" to the "ringleaders responsible for the organized murder of thousands of innocent persons and the commission of atrocities which have violated every tenet of the Christian faith."

And last week the president gave sympathetic consideration to a proposal of a committee of Jewish organizations in this country, headed by Rabbi Stephen S. Wise, for a United States commission to consider the persecution of the Jews and to act in conjunction with the United Nations in the matter. ◆

JANUARY 3, 1943

FRENCH RIVALRY LEAVES TANGLE IN NORTH AFRICA
De Gaulle's Demand That Giraud Oust Vichy Aides Complicates Plan To Maintain Present Sovereignty

WARNING BY U. S. SUGGESTED

By ARTHUR KROCK

WASHINGTON, Jan. 2—The announcement in London by a spokesman of the Fighting French—that General de Gaulle cannot consider making an alliance with General Giraud in North Africa until and unless the Imperial Council, deriving from Vichy, is abolished—has further complicated the problem of effecting French unity against the Axis. There is some hope here that, as the military phase of the United Nations in North Africa enters a major dimension, some accommodation may be found between General de Gaulle's newly announced position and what General Giraud has considered his legalistic necessities. But, should that hope be too long deferred, Washington authorities are prepared with a set of legalisms of their own which would illuminate a perilous post-war alternative to current unity among the anti-Axis French leaders, and thus perchance make unity simpler to attain than, despite the efforts expended, it has been so far.

This set of legalisms has its source in that section of the Atlantic Charter in which the President and Prime Minister Churchill jointly declare that "they respect the right of all peoples to choose the form of government under which they will live; and they wish to see sovereign rights and self-government restored to those who have been forcibly deprived of them."

NATIVE DEMANDS A FACTOR

The reference, of course, is to those sovereign rights and self-governments of peoples which were forcibly taken away by the Axis powers since they began their campaign of aggression. But the fact remains that previously the French forcibly took away those very freedoms from the natives of North Africa and are in a small minority in that region. A historian of French expansion in Africa has said that "it had to be wrested from the natives, literally yard by yard." And there are native irredentists in those lands whose aspirations have been stimulated by the advent of war and the war-induced collapse of French metropolitan power.

Therefore, if, during the peace conferences that will begin with a long armistice—assuming the victory of the United Nations—native majority elements demand the restoration of their sovereign rights and self-government, an issue might be presented under the Atlantic Charter that would embarrass a good deal the peace-makers of Great Britain and the United States.

THREAT OF HOLY WAR

Should such a demand be made, and get the support of the Moslem world to which the vast majority of the North African natives belong, embarrassment might develop into the threat of a holy war, with the green flag of Islam raised on both sides of the strategic Mediterranean.

An irredentist demand could not possibly present the legal and political difficulties it could if French sovereignty in the area had been suspended during a formal military occupation. If the present arrangement between General Eisenhower and General Giraud is maintained there will be no such suspension, since General Giraud represents the legitimist French Government of the territory. To ask the peacemakers to revert to the status of half a century ago in North Africa would be almost equivalent to a demand from Mexico that Texas be restored to that republic. So many reversions would be involved, including some which would affect Moslem states, that the peacemakers would have no great difficulty in rejecting such a proposal But if North Africa had been formally occupied by the United Nations, with military government superseding civil (as necessarily it would), then the continuity of French sovereignty would have been both suspended and interrupted. The claims of the native irredentists would attain a legal validity which otherwise they could not, and a most vexatious problem would afflict the peace conference, as well as a threat of valuable loss of territory to post-war France and disturbances in the Moslem world.

EISENHOWER'S POLICY

It was to avoid the rise of such a situation that General Eisenhower was instructed to seek, and found, a legitimist French civil government in North Africa with which, through the offices of the late Admiral Darlan, he was able to collaborate. That legitimacy has now passed to General Giraud, and it operates through the Imperial Council which General de Gaulle says must be abolished before he can himself collaborate with General Giraud in the tasks of war and eventual peace.

It is therefore believed by some officials here that the United States and Great Britain may be obliged to warn the anti-Axis French leaders that, unless they can settle their differences over procedure and achieve unity in military effort, it may become necessary for the United Nations to break the chain of French sovereignty with a formal military occupation of North Africa and West Africa, thus stimulating a post-war native irredentist movement and clouding the legal claims of France to this vast area of the old French empire in North and West Africa.

Even if military occupation were made with the specific statement that the region would be restored after the war to a French government of that people's own choosing, title to the area would be clouded, since the lands were won by force and their population is, after all, overwhelmingly non-French.

PRODS TO UNITY

The purpose of such a warning would be to provide a powerful prod to the non-Axis French leaders toward unity under some form of legitimist government that would maintain a link in the chain of continuous French sovereignty.

The purpose would not be to prevent or discourage General Giraud from purging the Imperial Council of pro-Vichy members if that should, in his judgment, help to assure local security and meet the basic objectives of the Fighting French General de Gaulle to unified action.

By very stern experience, in which some American lives were lost, General Eisenhower discovered that French and native military and civil officials in North Africa were unwilling to take orders save from the representative of a form of continuous government. One reason for this is that their appointments came from Vichy. But another is the legalistic type of the French official mind and that of natives who have lived and thought under French tutelage.

GIRAUD'S DILEMMA

This preoccupation with legalisms has already made difficulties for General Giraud because, unlike Darlan, there is a hiatus between his new authority and the formal delegation of power from an established source. If he should abolish all established forms, and break the chain completely, there is fear in Washington that his government would lose its influence at a most critical time, and that civil and military troubles would arise across the North African littoral behind the advancing lines of the United Nations.

When General Eisenhower landed in North Africa he had two sets of orders, with the privilege of using that which seemed more likely to further his objective. One was to set up a military government and break the chain of French sovereignty. He chose the other—to leave civil government to constituted authorities. The reasons for his choice still, in great measure, exist, ◊

General de Gaulle in Tunisia, 1943.

JANUARY 19, 1943

The War in Russia

Red Army's Advances Are Remarkable Because of Winter's Severe Hardships

By HANSON W. BALDWIN

The week-end news from Russia may eventually prove to be some of the most dramatic of the war.

Moscow claimed that the sixteen-month siege of Leningrad had been lifted and on all fronts the Russians still held the initiative and were still driving deeply into the German lines. The claims from Moscow are now at least partly borne out by back-handed admissions from Berlin and by the greater freedom given by the Russians to American newspaper men in the coverage of the fighting.

The Russian special communiqué describing the encirclement and gradual reduction in strength of the German garrison at Stalingrad must be coupled with the official Nazi admission that this garrison has long been engaged in repulsing attacks "from all directions."

And the Voronezh offensive apparently has had early and spectacular success. The reported capture of the railroad towns of Rossosh, Miilerovo and Kamensk should do much to expedite the supply of the Russian push toward Rostov, and at the same time will pose an indirect threat to Nazi-held Kharkov. Yesterday's reported crossing of the Donets near Kamensk is, if verified, of considerable importance, for it means that the battle for Rostov, the key to the whole German southern position, is starting.

RUSSIANS DEFY HARDSHIPS

The Russian advances are all the more remarkable in that they are being accomplished despite the snow and ice and incredible hard-ships of the Russian Winter. The difficulties of campaigning in Russia—when the frost is so severe that ungloved hands are instantly frozen to whatever metal they' touch—were sufficiently emphasized last Winter, which was one of the most severe in Europe's history, but the influence of weather upon war can never be neglected.

This Winter, according to reports from Russia, is far milder than last

Winter; the snow drifts are not so deep and permit greater manoeuvrability; the frost is not so severe. But in so far as manoeuvrability is concerned, this is not all net gain, for in Southern Russia, in places where frost comes but briefly, the rutted roads may become mud; rain may substitute for snow, as it did last week when the packed snow of the steppes was drenched with a cold downpour, and the going for both armies became heavy.

Russia excels in extremes—space, distance, heat, cold and mud or ice.

Captain Elzéar Blaze, in his "Recollections of an Officer of Napoleon's Army," gives a good description of the difficulties with which both armies must contend. He wrote, in part, of Poland and of other areas of Europe, but his remarks apply with even greater validity to Russia.

"In Poland," he said, "the roads are not paved; the trouble has been taken of tracing them through the forests, that is all. During the Winter, and when the French Army tracked over that country in all directions we encountered oceans of mud which it was impossible to cross. The mud, of Pultusk has become unhappily celebrated; mounted men have been drowned in it with their horses; others have been seen to blow out their brains, despairing of ever getting out.

"An officer of engineers found himself stuck in mud up to the neck and could not get out A grenadier appeared:

"'Comrade,' calls out the officer, come to my aid, I am lost, I am drowning, the mud will soon choke me.'

"'Who are you?'

"'I am an officer of engineers.'

"'Ah, you're one of those who solve problems; well, draw your plan.'"

And the grenadier went on his way. The soldiers did not like the officers of grenadiers because they never saw them fighting with the bayonet. They found it difficult to understand that one could render services to the army with a pencil and compass.

MUD'S TERRORS DESCRIBED

Coignet and Baron Percy also speak of the terrors of "General Mud":

" ... the roads have disappeared beneath the waters and mud, one sees only wrecked carriages and horses buried to the belly; the six-horse coaches of the Emperor, in spite of all precautions, upset in frightful bogs ...

"As to the army, it was never so wretched; the soldier, always on the march, bivouacking every night, spending entire days in mud up to the knees, without bread, without brandy, falls with fatigue and ▶

exhaustion. Many die in the ditches."

Today, in most of Russia, it is the snow, the cold, the frost, rather than the mud that slows the fiery pulse of battle. In January in the North Caucasus area the temperature usually averages about 23 degrees, sometimes considerably lower, but the mercury does not start a slow climb until well into February. Farther north it is much colder; the mouth of the Don River at Rostov is usually frozen from about Dec. 6 to March 21; farther north the period of frost is even longer.

Though the snow and the cold are in one sense a handicap to military operations, the freezing of the rivers and marshes makes highways out of what normally are military obstacles; if the Russians reach the mouth of the Don, the ice may facilitate their passage.

There is, as yet, no such rout as the Grand Army experienced a century ago. But Winter is unquestionably on the side of the Russians today as it was a century ago. And the same hardships and deprivations, the same snow and cold and mud and frost are helping to wear down the Wehrmacht of Adolf Hitler. ◊

JANUARY 23, 1943

Editorial
THE MARINES WRITE A CHAPTER

When news comes that the Marines are leaving Guadalcanal for a well-earned rest we know that this is not because they asked to he relieved of their assignment. They have been on Guadalcanal since Aug. 7, and at no time have they asked relief from any duty or respite from any risk. They landed with no certainty that any single landing boat would reach shore. They marched into a tropical forest infested with Japanese, the world's most experienced and savage jungle fighters. They took what is now Henderson Airfield and held it for two weeks without air support For weeks, until the Navy had considerably abated the Japanese menace at sea, they were exposed to naval shellfire. Again and

again the enemy attempted landings; some of these landings were successful, and some of them, like the one at the Tenaru River, resulted in the attacking force being completely wiped out.

The Marines were presumably as well trained as soldiers could be, short of actual battle experience. They learned the rest as they went along. They learned it the hard way during perilous days and sleepless nights. Their aviators kept the air by stretching human endurance to the breaking point. Before six weeks had gone by the Marines were not only as good as their enemies: as the ratio of casualties shows, they were better. Let no one suppose that this was gay or easy. The Marines on Guadalcanal went through hell and came up smiling, but the joke was tough and grim. The soldiers who replace them will have something to live up to—and are already living up to it. The Marines can write Guadalcanal into their song, along with the Halls of Montezuma and the Shores of Tripoli. We hope they can find something to rhyme it with: the story will never die as long as we need Marines. ◊

JANUARY 24, 1943

With Women at Work, The Factory Changes

Mrs. Herrick describes some of the problems created by the rush of women into industry. She sees lasting gains for all concerned.

By ELINORE M. HERRICK

There are many deterrents—largely psychological—to the increased employment of women in industry. Many of them spring from prejudice, lack of information, fear of change. Others arise simply from inertia. It is rather like going swimming off the coast of Maine—one has always heard that the water is cold, even though invigorating, but the latter remains to be proved. Toes first, gingerly. The water is cold, but the invigorating tingle after the reluctant plunge warms the blood stream.

I wager that every employer who has made his first plunge into the employment of women made that plunge with many misgivings, but in adding up the final score he finds that it is a success. And feels that way in spite of the laws that regulate working conditions for women, with which he is having his first experience. He may have to rearrange

work schedules for men in order to meet the State standards for women. He may have to go to a stagger shift system to avoid working the women over the legal maximum. But he will find that the shorter hours mean more regular attendance and better production.

Rest periods for women are required in most States. Employers fear this will encourage the men to loaf. Production is all that matters. Why should the women be pampered? But when they find the women returning refreshed to the job and the work going faster after the rest period, the last objector is apt to be silenced. It might even be better, they concede, to give everyone a regular rest period.

Often the company's first introduction to State sanitary codes may come through the employment of women. I know the men of the Todd Shipyard organization thought I had an obsession

over plumbing. I poked around the shipyards, looking not at the great vessels laid up for repairs, but looking for a corner where I could install lavatories and rest rooms for the women who were shortly to come to work in the shipyard. I was far more interested in the location of drains and sewers than in the thrilling spectacle of men tearing apart and rebuilding the boats to keep the life lines open for our armed forces abroad. I wanted this machine and that tool bench moved to make a little more space for a toilet.

The men were patient and let me poke around. Blueprints were produced to show why I could not have the desired space, but to the credit of the men, be it said, they always found some other space which I, in turn, decided could be used just as well. They were tolerant even of my insistence that the State sanitary codes were minimum standards and that we ought to have more toilets, more washing facilities, than the law required if we were to meet the really best standards of modern factory construction.

The purchasing department, accustomed to buying wire, rope, steel, motors, heavy machinery of all kinds, had as much fun as I picking the color scheme and fabrics for the furniture in the new rest rooms. I suspect some of their helpful suggestions came from their wives—but perhaps that sounds

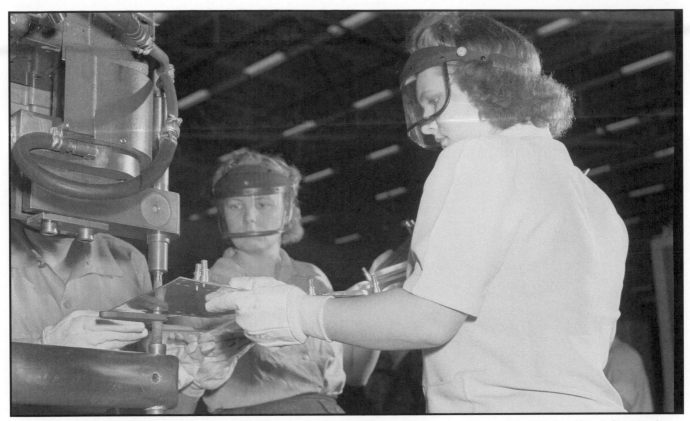

Women operating a spot welding machine at Ford's giant bomber plant at Willow Run, Michigan.

ungenerous. The point is that they were equally interested in finding the fabric that was colorful but serviceable. Showers for the men were already an institution, but the idea of shower curtains for the women seemed a little startling, not to say unnecessary. Hand creams for the women was another innovation that seemed a trifle "fussy." I pointed to the practice of the experienced men doing spray painting who always greased every inch of exposed skin heavily, which was also a protection against lead poisoning. So the purchasing department investigated hand creams.

The necessity for feeding women properly to enable them to do the hard day's work that is inevitable for a shipyard worker is rapidly branching out into a program for feeding all the workers. And not a diet of salads—for either sex—and with emphasis on vitamins. With food rationing on a wide scale sweeping toward us, the importance of mass feeding in factories here, just as in England, becomes a very practical necessity in keeping men and women fit for the long, hard war production battle.

What kind of clothing should the women wear? That is another new problem for the new employer of women. You don't have to think about what the men will wear, except in terms of safety equipment, helmets, safety shoes; gloves, goggles and the like. Women have to have those things too. Every industry has a different type of problem

where women's working clothes are concerned, I find. It is important to the women's approach to her job to have requirements for practical, workmanlike clothing, however. Fancy clothes, dangling jewelry, shoulder "bobs" are not conducive to wholehearted attention to the work at hand.

In shops where delicate, dainty precision work is done amid clean surroundings, Lilly Dache can design a fetching bonnet to keep the hair from catching in the machinery. Molyneux can do a dashing uniform in gay colors and light fabrics. But in a greasy machine shop—and they all have some grease—or in a shipyard where most of the women's work like the men's must be out-of-doors no matter what the weather, the problem is different. There warmth, dark colors, grease resistant non-inflammable fabrics are all important. Despite all the most conscientious planning in the world, you will find the women workers have their own ideas. We did, when after much long-distance telephoning and frantic pleas to the manufacturer of the best so-called safety shoe for women factory workers, the shoes finally arrived on the day the first class graduated from the training school. The women flatly refused to wear them. Why?

"The soles aren't heavy enough, oxfordcut low shoes aren't safe enough; we want them over the ankles too. And we want steel toes like the men," they cried. So the long-suffering purchasing

department sent the shoes that had been flown from the Middle West back to the manufacturers and we started searching the city for men's heavy, bulky safety shoes in the smallest sizes made for men. And we wondered whether they would ruin the women's feet, with their higher arches and their long use of relatively high heels.

A prominent orthopedic surgeon was consulted, a supply of arch pads bought, the girls were warned to wear an extra pair of wool socks over their usual hose to help cushion their feet. But the women were right, only it had never occurred to us who were planning that they would be willing to wear those unshapely, hulking men's shoes. The thing we learned was that the women really cared about doing the job safely even at the expense of attractiveness.

Insistence upon the women wearing all the necessary safety equipment plus the women's own fear of injury in the new and unfamiliar terrain of a shipyard has spurred the drive for safety among the men. The men who had become accustomed to the environment and had persuaded themselves that "no hammer will drop on my head" have begun to wear their helmets more faithfully and with less resistance. The safety engineers are having an easier time in that respect at least.

Employment of women has made new problems for the engineers. Jobs that required heavy lifting were no problem when only men were involved. Now the relationship of supplies to the height of the machine to make a long lift unnecessary has to be studied. But it pays in the long run, whether for men or women, to let brains supplant brawn. And so, if new engineering ideas are developed to lessen lifting hazards of heavy work for women, the men will be the gainers in the long run.

Selecting the women presented new problems. We asked the foremen what kind of women, what physique, what previous experience would be needed, in their judgment, for a woman on a particular type of machine or job. Many foremen have changed their minds. They would have scoffed at the idea of a college degree as being useful in the machine shop in the operation of a turret lathe. The men who were working these machines had not been to college. But one of the most skillful workers in the machine shop today is a woman who has not one but several college degrees. Another was the head mistress of a fashionable girls' school.

The clamor was for big, husky women—accent on young. Yet slender, deft-handed women of all ages are among our best welders and shipfitters. A Danish woman welder of 53 can match the record of the best man, we have found. Our emphasis has now been placed on the physical condition of the woman

rather than her age. And this is leading us to a more careful preemployment physical examination, which, starting with women, is influencing also the standards for selecting men.

New standards of physical examination, new records of first-aid service have to be kept, in order that we may be sure the women are not being harmed by these new and unfamiliar and strenuous tasks. There is a new emphasis on toxic poisoning, because this is often disastrous to the woman of child-bearing age. This will undoubtedly bring many a company to study the health problems of men with a new understanding of their importance to morale, to effective production and to lessened absenteeism among the men. In the States which have sound legislation on workmen's compensation and occupational diseases employers are already accustomed to methods of mitigating occupational hazards. But in other States, where this type of legislation is less advanced, the employment of women will serve to turn attention to this type of planning.

The new employer of women looks at the statistics of absenteeism among women, which over the country are concededly higher than among men. He visualizes the women as being out sick a lot of the time or at home taking care of ailing children. But the employer who has considered this problem and has planned a careful pre-employment interview will find that the picture is not as dark as the statistics seem to indicate.

To his surprise the women are not out sick a great deal, and they aren't at home taking care of ailing children.

This reflects the greater thoroughness of the pre-employment interview at the personnel office which inquires into the home conditions of the applicant. If there are children, what are their ages? What plan has been made for their care? Has the prospect had many colds during the Winter? Does she have sinus trouble? The rigid physical examination supplements the answers given by the women. Absenteeism can be reduced by attention to these conditions before employment and by proper coordination of first aid and dispensary service with the personnel office.

We have found the women punctual on the job. They get to work on time. In our first two and a half months' experience at the first Todd Shipyard to employ women, not a single woman has been tardy even once and the foremen noted it, appreciatively. Perhaps, it is long habit of getting the children off to school on time.

There is uniform agreement that the women do a swell job—that they work conscientiously and well and are anxious to learn. They are amenable to discipline. Their interest in their work is typified by an incident that happened to me recently. A foreman sent for me, saying he wanted me to see "the two best men I have." Both were attractive young women, working on a big armature. They told me. "This is such responsible work. We know it must

---

JANUARY 25, 1943

LEADERS GO BY AIR
Aim at 'Unconditional Surrender' By Axis, President Says

MILITARY AIDES TALK
French Chiefs Declare Groups Will Unite to Liberate Nation

By DREW MIDDLETON
Special Cable to The New York Times.

CASABLANCA, French Morocco, Jan. 24 (Delayed)—President Roosevelt and Prime Minister Churchill today concluded a momentous ten-day conference in which they planned Allied offensives of 1943 aimed at what the President

called the "unconditional surrender" of the Axis powers.

The President flew 5,000 miles across the Atlantic with his Chiefs of Staff to confer with Mr. Churchill and British military, naval and air chieftains in a

sun-splashed villa within sound of Atlantic breakers. Every phase of the global war was discussed in conferences lasting from morning until midnight. Both war leaders emphasized that the conference was wholly successful and that complete agreement had been reached on great military enterprises to be undertaken by the United Nations this year.

General Henri Honoré Giraud, High Commissioner for French North Africa, and General Charles de Gaulle, leader of Fighting France, met at the conference and found themselves in accord on the primary task of liberating France from German domination. President Roosevelt predicted that French soldiers, sailors and airmen would fight beside the Allied armies in the liberation of France.

STALIN KEPT INFORMED

The President and Mr. Churchill expressed regret for Premier Joseph Stalin's inability to leave the Russian

be done just right else the motor of this ship might fail and the men aboard would be at the mercy of a German submarine," and they turned back to their work with frowning attention.

Employment of women in industries hitherto accustomed only to men does involve new problems. The solutions are to be found in analysis of the problems and ingenuity in meeting them. If more attention is paid to pre-employment interviewing at the personnel office, resulting in a steadier type of employee, and if more attention to physical requirements results in a better integrated medical service, the benefits that flow from these changes will help the employment problems of men as well. Lessons learned during the war emergency will remain as standard practice after the war.

Work places where heretofore too little attention has been paid to sanitation will be better places now and after the war. Changes in working hours that produce steadier employment will likewise remain as post-war practice. Improved methods of work which reduce fatigue for women will help the men and make for more efficient operation after the war. too. The very necessity for devoting time and thought to the problems affecting women cannot but result in a more alert and quickened attention to the whole process of manufacturing methods. The necessity for maximum efficiency in winning the war will have long-range results in our whole industrial system. ◆

offensive, which he is directing personally, but emphasized that all results of the conferences had been reported to the Soviet leader. [Generalissimo Chiang Kai-shek was similarly advised, The Associated Press reported.]

Assurance of future world peace will come only as a result of the total elimination of German and Japanese war power, the President declared. He borrowed a phrase from General Grant's famous letter to the Confederate commander at Forts Donelson and Henry—"unconditional surrender"—to describe the only terms on which the United Nations would accept the conclusion of the war.

He emphasized, however, that this did not mean the destruction of the populace of Germany, Japan and Italy, but the end of a philosophy based on the conquest and subjugation of other peoples in those countries.

Sitting side by side in the bright sunlight on the grassy lawn of the villa, the President and the Prime Minister reviewed

American and British military leaders at the Casablanca conference, Morocco, 1943.

the work of the conference, in which the Chiefs of Staff conferred two or three times a day, reporting at intervals to them.

The President saw three objectives before the United Nations in 1943.

The first of these is maintenance of the initiative won in the closing days of 1942, its extension to other theatres and an increase in those in which the Allies now hold the upper hand.

Second, the dispatch of all possible aid to the Russian offensive must be maintained with the double objective of whittling down German manpower and continuing the attrition of German munitions and material on the Russian front.

Third, Mr. Roosevelt called for assistance for the Chinese armies, now in their sixth year of war, with Japanese domination ended forever.

BOTH LEADERS SATISFIED

To gain these objectives the military and political leaders of the United Nations are determined to pool all their resources, military and economic, in 1943 to maintain the initiative wherever it is now held and to seek every opportunity to bring the enemy to battle on terms as unfavorable as those now prevailing in Tunisia.

Both leaders were extremely satisfied at the successful conclusion of the fourth meeting between them since the beginning of the war. Cooperation between the American and British Chiefs of Staff was described by Mr. Roosevelt as the closest possible, with the military leaders living together and working as personal friends more than as allies.

President Roosevelt predicted that the war would proceed according to schedule, with every indication that 1943 would be an even better year for the United Nations than 1942.

The conference, which probably

made more important decisions than any other called by the United Nations, was held in a lush tropical setting in conditions of greatest secrecy. The President's villa was shaded by palm trees, with Bougainvillaea climbing on trellises around the house, and oranges nodding on trees in the yard. A swimming pool in the back yard had been turned into an air raid shelter, but no German planes approached Casablanca during the conferences, and if any had come they would have been greeted by squadrons of British and United States fighter planes flying guard over the region.

TALKS CLOSELY GUARDED

Many acres of the resort were enclosed in two lines of barbed wire, on which tin cans were hung. If anyone had been foolhardy enough to approach these lines he would have been riddled by bullets from machine guns or bayoneted by some of the hundreds of American infantrymen who stood helmeted atop roofs or patrolled the shady walks around the area.

Both the President and the Prime Minister seemed confident and satisfied when they appeared at the noon press conference today. The President wore a worn gray suit and the Prime Minister was dapper in a gray pin-stripe suit topped by a somewhat battered gray Homburg hat. The sunshine winked in a jeweled "V" and an American Distinguished Service Order bar in his lapel buttonhole.

The two unmilitary-looking men, who lead half of the strongest coalition in history, were accompanied by General de Gaulle and General Giraud. For the benefit of camera men the two generals shook hands.

"A historic moment," President Roosevelt commented.

The sun beat fiercely on the ❯

group. Mr. Churchill asked the President, "Don't you want a hat?"

"I was born without a hat," Mr. Roosevelt replied.

While the President and the Prime Minister talked, guards silhouetted on nearby rooftops never relaxed their vigil and tight formations of fighters roared overhead.

Mr. Roosevelt revealed that the Allied victories in North Africa had made his fourth meeting with Mr. Churchill necessary. The situation had been reviewed in the meeting and plans made for the next steps in 1943, he said.

Both he and Mr. Churchill expressed deep regret for Premier Joseph Stalin's inability to leave the Russian offensive which he is directing personally, but emphasized that all the results of the conferences between the President, the Prime Minister and their Chiefs of Staff committees had been reported to the Soviet leader.

Mr. Churchill agreed with Mr. Roosevelt that the conference was unprecedented in history. Describing himself again as the President's ardent lieutenant, Mr. Churchill declared they worked together as partners and friends and described their cooperation as one of the sinews of war of the Allied powers.

The Prime Minister began to speak slowly, but gradually raised his voice as he described the frustration of the enemy by the men Adolf Hitler had called incompetents and drunkards. This brought a laugh. Mr. Churchill beamed.

The events in North Africa have altered the whole, strategic aspect of the war, making the Germans and Italians fight under conditions of great difficulty, he declared. He described General Field Marshal Erwin Rommel as a fugitive from Libya and Egypt now trying to pass himself off as the liberator of Tunis. But he reminded the correspondents that General Sir Bernard L. Montgomery was hot on Marshal Rommel's trial and that everywhere that Mary went the lamb was sure to go.

PURPOSE IS UNCONQUERABLE

Design, purpose and an unconquerable will lie behind all that is being done by Britain and America, the Prime Minister said solemnly. These will be applied to enforce unconditional surrender upon the criminals who plunged the world into the war, he concluded.

Both the President and Mr. Churchill seemed hopeful on the results of the de Gaulle–Giraud meeting, in which the two French leaders found themselves in "entire agreement" on the end to be achieved, which is the liberation of France and defeat of the enemy. Yet although a joint communiqué issued by the two generals

said this could be achieved only by union in war on all Frenchmen fighting side by side, it gave no clue as to how the present difficulty in the North African political situation is to be adjusted.

It is felt, however, that the conference between the generals and their talks with Mr. Churchill and Mr. Roosevelt had cleared the way for an agreement of some sort between Generals Giraud and de Gaulle on the political aspects of their crusade for the liberation of France. The mere fact that they were seen talking together and were photographed shaking hands should do much to unite the French all over North Africa and to emphasize that a union of General de Gaulle's followers with the other factions must be carried out swiftly if the French are to bulk large in the United Nations' war plans.

FIRST FLIGHT OF PRESIDENT

Mr. Roosevelt, the first President to leave the United States in wartime, became the first to inspect United States troops in the field since Abraham Lincoln when he reviewed armored and infantry units in a day snatched from the long series of arduous conferences. Riding in a jeep, the President inspected camps, talked with dozens of men and officers and ate "chow" with the soldiers.

"We had a darn good lunch," he said. "I wish the people back home could see the troops and their equipment. They have the most modern weapons we can turn out. The men are in good health and high spirits and I found the officers and men most efficient. Their morale is splendid and I know they will keep it up. Tell the folks back home that I am mighty proud of them."

The President visited Port Lyautey, scene of heavy fighting during the American landing, and placed wreaths on the graves of American and French soldiers buried there. He also directed that a wreath be placed on the grave of Edward Baudry, Canadian Broadcasting Company war correspondent, who was killed by a Spanish anti-aircraft bullet on a flight to cover the conference.

Among the happy features of his visit were talks the President had while here with two of his sons, Lieut. Col. Elliott Roosevelt, who is with the Allied Air Force, and Lieutenant Franklin D. Roosevelt Jr., who is on duty with the Navy.

Mr. Roosevelt had one other break from the conferences. This came when he dined with the Sultan of Morocco, Sidi Mohammed, at "a delightful party." According to the President, they got along extremely well and he found the Sultan deeply interested in the welfare of his people.

The President flew to Africa in two aircraft, switching from one to the other at a point on the journey. It was his first flight since his historic trip from Albany to Chicago in 1932 when he accepted the presidential nomination. He was accompanied by Mr. Hopkins on the flight, the first ever made by a President of the United States.

[The President flew by Clipper to a point in North Africa, then changed to a four-motored bomber especially fitted for comfort, The United Press reported.]

SERVICE CHIEFS IN TALKS

The United States Chiefs of Staff, General George C. Marshall of the Army, Admiral Ernest J. King of the Navy and Lieut. Gen. Henry H. Arnold of the Air Forces, preceded the President and already had begun conferences with their British "opposite numbers," General Sir Alan Brooke, Chief of the Imperial General Staff; Admiral Sir Dudley Pound, Chief of the Naval Staff, and Air Chief Marshal Sir Charles F. A. Portal, Chief of the Air Staff, when the rest of the party arrived. W. Averell Harriman, United States Lend-Lease Expediter, joined the conference from London.

The Chiefs of Staff were assisted by Lieut. Gen. Brehon B. Somervell, chief of the United States Services of Supply; Field Marshal Sir John Dill, chairman of the British military mission to the United States; Lord Louis Mountbatten, chief of the operational command, and Lieut. Gen. Sir Hastings Ismay, Chief of Staff to Mr. Churchill as Defense Minister, Conferences took place two or three times daily, with constant reports going to the President and the Prime Minister.

The Prime Minister, who arrived first at the rendezvous, was accompanied by Lord Leathers, British Minister of War Transport. The President had just settled in his spacious white villa when Mr. Hopkins ushered in Mr. Churchill and the first of their many conferences began. It lasted through dinner and continued until 3 o'clock the next morning.

The Chiefs of Staff, the President and the Prime Minister conferred with Allied military and political leaders from all over the African theatres. Lieut. Gen. Dwight D. Eisenhower, commander of Allied operations; his deputy, Lieut, Gen. Mark W. Clark, and General Sir Harold R.L.G. Alexander, Commander in Chief of the Middle East forces, represented the ground troops. Admiral of the Fleet Sir Andrew Browne Cunningham, Allied naval Commander in Chief in North Africa, gave the naval views on what Mr. Churchill described as the great events impending, while Major

Gen. Carl A. Spaatz, chief of Allied air operations; Air Marshal Sir Arthur William Tedder, vice chief of the air staff, and Lieut. Gen. Frank M. Andrews, United States Middle East commander, discussed the air situation.

Not the least interesting of these conferences were those between Mr. Churchill, Mr. Roosevelt, Harold Macmillan, British Resident Minister in North Africa, and Robert D. Murphy, civil affairs officer on General Eisenhower's staff, in which the tangled political situation was reviewed.

It is impossible to assess the value of the conference as yet, but it may be said that its close probably heralded the end of the long lull in Tunisia. Both Mr. Churchill and Mr. Roosevelt gave every indication that the Allies' watchword is "get on with the job." The Casablanca "unconditional surrender" conference was a directors' meeting of one-half of the mighty coalition now definitely on the offensive.

Two chief results of the conference appear to be, first, full admission that the Allies intend to press home the present strategic advantage during their campaigns in 1943, and, second, the fact that Generals de Gaulle and Giraud have been brought together in a meeting that, if barren of definite political agreement, at least showed France and French North Africa that they have agreed in principle and are ready to work together.

The President's use of General Grant's famous cry, "unconditional surrender," gives the key to the Allies' political strategy in the closing months of the war and indicates that, although mercy may be shown to the Axis peoples, none will be shown to their leaders.

This warning should do much to hush the German propaganda that claims that events in North Africa show that the Allies have been willing to cooperate with "Quislings" here and may be expected to do so again when the Continent is invaded.

There is no doubt that the conference was the most important of the four held by the two leaders, for this time they were not occupied by expedients to gain time or hold the enemy in check, but to fashion a crushing offensive against the Axis.

Although the meeting took place in Africa, it is unwise to believe that the Mediterranean is the only war theatre that will figure largely in the war news in the next six months. Every front was reviewed and discussed in the conferences and plans were made for new operations, and above all for maintenance of the precious initiative. ◆

Hitler and Goering Warn Europe Faces 'Red Peril'

LONDON, Jan. 30—Adolf Hitler failed to appear today at a gloomy party celebrating the tenth anniversary of his accession to power, and British bombs twice upset the broadcast explanations of Reich Marshal Hermann Goering and Propaganda Minister Joseph Goebbels as to why the German Armies were meeting reverses in Russia.

Herr Hitler was reported off somewhere "with his soldiers." His proclamation, read by Dr. Goebbels, warned the German people that they faced enslavement to bolshevism unless they fought on to the end.

Marshal Goering, whose speech suffered an hour of confused delay, talked for ninety minutes on the perfidy of the Russians, of their long war preparations, "camouflaged" by their inept 1939–40 Winter war against Finland, and of Stalingrad, which he distorted into a token of ultimate German victory.

[A British broadcast heard in New York by the Columbia Broadcasting System said Marshal Goering was interrupted several times by a ghost voice heckling him on the same wavelength, saying: "You surely don't believe that."]

Dr. Goebbels read the Hitler proclamation several hours after the Goering speech, and introduced it with a talk of his own in which he said, "capitulation has never existed in our vocabulary and it never will. If they think we have no reserves left, they will soon see them."

Marshal Goering sought to explain why Germany attacked Russia, and in the opinion of observers his speech was contradictory in this respect.

"It required all the hardships of last Winter to realize that Russia's war against Finland [1939–40] was perhaps the cleverest, greatest camouflage in world history," he said. "We had seen a small but gallant nation fight heroically for many months against this vast empire and we thought, 'What danger can possibly come from that empire in the East?'"

Later, after making this reference to the "camouflaged" Russian war against Finland before Germany attacked Russia the following year, he said:

"While the Russians had few armies fighting Finland with obsolete arms, they spent the last decade and a half building up the most powerful armaments which ever had been made by any nation."

Still later he said, "The strength of the Russians was known, but the Fuehrer's intuition warned him we must attack all the same."

He recounted the hardships encountered in the Russian campaign a year ago—when "the Fuehrer, with his display of toughness, held the whole German front himself."

He kept emphasizing Russia's strength and the need of German unity to combat it.

"Russia hardly had pencils for ›

A still image from a film captured from the Nazi government showing Hermann Goering (center) and Adolf Hitler with advisers in 1943.

{ the people in general," he said. "The whole industry worked with a single aim and Russia placed emphasis only on the four branches of her arms—namely, tanks, antitank guns, airplanes and antiaircraft defense.

"It is not easy to fight Russia. Our enemy is hard, his leadership barbaric, and disobedience means death."

He kept stressing, too, what he said was the danger to all Europe of a Russian victory. This was seen as an appeal to Axis allies to stand firm and also an attempt to recruit neutral States against Russia. Marshal Goering also said: "This is a fight of philosophies and races. Though some may say it is imagination, we believe in it: Our Nordic, Germanic race is the bearer of the highest culture and the highest values, and the German Reich is the first representative of the Nordic-Germanic conception." ◇

JANUARY 31, 1943

OFFENSIVE STRATEGY LAID DOWN AT CASABLANCA

By HANSON W. BALDWIN

The grand strategy of the United Nations for the year 1943 was undoubtedly beaten out on the anvil of discussion during the Roosevelt-Churchill meeting at Casablanca. Just as the June meeting of the two leaders in Washington and the subsequent visits of General George C. Marshall and other high-ranking American Army officers to London in July preceded the launching of the African offensive, so the meeting in Casablanca heralds additional offensive operations on the part of the United Nations.

But more than that, it produced a plan, perhaps a plan limited in scope and time and one still to be modified and implemented, but a plan.

It could truthfully be said before the Casablanca meeting that the United Nations had no strategic plan in the sense of a program of operations agreed to and accepted by all and intended to chart our future movements. Our strategy in the past has been painfully and obviously opportunistic. It was a hand-to-mouth strategy; events were shaping it; we were not masters of our fate.

PLANS LONG IN THE MAKING

This is not to say that there were not any war plans. Obviously, plans had been worked out in detail long before the war covering nearly all possible contingencies; equally obviously, these plans have been revised, brought up to date, expanded and modified since we entered the war. There is no question that the planners of the Army, the Navy and the Combined Chiefs of Staff had considered and worked out in detail every possible plan from a landing on the coast of Norway to an attack upon Japan from the air.

It is also probable that some tentative agreement had been reached on the highest echelons between our own military representatives and those of Britain as to which of these plans should be adopted. This was not necessarily true, however, for it is rare to find perfect agreement among the representatives of different powers in a coalition war.

But whether there was agreement on the military level or not, such agreement meant nothing unless implemented by the political heads of at least the great Anglo-American powers. And it is al-, most certain that there was not final agreement to move into North Africa on the parts of these political heads until last July, although plans for such an expedition—indeed, for any one of many different expeditions—had been made at least in general outline much earlier. The same situation has existed in recent months. The Casablanca meeting shows more graphically than ever that Prime Minister Churchill and President Roosevelt are running this war, in so far as the Anglo-Saxon powers are concerned, with Stalin very clearly the dominant figure in Russia and with Chiang Kai-shek important in China. It was necessary to have a meeting of the Churchill and Roosevelt minds—and if possible of the Stalin and Chiang Kai-shek minds—before one of any number of different plans could be decided upon.

Stalin and Chiang were not in Casablanca in person and, so far as is known, were not even represented. This was not because of the lack of an invitation. The Russians were almost certainly invited to come. The Chinese, because the discussion primarily concerned the European phase of the war, may not have been but it is probable that they were.

That Stalin could not in person accept the invitation is understandable. He is truly Commander in Chief; from day to day the tactical and strategical moves of the Russian Army are directed by him, and the conference came at a time when that army was in the midst of winning its greatest victory. And in a real sense no one can represent Stalin—or Generalissimo Chiang Kai-shek.

LIAISON EXISTS

Their absence, though disappointing because a true global strategy could not well be completely evolved without them, is not as serious as some critics would make it appear. For, despite the lack of a Supreme War Council of all the United Nations powers, the mechanism for liaison among Russia, China and the United States exists in Washington in the form of diplomatic representatives, military missions, etc. And the representatives of Russia and other United Nations powers either have offices in the same building with the Combined Chiefs of Staff or have ready access to that committee or some of its subordinate groups. These facts, coupled with the joint letter sent to Mr. Stalin by the President and Mr. Churchill, make it clear that Russia and China were rather fully informed of the deliberations and results of the Casablanca conference.

Moreover, that conference had really only one major task—to map the course of action the United States and the British Empire should follow in the months of 1943. Russia's course is quite clear; so is China's. Both are engaged in a bitter struggle to rid their own soil of invaders.

THE CHOICE OF ACTION

There has been a certain choice open to Britain and the United States. Should we concentrate our efforts upon a major assault upon Germany through the air? Should we strike northward from Africa across the Mediterranean? Should we invade the coast of Western France or that of Norway? What should we do in the Pacific and in Asia and against the submarine?

The rains in Tunisia end shortly, and with their end will undoubtedly come an intensive effort to root out the Axis from their last foothold in Africa. What should we do then?

There were many plans, but it is almost certain that no one, or several, of the plans had been implemented until the Casablanca conference. Until the President and Mr. Churchill met, we had no defined strategical program. Today, we have a program. What it is, future events will soon show. For the present only speculation is possible.

The principal issue at the Casablanca meeting involved a decision as to what sector should be chosen as the first point of the attack on Hitler's European fortress. The Churchillian conception of strategy always has centered about the Mediterranean; the British Prime Minister and many other Englishmen who remember the bloody business of Dunkirk and Dieppe have apparently favored a blow toward the outer segments of the enemy's position—not toward the well-defended heart. Others, including some American opinion, have envisaged the coast of France or Norway as the best point of attack; some have favored multiple attacks, with that one exploited to the full which promised— after the actual landings were made— the greatest hope of success.

Prime Minister Churchill is said to have repeated after the Casablanca conference the remark he made after the North African landings, that he was the President's "ardent lieutenant." Yet Mr. Churchill's influence is written large on present strategy, and whether or not he is the dominant partner in the Churchill-Roosevelt combination, his influence will continue to be of major importance in shaping things to come.

REACHING THE DECISION

If after cleaning up North Africa, we attack northward across the Mediterranean—toward the Balkans, or Italy— the program probably will have been largely Churchillian in concept and support. If we attack the western coast of France or Norway, it might be said to be Rooseveltian. Actually there is no such sharp cleavage in strategical opinion as these oversimplifications seem to imply, but the main decision that had to be made at Casablanca, and one that has been made, was the decision as to where Germany should be attacked.

All other decisions, though important, were unquestionably subordinate to this. The question of command in North Africa and in the European theatre (reports still persist that General Marshall, American Chief of Staff, is to assume command of the whole European theatre) was undoubtedly decided. An attempt was made, with only minor success, to reconcile French differences. Means, methods and organization for meeting the submarine menace were probably discussed. The role of China and the next step in the Pacific were doubtless on the agenda.

The results were legion, and we shall see their effects upon all phases of the war in the months to come. For it is only by a face-to-face meeting such as that at Casablanca that the two men primarily responsible for molding the course of the future can turn the military plans of their subordinates into decisions—decisions which will soon become strategical realities. ◇

Chapter 14
"WAR ON ALL FRONTS"
February–May 1943

On February 7 The Times carried an editorial titled "War on All Fronts." It was a play on words. Alongside the "gratifying victories" in Russia and the South Pacific, there were areas still in crisis where arguments went on between allies about the distribution of American resources and reinforcements. The war for resources, continued The Times, could not be solved overnight but required hard thinking about priorities. Moreover, the resources themselves were vulnerable in transit.

The spring of 1943 was full of bad news from the Battle of the Atlantic, a conflict that German Grand Admiral Karl Dönitz was determined to fight to the finish. In 1942, 7.8 million tons had been sunk on the high seas, just a little less than the 8 million tons built in American shipyards. The submarine "wolf packs" were restricted now to the so-called Atlantic gap as air cover spread over the ocean. In March large convoys were heavily mauled, but in April Secretary of the Navy Frank Knox announced a sudden fall in sinkings. In May only 160,000 tons of shipping was lost at sea while forty-one German submarines were sunk. Thanks to breaking the German naval codes, the use of long-range aircraft, advanced new radar equipment and naval support groups, the submarine threat was finally defeated. At the end of May Dönitz admitted defeat and withdrew his force. The same month the operation of Allied submarines and aircraft against Axis shipping in the Mediterranean starved Axis forces in Tunisia of resources and oil. The naval war on all fronts had gone the Allied way.

The struggle in North Africa had nevertheless been longer and tougher than expected. For American forces it was a harsh learning environment as they pressed across Northwest Africa toward Tunis. On February 20 Rommel inflicted a sharp blow at the Kasserine Pass, but was unable to exploit the breakthrough once British and American reinforcements arrived. The Times observed that American soldiers had to learn in order to survive. "The Doughboy," ran one headline, "is, in Turn, Cocky, Scared, Dazed, Damn Mad and Effective." By mid-April Axis forces were bottled up and, on May 13, 240,000 German and Italian forces surrendered, a larger number than had been captured at Stalingrad. Far away from the action, American forces stationed in the Aleutian Islands began the difficult task, in appalling conditions, of dislodging the small Japanese force from the island of Attu. This was indeed war on all fronts.

The long years of war took their toll on domestic peace. In America there were grumbles about rationing. In April the National Negro Congress called for an end to race discrimination and the right of blacks to be hired for any job. In early May a major strike for higher wages was called in American coal and anthracite mines. The strike rocked the Roosevelt administration, and the president himself intervened to get the men back to work, while hard-liners in Congress demanded tough legislation against the right to strike in wartime.

In India the political challenge from Gandhi reached a new crisis. He went on a prolonged fast to protest his imprisonment and the British rejection of self-rule. The Times followed the drama closely. Readers were warned that "India Faces Violence If Gandhi Dies," which was almost certainly the case. Gandhi gave up his fast in early March but the struggle for independence continued to challenge the British Empire's war effort in Asia.

Resistance was also growing in German-controlled Europe, where efforts to recruit forced labor and the expropriation of property and artwork propelled more Europeans toward active opposition. On May 2 The Times announced that the Norwegian Norsk Hydro plant, which produced "heavy water" used in nuclear development programs, had been successfully sabotaged. The raid had taken place on February 27 and 28, but the details could not be revealed. The Times did suggest that the Germans were not yet at a stage to produce a weapon of "devastating power," a judgment that was closer to the truth then they could have hoped.

Doenitz Pledges U-Boat Warfare Backed by Total Nazi Sea Power

By The Associated Press.

LONDON, Jan. 31—Grand Admiral Karl Doenitz, Nazi Germany's wily submarine warfare wizard, assumed command of the German Navy today with the prompt declaration that every ounce of German sea power was to be thrown into the submarine war against the Allies.

Raising his new Commander in Chief's flag—a black cross on a white field—over his headquarters, Admiral Doenitz was quoted by the German radio in a broadcast recorded by The Associated Press as saying:

"I will put the entire concentrated strength of the navy into the submarine war, which will be waged with still greater vigor and determination than hitherto.

"The entire German Navy will henceforth be put into the service of inexorable U-boat warfare.

The German Navy will fight to a finish."

The declaration was regarded here as a substantiation of views expressed previously that Admiral Doenitz's appointment yesterday as successor to Grand Admiral Erich Raeder was a forecast of a greatly intensified U-boat campaign that already is causing marked concern in Allied war councils.

Stockholm dispatches said the elevation of Admiral Doenitz, originator of the "wolf pack" method of U-boat fighting, was regarded by observers there as a sign that Reichsfuehrer Hitler was pinning all his hopes of winning the war on the submarine weapon. Admiral Raeder, it was reported, would become a sort of honorary "first adviser on naval affairs" to Herr Hitler.

Even as Admiral Doenitz was assuming command, the German radio today announced, without verification from Allied sources, the sinking of 450,000 tons of Allied shipping in January. Included in this claim were nine Allied merchant ships of 45,000 tons which the German High Command said today had just been sunk in the North Atlantic, Arctic and Mediterranean.

Allied sources have estimated that the Germans have anywhere from 300 to 700 submarines available for duty, a third of which might be on the hunt at any one time. ◇

YOUNG GIRLS FOUND MENACE TO TROOPS
Outnumber Prostitutes 4–1 in Spreading Venereal Disease, Health Officers Say

Girls of teen age picked up in this area by service men outnumber professional prostitutes by a ratio of 4 to 1 as spreaders of venereal diseases among our armed forces, a conference on wartime control of venereal disease was informed yesterday by representatives of the Army, Navy and the United States Public Health Service.

The meeting, held at the Hotel Astor, was one of three simultaneous sessions of the eleventh regional conference on social hygiene under the auspices of the New York Tuberculosis and Health Association's Social Hygiene Committee and 116 other sponsoring organizations. The conference was attended by nearly 1,000 representatives of the Army, Navy, Public Health Service, New York State and City Departments of Health and by doctors, nurses, magistrates, and educational and social workers from the metropolitan area.

The annual meeting and conference on tuberculosis of the New York Tuberculosis and Health Association was also held yesterday at the Astor, jointly with the Tuberculosis Sanatorium Conference of metropolitan New York. All the various groups attending the sessions met jointly at a luncheon session.

'LOCAL TALENT' IS BLAMED

"In the present war," said Dr. Robert E. Heering, past assistant surgeon, Public Health Service. "We find that local talent—so-called charity girls or 'chippies'—is figuring more and more prominently in the spread of venereal diseases. This prominence is due in part, at least, to the fact that many communities, having finally come to the realization of their responsibilities, have made it uncomfortable for commercial prostitution, with the result that relatively fewer infections are acquired from this source.

"Professor John H. Stokes of the University of Pennsylvania has recently reported a loosening up of sex standards, citing as evidence a shift of the infection source from professional prostitute to casual."

Quoting Professor Stokes, Dr. Heering continued:

"We find the girl-friend or pick-up performing her uncertain offices without cost, which confounds the police attack on prostitution; and we find among women and girls of the most unexpected types an almost avid desire to show the boys a good time.

"We are concentrating troops overwhelmingly in the South, in areas where both white and colored races have a phenomenally high incidence of venereal disease. The color-line is thinning, drawing on the Negro reservoir of infection, the highest in the country. The population as well as the armed forces is on the move, and civilians, equally with the soldier and sailor, are swept into the morale-wrecking effects of the change. And now, scientific discovery, the one-day cure of the maligned but often effective fear-producing deterrents of disease, is knocking the props out from under our platform." ◇

FEBRUARY 4, 1943

ROMMEL'S FORCES BATTLE AMERICANS

Marshal's Best Armored Units Thrown Into Struggles on Central Tunisia Sector

By FRANK L. KLUCKHOHN
Wireless to The New York Times.

ON THE TUNISIAN FRONT, Feb. 2 (Delayed)—The American Air Force fought the Germans today over the expanding battlefield in Southern Tunisia as Field Marshal General Erwin Rommel succeeded in getting some of his prize armored units into the fighting in this sector.

Both at Sened Station, on the way to Maknassy, and opposite Faid Pass, American armored units and what infantry support they could muster ran into units that Marshal Rommel—"the professor" to the American troops—has been able to rush north in an attempt to break the British First Army's communications southward and clear the way coincidentally for his own advance to the north.

The infantry—green two days ago—succeeded today in taking the high hills east of Sened Station, giving it a commanding position there. Our tanks beyond Sened backed an estimated twenty German tanks against the mountains and captured them in heavy fighting.

But today was devoted primarily to air battles as dive-bombers raked the American positions, Messerschmitts cannonaded them and Focke-Wulfs did both. In 150 sorties, the numerically inferior planes of Major Gen. James H. Doolittle's command sought to break up the air attack that the enemy had held in leash for such a moment.

MARETH LINE GETS MORE GUNS

Besides rushing troops and tanks to halt the American operating in the south under Lieut. Gen. Kenneth A. N. Anderson's orders, Marshal Rommel is reportedly reinforcing the Mareth Line, which runs fifty miles between the sea and the mountains, with medium and heavy artillery—88-mm. guns and long-range 105s. Col. Gen. Dietloff von Arnim's

forces around Tunis and Bizerte also were making demonstrations southward against our communications lines as their air force cut loose after a week of inactivity on the ground. As was the case earlier on the northern front, where the British form the bulk of the force, as soon as our light fighter swoops dis appeared, the enemy swooped in, his bombs making it tough for our infantry. It was a measure of what the green American troops could take before giving it back that our infantry units could capture the hills beyond Sened today. I saw these troops dive-bombed time after time on their way to battle. Yesterday they were attacked by tanks but they counter-attacked. Today they moved forward despite their casualties.

BATTLE OF FAID DESCRIBED

For two days, American armored forces attached to General Anderson's First Army have been battling to check the German breakthrough near Faid Pass. From an Arab rug tent camouflaged around the sides with brush I watched preparations for a counter-attack in which, as this is written, twenty-two enemy tanks have been reported destroyed against five of ours knocked out by German 88-mm. artillery. ◆

German Field Marshal Erwin Rommel (third from left) on the Tunisian front, 1943.

FEBRUARY 5, 1943

MIKHAILOVITCH SET TO MOBILIZE 200,000

By C. L. SULZBERGER
Wireless to The New York Times.

LONDON, Feb. 4—General Draja Mikhailovitch, Serbian-born de Gaulle of the Balkans, has reported by wireless to the Yugoslav Government in London that he is prepared to mobilize an army of more than 200,000 men in occupied Yugoslavia and that he is now in constant touch with Greek and Bulgarian sympathizers who are prepared to act with him when the United Nations second front opens up in the Balkans, it is stated by General Mikhailovitch's admirers in the Yugoslav Cabinet here.

This correspondent makes no pretense to verifying these claims. That is impossible. However, this is a tale of "Draja" as told by his adherents and, like previous accounts of the Partisan movement, it should be accepted as a one-sided version in a two-sided dispute.

General Mikhailovitch can be regarded as preeminently a Serb, who wants to liberate his country and restore the pre-war Kingdom of Yugoslavia under the Serbian Karageorgevitch dynasty. At the time the present war started in 1939 he was charged with planning new fortifications along the Italian-German frontiers, and he recommended that it was a foolish and wasteful expenditure because in case of attack the Yugoslav Army must be withdrawn nearer to the center of the country and there try to hold, first, in the region of the Sava River.

General Mikhailovitch, then colonel, was disapproved by the General Staff of the time and withdrawn to Belgrade, where he received a relatively unimportant job. In this sense of disagreement with his superiors on the basis of military opinion, General Mikhailovitch's career was much like that of General Charles de Gaulle. Both have been proven right by events.

While he was in Belgrade General Mikhailovitch participated in occasional secret talks held at Zemun, across the Sava from Belgrade, in which patriot officers discussed possible action in case the government knuckled under to Axis pressure. Others who took part in these talks were General Borivoye Mirkovitch, who was a major directing force in the Yugoslav coup d'etat; General Simovich, former Prime Minister, who was selected by General Mirkovitch to be titular head of the coup, and various air force and army officers, some of whom are now abroad helping the Yugoslav cause.

AMONG FIRST TO RESIST

When the bewildered government gave its shattered army the order to surrender to the Axis, General Mikhailovitch was one of many officers who disappeared into the mountains, as had patriotic South Slavs for centuries before when they

FEBRUARY 7, 1943

Editorial
WAR ON ALL FRONTS

The nature of this total and global war brings it about that while the United Nations are able to hail gratifying victories on some fronts, there are stalemates and touch-and-go battles on others, and there are also cries of distress and urgent appeals for help from some of our allies exposed to an immediate menace.

Such outcries and appeals, combined with foreign and domestic criticism of our conduct of the war, arose during those dark days some months ago when the Russians were apparently holding on to Stalingrad and the passes of Caucasus with little more than the skin of their teeth and grim determination, and when our Marines were fighting for their little beachhead in the Solomons. There were cries for the second front, for more lend-lease aid to Russia, for more troops and supplies for our hard-pressed forces on Guadalcanal. As soon and as adequately as it was humanly possible, supplies were sent to Russia at great risk and cost, a second front was established in Africa, and the German disaster in Russia began to take shape. Likewise, our troops in the Solomons received reinforcements and drove back the Japanese.

Now there come similar outcries and appeals from both Australia and China. The first is menaced by a Japanese invasion, the second is pictured as being close to an economic collapse. Nobody will deny the justification of these pleas, or minimize the dangers which they picture. If either of these dangers should materialize it would be a catastrophe of great magnitude for all the United Nations.

Yet, in answer to frequent criticism that our aid to China or Australia is still inadequate, it must be pointed out that what we can send is determined in large part by circumstances at present beyond our control, and that the battles fought in Russia, in Africa or in the Solomons are as much battles for China and Australia as for any other country. Unfortunately, despite the American and British production miracles, there is just so much to go around. There are just so many planes, and tanks, and guns, and there are just so many ships to transport them to the front lines. In the Pacific all our available forces are in there fighting to protect Australia. And in North Africa all available United Nations forces are likewise fighting, not only to drive out the Germans and Italians and thereby blast a way for an invasion of the European continent, but also to open up the Mediterranean as a supply route to India, Burma and China, without which a major campaign from these regions is impossible.

In this global warfare it is a question of nice military judgment as to just where the available manpower and resources should be utilized to obtain maximum results. Nobody will today challenge the wisdom of the aid to Russia or the African landing which averted a German-Japanese junction in the Middle East. And if there was not enough left to provide more aid to the Far East than was actually sent, that was not a fault of distribution but a result of the original sin of all democracies—the sin of being unprepared for war. ◊

fought occupying troops in Hajduk and Chetnik bands. Already the first shots of guerrilla resistance had been fired in Hercegovina by an independent peasant band by the time General Mikhailovitch began to organize his forces.

In the remote mountains he found Major Paloshevitch, who had refused to demobilize his battalion, and together they planned the future fight. Word of their plans began to filter through the land. Although all Yugoslav generals, good as well as bad, had lost their popular reputations as a result of the army's collapse, General Mikhailovitch was the only colonel who did not suffer from this blot. He worked slowly, gathering recruits and cached arms and limiting himself to small skirmishes and sabotage until Germany invaded Russia, when the feeling spread through Slavophil Yugoslavia that the moment had come to arise.

According to the Yugoslav War Minister, who was promoted to general by the emigre government after his first successful attacks, his army is being thoroughly trained on a basis of regular officer cadres and a large number of noncommissioned officers, but with small irregular groups of Chetniks under them conducting limited raids. In other words, he claims to be retaining command of the nucleus of a large force while keeping many of his sworn followers in their native villages and towns prepared to rise on a given signal from his secret agents.

In this connection it is reported here that the Axis is busily trying to round up his clandestine supporters and break this organization and their agents traveling about occupied Yugoslavia, pretending to collect funds in General Mikhailovitch's name and arresting all contributors. Between Dec. 9 and 13, 3,000 are believed to have been arrested of which number 300 were shot on Christmas Eve, and later 3,900 more were rounded up and executed. ◇

FEBRUARY 10, 1943

U.S. Submarine Flaunts a Broom For Clean Sweep Off New Guinea

By ROBERT TRUMBULL
By Telephone to The New York Times.

ABOARD THE U.S. SUBMARINE WAHOO, at a Pacific Base, Feb. 9—An engagement with a Japanese destroyer in a finger-like bay of Mushu Island, north of New Guinea, followed by a running torpedo and gun battle with a four-ship convoy the next day, gave this new submarine of the Pacific Fleet the right to wear a broom tied to her periscope when she came into port. The broom, by naval usage, denotes a "clean sweep." The Wahoo earned the unofficial decoration by sinking all four ships of the convoy, in addition to the destroyer.

The Wahoo's captain, Lieut. Comdr. Dudley W. Morton, 35 years old, of Miami, Fla., and his executive officer, Lieut. Richard H. O'Kane, 32 years old, of San Rafael, Calif., told the story of this and later engagements that took place after the Wahoo had fired all her torpedoes. Regarding one of these, Lieut. Comdr. Morton remarked: "It was another running gun battle—destroyer gunning, Wahoo running."

FIVE CROWDED DAYS OF PERIL
The Wahoo's adventures on this patrol in the New Guinea area were compressed into five days crowded with peril. Once two members of the crew were wounded "as a result of enemy action."

A pharmacist's mate had to amputate two toes of one of the men while the submarine was still under fire. Lacking surgical tools, he used a pair of wire-cutting pliers for the operation. The patient, Fireman H. P. Glinsky, is now doing well.

This pharmacists's mate, L. J. Lindhe of Wisconsin, affectionately dubbed "the Quack," has been giving the back of Lieut. Comdr. Morton's neck a daily massage for the past five days to relieve tenseness of muscles resulting from the action.

"A form of being scared, gentlemen," Lieut. Comdr. Morton told the press, explaining how he got the sore neck.

At the time of the action Lieut. Comdr. Morton was exploring the new Japanese harbor of Wewak on the northern coast of New Guinea. Wewak is one of the advance bases being established by the Japanese as General Douglas MacArthur's conquering forces drive them from their former strongholds in the regions of Buna and Gona. Wewak Harbor was then uncharted, but one of the enlisted men on the Wahoo had a 25-cent atlas that shows the location. Lieut. Comdr. Morton's officers traced the area from the atlas and enlarged this by photography to obtain a satisfactory map.

Mushu Island lies a short distance off Wewak. While nosing around there submerged, Lieut. Comdr. Morton spotted a ship in Mushu's narrow bay. It was a Japanese destroyer at anchor, possibly an escort for the convoy the submarine wiped out the next day farther north.

As the Wahoo fired a torpedo and missed, the destroyer upped anchor and drove in to attack. The Wahoo fired several more torpedoes, but all missed because the range was too long to hit a fast target. The last immediately available torpedo was fired at a range of 800 yards The destroyer steamed on, firing her guns and met the tin fish almost half-way, or at 500 yards.

The torpedo hit amidships, scrambling the destroyer's vital installations, and she burst in two. Into the sea went a large number of white-clad Japanese sailors who had been acting as lookouts in the riggings, on the yardarms, on top of the turrets, every place a man could hang on. The warship went down in two sections, bow first, in five minutes.

Two days later, on Jan. 26, the Wahoo sighted the convoy of two freighters of 7,000 to 9,000 tons, a 7,000-ton transport and a tanker of about 6,000 tons. The transport was loaded with troops, of whom Lieut. Comdr. Morton believes there were no survivors.

The Wahoo torpedoed and sank a freighter first, then the transport. It wounded the other freighter, then knocked off the tanker before pursuing the crippled ship. There ensued a running battle.

"We were inclined to laugh at the freighter's erratic firing," Lieut. Comdr. Morton said, "but a shot that landed right in front of us wiped the smirks off our faces."

We finally sank the freighter at about 9 P.M. ◇

FEBRUARY 11, 1943

GANDHI STARTS FAST TO PROTEST ARREST
Plans to Subsist 21 Days on Fruit Juice and Water

BOMBAY, Feb. 10 (AP)—With India apprehensively alert, Mohandas K. Gandhi started a twenty-one-day hunger strike today, to subsist on citrus fruit juice mixed with water, but not to "fast unto death" as he threatened on previous abstentions. His fast is in protest against his confinement behind barbed wire in the palace of the Aga Khan at Poona.

The 73-year-old independence leader imposed the limited diet upon himself after long correspondence with the Marquess of Linlithgow in which the Viceroy advised against it for reasons of health. The Viceroy asserted it constituted "political blackmail for which there can be no moral justification."

Mr. Gandhi went ahead, however, with the objectives of compelling the government to alter its policy of locking up members of the All-India Congress party "for the duration" and to protest against the "leonine violence" which he accused the government of using to suppress the civil disobedience campaign.

REFUSED FREEDOM FOR FAST

The correspondence of Mr. Gandhi and the Viceroy was published by the Government of India today with an accompanying statement that the government had informed Mr. Gandhi he would be released for the purpose and for the duration of the fast and, with him, any members of his party who wished to accompany him.

"Mr. Gandhi," the statement added, "has expressed his readiness to abandon his intended fast if released, failing which he will fast in detention."

The government statement said "it is now clear that only his unconditional release could prevent him from fasting."

"This the Government of India is not prepared to concede," it added.

Mr. Gandhi in his letters to the Viceroy denied that the Congress party was responsible for slayings, train-wreckings and other violence of the past few months. He demanded his unconditional release from the palatial surroundings where he has been confined since last Aug. 9 after a new civil disobedience campaign broke out against British rule.

This is Mr. Gandhi's ninth fast in twenty-five years. The first in October, 1918, lasted three days in support of a cotton mill workers' strike at Ahmedabad. The second, in February, 1922, lasted five days, in condemnation of his Indian followers for burning a policeman alive. The third, of twenty-one days, was in September, 1924, on behalf of Hindu-Moslem unity.

In Yerawada jail he undertook a "fast unto death" which lasted thirteen days in September, 1932. It ended when the British Cabinet withdrew its decision to have separate elections for Untouchables, which Mr. Gandhi contended would split Indian ranks.

His fifth fast lasted twenty-one days in May, 1933, and was undertaken as a form of purification for his followers. The sixth, in August, 1934, was directed against over-zealous reformers. His seventh, in the same month, lasted a week. He undertook it to compel the British to permit him to edit his weekly publication Harijan from jail. He went without food again for four days in April, 1939, over a local political problem.

The hunger strike has also been used against Mr. Gandhi. In October, 1934, he declared himself "a dead weight" on the Congress party and offered his resignation. Seven of his followers fasted until he changed his mind. ◇

Mohandas K. Gandhi in 1943.

FEBRUARY 17, 1943

Editorial
ACTION IN THE SOLOMONS

An official summary of extensive air and naval operations in the Solomons area from Jan. 29 through Feb. 7 reveals at least part of what happened during the Japanese evacuation of Guadalcanal. No ships met in battle except some torpedo boats and destroyers. Those lost on both sides went down under air attack. We did not prevent the evacuation, and suffered substantial naval loss. The American heavy cruiser Chicago was sunk by torpedo planes on the second day of continuing engagements in which we also lost an unnamed destroyer and three PT boats. Against this we claim two enemy destroyers certainly sunk, four probably sunk and eight others, with three smaller craft, damaged.

Our loss was not "extremely light," as first reported. The Chicago was a fine 9,300-ton vessel, mounting nine 8-inch guns. She is undoubtedly the "battleship" which the Japanese announced they had sunk off Rennell Island, together with another "battleship" and three cruisers. The Chicago was damaged by aerial torpedoes and succumbed to torpedo plane attack the next day while under tow. Fortunately, most of her crew were saved. Exaggerated Japanese claims may be based on other damage inflicted on our ships, but not yet reported by us.

Apparently the descent of the Japanese rescue fleet with battleships and carriers on Guadalcanal almost coincided with the approach of an American task force convoying transports to our island base. The troops were safely landed; but at dusk, south of Guadalcanal, our fighting ships were sharply attacked by enemy carrier planes and dispersed. Meanwhile, twenty enemy destroyers were taking the remnants of their beaten force from Cape Esperance. One at least was sunk in this attempt. When our main naval forces swept northward the Japanese capital units, which had come down from Truk, withdrew to safer waters, pursued by our ships and planes. In this flight the Japanese suffered their chief loss, not too heavy from their standpoint, considering the risk involved. Apparently our battle fleet was ready and eager to engage the enemy, but that opportunity still lies ahead. ◇

A German U-Boat in 1943.

FEBRUARY 21, 1943

The Battle of the Wolf Packs

By Rear Admiral Emory S. Land, Chairman,
U.S. Maritime Commission, and Administrator, War Shipping Administration

The greatest threat confronting the Axis is the steady translation of American resources and industrial might into fighting power. Germany, Italy and Japan know that the strength of this nation, added to the already fully mobilized forces of our Allies, will eventually crush them unless by some means they can prevent complete utilization of that power in the grand strategy of the United Nations.

This is the reason for Germany's intensive submarine campaign in the Atlantic. If the Nazis are to avert the full impact of American productive power on the battlefront, they must neutralize that power before it can be hurled against them. Since they have not destroyed our cities, shipyards and factories, they must concentrate on attempting to send our ships to the bottom.

The "Battle of the Atlantic" is but one phase of our efforts to meet the challenge. It has been a spectacular phase, and one in which the naval forces, the air forces and the merchant marine of the United States and Great Britain have distinguished themselves. But other phases of the war of production and transportation have been carried on with equal intensity and are having their effect in gradually wearing down the power of Germany's undersea "wolf packs."

The submarine threat to the maintenance of our transatlantic lifelines is being met in three ways: (1) by striking at enemy submarine construction, repair and servicing bases, (2) by accepting the challenge at sea through convoy and patrol operations and (3) by building new merchant ships to replace our losses and to increase our available tonnage. Information about the first two items is restricted, for reasons of military censorship and security. Concerning the third item, one may express some very definite views.

The question most frequently asked of those administering the merchant shipbuilding program is: "Are we building ships at a rate faster than the rate of sinkings?" The implication is that the United States has set out to solve the sinking problem by sending out more ships than the Nazis can sink. The question seems to imply the placing of an unfair burden of responsibility upon the shipbuilder when, in fact, the answer to the problem is only partly in his hands.

The fortunes of war are subject to much more rapid change on the battlefront than on the production front. The rate of sinkings can rise or fall more quickly than the rate of shipbuilding. Moreover, as I have frequently emphasized, you can sink a ship far faster than you can build one—even in these times when we are turning out Liberty Ships in an average time of fifty-five days.

Whether submarine activity will grow worse in the future is something one cannot predict. It is a fact, however, that this type of naval thrust at our shipping is more active in the Winter months, when nights are longer and conditions at sea are less favorable to surface craft and more favorable to submarine operations. With the coming of Spring and Summer it is possible that we may see some slackening off in the activity of German U-boats. But that will be governed by the exigencies of war. The Nazis, we may be sure, will send their submarines wherever they are most useful as the United Nations press onward with the offensive begun in the closing weeks of 1942. Submarines go where "the fishing is best."

The amazing progress of shipbuilding in the United States during the last year is an indication of the ingenuity and enterprise of the American people and our determination to win this war. Fortunately, a fair start had been made on the Maritime Commission's long-range building program when the call for sudden expansion of facilities and stepping up of the program came with the outbreak of war in Europe in 1939. At that time the commission was working on its schedule of building fifty ships a year for ten years, and some of these vessels had already been turned out.

The start was slow, but the progress has been rapid and gratifying—if not startling. To speed production and utilize the type of engines that could be produced in large numbers, the commission settled on a standardized design in the Liberty Ship of 10,500 deadweight tons. It took an average of 235 days to build the first two of these vessels, which were delivered in December, 1941. In December, 1942, when eighty-two Liberties were delivered, the average building time was reduced to fifty-five days. Performance like this, combined with an increase of more than 600 per cent in shipbuilding facilities, made it possible to turn out 746 ships, totaling 8,090,800 deadweight tons, in 1942.

The commission's directive from President Roosevelt was to build 8,000,000 tons of ships last year. Our directive for 1943 is for at least 16,000,000 tons, which will give us a total of about 2,300 vessels, totaling 24,000,000 tons, in the two years. I am confident that we will fulfill the President's directive this year. ◆

FEBRUARY 21, 1943

The ABC of Point Rationing

By JANE HOLT

The point rationing of processed foods, according to the Office of Price Administration, is the most far-reaching rationing yet imposed by war necessity. It affects almost every man, woman and child in the nation

Only A, B and C stamps may be used during the first month. Point values will fluctuate as food supplies vary nation. Here, briefly, are some questions that may occur to you in connection with the program, together with answers that are intended to help you adjust yourself to the regimen:

Q: How does point rationing differ from other methods of rationing?

A: This is best answered by a brief definition of the three systems now in use. The simplest is coupon rationing, which is used in rationing single commodities—sugar and coffee, fuel oil and gasoline. By this time you are thoroughly familiar with its workings.

The second system, rationing by purchase certificate, is the one now in use for the rationing of automobiles, bicycles, heating stoves, heavy-duty rubber footwear, tires, tubes and typewriters. Here is how it functions: A person desiring one of the items listed applies to his local Rationing Board, which issues a form for him to fill out. The applicant supplies the information, and if this complies with the requirements the board issues a Purchase Certificate, which the consumer must present when he purchases the item.

The third point rationing is a method for rationing many articles in one group of related commodities, which may be used interchangeably. The remainder of this column is devoted to an explanation of how point rationing operates.

Q: Why do we need point rationing? A: Point rationing is a system for rationing all items in a group of closely related commodities. If only some of the goods in such a group were rationed—the scarcest ones, for example—consumers would rush to buy the others and they would soon disappear from the stores. On the other hand, if all the goods were rationed separately—as coffee and sugar and gasoline have each been rationed—different stamps for every individual product would have to be issued. This might mean hundreds of various ration stamps, which, in turn, would mean endless confusion for all concerned.

Q: What is a point?

A: A point is a ration value, much as dollars and cents are money values. Each rationed food will be worth so much in currency and so much in points. The size of the supply will determine the number of points given to an article; the price and quality will have no bearing. Thus, for example, if peas are more plentiful than beans, peas will have a lower point value than beans. You can see that this system enables the government to steer consumers away from buying scarce items and encourages them to purchase those that are comparatively abundant.

Naturally, a large can of corn—or anything else for that matter—will be worth more in points than a small one. In establishing the point values of varying amounts of the same food the net weight of the contents of the can will be the deciding factor.

Q: What sort of foods will be point rationed?

A: Processed foods: canned and glassed fruits, vegetables, soups and juices; dried fruits; frozen fruits and vegetables; chili sauce and catsup. Processed baby foods—strained or chopped preparations made of fruits, vegetables or meats—also will be included.

Q: When will the point rationing of processed foods go into effect?

A: On March 1. This week retail sales of these foods will be suspended to permit wholesalers and storekeepers to prepare for the program and to allow civilians to apply for War Ration Book No. 2.

Q: What is War Ration Book No. 2?

A: This is the book containing the stamps that will be necessary in procuring processed foods. Later it will be used in meat rationing.

Q: Would you indicate how War Ration Book No. 2 is to be used by describing its contents?

A: You will find that Book 2 contains blue and red stamps. The blue stamps are to be used in purchasing processed foods; the red stamps are to be reserved for meat rationing, which is expected to start April 1. In addition, each stamp is lettered and numbered. The letters tell you when the stamps may be used—only A B and C stamps may be used during March, the first ration period—and the figures tell you the point value of each stamp.

Q: How will I know the point value of a rationed food?

A: Toward the end of this week the government will issue an official table of point values, which your grocer must post where you can see it. This will tell you exactly how many points each rationed food is worth. Modifications, probably not oftener than once monthly, may be made in the table, which will be the same throughout the country.

Q: Does it make a difference how I spend my stamps?

A: Yes, to a certain extent it does. Using the high-point stamps first means that you won't be left at the end of a month with anything but an eight-point stamp to exchange for a six-point purchase. You should avoid such a situation, because your grocer isn't permitted to make "change" in stamps. If what you buy is lower in point value than the stamp you present, you'll lose some of your points.

Q: How can I best budget my points?

A: One way to do it is to figure out your family's approximate weekly point allowance. Each person is allowed forty-eight points a rationing period, which means that, if your family consists of two, you have approximately twenty-four points a week to spend. Then list the point-rationed foods and the quantities you expect to buy for the week, jotting down the point value beside each

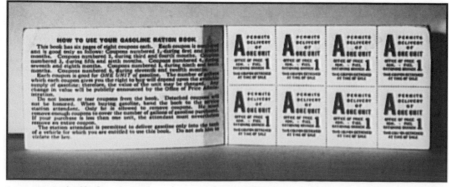

A gas rationing booklet from the 1940s.

item. Add up the points and compare the sum with your family's point allowance for the week.

If your total is less than the weekly budget, then, obviously, no changes are necessary. If it is more, you will have to modify your list. This can be done by substituting low-point foods for those that have a high-point value, and by shifting to fresh fruits and vegetables in some instances.

Q: What happens when my son, who is in the Army, and has no ration book, comes home on furlough?

A: If your son is on furlough for seven days or longer he presents his leave pa- pers to the local rationing board, which will issue a point certificate, allowing enough points to cover his leave period. Your grocer will accept this point certificate instead of point stamps.

Food ration stamps must be torn out of the book in the presence of your grocer or in the presence of the delivery boy. ◊

FEBRUARY 22, 1943

ANOTHER SETBACK FOR THE ALLIES IN MID-TUNISIA

GERMANS ADVANCE
Tanks and Infantry, with Artillery, Break U.S. And British Lines

By DREW MIDDLETON
Wireless to The New York Times.

ALLIED HEADQUARTERS IN NORTH AFRICA, Feb. 21—German tanks and two battalions of infantry cracked the stubborn Allied defense yesterday and occupied the highly important Kasserine Pass, twelve miles from the nearest point on the Algerian frontier, as the second phase of the German offensive in Central Tunisia got under way.

Veteran British armored units that had rushed south during the past week joined an American combat command in heavy fighting that continued through yesterday and early today. American and British tanks lunged forward together, leading their infantry comrades in counter-attacks against the steel fingers of Field Marshal General Erwin Rommel's army reaching for Tebessa, Algeria, the junction of four main roads and two railroads.

Defying heavy clouds that hung over the battlefront, Airacobras of the Twelfth United States Army Air Force harried enemy supply columns winding toward the front. A number of trucks were damaged by cannon and machine-gun fire in attacks that followed a night raid by Royal Air Force Bisleys against targets on these roads and others farther south in the Gafsa area. German communications were also attacked by these medium British bombers Friday night, but bad weather prevented accurate observation of the results.

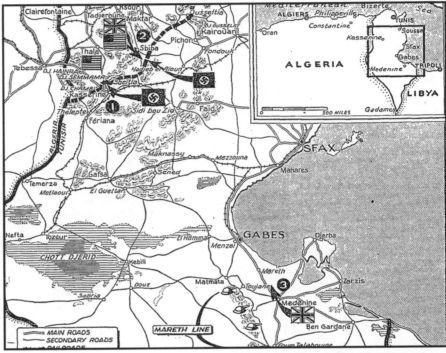

Besides the successful attacks on the Kasserine Gap, the enemy made one other offensive movement. For the second time in two days a strong armored reconnaissance force probed the British positions near Sbiba. Again they were met by the ubiquitous guards; who knocked out two tanks and severely damaged two more. [The French also claimed a role in this action.]

Enemy losses in the fighting at Kasserine are believed to equal the heavy ones suffered in the first attack Thursday. The second push, however, was preceded by much heavier fire from heavy and medium artillery, which reportedly silenced American guns in the gap and on the hills to each side.

Dive-bombers, which played a major part in the break-through at Faid just one week ago, did not have an important role in this attack. The gap was won mainly by guns, tanks and infantry after hours of severe fighting in which the Americans and British counterattacked with reckless abandon.

The entire Allied position in Western Central Tunisia is affected by the smash through the gap northwest of Kasserine, which showed again that

Another Setback for the Allies in Mid-Tunisia: Marshal Rommel's infantry and tanks captured the pass northwest of Kasserine (1). He may now turn to the right and make for Thala or turn to the left, force his way through the pass at Djebel Hanira, break into the comparatively flat country beyond Tebessa and strike for Constantine (shown on the inset). East of Sbiba (2) a new German thrust was smashed back. The British Eighth Army drove eight miles beyond Medenine (3) on the road to Mareth and the railhead at Gabes.

the enemy was willing to commit large forces for taking geographical positions essential in that country. Should Marshal Rommel swing west on Tebessa, the communications of all American and British forces in that area would be seriously threatened. If he turns northward against the rear areas of the British First Army, a further adjustment of the Allied line will be necessary to meet this attack on the open flank.

But all the indications are that Marshal Rommel intends to pursue his attacks against the American and British troops in the Tebessa region. It must be noted that the movements of the last few days have left the German forces open to a counter-attack from the north. Whether General Sir Harold R.L.G. Alexander, commanding the Allied ❯

land forces, can risk committing the First Army's reserves to such an action while Col. Gen. Dietloff von Arnim waits at the head of the Medjerda Valley in Northern Tunisia is a difficult problem for the Allied commander.

The bulk of the best German troops is being used in the present offensive, the future of which will be dictated by the German losses in tanks. If the enemy can recover enough Allied tanks to replace his own losses and give him reasonable

security for the coming battle with General Sir Bernard L. Montgomery's British Eighth Army, the battle of Kasserine Pass is only the first step in a serious and very threatening offensive. ◊

MARCH 2, 1943

SAVE DOOMED JEWS, HUGE RALLY PLEADS

Immediate action by the United Nations to save as many as possible of the five million Jews threatened with extermination by Adolf Hitler and to halt the liquidation of European Jews by the Nazis was demanded at a mass demonstration of Christians and Jews in Madison Square Garden last night.

The demand by religious, civic, political and labor leaders was heard by an audience of 21,000 that filled the huge auditorium, while several thousand others were unable to get in.

By 8 o'clock, shortly before the meeting opened, the approaches to the Garden were closed by the police, but 10,000 persons remained standing in Forty-ninth Street, between Eighth and Ninth Avenues, and heard the addresses through amplifiers after many thousands of others who were unable to get in had dispersed. Rabbi Stephen S. Wise, president of the American Jewish Congress, who presided, announced from the platform, on the basis of police estimates, that 75,000 persons had tried to make their way into the Garden in the three hours before the meeting opened.

Joining in support of the demonstration from overseas in messages read at the meeting were the Archbishop of Canterbury, Cardinal Hinsley, Archbishop of Westminster, who is gravely ill in London, and Chief Rabbi J. H. Hertz of Great Britain. Sir William Beveridge, author of the Beveridge plan for social security, addressed the meeting by radio from the British capital.

The "Stop Hitler Now" demonstration was under the joint auspices of the American Jewish Congress, the Church Peace Union, the Free World Association, American Federation of Labor and the Congress of Industrial Organizations and other Christian and Jewish bodies.

A resolution offered by Louis Lipsky, chairman of the governing council of the American Jewish Congress, and

adopted unanimously, proposed an eleven-point program of action to achieve the purposes of the demonstration.

The resolution will be submitted to President Roosevelt and through him to the United Nations.

LA GUARDIA SPEAKS FOR CITY

Mayor La Guardia spoke in the name of the people of New York. Dr. Chaim Weizmann, president of the Jewish Agency for Palestine, spoke in behalf of the entire Jewish community.

Governor Dewey addressed the meeting by radio from Albany. From Washington came radio addresses by Supreme Court Justice William O. Douglas and Senator Robert F. Wagner. A message was read from Wendell L. Willkie, who declared that "practical measures must be formulated and carried out immediately to save as many Jews as possible."

The keynote of the meeting was struck by Herman Shulman, chairman of the special committee of the American Jewish Congress on the European situation, who in introducing Dr. Wise as presiding officer of the meeting called attention to the fact that "months have passed since the United Nations issued their declaration denouncing the unspeakable atrocities of the Nazis against the Jews and threatening retribution," with the promise that "immediate practical steps would be taken to implement it," but that nothing had been done as yet.

PRAYERS FOR THE DEAD

The climax of the meeting was reached after Cantor Morris Kapok-Kagan had sung "El Mole Rachmim," Hebrew prayer for the dead, memorializing the Jewish victims of the Nazis. This was preceded by the blowing of the shofar, the ram's horn, by Rabbi Maurice Taub, and as the sounds subsided and Mr. Kapok-Kagan began the prayer the huge audience wailed and wept, while the thousands outside, who

heard the proceedings through amplifiers, joined. There followed the reading of the Kaddish, another prayer for the dead, by Rabbi Israel Goldstein, and the reading of a passage from the Psalms by Rabbi Jacob Hoffman, ending with the words, "Save, Lord: Let the King hear us when we call."

PLEA BY CHIEF RABBI

The message from Chief Rabbi Hertz read:

"It is appalling to think that Whole of mid-European Jewry stands on brink of annihilation and that millions of Jewish men, women and children have already been slaughtered with fiendish cruelties which baffle belief, but equally appalling is fact that those who proclaim the Four Freedoms have so far done very little to secure even the freedom to live for 6,000,000 of their Jewish fellow men by readiness to rescue those who might still escape Nazi torture and butchery. May God grant that your great demonstration of American Jewry be the means of overcoming the strange and calamitous inertia of those who alone can initiate the sacred work of human salvage."

Dr. Weizmann called upon the United Nations to implement their expressions of sympathy for the Jews by deeds.

"Two million Jews have already been exterminated," he said. "The world can no longer plead that the ghastly facts are unknown and unconfirmed. At this moment expressions of sympathy, without accompanying attempts to launch acts of rescue, become a hollow mockery in the ears of the dying.

"The democracies have a clear duty before them. Let them negotiate with Germany through the neutral countries concerning the possible release of the Jews in the occupied countries. Let havens be designated in the vast territories of the United Nations which will give sanctuary to those fleeing from imminent murder. Let the gates of Palestine be opened to all who can reach the shores of the Jewish homeland. The Jewish community of Palestine will welcome with joy and thanksgiving all delivered from Nazi hands." ◊

MARCH 3, 1943

GANDHI FAST ENDS; AIM NOT ACHIEVED

He Failed to Win Release or to Get Much Notice, Except When Near Death

By HERBERT L. MATTHEWS
Wireless to The New York Times.

POONA, India, March 3—Mohandas K. Gandhi's twenty-one-day fast ended in defeat and failure at 9 o'clock this morning [11:30 last night in New York].

His life has been saved against all belief, but politically it has been a blow, to his reputation and to the Congress movement. He pledged a fight to the finish against the British last August; now he has lost the second round.

The government forbade any demonstration in connection with the breaking of the fast, only Devadas and Ramdas Gandhi, sons, and a few fellow-prisoners were present. This is the first time Mr. Gandhi has failed to achieve his object by fasting. This has disappointed and discouraged him. Therefore, he is hardly likely to let things rest as they are.

His first task is to regain some of the strength he has lost by his astonishing ordeal. Anxiety for his health will continue for weeks.

To what extent his faith and that of the Hindu community is shaken by this defeat cannot be ascertained yet. The Hindus still assert that they had tremendous popular backing in their pleas for Mr. Gandhi's release and that there will be an aftermath of bitterness that will make reconciliation more difficult than ever.

The British, on the other hand, are pleased at what they consider to have been a brilliant stroke of judgment by the Viceroy, the Marquess of Linlithgow, who for the second time in less than a year has demonstrated that the Congress party is not nearly as strong as it claims to be.

There was little mass expression of sympathy, concern or even interest, except when Mr. Gandhi appeared to be dying. The bulk of the Moslems and all the princely States remained on the sidelines. Even the Hindu Mahasabha, the most important Hindu political organization other than the Congress party, deplored the fast.

Mohammed Ali Jinnah, head of the Moslem League, again profits by Congress blunders. Although he has carefully refrained from rubbing it in during Mr. Gandhi's fast, he must be delighted at the turn events have taken.

World reaction to his fast has also disappointed the Hindus. Neither they nor Mr. Gandhi seems to have taken into consideration that the rest of the world is absorbed in the war. In general the consensus here is that Mr. Gandhi has made the greatest mistake of his career and primarily because he overlooked the war factor. That made the British willing to face the risk of his death with all its consequences. One result of this failure is that it should be his last attempt to gain anything from the British by fasting.

In any event it is the war that will determine the government's reaction to any Congress move, just as it has to Mr. Gandhi's fast. India is going to be a base for one of the main attacks against the Japanese one of these days when the reconquest of Burma takes place. Meanwhile the British feel that India must be kept peaceful and under control. ◇

MARCH 28, 1943

AMERICANS OPEN NEW TUNISIAN DRIVE AS BRITISH CONTINUE MARETH GAINS; FONDOUK IS GOAL; U.S. TROOPS THRUST ON

By The Associated Press

ALLIED HEADQUARTERS IN NORTH AFRICA, March 27—American troops launched a surprise offensive toward Fondouk in Central Tunisia today and met with initial success as the British Eighth Army, doggedly fighting its way into the Mareth Line fortifications, was reported to be "proceeding according to plan in spite of stiff resistance by the enemy.

[The Axis-fed Paris radio said yesterday that a strong British push against the southeast flank of the Mareth Line had forced Axis troops to "withdraw from their forward positions," The United Press reported.

[Berlin, broadcasting a D.N.B. dispatch, said that British and American troops appeared to be preparing to launch offensives in both Northern and Central Tunisia and that detachments of crack British troops had recently reached the Medjez-el-Bab area from England, British and American movements were described as "considerably stronger" in both sectors and the Allies were reported to be bringing up heavy concentrations of artillery.]

The American push on Fondouk, which is fifteen miles southwest of an important Axis air base at Kai-rouan, was reported to be making "good headway." The drive began after a German infantry attack had been repulsed east of Maknassy, more than 100 miles south of the scene of the new fighting.

On the Maknassy–El Guettar front, where Lieut. Gen. George S. Patton Jr.'s main concentrations of men and armor are probing for a passage through the rugged hills to the Mediterranean, there was only local activity yesterday as rainstorms swept across Tunisia. ◇

NAZI 'HEAVY WATER' LOOMS AS WEAPON
Plant Razed by 'Saboteurs' in Norway Viewed as Source of New Atomic Power

Special Cable to The New York Times.

LONDON, April 3—"Heavy water," derived by an electrochemical process from ordinary water, with hidden atomic power that can be used for the deadly purposes of war as well as the happier pursuits of peace, apparently has become a source of anxiety for those Allied leaders who plan attacks against enemy targets.

Reports reaching Norwegian circles in London cite German sources as having announced on Wednesday that as a result of the work of "saboteurs," a big electrochemical plant at Rjukan, Norway, had been blown up in what is said to have been one of three recent raids against that enemy-occupied country.

The importance of Rjukan as a target for destruction is that it is a huge plant on a wild river, from the waters of which a queer chemical known as "heavy water" the discovery of which won a Nobel Prize in 1934 for Professor Harold Urey of Columbia University, is produced, and it can be used in the manufacture of terrifically high explosives.

USE IN EXPLOSIVES SEEN
Heavy water or, more correctly, heavy hydrogen water, is believed to provide a means of disintegrating the atom that would thereby release a devastating power. While it is not believed here that the Germans, even with all their expert chemical knowledge, have developed some fantastic method of hurling the shattering force of split atoms at Britain, it is known that heavy water, when added to other chemicals, gives a powerfully destructive force, just as it can help in the production of new types of gasoline, new sugars, new textiles and numerous other utilitarian as well as medical developments.

OUR SOLDIERS IN BATTLE SOON LEARN ART OF WAR
Doughboy Is, In Turn, Cocky, Scared, Dazed, Darn Mad and Effective

By C. L. SULZBERGER
Wireless to The New York Times.

ALGIERS, April 3—The average American infantryman is somewhat cockily overconfident when he approaches his first battle experience, pretty damned scared when he actually gets in the thick of things and slightly bewildered for a time, then sore as hell and anxious to do something effective to an enemy who is causing him all sorts of discomforts such as having to spend a good deal of time dodging in and out of slit trenches.

After the first wind is taken out of his sails by initiation into the arts of dive-bombing and drumfire and he finds he is still alive, he is likely to become a veteran moderately quickly and by and large to develop considerable offensive-mindedness. He also begins to appreciate the skill of his veteran German enemy and the pluckiness of the British Tommy who fights beside him, and the reason for all the discipline of the toughening processes he has been subjected to in months of tedious training.

AS OBSERVERS SEE THEM
In other words, the green Yankee soldier going into action for the first time is certainly not as good as he thinks he is but he has enough horse sense to realize quickly his own deficiencies and to try to do something about it. He is just as likely as not to learn the hard way by burning his fingers, but he does learn.

These in a broad sense are the opinions of qualified observers who have had a chance to observe the development from draftees of doughboys at the front and make comparisons with some of the more experienced soldiers of other armies.

The American is a good scrapper but he has to learn the technique of modern warfare and he is generally doing that by tasting battle first. When the newcomer arrives in the line he is much in the position of the tough street fighter facing a skilled heavyweight and he has got to learn the tricks fast.

The first time a unit enters battle it is likely to get the shakes, and such cases of shellshock as are likely to develop will start then. Frequently green units do not do terribly well in the initiation, partly because those that have come here so far are insufficiently trained in such hard courses as British battle schools for getting used to actual fire.

Sometimes the mere noise gets them down at the start. But once they have been in action, especially the hard ones such as Kasserine, and have discovered that lots of shooting does not mean they will be killed, they begin to gain confidence, and if they lose a pal they get very sore indeed.

THE HARDENING PROCESS
Frequently it takes more than one or two actions to get the doughboys working in cohesion, and even after five or six battles they do not function as smoothly as the Germans: they have not learned to do things automatically and without considered thought.

The way a unit learns can be exemplified by the experience of one unit that was brought up absolutely green for the second battle at Sened Station. They were dive-bombed four or five times the first afternoon and deserted their trucks, but returned when their officers called them back. About the fourth occasion one of the soldiers was heard to say, "They cannot stop American infantry that way."

The next day in their first real action they broke under combined infantry and tank attack. However, they managed to re-form and counter-attack. They eventually took their objectives.

Another example of quick learning was demonstrated in the case of another outfit which, although it broke at Kasserine Pass, only a few weeks later at the last battle of El Guettar, stayed in its fox holes calmly, let the German tanks pass

Consequently, Norwegians living in London studied with interest the report emanating from Stockholm Wednesday that Rjukan had been so heavily attacked by "saboteurs" that the Germans had declared a state of emergency. They considered that if the plant had been destroyed the Germans had suffered a severe loss in their output of ammunition.

At Rjukan one quart of heavy water can be produced from 6,000 gallons of ordinary water by an electrochemical process, the formula for which was given to the world by American scientists.

Rjukan is just south of a 3,500-square-mile area in a barren mountain plateau region known as Hardangervidda, which the Germans shut off to all civilians April 1. Recent German reports have said that R.A.F. transport planes towing gliders have dropped parachutists around that area. ◇

through to he taken care of by the artillery, then smashed the enemy infantry like old hands.

Our troops are learning that mobile warfare is entirely different from trench fighting and it is hard for them to master the cohesion between arms and units. For this instruction under battle conditions is absolutely essential. It has also been discovered in this great and bloody African war school that we definitely lack sufficient training in small units, although this has been stressed in all the Army's recent peace-time manoeuvres.

A sample of how this is mastered the hard way by American soldiers may be instanced. One combat team of the First Armored Division realized through bitter experience that you cannot advance against established enemy positions directly because the artillery will knock you to pieces. Although that lesson was stressed to two other combat teams, they each made the same mistake and had time to learn the hard way—but they did learn.

Instinctively that average soldier is beginning to realize how to appreciate automatically when to stand, when to fall back, and when to wait for the artillery to take care of things.

While the biggest thing acquired in this literal school of battle is realization by the doughboy that he must learn how to win, he also had psychological experience in the realization of the true value of previously accepted luxuries. He is beginning to wonder if people back home actually appreciate what he is up against and are taking the war seriously enough. ◇

APRIL 7, 1943

U-BOAT TOLL RISES; 'TOUGH,' SAYS KNOX

Special to The New York Times

WASHINGTON, April 6—With an increased number of U-boats now operating against Allied shipping and apparently employing new tactics, the Battle of the Atlantic swung in favor of the Germans last month and the submarine sinking toll was "considerably worse" than in February, Secretary of the Navy Knox declared today at his press conference.

Declaring that the situation was both "tough" and "serious," Mr. Knox asserted that "nobody is a bit complacent about it or should be."

He hinted that the U-boats, reported to be operating in "wolf packs," with various packs apparently cooperating with one another, had adopted different tactics lately. He did not elaborate on this point.

The present danger zone is sweeping in its scope, the Secretary declared. The U-boat packs are operating in mid-Atlantic, he said, with emphasis on the North Atlantic route to England. Activity also has occurred on the Mediterranean route.

The brightest ray of hope held out by Mr. Knox, who repeatedly has warned that the submarine menace would be heightened this Spring, was "a very marked improvement" in the production pace of the Navy's destroyer escort program. The Navy is banking heavily on the effectiveness of this new type of submarine-chaser, which is relatively quick and economical to make and is highly manoeuvrable.

The program is still being retarded by a scarcity of motors for the vessels, Mr. Knox said, but even that aspect is "getting better in every respect." On April 17, he announced, he plans to make a speech at a General Electric plant in Syracuse which less than a year ago was "nothing but a hay field." Now it is turning out fifty turbogenerators a month for Navy escort vessels.

Mr. Knox said it was difficult to assess the results of the Royal Air Forces' heavy raids on submarine pens at St. Nazaire and Lorient in France and elsewhere. Navy men recognize the difficulty of penetrating with bombs the thick slabs of concrete with which these pens are protected, but Mr. Knox said it might be "assumed" that the raids were "embarrassing" the Germans, even if the damage was confined to the plants and towns around the pens. ◇

APRIL 7, 1943

Text of the Treasury's Proposal for International Fund to Stabilize Currencies

By The Associated Press.

WASHINGTON, April 6—Following is the "preliminary draft outline of proposal for a United and Associated Nations Stabilization Fund" announced by the Treasury:

I—PURPOSES OF THE FUND

1. To stabilize the foreign exchange rates of the currencies of the United Nations and nations associated with them.

2. To shorten the periods and lessen the degree of disequilibrium in the international balance of payments of member countries.
3. To help create conditions under which the smooth flow of foreign trade and of productive capital among the member countries will be fostered.
4. To facilitate the effective utilization of the abnormal foreign balances accumulating in some countries as a consequence of the war situation.
5. To reduce the use of foreign exchange controls that interfere with world trade and the international flow of productive capital.
6. To help eliminate bilateral exchange clearing arrangements, multiple currency devices, and discriminatory foreign exchange practices.

II. COMPOSITION OF THE FUND

1. The fund shall consist of gold, currencies of member countries and securities of member governments.
2. Each of the member countries shall ▸

subscribe a specified amount which will be called its quota. The aggregate of quotas of the member countries shall be the equivalent of at least $5 billion.

The quota for each member country shall be determined by an agreed-upon formula. The formula should give due weight to the important factors relevant to the determination of quotas, e.g., a country's holdings of gold and foreign exchange, the magnitude of the fluctuations in its balance of international payments, and its national income.

3. Each member country shall provide the fund with 50 per cent of its quota on or before the date set by the board of directors of the fund on which the fund's operations are to begin.

4. The initial payment of each member country (consisting of 50 per cent of its quota) shall be 12.5 per cent of its quota in gold, 12.5 per cent in local currency and 25 per cent in its own (i.e., government) securities. However, any country having less than $300,000,000 in gold

need provide initially only 7.5 per cent of its quota in gold, and any country having less than $100,000,000 in gold need provide initially only 5 per cent of its quota in gold, the contributions of local currency being increased correspondingly. A country may, at its option, substitute gold for its local currency or securities in meeting its quota requirement.

5. The member countries of the fund may be called upon to make further provision toward meeting their quotas pro rata at such times, in such amounts and in such form as the board of directors of the fund may determine, provided that the proportion of gold called for shall not exceed the proportion indicated in II-4 above, and provided that a four-fifths vote of the board shall be required for subsequent calls to meet quotas.

6. Any changes in the quotas of member countries shall be made only with the approval of a four-fifths vote of the board. ◊

OUR PRIZED RELICS SAFE FROM BOMBS
Declaration of Independence, On Display Tuesday, Comes Out of Secret Refuge

Special to The New York Times.

WASHINGTON, April 10—An indication of the extraordinary steps taken to safeguard the nation's treasure of historic documents, valuable paintings and other important mementos was given this week in an announcement that the Declaration of Independence would be taken from a secret place of safekeeping for display Tuesday when the Jefferson Memorial will be dedicated at the celebration of the bicentennial of Thomas Jefferson's birth.

Among other articles taken from

Washington to secret depositories since Pearl Harbor are the Constitution, the Lincoln Cathedral Copy of England's Magna Charta, entrusted to the United States for safekeeping by the British Government, the Articles of Confederation and the Gutenberg Bible.

SPECIAL FUNDS PROVIDED

All of these are in custody of the Library of Congress, which obtained Congressional appropriations of $130,000 to make its valuables secure. The library has shipped out 4,723 boxes of rare and irreplaceable materials.

The National Archives, recently adjudged the most nearly bombproof building in Washington, has felt it necessary to evacuate nothing except highly inflammable nitrate-based films.

The Smithsonian Institution, under twenty-four-hour guard like the other depositories, has evacuated what a spokesman called "absolutely Grade A material" which would serve as a nucleus for rebuilding its collection if everything else was destroyed. The material includes a few highly important paintings from the National Gallery of Art and "a vast number" of scientific specimens such as the first example of each species made known to science. ◊

NEGROES ASK END OF DISCRIMINATION

A national campaign against all types of discrimination against Negroes in the armed forces and in industry was approved yesterday at the closing session of the two-day meeting of the Eastern Seaboard Conference of the National Negro Congress at the Abyssinian Baptist Church, 132 West 138th Street.

Urging the establishment of a mixed military unit containing both white men and Negroes, a resolution adopted by the conference said such a grouping would enhance the Negroes' morale, "which is fast waning due to undemocratic conditions in this democratic country." Such a mixed unit would let Negroes and whites partake together of that democracy for which both are fighting, the resolution declared.

The same resolution pointed to the shortage of manpower in war industries and on the farms and asserted that "in spite of this acute problem there remains virtually an untapped source of manpower, the Negro, who is trained and stands ready to answer the call."

"We further believe," the resolution

KNOX NOTES SLASH IN APRIL SINKINGS

Special to The New York Times.

WASHINGTON, April 30—Qualifying his statement with a warning "not to attach too much significance to it," Secretary of the Navy Frank Knox announced at his press conference today that losses from enemy submarine sinkings had been "much lower" in April than during the previous month.

Mr. Knox said he made the statement with his "fingers crossed" and that he did not want anyone to draw overly important conclusions from it "because figures in that type of warfare can—and do—go up and down."

Nevertheless, April did show an improvement in the Battle of the Atlantic, and the Secretary of the Navy said he shared the hope of Admiral Ernest

continued, "that the ultimate victory can be won only through the working in unity of all the people in America with full integration of the Negro in our nation's production forces."

The delegates urged the establishment of a second land front in Europe and the prosecution of the war until the "unconditional surrender" of the Axis. "We urge that the right of self-determination for all colonial peoples be the stated policy of the United Nations," the resolution continued, "and that the Atlantic Charter and the Four Freedoms be immediately applied to India, Africa, the Carribean and other colonial peoples. "The plight of the Jewish people in foreign countries is the concern of all the United Nations and we therefore advocate that Government of the United States initiate and undertake immediately all possible rescue measures.

"We are unalterably opposed to any force which attempts to disrupt the unity and sympathetic cooperation of this nation with the Soviet Union, China and other members of the United Nations."

James B. Carey, national secretary and treasurer of the Congress of Industrial Organizations, told a mass meeting that ended the conference that when peace came 35,000,000 men and women might be without work unless a full employment and social security program was enacted. ◇

MAY 2, 1943

Anthracite Mines Closed; 80,000 Standing By Lewis

Hard-Coal Miners Join Bituminous Strike

By WALTER W. RUCH
Special to The New York Times.

WILKES-BARRE, Pa., May 1—The entire anthracite field in Eastern Pennsylvania was made idle today by a walkout of about 80,000 miners who remained unmoved by the announcement that the Federal Government had taken control of the mines which they quit last midnight at the expiration of their contract.

Not a shovel of coal was turned in the hard coal region, forming a rough triangle bounded by Scranton, Shamokin and Pottsville, and it was obvious that the miners were looking toward New York rather than Washington for the cue to return to work.

Although the miners were looking forward to President Roosevelt's radio address tomorrow night, their leaders who were available for comment declared that nothing he could say would induce the men to resume operations Monday morning.

The only thing that could persuade the men to return, these leaders said, would be word from New York that a new contract had been signed or that the old one had been extended, with wage provisions retroactive to April 30.

There was no disorder in the hard coal field during the day. The men simply failed to appear for work, many of them turning up later on the street corners instead in their Sunday best to discuss the action they had taken.

Spokesmen at the union headquarters in the three hard coal districts of the United Mine Workers of America reported this morning that everything was down tight and not a wheel was turning.

The only ray of hope visible to mine leaders here was the fact that the U.M.W.A. representatives and the operators had resumed their negotiations in New York this morning and might reach some basis for a settlement.

Union leaders were reluctant to discuss the strike, choosing that word should come from New York, and those who did so insisted that their identity be withheld. One of these was a member of the scale committee of the U.M.W.A. who returned today from New York to make a survey of the situation in this field.

VIEW OF CONSERVATIVE LEADER
This man, regarded in the area as a conservative, insisted that the miners now were 100 per cent behind John L. Lewis and would turn a deaf ear to pleadings or orders to return to work in the absence of a new contract or an extension of the old one.

"These men won't go back to work without a contract," he said.

"They will not accept a promise from the government or from anyone else. They will only be satisfied when the anthracite operators put their John Hancocks on the agreement.

"I do not expect any change in the situation as a result of the President's address tomorrow night. All the President can do is to ask the men to go back to work and guarantee them protection. This will be meaningless." ❭

J. King, Commander in Chief of the United States Fleet, that the submarine menace would be brought under control within four to six months.

Sinkings in March had been higher than in the previous two months, Mr. Knox said, but he declined to disclose the percentage of the improvement in the month just ending.

"During the past four months," he commented, "we have added steadily to the number of surface craft and aircraft being used to combat submarines."

Commenting on the fact that United States merchant ship losses in the Pacific from submarine action were practically nil, Mr. Knox explained that the Japanese used their submarines for entirely different purposes—service with the fleet, patrol duty and observation, and so forth.

In the Pacific the situation was somewhat reversed in comparison with the Atlantic, for there it was American submarines that were taking the toll of warships and merchant vessels, he said.

There had been no evidence yet that the Japanese were using their developing air bases in the Aleutian Islands, Mr. Knox asserted. ◇

Secretary of the Navy Frank Knox, 1942.

Soldiers with an anthracite miner in 1943.

Editorial
EUROPE'S IMPERILED ART

When the United Nations troops march across Europe on the final stages of their journey they may carry with them maps showing where buildings with a historic or artistic interest are located and where paintings and other cultural treasures are likely to be found. So much is indicated, though not precisely stated, in the announcement of a committee formed by the American Council of Learned Societies under the chairmanship of Dr. William Bell Dinsmoor of Columbia University. The committee has been in existence since January, working quietly and not putting out any superfluous information.

The nature of its problem is obvious enough. It is also obvious that the problem has military as well as artistic phases. How much is a museum or a cathedral worth in terms of human life, if that question has to be answered? Shall such an edifice be bombed or shelled if

erators.

He said that the members of the scale committee had been directed to remain in their respective fields until the international officers of the union had worked out an agreement with the op-

"When and if that is done, the international officers will summon the scale committee back to New York to approve the agreement," he added. "If a contract is signed then, work will be resumed." ◇

MINERS HEAR NEWS; READY TO GO BACK

Some May Resume Work This Morning Despite Need for Ratifying of Decision

By CRAIG THOMPSON
Special to The New York Times.

PITTSBURGH, May 2—A large part of the 125,000 bituminous coal miners in this area tonight heard the news that will send them back into the mines, discontinuing a stoppage that had already

resulted in the United States Government taking over the operations of the mines.

In some small communities they gathered in knots around radio sets through which they heard the speech of President Roosevelt.

More important to them, however, was the announcement of John L. Lewis, head of the United Mine Workers Union, that a fifteen-day truce pending further negotiations, had been agreed to by him and Harold L. Ickes, Fuel Administrator.

Through a day of waiting while they listened to radio news bulletins on the movements of Mr. Lewis; they had been grimly determined not to return to their jobs unless Mr. Lewis told them to. After he had authorized a return on Tuesday—apparently deferring resumption of operations an extra day so as to give local union leaders an opportunity to notify the full membership—many of them appeared ready to report for the shift beginning at 7 A.M. tomorrow.

IMPRESSED BY THE PRESIDENT
It was not believed possible to get the mines in full operations before Tuesday morning, or possibly Monday evening. Meanwhile, the miners had accepted a decision by Mr. Lewis, although impressed by the President.

The miners had taken a pretty bad beating from public opinion in this area and were smarting under it. At a little place called Library, near here, about fifty had assembled in the local firehouse around the radio. When reporters showed up to watch their reactions and to report the manner in which they received the decision the men ordered them out.

In other places there was a small amount of criticism directed against Mr. Lewis and a great deal directed against the President. Although some of the miners appeared to have been moved by what the President said, they were determined to string along with Mr. Lewis and said so.

It developed fairly rapidly that the

it happens to adjoin a railway station or fortified point? Or shall infantry flow around it at greater human cost? We don't suppose Dr. Dinsmoor's committee wants to say, but the generals will wish all the information they can get. Another aspect of the subject is the discovery and identification of looted works of art. The Nazis in a thousand years would create nothing worth crossing the street to look at, but as thieves they show some discrimination.

One thinks of all the centuries of Europe: the Romanesque, the Gothic and the Renaissance; the builders of Notre Dame and Chartres; the genius of stonecutters flowering in the day's work; the painters of religious ecstasy and tavern vulgarity; the masterless men who plied their noble trades in the shadow of tyranny and war; the young who dreamed dreams, the old who saw visions; the passion and revolt which expressed themselves, not in blood but in creation; the growth of a majestic continental culture through slow generations, out of multitudinous lives. This is the foundation on which the future will have to be built. The future will be surer if the visible objects remain. Dr. Dinsmoor and his colleagues can play as significant a role as the generals do. ◇

full resumption of operations would involve meetings of the local unions and a ratification of the truce, which was expected to take up most of tomorrow.

During the day while they waited to be told what to do, the miners had been determined that they would not call off the strike unless ordered to do so by Mr. Lewis.

Last night in his radio address the President said: "Tomorrow the Stars and Stripes will fly over the coal mines. I hope every miner will be at work under that flag." This flag was raised over the Pittsburgh Coal Company at Pricedale Pa., on the day the miners walked out.

How much they might have been influenced by President Roosevelt had not a truce been reached became an academic matter, but there were signs that he probably would not have swung much weight. ◇

MAY 16, 1943

LANDING ON ATTU OPENS NORTH PACIFIC OFFENSIVE
Army and Navy Act To Remove a Longstanding Menace to Our Position

By SIDNEY SHALETT

HEADQUARTERS ARMY AIR FORCE OF APPLIED TACTICS, Orlando, Fla., May 15—After nearly a year of sparring, the American landing at Attu Island on Tuesday finally elevated the North Pacific theatre from the side-show category and raised the curtain on a great forthcoming battle. At last American forces are in contact with the Japanese in the North Pacific and the issue is joined.

Details of the fighting were scarce in the early hours after the invasion was confirmed, but it was obvious that the fighting was bitter and that it was going to require a full-scale effort to expel the entrenched enemy. The invasion did not come as a surprise in Washington, for, within the past month, there has been an increasing belief in military and naval circles that we might strike soon at the enemy with something heavier than bombing raids. There was something of an element of surprise, however, in the fact that the first blow was struck at Attu, as Kiska is the main Japanese base in the Aleutians.

JAPANESE SEEM STRONG

There is good reason to believe that the Japanese strength on Attu and Kiska is considerable—probably more than the meager reports concerning that area have indicated. Thus the attack on Attu indicated that our North Pacific strategy is based on the plan of cleaning out the weaker enemy nest first, then probably coming to grips with the main body on the stronger and the strategically located island of Kiska.

As the long-awaited counter-offensive in the Aleutians began, there was much speculation as to how the Aleutians, once restored fully to American hands, might figure in the general war program now being discussed by President Roosevelt and Prime Minister Churchill. There were so many imponderables—the enigma of Russian cooperation in the Pacific war and the ultimate decision as to how air power may be best used against the heart of the Japanese Empire—that there was little clarification of the question.

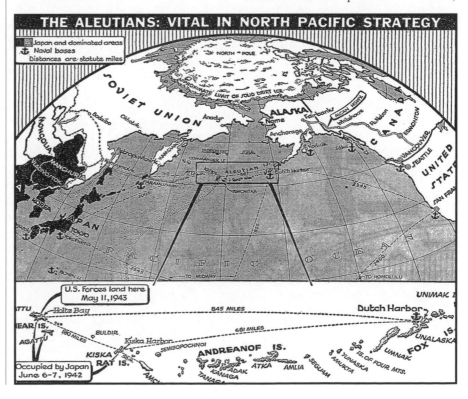

THE ALEUTIANS: VITAL IN NORTH PACIFIC STRATEGY

U.S. Forces land here May 11, 1943

Occupied by Japan June 6-7, 1942

◀ The two big questions in regard to the Aleutians situation were these:
(1) Could we afford to let the Japanese continue to develop their airfield for bombers on Attu? By now, perhaps, these air bases are nearing completion, or possibly have been completed, although there have been no reports that land-based fighters or bombers have been aimed at our Aleutian bases. The location of these fields indicated that the Japanese were hoping to send out planes against us, starting out their bombers from Attu and letting the fighter escort pick them up at some rendezvous near Kiska.

WEATHER A MAJOR FACTOR

Whatever course the Aleutians situation takes, the occupation of Adak and Amchitka, particularly the latter, is of extreme importance to America's strategy in the North Pacific. The great enemy of the air offensive in the North Pacific is the weather, which may be best described as vile. When American forces had to operate at greater distance, it was impossible to do much damage to the Japanese. Establishment of the Amchitka airfields, however, makes it possible for our fliers to throw heavier and more frequent punches.
(2) Could we afford, at this stage of the war, to expend the effort necessary to throw them out?

Apparently, by moving on Attu, our chiefs of staff provided the answers to both questions.

If the Aleutians situation develops favorably, one possible use of the Amchitka and Attu airdromes might be against Paramu shiru, the big Japanese naval and air base below Kamchatka.

That the Japanese feared the offensive possibilities that Amchitka opened against them was indicated by the manner in which they attempted, with the limited air strength they can muster in that area, to interfere with establishment of the American base, once they discovered we had moved in. Their raids, however, were mere gnat stings, easily repelled. ◈

MAY 17, 1943

BRITISH BELLS HAIL VICTORY IN TUNISIA
Celebration at Its Peak When von Arnim, Axis Commander, Arrives as a Prisoner

By JAMES MacDONALD
Wireless to The New York Times.

LONDON, May 16—Throughout Britain and Northern Ireland church bells pealed today in celebration of the big Allied victory in Tunisia, but there was at least one man whose heart was not gladdened by their joyful sound, Col. Gen. Jurgen von Arnim.

The German general, who was captured in Tunisia last week, arrived by airplane to be a prisoner for the rest of the war as the church bells were ringing their thankfulness for the Allied triumph.

From spires and domes of Britain's great cathedrals and from belfries of little parish churches throughout the land the bells sounded. At some railroad stations train travelers heard recordings of church bells being played over loudspeakers.

Radio listeners heard the bells of St. Paul's Cathedral, of Westminster Abbey, of St. Cuthbert's in Edinburgh and of Armagh Cathedral in Northern Ireland. At night there were broadcasts to European listeners of the bells of Tunis Cathedral and of a recording of the bells of Carthage Cathedral.

When the chorus of bells was swelling, General von Arnim alighted from a Royal Air Force plane at an airfield in South England. He was brought to London and later taken to an undisclosed destination.

During his captivity General von Arnim, who harbors a bitter hatred against Britain, will receive the courtesies due his high rank as a colonel general. His accommodations at his place of detention, which will be kept secret, will be more comfortable than those of ordinary war prisoners. ◈

MAY 22, 1943

Yamamoto Death Called Mystery; One Authority Suspects Suicide

Two versions of the death of Admiral Isoroku Yamamoto, said by Tokyo radio to have been killed in action while directing a naval operation from an airplane, were advanced in the United States yesterday.

One of these, put out by the Office of War Information, raised the possibility that he might have been killed in the crash of a passenger airplane. The other was that he might have killed himself over the realization that Japan's far strung seizures in the Pacific were beginning to be rolled back.

The OWI revealed that the Tokyo radio had beamed to Burma in the Burmese language on April 18 the announcement that a large passenger plane, carrying fourteen persons including "very high ranking officials," had crashed into the sea between Singapore and Bangkok on April 7. The OWI said that no other reference to this crash was heard. The delay in the announcement of Admiral Yamamoto's death could be explained by the fact that it might have taken time to verify it or to lead to the conclusion that he was dead.

PROMOTED WHILE DYING

The Tokyo radio indicated Admiral Yamamoto was not killed outright in combat but died later of injuries. Several hours after the original announcement of the death Tokyo broadcast, according to The United Press:

"When His Imperial Majesty the Emperor received word of the grave condition of the late Fleet Admiral Yamamoto on April 20, he elevated him from the post of Commander in Chief of the Combined Fleets to Fleet Admiral. This gracious gesture on the part of His Imperial Majesty failed to rally the condition of Admiral Yamamoto."

The Tokyo radio announced that the state funeral to be given the admiral would be the twelfth ever accorded to a Japanese and the second to be given a navy man. The other state funeral for a naval officer was for Admiral Heihachiro Togo.

The supposition of suicide was advanced by Robert Bellaire, former United Press bureau manager in Tokyo, who

Japanese Admiral Isoroku Yamamoto in 1943.

Americans. These, he was told, were the barbarous people who had come "in their black ships, broken down the doors of Japan, threatened the Son of Heaven and trampled upon the ancient customs of Nippon." Admiral Yamamoto was said to have determined upon a naval career because he "intended to return the visit of Commodore Perry."

The Japanese were responsible for the publication of a letter said to have been written, by the admiral. In this he said:

"I shall not be content merely to capture Guam and the Philippines and to occupy Hawaii and San Francisco. I am looking forward to dictating peace to the United States in the White House at Washington."

Admiral Yamamoto was 59 years old. He came out of the Japanese Naval Academy in 1904 in time to take part in the Russian-Japanese war. He had two fingers shot off while serving on Admiral Togo's flagship in the Battle of Tsushima.

He was a poker player, a heavy drinker and a hard fighter. He apparently was not far from Pearl Harbor on Dec. 7, 1941, and his report of what happened there was couched in this language: "America had a full house, but we had a royal flush." He believed, he told Mr. Bellaire on one occasion, that the American Navy was "a social navy of bridge players and golf players—a peacetime navy." He always argued that the Japanese were so high in morale that they "would take their own lives rather than live in disgrace after defeat." ◆

was interned at the start of the war.

"I suspect," Mr. Bellaire wrote, "it may have been hara-kiri. Yamamoto frequently said that he would rather take his own life than lose any Japanese territory. He repeated that when General Douglas MacArthur came out of the Philippines."

HIS FLIGHT NOT EXPLAINED

While the Tokyo radio limited itself to the simple statement that the Japanese admiral, who was the author of the sudden attack on Pearl Harbor and commanded the Japanese naval operations against the Philippines, has been killed in an airplane on a "far southern front," an effort to analyze such operations during April, when he was stated to have died, led observers in Washington to the conviction that nothing occurred in that theatre during that month to require his presence in such a dangerous role.

He might have been in a minor air raid, for he was regarded as perhaps the boldest, most imaginative and—where the United States was concerned—the most unscrupulous of the Japanese offensive fighters. He hated the United States.

One commentator, writing for The Associated Press, ascribed his hatred to the fact that in his youth Admiral Yamamoto was taught by his father to hate

Chapter 15

"EISENHOWER RUBS HIS SEVEN-LUCK PIECES"

June–July 1943

News in the summer months was dominated by the invasion of Sicily, which began on July 9 following the bombing and capture of the smaller island of Pantelleria on June 11. It was, Roosevelt announced, the "beginning of the end" for the Axis nations. This was just as well, since on the home front there were signs of growing impatience with the war effort. In June the Smith-Connally anti-strike bill was introduced into Congress to try to outlaw wartime union activity. Although Roosevelt thought the measure too extreme and vetoed it, Congress on June 26 overrode his veto and the bill became law. The domestic squabbles were soon overshadowed by the massive military undertaking in the Mediterranean.

After a news embargo, The Times finally reported on July 11 the start of the invasion. Eisenhower, noted the report, "Rubs His Seven Luck Pieces," seven old coins (including a gold five guinea piece) that he kept in his pocket as a talisman. Times correspondent Hanson Baldwin later described the Sicily campaign as a strategic compromise, "conceived in dissension, born of uneasy alliance . . . unclear in purpose." It was, nevertheless, an immediate success as Allied soldiers swarmed onto the south and east coasts of the island. Ernie Pyle, the veteran war correspondent, went ashore with the Army on a section of coast with no enemy opposition and found that the American soldiers were "thoroughly annoyed" that there was no fighting after days with their adrenalin pumping. Italian soldiers gave up quickly. Pyle thought they looked like people "who had just been liberated rather than conquered." By mid-July General George Patton's U.S. forces were pushing toward Palermo while Montgomery's Eighth Army was approaching Catania, hoping to cut off the remaining German and Italian troops. Progress in the mountainous zones was slow; though Italians surrendered by the thousands, the German Army fought with its trademark skill and tenacity.

The Sicilian campaign temporarily overshadowed the Pacific and Soviet campaigns, but there was evidence in both theaters that the "beginning of the end" was no exaggeration. General MacArthur launched the start of his South Pacific campaign against the Japanese in New Guinea on June 29, hand in hand with further advances in the Solomons after the victory on Guadalcanal. On the Eastern Front Hitler's armies launched Operation Citadel on July 5 against a large Red Army salient around the Russian city of Kursk. After making slow progress on both sides of the salient, Hitler terminated the operation when news arrived of the invasion of Sicily. The Red Army had held back large reserves that were suddenly released against the retreating Germans. The result was a devastating defeat, as German armies were ejected from Orel, Bryansk and Kharkov by late August. This was the first major defeat inflicted on German forces in good summer campaigning weather and it marked a decisive turning point in the Eastern war.

Meanwhile, the bombing of German and Italian targets continued relentlessly. Operation Gomorrah against Hamburg left 37,000 dead after a week of bombing, which included a deadly firestorm on July 27–28 that incinerated 18,000 people. In Italy the decision was finally taken to bomb Rome, the Eternal City, which had been left unscathed because of the political risks of damaging its cultural heritage or accidentally striking Vatican City. On July 19 a Times correspondent, Herbert Matthews, flew in one of the bombers to record the operation against the San Lorenzo and Littorio marshaling yards and the Ciampino air base. The headline the following day ran "Times Man from Air Sees Shrines Spared," though Rome's Basilica of San Lorenzo was, in fact, badly damaged. Six days later Mussolini was overthrown by a revolt of the army and some Fascist Party leaders. The Times, like many other papers, assumed that the bombing must have accelerated the decision to stage a coup, but it did not yet mean that Italy would surrender.

JUNE 2, 1943

MANY WOMEN SHOW WAR WORK STRAIN

Signs of Fatigue, Loneliness and Sense Of Instability Noted in USO Survey

HOUSING HELD BIG FACTOR

Also Sanitation, Recreation—Trailers Present A Variety of Special Problems

Women in war jobs in various areas are beginning to show signs of fatigue and emotional strain, according to Miss Florence Williams, director of health and recreation for the United Service Organizations division of the National Young Women's Christian Association, who returned yesterday from a six-month field trip through centers in the East, South and Midwest. She is now drafting a program to aid women white collar and factory workers.

That old adage about "all work and no play" is in evidence among women workers in factories and offices, Miss Williams said. She has noted distinct signs of loneliness and a sense of instability.

"Last year," she continued, "most women regarded taking war jobs as a game. Today it has become a serious business. Women are showing visible signs of fatigue. In many communities, they just work and go to bed; work and go to bed. They aren't living right or eating right. And many are working under the misapprehension that it is unpatriotic to have a good time."

THE PRINCIPAL PROBLEMS

Chief problems noted by Miss Williams were inadequate housing facilities, with girls having to do their laundry in a tiny cubicle that is also the only place where they can receive men visitors: lack of washrooms and adequate cafeterias in both dormitories and plants; locations that offer no form of amusement or relaxation; high cost of food; long hours and too frequent changes of women workers from "graveyard" shifts to swing shifts.

Another problem arises from trailers that wind their way across the country. As many as 350 were found in one Kansas war plant community, with only seventy of these units filled.

Miss Williams, in consulting some of these families, found a distinct contrast between their point of view and that of the community. The trailerites consider themselves modern pioneers, carrying on the tradition of the covered wagon. Towns where they set down their caravans, however, frequently frown upon them. Consequently the women in the trailer colonies are lonely and unhappy, with difficulty in obtaining food added to their social problems.

The USO, Miss Williams said, is helping these colonists set up their own community law and planning committees. For those whose knowledge of child care and sanitation is deficient, the USO conducts child-care classes and teaches mothers, some as young as 16, how to enforce sanitary laws.

CONTRIBUTIONS TO 'MELTING POT'

Miss Williams stressed, however, that persons of widely differing cultures are living in trailers parked right beside each other, and that with each group contributing its native games and customs, the trailer colony is adding to the melting pot qualities of American democracy.

Housing conditions in certain areas of Texas are so poor that women war workers have to wade through mud to get to and from their dormitories. In one part of Ohio, the only recreational center is a USO clubhouse, consisting of two rooms over stores twelve miles from the industrial dormitories. ◇

Working the file room of the FBI, 1943.

JUNE 6, 1943

JAPANESE EXCEL IN U.S. COMBAT UNIT
American-Born and Nizei from Hawaii Are Setting Mark at Camp Shelby, Miss.

GROUPS ARE SHOCK TROOPS
Officers Praise Highly Their Zeal for Military Training, Sports and Sociability

Special to The New York Times.

CAMP SHELBY, Miss., June 5—Spiritedly conforming to its regimental motto, the Japanese-American Combat Team is rapidly taking shape here on the red clay drill fields of southern Mississippi. Japanese by ancestry but Americans by speech, customs and ideals, the several thousand Nisei from Hawaii and War Relocation Centers on the mainland are training for the day when they can fight shoulder-to-shoulder with other Americans against a common enemy.

"Go for Broke" is the motto they have inscribed on their self-designed and officially approved coat of arms. It is soldier slang born of dice games, and it means "shoot the works," or risk all on the big venture before them. It was no idly chosen phrase. The Japanese-Americans realize they have perhaps more at stake in this war than the average soldier. They have known from the beginning they would be under close public scrutiny, each soldier—in the words of their commanding officer—"a symbol of the loyalty of the Japanese-American population" in our country.

WELL SUITED TO COMBAT TEAMS
By temperament, character and zeal they are admirably suited for a combat team. A combat team is a small, streamlined army able to fight its own battles without aid from other forces. The Infantry calls them combat teams, the Armored Forces call them combat commands and the Navy calls them task forces. They do essentially the same thing—specific jobs, operating often independently of other units.

The Nisei are proud to be chosen for a combat team. Young, mostly unmarried and with all the makings of combat team troops, they are keen for action and anxious to make good. Among themselves they boast they have "a year and three minutes to live—a year of training and three minutes of action." Already they have the psychology of shock troops.

Officers training the Japanese-Americans without exception praise the attitude and early soldierly bearing of the Nisei. For the most part these officers are having their first contact with soldiers of Japanese ancestry. Said one lieutenant: "Once in a while you may have to tell them something twice, but not often. They are so eager to learn they are constantly attentive and usually get it the first time." Another company officer commented: "I've been in the Army twenty-six months and I've never seen a group of soldiers with less griping than this organization. And as for profanity, it simply doesn't exist."

About thirty company officers are Nisei, the rest Caucasian.

AVID FOR MANUAL OF STUDY
Even off the drill field, the Nisei constantly seek to better themselves by study of manuals and technical books. One bookstore in nearby Hattiesburg is reported to have done about $2,000 worth of business during the first month after the arrival of the Japanese-Americans, selling them textbooks and other works on military subjects, some at prices ranging up to $5 apiece. Recently during a weekend visit of 100 Japanese-American girls from a Relocation Center in Arkansas a sizable group of Nisei were observed in a nearby field practicing grenade throwing, entirely aloof to the presence of femininity.

The Nisei are proud, too, that the Combat Team is 100 per cent an organization of volunteers. In fact, thousands more volunteered than the prescribed quota. Many applicants who were turned down actually wept in disappointment. Many quit high-paying jobs in Hawaii to enlist, and some left wives and children in the islands.

Typical, too, is the reasoning of Private Tadashi Morimoto of Honolulu, a social worker, a graduate of the New York School of Social Work. Private Morimoto in 1940 served six months in the Psychiatric Clinic of the Manhattan Children's Court in New York. "In Hawaii," he said, "I met a soldier from New York. He was homesick for his wife and children. He said he hoped for nothing more than an early victory so he could return to civilian life, enjoy his family and his old job. Suddenly it occurred to me that this soldier not only wanted the very things I did, but he was willing to fight for them. Why then should I sit back and let someone else fight for the rights and privileges I myself cherish? I didn't want anyone else to do my fighting for me. My wife concurred, so I enlisted for the Combat Team."

From a mainland volunteer came this succinct statement: "We are anxious to show what real lovers of American democracy will do to preserve it. Our actions will speak for us more than words."

On the post the Japanese Americans already have made a name for themselves in athletics, with their musical talent and in war bond buying. The Combat Team, in two days and with no more than a suggestion from company commanders, bought $101,550 worth of war bonds, putting their cash on the barrelhead.

The Combat Team has two baseball teams, both near the top of one of Shelby's leagues.

Sentiment, too, runs high among the troops from Hawaii. On Mother's Day they sent 247 telegrams to the islands at an average cost of $2 a message. A thousand more sent air-mail letters, and many others inquired about personal telephone calls.

Commanding the Combat Team is Colonel Charles W. Pence, who was born in Illinois and served overseas in the First World War in the Fourth Division. Colonel Pence also served for four years with the famous Fifteenth (Can Do) Infantry Regiment in China. Before coming here last February he commanded a regiment at Fort McClellan, Alabama.

Second in command is Lieutenant Colonel Merritt B. Booth, also born in Illinois but who entered West Point from New York and came to the Combat Team from foreign service. ◆

JUNE 12, 1943

ALLIES PLANT FLAG ON FIRST MEDITERRANEAN STEPPING-STONE

ISLAND IS OCCUPIED
The Italian 'Gibraltar' is Knocked Out By Record Avalanche of Bombs

ALL GUNS SILENCED
Troops Take Over in 22 Minutes as New Design in Warfare Emerges

By DREW MIDDLETON
By Wireless to The New York Times.

ALLIED HEADQUARTERS IN NORTH AFRICA, June 11—Blasted into ruins by hundreds of tons of bombs, the Italian island of Pantelleria, the last Axis stronghold in the Sicilian Strait, surrendered to overwhelming Allied air power this morning rather than endure another day of death and destruction under the most concentrated aerial attack in the history of warfare.

Allied assault craft darted ashore at noon soon after air crews had sighted a white cross of surrender on the airfield and cruisers and destroyers that supported the landing had spied a white flag flying from Semafore Hill, 2,000 yards from the Harbor of Pantelleria. There was slight resistance from Axis troops, dazed by thirteen days of continuous bombing, and all primary objectives were reached by 12:22 P.M. [London estimates placed the garrison at 8,000 Italians, The Associated Press said.]

It was evident that the island was so disorganized by the bombing and frequent shelling by British cruisers and destroyers that news of the surrender had failed to reach all the enemy troops on the island although the commander had surrendered by displaying the white flag and white cross.

GERMAN DIVE-BOMBERS ROUTED
British troops scrambled up the rocky beaches past wrecked gun batteries—the last enemy gun was silenced by dusk yesterday—and the people of the island crept from shelters to watch with eyes dulled by fear.

[Within an hour after the surrender of Pantelleria, fifty to sixty German dive-bombers attempted to break up the landing forces, but Americans in Lightning fighters routed the Germans, forcing them to jettison their bombs haphazardly in flight, The Associated Press reported. An Algiers broadcast said that naval and infantry casualties in the occupation were negligible.]

The major share of credit for opening the first breach in Italy's chain of island strongholds goes to air power, such air power as never before had been concentrated on a target of similar size.

The climax came yesterday when more bombs were dropped on the island than were dropped in the entire month of April on all targets in Tunisia, Sicily, Sardinia and Italy.

As great a weight of bombs was unloaded on the island in the intensified aerial offensive from May 29 to June 10 as was dropped on all targets in the African theatre in the month of May. And this round-the-clock assault was preceded by six days of heavy intermittent attacks.

YIELDED AFTER THIRD DEMAND
The capitulation in the form of the white cross on the airfield came as formations of Flying Fortresses, Mitchells and Marauders were over the island. Two previous requests to surrender were ignored by the commander of the Axis garrison. Once emblems of surrender were sighted by the Allied air and naval forces [at 11:40 A.M., according to The Associated Press], the Allied military commander started occupation of the island.

[The surrender also was made known by Admiral Paresseni, senior Italian officer on the island, in a message to an American air base, saying, "Beg surrender through lack of water," The Associated Press said.]

Lieut. Gen. Dwight D. Eisenhower, Commander in Chief of the Allied forces in North Africa, and Admiral Sir Andrew Browne Cunningham, Naval Commander in Chief for the Mediterranean, were on the bridge of the famous British cruiser Aurora when she led a fleet of four other cruisers and eight destroyers in the bombardment of Pantelleria on Tuesday. The Aurora steamed close inshore to test the fire of the Italian shore batteries.

SHELLS HIT NEAR CRUISER
The Allied Commander in Chief and Admiral Cunningham watched the dramatic naval and air assault, which came to a climax at noon when motor torpedo boats dashed into the harbor of Pantelleria on a test run. While the squadron was waiting for the small craft to reappear, shells from the big Italian shore batteries fell within 300 yards of the Aurora.

When the naval bombardment and aerial pounding were over for the day, General Eisenhower said there was "no doubt" that the island would fall "once the infantry gets in their part."

The surrender was the first in the war by a fortress of the size of Pantelleria to air power supported by sea power, without serious action by ground forces.

American bombers and fighter bombers, which bore the main weight of the Allied attacks on Pantelleria, also contributed heavily to the campaign of attrition against the Axis fighters in this theatre. Thirty-seven enemy fighters were shot down by American airmen over Pantelleria yesterday. In the last thirteen days of the offensive seventy-eight enemy planes were destroyed in combat against an Allied loss of twelve.

The shattering attack delivered yesterday eclipsed anything done before in this theatre. The greatest number of Flying Fortresses ever employed in this area led the attack on the island, dropping hundreds of thousand-pound bombs. It is estimated that well over a thousand sorties were flown by the Allied airmen. The assaults, which started with dawn and ended at the approach of dusk and a thunderstorm, dropped a load of bombs that no other target of similar size ever sustained in one day. The night before heavily loaded Wellington medium bombers and Hurricane fighter-bombers of the Royal Air Force had hammered the island as a prelude to the great assault to come.

During the day traffic over the island, which was marked by a heavy

British troops in Sicily, 1943.

cloud of smoke that lay above it, was so heavy that the bomber formations had to circle the island waiting their turn to make "a pass" at the target.

The aerial offensive against Pantelleria was "a test-tube attack" that went beyond the original objective of battering the island defenses to a point where Allied troops could land to force complete surrender of the island. Although sea power gave valuable support and the ground forces were ready when the time came, it was air power that conquered the vital, strongly defended fortress.

GREAT POWER THROWN AT TARGET

In the culmination of the air attack yesterday Flying Fortresses, Marauders, Mitchells, Bostons, Baltimores, Lightning and War-hawk fighter-bombers and Spitfire fighters from the Allied air forces took part in day-long attacks.

The progress of the offensive was worked out on a mathematical pattern, with the weight of bombs and number of aircraft gradually increased each day from May 29 until the knockout punch was delivered yesterday and this morning following the refusal of the island's commander to surrender. Another request for unconditional surrender had been dropped on the island yesterday after the two previous ones had been ignored.

Hundreds of hits were made on military installations, batteries, range finders, barracks and gun positions all during yesterday's bombing. Several large explosions, probably the result of bombs hitting ammunition dumps, were reported.

When the Boston, Baltimore and Mitchell bombers of the United States Army Air Force and Royal Air Force began their attacks yesterday morning they found antiaircraft fire was negligible and encountered no enemy fighters. Between sorties by light and medium bombers, fighter-bombers attacked targets at fifteen-minute intervals, sweeping in at low level to top off the destruction started by high-level attacks.

Pilots and crews returned from Pantelleria impressed by the destruction down below. First Lieutenant Melvin Pool of Durant, Okla., called it "a damned good show" and said he believed the Fortresses "had the bases loaded and knocked a home run." Wellingtons attacking the night before had started several fires, some of them very large, in the Pantelleria harbor area.

Studded with heavy gun batteries well concealed in and behind cliffs along the coast, Pantelleria was believed impregnable by the Italians. Benito Mussolini wrapped the island in a cloak of secrecy after 1937, when he announced that naval and air bases were being built there. Landings were forbidden on the island except for Italian military, naval and air personnel, and a decree forbade flight over it or adjoining territorial waters.

Bit by bit this island fortress, two-thirds the size of Malta, was knocked apart. Bombers, began by wrecking the airfield in the early days of the offensive, destroying numerous planes on the ground.

Then every ship in the harbor either was sunk or damaged so severely that she was useless.

Gun batteries were next. One by one the emplacements were bombed by Flying Fortresses and medium bombers, while fighter-bombers attacked from lower levels. Meanwhile, a complete sea blockade was achieved and the enemy fighter fleet based on Sicily was unable to check the steady progress of the offensive.

The enemy made his greatest defensive effort yesterday in the day of aerial operations that undoubtedly will become a classical example of the exertion of air power.

ENEMY ATTACKS FROM SICILY

Drawing from fighter squadrons based on-Sicily, the enemy attacked Allied bombers heavily from mid-morning to dusk. Marauders of the Strategic Air Force and an escort of Warhawks were intercepted over Pantelleria by Axis fighters. The Warhawks got five enemy planes and the bombers destroyed one in a running fight that lasted from the target to near the African coast at Cap Bon.

Captain Ralph Taylor of Durham, N.C., shot down two Messerschmitt 109's in this engagement.

American Spitfire pilots of the Tactical Air Force destroyed twelve Italian and German aircraft. One squadron knocked five enemy planes out of the skies in the morning while another squadron of the same group shot down seven more in the late afternoon. The group as a whole destroyed seventeen aircraft June 9 and 10, and lost only one plane.

Thirteen Macchi 202's dived on Allied bombers that the Spitfires were escorting to open the afternoon battle. The Spitfires gave chase and intercepted the Italians before they reached the bombers. The dogfight was joined by six Messerschmitt 109's and three Focke-Wulf 190's.

The Italians were being knocked down so fast that the Spitfire squadron commander, Major Frank Hill of Hillsdale, N.J., said he counted four enemy parachutes in the air at one time.

"And down below us," he added, "I could see I don't know how many splashes in the Mediterranean where their aircraft were crashing," Major ❯

◄   Hill destroyed a Macchi 202, his sixth victory of the war.

Lightning fighter-bombers led by Lieut. Col. John Stevenson, West Point graduate from Laramie, Wyo., fought a brief action with several Messerschmitts, destroying one. So many pilots pumped lead into an enemy plane that it "went down as a squadron victory, and that makes everybody happy," according to Colonel Stevenson.

Altogether twenty-six of thirty-seven enemy aircraft destroyed over Pantelleria were knocked down by the Tactical Air Force. Marauders of the Coastal Air Force operating near the coast of Italy yesterday shot down two Messerschmitt 109's, increasing the day's victory total to thirty-nine. Six Allied planes were lost.

The highest scorer in the American Spitfire unit is Lieutenant Sylvan Feld of Lynn, Mass., who on June 6 shot down a German plane to bring his total of victories to nine, all scored since March 22. ◊

JUNE 20, 1943

CRITICAL PERIOD AT HAND IN HOME-FRONT CONFLICT
War Crises in Mining, Wages, Food and Inflation Reflect Uncertainties Of the National Effort

BYRNES, BARUCH TO THE FORE

By ARTHUR KROCK

WASHINGTON, June 19—The most critical period on the home front since the United States entered the war is at hand. Whatever may be the immediate solutions of such emergent matters as the wages of the United Mine Workers, some weeks must elapse before it will be possible to determine with certainty whether the Administration will be able to support the military forces with supplies produced at an expanding rate and at anywhere near the present levels of cost.

On the outcome of the group conflicts now raging depend also the morale of the home front and, to some extent, that of the armed services. Conditions in the various areas of dispute which constitute a battlefield on which the struggle will, in the next few weeks, be won, lost or compromised—harmfully or destructively—are about as follows:

Food—Unfavorable weather, a price system in several respects ill-conceived, depletion of farm manpower, restriction of farm machinery and of the reproductive elements in agriculture have combined with a loose and confused administration of food controls by Washington to bring about a menacing situation. Among examples of what is happening in this sector is a report by Senator Scott Lucas of Illinois that farmers are holding 900,000,000 bushels of corn in their bins awaiting a price adjustment; a depressing crop report by the Department of Agriculture, and an assertion by Chester C. Davis, Food Administrator, that serious food shortages are certain. It has been predicted that between the time of the next spring planting and the 1944 harvest some of these shortages will be acute.

REFORMS MAY BE FORCED

Many remedies have been proposed, and some will be attempted during the critical period on which the nation is now entering. There are definite signs that the War Department has revised downward the size of the Army planned for the end of 1943, which should relieve the drain on the manpower that produces and processes food. The President has rejected proposals that all Federal food controls be merged under the Secretary of Agriculture, replacing the incumbent, Claude Wickard, with Mr. Davis; and he has also declined to break up the Office of Price Administration or cause a revolutionary change in its pricing policies.

Plans are proceeding to institute a broad system of Federal subsidies to maintain consumer prices of certain foods and push down the prices of others to the level of several months ago. No one authority agrees with another as to the ultimate cost of such a program, the guesses ranging from Price Administrator Prentiss Brown's of less than a billion to the President's of a three billions maximum. Food-producing groups, their spokesmen in Congress and outside citizens who fear that politics will mix with economies in the use of subsidies are resisting the project But the general belief is that the present limited subsidy program will be expanded by the Administration in an effort to win the adherence of organized labor to the President's hold-the-line program.

Wages—Despite the common national peril and military effort, the attitude of organized labor toward legal restraints invited by its own excesses and toward the employing group remains hostile. Only this week A. F. Whitney, president of the Brotherhood of Railway Trainmen, denounced the railroad managers as swollen with war profits and conspiring to create the greatest monopoly in American history after the war has ended. He said that in opposing wage increases and rate decreases at the same time, the managers are about "as reasonable as an alley-cat with a hunk of raw meat."

A store clerk next to a sign supporting government-controlled prices during the war.

ATMOSPHERE OF HOSTILITY

This same atmosphere of hostility between employees and employers surrounds other industrial areas in a time when good-will would amount to a military asset. Mr. Whitney is known as a "maverick," not representative of the general attitude of railway labor.

Yet his outburst, coming from a source where labor relations have been more harmonious than in any other, emphasizes the spread of ill-feeling. The President has done much to foster economic and social class resentment, and in this respect his own chickens are coming home to roost. But it is the whole country and the war program that must pay the price.

The philippics of John L. Lewis toward the employers of coal miners have been almost a part of the daily news record for the last few weeks. In purple phrases he has drawn a picture of hungry workers and undernourished children, victims of rich and heartless coal operators who would be complimented by the names of war profiteer, cormorant or vulture. This language is only part of Mr. Lewis' tactics when he is fighting for a wages rise. But the effect on the workers is to stimulate a feeling of bitterness toward those who pay their wages, and this contributes to the critical situation in which the nation finds itself. How much it is ameliorated by the reiteration Friday of the "no strike" pledge by Van Bittner, Daniel Tobin and other labor leaders remains to be seen.

WEIGHING THE REMEDIES

As this is written, and probably when it shall have been published, the ultimate solutions of the conflicts over mine wages and the anti-strike bill are not in sight, though stop-gap methods may be discovered in the interim. But not for some time will it be possible to measure the effects or durability of the remedies. And only when that measurement can be made with some accuracy will it be discerned whether the American people have passed from a most critical period into a worse one, or into improved conditions that will make it possible to hasten victory and keep down the cost in life and treasure.

Mr. Lewis defied the jurisdiction of the War Labor Board, and, braced by the President through the Office of War Mobilization, by Congress with the anti-strike bill and by many evidences of popular support, the board stood firm against Mr. Lewis. If he is routed by the various processes, his power as a labor leader will be destroyed for some time, perhaps forever. But his tactics have

brought him to the point where his rout must be total or he will continue to make difficulties in labor ranks and prolong the critical period. He has won every other battle in which he has engaged since the President took office, at first within and then without the political structure of the Administration. This fact will impel sound observers to make more than an instant test of the effects on Mr. Lewis' influence of events in the next few days.

THE BATTLE OF INFLATION

Inflation—This dubious battle will be decided in the areas of conflict over food, prices and wage controls as out-

lined above. As they go, it will go.

Next to the President, the burden of resolving the critical period into one of progress falls upon James F. Byrnes, chairman of OWM. But signs are innumerable that the country is looking behind him to his eminent official adviser, B. M. Baruch. If the line holds and goes forward, the pair will be given credit for much of the victory, and vice versa. But if the line is broken, by Presidential concessions and related causes, Mr. Baruch will be expected either to accept a share of the blame or divest himself of it by retiring from his first official post since 1920. ◆

JUNE 21, 1943

Escort Carrier Helps Convoys Win Five-Day Battle with U-Boat Packs

New Type of Protective Vessel Instrumental In Destruction of Enemy Raiders—Land-Based Planes Also Play Big Part

By JAMES MacDONALD
By Cable to The New York Times.

LONDON, June 20—Illustrating why the month of May was one of the best for Atlantic convoys to Britain since the closing days of 1941, officials gave out today an exciting account of a bitter five-day fight against enemy U-boats in which warships and planes from a carrier and shore stations sank two submarines, probably destroyed three more and are believed to have damaged many others.

Ranging over hundreds of miles of ocean, including the particularly dangerous area in mid-Atlantic beyond the reach of land-based planes, the struggle marked one of the fiercest and most sustained attempts ever undertaken by U-boat packs to prevent ships and supplies from reaching this country. The ships were so well protected that the majority of the U-boats were kept well out of the range of their intended victims. Some did get within range, however, but they scored on only 3 per cent of the vast merchant fleet involved.

A new technique in anti-submarine warfare was responsible for the fact that the losses were small, considering the intensity of the attack. An important role was played by one of the British Navy's newest weapons—the pocket aircraft car-

rier, known officially as the escort carrier.

This vessel was H.M.S. Biter, a former merchant ship built in the United States and transformed into a floating air base for the special purpose of closing the "air gap" in mid-Atlantic where U-boats were formerly immune to blows from the air. The Biter was commanded by Captain Abel Smith, a kinsman of Queen Elizabeth and former equerry to King George. He was a member of the royal party on its tour of Canada and the United States in 1939.

The fight began, according to a joint communiqué issued by the Admiralty and the Air Ministry, when two U-boats in a big pack were sighted far out in the Atlantic by navy planes that had taken off from the Biter. The planes attacked the submarines with depth charges and machine-gun fire, forcing them to dive.

Later, after the convoy had proceeded so far that it was within reach of land-based planes, its protection was increased by Royal Air Force Coastal Command forces. First blood was drawn by an RAF Liberator, which disabled one U-boat while it was fifteen miles from the surface ships.

Meanwhile, Navy planes were ▶

◀ busy with another U-boat. They sent word to H.M.S. Broadway—formerly the U.S.S. Hunt, one of the fifty destroyers transferred to Britain in 1940—and the frigate Lagan, one of Britain's latest-type special-duty warships, and guided them to the scene. The destroyer and the frigate took turns attacking the submarine. The Broadway struck twice, and, after its second attack, there were muffled undersea explosions that shot wreckage bearing German markings to the surface. The communiqué said that the U-boat was considered sunk.

As the hours wore on, more Coastal Command planes, including Flying Fortresses, Catalinas and Sunderlands, arrived to protect convoys. Further fights with submarines followed in quick succession. In one of these actions, the destroyer Pathfinder hurled depth charges at a U-boat that surfaced for a brief moment and then disappeared beneath the waves. Its fate was not determined. Later, a Sunderland plane guided the Lagan and the Canadian corvette Drumheller, which has been on active service in the Battle of the Atlantic for three years, to a U-boat that received similar treatment. The spot where that submarine had been seen going down was covered by wreckage and a steadily widening oil slick that covered an area of almost four square miles the next day.

While these scraps were going on, another convoy found itself threatened by a U-boat pack ahead of it. The destroyer Hesperus sighted one enemy submarine on the surface, steering straight for the convoy. The Hesperus commenced an attack with gunfire, scoring repeated hits and blowing the U-boat's gun-crew into the sea.

Closing in for the kill, the Hesperus let go depth charges. The U-boat either dived or sank out of control. The destroyer threshed across the spot where the enemy had last been seen, dropping a final "pattern" for good measure. The submarine's fate was uncertain.

Soon afterward the Hesperus spotted another U-boat on the surface. She attacked the enemy with gunfire, then rammed him and probably destroyed him. While the submarine was being gunned, several members of its crew were seen jumping overboard. Whether they were rescued was not reported. The next day the Hesperus attacked still another U-boat, which disappeared amid an oil slick and floating wreckage. Meanwhile, aircraft maintained unceasing patrol over and in the vicinity of the convoys, compelling the undersea raiders to remain submerged well out of harm's way and to lose track of the prospective victims. ◆

JUNE 26, 1943

CONGRESS REBELS

President Is Defeated by 56 to 25 In Senate, 244–108 in House

SWIFT VOTE TAKEN

Criminal Penalties Are Made Law, But 30-Day Strike Vote Is Set

By W. H. LAWRENCE
Special to The New York Times.

WASHINGTON, June 25—A rebellious Congress, angered by three coal strikes and other sporadic interruptions of war production, quickly overrode President Roosevelt's veto today and enacted into law the Smith-Connally anti-strike bill requiring thirty days' notice in advance of strike votes and providing criminal penalties for those who instigate, direct or aid strikes in government-operated plants or mines.

The Senate voted 56 to 25 to make the bill law despite the Chief Executive's disapproval. The House voted 244 to 108 immediately afterward. Both votes were well over the constitutional requirement of a two-thirds majority to override a veto.

Both Houses acted not only quickly, but with a minimum of discussion to reject the President's warning that the measure would stimulate labor unrest, give governmental sanction to strike agitation, and foment slowdowns and strikes.

HOW THE PARTIES DIVIDED

In the Senate, twenty-nine Democrats, including the acting Majority Leader, Senator Lister Hill of Alabama, and twenty-seven Republicans voted to override the President's veto, and nineteen Democrats, five Republicans and one Progressive voted to sustain it.

Of the Senators who voted after the veto message had been read and who had been recorded on the conference committee report, not one changed his vote

as a result of Presidential disapproval of the measure. Senator Joseph Ball, Republican, of Minnesota, who had been paired for the bill but did not vote at the time the conference committee report was taken up, voted to sustain the veto.

In the House 130 Republicans and 114 Democrats voted against the President. Of those who voted to sustain the veto, sixty-seven were Democrats, thirty-seven were Republicans, two Progressives, one Farmer-Laborite and one member of the American Labor party. Advocates of the bill gained twenty-five votes between approval of the conference committee report and the veto action, while opponents of the measure lost twenty-one supporters.

LAW GOES INTO EFFECT AT ONCE

The measure, which had been bitterly opposed by all organized labor, is effective immediately and until six months after the conclusion of the war, and contains these provisions:

The President receives authority to take immediate possession of plants, mines or other production facilities affected by a strike or other labor disturbance.

Wages and other working conditions in effect at the time a plant is taken over by the Government shall be maintained by the Government unless changed by the National War Labor Board at the request of the Government agency or a majority of the employees in the plant.

Persons who coerce, instigate, induce, conspire with or encourage any person to interfere by lockout, strike, slowdown or other interruption with the operation of plants in possession of the Government, or who direct such interruptions or provide funds for continuing them shall be subject to a fine of not more than $5,000, or to imprisonment for not more than one year, or both. The penalty clause does not apply to those who merely cease work or refuse employment.

SUBPOENA POWER FOR NWLB

The NWLB receives subpoena power to require attendance of parties to labor disputes, but NWLB members are forbidden to participate in any decision in which the member has a direct interest as an officer, employee or representative of either party to the dispute.

Employees of war contractors must give to the Secretary of Labor, the NWLB and the National Labor Relations Board notice of any labor dispute which threatens seriously to interrupt war production and the NLRB is required on the thirtieth day after notice is given to take a secret ballot of the employees on the question of whether they will strike.

Labor organizations, as well as national banks and corporations organized by authority of Federal law, are forbidden to make political contributions in any election involving officials of the National Government, with the organization subject to a fine of not more than $5,000 for violating the act and the officers subject to a fine of not more than $1,000 or imprisonment for not more than one year, or both.

The President waited the full ten days of the constitutional period before vetoing the measure which was sent to him by a 219-to-129 House vote and 55-to-22 Senate vote. At 3:13 P.M. his veto message was read to the Senate, and by 5:28 P.M. the measure was law.

SENATE IS FIRST TO ACT

The Senate acted first, with Senator Connally of Texas taking the floor to say:

"I am sorely disappointed. The Senate is sorely disappointed. The House, I am sure, is disappointed. The people of the United States by an overwhelming majority are disappointed. The soldiers and sailors wherever they may be, on land, on the sea, in the air, all over this globe are disappointed.

"The section of the bill to which the President objected was in the House provisions.

"The President has a right to veto legislation. The Senate has a right to pass a bill over the veto.

"I hope that the Senate now will exercise its constitutional privilege."

Senator Carl Hatch, Democrat of New Mexico, seconded the motion, and the roll-call began.

When the vote was announced as 56 to 25 to override, there was applause from the galleries, led by men in uniform.

The large House majority in favor of overriding was apparent as soon as word of the Senate action reached it. A Commodity Credit Corporation extension and modification bill was up for consideration and members immediately began to move that this either be laid aside or that debate close and immediate action be taken on it, thus to clear the way for consideration of the veto.

APPEAL FOR ACTION CHEERED

Representative Clifton Woodrum, Democrat, of Virginia, received repeated applause and cheers for his plea for "action, not tomorrow, not Monday, but today, so that we can send the message to our boys in the foxholes that the American people are behind them."

Chairman Andrew J. May of the House Military Affairs Committee, which brought out the original draft of changes in the Senate bill to which the President objected so vigorously, repeated the same thought, bringing objections that he was out of order and "trying to create a lynching spirit in the House." The latter assertion came from Representative Vito Marcantonio, American Labor, of New York.

Apparently sensing the House insistence on action today, Representative John W. McCormack of Massachusetts, the majority leader, quickly promised that the veto message would be taken up as soon as the pending bill was disposed of. Delaying tactics by other Administration supporters in seeking record votes on amendments to the CCC bill failed to find sufficient House support to be effective and a motion made at 4:50 that the House adjourn was overwhelmingly shouted down. The veto message was then read, and the vote taken immediately.

SAYS STRIKES WON'T BE TOLERATED

The President's veto message firmly declared that the Executive would not countenance strikes in wartime and was conciliatory in its approach to Congress.

Declaring it was the will of the people that for the duration of the war all labor disputes shall be settled by orderly, legally established procedures, and that no war work shall be interrupted by strike or lockout, the President said that the no-strike, no-lockout pledge given by labor and industry after Pearl Harbor "has been well kept except in the case of the leaders of the United Mine Workers." During 1942, he said, the time lost by strikes averaged only 5/100ths of 1 per cent of the total man-hours worked, a record which he declared had never before been equalled in this country and which was as good or better than the record of any of our allies in the war.

He conceded that laws often are necessary "to make a very small minority of people live up to the standards that the great majority of the people follow" and in this connection he cited the recent coal strike.

FAVORS FIRST SEVEN SECTIONS

Analyzing the bill, section by section, he said that the first seven sections, "broadly speaking," incorporate into statute the existing machinery for settling labor disputes and provide criminal penalties for those who instigate, direct or aid a strike in a government-operated plant or mine. Had the bill been limited to this subject matter, he said that he would have signed it.

His principal objection was to the eighth section, which, he said, would foment slowdowns and strikes. That section provides a thirty-day notice before a vote to strike can be taken under supervision of the National Labor Relations Board, and, while Congressional sponsors called this a "cooling off" period, Mr. Roosevelt contended that it "might well become a boiling period" during which workers would devote their thoughts and energies to getting pro-strike votes instead of turning out war material. "In wartime we cannot sanction strikes with or without notice," he declared. "Section 8 ignores completely labor's 'no-strike' pledge and provides, in effect, for strike notices and strike ballots. Far from discouraging strikes, these provisions would stimulate labor unrest and give government sanction to strike agitations."

DRAFT CHANGE RECOMMENDED

The President was highly critical also of Section 9, which prohibits, during the war, political contributions by labor organizations. This section, he remarked, "obviously has no relevancy" to an anti-strike bill. If the prohibition on trade union political contributions has merit, he expressed the belief that it should not be confined to the war. Congress, he added, might also give careful consideration to extending the ban to other non-profit organizations.

The President reiterated his recommendation that the Selective Service Act be amended to provide noncombat military service for persons up to the age of 65, declaring that "this will enable us to induct into military service all persons who engage in strikes or stoppages or other interruptions of work in plants in the possession of the United States."

"This direct approach is necessary to insure the continuity of war work," he said. "The only alternative would be to extend the principle of selective service and make it universal in character."

Whether enactment of the bill would cause the withdrawal of labor representatives from NWLB was an open question. Many persons in Washington thought that it would, but no responsible leader of labor would commit himself on this question tonight.

A NEW BILL AIMED AT EMPLOYERS

After Congress, by overriding the veto, had enacted into law the section banning contributions by labor organizations to which the President had objected, Senator Hatch introduced a measure forbidding similar political contributions by associations of employers.

It was the eighth time that Congress had overridden President Roosevelt by a veto during the more than ten years he has been in office, and it was the most important measure on which the ❯

(Congress acted independent of the Executive since payment of the soldiers' bonus was authorized, January 27, 1937.

Observers on Capitol Hill believed that the continued absence from work of a large number of coal miners, despite the back-to-work order of the UMW policy committee, and the lukewarm reception by Congress to the President's draft proposal, played a major role in the decisive

votes. There was a roar of protest on the floor of the House when the President reiterated his proposal to increase the draft age to 65 to deal with strikers.

Many members of Congress expressed dissatisfaction, saying that coal mine owners were being punished by being deprived of their property, although it was the union, and not the employers, which had defied the NWLB and called strikes.

Another cause of restiveness among members was the fact that John L. Lewis, in ordering the miners back to work, set another deadline for Oct 31, and said his decision to work on the Government's terms was predicated on continued Governmental operation of the mines. ◊

JULY 1, 1943

M'ARTHUR STARTS ALLIED OFFENSIVE IN PACIFIC; NEW GUINEA ISLES WON, LANDINGS IN SOLOMONS; CHURCHILL PROMISES BLOWS IN EUROPE BY FALL

UNITED NATIONS FORCES MOVE FORWARD IN THE SOUTHWEST PACIFIC

By SIDNEY SHALETT
Special to The new York Times.

WASHINGTON, July 1—Combined Army and Navy forces under General Douglas MacArthur have opened the long expected offensive against the Japanese in the south and southwest Pacific.

Fighting was in progress on Rendova and New Georgia islands, which were hit by ground, naval and air forces in "closest synchronization," a communiqué from General MacArthur's headquarters in Australia reported today. Nassau Bay, ten miles south of the

big Japanese base of Salamaua in New Guinea, fell to the Allies after a slight skirmish, and the Tobriand and Woodlark island groups, 300 to 400 miles west of the New Georgia group, were occupied without opposition.

The Allied push—aimed, observers here believe, at the major Japanese base of Rabaul, on New Britain Island—got under way yesterday, Solomons time, which was Tuesday here.

NUTCRACKER MOVE SEEN

It was believed here, on the basis of early reports, that the fighting and occupations reported so far were preliminary to major actions to come. If bases in the New Georgias are consolidated, a two-way push against Rabaul might be developing, with one arm advancing northwestward from the Central Solomons and the other swinging across eastward from new bases in New Guinea.

United States heavy bombers carried out an attack on Rabaul during the night, dropping nearly twenty-three tons of high-explosive, fragmentation and incendiary bombs throughout the dispersal areas at the Vunakanau and Lakunai airdromes, the communiqué from Aus-

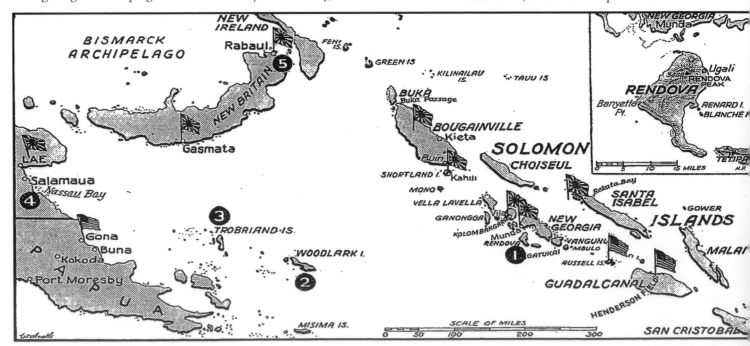

tralian headquarters reported. "Several explosions" and "numerous fires" were observed, one of which was visible for 100 miles, the announcement said.

The big bombers, which have punished Rabaul extensively in recent weeks, ran into heavy Japanese anti-aircraft fire and interference from some enemy night fighters. One American bomber was missing after the raid.

The Tobriand and Woodlark islands will be valuable as stepping-stones in a chain of fighter-plane bases from the Allied stronghold of Milne Bay, on the tip of New Guinea. Japanese-held Gasmata and Rabaul may be raided with comparative ease with the aid of these bays.

NAVY GIVES FIRST NEWS

The first report of landing actions came early yesterday when the Navy announced here in a communiqué that combined United States forces had landed June 30 (Solomons time) on Rendova Island, in the New Georgia group, which is only five miles from the important Japanese air base of Munda, on New Georgia Island, but that communiqué said, "No details have been received."

A hint that the fighting had extended came later from Secretary of the Navy Frank Knox in Los Angeles, where he is inspecting Pacific Coast installations. The Secretary declared that the Rendov attack was the beginning of "an offensive against the Japanese base at Munda and surrounding bases." Navy officials in Washington yesterday declined, however, to confirm that the attack had been extended to New Georgia.

General MacArthur's announcement of more sweeping actions in the Pacific seemed to confirm impressions that the American forces were running into opposition on Rendova and were not making a bloodless conquest as had been the case in the occupations of Funafuti, in the Ellice group, and in the Russell Islands, northwest of Guadalcanal, which were the last two places in the South Pacific revealed by the Navy as occupied by our forces.

On March 27 American planes bombed and strafed Japanese positions at Ugali, which is on the northeast coast of

United Nations Forces Move Forward in the Southwest Pacific: American troops landed on Rendova and New Georgia Islands (1), in the vicinity of the enemy air base at Munda, and engaged the Japanese. The inset shows this area in detail. To the west, the Allies occupied Woodlark Island (2) and the Trobriand Islands (3) without opposition. In New Guinea they occupied Nassau Bay (4), just below Salamaua; the landing craft encountered only slight resistance. Apparently these widespread operations have as their ultimate goal the reduction of Rabaul (5), which was bombed.

Rendova, a previous Navy communiqué disclosed. This indicated that there were enemy forces on the island, which, if they still were there, undoubtedly were resisting.

Observers here have been expecting action in the South and Southwest Pacific for some time. Attention, however, had been focused on spots other than obscure Rendova, a twenty-mile-long, densely wooded island, 195 air miles northwest of Guadalcanal.

Munda was for a while the "Japanese Malta" of the central Solomons. It has been bombed at least 150 times since last November, and the attack on Rendova was preceded by four bombings of Munda within four days. For a brief period a few months back our South Pacific fliers let Munda alone and the impression arose that it had been knocked out by the severe punishment it had received. Then, apparently, the Japanese put it in commission, for the poundings were resumed.

It is believed that American strategy, now that the southern Solomons are safely consolidated, is to move northward through the central Solomons, up to the northern Solomons, where the Japanese are believed to have heavy troop concentrations, and then, if things go well, to the more important objective westward and northward.

It is regarded as entirely likely that the immediate objectives, if Munda is knocked out, are Bougainville Island, about 155 air miles to the northwest, where the important harbor and air base of Kahili is situated, and Rabaul, on New Britain Island, one of Japan's strongest air and sea bases in the southwest Pacific.

Rendova in American hands will give our forces a base 195 miles nearer Japanese targets than Guadalcanal. Rendova is 103 miles from Rekata Bay, submarine and seaplane base; only twenty-five miles from Vila, an air base; 137 miles from bases in the Shortland area, and 410 miles from Rabaul.

Rendova is described by the Navy as "entirely mountainous and densely wooded." It gradually increases in height from its southeastern extremity, where it is 1,021 feet high, to its summit, a precipitous volcanic cone called Rendova Peak, which is 3,488 feet high. This peak, only four miles from the northern end of the island, has been a conspicuous landmark in air flights over the island. Its summit, an extinct crater, is frequently obscured by clouds.

There is a black sand beach called Banyetta Point at the western extremity of the island. Tidal currents there are strong. The coast rises steeply and is thickly wooded.

From seven miles above Banyetta Point to the northern point of the island, a barrier reef parallels the coast. It extends out a maximum distance of two and one-half miles. There are six deep passages through the reef, and several islands are located on the northern part of the reef. The lagoon inside the barrier is shallow and is encumbered by several reefs ◊

PUBLISHER VISITS KREMLIN
Sulzberger and Molotoff Confer For an Hour In Moscow

MOSCOW, July 5 (AP)—Arthur Hays Sulzberger, president and publisher of The New York Times, spent an hour today in the Kremlin with Foreign Commissar Vyacheslaff M. Molotoff.

Mr. Sulzberger said later he could disclose no details of the interview. He was introduced to Mr. Molotoff by William H. Standley, United States Ambassador.

The publisher has been here as a special Red Cross representative and expects to leave Moscow within a few days. ◊

Eisenhower Rubs His Seven Luck-Pieces As Allied Invasion Fleet Approaches Sicily

By EDWARD GILLING
Representing the Combined British Press.

ALLIED HEADQUARTERS IN NORTH AFRICA, July 10—Gen. Dwight D. Eisenhower always carries in his pocket seven old coins, including a gold five-guinea piece.

As the Allied invasion fleet ap- ❱

proached Sicily last night to begin the great assault on Europe, the General gave them a good rub for luck. In fact, as one of his aides said, he gave them several good rubs.

In the early hours of the morning the General heard that the landing had been made and that everything was going according to plan. General Eisenhower spent all night at headquarters, except for one brief period when he drove out to the coast with a small party of his staff to watch an Allied air fleet leaving.

Climbing out of his car, he stood in moonlight with his hand raised to salute the air armada. The period of waiting between the planning of the assault and its realization was over.

Returning to headquarters, General Eisenhower went at once to the naval section, where he joined his staff in following closely the movement of the operations on charts. He spent some time in the Fighter Command room, from which the air umbrella covering the operations was controlled.

At 1:30 A.M. General Eisenhower, apparently satisfied with the progress of operations, went to bed on a cot in a room next to the war room. He slept soundly for three hours until awakened at 4:30 A.M. by an aide who informed him that assault troops had landed and that everything was going according to plan.

The Royal Navy served the General a cup of hot tea and he then returned to the war room, where reports were now

General Dwight D. Eisenhower, commander in chief of Allied Armies in North Africa, and General Honoré Giraud, commanding the French forces, saluting the flags of both nations at Allied headquarters, 1943.

coming in regularly. He remained there until he heard the British Broadcasting Corporation broadcast his message telling the people of France that this was the first stage of the invasion of the Continent, which would be followed by others.

General Eisenhower then left the war room, but only for a change of clothes. He returned soon to follow with his commanders the progress of operations. ◊

JULY 11, 1943

ROOSEVELT SEES 'BEGINNING OF END'
President Reassures Pope on Sparing of Churches and on Respect for the Vatican

By BERTRAM D. HULEN
Special to The New York Times.

WASHINGTON, July 10—The Allied invasion of Sicily looks to President Roosevelt like "the beginning of the end" for Adolf Hitler and Premier Mussolini.

This was revealed by the White House today as an intimation was given that success in Sicily would be followed by the invasion of Southern Italy.

President Roosevelt stated his views in a dramatic announcement when he received word of the invasion during a dinner at the White House last night in honor of Gen. Henri-Honoré Giraud, the French Commander in Chief.

The intimation that Southern Italy might be the next objective was contained in a communication given out by the White House today from President Roosevelt to Pope Pius XII.

In it the President promised that during the invasion of Italian soil churches and religious institutions would "be spared the devastations of war" and the neutral status of Vatican City, as well as of Papal domains "throughout Italy," would be respected. Mr. Roosevelt assured the Pontiff that the United States was seeking "a just

and enduring peace on earth."

Mr. Roosevelt's views concerning the campaign in Sicily were echoed at noon by Senator Tom Connally, Democrat, of Texas, chairman of the Senate Committee on Foreign Relations, who discussed it with the Chief Executive when he called to say good-bye before leaving for Texas.

"Our forces will sweep through Sicily," the Senator declared as he was leaving the White House. "Already on the land, I don't believe they can be stopped. The curfew has rung for Italy."

Nevertheless, there was an air of caution here today until the fighting had developed further, because of reports that the Axis has concentrated in Sicily 300,000 troops, including at least two German divisions. The rest are Italians.

The Allied forces consist of British, Canadian and American units. The Americans, from indications given by military experts, are grouped in the Fifth Army under the immediate command of Lieut. Gen. Mark. W. Clark, with Gen. Dwight D. Elsenhower in over-all command from North African headquarters. The British and Canadians are reported probably to outnumber the Americans.

It is considered probable that some days may elapse before definite conclusions can be reached concerning the progress of the campaign, but it is clear that Allied success would mean air and sea control of the Mediterranean and open the way for the conquest of Southern Italy, Sardinia and other Mediterranean points.

Although the operation is not a second front in Europe, it could open a way for such an undertaking.

These considerations were apparently in the mind of President Roosevelt when he made his dramatic announcement at the dinner last night. The details were revealed by Stephen F. Early, Presidential Secretary, today.

The guests included Secretary of State Cordell Hull, Gen. George C. Marshall, Army Chief of Staff; Admiral William D. Leahy, the President's Chief of Staff; Admiral Ernest J. King, Commander in Chief of the United States Fleet, and other military and naval officials.

ANNOUNCES NEWS OF ATTACK
President Roosevelt began receiving reports of the invasion of Sicily at about 9 o'clock. Just before 10 o'clock, as the dinner was nearing its close, he made the dramatic announcement:

"I have just had word of the first attack against the soft underbelly of Europe."

He then asked the guests to say nothing about it until midnight, when simultaneous announcements would be made in North Africa, London and Washington.

He stressed that the major objective was the elimination of Germany, for once ashore our forces could go in different directions, that it certainly was to be hoped that the operation was the beginning of the end, and it could almost be said that it was.

In a toast to unified France, he promised that while this invasion was not directed at the shores of France, eventually all of France would be liberated.

After telling of the attack and landing, the President said:

"This is a good illustration of the fact of planning, not the desire for planning, but the fact of planning. With the commencing of the expedition in North Africa, with the complete cooperation between the British and ourselves, that was followed by complete cooperation with the French in North Africa.

"The result, after landing, was the battle of Tunis. That was not all planning; that was cooperation and from that time on we have been working in complete harmony.

"There are a great many objectives, of course, and the major objective is the elimination of Germany. That goes without saying, as a result of the step which is in progress at this moment. We hope it is the beginning of the end."

"Last autumn the Prime Minister of England called it 'the end of the beginning.' I think we can almost say that this action tonight is the beginning of the end.

"We are going to be ashore in a naval sense—air sense—military. Once there, we have the opportunity of going in different directions and I want to tell General Giraud that we haven't forgotten that France is one of the directions. One of our prime aims, of course, is the restoration of the people of France and the sovereignty of France.

PLEDGES LIBERATION OF PARIS
"Even if a move is not directed at this moment at France itself, General Giraud can rest assured that the ultimate objective— we will do it the best way—is to liberate the people of France, not merely those in the southern part of France, but the people in northern France—Paris. And in this whole operation, I should say rightly in the enormous planning, we have had the complete cooperation of the French military and naval forces in North Africa.

"Gradually the opposition has cooled. The older regime is breaking down. We have seen what has happened or is happening at the present moment in Martinique and Guadeloupe. That is a very major part toward the big objective.

"We want to help rearm those French forces (the President referred to the French forces in North Africa) and to build up the French strength so that when the time comes from a military point of view when we get into France itself and throw the Germans out there will be a French Army and French ships working with the British and ourselves.

"It's a very great symbol that General Giraud is here tonight, that he has come over to talk to us about his military problems and to help toward the same objective that all of the United Nations have—freedom of France and with it the unity of France."

GIRAUD THANKS ROOSEVELT
General Giraud, in responding, thanked the President for the support being given France and expressed gratification for American assistance in rearming the soldiers of France.

He then raised his glass in a toast to the President and "the glory of the United States," referring to this country as "that great nation through which peace and freedom will be restored to the world." ◆

JULY 11, 1943

GIRAUD'S VISIT REVIVES CONTROVERSY
Americans Caught Up In Emotional Storm That Has Swept Over Frenchmen—President Disappoints Both Sides

By HAROLD CALLENDER
Special to The New York Times.

WASHINGTON, July 10—The visit to Washington this week of General Henri-Honoré Giraud, who is commander of the French forces in North and West Africa and shares with General Charles de Gaulle the chairmanship of the new French Committee of National Liberation at Algiers, has revived the impassioned controversy that has raged around those two men and the situation in North Africa for six months.

It has raged in North Africa, in London and in Washington, with echoes in remoter places like Moscow and Tahiti and New Caledonia. Although Algiers has not been' silent—it never is—the storm center this week has been Washington.

At a huge reception for General Giraud yesterday the ballroom of one of the largest Washington hotels glittered with French, British and American uniforms. In that room this correspondent listened to a de Gaullist who felt sure the United States had ruined its reputation in Europe by interfering in French affairs so far as to insist that General Giraud be retained as French commander.

CLASHING OPINIONS
A few feet away he met a Giraudist who warmly praised the official American policy and said the de Gaullists were about as important as their armed forces in North Africa, which numbered 11,000 in a total French force of about 70,000.

Both de Gaullists and Giraudists expressed consternation at the remark made earlier that day by President Roosevelt to the effect that the French were under Germany's heel and therefore there was no France now.

What, undoubtedly, Mr. Roosevelt meant was that there was no French ▶

State to speak for France. If he had said that, his words would have caused less astonishment, but perhaps not much less disappointment; for Frenchmen of both groups have hoped the committee at Algiers would be recognized by the Allies as the ad interim French authority that might speak for France in Allied councils and hold as trustee for France all available territories, including Martinique.

Americans too have been drawn into the emotional torrent. There are Americans sitting at desks in Washington who lose their tempers at the mere mention of de Gaulle or Giraud. Some who were ardent for General de Gaulle have gone to North Africa and come back ardent for General Giraud, or vice versa.

Correspondents here who think it their duty to tell their readers of the official coolness toward General de Gaulle and why it exists are swamped with letters denouncing them for maligning General de Gaulle.

There is something about this controversy that upsets the emotional and perhaps the intellectual equilibrium not only of Frenchmen but of Americans and Britons. It is certainly not the quiet, composed, gentle personality of General Giraud, whose only or at least whose main desire seems to be to kill Germans in a systematic, professional and mechanically efficient manner so as to liberate France and restore French institutions, including, no doubt, the right of Frenchmen to quarrel endlessly among themselves as they have traditionally done.

EMOTION UNLEASHED

General Giraud's appearance in Washington happened to unleash a new flood of emotion because it was a logical occasion for defining what our officials would describe as the de Gaulle problem and the present attitude of the principal Allies toward it.

The emotionally provocative qualities of the controversy derive from two assumptions on the part of the de Gaullists and the reactions to those assumptions in other quarters.

The first assumption is that General de Gaulle or his movement represents the French people in a special sense—the "petits gens" or little fellows or forgotten men who work hard for a living and have no family estates or distinguished ancestors—the masses who live what may be called the left side of the line of demarcation that has run through the French nation without much variation since the Revolution of 1789.

According to this view Marshal Henri Philippe Pétain and his circle sinned not only by too readily accepting defeat and collaboration, but principally by being politically and socially reactionary—by representing those who never accepted the French Revolution; and de Gaullism is therefore depicted as the youthful, progressive, democratic side of France.

DYNAMIC NATIONALISM

The second assumption is that de Gaullism embodies a dynamic French nationalism indispensable to the revival of a ravaged nation, a nationalism the arteries of which have not begun to harden.

It is a ruthless nationalism calling for purges on all sides and even whisperings of guillotines. It is directed not only against the Germans but just now also against the Allies, who are accused of unnecessarily infringing French sovereignty by taking possession of ports and communications in North Africa and by dictating who shall command the French forces.

It probably will be directed in the future against all foreigners and may verge upon xenophobia, as nationalism in its extreme forms usually does.

Meanwhile, in less friendly quarters the first assumption mentioned above was flatly rejected on the ground that none could tell who, if anyone, represented the imprisoned French people of today. Some frankly feared that General de Gaulle and his underground Allies within France might turn out to be communistic. Had not a Communist Deputy joined General de Gaulle in London? In the same quarters the second assumption was angrily denounced as calculated to interfere with the military operations of the Allies, since it was accompanied by a demand for a purge of French Army officers that our military authorities thought would impair the efficiency of a force which had fought extremely well against the Germans.

ALLIED RESPONSIBILITY

Moreover, it was regarded as absurd for Frenchmen to squabble over technicalities of sovereignty at a moment when Allied armies were preparing to liberate France, whose sovereignty could not be said to exist unless those Allied armies won the war. The Allies had a right to determine how the French could best cooperate in that common task, since the Allies were bearing the major burden and expense and were responsible for the high command.

The two assumptions apparently have generated in General de Gaulle supreme confidence in his popularity and his destiny and a sense of having a kind of Joan of Arc mission to save France. All men with missions tend to inspire boredom or distrust or both in those who do not share their enthusiasm; and de Gaulle, by frankly expressing his aspirations, seems to have put some people's backs up, notably at the conference at Casablanca.

Moreover, General de Gaulle for three years has carried on a campaign that necessarily clashed all along the line with American policy. For he was denouncing as unworthy and traitorous the government of defeat which the United States recognized and dealt with—although with constant misgivings—as the government of France. It therefore seemed to Washington that de Gaulle's mission was to frustrate our policy; and for that there was no quick forgiveness.

The recognition of the Vichy Government is now gone, but General de Gaulle is still sabotaging our policy, this time our military policy which alone can save France—so it seems to Washington officials. If he wants to dispel distrust, why does he not stop arguing and start fighting Germans, since he is a military man, ask his critics.

OUR INTERVENTION

American emotions are stirred mainly by the first assumption—that de Gaullism is democracy and all that opposes it is toryism. Prime Minister Churchill's acceptance of what is described as an antide Gaullist policy is explained by recalling that he is a Tory. President Roosevelt's adoption of the same attitude is not so easy to explain, but the critics attribute it to some of his advisers in North Africa and here.

From Algiers this week comes the report that many Americans object to Allied intervention in French affairs "to frustrate de Gaulle." Others think it would be more logical to object to intervention as such, whomever it might frustrate.

The invitation to General Giraud to come here was interpreted as designed to increase his prestige not only with the Army but with civilians in North Africa. His visit is now officially described as strictly military, although it would be rash to suggest that in the General's conversations here no mention will be made of the committee that aspires to rule the French Empire and its armed forces.

UNITY STILL ABSENT

The status of that committee remains obscure pending definition of the Allied attitude toward it. The case of Martinique, where the Vichy regime has collapsed, offers the opportunity for such a definition.

Meanwhile, the extent of de Gaulle's influence in the committee and in the French Empire, and the somewhat unbending nature of de Gaulle, seem to preclude at least for the present that French unity which everybody has professed to desire. ◇

JULY 11, 1943

FOURTH-TERM RACE TAKEN FOR GRANTED

But Recent Washington Rows Suggest Re-election Is Far From Certain

POLITICAL TACTICS SHAPED

By TURNER CATLEDGE

WASHINGTON, July 10—Regardless of the political strain which the intramural feuding and clashes between the White House and Congress undoubtedly have imposed lately upon the Administration, the nomination of Franklin D. Roosevelt for a fourth term as President is still taken for granted here.

Reports from the country as to reactions to the continuing squabbling in Washington suggest the advisability of a recheck by those who would make Mr. Roosevelt a heavy-odds favorite for re-election against the entire field, Democratic and Republican. There appears no evidence that he will be seriously countered in his own party, but a general disgust with the Washington rows, as reported, especially from the Middle West, may, if the quarrels continue, bring about a tightening up of the winter book quotations for 1944.

SIGNS OF WANING SUPPORT

Regardless of the belief that Mr. Roosevelt will be nominated again—assuming, of course, that he wants to be—he perhaps will have less emotional support than ever before from the rank and file of the heterogeneous aggregation that has occupied the Democratic wigwam for these last ten years.

Ardor for him has cooled and is cooling perceptibly among his partisans in some regions. Feeling has run pretty deeply in the South over the activities of the Administration, and particularly of Mrs. Roosevelt, in relation to the delicate racial problem, and in the Middle West over efforts to control farm prices.

Realizing all of this, the White House political high command headed by Harry Hopkins, with David K. Niles as first assistant, is not expected to try to give the fourth-term nomination the semblance of a "draft," as they did the third-term nomination in 1940. They are expected, on the other hand, and in their own time, to go after the plum by direct and obvious means, always with this legitimate question: "Pray, who else?" And, if the fighting is still under way in the fall of 1944, they can be expected to present the case of Mr. Roosevelt's fourth-term election as a military necessity to assure victory for the United Nations, and as a means for insuring a more lasting peace for the whole world.

PREPARATORY STEPS

The fourth-term planners are letting no grass grow under their feet. The recent appointment of George E. Allen as secretary of the National Committee can be considered as in line with the purpose of the planners to become more active, especially in appeasing the virulent opposition within the party. Mr. Allen is what is known in his native Mississippi as "a smooth operator."

While the fourth-termers have made no outstanding open moves to date, they have been laying the groundwork. Proof of the skill with which they have been laying it may be found in some degree in the fact that until now no opponent of the fourth term has stuck his head very high within the party. At this stage four years ago at least two—John N. Garner and James A. Farley, then respectively Vice President and Postmaster General—were offering themselves as rallying points for antithird term Democrats.

Politics is an ever-present element in Washington. It has its influence, one way or another, on practically every major action taken here. The war has brought no exception to that rule—in fact, politics is more present in current measures than at any time for several years.

Yet it is difficult to see the influence of the fourth-term campaign, so far as the "fourth term" is concerned, in these actions and discussions. The question of the two-term limitation seemed to have been disposed of quite definitely in 1940 so far as it involved Mr. Roosevelt. Opposition to him and his measures now is based on other things than his threat further to shatter tradition.

RECENT DEVELOPMENTS

Recent Washington developments, particularly the action of Congress in running roughshod over some of the projects of the President, have underscored the view that Mr. Roosevelt's strength politically is not what it used to be on the domestic front. It may not be basically what it used to be on any front, but Congress, being uncertain of itself and lacking information on international issues, used home ground on which to make its stand.

The trouble between the White House and the Capitol cannot be ascribed altogether to a difference on issues. Of political importance from an intraparty political standpoint is the method which the President and the little inner-circle group around him have used for several years now in dealing with their sensitive partisans on The Hill. So far as the trouble to the White House is concerned, it is a case in large degree of chickens coming home to roost.

One thing which many Washington observers seemed to think settled by the recent feuding was that Vice President Henry A. Wallace would be off the ticket for 1944. Mr. Wallace's chances already were considered to be dimming, what with his own failure to strike political fire and the availability of other highly placed and more romantic figures. But his row with Jesse H. Jones, Secretary of Commerce and Chairman of the Reconstruction Finance Corporation, undoubtedly set off active opposition. It will be remembered that Mr. Jones was one of a long string of possible Vice-Presidential nominees who, under White House pressure, withdrew their names in favor of Mr. Wallace at the Chicago Convention in 1940. ◊

JULY 14, 1943

Editorial
HITLER IN COMMAND?

There are reports by way of London that Hitler is back in command on the Eastern Front. Good news, if true. There are excellent reasons for believing that the overvaulting ambition of this self-infatuated man played an important part in the disasters which overtook the German armies at the end of last year's campaign in Russia. It was his decision, most accounts agree, that split the German forces when they should have been united, in a too greedy effort to grab both the Volga and the Caucasus, thereby bringing on the catastrophe at Stalingrad. In the earlier stages of the war, when Germany's neighbors were unprepared for sudden treacherous attacks, Hitler's "intuition" frequently worked wonders. In the present stage of the war, with the supremacy of power shifting to the Allied side, any enemy of Germany would prefer to have Hitler's "intu- ❯

ition" substituted for the cool competence of the German General Staff.

Moreover, if Hitler is now back in command on the Eastern Front, the German people will be reminded, at an inconvenient stage of the war for such remembrances, of past promises about performances in Russia that failed to come off. There was Hitler's confident declaration, as early as Oct. 3, 1941, that "This enemy is already broken and will never rise again." There was his promise, on Dec. 11 of the same year, that "With the return of summer weather

there will be no obstacle to stop the forward movement of the German troops." There was his iron-bound guarantee, on March 15, 1942, that "The Russians will be annihilatingly defeated by us in the coming summer." And there was the famous declaration of last Sept. 30 that Stalingrad would stay in German hands: "You can be of the firm conviction that no human being shall ever push us away from that spot."

Hitler's record as a military commander on the Russian front is strewn with pledges he has not redeemed. ◊

JULY 15, 1943

BRITISH ADVANCE NEAR CATANIA; AMERICANS SEIZE KEY AIRDROMES; 12,000 AXIS PRISONERS CAPTURED

U.S. TROOPS LANDING IN SICILY UNDER ENEMY FIRE

By The Associated Press.

ALLIED HEADQUARTERS IN NORTH AFRICA, July 14—The British Eighth Army bore down tonight on Catania, the port city halfway along the eastern Sicilian coast toward Messina, opposite the toe of Italy. Late dispatches said that Catania's fall was imminent.

[The Eighth Army stood on the plain before Catania, The United Press reported. According to an Algiers broadcast recorded in London by The Associated Press, the British had driven a wedge into the city's defenses. A Madrid report quoted by The United Press said that German sources had told of a large-scale landing of British paratroops in the plain, though the Germans claimed that they had wiped out the attackers.] In the southwest a powerful force of Americans, which has already taken more than 8,000 prisoners, scored a fifteen-mile advance on the left flank, captured two more key airdromes and struck inland toward Caltagirone, the southwestern gateway to the Catania Plain. More than 12,000 prisoners altogether have been captured on Sicily, it was announced tonight. On the fifth

day of the campaign the Axis defenses appeared to be still paralyzed.

The American middle column, headed toward Caltagirone, was last reported only a few miles from there, fighting a German unit at Niscemi.

MEET NO 'SERIOUS OPPOSITION'

But an Allied commentator said that, in the over-all picture, the Allies "are not really meeting any serious opposition." Dispatches made it clear that the invaders were ahead of their timetable.

British troops and the Canadians attached to the Eighth Army were reported to be within fifteen miles of Catania during the afternoon after a swift twenty-mile advance from Augusta. At this rate the Eighth Army should be nearing Catania, unless serious opposition had developed at the intermediate inland cities of Lentini and Carlentini, on the edge of the Catania Plain below Mount Etna. Catania itself has no natural defenses.

The British were moving along a road that curves inland toward

Lentini and may already have taken that city. Catania is thirty-five miles from Augusta along this winding route.

The Americans captured airdromes at Comiso, six miles west of Ragusa, and at Ponte Olivo, nine miles inland from Gela. Plunging west and north from Licata, the Americans overran Palma and Naro. The latter is only twelve miles from Agrigento, where the Axis was said to have concentrated heavy forces for a counter-attack. Hundreds of prisoners were swept up in this fifteen-mile drive.

The American sector of the 150-mile bridgehead was a long, shallow one, with the invasion plan apparently calling for the Americans to deepen and protect the Allied left flank while the British raced up the eastern coast to Messina.

French forces have landed in Sicily and are participating in the Allied campaign, it was officially announced at the headquarters of French forces in North Africa. ◊

JULY 15, 1943

GEN. PATTON WADED ASHORE TO BATTLE
Leader Leaped into Surf from Landing-Craft as Tanks Periled U.S. Force

BY NOEL MONKS
London Daily Mail Correspondent
(Distributed by The Associated Press.)

ABOARD A DESTROYER, Off General Montgomery's Sicilian Headquarters, July 13 (Delayed)—Lieut. Gen. George S. Patton Jr., commander of the United States Seventh Army invading Sicily leaped into the surf from a landing barge and waded ashore to take personal command of bitter fighting against German tank units opposing the landing.

JULY 18, 1943

SUCCESSES ELATE MOSCOW
Failure of Vast German Effort Is Potent Russian Tonic

By Wireless to The New York Times.

MOSCOW, July 17—Today there is a feeling of excitement and exaltation in Moscow unequaled since the height of last winter's victories. Everyone has become more aware than ever of the enormous change that has occurred since last year.

The Germans' failure to cut off the Kursk salient had become increasingly clear since July 5, when the Nazis launched their offensive. It was clear that the Russians had devised, through months of careful training and preparation, means of breaking any Blitzkrieg attack the Germans could devise with their shock tactics and Tiger tanks.

The Russian Army was trained to withstand what seemed impossible, first

At General Patton's American bridge-head at Gela I heard the story of General Patton's great personal courage and the magnificent fighting quality of his troops.

When the Americans landed at Gela they found the town in control of two German tank regiments. During the next twenty-four hours the fiercest fighting of the whole Allied invasion took place. Twice the Germans were driven from the town and twice the Americans were forced right back on to the beaches.

At this stage General Patton leaped into the surf.

Step by step the Germans were driven back from the beaches as wave after wave of Americans landed from the troopships. By sunset Sunday the bridgehead was well established and the Americans had pushed the Germans back to a few miles beyond town.

When Gen. [Dwight D.] Eisenhower visited General Patton's headquarters yesterday he warmly congratulated his old colleague on his splendid fighting achievement. ◇

Lieutenant General George S. Patton during the campaign to liberate Sicily, Italy, 1943.

JULY 21, 1943

ROME BOMBED: FIRST PHOTOGRAPHIC REPORT OF ALLIED RAID

By The Associated Press.

ALLIED HEADQUARTERS IN NORTH AFRICA, July 20—Reconnaissance photographs today showed vast sections of Rome's great railway yards in twisted, smoking ruins from the terrific blasting inflicted yesterday by hundreds of American bombers. The initial raid on the Italian capital was officially labeled an "outstandingly successful operation."

While more than 500 heavy and medium bombers, escorted by fighters, struck the city in wave after wave beneath a bright midday sun, Allied communiqués disclosed today, the entire two-and-a-half-hour assault was carried out with the loss of five planes. All the losses were suffered by Maj. Gen. James H. Doolittle's Strategic Air Force. Ninth United States Air Force headquarters in Cairo announced that all the Liberator bombers participating in the raid had returned safely to bases in the Middle East.

The Ninth Air Force formations alone dumped nearly 330 tons of high explosives on Rome, the Cairo communiqué said, declaring that the Littoria railway yards had been "completely destroyed."

"String after string of bombs criss-crossed the yards, and photographs indicate that an area 400 yards by two miles long is a mass of twisted steel rails, gaping bomb craters and wreckage of rolling stock and buildings," the bulletin said. "An ammunition train moving through the yards received several direct hits and exploded, contributing to the destruction."

An Allied headquarters communiqué said that "very severe damage" had been caused to all the targets, including the Littoria and San Lorenzo rail yards, both within the limits of the city, and near-by airdromes and industrial plants.

Allied aerial chieftains, apparently pleased that the outcome of the attack had surpassed expectations, were lavish in their praise of the airmen responsible for its execution. Lieut. Gen. Carl A. Spaatz, commander of the Northwest African Air Forces, sent congratulations to General Doolittle, saying: ▶

an artillery barrage of enormous intensity, then an intensive air bombing, and finally vast waves of tanks, including a high proportion of Tigers. When these broke through, still nothing was settled for the Germans. Through remarkable coordination of weapons, the Russians always succeeded in limiting the damage of the break-through and usually managing to destroy the broken-through tanks after detaching them from their infantry or forcing them to turn tail.

The magnitude of the attack may be gauged from the fact that the Russians in many cases succeeded in a small sector in repelling, dispersing and partly destroying as many as 6,000 tanks attacking simultaneously.

This is explainable by several factors working together—the cultivation of Russian iron nerves, for it takes iron nerves to crouch inside a trench, allow a Tiger tank to cross beyond it and then fire from an anti-tank rifle into the tank's vulnerable rear; iron discipline and an unlimited spirit of self-sacrifice; all this, together with admirable coordination of weapons, an extraordinarily rich endowment of infantry with all types of anti-tank weapons and a general richness in automatic and semi-automatic weapons; failure of the Germans to gain air control in the Kursk-Orel

and Belgorod battles, the effectiveness of Russian aviation and above all the high power and skill of the Russian artillery, which bore the brunt of the German onslaught.

Finally, the high quality of Russian tanks, which counter-attacked effectively, proved, according to all reports, that the KV tank is more than equal to the Tiger.

In the Kursk-Orel sector the Germans, who had not made any real progress, gave up hope of achieving anything some days ago. In the Belgorod sector they are still attempting to press forward and enlarge their ten- to fifteen-mile penetrations, but still without success, and above all without that "conviction" with which the Germans started their July 5 offensive, which in the words of Adolf Hitler's order to his troops, was to become the battle that would decide the war's outcome.

The moral effect of the failure of the biggest German armored attack ever launched along a relatively narrow front was immense in Moscow. Here, more even than in the Stalingrad battle, was a demonstration of a fundamental improvement in Russian defense tactics immensely greater than the perfection in German attack tactics. ◇

"It is one of the many accurate attacks which your forces have carried on during the present battle, all of which had a marked significance in their successful outcome."

The Tabonelli steel plant and a large chemical works were battered by the raiders, which met what was described officially as only "slight opposition" from enemy fighter planes. Two enemy interceptors were shot down by Lightning fighters.

The official pictures of the havoc created by the bombers showed that the Ciampino airport had been severely damaged. A number of hangars were blasted or set afire and a large number of parked aircraft near by were hit by fragmentation bombs. The Littoria airport, near the railway yards, also was hit hard. ◊

Vatican apartment of Pope Pius XII after one of the later raids on Rome.

JULY 21, 1943

TIMES CORRESPONDENT BROADCASTS TO ITALY

Matthews Explains Why Allies Had to Raid Capital

LONDON, July 20 (AP)—Herbert L. Matthews, Rome correspondent of The New York Times from 1939 to 1941, said in an Algiers broadcast to Italy today that "it was hard to have to bomb Rome but war is like that."

Mr. Matthews, who accompanied the Allied bombers, told Italy:

"Neither as an American citizen nor as an individual did I feel any satisfaction when I flew over Rome yesterday. Believe me, this raid was undertaken after long and careful consideration and preparation. There are more than 25,000,000 Catholics in America whose opinion we have to take into account.

"The San Lorenzo marshaling yards are of greatest strategic importance and had to be considered a military target. It was hard to have to bomb it—but war is like that.

"It is the Duce and the Fuehrer whom you have to blame for that.

"Rome's anti-aircraft defense was feeble and ineffective. Was that all Musso and Hitler could do for you?" ◊

JULY 24, 1943

LUFTWAFFE'S LACK SEEN AS STRATEGIC
British Experts Say Faults Basic in its Creation Are Now Showing Up

NUMERICAL POWER FAILING
Udet's 'Second-Rate Planes' at Loss—Flying Fortress Gets New Praise In London

By FREDERICK GRAHAM
By Cable to THE NEW YORK TIMES.

LONDON, July 23—A study of one phase of military air power is offered in the present position of the Luftwaffe. Reich Marshal Hermann Goering's once awe-inspiring warbirds now seem to be perched on the edge of the nest uncertain what to do.

The fact that the vaunted Nazi Air Force, which started the war as the most powerful aerial armada in the world, was unable to halt or even to hinder the Allied seaborne invasion of Sicily over 100 miles of open ocean and that the Germans with vaster aerial might proportionally could not beat down the Royal Air Force in 1940 for a Nazi invasion of Britain across twenty miles of water must contain a meaningful lesson for future strategists. Although the full answer belongs to the future, at least a partial solution seems indicated now.

To the frequently asked question, "Where is the Luftwaffe?" the often implied reply, either that it is "stretched too thin" to be really efficient or that it is awaiting the proper moment for a bold counterstroke, is thought here not to be the full, real answer. Even now the Luftwaffe is undoubtedly stronger in both planes and personnel than the RAF was during the Battle of Britain.

Some experts here believe the truth of the matter is that the builders of the Luftwaffe never grasped the real meaning and function of air power. Basically, the Luftwaffe was created to cooperate with the German Army, supporting it in ground operations with hard-hitting, highly mobile units striking a concentrated blow against a single point.

FAILURE IN CONCEPTION

Against defenseless cities and untried troops and without real aerial opposition, it worked out almost exactly as Marshal Goering, Col. Gen. Ernst Udet, technical chief of the Luftwaffe who was killed in 1941, and the others planned. But as a strategic bombing weapon and as a fighter destroyer it must be considered a failure.

Another related reason that is believed to contribute to the comparatively poor showing of the Luftwaffe now was the German idea that quantity was more important in aerial warfare than quality, as remarked in the latest edition of Jane's "All the World's Aircraft," by J. M. Spaight, former Assistant Secretary of the British Air Ministry.

Col. Gen. Udet, who had a large role in building up the Luftwaffe, once told friends in the United States that he did not want the best planes in the world; he wanted overwhelming numerical superiority of the second best. Germany surely had them during 1940 and part of 1941, but they did not achieve Colonel General Udet's aims.

The current Issue of The Aeroplane, British aeronautical journal, scathingly declares one of the Luftwaffe's most serious blunders is in the use of fighters, noting that the Germans are no weaker in fighter strength in Sicily or at Orel than the RAF was over southeast Britain in 1940. The RAF, in 1940, fortunately had superior fighters in the Spitfire and the Hurricane.

THE B-17'S ABILITIES HAILED

The big Flying Fortress of the United States Eighth Air Force here and Twelfth Air Force in North Africa, in which American air officials believed as a powerful weapon even when some British experts shook their heads and wrote sour articles for aviation magazines about, is also revealing the weakness of the Luftwaffe's foundation.

In the first place, the B-17 Fortress is showing its ability to hit important targets from a high altitude and, second, it is proving it can more than hold its own with enemy fighters trying to intercept it. One of the biggest boosters of the

Fortress now is the RAF, which has seen and marveled at its precision bombing and its toughness against fighters and anti-aircraft fire.

German plane plants are known to have shifted production from bombers to fighters to meet the battering Allied aerial assaults, but it is probably too late for the Nazis to correct their original mistakes in conception of airpower to win this war or even to stave off defeat.

As to the Flying Fortress, The Aeroplane, whose co-founder and former editor, C. G. Grey, once dubbed the Boeing bomber "the Flying Baloney," pays high tribute to it in the issue dated tomorrow.

In an article entitled "Bomber Self-Defense," the magazine states that the Fortress has "reduced the enemy's fighter attacks to snap-shooting," and adds that "no bomber could be treated with greater respect" than the B-17 is now by German fighters.

Praising the heavy firepower and the gun turrets of the four-motored Boeing, the article concludes:

"We will gladly offer our thanks to those Fortress crews who showed us what a little more weight and a little more range in turret armament might mean." ◆

As war wore on, the Luftwaffe was stretched thin.

JULY 25, 1943

LETTERS TO THE TIMES
Rome Bombing Upheld

Attack Regarded As Regrettable But Highly Necessary

To The Editor of the New York Times:

The letter from Pope Pius XII to his Vicar General for the District of Rome is interesting and a worthy document. As always, it again shows his yearning for peace and his noble humility. It deserves careful study by those who are inclined to advocate a ruthless treatment for the Axis nations when the conflict is over.

As could be expected, his message has given Nazi and Fascist leaders the opportunity to make a feature of the Pope's expressed anxiety for the preservation of ancient works of art and of historic value—not overlooking even Christian civilization, which during four long years they have done everything to destroy.

The high esteem in which His Holiness is held throughout the world has led not a few good people among us to indicate their approval of his declaration. However, all such well-meaning people should be reminded that the greatest and the most precious "work of art and of ancient historic value" is man, who, as the Holy Writ has told us "God created in His own image—in the image of God He created him."

Again, the great philosopher and Apostle St. Paul declared that "Man is the Temple of God." Then note with what scrupulous care our armed forces have carried their attack on the Eternal City, which has been an important Axis base for action against the Allies!

Bearing all this in mind, if some great art objects—the handiwork of man—must be destroyed in order to save the lives of our men, the attack on

Rome is fully justified. While millions of Allied soldiers are battling for human rights in a war for which they are in no way responsible the method and conduct of war must be left in the control of our humane military leaders and not to the judgment of spiritual advisers, whose turn will come—let us hope soon.

When mankind is freed from the ravages of war, and the great leaders of the present generation establish a lasting peace founded on justice and righ-

teousness, there will in time arise great men and women in all walks of life, in all lands and among all nations, to more than make up the terrific losses of every nature sustained in this war. The greatest leaders of the future, however, will be those who will render real service to their peoples—a situation quite different from what the great mass of humanity has been accustomed to in the past.
S. KENT COSTIKYAN.
Montclair, N.J., July 23, 1943. ◇

JULY 26, 1943

MUSSOLINI OUSTED WITH FASCIST CABINET;

ARRESTS REPORTED

Berne Hears the Fascist Leaders Are Being Held in Homes

'PEACE' CRY IN ROME

Nazis in Milan Said to Have Fired on Mob of Demonstrators

By DANIEL T. BRIGHAM
By Telephone to The New York Times

BERNE, Switzerland, July 25—King Victor Emmanuel announced to Italy tonight that he had accepted the "resignations" of Premier Benito Mussolini and his entire Cabinet. He ordered Marshal Pietro Badoglio to form a military government "to continue the conduct of the war."

The announcement was made in a proclamation that was broadcast to the people of Italy from Rome at 11 P.

M. Rome time. The Rome radio then signed off for twenty minutes, resuming its broadcast at 11:20 to carry a proclamation by Marshal Badoglio. Before giving this, however, the announcer said:

"With the fall of Mussolini and his band, Italy has taken the first step toward peace. Finished is the shame of fascism! Long live peace! Long live the King!"

BADOGLIO SAYS HE'LL FIGHT
Marshal Badoglio's proclamation was then read. It appealed to the nation for "calm" in this hour of trial, saying:

"Italians! On the demand of His Majesty the King-Emperor, I have assumed the military government of the country with full powers. The war will continue. Italy bruised, her provinces invaded, and her cities ruined, will retain her faith in her given word, jealous of her ancient traditions.

"We must tighten our ranks behind the King-Emperor, the living image of the country, who stands as an example for all today. The task I have been charged with is clear and precise. It will be executed scrupulously, and whoever believes he can interrupt the normal progress of events or whoever seeks to disturb internal order will be struck down without mercy.

"Long live Italy! Long live the King! PIETRO BADOGLIO."

For the first time in twenty-one years the Italian radio signed off a nation-wide program by playing only the royal march. "Giovinezza," the fascist anthem, like fascism, is dead.

[Field Marshal General Albert Kes-

Italians in Rome, celebrated the downfall of Benito Mussolini with pictures of King Victor Emmanuel, July 1943.

selring. German Commander in Chief in Italy, and Hans-Georg I Viktor von Mackensen, the German Ambassador, negotiated with Marshal Badoglio in Rome last night, according to a Rome radio bulletin picked up in Stockholm, Sweden, by Reuter.]

Following the proclamation broad cast demonstrations broke out in many parts of the country as Italians went to the streets to celebrate the end of fascism. A Milan report, received here by telephone just before telephone communications were cut at 11 o'clock, told of bloodshed there when German anti-aircraft units had apparently fired on a mob. No further details were given.

With half of the Italian population fleeing in an evacuation greater than that in France and those still at home "looking for Blackshirts," the situation inside Italy is developing rapidly. Frontier reports tell of a state of "latent revolution," leaving the country still looking for a Government with which to sue for peace. Marshal Enrico Caviglia may be the spokesman, but Marshal Badoglio will be the leader-and the King will remain as long as he can.

As troubles spread in Rome, more than an hour before the rest of Italy, fears were expressed for the safety of Signor Mussolini, Carlo Scorza, the Fascist party secretary, and the entire Cabinet, which was being detained under house arrest. They were therefore transferred to a place outside the capital, the approaches to which are being guarded by the army.

The first details received here of the origin of the Cabinet Crisis—heavily censored, for the movement was still in full swing—say it began in this morning's special Cabinet session of the key Defense Ministries.

Premier Mussolini outlined "propositions" Adolf Hitler had made for the "salvation of the new European order" during their last meeting. They called for such great Italian sacrifices that the Under-Secretaries of War, Air and Navy refused to accept the responsibility for their execution without consultation with the full Cabinet.

When the Cabinet met the debate was lively until it was decided to submit the entire problem to the King and his councilors, who in the last analysis would be alone responsible to the nation.

The principal "proposition" was said to be the immediate withdrawal of all possible manpower and materiel from the Sicilian front, accepting enormous losses during that operation as inevitable. The Catania front, defended by the Hermann Goering Division, was to

be taken over by "sufficient Italian rear guard" to enable its withdrawal first.

Italian forces would then be called upon to fight a "retiring rear-guard operation up the entire length of the Italian mainland from Naples, Calabria and Puglia to a line running approximately east west through the southern limits of Tuscany, which would leave the Axis nations "a line of elastic defense while final preparations were being completed in the Apennines."

This operation would be entirely Italian, aided only by German matériel. It was suggested the operation should be exclusively in the hands of the Italian military, while the slightly more trained Blackshirt militia formations would be reserved for "advanced line defense" in

front of the Apennine positions.

Rome would be abandoned, while such matériel as could not be moved northward would be destroyed, mainly ammunition and explosives, several very big shipments of which are believed to have just arrived for the Germans.

As presented to the King, the alternative to defeat left little of his already shriveled empire and meant the abandonment of more than half of his country. His refusal was emphatic: the nation stood or fell, but it did one or the other together "despite the lacerations the nation has suffered" at the hands of the Fascist party.

The King then "accepted" the resignations of the Fascist government. ◇

JULY 26, 1943

Biggest RAF-U.S. Raids on Reich Blast Hamburg, Hit Baltic Cities

By The United Press.

LONDON, July 26—United States heavy bombers struck deep and hard into Germany by daylight yesterday, hammering aircraft factories at the Baltic port of Warnemuende and showering hundreds of high explosives into the smoking ruins of Hamburg, gutted by the British Royal Air Force's night bombers twelve hours earlier in the greatest bombing assault of the war.

At the same time, other American heavies struck in force at the great German shipyards in Kiel and raided the Baltic industrial center of Wustrow, twenty-five miles west of Rostock.

The attack marked the biggest around-the-clock aerial assaults yet made by the American-British bombing teams. The raid on Warnemuende, seaport for the big manufacturing center of Rostock, was the deepest penetration of Germany yet made by the United States Eighth Air Force.

The RAF's night bombers in fifty blazing minutes blasted Hamburg with 2,300 tons of explosive and incendiary bombs, a far greater weight of bombs than ever before had been dropped in a single operation. [The British Air Ministry gives its figures in tons of 2,240 pounds; at 2,000 pounds to the ton, the RAF blasted Hamburg with 2,576 tons of bombs.]

RAF heavy bombers returned to the

assault on Germany during last night, British officials reported early today. Channel coast watchers reported that a ninety-minute procession of heavy bombers flew out of Britain toward occupied Europe just after midnight.

Large formations of American Flying Fortresses staged the follow-up daylight raid on Hamburg, raining hundreds of 500-pound bombs in mid-afternoon through great clouds of smoke rising thousands of feet from the fires started by the RAF armada.

Nazi fighters swarmed up to attack the American raiders before they completed their crossing of the North Sea en route to the targets, and German ground batteries in every town on their route threw up barrages of anti-aircraft fire and smoke screens.

Returning American crewmen reported that as many as 300 Nazi fighters intercepted their formations as the German defenders, apparently angered and shaken by the fury of the RAF's Saturday night attack, strove desperately to prevent further damage to the vital port of Hamburg.

HAMBURG RAIDS COORDINATED

Brig. Gen. Frederick L. Anderson, chief of the Eighth Air Force Bomber Command, described the day's operations as the biggest ever undertaken by the American bombing fleets. The Hamburg assault, he said, was "coordination with the RAF, both in the planning and execution."

The four-pronged American heavy bomber raids were made at a cost of nineteen planes missing. The RAF over Saturday night, operating in what the Air Ministry called "very great strength" [an Associated Press account from London cited an estimate of ▸

{ 1,000 British planes used], lost twelve bombers. Paced by the Flying Fortresses' major raids, medium bombers of the Eighth Air Force and RAF bombers and fighters delivered many other blows at the Nazis in the occupied Low Countries and France.

The American medium bombers pounded factories near Ghent, Belgium, returning without loss. Escorted Mitchells of the RAF wrecked a Fokker aircraft factory at Amsterdam, while American Thunderbolts and Allied fighters swept over France and Belgium. Four Nazi fighters were destroyed.

Typhoon bombers attacked the enemy airfield at Woensdrecht, north of Antwerp. Boston bombers hit the Schipol airfield near Amsterdam.

FORTRESS GUNNERS DO JOB

The Flying Fortress gunners were credited with shooting down a "large number" of the Nazi fighters.

Official reports on the series of American heavy raids stated that bomb bursts were observed flush on the targets of Hamburg, Kiel, Warnemuende and Wurtow, with the weight of the American attack apparently centered on Hamburg.

In the Saturday night blow, far exceeding history's previous heaviest air attack, the RAF dropped an average of nearly fifty-two tons of explosives and incendiaries every minute on Hamburg harbor and its shipbuilding yards and vital industrial plants, smashing ground defenses and scattering them.

The Allied air offensive against the Nazis in Western Europe was in high gear again. It was resumed after eight days of bad weather when large formations of American Flying Fortresses attacked U-boat installations at Trondheim and an aluminum and magnesium plant at Heroya, Norway, by daylight Saturday.

The Air Ministry announced that the RAF's Hamburg assault began at 1 A.M. yesterday and soon afterward "dense black smoke rose four miles into the air and there were many reports of violent explosions."

Fierce, fast-spreading fires roared through the city, illuminating the inky sky with a brilliant yellow glow.

One flier, who had participated in the last seven raids on the Ruhr, said the Nazis, ground defenses at Hamburg were quickly swamped. The raid set a record for concentration as well as for weight. In attacks on Dortmund, Muenster, Bochum and Duesseldorf, the RAF had dropped 2,000 tons of bombs in a little more than an hour. ◊

Hamburg in ruins after being heavily bombed by the RAF in July, 1943.

JULY 26, 1943

PRESIDENT PLEDGES AID TO SAVE JEWS

President Roosevelt, in a message read last night to the Emergency Conference to Save the Jewish People of Europe, promised that this Government would not cease its efforts to save those who could be saved.

This message and another from Secretary of State Cordell Hull, with which the President concurred, were read at the closing session of the conference in the Hotel Commodore. Mr. Hull said the final defeat of Hitler and the rooting out of the Nazi system were the only complete answer to the problem of saving the 4,000,000 Jews in Europe.

Former President Herbert Hoover, speaking by telephone from San Francisco, suggested development of the uplands of Central Africa as refuges for the oppressed minorities of the Axis-dominated countries.

Mayor Fiorello H. La Guardia, at the afternoon session, urged the United States and its Allies to serve notice on the Axis that all persons responsible for the deaths of Jews or non-Jews would be tried for murder. Meanwhile there would be practical steps taken for re-settling those who desired to emigrate from Europe, he said.

THE PRESIDENT'S MESSAGE

The message from President Roosevelt, addressed to Dr. Max Lerner, read:

"In reply to your telegram of July 15, 1943, asking a message to the Emergency Conference to Save the Jewish People of Europe, I am glad to transmit a message from the Hon. Cordell Hull, Secretary of State, which has my full concurrence. You are aware of the interest of this Government in the terrible condition of the European Jews and of our repeated endeavors to save those who could be saved. These endeavors will not cease until Nazi power is forever crushed."

Mr. Hull's message read: "The rescue of the Jewish people, of course, and of other peoples likewise marked for slaughter by Nazi savagery, is under constant examination by the State Department, and any suggestion calculated to that end will be gladly considered. An inter governmental agency has been created designed to deal with these problems. You will readily realize that no measure is practicable unless it is consistent with the destruction of Nazi tyranny; and that the final defeat of Hitler and the rooting out of the Nazi system is the only complete answer. This Government in cooperation with the British Government has agreed upon those measures which have been found to be practicable under war conditions and steps are now being taken to put them into effect."

The messages were addressed to Dr. Lerner in his capacity as chairman of the panel on international relations.

GREAT PROBLEM, SAYS HOOVER

Mr. Hoover declared that to find relief for the Jews in Europe was one of the great human problems and that it required temporary and long-view measures.

"There should be more systematic temporary measures," he said. "There are groups of Jews who have escaped into the neutral countries of Europe. They and any other refugees from the persecution of fascism should be assured of support by the United Nations. This step should go further. Definite refugee stations should be arranged in these neutral countries for those who may escape. But these measures should be accompanied by arrangements to steadily transfer them from these refugee stations in neutral countries to other quarters. Possibly the release of greater numbers of refugees could be secured from the Nazi countries by European neutrals."

He said he had been urging for more than two years systematic food relief for the starving in the occupied countries. Referring to the aid given to Greece he asked: "Does not this experience warrant its extension to other occupied countries? It would save the lives of thousands of Jews."

THE LONG-RANGE VIEW

The long-view solution, he said, resolves itself into two phases—where to move these people so as to give them permanent security and how to establish them there.

"We must accept the fact that the older and more fully settled countries

have no longer any land and opportunity to absorb the migration of the oppressed," he said. "Most Jews recognize that it is not in their interest to force such an issue. Palestine could take more of them. But after all, Palestine would absorb only a part of the three or four millions whom this conference has been discussing as needing relief. That could be accomplished only by moving the Arab population to some other quarter. These are problems impossible to settle during the war.

"But I am one of those who do not believe in half measures. And I believe in realism in physical problems.

"The world today needs an outlet for the persecuted of all lands and all faiths, not Jew alone. There should be some place where they may build a new civilization, as they did on this continent during the last century. The newest continent, from the point of view of development, is Africa. It is as yet comparatively unsettled and underdeveloped.

"Particularly in the uplands of Central Africa. Large areas of this upland are suitable for a white civilization. They are rich in material resources. But if we are to make use of them, there must be vast preparation. Men, women and children today cannot be dumped into new lands. There must be definitely organized advance preparation of housing, transportation, industrial establishments and agriculture on a huge scale. Many of these great African areas are mandates established from the last war,

in trust for all the world. Such an area in Africa could be considered sentimentally an annex to Palestine.

"At least the time has arrived when we should demand that a real solution be found, and further that the United Nations undertake to finance and manage a real solution as part of the war. And that the enemy countries after the war be required to restore the property of these persecuted peoples and help financially their new settlements.

"After all, it is a great human problem that ranks with the other human problems we must meet as part of the reconstruction of the world."

MAYOR URGES UNITED STATES TO ACT

The Mayor, in proposing that the United Nations serve notice that those responsible for the slaughter of the Jews would be held strictly accountable, said:

"With regard to this action and other actions which might be taken, I have to point out that our own Government cannot urge other nations to take the initiative before it takes action of its own.

"I refer here also to plans of emigration and colonization which have been put forward. We cannot tell others to take in the doomed while we keep our own doors closed. While we consider emigration and colonization, however, we must realize that taking the Jews and other minorities out of terrorist-ruled lands is not really the solution. The rights of the Jews and other minorities must be made safe in every country

in the world. Therefore I can tell the Emergency Conference to Save the Jews of Europe that what it is striving for is an important part of what the United Nations are fighting for."

Francis B. MacMahon, Professor of Philosophy at the University of Notre Dame and president of the Catholic Association for International Peace, characterized the plight of the Jewish people in Europe under Hitler as "the most terrible single tragedy of the present war." "Passive acquiescence will make us moral participants in the crime of the Nazis," he said.

Professor MacMahon said that Pope Pius XII had sought in many ways to save the Jews and that the full story could not be told today about the action of the Vatican. "It will be revealed when Germany is conquered," he added.

Sigrid Undset, author, after denouncing anti-Semitism, said:

"It is the right of the Jewish nation to get the opportunity to defend itself in the future from a national stronghold, as an independent nation, in possession of all the organs of a national life of its own," she added.

The conference adopted resolutions regarding ways to rescue the Jews of Europe and post-war aid based on previous findings by its various panels. ◆

Chapter 16

"RUSSIA STILL ASKS FOR SECOND FRONT"

August–September 1943

The popular interest in the Italian campaign continued to dwarf all other news. American and British forces were winning there while news from the Russian Front and the Pacific was patchy and unclear. On August 17 the conquest of Sicily was over, though one-third of Axis forces managed to escape across the Straits of Messina before the Allied trap could be closed. There were around 20,000 Allied casualties while the Axis lost 160,000, most of them Italian soldiers only too willing to be captured. The Allies pursued what seemed to be a beaten enemy onto mainland Italy, their first steps on European soil. The new government in Rome, led by Marshal Pietro Badoglio, kept fighting out of fear of what the Germans might do if Italy surrendered. Within weeks of Mussolini's fall in late July, the number of German divisions in Italy increased from six to eighteen. Continuous bombing forced Badoglio's hand and on September 3 an armistice was signed.

Montgomery began to move his army to Calabria and on September 9, the day after the armistice was formally announced, General Mark Clark led a combined Anglo-American force to storm the beaches at Salerno, in the Bay of Naples. The landing was strongly opposed by a German Army now occupying its former ally's territory. Mussolini was rescued from prison by a unit of German commandos and an Italian social republic was declared at the northern Italian city of Salò, establishing what The Times called a "New Kind of Regime." The fight for Salerno was the toughest so far, but by September 20 the German counterattack had been repulsed. The German Army retreated to a line north of Naples, after first wrecking the port. The city was liberated on October 1.

The invasion of Italy, even more than the invasion of North Africa, posed complicated challenges for American diplomacy. "It was a test," wrote Times correspondent Harold Callender, "of our ability to comprehend as well as to liberate Europe." From Washington it was difficult to grasp European realities. The long arguments about whether to support de Gaulle or Giraud continued to take up column inches in The Times. On August 27 Roosevelt finally made a halfhearted gesture by agreeing to recognize the French Committee of National Liberation, dominated by de Gaulle, as representative of French overseas territory, but not as a potential government for France. The situation in Italy was also complex, since Badoglio was a former supporter of Fascism and the king, Victor Emanuel III, was widely unpopular. No commitments were made this time to the conquered regime, but with Rome still in German hands it was hard to come up with an alternative.

The Times took a strong stand on the need to ensure that America would play its part in restructuring world politics after the war. In an editorial on September 14 The Times reminded readers that "this time the United States intends to help enforce a world peace when it is won." This was easier said than done, and there was a long road ahead before peace could be certain. Stalin in Moscow repeated his demands for a second front in Europe to take the pressure off Russian armies. The Soviet leadership regarded the Italian campaign as a sideshow, as did many Americans. By this time the Red Army had consolidated its victory in the summer at Kursk and pushed the German Army back on every front. Smolensk was liberated on September 25 and bridgeheads were made over the Dnieper River toward the city of Kiev. On September 26 The Times ran another article by the famous Soviet correspondent, Ilya Ehrenburg, who had popularized the propaganda of hate against the Fascist enemy in 1942 and 1943. In "Hate Marches with the Red Army" Ehrenburg explained that a war like this "plows up men's souls."

AUGUST 2, 1943

PLOESTI SMASHED
300 Tons Rain On Major Gasoline Source of Reich Air Force

RAID MADE AT LOW LEVEL
Delayed-Action Bombs Enable 2,000 Fliers to Get Away, Leaving Great Fires

By A. C. SEDGWICK
By Cable to The New York Times.

CAIRO, Egypt, Aug. 1—A day-light air attack that "may materially affect the course of the war" smashed the oil refineries and dependent installations at Ploesti, Rumania, where fully one-third of the Axis' petroleum supplies for use in aircraft, tanks, transport vehicles, submarines and surface hips is believed to originate.

[The area produces 90 per cent of the German Air Force's gasoline, according to The United Press. The distance flown by its attackers was believed to have set a record for aerial warfare.]

The raiders, numbering more than 175, were all Liberators of the Ninth United States Air Force. The 2,000 men in their crews had been trained especially for this all-important mission and the machines were equipped with special low-altitude bomb-sights.

300 TONS OF BOMBS DROPPED

The planes were over their target at about 3 P.M. today. They remained not more than a minute and then were off, having dropped their great load of bombs with what, judging by first reports, seemed to have been highly satisfactory results. The pilots reported that, according to every indication, many fires and explosions had been caused. In all, some 300 tons of high-explosive bombs, mostly of the delayed-action type, were dropped. Clusters of incendiaries by the hundreds were also dropped, all from altitudes of less than 500 feet.

Brig. Gen. U. G. Ent led the formations. His plane was among the first to return. All the aircraft had been expected about an hour earlier and there had been a period of the greatest tension. Lieut. Gen. Lewis H. Brereton, American Commander in the Middle East, was among the anxious crowd. He was the first to welcome General Ent and to hear reports from a number of officers.

Col. Keith Cropton said "We got them completely by surprise." Capt. Harold A. Wickland, who also took part in the recent Rome raid, said: "I saw a lot of smoke and we did some damage, but it all happened so quickly I don't know what it was we hit." Many others gave testimony that tended to show the general impression that widespread damage had been done.

RUMANIANS SEEM FRIENDLY

Particularly interesting at this time was the testimony of several of the air crews. They said that the Rumanian peasantry had shown the greatest friendliness. Rumanian girls were said to have waved "a great welcome." A Rumanian soldier, gun on shoulder, was described as completely unconcerned.

It was said at Ninth Air Force headquarters that months of planning and preparation had gone into this attack on Ploesti. Not only military specialists but authorities on oil refining were consulted.

It was explained that, for several reasons, no large-scale bombing of the Ploesti refineries had been attempted before. The nature of the target makes it particularly invulnerable to attack by small formations.

There were too few long-range heavy bombers based within striking distance of Ploesti. The distance to the target from any Allied airdromes rendered it impossible to attack with large forces of medium bombers.

As soon as it appeared feasible to the Allied commanders to destroy Ploesti, a plan for doing so was formulated and its execution fell to General Brereton, the first commander of heavy bombers in the United States Army Air Forces to see action in this war. General Brereton supervised all phases of training and practice for the raid.

Repeated high-level attacks on Ploesti would undoubtedly have accomplished its destruction, but such a process would have meant heavy losses to the attacking force. It would also have enabled the enemy to protect his installations.

Oil storage tanks at the Columbia Aquila refinery in Ploesti, Rumania burning after the raid of American B-24 Liberator bombers, 1943.

EXTREMELY VITAL TARGET

The city of Ploesti, with its adjoining oil fields, refineries and transportation facilities, is generally conceded to be one of the most vital targets in Europe. Perhaps as much as half the entire German war machine would be halted if it were obliterated.

In 1911 the Russians realized its importance but were unable, in two raids, to do more than a modicum of damage. In June, 1942, a small force of

Ninth Air Force Liberators attacked but had little success, largely because of foul weather.

Ploesti and its vicinity have thirteen refineries, seven of which are said to produce almost 90 per cent of all Rumania's oil. The rest are all small and some are obsolescent. The Ploesti refineries can produce annually approximately 11,500,000 tons, but, since the German occupation, the flow of crude oil from the ground has dropped to a point at

which it can supply scarcely more than half the capacity of the refineries.

Nevertheless, it is estimated that the Ploesti area still supplies at least 35 per cent of Germany's petroleum demands, including, besides aviation fuel, ordinary gasoline for motor transport and lubrication and Diesel oils. Including its refineries and pump stations, which encircle the city, the Ploesti area approximates nineteen square miles. Most of it is an enormous rail ganglion. ◇

AUGUST 4, 1943

AXIS POSITION IN SICILY GROWS MORE PERILOUS
Americans Sweep Past Troina— Canadians Take Regalbuto

EIGHTH ARMY FLANK GAINS
Catania Now Faces Multiple Drive as Ships and Planes Help Land Advance

By MILTON BRACKER
By Wireless to The New York Times.

ALLIED HEADQUARTERS, NORTH AFRICA, Aug. 3—Converging inexorably on Mount Etna and northeastern Sicily, the Allied forces have battered down increasingly stubborn opposition to capture Regalbuto, Centuripe and Troina.

While the Canadians smashed their way into Regalbuto and the British Seventy-eighth Division took Centuripe, the Americans continued eastward from the Nicosia-Mistretta road line to sweep

beyond Troina, the last German bastion directly west of the inner ring around Mount Etna. With the offensive mounting in power and the bases ahead, as well as ports in Italy, undergoing constant aerial pounding, the Allies now appear to be thrusting out one steel prong north of Mount Etna, possibly by way of Randazzo, while the other cuts its way forward toward Catania.

[Some American units are reported to be less than twenty miles from Ran-

dazzo, the British radio said, according to the Columbia Broadcasting System.]

MULTIPLE DRIVE ON CATANIA

The drive against Catania is a multiple offensive in itself. British Eighth Army artillery is hammering the German positions along the coast, while the captors of Regalbuto and Centuripe clearly menace the city from the rear, via Paterno. Within twenty miles of Regalbuto and fifteen miles of Centuripe, Paterno would be the last obstacle confronting the Army sweeping down on Catania from the northwest. Besides Paterno, the Allies threaten Adrano, from which Catania could be cut off or reached via Biancavilla and Belpasso.

[The Allies were within six miles of Adrano, The United Press said.] The advance has averaged about ten miles on a broad front. The situation is bound to be uncomfortable for the reformed Hermann Goering Division and the German paratroopers around Catania. To the right of the British Seventy-eighth Division—veterans of the entry into Tunis—the Fifty-first Highland Division is forging its way ahead against opposition that includes the Twenty-sixth Italian Division—apparently the only major Italian unit still battling for Sicily—and the German Fifteenth Armored Division.

TWO NORTHERN TOWNS TAKEN

In the north, the Americans' success around Troina was preceded two days ago by the capture of Capizzi and Cerami. The fall of the two towns had previously ⟩

American advances that overran Capizzi (1) and, to the southeast, Cerami and Troina (2) threatened to throw a ring around the enemy's Mount Etna positions. These positions sixere further jeopardized when the Canadians broke through to Regalbuto (3) and units and units of the British Eight Army smashed forward to Catenanuova and Centuripe (4). In addition, British troops above Rammacca entered the western end of the Catania Plain (5) and kept up their pressure near the city of Catania itself (6) with heavy Eighth army artillery bombardments.

been announced, but their names were made public only today. The Americans have been progressing against the German Twenty-ninth Motorized Division.

[The Germans were trying to establish a temporary anchor at San Fratello, The Associated Press said, but the occupation of the Troina area would make San Fratello strategically untenable.

[Off both the north and east coasts, The Associated Press added, warships continually swept behind the enemy front to batter rear communications and troop movements.] The Axis troops face the weight of extensive Allied reinforcements brought up during the period of apparent inactivity before the opening of the great new drive on Sunday. Although the enemy resistance has continued to stiffen as the means of escape narrows, the Germans in particular have paid a heavy toll.

But the Allies have recently had to fight over some of the most difficult terrain imaginable. Guns and tanks have been doing their share, but basically it has been an infantry job.

Before the announcement of the fall of Regalbuto, Centuripe and Troina, the communiqué issued here filled in the details of previous operations. The advance on the plain of Catania continued generally north and northeast from Rammacca and Raddusa. These towns formed the lower corners of an irregular oblong, with Regalbuto and Paterno at its upper ends.

At the same time a substantial bridgehead was established north of the Dittaino River in the vicinity of a captured town that has not been identified. After a laborious advance through rocky country other British and Canadian troops gained positions overlooking Agira, west of Regalbuto, and now plainly behind the lines. [The Eighth Army has captured Catenanuova, Reuter reported.]

PLANES COOPERATE CLOSELY

Operating with the ground forces, Bostons, Mitchells and Baltimores of the Northwest African Air Forces concentrated on Adrano, Randazzo, Milazzo and Messina in Sicily and on Reggio Calabria in Italy. Fighters cotinued their sweeps and patrols over the island.

In other operations, Beaufighters strafed a destroyer and three motor torpedo boats off Cagliari, Sardinia. Lightnings shot down three enemy aircraft and damaged two while assisting flying boats in an air-sea rescue.

Naples was attacked for the second successive night. ["Block-busters" and incendiaries were dropped in railway areas, The Associated Press said.] During all these operations, seven Allied craft were lost. ◇

FLAME THROWERS DECISIVE
Account for Many Pillboxes In Final Drive on Munda

By GEORGE JONES
United Press Staff Correspondent.

MUNDA AIRPORT, New Georgia Island, Aug. 3 (Delayed)—The battle for Munda airfield virtually ended today, except for mopping up, when sweat-stained American jungle troops poured onto this strategic airstrip, an objective toward which they had struggled yard by yard for thirty-five days.

For the past three days the Japanese defenses have cracked wide open. It is believed now that they began evacuating high-ranking officers and some troops by destroyer to Kolombangara Island to the northeast several days ago, leaving a rear guard to protect the evacuation.

These battered Japanese were instructed to "fight to the death" for their Emperor. They are still hurling a weak challenge from Kokengolo Hill extending from the airport in a northwesterly direction.

American artillery, which has tormented the Japanese since the start of the campaign, poured hundreds of shells on this position in preparation for the final extermination of the enemy remnants.

Other American troops moved north, attempting to cut off the would-be evacuees. Small craft last night sank a small Japanese ship in narrow Blackett Strait and damaged two barges in early stages of the Japanese flight from New Georgia.

The writer has just visited the airport, where he surveyed the ravaged face of Munda. Americans and Japanese were exchanging mortar and rifle fire across the western edge of the airstrip. Half a dozen enemy Zeros and Mitsubishi two-motored bombers were scattered about the revetments. Souvenir hunters already had started stripping them.

The United States forces were now inside the airport at the eastern edge and along the field on the east and south boundaries. These troops advanced 2,000 yards on Aug. 1 and 2 past battle-scarred Lambeti plantation, along the coast, while in the interior our forces were temporarily held back in their southward advance by remaining Japanese resistance.

The Americans encountered little opposition during the last three days of the advance.

The Japanese evidently were demoralized by the continued artillery and aerial assaults. They left huge stores of rice, damaged field pieces, clothing and blankets.

The Americans easily took the dominating Bibilo Hill, 400 yards northeast of the airport, where it had been anticipated the Japanese would attempt to block our entrance into Munda.

Instead, enemy remnants retreated farther westward behind Kokengolo Hill, where they proved unable to halt our coastal advance into the airport.

TWENTY YARDS FROM THE GOAL

Last night we were twenty yards from our goal. With mortars and one or two 77mm. dual-purpose field pieces of the type fondly called "Pistol Petes," American artillery was instructed to shell the Japanese.

A few minutes later smoke bombs were dropped on enemy positions. Batteries then began to lay in salvo after salvo of explosives. The barrage lasted all morning.

Pistol Pete was silent this afternoon, his work done.

The airport was in reasonably good shape considering the continuous shellacking it had taken since last December. It shouldn't be long before the airport is being used by American planes.

This correspondent has examined pillboxes in which the Japanese chose to die rather than surrender. Some were eight feet deep, reinforced with coral and divided into compartments by thick coconut logs. They dotted the hillsides and hilltops.

Only a direct hit could destroy such defenses. Blanket artillery fire and bombings often destroyed the personnel, but the Japanese either replaced casualties or left one machine gunner in each pillbox.

It was in the latter stages of the campaign that we found the answer: flame throwers, which poured in streams of fire and fumes through the apertures of the pillboxes from fifty feet. Flame throwers were credited with destroying thirty-three pillboxes in the past seven days. ◇

AUGUST 8, 1943

Rome Seeks Open City Role; Hitler's Demands Presented

By DANIEL T. BRIGHAM
By Telephone to The New York Times.

BERNE, Switzerland, Aug. 7—The Italian Government has begun preliminary operations connected with the declaration of Rome as an open city. The Premier, Marshal Pietro Badoglio, according to travelers from Italy, is taking this measure to prevent Rome from suffering the fate of Warsaw, Rotterdam and Belgrade should Italy become a battlefield.

In this connection the key ministries of defense—War, Navy and Air—have already been removed to other points, while the evacuation of military stores from the capital area is being speeded.

Meanwhile, Italian-German conversations between the Foreign Ministers, Joachim von Ribbentrop for Germany and Raffaele Guariglia for Italy, in Verona, took a new turn late this afternoon when Field Marshal Gen. Wilhelm Keitel, accompanied by many technical experts, arrived by plane from Vienna with Adolf Hitler's demands for an immediate clarification of the Italian position.

Gen. Vittorio Ambrosio, chief of the Italian General Staff, arrived in Verona last night on the Germans' invitation to sit in on "important discussions," which got under way immediately.

While these discussions were extending their scope, the government in Rome demonstrated its internal policy of "pacification" by decreeing a state of war throughout the peninsula, a measure hitherto applied only to the coastline and the Northern Provinces. Believed to be a measure with which to impress the Allies and the Axis, the new move indirectly stiffens the regulation of the martial law decree following the downfall of Benito Mussolini.

Under a state of war decree any civilian "resisting or obstructing the public authority in the performance of its duty" is liable to the death penalty for treason. The Government, therefore, has put teeth into its threats against those who continue in their peace manifestations and strikes throughout the industrial north.

Effective from midnight tonight the new decree comes into force exactly three days before the scheduled completion of the mobilization of all classes born between 1907 and 1922. Both of these measures, the Rome radio said, will "prevent any surprise developments from any quarter that might hinder the Government in its action of conducting the war to an honorable conclusion." ◊

AUGUST 8, 1943

HARLEM UNREST TRACED TO LONG-STANDING ILLS
Basic Racial Problem Seen Sharpened By New Complaints Born of War

By RUSSELL B. PORTER

Last week's riot in Harlem, with its toll of five dead, 500 injured, 500 arrested, and an estimated $85,000,000 in property damage, was a social explosion in a powder keg that has been years in the offing.

The Harlem problem is a racial one, rooted in the Negro's dissatisfaction with his racial status not only in Harlem but all over the country, and exhibited in his efforts, sometimes intelligent and moderate, sometimes blind and extreme, to break down the economic and social discriminations, barriers and frustrations which at times seem unbearable.

In Harlem and other Negro districts where all told 500,000 persons live, there is no question that an ugly mood has existed for some years, especially among the younger Negroes. This condition is not peculiar to New York. As all reports make clear, it is a reflection of a nation-

The cleanup after the Harlem riots of 1943.

wide attitude—a feeling of resentment and bitterness which came to a head in the depression years and has been nourished by a variety of old and new grievances, many of them real, some fancied or exaggerated, but all being exploited by pressure groups and subversive, antidemocratic elements.

LONG-STANDING COMPLAINTS

The tinderbox of Harlem was started many years ago when Negro segrega- tion and overcrowding gradually transformed much of that historic community into a slum area—a "black ghetto." These conditions were terribly aggravated in the depression years. Negroes were among the first to lose their jobs. Poverty, misery and crime increased rapidly. Later, when New York became known all over the country for its relief system, new waves of immigrants began arriving from the South, and Harlem became more overcrowded than ever. ❯

The start of the war in Europe brought new problems and accentuated old ones in Harlem. Since Pearl Harbor the principal cause of unrest in Harlem and other Negro communities has been complaint of discrimination and Jim Crow treatment of Negroes in the armed forces, according to responsible Negro leaders. Visits and letters from Negro soldiers and articles in the Negro press keep Harlem continually reminded of the tension in Southern States where Negro troops are stationed.

WAR JOBS A FACTOR

Closely linked to the status of the Negro in the armed services in breeding resentment is that of his status as a worker, particularly in war plants. Not until labor shortages began to threaten war production, Negro leaders say, could Negro workers break down the reluctance of many employers and labor unions to give them jobs in any large number. Even now, they charge, the Negro worker has to contend with many subtle discriminations, especially in upgrading for better jobs.

Students of the problem agree that the most important long-range factor is that of employment, for the refusal to give work to Negroes, or their confinement to menial, low-paid jobs regardless of merit, not only breaks down morale and increases disillusionment but also aggravates the other basic causes to which Negro leaders attribute trouble in Harlem—bad housing conditions, inadequate educational and recreational facilities, substandard health and hospital service, and crime and delinquency.

Much has been done and is being done to improve the situation. After the 1935 riot, the Mayor's Commission on Conditions in Harlem made a report which was critical of certain aspects of the way the problem had been handled. Although the report was never released, the Mayor has put many of its recommendations into effect. There has been improvement in police methods, housing, health, educational and recreational services. Steps taken against discrimination in civil service examinations have brought more Negroes into the city departments.

OTHER CORRECTIVE STEPS

The City-Wide Citizens' Committee on Harlem, organized in 1941 with outstanding white and Negro leaders among its officers and directors, has succeeded through cooperation with city officials and private employers, in persuading some large department stores, insurance companies and public utilities to employ Negroes in larger numbers and in better jobs than ever before.

One of the outstanding Negro leaders of the community, Lester B. Granger, executive secretary of the National Urban League, is convinced that much more could be done if there were better leadership among both the whites and Negroes who are actively interested in the problem. He thinks the Negro leadership should return to the more moderate hands in which it was held before 1934 and 1935, when Communists and other extremist advocates of "mass pressure" took over, and that the white leadership should include more practical business men and labor leaders and fewer sentimentalists, professional liberals and the like. ◆

AUGUST 11, 1943

RUSSIA STILL ASKS FOR SECOND FRONT
Sicilian Campaign Considered Fine But Not a Substitute for Major Operation

PESSIMISM IS APPARENT
Many Believe Allies Have the Power To Open Big Drive, Yet Are Not Willing To Do So

By Wireless to The New York Times.

MOSCOW, Aug. 10—The Russian people do not dispute that the campaign in Sicily is a grand show, but they consider it a small show compared to the military power represented by the combined British Empire and the United States.

It was with some bitterness that a Russian friend said to the writer:

"Of course, our troops would have preferred to take a well-deserved rest after winning the two colossal battles of the Kursk salient and Orel."

Then he added: "If they are still going ahead, perhaps it is because our high command no longer believes in the early opening of a second front, and we want the war to end soon, anyway. But it would be infinitely easier if a second front were there. Then we really could cut like a knife through butter.

"Today, in addition to the bulk of their land forces, the Germans have every available bomber on this front, That's why Goebbels had to apologize to the Germans for the German Government's inability to retaliate against the Allied bombings of Hamburg and the Ruhr, and so on."

That attitude is fairly typical of the general mood, and it is reflected also in the press. With unconcealed bitterness, Ilya Ehrenburg wrote the other day:

"How soon will the British and Americans move from Italian psychology to the German fortifications?"

There is also some suspicion that, whereas the Allied argument last year that they could not open a large-scale second front was more than plausible, now the Allies "can, but don't want to." There also is a tendency to disbelieve the view that the French coastline is impregnable. If we broke through the Orel defenses, why can't you break through the Atlantic wall? is the attitude. ◆

QUEBEC PLANS LAID FOR RUTHLESS WAR
Military Decisions Covering Germany and Japan Stress Increased Aggressiveness

By P. J. PHILIP
Special to The New York Times.

QUEBEC, Aug. 16—Until today the Quebec conference has been engaged mainly with the gigantic military and joint operational measures that must and can be taken at this stage toward winning the wars in Europe and the Pacific. All accounts from inside the Chateau Frontenac, where the general staffs have been at work, are that by intense application and goodwill on every side the problems entailed have been largely solved.

The plans for attack and the invasion of enemy and enemy-occupied territory in every war zone have been studied from every angle and a blueprint of the course of the war during the next months—and years, if necessary—has been prepared.

What these plans are will, of course, only become known when they are set in motion. The one thing that can be said about them is that they have been made in a ruthlessly aggressive spirit. What is being sought is the defeat of the enemy in all war zones in the shortest possible time. To that end it is certain that every one of the United Nations will be called upon to fight harder and work harder.

In the discussions of the Chiefs of Staff there have been, of course, no questions of politics. Their job was to plan how to win the war in the shortest time.

POLITICAL ISSUES TO THE FORE

This week the second task of trying to solve the political questions that attach to the military problems must be tackled. A beginning has undoubtedly been made already in the conversations at Hyde Park between President Roosevelt and Prime Minister Churchill to which W. L. Mackenzie King, Canadian Prime Minister, also added his quota of council. Before the conference here ends it is expected that Anthony Eden, British Foreign Secretary, will arrive from London,

Like their military chiefs, the political heads of the governments assembled here will have to face their problems re-alistically. Prejudices and even past policies, it is said, may have to be set aside if sound solutions are to be reached.

The foremost of these problems is how to treat the Italian Government and people. It is now clear that the action of King Victor Emmanuel and Marshal Pietro Badoglio in getting rid of Benito Mussolini and trying to break the fascist regime came too soon. Perhaps some will say that the Allies were not quick enough and powerful enough to take advantage of it.

The German resistance in Sicily has succeeded in gaining time for the application in large part of the plan to which Mussolini gave his assent and to which the King refused his. For all practical purposes the Italian King is as much a prisoner of the Nazis as King Leopold of the Belgians, and the Badoglio government is powerless.

This is a problem that obviously calls for a combination of firm and delicate treatment.

Next, in order of public interest at least, is the question of the recognition of the French National Liberation Committee as the provisional government of France. Here in Quebec and throughout Canada feeling runs high on this issue, with opinion strongly in favor of immediate recognition as a proof on the part of the Anglo-Saxon powers of their intention to respect their past promises with regard to the entire sovereignty of France and incidentally of all those nations which have been occupied by the enemy.

SUSPICIONS OF IMPERIALISM

It may be said that the publicity given to "AMGOT" has created a suspicion here as well as among some of the governments in exile that the post-war policies of the Anglo-Saxon governments have a flavor of Imperialism that is considered both unwelcome and unbecoming in Allies fighting for the preservation of international as well as national democracy. The third problem on which there is a public demand for clarification is that of the relationship between the Government of the Soviet Union and the other governments engaged in the war.

All these questions of the policy to be followed with regard to Italy, to the French Liberation Committee, to the various governments in exile, and to Russia's attempts at independent political action are regarded by many here as so closely interlocked that a solution for all of them can be best found in the formulation of a clear statement of joint policy by the governments which are and will be represented here. ◇

CHINA COMMUNISTS FIRM IN DEMANDS
But Chungking Refuses to Give Approval to the Party Or to the Organization's Armies

CIVIL WAR SEEN UNLIKELY
Some in Government Believe Differences Can Be Removed By Compromises

By BROOKS ATKINSON
By Wireless to The New York Times.

CHUNGKING, China, Aug. 16—No change is expected in the relations between the central government of China and the Chinese Communists, at least for the present. Although relations are strained, as they have been for years, they seem not to be any better or worse and both sides have many reasons for wanting to avoid violence.

When Gen. Chou En-lai, unofficial liaison officer between the Communists and the central government, started for Yenan, the communist capital, about two months ago with the consent of the central government, many persons hoped that he was carrying information or at least a point of view that would result in a settlement or hold out the promise of a settlement. But by the time he arrived at Sian, the situation had begun to deteriorate.

Now a war of words is going on. From Communist-controlled areas in Shansi and Shensi come bulletins accusing the central government of inefficiency in the war against the Japanese and of preparing to dissolve the Communist party by force. Newspapers in the rest of free China print petitions to Mao Tse-tung and Chu Teh to dissolve the Communist party and turn over the Communist armies to the control of ❯

❨ the central government in the interests of a completely united China.

CENTRAL GOVERNMENT'S VIEW

For several years no journalist has been to the region where the Communists are in control so there is no disinterested information on what is going on there but it is easy to discover what the point of view of the central government is. The Ministers and political leaders interviewed in recent weeks agree on one point: There will be no civil war unless the Communists start it.

The Communist representatives here have political and military reasons against civil war. Despite reports of occasional skirmishes all is quiet in the border region with no fundamental change in the political and military situations.

The People's Political Council and the central executive committee of the Kuomintang, the Government party, are scheduled to meet soon and it will be interesting to see whether they arrive at a decision respecting the Communists.

The differences between the central government and the Communist party are fundamental. The central government cannot tolerate one section of the country that has its own government, army and currency and collects its own taxes. As long as the Communist party remains outside the law of the central government it cannot be recognized as a legal party.

The Communist party asks nothing except recognition as a political party.

But it is unwilling to give up its military force on the speculation that the Government and the Kuomintang will accept it as a legal party. It also distrusts certain aspects of the Government.

BOTH LACK UNDERSTANDING

Apart from these fundamental differences, there is a fundamental lack of understanding on both sides which possibly is more serious than the chief points at issue. The minor accusations are bitter.

Some members of the Kuomintang and of the Government think the differences can be resolved by a series of compromises. Since it would be to everyone's advantage to remove this flaw in national unity, they believe in compromises without violence.

Although the Communist party is not recognized in law, it is recognized in fact. There are seven Communist members of the People's Political Council. The Chungking Communist party publishes a daily newspaper that can be bought on the street.

To a foreigner who enjoys the paradoxes of Chinese life the only entertaining aspect of the current situation is the presence of Communist headquarters in the former dormitory of the Executive Yuan. On the second floor still live some high officials of the Executive Yuan and near by is the youth hostel of the central government's political training department. ◊

AUGUST 21, 1943

NAZI SECRET WEAPON DUE
Goebbels Tells Germans It May Halt Allied Raids

LONDON, Aug. 20 (AP)—Dr. Joseph Goebbels, Adolf Hitler's propaganda chief, told the German people today a new secret weapon might soon give them relief from Allied air raids.

"The new weapon against the aerial war imposed upon us by the enemy is under construction," he wrote in his article in the propaganda publication Reich. "Day and night innumerable busy hands are engaged in its completion."

The text was broadcast by the German radio and recorded by The Associated Press. ◊

AUGUST 22, 1943

Cold, Fog, Mud-Life In the Aleutians

By Foster Hailey

LIFE in the Aleutians in the good old summertime is like this: You crawl out from under the blankets about 7:15— that is, if you want breakfast—hurriedly pull on your heavy underwear, G.I. trousers and close the ventilators. Then you take the rest of your clothes and go into the front room—shut off from the sleeping quarters by a cardboard partition— and complete your dressing there by the little Diesel stove. If you're finicky about such things you then grab your towel and a bar of soap and head for the washroom, a block away. Careful of that slope there, because the mud is like grease and you're liable to end up in a slit trench or on top of the quonset at the foot of the slope.

The washroom is warm and steamy from the heat of the Diesel water-heater and the hot water running from ten faucets at which twenty or thirty men are trying to brush their teeth or wash their faces at the same time. You take your turn in line and then gallop back to your

American soldiers trudge through muddy ground near the American base at Attu in the Aleutian Islands, Alaska, 1943.

quonset to brush your hair and slip on a fur-lined flight jacket or parka.

By this time the sun may be shining, or more probably not shining One thing the sun never does is rise. It just starts coming through the mist or a hole in the clouds, some time during the morning. It never sets, either. There always seems to be fog or clouds in the way. Down south you get so you hate the sight of the sun, a brassy furnace mouth that sears your eyeballs. Up here when it shines you open the door and haul a chair to the lee of a building and bask in it.

The trip to the mess hall, a quarter of a mile away, is a wandering course around mud puddles or through them, if they can't be avoided. A loblolly of yellow mud six inches thick spreads over the main road. You catch a break in the line of trucks and jeeps and ambulances and dash across. The Lord help you if a truck catches you within twenty feet of the road. You will be spattered from head to foot as it passes.

You pay your 30 cents at the window as you enter the transient Navy mess (luncheon is 40 cents and dinner 50 cents) and sit down on a bench to a breakfast of canned fruit juice, a dish of peaches or apricots or figs, dry cereal with powdered milk (which tastes like chalk, incidentally), eggs and bacon or French toast or hot cakes and coffee. There is plenty of butter and you can have three or four cups of coffee if you like. Luncheon and dinner are in proportion, with fresh salads and dessert and a soup at night. There are no napkins, but, then, what are trouser legs for?

If you are in the Navy or Army you go to work at the change of the watch at 8 o'clock; or, if you have been on duty during the night you go to your quonset and go to bed. If you are a newspaper man you go back to your hut, called the "Press Club" and match quarters for the jeep the Army has furnished and start the rounds of Fighter Command, Bomber Command, Air Force, Island Command, Navy Headquarters; or perhaps you catch the crash boat for a ride out to some ship that has been bombarding Kiska or is just back from the States or Attu.

If there has been a promise of a clear day you won't have needed an alarm clock. The planes will have been taking off at daylight, seeming almost to scrape the ventilators off the roof of your quonset as they roar over, fighting for altitude to clear the encircling, snow-covered hills.

A visit to the area where Vice Admiral T. C. Kinkaid and Lieut Gen. Simon Bolivar Buckner have their headquarters involves a round of dog patting. General Buckner and Maj. Gen. W. O. Butler, commanding general of the Eleventh Air Force, both have springer spaniel pups. Lieut Col. W. J. Verbeck, General Buckner's intelligence officer, has a magnificent big Irish setter and also is taking care of a retriever for a fellow-officer who is in the hospital. There are many other dogs around the base.

For the men assigned to the base it is a not too uncomfortable life. The temperature generally is in the forties or fifties and everyone has a sufficiency of foul-weather clothing, heavy underwear, wool shirts and trousers, boots, woolen hose, slickers, waterproofed parkas and fur-lined jackets.

The weather is not too bad and probably would go unnoticed in San Francisco. It is the lack of paved roads and sidewalks amid the mud, the long treks to the washroom or the mess hall in the rain that makes it so disagreeable at times. And the lack of sun makes you sympathize with Oscar Wilde's feeling in "The Ballad of Reading Gaol" when he spoke of "that bit of blue that prisoners call the sky." A rift in the clouds with the blue sky showing through has everyone pointing and looking and enjoying it

The fliers are really the only ones who see the sun with any regularity. They have a bad time taking off and landing, but once they get "upstairs"—and it often is not far—they have the sun and blue sky above them and below the blanket of fog, white as snow, with the volcanic peaks of the Islands poking through it.

All this, of course, of just one base, but I am told it is very similar all the way along the Aleutian chain. The weather here is not to be confused with that in Alaska, where it is much warmer in the summer and colder in the winter, but where the sun shines more frequently and there are trees and frequent evidences of civilization.

This description of life at this base does not cover, either, the life of the infantry. Nobody loves them. All they do is fight. They bivouac out in the hills, miles from the PX's and theatres, or on the lonely beaches. They eat from field kitchens and sleep, a lot of the time, in pup tents and on the ground. Occasionally they march in to take a bath or see a movie or go to church, but the buses don't run to their camp and getting a ride back home often is a difficult assignment. As a result they seldom come to "town," as the main Army and Navy camps are called.

Does anyone like it? Of course they don't. But the great majority of them recognize that it is something that has to be done and they want to get along with the doing. Their chief complaint is that it seems to take so long.

I overheard a conversation the other day that seemed to cover the majority attitude. It was two Navy chief petty officers talking. One apparently had just got his orders for some other base or ship.

"Wish you were going back to the States, Joe?" the other asked him.

"No," he said, "as long as this war is going on I would rather be out here helping fight it. When I go back I want to go back to stay." ◆

AUGUST 27, 1943

The Roosevelt Statement

WASHINGTON, Aug. 26 (UP)—The text of President Roosevelt's statement on United States recognition of the French Committee of National Liberation:

The Government of the United States desires again to make clear its purpose of cooperating with all patriotic Frenchmen, looking to the liberation of the French people and French territories from the oppressions of the enemy.

The Government of the United States, accordingly, welcomes the establishment of the French Committee of National Liberation. It is our expectation that the committee will function on the principle of collective responsibility of all its members for the active prosecution of the war.

In view of the paramount importance of the common war effort, the relationship with the French Committee of National Liberation must continue to be subject to the military requirements of the Allied commanders.

The Government of the United States takes note, with sympathy, of the desire of the committee to be regarded as the body qualified to ensure the administration and defense of French interests. The extent to which it may be possible to give effect to this desire must, however, be reserved for consideration in each case as it arises.

LIMITED RECOGNITION

On these understandings the Government of the United States recognizes the French Committee of National Liberation as administering those French overseas territories which acknowledge its authority.

This statement does not constitute recognition of a government of ▶

France or of the French Empire by the Government of the United States. It does constitute recognition of the French Committee of National Liberation as functioning within specific limitations during the war. Later on the people of France, in a free and untrammeled manner, will proceed in due course to select their own government and their own officials to administer it.

The Government of the United States welcomes the committee's expressed determination to continue the common struggle in close cooperation with all the Allies until French soil is freed from its invaders and until victory is complete over all enemy powers.

May the restoration of France come with the utmost speed. ◆

SEPTEMBER 5, 1943

BADOGLIO POLICY MAKES ITALY A BATTLEGROUND
Country Is Invaded After Mussolini's Successor Tries to Carry On War as Partner of Nazi Germany

BIGGER ORDEAL IS ON THE WAY

By EDWIN L. JAMES

If ever anyone asked for it, Badoglio did. When Mussolini, the bombastic partner of Hitler, went into the limbo as the United Nations were cleaning up in Sicily, the way was open to Italy for the best sort of peace she could get. Badoglio passed up the chance. Whether or not the presence of German troops in Italy influenced his decision is beside the point from a military point of view. He declared he would fight on against the Allies.

Surely Badoglio knew that the Italian Army could not save his country from defeat. It was apparent that he was counting on German help, and the truth is that he had the evidence of the presence of the Nazis all around him. But that did not change the basic fact that he did not make peace and elected to fight

Now Italy proper has been invaded. And that is but the beginning. It is perfectly plain that Italy is fighting Germany's war. Hitler has evidently decided to make a battleground of Italy. There he intends to fight a delaying battle against the advancing Allied armies. It is too early to tell to what degree the Italian troops will fight a last-ditch battle, but it is not too soon to say that the battle in Italy is primarily a German battle. Italy has nothing to gain from it; tactically, Germany has a good deal to gain. If she could make the Americans and British fight their way all along from the toe of the Italian boot to the Alps she would perhaps have

Marshal Pietro Badoglio in 1943.

gained months of delay in any other big attack against her "European Fortress." Italy is being a sucker for the Nazis.

MISSING A PEACE CHANCE

As the Allies invade Italy proper there is still talk from Italian sources of a "reasonable" peace. These statements are always linked to the statement that the United Nations' demand for unconditional surrender is impossible because it would be undignified for Italy to accept such terms. Looking over the various emanations from Rome on the subject of peace one finds the idea that the Allies should agree not to occupy Italian soil if Italy should surrender. The Allies could not listen to such a proposition because they intend to use Italian soil and port facilities for the war to beat Hitler. One may imagine that perhaps the chief reason for which the Nazis are planning to defend the north of Italy, where they have sent forces estimated at from fifteen to twenty-five divisions, is to prevent the United Nations from using airfields south of the Alps.

The possession of such fields would bring a large part of southern Germany, including Munich, and a large part of Central Europe, including Vienna, Budapest, Linz and Innsbruck, within easy reach of United Nations bombers. If Italy could obtain a peace which would prevent the use of such airfields and prevent the Italian Adriatic coast from being used for a drive into the Balkans, should the Allies decide on such a campaign, it would spell a German victory of no small importance. Therefore the idea made no headway whatsoever in Washington and London.

Badoglio had a chance to surrender and get his country out of the war. He missed the chance. His country will suffer. The longer he holds on to a forlorn hope, the more his country will suffer.

ONLY A BEGINNING

The landing of Montgomery's men on the Messina Straits is but the beginning. The Americans have not yet been heard from. In view of the long distance between the toe of the boot and North Italy, it would be no surprise if there were other Allied landings up the coast. Naples has been softened by repeated bombings. The railroads have been crippled.

And in considering the possible strategy of the attackers, it is not to be forgotten that Rome has been declared an open city. That means it is not to be used for military purposes. All of the railroads from the south, with one minor exception, run through the capital. Will the Germans use those roads through Rome? One guesses that the Allies have means of finding out. Furthermore, if Rome is an open city it is not to be defended. This does not mean that the Allies may not occupy it. Under such conditions the capital region looks like a soft spot.

The Germans have made it evident that they will try their big defense in the region of the Po River, running across northern Italy. Their fighting south of that position probably represents a delaying action, and, of course, if the Allies undertake to fight their way all the way up from the Messina Straits to Milan, the Nazis can accomplish a good deal of delay.

THE FIFTH YEAR BEGINS

It is not without interest that as the fifth year of Hitler's war begins, the Germans are fighting a defensive war everywhere. They are fighting to delay the Russian advance to the east and they are fighting to delay an Allied advance to the south. Even in the war of the air, which they started in their attacks against England, they are on the defensive.

The Germans make it plain that such is the kind of war they intend to fight from now on. One imagines that even Dr. Goebbels has given up hope of conquest in Russia. Germany is driving ahead nowhere; she is now trying to hang on to what she has stolen in the hope that the effort to take it away from her will tire her enemies so that she can keep her frontiers intact and hold on to some of her loot. It is in such an effort that Badoglio is giving aid and assistance to Hitler.

But it will be no fun for Italy and the Italians. The question will surely soon arise as to whether the repressive measures taken by the King and Badoglio will suffice to hold in line all of the Italian people, who must by now realize what sort of a fight they have undertaken. One may imagine that if and when Rome is occupied a crucial situation for Badoglio may arise. And a King in flight loses much of the dignity of his office.

A VERY BIG CAMPAIGN

The Italian campaign is a major undertaking. It is the biggest thing the British and Americans have started in this war. They know they face a formidable foe in the north of Italy. But they have cards to play. Although the Germans in the past three weeks have sent large air forces into Italy, there is every prospect that the United Nations will retain air supremacy during the whole campaign. That is of tremendous import.

Furthermore, the Germans have a bad line of communications. The main support runs through the Brenner Pass, where the railroad and the roads are vulnerable. It is reported that Allied bombers have already wrecked a vital bridge on the railroad. There are many bridges over the mountains and there are many spots where damage to the railroad can be most difficult of repair. The closer the Allies can put airfields, the more attacks can be made on the Brenner Pass.

There are other minor lines for supplies running north of Trieste. But they are not large and are also open to attack from the air and possibly from the land by forces sympathetic with the Allies.

On the other hand, the Allies' lines of communication are not easy. They are long—running back to the United States and Britain. They are, too, subject to attack. But the large difference exists in the circumstance that the basic sources of supplies for the Allies are much more safe than the German sources.

And, taking into consideration the size of the Italian campaign and its importance, Stalin should realize, and, of course, he does, that it constitutes a great aid to the Russian front. The troops and planes which fight the British and Americans in Italy cannot fight Stalin in Russia. ◊

SEPTEMBER 5, 1943

What About Women After the War?

By Elinor M. Herrick
Director of Personnel and Labor Relations, Todd Shipyards Corporation

I have no idea what the women of America think should be their place in the post-war world. And I am a trifle irked when a "special interest" woman's group states with what appears to be authority that "American women want this" or that. Too many men, likewise, think they know what is good for women. The truth is that there is no common denominator for women and no spokesman for American women—or for men, either.

Different women want different things. I think most of them—whether they will admit it or not—want only to marry, have a home and children and a man to do their worrying (and sometimes their thinking) for them. Some marry wanting children and can't have them. Some simply want a life of ease—with a marriage license.

And, of course, there are other women who want Careers—capital C. Others want to be "socially useful." A lot of women have to earn their living whether they want to or not, either because they have no one to support them or because they are suddenly thrown on their own resources when husbands die or divorce them. A lot of women want homes, children and careers—all three.

So, you see, it's all very mixed up. The solution won't be easy. We need a clear-cut social and economic plan. When I say "plan" I certainly don't mean that we should fall back upon the easy old-fashioned economic solution mouthed so piously after the last World War: "Woman's place is in the home"; "married teachers must be dismissed"; "no married women hired." That campaign brought nothing in its train but secret marriages deception and sordidness. It didn't work. It couldn't work.

We've got to tackle the problem now. Unless some tough-minded thinking is done soon the war will end with women a drug on the market, as they were twenty-five years ago. Any solution will have to cover such basic questions as:

Are we going to plan so that there will be a job for everyone who wants to work? Or only for those who need to work?

Are we going to bar men of independent income from jobs when the war is over? If not, then why should we bar women who don't need to work but want to?

Are we going to build a system in which everyone must work, produce to justify his existence?

Are we going to say that everyone, regardless of sex, who wants to work must have the opportunity?

What employment conditions will we face when this war ends? There are many more men in the armed services today than at the peak of the last World War, and many more women in industry today than ever before. The Selective Service Act of this war makes it mandatory for employers to re-employ the returning soldier if there is any job at all for him, ejecting employees hired since the soldier left in order to make ❯

room for him. This is only fair. Even the temptation to retain women because they are cheaper labor has been largely removed in this war by the government policy of "equal pay for equal work," and most employers have not even used the loophole in that policy.

Many women who have become accustomed to the independence of having their own money will want to continue in their jobs. Others are already finding the strain of double duty at home and in the factory too hard. Those women who are bored by housework and have found excitement and companionship in the factory will not want to give this up. Some women will want to keep their jobs in order to ease the economic strain until their men, back from the war, find their places. Thousands of soldiers will never return and it is important and only fair that their wives or daughters should have the chance to work.

It is wishful thinking to believe that the majority of America's newly recruited woman power will flock back into the home. Many will because of their children. Many will not who should. On the other hand, there are already indications that a substantial number of the women war workers will choose voluntarily to give up their jobs. I venture to say that the most frequent reasons for this decision will be that many women left their homes to meet a goal—pay off the mortgage, earn enough for a college education for a child, or buy a new parlor suite or a fur coat. Their objective attained, they quit the job. Many others will undoubtedly leave because they have been unable to maintain proper conditions for their children or have found the physical strain of the combined home and factory job too great.

There will be more unmarried women in the post-war generation. What of them? Will not the increase in their numbers offset the married women who elect to return to their homes? The majority of these single women must work to live. For those who need not work there is plenty of useful, important community service to be rendered, but we have always put the dollar sign as the valuation of work. Volunteer social work will not have much appeal even to those who do not need to earn and who, during these busy war years, have been engaged in exciting war work, driving ambulances or driving generals.

Then there is the vast army of professionally trained women who have been given a place in the sun—at least temporarily. The professionally trained woman has always found it notoriously difficult to secure adequate opportunities

in her chosen field and to advance therein. American women have had greater educational opportunities and have used them more widely than the women in any other country. Yet after receiving this expensive education, too often they find themselves frustrated by the professional caste system. And too often they have failed to maintain their sense of perspective and sense of humor. But they have had an uphill fight when there should have been no necessity to fight.

The woman past 40 also will present a problem. Her children have grown up, gone off to school or college. She feverishly throws herself into a round of bridge games, a literature or music club, with Wednesdays for the local charity organization, and becomes dissatisfied because there is no reality, no substance to the occupations at hand. Should she not be offered a chance to train herself for useful employment? Can't we break down the taboo upon employment of women over 40?

On the one hand, we have urged that women stay at home and raise their families. That job done—what is there left for them to do? Still young and vigorous, they find themselves not wanted in a busy, active world. Pearl Buck has said that if American women were not to be allowed to fulfill their bent, whether it be for home making or professional life, they should not be given the educational opportunities they now have. I think she is right.

The woman past 40 is far from useless. As the records show, she can achieve much after 40—giving the first years of her life to her family. But the way is not easy. Society ought to make it uniformly possible for such women to use their talents, and this applies not alone to the professionally trained women.

Finally, what of the children of women workers? We all have heard or read of children locked in parked cars while their mothers work in war plants; children sitting through repeated performances in the movies until their mothers get home from the second shift; children locked in or out of homes day after day while both parents work. No one can deny that juvenile delinquency and destruction of home standards are rampant where you have such an emergency mass employment of women as the war machine has required. But need these things be? In a few communities where the labor market has been very tight the community has started nursery schools, food kitchens or other communal feeding, and supervised play periods, to make it possible for the mother of even small children to work. I think the whole situation should receive

more intensive study.

Some people question whether children should be turned over to nursery schools and playground supervisors. There is plenty of precedent which will be cited. It will be said that children's institutions are everlasting proof that even a poor mother is better than no mother. Social welfare organizations have learned this and instituted the system of "foster homes."

But the fact remains that some women are temperamentally unsuited to caring for children, or untrained for housework, and having been in the business world before marriage, find themselves happiest in that life. Many children would be better off in a good nursery school than under the constant nagging of an irritable, because unadjusted, mother.

Many mothers come home to their children better able to give them affection and intelligent care because they have not had them all day long. But it is the rare woman who can successfully swing a job and a home with children. The problem pretty well boils down to one for individual decision. Although I believe most women will put the welfare of their children first, it seems only fair that society should provide a job opportunity for all who want to work or for all who must work irrespective of sex.

There are three courses we can follow. First, the Russian system, where all family life is subordinated to the needs of the State. Second, we can cling to the old idea that woman's place is in the home and waste a lot of good citizens and make for more unhappy homes. Third, we can leave it to the individual choice and see to it that there are jobs for all who want them. This is a middle ground.

If we take this middle course there is still the need to emphasize that most young children will fare better in their homes—though the Russians might dispute this. But the important psychological element in this picture is that women would stay home only if that were their choice. If they wanted to work or had to work, the way would be open.

If Mme. Curie had not made such a choice the world might have lost one of its most distinguished scientists. I know it is not easy to do all three things. But I do not believe the children suffer under such circumstances as they are popularly supposed to. Mme. Curie's children have achieved their own distinction, helped by the richness of the lives of their parents. All women should have a chance to make their choice of home, children or career—or all three. ◊

SEPTEMBER 9, 1943

GEN. EISENHOWER ANNOUNCES ARMISTICE
Capitulation Acceptable to U.S., Britain and Russia Is Confirmed In Speech by Badoglio

TERMS SIGNED ON DAY OF INVASION
Disclosure Withheld by Both Sides Until Moment Most Favorable For the Allies—Italians Exhorted to Aid United Nations

By MILTON BRACKER
By Wireless to The New York Times.

ALLIED HEADQUARTERS IN NORTH AFRICA, Sept. 8—Italy has surrendered her armed forces unconditionally and all hostilities between the soldiers of the United Nations and those of the weakest of the three Axis partners ceased as of 16:30 Greenwich Mean Time today [12:30 P.M., Eastern War Time].

At that time, Gen. Dwight D. Eisenhower announced here over the United Nations radio that a secret military armistice had been signed in Sicily on the afternoon of Friday, Sept. 3, by his representative and one sent by Premier Pietro Badoglio. That was the day when, at 4:50 A.M., British and Canadian troops crossed the Strait of Messina and landed on the Italian mainland to open a cam-

paign in which, up to yesterday, they had occupied about sixty miles of the Calabrian coast from the Petrace River in the north to Bova Marina in the south.

The complete collapse of Italian military resistance in no way suggested that the Germans would not defend Italy with all the strength at their command. But the capitulation, in undisclosed terms that were acceptable to the United States, the United Kingdom and the Union of Soviet Socialist Republics, came exactly forty days after the downfall of Benito Mussolini, the dictator who, by playing jackal to Adolf Hitler, led his country to the catastrophic mistake of declaring war on France three years and three months ago this Friday.

NEGOTIATIONS BEGUN SEVERAL WEEKS AGO

The negotiations leading to the armistice were opened by the war-weary and bomb-battered nation a few weeks ago, it was revealed today, and a preliminary meeting was arranged and held in an unnamed neutral country.

The Italians who had approached the British and American authori- ›

U.S. General Walter Bedell Smith (future director of CIA) signs the armistice between Italy and the Allied forces in Siracusa, September, 1943. Looking on, from left, English Commodore Royer Dick, U.S. Major General Lowell Rooks, English Captain De Haar, and the Italian General, in civilian clothes, Giuseppe Castellano, U.S. Brigadier General Kenneth Strong and the Italian officer of the Ministry of Foreign Affairs, Franco Montanari.

ties were bluntly told that the terms remained what they had been: unconditional surrender. They agreed, and the document was signed five days ago. But it was agreed to hold back the announcement and its effective date until the moment most favorable to the Allies.

That moment came today, when the Allied Commander in Chief, in a historic broadcast, announced the armistice. He concluded with the reminder that all Italians who aided in the ejection of the Germans from Italy would have the support and assistance of the United Nations.

One hour and fifteen minutes after the General's voice had gone out over the air, Marshal Badoglio faced a microphone in Rome and confirmed the armistice. He concluded with the promise that the Italian forces would oppose attacks "from any other quarter," although they were laying down the arms that they had taken up against the Anglo-American armies.

MILITARY ASPECT EMPHASIZED

Although it was emphasized that the armistice was a strictly military instrument, "signed by soldiers," it was disclosed that it contained a clause binding Italy to comply with political, economic and financial conditions to be imposed at the Allies' discretion.

[It was believed that the armistice conditions were substantially the same as those imposed on France in 1940, which allowed the Germans to use all strategic French ports and military bases to wage war against Britain, The United Press reported.]

Immediately after the announcement of the armistice, the Allies made two appeals—one to the Italian people and one to the Italian Fleet—urging them to rally to a cause that was, in effect, the liberation of their own country. The appeal to the people was disseminated by radio and airborne leaflet, while that to the Navy was broadcast by Admiral Sir Andrew Browne Cunningham, the Allies' Mediterranean naval commander.

The Italian people, particularly transport, railroad and dock workers, were asked not to give the slightest aid to the Germans. The men who man Italian ships received specific instructions how to bring their vessels into the protection of the United Nations.

Although the fear was proved un-

justified by Marshal Badoglio's broadcast, the Allies had taken no chances of a German move to forestall his giving the news to the people. As a safeguard, they had obtained from the Italians an agreement to leave one senior military representative behind when the others returned to Rome. This man is now in Sicily and presumably, had Marshal Badoglio not gone on the air, his representative would have broadcast the decision to the Italian public. As a further earnest of good faith, Marshal Badoglio had arranged to send the text of the proclamation that he made this evening to Allied Headquarters here. He kept his word.

1,181 DAYS AT WAR AND LOSSES

Italy quit the war after 1,181 days, during which she steadily lost territory and prestige. Last May 7, with the fall of Tunis and Bizerte, the last Italian soldier in North Africa was doomed. Since then, Sicily, part of Metropolitan Italy, was occupied in thirty-eight days.

The Italians endured two raids on military targets in Rome and felt the weight of 20,000 tons of bombs on the mainland in the past six months. Of this total, 11,300 tons fell in August alone.

But, despite the abject condition of the nation today, it was emphasized here, the Germans were still expected to fight on in the worst way. It would be wrong and dangerously foolish to regard Italy as geographically out of the war, even though she is so politically. Thus the Allies kept up the air war against Italian airdromes yesterday even though the effective time of the armistice was almost at hand.

Despite rumors of negotiations of one kind or another ever since the fall of Benito Mussolini, it may be said that the news of the capitulation struck this area with stunning impact. It was known that Italian resistance and morale, as evidenced by the Sicilian and Calabrian campaigns, were dwindling, but complete capitulation was something of which few persons outside General Eisenhower's immediate circle had any idea.

Maj. Gen. Walter B. Smith, General Eisenhower's Chief of Staff, said at the close of the Sicilian campaign that one lesson had been never to give up the possibility of achieving surprise. That apparently applied to the news of the armistice as well as to that of military developments. ◆

MAFIA CHIEFS CAUGHT BY ALLIES IN SICILY
Coup, Led by U.S. Soldier, Helps to Break Black Market

Distributed by The Associated Press.

WITH THE AMERICAN FORCES IN SICILY, Sept. 9—The Mafia, Sicilian extortionist gang that fascism tried for years to rub out and then incorporated as one of its own criminal appendages, has been smashed from the top.

Two of its notorious leaders, Domenico Tomaselli and Giuseppe Piraino, and seventeen district bosses were nabbed in a joint British-American coup in which Scotland Yard had a hand.

All of them are behind bars, and the responsible Allied authorities have enough leads on the other regional chiefs to insure their capture.

The Mafia men already jailed and those on the way to joining them controlled the black market, which still has a stranglehold on Sicilian life. It follows that breaking the Mafia gang means breaking the black market.

Within the secret society are men who have fought fascism since its inception, men of unquestionable integrity who shunned all ties with the sprawling majority of the fascistized profiteers. This group, genuinely interested in the future of Sicily, aided the coup.

Operations that led to the roundup began when the American Third Division, then on the Messina drive, chose Castel d'Accia, inland from Trabia, which is about twenty-two miles from Palermo, for its rear echelon headquarters.

Louis Bassi of Stockton, Calif., a technician in the special service staff, discovered that the tiny hamlet was nothing more or less than the Mafia fortress. He reported to his colonel, investigated by day and by night alone and reported again and again until he had accumulated enough evidence for an open and shut case against the racketeers. ◆

1943

to

1946

▲ The Casablanca Conference, January 1943. From the left, French General Henri Giraud, U.S. President Roosevelt, French General Charles de Gaulle and British Prime Minister Winston Churchill.

▼ Mary Saverick stitching harnesses for the Pioneer Parachute Company Mills in Manchester, Connecticut, 1943.

▲ General Douglas MacArthur, 1943.

▲ American war propaganda poster from 1943.

▲ A field hospital run by the U.S. Army
10th Mountain Division in Italy, 1944.

▲ A squadron of Stukas (German dive
bombers) over the Russian front, April 1943.

▲ A soldier from the 92nd Division, one of two all-Black Infantry
Divisions, exploding anti-tank mines at Viareggio, Italy, 1944.

▲ Axis prisoners at a temporary holding camp for POWs in Tunisia during
the North African campaign, May 1943.

▲ An American Sherman tank passing through a town in Southern Italy, 1944.

◄ Sergeant William
H. Bass of Memphis,
Tennessee gives food
to two Italian girls,
1944.

▲ American soldiers await the signal to begin the D-Day invasion, England, June 1944.

▲ Troops of the 3rd Canadian Infantry Division landing at Juno Beach on the outskirts of Bernieres-sur-Mer on D-Day, June 6, 1944.

▲ A D-Day planning session in February, 1944. From the left, U.S. General Omar Bradley, Admiral Bertram H. Ramsay, Marshal of the Royal Air Force Arthur Tedder, General Dwight D. Eisenhower, Field Marshall Bernard Law Montgomery, Royal Air Force Chief Marshal Sir Trafford Leigh-Mallory and U.S. General Walter Bedell.

▲ American troops boarding an LCVP (Landing Craft, Vehicle, Personnel) in Weymouth, England on June 5, 1944, in preparation for the invasion of France.

▲ The ruins of the town of Monte Cassino, southeast of Rome, 1944.

▲ American troops of the 7th Navy Beach Battalion training in Britain before their deployment at Omaha Beach during the D-Day landings, 1944.

▲ Allied troops landing in Normandy, France, 1944.

▲ Allied soldiers viewing their position in Normandy with two French policeman policemen, June 1944.

▲ Allied soldiers under the Arc de Triomphe during the French liberation celebrations at the end of World War II, August 1944.

▲ Ruins of the city Dresden after the Allied bombings in February, 1945.

▲ U.S. Army vehicles driving through the ruins of Saint-Lo in Normandy, 1944. The town was almost totally destroyed by 2,000 Allied bombers when they attacked German troops stationed there during Operation Overlord.

▲ From left, Chief of the Imperial General Staff Field Marshal Sir Alan Brooke, British Prime Minister Winston Churchill, and commander of the 21st Army Group, Field Marshal Bernard Montgomery in Normandy, June 12, 1944, six days after the D-Day landings.

▲ A young Holocaust survivor of the Buchenwald concentration camp shortly after the liberation of the camp by U.S. Army Forces, Germany, April 15, 1945.

▲ An American solder of the 42nd Rainbow Division reacting to the conditions of the Dachau concentration camp, April 1945.

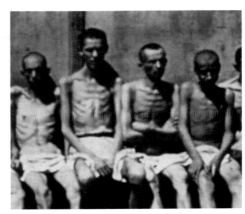

▲ A group of inmates after liberation of Dachau concentration camp by the 42nd Rainbow Division and the 45th Thunderbird Division, Germany, May 2, 1945.

▲ An American Sherman M4 tank in the Ardennes Forest during the Battle of the Bulge, the last major German offensive of World War II.

▲ U.S. Army soldiers near the Cologne cathedral, 1945. The last tank battle took place March 6, 1945 and it took another five weeks to take the city.

▲ The funeral procession of President Roosevelt moving from Union Station to The White House, April 14, 1945.

The ruins of the Hiroshima ▶ Prefectural Industry Promotion Building, known as the Atomic-Bomb Dome, in September 1945.

▲ Crowds gather in Times Square to celebrate the end of the war in Europe, New York, May 7, 1945.

▲ Soldiers and sailors on the decks of the USS Missouri watch the Japanese surrender which was signed on board, September 2, 1945.

▲ American Marines raising the United States flag at Iwo Jima, February 23, 1945.

▲ Students at a camouflage class at New York University in 1943 made models from aerial photographs.

▲ Crowds of French citizens line the Champs Elysees during a parade in celebration of the liberation of Paris, August 1944.

◄ American soldiers march through the streets of Rome shortly after the arrival of General Mark Clark and Secretary of War Henry L. Stimson, July 4, 1944.

▲ U.S. warships in the Fast Carrier Task Force (Task Force 58), under the command of Rear Admiral Marc Mitscher, in the Pacific Ocean, 1944.

▲ Members of the United States 69th Infantry Division meet a Russian patrol south of Torgau, April 25, 1945.

▲ Crewmen playing poker in the cramped quarters of the USS New Mexico during Pacific operations, 1944.

▲ American troops with local residents at Guadalcanal Island in the Solomon Islands, 1943.

American troops playing ▶ softball on the island of Tarawa in the Pacific, 1943.

▲ The Nuremberg Trials, 1946. In the first row, from the left, Hermann Goering (with hand on his chin), Rudolf Hess, Joachim Von Ribbentrop, Wilhelm Keitel, Ernst Kaltenbrunner, Alfred Rosenberg, Hans Frank, Wilhelm Frick, Julius Streicher, Walther Funk and Hjalmar Schacht.

▲ Hermann Goering during his cross-examination at the Nuremberg Trials, Germany, 1946.

▲ Representatives of the Allied powers establishing a War Commission for the trial of European War criminals. From the left, seated, Professor Trainin of Russia, General Nikitchenko of Russia, Lord Jowitt of the U.K. and Justice Jackson from the U.S.

▲ General Alfred Jodl, Hitler's military adviser, controller of German High Command and chief of the Operations Staff (center), signs the document of surrender of the German armed forces at Reims in General Eisenhower's headquarters, May 7, 1945. Major Wilhelm Oxenius is on his left and Hans-Georg von Friedeburg, Admiral of the Fleet is on his right.

SEPTEMBER 14, 1943

Editorial
AMERICAN POST-WAR POLICY

We hope that Congress, returning to work today, will lose no time in putting itself on record regarding the main outlines of a post-war settlement. The stage is set for such a declaration. A clear statement of policy, made at this time with overwhelming bipartisan support, could help both to shorten the war and to win a better peace.

Before Congress adjourned for its midsummer recess the House had before it a resolution which had received the unanimous approval of its Foreign Affairs Committee. This resolution, introduced by Representative Fulbright of Arkansas, proposed that Congress go on record as "favoring the creating of appropriate international machinery with power adequate to establish and to maintain a just and lasting peace and as favoring the participation by the United States therein." Since then an almost identical declaration has been adopted, again unanimously, by the Republican policy-makers in their conference at Mackinac Island. Republican support of the Fulbright resolution is thereby assured.

The great merit of adopting such a resolution now is that it would tell the world, before the fighting ends, that this time the United States intends to help enforce world peace when it is won. Such a declaration would strengthen the ties that now bind the United Nations. It would thereby help win the war. By encouraging our allies to put their faith in a new post-war alliance or a new league of nations, instead of attempting to find an independent and precarious security in the acquisition of new territory, it would help win a better peace. ◆

SEPTEMBER 14, 1943

HARD-FIGHT RAGES IN SALERNO ITSELF
City Changes Hands Several Times in Day, But Allies Break Counter-Blow

TOWN FOUND DESPOILED
Germans Had Looted It of All That They Could Take in Earlier Withdrawal

By L. S. B. SHAPIRO
For the Combined Allied Press

IN THE SALERNO AREA, Sept. 14 (UP)—The town of Salerno was the scene of a violent battle yesterday and changed hands several times as the Germans fought with desperation.

German "ghost" formations, built around a nucleus of the battered remnants evacuated from Sicily, flung themselves against the advancing Allied forces in a desperate effort to prevent the exploitation of our beach-head. The effort failed against a quickly mounted Anglo-American defense line that sealed the Allied foothold.

Thus far in the battle, it is estimated that more than forty German tanks, mostly Mark V's, have been destroyed in this area. The attack has been held off, after the bitterest of fighting, at some cost to the Allies. Warships off the coast have joined with the land forces to fling a withering barrage along the line of the German counter-attack.

Over the battle area the air fighting is the most violent that has been experienced since the closing days of the North African campaign. Dogfights swirl overhead continuously during the daylight hours, and the nights are filled with the flash of multi-colored tracer bullets reaching up at attacking planes.

Allied planes are gradually gaining domination over the area, but the German air force is battling with a daring that matches the desperate resistance of the German land forces. ◆

An explosion during the invasion of Salerno.

SEPTEMBER 16, 1943

'MUSSOLINI' SETS UP NEW KIND OF REGIME

Broadcast from Reich in His Name Creates 'Republican Fascist Government'

TERROR REIGN INDICATED

Seizure of 'Traitors' Called for in Radio 'Orders of Day'—Militia to Be Formed

LONDON, Sept. 15 (AP)—Italy's ousted and invisible "Premier," Benito Mussolini, apparently attempted to dethrone King Victor Emmanuel today in a proclamation) read in his name by a radio announcer, recasting defunct Fascism in Italy as the "Republican Fascist Party," with Mussolini as its supreme leader.

The manifesto, read over a German-controlled "Fascist government radio" failed to mention the King by name, but the reconstitution of the party under the "Republican" label obviously meant that the King no longer ruled in the eyes of the Nazi-sheltered ex-Duce.

This action was in line with predictions that the new German-nurtured government would disestablish the House of Savoy and establish a republic. There was little likelihood, however, that the population, which joyously welcomed the end of Fascism, would assist in re-establishing the old regime.

REIGN OF TERROR INDICATED

The threat of "exemplary punishment of traitors and cowards" signaled that a reign of terror might be expected in Italy.

The appointment of Gen. Count Carlo Calvi di Bergolo as Governor of Rome—with German consent—to carry on the government failed to square with the previous German announcement that the "national fascist government" had been placed in charge.

Mussolini remained in the shadows. At last accounts he was reported to have gone to Berchtesgaden for treatment of a gastric disorder. Only yesterday the Germans said he was a very sick man whose condition had been greatly aggravated by his recent experiences.

NEW CABINET IS SET UP

German broadcasts reported to the Office of War Information by the United States Foreign Broadcast Intelligence Service asserted that Gen. Calvi di Ber-golo, puppet commandant of Italian forces in Rome, had formally liquidated the Badoglio Cabinet and named commissioners—all of them well known in the fascist regime—to take the functions and responsibilities of the Ministries.

The Mussolini decrees, said to be signed by the former Premier, were read over the German radio station Zeesen. They were read, not by Mussolini but by Alessandro Pavolini, former Italian Propaganda Minister, who was named in one of the decrees as "temporary secretary" of the new Fascist party.

A short time later the Italian agency Stefani, now under German control, broadcast a dispatch containing an ordinance signed by Calvi di Bergolo naing Dr. Augusto Rosso, former Ambassador to the United States, as Commissioner of the Foreign Ministry, to replace Raffaele Guariglia, the Badoglio Foreign Minister.

A Swiss broadcast, also reported to the OWI, said that Signor Guariglia had been placed under arrest in Rome and that other Ministers of the legal Cabinet still in Rome also were reported under arrest.

The Stefani broadcast listed these appointments by Calvi di Bergolo in addition to that of Rosso:

Presidency of the Council of Ministers—Dr. Gian Giacomo Bellazzi.
Interior—Dr. Lorenzo Lavia.
Italian Africa—Dr. Enrico Cerulli.
Administration of Justice—Dr. Giovanni Novelli.
Finance—Dr. Ettore Cambi.
National Education—Dr. Giuseppe Guistini.
Public Works—Engineer Paolo Saltino.
Agriculture—Professor Vittorio Ronchi.
Communications—Engineer Luigi Velani.
Industry and Commerce—Dr. Ernesto Santoro.
Popular Culture—Dr. Armedeo Tosti.
Foreign Currency and Exchange—Dr. Francesco Cemonese.
War Production—Dr. France Liguori.

TEXT OF BROADCAST

The text of the alleged order of the day by Benito Mussolini as broadcast yesterday by the German Transocean news agency and recorded by The United Press in New York follows:

Order of the Day No. 1

To all loyal comrades in the whole of Italy: From today, Sept. 15, 1943, I again assume the supreme leadership of fascism in Italy.

Order of the Day No. 2

I appoint Allessandro Pavolini provisional secretary of the Fascist National party, which from today will be known as the Republican Fascist party.

Order of the Day No. 3

I decree that all military, political, administrative and educational authorities, as well as all others who were dismissed by the capitulation of the Government, shall immediately be reinstated.

Order of the Day No. 4

I decree the immediate re-establishment of all party organizations on which the following duties will be incumbent: (1) To actively assist the German armed forces that are fighting the common enemy on Italian soil; (2) to afford immediate and effective moral and material assistance to the people; (3) to revise the lists of party members with the aim of ascertaining the attitude taken by members toward the coup d'etat capitulation and dishonor and of inflicting exemplary punishment on cowards and traitors.

Order of the Day No. 5

I decree the re-establishment of all formations and special sections of the voluntary militia of national security. Mussolini. ◇

SEPTEMBER 17, 1943

WAR PRISONERS AT WORK 110,000 Axis Men Are Filling Farm And Other Jobs

WASHINGTON, Sept. 16 (AP)—Many Axis prisoners in this country were being used to relieve manpower shortages, the War Department reported today, announcing that 110,000 of the nearly 141,000 captives were at work on farms and elsewhere.

SEPTEMBER 19, 1943

PROPAGANDA BATTLE JOINED
We Try to Bolster Italian Morale, While the Germans Play Up Mussolini's Rescue

By HAROLD CALLENDER

WASHINGTON, Sept. 18—The propaganda battle in the Mediterranean this week has been in its own way as intense and as continuous as the land, air and sea tussle around Salerno, each side making full use of its military achievements to encourage its own people and to depress the morale of the enemy.

The surrender of Italy was not only a great military achievement. It was—or so our propagandists like to think—partly a propaganda achievement, and it certainly was a propaganda opportunity. As such it was exploited to the full in broadcasts to Italy, Germany, the Balkans and Europe generally.

The theme of these Allied broadcasts this week has been that while Hitler has got Mussolini, the Allies have got the Italian fleet and thus in effect Increased their already overwhelming naval power by eliminating the only naval opposition in the Mediterranean and releasing surface ships for use elsewhere.

For the edification of Europeans generally our propagandists emphasized the value to the Allies of the air bases they hold or will capture in Italy, from which they can readily bomb within a radius extending to Central Europe, to which Germany has moved some of her war industries in order to get them out of the range of Allied bombers striking western Europe from Britain.

MORAL FOR GERMANS

In addressing the Germans, our broadcasters have dwelt upon the fact that the initiative is now on the side of the Allies who, first, by invading North Africa and then by moving into Sicily and Italy, themselves decided where the present major campaign would be fought. Moreover, the Germans are told, the geography of the present phase of the war favors the Allies because they have virtually the same sea communication lines to Italy that they had to North Africa, not more extended lines.

Meanwhile, continue the German-language broadcasters, the German forces in Italy are handicapped by having to get their reinforcements and supplies through mountain passes and along railways that can be bombed. Italy is described as a "sink hole" into which the Germans will drop, never to return.

In talks to Italy, where the Germans have instituted a reign of terror apparently worse than in France, the effort has been to sustain Italian morale—odd as that now sounds in the reversed situation—pending Italy's liberation by the Allies, to turn fear of the Germans into hatred of them and resistance to them and to stimulate the normal Italian desire to get back at the Germans by sabotage.

The German propagandists also have had their innings this week and made their score, principally with the reports of the rescue of Mussolini and with the battle for Italy in which they have given the Allies a hard fight.

Their aerial salvage of Mussolini was depicted by the German radio as a great stroke, tantamount to a major military victory. Mussolini's value to anybody appears at this stage highly doubtful. The Germans' repulse of earlier Allied advances around Salerno was described as "a Dunkerque," and that ominous story was heard and momentarily believed at least as far as Washington—which was a tribute to German propaganda, as obligingly relayed by American radio speakers.

'A DARING DEED'

Having had no victories to talk about for a long time, the Nazis let themselves go on the Mussolini rescue. Their press and radio called it "one of the most daring and sensational deeds of history" and a "touching demonstration of friendship" between two dictators. "A nation capable of such deeds must win the war," they said.

Mussolini, said the Nazis, was transferred on Aug. 28 from the island of Santa Maddalena to the Abruzzi Mountains. The Nazis followed him, they say, as he was sent by motor car, motor boat, airplane and battleship from place to place. Finally, when an S.S. captain reached the mountain retreat and told Mussolini, "The Fuehrer sends me to deliver you," Mussolini embraced him and said he had known the Fuehrer would save him. Just then a German plane, a helicopter, according to some versions, picked up the fallen Duce and "the rebirth of fascism" was assured.

This action, or the story of it, was a propaganda stroke of great value, and a Swiss commentator in the Neue Zuericher Nachrichten thought it would divert German attention from the Russian front and even make the war in Italy popular. It is believed here to have ministered considerably to Hitler's much injured self-esteem and it did not dismay the neutrals whom President Roosevelt had warned not to let Mussolini cross their frontiers.

The Nazis professed to have cheated the Allies of a victim in rescuing Mussolini who, they said, was to be led in chains before President Roosevelt and Prime Minister Churchill in Washington and then executed. It was for this that Mr. Churchill had remained here, they said. Morever, the capture of Mussolini was to be "a trump card in Roosevelt's election propaganda" and Elmer Davis, Director of the Office of War Information, was all set to publicize it, said the Nazis.

DISSENTING VOICE

Allied propaganda sought to minimize the Mussolini rescue by saying he was of no use to the Germans and that, having been a dictator, he had now sunk to the level of a puppet, like the Frenchman Laval.

In telling of the battle for Italy, the Nazis began on Monday by reporting repulses of the Allies; on Tuesday they spoke of a "decisive defeat," a "collapse" and "a Dunkerque"; the next day they magnified their story but gave the impression of a finished action in which the Germans had definitely triumphed. ◇

The department said the war prisoners had helped relieve labor shortages in many States, adding:

"They have harvested peanuts in Georgia and South Carolina, tomatoes in Indiana, corn in Iowa, have picked cotton in Texas, dug potatoes in Missouri and worked on a variety of non-agricultural jobs in several sections. One group now is engaged in constructing a dam for flood control in Oklahoma."

All prisoners, except officers, may be required to work on projects having no direct relation to war operations under the terms of the Geneva convention. They receive 80 cents a day, the money being credited to them regardless of whether the work is done for a Federal, State or private contractor. ◇

SEPTEMBER 21, 1943

In the Nation

The Rumored Transfer of General Marshall

By ARTHUR KROCK

WASHINGTON, Sept. 20—If the rumors prevalent in high military circles prove correct, and General Marshall, Chief of Staff of the Army, is sent abroad in a post of supreme combat command in the European theatre, the event will shock and disturb a great many people who have observed his work at first hand and are qualified to evaluate it. The discussion, private and public, which has followed an editorial in The Army and Navy Journal opposing the replacement, demonstrates this statement to be a fact and not an opinion.

PERSHING'S APPREHENSION

The discussion has been all the more earnest because of the source of the editorial, a military newspaper known to be close to the services and especially to General Pershing, whose aide General Marshall was in World War I. It is accepted here, though there is no public evidence to support the view, that the editorial, as often before, expressed General Pershing's sentiments and reflected apprehension on his part that the transfer is being seriously considered by the President.

The President is the Commander in Chief of the armed services, and in time of war his activity in that field is very great. He is ultimately responsible for the military conduct of the war and personally selects the commanders. The qualifications and records of none come into the President's purview more intimately than those of the Chiefs of Staffs of the Army and the Navy.

This being so, the President alone must decide who shall be the Chiefs of Staffs and when they shall be replaced. If Mr. Roosevelt has determined, or shall determine, that military objectives can better be served by transferring General Marshall to command the European invasion zone than by retaining him in Washington, his decision will be accepted in dutiful silence by the Army, including Generals Marshall and Pershing.

PROTEST REGARDED AS LIKELY

But Congress, which has a legal responsibility second to the President's for the conduct of the war, would probably not bow in silence to such a decision. And when the points against it which are being made here were circulated throughout the country, as they would be, the chorus of dissent could be expected to grow.

These points are several, among them the following:

1. In World War I the best-known Army officer, and rated by the public as

---

SEPTEMBER 24, 1943

NAZIS WRECK NAPLES PORT, SINK SHIPS; ALLIES SWING THEIR LINE NORTHWARD; POLTAVA TAKEN, RUSSIANS AT DNIEPER

RETREAT REPORTED
Enemy Quitting Naples Area After Scuttling 30 Vessels, Berne Hears

ALLIES MAKE WIDE GAINS
Advance Up to 14 Miles in Some Sectors—Our Fliers, Unopposed, Smash at Foe

By MILTON BRACKER
By Wireless to The New York Times.

ALLIED HEAD QUARTERS IN NORTH AFRICA, Sept. 23—The Germans have sunk at least thirty ships in the harbor of Naples to block Allied use of the port. The city is ringed with fire and palled with smoke from the enemy's demolition of harbor installations and possibly valuable military installations.

"Practically every usable berth along the docks has been blocked," an official statement said. "Fires have been burning along the docks for several days. Charges have been seen to explode."

The destruction carried on in the last few days is designed to make Naples, one of Europe's largest and best peacetime harbors, completely useless to the Allies when they occupy it, military leaders say, but they are inclined to doubt that the Germans are sacking the city.

[The Germans in the Naples area, totaling seven divisions, were forced last night to abandon their lines and retire to new positions, according to reports received in Berne, Switzerland, from Rome.

[Field Marshal Gen. Albert Kesselring was compelled to pull out his infantry because of lack of artillery ammunition, which was due to the cutting of his communication lines by Italian troops, it was said.]

GERMANS STILL USING TANKS

Meanwhile the Allied front in Italy moved up rapidly yesterday as the opposing armies, getting ready for the next stage of the campaign, remained locked in bitter fighting only at the "hinge" of the back-swinging German line north of Salerno.

The advance reached as much as fourteen miles in some sectors, with probably the most important gains being from Sala Consilina to Caggiano and from Potenza to Avigliano. The Fifth Army also captured Acerno, five miles northeast of Montecorvino Rovella, while the British Fifth Corps driving forward from Taranto took Ginosa, fifteen miles southwest of Gioia del Colle.

On neither the Eighth Army nor Fifth Corps front was there any action comparable to that which kept Lieut. Gen. Mark Clark's Americans and British busy in the difficult German-domi-

chief American military factor in the victory over Germany, was General Pershing. The Chief of Staff, General March, though his contribution was very large, was nothing like so well known. The fame and glamour of field command that surrounded General Pershing were of essential value in stimulating and maintaining home front morale.

But in that war there was only one important, or at any rate conspicuous, war theatre—the Western Front. The general in the field was far more important, and was required to make the great and immediate decisions. In this war Army fighting covers the whole planet; it must be closely integrated with the work of the Navy; its direction must be from a central point, which has been and will be Washington; and that direction by General Marshall has been notable, as his recent report brilliantly reveals.

A LIMITING ASSIGNMENT

Therefore, to transfer him to just one theatre of combat, however vital, and even though he might lead the successful invasion and conquest of Germany, would be to confine his great talents and deny them to commanders in other combat zones, including our fronts in the Orient.

Another invasion commander can be found, but not a Chief of Staff of General Marshall's caliber; also, he does not aspire to this field command.

2. Never have two Chiefs of Staff worked together more closely and harmoniously than General Marshall and the Navy's leader, Admiral King. They have been sedulous in asserting national interests whenever they believed that these were being subordinated to those of an ally without benefit to anti-Axis military operations as a whole.

POLITICS KEPT OUT

They have collected some of the same detractors and aroused opposition from the same outside sources. They have been as one in keeping politics out of their considerations. They have repelled civilian attempts, however high the source, to interfere with the discipline for which they are responsible. They have adopted the same general pattern of war and, though occasionally overruled, continue to advocate it.

To break up this team would produce a loss that could not be canceled by General Marshall's exploits in Europe, however sensational.

3. If the Army's Chief of Staff is replaced, those who have urged it will the more easily be able to displace Admiral King.

It may be the President has not been considering a transfer for General Marshall. But, if he has, many influential persons, in and out of the war program, who have developed unbounded admiration for this gifted and high-minded officer hope these reasons will induce Mr. Roosevelt to decide in the negative. ◇

nated heights above Salerno.

Here the Germans still called on tanks in small numbers and more mines and demolitions to hold off the Allies pressing them back toward the region of Mount Vesuvius. [A British Broadcasting Corporation correspondent reported that Allied guns opened a thunderous barrage in the direction of Naples.]

ALLIED FLIERS BATTER FOE

The Allies' continual air war went on in the Naples area although targets within the city itself were spared. Medium bombers did some pinpoint bombing behind the battle lines in the mountainous defiles north and east of the battered city while fighter-bombers continued their personal war against enemy truck convoys and Wellingtons flew beyond Naples to Formia on the Gulf of Gaeta.

Tactical operations largely concerned the area just beyond the embattled pivot of the German line but, as has often been the case in recent weeks, the line between strategic and tactical bombing was not precise and the general objective remained the same: to make the entire area north and east of Allied bridgehead useless to the Germans while destroying as many as possible of them at the same time.   ❭

Hundreds of Neapolitans used caves like this one which once housed supplies of the Italian Navy, as shelter to escape German demolition bombings in 1943.

The day's warfare was largely one of the armies regrouping and shifting in position for the struggle both know is due soon to break out in renewed savagery. Meanwhile the Allied force in Italy kept growing stronger, with Taranto, Bari and Brindisi available for shipping as well as Salerno, itself.

The line now runs from the heights of the Sorrentine Peninsula to Salerno then irregularly inland to San Cipriano, Montecorvino Rovella, and Acerno. There it cuts inland to Contursi, which is eleven miles southeast of Acerno, and twenty miles from the shore of the Gulf of Salerno.

The front then dips down through Contursi and Caggiano to Avigliano above Potenza, which is the most important point held by the Eighth Army in south-central Italy.

The spot farthest south is now Montalbano, nearly sixty miles southeast of Avigliano and barely ten milos beyond the coast of the Gulf of Taranto.

Finally, the line parallels the western shore of that gulf through Ginosa and Gioia del Colle and then swerves up to Bari, the Adriatic terminus.

Although the Allied forces were following up the yielding left flank of the Germans, only occasional sharp clashes with rear guards were reported. Allied planes had even less resistance as they carried out the day's varied program with scarcely any aircraft opposition.

One of the heaviest blows was that struck by Wellingtons last night at Formia. The coastal rail route linking Naples to Leghorn was again battered and one Wellington, taking a leaf from the fighter-bombers' book, dove beneath the haze to shoot up a line of transports huddled at the roadside.

The day's targets also included enemy positions near Avellino Nocera, Pagani and Montella, where A-36 Invaders did their stuff at the expense of slow-moving trucks.

The Allied planes encountered some flak but suffered no losses. ◇

SEPTEMBER 26, 1943

Editorial
THE YEAR OF THE TOMATO

It won't go down in the history books under that name, but 1943 might well be called The Year of the Tomato. Is there any gardener within sight or hearing who hasn't all but buried himself under tomatoes? Of course not. They have even been harvesting tomatoes from window boxes. And right now suburbanites in frost-haunted regions are rapidly burying themselves under green tomatoes while they frantically scald, crush and strain the last high tide of ripe ones and fill the ketchup and chili sauce kettles. Our own carefully unconfirmed statistics show that two of every three jars sold for home canning this year are now full of tomatoes and looking around for a place to park themselves. Maybe even more.

Nobody would say anything but the kindest words for the tomato. It is a friendly, healthful vegetable, or fruit—and let's not quibble about classifications. It oozes vitamins, and even more delectable things. It has flavor and substance and color. If it doesn't help you to see at night, it ought to, for it outsells carrots on most tables. And it certainly helps you to see on the morning after.

In any normal season there are just about enough tomatoes to go around, generously. Somebody sees to such things. But this season everybody with a spade blister on his hand set out tomato plants, and the season, in these parts anyway, was just right for tomato culture. We've been stuffed to the ears with them for two months, and now we've stuffed every jar in sight with them. We're about ready to call it quits. Until along about Thanksgiving. By that time we'll be back to our normal vitamin deficiency and ready to say, from the heart, "And we are thankful, too, for all those jars of wonderful tomatoes—if they haven't spoiled." ◇

M'ARTHUR'S ISSUE ONE OF STRATEGY
General's Statement Indicates That He Wants to Fight His Way Back to Philippines

AGAINST 'ISLAND HOPPING'

By FRANK L. KLUCKHOHN
By Wireless to The New York Times.

ALLIED HEADQUARTERS IN NEW GUINEA, Sept. 25—The statement issued this week at his battle headquarters in New Guinea by Gen. Douglas MacArthur raised the issue of general Pacific strategy. The ranking United States four-star general put himself on record as opposed to any Allied strategy calculated to take years to beat Japan and costing heavily in men and materiel meanwhile. He made it clear that he was confident that the job could be done quicker and with relatively light cost if the proper strategy were adopted and followed.

Although no official statement has yet been made either by Washington or London, it appears likely that Lord Louis Mountbatten is not to be over MacArthur, but the general left little doubt that he thinks that Mountbatten is to get the men and implements of war and he is not to get them.

NEW PLANS SEEN

If this is true, it would seem to mean that MacArthur cannot return to the Philippines, as he has not the strength to do it now. It means instead that the strategy is to include a drive via Burma, Malaya and Indo-China as well as China itself.

This must be a bitter blow to MacArthur, but he insists he is not so much interested in what happens to him personally as in the way the Pacific war is to be conducted.

The statement was carefully phrased, MacArthur basing it upon "press reports" from England and the United States, but there is every reason to believe that he was not seeking a clarification of his position, the entire implication of the statement being that he was aware he had been sidetracked to a "secondary position."

MacArthur went about as far as a ranking officer in active service could in bringing the strategy issue into the open. Whatever the merits of the statement, it seems to give away no information that was not already in general possession after the Quebec conference.

MacArthur's idea always has been that if a firm position could be established in the Philippines it would flank and cut off Japanese sea routes to the Netherlands Indies as well as eastward to the Carolines and Marshalls. With Australia's food and limited industrial production aiding the support of such a position, there then would be a sound base for operations against Japan proper.

The general emphasized in the statement that his proposed strategy calls for flanking operations involving air and sea power plus the unusual military tactics he employed successfully in the Lae operations, not "island hopping" which requires taking numerous islands. In fact, strategy of a different sort would require such hopping.

THE RECORD CITED

MacArthur's supporters assert in defense of his plan that the general has not yet failed to carry out any assignment. They say he immediately realized that the battle for Australia must be fought in New Guinea and the Solomons and that he was successful in changing the trend from defense to offense with an amazingly small force while employing the flanking tactics he advocates. They note that the flanking attack on Lae forced the fall of Salamaua farther east, and this week the general can point to a new success at Finschhafen sixty miles farther up the New Guinea coast.

They note also that if MacArthur's strategy is followed the Japanese would have to support their defense by sea, making impossible the employment of more than limited forces, whereas any land bloc strategy permits the Japanese to bring their full strength to bear.

The General was careful not to criticize any specific strategy, yet what was in his mind appears fairly apparent. It may be seen as something like this:

The Nipponese have numerous divisions in Burma with a land route for sending more. The terrain is most difficult. Even if the Burma Road is reopened the amount of supplies which can be sent to China probably would be insufficient for large-scale operations against the large Japanese Army.

The Japanese also have interior lines of communication in Malaya and Indo-China.

Admiral King addressing the American Legion convention this week, asserted that recent United States naval attacks on Marcus and the Gilbert Islands were only the shape of things to come. In case of any attack based on Pearl Harbor it is obvious that the flanking Marshall, Gilberts, Carolines and other islands would have to be cleared first. Moreover, Hawaii itself is not self-supporting, and the real base of operations may be the west coast of the United States.

There are also political considerations in respect to battered China, still the principal land front against Japan, which those making policy decisions can not ignore. China's air bases are the closest available to Japan.

What General MacArthur has done is to make his own views clear to the American public and raise questions on a matter of intense public interest and concern. It was implied in the statement that MacArthur wanted a minimum loss of men and material, and that he believed he could do the job his way without an overwhelming mass of war implements, although he needs considerably more than he has now.

AUSTRALIAN VIEWS

In any full and accurate report of the matter it is necessary to note that many Australians and some long-time observers here believe that, because of the tremendous popular acclaim he obtained in the glorious epic of Bataan, General MacArthur has been penalized for domestic political reasons by having the sinews of war withheld or meted out in such a manner as to make possible only limited operations. They express the opinion that this is one of the reasons he is allegedly being bypassed by the authorities now.

A year ago, General MacArthur, commenting on press reports, said that all he wanted was to retire at the end of the war. In this week's statement, devoted exclusively to military affairs, he emphasized that he had no "military ambitions." ◆

SEPTEMBER 26, 1943

Hate Marches With the Red Army

By Ilya Ehrenburg
Soviet Author and Correspondent
(By Wireless)

MOSCOW—In September, 1941, I happened to be in the forest near Bryansk. That was a bitter time. The tragedy of Kiev had begun. Every day the Berlin radio announced the fall of new cities and the communiqués were accompanied by the rolling of drums, Tyrolean yodels and roars of "Heil!" Peasant women gazed after the retreating Red Army with hard eyes. Terrifying rumors were rampant. Sweaty Germans in their undershirts and with their caps perched jauntily to one side cold-bloodedly shot refugees. Carts creaked—how I remember that mournful creak. The Germans wrote, "Russia is a colossus with feet of clay."

That is worth recalling now, when Russia is striding westward. Her feet proved sturdier than many thought. And her heart proved sturdy too. It is vain for Hitler to try to reassure the Germans by saying. "We're shortening our line of our own accord." One has only to take a look at the scorched, shell-riven fields to realize what stubborn resistance the Germans are putting up. Elastic defense? They'll have to take care the elastic does not break.

The Red Army is catching the Germans unprepared. Here, for example, is an announcement of Lieutenant Colonel Lenz, former German commander of Stalino, to the Russian inhabitants of that city:

For some time rumors have been circulating in the city, alarming the inhabitants, to the effect that the position of the German troops at the front is hopeless and that the arrival of the Bolsheviks is only a matter of a few days. Increased movement of vehicles in the streets are taken to mean that the German troops are retreating. The enemy has thrown his last forces into the field. Anyone who gives credence to such rumors is helping spread panic. Everyone must calmly and conscientiously continue at his work.

The Germans had no time to display this announcement; the posters were found lying in a print shop.

In an attempt to explain the reverses in Russia, Berlin is letting it be known via Stockholm and Berne that German divisions are being shifted from Russia westward. But at the same time reinforcement battalions are speeding from Germany to Russia. I have spoken to many prisoners of war who came to Russia last month. What do these reinforcement battalions consist of? Men mustered under the total mobilization scheme [munitions workers, men with physical defects] from Alsace-Lorraine and Slovenia, and also wounded men discharged from hos- ❯

◀ pitals. Poor fighting material.

One German prisoner—an officer—said to me, "I prefer a platoon of seasoned soldiers to a company of such fellows." But seasoned soldiers are not to be had—they are all under ground. For two months sanguinary battles have been raging. Many German regiments in this period have been replenished twice, even thrice, yet they count only fifteen to twenty men to a company. In many tank divisions there are only thirty to forty tanks left instead of 200. The Greater Germany Division which has not suffered as badly as most has sixty tanks. German bombers often fly without fighter protection. All this testifies that the German war machine is badly debilitated.

Formerly the Germans used to drag away their disabled tanks and get them repaired quickly. Now they often leave them where they are. This is more a matter of heart than of machinery: "The German isn't what he used to be," is the way our soldiers put it.

Corporal Fechner of the German Tenth Motorized Division, recently taken prisoner, complained: "The German soldier is used to fighting when results are to be felt at once. But there is no end to war here. And so our fellows are giving way. Do you want facts? Well, look at the number of prisoners here. They

Exhausted German troops surrendering outside of Moscow in 1943.

all surrendered like me, but they might not have surrendered. They might have fought back. In these two years of Russian war the Germans have changed. We have not got our old fighting spirit. Every man is thinking of his own skin."

THAT is the way many Germans think now. The Red Army's summer offensive not only smashed the German's fortifications; it smashed the German's self-confidence. The Conquistadores don't feel so sure of themselves.

I don't mean by this that all Germans have in their hearts capitulated. The Germans are not Italians. They are not the supers, but the authors and directors of war. Italian fascism was a sort of eczema—a skin outbreak. German fascism is a cancerous tumor. Among prisoners you still find many who believe in Der Fuehrer's star.

There is Lieut. Hans Lucke, for instance. He says, "It's true the old fellows at home are grouching. It's true Italy has let us down. It's true the Red Army is now very strong. But I am convinced we will win. If we manage to finish off Russia, we'll go for England. Some, however, think we'll build an 'eastern wall' and then turn against the Englishmen. As regards our post-war aims, most likely we'll settle German colonists in conquered regions who at the same time will be soldiers, as Austria-Hungary did when she defeated Turkey at the beginning of the eighteenth century."

Another prisoner, Lieut. Johann Bechtel, put it more simply: "We believe we'll win because we've got to win. I am talking of the officers and noncommissioned officers. We all understand that victory will mean for us a fine life and a chance to get rich quick."

Prisoners have become more numerous. German Army discipline is not yet undermined, but the Germans surrender more freely. That is a sign the end is near. Having fought in Russia for two years, the German suddenly feels he is a civilian at heart. He yearns for the quiet life. He is profoundly disillusioned. He keeps repeating "We failed." Deal him one more blow and he will cry "Pass, I throw in."

On the other hand, the Russians after two years of war have become a warlike people. Their new spirit finds its expression in many ways. In language, in discipline, in the cult of decorations, shoulder straps and insignia, and in the urge every officer feels to improve his military education.

Our people have changed profoundly in these two years; they have fallen in love with much which they formerly condemned, and learned to dislike much they formerly liked. A war like this plows up men's souls. The Red Army is more of an army today than it was in 1941.

The artist learns a new process of creation. No military academy can replace actual fighting experience. Soviet officers have progressed. There was too much

routine in our army at first. Many were under the spell of the civil war. They had to learn the strategy of a new epoch. In 1939 the Germans were military innovators. They have now become academics—such is the nature of the German character. In a military sense we were backward. Now we have outstripped the Germans. We have a more lively intelligence, more elasticity. I do not mean by this that the Red Army has become a professional army. It is a people fighting.

What force has converted the Siberian farmer into a fierce fighter? What force enables our infantrymen to march forty kilometers a day and smile contemptuously when German bombers hover over their heads? There is something in this war which distinguishes it from all other wars: its motive power isn't intelligence or even ardent love of country but the outraged conscience of the people.

As it advances the Red Army sees all the horrors of "the desert zone." Who would believe that this was once the city of Karachev? Makeyevka, Stalino are in flames. In Taganrog the Red Army saw the horror of the Petrushina Ravine, where lie buried 38,000 inhabitants shot by the Germans. Thirty five thousand inhabitants were carried, off to Germany. And the city had a total population of 200,000. Between Orel and the River Desna stretches a desert waste. Before me lies an order of the German Command for the depopulation of the entire district. It reads:

"Every inhabitant together with his family, cattle and movables shall leave in a westerly direction. Anybody attempting to move eastward will be shot."

When you listen to accounts of survivors, when you look into their eyes dimmed with terror and humiliation, you see a second desert zone—in the hearts of people devastated by two years of arbitrary tyranny.

I know a battalion consisting mainly of men from the Kursk region. Officers and men eagerly awaited news. News came. Eleven learned that their relatives had been hanged or shot, nine learned that their families had been carried off to Germany. Thirty-two learned that their homes had been burned down What force can hold a battalion like this when it is marching westward?

A German officer, Ziegfried Manzke, a war prisoner, said to me, "To continue this war is senseless." Yes, war had sense for the Germans when they set out on a grand robber campaign. War then meant bacon for the German soldier, oil for the German officer. Now war has lost its meaning for them. But it is full of meaning for us—we are teaching them to stop making raids on others' property every quarter of a century. Let their children reflect what a pound of bacon and a ton of oil cost.

The military successes of the last few weeks are a spur to the Russians. But we are not intoxicated by them. We are aware of Germany's strength and are waiting for large-scale military action on the part of our Allies. Much can now be saved—swift coordinated blows may save a large part of Europe which otherwise would be converted into a "desert zone."

I would advise our friends to listen to the voice of Germans themselves. Take Lieut. Arnold Klassen, who says, "It's all up now. In the fall British and Americans will invade Germany. Germany was to have gained decisive results in Russia this summer. But nothing came of it. That means the end is disaster when winter comes. Yet my people were so near the realization of their century-old dreams!"

Let us leave Lieutenant Klassen to sigh over the "century-old dreams" of bandits, but let us realize that within his words is to be found Germany's mortal fear. ◊

Chapter 17

"THREE MEN OF DESTINY"

October–December 1943

By late autumn of 1943 it was evident that the Western Allies were at last preparing to open up a major front in Western Europe. Speculation spread in The Times and elsewhere that George Marshall, Army chief of staff, would be posted to Europe to lead the final campaign to destroy Hitler's Reich. "Soldier without Frills," The Times called him, a modest, hardworking, sensible commander, but one who had yet to head up a field command.

The "Big Three" Allied leaders quietly planned two major summits to discuss the future military and political course of the war. While the meetings were being prepared, the campaigns continued, stuck—often quite literally—in the mud and sand of Italy, Ukraine and the Pacific. In the Soviet Union, the Red Army drove on through the harsh winter rains and snow to seize Kiev on November 7. By the end of the year Soviet troops had marched more than a hundred miles closer to the Polish frontier. Conditions in the Mediterranean theater were just as grim. "The front-line soldier I knew," wrote the famed war correspondent Ernie Pyle in late 1943, "lived for months like an animal," but one haunted by the "cruel, fierce world of death." American troops were short of news from home, but anxious when it arrived. With an eye toward issues of morale, The Times published an article on "What to Write to Soldiers Overseas," which concluded that regular hometown news and a good deal of affection were needed most. For soldiers whose wife or girlfriend wrote to say that she had met someone else, there were informal " 'Dear John' Clubs" where the jilted men could drown their sorrows.

Conditions in the Pacific were, if anything, worse. Dogged Japanese resistance on small islands a long way from the mainland dimmed prospects of reaching the Japanese heartland. On November 1 American and New Zealand troops invaded the island of Bougainville. On November 20, some 35,000 Marines and soldiers tried to capture the atoll of Tarawa in the Gilbert Islands in Operation Galvanic. The battle was fierce and for once American casualties were high compared with Japanese—1,140 Japanese against 4,700 Americans. The battle, one correspondent recorded, was "infinite and indescribable carnage," with bodies and broken vehicles strewn across the narrow stretches of sand and coral.

Against this backdrop, President Roosevelt and Prime Minister Churchill traveled first to Cairo, where they met with the Chinese leader Chiang Kai-shek to discuss the war in Asia, then, on November 20, to the Iranian capital of Teheran, where they met Stalin and his military staff. The "Three Men of Destiny," as The Times called them, without exaggeration. Roosevelt, Churchill and Stalin discussed the course of the war and its political consequences, which assumed increasing importance as the prospect of victory began to seem more likely. Stalin at last got a commitment from his Anglo-American Allies to launch a major invasion of Western Europe, relieving considerable pressure on the Red Army. Cyrus Sulzberger, reporting a few days after the final communiqué was issued (only two correspondents were allowed at the conference), noted in The Times that "Moscow's long pleas for a second front are entirely answered." Churchill had been less enthusiastic than Roosevelt about the prospect of invading Western Europe, but there was nothing he could do to stop the commitment.

By December The Times could report that the invasion plan in Britain was taking shape. Speculation about Marshall as the top field commander was shown in the end to have been just that. He remained in Washington, viewed as indispensable to the overall American war effort, and Eisenhower was transferred from the Mediterranean to take charge of the invasion, code-named in secret Operation Overlord. Facing him was his old enemy from North Africa, Field Marshal Rommel, who in December was put in charge of organizing the defense of the French coast.

OCTOBER 3, 1943

Marshall: Soldier Without Frills

By Sidney Shalett
WASHINGTON.

GEN. GEORGE CATLETT MAR-SHALL is moving toward the climax of his career. As one looks at the man and his record—a record of slow but steady progress—one senses clearly the reasons for his rise to eminence.

Not long ago occurred an incident which gives a sharp clue to the man's character and methods. General Marshall was returning from Algiers. He took a look at the partly empty transport plane which was carrying him and a couple of other high-ranking generals and their aides back to the United States, and observed that it was a "crime" for those seats to be empty when there were so many wounded men who could be saved a trip back home on a slow boat.

In three minutes a young staff officer (the general had no aide de camp) was on his way to an Algerian hospital with orders to pick up some wounded enlisted men who would be able to travel sitting up. He came back with a couple of privates—one with his arm in a sling and the other with his head swathed in bandages. They got in and sat down. Just before the transport took off the general, who still has the powerful shoulders which helped make him an All-Southern football tackle in 1900, hopped into

General George C. Marshall in the 1940s.

the plane, went over to the soldiers and, putting out his hand, said: "I'm General Marshall. Glad to have you with us."

At the next base he heard of an injured second lieutenant who had been awaiting transportation home, so he loaded him into the plane, too. The somewhat awed patients all went to Walter Reed Hospital on their arrival in Washington. Three days later General Marshall, whose mind at the time was full of long-range plans for dislodging the Italians and Germans from Sicily and points north, took time off to call in a staff officer and have him check with the hospital on the condition of the two privates and the shavetail.

The tall, muscular soldier, who will be 63 years old next Dec. 31, is like that. He can be tough as the skin of a General Sherman tank; he can roll a head for incompetence as quickly and inexorably as the bite of a guillotine, yet he is one of the most considerate men in the Army concerning the welfare of his subordinates. His mind is a ready filing system of a vast amount of technical and personal knowledge, and by consulting this filing system he makes rapid decisions concerning men and matters. Dilly-dallying—either mental or physical—and General Marshall just don't mix.

General Marshall also is one of the most untheatrical men in the Army. He has almost a fixation for unornamented language, and he never courts publicity. Men who work closely with him say that he has no phobias against publicity, but that (1) he does not want his work slowed up by the loss of time which would be consumed by posing for pictures, making numerous speeches or granting interviews, and (2) he does not want any monkey wrenches thrown into his delicate job by misconstruction, accidental or otherwise, of what he might say. He is reputed once to have remarked: "No publicity will do me no harm, but some publicity will do me no good." If he wished, however, he could become a constantly publicized figure, for, in addition to his position, now one of the most important in the world, he has the background, the wit and the striking appearance necessary to capture the public fancy.

General Marshall's habits on his frequent inspection trips are another clue to his character. He dislikes guards of honor and formal reviews, and will have nothing to do with either except when absolutely necessary. He likes to drop in unannounced on installations as he wants to see things as they really are. If a division commander, for instance, wants

to show him a rifle range, he asks if any men are shooting on it. If the answer is no, he explodes: "Hell, I've seen a thousand rifle ranges—what I want to see is the men using it."

He has a disconcerting habit of dropping in on mess halls and picking out his own mess hall for inspection so as not to be led into one that has been especially shined up for him. He has a passion for food conservation, and almost inevitably hops behind the counter to check up personally on how much food is coming back uneaten; if anything is wrong, he finds out what and sees that something is done about it. Similarly, if he learns in North Africa, for example, that a jeep motor is knocking because of slowness in delivery of certain parts, he will order an investigation of American camps all over the globe to see if those parts are generally slow in reaching the camps. And when he tells an officer he wants action on something, he doesn't want to hear from the officer that that thing will be corrected next Tuesday; he wants to hear that it was done yesterday.

General Marshall was born at Uniontown, Pa., where his father, a Kentuckian, was a coal and coke operator. The young Marshall wanted to be a soldier as far back as he can remember, although he does not know just what influenced him. His father approved of his ambition, but, being a Southern Democrat in a period when the Civil War was still a strong issue, couldn't get the local Congressman to send young George to West Point. So he went instead to the Virginia Military Institute, where, aside from his football prowess, he was First Captain of the Corps of Cadets. He distinguished himself during his freshman year by stoically keeping his mouth shut after a sophomore hazer ran a bayonet into his body and almost killed him. This same reticence still prevails, for none of the men who work with him (unless it be his most intimate colleagues, who won't tell) ever heard him express himself on whether he would prefer to get out from behind his desk and into the field of action.

He was graduated in the class of 1901 and became a second lieutenant of infantry in the United States Army in February, 1902. He served with great distinction in numerous posts in the first World War, including the important job of Chief of Operations for the First American Army.

Something of his ability for organization and handling great bodies of men was shown in that post; he was responsible for the transfer of several hundred thousand men and their equipment from

St. Mihiel to the Argonne in less than two weeks. He directed their movements by night and handled them so adroitly that the Germans were completely surprised by the presence of this large force when the Argonne offensive began.

He was extremely close to General Pershing, whom be served as aide de camp for a number of years. General Pershing, still one of General Marshall's closest friends, recommended him in France for promotion to a brigadier generalship, but Marshall never rose higher during the war than his temporary rank of colonel, and, indeed, it took him nearly thirty-two years of Army life to achieve the permanent rank of colonel. In September, 1939, however, by which time he had become a brigadier general, President Roosevelt jumped him over the heads of thirty-one senior generals to become Chief of Staff. Five of the preceding fourteen Chiefs of Staff had been non-West Pointers, but General Marshall was the first V.M.I. graduate to fill the post.

General Marshall stands 6 feet and weighs 180 pounds.

SOLDIER WITHOUT FRILLS

His rather stern face has strong lines, more muscular than creased. His eyes are a pronounced blue. One of his great personality talents, particularly during the prewar years when Congressmen still were backward about voting large appropriations for the Army, is his ability to get along well with all kinds of men. He impressed Congressmen by his serious but courteous manner, by his willingness to give them what information they wanted; by the way he could pour out a flood of facts and figures in response to whatever questions they may have sprung upon him, and by the fact that he has the unmistakable air of a man who is telling the truth. The respect which General Marshall won from Congress has had a great deal to do with the rapid manner in which the peacetime Army of 174,000 troops which he took over in 1939 grew to its present status of nearly 8,000,000.

General Marshall is not the kind of man who can delegate all his responsibilities to his staff. However, he has sense enough to know he cannot personally handle thousands of details, so he has evolved a two-point system for meeting the situation: First, he selects as staff officers men who know his methods and in whom he has complete confidence, and, second, he has developed a way of having these men give him thumbnail outlines of current problems so he can grasp a situation without too much waste of time.

When an aide reports to General Marshall on a matter the general listens, then says, "Do it," or, "Don't do it." He makes his decisions with lightning quickness and rarely explains why, and he expects them to be carried out immediately.

He has an incredible knowledge of the personal qualities of hundreds of generals, and his selections have been largely good. It is a tribute to his character that he has placed in high positions a number of men whom he does not care for personally but whom he knows to be good officers.

General Marshall is scrupulous about not granting favors in behalf of service men or officers requested of him by acquaintances or even close friends. He gets hundreds of letters asking such favors, but he replies, in effect, that "it would not be fair to the hundreds of people I have to turn down every day for me to grant this favor to you."

The general has such abhorrence of any frills or excess verbiage in writing that it is not easy for any aide even to write a thank-you note for him. If anyone sends him a letter draft beginning, "Permit me to thank you," the general will scratch it out and substitute, "I thank you."

Almost everything that goes in to him for his signature comes back completely blue-penciled.

He insists on writing at least the bulk of his speeches and reports himself—and his recent 30,000-word biennial report to the Secretary of War was no exception. He once was so impressed by the clear, simple manner in which Maj. Gen. Terry Allen wrote an order during the Tunisian campaign that he sent a copy to President Roosevelt.

General Marshall has always worked very closely with Secretary Stimson. Their traits of integrity and devotion to duty undoubtedly have brought them near together. The general has also spent a good many of his luncheon and afternoon hours with President Roosevelt. There seems to have evolved a smoothly working relationship between the White House and the general, and some observers report that the White House has rarely suggested anything that is counter to War Department policy.

General Marshall has the happy faculty of being able to relax when he is away from his job. In Washington he has enjoyed long walks or canoeing on the Potomac with Mrs. Marshall. He also likes horseback riding and, on the rare occasions when he could get to his own home at Leesburg, Va. he has done hard physical work in the garden. He is an inveterate reader, not restricting

his reading to military subjects. He can relax and read on his long plane trips. He admires the writings of Benjamin Franklin. He enjoys Sherlock Holmes, but not the ordinary whodunit, and he likes to reread books he has enjoyed. One work he recently reread was "The Three Musketeers."

There are two other facts affording insight into the general's character. One is that, while he is the holder of enough United States and foreign military decorations to fill a hat, he does not wear many. Among those always on his blouse, however, are the yellow pre-Pearl Harbor ribbon which every soldier who was in the Army before Dec. 7, 1941, is entitled to wear, and the Victory Ribbon, awarded to everyone who participated in the last war.

The other fact is that he employs no elaborate map system. He has a big globe and a few relief maps of the theatres where American armies are currently in action, but nowhere on any of them is stuck a flag, a symbol or so much as a colored pin.

The general doesn't need flags and colored pins. He carries that information in his head and can tell you, right down to the last division, just what commander is leading what division behind what hill. ◊

OCTOBER 3, 1943

What to Write the Soldier Overseas

By Milton Bracker
By Wireless from Allied Headquarters, North Africa.

Do's and don'ts for those who want to give the news from home and keep up morale at the front.

The dourest dogfaces in Africa these days are strictly non-dues-paying members of the "Dear John" club. That the depth of their despair is matched by members of other chapters throughout Uncle Sam's Army is entirely probable; but that does not matter. In this theatre their melancholy is supreme.

"Dear John" clubs are composed of G.I.'s—and officers, too—who have received letters from home running something like this:

"Dear John: I don't know quite how to begin but I just want to say that Joe Doakes came to town on furlough the other night and he looked very hand- ▶

some in his uniform, so when he asked me for a date—"

Obviously the letter has infinite variations, but the impact on the recipient is always the same. He is "browned off"—and a deep, dark, blackish sort of brown it is.

This cropping up of "Dear John" clubs is symptomatic of the effect mail has on a soldier, no matter where he serves and what his job. Probably the one most dominant war factor in the lives of most people these days is separation—a concept which to many who grew up in traditional American homes was virtually unthinkable before the war. Now sons, brothers, sweethearts, husbands and fathers from Maine, Carolina, Utah and Texas abruptly find themselves in places as unimaginable as Algiers. And the link between them and what they know and love best is much less an abstract patriotic ideal than a very tangible if often humbly written letter from home.

A long-legged G.I. lounging in front of the Red Cross club here the other evening was asked what kind of letter he liked most to receive. "Brother," he said, and you knew at once he came from Carolina, "all Ah evah want is a lettuh." As a matter of fact, soldiers repeatedly tell you they would rather have bad news than no news.

Recently an OWI bulletin was credited here with giving these suggestions for the kind of things to write soldiers: (1) How the family is doing everything to help win the war. (2) How anxious the family is for the soldier's return. (3) How well the family is—giving details. (4) How the family is getting along financially. (5) What is doing in the community, news about girls, doings of friends, who's marrying whom, exploits of the home team, social activities, effects of the war on the home town.

When Private John Welsh 3d of Houston. Tex, saw the bulletin he did a little letter writing himself, and what he did to the suggestions approximated what Allied blockbusters have been doing to German cities. Sgt. H. Bernard Bloom, a former Indianapolis advertising man, has some equally strong opinions on "type letters," although the categories are his own, not ours.

Like his buddies, Bloom regards the "Oh, you poor boy" type as one of the commonest and "most disgusting." This is the kind in which the correspondent "weeps over your body" before anything happens to it. He is equally bitter about the "I'm having fun" type. This is the kind of letter, first cousin to the "Dear John" species, in which the sender tells all about her gay whirl of parties,

dances, cocktail parties, romantic walks in the park with Air Force officers on leave, etc. Bloom goes on to list the "Gee, things are terrible," "I'm sorry to tell you," "I wish I could be with you" and "Look up Cousin Zeke" type as others which plague him and his comrades.

But it would be grossly misleading to suggest that men in uniform are more critical of mail than appreciative. On the contrary, it means everything to them, and certain types of mail in particular can buck up a soldier more than any pep talk by his general. Soldiers carry their letters around with them, save them in footlockers, pull them out at mess table. Their faces light up when letters come, and drop when they don't.

At the risk of attempting a formula, just as OWI did, it would appear safe to say most soldiers and Wacs like to get letters from their loved ones telling, first, that all is well at home; second, that the folks are proud of them—without laying it on thickly—and, third, amiable, chatty details of things close to the soldier's peacetime way of life. And they like answers to direct questions they have written home; nothing is more exasperating than to ask for the specific address of a friend or how certain crops are doing and to have the query completely ignored.

In letters from their sweethearts and wives, soldiers want what every lover since the world began wants—that he is still the sole object of the girl's affection, that she misses him and will wait till kingdom come. There is a difference of opinion on love letters as such, some soldiers saying they don't trust girls who "give out a lot of that goo." But they are not representative of those who have left behind sweethearts, fiancées and wives who mean the world to them.

There was a sergeant named Eddie whom I met in a London restaurant last spring, because they always double up male patrons who come along. He began telling me of the woman he had married just a month or so before leaving. He had a letter with him and in the few paragraphs he read aloud he somehow communicated more of the terror and beauty and solemn anguish of separated lovers than I have ever heard: "And so I don't really worry about you, my darling," his girl wife had written, "because I know that my husband is the best and the bravest and the strongest of all the men who have gone out to fight. Yes, and the gentlest. And I know God will not let anything happen to him because he is like that and because he isn't anyone else's husband. And that makes me very happy."

Maybe the impact is not in the words

themselves; perhaps it was in the way the boy read them, eyes aglow, his voice low. And perhaps you had to realize that he was a rear gunner in a Flying Fortress assigned to a station that had had and was having particularly heavy casualties.

Soldiers are more likely to be inspired and bucked up by personal things—how a namesake nephew is growing up or how the girl friend loved his picture in uniform—than by impersonal notes. They like to know how the war effort is continuing at home, but prefer to take for granted that it is going smoothly than to hear about strikes and wage arguments. They hate complaints about shortages of gasoline, rubber, candy, silk stockings or anything else.

One soldier here was infuriated the other day by a letter from a friend complaining that you could no longer get a hot dog big enough to see for a dime, while on meatless Tuesday you had to eat, etc., etc. "That so-and-so should have had what we had to eat in Kasserine Pass," the soldier said, "and the sound effects, too."

In general the men dislike the approach of those who write, "Don't let anyone tell you we at home don't know there is a war going on." He doesn't like to hear of his girl friend going out with other men, but he is likely to be pleased and amused by her lament that the only men left in town are "4F's, old men and babies." And he is also a sucker for all sorts of photographs of his family, his girl friend, his pets and friends, as well as for any clippings about him that may have broken into the local newspaper. Pictures and clippings never fail where written words may. One soldier said candidly his girl friend wrote him eight pages twice a week—and "frankly, after the first two pages I don't know what the hell I'm reading." He said he would prefer one V-mail letter every day and a longer letter every week or ten days. ◊

OCTOBER 11, 1943

INDIAN CITIES MARKED BY SIGNS OF FAMINE

CALCUTTA, Oct. 10 (Reuter)—It is impossible to go from one place to another in famine-stricken Calcutta and Bengal without steeling one's self to the indescribable sight of men, women and children ly-

OCTOBER 4, 1943

DANISH JEWS POUR ACROSS TO SWEDEN

Many Fugitives Are Pursued Through Jutland—1,600 Reported Already Arrested

FIGHTING IN COPENHAGEN

Stockholm's Offer Of Haven, Ignored By Germans, Bars 2,000 Earlier Refugees

By Wireless to The New York Times

STOCKHOLM, Sweden, Oct. 3—Fleeing the Gestapo terror introduced into Denmark on Thursday, more than 1,000 Danish Jews reached Sweden, most of them last night.

Braving the icy Oeresund, Jewish refugees of all ages and conditions arrived on the Swedish coast. Some even swam the strait—two miles wide at its narrowest point. Others were rowed across by Danish fishermen, who charged $375 to $750 for the passage.

Not all those who have tried to cross have succeeded. It is thought probable that most swimmers were seized by cramps and sank. Others crossing in boats were surprised by German Navy mosquito craft patrolling the strait and

Jewish refugees in Malmo, Sweden, 1943.

their boats were sunk by gunfire.

The refugees said that when the Gestapo intruded on their new year celebrations, some Jews had resisted and both sides had had many killed. [Many are being hunted through Jutland, The Associated Press said.]

Municipal authorities and Red Cross branches in coastal communities in southern Sweden are lodging and feeding the refugees in schools and other available buildings. Many are destitute. Copenhagen reports said that the Gestapo had concentrated on poorer Jews, apparently giving those who could afford to pay huge ransoms a chance to negotiate.

Travelers reaching Sweden tonight said that Heinrich Himmler had arrived in Copenhagen to superintend the round-up of Jews but this was not confirmed by any other source. ◇

OCTOBER 12, 1943

BISHOP DESCRIBES HONG KONG HORROR

O'Gara Gives Details Of His Escape From Execution And Suffering In Japanese Camp

MAKES PLEA FOR CHINESE

Urges Repeal of Exclusion Act and Wants U.S. to Exercise More Influence After War

Recounting the story of his narrow escape from execution and subsequent ordeal as a prisoner of the Japanese, Bishop Cuthbert O'Gara, the Vicar Apostolic of Yuanling and head of the Passionist Missions in western Hunan, China, urged in an interview yesterday that the Chinese Exclusion Act be repealed and also advocated greater American influence in China through offering "cultural and technical assistance to Chinese institutions of learning."

The interview took place in the offices of the Society for the Propagation of the Faith, 109 East Thirty-eighth Street. Bishop O'Gara, who was born in ▶

ing where they fell from starvation, either dead or too weak to utter a sound.

There are fewer beggars in the streets, compared with several weeks ago, but thousands more are too ill to beg or drag themselves about. The Calcutta hospitals, which started to take in "sick destitutes" nearly two months ago, are now mostly overcrowded. Many doctors say that they have seen more suffering in the past month than in the past twenty years.

In the week ended last Thursday there were 527 deaths in the city's hos-

pitals. Countless bodies were picked up in the streets. From Aug. 1 to Oct. 6 two public organizations, one Hindu and one Moslem, together with police squads, disposed of 4,152 bodies, though they were not all starvation cases.

All care of the sick is being coordinated. At free rice kitchens, rice and vegetables are ladled out from huge spoons into the earthen bowls that are the only possessions of the thousands who crowd the kitchens. Some 1,350,000 persons are being fed by free kitchens in the province. ◇

Ottawa, Ont., and is 57 years old, has recovered from his six months of internment by the Japanese at Hong Kong. He expects to return to his post in Yuanling after a stay of two or three months here.

20 YEARS IN CHINA

Bishop O'Gara has been connected with the missionary work of American Passionist priests in China for twenty years and has received high praise from the Chinese Government for his relief activities on behalf of the refugees driven into the interior by the Japanese invaders.

He told of the "fine impression" American airmen and soldiers have made on the Chinese population, both for their fighting ability and faithfulness to their religion.

The Bishop explained that he had flown from Yuanling to Hong Kong for medical treatment eight days before the attack on Pearl Harbor.

"I was at our Catholic hospital in Stanley, just outside Hong Kong, on Christmas morning, 1941," Bishop O'Gara continued, "when the Japanese took me prisoner along with thirty-two of our missionary priests and brothers. We were stripped to our underwear and our hands were bound behind our backs.

"We were taken to a firing line and kept there for about an hour and a half. Then we were questioned and afterward we were put in a garage near by, with our hands still bound.

"I don't know why we were not executed unless it was because Hong Kong surrendered that afternoon—a few minutes after six British officers were bayoneted to death. We expected it to be our turn next.

REMAINED BOUND FOR TWO DAYS

"For four nights and three days we were kept in the garage, still in our underclothes, and for two of those days our

---

OCTOBER 15, 1943

ARMY GETS BOMBERS DWARFING FORTRESS

B-29 Carries More Explosives and Can Range Deep Into Enemies' Territories

FULL REIN IN 1944 LIKELY

Output Rate Rising But No Let-Up in Liberator and Boeing Production Is Planned

By The Associated Press.

WASHINGTON, Oct. 14—A new American super-bomber carrying more explosives and having greater range than any existing war-plane is in actual production.

An unspecified number of the new giants have been delivered to the Army within the last few weeks. An increased rate of output is scheduled for this month.

Dwarfing the Consolidated Liberator and the Boeing Flying Fortress, the new dreadnaught of the sky is reckoned to be capable of bringing the innermost production centers of Hitler's European fortress and the Japanese Empire within reach of United States bombardiers.

The plane has been identified as the B-29 by the Army weekly newspaper Yank in a recent article which said:

"A new super fortress, the B-29, is being built which will have a greater bomb capacity and longer range than any existing bomber."

From previous guarded reports which have cleared military censorship, it appeared that officials did not expect to see the new airplane in combat before 1944. This is presumably because of the time required to attain full-scale production, train crews and eliminate any "bugs" which may show up in the early models,

A prediction that the new heavyweight puncher would be "the determining factor in crushing Germany" came last summer from Capt. E. V. Rickenbacker, World War ace. In June he told the Tenth United States Army Airforce in New Delhi, India, that the new bomber would join the Liberators and Fortresses in 1944.

He also told the American pilots and crewmen that the super-bomber would have double the load and fighting power of the planes they were flying and was especially designed for bombing Europe.

"No nation could survive the pounding a fleet of these planes can deliver and they will be out in mass production next year," Captain Rickenbacker said.

Any statistical comparison of the new plane with the flying fortress is unobtainable at this stage, but Gen. H. H. Arnold, commander of the Army Air Forces, several months ago gave a tipoff to the difference in his remark that Liberators and Fortresses are "the last of the small bombers."

Introduction of the new bomber into the United States' aerial arsenal will not mean the tapering off of production schedules of present-day bombers, it was made clear recently by Charles E. Wilson, executive vice chairman of the War Production Board. Revealing in May that heavy bomber output by April would be eight times greater than in April, 1942, Mr. Wilson added:

"This does not include the scheduled output of the new super-bombers."

Production of Liberators and Fortresses reached a righ record in August, the WPB revealed more recently, with a gain of 11 per cent from July. Over-all aircraft output in August was 7,612 military planes.

It was recently disclosed, also, that the Flying Fortress was undergoing changes to increase its bomb load to ten tons, making it, the heaviest in the world—until, presumably, the super-fortress gets into the fighting. ◆

A B-29 bomber takes off from the air base at Saipan destined for Tokyo in 1944.

wrists remained bound behind our backs, while we were given nothing to eat. On the third day our captors gave us a little milk and hardtack.

"Then we were given outer garments and taken to a dark, filthy Chinese hotel, exactly thirteen and a half feet wide and four stories high. For three weeks we were interned in this place, four prisoners to a cubicle measuring 8 by 10 feet and crawling with vermin.

"After that horror we were moved to a big concentration camp, which hardly deserved its designation by the Japanese as the Stanley Civilian Recreation Cen-ter, although it was a great improvement in our lot as prisoners."

Bishop O'Gara said he believed his release, after more than five months in the internment camp, was brought about "through the good offices of the Holy See." His physical condition then, he said, made it necessary to remain in Hong Kong another month as the guest of the Italian bishop there, Enrico Valtorta.

Asked how he felt about the Chinese Exclusion Act, the Bishop replied: "I feel rather keenly that if relations between China and the United States are to be built on mutual admiration and respect, obstacles such as the Exclusion Act should be removed from the way of a better understanding.

"In the reconstruction period after the war there is much that the United States can do to aid the Chinese. It can give cultural assistance in the way of educational facilities and technical development."

Sun Yat-sen, the founder of the new China, turned to Russia for aid after his first appeal to the United States was virtually ignored. Consequently there has been a strong Russian influence in the new China's development, especially in the last twenty years. ◇

OCTOBER 20, 1943

Editorial
THE BATTLE OF THE DNIEPER

It was just about three weeks ago that Hitler reappeared on the Russian front and supposedly gave orders that the Dnieper line must be held at all costs. And for three weeks now that river has been witnessing one of the fiercest battles of the whole war, in which the resources and the endurance of both sides are being tested to the utmost. The Russians, with a stamina that is all the more remarkable because they have been fighting in a victorious advance since the middle of July, have succeeded in crossing the river at four points and have established bridge-heads which all the German counter-attacks have been unable to eliminate. This drive is synchronized with another farther south, against Melitopol, where bitter street fighting is proceeding now. Together, the two great drives constitute a pin- cer movement which, unless checked, would endanger the whole German position in the Crimea and force a further precipitate retreat.

Yet it is also evident that, having determined to make a stand, the Germans have been able to put up a resistance which testifies to their continued strength and dampens hopes for their quick defeat. We have still to see the whole sig-nificance of the Dnieper River battle. Did the Germans actually decide to hold the Dnieper line "at all costs"? Or did they seek to hold it only to gain time in order to extricate their armies from the Crimea and then continue their retreat to the so-called Moltke line from Lake Peipus, or possibly Riga, to Odessa?

Only the result of the battle can provide the answer, and any indications of what the answer will be are undoubtedly being watched with the keenest interest by the three-Power conference in Moscow. For to the Russians a crumbling of the Dnieper front would be a demonstration that all that is necessary for a quick victory is another front in the west, since the Germans would be shown to be no longer able to stem any determined assault in force. ◇

NOVEMBER 1, 1943

DIMOUT ENDS TODAY EXCEPT BY THE SEA
Police Get Rules for Voluntary Compliance— Street Lights to Be 90% Normal

New York Police Commissioner Lewis J. Valentine issued to all borough commanders yesterday a ten-point set of instructions for their guidance in obtaining voluntary compliance with the "brownout" that is to go into effect today to conserve electricity as a substitute for the dimout that has been in effect for eighteen months.

These instructions revealed that shields would be removed from all traffic lights except those visible from the sea; that street, parkway and bridge lighting would be restored to 90 per cent of normal except where visible from the sea; that masks might be removed from automobile headlights and that the Police Department would take many steps to conserve electricity and thereby reduce the consumption of coal.

OBSERVANCE TO BE VOLUNTARY
The orders issued by Mr. Valentine made it plain, however, that observance was to remain on a strictly voluntary basis. They provided that when a member of the department discovered a violation of the recommendations for business establishments and electric display signs, he was to warn and admonish the offender when possible.

Under no circumstances is a summons to be served or a summary arrest made of any offender, according to the orders. Instead, reports of violations are to be filed in alphabetical and numerical order of the streets and avenues in each precinct. The orders provide that the precinct commander "shall take such further action as may be necessary to insure compliance with these instructions."

The instructions set forth that the engineering bureau of the Police Department was removing shields from traffic lights as rapidly as possible, and that street, parkway and bridge lighting would be restored to 90 per cent of the pre-war normal as measured in kilowatt hours. The excepted areas include those parts of the Rockaways, Coney Island, ❯

{ the south shore of Brooklyn, and the east and southeast shores of Staten Island that are visible from the sea.

AUTO HEADLIGHT INSTRUCTIONS

Masks may be removed from automobile headlights, according to the instructions, but under no circumstances will other than parking lights be permitted along the coast showing seaward. In all other areas low-beam headlights will be permitted, Mr. Valentine noted, as already announced, that subway and elevated trains, surface cars and buses would return to normal prewar lighting.

Outdoor advertising, promotional and display sign lighting will be eliminated in the daytime as well as at night, the instructions disclosed. Electric signs necessary for the identification of places of public service, however, such as shops, stores, theatres, restaurants, public lodging establishments and transportation terminals, may be operated for two hours between dusk and 10 P.M.

Show window lighting must remain as at present and not be increased in intensity, according to the Commissioner's instructions, but the issuance of (A) and (B) certificates for show windows will be discontinued.

Lighting of marquees and building entrances will be eliminated completely in the daytime, and will be reduced as much as is consistent with public safety

at night, according to Mr. Valentine. He also directed that lighting of outdoor business establishments be eliminated completely in the daytime and reduced as much as possible at night.

"Occupants of residences and hotels are to turn off lights when not actually needed and eliminate waste in the use of various electric appliances in homes," the instructions continued.

"Commercial and industrial customers are to turn off lights and appliances when not actually needed. Note: Army air raid regulations require that, at all times, during the hours of darkness, occupants of premises and operators of road vehicles and other conveyances shall not have any unattended lighting."

The police commissioner also announced that the present speed laws of twenty miles an hour at night and twenty-five miles an hour in the daytime would remain in effect except where properly authorized signs indicating greater or lesser speed limits were posted.

MAYOR SOUNDS A WARNING

Mayor La Guardia, in his weekly radio talk over Municipal Station WNYC yesterday, warned that it might be necessary at any time to return to the dimout regulations and that "we will continue to have air raid drills."

The public was told not to expect street lights to return to their former brilliancy immediately. The Mayor cautioned that it would be some time before the entire 70,000 bulbs that are required would be obtained. He said the first batch would be delivered next Monday.

The Mayor disclosed that he was now receiving in his mail "kicks" against the suspension of the dimout, some complaints going so far as to say the dimmed-out lights in subway trains were good for the eyes.

"How would you like to be Mayor of New York?" he asked. "Well, let's say it's funny, because if you didn't think these things were funny you'd just go plain crazy. No matter what we do, the mail continues and the protests continue." ◆

The Statue of Liberty lit only by her torch of two 200-watt lamps instead of the usual thirteen 1,000-watt lamps and pier lights, on Bedloe's Island during New York City's wartime lighting dimout to conserve energy costs.

WAR-CRIME TRIALS SETTLED BY ALLIES
Russia, for First Time, Takes Definitive Stand With the Other Major Powers

Special to The New York Times.

WASHINGTON, Nov. 1—The three-power declaration on German atrocities, the most strongly worded yet issued on the subject and the only one in which Premier Stalin has directly participated, defined today for the first time the jurisdiction over the responsible individuals and the time for their trial and punishment. Those questions were left unsettled in a similar Anglo-American declaration published last Aug. 29 and in earlier warnings made individually by the President and Prime Minister.

While the Russian Government, by various means, had previously made plain its agreement on the general principle of the punishment of war criminals, the lack of complete mutual understanding had been reflected in such incidents as Russia's demand for the immediate trial of Rudolf Hess, Deputy Fuehrer of Germany, after his capture in England.

Today's statement made it clear that Russia now agreed with the United States and Britain that the punishment of war criminals should await the armistice and that jurisdiction would be delegated to the respective countries wronged instead of to an international tribunal, as had been suggested unofficially. The statement mentioned various atrocities perpetrated by the Germans in countries that they have overrun, emphasizing particularly the "monstrous crimes on the territory of the Soviet Union." In the name of the thirty-three United Nations, it gave "full warning" to the Germans.

Detailed lists will be compiled in all the wronged countries, especially the overrun parts of Russia, Poland, Czechoslovakia, Yugoslavia, Greece, Crete and other islands, Norway, Denmark, the Netherlands, Belgium, Luxembourg, France and Italy.

Thus, the statement pointed out, the war criminals will know that they will be brought back to the scenes of their crimes "and judged on the spot by the peoples whom they have outraged." ◆

NOVEMBER 4, 1943

Platoon of Dogs Helps Marines On Bougainville

By The United Press.

WITH UNITED STATES MARINES ON BOUGAINVILLE, Nov. 1 (delayed)—The first Marine dog platoon went into action when the Marines landed today on Bougainville Island, last major Japanese stronghold in the Solomons.

The dogs included twenty-one Doberman pinschers and three German shepherds under the "command" of Lieut. Clyde Henderson of Breckville, Ohio.

Part of the platoon was divided into scout, messenger and first aid units. The first unit will be employed to smell out enemy nests. The second will carry messages to rear headquarters. The third searches out wounded who have crawled to cover.

Lieutenant Henderson said this was the first time a trained dog unit had been employed in this war by American armed forces. ◊

NOVEMBER 21, 1943

Three Men of Destiny
On Roosevelt, Churchill and Stalin depend the shape of things to come— three men of sharp contrast, but alike in the power they wield.

By Anne O'Hare McCormick

The stage is set for one of those great occasions on which history hinges. Preparations have long been under way for a meeting of the three men who are the spokesmen and the symbols of the three most powerful nations on earth. Since the Moscow conference of their Foreign Secretaries it has been clear to all the world that they have an appointment with one another—and with destiny.

It is easy to visualize a meeting of the men, from points very far apart in time and space and ideology, sitting down for the first time at the same table to discuss the future of the world. In the background is a vast panorama of battle— the pounding of the Red Armies driving the Nazis out of Russia, the roar of German cities going up in smoke, the fire of Anglo-American guns blasting the road to Rome. As war commanders, Franklin Roosevelt, Joseph Stalin and Winston Churchill are acutely conscious of these mighty movements in the field. They know that a decisive shifting of pressure from the Eastern to the Western front is in full progress. But though war has made them allies, almost without their own volition, the primary purpose of their meeting is not to discuss war strategy. The military plans are made and the issue of the conflict is beyond doubt. What at last brings the three leaders together in person is the certainty that the war is won.

This is the great significance of the conference. It is a peace conference, held to confirm and fill in the outlines of the agreements signed by the Foreign Ministers in Moscow. Since it could not take place until a basis of agreement was reached, it is a dramatic notification to the world that the victors are resolved to perpetuate their partnership and work out a joint strategy for victory.

Here is a scene that will live as one of the famous conversation pieces of our epoch. The table is likely to be smaller and the conversation more private and informal than in the Hull-Eden-Molotoff meeting. In the most important talks the three men will probably be alone except for an interpreter or two. Stalin always provides his own, and while the necessity of translation will slow up the give-and-take, it will not dam the flow of discussion. The President and the Prime Minister are fluent, highly expressive men who relish the flavor of their own phrases. Stalin, for all his reputation as a man of mystery, is by no means a man of silence. He has the blunt decisiveness of a leader who is never contradicted, but he was trained in the Marxist dialectic and he is given to embroidering his points with copious arguments.

Even the shapes of the faces are a study in contrasts. The round, cherubic countenance of the Briton differs as sharply from the square, pock-marked visage of the Georgian as both do from the oval, smiling face of the American. Stalin's cool eyes are watchful under a grizzled brush of hair. As he sits calmly smoking his pipe, the effect of power in repose heightened by occasional slow, lithe, panther-like movements, he does not miss a gesture or expression.

The President's eyes are cool, too, and slightly quizzical. He makes large gestures with his long-holdered cigarette, and appears more casual and at ease than the others, but his unquenchable curiosity and his interest in this encounter, which he has desired for years, make him as alert as Stalin. Churchill listens with half-closed eyes, slumped in his chair. He chews his fat cigar more than he smokes it, and this gives him a slightly ruminant air. But nothing escapes him either, and his opinions are delivered with a flash and vigor that show the high tension of his mind.

These are the men cast by destiny to play stellar roles in the tremendous drama of war and peace. They are alike in the power they wield and the massive self-confidence with which each in his different way exercises his authority. Stalin is the absolute dictator, master of a party machine that has welded "all the Russias" into a unity and force they never knew before. He stands guard over the biggest land mass on earth, a living Colossus of Rhodes who straddles two continents and links them into one.

There is not the slightest prospect that he will modify the system which has proved stronger under the test of war than even he could have predicted. Obviously it gives him an advantage in negotiation over the heads of democratic governments, who can never decide anything with the same finality, or speak without looking behind their shoulders at their parliaments and their public.

Yet the war, while it has increased Stalin's popularity, has in some degree diminished his power. It has obliged him to take more people into council— the military chiefs, the directors of the war industries, the spokesmen of soldiers, refugees, peasants—and the effect of this wider consultation, plus the force of events, is clearly visible in the changes that are taking place within the Soviet system while the fighting goes on.

By the same logic the war has given authority very like that of a dictator to Mr. Roosevelt and Mr. Churchill. They have been obliged to assume extraordinary powers, to make secret plans and decisions, to impose military censorships that often lap over into civilian fields. Total war applies its own rules, its own uniformity. Hence, as war leaders, the three statesmen meet on a basis nearer equality of function than would be possible in peacetime.

All three, moreover, are by nature men of strong will who are irked by interference. Roosevelt cloaks his masterful temperament in an amiable manner. Stalin's steely hardness is hardly concealed by his level voice, his lusty humor and the genial prodigality with which he dispenses Oriental hospitality. Churchill is much more the bulldog type than either. He is John Bull in person, short, round, rosy, a mighty trencherman and a mighty talker, whose eloquent tongue lisps in private conversation, but not in hesitation, and always in the ringing rhythms of Milton and the King James Bible.

Such likenesses are not strange in leaders who are not where they are by accident. They have forged their way to the top because they are rulers by will and temperament. What is strange is that they have reached their present eminence, truly awful in its responsibility, from such different backgrounds and by such different processes. The representatives of democracy are both aristocrats. Churchill likes to think he is half American, but he is English in every fiber of his being and every turn of his thought.

He has not always belonged to the Conservative party, but he is nevertheless a true Conservative and a professing imperialist in the British style, which is ample enough to adapt itself to new conditions. He has not always held office, and but for the war would never have realized a lifelong ambition to be Prime Minister. Yet he has always been in politics, a passionate parliamentarian. In their lives and thought and view of government there is no common meeting ground between Winston Churchill and Joseph Stalin.

Roosevelt and Stalin have a point of contact in that both are more adept politicians than Churchill. They share a relish for politics as a game. The Soviet leader gained control of the Communist party and changed its direction by adroit and patient manipulation: Under entirely different conditions, the President's skill as a political maneuverer has changed the political alignments in this country without changing the party labels.

But there the likeness ends, Roosevelt typifies the oldest and solidest America. His Groton-Harvard-Hyde Park background is near Mr. Churchill's, but as remote from Stalin's as the White House is from the Kremlin. Neither Churchill nor Roosevelt can have even an imaginative conception of the life of the cobbler's son of Tiflis who grew up as a conspirator, holding up banks and organizing underground revolution in Czarist Russia while Lenin and the intellectual leaders of the revolution were producing its literature abroad.

The two democratic statesmen are types and products of a world that Stalin has never known, and he is the product of a world that they have never known. Roosevelt and Churchill have flourished in the upper strata of a free society, have traveled widely, have reached their present position through the smooth working of a well-established democratic system. Stalin fought his way up from the underground; he is the first guerrilla leader come to power. Perhaps the most vital hiatus between them as they talk is that the Englishman and the American know the world and do not know Russia, while the Russian knows Russia and does not know the world.

The President, asked not long ago what he would say to Stalin when they met, replied that to begin with he would announce that he was a realist and intended to discuss the problems that had to be dealt with in common on the basis of realism. This is a tribute to Stalin as the "great realist." But it implies that his definition of realities is the same as ours. On the question of Russia's western borderlands, for instance, the Soviet position is very clear. Not only the Moscow press and other Soviet spokesmen but Stalin himself has announced that the frontiers they claim are beyond discussion. This may be true for Russia, but the President and the Prime Minister are uncomfortably aware that they are not beyond discussion in Great Britain and the United States.

This is only one of many ticklish questions on which there will be one mind in the Soviet Union and opinion will be divided in the democracies. It illustrates the difficulties that will have to be faced and surmounted in these conversations. For agreement must be reached on some terms if the coming victory, purchased at a price that is still far from paid, will lead to the peace and order the three powers and their representatives are working for. The quest for peace is the reality overshadowing all lesser considerations, and if the three statesmen convince one another that this

is the paramount aim of all, they will proceed in an atmosphere of confidence in which all problems are arguable—and soluble.

Can men coming together from points so far apart, shaped by personal experiences and systems of life so different, driven together only by the attack of a common enemy and carrying with them so many old suspicions and reservations, create the atmosphere of agreement?

The answer is threefold. In the first place they have sought this rendezvous. Slowly, even reluctantly, it has grown out of a decision that must be a tripartite decision or the meeting would not take place. The decision is that the safety of Russia, Great Britain and the United States requires that they shall work together to win the peace as well as the war. Stalin, Roosevelt and Churchill are above all representatives of the supreme national interests of their respective countries. They are convinced that the cooperation they seek from one another constitutes the minimum guarantee of "peace in our time."

The second part of the answer is to be found in the aspirations of the statesmen themselves. It is a fact of prime importance that all are inclined to view themselves in the light of history. Churchill is a historian. He has studied with minute care the career and character of his ancestor, the Duke of Marlborough, and he can hardly help thinking of himself as the second of his line to take his place among the immortals in the story of England. Certainly his speeches are addressed as much to the reader of tomorrow as to the listener of today.

In the first year of the war, while waiting to see Churchill in the library of Admiralty House, I picked up from the table the book in which he describes his early life. When my turn came I told him I found the story so interesting that I was almost sorry to be interrupted. Immediately he offered to give me a copy of the book. "But no," he said on second thought, "if I give you a book it won't be that one. I'll give you a volume of my speeches because they are historic documents. It is by my speeches that I shall be remembered in history."

To listen to Stalin talking of Lenin, and of himself as the successor of the founder of the Soviet State, is to understand that he, too, considers himself a chosen instrument of history. The true Communist sacrifices himself to posterity as eagerly as the true Christian bears the sufferings of this life in anticipation of rewards in heaven. If Stalin is no longer the single-minded Communist, it is because he has become the heir of Peter the Great. He has banished the Old Bolsheviks in favor of the heroes of imperial history beause he beholds Russia today as a great, perhaps the greatest, power in the world and himself as a towering figure in the pageant of that greatness.

The President's sense of history is very strong. Long before the war, from the beginning of his administration, in fact, he thought of himself as one of the small company of American Chief Executives destined to loom large in the record because they preside over periods of convulsive change. Perhaps this premonition of immortality came from his triumph over physical disability; perhaps from the crisis in which he was inducted into office. As time passed, at any rate, it grew stronger. The part he felt elected to play became not simply an American but a world role.

Neither Stalin, the triumphant revolutionary who revitalizes the power of Russia, nor Churchill, the triumphant Conservative who restores the prestige of the British Empire, has a greater sense of mission and of destiny than Franklin Roosevelt. Perhaps he thinks in even larger terms than they do. Certainly he is more attracted by large ideas and global plans. His field for the Four Freedoms is "everywhere in the world." So he is likely to be more stirred than the others by this meeting not merely because he responds to drama but because he is playing there the role he most covets. Roosevelt would like to go down in history as the great peacemaker. For a long time he was lukewarm to the Wilsonian dream, and he is much readier than Wilson to compromise with the ideal. Yet in a strange way—strange because it shows that in spite of our defection it is indigenous to America—it is still the same dream. Roosevelt also yearns to be the founder of a world peace system.

On two counts, therefore, because the three men aspire to a large niche in history, and because they believe cooperation is a safer national policy than isolation, there is reason to hope that they will strive hard to agree on the concrete decisions left suspended at the Moscow conference.

The unanswered part of the question depends on more imponderable factors. It depends in no small part on what might be called the intra-relations within the Big Three, the personal impressions they make, the impact of the mind and manner of each upon the others. The Prime Minister and the President are already friends. Churchill did not get on too well with Stalin when he went to Moscow at the height of the Russian dissatisfaction at the failure to open the second front. The picture is different now. But what effect will the Roosevelt charm have on Stalin?

Winston Churchill has frequently mused aloud on the fate that has pushed the President, Stalin and himself into a relationship none of them could have foreseen when the war began. It strikes him as extraordinary that this oddly assorted trio should be brought into conjunction and given a joint control of a great crisis in the destiny of mankind.

It is extraordinary that a few men should exercise so much power that the interplay of their ideas and their personalities should be so important as it is. It is extraordinary that so much should depend on how they get on together at this historic parley. But that is so only because they are all alike instruments of great forces and symbols of the desperate hopes of peoples that these forces can be controlled and used henceforth for construction instead of destruction. Whether they can work together depends, finally, not on three men, however powerful they are, but on the will of the great nations they represent. ◊

SCENE OF PARLEY LIKE ARMED CAMP
Each Delegate's Villa and Hotel Where Sessions Were Held Under Heavy Guard

By Cable to The New York Times.

CAIRO, Egypt, Dec. 1—Not since the days of the Ptolemys has Egypt been such a cynosure of attention from the civilized world.

The fact that something big was about to happen was a wide-open secret in the rumor-ridden cities of the African periphery for weeks. Finally, after a flood of rumors, it was blandly announced on the morning of Nov. 22 that Prime Minister Churchill, President Roosevelt and Generalissimo Chiang Kai-shek, accompanied by their principal military advisers, had arrived here.

CHIANG FLIES IN AMERICAN PLANE
Dr. Hollington Tong, the Chinese Vice Minister of Information, then told about the Generalissimo's first visit thus far west except for his trip to Moscow several years ago. The Chinese party came in two four-engined American planes with American crews. General Chiang's plane arrived at 7 P.M. on Nov. 21. Mme. Chiang was not in good health but felt that her presence was needed. Only two long stops were made on the four-day journey, General Chiang's first from China since his trip to India in 1942.

Major George Durno, a former White House correspondent who is handling Mr. Roosevelt's press relations, then spoke of the President's trip. There was a sudden hush when he quietly stated that not only the President but the Army and Navy staffs were here. "The President requests you fellows to have lots of fun for three or four days, then get your answer at a press conference," he said.

Mr. Roosevelt arrived on the morning of Nov. 22 by plane. Rear Admiral Wilson Brown, his naval aide; Rear Admiral Ross McIntyre, his physician: Harry Hopkins, Rear Admiral William Leahy and service men came with him. The plane was protected by fighters.

PLANE BROUGHT SPECIAL JEEP
It taxied up to an enormous concentration of jeeps, armored cars and guard patrols blocking all points as Mr. Roosevelt's special jeep was unloaded from the huge plane. The President then drove off past lines of soldiers guarding the road with their faces sternly pointed to the desert. Not a single eye peeked at the road for a glimpse of the visitor as the armored cars swirled protectively through the desert.

Mr. Churchill, who had arrived the previous evening by warship at Alexandria, having called at Gibraltar, Algiers and Malta, was accompanied by a party that included his daughter, Sarah Oliver, and Ambassador John G. Winant. The ship had a special cipher staff and map room, permitting the Prime Minister to carry on his regular work. ▸

❧ The three Allied leaders took time from their talks to visit the Pyramids and the Sphinx.

The President stood the journey well. He had never been so far east, Major Durno said.

The President saw Mr. Churchill first on the afternoon of Nov. 22 in his villa. All the leaders met in their villas, compared to the general conferences.

34 VILLAS, ALL GUARDED

At 10 A.M. on Nov. 23 the chief of the Office of War Information in Asia took up the story with a description of the physical set-up of the conference. "There are thirty-four villas in the hotel's general vicinity," he said, "with its own guards around each one in which the 'big shots' live. Each villa can be considered a separate defensive area protected by British and American guards. The whole region is a general defense area protected by its own guns and searchlights.

"Right alongside the peasants laboring in the cabbage and corn fields, there are ack-ack batteries. Near the road turn-off British and American M.P.'s are on sentry duty. One needs two passes to penetrate beyond there— a special delegate's pass and your own identity paper. After that, accredited visitors are again stopped twice before they are admitted to the hotel."

Within the hotel were the service agencies: billeting, transportation and information desks. Observers' desks, for those officials reporting the occasion to the world, were in the corner. On the left was the bar.

The main conference room was back near the dining room, in a former salon. Other conference chambers were on the left. An American Army post exchange was set up in a corner. Conference Room No. 1 was a big private dining room with twenty-eight seats grouped around a green-baize-covered table.

Both the dining room and the bar were much in use by the delegates, who did not pay cash but merely signed chits.

CONFERENCES BEGUN NOV. 22

At 11 A.M. on Nov. 22, the conference began. Gen. George C. Marshall entered the central lobby. Shortly thereafter, papers and pencils were rushed into Conference Room No. 1 and soon the military chiefs entered the chamber. A little later Lieut. Gen. Joseph Stilwell

The Cairo Conference, in 1943. From left, Chiang Kai-shek, Roosevelt, Churchill and Mme. Chiang Kai-shek.

came up and asked where Conference Room No. 4 was. At 3 P.M. a general conference began, after the staff talks, the OWI official said.

At this point the correspondents rushed in with a series of questions regarding the details and color surrounding the meeting. The following unrelated facts emerged:

On Sunday night, Nov. 21, General Chiang called on Mr. Churchill and at 11 A.M. the next day the Prime Minister called on Mr. Roosevelt.

The entire ground floor of the hotel was devoted to conference rooms, of which there were five. There were offices on the first, second and third floors. About eighty offices were prepared in advance.

Maps posted in the main corridors listed the offices. Special telephone directories and exchanges were prepared, each national delegation having its own differently colored directory.

The British Government acted as host for the conference, footing all the bills. The preliminary arrangements for this meeting began some time ago, with about twenty specially sworn officers and more than 200 soldiers making preparations.

Outside the hotel, in the garden, British medical and dental posts were erected in special tents with tiled floors. Serious medical cases would have been

sent off immediately by ambulance to the Fifteenth General Hospital.

The first call on the medical officers was made by Mme. Chiang shortly after her arrival on Sunday. She had her own doctor with her, but was bothered by serious eye trouble and her face was swollen. After a consultation between a conference medical officer and the Chinese doctor, specialists were called and Mme. Chiang was treated for a painful, but not serious, illness.

A special deep air-raid shelter and many slit-trenches were built around the hotel and the villas.

The make-up of the British delegation was announced after these details had been given. Mr. Churchill brought, as his aide-de-camp in his capacity of Minister of Defense, his daughter, Section Officer Sarah Oliver of the Waaf, the wife of the well-known comedian.

His party included Lord Moran, president of the Royal College of Physicians, as his doctor; Comdr. C.V.R. Thompson, his personal assistant, and two private secretaries.

On Monday, after his call on Mr. Roosevelt, Mr. Churchill repaid a call by General Chiang at noon in the latter's villa.

At 3 P.M. on Monday the first big meeting in Conference Room No. 1

commenced. British marine guards were posted at each door.

The room looks out on a path leading to the hotel's drained swimming pool, which was also blocked off and guarded.

British, American and Chinese delegates attended the session. They included the service chiefs of all three nations. The sitting lasted one hour.

The British delegation's offices were on the first floor, the Americans' on the second.

On Monday afternoon the hotel was like a railway station. World-important figures were milling about, shouting "Hello, how are you? I haven't seen you for a long time." Numerous beribboned generals were moving around in clusters.

As one American observer put it, the interior of the conference room was very depressing and filled with gaudy furniture. The lobby was like a college-town hotel during a class reunion.

On Nov. 23, two conferences took place in the hotel. A British staff meeting occurred between 9:45 A.M. and 12:30 P.M. and an American counterpart lasted from 11 A. M. to 12:30 P.M. This, it was explained, was the normal procedure for staff talks.

On Sunday evening, according to later disclosures, Mr. Churchill had all the British staff chiefs to dinner in his villa, and informal talks followed. On Monday morning he conferred with Sir Archibald Clark-Kerr, Ambassador to Russia, then called on Mr. Roosevelt and General Chiang. Gen. Carton de Wiart was present at the latter call. Mr. Churchill lunched privately with Mr. Roosevelt at the latter's villa, rested during the afternoon and then dined with him. After dinner the two statesmen held a discussion with their military staffs. No Chinese were present. The Prime Minister returned to his villa with the British chiefs and worked until 2 A.M.

On Tuesday morning a plenary conference was held among the political chiefs at President Roosevelt's villa. Chinese representatives attended. Mr. Churchill and Mr. Roosevelt again lunched together.

During the conference Mr. Churchill and Mr. Roosevelt visited the Pyramids. Mr. Roosevelt sat in a large brown car while Mr. Churchill, his daughter and staff walked about at the base of the Sphinx.

The statesmen remained a half hour. As the sun began to set in the western desert they moved on to a point from which the Pyramids could best be viewed with security. Officers rattled

behind on jeeps and a few British antiaircraft gunners manning the nearby defenses gazed on in awe.

IMPORTANT TALK ON ASIA

On the afternoon of Nov. 23 an important conference concerning Allied strategy in Asia was held. At 3:20 P.M. word ran through the hotel that General Chiang was coming. Large colored maps of Asia were placed on the walls of the conference rooms and place-cards were affixed to the green table.

General Chiang was placed at the north end and Admiral the Lord Louis Mountbatten at the south, with various generals and admirals between. The Chinese were all handsomely uniformed and included China's only admiral, C. S. Yang.

This key talk began at 3:30 P.M. and ended a half hour later when the delegates, preceded by Admiral Leahy, emerged with earnest, grim expressions. Admiral Leahy led a group of high officials upstairs with Maj. Gen. Claire L. Chennault to the American secretariat, while five Chinese officers waited in the lobby.

The arrival of Ambassador Laurence A. Steinhardt indicated that Turkey's position would be reviewed.

On the morning of Nov. 24 three important meetings took place:

The British staff chiefs met in Room 1 for an hour, other British experts met for a short time in Room 5, and all morning long the American chiefs of staff as well as some Chinese conferred in Room 4.

The delegates were working excessively hard by midweek. There was much shuttling about, with sixty-four jeeps making more than 150 trips daily. By Wednesday evening it was established that Mr. Roosevelt, Mr. Churchill, General Chiang and their staff chiefs were in constant daily contact. General and Mme. Chiang saw Mr. Roosevelt on Nov. 22 and dined at his villa the next evening. General Marshall had dinner alone with Mr. Churchill on Nov. 23.

At 11 A.M. on Wednesday a plenary conference was held in Mr. Roosevelt's villa among the Government chiefs and their staffs. The President lunched with Mr. Churchill afterward.

By the morning of Nov. 25 a galaxy of famous Allied figures had appeared. Virtually every famous United Nations military leader was here.

Dr. Tong revealed details of General Chiang's daily routine, pointing out that it was unchanged by the African atmosphere and the press of new work.

The Generalissimo rises at 5 A.M. and spends a half hour at his devotions. After breakfast he starts his work.

Both Generalissimo and Mme. Chiang atended the plenary conferences with the heads of states, where Madame Chiang interpreted for her husband. But neither attended the strategic staff talks.

General Shan Chen, director general of National Military Council, represented China as senior military officer, with Admiral Yang as chief of intelligence, since the only navy that he has is Yangtze River gunboats. Gen. Shih Ming, military attaché in Washington, acted as interpreter.

On the evening of Nov. 24 there were new arrivals. Harold Macmillan, British member of the Italian Advisory Council, flew in. Then Foreign Secretary Anthony Eden arrived with Sir Alexander Cadogan.

EISENHOWER AND MURPHY ATTEND

On Nov. 25, Gen. Dwight D. Eisenhower and Robert D. Murphy arrived. This indicated obvious preparations to include European aspects in what had hitherto been primarily Asiatic talks.

Although Thursday was Thanksgiving, the conferences continued, with two American talks in the morning as well as one British staff talk. But during the afternoon the conferences were largely limited to lesser officers. A new world map was placed in the main meeting room.

On Thanksgiving Day, General Eisenhower received the Legion of Merit from Mr. Roosevelt at his villa before General Marshall. The award was made for his "outstanding contributions to the Allied cause." Mr. Roosevelt dined the previous night with Mr. Churchill, Mr. Eden, Mr. Hopkins, W. Averill Harriman, Mr. Winant, Col. Elliott Roosevelt, Maj. John Boettiger and others.

All during Nov. 26, Mr. Eden worked steadily, conferring often with Mr. Winant and lunching with several Allied dignitaries. In the afternoon, in Conference Room 1, there was an important meeting of the staff chiefs and the Mediterranean commanders. After an hour the Mediterranean experts left but the conference continued.

After some time the most secret talks, among staff chiefs only, commenced. All others left the room and the Marine Guards were ordered to permit no entries, regardless of rank. ◆

DECEMBER 2, 1943

1,026 MARINES LOST IN TARAWA CAPTURE

2,557 Wounded, Nimitz Reveals— 65 Soldiers Died On Makin, 121 Injured In Assault

ONE SLAIN ON ABEMAMA

Our Total Casualties Of 3,772 Compare With Japanese Dead Numbering 5,700

By GEORGE F. HORNE
By Telephone to The New York Times.

PEARL HARBOR, Dec. 1—Our total casualties among assault forces in the Gilberts occupation numbered 3,772 men.

Admiral Chester W. Nimitz, commanding the United States Fleet and Pacific Ocean areas, in a communiqué issued before noon today, listed total casualties on the basis of preliminary reports that have come in from Vice Admiral Raymond A. Spruance, commander of the Central Pacific force; Maj. Gen. Ralph C. Smith, USA, commanding the Twenty-seventh Division, elements of which made the landing on Makin, and Maj. Gen. Julian Smith, United States Marine Corps, commanding the Second Marine Division, which took Tarawa.

The figures reveal that at Tarawa 1,026 men were killed in action and 2,557 wounded; at Makin sixty-five were killed in action and 121 wounded, and at Abemama one was killed in action and two were wounded.

The figures noted in the communiqué are approximate and cover events up to today. Final and conclusive reports, which will take some time in preparation, are not expected to vary greatly from these estimates, which have been released with unusual promptness following the termination of the engagement.

WARNINGS RECALLED

In the light of stern warnings issued in high quarters here and in Washington and equally in view of the tremendous value that will accrue to us in possession of the islands, the losses are not considered too extreme.

The losses might well have been much higher, considering the surprising strength of the Japanese defenses at Tarawa, and they may be compared favorably with Japanese losses. In assault operations of this kind it is almost invariably the case that the attacking troops lose more than the defenders. Tarawa was taken by less than a division

of marines, against about 4,500 Japanese defenders, of whom approximately 3,500 were fighting men and the rest laborers.

At Makin there were fewer than 1,000 Japanese. The assault there took fifty-four hours. Landings on Abemama, which took place after the other battles were well under way, met virtually no resistance and the marine raider force cleaned up the island in a matter of a few hours. Abemama was defended by fewer than 200 men.

The figures released today include a few Navy and Coast Guard casualties among the men of these elements who engaged in the landings as part of the medical forces and landing boat crews.

Against our losses it is now possible to set fairly accurate figures of Japanese losses. We all but wiped out the garrisons of the enemy on these islands, for few prisoners were taken. Including the laborer-prisoners mentioned in the overall figures, the Japanese had approximately 5,700 men on the three atoll groups.

In the absence of any indication of severe losses among our sea forces—and Secretary of Navy Frank Knox has been quoted in Washington to the effect that they were "light"—it is fair to compare our total killed in action—1,092—with the total Japanese strength of 5,700.

No attempt is made in the comparison to gloss the rugged truth. Admiral Nimitz, in his stark communiqué says merely, "Preliminary reports of the Gilbert operations indicate that our landing forces suffered the following approximate casualties," and then comes the table.

A few remaining enemy stragglers in the north of Tarawa atoll were mentioned two days ago. There are no more now. The last sniper has been ferreted out and the last foxhole purged. No Japanese are left in the Gilberts.

2 CARRIERS SUNK, FOE CLAIMS

A Tokyo broadcast recorded by The Associated Press in New York quoted a Japanese Imperial Headquarters communiqué as saying that Japanese naval aircraft had sunk two Allied aircraft carriers and another unidentified warship east of the Gilbert Islands on the night of Nov. 29. A large cruiser also was set afire, said the communiqué, which was wholly unconfirmed by any Allied reports. The Japanese acknowledged the loss of six planes. ◈

The aftermath of the Battle of Tarawa.

DECEMBER 3, 1943

AMERICANS BATTLE THE MUD IN ITALY
The Going Against Germans Is Also Tough—Foe's Boots Held Superior to Ours

By HERBERT L. MATTHEWS
By Wireless to The New York Times.

WITH ALLIED FIFTH ARMY IN ITALY, Dec. 1 (Delayed)—It is slow, hard going in the hills north of Venafro, where the American force is slogging its way from hill to hill, the writer learned today on a visit to the front.

The Germans are contesting every mountain top and for two days they have been fighting vainly to get back one mountain west of Montaquilo. On Monday they attacked it four times and last night they went for it in earnest with a few companies of infantry, preceded by artillery and mortar fire.

This afternoon we were still holding that hill and another one south of Castelnuovo, which the Germans hung on to grimly and have been trying to take back ever since it was lost. It was tough, close fighting on that mountain, with soldiers within less than a hundred yards of each other, throwing hand grenades. In repulsing last night's attack west of Montaquilo grenades were also used along with everything else that the Americans had, from artillery down to rifles.

With weather still bad and the Germans contesting every summit, the troops cannot advance quickly. All morning there was a cold, driving rain, with oceans of mud under foot—mud in which you flounder, slide and often fall, mud that splashes you from head to foot, mud in which even a four-wheel drive jeep skids as if on ice. It is miserable for the soldiers, but with pup tents and sometimes caves, with overcoats, extra blankets and sometimes overshoes, it becomes bearable.

The Germans, incidentally, are dressed as well as American soldiers and with even better boots. They are a good type of soldier along this whole sector and they are fighting well.

Around Venafro itself the front has been static for both sides, which have had each other pinned down so that, as one officer put it to me, "If Jerry as much as raises his head during the daytime it comes off, and the same goes for our boys."

So all the fighting is done at night, and sometimes units go astray in the dark, which happened yesterday just before 10, near Mignano, when a German company, evidently moving into line, came under our observation and was heavily shelled.

Today the communiqué mentions reconnaissance in force that took place northeast of Mignano. Our unit went out night before last and stayed all day yesterday, returning safely, its mission accomplished. ◆

DECEMBER 4, 1943

AMERICAN FORCES HELPING TO WRITE THE EPIC OF MAKIN AND TARAWA
Grim Tarawa Defense a Surprise, Eyewitness of Battle Reveals Marines Went in Chuckling, To Find Swift Death Instead of Easy Conquest—Writer Senses 'Something Wrong'

This eyewitness account of the conquest of Tarawa was written by the first Marine Corps combat correspondent to land on Tarawa Atoll, in the Gilbert Islands:

By SGT. JAMES LUCAS

TARAWA, Nov. 23 (Delayed) (AP)—Five minutes ago we wrested this strategic Gilbert Island outpost and its all-important air strip from the Japanese who seized it from a few missionaries and natives weeks after they had attacked Pearl Harbor.

It has been the bitterest, costliest, most sustained fighting on any front. It has cost us the lives of hundreds of United States Marines. But we have wiped out a force of 4,000 Imperial Japanese Marines—we expected to find only 2,000—mostly dead.

Before we started it was great fun. We grinned and chortled. We said, "There won't be a Jap alive when we get ashore."

That was the plan. Naval and air bombardment was to all but destroy the island.

But something suddenly appeared to have gone wrong. We learned H hour had been delayed thirty-one, then forty-five minutes. The pounding continued. There was little doubt there were still living—and fighting—Japs on the island.

Fifteen minutes later, we climbed into our tank lighter, sharing it with many other marines, and a truck and a trailer.

"We have landed against heavy opposition," came the first word from shore. "Casualties severe."

It came over our radio as we moved in. We looked grimly at each other.

A control boat roared by, a naval officer screaming at us to "stay back" until we received word it was safe to go in. That was 10:30 A.M.

TURNED BACK TWICE MORE

At 1 P.M. we started in again, moving toward the pier which appeared undamaged. We were stopped by machine gun fire.

At 3 P.M. we tried again. Shells tore the water on all sides. Two more boats went down, and more marines died. We backed out again, unable to pick up the survivors. Many of them swam to us, and were later moved back to their ❯

transports. Many of the wounded drowned.

The sun was punishing. There was no shade. We broke out our rations and nibbled at them.

At midnight the control boat appeared out of the darkness. We were to try again.

We inched toward the dock, partly wrecked by our own shelling. The hulk of a Japanese merchantman loomed to the right. Two direct hits from our destroyers had put it out of action. On the lookout for snipers, we covered it with our machine guns.

When we reached the dock snipers in the wrecked ship opened up, but they were firing over our heads. We climbed on the dock and more snipers fired. We hit the deck. We moved down the docks ten feet. Japs on the beach began throwing mortars our way. We hit the deck again.

Minutes later a second mortar hit directly beneath us. I felt the blast and was sprayed with salt water.

Someone yelled:

"Get to the other side! The next one will be right on!"

We were uncertain where to go. The Japs' lines were only fifty yards past the end of the pier, and there was no command post.

The last seventy-five yards of the pier was white coral grit. There was a brilliant moon—at home I would have called it beautiful. We swore at it viciously. We were perfect targets.

Crouched, we sprinted down the pier, silhouetted against the coral. Snipers opened up, and six men fell, screaming in agony. We lay like logs.

"We can't stay here," someone said up the line. "They'll shell hell out of us and we'll all be gone."

"Advance slowly. Five feet between each man. They won't get us all that way."

FIRST FOXHOLE ON ISLAND

We started. Three more marines fell, and we hit the ground. Inch by inch we moved up. Each ten yards cost us the lives of more marines.

On the beach, the fire was still hot. We ducked behind the wreckage of a Japanese steam roller which appeared to be between us and the enemy. I found a shovel and began frantically to dig. Within five minutes we had our first foxhole on Tarawa.

There we spent the night. It was 4 A.M. when we got to lie down.

At dawn we found our position precarious. Our own men were on the left of us, the Japs not more than fifty yards on the right. We were in No Man's Land.

At 6 A.M. a fight began over our foxhole. Scores of bullets nicked off the big steam roller, while we burrowed deeper.

Shortly before noon the Japs were driven back, and we came out of hiding.

Our cruisers and destroyers resumed their shelling of the Jap half of the island, knocking out the last remaining big guns. The concussion was terrific, for the shells were landing not more than 100 yards away. Our planes came in strafing.

I waded and swam through a small bay to reach the opposite shore but was unable to find anyone. Virtually everyone I knew was reported dead or missing.

REPORTED KILLED IN ACTION

Far down the beach (not more than fifty yards but it took me two hours to cover it), I saw a marine with a camera. Painfully I crawled to him, for my body was one mass of bruises.

He was a stranger.

"Where'd you get it?" I asked.

"From Lucas," he replied.

"Where is Lucas?" I asked.

"Over there," he replied. "Dead."

"I'm Lucas," I told him.

I left my foxhole at noon, went 100 yards and returned at 6 P.M. It was that tough.

The night was hellish. More men came in, and more were killed on the pier.

At dawn the enemy sent its first bombers. There were only two of them, and five men were killed.

We awoke to one of the strangest sights in history. We badly needed replacements. Men were being landed 500 yards from shore in the surf at low tide and were wading in past enemy machine gun emplacements. Many men fell before they reached shore. In the afternoon marines were still staggering ashore, carrying the limp forms of buddies between them.

By now, however, the Japs were being forced steadily back. We were able to move about. Snipers continued, but we ignored them. One was killed in a coconut tree fifty feet away.

Still our naval and air poundings continued. On the third day the heaviest fighting took part in a cleared space around the air strip.

Suddenly there was firing at our rear. Seven Japs had been found in the ruins of a dugout less than ten feet from the command post from which our officers were directing the operations. They were wiped out.

PRISONERS KILLED BY SNIPERS

I returned to the beach to find snipers again sweeping the pier where ammunition was being unloaded. They fired from the wreckage of one of our boats fifty yards away. I ducked into the water on the opposite side, and found five husky military policemen herding a convoy of Japanese prisoners toward the beach in water up to their waists and up to the Japs, shoulders. Three dead marines were in the water. The MP's herded the Japs out to a waiting landing barge. As the frightened prisoners climbed aboard, they were subjected to murderous fire from their own snipers. Three were killed.

I got back in time to be in on the battle that broke Japanese resistance on Tarawa. Several hundred Japs were holed up for two days in a bomb-proof shelter at the end of the airstrip, holding up our advance.

Pfc. Robert Harper, 22, of Houston, Texas, and Sgt. John Rybin, 25, of Laurel, Mont., dashed forward with their flame-throwers while automatic riflemen covered them. At the entrance of the bomb shelter Harper threw his flame on a Jap machine-gun nest, charring three enemy marines beyond recognition. He poured on more fire. There were screams inside the shelter, and the marines rushed forward to capture their objective. Harper returned to our post.

"They were all huddled in there scared to death," he said. "I turned on the heat and that was all."

From this point on our advance was rapid. Following our advancing troops, I came upon one position we had held less than five minutes and counted twenty-seven Japanese who had committed suicide by strapping their feet to the triggers of their rifles, placing the muzzle to their chests and pulling the trigger with a kick.

Under heavy guard, some of the few prisoners captured on Tarawa are marched along a beach. They are ordered to walk in a stooped position to safeguard against their making a surprise attack or an escape. ◆

BARI IS ATTACKED BY GERMAN PLANES
Use of Glider Bombs Seen as First Air Assault on City Takes It by Surprise

By WALTER LOGAN
United Press Correspondent

BARI, Italy, Dec. 3 (Delayed)—This city experienced its first air attack of the war today. What was probably the first bomb to fall knocked me flat.

The last thing that I remembered was walking toward the docks before the sirens sounded. The next thing I knew was my asking a British army lieutenant "Where am I?" He replied: "In a truck en route to the hospital." This conversation was punctuated by heavy anti-aircraft fire and the bursting of bombs.

[A German communiqué issued yesterday said that strong formations of German aircraft had attacked Bari on the night of Dec. 3. According to "defi-nitely established figures," the German communiqué said, four cargo vessels totaling 31,000 tons, among them a large tanker, were sunk. Nine other vessels were hit, the Germans claimed. Two German planes were said to have been lost.]

The attack lasted for an hour and eyewitnesses told many tales of heroism. One of them concerned members of the Merchant Marine who volunteered to load stacks of Allied 500-pound bombs on trucks so that they could be removed from the danger zone. A British naval commander and a lieutenant in the Royal Navy Volunteer Reserve took a volunteer crew aboard an abandoned Italian tug and towed to safety a tanker laden with hundreds of thousands of gallons of high-octane gasoline.

USE OF GLIDER BOMB LIKELY

The possibility that the Germans' radio-directed rocket, or glider, bomb had been employed in the attack on Bari was seen here yesterday in the reports indicating that the city's defenses had been caught napping by the suddenness of the attack.

The Germans' use of the rocket bomb, which is released as a glider directed toward its target by a parent aircraft, was first disclosed by Prime Minister Churchill on Sept. 21. Mr. Churchill declared, however, that the new weapon was being used principally against nautical targets.

Some circles have believed that the Italian battleship Roma was sunk by some sort of glider bomb, since a modern battleship, properly protected, should not have been sunk so easily as she appears to have been. ◆

American ships ablaze after a Nazi attack on the Adriatic port of Bari, Italy. First reports estimated, 1000 casualties and five U.S. vessels lost.

DECEMBER 7, 1943

BIG THREE CHARTS TRIPLE BLOWS TO HUMBLE REICH

ATTACK PLANS SET

Dates Fixed for Land Drives From the East, West and South

IRAN TO BE FREED

Allied Leaders Say 'No Power on Earth' Can Balk Our Victory

By C. L. SULZBERGER
By Cable to The New York Times.

CAIRO, Egypt, Dec. 6—Final concord on a campaign to destroy the German military power by land, sea and air and to erect an enduring peace in which all nations, both great and small, shall participate, was agreed upon in the momentous Teheran meeting between President Roosevelt, Premier Stalin and Prime Minister Churchill.

Simultaneously, the three leaders, as a sign of their faith in each other and as proof of the validity of their intentions toward little nations, guaranteed the post-war independence, sovereignty and territorial integrity of Iran.

These Allied agreements were announced to the world today in two joint declarations signed in order by President Roosevelt [the only titular Chief of State among the three], Premier Stalin and Prime Minister Churchill. They were issued in Teheran Dec. 1 after a long final sitting of the leaders and their innermost circles of advisers in the magnificent Soviet Embassy where President Roosevelt lived as a guest.

3-PRONGED ATTACK PLEDGED

Their military promises can be summed up accordingly: the three powers will work together throughout the war; their military staffs have concerted plans for the destruction of German forces; these staffs have reached a "complete agreement as to the scope and timing of operations which will be undertaken from the east, west and south."

Guarantees satisfactory to the three chiefs now exist that the final victory will rest with the United Nations. "No power on earth can prevent our destroying the German armies by land, their U-boats by sea and their war-plants from the air," says one of the joint declarations. "Our attacks will be relentless and increasing."

SEAL DOOM OF HITLER

Thus in four days of deliberation in the romantic Iranian capital the "Big Three" laid the second half of the plans for ending the global war and establishing lasting peace for the benefit of all in its ruins. The Asiatic talks in North Africa between Mr. Roosevelt, Mr. Churchill and Generalissimo Chiang Kai-shek already had laid the program for accelerating the defeat of Japan and for building up a new Asia.

Now European talks of exactly the same length have rounded off the final plans for smashing Hitler which obviously must precede the destruction of Japan in the over-all scheme of the Allied grand strategy planners. Britain and America have clearly coordinated their ultimate schedule for the invasion of Europe from several points from the west and south with a program for new Russian offensives against the Reich.

It may be assumed that once the fulfillment of these plans comes about and Moscow's long pleas for a second front are entirely answered that the Soviet Union might conceivably alter its present neutral attitude toward Japan. This certainly was discussed at Teheran but the outcome of these discussions is not known.

It would seem a fair assumption from a complete survey of both the present wartime and future post-war problems indicated in the latest declarations that the three powers must now have agreed on specific terms within the framework of unconditional surrender on which

Germany can and must eventually sue for surrender. In this sense, the Teheran meeting may have proved to hold the same historical significance against Germany as the Quebec conference held against Italy.

LASTING PEACE FORESEEN

Concrete guarantees of world peace, prefaced by the flat promise the powers will work together, insure their efficacy. The peace envisioned will be enduring, will eliminate the dangers of war and will be based on a popular desire for good-will. And its mechanism will be the responsibility of the United States, Britain, Russia and all the United Nations.

Cooperation and active participation by both large and small nations will be encouraged to eliminate tyranny, slavery, oppression and intolerance in a democratic world based on the architectural plan of the Atlantic Charter.

In conclusion, the friendly conferences summed up:

"We look with confidence to the day when all peoples of the world may live free lives untouched by tyranny and according to their varying desires and their own consciences.

"We came here with hope and determination. We leave here friends in fact, in spirit and in purpose."

That spirit of friendly peacetime cooperation was revealed in their pledge to Iran, which was based on the broad principles of the Atlantic Charter.

Iran [the only nation jointly and severally occupied by the "Big Three"] is of vital importance to the present and future welfare of the United States, Britain and Russia. Lying athwart the lifelines of Britain's eastern empire, Iran also controls many of the most important mid-Asian air bases in which the United States is so interested and blocks any access to the Indian Ocean toward which the Soviet Union might gradually be tending in the traditional search for a permanent open seaport.

Red Army troops already are in control of the northern portions of Iran into which they marched in August, 1941, in consort with Britain, which took over the southern section. America's Persian Gulf Service Command, with thousands of troops, operates the present supply lines to Russia. Thus all three nations have agreed in the Teheran declaration to recall their troops when the war ends, restoring to Shah Mohammed Riza Pahlevi that which is his.

The so-called Iranian problem, though little mentioned in censored press these days, thus is eliminated by the pledge of the United Nations leaders. This is urgently important, first in its obvious elimination of a possible point of friction between themselves and, secondly, as an example of the great powers' honesty in their promises to respect the territorial claims of small lands and, furthermore, to assist them in recovering from the scourge of war.

INVITE ALL TO JOIN PEACE

Encouraging as such straightforward pledges may be to the conquered peoples of Europe, still greater hope can be injected into their presently heavy hearts by those other promises of freedom and happiness in a "world family of democratic nations" resolved on by the statesmen and their political staffs.

These forthright announcements should be calculated finally to knock the stuffings out of Hitler's frantic efforts to assemble his weird collection of satellites, puppets and shadow allies into a flimsy new order, which would fight to the death against the United Nations on Propaganda Minister Joseph Goebbels' warning that otherwise they would be destroyed.

It is hard to see how the desperate Governments of Finland, Rumania and

Bulgaria can instill much fighting spirit into their bewildered armies now in the face of the cocky Allied assumption of their imminent defeat and the deliberate Allied planning for the future, which any European peasant can see will be for his own good.

Regarding the post-war future of Europe, nothing specific was said, Iran being the only absolutely concrete subject published in the statements. However, within the general lines of the declaration the obvious entire question of eastern Europe, including Finland, Poland and the Balkans must have been reviewed.

Both the Polish question and the Balkans were discussed at the previous Moscow conference of Foreign Ministers and one result of those talks, it would seem, was an obvious alteration of the line of Allied propaganda toward Yugoslavia, showing an increasing tendency to support the Partisan movement there.

POLAND REMAINS QUESTION

Poland, however, remains a question. Moscow always has been adamant that part of Finland, the Baltic States and Bessarabia rightfully belong to the U.S.S.R. It is this correspondent's guess that there has been absolutely no alteration of that view, which means ultimate

agreement to it by Washington and London, especially in view of what was clearly a Soviet concession in agreeing to the postwar evacuation of northern Iran.

The Iranian matter was agreed upon during the Foreign Ministers' conference at Moscow and Premier Stalin stuck by his guns in signing the Teheran declaration. Moscow is clearly sticking by a consistent and steady policy she has had since the earlier days of the war, in which it has been constantly announced that the U.S.S.R. has no territorial ambitions. It was within this framework, one can assume, that Britain and America promised to give China Manchuria after the defeat of Japan, since Russia has never proclaimed an interest in that rich territory since giving over to the Japanese her share of the Chinese Eastern Railway.

However, the question of Manchuria was not discussed at the Moscow meeting and it may be assumed the first time it could have been brought up between the "Big Three" powers was at Teheran.

On the assumption that Moscow's policy remains the same as it has been consistently since the last territorial acquisition before the German attack—and there is every indication this is a safe ground on which to work—one may draw the following conclusions: ❯

The Teheran Conference of the Big Three in 1943. Russia's Joseph Stalin, U.S. President Franklin Roosevelt and British Prime Minister Winston Churchill.

◀ 1. That the U.S.S.R has no desires to expand at Turkey's expense and that on the one hand the Caucasian frontier with Turkish possession of Kars and Ardahan will remain unchanged and on the other hand there is no territorial menace to Turkish possession of the Straits and Dardanelles, despite German propaganda to the contrary.

2. That Moscow, while not admitting in any sense her policy of seeking gain, will seek expansion to her pre-1939 borders in Eastern Europe. She has always openly stated the need of a small portion of Finland in order to protect Leningrad as well as certain strategic Baltic bases. She also desires a portion of East Poland, roughly according to the Curzon line. From Rumania she desires North Bukovina and Bessarabia and possibly a small strip across the Danube delta controlling the mouth of that river. She may also desire some bases in Bulgaria, although the latter is quite uncertain.

Moscow continually insists that all territory mentioned above, saving speculation regarding the area south of the Danube, was once and for a long time Russian and the U.S.S.R. has every right to have it back.

Beyond that in Europe it is evident that Moscow wants closest ties with eastern lands, based on the formula of the imminent Czecho-Russian treaty. But aside from preventing the formation of any "cordon sanitaire" under the guise of an Eastern European Federation led by the Poles and inspired from the west, Russia apparently wishes no other territorial gains.

This correspondent can only say on the basis of the above statements that these are the impressions of the Anglo-American delegates to the Teheran conferences, and there is every reason to believe they are the most accurate statements of fact available at present. ◇

Only 3 Anglo-U. S. Writers in Teheran During Parley

By Cable to The New York Times.

CAIRO, Egypt, Dec. 6—The only three Anglo-American newspaper men in Teheran, Iran, during the tri-power talks there were John Wallis, regular Reuter correspondent in Iran; Edward Angly of The Chicago Sun and Lloyd Stratton of The Associated Press.

All the correspondents in Cairo were under military orders not to leave the town, although many of them had tips ahead of the time as to where the second phase of the conference would take place and some of them actually had their air transport arranged.

Mr. Wallis is permanently stationed in Teheran. Two Americans were en route to Moscow, but were waiting for a plane when the talks started. They were ordered back to Cairo to conform with instructions given to the correspondents here, but these instructions were rescinded by President Roosevelt's son-in-law, Maj. John Boettigre.

The only time they glimpsed the principals was once when they were photographed. For the rest the reporters were forced to depend on observers for information, as were those reporters remaining in Cairo. ◇

The 3-Power Declaration

TEHERAN, Iran, Dec. 1 (UP)—The text of a declaration by President Roosevelt, Prime Minister Churchill and Premier Stalin:

A DECLARATION OF THE THREE POWERS
We, the President of the United States of America, the Prime Minister of Great Britain, and the Premier of the Soviet Union, have met in these four days past in this the capital of our ally, Teheran, and have shaped and confirmed our common policy.

We express our determination that our nations shall work together in the war and in the peace that will follow.

As to the war, our military staffs have joined in our round-table discussions and we have concerted our plans for the destruction of the German forces. We have reached complete agreement as to the scope and timing of operations which will be undertaken from the east, west and south. The common understanding which we have here reached guarantees that victory will be ours.

And as to the peace, we are sure that our concord will make it an enduring peace. We recognize fully the supreme responsibility resting upon us and all the nations to make a peace which will command good will from the overwhelming masses of the peoples of the world and banish the scourge and terror of war for many generations.

With our diplomatic advisers we have surveyed the problems of the future. We shall seek the cooperation and active participation of all nations, large and small, whose peoples in heart and in mind are dedicated, as are our own peoples, to the elimination of tyranny and slavery, oppression and intolerance. We will welcome them as they may choose to come into the world family of democratic nations.

No power on earth can prevent our destroying the German armies by land, their U-boats by sea, and their war plants from the air. Our attacks will be relentless and increasing.

Emerging from these friendly conferences we look with confidence to the day when all the peoples of the world may live free lives untouched by tyranny and according to their varying desires and their own consciences.

We came here with hope and determination. We leave here friends in fact, in spirit, and in purpose.

Signed at Teheran, Dec. 1, 1943. __ Roosevelt, Stalin, Churchill. ◇

Tito's Influence Growing

By Wireless to The New York Times.

CAIRO, Egypt, Dec. 8—Unofficial contact of a political nature has now been established between the Allied authorities and the new temporary government headed by Marshal Tito in Partisan Yugoslavia. It is possible the confused Yugoslav situation may be somewhat crystallized as the result of conversations now taking place.

Some contact, direct or indirect, presumably will be established for the purpose of the talks between Partisan spokesman and the emigre regime of King Peter II. King Peter's Government is out of the picture as far as Partisans go. Thus the Allied task in maintaining proper relations is somewhat difficult, for their formal diplomatic exchanges are with King Peter's Government, although the bulk of material aid to Yugoslav Patriots now goes to Marshal Tito.

Meanwhile, there is every indication that the most important diplomatic and political crisis since that country was overrun by the Axis is now brewing. King Peter's Ambassadors to Washington, London, Ankara and Moscow have been summoned here for consultation.

Dr. Berislav Anjelinovitch, Minister of Posts and Telegraph in the present exiled Government, handed in his resignation to Prime Minister Bozidar Pouritch today. His resignation emphasized that the Government should be enlarged.

A delegation of Yugoslav soldiers being organized into a Free Army that is slowly forming in the Middle East informed Yugoslav political leaders that they would be happy to fight for the King,

Josip Broz, also known as Marshal Tito, leader of the Yugoslavia resistance in 1944.

but not for Mikhailovitch. All these soldiers were once in the Italian Army, being almost entirely made up of Slovenes from the Trieste region and Istria.

The statement of Mr. Law regarding Britain's view on Yugoslav matters and the share of aid Tito is getting tended to impress Yugoslav official circles here.

There has been much regret in some moderate circles over the sharp wording of the Yugoslav Government's statement Sunday condemning Marshal Tito's temporary government, and, indeed, an effort was made twenty-four hours too late to withdraw it.

The Yugoslav Government press office today published a series of communiqués purporting to emanate from General Mikhailovitch's headquarters on Dec. 3. It was stated therein that "apart from the Communist party, which never has been particularly powerful in Yugoslavia, no political organization supports this government [Tito's]. All Serb political parties decided to support the National Committee of Resistance, which also supports the Yugoslav Regular Army [Mikhailovitch's]." It is further claimed that no Slovenian or Croatian political parties back Marshal Tito. ◇

INVASION PROGRAM SHAPING IN BRITAIN

Phases of Allied Supply and Transport, Air Support and Striking Force Take Form

FEBRUARY A TIMING POINT

Weather in Western Europe Is Major Factor—Britons Due For Big Part in Opening

By Cable to The New York Times.

LONDON, Dec. 10—The organizing of the prospective Anglo-American invasion of northwestern Europe is progressing swiftly, despite the magnitude of the task set for officers and men of the Allied armies, navies and air forces, it was indicated today.

Difficulties of supply and transport are being overcome, command personnel problems are being worked out and the planning stage appears to be over. The American and British staff officers are clothing the bones of the great enterprise with blood and iron.

A very considerable fighting force amassed in Britain has been going through extensive training in combined operations.

WEATHER A FACTOR IN TIMING

Security necessarily blurs the outline of the plan, yet conditions here and Allied experiences in other theatres give partial guidance to speculation on the invasion. Consideration of these factors leads to the following conclusion:

The weather conditions needed to apply the maximum pressure at a time when the enemy is hard pressed on the eastern and southern fronts may delay operations on a large scale until after the middle of February.

The two allies are well aware of the strength of the German bomber force lying in wait in western Europe and are extremely unlikely to launch the invasion without overwhelming air support, which means the blow will be directed at some section of the European coast line within effective range of land-based Anglo-American fighters.

Initial landings will probably be spread over a considerable section of the coast, with the troops uniting for operations inland once the Germans' coastal defenses have been penetrated.

One of the many suitable ports of northwestern Europe is probably among the primary objectives so that the invading forces can get reinforcements and supplies from Britain and, as was ❯

◀ the case in Sicily, directly from the United States.

Since the British have the greater number of veteran divisions available, despite the greater numerical strength of the United States Army, it is possible Britons will form half or more of the original ground force that will encounter the severest fighting.

AIR-BORNE ATTACK LIKELY

The success of the Allied airborne troops in Sicily points to a possible, further-expanded use of air-borne forces in this operation, principally to seize airfields upon which to base fighter support in the second phase of the invasion and to bar routes to the battle areas over which enemy reinforcements could travel.

The problem of supply of the forces that ultimately will total well over 1,000,000 men is at present as important as these strategic and tactical problems. Another difficult task is coordination of the ground forces with the Allies' tactical air force.

Moreover, strategy, tactics and logistics—the trilogy of war—have been joined by propaganda. The machinery for political warfare is already being organized.

The supply position in certain categories of quickly expendable material, such as ammunition, is excellent. Great concentrations of all stores have been piling up here. The fighting men on the "second front" will be lavishly equipped.

Maritime transport remains an all-important matter. For some months the Allies have had to switch from one operation to the next, the type of transport used before a port is captured. The invasion of northwestern Europe will require a far greater number of landing craft and small, fast transports than in any previous Allied overseas adventure.

The British figure a combat division requires 400 to 600 tons of supplies a day. Considering the stubbornness of the Nazi resistance in Sicily and Italy, it seems probable that the maximum amount for each division will be needed and that most of it will have to be taken to the beaches by landing craft or by small, fast transports with strong anti-aircraft armament

A considerable proportion of the Allied heavy bomber strength will presumably be diverted to the bombing of the enemy's communications and strong points as part of the air preparation. This is another reason for believing the invasion will not come until mid-February, although the Allies may make several diversionary landings earlier to pin down the Germans. ◆

Rommel Reported Switched to West

Marshal Said To Be in Charge Of Anti-Invasion Defenses

LONDON, Dec. 12 (AP)—German reports reaching Stockholm today said that Field Marshal Gen. Erwin Rommel had been named anti-invasion chief to prepare for the Allied attack on western Europe.

Marshal Rommel, who has been directing the over-all command of German troops in both the Balkans and Italy, has been reported to be inspecting Denmark's coastal defenses all week.

Berlin dispatches said that, although the tension was still great in the Balkans over a possible Allied invasion, German military experts expected the biggest Allied attack in the west. The Scandinavian Telegraph Bureau, reporting Marshal Rommel's appointment, said that German commanders viewed the defense of western France and northern Germany as more important than that of Italy. Vichy reports, via Madrid, confirmed this report and said that the Germans in France believed that the Allies had withdrawn some of their best troops from the Italian front and many warships from the Italian area for use on another front. The Germans were said to believe that a major Allied attack would come soon but apparently could not decide whether it would come only in the English Channel or simultaneously with a thrust in the Mediterranean. ◆

AMERICANS ASHORE
Landing Made Without Loss of Ship Or Plane on Southwest Coast

GOALS QUICKLY WON
MacArthur's Men Take Peninsula, Seize Rule of Vitiaz Strait

By Wireless to The New York Times

ADVANCED ALLIED HEADQUARTERS IN NEW GUINEA, Dec. 17—American forces have landed on New Britain Island and established a firm bridgehead.

Large elements of Lieut. Gen. Walter Krueger's Sixth Army made a seventy-mile jump north from New Guinea and swarmed ashore near Arawe Wednesday from all types of landing craft. This important barge base on the southeast corner of the biggest island of the Bismarck Archipelago is about 270 miles from Rabaul, Japan's New Britain naval plane base protecting the southern approaches to Truk, the enemy's Pacific bastion 798 miles to the north.

With the landing in New Britain, Gen. Douglas MacArthur is squeezing Rabaul from two directions, since marines and soldiers under his command landed on Bougainville last month.

ONE FORCE IS REPULSED

The green-clad soldiers hit the beaches at two points on narrow Cape Merkus and one on Pilelo Island, just offshore, in amphibious tanks and rubber boats after a naval bombardment in which hundreds of shells exploded in the main landing area at Orange Beach.

One of the three landings made by a commando-trained party was repulsed with heavy loss in lives, the Japanese puncturing the rubber boats with machine-gun and mortar fire. Despite counter-fire other commandos captured the radio station at Pilelo. But after naval bombardment and intensive strafing by American planes there was no opposition at the main beach. Troops were able to beat off, with only two casualties and no damage, a fierce attack launched by more than twenty Japanese planes while the landing was still progressing.

United States soldiers arriving ashore at Cape Gloucester, New Britain Island, Papua, New Guinea 1943.

Ack-ack crews ashore and guns of the landing craft drove off the raiders and knocked down two enemy planes.

TEXAS FLAG FLIES FROM BEACH

Two commando parties neared shore at 5:20 A. M. in moonlight, but the first tracked "alligator" did not hit the main beach with its fighting men until 7:49 in the morning, since a treacherous, narrow passage only a few feet wide had to be traversed between Pilelo Island and Cape Merkus. One group planted the flag of Texas on the beach.

Soldiers equipped for jungle fighting immediately pressed up the three-mile peninsula, which, if entirely occupied by the force that landed, is virtually impregnable against attack because of a narrow neck joining it to the mainland.

Because of shoals and currents, the operation was most delicate.

Only careful preparation and the closest cooperation between sea, ground and air forces made this amphibious operation successful.

The task force was commanded by Rear Adm. Daniel E. Barbey and the landing force by Brig. Gen. Julian W. Cunningham. General MacArthur is with General Krueger at headquarters, a point north of New Guinea, generally directing operations. The good weather, which was bad for this operation since the moon shone brightly, was probably responsible for the disaster that befell one commando force. It made impossible what was expected to be a surprise foray to obtain control of a roadblock. The Japanese atop a 250-foot cliff over the beach poured on a withering fire at point-blank range, not opening up until the fragile rubber craft were nearly ashore. Some men were in the water three hours, some were wounded, some died and some few who got ashore probably were wiped out or captured. Nevertheless their sacrifice was not in vain for the Japanese apparently thought this effort on Blue Beach was the main landing.

VITIAZ STRAIT CONTROLLED

Little is known about the fight on Pilelo Islet except that we received messages from the radio station at the appointed time.

This jump away from New Guinea where the fighting has been going on so long was the first all-American show in the Southwest Pacific theatre.

It gives the Allies effective control of Vitiaz Strait between New Guinea and New Britain, only forty miles wide at its narrowest point.

The landing followed the establishment of airfields on the Huon Peninsula following the capture of Lae and Finschhafen, the air cover from the fighters on the operation being excellent as we had an overwhelming number of planes.

This correspondent has flown over most of New Britain. It is about 320 miles long but only fifty miles across at its widest point. Its jungles are, if anything, denser than those of New Guinea and Guadalcanal and others in the Solomons.

The coastal range runs the length of the volcanic island where live volcanoes still play, particularly around Rabaul, where a 600-foot island was shoved up during the cataclysmic 1937 earthquake and volcanic eruptions. ◇

DECEMBER 19, 1943

De Gaulle— Enigma and Symbol
He puzzles critics and friends alike, but there is little doubt that he speaks for France.

By Milton Bracker
ALGIERS (By Wireless).

THROUGH the skylight of Gen. Charles de Gaulle's borrowed villa here, you can see the Tricolor on the roof whipping in the breeze from the harbor far below. On brisk days you can actually hear it, too. It is said by his intimates that the general himself always hears it, that he is as closely attuned to the needs of his oppressed homeland as if he maintained telepathic connection.

Whether or not this is true de Gaulle has now emerged as the single most important Frenchman in the world and his somewhat enigmatic personality is a factor Allied statesmen are likely to have to reckon with for an indefinite period in the future. That some of them do not like him is not news to the general or to any one else, but that all of them now accept him as the dominant spokesman for his people is increasingly obvious. And it is perhaps an indication of the whole trend of the de Gaulle movement that the general remains more a "spokesman" or symbol than a personality.

De Gaulle is a complete introvert. He is shy, gauche and without warmth. He has never learned to smile easily. His oval face has the faintly yellowish look of a man who works primarily indoors and doesn't sleep too well. His deep-set eyes, underlined with blue, reveal a combination of sensitivity and shyness, uncertainty and caution, impatience and purpose.

De Gaulle's height (6 feet 3) is his most obvious physical characteristic; it is accentuated by his high-crowned olive-drab field cap. He isn't fluid or graceful, like an athlete.

Even those closest to him are prone to talk more of his ideas, his "role" than of his personal idiosyncracies. De Gaulle himself despises detail and trivial matters and relegates such things to subordinates who, he earnestly hopes, will dispose of them without bothering him. His aide de camp usually calls for him in a car about 9:45 A.M. and at 10 ❯

◀ they arrive at the Villa des Glycines, one of the many modern Moorish establishments overlooking the harbor from the vast hill into which Algiers is built.

The Glycines has only two floors and the general's staff, including secretaries and clerks, counts not more than twenty-five. De Gaulle has a way of virtually gliding in on silent feet, darting his eyes nervously here and there, taking everything in. He says little. His private office in the rear of the ground floor is dominated by a highly polished desk and six brown leather chairs. The general welcomes some visitors from his place behind the desk; with others he wants to put at their ease, he comes around in front and takes one of the outer chairs himself.

Everything about the setting in which he works is businesslike. No family pictures or gadgets are about. The only touch of sentiment is steeped in the present struggle of France. It is the original pen-and-ink eight line ultimatum sent to Gen. Josef Koenig at Bir Hakim by Marshal Rommel. It hangs on the wall over the general's left shoulder.

The general usually spends his mornings receiving people. But on Tuesdays, Thursdays and Saturdays he drives to the Lycée Fromentin, formerly a girls' school, where he presides over meetings of the French Committee of National Liberation. He sits at the south end of a big square table. A quaint rocking-chair blotter is the only thing at his place not at the other members' places. A vase on the high ledge near the window has come to be known as "the general's ash tray." He smokes while he paces.

De Gaulle breaks his day at 1:30, when he returns home for lunch. Usually he has two or three guests. The table is simple and so is the fare. Like everyone else in Algiers, he has no butter. His one luxury is an after-lunch cigar. Mme. Yvonne de Gaulle, an intensely French woman of still recognizable charm, fits into the general scene like a picture in a frame.

Back in the office, de Gaulle is likely to spend the afternoon alone. His closest aide perhaps is Gaston Palewski, who is de Gaulle's chef de cabinet as he was formerly Paul Reynaud's. Palewski speaks of de Gaulle in hyperbole. During the Corsican campaign he told the writer that while France defined General Giraud as a "good soldier, a fine and upright man," it saw in de Gaulle "the will of the nation to live in its greatness."

The general goes home for dinner, usually again with guests, and he is in bed by 11, if possible. He does not like people as such, but he regards them as part of his job. He is hospitable with-

French General Charles de Gaulle delivering an address at the end of the Allied Armistice Day parade in Algiers, 1943.

out being genial, thoughtful without being warm. He keeps his distance and expects you to keep yours. He never really relaxes and nearly always gives the impression of being under strain. Politically of course he is.

BUT there is no question that he has enlarged his stature since June, 1940. In those days he was not only shy and uncertain but utterly lacking in even elementary diplomatic sagacity. He would walk into a press conference and open it gravely with a long set speech. He would tolerate a question or two, then stand up and stride out at his own convenience.

Now he sits back and is complete master of the situation. He is ready for any question that comes along and when someone asks a rather embarrassing one about his attitude toward becoming first President of the new Fourth Republic he smiles wanly and says, "You're the first to offer me the job."

Similarly he has taken on more and more the external attributes of the politician. He still wears a uniform—except on Sunday when he invariably drives with Mme. de Gaulle in a flagless car to attend mass at near-by Le Biar—but on ceremonial occasions he is as much the politician as the general.

On Armistice Day, for instance, he and General Giraud (who had just signed his political death warrant as co-president of the French Committee of National Liberation) climbed one of the interminable flights of stairs leading to the war memorial they were about to decorate.

At every single landing de Gaulle paused and went out of his way to shake hands with men and women along the route. While Giraud stood by plainly uncomfortable, de Gaulle did his hand-shaking and murmured grave pleasantries. And this went on all the way up and again all the way down after the observance.

A man extremely close to de Gaulle and ardently devoted to his cause says things like this are not "the real de Gaulle" but represent a conscientious and still rather graceless effort to live up to the new position in which he finds himself.

This may well be true. For the general is certainly not by nature a "glad-hander." Routine physical ceremonies seem to oppress him. But more and more he has become oppressed with what he concedes to a sense of duty— the duty of representing the people of France in and out of Hitler's clutches. In essence, however, he remains stubborn and uncompromising. Even his critics allow that he is wholeheartedly sincere, that his motives are from his own viewpoint the best.

A standard gibe at de Gaulle, and one whose origin has been attributed to a very high official, charges him with trying to be both a latter-day Clemen-ceau and a latter-day Joan of Arc, while actually he is unsuited to be either.

De Gaullist sympathizers retort that the general seeks to be neither and that the Joan of Arc parallel in particular is bunk. The fact remains that there is a strong strain of mysticism in de Gaulle which is evident in almost every speech and every piece of correspondence.

When Harold Macmillan and Robert D. Murphy, respectively for Britain and the United States, had the rather embarrassing task of formally notifying the general that an armistice with Italy had been concluded without the Committee of National Liberation being informed, Macmillan hopefully suggested that "as a military man you will surely understand."

"You forget," said de Gaulle, "that I hold the political destinies of France in my hand."

Whether he holds these destinies as custodian or as molder remains the big question. Taking a leaf from the general's own tendency to deal in figures of speech—he loves poetry and can quote Racine and Chateaubriand in great gobs—his adherents say he is like a glass vessel taking on the color of the liquid poured into it. That liquid, they say, is the living sentiment produced by the quick and precious heartbeat of France.

Anti-de Gaullists counter that the figure is put backward—that France is a glass into which the general is trying to pour the color of his own ambition and his own personality.

How will this son of the "petite nobilité," who in 1940 was criticized as being a Fascist and is now being criticized as being Communist, sit with the leaders of the post-war Allied world?

Assuming that Winston Churchill stills speaks for Britain there is much more likelihood of bringing about political harmony between Britain and France than personal harmony between Churchill and de Gaulle. In every way the two men grate on each other, though each is big enough to acknowledge the basic sincerity of the other when each praises the ideals and aspirations of the other's country.

While he headed the French National Committee in London de Gaulle frequently visited 10 Downing Street. Mr. Churchill once told him in French as poor as de Gaulle's English would have been, "You may be France—but you're not all France." De Gaulle returned to his headquarters in Carlton Gardens pale and pent up. He strode by the sentry and disappeared into his private office.

But later he learned to suppress his anger or at least to control it to his own advantage. At the time of the North African invasion only the faintest inkling trickled to his ears. Finally on a Sunday morning in November he was confronted with the reality of the presence of Allied troops.

So the general went to 10 Downing Street again, and according to a member of his staff at the time he "took a leaf out of Churchill's book and pretended to be angry when he wasn't." As a result, according to this version, he got British recognition and sovereignty of the Fighting French in Madagascar.

All through his extremely trying period in London de Gaulle unquestionably learned more of the ways of statesmen and politicians. He was a good student. But probably his lowest moment was when just as he was about to leave for North Africa he was halted by a last-minute request—in fact a command—from General Dwight D. Eisenhower. He went to the English countryside and wrote sad and eloquent letters. Finally he was re-invited—or rather permitted—to come here.

De Gaulle's present political situation tends to obscure his really brilliant military record. Son of a college professor he went to St. Cyr and was both wounded and imprisoned during the First World War. He later served as aide de camp to Marshal Pétain, toward whom his present attitude is one of utter forgiveness. Ironically when in 1924 he wrote "La Discorde Chez' Ennemi" it was Pétain who inscribed the preface, "The day will come when a grateful France will call upon him."

In the Thirties de Gaulle began to write about mechanized warfare. It was his intense conviction that the nation's safety depended upon modern mechanization that built up his reputation before the fall of France. He was made a general on the battlefield on May 15, 1940. Three weeks later Reynaud summoned him to Paris and made him Under-Secretary of State for National Defense and War. De Gaulle did not know it, perhaps, but the political phase of his career had begun. That phase was thrust before the public when he made his speech at the BBC in London on June 18, 1940, and soon after when his reminder that "France has lost a battle, she has not lost the war" became a watchword which has retained its punch.

Some think that de Gaulle's troubles began when he refused to allow the Free French Forces to become a sort of "French Foreign Legion in the pay of the British." At the same time he was largely in British power and the fiasco at Dakar did nothing to help his prestige.

But de Gaulle survived. He is now riding his highest. He has claimed for the committee he heads sole authority to speak for France and no one has seriously contested his claim. But he is still subject to Allied military control. De Gaulle knows that and is concentrating on so solidifying his support within and without France as to make any such Allied interference ridiculous. He has said that going back to France will be just like going back to one's slippers. ◇

DECEMBER 25, 1943

NEW INVASION COMMANDER IN CHIEF

GENERAL IS SHIFTED

Choice of 'Big 3' Parley, He Has Montgomery as British Field Leader

WILSON IS SUCCESSOR

Mid-East Head Honored—Spaatz To Direct U.S. Air Strategy

Special to The New York Times.

HYDE PARK, N.Y., Dec. 24—President Roosevelt announced today the appointment of Gen. Dwight D. Eisenhower to lead the invasion of Europe from the north and west, and from London came word that Gen. Sir Bernard L. Montgomery of North African fame would head the British troops under General. Eisenhower to form a proved and hard-hitting team to lead the assault on Adolf Hitler's "Fortress Europe."

The President's announcement of General Eisenhower's selection at the recent Teheran conference to lead the main attack against Germany also set to rest the old rumors regarding the probable appointment of Gen. George C. Marshall, Army Chief of Staff, to that post.

The President, in his radio report today on the recent conferences at Teheran and Cairo, also named Lieut. Gen. Carl A. Spaatz as commander of "the entire American strategic bombing force operating against Germany."

This was taken to mean that while General Eisenhower will confine his command to the mass attack on Europe from the north and west, General Spaatz' command over all American strategic bombardment of Germany extends to operations against Germany from all neighboring bases. ▸

QUASHES MARSHALL RUMORS

The President gave a vivid picture in his radio report of complete agreement between Prime Minister Churchill, Premier Stalin and himself regarding a detailed program for the annihilation of Germany by land and air from all directions.

He also paid high tribute to General Marshall, presumably to set old rumors at rest. Some persons have argued that the position to be occupied by General Eisenhower is of greatest importance, but the official decision now revealed seems to give credence to the opinion that the most important position in the Army is that of Chief of Staff, just as Washington is the only place from which the whole global operation can be commanded.

"To the members of our armed forces, to their wives, mothers and fathers, I want to affirm the great faith and confidence that we have in General Marshall and Admiral King (Chief of Naval Operations), who direct all of our armed might throughout the world," the President declared.

THEIR MILITARY GENIUS STRESSED

"Upon them," he said, "falls the responsibility of planning the strategy; of determining where and when to fight. Both of these men have already gained high places in American history; places which will record in that history many evidences of their military genius that cannot be published today."

The announcement from London told not only of General Montgomery's appointment to head the British invasion forces under General Eisenhower but also of Gen. Sir Henry Maitland Wilson's appointment to replace General Eisenhower as commander of the Mediterranean Theatre and Gen. Sir Harold R.L.G. Alexander's appointment to command all Allied forces in Italy.

The Teheran military decision announced by the President proved as much as anything else that the American handling of the invasion of North Africa and of Italy had deeply impressed the United States allies. Those invasions may now be regarded as the testing phase of the main European invasion, since the American officers identified with their command have now received key positions in the final stage of the war, which is about to begin.

General Eisenhower's prestige with the Allied leaders has received frequent testimony, and it is almost axiomatic that General Montgomery is the best and most proven tactical field general the Allies, possess, just as General Eisenhower is the best strategical commander for big operations in the European theatre.

DECEMBER 26, 1943

POLISH FRONTIERS TEST ALLIED STATESMANSHIP

Russian Claims Come Right Up Against Enunciated Principles, Including Those of Atlantic Charter

STALIN'S PROPAGANDA CHANCE

By EDWIN L. JAMES

A Pole would put it this way: "It would be a travesty of justice if after an Allied victory in a war which started when Britain and France declared war on Germany because Hitler attacked Poland, Poland should come out of it worse off than if Hitler had been left to complete his designs." The Pole would be referring, of course, to Moscow's claims concerning the western borders of Russia, which means naturally the eastern frontiers of Poland.

Moscow has made no official statement regarding the Polish frontiers. In most Polish quarters there is real fear that Russia is going to demand parts of what was Poland before 1939. It is recalled that in commenting on a statement that Stalin's armies were so many miles from the Polish frontier, Ambassador Ouman-sky in a speech in Mexico City made a "correction" by giving a distance which indicated he, at least, regarded the line drawn by Germany and Russia in 1940 as the real Russian frontier. Recently, at the UNRRA meeting in Atlantic City, a Russian film was shown which pictured Lwow as "returning to the motherland." The Poles regard Lwow as the oldest of Polish cities.

In any event, the Poles draw the conclusion that their eastern frontiers are in danger. They are worried. Their worry is not decreased by the circumstance that in the conferences with the Russians the Americans and British have not discussed Russian frontiers, and they have noted the Russian statement that Russian frontiers are "inviolable," which doesn't mean much until one knows what it is that is inviolable.

THE UKRAINIAN ISSUE

Any consideration of the Polish frontier problem at once raises the issue of Polish Ukraine. In other words, Poles fear that the Russians will wish to incorporate that part of Poland, with a population of some 4,000,000, into the Soviet Union. The Russians have intimated that such was their desire; certainly they have not denied it was in all the discussions of the matter.

Now Ukrainian nationalists, outside of Russia, preach much of the unity of the Ukraine. But these leaders, especially those in the United States, look toward a united Ukraine which would be neither Russian nor Polish—just Ukrainian. It is possible that if Russia—which is not expected—would entertain the idea of an independent Ukraine some Poles might not object to the Polish Ukraine being included in such a country, provided it was not a part of the U.S.S.R. But there is little likelihood of the fruition of any such plan.

The Poles think they see some indications, such as talk of a common frontier between Russia and Czechoslovakia, of Moscow's intention to try to take over Galicia, the richest part of Poland.

In the absence of any definite declaration by Moscow the issue is difficult to draw clearly, but, to repeat, the Poles are worried about Russia's intentions. They are afraid Moscow may choose the line the Russians held after Hitler and Stalin partitioned their country.

WHERE POLISH HOPES LIE

The Poles put their hopes in the United States and Britain. They are frank about some doubts of the official British attitude, and so their hopes turn particularly to the United States. They say they think the Atlantic Charter meant to guarantee the restoration of their country as it was before Hitler attacked them in 1939. They hope that the Washington Government when the time comes—and they think the time is near—may be able to bring cogent arguments to bear on Stalin. They would like to see a proposal put forward for the drawing of a line around undoubtedly Polish territory, with a provision for plebiscites in disputed territory. They have not as yet got much encour-

They worked together in Africa and Italy and will now begin a new chapter of teamwork in the vaster task of invading Eurone at its most strongly defended positions.

Likewise, General Spaatz was a product of the North African testing period, having directed American air operations in the Mediterranean under General Eisenhower. Air Marshal Sir Arthur W. Tedder, a British air commander, stood between General Spaatz and General Eisenhower as air commander of all Allied air forces in the Mediterranean Theatre.

General Wilson's injection into the western Mediterranean picture is significant as suggesting the abandonment by the Allied chiefs at Teheran of plans for an Anglo-American invasion of the Balkans, an area that the Russians have been reported as wanting to act in militarily when the time comes.

General Wilson, who established his reputation in this war during the early stages of the first British African campaign, has been commanding the Tenth British Army in the Middle East, which stood ready for a Balkan campaign if one was ordered.

Of General Eisenhower, the President said:

"His performances in Africa, Sicily and Italy have been brilliant.

"He knows by practical and successful experience the way to coordinate air, sea and land power.

All of these will be under his control."

To General Wilson, the President pledged that "our powerful ground, sea, and air forces in the vital Mediterranean area will stand by his side until every objective in that bitter theatre is attained." ◆

---

agement, but they are still hoping.

The situation is rendered somewhat difficult by the fact that Moscow does not like the present Polish Government-in-Exile; in fact has broken off relations with it. However, over against that one might place the statement by President Benes of Czechoslovakia, made in Moscow the other day, that he hoped to see a treaty made between Russia and Poland along the lines of the pact of friendship and mutual protection which has been signed by Russia and Czechoslovakia. Benes is an experienced politician, and he must have had something to go on.

IS STALIN ADAMANT?

The Poles have no illusion about their future depending on what Stalin is willing to do or what he may be persuaded to do. They realize quite well that American and British armies are not going to fight the Russians over Poland. But they feel that the other United Nations can bring pressure to bear on Russia in their favor.

No one can say today what merit lies in this idea. There are reports which tell of a different attitude in Russia in recent months. There are evidences that Stalin the nationalist is proud of the position he has won for Russia in this war, and there is a chance that after the fighting is over he may wish to keep Russia in polite company. That might form the basis of an approach to him in behalf of Polish territoriality.

An argument could be made that Russia would heighten her stature by not demanding Polish territory. That would give a picture of Russia which, if unexpected, might well reflect changes in the Russian outlook. While Stalin has never said what frontiers with Poland he desired, he has stated that he desired a "strong and independent Poland." The question would be whether his conception of such a state would agree with that of the Poles, who wish their complete independence re-established in the territory they had before this was started.

A MOST THORNY PROBLEM

Sooner or later the Polish issue has got to be dealt with. It may or may not be the best time now to try to do it. The Russian armies are not yet on the soil of what was Poland. In other respects the war is far from over. Even when Germany is defeated Japan has got to be whipped. Stalin may or may not take part in the war against Japan. It is more likely that once Germany is defeated he will do so than that he will not. If for no other reason, the Russians will surely wish to be in on the peace settlement if and when Japan is beaten.

One does not like to suggest that after a war fought for freedom there will be widespread trading of territorial advantages, but it does stand to reason that in the bargaining among victors, which has always taken place after a war and which will take place after this one, there may arise the opportunity to give Stalin concessions which might well weigh against any desires Russians may have with respect to territory that was Poland's prior to Hitler's invasion of that country.

Perhaps in that direction lie the best prospects for Poland. ◆

Chapter 18

"THE DOUGHBOY'S GRIM ROUTE TO ROME"

January–May 1944

The whole world waited during the first half of 1944 for the expected invasion of France. "Plans Are Perfected," The Times reported in early January, but the plans were difficult to realize with millions of men and thousands of ships to transport across a waterway with notoriously unpredictable weather.

There was not much to cheer in the news from other theaters, either, as the German defensive lines held in Italy and Ukraine. To circumvent the stalemate in Italy the Sixth U.S. Army Corps, under Maj. General John Lucas, tried a landing farther up the coast at Anzio to outflank the German line, but it stalled at the beachhead and became as bogged down as the rest of the line. The real key to unlocking the German front lay in the mountains and valleys around the town of Cassino, dominated by the ancient Benedictine Abbey of Monte Cassino. Efforts to dislodge the Germans from the town and the heights were frustrated by the terrain. On February 15 the Mediterranean Allied Air Forces, commanded by General Ira Eaker, flew in to demolish the abbey in the mistaken belief that the Germans were using it. Instead, the bombing created in the ruins a perfect fortress for the Germans who now took it over. Not until May was Cassino and its destroyed abbey overrun, with exceptionally high casualties. The Polish divisions that finally stormed the heights on May 17 lost 3,500 men in the process.

The Germans now began to withdraw and the road to Rome lay open. But as it turned out, it was a road, Cyrus Sulzberger wrote, of "endless sticky mud . . . forbidding mountain crags." Beside the freezing rivers and shattered bridges, he saw "gutted villages peopled with tattered scavengers." "The Doughboy's Grim Route to Rome," The Times called it, the very opposite of the popular image of a sunny, art-lover's paradise.

To ease the way for the invasion of France, the Western Allies decided in March 1944 to use the heavy bombers to pulverize the transport network in northern France and the Low Countries. This was not how RAF Bomber Command or the Eighth Air Force wanted to proceed. In April The Times gave Air Chief Marshal Arthur Harris several pages to describe the bombing campaign he had commanded since February 1942. Of thirty German industrial cities subjected to RAF area bombing, only five, Harris claimed, had not been heavily damaged. He made no pretense that the RAF was doing anything other than destroying half or more of the built-up areas of the target cities, with the aim of stopping production by killing workers and obliterating their houses. Harris hoped that Allied bombing might end the war without the need for invasion of the Continent. But Eisenhower insisted that tactical bombing against transportation networks was now a priority, so the bombers were diverted for five months, first to destroy the rail system, then to support the land battle in France once the invasion had taken place.

While the waiting went on, Eisenhower assured the press that they would get good coverage of the invasion when it happened. At the annual convention of the American Newspaper Publishers' Association, a letter from the supreme commander was read out loud, in which Eisenhower hailed the war correspondents now crowding into London as part of "the great team seeking an early victory." He promised them access to news because, in his view, "public opinion wins wars." In this case, however, public opinion was growing increasingly impatient. Neither the defeat of a Japanese offensive on the Indian border at Kohima and Imphal in April 1944 nor the news of further advances in the Pacific could compensate for the long wait for an invasion and a second front against the Germans. From London, Times bureau chief Raymond Daniell wired the paper to expect something big.

JANUARY 1, 1944

ARMY PERFECTS JUNGLE FIGHTERS
Intensive Courses At the New Hawaiian Center Turn Out Thousands Every Week

By GEORGE F. HORNE
Special to The New York Times.

U. S. ARMY HEADQUARTERS, Central Pacific, Dec. 29 (Delayed)—The nature of the coming war in the Pacific has been brought into clear focus in 1943, and the weight of our military and naval might is shifted like that of a boxer who alters strategy to fit his opponent's style.

New Army training courses, adapted to the lessons learned in recent engagements in the Central Pacific, are now in full swing here in the world's greatest military training area, the Hawaiian Islands, and they are equipping soldiers thoroughly with such a variety of deadly skills that officers in charge say there is no doubt that our Army is becoming the most terrific force of any in our history.

Lieut. Gen. Robert C. Richardson Jr., commander of Army forces in the Central Pacific area, sent correspondents on a day's inspection tour of his new unit jungle center, where thousands of men are now turned out every week after an intensive study of living and fighting in the jungles.

GENUINE COMBAT CONDITIONS
The conditions are not of mock-up caliber, for these islands afford every type of terrain, every kind of problem and obstacle to be found in the islands of the Pacific where we are going to attack and oust the enemy.

There are matted jungles through which the students hack their way under simulated fire. Behind them nature swiftly closes the man-made gaps, making a new jungle in a few weeks for coming classes.

There are streams where the men cross by their own devices under fire; there are cliffs and mountains; there are the average jungle fruits and roots on which they may live.

The program is under the direction of Col. William C. Saffarrans, of Atlanta, Ga., a former athlete and football coach and until recently instructor at the Ranger training school in Tennessee. From his schooling the outward-bound soldier, he is a tough customer, tougher than the average Japanese and better equipped to defend himself and take a personal offensive than any average American soldier has ever been.

These men are not Commandos and not Rangers. They are average American infantrymen. They go through a dozen courses at the center. Thousands of men have already gone through, and General Richardson said this afternoon that "not a single man will go out to fight in the areas under my command until he has had this training."

In the stream-crossing course, under Lieut. William L. Fornwald of Scranton, Pa., one of the center's fifty instructors, the men are thrown on their own to get over and attack "the enemy." They use flotation bladders, or make rude rafts of shelter halves and poles and swim behind them.

They take a twelve-by-twelve camouflage net, fill it with coconuts and float a 30-caliber machine gun across. They take a 2 1/2-ton truck tarpaulin and float twenty-four men or two tons of equipment in it. They can wrap up a jeep in a tarpaulin and push it over.

They also cross streams by net bridges, with explosives being set off under them. They learn how to jump into oil-soaked water aflame, come up splashing and swim through, pushing the fire away with their hands.

Under Lieut. Lloyd A. Behymer of Cincinnati, they are taught the handling of booby traps and demolitions including special charges now designed to meet the challenge of the palm tree shelters found on Tarawa. Special engineer classes get advanced training in this field.

There is an open hut, with three sides, equipped with chairs, tables, bottles of sake and a light extension. The instructor selects a soldier to enter the building. His nickname is "Alamaba."

He walks gingerly up the steps. The first two are safe, but on the third a booby trap goes off. Turning on the light sets off an explosion and picking up a bottle detonates another. So they learn.

HAND-TO-HAND TACTICS TAUGHT
Under Lieut. William E. Vazzani of Monongahela, Pa., the men get hand-to-hand combat experience, the hard way. A special demonstration was given by Sgts. John R. Compton of Perry, Mich., and Barney Bernard of Grand Rapids, Mich., professional wrestlers.

They came at each other with knives or bayonets and showed how to eliminate the attacker in a painful, deadly and seemingly simple style which is best not described. They teach every soldier how to gouge and choke most efficiently. ◆

JANUARY 2, 1944

Editorial
Invasion Year Plans Are Perfected

The new year opened yesterday on a note of great expectations. In the East German armies, their lines of retreat into Poland endangered, were reeling back under the hammerblows of the Russians. Allied air fleets—more than 3,000 planes strong on one day—roared through German skies, battering at German cities. British and American armies were moving doggedly forward in Italy despite the stiffest resistance the Wehrmacht was able to offer in any theatre. All these signs seem to point to ultimate Allied victory in Europe.

The primary task for 1944 had been set at meetings of the United Nations leaders in 1943. The Allies must drive over the plains of Poland from the East, over the Alpine mountain passes from the south, over the beaches from the West into the German heartland. The vitals of

JANUARY 2, 1944

Our Hard-Hitting Invasion Chief

General Eisenhower brings to his new task the qualities of steel—coolness, precision, power.

By Milton Bracker
ALGIERS (By Wireless).

Since November, 1942, Dwight D. Eisenhower has been directing the gigantic task of kicking in the southern door to Germany. Now he is about to shift his approach to "other points of the compass," as President Roosevelt put it. But his primary objective will remain the same—to kill Germans.

The general, himself, reduced his job to these terms, and they cannot be improved upon. When the glorious and terrible moment of the invasion comes,

Nazi war power—the industries of the Ruhr and Rhine valleys, the Lorraine coal mines, the coal and iron of Polish Silesia, the Rumanian and Galician oil fields, the minerals of Yugoslavia—must be taken. It would not be easy. It would be costly in lives, in effort and material.

CHANGES IN COMMAND

In preparation for these drives the Allied commanders were being assigned last week to the invasion tasks that lie ahead, The importance air power will play—it is now axiomatic that a bridgehead cannot be secured on a hostile shore without almost complete air cover—was indicated in the appointment of Air Chief Marshal Sir Arthur Tedder as second in command under Gen. Dwight D. Eisenhower in the West. In the South Gen. Sir Henry Maitland Wilson will have as his assistant the American Lieut. Gen. Jacob L. Devers.

There were other shifts. Air Chief Marshal Trafford L. Leigh-Mallory, once head of the RAF's School of Army Cooperation, was named head of Allied air forces in the West, with Maj. Gen. James H. Doolittle and Lieut. Gen. Carl Spaatz in charge of the American forces under him. The American Lieut. Gen.

Ira C. Eaker was named head of all Allied air forces in the South. Admiral Sir Bertram Ramsay was named to command the great sea armada that will carry the forces of the Allies across the western seas to Europe's shores.

On all fronts the tempo of preparation was being speeded. At home Charles E. Wilson, executive vice chairman of the War Production Board, warned industry that supplies in quantities dwarfing those assembled for the invasions of Africa and Italy will be required to launch and sustain the operations of the coming year. "The $61,000,000,000 of munitions we made in 1943 must be greatly increased in 1944" he said, "without the help of new plant facilities." President Roosevelt has declared that the 3,800,000 American troops now abroad must be increased to more than 5,000,000 by July.

Where along the walls of Festung Europa the attack will be hurled remained the secret of the Allied High-Command. In the West, where already Germany has reported increased probing thrusts by British commandos, General Eisenhower has a choice of many possible landing places ranging from the

rugged coasts of Norway and the highly fortified shores of Germany, the Low Countries and northern France to the sandy beaches of western France. Some military experts have thought the possibilities might be restricted to those areas which can be reached effectively by fighter aircraft, the areas directly across the Channel. The likelihood seemed to be that on D-day blows would be aimed at many points, leaving the German High Command to guess which was the thrust with full power behind it.

When this great operation will start was also a secret of the Allied High Command. All the Germans could be sure of was that it would come some time in 1944. Meanwhile the pressure would increase. The Russians, with prospects of great victories of entrapment immediately before them, were straining to exploit their superiority to the utmost. The air war was growing in strength and the pressure from the South continued.

Looking into the future, Adolf Hitler delivered gloomy messages to the German peoples and armies. He saw a "second year of great crisis." "In this war," he said, "there will be no victors and losers, but merely survivors and annihilated." ◇

---

greater Allied land, air and possibly sea forces than have ever struck a blow together, will combine to do just that—kill Germans. And General Eisenhower is the kind of man who is prepared to kill just as many of them as is necessary to beat Hitler's Nazis to their knees.

In his position as Allied Commander in Chief for the invasion, General Eisenhower becomes the symbol of all Allied hope—and confidence—in an Allied victory this year, if possible. He is the arm that swings the hammer, and it will strike a terrible blow.

In the job he is about to assume, Eisenhower will find many problems paralleling those he has solved in North Africa, Sicily and Italy. For the supreme commander of any striking force remains fundamentally the point of liaison between the will of his Government and the armed forces themselves. Men like President Roosevelt, Prime Minister Churchill and General Marshall may do much of the larger planning, but there will be a complex substructure of planning for Eisenhower, himself.

It will be he, for instance, who will figure out the proper relationship between the air, land and sea power at any given place and time, the necessary allocation of men and materials. It will be

he who will decide whether plan A or B must be invoked to meet a given situation, and he who must fully exploit a sudden advantage.

It will be Eisenhower to whom the surrender of defeated Germany will be addressed. This will be a supreme moment for a man whose ancestors fled religious persecution in Germany in the seventeenth century.

General Eisenhower's character is in his face. It is a roundish, imperturbable, candid face with wide-set gray-blue eyes and a hard compactness about the features. He can snap his jaw like a steel trap, and the implication that he may do so at any moment is never lacking.

If there is one thing certain about his approach to his new job, it is that the qualities of steel—which include the ability to get white hot and cut through almost anything—will go with it. Yet there will be a minimum of sparks, a maximum of smooth, deadly driving power. That is the impression "Ike" inevitably gives—coolness, precision, speed, power and potential ruthlessness.

He is always canny and he can be tough—with his best friends if necessary. But like so many of his fellow-American soldiers, he is shot through with sentiment and with humor. His devotion to

General Dwight D. Eisenhower in January, 1944.

his Scotty, called Telek, is something of a legend, and it goes back to his boyhood when he found a terrier with a broken leg and coaxed it back to health.

Sentiment on a nobler plane was demonstrated by Eisenhower on the shores of Malta in July. His second tremendous D-day was about to dawn. The plans were made, the ships were en route. The very heavens themselves could not have called back the armada the one-time Kansas cowboy had ▸

launched. Through the night the planes droned toward Sicily bearing the paratroopers, many of whom were to be shot down while still hanging in their shrouds, as the general must have known they would be. As he looked into the darkness after them, the general's eyes misted.

General Eisenhower has never forgotten that while the general staffs map larger strategy and men like himself carry it out, it is the ordinary foot soldier who imposes it with gun and bayonet upon the stubbornly resisting foe. When he recently decided it was time to "plug" one specific branch of the service, it wasn't the glamorous Air Force or the tank troops he had schooled in World War I that he singled out; it was the mudstained and weatherbeaten infantrymen, of whom the general said:

"We realize it in our own consciousness but does the man in Abilene, Kan., or in some little village in England? Does he realize just exactly what these people are doing, how they are performing?"

The general loves a good soldier and deplores a bad one and he has no difficulty in talking to the ordinary G.I. because he is as blunt as a chin and the antithesis of bunk. On his tours of the front, Eisenhower talks to everyone and manages to do it more naturally than most multiple-starred officers.

He speaks a language his men can understand. He never says "We'd better do something to remedy the situation." He simply snaps "Hell, we'll change that." His political view of the war is as simple and direct: "What the hell are we in this war for but to beat fascism and autocracy?"

His daily routine involves a lot of deskwork; any commanding general's does. But paperwork is the phase of his job that he likes least, so he breaks it with periodic trips to advance headquarters and the front. Within a few weeks of the establishment of the new western land front, it is a safe bet that he will be flying again to be among the men who are doing the actual fighting. And this process is sure to continue as the march toward Berlin gets under way.

He has assumed the most colossal task ever assigned to any man in American military history. He has become the single most dramatic and most important figure in the Allied military scheme. Yet with it all he remains the Texan from Kansas, or perhaps more accurately the Kansan from Texas, who reads "Ivanhoe" and Cromwell and who quotes Lewis Carroll's philosophical walrus. ◊

POLISH ISSUE SHARPENS AS REDS CROSS BORDER
Moscow Shows Resentment Over Any Discussion of Future Boundaries of Russia to Westward

By EDWIN L. JAMES

As the Russian armies, driving against the Germans, cross the frontiers of Poland, the issue of the future frontiers between Russia and Poland comes to the front with an accentuated sharpness. The complication of the situation may well be illustrated by saying that the statement that Stalin's armies have crossed Poland's frontiers means a reference to the borders of Poland before Hitler attacked her in 1939. But at the same time the Russians do not say they have crossed the frontiers of Poland. The frontier does not appear on new Russian maps. That leads to the logical assumption that the Russians consider that, where others think they have crossed the Polish border, they think they are fighting on Russian soil there.

To illustrate: Last week, when most American newspapers announced the Russian crossing of the Polish border, New York's Communist paper The Daily Worker came out with a front-page box entitled "A Lesson in Geography," the gravamen of which was that the Polish border lay a long way ahead of where the Red armies had reached. The reference was ostensibly to the line fixed by Hitler and Stalin when they divided up Poland in the fall of 1939. That was, it will be recalled, when Berlin and Moscow were working under a treaty of friendship. Now, of course, the Comin-

---

QUIRKS OF CENSORS PUZZLE TO WRITERS
Correspondents in The Field Astonished When Home Press Reveals Guarded Secrets

By FRANK L. KLUCKHOHN
By Wireless to The New York Times.

ALLIED HEAD QUARTERS IN AUSTRALIA, Feb. 1—The question of censorship in the war theatres remains a subject of key importance—as it has been since the war started—to the American people, who are anxious for accurate news.

American war correspondents in the field during various operations recently were astonished by printed disclosures at home blueprinting not only with words but maps future moves about which the men on the spot have maintained oral as well as written silence; for there is no man in the world more security-minded than a correspondent about to risk his life with a landing, whether it be in Sicily, Europe or the Pacific area. Correspondents in some theatres—principally the European—after agreeing to security censorship, have been amazed to have censors tell them bluntly, "This is being halted for political reasons."

STORIES NOT ALWAYS OFFICIAL

But there is not one news writer in the field who would write a word that would cost the life of one American fighting man. Starting on expeditions in which they know they share the risks, correspondents have been amazed to see home magazines and newspapers forecasting exactly what is going to be done and giving the enemy a chance to get set.

One example of this—although it was not the primary cause of the heavy loss of life, as it turned out—was an accurate prediction of the Navy's move into the Gilbert

tern is abolished and perhaps theoretically The Daily Worker is no longer getting its orders from Moscow. So perhaps the lesson in geography represented a bit of mental telepathy. Perhaps not.

At any rate there are ample indications that the Russians do not feel bound by the old frontiers of Poland, although, interestingly enough, there is no official Moscow statement that Russia adheres to the line drawn in her bargain with Hitler.

SOME CHANGES DUE

It is a perfectly good guess that the Russians will desire to make some changes in the eastern border of Poland, and that at the expense of Poland. Most students of the situation think that Poland will lose the Ukrainian region that was within her frontiers and also, further to the north, the region known as Byelo-Russia. Not that the Ukrainians are burning with any desire to join Russia, but it can be argued that the Russians regard the larger part of Ukraine as theirs and that the Ukrainians who were in Poland form a natural part of this territory.

It may, of course, be true that the Russians are thinking of the line which was drawn by them and Hitler and which would take away about 40 per cent of Polish territory. But there is no official evidence that that is true. There has also been some talk of Moscow's taking over Galicia to make a common frontier with Czechoslovakia. But Stalin has not said so, and it is to be borne in mind that this region did not belong to Russia prior to 1914, it was a part of Austria.

Attention may also be given to the fact that the Polish Committee set up in Moscow under the aegis of the Russians has been talking of compensating Poland by giving her German Galicia and perhaps East Prussia. East Prussia might prove hard for the Poles to digest, but the fact that there is talk of compensating Poland in other directions for what she may lose to the east is to be kept in mind.

DIFFICULTIES FOR POLES

It would be difficult to imagine a more complicated situation than that in which the Poles find themselves. Moscow has broken off relations with the Government-in-Exile. Even when that Government urges its underground not to fight the Russians on Polish soil, a gesture that should please the Russians, the circumstance that the Poles, as perhaps they felt obliged to do, spoke of their right, territorial and political, has brought upon them no end of criticism from Moscow and from Russian advocates outside Russia.

There is in this country a large mass of sympathy for the Poles—due in part to the presence on our soil as good citizens of so many persons of Polish blood. That is a circumstance that certainly weighs with our President. Yet the biggest job there is before Mr. Roosevelt is the conquest of Germany, and Stalin has done more militarily against the Nazis than any other United Nations leader. And he is expected to do more. Whether or not the Poles consider Russia as their ally, certainly our Government considers Russia as an ally of this country and a very powerful and therefore valuable ally.

No one blames the Poles for being worried and for fearing what they will regard as injustices. But the idea may be advanced that until after President Roosevelt and Premier Mikolajcyzk have their talks it might be a good thing for the Poles to make fewer statements that might increase the difficulties of the situation. ◇

Islands. Sometimes, fortunately, these predictions are inaccurate, so the enemy cannot be sure they are absolutely correct.

Some serious critics believe that one reason for disappointment in the Italian campaign was that the American landing at Salerno was so well "telegraphed" that the enemy was set to meet it.

But the mere assumption that because a news article passes military censorship it has the stamp of official approval is incorrect. For example, in this theatre Gen. Douglas MacArthur confines censorship to what he regards as primary military security. Anyone can write anything he wishes to about political matters and about military matters where security is not involved. The reports may not accord with official desires, to say nothing of having official endorsement. Anyone here, for instance is free to do any speculating he likes about General MacArthur's position vis-a-vis home policy.

CONDITIONS ALTER REGULATIONS

The views this correspondent, or any correspondent, expresses on General MacArthur's political stands are his own deductions and are not official and this will continue to remain true.

As far as military matters are concerned, this correspondent today passed a news report through censorship that Rabaul, a key Japanese base, was not neutralized. Several months ago General MacArthur said it was neutralized, but he was speaking of a temporary situation at the time. On the other hand, if this correspondent wrote an article predicting this theatre's next move, his story would be halted.

As far as this theatre is concerned, censorship, it is believed, will continue to be held to a minimum, and what leaves here through censorship does not necessarily have the stamp of official approval.

Security is the only type of censorship to which the war correspondents have knowingly agreed. Correspondents covering current actions, however, have been amazed by the "spilling" of prospective moves in home publications. In the long run this will lead to tightening the censorship rules, which, with many faults, have permitted a large measure of truth to reach the American people. ◇

FEBRUARY 3, 1944

SWIFT SUCCESS CROWNS THE KWAJALEIN CAMPAIGN

ATOLL ISLETS FALL

By GEORGE F. HORNE
By Telephone to The New York Times.

PEARL HARBOR, Feb. 2—The marines have captured Roi Island, primary objective in the northern portion of Kwajalein Atoll in the Marshall Islands and the first prewar Japanese territory to fall to United States forces.

Without a single naval loss and with "very moderate" casualties, we have accomplished what no one apparently believed we could do. We have taken the Japanese by surprise, overwhelmed them with unprecedented striking power and in two days of fighting have captured one of the three principal objectives in the atoll.

▸

American forces have landed on Namur, an island connected with Roi by a causeway, and pushed the enemy back to its northern extreme. In the southern part of Kwajalein Atoll troops of the Seventh Infantry Division under Maj. Gen. Charles H. Corlett are well established on Kwajalein Island and are forcing the enemy back.

Our marines and infantrymen have demonstrated to the enemy that we also can strike with terrific force when and where he least expects it. The astonishing early success of the Marshalls operation may well shorten by many weeks a campaign thought of in terms of months.

ATTACK LONG PLANNED

Admiral Chester W. Nimitz, Commander in Chief of the Pacific Fleet and Pacific Ocean Areas, who, with other naval and military authorities conducting the Central Pacific war, planned the campaign months in advance and with precious attention to every detail, issued information on the successful early stages at 11 A.M.

His communiqué says it is "now apparent that the attack took the enemy completely by surprise."

Presumably the enemy considered the Saturday carrier attack as another heavy task force blow and prepared to meet it as best they could, as they had met the one last December. When the carriers continued the attack on Sunday, the enemy was unable to maintain his defenses. The following morning when American assault forces stormed ashore on small islands near the objectives, the enemy realized it was an all-out invasion assault.

A significant sentence in Admiral Nimitz's communiqué may contain one clue to the remarkable operation: "Continuous bombardments of beaches by our warships, planes and land-based artillery enabled our forces to make landings on the three principal objectives with little resistance."

A spokesman at fleet headquarters disclosed supplementary details. After the initial landings on Kwajalein Island, which probably came yesterday, troops of the Seventh Division encountered considerable rifle and machine-gun fire and some mortar fire. It was explained, however, that the most formidable immediate obstacle to our troops seemed to be huge fires started earlier by our heavy bombardment, both by surface and aircraft.

SEVERAL DOZEN CAPTIVES

We have captured "several dozen prisoners" at Kwajalein Island, and there are indications that we may take more than we did in the Gilbert Islands. The enemy military strength is unknown, although probably considerable.

It was also disclosed at fleet headquarters that neutralization of the enemy's other defense points throughout the Marshall Islands was continuing unabated, with planes of the Seventh Army Air Force and Fleet Air Wing 2 carrying out systematic attacks.

Carrier-based planes were coordinating bombing attacks with artillery and naval shelling to cover the main landing. The carriers have been in almost continuous action for four days now, and today would be the fifth. The ability to carry on such heavy action may offer a clue to the size of the carrier force used.

With possession of the excellent, though small, airfield on Roi Island so early we will be able to consolidate our position in the Marshall Islands more quickly than was anticipated. When we get the air strip on Kwajalein we will be further strengthened for the counterattacks the enemy is almost certain to launch.

Roi Island's two runways are 3,600 feet and 4,300 feet long and are excellent for smaller planes but short for heavy craft. On Kwajalein there is a runway of 5,000 feet that can be extended.

These strips are probably not in the best condition, but our forces are able to put them in fair shape in a brief time. ◊

Roi Island (1), site of an air base, has been captured by American marines. The invaders first took Mellu and Boggerlapp (2), then crossed over to Ennugarret, Ennumennet and Ennubirr, thus flanking Roi. The Japanese have now been herded into the northern corner of Namur, just east of Roi. In the southern part of the atoll (3) American infantrymen captured Gea—by mistake in the dark—then crossed to their intended objective, Ninni. They also occupied Ennylabegan and Enubuj; in Kwajalein (4) they are pushing the enemy back. The entire campaign was supported by an armada gathered from far-flung bases in the Pacific (inset).

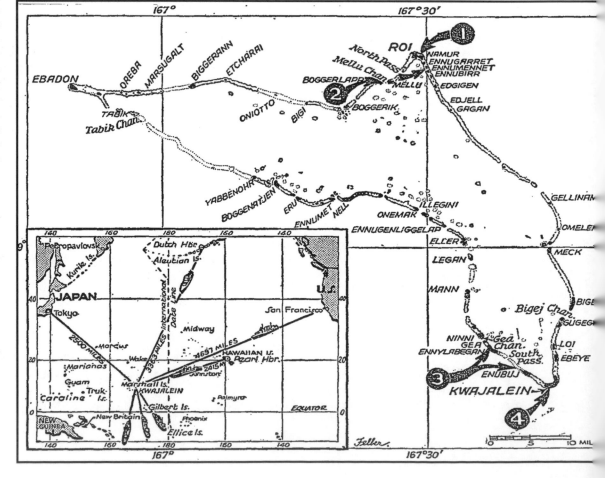

FEBRUARY 8, 1944

Smoke rising from Castle Hill during the Battle of Monte Cassino, Italy, February 6, 1944.

CASSINO DEFENSES LIKE STONE WALL

By C. L. SULZBERGER
By Wireless to The New York Times.

WITH THE FIFTH ARMY IN ITALY, Feb. 7—In the sixth successive day since they first crept into the outer ridge of stone houses of the little mountain town of Cassino, American troops kept up their stubborn fight, trying to expand their hard-won toehold.

But, despite the continual Allied shelling that is crumbling many of their defenses around them, the Germans are still desperately beating back all major assaults designed to force open the gateway into the broad Liri Valley and the highway to the Anzio beachhead and Rome.

The grimy, unshaven infantry squads in the small cluster of ruined buildings are still virtually on the outskirts of Cassino. They are maintaining themselves against all counter-attacks, but they are finding it still virtually impossible to break through toward the town's main square past the enemy tanks and self-propelled guns continually dodging about behind the wrecks of houses and supported by hidden artillery ensconced in concrete cellar bunkers and steel pillboxes manned with machine guns.

GUNNERS STILL IN OLD CASTLE

Despite the terrible pounding of the medieval castle on the hilltop above the town, which continued today, the German gunners there still opened up against the Americans whenever they sought to cross the gully separating them from the rise and storm the height. It dominates the position today as much as when its engineers conceived its military use centuries ago.

Although the present struggle has been one of house-to-house fighting for six days, the actual battle for Cassino may be said to be twenty-three days old. It started with the main attack on the Trocchio feature before the town. The Rapido River was crossed by tanks on Jan. 29.

The Germans are making every effort to stave off as long as possible, by their stone-wall defenses, the completion of the breach of the Gustav Line and the Allies' entry into the Liri Valley. Nevertheless, behind Cassino, Allied infantry units won control of three new elevations. Behind Mount Cassino and its famous abbey they have established forward points only a mile from the Via Casilina, possibly menacing the eventual route of the German withdrawal if they can consolidate and reinforce their gains.

Constant small attacks against Mount Cassino continued all last night and today, but the ban on shelling the abbey's grounds made it exceedingly difficult for the artillery to give any support, since American patrols are only about 300 yards from the abbey. Nevertheless, some careful concentrations were aimed at the zigzag road leading up to the monastery from the town. Over this route the Germans must supply their units defending the height. Our troops are so near the landmark that they can easily read the sign posts warning that it is neutral territory of the Vatican. ◇

FEBRUARY 16, 1944

PRELATES DEFEND BOMBING OF ABBEY
Blame Germans For Employing Monastery As Lookout

BALTIMORE, Md., Feb. 15 (AP)—The Most Rev. Michael J. Curley, Archbishop of Baltimore and Washington, expressed regret today at the necessity for bombing the Benedictine monastery at Mount Cassino, but said that "every Catholic throughout the world, I am sure, will understand..."

"If it had to be bombed, I am very sure that our American fighting men had no desire whatever to destroy that glorious symbol and fixed sanctuary of Christianity," he said. "The Germans evidently took advantage of the American attitude toward such a monument and, according to all information, they took possession of that sacred place in order to carry out their nefarious warfare." ◇

FEBRUARY 20, 1944

The Doughboy's Grim Road To Rome

By C. L. Sulzberger with the Fifth Army

SUNNY Italy, land of rich tourists and eternal bright blue sky, is to the average American doughboy an endless road of sticky mud dotted with minefields, a series of forbidding gray mountain crags filled with almost inaccessible gun pits; murky, freezing rivers rushing past shattered bridges; a collection of barren, gutted villages peopled with tattered scavengers—all set beneath gray, cloud-filled sky dripping rain, sleet and more rain. In the vernacular he has borrowed from his British ally, the American doughboy says that so far as Italy is concerned, "I've had it." ⟩

◀ It was a captured German general who told his interrogators that the western desert was a tactician's paradise and a quartermaster's hell. Italy is a tactician's hell and a quartermaster's purgatory. For the United States Army, from its commander to its smallest squad of infantry men, this campaign is like something out the lower reaches of Dante's "Divine Comedy," and there is nothing either divine or comic about it. General Sherman's description of war in general, rather than Baedeker's description of Italy, is applicable in this festering, bewildered land today.

The peculiar, peak-serrated front stretching between the romantic Tyrrhenian and Adriatic Seas is a scene of heroism and disaster, of hope and gloom and suffering by a potpourri of troops representing the actuality of the United Nations in its fullest sense. Here are British, New Zealand, Indian, French, Japanese-American, Moroccan, Tunisian, Algerian, American and even a handful of Italian soldiers.

The American doughboys now in the line, determined and brave as they unquestionably are, nevertheless are a weather-beaten, weary group of men who are surviving in their dreary, tedious, costly push forward merely by the skill instilled within them by that hardest school of all—battle. These men have fought with dogged courage equal to anything their ancestors demonstrated in their so-called harder days. They have fought with a canniness mindful of the forays by the first Continental pioneers against Indian tribesmen. And they have fought against odds and determined opposition certainly equal to those of any battle of World War I. There are many veterans of the last war who still reminisce by their firesides in terms of the huge catastrophes of those days—the terrors of a creeping barrage and massed infantry assaults with bayonet. Certainly such features on such a scale do not prevail along the contested central belt of Italy. But artillery these days is ingeniously more accurate than ever before, thanks to new devices and new methods of observation. And artillery supported by air is devilishly powerful.

Added to artillery now are new types of mortars; swifter, stronger tanks; self-propelled guns; rocket projectiles, such as the Nebelwerfer and the bazooka.

These American men have great quantities of almost all of these weapons, but it would be most foolish to get the idea that we have the fastest planes, the best tanks, the most powerful guns in the world—because we haven't. On this front the Germans can match almost any weapon we are using, and it is only the grim, wary, brave capability of the doughboy, tankman or pilot which enables him to surmount obstacles erected by a nation whose peacetime profession was preparation for war.

American soldiers are going into tank battles with the knowledge that the model opposing them has armor over its Achilles heel almost as thick as the best protection their own vehicle may have; that they are outgunned both in the sense of range and muzzle velocity and that it will be their own fighting skill, acuteness and daring which will have to see them through if the odds are equaled.

Artillerymen pound away with huge concentrations of guns—batteries sometimes landing more than 100 projectiles simultaneously on the same target knowing full well that when the counterbattery work begins and those 32,000-yard Nazi 170's start slowly feeling for them with shells traveling so fast that the whine is almost simultaneous with the burst, they have no single gun able to reach the enemy's batteries.

Fighter pilots often go into action with outmoded aircraft, knowing that only the greatest cunning can give them victory. But none the less they take off full of confidence.

And then the infantrymen, whose job isn't, as some theorists seem to suppose, merely to march in and occupy territory evacuated under pressure from massed armor and aerial assaults. They go crawling forward toward enemy pillboxes, tired, cold and sometimes scared, entirely aware that the German, far from being a beaten man, remains a tough, resourceful soldier—one of the best in the world.

As if to add to these difficulties there is the question of forbidden territories—those clerical monuments with which in the words of the G.1. "Italy is just lousy." In the bloody battle for Cassino, it is the opinion of many an officer and private that had we started the attack by shelling the famous Abbey of Mount Cassino, which dominates the chewed-up town, and wiped it off the map at once, the tide of battle might have turned during the first week of February.

"I am a Catholic," says one lieutenant colonel, "but this thing didn't make much sense. We lost lives rather than destroy stones. If you would just let the Catholic boys in the artillery shell away at the monasteries, I think they'd do as good a job as anyone." Why, you may ask when all these gloomy facts are pointed out, are we able to advance at all? The answer is that something which enables these Americans despite their many dis-advantages to climb forward over frozen peaks, inch across mine fields and batter their way through villages, which are shambles of fallen stone.

In the first place, these men are now experienced, hard-bitten soldiers who not only have been able to utilize to the fullest that fighting mechanical capacity with which the American nation is gifted, but also have developed the instinctive scouting and sharpshooting ability of their forebears.

Secondly, they possess a vigor. health and youthfulness in its fullest and best sense that Germany no longer is able to muster among its wayward decimated menfolk drained of blood and energy by more than four years of what was meant to be a Blitzkrieg.

Thirdly, the Americans know not only that they already have definite quantitative superiority in all the necessary tools of war, but that there are more where they came from in the bomb-free factories back home. Their quantity of weapons, their vigor, youth and fine health cared for so exactingly by medical and feeding organizations, are slowly proving the answer to what is actually a mercenary Nazi army defensively entrenched in some of the most difficult military terrain a major engagement has ever been fought over. Mud like thick soup, mountains like barren limestone teeth, and a ravaged landscape of torn-up roads, uprooted railways, blown-up bridges—difficult as they may be, these are merely tests of the engineering ingenuity of those supply geniuses on whom the success of this or any other campaign must eventually depend.

The backbone of this American Army, as it always has been, remains the infantry. They are used to the ghastly sight of death; they are used to its strange, slightly sour, fetid smell.

They know where a shell is going to burst from its sound. They know how to follow a mine tape in the darkness and cut wire on patrol.

These generally sentimental and, in its best sense, simpleminded youths have attained a somewhat remote connection with their former selves. This writer has seen them slogging silently with impassive, grimy faces past slit trenches containing the awkwardly sprawling bodies of their fellows, regarding them, if at all, as if they might be stones. Not that this unfeelingness has made them automatons, but in war it is necessary to compartmentalize the mind, and softer thoughts remain very much in the innermost compartment.

In spite of the bitter cold at night and the steep terrain, topped by precipitous rock formations and coated with snow and slippery frozen mud, our infantrymen prefer to fight on these heights. Generally, such actions comprise a modern kind of American-Indian warfare, with careful probing of the enemy from behind cover until contact is established.

When the two armies meet in close-up fighting, Allied artillery generally is able to give the infantry only a modicum of support because infantry units are too closely intermixed with our own men. It then becomes a question of small arms and as many grenades as a man can pitch. Then the plodding doughboy, sweating despite the crisp wintry climate, is likely to pound the side of a friendly tank with his rifle butt and holler, "Come on over here. We've got some Kraut holed up. Dig them out, will you?" Or there will be a shout. "Don't fool with that. Throw in a grenade."

These actions will never go down in history as battles any schoolboy ever will be expected to study, but the rate of casualties here is high. and from such pushes one gets an idea of what the ordinary, unglamorous infantryman goes through in this war.

The best example of this terrible process of troops bleeding their way forward was our attempt to cross the little Rapido River. Under cover of the heaviest type of shelling and combined night and smoke screening, the infantry led the engineers to the river, where the latter put up a flimsy, railless little foot-bridge. Spray from the swift, swollen stream froze on the bridge.

Infantrymen staggered toward the river carrying heavy boats loaded with equipment, while other small units began crawling across the bridge, gripping its icy sides with bleeding fingers. A hail of enemy fire from fixed positions broke through the smoke.

The first group lost sight of the mine tapes, and the boat and its crew blew up in a cascade of frozen earth.

Thick fire of all sorts burst about the bridge to the contrapuntal accompaniment of screaming rocket projectiles. Some units penetrated to the enemy's second line wire defenses while the Germans coolly opened up fire from their hitherto silent hidden positions. This pressure on the exposed attackers was too much. and the effort had to be given up after excessive losses.

Northward along the Tyrrhenian coast the infantrymen fighting at the Anzio-Nettuno beachhead have had better fighting weather and better terrain than those in central Italy. Here the original emphasis was laid on naval operations, supply and weather being the two big questions during the initial phase of any such battle. Clear skies afforded a much better fighter plane cover over the crowded harbors and beaches as well as improved vision or heavy bombers droning inland with their cargoes of explosives.

When the writer went into Anzio with Gen. Sir Harold R. L. Alexander the other day the usual air raid was going on under a light cloud blanket. It was rendered somewhat dramatic by the sudden plummeting to earth of a sheet of flame that was once a fighter plane, followed by the lackadaisical silver parachute of its pilot. Everyone in the harbor region was working like a beaver disregarding the invisible dogfighting above the clouds. They were unloading truck after truck of supplies from the ships, while tarpaulin-covered "ducks" were chugging in over the beaches with cases of ammunition.

Long lines of heavy guns rumbled inland past laurel groves toward the critical battlefield. Despite the marshland spreading about inshore from the beachhead, this is by far the best tank country on both Italian battlefronts and the ugly monsters crawled steadily toward the highlands in support of the infantrymen who had already fought their way inland.

These then are Italy's two fronts. Fighting on either of them is a tough job. Before we achieve victory on either or both of them, as one general put it, "We're bound at least to get a bloody nose." As still another commander sees it, "We will have to put out plenty" before the battle is over.

But in this discussion, just as in the fighting, it is the infantrymen who have the last word. "If all roads lead to Rome," the doughboys ask, "why in hell don't the Krauts just pack up and follow them?" ◊

APRIL 10, 1944

PRAVDA RIDICULES TIMES WAR WRITER

Hanson W. Baldwin Is Termed 'Admiral Of Ink Pool' Who Uses German Data

By Wireless to The New York Times.

MOSCOW, April 9—Pravda published today a sharp, satirical personal attack upon Hanson W. Baldwin, military commentator of the New York Times, labeling him "admiral of the ink pool." Mr. Baldwin, according to Pravda, relies exclusively upon German information for news of the Soviet-German front, and thereby has put himself and his newspaper in a ridiculous position.

The author of the 1,100-word dispatch concerning Mr. Baldwin is David Zaslavsky, one of the Soviet Union's leading writers, who recently attacked Wendell Willkie and William R. Hearst.

Mr. Zaslavsky quoted from Mr. Baldwin's dispatches over the period since the Soviet-German war began, and concluded that Mr. Baldwin had made a number of incorrect appraisals and forecasts of the true situation on the Eastern Front.

"You can't explain the systematic failures of Mr. Baldwin only by his lack of information or by his limitations," Mr. Zaslavsky said. "The source of his mistakes is different, and he has disclosed it himself. On April 26, 1942, he wrote that he did not trust Soviet information and that he operated only on the basis of German information. To this he has remained inevitably true. And that's exactly why his 'prognoses' are suffering defeats, together with Germany.

"German information is misinformation. Speaking simply, it is lies. The Germans try to deceive everybody—their adversaries, the neutrals and their own people. They are deceiving very crudely, and only those who want to be deceived.

NAVAL EXPERIENCE CITED

"The ink pool admiral—Hanson Baldwin—can say that he is also a sort of victim of German atrocities. The Germans have atrociously deceived him and put him in wrong. But he wanted it himself. The fact that he is attracted to false German sources is really a kind of political disease, so let him blame himself if he has put himself and his newspaper in a ridiculous position."

SOME PROPHECIES ASSAILED

"All through 1941 and the greater part of 1942, Mr. Baldwin in his surveys was forecasting the defeat of the Red Army," Mr. Zaslavsky said. "On paper he ▶

himself was defeating the Red Army, and about him you could say, in the words of an old Russian song: 'Here, in militant zeal, Mister Hanson Baldwin defeats Russia on a map by his forefinger.'"

Mr. Zaslavsky quoted a number of Mr. Baldwin's forecasts that he said did not turn out right, and that Mr. Zaslavsky said should have persuaded The New York Times commentator to "at once and forever give up making brash prophecies." But, Mr. Zaslavsky added, Mr. Baldwin's "tongue is his enemy, and he forecast with all the authority of an old seawolf that the Russians

wouldn't have any big victories" in the winter of 1942–43. The Soviet author said that prophecy was faulty navigation.

Mr. Zaslavsky concluded with the assertion that if Mr. Baldwin had commanded a naval ship "along such a course, with such skill, and with such brains, he would have smashed the ship long ago, and would have been thrown out of the Navy in dishonor.

"But an inky sea has its own laws," Mr. Zaslavsky said. "Its admirals can for years flounder around in the pool and feel no shame at all." ◆

APRIL 14, 1944

Bong Downs 27th Japanese Plane and Becomes U.S. 'Ace of Aces'

By FRANK L. KLUCKHOHN
By Wireless to the New York TIMES.

ALLIED HEADQUARTERS IN THE SOUTHWEST PACIFIC, April 13— Capt. Richard Ira Bong, 23-year-old farm youth of Poplar, Wis., became the leading United States combat ace yesterday when he shot down his twenty-seventh Japanese plane over Hollandia, New Guinea.

Captain Bong is now "the American ace of aces," an announcement from Gen. Douglas MacArthur's headquarters stated. [Meanwhile, Capt. Don S. Gentile, leading American ace in the European theatre with a record of twenty-three planes shot down in combat and seven destroyed on the ground, has been put out of action for a few days as the result of a crash landing in his Mustang at his home base in England, it was disclosed Thursday.]

Quiet Captain Bong, an Army fighter pilot, exceeded Capt. Eddie Rickenbacker's World War I American record of twenty-six planes shot down, which had been equaled in the present war by Maj. Joe Foss of the Marine Corps and Maj. Gregory Boyington, also a marine, who is missing. Captain Bong yesterday shot out of the sky his twenty-sixth and twenty-seventh.

Flying the two-engined Lightning in which he has made combat air history, Captain Bong won official credit for the two additional planes, which he coolly shot down as wing men "covered" him to give his remarkable marksmanship full play.

A JINX IS SHATTERED

Captain Bong not only broke the record but shattered a "jinx"—the twenty-six mark that had seemed an impassable limit to American pilots; particularly since Major Boyington was reported missing in January. Major Foss, who recently returned to duty in the South Pacific area after an interval in the United States, has been grounded.

Col. Neel E. Kearby, Thunderbolt ace, of San Antonio, Texas, who won the Congressional Medal of Honor for shooting down six Japanese planes recently, was declared missing within a week after winning America's highest military decoration. Within a few hours, Maj. Thomas R. Lynch, another ace, was killed in New Guinea. Colonel Kearby was officially credited with twenty-one planes, Major Lynch with nineteen.

HAS TWENTY DECORATIONS

Captain Bong, with twenty decorations, including the Distinguished Service Cross, Silver Star with oakleaf, Distinguished Flying Cross with four oak leaves and Air Medal with eleven oak leaves, looks less like an ace than any of them.

He looks to be just what he is, a lad off the farm rather than a killer. But in the air he is a top flier as well as a man who can shoot from any angle with cold precision whether coming out of a roll or screaming down on the enemy. ◆

APRIL 16, 1944

The Score—By Air Chief Marshal Harris
RAF bomber commander sums up the results of persistent attacks on two priority targets—industrial cities and plants making fighters.

By Air Chief Marshal Sir Arthur Harris
Air Officer Commanding-in-Chief
Bomber Command, Royal Air Force
London (By Wireless).

Half of the German Air Force now faces westward toward Britain and toward the bombers of the Royal Air Force and the United States Army Air Force; each of which can now send out a thousand bombers by day or by night in a major attack. Included in this western half of the German Air Force there are about 400 bombers whose function at the moment is to carry out sharp raids on London which have no strategic value but are meant to give the German people the illusion that England is being hit as hard as Germany. Such operations are essentially defensive—a mere reaction to pressure exerted by the other side.

There is also a comparatively small number of aircraft cooperating with the German U-boats in the Battle of the Atlantic—a battle which the Germans are steadily losing. But all the rest of the German Air Force in the west consists of fighters, single and twin engined. The result of this disposition, with the emphasis enormously on defensive action against the Anglo-American bombers, is that there are now four times as many fighters on the western as on the eastern front.

The Luftwaffe was designed to cooperate with the Germany Army, first, by destroying any air force that opposed it, then by blasting the path for the advance of the Panzer divisions. One result of the bomber offensive by Britain has been to smash cooperation between the German Army and the German Air Force, compelling each to fight by itself in a manner for which the Oberkommando of the Wehrmacht had laid no plans. The German armies in Italy are without adequate air cover or air support. The order of battle of the Luftwaffe shows that this must be so on the eastern front.

Even these figures of relative strength of the German Air Force on three different fronts—one-half on the Western front, one-third on the Eastern and one-sixth on the Mediterranean, with fighters in the west outnumbering those in the east by four to one—give no complete picture of the extent to which the air offensive in the west has disorganized the plans of the German air staff and with them the plans of the German Army. To a considerable extent the aircraft of the Luftwaffe is interchangeable in function: bombers can serve as night fighters and fighters as bombers. Therefore the proportion of bombers to fighters in the Luftwaffe does not expose the full extent to which the Germans have been forced onto the defensive in the air.

To get this large defensive fighter force the Germans have not only had to cut their bomber production and convert many factories to making fighters; they have also had to convert many actual bomber types into defensive fighters. All of the twin-engined fighters which until recently provided almost the whole of the air defense of Germany by night were originally bomber types. The Junkers-88 and the Dornier-217 were essentially bombers, while the Messerschmitt-110 is a very efficient fighter-bomber and would be used as such if it was not required to guard the industrial cities of Germany.

Two years ago Hitler was already so much alarmed by the prospect of the great air offensive which was then threatened from the west that he personally gave an order for the production of fighters to be given priority over all other weapons. Since then fighter production has greatly increased, but at a cost of violently wrenching the whole German aircraft industry away from the production of the offensive weapons with which Germany originally planned to win the war.

After two years of ceaseless effort, combined with a policy of starving Germany, even at the height of the Russian offensive, of really effective air cover and support, the Germans have now built up a very formidable defensive air force, which the two bomber commands of the RAF and of the United States Army Air Force in Britain have to face.

There have been moments, especially during the battle of Hamburg, when the German air defenses seemed on the point of collapsing. There have been other moments, especially during February, 1944, when sudden reductions in Anglo-American bomber losses proved how near the Luftwaffe was getting to exhaustion after fighting a whole run of defensive battles

Arthur "Bomber" Harris, commander-in-chief of the Bomber Command RAF, shown here in 1943.

both by day and by night.

This exhaustion comes more quickly nowadays because the pressure of the Anglo-American bomber offensive caused the Germans in the summer of 1943 to give up the old plan of keeping their twin-engined fighters for use by night and their single-engined fighters for use by day. At present the RAF's night bombers have to contend with a considerable number of single-engined as well as twin-engined fighters. Especially over Berlin there are crack squadrons of flying Focke-Wulf-190's and Messerschmitt-109G's, Germany's best single-engined fighters, whose specialized task is to intercept night bombers while actually over the target. The day bombers of the USAAF also encounter numbers of twin-engined night fighters equipped with rocket projectiles which they fire at massed bomber formations in an attempt to break them up.

In this way many German fighters have worked double time, and after a whole series of battles the crews get more quickly exhausted while aircraft becomes more rapidly unserviceable.

The decline of seventy-nine RAF bombers missing in the attack on Leipzig on the night of Feb. 19 to twenty-four missing from an equally heavy attack on Augsburg on the night of Feb. 25 reflects the strain put on German air defenses by successive coordinated Allied attacks. But these figures also show how necessary it is to outmaneuver the enemy's great force of fighters at every stage, to deceive and perplex the German air staff by a multiplicity of attacks, to vary the tactics of the offensive on every possible occasion. ◇

APRIL 20, 1944

KOHIMA SIEGE ENDS
British at Imphal Also Gain Against Enemy At Three Points

By The United Press.

SOUTHEAST ASIA HEADQUARTERS, Kandy, Ceylon, April 19—British and Indian troops, in bayonet fighting, have broken through Japanese road blocks and relieved Kohima where a surrounded English Home Counties regiment held out against enemy attacks for a week, it was announced tonight.

Tanks and artillery reinforcements for the Kohima garrison were reported moving down the road from Dimapur after the initial break-through to the East Indian base was accomplished by an Indian Rajputi patrol and British specialist units.

A strong artillery barrage, fired from 700-yard range against a 150-square-yard area of the siege ring, paved the way for the relief attack, and when the infantrymen broke through they found many of the Japanese dead or too dazed to offer effective resistance.

Sixty miles to the south, tankled British Imperial troops were driving the Japanese invaders of Manipur farther beyond the Imphal plain, seizing three enemy defensive positions and threatening to throw the entire Japanese expedition to India into reverse.

FOE FIRM TO SOUTHWEST

Only at a point southwest of Imphal, where the Japanese had developed a threat to Imphal's dirt road connection with the Assam-Bengal railroad, was the enemy still maintaining strong pressure. A battle had been under way in that sector for two days, but the British were holding firm.

Belated dispatches from the Kohima front revealed that the garrison was relieved over the weekend after fighting for a week against repeated Japanese attacks from all sides. Fighting was particularly heavy in the western quarter of the city where the British, barricaded in the ruins of English colonists' houses atop a 500-foot ridge, threw back waves of artillery-supported Japanese.

With the breaking of the siege from the northwest the Japanese pulled ❯

back their exposed flank, but military observers said they probably would attempt to reestablish their forces across the forty-six-mile road to Dimapur.

The Japanese infiltration tactics, which proved so successful in the initial stage of the drive into India, were of no use to the enemy when he reached the Imphal plain. One enemy column had reached the Nunshigum hill feature on the edge of the plain northeast of Imphal, but exposed itself to Imperial artillery, which killed 400 Japanese as British and Indian infantry swept forward and regained the position.

Sharp fighting continued in the Indo-Burmese border area east and south of Imphal. In one clash Gurkhas killed more than 250 Japanese.

ATTACKS NEAR PALEL FAIL

Japanese attacks Monday night on Allied positions near Palel, road junction, twenty-five miles southeast of Imphal, were repulsed, it was announced. Enemy planes dropped bombs on the Imperial defenders, but intercepting RAF Spitfires shot down one of the enemy aircraft and damaged four. Allied fighter-bombers destroyed three more Japanese fighters and damaged three others over the Tamu area, thirty miles southeast of Palel.

In northern Burma, meanwhile, Lieut. Gen. Joseph W. Stilwell's Chinese forces continued their successful advance southward in the Mogaung Valley, driving beyond Tingring, twenty-two miles north of Kamaing.

American heavy bombers made a successful daylight raid yesterday on oil plants at Yenangyaung, southwest of Mandalay, while medium bombers blasted a sixty-mile stretch of the railroad north of Mandday, scoring at least thirty-five hits on the track.

Not a single Allied plane was lost during the past two days. ◇

CHINESE CENSORSHIP DEFENDED BY OFFICIAL
Tells Correspondents Caution Has Been Necessary in War

CHUNGKING, China, April 19 (AP)— Chinese censorship was defended by Information Minister Liang Han-chao today on the ground that it had been necessary to "exercise a good deal of caution and precaution in the interests of national survival, particularly since the outbreak of Sino Japanese hostilities."

He told foreign correspondents, who have become outspoken in their dissatisfaction with restrictions on their dispatches, that censorship in the interest of security existed elsewhere, and cited the recent censorship controversy in Australia and England's action in imposing restrictions on diplomatic pouches.

The foreign correspondents have protested, however, that the Chinese restraints are not confined to news likely to be of military value to the enemy, but apply also to criticism of the government and its policies, exposition of the Communist differences with the gov-ernment, and coverage of events tending to suggest military or political disturbances. ◇

The Battle of Imphal-Kohima: An M3 Lee tank crosses a river north of Imphal to meet the Japanese advance, March 1944.

BRITISH ISLES GUARD VITAL INVASION SECRETS
Drastic Measures May Conceal Time And Place But Not Allied Purpose

By RAYMOND DANIELL
By Wireless to THE New York Times.

*LONDON, April 22—*Some day an Anglo-American Army from Britain is going to descend on the Continent, which for four years has been under German domination. That much is known to Hitler and his general staff. It has been shouted from the housetops of all Allied capitals since Teheran. Strategic surprise, therefore, is impossible, but the success or failure of the expedition might well depend upon that slight advantage which always goes to the army which enjoys tactical surprise. That is just another way of saying that, while Hitler and his generals have been told what they probably had figured out for themselves, they still don't know when or where the blow will fall.

That they do not find out that vital secret of war is one of General Eisenhower's chief concerns. It isn't easy to keep such a secret these days when huge masses of supplies and equipment, such great armadas of ships must be assembled almost under the eyes of enemy observers in reconnaissance craft. But some things cannot be seen from the air and there are others which when seen may merely serve to confuse the enemy: unless he has agents working for him here to interpret the meaning of the preparations and tell him such important secrets as what kind of weapons and how many of them are being gathered for use against him.

GREATEST IN HISTORY

The invasion, when it comes, will be the greatest expedition of its kind in history. Upon its outcome the fate of the world for generations may well depend. Not since Wellington landed his army in Portugal has anything comparable been attempted from this island and even then the British General was assured of landing on friendly soil. This time the Anglo-American armies must batter a hole in the wall of Hitler's fortress against the greatest defensive armament ever known and they must take with them not only food and ammunition but gasoline and every other conceivable thing they may need, down to locomotives, rolling stock and track for railroads.

In his undertaking General Eisenhower will be attempting in reverse a feat which Julius Caesar and William the Conqueror managed to bring off successfully but which Napoleon and Hitler at the crucial moment found beyond their power. All the hazards and difficulties which caused these two would-be rulers of the world to hesitate—twenty miles of salt water, the fog and swell of the Channel, and the peril of landing on a hostile shore—have been considered and as far as can be told in advance, surmounted.

Even if all the statesmen who have proclaimed Allied intentions of invading Europe had held their peace, the Germans would still have known the assault was coming. It is the only way the Nazi hold on Europe can be completely and finally broken. Nor could the approximate time be kept entirely secret, for it is impossible to gather an army big enough for the job in hand without knowledge of the enemy. But while German reconnaissance pilots can probably see themselves when British harbors are glutted with ships, and huge stockpiles disclose themselves in spite of elaborate camouflage, only a mind reader can tell when those supplies have reached the point which the Commander in Chief himself regards as sufficient.

Despite this fact, however, there are weather conditions, the state of the moon, the tides and the season, which any prudent military man would have to consider. The Germans know that as well as we do, and so they probably know when it is safe to relax and when it is advisable to stand on guard. But it is a large coast line that they are defending and unless they are told they cannot tell just where we will strike.

UNPRECEDENTED PRECAUTIONS

The British Government has made an elaborate effort involving drastic and unprecedented action to insure that no leak from here imperils the safety of the expedition. These precautions begin at supreme headquarters and affect every individual on this island. Only a handful of men close to General Eisenhower know just what is being planned. Everyone in the services has been impressed with the necessity for keeping his lips buttoned up and not even making guesses aloud for the sake of his own safety.

The garrulous soul who might be tempted to so much as mention anything to do with military matters in a public place is restrained by the knowledge that he is likely to have an anonymous note passed to him by the bartender, waiter or tram conductor, reading something like this: "Do go on with your story. We're all listening. So is Hitler."

Not to emphasize the seamy side of life but for the sake of the record it is true that among those ladies of the evening with whom soldiers, sailors and airmen sometimes spend their leisure there are many who came to this country from the Continent with other refugees some years ago. Scotland Yard has not overlooked them and those whose loyalty, regardless of virtue, is doubted have been placed beyond temptation. There has been a general checking up all over the country until officials now are reasonably sure that all those who might want to help the enemy are either under surveillance or where they cannot do any damage.

Much that has happened on this island in the past few weeks must be regarded as part of the general campaign to make this country spy-proof. The recent round-up of labor agitators was not undertaken solely in the interest of industrial peace and harmony but was partly dictated by security considerations. Of course, at the time when the crucial battle begins, strikes and other stoppages cannot be tolerated and the Government has taken strong action to discourage them. But a good deal of the fanfare about agitators was designed to make the public even more security-minded than they were.

KEEPS ENEMY GUESSING

Many of the things that have been done were of the nature that Germany in the past has left to the last moment before attacking some unsuspecting neighbor. But for the British to adopt the same policy and wait for zero hour would be a sure way of notifying the enemy that now at last the hour had struck. So, in accordance with Prime Minister Churchill's policy of keeping the enemy guessing with many feints and false alarms, the necessary steps have been taken one by one and nobody on either side of the Channel knows from day to day whether the event that the whole world is waiting for so anxiously is near or far away.

In this category falls the ban on travel to coastal areas by any but those who have good reason for being there. So, too, does the warning to the public that if they embark on long rail journeys they may find themselves cut off from the rest of the country for days and weeks. The repeated warnings to the people of the Continent to prepare for invasion helps keep the Germans guessing.

The recent American note to Eire calling on that country to close German and Japanese legations provided the British with a good excuse for tightening restrictions on travel and communication with that neighboring neutral member of the British Commonwealth of Nations after President de Valera had rejected this demand. Now it is almost impossible for anyone to travel between the two countries; telephonic communication is cut off and the mails are slow. It is true the border between northern and southern Ireland is open but it is about as well controlled as it would be if it were closed.

The most drastic action this country has taken to insure against leakage of military secrets was the order restricting movements of foreign diplomats, making diplomatic bags subject to censorship, and directing that all cables and messages to their Governments be sent in plain English or in British code. Only those dominions fighting at Britain's side and the United States and Russia are exempt from the order abrogating the privileges diplomats have enjoyed since earliest times. Not even those other foreign Governments which are members of the United Nations were exempt from the order which is designed to prevent secret information from reaching Germany by accident or design. It will cause some inconvenience to many neutral and Allied Governments but where so much is at stake the British are confident their action will be understood and accepted with protests. ◆

EISENHOWER TELLS PUBLISHERS OF AID ON INVASION NEWS
Message Says Correspondents Are Part of the Great Team Seeking Early Victory

By FRANK S. ADAMS

A message from Gen. Dwight D. Eisenhower declaring that public opinion wins wars and pledging his help in facilitating the flow of news from the invasion was read yesterday at the opening session of the fifty-eighth annual convention of the American Newspaper Publishers Association, held at the Hotel Waldorf-Astoria.

"Public opinion wins wars—that is as true now as ever," said the message, which was read by Buell W. Hudson of The Woonsocket (R.L) Call, chairman of the session. "In order to facilitate the flow of news to the public in the impending operations we are drawing upon past experiences and hope to profit from them.

"I have always considered as quasi-staff officers those correspondents who are accredited to my headquarters. These correspondents are a part of the great team striving to conclude this war successfully at the earliest moment."

Five hundred and seventy-five delegates, a record number for the opening session of the ANPA, were on hand yesterday for the first meeting, which, in accordance with the custom of the organization, was devoted to a discussion of the problems of dailies of less than 50,000 circulation. It is expected that the number of delegates will pass the 700 mark today, when the first general session is held.

FINDS PRESS PRESTIGE RISING

Arthur S. Hodges, editor of The Nassau Daily Review-Star of Rockville Centre, L.I., reported on the results of a questionnaire circulated among editors, publishers, deans of schools of journalism and managers of newspaper associations. He said that it was the consensus among them that newspapers would have the highest prestige at the end of the war they have ever known.

"We found a widespread disposition to make the press more independent and do a better job for the people," he said. "We found that there is no serious fear of interference with freedom of the press by the Government and a sober conviction that the newspaper can meet any kind of competition from other media that may develop."

Nelson R. Poynter of The St. Petersburg (Fla.) Times expressed the hope that not only worldwide freedom of the press, but absolute freedom of information and communications would be established by the peace. He expressed hope that Congress would adopt a joint resolution declaring this to be our national policy.

HOWARD HANDLEMAN HONORED

The award of the annual George R. Holmes prize for war correspondence to Howard Handleman, author of "Bridge to Victory," an account of the Aleutians campaign, was announced by Barry Faris, editor in chief of International News Service, at the twenty-fifth annual Banshees luncheon given by King Features Syndicate for visiting publishers.

In the absence of Mr. Handleman, Richard Tregaskis, last year's winner of the award, accepted it in his behalf. Mr. Tregaskis, who has been recuperating from a severe head injury suffered while covering the Italian campaign, urged those at the luncheon not to forget, in their merrymaking, the men at the front who were actually doing the fighting. ◊

MacArthur and Nimitz Meet And Agree on United Efforts

By FRANK L. KLUCKHOHN
By Wireless to the New York Times.

ALLIED HEADQUARTERS IN NEW GUINEA, April 28—Gen. Douglas MacArthur and Admiral Chester W. Nimitz, America's two theatre commanders in the Pacific, have conferred at General MacArthur's Australian headquarters and worked out "completely integrated" plans for the campaign against Japan, according to a joint announcement made simultaneously here and at Pearl Harbor.

The statement issued here said:

"General MacArthur and Admiral Nimitz recently conferred regarding future operations in the Pacific on their two commands. Plans were completely integrated so that a maximum cooperative effort might be exerted against the enemy."

It was authoritatively asserted that the geographical division of the two commands had not been changed, and the wording of the announcement made it clear that neither the admiral, who is Commander in Chief of the Pacific Fleet and Pacific Ocean Areas, nor America's senior general would have authority over the other.

The fact that the announcement came after the Humboldt Bay campaign, although the meeting was held prior to it, as well as the phrasing of the statement, made it apparent that the two Pacific leaders were prepared to work together in the future and not merely for the one operation. More important, however, was the fact that Admiral Nimitz and General MacArthur got along splendidly together when they met, according to a number of those present. The basis for a personal relationship was established, which, it is felt, will have a greater effect upon the unity of future operations than any formal agreement might have.

General MacArthur has made no secret of the fact that his primary objective is to return to the Philippines as rapidly as possible, and it is certain that no such agreement as the one announced would have been possible unless the commander of the mighty and fast-growing United States Fleet had concurred.

Some service-proud officers have in the past taken the stand that one service or another should take the lead in beating Japan. Some extremists have even argued that one service could do it alone. General MacArthur and Admiral Nimitz have now in effect expressed their agreement that the sea, land and air forces should work together. ◊

MAY 4, 1944

NAZI RAIL LINES IN CHAOS IN 100-MILE COASTAL ZONE
Every Major Yard From Bay of Biscay To Cologne Blasted, Says British Ministry Aide

By DAVID ANDERSON
By Cable to The New York Times.

LONDON, May 3—Across western France and the Low Countries to Germany in a coastal zone roughly 100 miles wide from the shores of the Bay of Biscay to Cologne, Allied air attacks have blasted every railroad yard worthy of the name, an expert on European communications for the British Ministry of Economic Warfare said today.

To keep this area in the desired state of chaos has been an objective of the British and American air commands in recent months.

Today, it can be said, there is not a single place where the Germans could handle even moderately heavy military traffic. Trains still run through the zone, but no longer is it possible for the enemy to mass reserves in the area for speedy disposition elsewhere by rail.

The result has been that the enemy has been forced to rely on road convoys, which are easier for the Allies to attack from the air, or to keep his troop trains well back of the coast. It seems unlikely that Nazi reserves would be stationed on top of the coastal defenses, since that would give them a minimum of mobility.

BIG STRIKE IN TRAIN BOMBING

As an illustration of what happens to Nazis within the belt of destruction the expert told of an incident at Vaires, a suburb of Paris, not long ago.

Allied bombers attacked two trains standing there. One of them was full of troops, the other carried ammunition.

So violent was the explosion that the Allied air crews did not know precisely what they had hit. Some time passed before the authorities here learned that more than 1,000 Nazis had been killed and a great mass of material destroyed,

During the past year sabotage in France has increased 1,000 per cent, incidents growing in volume from a few to dozens daily. The damage is often slight, yet the cumulative effect is great.

One of the most effective forms of sabotage has been the blowing up of rails, which the Germans have difficulty in replacing now that Russian manganese is

A railway viaduct destroyed by the Allies at Mornesnet, Germany in 1944.

lost to them and the supply of French tracks has been so heavily drawn upon—no less than 30,000 miles of steel right of way has been transplanted by the enemy.

REICH DRAINED OF RAIL WORKERS

The labor shortage is an even graver problem for Nazi transport officials. The British Ministry estimates that 50,000 German railroad men have been sent into occupied territories in the last twelve months, and nearly that num-

ber has been employed in France alone. Today there is one German for every Frenchman on the railroads of France.

Close observation of western Europe's rolling stock at the present time has convinced the British experts that Germany simply cannot count on the railroads to stand the strain Allied invasion of the Continent will bring. ◊

MAY 7, 1944

GANDHI'S RELEASE WIDELY APPROVED

NEW DELHI, India, May 6 (AP)—Widespread satisfaction greeted the release today of Mohandas K. Gandhi, Indian Nationalist leader detained for

twenty-one months as a political prisoner in Aga Khan's summer palace in Poona, but intimates feared it marked a new crisis in the illness of the frail disciple of India's masses.

The press of all shades of opinion, Nationalist as well as English-owned, welcomed the freeing of Mr. Gandhi. The Government released the 74-year-old leader unconditionally, citing failing health, after having confined him in August, 1942, for political activity that it regarded as hampering India's ⟩

resistance to Japan.

His intimates here said that Mr. Gandhi would depend for recovery on a spiritual source of strength "beyond the conception of the Western World." His son, Devadas Gandhi, expressing the opinion that his father was seriously ill and possibly near death, said that Mr. Gandhi would scorn most medical ministrations.

FOUR OTHERS RELEASED

Mr. Gandhi's release came without untoward demonstration by his followers but crowds of them, acting on an earlier announcement that their leader would be freed, gathered at the gates of the palace to greet him. He looked cheerful but tired and was taken immediately to "Parnakuti," palatial residence of Lady Vitall das Thackersey. She is the widow of a Bombay merchant and an old friend of Mr. Gandhi. It was understood that Mr. Gandhi would be taken to Bombay Monday.

At Parnakuti," Dr. Gilder and Dr. Nayad issued a bulletin declaring that Mr. Gandhi had "become very weak and there is physical and mental exhaustion, though he keeps cheerful."

The bulletin revealed that Mr. Gandhi has had recurring malaria fever since April 14, and as a result his blood pressure was persistently low. He is delirious whenever his temperature goes up, the bulletin said.

His medical advisers urged friends and followers to "spare him all strain for some time to come."

Mr. Gandhi's son said he was not disposed to adopt an attitude of complete optimism because of the lack of definite information about his father's condition, but expressed the belief that he would survive. Through long years, by rigorous discipline, Mr. Gandhi has been able to control bodily functions almost completely through the mind and prayer, his son said.

He added that Mr. Gandhi would certainly oppose blood transfusions or administration of any drugs with animal derivatives. He said his father was opposed to medicine generally, relying mainly on a water and a vegetable diet and massage.

He said Mr. Gandhi especially frowned on blood transfusions on the grounds that the essential life stream of one human being should not be used to extend the life of another. The son added, however, that this belief would not extend to the case of a wounded soldier because "a man injured in such a way has a right to employ every legitimate means in saving his life to continue its work." ◇

MAY 8, 1944

'GUSVILLE' THRIVES IN ANZIO FRONT LINE

By MELTON BRACKER
By Wireless to The New York Times

ON THE FIFTH ARMY ANZIO BEACHHEAD, May 7—The road signs say "Roma—58 kilometers" but it is not nearly that far to "Gusville." All you have to do is to give your jeep its head and sooner or later some one will say:

"Gusville is down that way. But from here on you gotta walk."

And it is most appropriate to amble into Gusville on foot, for it is the most rural community imaginable. The incredible thing about it is that besides having its own cow, Daisy, its own chickens and its own G.I. mayor, Gusville is an infantry outpost in one of the most sensitive sectors of the beachhead front.

As one uniformed citizen put it, "Brother, this is the front."

If you have any doubt, walk down Gusville's main street, which goes by one of the loveliest little churches in the world and takes you right up to a line of tank mines protruding from the roadway like push buttons.

"They'll stand your weight, all right," a soldier will say, "but they ain't so chummy with Mark IV's."

Gusville actually is a pleasant little town where farmers used to come to do their shopping. It is something like a county seat waiting for Saturday night—except that these days Saturday night never comes.

GUNS EXCHANGE DEATH

Every day and every night are the same;

MAY 11, 1944

FREED SEVASTOPOL QUICKENS WAR PACE
Red Army Victory Won Over Strong German Resistance in Mountain Forts

By W. H. LAWRENCE
By Cable to The New York Times.

MOSCOW, May 10—All Russia celebrated today the liberation of Sevastopol, mighty fortress and former main base of the Soviet Black Sea Fleet, whose recapture took three days' fierce battles compared with 250 days required by German and Rumanian troops to overcome the resistance of the Russians when the city was under siege in 1941 and 1942.

The doomed German and Rumanian garrison, which had little hope of escape once the Russians had started breaking through the strong concrete fortifications on the steep cliffs and hills surrounding the port, fought back with intensity, launching more than twenty counter-attacks in a desperate effort to halt the mighty Soviet force of infantry, artillery and aviation commanded by Gen. Fedor I. Tolbukhin.

No estimate is available here of the size of the opposing armies in the final battles for Sevastopol, but front-line dispatches in Moscow newspapers leave no doubt that the battles were on a large scale, with aviation playing a particularly outstanding role in reducing the German fortifications.

USE OF BLACK SEA WIDENED

Clearing the enemy from Sevastopol and the whole Crimea is of military, historic and sentimental significance.

On the military side it means that Russia's Black Sea ports now are cleared of the enemy as far as the Dniester estuary, opening up greater possibilities for the use of the Black Sea Fleet in raiding Rumanian ports and attacking enemy communications in the Black Sea, which in the future will probably be on a highly restricted basis.

From historic and sentimental viewpoints a Red Star editorial struck the keynote evident in the comments of all Russians:

"Millions of hearts thumped with joy when they heard the news about the exquisite victory of the Red Army and Sevastopol again is on the tip of every-

shells lob in and shells lob out, and during lulls Gusville's American and Canadian population drinks Daisy's milk and keeps one eye on "Jerryland."

From Jerryland jagged death has hurtled into bodies of boys in Gusville and Gusville is studded with guns that keep paying back in kind.

Gusville got its name from First Lieut. Gus Heilman, who every University of Virginia man will know as the former proprietor of the Cavalier, student hangout at Charlottesville.

Actually Lieutenant Heilman is company commander, but as civic pride in the incredible little community began to grow, one Canadian insisted it had to have a Mayor.

"Gus being the C.O., they made him Mayor," it was explained.

So a deserted farm house became the city hall and Tech. Sgt. John Walkmeister became, in effect, city clerk. He has the biggest mustache in the Fifth Army.

The reason Gusville soon acquired livestock and poultry was simple: no civilians were left in the town and cow and chickens were left to themselves. Mess Sergeant Roland Uecker of Grand Rapids Mich., found Daisy, a black and white Holstein (he thinks) lolling innocently through minefields that hem in the town.

MINES PROVIDE MEAT

Uecker pleaded and cajoled until Daisy swishtailed into a corral; members of Daisy's family have not been so lucky. Mines go off with a great whoosh of soil and Gusville has a new stock of fresh meat.

Sergeant Granville Harper of Gallup, N.M., old rodeo man, swears Daisy would be worth $200 at home. But over here $200 wouldn't buy the tip of her tail.

"Do you know how long it is since most soldiers have seen fresh milk?" one might ask. ◇

---

body's tongue. Sevastopol has lifted its proud head. Sevastopol is sacred to Russia. It was the cradle of Russian might and heroism in past centuries, a school for the valorous Black Sea Fleet. It created the giant image of the Russian sailor during the Crimean wars.

"Together with the crushing of the German defenses on the northern flank of the Soviet-German front—at Leningrad—the Perekop operation was one of the outstanding events of the war. The

importance of the event is enormous. The entire Black Sea shore, from Novorossiisk to the Dniester Estuary, is liberated and cleared and now in our hands. The Black Sea main base has returned to our hands. The Sevastopol victory opens new, wide horizons for the operations of our troops. Glory to immortal Sevastopol!" ◇

Russian soldiers entering Sevastopol after ousting the German forces in May, 1944.

MAY 15, 1944

TITO, IN INTERVIEW, CITES NAZI TACTICS
Allied Newsmen Have Dinner with Yugoslav Leader in Mountain Fastness

By JOHN TALBOT Reuter Correspondent For the Combined Allied Press.

MARSHAL TITO'S HEADQUARTERS in the Yugoslav Mountains, May 10 (Delayed)—High up in the Yugoslav mountains, less than twenty miles from where the Partisans are putting up a magnificent fight against the Germans, Marshal Tito has the most impregnable headquarters of any commanding general in the world. The Germans have tried to get it.

Some time ago fifteen German dive-bombers tried to blast the Yugoslav marshal from his eyrie. They failed completely.

The headquarters are a series of natural caves running in a gallery straight into the sides of a deep ravine.

Last night my American colleague, two Allied cameramen and I had dinner with Tito in his incredible lair. Also present were Gen. Arsu Yvanovitch, his chief of staff; M. Chokaloviteh, secretary of the Anti-Fascist Council, and M. Kardelz, Vice President of the Yugoslav National Committee.

To reach Tito's headquarters our guards, who were changed three times during the journey from our billets, led us along a rough path cut out of the rock and up the side of a ravine. Besides us, for part of our journey, a great waterfall plumed down in a thundering white cascade into the dim, moonlit valley far below. At times we clung to rocks as the path twisted and turned round jutting spurs and ledges.

At length we arrived at the top to find the Marshal waiting to welcome us. He led us into the study of a small, simply furnished apartment.

A long dining table stands against a wall facing two windows which look directly down over the ravine and out into the valley. The chairs are all simple, wooden affairs. On three walls are maps, including a large-scale one of Yugoslavia. The meeting with the marshal was completely informal, and we discussed a variety of topics. The marshal does not like to talk in English as he does not consider himself sufficiently ❯

fluent. He can, however, read it easily. We spoke with him mostly through the American correspondent, Stoyan Pribichevich (Time and Life correspondent), who is a Serbian by birth.

The marshal wore the blue-gray uniform of the National Army of Liberation, with his marshal's insignia on his sleeves and collar. He is some 5 feet 8 inches tall, very strongly built and has an exceedingly strong face, which at first strikes one as being stern until one sees the lines of laughter at the corners of his eyes and mouth.

I asked him if he thought that German and Quisling troops had any plans for another offensive against the Partisans.

"No," he answered. "I do not think

they have.

"The main German concern at the moment is to keep the forces of the National Army of Liberation split into groups throughout the country.

"German tactics at present consist of minor thrusts in various localities, with the idea of making the Partisan soldiers use up their scanty stores of ammunition and thus immobilize them.

"We are finding now that the German soldier is deteriorating as a fighter and is not what he used to be a year ago. By far the best soldier the enemy has is the Ustashi (Yugoslav puppet troops). I think one Ustashi is two Germans against us. Chetniks definitely are bad soldiers." ◇

MAY 18, 1944

LETTERS TO THE TIMES
De Gaulle Stand Questioned

To the Editor of The New York Times :

I have no doubt that many of your readers felt as I did that your editorial of May 9, "French Realities," laid stress upon a vital point, namely, that while it is in the clutches of the most cruel of enemies, none should discount the will of the French people in the selection of its government until it is able at last to exercise that will. And you stressed another fact: that the liberation of France necessarily depended upon the exertions of the British and American armed forces now awaiting the signal to attack France's invader from the north, east and west as the foe is now being attacked on the Italian front.

My good friend Oswald Chew argues in your columns today that General de Gaulle and the Committee of National Liberation are "the ones to administer the rights of the French civil population" during the process of liberation. He supports this by the claim that "they have the complete confidence of the French underground movement, representing 90 per cent of the French people." Of course, Mr. Chew's authority for that assertion is that of the Committee of National Liberation and its

various organs of propaganda. But why should any American assume that his own Government with its intelligence facilities is not informed as to the sentiments of the French people?

DE GAULLE SELF APPOINTED
General de Gaulle was self-appointed when he asked the French people to continue to fight notwithstanding the Hitler-Pétain armistice. He asked them to rally to him as a military leader, and his fame rests on that. The British Government thereupon reached an agreement with him dated Aug. 7, 1940, in which he was recognized as "leader of all Free Frenchmen, wherever they may be, who rally to you in support of the Allied cause."

There were Frenchmen in Africa, under the Pétain regime, who not only had not rallied to General de Gaulle but had fought him. To have resorted to him for the landing in Africa in November, 1942, after the experience at Dakar, would have been fatal to the undertaking and perhaps to the outcome of the war. Our Government sought a leader who might prove acceptable to the Frenchmen in Africa.

If General de Gaulle will devote himself to the common task of defeating the Boche and leave aside the idle question whether he is the head of the Government of France, he will render the greatest service which it is in his power to render to the common cause which he served so nobly in July, 1940.

Maurice Leon
New York
May 15, 1940 ◇

MAY 21, 1944

EDUCATION IN REVIEW
UNRRA School Is Training Workers For the Grim Job Of Relief in War-Stricken Countries

BY BENJAMIN FINE

In what is probably the only school of its kind in the world, a group of carefully selected men and women have returned to the classroom for a concentrated eight weeks' program dealing with the salvaging of human lives. The school, located on the peaceful University of Maryland campus, is the United Nations Relief and Rehabilitation Administration Training Center. From early morning until far in the evening, these men and women—there are fifty of them on the campus now, and they are called "members" rather than students—sit in classrooms, listen to lectures, pore over maps and books, and tackle "homework."

Operated by UNRRA, under the immediate supervision of Dr. Frank Munk, a Czech refugee who has been a lecturer

---

MAY 23, 1944

ALLIES PREPARED TO MEET NAZI GAS
Its Use by Enemy Doubted, but Our Troops Are Equipped For 50-to-1 Retaliation

By DREW MIDDLETON
By Cable to The New York Times.

LONDON, May 23—Retaliation swift and sure, on an unprecedented scale, will follow any use of poison gas by the enemy, either against the invasion ports or the Allied armies invading the Continent.

in economics at the University of California since 1941, the training center has been in operation since May 1. A continuous flow of members is expected, as UNRRA will need many hundreds of field workers in devastated countries of the world before the full job of rehabilitation is completed. The Maryland project can accommodate as many as two or three hundred at any one time.

This is not an academic institution in the accepted sense of the term. The "students" are all employes of UNRRA or of the voluntary agencies collaborating with it. At present the center is emphasizing the "Balkan Mission." Following their training the men and women will go to Cairo, there to get practical experience in dealing with refugees. Several camps are located in Egypt. When the time is ripe they will take their posts in Greece, in Yugoslavia, and wherever else they may be needed.

CURRICULUM OF FIVE PARTS

Although the course of studies is rather flexible, the curriculum can be divided into five major headings: a study of regions, languages, instrumentalities, people and operational programs. The students learn about the region to which they are to be assigned—the economic, political, social or cultural background. They study the languages of this region; each member of the training center is required to select one language for extensive study. Instrumentalities of services—such as the agencies that are to operate in the field, especially the functioning of UNRRA itself—are stressed.

A typical week's work may include such topics as "People in Need," "What UNRRA Expects from Its Representatives in the Field," "Simple Living," "Balkan Mission," "Displaced Persons in the United States of America," "How to Get Along in Greece," "Work of Division of Industrial Rehabilitation," "Impact of Nazism" and "Allied Military Government in Sicily and Italy." Each student gets two hours of language daily.

In a sense, the training school is a point of embarkation. Even before their eight weeks are up, many of the members are "alerted" and then called into active service. They know that they may be sent abroad on twenty-four hours' notice. While at the school they live in dormitories, eat in the cafeteria "army style," take toughening exercises, and follow a semi-military discipline.

"You are going to see things that will be awfully hard on you physically and emotionally," their lecturers warn. "You will need strong stomachs; it will not be an easy job. You'll have to learn to take it."

Dr. Munk summed up the purpose and objectives of this unique school in these words:

"I'm trying to make them understand the country that they are going to, the people that they will work with, the purpose of UNRRA and their particular place in it." ◆

Responsible opinion here is that the employment of gas as an anti-invasion measure is possible but not probable inasmuch as the German General Staff is aware of the Allies' ability to retaliate with at least fifty cubic feet of gas for each one loosed by the Germans.

Nevertheless, every precaution is being taken, and Gen. Dwight D. Eisenhower's invading armies will be equipped both to withstand gas attacks and to retaliate.

It is thought here that the enemy will use gas only if he hopes to achieve a victory so important that the use of gas would outweigh the long-term effects of retaliation. The two periods when the enemy may use gas are the pre-invasion period, when the Allied armies are embarking, and when the Atlantic Wall is being assaulted.

Gas attacks on British ports by the Luftwaffe bomber force, which has had little employment lately, would have as their objective the dislocation of the invasion timetable to such an extent that the enemy might be able to deal, in the initial onslaught, with smaller forces than they now contemplate facing.

It is more likely, however, that the enemy would employ gas to strengthen his static defenses along the coast. It would certainly increase the difficulties of attack, especially if mustard gas were sprayed over the areas across which the assault against the Atlantic Wall were to be launched. The best anti-gas precautions in the world cannot entirely nullify the effects of mustard gas.

Although gas has not been used by the Allies, experimentation in its use has not ceased. ◆

Chapter 19

"THIS IS THE EUROPE WE CAME TO FREE"

June–July 1944

While an estimated 350 correspondents waited patiently in London for news that the invasion of France had begun, Herbert Matthews of The Times was with the U.S. Fifth Army ducking German bombs and snipers while battling into the suburbs of Rome. By June 4 the Italian capital was in American hands. This symbolic triumph was overshadowed two days later when the news blackout imposed in Britain was finally lifted. Just after dawn on June 6, a fleet of 7,000 ships and landing craft of all sizes, supported by 12,000 aircraft, transported the first American, British and Canadian troops—more than 130,000 in all— across the English Channel to five beaches in Normandy. The news first reached The Times in New York City from the German broadcasting service just after midnight. Ninety minutes later, the paper was on the street, the first announcement of the invasion the world had been anxiously awaiting. A few hours later General Eisenhower released a formal communiqué, but it was brief and short of hard facts .

Although The Times sent seven newsmen ashore in Normandy, reports of the battle lacked real detail. The Times used the first week of the campaign to renew its enthusiasm for the liberation of France. "The love of France," claimed one editorial, "of the French culture, of the French landscape is shared by all civilized men." Among the first reports, "The Europe We Came to Free" declared that Europeans were "hungry and rebellious," alternately animated by "hope, depression and exaltation." The struggle to free them went more slowly than anticipated, "Hedge to Hedge" as one headline put it.

The beachhead was well-established by mid-June and by June 26 the port of Cherbourg was captured by General Omar Bradley's forces. But the city of Caen, opposite Montgomery's British and Canadian forces, was strongly defended; when the Germans finally withdrew to a line south of the city, a British assault, code-named "Goodwood," failed to dislodge them. To make matters worse, on June 13 the German secret weapon, long threatened by Goebbels's propaganda, became real. The first V-1 "flying bombs"—unmanned cruise missiles—landed on London, the opening of an assault in which 10,000 bombs were fired, though only 2,419 reached the British capital. Not until the end of July was the deadlock in Normandy finally broken, a week after a group of senior German army commanders had tried unsuccessfully to assassinate Hitler and seize power. Hitler remained in control, ordering fanatical resistance in France as German forces grew weaker. On July 25 Bradley finally unleashed Operation Cobra for a breakout from Normandy toward the port of Avranches. The German Front crumbled at once, the start of a two-week retreat that left much of France in Allied hands.

The news from France once again eclipsed battles elsewhere. In Belorussia the Red Army mounted one of the largest operations of the war, code-named "Bagration," against German Army Group Center, the major front in the East. It began on June 22, when 2.4 million soldiers, 31,000 guns and 5,200 tanks smashed forward into the German line. Unlike Normandy, the Soviet offensive worked like clockwork. Minsk was captured by July 4, and Brest-Litovsk, where German forces had launched Barbarossa three years before, on July 26. Army Group Center was destroyed. That summer the German Army lost 589,000 men in the East, the biggest defeat inflicted on German armed forces.

Progress was also rapid in the Pacific,. On June 15 American forces stormed ashore on Saipan in the Marianas, supported by a huge fleet that included fifteen aircraft carriers. The Japanese responded by sending a large task force with nine carriers to intercept the invasion. The Battle of the Philippine Sea began on June 19, the largest carrier-to-carrier engagement of the war. The result was a decisive defeat for the Japanese Fleet. Despite Japanese successes in China in the so-called Ichi-Go offensive, on July 20 General Hideki Tojo resigned as premier, following his country's defeats in the Pacific. By the end of July not only Saipan but also Guam was in American hands.

In the United States, President Roosevelt was named the Democratic Party's candidate for president for an unprecedented fourth term with The Times now in support of his candidacy. Arthur Sulzberger thought Roosevelt was more likely to guide the nation to "ultimate victory" than any other choice.

JUNE 5, 1944

CONQUERORS' GOAL REACHED BY ALLIES
Fifth and Eighth Armies Drive Up From South on Rome In a Historic Campaign

By HERBERT L. MATTHEWS
By Wireless to The New YorkTimes.

ROME, June 4—The Allies' troops fought their way into Rome this morning and at nightfall they were still fighting on the outer edges, which the Germans were defending despite all their protestations about considering Rome an open city. Other large German units faced entrapment south of Highway 6 unless they could be pulled back across the Tiber or through Rome.

But Rome has been reached—the goal of conquerors throughout the ages, though none was ever before able to make the almost impossible south-north campaign. What Hannibal did not dare to do, the Allies' generals accomplished, but at such a cost in blood, matériel and time that it will probably never again be attempted.

Mark Clark, Commander of the U.S. Fifth Army, rides through Rome following the liberation of the city in June 1944

FIRST TANK SET AFIRE

Early today Rome was just a few yards in front of us and a road sign, "Roma," faced us tantalizingly. On the other side the Allies' first tank to penetrate Rome proper was blazing fiercely, while a German self-propelled gun, some tanks and machine-gun snipers held up the triumphal entry into the greatest prize of the war thus far. Here is the story of our getting to that point.

It was the break-through on the Fifth Army's right wing yesterday that did the trick. That thrust into the mountain ridge behind Velletri three days ago that permitted the flanking of Rocca di Papa cooked the Germans' goose. Faced with the certainty that their positions along the coast would be quickly flanked, the Germans fell back swiftly to positions just before Rome, playing desperately and successfully for time until darkness had fallen. Meanwhile their right wing began falling back, but they are going to lose plenty, for they have delayed overlong.

Evidently they underestimated the Allies' drive. They started massing tanks north of Highway 6 to throw against our advancing columns, but they could not even get those up in time.

HEADQUARTERS QUICKLY SHIFTED

Correspondents started for Rome at 5 P.M. yesterday. Divisional headquarters were moving so quickly that we had trouble finding the one that we wanted. There they told us that their force was moving quickly.

Prisoners were filing back by the dozens. The Hermann Goering Armored Division was really steam-rollered this time, but everyone available was thrown in, even veterinaries, in the vain effort to stem the Allies rush.

We knew that there would be strafing, bombing and perhaps shelling by dark, but we had to get up there on Highway 6. A three-quarter moon was a blessing, just as it was the night before we took Messina. There was an eerie tenseness in the air as darkness came on. We got over the Alban Hills in the dusk and our eyes searched vainly through the haze for Rome, which, we knew, lay on the Campagna right before us. Excitement had gripped everybody, but it was a grim, silent and deserted countryside, except for our advancing columns.

Our little jeep wound in and out among the cars and soon we reached the infantry filing along both sides of the road. The wounded were coming back steadily, and so were the prisoners, but otherwise this was like all the roads that led to Rome, not far away.

Every moment we expected the Germans to react, but still we kept going. At Kilometre 18, dead bodies began cluttering the landscape—ours as well as theirs. Suddenly we struck a clear patch and rushed on alone through the darkness, almost holding our breaths. But we knew that there were some reconnaissance units ahead and perhaps the way into Rome was clear, after all.

THROUGH FIELDS OF GERMANS

At last we reached the leading reconnaissance unit; "You'd better watch out," an officer said. "You've come through lots of Jerries. They're all over these fields and there's nothing up here except armored cars."

Kilometer post 13 was right there. That meant that we were little more than ten miles from the center of the city and five miles from the outskirts. A tank fight was going on just a mile ahead, the nearest that our forces were to reach during the night. There was a little side road to a group of three houses. We went in there, and none too soon. Within a few minutes we heard the German planes come over. They took their time, tantalizingly flying around and around to get their bearings. An important crossroads was only 100 yards away, and we knew that we were in for it

They began dropping flares. Then came strafing, then bombs. We flattened ourselves on the floor of the peasant's stone house. One flare dropped next to it and, for what seemed like ages, we dug our heads into the ground and held our breaths, waiting and waiting. And then it came. Two bombs crashed beside the house, which shook dizzily as plaster fell from the ceiling.

Only then did we learn that the farmer had built a refuge just outside the house and we dashed into it. There we were relatively safe. Within a few minutes, four jeeps loaded with ammunition dashed up. The men jumped out of them and into our refuge. Then began a strange night.

We were surrounded by Germans, and we knew it. We dared not move. Two soldiers came in with us, while their comrades went up the hill to another refuge.

Acrid smoke still filled the refuge, coming from the bombs that had been dropped almost squarely on it. Outside, more armor was trundling down the highway. This gave us some comfort, but our worry was the Germans who had been left behind, scattered in the fields.

Somehow the night dragged its weary length. A peasant woman heated us some water for our coffee, which we hastily downed. Then we went on.

Tanks with infantry were now ahead of us. Tough, bearded, dirty youngsters sat astride them as we passed, again aiming for the head of the column.

NO CHEERS FROM PEASANTS

The peasants were beginning to line the roads, but they were not cheering, as they had done before Naples. They were stolid and curious. Rome was being conquered again, but they showed no emotion at first. Then, as we got nearer to the outskirts, enthusiasm began to rise and a few peasants threw flowers at the tanks.

It was 6:30 A.M. and we were almost at the head of the column. Two tanks were in front of us and there at last was the road sign, "Roma," just at a bend in the highway.

The first tank clanked around it and then came a crash and a vivid flash as it was hit by an 88mm. shell from a self-propelled gun that had undoubtedly been waiting. The tank driver was killed and two others were wounded. Everybody else dashed for the ditches. The infantry deployed and went forward.

Civilians were foolishly running into and out of their houses, oblivious to danger but scattering wildly when shells came over. Then a sniper got going. He could not have been there before, but now he had a bead on us with a machine gun straight down the road.

This will be a great day in history, but one would not have thought so from the demeanor of the Romans and the strangely peaceful sounds of Sunday morning in the spring. Church bells tolled and even a wedding procession walked solemnly to one church within range of the German guns. A train chugged and whistled along the tracks inside the city. An Italian rode up on a bicycle, not even hurrying as snipers' bullets whined overhead. ◇

JUNE 5, 1944

AMERICANS IN FIRST
U.S. Armor Spearheads Thrust Through Last Defenses of Rome

By The United Press.

NAPLES, June 4—The Fifth Army captured Rome tonight, liberating for the first time a German-enslaved European capital. German rear guards were fleeing in disorganized retreat to the northwest.

Except for the railway yards, smashed by the Allies' bombs, the city is 95 per cent intact, United Press correspondents reported after their arrival in the city.

Late tonight, the British Eighth Army, rushing into Rome from the southeast along the Via Casilina, was reported to be joining the Fifth Army in close pursuit of the hard-pressed enemy remnants, under orders to destroy them to a man if possible. Only enough troops to maintain order and ferret out any German snipers or suicide nests were to be left in Rome as the Allies' main armies pounded on without pausing to celebrate their greatest triumph, coming 270 days after the start of the Italian campaign.

FINAL STAND AT ROME'S GATES

At the very gates of Rome, the Germans had made a final stand but Lieut. Gen. Mark W. Clark, after having waited three hours for the enemy troops to withdraw in accordance with their own declaration of Rome as an open city, ordered a violent anti-tank barrage. Then masses of Fifth Army men and weapons crashed into the city and began mopping up enemy snipers and a few tanks and mobile guns trying to cover the retreat.

More of the enemy survivors of the Allies' whirlwind offensive were streaming in congested retreat to the northwest at the mercy of the Allies' planes, which, during the day, destroyed or damaged 600 enemy trucks and other vehicles. The Germans' jammed traffic columns stretched fifty-five miles to Lake Bolsena.

Direct radio contact with American correspondents in Rome was established tonight. A United Press reporter said that the main entry into the city had been made along the Via Casilina, which passes through the Porta Maggiore at the southeastern edge of the city. Other Allied troops were reported to have fought their way through the Ostiense freight yards, just south of St. Paul Gate, the main entrance to the city from due south and only one and one-quarter miles from the Venice Palace.

The entry into Rome came with dramatic suddenness after the Allies, spearheaded by American armored forces, had shattered the last German defenses below the city in the Alban Hills. The final advance covered almost fifteen miles in twenty-four hours and was so rapid along the last miles that large pockets of Germans were believed to have been cut off. There was a furious battle in the workers' district, where the Germans fought from streets and buildings before their ranks broke.

The final breakthrough, the result of an overwhelming assault by the Allies' arms, came in the twenty-four hours beginning on Saturday evening. After having outflanked enemy strong points in the southern Alban Hills the Allies smashed through those formidable peaks and burst out on the plain before Rome. They then drove on into the city. ◇

NEWSMEN AWAIT INVASION CALMLY

By FREDERICK GRAHAM
By Wireless to The New York Times.

LONDON, June 4—As nearly as can be determined there are more than 350 assorted British and American newspaper, magazine and radio correspondents and photographers in the European theatre of operations now waiting to cover the coming invasion. Most of them are men and the majority of them represent the three major news agencies and daily newspapers.

Correspondents who have been in this theatre for two, three or even four years seem to have absorbed the wisdom of patience—or maybe it is the British wartime diet that makes them appear patient as they wait for the invasion. A good many in this category have put down roots of a sort here. Admittedly these roots usually are pretty shallow but, even so, the correspondents appear to be in no high fever to tear them up and follow an invasion that may be less pleasant, comfortable and convenient than London.

Correspondents who have been here one year or short of two years appear no more impatient to get the invasion under way than their older colleagues.

The newcomers—those who have been here from three to six months—hardly give the impression that they are all keyed up, either. Most of them are still getting used to wearing a uniform and taking salutes from misled G.I.'s.

Many of these never had been outside the United States before and would like to see more of London before leaving it. They want to see France, Belgium, the Netherlands and Germany, too, but they would prefer to see Britain before moving on.

Correspondents, like military police, seem never to travel alone. In pairs or larger groups you see them almost everywhere in London: in small local pubs, in the cocktail lounges of swank West End hotels and in the bars of scrubby Bloomsbury, in pubs and restaurants around Fleet Street and in the better Mayfair establishments.

The better-known correspondents—the "name" correspondents—and those representing the well-heeled publications can usually be found in the costlier and more exclusive bars and eating places. But there are enough correspondents who have tough expense accounts and less than magnificent salaries to provide business in great measure to the smaller and cheaper ones. ◆

War correspondent Frank Gillard at work in early 1944, during a mock battle to rehearse the reporting of the D-Day landings for BBC radio.

U. S. BOMBS REDUCE NAZIS' 'ERSATZ' OIL

By Wireless to The New York Times.

LONDON, June 4—Germany's synthetic oil industry, which has become the Wehrmacht's main source of supply since Rumania's Ploesti oil fields were bombed, was crippled in three days of operations in May by the Eighth United States Air Force.

During these three days the Zeitz plant, twenty miles south of Leipzig, was put out of production indefinitely. Other plants at Poelitz, outside Stettin, and Bruex, in Czechoslovakia, were so badly damaged it is unlikely they will be able to resume production.

Five other synthetic oil factories at Merseburg, Magdeburg, Bohlen, Lutzkendorf and Ruhland were badly damaged by attacks.

In addition American bombers and fighters destroyed 343 enemy fighters. On May 12, 150 enemy planes were shot down, on May 28, ninety-three, and on May 29, 100.

Of the thousands of American aircraft dispatched to these targets, 145 were lost.

In the attack on Poelitz, on May 29, large fires broke out throughout the plant and smoke rose to a height of more than 10,000 feet.

Zeitz was even more heavily hit. Building after building was either blasted flat or burned out. ◆

JUNE 6, 1944

FIRST ALLIED LANDING MADE ON SHORES OF WESTERN EUROPE

EISENHOWER ACTS
U.S., British, Canadian Troops Backed by Sea, Air Forces

By RAYMOND DANIELL
By Cable to The New York TimEs.

SUPREME HEADQUARTERS ALLIED EXPEDITIONARY FORCES, June 6—The invasion of Europe from the west has begun.

In the gray light of a summer dawn Gen. Dwight D. Eisenhower threw his great Anglo-American force into action today for the liberation of the Continent. The spearhead of attack was an Army group commanded by Gen. Sir Bernard L. Montgomery and comprising troops of the United States, Britain and Canada.

General Eisenhower's first communiqué was terse and calculated to give little information to the enemy. It said merely that "Allied naval forces supported by strong air forces began landing Allied armies this morning on the northern coast of France."

After the first communiqué was released it was announced that the Allied landing was in Normandy.

CAEN BATTLE REPORTED
German broadcasts, beginning at 6:30 A.M., London time, [12:30 A.M. Eastern war time] gave first word of the assault. [The Associated Press said General Eisenhower, for the sake of surprise, deliberately let the Germans have the "first word."]

The German DNB agency said the Allied invasion operations began with the landing of airborne troops in the area of the mouth of the Seine River.

[Berlin said the "center of gravity" of the fierce fighting was at Caen, thirty miles southwest of Havre and sixty-five miles southeast of Cherbourg, The Associated Press reported. Caen is ten miles inland from the sea, at the base of the seventy-five-mile-wide Normandy Peninsula, and fighting there might indicate the Allies' seizing of a beachhead.

[DNB said in a broadcast just before 10 A.M. (4 A.M. Eastern war time) that the Anglo-American troops had been reinforced at dawn at the mouth of the Seine River in the Havre area.]

[An Allied correspondent broadcasting from Supreme Headquarters, according to the Columbia Broadcasting System, said this morning that "German tanks are moving up the roads toward the beachhead" in France.] The German accounts told of Nazi shock troops thrown in to meet Allied airborne units and parachutists. The first attacks ranged from Cherbourg to Havre, the Germans said.

[United States battleshipsand planes took part in the bombardment of the French coast, Allied Headquarters announced, according to Reuter.]

The weather was not particularly favorable for the Allies. There was a heavy chop in the Channel and the skies were overcast. Whether the enemy was taken by surprise was not known yet.

EISENHOWER'S ORDERS TO TROOPS
Not until the attack began was it made known officially that General Montgomery was in command of the Army group, including American troops. The hero of El Alamein hitherto had been referred to as the senior British Field Commander.

In his order of the day, made public at the same time as the first communiqué, General Eisenhower told his forces that they were about to embark on a "great crusade."

The news that has been so long and so eagerly awaited broke as war-weary Londoners were going to work. Hardly any of them knew what was happening, for there had been no disclosure of the news that the invasion had started in the British Broadcasting Corporation's 7 o'clock broadcast.

Even the masses of planes roaring overhead did not give the secret away, for the people of this country have grown accustomed to seeing huge armadas of aircraft flying out in their almost daily attacks against German-held Europe.

Details of how the assault developed are still lacking. It is known that the huge armada of Allied landing craft that crept to the French coast in darkness was preceded by mine sweepers whose task was to sweep the Channel of German mine fields and submarine obstructions.

Big Allied warships closed in and engaged the enemy's shore batteries.

Airborne troops landed simultaneously behind the Nazis' coast defenses. ◆

An array of sea craft at Omaha Beach, Normandy, during the first stages of the Allied invasion.

JUNE 6, 1944

WASHINGTON WAITS 3 HOURS FOR FLASH

Special to The New York Times.

WASHINGTON, June 6—Washington learned officially of the invasion of Europe at 3:32 A.M. today when the War Department issued the text of the communiqué issued by the Supreme Headquarters, Allied Expeditionary Forces.

This flash was the climax of three hours of tense waiting that followed first German radio reports that hostilities off France had begun. Before that both the War Department and the Office of War Information said they had no information to confirm or deny the German reports.

The communiqué was handed newspaper men in the War Department by Maj. Gen. Alexander D. Surles, chief of the Army Bureau of Public Relations. With the communiqué was issued a statement by General of the Armies John J. Pershing which declared the sons of the American soldiers of 1917 and 1918 were engaged in a "like war of liberation" and would bring freedom to people who have been enslaved.

The capital awakened rapidly after the initial broadcasts. Lights flashed on and radios began to blare. Newspaper men hurried to their offices. Everybody was demanding to know whether it was "official."

If the White House was aware of the report, there was no outward indication. Only a few lights glowed there and the customary guards patrolled up and down monotonously.

Only a few hours earlier—at 8:30 P.M.—Mr. Roosevelt had addressed the world for fifteen minutes on the fall of Rome.

By 1:45 A.M., almost the entire public relations staff at the War Department had reported for duty.

Elmer Davis, director of the OWI, met about half a dozen news men in his office about 4 A.M. and told them the OWI had no assurance that the invasion was coming off this morning but thought that it might be. He said that OWI did not put out any of the German broadcast reports prior to official confirmation from General Eisenhower's headquarters.

Between the official flash and the time General Eisenhower began his talk, the OWI was transmitting the text of the communiqué. ◆

JUNE 7, 1944

LANDING PUTS END TO 4-YEAR HIATUS
Fiery Renewal Of Battle for France—Britain Recalls Grimness of Dunkerque

By RAYMOND DANIELL
By Cable to Tax New York Times.

LONDON, June 6—This was D-day and it has gone well.

At daybreak Anglo-American forces dropped from the skies in Normandy, swarmed up on the beaches from thousands of landing craft and renewed the battle for France and for Europe, broken off four years ago at Dunkerque.

And when darkness fell, on the word of no less than Winston Churchill, the King's First Minister, who is still this country's best reporter, they had toeholds on a broad front and were fighting as far back from the coast as Caen, which is eight and a half miles behind the Channel beaches and 149 miles from Paris.

At the time he spoke the Prime Minister said that the battle which was just beginning was progressing in "a thoroughly satisfactory manner." But even he, like most people in this island, had his fingers crossed.

The Germans' resistance until now has been surprisingly, perhaps ominously, slight. Several obstacles to any amphibious operation have been surmounted. The concentration of ships has escaped serious bombardment from the air and the huge armada has crossed the Channel without encountering real enemy naval opposition. Submarine obstacles and shore batteries, which had been pounded relentlessly by the Allied air forces, were less lethal than had been expected.

WEATHER NOT FAVORABLE

The weather was uncertain but possibly a decisive factor. It was not favorable to the attacking forces. It was revealed at the Supreme Headquarters of the Allied Expeditionary Force that the great blow had been postponed one day because the barometer had started to fall—not an unusual occurrence in this land of fickle weather.

On the basis of reports from his meteorologists, General Eisenhower postponed the launching of his attack twenty-four hours. Then the weather men assured him that an improvement was coming and he was faced with the problem of gambling on their science or postponing the attack another month. His was a grim decision, for it waslearned at Supreme Headquarters that had the meteorologists been wrong the whole expedition might have met with disaster.

As it was, the weather was not good, but it improved. At the start clouds obscured air targets and winds swept the Channel into one of its hellish moods, so a large part of the invading force must

JUNE 9, 1944

Editorial
IN JUSTICE TO FRANCE

Two great phases of history are unfolding today on the new Western Front. One is the destruction of the Nazi power. We cannot come to grips with that power today on the soil of Germany itself. We must encounter it first on the soil of France, where if we could avoid it we would not shatter one ancient wall, cut down one tree or trample a single poppy under foot. The love for France, for the French culture, for the French landscape, is shared by all civilized men. It is pitiful that we must hurt what we love in order to kill what we hate.

This awful necessity must burden everyone in authority, from President Roosevelt and Prime Minister Churchill down to the company commander who has to open fire on a Norman farmhouse in order to clear out snipers. If it so weighs on us, how heavy must be the burden on all true Frenchmen. No doubt freedom is greater than Paris and honor outbalances even a village whose houses may have seen Joan the Maid pass by. But we should have reverently in mind the agony that is mingled at this moment with French hopes.

And surely the two great Governments which are chiefly responsible for Allied military and political policy in

U.S. troops disembarking from landing crafts during the D-Day invasion, June 6, 1944.

have been seasick when they landed to do battle with the enemy.

The tides of the Channel, which in the days of the Spanish Armada favored England, changed in the crucial hours between dark and daylight. Minesweepers had to switch their gear from one side to the other and never slow down or stop lest the cutting tools they drag behind them sink to the ocean floor.

The first communiqué merely said Allied troops had landed in northern France. Later this was expanded unofficially to mean Normandy, where the apple trees have just shed their blossoms and begun to bear fruit.

The attempt at liberation of the Continent has begun auspiciously. Later the Allies will count upon the help of the resistance movements of Europe, but radio broadcasts by Gen. Charles de Gaulle, head of the French Committee of National Liberation; Dr. Pieter S. Gerbrandy, Netherlands Premier; Hubert Pierlot, Belgian Premier, and General Eisenhower have made it clear that the time is not yet. All these speakers advised the people of occupied Europe to wait for orders to rise against the Nazi occupation. ◆

France should go as far as they possibly can to spare the feelings of those Frenchmen, in and out of France, who did not surrender in 1940. Some progress has indeed been made toward full cooperation with the French Committee of National Liberation. General Eisenhower and General de Gaulle are now "in complete agreement on the military level." That is good news. But military agreement is not sufficient. As soon as battle conditions permit we shall want and need to hand over liberated French territory to Frenchmen, To what Frenchmen shall we hand over the guardianship of French soil until the French people themselves by popular choice have created a new Government? Obviously to those, both inside and outside of France, who have been loyal to their country and to liberty.

We do not believe there is any basic difference of opinion on this score either in Washington or in London. Yet there has been a shocking lack of preparation for this political emergency. There may have been good reasons for our present uncertain policy toward the National Committee, but, if so, they have been kept inexcusably secret.

Our soldiers need the eager support of every French civilian. How much easier would their task be if there could now be awakened in France the spirit that brought the Marseillaise marching to Paris in 1792! The Fourth Republic is about to be born in fire and pain. Cannot it be welcomed into the world with something more stirring than a business-like agreement between two generals? ◆

JUNE 11, 1944

Allies Landed Men Months Ago To Dig Sample Of Normandy Soil

By Cable to The New York times.

SUPREME HEADQUARTERS, Allied Expeditionary Force, June 10—A "commando" raid by a group of civilian scientists, a search through obscure seventeenth–eighteenth-century French manuscripts, months of study of geological reports, experiments with model beaches—all these were a part of the Allied preparations for the invasion of Normandy that is one of the most remarkable stories of the war.

Months before the invasion parties of civilian scientists, not all of them young or signally muscled, landed on the beaches up which the Allied infantry were to scramble last Tuesday. Wriggling along on their bellies, within range of German guns, they obtained samples of sand soil so when the tanks and trucks bustled ashore the drivers would be prepared for the terrain and equipment would be on hand to bridge the worst spots.

The dramatic story of the preparations, which began in musty libraries, shifted to laboratories and ended on the shell-swept beaches, was told today by a mild-mannered professor in baggy clothes.

When the invasion was planned he was consulted by the Allied staff on the character of the beaches. He referred the officers to the old manuscripts, which, he said, stunned the staff officers. "But I convinced them they were worth studying so we went to work," he said.

"The geologists expected trouble because the area had been an Ice Age forest," the scientist added. "But the military people did not like all this book talk. So the only thing to do was to go and see."

Photographs and pre-war reports helped in the study of the beaches, but the final investigation had to be carried out on the spot. According to the scientist, a few months before the invasion "some very bright lads got over nicely and quietly by night, causing no disturbance and attracting no notice.

"They crawled half a mile on their bellies on the beach, with special instruments taking samples and charting the positions of the soft clay patches on the beaches, then brought the results to England." ❭

◀ With the samples to go on, the scientists recommended the type of vehicles that could best be used on the beaches and marked the points where steel carpets would have to be laid over the soft spots.Then the team of scientists got to work on the enemy's beach defenses. These were copies, and the experiments showed the troops how they could best be dealt with on landing.

Most of the defenses were reconstructed from photographs and other intelligence reports.

In the same painstaking manner the scientists assembled data on flooded areas around Carentan. Every scrap of information was gathered. Here, too, there were manuscripts to be studied as well as military references to the French-flooded area in the Franco-Prussian War seventy-four years ago.

Carentan lies in the center of the whole series of tidal river valleys. By the simple process of openingthe sluice gates at high tide andclosing them at low tide, the Germans converted the entire area into a mass of shallow lakes and ponds. ◇

JUNE 11, 1944

This Is the Europe We Came to Free
The ordeal of Nazi rule has created a welter of hungry, rebellious peoples.

By PIERRE MAILLAUD
LONDON (By Wireless).

What kind of Europe are the Allied armies going to discover as they penetrate the areas of German conquests in Western Europe? One may well say "discover" rather than "rediscover," for long years of ordeal have wrought such deep changes that even former visitors to the old Continent won't be able to retrace their steps on once familiar paths.

To such a Europe there is no available Baedeker. Its national traditions, beliefs, basic ways of living, even its frontiers, have all been thrown back into the melting pot. The old molds have been broken; Europe has refused to be cast into the new German one. Nothing quite similar has happened in history since the tenth century, when, through the dismemberment of Charlemagne's empire, the first European framework was shattered and the Continent fell back on feudal anarchy.

Our contemporary Europe, to be sure, had several hundred years of national traditions behind her, but these traditions, deep-rooted in the West, were less settled in eastern and Balkan Europe, where frontier and minority feuds had never ceased and have lately been deliberately fanned by the Germans. In the West the foundations of social life and many tenets of national life have been shaken. For more than four years Europe has existed chiefly on negative sentiments—hatred of German rule and a burning will to free herself from the German yoke.

This is not to say there are no currents of thought, no political tendencies, no valuable trends of social evolution, no ethical life in shackled Europe. That would be far from the truth. But there is no means of coordination among these diverse tendencies so that the general pattern of the Continent is infinitely variegated and confused not only to the onlooker but equally so to the citizen of any occupied nation who cannot communicate either in thought or deed with his fellow countrymen or his fellow Europeans. From tales of the experiences of travelers, fugitives and combatants one can form a general picture of the Continent.Let us paint it in broad strokes:

It is a hungry, rebellious, touchy, hypersensitive welter of peoples, among whom all contradictions can coexist and even be somewhat reconciled or merged.

JUNE 14, 1944

ALLIES' CENSORSHIP WORKS WITH SPEED
Average Time for Dealing With Invasion Story 11 Minutes— 3 Nations Take Part

By E. C. DANIEL
By Wireless to The New York Times.

LONDON, June 13—At one of the touchiest moments of the war, it still takes an average of only eleven minutes apiece for invasion news dispatches to be read and censored by the three-nation military censorship at Supreme Headquarters of the Allied Expeditionary Force.

These dispatches are pouring through London at the rate of 500,000 to 750,000 words a day. Front-line dispatches generally consist roughly of 300-word "takes," or sections, each.

On the stroke of D-day, the special SHAEF censorship force representing the United States, Britain and Canada and the ground, sea and air forces was at "action stations" in London. Sixteen field censors with three radio transmitters crossed the Channel with the fighting forces to handle dispatches under fire.

They had received not only full training in censorship but also field training to fit them for the rigors of the front, and they had thoroughly studied the organization, personnel and secret weapons of the invasion units about which the correspondents would be writing. Several of them served in Africa. The censors have already started functioning and news dispatches are being sent by wireless from the beachhead to London, ready for immediate publication or transmission overseas.

HEADED BY BRITISH OFFICER
At headquarters the news censorship consists of a vast enlargement of an American organization that has been functioning for months as an advisory and auxiliary body to the highly geared press censorship operated by the British Ministry of Information since the beginning of the war. The SHAEF cen-

It is idealistic in its long-term aspirations, often cynical in the attempt to satisfy its daily needs. It believes in man's future, yet often sets little store by human life. Large sections of the population cling to past memories as antidotes to present sufferings, while iron-hard groups of resistance live only for the future in ruthless indifference to their own temporary plight or their own lives.

It is apt to be parochially nationalistic in its sentimental reactions, through years of national humiliation, yet its hopes are broadly European and even world wide. Its men and women folk, who queue up for hours for a few ounces of bread and live for days on end on the single obsessive thought of getting food, suddenly stake their own and their children's lives on an act of defiance of the enemy or charity to a friend. They chafe under Allied bombings, if they feel they have more than their share, but they will take any risks to save an Allied pilot.

Hunger, hope, depression and exaltation, the overpowering pressure of daily needs, acts of utter self-denial, contrasts between the urgency of the small problems of life and the general yearning for great accomplishment, contradictions between the narrowness of the day-to-day outlook and the broadness of long-term conceptions which is the reaction against moral and intellectual servitude, greed and generosity, brutal realism and idealism—such are the elements of the European make-up. It is at once soft and hard. Life is spasmodic. Such a Europe, for which emergency has become a habit, is in many respects incalculable. In it the largest allowances must be made for the unexpected.

More than any other event in history, the invasion will be, above all, for better or for worse, a meeting between peoples on which lasting impressions will be formed. This is not to suggest that responsibility for the consequences will lie solely with Allied soldiers and not with the continental peoples as well.

But it must be realized that humiliated nations are nationally touchy, that their pride has been deeply hurt, that anything suggestive of a patronizing attitude toward them would touch a very sore point. They are purchasing at a very high cost the right of being treated as equals.

What inferiority complex the western nations of the Continent may therefore have suffered since June, 1940, has been largely redeemed by their share in the struggle, both in the internal and external theatres of war. British and American soldiers will find themselves among people who will be oversensitive to their behavior for good or evil.

It is impossible for the average American citizen, or for that matter for the British, to form an approximate picture of the appalling misery inflicted, and inflicted with ruthless and perverse deliberation, by the German invader. To cause enduring, and if possible irreparable, damage to the body and soul of Europe was, and still is, a part of the German—and not only the Nazi—policy. So that underfeeding, destitution, political and literal slavery have been dominant notes in the lives of the occupied peoples for more than four years. The spectacle of physical fitness, relative abundance and freedom which their allies will present, in striking contrast to the continental plight, will therefore be all the more welcome if it is not coupled with the display, conscious or not, of superiority in wealth or conduct.

Readers may, perhaps, find the above picture too gloomy, or feel that if the outlook of the occupied nations is such as I have tried to describe it, it shows a degree of ingratitude. They must, however, understand that nations cannot endure appalling physical and moral sufferings without finding some compensatory element This can only be found in the hardening of national pride, which in itself entails a strain on relationships with others—including friends.

To take this into account and turn the present operations into a reunion of peoples as well as a military victory is the great ambassadorial task not of statesmen only but of every citizen-soldier who sets foot on the Continent. No task was ever worthier, nor its fulfillment more fatefully decisive. ◇

---

sorship, which does not cover political matters, is a branch of the Supreme Headquarters public relations department, under a British officer, Lieut. Col. George Warden, formerly a military adviser to the British censorship. He has as his operations officer an American, Lieut. Col. Richard H. Merrick, who was for several months the United States Army censor in this theatre.

Colonel Merrick commands an organization with the unwieldy name of "SHAEF Joint Press Censorship Group." Its battleground is known to every correspondent as "Room 16" in the Ministry of Information Building. Its personnel consists of 138 censors, including the sixteen in the field, from the British, American and Canadian armed services.

The censor makes any necessary emendations, stamps the copy "Passed for publication as censored," and marks it with his initials and number. The dispatch is then returned to the senior censor, who, if he has time, inspects it for too much or too little censorship. Of fifty representative dispatches recently passed—dispatches of all types and lengths—it was found that two minutes was the shortest time for censorship and thirty-eight minutes was the longest. This record can be expected to improve as the first rush of dispatches subsides and the censors become more familiar with the material.

Dispatches written in the London offices of American newspapers and news agencies and sent to cable companies for transmission in the usual routine are referred, usually by telephone, to the SHAEF censorship if they contain disputable points about operations in France. The censors at the cable companies are the same British censors who have functioned there for years, augmented by eighteen American censors "lent-leased" to the British for the rush. ◇

JUNE 16, 1944

STUNNING BLOWS STRIKE FOE IN PACIFIC ARENA; SAIPAN IS STORMED

By GEORGE F. HORNE
By Telephone to The New York Times.

PACIFIC FLEET HEADQUARTERS, June 15—American troops who fought their way ashore on Saipan Island in the Marianas Islands on Wednesday have firmly established their beachheads and are making good progress in an advance inland against heavy opposition, Admiral Chester W. Nimitz said in a communiqué tonight.

The enemy is fighting bitterly and ❯

has attempted several counter-attacks with tanks, but they have been broken up by our troops with the support of aircraft and warships lying offshore. Thus the most important battle fought so far in the Pacific offensive, now reaching to within 1,465 statute miles of Tokyo and a threat to the Japanese homeland itself, was going well for the invaders.

Tonight's communiqué was the second of the day issued by Admiral Nimitz. The first confirmed previous Japanese reports that Saipan was being invaded.

ENEMY BATTERIES SILENCED

Tonight's communiqué follows: Assault troops have secured beachheads on Saipan Island and are advancing inland against artillery, mortar and machine gun fire. Virtually all heavy coastal and anti-aircraft batteries on the island were knocked out by naval gunfire and bombing. Our troops have captured Agingan Point. In the town of Charan-Kanoa brisk fighting is continuing.

The enemy has attempted several counter-attacks with tanks, but these attacks have been broken up by our troops with the support of ships and aircraft.

In general, fighting is heavy, but good progress is being made against well-organized defenses.

In the earlier announcement Admiral Nimitz told how under cover of supporting bombardment by air and surface forces, following an unprecedented four-day battering of Saipan and other islands throughout the Marianas group, our forces were still pouring ashore. He said reports thus far indicated that our casualties in the initial stages were moderate.

The first assault troops went in yesterday and were supported in their battle on the beachheads by a naval bombardment maintained all last night.

STAKES ARE HIGH

Saipan is the largest island central Pa-

American Marines attack Japanese defensive positions during the Battle of Saipan in the Northern Mariana Islands, 1944.

cific forces have ever assaulted and perhaps the best defended, for it is believed to have been reinforced with materiel and fighting men in recent months. The Japanese, obviously aware of the stakes involved, are going to defend it bitterly and they are in a position to inflict severe punishment on landing forces.

There is no question that the operation is the most important yet staged in the central Pacific area. Because of the land mass involved—Saipan is twenty and three-quarters miles long and five and one-half wide with an area of seventy-five square miles—and the heavy defenses, it will be the scene of the first encounter between large numbers of amphibious attackers and large numbers of land troops of the enemy's army.

Its importance is heightened by the proximity to Japan itself and the fact that victory will bring at an early date the next phase of the crushing of Japan, concentrated air attacks by land-based bombers from all sides. Possession of Saipan would bring to the enemy with shocking emphasis the realization that the final phases of our advance are near at hand.

It would sever communication lines with its many bases eastward and to the south and leave to the withering process thousands upon thousands of men and tremendous quantities of materiel that Japan cannot afford to lose.

The effect upon the morale of the Japanese people cannot fail to be staggering.

Coming with the bombing of Japan itself by land-based Superfortresses, the assault in the Marianas, if it is as successful as it is expected to be, will be difficult for the enemy propagandists to explain away and to convert by their own special type of sophistry into another Japanese victory. ◆

JUNE 16, 1944

B-29'S MAKE DEBUT
Tokyo Reports Assaults on Industrial Heart Of Kyushu Island

By SIDNEY SHALETT
Special to THE NEW YORK TIMES.

WASHINGTON, June 15—The air war against the heart of the Japanese Empire has begun, the War Department announced this afternoon. B-29 Superfortresses of the new Twentieth Air Force, which is part of a new "super-air force" under the personal command of Gen. H. H. Arnold, bombed Japan today, a special communiqué revealed.

There are three epochal factors in the announcement:

First, that the monster B-29, half again as big as the Flying Fortress, is in operation.

Second, that the type of aerial attrition that reduced Germany to the stage where an invasion of Europe could be launched has commenced against Japan proper.

Third, that, in creating the Twentieth Air Force, a special organization that is not subject to the jurisdiction of any theatre commander, the Joint Chiefs of Staff have set up what virtually amounts to a separate air force.

The importance of this new phase of the Pacific war was emphasized by statements from Gen. George C. Marshall, Chief of Staff, who termed it the beginning of "a new type of offensive against our enemy"; from General Arnold, commanding general of the AAF, who declared it was "the fruition of years of

planning for truly global warfare," and Secretary of War Henry L. Stimson, who asserted that the action had "shortened our road to Tokyo."

The history-making communiqué was confined to the following bare statement, personally handed out by Maj. Gen. Alexander D. Surles, War Department Director of Public Relations, at 1:39 o'clock this afternoon:

"B-29 Superfortresses of the United States Army Air Forces Twentieth Bomber Command bombed Japan today."

No details of where we struck the enemy, or how hard we hit, were revealed, although it was understood that the War Department would release this information as quickly as it felt the story might be told without imperiling security.

While the War Department did not disclose the location of the necessarily huge bases from which the "Superforts" flew, it was revealed by James Stewart, Columbia Broadcasting System Far Eastern correspondent, in a broadcast from Washington today, that the B-29's had flown from "somewhere in West China." Mr. Stewart, recently returned from Chungking, said the B-29's "took off and landed on Chinese bases" constructed entirely by the hand labor of 430,000 Chinese farmers.

Additional historical significance was added to the bombing, our first air attack on Japan proper since the small-scale raid on April 18, 1942, by carrier-based planes led by Lieut. Gen. (then colonel) James H. Doolittle, by the fact that it occurred on the same day that American landings on Saipan in the Marianas,another step on the road to Tokyo, were announced.

WE GET THE NEWS FIRST

For once the Tokyo radio failed to beat us in announcing the news of the B-29 raid.The Tokyo radio was on the air twenty minutes after the War Department told the story, but it talked only about its version of the Saipan landings. Elmer Davis, Office of War Information director, congratulating the Army both on bombing Japan and "scooping" the enemy on the story, suggested that the Japanese might be "trying to cook up a story that will gloss over their losses." ◇

A B-29 Superfortress, 1944.

JUNE 17, 1944

Winged 1-Ton Bomb Bared; German Weapon Is Erratic

By RAYMOND DANIELL By Wireless to THE New York Times.

LONDON, June 16—For the last twenty-four hours parts of England south of a line drawn from Bristol to The Wash have been bombarded intermittently by robots. Most of the night and in daylight these one-ton bombs with wings and engines but no pilots have sailed in to blow up in haphazard fashion.

There is little doubt that this is Adolf Hitler's "secret weapon." In fact the Germans say it is. This is their answer to the breach that Anglo-American armies of liberation have made in their Atlantic wall, but whether it was dictated by a spirit of revenge or by necessity, providing some comfort for their own suffering people, is speculative. Maybe it is a combination of both, but the military value of the new weapon remains to be proved.

In announcing to the public several hours before the Germans got around to it that the Nazis were using their secret weapon at last, Home Secretary Herbert Morrison advised the country to carry on with its war work until danger was imminent and to duck as fast as possible when the broken thrumming of one of Hitler's newest engines of destruction ceased and its light died out.

"There is no reason to think that the raids will be worse than, or indeed, as heavy as the raids with which the people of this country are familiar and which they have borne so bravely," he said.

There is something a little eerie and unsettling about the idea of 2,000 pounds of TNT whizzing around the sky with no direct human control, but after the experiences of these peoples with the indiscriminate bombings in 1940, that idea can be accepted with reasonable equanimity.

These veterans of the air raids knew last Tuesday night that the war in the air had entered a new phase, although security considerations kept their newspapers from telling them so. When Mr. Morrison announced in the House of Commons today that this country was being bombarded by pilotless aircraft sent into the air by Germany, everyone breathed more easily. That was something everyone could accept even if he did not understand it.

The robot planes first made their appearance in the skies over southern England on Tuesday night. They were so few and the evidence was so scanty it was decided to keep silent and let the enemy show his hand. That he did last night to a point where silence had lost its virtue. So, with admirable timing, Mr. Morrison made his statement.

Since it seems likely that the Germans guide their gadgets on some sort of radio beam it is interesting to note that tonight the British Broadcasting Corporation announced that its programs were liable to interruption or cancellation without notice.

Pinpointed in searchlights, the Germans' new toy looks a little like a miniature fighter plane. It flies on an undeviating course at about one thousand feet and gives a telltale glow from its tail. Its engines, which have an ominous, rhythmic throb, die out a few seconds before the whole mass plunges to earth and explodes with a terrific lateral blast.

These infernal flying machines are believed to be designed for launching from a roller coaster, like tracks suddenly halted on the upgrade, so they are airborne at a terrific speed and at an altitude of about two hundred feet

They seem to attain an altitude of 1,000 feet or so and hold it until they blow up either by accident, design or contact.

Last night the Germans sent along a small number of ordinary bombers, apparently to observe and report where the mystery missiles were landing. ◇

JULY 2, 1944

JAPANESE LAUNCH SOUTH CHINA DRIVE

By The Associated Press.

CHUNGKING, China, July 1—The Japanese have launched their long-expected general offensive northward from the Canton area, the Chinese High Command announced tonight, with the enemy making an effort to join with forces driving down the Canton-Hankow railway through battered Hunan Province which, if successful, would be a disaster for the Chinese.

The general northward advance began in Kwangtung Province June 28, the Chinese said, reporting that heavy fighting was in progress along the route. The invaders lunged forward in striving ❯

to accomplish the juncture with their forces at Hengyang, about 225 miles from the Japanese-held Canton area and ninety-five north of the Kwangtung border.

An unconfirmed report said Japanese forces had landed on the coast of Fukien Province and were heading for Foochow, a few miles inland. Such a landing might be another Japanese move to prevent an American landing on the China coast and to neutralize all Allied air bases between the coast and the Peiping-Hankow and Canton-Hankow railroads.

There also was an unconfirmed report of a Japanese landing at Pakhoi, on the southwestern coast of Kwangtung, which might presage a thrust through Kwangtung into Kwangsi Province.

The High Command, aware of the gravity of the situation, was known to be rallying forces for a stand to prevent a junction of Japanese forces, but doubts were expressed openly as to ability of the Chinese to arrest the onslaught.

In the new drive from the Canton area, first three, then six Japanese columns were reported to have driven northward, their main weight apparently thrown in the direction of the important highway and river junction of

Tsingyun, about 110 miles south of the Hunan Province border. This offensive began a few days before the Chinese mark the beginning of the eighth year of hostilities on July 7.

The Chinese High Command claimed battered Hengyang, vital rail junction of the Canton-Hankow route, with lines to Kwangtung and Kwangsi to the south, still was in Chinese hands. Evidently fighting raged within the city.

A rail station apparently has fallen to the slashing attack by three Japanese divisions besieging the city, for a communiqué of Lieut Gen. Joseph W. Stilwell's headquarters told of its bombing by American planes. Two days ago a Stilwell headquarters bulletin reported American bombs had been hurled against Japanese positions at Hengyang.

Junction of enemy forces with the Hengyang troops would give the Japanese virtually complete control of 1,000 miles of railway north and south all the way from Peiping through Honan, Hupeh, Hunan and Kwangtung Provinces to Canton. Such an unbroken rail route would solve the supply problems of the Japanese, heretofore dependent upon sea lanes and river and overland routes, all open to attack.

It also would slice China in two, sealing the eastern coast against the eventuality of American landings, and appeared to be aimed at the same time at neutralizing established American air bases in the country.

The Chinese claimed to have smashed another Japanese attack, this one from Chekiang Province, and aimed at supporting the drive in Hunan, 300 miles to the west, and to have seized the enemy base of Chuhsien, about twenty-five miles east of the Kiangsi border.

This drive, the Chinese said, had been knifing westward along the Chekiang-Kiangsirailway. The High Command said all positions taken by the Japanese since they began the campaign June 11 had been retaken, and that more than 4,000 of the invaders had been killed, including a brigade commander, Maj. Gen. Takahiku Yokoyama.

American planes struck savagely throughout the Hengyang battle area in a wide radius, slashing at Japanese river transport, troop and cavalry concentrations, gun emplacements and installations, in an effort to stem the enemy drive along the railway. ◆

JULY 4, 1944

NORMANDY BATTLE IS HEDGE TO HEDGE

U.S. Troops in La Haye du Puits Area Find Enemy Using Bicycle Transport

By Harold Denny

WITH THE AMERICAN FORCES, In France, July 5—Today's fighting in this sector was just hard slugging for small gainsagainst stiffening German resistance.

Almost everywhere on our twenty-five-mile front it was a continuation of the hedge-to-hedge fighting. Our men were digging out their cunningly concealed enemies.

The Germans were making much use of bicycles for troop movements to counteract the interference with the railways and the apparent shortage of motor transport or gasoline.

Daily we see the highways from which fighting has been heard dotted with dead Germans lying near their bicycles. The French are gathering these cycles and we see them everywhere pedaling along the roads.

A curious and fortunate feature of the fighting on this front is the scarcity of German artillery. The Germans gambled on dive-bombers to take the place of field artillery in the beginning of the war. They subordinated the manufacture of artillery and the training of artillery staffs. Now that the Allies have mastered the German dive-bombers and have gained command of the air, the Germans are badly outclassed in supporting fire for infantry. A considerable amount of the enemy artillery that our forces have overrun is captured Russians guns. Around La Haye du Puits, however, they had massed a number of guns. As they had direct observation over the town's northern approaches, they raked the roads and our infantry positions. Their artillery is manned entirely by real Germans, in contrast to the impressed troops in many of their infantry units.

The path of our troops who got into La Haye's railway yards today and of the others who swung around the town from the west was hard all the way yesterday afternoon and today. The enemy threw seven tanks against our men west of La Haye late yesterday.

While two of them made a demonstration to draw our fire, the five others lay hull-down behind a ridge and raked our men in the open fields with machine guns. Our forces rushed anti-tank guns into action, however, and drove the German tanks off.

Another brisk fight last night raged around a farm near Denneville. Our forces finally drove out what Germans were still alive. Our troops were finding many mines, though often they had been hastily laid. One variety appearing now is the "mustard pot," which can blow a foot off any unwary soldier.

The crew of an American long-range large-calibre artillery piece and a mischievous American fighter pilot had sport this morning with a German command post that had been discovered last night. Today this gun made a direct hit on the building housing the German staff. The Germans came boiling out and started to flee in a command car.

The fighter pilot, seeing this, dived down and machine-gunned the car. It careened off the road and smashed against a stone wall. ◆

JULY 3, 1944

INQUIRY CONFIRMS NAZI DEATH CAMPS 1,715,000 Jews Said to Have Been Put to Death By the Germans

By DANIEL T. BRIGHAM
By Telephone to The New York Times.

GENEVA, Switzerland, July 2—Information reaching two European relief committees with headquarters in Switzerland has confirmed reports of the existence in Auschwitz and Birkenau in Upper Silesia of two "extermination camps" where more than 1,715,000 Jewish refugees were put to death between April 15, 1942, and April 15, 1944.

The two committees referred to are the International Church Movement Ecumenical Refugee Commission with headquarters in Geneva and the Flucht-lingshiie of Zurich, whose head, the Rev. Paul Voght, has disclosed a long report on the killings.

This report says national "clean-ups" are periodically ordered by the Nazis in various occupied countries and when they are enforced Jews are shipped to the execution camps. Totals compiled two months ago show the following number of Jews "eradicated" in the two camps, excluding hundreds of thousands slain elsewhere:

Poland	900,000
Netherlands	100,000
Greece	45,000
France	150,000
Belgium	50,000
Germany	60,000
Yugoslavia, Italy and Norway	50,000
Bohemia, Moravia and Austria	30,000
Slovakia	30,000
Foreign Jews from various camps in Poland	300,000

HUNGARIAN JEWS SLAUGHTERED

To this total must now be added Hungary's Jews. About 30 per cent of the 400,000 there have been slain or have died en route to Upper Silesia. Discussing "malicious, fiendish, inhuman brutality" in the treatment of Hungarian Jews, the Ecumenical Commission says:

"According to authenticated information now at hand, some 400,000 Hungarian Jews have been deported from their homeland since April 6 of this year under inhuman conditions to Upper Silesia. Those that did not die en route were delivered to the camps of Auschwitz and Birkenau in Upper Silesia, where during the past two years, it has now been learned, many hundreds of thousands of their coreligionists have been fiendishly done to death."

After a fortnight to three months' imprisonment, during which they were "selected" or worked to death, the Jews were led to the execution halls, it was said. These halls consist of fake bathing establishments handling 2,000 to 8,000 daily.

CYNANIDE GAS CAUSED DEATH

Prisoners were led into cells and ordered to strip for bathing. Then cyanide gas was said to have been released, causing death in three to five minutes. The bodies are burned in crematoriums that hold eight to ten at a time. At Birkenau there are about fifty such furnaces. They were opened March 12, 1943, by a large party of Nazi chiefs who witnessed the "disposal of 8,000 Jews from 9 o'clock in the morning until 7:30 that night," according to the report. ◇

JULY 5, 1944

Nazis Continue To Guess About Gen. Patton's Army

The Nazis continued yesterday to fish for information regarding the where-abouts of Lieut. Gen. George S. Patton Jr. and the American seventh Army.

A German DNB broadcast for the European press outside Germany, reported by United States Government monitors, speculated that General Sir Bernard L. Montgomery, Allied ground commander, intended "to coordinate resumption of large-scale operations with employment of a United States Army group under General Patton." DNB said "it can be expected" that this group will attack "another sector of the Atlantic front in the very near future."

"The group may attack the adjoining sector between the Seine and the Somme, the Pasde Calais area, or the Breton Peninsula, the occupation of which must be a very tempting prize to the Allied High Cornmand," the Nazi broadcast continued. "Possession of Brest would provide them with another deep-sea port." ◇

JULY 10, 1944

JAPANESE CRUSHED Americans Are Rapidly Mopping Up Scattered Remnants On Saipan

By GEORGE F. HORNE
By Telephone to The New York Times.

PEARL HARBOR, July 9—The furious battle for Saipan is over after twenty-five days. "Our forces have completed the conquest," Admiral Chester W. Nimitz announced this morning.

The Commander in Chief of the Pacific Fleet said that the island was secured yesterday afternoon.

"Organized resistance ended on the afternoon of July 8, West Longitude date, and the elimination of scattered disorganized remnants of the enemy force is proceeding rapidly," he stated.

The battle lasted nearly a month, including the preparatory carrier-aircraft assaults and pre-invasion bombardments. It was on June 10, before dawn broke over the Western Pacific, that the first attack began. For four days the well-entrenched defenders of Saipan, estimated at 20,000 to 30,000 Japanese troops, and other enemy garrisons and defense installations from Tinian to Rota, Guam and Pagan were shattered by powerful carrier-plane raids or bombardment by the big guns of the surface fleet, in some cases both.

FIERCE COUNTER-ATTACK BROKEN

The marines stormed ashore on Saipan's western beaches to come finally to grips with the largest and strongest enemy force yet encountered in the Central Pacific offensive.

▸

The end came sooner than observers here had expected, for only yesterday the Admiral disclosed that an enemy counter-attack had plunged through our left flank for a distance of 2,000 yards. It was one of the bitterest battles and casualties on both sides were believed to have been heavy.

And at the last report yesterday we had regained only about a third of the lost ground.

Apparently, however, the troops on the western anchor of our line advanced rapidly again, slashing forward north of Tanapag town to retrieve the losses and carry the battle forward to the island's northeastern extremity.

Meanwhile, on the right flank marine forces advanced to their objective.

No official announcement has been made of the number of enemy prisoners taken, but it will probably be small, for the Japanese have fought all the way through with their traditional fanaticism and determination to stand or die. It can be assumed that the majority of the garrison was wiped out.

Up to the middle of last week our own forces had buried nearly 10,000 Japanese.

For our part the story of Saipan will live as one of sacrifice, for the price paid has been in keeping with the importance of the island to us. There has been no announcment of our casualties since June 30, when Admiral Nimitz disclosed that 1,474 Americans had been killed between June 14 and June 28.

Our total casualties, including dead, wounded and missing up to that date, were 9,752.

Admiral Nimitz said later he expected our losses would be relatively smaller in the final stages of the battle, and it is likely that they were during the next ten days, for we had then taken commanding positions, we had captured much material and supplies and had given the enemy fatal blows.

Nevertheless, the significance of the casualty lists should not be overlooked, particularly by those who may be inclined to misinterpret our unbroken roster of victories from the Gilberts to the Marianas.

Before the seizure of Tarawa and Makin back in November the island-spotted sea stretching toward Japan looked discouragingly wide and probably few people dreamed we would go so far so fast.

At Saipan we are 1,465 statute miles from Tokyo and although the end is in sight there is still many a bitter story to be told.

Possession of strong air and sea facilities in the Marianas will, as Admiral Nimitz explained, permit us to employ our sea strength relatively near to the heart of Japan.

And then perhaps, when the entire inner defense of the enemy falls within the arc of which the Marianas form the center, sea and air power can be brought to bear on the enemy's homeland from the north through the Kuriles and from the Asiatic mainland whence the mighty Superfortresses are already beginning to come. Admiral Nimitz and Gen. Douglas MacArthur can batter at arm's length against the Philippines, against Japan itself, and against the China coast where Pacific forces will land for the final stages. ◇

JULY 13, 1944

ALLIES SLOWLY BATTER DOWN GERMAN RESISTANCE IN NORMANDY

A grinding advance toward Lessay carried the Americans to Angoville-sur-Ay and gave them possession of the entire Forest of Mont Castre (1). Although they were still four miles from the Feriers junction they widened their spearhead by taking Blehou (2). A German counter-attack forced our troops out of Le Desert, but to the west they occupied most of St. Andrés de Bohon (3).

As one American column smashed to a point one and a half miles from St. Lo, another "began outflanking the junction by seizing St. André-de l'Epine, Le Calvaire and St. Pierre-de Semilly (4). Heavy fighting raged near Hottot les Baques (5). Around Caen the British repelled attacks southwest and the Germans clung to recaptured Louvigny (6) and battled for Colombelles (7). ◇

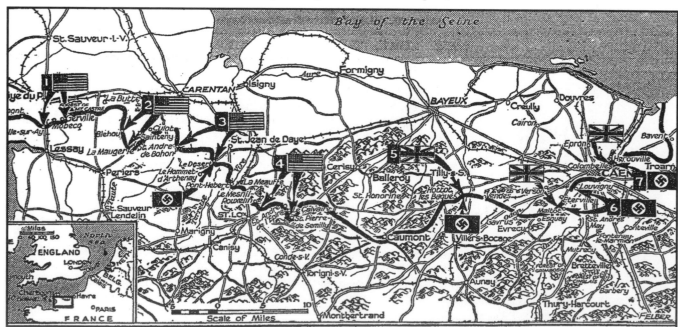

TOJO REGIME QUITS
Failure to Win Goals Is Cited As Cause for Stronger Executive

HIROHITO IS 'CONCERNED'
Emperor Calls Home Minister Kido To Audience
To Discuss New Cabinet Formation

Premier General Hideki Tojo's "entire Cabinet" has resigned, the Japanese Domei agency announced last night in a wireless dispatch to Japanese-occupied areas.

The dispatch, reported by the Federal Communications Commission to the Office of War Information, quoted a statement by the Japanese Board of Information.

The Japanese announcement said that "it has been decided to strengthen the Cabinet by a wider selection of the personnel."

"By utilizing all means available the present Cabinet was not able to achieve its objective." the statement declared.

It said that "the Government has finally decided to renovate its personnel totally in order to continue to prosecute the war totally."

The announcement came a day after Tojo had been divested of his concurrent post as Army Chief of Staff in continuation of a Japanese High Command shake-up that began two days ago.

DELAY NOT EXPLAINED

Last night's Domei dispatch carried this introduction:

"Tojo's Cabinet resigns: Premier Tojo's Cabinet took a resolute step on July 18 and effected the resignation of the entire Cabinet."

A Domei transmission last night at 11 o'clock [Eastern War Time] to newspapers in Japanese-occupied areas, said that on July 18 the Emperor had ordered Marquis Koichi Kido, Home Affairs Minister, into audience, with a view to forming a new Cabinet.

Marquis Kido, who, as Lord Keeper of the Privy Seal, is the highest adviser to the Japanese Emperor, called a meeting of former Premiers the evening of July 18 to deliberate on the personnel of the succeeding Cabinet, Domei said.

One Domei broadcast, referring to the Cabinet resignation, said:

"The reason, to put it straightforward, is that the individuality of the Tojo Cabinet was unable to keep up with the intensity of the burning war spirit of the people. The Board of Information announcement was issued July 20 (Japanese time). No explanation of the delay in making known the resignation was offered immediately.

The board's announcement follows:

Since the outbreak of the (Greater East Asia) war the Government has been cooperating closely with the Imperial Headquarters as one unit and has exerted every possible effort for the prosecution of the war.

At present, in face of a grave situation and realizing the necessity of a strengthened personnel in time of urgency for the prosecution of the war, it has been decided to strengthen the Cabinet by a wider selection of the personnel.

By utilizing all means available the present Cabinet was not able to achieve its objective; here, then the Government has finally decided to renovate its personnel to continue to prosecute the war totally and, having recognized the fact that it was most appropriate to carry out a total resignation of the Cabinet, Premier Tojo gathered together the resignations of each member of the Cabinet and presented them to the Emperor on July 18 at 11:40 A.M. (Japanese time) when he was received in audience.

At this time of decisive war, to have reached the stage existing today is causing the Emperor much concern, because of which the present Cabinet is filled with trepidation, and in apologizing for the Government's meager power to the men on the fighting front and the 100,000,000 people of Japan who continue to work toward certain victory, it has been decided that this Cabinet should be dissolved.

Thus, for the purpose of assuring a successful prosecution of this war, we anticipate with great anxiety the appearance of a new strong Cabinet at this time without loss of opportunity.

Meanwhile, Japanese propagandists, in their output for domestic and overseas consumption, continued to focus attention on the loss of Saipan as a means of whipping up the people's fighting spirit. The propagandists appealed for still greater efforts on the "production front" and urged the Japanese to achieve a "protracted war," dismissing any ideas of a war of comparatively short duration.

Tojo, known among his colleagues as the "razor blade" because of his sharp tongue, held office since the fall of the Konoye Cabinet Oct. 17, 1941, and headed the Government that ordered the Japanese attack on Pearl Harbor on Dec. 7, 1941. ◊

FUEHRER 'BRUISED'
Bomb Wounds 13 Staff Officers, One Fatally— Assassin Is Dead

Adolf Hitler had a narrow escape from death by assassination at his secret headquarters, the Berlin radio reported yesterday, and a few hours later in a radio broadcast to the German people he blamed an "officers' clique" for the attempt to kill him. His address disclosed a movement in the armed forces to overthrow him and his regime. He announced that a purge of the conspirators was under way.

Thirteen members of his military staff were injured, one fatally and two seriously, by a bomb set off at an undisclosed place while many of his highest advisers were assembled around him. The man who played the role of assassin, Hitler said, was Colonel Count von Stauffenberg, one of his collaborators, who stood only six feet away from him as he hurled the bomb. Von Stauffenberg is dead, Hitler announced.

Waiting to see Hitler before the assassination attempt was Benito Mussolini. Reich Marshal Hermann Goering, who rushed to Hitler's side, was in the immediate vicinity. Hitler escaped with singes and bruises.

▸

ARMY CLIQUE BLAMED

While Dr. Joseph Goebbels and Nazi radio propagandists at first tried to put the blame for the attempt to kill the Fuehrer upon the Allies, Hitler himself exploded the bombshell by announcing that the culprits were a group of German Army officers. He thus confirmed reports of a serious rift between the Nazi High Command and German military elements.

In his broadcast, recorded by the Federal Communications Commission, Hitler told the German people: "If I address you today I am doing so for two reasons: first, so that you shall hear my voice and know that I personally am unhurt and well, and, second, so that you shall hear the details about a crime that has no equal in German history.

"An extremely small clique of ambitious, unscrupulous and at the same time foolish, criminally stupid officers hatched a plot to remove me and, together with me, virtually to exterminate the staff of the German High Command. "The bomb that was placed by Count von Stauffenberg exploded two meters [slightly more than two yards] away from me on my right side. It wounded very seriously a number of my dear collaborators. One of them has died. I personally am entirely unhurt apart from negligible grazes, bruises or burns.

"This I consider to be confirmation of the task given to me by Providence to continue in pursuit of the aim of my life, as I have done hitherto. ... "In an hour in which the German Army is waging a very hard struggle there has appeared in Germany a very small group, similar

Members of the German High Command, including Hermann Goering (third from left) survey damage to Hitler's bunker after the failed assassination attempt.

to that in Italy, that believed that it could thrust a dagger into our back as it did in 1918. But this time they have made a very great mistake." Hitler concluded by saying that the "criminal elements" would be exterminated ruthlessly. He spoke for only six minutes, shrieking in maniacal rage as he described the circumstances of the attempted assassination that nearly killed him and his entire staff.

He said that the annihilation of what he called the criminal clique behind the attempted assassination would give to Germany the "atmosphere" that the front and the people needed.

That the attempt to kill him was coupled with efforts to provoke a report in the German Army was indicated in Hitler's address when he called upon German troops and civilians to refuse to obey the orders of the men he called "usurpers" and to kill them. He revealed also that Heinrich Himmler, his Minister of the Interior and chief of the Gestapo, had been put in charge of the home front army, with special powers to deal with the emergency. The vesting of Himmler with special powers even beyond the authority he already enjoys was taken as an indication that Hitler and his immediate Nazi entourage were squaring off for a possible life and death struggle with the Army.

How serious was the clash between the Nazi ruling circle and the "usurpers" of whom Hitler spoke was evident also from his statement that "accounts would be settled in a National Socialist manner" with his enemies in the armed forces.

Hitler's own characterization of the situation compared it to 1918, when Germany was making her last vain effort to hold back the deluge. He spoke of the "stab in the back," a slogan he used so

successfully in stirring up the German masses against the Weimar Republic, whose leaders he had accused of bringing about the German defeat in World War I by undermining morale and letting down the armed forces in the field. The specter of 1918 hovered ominously over Germany in yesterday's developments.

A telephone dispatch from The New York Times bureau in Berne, Switzerland, last night noted that telephone communications between the Reich and the outside world had been cut since midnight Tuesday. All attempts to reach the Reich by telephone through neutral quarters last night received the answer "gespert"—closed.

After Hitler, Doenitz and Goering had spoken on the radio a mysterious broadcast was picked up in London on the Frankfort wavelength by a "Wehrmacht officer" who appealed to like-minded men to help "save our cause." ◊

JULY 21, 1944

MOTHER SAYS TRUMAN SHOULD STAY IN SENATE

KANSAS CITY, July 20 (AP)—The 91-year-old mother of Senator Truman does not want her son to be Vice President. She believes he should stay in the Senate where "he can do more good."

"His investigating committee is doing fine work," she said. "He ought to stay there."

Mrs. Martha E. Truman, who will be 92 on Nov. 25, recalled that she told her son last week, just before he left her home in suburban Grandview, Mo., for the Democratic Convention that he should remain a Senator. She added:

"Harry said, 'I'd rather be.' And he meant it."

Mrs. Truman sat in her old-fashioned rocker last night and listened to the convention by radio.

"I listened to all the Republican Convention, too," she said. "They keep predicting that Roosevelt will die in office if he's elected. The Republicans hope he will. They keep saying that I'll die, too, and I'm almost 92. I hope Roosevelt fools 'em."

Mrs. Truman said that if her son were nominated for Vice President. "I'll be for him." ◊

AGAIN NAMED FOR PRESIDENCY
Roosevelt's Acceptance

Following is the text of President Roosevelt's acceptance speech from a Pacific Coast naval base, as recorded and transcribed by The New York Times:

Mr. Chairman, ladies and gentlemen of the convention, my friends:

I have already indicated to you why I accept the nomination that you have offered me, in spite of my desire to retire to the quiet of private life.

You in this convention are aware of what I have sought to gain for the nation, and you have asked me to continue.

It seems wholly likely that within the next four years our armed forces, and those of our Allies, will have gained a complete victory over Germany and Japan, sooner or later, and that the world once more will be at peace, under a system, we hope, that will prevent a new world war. In any event, whenever that time comes new hands will then have full opportunity to realize the ideals which we seek.

In the last three elections the people of the United States have transcended party affiliation. Not only Democrats but also forward-looking Republicans and millions of independent voters have turned to progressive leadership, a leadership which has sought consistently, and with fair success, to advance the lot of the average American citizen who had been so forgotten during the period after the last war. I am confident that they will continue to look to that same kind of liberalism, to build our safer economy for the future.

I am sure that you will understand me when I say that my decision, expressed to you formally tonight, is based solely on a sense of obligation to serve if called upon to do so by the people of the United States.

NO CAMPAIGN
'IN THE USUAL SENSE'

I shall not campaign, in the usual sense, for the office. In these days of tragic sorrow, I do not consider it fitting. And besides in these days of global warfare, I shall not be able to find the time. I shall,

however, feel free to report to the people the facts about matters that concern them and especially to correct any misrepresentations.

During the past few days I have been coming across the whole width of the continent to a naval base where I am speaking to you now from the train.

During the Nineteenth Century, during that era of development and expansion on this continent we felt a natural isolation, geographic, economic and political, an isolation from the vast world which lay overseas. Not until this generation, roughly this century, have people here and elsewhere been compelled more and more to widen the orbit of their vision to include every part of the world. Yes, it has been a wrench perhaps, but a very necessary one.

SAYS ISOLATIONISTS
ARE BECOMING EXTINCT

It is good that we are all getting that broader vision. For we shall need it after the war. The isolationists and the ostriches who plagued our thinking before Pearl Harbor are becoming slowly extinct. The American people now know that all nations of the world, large and small, will have to play their appropriate part in keeping the peace by force, and in deciding peacefully the disputes which might lead to war.

We all know how truly the world has become one, that if Germany and Japan, for example, were to come through this war with their philosophies established and their armies intact, our own grandchildren would again have to be fighting in their day for their liberties and their lives.

Some day soon we shall all be able to fly to any other part of the world within twenty-four hours. Oceans will no longer figure as greatly in our physical defense as they have in the past. For our own safety and for our own economic good, therefore, if for no other reason, we must take a leading part in the maintenance of peace and in the increase of trade among all the nations of the world. ◊

Analysis by Morgenthau of Monetary Agreements

Special to The New York Times

BRETTON-WOODS, N,H., July 22— The text of Secretary Morgenthau's radio broadcast tonight marking the completion of the international conference was as follows:

I am gratified to announce that the conference at Bretton Woods has completed successfully the task before it.

It was, as we knew when we began, a difficult task, involving complicated technical problems. We came here to work out methods which would do away with the economic evils—the competitive currency devaluation and destructive impediments to trade—which preceded the present war. We have succeeded in that effort. The actual details of a financial and monetary agreement may seem mysterious to the general public. Yet at the heart of it lie the most elementary bread and butter realities of daily life. What we have done here in Bret-ton Woods is to devise machinery by which men and women everywhere can exchange freely, on a fair and stable basis, the goods which they produced through their labor. And we have taken the initial step through which the nations of the world will be able to help one another in economic development to their mutual advantage and for the enrichment of all.

'FACED DIFFERENCES FRANKLY'

The representatives of the forty-four nations faced differences of opinion frankly, and reached an agreement which is rooted in genuine understanding. None of the nations represented here has had altogether its own way. We have had to yield to one another not in respect to principles or essentials but in respect to methods and procedural details. The fact that we have done so, and that we have done it in a spirit of goodwill and mutual trust, is, I believe, one of the hopeful and heartening portents of our time.

Here is a sign blazoned upon the horizon, written large upon the threshold of the future—a sign for men in battle, for men at work in mines, and mills, and in the fields, and a sign for women whose hearts have been burdened and anxious lest the cancer of war assail yet another generation—a sign that the ❯

peoples of the earth are learning how to join hands and work in unity.

There is a curious notion that the protection of national interest and the development of international cooperation are conflicting philosophies—that somehow or other men of different nations cannot work together without sacrificing the interests of their particular nation. There has been talk of this sort—and from people who ought to know better—concerning the international cooperative nature of the undertaking just completed at Bretton Woods.

NATIONAL INTERESTS CITED

I am perfectly certain that no delegation to this conference has lost sight for a mo-

ment of the particular national interest it was sent here to represent. The American delegation, which I have the honor of leading, has been, at all times, conscious of its primary obligation—the protection of American interests. And the other representatives have been no less loyal or devoted to the welfare of their own people.

Yet none of us has found any incompatibility between devotion to our own country and joint action. Indeed, we have found on the contrary that the only genuine safeguard for our national interests lies in international cooperation. We have come to recognize that the wisest and most effective way to protect our national interests is through international cooperation—that is to say, through united ef-

fort for the attainment of common goals.

This has been the great lesson taught by the war, and is, I think, the great lesson of contemporary life—that the peoples of the earth are inseparably linked to one another by a deep, underlying community of purpose. This community of purpose is no less real and vital in peace than in war, and cooperation is no less essential to its fulfillment.

To seek the achievement of our aims separately through the planless, senseless rivalry that divided us in the past, or through the outright economic aggression which turned neighbors into enemies would be to invite ruin again upon us all. Worse, it would be once more to start our steps irretraceably down the

---

JULY 23, 1944

RED ARMY DRIVES SHOW NO SIGNS OF FLAGGING
German Debacle Worse Than That Of Russians in First Month of War

By W. H. LAWRENCE
By Wireless to The New York Times.

MOSCOW, July 22—The Soviet summer offensive was one month old yesterday and still increasing in intensity, each new advance adding to the threat it holds to the bulk of the German Army and that army's rapidly diminishing prospects of keeping land fighting away from German soil for more than a few months.

In thirty days Soviet forces, mounting the greatest offensive yet thrown at the battered, reeling Wehrmacht, already have achieved results which stagger the imagination, and every indication is that next month will bring even more bad tidings for German soldiers who try to stand on eastern ground, obeying Hitler's personal order not to retreat

CAPTURE TWENTY GENERALS

In the first month of this offensive, armies operating under seven front com-

manders and spread over more than 600 miles have liberated a total of 70,000 square miles of Soviet territory and, more important—from a strategical viewpoint—have knocked out a large section of the best part of the German Army, capturing more than twenty generals. They have pushed the front back 317 miles toward Warsaw and Germany in at least one sector, moving at a rapid pace, and the offensive up to now has given no indication of lagging.

Not only has the Red Army been destroying German soldiers and equipment on a vast scale and regaining thousands of square miles of territory but it has also been systematically knocking out the lines of supply and retreat for German forces with which it has not yet come into contact.

Specifically, these are the major front advances which have occurred since the Soviet-German war was three years old, on June 22:

Along the Moscow-Riga railroad in the area west of Velikiye Luki—forty-four miles.

From Vitebsk area to the suburbs of Kaunas—226 miles.

From slightly east of Mogilev to a point west of Grodno—317 miles.

From east of Bobruisk to east of Bialystok—260 miles.

In the sector east of Brody to the western Bug north of Lwow—62 miles.

Thus it is easy to see and realize that the position of the German Army in the first month of the fourth year of war with the Soviet Union is even worse than that of the Soviet soldiers in the very first month of the war. All territory for which fighting is now going on was taken by the

steep, disastrous road to war.

That sort of extreme nationalism belongs to an era that is dead. Today the only enlightened form of national self-interest lies in international accord. At Bretton Woods we have taken practical steps toward putting this lesson into practice in monetary and economic fields.

I take it as an axiom that after this war is ended no people—and therefore no government of the people—will again tolerate prolonged or widespread unemployment. A revival of international trade is indispensable if full employment is to be achieved in a peaceful world and with standards of living which will permit the realization of man's reasonable hopes. ◊

then unbeaten German Army in their first thirty days on Soviet soil.

EXTENSIVE PREPARATIONS

Allied military observers who have been at the Soviet front since this drive began are high in praise of the preparations which preceded it. Perhaps the best testimony of the effectiveness of the Soviet offensive comes from captured Germans themselves, who say simply "they swamped us."

Several things are apparent about the Soviet summer campaign. Before launching these drives the Soviets amassed an imposing force, both in terms of manpower and equipment and air-power. This they have used with deadly effect through a series of quick jabs here and there all along the broad front, drawing German reserves first to one place, then to another, beforestriking at a third. Invaluable aid in these campaigns has been given by Partisan forces, whose ability to supply up-to-the minute first-rate information about the disposition of the enemy's forces has been even more important than sabotage and other guerrilla activity carried out behind the enemy lines.

The Red Army's present campaigns are being waged with both the most modern and most ancient of weapons. Modern American trucks carry supplies alongside horsecarts, which are invaluable in the wooded, marshy territory over which much fighting is now being conducted. Correspondents at the front have also reported large-scale use of horse cavalry, including the colorful, relentless Don Cossacks. ◊

JULY 24, 1944

Rival Polish 'Government' Set Up in Liberated Area

By E. C. DANIEL
By Wireless to The New York Times.

LONDON, July 23—The Moscow radio announced tonight the creation of a Polish Committee of National Liberation designed to perform all the functions that the exiled Polish Government in London had hoped to undertake in territory liberated by the Red Army. This announcement seemed to indicate an utter lack of Russian interest in the eleventh-hour proposal, cautiously put forward last week by Polish circles here, that Premier Stanislaw Mikolajczyk should go to Moscow to settle the differences with Premier Stalin. The Russians, apparently, are not interested in conversations. Three decrees were announced by the Moscow radio as having been issued in Warsaw by the Polish National Council, a pro-Soviet movement that does not recognize the authority of the Government in London. These decrees created the Committee of National Liberation to take charge of the civil administration in the liberated areas of Poland, placed the National Council in charge of the Union of Polish Patriots and the union's activities in Russia and consolidated the Polish Army in Russia with the council's underground forces in Poland, under a single command.

The result is to create in Poland an administration rivaling that of the London Government, which claims to have an organization of 30,000 underground civil servants and a large guerrilla army in the country.

The creation of such a "provisional government" had been anticpated as the logical outcome of the quarrel between Russia and the Polish regime here. A Polish spokesman here quoting the similarity between the Polish liberation movement and that of Marshal Tito in Yugoslavia, expressed the belief that there was still a possibility for reconciliation with Moscow that would result in combining the rival Polish governments.

Polish quarters in London clung to their contention that the Polish National Council was simply a small group of radical intellectuals without any broad basis of support among the masses of Polish peasants and workers and the underground forces. ◊

JULY 28, 1944

McNair Killed in Normandy Watching Push on U.S. Front

General Trained Our Ground Forces and Developed Tank Usage—Marshall Called Him the 'Brains of the Army'

Special to The New York Times

WASHINGTON, July 27—Lieut. Gen. Lesley J. McNair, one of the "big four" of the United States Army, who, as commanding general of the Army Ground Forces, directed the greatest military training and conditioning job in history, was killed by enemy fire while observing action of our front-line troops in the new Normandy offensive, the War Department announced today. The news of the death of General McNair, who was 61 years old, came as a personal blow to officials of the War Department. High-ranking officials, including the Chief of Staff, Gen. George C. Marshall, who once was reputed to have described General McNair as "the brains of the Army," issued statements deploring the Army's great loss.

General McNair, who recently relinquished his command of Army Ground Forces to go overseas on an important assignment, the nature of which was not disclosed, apparently was killed shortly after his arrival in Normandy. Hard luck had dogged the quiet but scrappy little general, who went through active service throughout the last war without receiving a scratch. In April, 1943, while on an inspection trip to the Tunisian battlefield, he was wounded on the first day he went out to observe American troops in action; now death came to him under somewhat similar circumstances.

General Marshall, in his statement on his colleague's death, revealed that it happened during the new offensive which the American First Army has opened on the front below St. Lo. He said:

"The American Army has sustained a great loss in the death of General McNair. Had he had the choice he would probably have elected to die as he did, in the forefront of the attack. His ❯

presence on the firing line with the leading element in the great assault which has just been launched on the American front in Normandy was indicative of his aggressive and fearless spirit, and should be an inspiring example to the forces of our great ground army which he organized and trained."

Under-Secretary of War Robert P. Patterson Jr. declared that the Army had lost "one of its great leaders."

One of the most striking speeches that General McNair ever delivered—and one that provided a perfect outline for the way he viewed his training job—was his famous Armistice Day address to Army ground troops on Nov. 11, 1942. Speaking over a nation-wide hookup, he declared:

"Our soldiers must have the fighting spirit. If you call that hating our enemies, then we must hate with every fibre of our being. We must lust for battle; our object in life must be to kill; we must scheme and plan night and day to kill. There need be no pangs of conscience, for our enemies have lighted the way to faster, surer and crueler killing; they are past masters. We musthurry to catch up with them if we are to survive." ◇

JULY 28, 1944

WE CHASE GERMANS
Race On to Trap Foe's Army After Stunning U.S. Break-Through

By E. C. DANIEL
By Cable to The New York Times.

SUPREME HEADQUARTERS, Allied Expeditionary Force, July 28—A smashing tactical success has been achieved on the western sector of the Normandy battle line by a daring American maneuver which late yesterday was within five miles of cutting the escape lines of German forces defending that side of the Cotentin Peninsula. The German defenses were already being described from the field last night as "chaotic" and 2,408 prisoners had been counted at the end of the second day of this offensive.

By bold and swift employment of tanks, Lieut. Gen. Omar N. Bradley had thrust west from the St. Lo area to within artillery range of Coutances, forty-two miles south of Cherbourg. The capture of that town of 7,000 near the western coast of the peninsula would bar Field Marshal Gen. Erwin Rommel's forces from using the roads leading south from Lessay and Periers, which the Americans occupied yesterday. General Bradley's swift armor was last reported in dispatches from the front last night to have reached Camprond, about five miles northeast of Coutances.

SEVEN DIVISIONS THREATENED

If—and that "if" should be underlined in view of the Germans' past powers of recovery—the First Army is able to extend and hold this line it will have trapped the best part of seven German divisions, including the Elite Second and Seventeenth Armored Divisions within the triangle from Lessay to St.

JULY 30, 1944

COMMAND POST HAS WILD GUAM DAWN
25 Marines Led by Senator Chavez's Son Kill 68 Japanese Intruders

By ROBERT TRUMBULL
By Wireless to The New York Times.

WITH THE FIRST PROVISIONAL MARINE BRIGADE, on Guam, July 24 (Delayed)—An audacious Japanese who walked boldly into an American command post near Agat and picked up a box of grenades touched off a dawn battle in which twenty-five Americans commanded by Lieut. Dennis Chavez Jr., son of the New Mexico Senator, slew sixty-eight Japanese.

The story is all the more remarkable because Lieutenant Chavez's outfit is part of a headquarters and supply company, which is not ordinarily expected to engage in rough-and-tumble combat, although it happens—in fact, Chavez's platoon sergeant, John Green, a big rugged West Virginian, was commended for a similar mix-up on Eniwetok in February.

The headquarters and supply company, commanded by Capt. Elliot Lima of Fallon, Nev., the night of D-Day dug in on a level stretch between two rugged knolls north of Agat. During the day they captured a Japanese Hotchkiss machine gun. Toward dawn a dark figure strode boldly past the sentry. Challenged, he said, "Watcha say, mate?" laid hold of a box of grenades and started to walk off toward the Hotchkiss.

A JAPANESE IS BLOWN UP

A marine noticed that the newcomer was a Japanese and fired. The bullet struck and detonated the grenades in the box, obliterating the Japanese. Captain Lima said a Japanese flag was found the next morning torn to small bits and ribbons and the Japanese's notebook was strewn like confetti over a fifteen-yard circle.

Shortly afterward, as the sky began to lighten, the marines relaxed, thinking they soon could get out of the wet foxholes. A group of men approached bearing boxes of ammunition. When they were almost inside the line guarding the command post of Col. Merlin F. Schneider someone spotted Japanese leggings on these men and opened fire.

Immediately the Japanese dropped into tall grass and deployed for an attack.

"Our position was good," Lieutenant Chavez said. "We were in foxholes, the Japanese in an open field of fire. But we had only two light machine-guns and a few automatic rifles, while they sounded like a full machine-gun company."

'LAST REEL OF HORSE OPERA'

The Japanese suddenly rose and charged, some swinging swords and bayonets. One officer ran toward Pfc. William Hurst yelling, "Marine, you die."

Hurst replied "The hell I will," and cut him down with an automatic rifle.

Lo to Coutances. The destruction of that force, the Eighty-fourth German Army Corps, which represents roughly half the divisions facing General Bradley's army, would materially reduce opposition to a further American push southward through the heartrending "bocage country" to the base of the Co-tentin Peninsula.

Space is still needed within the peninsula for Gen. Sir Bernard L. Montgomery to deploy his numerically superior weapons and men, and the Germans reported last night that the British Army on General Bradley's left had also set out to gain more ground. "The Allies have launched a new major offensive on the whole British front," said the German Trans-ocean News Agency. This front runs from around Caumont to Troarn on the eastern end of the line.

While Allied verification of this report was awaited, there was little doubt of the tremendous import of the multi-pronged American advance slicing south and west through German defenses and communications. It was the greatest battle the Americans have yet fought in France. ◆

Another officer, "a story-book Jap with buck teeth," rushed at Lieutenant Chavez.

"He grinned kinda toothily just as I shot him," Chavez said, "and I kinda hated to do it."

"The end of it was like the last reel of a horse opera," Captain Lima said. "Two wounded Marines crawled to me and said Lieutenant Chavez's outfit was running out of ammunition, lobbing grenades from foxholes and shooting like wild men. Meantime I had sent in another platoon under Lieut. Reginald Fincke of New York to back em up. By sun-up there were sixty-eight dead Japs against one Marine killed and five wounded."

Lieutenant Chavez, who is 31 but looks 25, discussed the engagement modestly and kept switching the conversation to New Mexico politics. It was some time before the writer wormed from him the reluctant admission that he had personally killed at least five Japanese with a tommy-gun. ◆

Guns on a U.S. Navy battleship shell the island of Guam during the Pacific campaign, July 1944.

JULY 31, 1944

GUAM PROCLAIMED UNDER RULE OF U.S.

By ROBERT TRUMBULL
By Wireless to the New York Times.

GUAM, July 27 (Delayed)—United States sovereignty was reestablished today on Guam through a proclamation by Admiral Chester W. Nimitz at a flag raising ceremony.

In the shadow of Mount Alifan the American flag was raised over the rich red and black soil of Guam at 4 o'clock this afternoon after two and a half years of Japanese occupation. As the Stars and Stripes were unfurled atop a white metal pole in the sultry air, artillery fire crashed from a meadow near by and shells whistled overhead into the Japanese lines near Sumay, two miles away,

where marines on a muddy plateau were poised for a drive on the Orote Peninsula airfield.

A PAUSE AMID BATTLE

It was a simple, affecting ceremony, witnessed by marines in mud-caked green uniforms, some with bandaged wounds suffered on this ground. Seabees, stripped to the waist, climbed off trucks and bulldozers to watch the historic ceremony.

On a deeply rutted highway along the beach, other trucks and tractors continued hauling ammunition and supplies to the fighting line.

Watching the ceremony from a tent nearby was a native of Guam, Juan Mateo, who joined the Navy at Guam four years ago. The bugle call ended, the grimy residents of this crude camp went back to work, utilizing the three remaining hours of daylight at dull, dirty, muscle-straining labor—the digging, moving, shoving, lifting and hauling that goes on in alternate rain and heat, and mud, always mud, just behind the fighting line. ◆

Chapter 20
"PATTON LASHES OUT"
August–September 1944

The progress of Allied forces in France after weeks of frustrating combat was impressive during August and September. On August 1 the U.S. Third Army was activated under General Patton, who had been chomping at the bit in Britain as commander of "First Army Group," a phantom operation used before D-Day to fool the Germans about the destination of the invasion. Patton needed no second chance. After a feeble German armored counteroffensive was defeated at Mortain on August 7 and 8, Patton raced eagerly into Brittany and then turned east toward Paris. "Patton Lashes Out" ran The Times's headline, as he left cleanup operations "to other commanders and to history." Bradley and Montgomery, who had finally passed beyond Caen, closed in on the retreating Germans in a drive toward the small town of Falaise. On August 19 the "Falaise Gap" was closed between the two Allied forces with the capture of 45,000 enemy troops, but most of the German Army escaped and hastily retreated any way it could back to the Seine River and beyond. In southern France a smaller Allied force landed on the coast on August 15 in Operation Dragoon, and a French force liberated Marseille and Toulon by the end of the month. Maj. General Lucian Truscott's Seventh U.S. Army pursued the retreating Germans toward Alsace-Lorraine.

Although Paris was not strategically important, it symbolized the liberation of France and Eisenhower detailed the French General Jacques-Philippe Leclerc to divert his division from the pursuit of the retreating Germans in order to take Paris. Three Times reporters entered the capital with French forces on August 24 under sniper fire, but with no large-scale resistance. The German commander surrendered the following day and the population flooded the streets, "shrilly and hoarsely hysterical" with the liberation according to The Times. The European war seemed to be nearing its final days. On September 1 The Times reported that Eisenhower, "brimming with confidence," thought "Germany could be beaten in 1944." The enemy army had been pushed back to the German frontier and into Belgium by the sudden rout, encouraging widespread hope in the West that the Allied advance would continue all the way to the Reich headquarters in Berlin.

The optimism was evident as representatives of the three major Allies began the conference at Dumbarton Oaks in Washington D.C. on August 21 to determine the shape of the organization needed to secure world peace after the end of the war. Times correspondent James (Scotty) Reston was secretly given the outline of the proposal and The Times published it on August 23. Arthur Sulzberger was asked to suppress further news of the negotiations but refused, since he saw the reporting as a matter of public interest. On August 30 a formal communiqué was issued from the conference, confirming the shape of what was to become the United Nations Organization.

The prospect of an imminent Allied victory encouraged resistance forces in occupied Europe to fight for their own liberation. In Yugoslavia, an estimated 300,000 pro-Communist partisans, led by Tito (Josip Broz), stepped up their campaign against the large German garrison there, holding down troops that might have been used on other fronts. In Warsaw, the Polish Home Army launched an uprising against the Germans on August 1 in hopes that the approaching Red Army might help to liberate their capital. The relationship between Poland and the Soviets, had become increasingly complex after the Soviet recognition of a Communist "Lublin Committee" as the future government of Poland, instead of the Polish government-in-exile in London. The Polish Home Army took its orders from London, not from the pro-Soviet Poles. This doomed the uprising, since the West could do little to help, while the Red Army claimed to lack the means—and certainly lacked the political will to advance any farther. By October 2 Polish resistance was over and Warsaw was systematically destroyed by the Germans. The incoming Communist political regime shackled the possibility of a Polish democracy and the country would vanish behind the Iron Curtain until the Solidarity Movement of the late 1980s bloodlessly brought down the Communist government.

Meanwhile, farther south, the Soviets advanced into Romania and Bulgaria, which surrendered in August and early September and then switched sides to the Allies. In the west, Montgomery planned a flanking attack to seize the Dutch city of Arnhem and open the way into northern Germany. But the operation that began on September 17 known as "Market Garden," was a costly failure for the Allies. Defeat there made it clear that the war would not be over by Christmas.

AUGUST 1, 1944

SELF-RULE IN INDIA PRESSED BY GANDHI
Agreement to Confer with Jinnah On Moslem Autonomy Indicates Determination

By TILLMAN DURDIN
By Cable to The New York Times.

NEW DELHI, India, July 30 (Delayed)—The agreement between Mohandas K. Gandhi and Mohammed Ali Jinnah, president of the Moslem League, to meet in Bombay on Aug. 8 to discuss the Moslem demand for an autonomous Moslem State in India has added momentum to Indian efforts to reach political settlements between themselves and with the British that would bring about an increased measure of self-rule for this country. Mr. Jinnah will confer with Mr. Gandhi in response to an invitation from the latter.

The arrangement for the Gandhi-Jinnah talks follows closely debates on India in the British Parliament, during which L. S. Amery, Secretary of State for India, announced that the British Government would not reopen formal negotiations with the Indian Nationalists on the question of Indian independence on the basis of the recent Gandhi proposals for a settlement.

Mr. Amery indicated that the Gandhi proposals, which advocated postwar independence for India, and in the meanwhile a regime in which Indians would control civil affairs and the British military, with a cabinet responsible to the Legislature and not to the viceroy, did not constitute a starting point for a profitable discussion and were "in no sense a response to Field Marshal Viscount Wavell's recent invitation to Gandhi to produce constructive proposals."

PROPOSALS REJECTED BY WAVELL

Mr. Gandhi's invitation to Mr. Jinnah indicates his apparent determination to continue pushing for a settlement of India's relationship with Britain despite evident British reluctance at this time to reopen the matter. Since his release three months ago, Mr. Gandhi has become steadily more active politically.

After an exchange of correspondence with Lord Wavell during which he received negative answers to requests for a meeting with the Viceroy and for release from prison of members of the All India Congress working committee, Mr. Gandhi advanced his plan for increased wartime Indianization of the national Government and post-war independence. Both Lord Wavell and Mr. Amery have now rejected the Gandhi plan even as basis for discussion. ◆

AUGUST 3, 1944

GERMANS ON RUN BEFORE AMERICANS
Tanks and Infantry Overrun Makeshift Defenses in Normandy

By DREW MIDDLETON
By Wireless to The New York Times.

WITH AMERICAN FORCES, in Normandy, Aug. 2—Churning up thick clouds of white dust, tanks and infantry of the American First Army rumbled across the bridge at Tessy-sur-Vire today and plunged into the base of the German salient between the First Army and the Second British Army.

The blow was prepared and struck within twenty-four hours of the repulse of a German counterattack made by some of the troops that were on the run today. And run they did as our shells shattered their hastily built defenses and our armor swept around behind the strongpoints, knocking them out with cannon. There is an electric quality to this advance. Its progress may slow down, as it did once or twice today, but, when the enemy position is broken, as it inevitably is, the columns leap forward and new plumes of dust rise above the roads.

TANK AND INFANTRY TEAMS USED

Tanks have "made" the fighting in the advance into Brittany, but in this sector it is the old reliable teams of tanks and infantry that make the fighting. Walking slowly and solidly, the infantry fanned out from the bridge across the Vire River at Tessy and pushed into the rolling farmland beyond.

The whole front was moving forward. Two columns striking out from the Percy-Gavray line rolled up the Germans after some savage fighting. One reached a point a mile north of the road into Juvignyle Tertre while the second force, farther south, also made considerable progress. The great Forest of St. Sever has been by-passed and German ammunition and fuel dumps in it are being hammered by artillery fire. Tongues of flame are leaping skyward as a result of the hail of shells that has fallen on the forest.

At intervals today the front was unpleasantly like that of 1940 in this same area. The Germans, trying desperately to halt the destruction of their divisions,

U.S. infantrymen take a brief respite in the taproom of a deserted house in the French town of Tessy-sur-Vire.

Hitler Assassin A Cripple, Bitter Over War Wounds

By Wireless to The New York Times.

ROME, Aug. 2—Col. Count Claus von Stauffenberg, who recently was executed for his attempt on Adolf Hitler's life, was seriously wounded on April 8, 1943, by a shell of the First British Armored Division at Nezzouna, Tunisia, it was disclosed today. He lost an eye and an arm. He had gone to Africa from the Stalingrad front, so he had seen two serious defeats and had reason to be embittered against Hitler.

He was then Chief of Staff of the Tenth Panzer Division, commanded by Maj. Gen. von Broich. Both men were cavalry officers of the old school and had no love for the Nazi regime. When next heard from von Stauffenberg was a colonel on the staff of the German High Command, where he had immediate access to the Fuehrer. Disillusioned, crippled and resentful, he was the ideal choice for the assassin. ◇

---

sent planes over in groups of twenty or thirty fighter-bombers. They skimmed in over the poplars to drop anti-personnel bombs and strafe our infantry. The bullets raised little puffs of dust as they spattered along the road.

Strafing is not the gay old game that it once was for the Germans. Streams of machine-gun bullets met the planes and I saw one suddenly plummet, flaming, into the midst of a field populated by angry cows and angrier American soldiers.

AMERICANS USE PLANES, TOO

Once three Mustangs dropped out of the sun on two Focke-Wulfs. The German planes were smoking when all five aircraft disappeared in the distance. This was all very nice, but, as one infantryman said while we lay in a ditch, "it sure scares hell out of you."

It seems unlikely that the Allies will be able to draw a noose around the Germans in the salient. The enemy formations there are first-class troops with plenty of mechanized equipment, which should enable them to withdraw swiftly. Some movement out of the salient has already been reported by our observation planes. ◇

OUR SPEARHEADS CUT UP GERMANS IN BRITTANY
Columns 75 Miles From Brest and 38 Miles From St. Nazaire

DRIVE AT FURIOUS PACE
Germans Report Withdrawal Between Vire and Caen After Fierce Fighting

By The Associated Press.

SUPREME HEADQUARTERS, Allied Expeditionary Force, Aug. 5—United States tank columns, dashing across Brittany to sever the peninsula, raced to within thirty-eight miles of St. Nazaire today, and other armored forces were within seventy-five miles of the great port of Brest, while comrades guarding their flank swept eastward unopposed across the plains in a new drive toward Paris.

Two columns were approaching the German U-boat base at St. Nazaire, and also the Loire River port of Nantes. One of the columns was thirty-eight miles from St. Nazaire in the vicinity of Derval; another, forty miles from Nantes, was west of Chateaubriant.

[The Vichy radio, in a broadcast heard Saturday by the Ministry of Information in London, said an American armored spearhead was only eighteen miles from Nantes, according to The Associated Press.] An Associated Press battlefield dispatch said the American advance southeastward had engulfed Fougeres, twenty-three miles southeast of Avranches and twenty-seven miles northeast of Rennes.

MOVE ON ST. MALO

Two other American forces were moving on St. Malo port on the northern coast of the Brittany Peninsula, one moving up on each side of the St. Malo estuary. Each column gained six miles yesterday and was only seven miles from the port city.

Tank spearheads thundered through the ripped-open defenses of Brittany so fast that they were a good twenty-four hours ahead of all official reports, and they were followed by speeding columns of trucks bearing the infantry.

The Germans, admitting setbacks wholesale, said the Americans had reached a point sixty miles west of Brittany's capital of Rennes, which fell only yesterday, and were within seventy-five miles of Brest, the second port of France.

Front line reports said forces driving for St. Nazaire had passed Pipriac and that the columns advancing in the Chateaubriant area had swept beyond Bain-de-Bretagne.

Pontivy and Loudeac were reported to have been passed by the forces rushing for Brest.

STRIKE OUT TOWARD PARIS

But the surprising development of the day came when American forces, moving to guard the left flank of this great force pouring down from Normandy, ranged out southeast of Avranches feeling for a German western flank that was not there.

The Americans apparently had two choices, both possibly disastrous for the Germans: To head directly eastward toward Paris, or to strike northeastward and cut behind the Germans who have been containing the British and Canadian forces along the Orne River. ◇

ALLIES IN FLORENCE; FOE WRECKS BRIDGES

By The Associated Press.

ROME, Aug. 4—Allied troops hammered through the last German defenses before the great Tuscan art center of Flor-
ence today and sent patrols stabbing into the heart of the historic city as far as the Arno River, beyond which the Germans had withdrawn after destroying five of six bridges spanning the wide stream.

The only bridge spared by the Germans was the historic Ponte Vecchio—"old bridge"—which they blocked effectively by demolishing houses at both ends. The bridge, regarded as a priceless example of Tuscan building, is lined on either side with craftsmen's shops and is ❯

familiar to thousands of tourists from all over the world.

Incensed at the destruction of the bridges of the city after the Germans had declared it open, Allied headquarters issued an official statement saying:

"The enemy has taken advantage of the situation, knowing full well that our undisputed air power could not be used to destroy the bridges in Florence behind him (while the Germans still were on the south bank of the Arno) without damage to architectural buildings of the city.

"He has thus enjoyed unlimited use of bridges over the Arno and has seen fit, when outfought south of the city, to destroy bridges of military value, to deny us use of bridges which up to now he has enjoyed."

ACT OF 'SADISTIC IMAGINATION'

The statement added that military bridges could be quickly thrown across the Arno inside Florence and that the destruction would not hold up the Allied advance for long or have any bearing on future operations.

The Allied statement threw but little light on the military situation inside Florence—not saying whether enemy troops had withdrawn entirely from the northern part of the city—but continued at length on German vandalism.

It called the "wanton destruction" of bridges "just another example of Field Marshal Albert Kesselring's order to his troops to carry out demolitions with sadistic imagination."

"No doubt those responsible for allowing Rome's bridges to remain intact have been reprimanded by the Germans and even stronger measures were taken to insure that the bridges in Florence should not fall into Allied hands and so be preserved for posterity," the statement said.

After yesterday's concerted advance by British, New Zealand and South African troops south and southwest of Florence, South African units crashed into the outskirts early today and sent patrols probing to the river bank. There was no indication they encountered resistance within the city.

German guns were reported flashing, however, from heights behind the city which comprise the first defenses of the enemy's so-called Gothic Line. Prior to the Eighth Army's entry into the city, Allied artillery had shelled crossings of the Arno just west of Florence.

FLORENCE'S HISTORIC BRIDGES

Historic bridges at Florence that dispatches indicate were destroyed by the Germans included the Ponte alle Grazie or Rubaconte, built in 1237 and modernized in 1874; the Ponte Santa Trinita, erected in 1252 and rebuilt in 1567–70; the Ponte alla Carraia, built 1218–20, destroyed by a flood in 1333, restored in 1337, partly rebuilt in 1559 and widened in 1867.

The two other spans of the five apparently wrecked were the Ponte in Ferro, built in 1836–37, and Ponte Sospeso, which stand at each end of the town bordering the Arno. ◇

AUGUST 6, 1944

PARTISANS CLAIM MUCH OF WARSAW

By SYDNEY GRUSON
By Wireless to The New York Times.

LONDON, Aug. 5—Detailed operational reports reaching the Polish Government today said a large part of Warsaw was in the hands of General Bor's underground forces, but as the Germans threw tanks and planes against the uprising grave concern was expressed in London that it must fail for lack of arms if the Russian assault on the city was delayed many more days.

Reports from the Russian front indicated that a halt had been made in the frontal attack on Warsaw while Red Army columns were reaching for Warka, thirty-five miles south, in a bypassing maneuver.

Polish underground forces were reported to have seized the East and Vilna railway stations (1) and Marszalkowska Street (2), the chief north-west thoroughfare, and to be attacking the main station. Their capture of the central post office, power station and gas works (3) had previously been announced. They were said to control almost all the western and central stations of the city despite German counter-attacks and bombings.

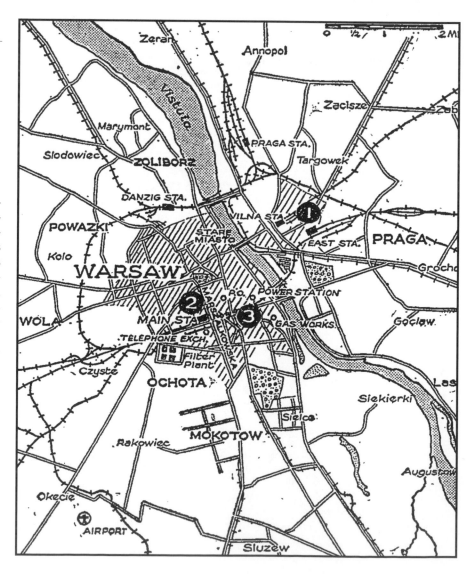

'Amphibious Miracle of Our Time'

Gen. Alexander Vandegrift tells how, in two years since he led
the Marines to victory in the Battle of Guadalcanal, we have evolved
a landing technique that cannot be stopped

JUST two years ago—a scant, incredible two years ago—we embarked on the first American ground offensive of the war. We undertook on a shoestring, so to speak, an amphibious operation against an enemy who, on the record, was the world's amphibious master of the day. Guadalcanal was a gamble, and no one knew it better than those of us who went in. But the gamble at Guadalcanal has swelled into the sure thing at Normandy and Guam. From our do-or-die beginning we have developed a great amphibious machine the power of which has amazed the warring world.

At Guadalcanal we concentrated our total effort on the single objective and still were outnumbered and outgunned by the enemy on land, in the surrounding sea and in the air. We moved in for the fight not with fear but with abundant anxiety. Less than two years later we threw overwhelming forces against both of our enemies almost simultaneously in amphibious attacks on opposite sides of the earth, and we moved in for both fights with utter confidence. There can remain no doubt anywhere, least of all in Germany and Japan, as to who now calls the amphibious tune and wields the weapons of decisive might. Normandy and Saipan have brought the realization home where it hurts most and with graphic effect. Japanese war lords who not long ago were strutting in the glory of their Pacific conquests have been ousted from power. The Fuehrer who assured his armies they would never have to fight on two fronts now faces insurrection of ominous scope among his own disillusioned armed forces.

Little did the enemy realize on Aug. 7, 1942, that the day of the turning point had come. Even as our men poured ashore to confront the surprised garrisons on Tulagi and Guadalcanal, the Japanese High Command expressed genuine confidence that we could be dislodged. Let us contrast what we threw against them then with what we can throw against them now, and we shall see why.

The Japanese commanders knew our covering fleet was relatively meager, but they did not know it was so sparse that after the battles off Guadalcanal in November, 1942, Admiral Halsey had only one aircraft carrier (which had been hit), one battleship, one cruiser and some destroyers. The Japanese knew that we lacked sufficient carrier-based and land-based planes to hold a continuous cover over our ground operations, and in the early stages they made vicious use of that advantage. But at Normandy and in the latest Pacific operations our naval and air forces have maintained complete domination over the battle areas and have been seriously challenged at sea only once in twenty months—at Saipan.

At Saipan, as Secretary Forrestal has pointed out, a great supporting fleet boldly stood guard off the island for more than one month, daring the enemy navy to attempt to interfere. Even though the fleet was 1,200 miles from its nearest base and 3,250 miles from Pearl Harbor, carrier-based aircraft held an ironclad umbrella over the invasion throughout the month of hostilities. Obviously the number of aircraft carriers taking part was large. It has been announced that we have at least one hundred carriers operating in the Pacific. And in November, 1942. Admiral Halsey was defending Guadalcanal with one damaged carrier.

Our amphibious troops at Guadalcanal were well trained, as well trained as any assault troops of this war. The Marine Corps has traditionally been the land arm of the Navy, and so we had studied the techniques of ship-to-shore attack and had equipped and trained our men for just such a task before this nation went to war. However, the number of men thus trained was not large and while our equipment was the best at that time, it was rudimentary in many ways compared with what we have now.

Wooden ramp boats and tank lighters were the major means of carrying men and equipment to the beaches. Tanks were few. Heavy equipment came in slowly. There were times, after we moved inland, when we could have used more supplies and ammunition than we had at hand.

In the past two months we have smitten the Axis with thousands of superbly trained amphibious troops in four big offensives which, in terms of coordinated pressure, were practically concurrent—Normandy, Saipan, New Guinea and Guam. In no instance has a force been put ashore which was not wholly adequate in size for the job. This of course, takes into account the fact that the French invasion was a combined British-Canadian-American strike.

In the two years since Guadalcanal an amazing variety of special landing craft has been developed to meet the needs of transporting men and material in these massive sea-borne invasions. Tracked landing vehicles now carry waves of assault troops over offshore reef formations on which the Japanese had depended to make long stretches of their island coastlines safe. The garrison on Saipan might well have expected us to avoid the southwestern coast of the island because of the treacherous reefs which fenced it in. But our forces went ashore there and while the securing of the beachhead was far from easy, it was firmly done before the defenders could mass the strength necessary for a major attempt to break our grip.

Tracked vehicles—amphibious tanks and tractors, armed and unarmed,   ▶

Apparently in full control of Warsaw's southern and central districts, the underground army, General Bor indicated in dispatches to his government, nevertheless had failed to hold the Kierbedz and Poniatowski Bridges, the only arteries across the Vistula River by which the Germans can keep supplies moving to the forces facing the Russians east of the Polish capital.

German efforts in the Warsaw fighting apparently were being concentrated on keeping control of the bridges and the city's most important thoroughfare, the Jerusalem Alley, which runs east-west and connects with the Poniatowski Bridge.

RAF DROPS WEAPONS

The underground army has been supplied mainly with British arms dropped by the Royal Air Force, but because of the method involved supplies have been necessarily minor compared with the Poles' needs. These have been augmented by what the Poles saved from their 1939 defeat and by what they have stolen and bought from the Germans. There is no indication that the Russians have given them arms, since they are opposed to the Polish London Government, which is acknowledged by the underground.

The Poles, it was said here tonight, timed their rising in the expectation of an imminent Russian assault on Warsaw. Bloody consequences for the Poles are foreseen here if the uprising fails. ◆

bearing both men and material—have become increasingly important in our ship-to-shore pushes, especially in the Pacific. Large amphibious craft which can carry men and machines from the embarking point over sea directly to the objective have come into wide use. Landing Craft Infantry and Landing Craft Tanks are two of many types of such vessels. Their shallow draft enables them to push their snouts so close to the beach that their disgorged men can wade and vehicles can roll from ship to shore. When the terrain permits, it is usually desirable to send tanks ashore as early in the landing as possible. From these large craft a surprisingly comfortable number of tanks can be put to work on enemy emplacements in a surprisingly brief period of time.

Those of us who watched the pre-invasion shelling and bombing of Guadalcanal thought we were seeing a deluxe show of fireworks, but actually we were seeing only a sample of the mighty bombardments to come. The relentless seventeen-day softening-up recently applied to Guam was beyond compare in the books of amphibious attack. We had ships and planes and shells and bombs for the job in such quantities as the Japanese never believed possible a few months ago.

There are many who seem to think it the duty of a pre-invasion bombardment to knock out all defending personnel, guns and emplacements so completely that the invading troops need only walk in and run up the flag. I will say that never once in the Pacific war to date has a pre-landing bombardment failed to do all that the Marine commanders expected it to do. But we have never yet taken the objective without a ground fight when there were troops there to defend it.

Bombardments will take out the large gun positions; but, no matter how long or intense, they will not take out all machine-gun positions and mortars. They cannot. It is the same in a wholly ground operation. You have heard of artillery being lined up hub to hub and fired until the enemy lines seemed pulverized, as at El Alamein, St Lô and numerous times in Russia. Yet when the infantry went forward they were invariably met by machine-gun fire. They found part of their enemy had survived and had come out of their holes, shaken but very much alive, ready to man their guns.

The amphibious successes of North Africa, Sicily, Italy and France may or may not be the whole of seaborne operations necessary to the reduction of the Reich. But of this we can be sure: if or when further amphibious operations

take place, the enemy will be as incapable of stemming the flood of Allied power as he was on the beaches of Normandy.

There can be no doubt that amphibious operations in the Pacific will continue until the day of final Japanese collapse.

In each succeeding ship-to-shore operation to date we have thrown more physical weight against the enemy's fortifications than before. There is no reason to believe this will not continue to be the rule.

If he is unable to stop us now what can he expect to do as our ever-increasing power drives his fleets from the seas, his armies from the land and his planes from the skies? His dilemma is complete: he dares not stand up and fight us toe to toe, but the longer he waits the stronger we become.

Japan's war lords expected to win the war in the Pacific by amphibious supremacy; Hitler's gang believed that Allied troops never could return by sea to the soil of western Europe. Today—two swift years after Guadalcanal—seaborne Allied forces are striking straight for the heart of Germany and the vitals of Japan. This is the amphibious miracle of our time. ◇

AUGUST 10, 1944

GEN. EISENHOWER MOVES TO FRANCE

Personal Headquarters Set Up in Normandy —Shift Made in Mediterranean

Combined American Press Dispatch.

GENERAL EISENHOWER'S ADVANCE COMMAND POST, Normandy, Aug. 9 (AP)—Gen. Dwight D. Eisenhower, Supreme Commander of the Allies' Forces, has established his headquarters on the Continent to maintain the closest possible contact with the Allies' fast-rolling offensive. The Supreme Command Headquarters unit, it was announced tonight, was moved to Normandy by air during the past few days. Officers and enlisted personnel—including Wacs—are living in tents in a camouflaged area under constant patrol by heavily armed military police.

The general is near an airfield from which he makes speedy trips daily for personal conferences with Gen. Sir Bernard L. Montgomery and Lieut. Gen. Omar N. Bradley. Instantaneous telephone communication with Supreme Headquarters in London is available from the general's trailer living quarters, which is under twenty-four-hour guard by M. P.'s who squat in a dugout behind a machine gun.

General Eisenhower's aide, Comdr. Harry C. Butcher, former Columbia Broadcasting System executive of New York, sleeps in a tent a few yards away. ◇

AUGUST 10, 1944

NEW ALLIED VICTORIES ENDANGER THE ENEMY IN FRANCE

By E. C. DANIEL
By Cable to The New York Times.

SUPREME HEADQUARTERS Allied Expeditionary Force, Aug. 10—American tanks have crashed into Le Mans and beyond in their drive toward Paris. The German radio reported last night that the fast motorized forces were only eighty-seven miles from the capital, though the latest dispatch from the American front put the distance at approximately 100 miles.

[An Allied spokesman said that the German report was undoubtedly true, if not even on the conservative side, in view of the average rate of advance, The United Press reported.]

South of the main thrust past Le Mans toward Chartres and the Seine

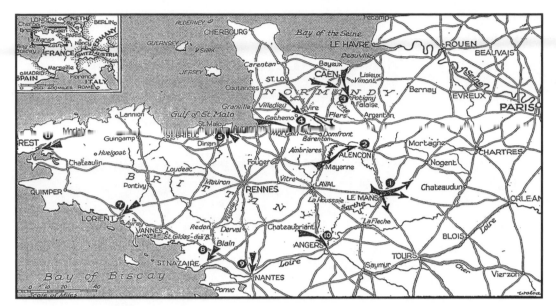

The Americans captured Le Mans (1) and were reported only eighty-seven miles from Paris as spearheads thrust toward Tours, Orléans and Chartres. Alençon (2) was threatened by another column. The Canadians advancing below Caen were only five miles from Falaise (3), forcing the Germans to pull back from the Orne, to the west. The Americans advanced near the Vire-Mortain road (4), but Mortain's fate remained in doubt. In Brittany, the Americans won St. Malo (5) and launched a heavy attack against Brest (6). They were still in the outskirts of Lorient (7) and no progress toward St. Nazaire (8) was reported. Our forces were said to have fought their way into Nantes (9) and Angers (10).

River, the Americans have spread out protective wings toward the Loire River, driving one column into the streets of Angers, fifty miles southwest of Le Mans on the Sarthe River, just above the Loire. A report that a second column had entered Nantes, a major port near the mouth of the river, has not been confirmed here. [Nantes has been captured, The United Press said.]

ST. MALO CAPTURED

On the north coast of Brittany, the Americans finally captured St. Malo. The German garrison of Brest refused an invitation to surrender yesterday and the Americans were assaulting the outskirts, while a second American tank force was reported from the field to be driving to their assistance from twenty-three miles away. [The last ramparts were under assault, The United Press reported.] Resistance was continuing at Dinan in the north and Lorient in the south, on which two American columns were converging from the east and northeast. No progress toward St. Nazaire was reported.

While the spearhead from Le Mans proceeded, evidently without encountering any well-organized German defense system, the Canadian forces bore down the road from Caen in the north to a point within five miles of Falaise through the best constructed German line in Normandy. Between Le Mans and Falaise a large portion of the tattered German Seventh Army was in danger of being trapped unless it desisted from counterattacks and pulled back.

The Allies' apparent objective is to decimate this army, the only sizable German field force southwest of the Seine River, and to merge the northern and southern branches of their own offensive, perhaps somewhere in the Chartres-Dreux area, for the storming of Paris. A Royal Air Force commander whose planes swept behind the battle lines yesterday reported that the enemy was tending to move east and southeast toward the Seine. The gap between the Seine and the Loire is already under persistent bombardment to discourage reinforcement or escape.

The Germans reported that the clean-up of Brittany was being left to infantry and that the tanks that had broken into the peninsula were being concentrated for a drive to the east. Ten divisions constitute the American striking force, the Paris radio said.

With unexplained persistence, the remnants of four German armored divisions continued to fight back twenty miles east of Avranches, where the Allies' line is thinnest, and retook Mortain yesterday for the third time. A "very strong force" of Germans was operating between Mortain and Vire, to the northeast, an American officer reported. [Each side held part of Mortain, other dispatches said.]

Northwest of Mortain, the Germans made several counterattacks at Chérence-le-Roussel. To the north, they struck around Gathemo with twenty-five tanks, five of which were knocked out. Between Mortain and Barenton, to the southeast, the American armor encountered resistance. Nevertheless, the Americans closing down on the Vire-Mortain road occupied three villages yesterday.

The German report that the Americans were within eighty-seven miles of Paris would place the advance elements in the vicinity of La Terte-Bernard, on the main railway and road through Chartres to Paris. [Other dispatches quoted German reports that the American drives were threatening Alençon, Orléans and Tours.]

In front of Le Mans, chief German resistance came from occasional strafing aircraft and sporadic fire from 88-mm. guns. The Germans acknowledged yesterday that no counter-attack on "any considerable scale" had been made against the American advance. To the north, the Canadian and British advance proceeded more slowly but crashed through the first and second lines of fixed defenses and forced the Germans to begin withdrawing between the Orne and Laize Rivers south of Caen. The Canadians, with British support on their left and right, were thrusting toward Falaise astride the road south from Caen, with two armored spearheads on a three-mile front.

As they drove within five miles of Falaise at Potigny, German tanks began to form up in the Laison River valley, one and a half miles to the east. Rocket-firing Typhoons ripped into them.

According to the latest reports the Allies' and the Germans' armor had clashed near St. Quentin de la Roche.

The Canadians plunging through the built-up German defenses found a network of inter-connecting trenches and dug-outs, reminiscent of those that their fathers had stormed around Amiens just twenty-six years ago. Clusters of machine guns, mortars and the ubiquitous 88's defended these lines.

West of this battleground the German forces were falling back under the threat of being outflanked by the bridgehead thrown across the Orne by the British Second Army south of the Grimbosq Forest. The Germans used most of their infantry and armor in that area in an attempt to batter back the tiny 300-acre bridgehead, but the British forces continued to ford the river and yesterday, behind a storm of 6,000 heavy mortar shells and artillery fire, struck out to enlarge it. This force was driving to link up across the Laize with the Canadians.

Most of the villages immediately along the east side of the Caen-Falaise road were overrun by the Canadians as they advanced throughout Tuesday night and yesterday. They were supported by the British to the northeast. Heavy fighting was reported last night just south of St. Sylvain.

The Allies' air forces continued their hot and close support of the drives on all fronts in improved weather. One wing of RAF Typhoons had shot up sixty-one tanks by early afternoon yesterday. On the previous day the United States Ninth Air Force claimed fifty-one tanks destroyed during 1,000 flights, besides other damage. ◊

AUGUST 15, 1944

WHERE THE ALLIES HAVE STRUCK NEW INVASION BLOW

FALAISE GAP CLOSING
Bombs, Shells Hit Foe Trying to Hold Open Highway of Escape

By The United Press.

WASHINGTON, Aug. 15—American, British and French troops are landing on the southern coast of France, a special communiqué from Allied headquarters in Italy announced today.

The communiqué, released simultaneously in Italy and by the War Department here at 6:10 A.M. EWT, reported that the landing forces were strongly supported by Allied air forces.

American, British and French fleets also are participating in the landing operations, which were preceded by heavy Allied bombings of German defenses on the Riviera last night.

The communiqué said:

AUGUST 17, 1944

PATTON LASHES OUT
Canadians in Falaise—Gap Cut To 6 Miles, but Many Escape

By E. C. DANIEL
By Cable to The New York Times.

SUPREME HEADQUARTERS, Allied Expeditionary Force, Aug. 17—In another swift and unexpected thrust, hard-riding

General George S. Patton in Normandy, August 16, 1944.

Lieut. Gen. George S. Patton Jr. was reported by the Germans yesterday to have whipped his tanks within a little more than forty miles of Paris in an effort to outrun and outflank German forces fleeing toward the Seine from the Argentan-Falaise trap. Reports from the front indicated the gap had been cut to six miles.

Leaving clean-up operations in Normandy largely to other commanders and to history, General Patton, according to the German Transocean News Agency, was pushing his armored forces along three roads into Chartres, forty-four miles southwest of Paris.

FIGHTING REPORTED NEAR DREUX
Earlier yesterday American Third Army tanks were reported on the authority of the German High Command to he engaged in "heavy fighting" against the Germans in the "Chartres-Dreux area." Dreux is forty-two miles west of Paris and only twenty-two miles from the Seine whose protection the defeated Germans in northwestern France are seeking.

As fighting ran fast and free again east of Alençon, the Allies imposed a ban once more on mention of place names and there consequently was no confirmation of the German reports. One veiled dispatch from the front, however, asserted that American forces had "another great day."

General Patton's sweep around the German flank, said Capt. Ludwig Sertorius, German commentator, possibly is planned to isolate German armies in Normandy from Paris and push them back into the estuary of the Seine. The estuary is some sixty miles down the river from Dreux.

There were indications from the front yesterday that the Germans were lining up barges on the Seine and organizing a hazardous evacuation across the river. If German reports are true the scene may be set there for a new battle of annihilation. All major Seine bridges northwest of Paris have either been broken by air attacks or are under repair.

The pocket west of Falaise was further compressed yesterday by concerted pressure all around the perimeter. Signs of disintegration inside the pocket increased. Clerks, cooks and other services troops were armed and put into the rearguards. The remnants of twelve units were counted in a single British operation, indicating all leftovers had been scraped together for a final fling.

Estimates of the number of prisoners that finally would be counted still were being scaled down, however. The latest guess from the British front was 40,000. At United States First Army headquarters it was stated officially that troops of eleven German divisions had been caught. What is left of these battered units remains to be determined.

Eight thousand prisoners so far have been penned and last night they were still coming back from the front by truckload. But still more also escaped yesterday under the cover of a morning fog that hampered air attacks. At one time 200 German transports were counted east of Falaise. ◊

"Today American, British and French troops strongly supported by Allied air forces are being landed by American, British and French fleets on the southern coast of France."

A statement by Gen. Sir Henry Maitland Wilson, supreme Allied commander in the Mediterranean theatre, addressed to the people of France, said the objective of the new invasion was to "join up with the Allied armies advancing from Normandy."

Rome broadcasts said the Allied landings began at 8 A.M., Rome time. The area bombed by our air forces included St. Tropez, St. Raphael, Marseille, Toulon and between Nice and Cannes.

The assault is meeting with initial success, reports from the beachhead said. Seven waves of infantry had been put ashore in the first two hours and one company reached its first objective within one hour after hitting the beach, the reports said. ◊

AUGUST 18, 1944

PARIS HEARS GUNS OF ITS LIBERATORS

By JOHN MacCORMAC
By Wireless to The New York Times.

LONDON, Aug. 17—One of the most uplifting items of news that exiled Frenchmen have heard since France fell they learned today from the German conqueror. It was that Paris today, for the first time since 1940, could hear the intermittent thunder of approaching gunfire.

"The roar of battle is approaching the French capital" was the first headline in the Paris radio news bulletin. The German Transocean News Agency announced that "the whole aspect of the capital is becoming that of a frontline city. For the first time the German command has appealed to the population to remain calm."

Tonight over the American forces radio a Supreme Headquarters spokesman told Paris policemen not to leave the capital "under any pretext" and to hide if Joseph Darnand, Vichy Secretary of State

for the Maintenance of Order, ordered them to Nancy, for the "day is not far off when you will have to rise and chase out the enemy and his accomplices."

Whether the American tank forces approaching the city will attempt to enter the city or outflank it, and whether or not the capital is their immediate objective, seemed to matter little tonight. What the news boded was the early liberation of Paris and that, to Frenchmen in London, was electrifying. Paris is not the whole of France but it is France's heart. "What are they saying in Paris?" used to be the chief anxiety of Napoleon on his campaigns.

It is in Paris that revolutions start and stop and wars begin and are ended. It was from there that Gallieni's taxi-cab army issued to win the Battle of the Marne that saved France, when in 1940 Paris was abandoned without a shot the doom of France was sealed. The tale since then for Paris has been one of humiliation and hardship—Hitler's posturings beside the tomb of Napoleon, bombings at the hands of France's friends, starvation and impoverishment by her captors.

But Paris, unlike Vichy, has never accepted the German. The underground there has remained strong. If the city is quiet, it is not because of German appeals or threats, but because Gen. Charles de Gaulle this week instructed the city to await his orders.

Electric current is now available for Parisians only between 10:30 P.M. and midnight, and from today there will be no more gas. Paris must therefore be supplied with meals from central communal kitchens.

The food position is reported by the Germans to be so serious that peasants have been asked to speed the threshing of wheat and cart it into the capital. The city, though hungry, is orderly. It is disciplining itself, since the Paris police struck against the appointment of an unpopular high police official.

Since the Metro, the only remaining public means of transportation, is now shut down, Parisians went to work today on foot or by pushbike after a three-day holiday marking the Feast of the Assumption. The "people listening to a concert in the square in front of the Palais Royale were in high spirits," the German Transocean news agency said yesterday, but it did not say why. ◊

AUGUST 24, 1944

FRENCH DIVISION SENT INTO PARIS

French Armored Division Sent into Paris by Bradley

The following dispatch by a representative of the Columbia Broadcasting System, the first American correspondent to enter Paris, was cabled to London and broadcast from there.

By CHARLES COLLINGWOOD

PARIS, Aug. 23—The French Second Armored Division entered Paris today after the Parisians had risen as one man to beat down the German troops who had garrisoned the city.

It was the people of Paris who really won back their city. It all happened with fantastic suddenness.

The American Army was occupied with the drive through Evreux to the mouth of the Seine, after which it planned to invest Paris. But yesterday a Frenchman burst into Lieut. Gen. Omar N. Bradley's headquarters. He was the chief of the French Forces of the Interior in Paris and he had a staggering, incredible story to tell.

He said that he had concluded an armistice with the German forces in Paris. The people of Paris had risen and had so hounded the Germans that the German commander had requested an armistice. He wanted to withdraw troops from the road blocks west and south of Paris, where they had been facing the Americans, and pass them through the city.

The armistice was to expire at noon today.

This news caused a sensation in General Bradley's headquarters because, although we had known that rioting had been going on in Paris since Saturday, we had not known that things had gone so far that obviously the French had given the Germans a terrific beating.

The whole operation was geared to the complete encirclement of the Germans west of the Seine, but General Bradley decided that we must go into Paris. It was short notice, for the troops had to be ready to enter at noon today. He ordered the French Second Armored Division out of the line and told it to start moving east toward Paris.

Certain American forces were sent ›

the same way. On a moment's notice the whole machinery was set in motion to occupy one of the world's largest cities.

It is no mean responsibility. Paris is in desperate straits. It is estimated that it needs immediately 3,000 tons of food and 3,000 tons of coal. After that, there must be a huge and steady supply.

But the decision had to be made, if only as a tribute to the tremendous fact that the French had reconquered their own capital. Every hand was raised against the enemy. For the first time in this war, the inhabitants of a city have wrested it from the enemy.

Paris would have fallen to our arms, but every American soldier in France would rather have had it this way. Paris, queen of cities, was freed by its own citizens, who proved that there was no such thing as defeat for them. ◊

AUGUST 30, 1944

U.S., Britain and Russia Agree On Outline For Security League

By JAMES B. RESTON
Special to The New York Times.

WASHINGTON, Aug. 29—The chairmen of the United States, British and Soviet delegations at the Washington Conversations on International Organization announced today that they had reached "general agreement" on the structure and aims of an international league to maintain peace and security.

In a general press conference at the Dumbarton Oaks Mansion Edward R. Stettinius Jr., Under-Secretary of State; Sir Alexander Cadogan, British Permanent Under-Secretary of State for Foreign Affairs, and Andrei A. Gromyko, Russian Ambassador, did not discuss the substance of the proposed security league or the means by which they would put force behind the league, but they made it clear that there was no disagreement among them on the creation of an assembly of all peace-loving powers, a world council of a restricted number of powers and an international court of justice.

"After a week of discussion," a joint communiqué stated, "the three heads of delegations are happy to announce that there is general agreement among them to recommend that the proposed International Organization for Peace and Security should provide for:

AUGUST 26, 1944

DELIRIOUS FRENCH MOB LIBERATORS
Milling Throngs Cry 'Thanks!' for Hours

By MAURICE DESJARDINS
Canadian Press War Correspondent.

PARIS, Aug. 25—For the last six hours we have been watching a tumultuous demonstration of gratitude by the liberated people of Paris.

After four years of German occupation, Parisians are putting on a show of sincere unbridled joy.

Thousands of delirious, happy people are massed along the boulevards and have been yelling hour after hour: "Merci, merci!"

This afternoon Gen. Charles de Gaulle drove past in a limousine and the cheers reached a new crescendo. Twenty-year-old patriots who were seeing him for the first time cried like babies.

One wonders when the fierceness of the demonstrations will abate. It shows no signs of doing so yet.

Upon approaching Paris this afternoon we saw two tired Germans in an American jeep. There was a crowd around them. Young French girls were spitting in one German's face. He just grinned sheepishly. ◊

The crowd cheering de Gaulle on rue de Rivoli, at the corner of the Hotel de Ville, during the liberation of Paris in 1944.

The delegates to the Dumbarton Oaks Peace Conference.

"1. An assembly composed of representatives of all peace-loving nations based on the principle of sovereign equality.

"2. A council composed of a smaller number of members in which the principal States will be joined by a number of other states to be elected periodically.

"3. Effective means for the peaceful settlement of disputes, including an international court of justice for the adjudication of justifiable questions, and also the application of such other means as may be necessary for maintenance of peace and security." ◆

SEPTEMBER 1, 1944

FIRST ARMY SWEEP BECOMES A ROMP
Infantrymen Stay In Trucks as They Rush Onward After Runaway Germans

By HAROLD DENNY
By Wireless to The New York TIMES.

WITH UNITED STATES FIRST ARMY in France, Aug. 31—Our drive is sweeping on at a breathless, incredible rate. Never in all warfare have troops advanced so swiftly and with such power. The Germans wanted a blitz war and now they have it.

The battle has become a full pursuit now, with our armored columns slashing deeply into the enemy's rear ranks and our infantry charging in trucks. So utter has become the enemy's defeat that our troops seldom need to dismount and deploy.

American troops are approaching the Ardennes Forest and already have forced several crossings of the Meuse River. They overran at a bound the Villers-Coterets Forest, scene of some of the bitterest fighting in World War I.

Vast quantities of munitions and of German transport are being captured with almost every hour of the present battle. Two airfields and supply dumps were seized intact near Fismes before the Germans had an opportunity to destroy them.

FIVE TRAINS DESTROYED

Five German railway trains carrying personnel and every kind of equipment from collaborationist women who dared not remain in France to Tiger tanks on flatcars have been destroyed as they tried to escape.

I came across the smoking wreckage of one today at Braine, east of Soissons. This train had consisted of a locomotive and twenty-three cars and coaches. Among the cars were four carrying Panther tanks. At the rear was anti-aircraft guns mounted on a flatcar. In between were cars carrying personnel, including a score of officers and women companions, one carload of liquor in barrels, and one carload of perfume. It is extraordinary the kind of things the Germans are trying to get out of this country.

An American airplane had spotted this train and had radioed an armored column in the neighborhood. Our armor sped down the highway to a point where it intersected the railway line. There it waited. When the train approached the crossing our tanks opened fire. The first shots riddled the locomotive and it blew up. The German tanks on the flat cars were manned. The crews swung their guns around and opened fire on our tanks, causing some casualties.

TANKS ON CARS FIGHT BACK

Perhaps never before had there been a battle like it, tanks on board a train fighting tanks on a road. It lasted only a few minutes. All four German tanks were hit repeatedly and all set on fire, Their ammunition blew up and then their gasoline. The crews never got out.

Our tanks turned their fire on each succeeding car and coach in rotation and riddled and set fire to every one. Many Germans were killed. Some fled to a railway embankment on the far side and were either killed or captured. And some died in the flames of the perfume, which burned furiously and with an unpleasant odor.

Now that we are immensely strong, General Bradley is turning the German defeat into a rout.

As one high First Army officer said tonight: "The boche is in a state of disorganization beyond comparison. The drive of the American First Army is actually a pursuit and exploitation."

The Germans have had to flee without a fight from geographically excellent lines on which they undoubtedly had expected to make a stand. That "defence in depth" of which Adolf Hitler and Field Marshal Gen. Erwin Rommel boasted before D-day has proved to be little more than lines on a map and much of it is already behind us now, with little fighting to take it.

The fighting since the liberation of Paris has been over battlefields of World War I, on many of which American troops shed their blood. This fighting has swept in an unchecked torrent across the Marne, Aisne, Ourcq and Vesle Rivers, and now has broached the Meuse.

MARNE JUST DAY'S BATTLE

The third battle of the Marne, along whose banks so many thousands died in 1914 and 1918, was but a day's episode in the present drive. Our engineers flung hasty bridges across that deep, still, little river and our tanks and infantry and artillery poured over it without pause. Town after town and city after city has been set free without marring beyond that of smashed German vehicles that clutter their streets where our forces caught and destroyed them.

I rode peaceably into Reims today and stopped for a quick cup of champagne, while crowds thronged the streets as on a holiday. The Reims Cathedral, where Joan of Arc crowned Charles and where so many other French Kings were crowned, has suffered no further damage since its vandalous pounding by German artillery for four years during World War I. It is just as it had been restored by John D. Rockefeller's beneficence. Many citizens were praying in thankfulness there today. ◆

Invasion of Reich Forecast In Eisenhower War Review

By Cable to The New York Times.

SUPREME HEADQUARTERS, Allied Expeditionary Force, Aug. 31—Gen. Dwight D. Eisenhower, supreme commander of the Allied expeditionary forces in France, forecast the invasion of Germany today when he declared that the American and British armies in France must follow the Germans into the Reich to defeat them decisively and completely.

Brimming with confidence, General Eisenhower declared that the campaign in France was five days ahead of schedule. Today on "D plus eighty-five" Allied positions were well in advance of the line where it was expected they would be on "D plus ninety."

Discussing the end of the war the supreme commander said he would stand by his prophecy of last Christmas when he declared that Germany could be beaten in 1944 if all on the battlefield and home fronts did their duty to the full.

MONTGOMERY CALLED GREAT SOLDIER

It is evident that General Eisenhower does not expect the Germans to be able to form a line in France, for he said he expected the American and British groups in the north and the invading forces in the south to continue their rapid progress.

The supreme commander confirmed reports that a new command set-up had been instituted in France under which Lieut. Gen. Omar N. Bradley and Sir Bernard L. Montgomery, just promoted to the rank of field marshal, commanding the Twelfth United States Army Group and Twenty-first British Army Group, respectively, are responsible to him. But he took great pains to explain that this did not mean a demotion for Marshal Montgomery.

Montgomery, who he said was one of the great soldiers of this or any other war, had been entrusted with the execution and direction of the battle in which from July 25 onward the first United States Army broke through west of St. Lô to Avranches and the Third Army exploited the break-through westward to Brest and eastward through Le Mans to the southeast of Paris.

BATTLE JOINTLY PLANNED

The planning of this battle, possibly the decisive one of the campaign in France, had been a joint affair, according to General Eisenhower.

The supreme commander emphasized that anyone who interpreted command changes as a demotion for Marshal Montgomery would not look the facts in the face, and declared that the change was part of a long-arranged plan under which Montgomery and Bradley would take command of the respective Army groups once the Allied forces had broken out of the Cherbourg Peninsula.

This break-out had occurred in a series of engagements starting from St. Lô during which Montgomery had exercised tactical command of the American land forces as well as the command of his own Twenty-first Group. It was the British general's job to coordinate the battle all along the line in Normandy, General Eisenhower said.

Once the break-out from Normandy was completed and the Twelfth Army Group organization activated, the final stage of the Allied command system, which had been settled since last January, was reached, and Eisenhower took over Montgomery's responsibilities for immediate control of the coordination of the Allied armies and Montgomery directed his attention to command of the Twenty-first Army Group.

STATEMENT CLEARS AIR

The statement that Montgomery had executed and directed the operations of both American and British armies in France during the great victories of July and early August was by far the most important news arising as General Eisenhower spoke to 150 newspaper correspondents. The allocation of command during those critical days has been argued over by hypersensitive soldiers and civilians of both nations in the last two weeks in London.

General Eisenhower's statement cleared the air. ◆

PARIS CONTINUES SEIZING SUSPECTS

3,000 to 4,000 Persons Herded into Bicycle Racing Arena To Await Their Trials

By Wireless to The New York Times.

PARIS, Sept. 1—The round-up of collaborationists and those suspected of having been too friendly with the Germans continued today. Already there are some 3,000 or 4,000 suspects interned in the Velodrome d'Hiver, a bicycle-racing arena. They all are awaiting trial. Some of them—perhaps 600—are women. Included among those detained is Sacha Guitry, famous playwright who tells all who will listen that he is being unjustly

Americans Smash Way Across the Moselle; Battle of Reich On

By DREW MIDDLETON
By Cable to The New York Times.

SUPREME HEADQUARTERS, Allied Expeditionary Force, Sept. 7—Mud-stained infantrymen of the American Third Army have fought their way across the Moselle River in face of fierce German fire to strike the first blow in the assault on Germany. They followed in the wake of armored reconnaissance units that darted across the enemy frontier and probed the Siegfried Line's outer works from the border of Luxembourg to a point south of Nancy.

The vanguards of two Allied armies nearest the German frontier to the northwest are moving steadily toward the Reich while infantrymen are mopping up big German pockets to the rear. Yesterday tanks of the American First

detained. According to the guards, he refused for two days to eat with a fork, gobbling his rice by piling it on bread with his fingers.

Many of those who are being detained fear that they will be shot. Actually there does not seem to be much danger of that. With one or two exceptions those gathered up at the Velodrome are small fry. The big shots got out to Germany or into enemy territory before the Allies' armies entered Paris. Most of these people who have been picked up on denunciation of neighbors are people who got to know the Germans, entertained them and accepted favors from them for the most part.

The round-up of suspects was still one of the major preoccupations of Paris today, along with food and transport.

While a demand arose for this new Provisional Government to abrogate the laws of Vichy formally, there was more and more evidence coming to light that the evils of German occupation did not end with the liberation of Paris. For instance, there is a whole section of Paris where the Jews still live in terror in a German-established ghetto.

There is currently a wave of denunciation in Paris. This Government is

A Nazi collaborator being arrested in Paris in August, 1944.

taking steps to see that while justice is administered mere vengeance does not prevail. Gen. Charles de Gaulle is determined that there shall be no terror.

The persons suspected and momentarily interned receive a preliminary trial by a committee of judges. If the judg-

cs find them guilty they are interned for a review of their cases by the Palais de Justice. ◆

Army rumbled across the Meuse at Namur, Dinant and Givet, pushing on north toward Liege and Aachen and in the south across the northern shoulder of the Ardennes Mountains toward a vulnerable section of the Siegfried Line.

FIRST ARMY CAPTURES 25,000

The First Army captured more than 25,000 prisoners in a pocket southwest of Mons on Sept. 3, 4 and 5. Except for the Falaise pocket, this is the largest bag of prisoners taken since the opening of the campaign.

The British Second Army, whose entrance into the Netherlands was confirmed by Supreme Headquarters forty-eight hours after it had been announced by the Premier of that country, also is extending its salient both to the east beyond Louvain and to the west toward Ghent. Ghent is thirty-one miles from the German forts at Zeebrugge, which, in conjunction with those at Flushing, prevent the Allies from using the great port of Antwerp.

The left flank of the British Second Army is moving steadily westward toward the Channel ports, while Canadians and Poles of the Canadian First Army are pushing in from the southeast. The Canadians have glimpsed England from the Channel coast around Calais,

and are pounding the stubborn German garrison in Boulogne. The Poles have smashed forward eight to ten miles from St. Omer to Cassel, seventeen and a half miles from Dunkerque. Three million surrender leaflets have been dropped on garrisons of Le Havre, Boulogne, Calais, Dunkerque and Ostend.

ALLIES ENTER YPRES

Meanwhile reconnaissance elements have pushed into Yprés in Belgium, twenty-six miles southeast of Dunkerque.

There is no longer any doubt that a stern and perhaps costly battle faces the Allies in their operations against the Siegfried Line. The American infantrymen that forced the Moselle were met by very heavy artillery fire while troops of the American First and British Second Armies, moving east, are encountering stiffer resistance as they near the German frontier.

A superiority in tanks has served the Allies well in their exploitation of victories around St. Lô and Caen, but it is clear that this stage of the battle is drawing to its close. For the next few weeks it will be up to the American doughboy and the British Tommy.

The stubborn German resistance in Brest is a reminder of how well the Germans can fight. More than 500 tons of

bombs rained on the city from sixteen waves of Marauders and Havocs yesterday, but the Germans still are holding out defiantly. The ability of these enemy troops to withstand unchallenged air and sea power, while fighting off ground attacks, should be a lesson to those who believe the Siegfried Line can be cracked easily.

AMERICAN BAG NOW 230,000

The American First Army's advance on the Siegfried Line has been speeded by the establishment of the three good bridgeheads across the Meuse at Namur, Dinant and Givet. Late last night armored formations had thrust some miles east, according to reports from the front. The left flank of this advance obviously was aiming at Liege and the open country of the Maastrict appendix. Liege is only twenty-four miles from Aachen in Germany.

The First Army infantry's capture of 25,000 men in the Mons pocket between Sunday and Tuesday brought that Army's total to date to 154,000. Counting the 76,000 Germans captured by the Third Army the American Twelfth Army group has now taken 230,000 German prisoners.

Two divisional commanders, Maj. Gens. Ruediger von Heyking and ⟩

Carl Wahle, were captured in the Mons pocket.

In addition to the heavy blow dealt the waning reserves of German manpower, the final cleaning up of the pocket has another significance. American troops employed there can now be moved eastward to join other units of the First Army in their advance on the Siegfried line. Compeigne and St. Quentin, two of the towns on the borders of the pocket have been liberated, it is believed.

In addition to the great bag of prisoners, fifty tanks and 1,500 other ve-

hicles were captured or destroyed in the final clean-up.

BRITISH DRIVE ON ROTTERDAM

A British armored column that left Brussels at 1 o'clock Tuesday afternoon raced through Louvain, twenty miles to the east, only two hours later. Since then little is known of the column's movements save that it is encountering increased resistance.

Other British troops, probably those that took Antwerp and according to the Dutch-occupied Breda Monday, are

now officially revealed as fighting in the Netherlands. Dutch sources report they have crossed the estuary of the Maas and are approaching Rotterdam.

The Canadian First Army is meeting stiff resistance in three areas. It is being checked at Le Havre and Boulogne and the forces moving on Calais evidently have split up and by-passed the port. Polish armored forces of this Army have struck northward to Yprés, ten miles inside the Belgian border.

The Canadians are now on three sides of Boulogne on a perimeter rough-

---

SEPTEMBER 8, 1944

War Against Robots Is Won; London Halts Evacuations

By E. C. DANIEL
By Wireless to The New York Times.

LONDON, Sept. 7—The second Battle of London has ended in victory—a victory that was in the making even before Allied armies overran the flying-bomb bases in France and Belgium, reducing to impotent pinpricks the effects of Hitler's vaunted Vengeance Weapon Number One.

"Except possibly for a few parting shots, the Battle of London is over," Duncan Sandys, chairman of the British Flying Bomb Counter-Measures Committee and son-in-law of the Prime Minister, told the press Monday.

It was a battle that lasted eighty uneasy days, employed 2,000 barrage balloons, 2,800 guns and vast fleets of Allied planes. The battle also required a wholesale rearrangement of London's entire antiaircraft defense system.

The British Government has signalized London's victory over the flying bombs by suspending tonight the evacuation schemes that are estimated to have taken more than 1,000,000 persons out of the danger zone since June 15.

Within less than one week after the last salvo of flying bombs was fired in London, the capital was already resuming its bustling aspect. Streets once more are crowded at dusk. Queues have reformed in front of movie theatres.

Opera, drama, ballet and musical shows that were driven to the provinces by flying bombs have returned in strength, with twenty theatres open, compared with thirty-four before the flying bombs and ten at the peak of the attack.

The Government, however, still wants thousands to stay away. There are 870,000 houses still awaiting the ministrations of a crew of 60,000 workmen engaged in flying-bomb repairs in London.

Many schools and hospitals have been extensively damaged. Users of these buildings are advised to stay away, and expectant mothers in the last month of pregnancy, as well as the aged, infirm, blind and homeless are still being sent away.

It was a battle in which American airmen and gunners fought side by side with the British to defend the homes in which they had been guests. Americans fought, Mr. Sandys said, "with just as much determination and enthusiasm as if New York or Washington had been the victim."

The result of their combined exertions was that in the last week of the flying bomb attacks only 9 per cent of the robots discharged actually hit London, whose sprawling reaches were their only feasible target. Of the total of 8,000 bombs launched—an average of 100 one-ton bombs a day—2,300 actually reached London, obviously far fewer than the German High Command had expected.

A queue composed mainly of American servicemen, waiting to go into the Windmill Theatre in London for a performance of the "Revudeville", September 1944.

ly two miles from the center of the city. Another force reached Marquise, six miles from Cap Gris Nez.

At Calais Canadian patrols are clearing the coast east and west of the port but have not entered the town itself.

CANADIANS TRAP 50,000

There are 50,000 Germans pinned against the Channel coast and the North Sea. Most of these are in ports where they are resisting stubbornly, but many units are striking northward in the hope they will be able to cross the mouth of

the Scheldt to safety. Some German troops escaped by this route but the number is not large.

Le Havre is garrisoned by 5,000 Germans. Tuesday night they were subjected to a 1,000-ton assault by heavy bombers of the Royal Air Force.

The fighting in front of Le Havre is fierce. British infantry of the Canadian First Army is moving through a strong defensive system of pillboxes, barbed wire and mines.

Pamphlets calling for surrender are being fired into Le Havre by artillery

and dropped by aircraft. These point out the hopelessness the local situation to the enemy and stress that as the war is drawing to a close it is useless to be killed in ineffectual action.

Meanwhile German engineers are destroying port installations in both Boulogne and Calais. The glow of fires can be seen and the thump of explosions heard by watchers on the English coast. German batteries in that area are still firing off their ammunition. Shortly after 8:30 o'clock last evening they opened fire across the Strait of Dover again. ◆

INVASION PLANS UNDISTURBED

This expenditure represented a tremendous wastage of German manpower and materials, which were diverted from the production of orthodox weapons and fortifications. For the Allies, the victory was accomplished without a single sign of faltering in the invasion of western Europe.

Asked whether the V-2—the rocket shell—would introduce a new phase in London's long struggle for survival, Mr. Sandys said:

"I am a little chary of talking about V-2. We do know quite a lot about it." But in any case, he added, the correspondents walking over the rocket sites in France will know a great deal more within a few days.

The youthful chief of the anti-flying bomb command told his fascinating story of the espionage work, secret bombing attacks, scientific research and battle dispositions in a setting that had all the pomp of a victory demonstration. He gave his press conference at the Ministry of Information, with an eighteen-inch model of a flying bomb, black and evil, on a table before him. Brendan Bracken, Minister of Information, presided, and chiefs of the services that won the battle were present.

SECRET SERVICE GOT THE FACTS

Mr. Sandys' story was told less than twenty-four hours after Great Britain had already received the cheering news of the relaxing of the blackout. The story began eighteen months ago, in April of 1943, when the Chiefs of Staff sent to Mr. Sandys four vague reports, received from secret agents, of a German long-range bombardment weapon.

The tales of Britain's renowned In-

telligence Services are rarely told, but the accumulation of information that followed these reports indicated that they were as resourceful as ever.

Puzzling photographs were taken in May, 1943, over the experiment station at Peenemuende.

But expert interpreters detected in a tiny blurred speck the shape of a miniture airplane sitting on an inclined ramp. In the vicinity of the ramp the ground was blackened as if by a hot blast. The secret of the flying bomb was all but divined.

Doubts were resolved last November, Mr. Sandys said, when 100 concrete structures like those at Peenemuende were erected along the French coast.

Beginning in December, American and British air forces destroyed every one of those sites. Unable to repair them, the Germans last March started constructing a new, simplified series.

SPEEDIEST PLANES USED

The new ramps were so well camouflaged that it was practically impossible to detect them until after they had been used. An intelligence officer sent to the Cherbourg Peninsula pitched his tent on one site before he found the launching rail.

The Allies already had invaded Europe when the attacks began in earnest on June 15.

The robots flew at from 350 to 400 miles an hour, and only the British Typhoon and the newest Spitfire fighters and American-made Mustangs could overhaul them in level flight.

They were fired in salvos, and on cloudy days as many as 200 were launched in twenty-four hours. But dur-

ing the first month 40 per cent of the bombs were downed.

The barrage balloon belt that dots the sky thickly south and east of London was increased to 2,000, and most balloons were fitted with extra cables. They stopped nearly 15 per cent of the bombs that reached their area.

In mid-July London's whole antiaircraft belt was moved down to the coast, requiring the resiting of 1,100 guns, which nevertheless were out of action for only two days.

20 CENT RANGE FINDER HELPED

With a clear view over the sea, gunners raised their scores until they were shooting down 74 per cent of the bombs entering the gun belt. Twenty American batteries, constituting one-eighth of the total of 2,800 guns, joined in the shooting. Special American equipment, for which President Roosevelt gave priority at Prime Minister Churchill's request, was imported for the battle.

Fighter pilots, aided by radio telephone spotters on land and sea during the daytime and by a simple 20-cent range finder at night, shot down more than 1,900 bombs.

Even from ground bases, however, only 29 per cent of the bombs got through to London. Twenty-five per cent were inaccurate. The remaining 46 per cent were brought down. Toward the end of the attacks, which with one exception were finished last Friday, the defenses were stopping 70 percent and only 9 per cent were reaching London. ◆

SEPTEMBER 15, 1944

Halsey Fliers Hit 84 Ships, Wreck Philippine Defenses

By ROBERT TRUMBULL
By Telephone to The New York Times.

PEARL HARBOR, Sept. 14—Carrier aircraft under Admiral William F. Halsey's command have "crippled" Japanese air forces, shipping and ground defenses in the Central Philippines in a three-day attack lasting from dawn Monday to sundown yesterday, a Pacific Fleet communiqué said today. Enemy air power in the area was apparently completely destroyed.

Sweeping over the four fortified islands of Panay, Cebu, Negros and Leyte, the American airmen shot down 156 Japanese planes in combat and destroyed 277 on the ground and sank or damaged eighty-four ships and "many" sampans. Enemy air opposition was described as "formidable" the first two days and "entirely non-existent" the third day.

Since Admiral Halsey's Third Fleet opened the naval campaign against the Philippines with an attack on Mindanao Island on Sept. 8, the enemy has lost 501 planes, at least 173 vessels sunk or damaged plus a great number of small craft not counted. These totals cover all the carrier raids on the Philippines bases. The communiqué said that these operations "inflicted crippling damage" on the enemy in the Central Philippines. Pacific Fleet communiqués are so carefully worded that such a statement may be accepted at its full value. It is inferred here that Admiral Halsey's bold raids have deprived the Japanese at least for the time being of their former defensive strength in the Philippines south of Luzon Island.

The attack on the central Philippines covered another heavy carrier attack Tuesday on the Palau Islands, 610 statute miles east of Mindanao. Carrier planes from another portion of the giant Third Fleet hurled ninety tons of bombs and 165 rockets at Angaur, Peleliu and Ngesebus Islands in the Palau group, damaging coastal gun emplacements, warehouses and a lighthouse at Angaur. This was the sixth attack on Palau in the past eight days and the fourth in the past four. There has been no air opposition at Palau since the Third Fleet opened its assault on Sept. 5.

Last Friday's attack on Mindanao Island in the southern Philippines cost the Japanese sixty-eight planes destroyed and forty-nine cargo ships definitely sunk in addition to many sampans sunk and a number of vessels probably sunk or damaged.

SEPTEMBER 16, 1944

AMERICAN TROOPS ON GERMAN SOIL

FALL OF METZ DUE

By DREW MIDDLETON
By Cable to The New York Times.

SUPREME HEADQUARTERS Allied Expeditionary Force, Sept. 16—Tanks and doughboys of the American First Army reached Stolberg, six miles east of Aachen and less than thirty miles from the outskirts of Cologne on the Rhine yesterday and, according to a late report from the front last night, American infantry broke through the main Siegfried Line. [Press services said the line had been breached at its strongest point east of Aachen.]

Reports from the front said the line was breached by infantrymen and combat engineers using flame throwers, dynamite charges on poles, grenades and secret weapons.

Armored reconnaissance units probed the northern outskirts of Aachen and the town itself and German strong points around it were being pounded into submission by American field batteries firing from high ground north, west and south of the town. Aachen's fall was said to be imminent

AMERICANS SEIZE MAASTRICHT

The German line was slowly disintegrating to the north and south as Aachen's defenses were crumbling. An armored column that crossed the German frontier east of Eupen fought its way through a chain of enemy pillboxes and took Lammersdorf, two miles southeast of Roetgen. Another American First Army force captured Maastricht, the first Netherland town to be liberated, and, according to reports from the front, it advanced across the Maastricht appendix and crossed the German frontier.

The penetration of the Siegfried Line, which has not yet been confirmed here but which on the basis of field re-

American soldiers of the First Army Division moving toward the city of Aachen, Germany.

AIRFIELDS BOMBED AND STRAFED

The three-day air assault on the four central islands resulted in the sinking of two large cargo vessels, one medium size transport, two destroyer escorts and thirty-five small ships. Damaged were five cargo vessels, one medium tanker, thirty-six small ships, two motor torpedo boats and "many" sampans.

The communiqué said "several" airfields were bombed and strafed. There are ten known air bases on the four islands. Fires were started among oil storage facilities, ammunition dumps, warehouses, barracks and other buildings.

"Enemy air opposition the first day was considerable and was reinforced during the first night so that its strength on the second day was also formidable," the communiqué declared. "Enemy planes rose to intercept our aircraft but no attempts were made to attack our surface ships.

"On the third day enemy air power was entirely non-existent and anti-aircraft fire was meager. Our losses in planes and flight personnel were relatively light." ◆

ports during the past forty-eight hours appears most likely, is the most portentous military news of the campaign since the break-through at St. Lô. The great enemy barrier has been forced in an area close to the Ruhr and its industry, still one of the principal citadels of Germany's armed might.

The momentous news from this sector of the American First Army front overshadowed all other operational reports yesterday. But the offensive also was progressing well to the south. An armored column of the American First Army that crossed the German frontier from St. Vith and advanced north of Pruem was pushing forward yesterday on a six-mile front through strongly fortified positions, including scores of anti-tank traps.

FALL OF METZ EXPECTED

Nancy, Charmes and Epinal, all on the right flank of Lieut. Gen. George S. Patton's American Third Army, fell in the past twenty-four hours and the German line on the Moselle River was blasted loose from its roots.

There was heavy fighting on the northern sector of the Third Army's front as well yesterday. Thionville is now largely held by General Patton's troops and the German situation at Metz is becoming more precarious hourly. ◆

SEPTEMBER 17, 1944

Feud Among Poles Growing Bitterer

Soviet-Sponsored Lublin Body Accuses London Regime Of Murder, 'Gangsterism'

By W. H. LAWRENCE
By Wireless to The New York Times.

MOSCOW, Sept. 16—With the Red Army at Warsaw's gates, apparently preparing to cross the Vistula River, the state of quasi-civil war that has broken out in sections of Poland threatens to further impair relations between the Soviet-sponsored Polish National Committee and the Polish regime in London.

Polpress, the news agency of the Polish Committee whose headquarters are in Lublin, charged Friday that at least four assassinations had been traced to adherents of the London group.

Behind the assassinations, according to Polpress, lies a planned campaign to frustrate the drafting of Poles under the mobilization order recently issued by the Lublin committee. The cleavage of the two groups was made further apparent by the Moscow radio.

Quoting front-line correspondents in Praga, Moscow said the writer had not found any evidence that General Bor's forces had played any role in the recent uprising there, although Praga was claimed by General Bor's forces to be one of their strongholds.

Meanwhile the apparently seething conditions behind the front lines in liberated Poland was bluntly laid by Polpress at the doors of the Polish Government in London. In addition to the direct method of terrorism, agents of the London group were charged with issuing appeals to the civil population to sabotage the Lublin Committee's mobilization measures.

Outright assassination of members of the Lublin Home Army is coupled with numerous other "gangster attacks," Polpress charges, attributing the trouble to the committee's mobilization decree of Aug. 15, which it says was issued "to form a new unit of the Polish Army, to increase its strength for the struggle against the Hitlerite invaders, and thus hasten the victory of the United Nations."

"All good Poles" greeted the decree with enthusiasm, says Polpress, but the "reactionary clique" in London, and its agents in Poland, "have proved incurable." ◆

SEPTEMBER 21, 1944

Fight at Arnhem Is Without Mercy

Our Sky Troops in Netherland Pocket Hold Off Nazis— Hear British Guns Approaching

By STANLEY MAXTED
For Combined Allied Press

WITH ALLIED AIRBORNE FORCES in the Arnhem Area, the Netherlands, Sept. 20 (UP)—Fighting is continuing bitterly throughout this area. There have been moments when our position looked very sticky, but you would never

Soldiers of the First Allied Airborne Army search a bomb-damaged school in the Netherlands for snipers during the Battle of Arnhem.

know it from the faces of our men, who are dug into hedges along the roadside, behind trees and where have you.

Hopes went up this afternoon because of the arrival on two separate occasions ❯

of Stirlings and Douglases with much-needed supplies. The planes flew through murderous flak to drop their loads.

This is the fourth day and our ears are wide open to the sounds of guns ten miles away, where the British Second Army is approaching from the south to relieve this surrounded bunch of fighting men who are hanging on and trading punches with a steadily reinforced enemy.

Sniping is going on continuously. It seems to come from the most unexpected places; but the mortaring is worst of all.

In a nearby town the Germans are sniping from the houses, firing even on medical parties.

Fighting is the most relentless I have ever seen. There is no quarter. ◊

SEPTEMBER 23, 1944

U.S. to Be 'Hard' With Germans

By JOHN H. CRIDER
Special to The New York Times.

WASHINGTON, Sept. 22—-The temper of American policy toward defeated Germany has already been set by President Roosevelt, it was learned today on unquestionable authority. It is definitely a very "hard" policy.

President Roosevelt's attitude, now well known to the officials who are busily spelling it out in various policies that should become known in the next few weeks, was stated in writing so that no one could misunderstand him.

He said that it was wrong, as some proposed, to attempt to restore Germany as Belgium and the Netherlands were to be restored. Some persons here and in England, he added, believed only the Nazis in Germany should be punished.

The fact is, the President said, that the whole German people must be made to understand that they have been defeated so that they will never again attempt to perpetrate a monstrous crime upon humanity. In thus making it clear that he had no patience with those who would be "soft" with Germany, the President laid the foundation of the policy that is now being implemented.

The President's attitude toward Germany, which has become the official Administration attitude, was reflected yesterday at a news conference held jointly by Elmer Davis, Director of the Office of War Information, and Robert Sherwood, Director of OWI Overseas Operations.

When Mr. Sherwood was asked what was the first problem facing OWI in Germany when the military situation permitted it to act, he replied:

"The first thing we must do is to convince the Germans that they have really lost the war."

"And," Mr. Davis put in, "to convince them that they would lose it if they ever start it again."

ARMY MANUAL IS CONDEMNED

The President took policy formation into his own hands about three weeks ago when he found evidences of "softness" in an Army manual prepared for guidance of Americans entering Germany. He let it be known that he thought the manual was "pretty bad."

Thus the formation of American policy toward defeated Germany, which had been developing tortuously from the ground up in various departments without any success at merging conflicting views into a solidified policy, is now being made under specific direction from the top.

A curious counterpart of the "hard" policy toward Germany adopted by the President is the feeling in official circles that German reparations should be relatively light, compared with those imposed following the last war. This time Germany will have been the scene of battle, with a large part of her industry destroyed. The reason for the stand for light reparations is that the Allies would have to provide money, materials and machines to restore her capacity to pay a large amount. ◊

SEPTEMBER 24, 1944

CHINESE COMMUNIST TELLS OF CIVIL WAR

By Wireless to The New York Times

YENAN, China, Aug. 15 (Delayed)—Taking sharp issue with the optimistic statement regarding the Kuomintang-Communist negotiations, made by Information Minister Liang Hanchao on July 26, Chou En-lai, Communist party leader who has taken a leading part in the relations with the Government said today that the negotiations have yielded no result.

Mr. Chou said that although Mr. Liang had repeatedly said China certainly would avoid civil war, many raids on the Shensi-Kansu-Ningsia border region had been made in recent months. He charged that Yen Hsi-shan's Sixty-first Army had attacked the Communist-led Eighth Route Army in Shansi Province in agreement with the Japanese, that Kuomintang troops under Li Pin-hsien had attacked New Fourth Army units in Hupeh who had rescued American pilots and at that time were attacking the enemy to divert them from campaigns on the regular fronts, and that Kuomintang troops under Lo Mao-hsun had attacked guerrilla detachments in the East River region of Kwangtung.

"These incidents," he said, "show that armed clashes still continue and that the danger of civil war is not yet past.

"To win final victory over Japan the Kuomintang and Communists must unite and the existing problems between the parties must be solved immediately. For this it is necessary that the ruling authorities in the Kuomintang immediately give up their one party dictatorship and their policy of weakening and exterminating those differing from it, must at once put democracy into practice and through democratic procedures reach a fair, just solution of the relations between the parties. Only thus can success be attained, and this is the heartfelt hope of the Communist party."

Mr. Chou said that the Communists, since the kidnapping of Generalissimo Chiang Kai-shek at Sian, had maintained that only democracy could strengthen China's defenses and that only democracy could provide a basis for a just settlement of the Kuomintang Communist and other political problems. He declared that this was the view not only of the Communists but also of 99 per cent of the Chinese people. ◊

SEPTEMBER 26, 1944

PEACE CONFEREES 90% IN AGREEMENT ON WORLD SET-UP

By JAMES B. RESTON
Special to The New York Times.

WASHINGTON, Sept. 25—The American, British and Russian Governments have decided to be satisfied, for the time being, with 90 per cent agreement on the kind of international security organization they wish to see established and to take up at "the highest level" the other 10 per cent at some future date.

It has not been possible for the three Governments to reach full agreement on the procedure for voting in the proposed Executive Council in the event of a charge of aggression against the United States, Britain, Russia or China, but on all other major points discussed at Dumbarton Oaks agreement has been achieved.

A "final draft" of the proposed agreement has been submitted by UnderSecretary of State Edward R. Stettinius Jr. to President Roosevelt, who is said to have approved it. Prime Minister Churchill is also understood to have approved the draft, and the Russian Government has indicated its support of all points contained in the "90-percent" draft. The Russian Government's final approval is expected tomorrow or Wednesday, when the Russian phase of the conference, now in its sixth week, is expected to end. The second half of the conference with the Chinese delegation will start probably Thursday.

WOULD SET UP COURT

The three Governments, as distinguished from their delegations at Dumbarton Oaks, are understood to have agreed to create:

An international court of justice to deal with justiciable disputes. The court would have competence to deal with any dispute referred to it by the Executive Council of the proposed League and an international commission would be established to codify existing international law and propose additional laws for the consideration of the member States.

A General Secretariat headed by a Secretary General who would act as Secretary General of both the League Council and the League assembly.

An assembly of all peace-loving countries with equal voting powers to deal with any questions referred to it by the Executive Council and with certain other general questions. This assembly would meet once a year and could be convened in cases of emergency. Its powers, however, would be mainly advisory.

An Executive Council composed of four "permanent members," the United States, Great Britain, Soviet Russia and China, and seven other non-permanent members, to be selected on a geographical basis. It is understood that the three powers engaged in the first phase of the conference also agreed that France should also become a "permanent member" when that country has a government freely elected by the French people.

This Executive Council would have primary responsibility for security and for the peaceful settlement of international disputes. Under the proposals understood to be accepted by the three Governments, this council would be empowered to determine the existence of any threat to the peace, or breach of the peace, and to decide on the action necessary to maintain or restore the peace.

It is understood that the three powers agreed to recommend to the other United Nations that, as soon as possible after the creation of the security organization, the member states should enter into a general agreement governing the number and type of forces each would be obliged to place at the disposal of the Executive Council for the purpose of preventing or repelling aggression.

Several weeks ago the question arose at Dumbarton Oaks as to what should be done in the event of charges of aggression against one of the permanent members of the council. One of the countries suggested that no party to a dispute should have the right to vote, regardless of whether it was a permanent member of the council. This proposal was opposed by Russia.

In the first place, the Russians pointed out that the country attacked as well as the aggressor nation was "a party to the dispute" and should not therefore be denied the right to vote in its own defense.

This discussion went on for days, and one of the proposals for solving it was that it should be left to the council to determine who should vote in the event of charges of aggression against a permanent member of the council. This proposal was said to have received considerable support at Dumbarton Oaks, but was finally rejected by the Soviet Government, which insisted that each of the permanent members should have the right to veto any proposed action by the League against any future aggressor.

When several additional sessions failed to produce full agreement on this point, it was finally agreed to defer final decision until some future date. Discussion on this point will, it is believed, be continued through regular diplomatic channels, and eventually it is hoped that Mr. Roosevelt, Prime Minister Churchill and Marshal Stalin may discuss it in another personal meeting ⌃

SEPTEMBER 28, 1944

Editorial
WITHDRAWAL FROM ARNHEM

The story of the British First Airborne Division is finished. As a division it no longer exists. Its dead lie in the woods west of Arnhem. Its disabled wounded are in German hands. About two thousand of its original eight or nine thousand fighting men have been "withdrawn" to safety. The circumstances of this "withdrawal" across a river that rescuing forces had not been able to pass must be imagined. Arnhem was a defeat, a red blotch on a brilliant page of victories, a reminder that the advance into Germany is no parade.

When the bold stroke fails, as this one did, we still have no right to criticize those who ordered it. The chance was worth taking. The airborne troops might have turned the German right flank. The official communiqué" says that they did enable "other elements to the south to hold the bridge at Nijmegen." They did detain some of the best Nazi units, probably far exceeding their own numbers. Their sacrifices were not in vain. They could not keep the ground on to which they were plummeted from the air, but they helped with their blood to buy ground for others. There will be no prouder men in years to come than those qualified to wear the Arnhem badge or ribbon.

Shall we say that these men were brave and let it go at that? The Nazis at Brest were brave. The "mad colonel" at St. Malo did not lack courage. But the airborne Britishers did not have the valor of fanaticism or desperation. They risked, and many of them endured, the hardest death the soldier has to die— when the flags are flying and the bells ringing in liberated cities, and the hope of victory and home makes life seem sweet. This is their tragedy and their everlasting honor. ◆

Chapter 21
"NUTS!"
October–December 1944

One sign that the end was approaching in Europe, if more slowly than the Allied public would have liked, was the transfer of correspondents to Eisenhower's new Supreme Headquarters Allied Expeditionary Force (SHAEF), set up in Paris. Correspondents were still subject not only to censorship but also to the limits of what the fighting forces would tell them. In the Soviet Union and on the Chinese Front reporters were constantly frustrated in what they could or could not publish.

On November 14 Arthur Sulzberger flew out to the Pacific theater to meet General MacArthur. MacArthur's forces had begun the reconquest of the Philippines on October 20, when four divisions landed almost unopposed on the southern island of Leyte. Sulzberger was too late to witness the great naval battle of Leyte Gulf, when three Japanese task forces, the last of the Japanese Combined Fleet, tried to engage the American armada off Leyte. Although able to inflict some damage on American escort carriers, the Japanese lost twenty-eight out of sixty-four warships, a decisive defeat from which the Japanese Navy never recovered. Sulzberger arrived after the costly occupation of Peleliu, secured by November 27, and went on to spend three days at MacArthur's headquarters before returning to the United States. Leyte surrendered on December 19 with the loss of 80,000 Japanese soldiers who fought to the death. On December 15 American forces reoccupied Mindoro as a stepping-stone to the reconquest of the main island of Luzon. MacArthur had made good on his promise of 1942: "I will return."

In Europe the confidence that the war would be quickly over ebbed away. On November 8 Roosevelt was reelected with a great deal still to be done to bring the war to an end. A few days earlier, Montgomery's Twenty-First Army Group had finally succeeded in clearing the estuary around the mouth of the River Scheldt so that Antwerp could be used as a port. But even before that a new German secret weapon, the A-4 rocket (or V-2), had begun to fall on the port. With no way to intercept or anticipate the rockets, their one-ton warheads did heavy damage, not only in Antwerp but in London and southern England as well. Meanwhile the problem of bringing a major port to full efficiency slowed down the advance to the German frontier as the flow of supplies failed to keep pace with the demand.

Then, contrary to all expectations, the German Army launched a surprise attack out of the Ardennes Forest to break open the Western Front and perhaps recapture Antwerp. Operation Autumn Mist came as a complete surprise against the weakest part of the Allied line. On December 16, in poor weather that kept Allied airplanes on the ground, half a million German troops and 1,000 tanks broke through toward the Meuse River, carving out a salient forty miles wide and up to sixty miles deep, which the Allies called the "Bulge." Eisenhower immediately ordered Patton and Montgomery to blunt the attack and to try to cut through both flanks to encircle the German force. German units began to run out of fuel and when the clouds lifted in the last week of December, thousands of Allied aircraft pounded the German positions. In the middle of the Bulge was a small fortress at Bastogne, held throughout the assault by the 101st Airborne Division against repeated German attacks. When on December 22 the commander, Brig. General Anthony McAuliffe, was invited by the Germans to surrender, he famously replied, "Nuts!" Four days later the embattled division was relieved by Patton's Third Army. By early February the Germans were back where they had started, but with little chance of being able now to defend the Reich.

WARSAW GIVES UP AFTER 63-DAY FIGHT

Losses Put Above 300,000—Bor Said to Have Fled—Some Poles Escape to Russians

By SYDNEY GRUSON
By Wireless to The New York Times

LONDON, Oct. 3—After sixty-three days of bitter resistance, the patriots of Warsaw have been forced to surrender and the Germans again are in control of the shattered Polish capital.

The rising, which began Aug. 1, when the sound of the Red Army's guns could be heard in the city, ended at 8 o'clock last night, it was announced by Lieut. Gen. Tadeusz Komorowski [General Bor], commander in chief of Polish forces, who is believed here to have escaped at the last minute.

In London tonight Prime Minister Stanislaw Mikolajczyk told why Warsaw had to quit fighting. The main reason was that "all hopes of relief from outside had vanished" with the failure of Soviet and Polish forces to forge the Vistula River in the Warsaw area, the Prime Minister said, and the Home Army laid down its arms after vain efforts to fight its way out.

Moscow reported that some units got through to the east bank of the Vistula held by Russians.

The decision to surrender was taken, M. Mikolajczyk said, with all food and water supplies exhausted, the garrison and the people starving and thousands of wounded lying in underground hideouts without attention and with no medical supplies or dressings available.

85 PER CENT OF CITY BATTERED

The saddened Poles in London estimated that the city suffered 200,000 casualties in the first six weeks of fighting and that another 100,000 had been imprisoned. This total is almost one-third of the capital's pre-war population. Half of Warsaw's buildings were destroyed and another 35 per cent damaged, the Poles said.

"Warsaw's fighting throughout August and September of 1944 is the only instance in the history of this war in which a great city has conducted such a long and isolated defense with her own means, without heavy equipment or considerable help from outside against a superior enemy having at his disposal the whole destructive might of modern warfare," M. Mikolajczyk declared.

He added: "The defense of Warsaw will remain forever a testimony to the invincible moral strength of the Polish nation and its unyielding will to independent life."

The Germans said tonight that the members of the Home Army who had surrendered "have been dealt with as prisoners of war instead of as franctireurs." Until the Allies warned that they would exact retribution, the Germans shot Polish captives as outlaws. ◇

NEWSMEN AT SHAEF TRANSFER TO PARIS

Last of Eisenhower's 'Family' Flown From London To Be Nearer to News Sources

SUPREME HEADQUARTERS, Allied Expeditionary Force, Oct. 10 (AP)— War Correspondents covering Supreme Headquarters wrote their stories closer to the scene of action tonight. Forty-five correspondents moved today from London to Paris—virtually the last of Gen. Dwight D. Eisenhower's official family to get across the English Channel.

Supreme Headquarters has been dribbling to the Continent for the last two and a half months. General Eisenhower moved his advance command post to an apple orchard on the edge of Cerisy Forest in Normandy early in August. The bulk of his staff had set up headquarters elsewhere in France by the first week in September. Now nearly everything is in Paris.

The war had run away from communications as long as a month ago and it had become increasingly difficult to keep abreast of developments from London, eighty miles from the fighting at Dunkerque, but 450 miles from the Seventh Army front before Belfort Pass.

The regular morning "briefing" for correspondents was held today at old SHAEF headquarters in Britain. Then the correspondents had an hour to write their stories before boarding special planes for France.

"Moving closer to the front will shorten our lines of communication many miles and should considerably speed up the relay of official news," a headquarters spokesman said.

On this first move, press associations were permitted to send two correspondents each; individual newspapers one. ◇

Soldiers of the First Polish Army attack a German position in the Warsaw suburbs in October, 1944.

OCTOBER 12, 1944

Correspondents Complain to Chinese On Censorship

By The Associated Press.

CHUNGKING, China, Oct. 11—Complaints against Chungking censorship of dispatches filed from the Communist area of China were voiced today by two correspondents at a government press conference.

Guenther Stein, correspondent of The London News-Chronicle, spent four and one-half months in the area. On his return, Mr. Stein said, he found that censors here had excised more than 5,000 words from seventeen messages.

Chungking is the relay point where messages from Communist territory are handled by the censor before retransmission abroad.

Brooks Atkinson of The New York Times, who recently returned from a fortnight in the area, also complained about the severity of censorship on news about the Communists.

K. C. Wu, Vice Minister of Foreign Affairs, suggested that the matter be discussed with government spokesmen at his office, rather than at a press conference. ◆

OCTOBER 15, 1944

NEW LEAGUE STARTING WITH GOOD PROSPECTS; 'UNITED NATIONS' AS NEW NAME

By EDWIN L. JAMES

As things stand now the new League of Nations, which will probably be called The United Nations, is off to a good start. The work of Dumbarton Oaks, which may be termed a subministerial plan, although it represents more than that implies, has been well received; even the isolationists have not had much to say against it—yet. It is presented by its authors as representing 90 per cent agreement on the many and difficult problems which arise in connection with any attempt at agreement by a number of nations with different Governments, different philosophies, different ambitions—but with the common purpose of preventing another world war. As Secretary Hull said so aptly, any such document can represent at best a highest common denominator and not the consecration of any one nation's plan.

Now the world has before it the initial plan of The United Nations. That plan resembles the old League of Nations in that it calls for a free association of national Governments rather than some form of superstate with powers independent of national Governments. However, it is evident that the rules will be somewhat different in that there is no sanctification of the political status quo in the world and therefore no guarantee of the political sovereignty and territorial integrity of the members as was contained in the much-mooted Article X of the League covenant. There will be other differences which are not yet in final form in some instances.

OFF TO GOOD START

Both Presidential candidates have praised the work at Dumbarton Oaks. When the text was given out it was accompanied by a statement from the White House in which President Roosevelt commended it in high terms. Governor Dewey has called it a fine beginning. Inasmuch as the platforms of both the Democratic and Republican parties call for world organization to preserve the peace, these statements by the two candidates must be regarded as highly important.

It has been held that the establishment of The United Nations will call for action by both Houses of Congress. There will be a treaty for the Senate to ratify and action by the House of Representatives may be needed in connection with the setting up of the limits of a force the United States might be called upon to supply. Both Houses of Congress are on record as favoring the participation of the United States in a world peace-keeping organization. The leaders of both parties approve the Dumbarton Oaks plan.

This ought to mean that when the isolationists start their effort to block the new League they will face a formidable undertaking. Of course, it is not to be forgotten that even Senator Lodge said the last time that the majority of the American people wanted the League and that was why he adopted the indirect method of killing it by reservations and amendments. It is up to the American people to see that they are not bamboozled the second time so that the path to World War III is not opened as the path to World War II was opened by the nationalistic isolationists of a quarter of a century ago. They were not all in this country, but we pointed the way along the tragic road.

SUPER-STATES ARE OUT

The praiseworthy interest of the American public in the proposition of preventing another world war has led to widespread and sincere study of many post-war plans. Some of these have been of a nature which must appeal sentimentally to almost anyone—the provisions for a real Parliament of Man, for a union of peoples rather than government—and such plans have been discussed by millions of our peoples.

These folks should now direct their attention to backing the Dumbarton Oaks plan and what will follow from it. Of course, it will not satisfy the pure idealists. But it represents what can be had, while their plans represent what cannot be had. The need is for something to be done while the iron is hot, for if there is delay until two or three years after the fighting is over nothing will be done.

The main idea is to get the nations of the world into an organization with a common purpose—that of preventing another war. The rules are, of course, important but not all-important. Rules can be changed in the years to come. But a world organization cannot be evolved in the years to come unless it starts while the United Nations are united.

The greatest advance which can be had now, or while most of us are living, is an organization of national governments. That is what Dumbarton Oaks provides. Those who believe in international cooperation should get behind the principle it represents. One may quarrel about details, but the quarrels should be about details. The main idea should stand. ◆

GENERAL M'ARTHUR FULFILLS A GALLANT VOW
Americans Seize East Coast of Leyte Isle, Are Widening Hold

By The Associated Press.

GENERAL MACARTHUR'S HEAD-QUARTERS in the Philippines, Oct. 20 (Army radio pool broadcast)—American invasion of the Philippines was officially proclaimed today by Gen. Douglas Mac-Arthur.

Two years and six months after he took sad leave of the islands and relinquished them to Japanese invaders, vowing "I shall return," he announced that his Navy and air-covered ground forces had landed in the archipelago.

[Japanese broadcasts, beginning some twenty-four hours previously, had listed at least three landings, all in the central sector where the invaders would be in position to split the archipelago's 150,000 defenders in half.]

General MacArthur, aboard a warship, went along with the huge convoy from New Guinea, and within four hours after his forces landed began making plans to go ashore.

EAST COAST SEIZED

The special communiqué text, in part, follows:

"In a major amphibious operation we have seized the eastern coast of Leyte Island in the Philippines, 600 miles north of Morotai and 2,500 miles from Milne Bay from whence our offensive started nearly sixteen months ago.

"The landing in the Visayas is midway between Luzon and Mindanao and at one stroke splits into two Japanese forces in the Philippines. The enemy expected the attack on Mindanao.

"Tacloban was secured with small casualties. The landing was preceded by heavy air and naval bombardment which was devastating in effect. Our ground troops are already extending their hold."

General MacArthur said supplies were rolling ashore.

225,000 OF FOE IN ISLES

Among participants in the action were the Sixth United States Army, Navy

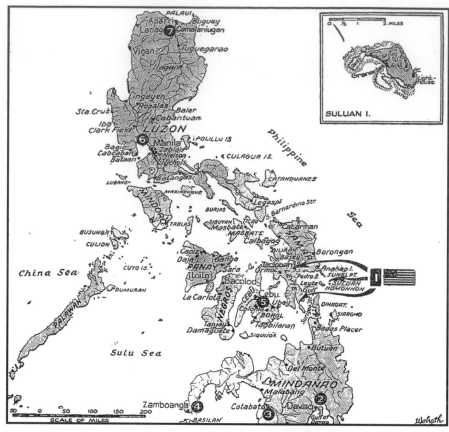

The return to the Philippines began at Leyte Gulf (1). Tokyo said the Americans had first invaded Suluan Island (shown in detail on inset). General MacArthur announced the capture of Tacloban in northern Leyte Island, a landing near Cabalian at the southern tip and occupation of the whole eastern side of island. Bombings were reported at Davao (2), Cotabato (3), Zamboanga (4), Cebu (5), the much-bombed area of Clark Field and Manila (6) and Aparri (7).

forces of the Seventh United States Fleet, the Third United States Fleet and the Far Eastern Air Force.

The landings pitted the invaders against Japanese Philippine defenders, estimated at 225,000 under command of Field Marshal Juichi Terauchi.

[The Japanese exulted exactly four days ago that their alleged naval-air victories off Formosa had set back "the impending invasion of the Philippines by at least two months." It turned out that they didn't score any naval-air victories either.] Eyewitness accounts from the scene reported the American Navy and airforce were on hand in such mammoth strength that the Japanese Navy was no-

where in sight and the Japanese air force, knocked out at all airfields in the Philippines, offered scarcely token resistance.

Every able-bodied man who escaped from Corregidor in Manila Bay before it surrendered May 6, 1942, went along on the invasion to liberate the Filipinos

---

HITTLERS CHANGE NAME
Cognomen Embarrassing, Butcher Now Becomes Hiller

Having suffered sufficient embarrassment with the name "Hittler," even with two t's, Jacob and Molly Hittler of 3478 Fish Avenue, the Bronx, and their two children received permission yesterday from Justice Ernest E. L. Hammer in Bronx Supreme Court to use legally the name "Hiller."

Mr. Hiller, a retail butcher at 1964 Amsterdam Avenue, said in his application that the name "Hittler" had been of particular embarrassment in his social and business life. He added he would have changed his name legally years ago but for the publicity. ◇

and their imprisoned fellow-Americans from bondage.

The preparation for the invasion included the destruction of more than 1,300 planes, the sinking of eighty-six ships, damaging of 127 ships and widespread devastation of airfields and reinforcement bases since Oct. 9 in task force blasts at the Ryukyus, Formosa and the Philippines.

An Associated Press war correspondent, reporting from the scene, said the invasion convoy stretched as far as the eye could see. ◇

OCTOBER 27, 1944

'17 Hours of Hell' Rage in Sea Battle Off Leyte

By RALPH TEATSORTH
United Press Correspondent

ABOARD ADMIRAL KINKAID'S FLAGSHIP, off the Philippines, Thursday, Oct. 26-The Tokyo Express rammed into the American Navy Limited today. The pride of Japan was wrecked so badly it may never make another long run. It was the day our Navy had dreamed about for considerably more than a year. It was seventeen hours of concentrated hell and the most amazing thing about the battle was that our Pacific Flight Carrier Force which nobody thought could deliver such a terrific punch-held off the bulk of the Japanese fleet all day and had it on the run all afternoon. When evening came and most of the pieces of the huge naval puzzle had been fitted together, a Navy spokesman announced "The enemy has been decisively defeated with heavy losses. Our fleet is without serious losses and fit to fight tomorrow."

It is yet too early to ascertain accurately the destruction and damage wrought on the Japanese fleet but the enemy's minimum losses are estimated at one Yamashiro class battleship sunk, one battleship knocked out and probably sunk, three battleships damaged "severely," several cruisers and destroyers sunk, three cruisers and several destroyers damaged. Four other warships were either sunk or very heavily damaged. ◇

OCTOBER 27, 1944

SUMMARY OF DESTRUCTION VISITED ON THE JAPANESE MAIN FLEET BROKEN
Halsey Force Inflicts a Staggering Defeat on Enemy Off Formosa

By GEORGE HORNE
By Telephone to The New York Times.

PEARL HARBOR, Oct. 26.—Japan's Navy was so decisively beaten in the two-day Battle of the Philippines it no longer figures as a major factor to be reckoned with in immediate American war plans.

Intercepted northeast of the tip of Luzon in a furious American assault that took the enemy by surprise, the main body of the enemy force was completely demoralized and crushed in a day-long series of air and surface actions so completely one-sided as to make questionable the use of the term battle.

The two smaller forces of the badly separated fleet were intercepted in separate actions, which raged with unprecedented fury involving enemy land-based air forces, elements of the Seventh Fleet, an assisting group of the Third Fleet and Australian sea forces serving under the Seventh Fleet.

FLEEING SHIPS PICKED OFF

Damaged units of the beaten enemy force are being pursued by air and sea and some of them have already been picked off.

An entire Japanese carrier force of three and possibly four carriers was wiped out by Admiral William F. Halsey's Third Fleet, which intercepted it. The Third Fleet is intact, having suffered no damage whatever.

There is no question that Japan has suffered the greatest blow in her history as a seafaring nation or that such damaged elements managing to get back home will be but ineffective fragments of the great force sent out to crush the Americans once more.

While no one claims that nothing escaped the deadly accuracy of American planes and guns, it can be claimed that not a single big ship went through unscathed, not a battleship, cruiser or carrier in the mighty force, which had at least sixty ships and perhaps sixty-seven.

It will be many months before the Japanese fleet can be repaired and reconstituted as a fighting force.

MANY DETAILS MISSING

There are still many details missing and the picture is complicated by the fact that action involving General MacArthur's forces is not being reported here. With air and sea battles swirling around the islands in the vicinity of Leyte, some of them involving Third Fleet forces cooperating in repelling the enemy attack, duplication may occur and is in fact expected.

A fairly accurate account of the entire action is now possible, however, beginning at the time the two smaller ❯

General Douglas MacArthur and his staff coming ashore during initial landings of U.S. forces at Leyte in the Philippines, October 1944.

enemy forces were discovered early Monday and ending at around 2 A.M. yesterday, when surface units of the Third Fleet caught up with a fleeing straggler cruiser and finished it off in the San Bernardino Strait.

In the three enemy forces, first, the small one with two fast new battleships first sighted coming eastward through the Sulu Sea; second, the middle force found moving eastward through the Sibuyan Sea, and, third, the northern force, coming down from Japan or the Yellow Sea, later smashed by the Third Fleet, were the following:

Three or four carriers, ten battleships, at least twenty-one cruisers and between twenty-seven and thirty-two destroyers. There may have been more destroyers than this figure. The total is at least sixty ships and probably sixty-seven.

The Third Fleet, in addition to its victory off Formosa, sent a carrier task group to assist units of the Seventh Fleet under Vice Admiral Thomas C. Kinkaid in striking a force of enemy battleships, cruisers and destroyers that had come through San Bernardino Strait and plunged southward to close range against escort carriers of the Seventh Fleet off the Leyte Gulf.

They were trying to get through the small carrier screen to the landing areas, where General MacArthur's troops are engaged on Leyte and Samar.

Admiral Nimitz reported that the Third Fleet Task group, which had been drawn down from the north Tuesday afternoon, shared with the escort carriers under Admiral Kincaid credit for inflicting the following damage:

One heavy cruiser was seen to sink, four battleships were heavily damaged by bombs and left the scene at low speed trailing oil; one destroyer was left dead in the water. Later around midnight this enemy force withdrew northward and tried to get back through San Bernardino Strait into the Sibuyan Sea. It was here that at least one cruiser was caught during the night by surface units of the Third Fleet. It was damaged and the American service units sent it to the bottom.

Carrier planes were continuing to carry the damaged enemy force yesterday through the Sibuyan Sea.

One of the fiercest battles was the

NOVEMBER 4, 1944

BATTLE TO OPEN ANTWERP IS WON; U.S. DRIVE EAST OF AACHEN GAINS; RUSSIANS 7 MILES FROM BUDAPEST

By DREW MIDDLETON
By Wireless to The New York Times.

SUPREME HEADQUARTERS, Allied Expeditionary Force, France, Nov. 3— The long, grim struggle to open Antwerp to Allied shipping is over. British marines and infantry overran most of Walcheren Island today, including the bulk of the important gun positions, and the Canadians mopped up the last German units holding out south of the Schelde estuary this afternoon, after the bulk of the German garrison had surrendered at 7:30 o'clock this morning.

With this pocket eliminated and the Germans on Walcheren Island fighting for their lives, the Schelde is free from German shelling and the dangerous task of sweeping the mines from the Schelde River can begin. By late this month Antwerp, the greatest port in northwestern Europe, may be open to convoys of the Western powers.

Between the Schelde and 's Herto-genbosch the Allies' battleline is slowly advancing. Three new bridgeheads, one American, one British and one Polish, have been established across the Mark River and Canal in the face of heavy enemy fire. Thus the two bridgeheads eliminated by the enemy on Tuesday and Wednesday have been replaced by three new ones and once again Allied forces are striking north toward the Moerdijk bridges over the Meuse (Maas) River.'

FIRST ARMY ADVANCES

American First Army troops, fighting what is described here as a "strong local action," took the town of Schmidt, about three-quarters of a mile east of a line drawn north and south through Vossenack, which was captured yesterday.

The American First Army had captured 199,834 prisoners up to midnight Thursday and may have passed the 200,000 mark today in the fighting in the Huertgen Forest. The American Third Army has now captured more than 100,000 Germans. Its total up to Oct. 31 was 102,340.

By the time the Canadians had stormed and mopped up Knocke, Heyst and Zeebrugge this morning, the clearing of the Schelde pocket had netted 12,344 prisoners, and perhaps another 1,000 were taken this afternoon. Lieut. Gen. Eberding and 1,800 prisoners were rounded up in the pocket Thursday. The captives taken in this area pushed the prisoner total of the Canadian First Army to more than 200,000.

ENEMY RESISTANCE COLLAPSES

German resistance on Walcheren Island dissolved today as battle-hardened British marines and infantry dug out sed-entary German fortress battalions from their positions with mortar, grenade and rifle. Flushing was entirely cleared of the enemy, and Lieut. Col. Rheinhardt, garrison commander, and several hundred of his men were taken prisoner. Most of Flushing had been taken by last night, and today the Tommies combed out the few snipers left in the town.

The marines, who landed at Westkapelle and pushed out to the north and south, advanced within about 3,000 yards of the infantry around Flushing, and almost the entire rim of the island, from Domburg around to Flushing, now is in the Allies' hands.

Two four-gun batteries of 250mm. coast defense guns north of Westkapelle, which has been held by the British for the past forty-eight hours, were taken today and others were captured Thursday. Domburg, a smaller but tactically, more important town than Flushing, was entered late yesterday from the rear, and the German garrison there dug out by an assault that swept down the cobbled streets from the east, instead of from the west, where the enemy expected it.

The prisoner "bag" today is believed to have been large, although no exact figures are available here. During Wednesday's fighting 600 Germans were captured.

The Germans have declared Arnemuiden, midway between Middleburgh and the Walcheren end of the causeway, an open area because of the hospitals located there. The Allies have agreed to this declaration.

The Canadian patrols that proceeded into the islands of Noord Beveland and Tholen to the north of Zuid Beveland and Walcheren took more

one late Monday when the small Sulu force penetrated almost to Leyte at the very eastern edge of the Mindanao Sea. The enemy apparently had succeeded in bringing in more land-based air power from the north, probably from Formosa and Ryukyu, and these planes joined in this battle, which nevertheless ended in a decisive defeat for the enemy, who finally turned back, routed.

It was probably in this and the other Seventh Fleet engagement off Leyte Gulf and the Surigao Strait that our escort carriers listed by General Mac-Arthur were hit.

He said one escort carrier was sunk and others were damaged.

It seems clear that the three enemy forces planned to go into action at the same time. The Sulu force, with two battleships, one cruiser and four destroyers, was sighted by submarines Monday and attacked by our carrier planes as it headed for Mindoro and Leyte.

The carrier force did not stop it, although they did considerable damage. The Sibuyan force was sighted west of the Palawan Islands at about the same time and was kept under heavy air attack throughout the afternoon in the Sibuyan Sea. Several of its ships, consisting of four battleships, ten cruisers and thirteen destroyers, were hit by bombs and torpedoes. Nevertheless, it kept coming, passed through the Sibuyan Sea and got out into the Philippine Sea, or Western Pacific, through the San Bernardino Strait. ◇

---

than 200 prisoners from a convalescent "stomach" battalion, all of whose soldiers were suffering from stomach trouble. The Germans form such battalions to facilitate dietary arrangements.

The most important sector between Walcheren and 's Hertogenbosch is on the Mark River, across which the three new bridgeheads have been thrown. [The Associated Press placed these bridgeheads northwest of Oudenbosch, immediately to the east and north of Oosterhout.] The Germans are shelling the new bridgeheads and also are counter-attacking all three, evidence of the importance they attach to the line of the Mark River and canal, their last defensive position south of the Meuse.

The Canadians are still held by the Germans south of Steenbergen, while the British grip on the south bank of the Meuse to the east of the sector is slowly expanding. Here, too, the enemy is fighting stubbornly and ably.

German artillery fire is delaying progress throughout the front. American engineers built a bridge across their sector of the Mark, only to have it destroyed by shell-fire.

Extensive minefields and machine guns firing on fixed lines are hindering the American advance in the Huertgen forest. Pillboxes encountered south of the minefields and the Vossenack position are being methodically wiped out by self-propelled guns and grenades. Generally the progress is slow and it would be unwise to expect any rapid advances in this sector.

Today's advance covered no more than two and a half miles through the forest.

SEVENTH ARMY PUSHES ON

Both the American Seventh and the French First Armies are making progress in the south. Baccarat was captured by French troops of the Seventh Army yesterday. Since then six other villages, Demeurve, Bazier, Noussoncourt, Menil-sur-Belvitte, Reclonville and Maxainville have been taken, the first two by the French and the others by the Americans.

These gains, won in the rugged country east of the forest of Mondon, followed some heavy fighting in the Grand Bois Glonville, where the enemy lost a number of tanks, three in one small action, and many men. The advance to Baccarat represented a five-mile gain.

East of Bruyere the Germans are being cleared from the forests despite heavy opposition from strong points.

The American drive toward Raon l'Etape is also progressing well. This advance toward the Schirmeck pass through the Vosges Mountains, was made in the Rambervillers and Mortagne forests and along the Rambervillers-Raon l'Etape road.

The weather broke enough this afternoon to allow the British Second Tactical Air Force to fly more than 400 sorties, most of them in support of the Canadian First Army. Spitfires and Typhoons harried the Germans north of Breda with rockets, bombs and machine-gun bullets attacking several buildings, one of which exploded.

The remaining heavy gun positions were attacked on Walcheren and two tanks were destroyed.

In the day's only important air clash a British Tempest probably destroyed a German jet-propelled Messerschmitt 262. ◇

NOVEMBER 5, 1944

GERMANS CHASED FROM ALL GREECE
Allies Report Enemy Fleeing into Yugoslavia— Only Stragglers Remain

By The Associated Press.

ROME, Nov. 4—British troops and Greek patriots have driven the Germans completely from Greece, Allied Headquarters announced today.

An RAF officer said it was believed the last German rear guards had crossed over into Yugoslavia Thursday night— thirty-eight days after British troops landed on the rocky western coast of the Peloponnesus Sept. 26. It took the Germans twenty-seven days to overrun the little country in the spring of 1941.

It was an almost bloodless victory for Allied arms, for so eager were the Germans to clear out, and so well did the guerrillas do their work, that British ground forces were unable to bring the rear guards to battle until they had overhauled the retreating columns in northern Greece.

Before that sharp, short engagement at Kozane, fifty-eight miles southwest of the port of Salonika, British and patriots had swept across the Peloponnesus and on Oct. 14 seized the capital of Athens by a combined assault from sea and air in which American transport planes took part.

An Allied announcement today said that additional British troops had landed near Salonika, which previously was freed by patriots, and other troops were moving up to the northern Greek port by land. These forces also reported that no German troops remained on the mainland except a few stragglers.

Tonight the Germans, who may never get back to the Fatherland in view of the strong Yugoslav and Russian Army positions in Yugoslavia, were still on the run out of Albania and Serbia.

A German broadcast said German troops had strong positions in northern Albania and were engaged in street fighting with "Communist elements" in the capital of Tirana itself.

Those Germans who fell back into Yugoslavia were under attack from Yugoslav partisans at Bitolj, thirteen miles north of the Greek border, and at Skoplje, seventy miles farther north, Marshal Tito's headquarters announced. Both towns were declared under siege.   ➤

❮ Reconnaissance pilots who went out looking for Germans in Greece were unable to find any, they reported, but in the last twenty-four hours small columns were spotted near Lake Prespa, just across the border in Albania.

The reconquest of Greece ended three years and six months of Nazi rule, during which it was estimated 500,000 Greeks had died from starvation, executions and mistreatment. ◇

NOVEMBER 8, 1944

ROOSEVELT AND TRUMAN ELECTED TO PRESIDENCY AND VICE PRESIDENCY

DEWEY CONCEDES

By ARTHUR KROCK

Franklin Delano Roosevelt, who broke more than a century-old tradition in 1940 when he was elected to a third term as President, made another political record yesterday when he was chosen for a fourth term by a heavy electoral but much narrower popular majority over Thomas E. Dewey, Governor of New York.

At 3:15 A.M. Governor Dewey conceded Mr. Roosevelt's re-election, sending his best wishes by radio, to which the President quickly responded with an appreciative telegram.

Early this morning Mr. Roosevelt was leading in mounting returns in thirty-three States with a total of 391 electoral votes and in half a dozen more a trend was developing that could increase this figure to more than 400. Governor Dewey was ahead in fifteen States with 140 electoral votes, but some were see-sawing away from him and back again. Typical of these were Wisconsin, where he overtook the President's lead about 2 A.M., Nevada where Mr. Roosevelt passed him at about the same time, and Missouri.

In the contests for seats in Congress, the Democrats had shown gains of 11 to 20 in the House of Representatives, assuring that party's continued control of this branch. In the Senate the net of losses and gains appeared to be an addition of one Republican to the Senate, which would give that party twenty-eight members—far short of the forty-nine necessary to a majority.

Despite the great general victories by the Democrats, the popular vote will evidently show a huge minority protest against a fourth term for the President. Tabulations by the press associations indicated that the disparity between the ballots cast for the two candidates will be so small that a change of several hun-

dred thousand votes in the key States, distributed in a certain way, would have reversed the electoral majority. At 4:40 A.M. the Associated Press reported 16,387,999 for Mr. Roosevelt and 14,235,051 for Mr. Dewey from more than one-third of the country's election districts. This ratio, if carried through, would leave only about 3,000,000 votes between the candidates.

One of the most interesting struggles for the Presidency was that in Wisconsin, where Mr. Dewey took an early lead, lost it and regained it again. Wisconsin is the State where the late Wendell L. Willkie made his stand for renomination, posing the issue of "isolationism" versus "internationalism." He ran last in the Presidential primary and expressed the belief, in then withdrawing from the race, that isolationism controlled the thinking of Wisconsin Republicans.

WALLACE PROVES RIGHT

The popular vote ran so close until after 11 o'clock that even the most optimistic supporters of the President were cautious in their claims. But Mr. Wallace was not so timorous. He established a national record as a forecasting statistician by announcing at 9:30 P.M. that the President had been re-elected by a large electoral majority, that he had been given a Democratic House with a "mandate" to carry out his war and post-war program and that "bipartisan isolationism has been destroyed."

When Mr. Wallace issued this statement few were ready to accept his conclusion. But an hour later he had become a major prophet. ◇

V-2 Is Aimed At Allied Armies; Speed Is '3,500 Miles an Hour'

By The Associated Press.

LONDON, Nov. 11—The German V-2 rocket bomb, described as a thirteen and one-half ton wingless projectile that cuts through space at a maximum speed of 3,500 miles an hour, has been falling in Allied sectors in Belgium and France as well as in Britain, front dispatches approved by Army censors said tonight.

A number of these new vengeance weapons, which cannot be heard coming because they are faster than sound, fell in one United States Army sector alone in less than two days, and the rate has increased at various intervals, said a dispatch from an Associated Press correspondent. The censor deleted the origin of the dispatch. In another dispatch, from which the censor also had deleted the dateline, a Canadian Press correspondent, in describing this "eeriest weapon yet

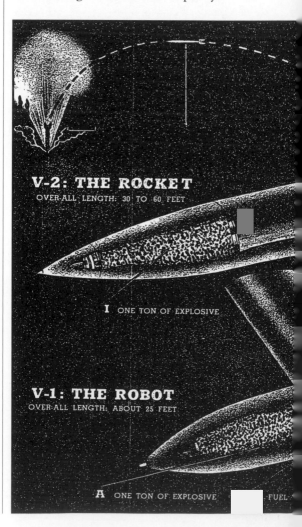

V-2: THE ROCKET
OVER-ALL LENGTH: 30 TO 60 FEET

I ONE TON OF EXPLOSIVE

V-1: THE ROBOT
OVER-ALL LENGTH: ABOUT 25 FEET

A ONE TON OF EXPLOSIVE   FUEL

produced in the war," said the Germans had been bombarding an Allied sector in Belgium. The correspondent was not allowed to say where the bombs fell, but the missile was termed poor in accuracy.

Today's German communiqué said the V-2 still was being fired at Antwerp in Belgium and at London.

The new German reprisal weapon was described by the correspondents as being about forty-six feet long and five feet wide, and less effective than the V-1, the robot bomb first used against England. The warhead contains almost a ton of explosive, and the fuel used to propel it weighs nine tons. It is shot from concrete ramps almost vertically, reaches a height of twenty miles before beginning a great arc toward its intended target. At the height of the arc it is fifty-five miles from the earth and attains a velocity of 5,000 feet per second, or approximately 3,500 miles an hour.

Allied experts were quoted as saying that the V-2 was not as effective in destructive power as the V-1 because of the huge crater it made, reducing the blast. The robot bomb digs hardly any crater, going off on contact with maximum effect.

The V-2 also is a much more complicated and expensive weapon than the robot bomb, a product which takes an immense amount of machining. The warhead is not encased in heavy metal and there is no shrapnel effect, the Canadian Press dispatch said.

ROCKETS ARE NOT ACCURATE

Field dispatches have reported the use of V-2 rockets in the battle zone, but correspondents indicated they were too inaccurate to have military value. V-1 robots have also been used at the front and against several captured cities in Belgium, France and Holland. Rockets fired at troops were reported to have been slightly smaller than those used against England.

At least thirty-six persons have been killed or badly injured by the V-2 bombardment of Britain, a check of casualties in reported incidents showed. The casualty figure is unofficial and incomplete because reports of some incidents did not include the fatalities.

In one case a rocket fell into a shopping crowd and "a number" of persons were killed. Nine children were killed at a birthday party.

One rocket exploded in an open area, and several ducks were the only victims. Still another rocket dug its deep crater in the open and killed only a pig.

The German radio continued its propaganda campaign on the effectiveness of the V-2, saying that one rocket damaged or destroyed 600 houses in London. The German home front was told that the new weapon "exceeded all imagination."

"Employment of V-weapons has just begun," German propagandists said, adding that the bombardment of London would increase.

Claims were made regarding the otherwise unsupported report that Antwerp, too, was under bombardment and that "a large part of the population has fled into the country." DNB, German news agency, said the V-1 and the V-2 were being fired against Antwerp and that dock and harbor installations had been heavily damaged. ◆

NOVEMBER 19, 1944

Editorial
V-1 AND V-2

THE second of Germany's "vengeance weapons," V-2, is now in action. V-2, the rocket, has much in common with V-1, the robot plane. Both are pilotless. Both are jet propelled—that is, they have "reaction motors"; they depend for their forward motion on the reaction to the explosive jets of gas that stream back from them at great speeds. But there are basic differences between them, too. V-1 looks like a small plane without a propeller. V-2 looks like a shell or a huge Fourth of July rocket. V-1 gets its oxygen (the essential element in combustion) from the air. V-2 carries its own oxygen supply and can therefore fly high into the sky, where there is little oxygen.

There are differences in performance, too. The robot plane has a speed of 350 to 400 miles an hour; the top speed of the rocket has been put at anywhere from 1,000 to as high as 3,500 ▸

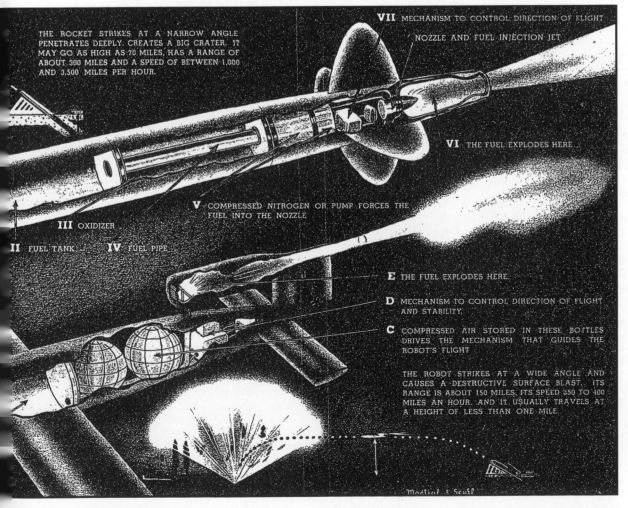

THE ROCKET STRIKES AT A NARROW ANGLE PENETRATES DEEPLY, CREATES A BIG CRATER. IT MAY GO AS HIGH AS 70 MILES, HAS A RANGE OF ABOUT 300 MILES AND A SPEED OF BETWEEN 1,000 AND 3,500 MILES PER HOUR.

VII MECHANISM TO CONTROL DIRECTION OF FLIGHT

NOZZLE AND FUEL INJECTION JET

VI THE FUEL EXPLODES HERE

V COMPRESSED NITROGEN OR PUMP FORCES THE FUEL INTO THE NOZZLE

III OXIDIZER

II FUEL TANK   IV FUEL PIPE

E THE FUEL EXPLODES HERE

D MECHANISM TO CONTROL DIRECTION OF FLIGHT AND STABILITY

C COMPRESSED AIR STORED IN THESE BOTTLES DRIVES THE MECHANISM THAT GUIDES THE ROBOT'S FLIGHT

THE ROBOT STRIKES AT A WIDE ANGLE AND CAUSES A DESTRUCTIVE SURFACE BLAST. ITS RANGE IS ABOUT 150 MILES. ITS SPEED 350 TO 400 MILES AN HOUR. AND IT USUALLY TRAVELS AT A HEIGHT OF LESS THAN ONE MILE

miles an hour. The range of the robot plane is believed to be about 150 or 200 miles; the rocket has a range of about 300. The robot flies low—the average height of those aimed at London was 2,300 feet: the rocket shoots up 60 or 70 miles.

The robot can be seen and heard and therefore can be fought very effectively by planes and anti-aircraft guns; the rocket travels faster than sound and therefore cannot be heard until it has struck; it travels so fast that the familiar methods of defense cannot be used against it.

How the rocket is launched and controlled is a question that has caused much speculation. The flying bomb can be launched from a plane, but the rocket is too big to be carried into the air and its exhaust is too dangerously hot. Platforms for launching flying bombs have been captured in France; they are necessary because the robot planes must have an initial momentum of 150 or 200 miles an hour before their engines work efficiently. The rockets however would not seem to need elaborate launching apparatus; they apparently get off under their own power and simply require plat-forms with guiding rails to start them in the right direction.

Once in the air, the flying bomb's direction of flight, altitude and stability are maintained by automatic pilots or gyroscopes—the "brains" of the robot. The bomb may also be controlled by radio. Its range may be determined by the amount of fuel or its motor may be cut off by radio. The rocket's range is apparently set in the same ways. Therefore by decreasing the amount of explosive or increasing the amount of fuel, the range of the rocket may conceivably be extended.

The drawing on these pages shows the differences in construction between V-1 and V-2; it was made by Martial & Scull, industrial designers, on the basis of the best available information.

V-1 is made up of five elements: the wings, the fuselage, the motor, the control mechanism, the explosive and the fuel. The explosive (A) is in the nose. The fuel tank (B) is placed between the wings. Compressed air, stored in spherical bottles (C) in the center of the plane, operates the mechanism (D) for controlling the direction of flight and the stability of the robot. The motor (E) is above the fuselage and in the rear. Air rushes through vents in the front of the motor, the fuel is mixed with the air and exploded, the resultant gases slam shut the vents and open the jet in the rear through which the gases escape.

V-2 is even simpler in construction, though more expensive to build and trickier to handle. It has four parts: the casing, the explosive, the fuel and the control mechanisms. The explosive (I) is in the nose. Behind it are the fuel tanks (II), which make up a chemical motor, one containing the explosive, the other the oxidizer (III). The fuel is forced along a pipe (IV) either by a pump or by the pressure of compressed nitrogen (V). It is exploded in a chamber (VI) at the end of the rocket. The mechanism (VII) that controls the flight of the rocket is in the rear.

Will either V-1 or V-2 be decisive weapons in the war? Goebbels is banking on them (or at least he tells the German people that they will make for victory in time) but no military expert believes that they will have any major effect on the course of the battle. Rather they are considered the weapons of the future. ◇

NOVEMBER 26, 1944

School of Battle for Doctors
The Surgeon General says that the lessons they are learning at the front will help us at home.

By MAJ. GEN. NORMAN T. KIRK
Surgeon General, U.S. Army

THE primary responsibility of the Army medical officer is to conserve the fighting strength of our Army. In discharging that task, however military doctors contribute in large measure to the general fund of professional knowledge in the fields of surgery and medicine. Lessons learned by application in the hard school of war under the whip of necessity become available to the medical profession generally, for the ultimate benefit of the civilian as well as the soldier.

The war has served as a vast clinic and laboratory in which thousands of doctors have obtained experience far exceeding in scope and variety the work which the civil practitioner might ex-pect to encounter in his private practice. After the war the public will be able to draw on the services of physicians and surgeons whose skills have been sharpened by intensive practice in caring for the sick and wounded. Many more American hospitals in the post-war period, it is safe to say, will be staffed by doctors competent, as a result of war experience, to deal with almost every conceivable type of surgical case.

War has given great impetus to research and new developments in the use of whole blood and its by-products, the sulfonamides and penicillin, both in medicine and surgery and their possibilities have by no means been exhausted. The results of much of this work already are available to the civilian population, but they undoubtedly will be used on a much wider scale when the military need is relaxed.

In preventive and curative medicine the civil population will profit by the application of new methods of treating disease developed during the war, by increased knowledge of sanitation nutri-tion and diet by more effective methods for control and destruction of disease-carrying insect pests and by advances in immunization. The recent announcement of the development of a vaccine to prevent the spread of influenza should the disease become epidemic within the Army, is only one example of progress in immunization that eventually will prove of immense value in protecting the general public against disease.

THE Army Medical Department for the time being, however, must devote itself to its principal task, the maintenance of the health of the troops and the rapid restoration to duty whenever possible of men who suffer wounds or disease. How well Army doctors are performing their jobs in this respect is best shown by two facts.

Ninety-seven per cent of all our war wounded recover, notwithstanding the terribly destructive power of modern weapons. Furthermore, the death rate from disease in the Army, many of whose members are fighting in the most plague-ridden sections of the world, has been reduced to less than 6 per 10,000 men annually, a rate below that prevailing in civilian life. The magnitude of these accomplishments may be better understood when it is considered that the death rate from wounds is more than 50 per cent below the level of the first World War and that the disease mortality rate is 95 per cent below that of the war of twenty-six years ago.

The excellent survival rate among our wounded may be attributed princi-

SUPPLY LAG DELAYS EISENHOWER DRIVE
Stimson Reveals Offensive Was Postponed By Bottlenecks in Shell Delivery

Special to The New York Times.

WASHINGTON, Nov. 30—Shortage of ammunition forced Gen. Dwight D. Eisenhower to hold up his general offensive just as the armies neared the Rhine, Henry L. Stimson, Secretary of War, announced at a news conference today in making a plea for greater production.

The War Secretary said the ammunition situation has been and is "extremely complicated and equally critical" and may continue so unless there is a great increase in output.

General Eisenhower's delay, Mr. Stimson explained, was partly attributable to the European railroad situation, but chiefly to the fact that limitations of ports prevented reception of the shells. Now, the Secretary added, we are nearing another limitation—the availability of ammunition in this country.

ANTWERP INCREASES FLOW

Opening the port of Antwerp will "tremendously" raise the possibility of delivering ammunition to the battlefront, Mr. Stimson said and will "therefore correspondingly increase the amounts" that must be made and delivered from this country.

"Last April," he said, "following our experiences in the mountain warfare in Italy, where artillery consumption tremendously increased beyond all previous estimates of theatre commanders or the War Department, a careful survey of the entire situation was made and it was then decided to increase greatly the heavy artillery, both as to guns and as to ammunition, and to make general increases in artillery ammunition throughout, anticipating an approach to a trench-warfare situation during periods of stalemate in the campaigns which had then been decided upon, notably the landing in France.

"Then following the breakthrough at Avranches and the rush across France, we experienced a series of artillery difficulties: first was the limitation imposed by disrupted railroad lines for the delivery of the ammunition available in the ports. As the railroad situation greatly improved, the next bottleneck was the incapacity of the ports to deliver the ammunition available in Great Britain.

"Following this we arrived at a situation as the armies approached the Rhine, where it became necessary for General Eisenhower to delay a general offensive until an adequate reserve of artillery ammunition could be accumulated. Rail deliveries were partially responsible, port limitations were principally responsible.

HOME SUPPLY NOW INVOLVED

"As both these two factors improve we are reaching another limitation, and that is the availability of ammunition in the United States. We could disembark more if it were available and we could transport across France more if it were available.

"However, the delay accepted by General Eisenhower has enabled us to accumulate the ammunition for the great offensive now in process. Even so, as a result of the transportation difficulties, portions of the front that otherwise would have been very active were forced to remain quiescent.

"The consumption of ammunition is necessarily on a tremendous scale. Throughout the Apennines, in Italy, and along the entire Western Front we are firing probably ten times the amount of ammunition the Germans are, but we are forced to use it to destroy concrete structures as well as to destroy the enemy himself.

"We insist on an overwhelming artillery power for the support of our infantry, not merely to gain success in ›

---

pally to five factors: Prompt and skillful surgery performed in the forward areas of the battle zones as soon as possible after a man has been hit; blood plasma and whole blood transfusions; the new drugs, including the sulfonamides and penicillin; a fast and efficient system of evacuating the wounded to fixed installations, where they receive definitive care, and a comprehensive program of immunization and other measures in preventive medicine.

The plan of the medical service in the fighting zones is based upon the principle, which was well learned in the last war, that the sooner a wounded soldier can receive surgical care the better are his chances for recovery. To implement this principle the Army is using highly mobile surgical teams composed of skilled surgical specialists, nurses and enlisted men of the Medical Department, who operate close to the front lines. Usually within ten minutes after a man has been hit a "medical soldier" is at his side to administer first aid, relieve pain, dress his wound and prepare him for evacuation to the rear.

In addition to saving lives, surgical specialists are performing wonders in reconstructive and rehabilitative surgery. Remarkable results that even a few years ago would have been considered impossible are being effected in vascular, nerve, plastic, brain and orthopedic surgery. The extensive use of land mines in this war has resulted in a relatively high number of amputations. Yet many who have lost one or more limbs will suffer comparatively little disability in civil life. Improvements in the manufacture, fitting and adjustment of appliances and the training the men receive in their use, so effectively conceal the amputations that these men are very unlikely to be the objects of morbid curiosity or to be publicly labeled as the "handicapped." The opportunity for normal, useful lives will be open to many of them.

Venereal disease, always important in military medicine, has been reduced to a rate of 30 per 1,000 men per annum, a record that is unmatched in an army at any time. Days lost from duty because of venereal disease have dropped from 1,278 per 1,000 men in 1940 to 400 per 1,000. In addition, more than 147,000 men with venereal disease have been inducted into the Army and successfully treated. Even greater improvement in venereal disease rates is anticipated as refinements in treatment with the sulfonamides and penicillin are perfected. ◇

❪ battles but more particularly to hold down the number of casualties. We foresee still further increased requirements, and it is for that reason that every possible measure should be taken to stimulate production in this country.

"The fanaticism of the enemy, who apparently has accepted the inch-by-inch destruction of Germany, has imposed additional requirements. Our determination is to smash the German Army and to give our troops every conceivable advantage of weapons and materiel. That, I think, should be the point of view of every American." ◇

DECEMBER 3, 1944

BOARD FACES HARD TASK IN SELLING WAR SURPLUS
Largest Store of Things Ever Amassed Must Be Disposed Of Wisely

By CHARLES E. EGAN

WASHINGTON, Dec. 2—Imagine a job in which one was ordered to find markets for 22,000,000 flashlight batteries, a dozen live monkeys, 1,000 garbage cans, 10,000 carrier pigeons and half as many dogs, and one will gain a slight conception of the range and variety of surplus property which the Surplus War Property Administration will be called upon to market over the next several years.

The items mentioned are only part of the more than $465,207,000 worth of war holdings already declared to be surplus. Of this amount $85,007,000 had been sold up to Sept. 30, this year. It does not include the twelve monkeys (seven of which have since been sold to the Columbus, Ohio, zoo), nor the 22,000,000 flashlight batteries which will go on sale to dealers soon.

The total already declared surplus and available for sales is but a small fraction of such war goods as aircraft, machinery, plants, real estate, ships and foodstuffs for which markets will have to be found at the end of the war.

HARD TO TELL VALUE
Officials of the Surplus War Property Administration, now headed by Will Clayton but soon to be directed by a board of three members under terms of the surplus property disposal law enacted this fall by Congress, say there is no way to give an accurate figure as to what the value of surplus property will be at the war's end. Until fighting actually stops, they explain, goods and equipment held in reserve cannot be regarded as surplus. When the cease-fire order is given, however, a large percentage will become surplus overnight.

Best estimates on Capitol Hill and in Government agencies place the probable value of surplus materials when the fighting ceases in excess of $100,000,000,000. Of this, $16,000,000,000 is represented by war plants and adjacent realty owned by the Defense Plants Corporation. This does not count the extensive war housing and other Government-owned realty which runs well above $1,000,000,000.

Until the war ends, only those items of equipment and plant which are declared to be no longer needed by the armed services, Maritime Commission, War Food Administration, National Housing Administration and others are officially regarded as surplus and allowed to be sold as such.

LARGEST STORE EVER
After V-E day, but particularly at the close of the war with Japan, the real task of the SWPA will open up. Then it will find on its hands the greatest collection of merchandise, machinery, real estate and other facilities of war that has even been assembled for disposition. Stocks of raw materials of all kinds, goods in a semi-manufactured state, canned and preserved foods of all kinds, electric appliances, cargo ships, aircraft numbered in the thousands from trainers to B-29 bombers, tanks, trucks marine engines and a seemingly endless array of other types of goods, will await disposal.

How best to dispose of this vast accumulation of goods without wrecking the normal channels of trade, stifling employment and creating a nation-wide depression in the post-war era, is the problem with which the Surplus War Property Administration and all responsible Government and business executives have been wrestling for months. Final solutions have not been reached yet but progress has been made and hopes are expressed that the task can be accomplished without jarring the economic machinery out of position.

The determination to find a solution stems largely from recollections of the sorry job made in surplus disposal following the last war.

At that time great quantities of raw and finished materials were dumped upon the country when the nation was trying to get its economic balance after a two-year spree of wartime spending. The results, in many lines of trade, were well-nigh catastrophic. Speculators grew rich buying consumer supplies from the Government for a fraction of the real value and marketing them at huge profits through retail outlets, while manufacturers of goods similar to the surplus items were forced to close the doors of their plants. Prices fell, employment dropped and the entire country suffered.

To guard against such occurrences after this war all goods owned by the United States and stored abroad will be sold only on guarantee that it will not re-enter this country, either in its original form or as part of a manufactured item.

One plan which is being tried out in the disposal of surplus cutting tools and some electronic equipment is to turn the goods back to the original manufacturer, letting him dispose of them for the Government on a commission basis. In such sales the plan is to have the goods marketed in a ratio of two surplus machines for each new machine sold. The ratio can be adjusted to conform to market conditions.

Even with all the precautions which will be taken, the marketing of so vast a quantity of merchandise, whether in finished form or as scrap (as in the case of some aircraft, dismantled artillery, etc.), will present a strain upon the economy.

The best that can be hoped for is that the impact will be softened through the proper timing of sales and by disposal in quantities which can be assimilated without disrupting the health of the nation's economy. ◇

DECEMBER 18, 1944

GERMAN ASSAULT IS A MAJOR EFFORT

By HAROLD DENNY
By Cable to The New York Times.

WITH AMERICAN FIRST ARMY, in Germany, Dec. 17—The German counter-offensive that started yesterday moved forward several more miles into our lines today and with increased power. It looks like the real thing.

It is too early yet to gauge its possible extent and scope and whether this is to be Germany's final all-out effort to stave off defeat. But the rate at which the Germans are throwing in divisions, including some crack ones, shows that it is a serious, major counter-offensive and serious exertions will be needed to meet it.

The Germans are supporting these divisions with everything in their arsenal—scores of paratroopers, who were dropped behind our lines in an effort to disrupt our supplies and communications, and tanks and aircraft in more lavish numbers than they have thrown at us at any one time since Normandy. And for the past two days they have been tossing over V-weapons in far greater numbers.

German troops, we learn from prisoners, were sent into this drive on a wave of do-or-die ballyhoo. The following order of the day was read to all troops before the attack:

"Soldiers of the west front:

"Your great hour has struck. Strong attacking armies are advancing today against the Anglo-Americans. I do not need to say more to you. You all feel it. Everything is at stake. You bear in yourselves the holy duty to give everything and to achieve the superhuman for our fatherland and our Fuehrer."

It was signed "Commander in Chief of the West Front von Rundstedt, Field Marshal."

Today surviving members of the German first waves had the satisfaction of crossing from German soil through the Siegfried Line into Belgium and Luxembourg at several points and our troops were seriously on the defensive for the first time since Normandy. The Germans were paying heavy, however. German dead were piling up in front of our forward positions. Some front-line commanders reported German casualties at 50 or 60 per cent of the attacking units.

As of yesterday, the total length of American front on which the attacks were occurring at various points was about seventy miles, which was in the First Army zone from the neighborhood of Monschau to near Echternach.

We had motored by jeep down a road that should have led us, without incident, to the Second Infantry Division. At another town en route, however, we learned that the Germans had cut the road ahead and were attacking toward this town. In front of this town were infantrymen of a division that cannot yet be identified as in the line. They had held off German attacks all day yesterday and until midnight when the German attack waned. It began again at 3:30 o'clock this morning, however, with a determined assault on this division's flank.

The Germans sent in forty to fifty tanks with infantrymen riding them pick-a-back. The infantrymen jumped down and tried to knock out our anti-tank guns and open a path for the tanks. By 6 o'clock this morning the Germans had penetrated this division's front three miles. Our men were out-numbered there and, except for some tank destroyers that were rushed up, they had to fight off these heavy attacks with rifles, grenades and bazookas.

Our troops in this town knew that reinforcements were coming up and they felt that they could hold off the enemy until the help arrived. We left for a headquarters farther back in the rear. When we reached it we learned that the town we had left had just fallen. ◆

DECEMBER 19, 1944

AMERICANS BATTLE TO STEM ADVANCE OF THE ENEMY; NAZIS STILL MOVING

By Wireless to The New York Times.

SUPREME HEADQUARTERS, Allied Expeditionary Force, Paris, Dec. 18—The American Ninth Air Force and the British Second Tactical Air Force dived through sleet and fog today to hammer the tank-tipped German columns pressing deeper into Belgium and Luxembourg as Field Marshal Gen. Karl von Rundstedt's counter-offensive continued to move westward for the third day.

The greatest enemy penetration revealed by the Allies was in the area west of Stavelot, which is eight miles southwest of Malmedy and twenty miles from the German frontier from which the northern arm of the offensive was launched. There, rocket-firing Typhoons of the British Second Tactical Air Force fell on a column of twenty German half-tracks, destroying three of them.

ALLIED PLANES BATTER FOE

The Allies' ground forces continued their news blackout today, but it is obvious from the reports of air battles, which involved three American tactical commands and two British fighter bomber groups, that the German counter-offensive was monopolizing the Allies' attention.

The air battles raged over this battle front, with American pilots destroying forty-five German planes and the British one. The Ninth Air Force, whose fighter bombers operated against enemy columns, claimed the destruction of ninety-five German tanks and other armored vehicles, 265 trucks and sixty railroad cars, while Marauders, Havocs and Invaders dropped more than 290 tons of bombs on five towns in the Schleiden area, well to the east of the German spearheads.

The Ninth Air Force also claimed that twenty-six tanks and other armored vehicles; sixty-five trucks and nineteen railroad cars had been damaged and that twenty fortified buildings had been destroyed and twenty gun positions silenced during the attacks today. German railroads were cut in three places.

BOMBERS HIT RAIL CENTERS

In a direct blow at the supply lines of ❯

the attacking German Armies, 1,800 American and British heavy bombers attacked major German railway centers including Cologne, Coblenz and Mainz last night and today.

The German thrust to the vicinity of Stavelot placed the northern arm of Marshal von Rundstedt's offensive in an area twenty-two miles southeast of Liege. There were no reports available here of the progress of the enemy drives into Luxembourg through Vianden and Echternach. The speed and depth of the penetration in the north, however, were disquieting.

The nature of all Allied measures taken to halt the enemy thrust cannot be revealed, but it is obvious that the two days of extensive air activity have failed to check the German offensive in the north at least. It is probable, however, that American divisions already are attacking the sides of the German thrust.

While the battle raged over the sodden hills of the Ardennes and through the stone villages of eastern Belgium,

far to the south two divisions of Lieut. Gen. Alexander M. Patch's American Seventh Army continued to push northward into the Palatinate from the German frontier in the area of the Wissembourg Gap.

Meanwhile, on the American Third Army front, the Ninetieth Infantry Division has cleared most of Dillingen, except for a single fortified area, knocking out five Siegfried Line pillboxes in the process. ◊

On the Ninth Army front our troops cleared Wuerm, Mullendorf and Beeck (1) and before Dueren they entered Roelsdorf and Lendersdorf (2). Although there was a blackout on news of the German offensive, it was indicated that the force was beyond Stavelot in Belgium (3), that the push at the northern tip of Luxembourg (4) had gained and that the thrusts below Viaden (5) and Echternach (6) had been stalled. The Third Army pushed to the eastern edge of Dillingen (7). The Seventh battered Maginot Line defenses near Bitche (8), entered Nieder Shlettenbach (9), west of which it gained, and passed Berg (10). Bombs show rail centers blasted.

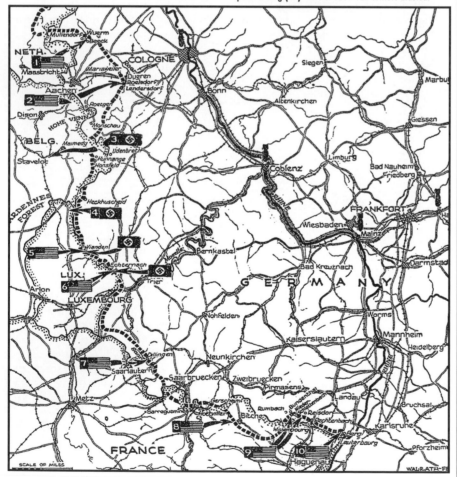

DECEMBER 19, 1944

COOKS AND CLERKS SLOW NAZI BLOW
Mustered When Foe Strikes Suddenly, They Hold Until Armor, Planes Arrive

By MORLEY CASSIDY
Of The Philadelphia Bulletin
North American Newspaper Alliance.

WITH THE AMERICAN SECOND DIVISION, Dec. 18—Here and elsewhere on a front of sixty miles the Germans are throwing what looks like a Sunday punch at American forces. For two days I have been watching the greatest German counter-attacks since Normandy against forward elements of this division.

Standing outside the division command post, I watched these veterans being forced, blow by blow, to give ground temporarily before enemy armored columns. German armored infantry forced its way over a hill less than three-quarters of a mile from this command post, while a column of German tanks poured withering machine-gun and artillery fire into the village streets for hours.

The command post mustered cooks, bakers and clerks of the headquarters personnel into posts as infantrymen until reinforcements arrived. The German tank attack gradually was slowed by these men, who later were aided by tank destroyers and tanks, which knocked out four German tanks and an armored scout car.

FOE USING GOOD UNITS

Barely a half mile from here the German attack continues with heavy concentrations of excellent divisions, including armored, infantry and panzer units. The enemy also is striking heavily in more than a dozen spots from the Monschau area in Belgium to Echternach in Luxembourg.

In some places these gains have been sizable, although the most ominous threats appear to be sealed off. One of the most dangerous of these was crushed—for a moment, at least—by the heroic stand of this division and its right-hand neighbor.

This furious assault broke with little warning. The command post here was shelled fiercely Saturday morning—it was the heaviest shelling in its history—and other divisions near by were shelled from unexpected areas, which was an indication of the wide scope of the German effort.

True to their tradition of Sunday attacks, the Germans hit with full strength yesterday morning, first in the air with V [robot] weapons and bombing missions. Shortly before dawn this whole division was alerted for the possibility of paratroopers. At about the same time came word that the Germans had broken into part of the division on our right with tanks and armored infantry and were sweeping toward our headquarters.

NEWS IS STARTLING

This news was startling, as this division had been in the midst of a terrific forward push and gained nearly two miles only the day before.

Our crossroads village was roaring with vehicles, racing to take positions. Cooks, kitchen police and headquarters clerks were jumping from pots, pans and typewriters to grab rifles, grenades and pistols. Many of these men had not fired a weapon since hitting the Normandy beach on D-day-Plus-One.

This job was too close for maps and telephones. Standing outside the command post Maj. Gen. Walter M. Robertson chain-smoked cigarettes as he directed the infantry into place. By this time German tanks had moved over the crest of a hill 1 mile across this little valley. They moved swiftly down the road in our direction, but suddenly there was a jet of flames when one tank was hit by a machine gun manned by Master Sgt. Melvin Brown and a jeep driver, Pfc. Alvin Taylor, both of Texas.

By now the hills east and south of our command post were flaming with streams of tracers fired by our men, and the Germans were criss-crossing in the curtain of red arcs. Enemy artillery fire was growing and high explosive shells and phosphorous bombs were landing across the street from us, but through it all General Robertson stood unmoved. He gave orders to headquarters personnel to defend the building until the last.

GENERAL LEADS THE WAY

With the first thrust held by these makeshift forces, thanks to the tank destroyers, our anti-tank guns arrived from another sector and rolled through the town. General Robertson mounted the lead scout car and rode to the lines to place the vehicles. He had barely returned when the German tanks hit with full force.

Five of them appeared on the road to our left. We watched breathless as a tank destroyer knocked off the first and set it blazing. A few moments later another was hit, then the third, along with a scout car. The other two turned and fled.

The vehicles burned brightly a few minutes, then burst into hundreds of flames as their ammunition exploded.

The danger was far from over, however. Infantry reinforcements had followed the lead tanks and other tanks were approaching up the valley to the south. With our command post ringed by machine-gun fire, we could see lines of fire moving down hills in our direction.

"If we could only get air," an officer kept repeating. Presently a dozen Thunderbolts of the Ninth Air Force circled overhead, spotting targets.

"Thank God they got through," seemed to be heard all around.

Diving, the planes dropped their eggs on troops and tanks. They were pinpointed to their targets by radio direction from Maj. J. P. Dunn of Chicago.

Mission after mission came over, but today the Germans had thrown in the Luftwaffe, too. From the east appeared a dozen Messerschmitt 109's. We saw one shot down by our ack-ack and another engaged by a Thunderbolt as it was dropping its bombs. There were two swift passes, then the Messerschmitt began trailing smoke and crashed.

The Luftwaffe returned. A dozen planes dive-bombed and strafed our command post. This time our AA guns got another. On its heels another fell to a Thunderbolt.

The situation at the command post was still desperate at noon and plans were laid for an escape route through a rear window. But again the doughboys turned up in scores of trucks. They dismounted to stream up the valley to the south. Grim-faced but cracking wry jokes, they plodded out to their posts, half a mile away.

Two battalions went through and some soon began coming back, some limping and some on litters. Others who went out won't come back, but they did a job.

The surprise attack on our flank had been held and sealed off, and General Robertson was able to set up a new line facing south instead of east. Then, and not till then, did he agree to move his command post to the rear—while he moved forward. ◈

DECEMBER 25, 1944

NAZI PUSH HALTED BY AIR AND GROUND BLOWS
Enemy Forced to Pause as Americans Strike Back in Force

By DREW MIDDLETON
By Wireless to The New York Times.

SUPREME HEADQUARTERS, Allied Expeditionary Force, Dec. 24—The mightiest tactical air assault of the war and a series of determined attacks by American troops have at least temporarily halted the German offensive in eastern Belgium.

The great battle neared its climax today when, with about 6,500 American and British bombers and fighters blasting the German divisions at the front, their supply lines and the airfields on which the Luftwaffe relies, the American forces smashed deeper into the southern flank of the enemy's salient in Luxembourg.

The halting of the enemy drive on which the Germans gambled so heavily—a Christmas gift for all who cherish freedom—may be only temporary, but it is apparent that the German smash has lost its first edge and that whenever his offensive is renewed the enemy will attack with greatly reduced forces against Allied divisions ready to resume their own offensive in the life-and-death struggle over the rugged, snow-covered hills and narrow valleys of the eastern Ardennes.

GERMAN MIGHT EBBS

The Germans, who attacked so confidently on Dec. 16 in the Indian summer of their military strength, suffered heavily in the air and on the ground today.

American and British pilots destroyed 116 German planes in air battles that covered the front from the Cologne plain to the Colmar area. While the doughboys, artillerymen and tank crews hammered the German flank on the south, more than 2,000 bombers of the Eighth Air Force, the greatest force of heavy bombers ever flown on a single mission by any air force, pounded enemy road, rail and supply lines and smashed airfields from which the Luftwaffe had been operating in support of the offensive.

◀ Meanwhile, a vast number of fighter-bombers of the Ninth Air Force and Spitfires, Typhoons and Mustangs of the British Second Tactical Air Force swept over the battle area.

HUNDREDS OF VEHICLES RUINED

American fighter-bombers reported that they had destroyed or damaged 116 German tanks and other armored machines and 778 motor transport vehicles and destroyed twenty-eight horse-drawn vehicles. Ten gun positions were silenced by fighter-bombers, which also destroyed or damaged fifty-six railroad cars, cut twenty railroad lines and eleven highways west of the Rhine and bombed seventeen fortified villages.

About 2,500 heavy bombers, including Lancasters and Halifaxes of the Royal Air Force Bomber Command, were in the fleet that hammered communications, dumps and airfields.

The most important development on the ground was a continuation of the American attacks on the southern flank of the German offensive, roughly in the area north of the line Arlon–Luxembourg City.

The Germans maintained pressure on the nose of their larger and more southern salient, but there has been no change of position here for forty-eight hours and the Allied forces are holding the enemy in check not only, as hitherto, on the flanks but in some areas on the western faces of the two salients.

FIVE FACTORS IN CHECK

The check of the German offensive, temporary though it may be, can be ascribed, in the view of this correspondent, to five causes. The first two, which are equally important, are the rapid reorganization of the Americans south of the German advance and their bite into the German side, reaching the area of Martelange, ten miles south of Bastogne, and the great aerial offensive, which for two days has hacked and hammered at the Germans from their armored spearheads in Belgium to their communications on the Rhine.

Since the opening of the offensive the Ninth Air Force alone has destroyed 288 German planes and destroyed or damaged 261 armored vehicles, 1,874 motor transport and 578 railroad cars. In the same period twenty-three locomotives have been disabled and forty-four enemy gun positions silenced. The American losses for that period are eighty-five fighter-bombers and thirty-six medium and light bombers.

The three other causes for the halting of the enemy offenses are, in the

American soldiers during the counter-offensive that would become known as the Battle of the Bulge.

opinion of this correspondent, the tank action fought by American armor at St. Vith, which averted a union of the two German salients, the gallant and bitter defense of their surrounded positions by American troops in a dozen towns or villages well behind the German spearhead and the pause in the offensive Thursday when, before pressure had been applied in great strength by the Allies on the ground or in the air, Field Marshal Gen. Karl von Rundstedt's columns began to regroup and the armor slowed its pace while his marching infantry divisions hurried to occupy ground won early in the week.

PANZERS IMPERILED

The advance into the southern flank of the German offensive, a "sensitive" area, where any deep penetration would imperil the panzer divisions to the west, has continued well. The Germans report that these forces are from Lieut. Gen. George S. Patton Jr.'s Third Army.

Martelange has been half cleared of the enemy by these forces and a brisk action is in progress in rugged country four and a half miles to the east of Martelange, near Rambrouch.

Doughboys pushing across the snow-covered hills have also made gains about two miles north of Grosbous, which is on the Arlon-Vianden highway, seven miles southwest of Eehternaeh.

NORTHERN AREA STABILIZED

The northern salient, too, is fairly quiet,

although the Americans at Maubach, nine miles south of Dueren, made local gains. From Monschau to the southwest the line still holds firm, and although the Germans continue to maintain pressure, they have made no important progress. Some enemy forces varying in size from a company to a platoon have infiltrated American positions in the Malmedy area with some success, but the position is not regarded as dangerous. Other enemy attacks have been repulsed.

Increasing artillery fire and continued German concentration and consolidation in this area, however, indicate that another strong attack is in the making.

St. Vith was occupied by the enemy after an attack Thursday night, thus ending courageous and skillful resistance there. Stavelot, despite persistent enemy attacks, is again in American hands, but the enemy is still trying to retake the town. More paratroops were dropped in the sector Friday night.

The Germans have withdrawn the spearhead of this salient, which formerly rested on Habiemont, to St. Oumont, three miles northwest of Stavelot. This is a stronger position.

Until Thursday noon, the last day on which the enemy enjoyed relative immunity from air attacks, German armor was still attacking hard south and southwest of Bastogne, where the American garrison is still clinging to its positions. ◆

Major Glenn Miller Is Missing On Flight from England to Paris

PARIS, Dec. 24 (AP)—Maj. Glenn Miller, director of the United States Air Force Band and a former orchestra leader, is missing on a flight from England to Paris, it was announced today.

Major Miller, one of the outstanding orchestra leaders of the United States, left England Dec. 15 as a passenger aboard a plane. No trace of the plane has been found.

His Air Force Band had been playing in Paris. No members of the band were with him on the plane. He last led his band in a broadcast Dec. 12. His band, scheduled to broadcast over BBC tomorrow at 7 P.M. [2 P.M., Eastern war time] in the "AEF Christmas Show," will be conducted by Sgt. Jerry Gray, deputy leader.

WAS TOP-RANK LEADER

Bespectacled and scholarly looking, Glenn Miller was one of the nation's top-ranking orchestra leaders before entering the Army as a captain in 1942. He not only established box-office records with his band but several times achieved first place in national popularity polls. In 1940 his gross income was $800,000. Almost 3,000,000 copies of his records were sold in 1940.

He was a trombonist and an arranger of exceptional talents. His theme song, "Moonlight Serenade," was internationally known.

Two-time winner of The Billboard's Annual College Music Survey, he was one of the earliest to understand the scoring of a swing arrangement. He contributed prolifically to the libraries of the nation's outstanding bands.

In 1942 he enlisted in the Army and was commissioned a captain. He trained and directed service bands, and entertained American troops here and abroad. He was commissioned a Major several weeks ago.

His wife, the former Helen Burger, was a university classmate. They were married on Oct. 6, 1928. They have two adopted children, a three-months-old daughter and a two-year-old son. He resided at Tenafly, N. J., with his family. ◊

MORE MASSACRES IN ITALY REPORTED

Members of the Nazi Elite Guard and Italian Republican Fascists have massacred approximately 300 Italian civilians at Monchio, in the Reggio Emilia region, "for sympathizing with the patriots," according to an overseas dispatch reported yesterday to the Office of War Information.

Italian Partisans arriving in Florence after a trip through enemy and Allied lines in northern Italy reported the massacre. They declared, according to the dispatch, that the Fascists lined their victims against a cemetery wall in groups of twenty and shot them. Then they set fire to the town.

"In the near-by town of Cervarolo another twenty-five civilians were also massacred by the Germans for unknown reasons," the dispatch said.

The Germans were said to have "devised new means of taking hostages and a new technique of killing."

In the town of Emilia they always "keep twenty civilian hostages at hand for instant reprisal," the dispatch said. It quoted the Partisans as having reported that the latest method of killing civilians was first tried in an "experiment against twenty-five civilians in the region south of the Po."

"The victims, with their hands tied behind their backs, are hung from a hook that is inserted into the back of the neck, the point directed toward the brain. Death is slow and usually occurs only after several hours," the dispatch said. ◊

OUR TROOPS REBOUND TO HAMMER AT THE GERMAN BULGE
Chase Foe Out of Towns Before Meuse—3,000 Planes Blast Enemy

By DREW MIDDLETON
By Wireless to The New York Times.

SUPREME HEADQUARTERS, Allied Expeditionary Force, Dec. 27—A strong American armored force has blasted a path through a ring of German tanks, guns and infantry surrounding Bastogne and relieved the weary, battered but unconquerable American garrison which since Dec. 18 had denied Field Marshal Karl von Rundstedt's columns the use of that important road and railway center.

The smash to Bastogne came soon after American forces in the town had beaten off three assaults, destroying thirty-one or thirty-two German tanks and inflicting heavy casualties on the enemy infantry. The advance covered approximately five miles from the last reported American positions around Chaumont and rolled through the village of Remichampagne, four miles south of Bastogne on the way to the beleaguered town.

The opening of this salient in the southern flank of the German bulge into eastern Belgium, coupled with the steady progress of other American troops along the southern flank east of Bastogne—progress that covered about a mile in most areas on Tuesday—has improved the general situation considerably.

GERMANS DRIVEN BACK ON WEST

German spearheads to the west are still within striking distance of the Meuse, but the enemy's tanks and armored cars have been driven from the area of both Celles and Ciney, four miles southeast and eight miles northeast of Dinant, on the Meuse, by sharp Allied attacks. The enemy continued to hammer the northwestern and northern perimeter of his bulge, but there were signs that American forces in these sectors have been reinforced.

The Germans are beginning to feel the tremendous weight of Allied air attacks on their supply lines. Seventeen tanks and self-propelled guns have been found abandoned because of lack of fuel, and the enemy seems to be using his tanks more sparingly than a week ago—which is probably due to heavy losses ❯

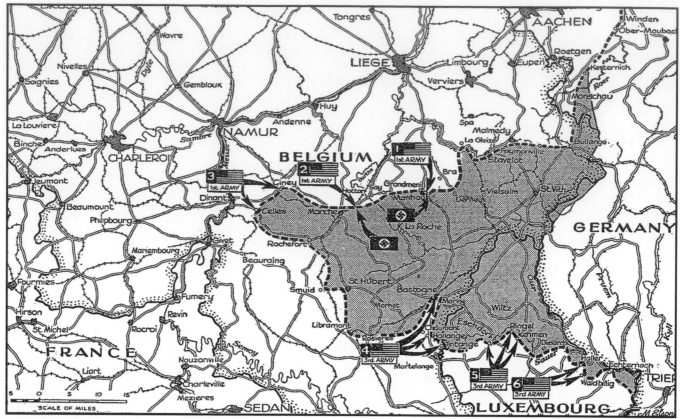

<(in armor as well as the cutting of supply lines. Today more than 3,000 sorties were flown by the Allied air forces, with fighter bombers pounding German forces on the battle line and to the immediate rear, and American and British heavy and medium bombers blasting the main railroads and roads to the battlefield.

MANY ENEMY VEHICLES DAMAGED

The Ninth Air Force, which flew over 1,200 fighter-bomber sorties today, destroyed or damaged 140 tanks and other armored fighting vehicles, 590 motor vehicles and 300 railroad cars. Thunderbolts and Lightnings darting down on enemy artillery silenced forty-one gun positions, including nine of twelve 88-mm. guns in the Bastogne area. Highways were cut at sixty places.

More than twenty villages were dive-bombed and strafed, and German troops were attacked in more than twenty places by fighter bombers.

The Luftwaffe once more made an extensive effort to check Allied air attacks on their ground forces. In air battles from the Ruhr to the Saar ninety-one enemy aircraft were destroyed. Twenty-eight Allied planes are missing, although the pilots of two are safe.

The salient that Americans have now hacked out to Bastogne continued advances into the enemy's southern flank from the Arlon Bastogne road east to the German frontier and the failure of German tanks to exploit their push to within four miles of the Meuse indicates that the Allies are slowly regaining control of the battle. The situation is still grave, for the enemy has committed the Fifth Panzer Army and one other armored army as well as the Seventh Army to the offensive, and the danger of a break-through to the Meuse has been by no means averted. Continuation of the pressure on the northern front indicates the enemy may mean to have one more try at pushing through into the Liege Verviers sector to the rear of the American positions along the Roer River on the Cologne plain.

GALLANT STAND AT BASTOGNE

The raising of the siege of Bastogne ended one of the most gallant stands in the European campaign, with an equally inspiring advance through an area heavily held by the enemy. German pressure on the town, which is a key to communications throughout the southern sector of von Rundstedt's push, reached a

On the northern flank of the enemy salient the Americans lashed out and retook Manhay (1). Between Hottom and Marche (2) they stood fast in the face of heavy Nazi pressure. The German tank columns that had driven to Ciney and Celles were expelled from the vicinities of both towns (3). On the foe's southern flank an American relief column broke into Bastogne (4) and to the southeast Hollange and Tintange were won. Fierce fighting raged at Eschdorf, Ringel and Kehmen (5). Closer to Echternach our troops took Haller and Waldbillig (6). The shading shows area taken by the enemy since his offensive began Dec. 16.

climax in the twenty-four hours before its relief yesterday.

The defenders were hit by three attacks, two of them on a large scale. Two regiments of German infantry, supported by a large number of tanks, made the first attack. They were driven back by doughboys in the town, who knocked out twenty-seven enemy tanks with anti-tank guns and bazookas and took 250 prisoners of war.

Soon afterward another attack on the same scale was launched, but this too was smashed after some initial gains by the enemy. Later the third assault on a smaller scale was repulsed and four or five German tanks were disabled.

The supply position in the town was growing rapidly worse despite supplies dropped from planes by parachute. But help was on the way. A strong American armored force flung into battle on the southern flank was hammering its way north. This force apparently broke through the crust of the German defenders around Chaumont, while other troops were biting through German infantry around Cobreville, seven miles to the southwest of Bastogne. According to enemy radio reports, both of these forces are under the command of Lieut. Gen. George S. Patton Jr., commander of the United States Third Army.

AMERICANS GAIN TO THE EAST

The column striking along the highway drove the Germans out of Remichampagne during the advance, and some time Tuesday its armored vanguard made contact with the exhausted but indomitable defenders of Bastogne.

The enemy, whose principal tank losses last week came from air attacks, is now beginning to lose heavily to Allied armor and antitank guns and by the cutting of his supply lines. However, von Rundstedt has committed about 1,200 tanks to the battle, and there is still enough German armor to do plenty of damage. ◆

'Nuts!' Retort by McAuliffe; Taken Up As a Rallying Cry

By The Associated Press.

BASTOGNE, Belgium, Dec. 29—The commander of Bastogne's valorous 10,000 who made history with a single word—"nuts"—was 46-year-old Brig. Gen. Anthony C. McAuliffe. He was acting commander of the 101st Airborne Division and odds and ends of the United States Third Army's Ninth and Tenth Armored Divisions that had been thrown in hurriedly to stem the German rush toward Sedan.

This soldier from Washington and his troops had been in tough spots before, such as the Normandy landings and the airborne penetration of the Netherlands. When the commander of the German forces drawn up in a siege ring around Bastogne sent an ultimatum to surrender, General McAuliffe sent back the reply that may rank with John Paul Jones' "We have just begun to fight!" It was simply: "Nuts!"

Then the general told his tough fighters what he had done, and this typical American retort became a rallying call for the garrison of 10,000.

OTHERS IN ON FIGHT

Besides the 101st (Screaming Eagle) Airborne and the Ninth and Tenth Armored Divisions, these Third Army divisions took relief roles in the Bastogne drama:

The Fourth Armored, the Eightieth (Blue Ridge) Infantry and the Twenty-sixth (Yankee) Infantry.

Two other units, the Fourth (Ivy) and Fifth (Red Diamond) Infantry Divisions, were named today as having aided in the Third Army's great offensive against the south of the German bulge, operating in northeast Luxembourg.

The answer "Nuts," went back to the German lines Dec. 22. Four days later, when the Eightieth Infantry and Fourth Armored Divisions broke through to their relief, the fields before the American lines around Bastogne were littered with the debris of 200 German tanks which had butted in vain against the doughboy positions. The Americans had been attacked by five German divisions.

More of the epic story of American courage at Bastogne was disclosed today. The stand well may have frustrated the well-laid plans of Field Marshal Karl von Rundstedt. Certainly the Germans could not keep the drive toward France going at full steam without Bastogne's seven highways and one railroad.

General McAuliffe and his troops told the enemy in terms that fighting men understand that they could not have the roads. The 101st Airborne had been spoiling for a fight, and got one when it was rushed into Bastogne by truck just before the waves of attacking Germans closed around the city.

"These parachute troopers were the best morale bucker-uppers we had," said Maj. Charles E. Fife of Los Angeles. "Those boys fought like hell from the word go." ◆

Bodies of German soldiers killed while trying to capture the American 101st Airborne command post at Bastogne.

Chapter 22

"JAPANESE EXPECTED TO WIN, POLL FINDS"

January–March 1945

With the German defeat in the Battle of the Bulge by January 1945, the way was open for the final push to bring Germany to accept the Allied demand of unconditional surrender. On the Eastern Front, after months of preparation, the Red Army renewed a major offensive. "Five Armies on the March" ran The Times's headline, but these were actually entire army groups. The Vistula-Oder operation from eastern Poland opened with attacks on January 12 by Marshal Ivan Konev's First Ukrainian Army Group, followed two days later by Marshal Zhukov's First Belorussian Army Group, which took Warsaw and drove toward Lodz. Against the Red Army's 2.2 million men and 7,000 tanks, the revived German Army Group Center had only 400,000 men and 1,136 tanks. The disparity explains the ease with which the Soviet armies swept across Poland into East Prussia and by February 2 across the Oder River.

The Times received little news of the campaign, but it was only a matter of time before Berlin would fall. There was no hint of the atrocious treatment meted out to the German civilian population by Soviet soldiers maddened by the destruction they had seen in the Soviet Union and the evidence of the extermination centers for Jews, one of which they liberated in January when Auschwitz was occupied. On the Western Front progress was again slower. Eisenhower favored the strategy of the broad advance and launched four separate operations against thin German resistance. On February 8, Montgomery began a campaign in the north to clear the area between the River Meuse and the River Rhine. The U.S. Ninth Army reached the Rhine at Düsseldorf on March 1, Bradley's Twelfth Army Group reached the Rhine six days later, while in the south the Sixth Army Group reached Mannheim in the south that same day. On March 7 American soldiers surprised German guards at the Remagen Bridge over the river and captured it intact, opening the way for speedy deployment to the eastern bank. By late March, crossings had been made all along the river and the drive into Germany could begin.

With the rapid progress made in early 1945, fighting in winter weather, the major Allies realized that there was real urgency now in reaching political agreements about the peace. The final wartime summit at the Crimean resort of Yalta was to be Roosevelt's last. The three leaders decided to set up the United Nations Organization and a conference was arranged for San Francisco in May 1945. Stalin agreed to intervene militarily against Japan once the war in Europe was over. Most important of all, the Western Allies finally accepted Stalin's plan for Poland: territory seized by the Soviet Union in September 1939 would remain Russian, while Poland would be compensated for its loss with territory carved out of eastern Germany. The London Poles rejected the Yalta decision but The Times, which had shown increasing impatience with Polish opposition, ran an editorial that regretted Polish intransigence in the face of a solution that "has much to recommend it." Tito, on the other hand, got everything he wanted. In early March he became the new Communist prime minister and would soon become dictator of a reconstituted Yugoslavia.

When it came to accepting Soviet help against Japan, the Western Allies had mixed feelings, since it was now evident that Japan could perhaps be defeated by American efforts alone. Bizarrely, however, a poll of captured Japanese showed that the majority still thought Japan might win the war in the end.

On January 9 the American Army landed on Luzon and by March 3 the capital, Manila, was again in American hands. On February 19 a force of 60,000 marines, brought by a fleet of eight hundred ships, landed on the island of Iwo Jima, within striking distance of the Japanese home islands. There were 22,000 Japanese dug into deep defensive positions and the battle was long and fierce, but on February 23 the iconic image of the Stars and Stripes flying on Mount Suribachi was photographed and two days later the photo appeared in The Times. By March 26 the island was secured at the cost of almost the entire Japanese garrison and 5,931 Marine deaths. At this point the Twenty-First Bomber Command, under Maj. General Curtis LeMay, had launched the first firebombing attacks on Japan, killing 100,000 people in the raid on Tokyo on the night of March 9–10, 1945. The Times had announced a few days before in an editorial that "Japan cannot be knocked out of the war with bombings alone," but the U.S. Army Air Forces commander, General Henry "Hap" Arnold, hoped it could.

JANUARY 5, 1945

BESIEGED AMERICANS MOVING OUT TO ENGAGE NAZIS AT BASTOGNE
Germans Now Threaten Alsace and Lorraine in New Offensive

By DREW MIDDLETON
By Wireless to The New York Times.

SUPREME HEADQUARTERS, Allied Expeditionary Force, Paris, Jan. 4 — Armored and infantry units of the American First Army, fighting over rugged terrain in the teeth of a snowstorm, smashed into the northern flank of the German salient in Belgium on a thirteen-mile front today, hammering out gains of three and a half miles in some sectors.

Lieut. Gen. George S. Patton's American Third Army, after having repulsed a series of ten heavy German counter-attacks in thirty-six hours, has regained the initiative and is again striking northeastward from Bastogne and toward St. Hubert on the west. At last reports only eleven miles separated the two American armies struggling to close the neck of the Belgian salient against bitter opposition from German infantry and tanks.

Meanwhile Allied troops striking from the west into the head of the salient have driven the Germans out of Bure, four and a half miles southeast of Rochefort, six and a half miles northwest of St. Hubert.

SEVENTH OUT OF REICH

The growing success of Gen. Dwight D. Eisenhower's counter-offensive against the German salient in the north must be balanced by an Allied withdrawal in the south.

American Seventh Army troops have now withdrawn from German soil from Sarreguemines east to the Rhine.

The Germans thrusting southward on the flat ground east of Sarreguemines have advanced five miles from their starting point and have reached the neighborhood of Achen, three miles southwest of Rimling and six to seven miles west of Bitche.

An American withdrawal from the Wissembourg gap, gateway to the German Palatinate, was forced by further German progress southeastward through the Bannstein forest southeast of Bitche. The Germans are attacking anew at Barrenthal and Philippsbourg, threatening to break through onto the plain northeast of Hagenau forest.

GERMANS GAIN ADVANTAGE

The American withdrawal back to positions, which in some areas are based on the Maginot Line, covered five miles and more in some areas. Although it may turn out to be an unimportant move strategically, it is tactically important at the moment and it is certainly a decided political advantage for the Germans, who have now cleared German soil of invaders on a wide stretch and once again have invaded Alsace, as important politically to the Germans as to the French.

The Allied armies attacking the German salient in the north fought without air support today for weather grounded

JANUARY 6, 1945

SPLIT OVER LUBLIN
Soviet Recognizes Polish Provisional Rule— U.S., Britain Back Exiles

By CLIFTON DANIEL
By Cable to The New York Times.

LONDON, Jan. 5—The Soviet Union extended diplomatic recognition to the self-appointed Provisional Government of Poland in Lublin today despite appeals by Prime Minister Churchill and President Roosevelt to defer this action until it could be considered in a joint meeting of all three great powers.

The British and American Governments had exchanged correspondence with Moscow on this question ever since the Lublin Committee of National Liberation had constituted itself a government. It is presumed that since the Big Three previously had been personally concerned with the Polish question the correspondence was between Messrs. Churchill and Roosevelt and Premier Stalin themselves.

The correspondence produced no agreement and the Soviet Union decided to act alone. Its decision was known in advance in both Washington and London.

[Washington and London reacted promptly to the Moscow announcement, reaffirming their recognition of the Polish Government in exile. France's position was described by Ambassador Henri Bonnet in Washington as the same as Britain's and the United States'.

A result of the Soviet recognition of the Lublin Government is that the "unhappy spectacle of rival governments in Poland, one recognized by the Soviet Union and the other by the Western Powers," of which Mr. Churchill warned in his speech Sept. 28 urging the Poles to accept Russia's frontier terms, has now come to pass.

The Soviet recognition of Lublin was no surprise, however, to anyone. It was inevitable since, as almost everyone here concedes, the Lublin Government was the creation of Communist party agents in Poland.

Moscow's decision is significant mainly for its bearing on inter-Allied relations and for the fact that it represents

A tank and other equipment from 212th Armored Field Artillery Battalion, sixth Armored Divisions under camouflage near Bastogne, Belgium, in January 1945.

the Ninth Air Force and only the British Second Tactical Air Force farther north and the Twelfth Tactical Air Command, American component of the First Tactical Air Force in the south, were able to maintain the aerial offensive against the German ground forces.

ALLIED OUTLOOK BETTER

It is perhaps too early to speculate on when the two American Armies will unite across the neck of the salient. It is, however, clear that the possibility of turning the German offensive into a costly defeat by cutting off and destroying some of the best German Panzer divisions is better today than it has been for the last week. ◆

one more unilateral action in a series that seems to grow longer each week that a Churchill-Roosevelt-Stalin meeting is delayed.

It is the general opinion here that the Polish question will top the political agenda of the tri-power meeting, which Mr. Roosevelt indicated today would be held after Jan. 20. Hope that the Big Three may agree to a common policy on Poland was encouraged by the fact that Moscow recognized the Lublin regime as the "provisional Government." This seems to leave the way open for a broadening of the Lublin Government or its amalgamation with elements of the Polish Government in exile here.

Meanwhile the policy of the British and American Governments remains unchanged. They still recognize the Polish Government here, although since the retirement of Stanislaw Mikolajczyk as Premier they find its composition distasteful.

LONDON, Jan. 5 (AP)—The London Poles officially expressed "regret from the point of view of United Nations unity" at the Soviet decision, but said they were not surprised at the development. Their spokesman said the Soviet action "makes more difficult our position and any hopes of reaching a settlement."

Diplomatic and military observers here believed that the Russians were now ready to launch their long expected offensive in Poland.

The Soviet Union severed relations with the London Polish Government in April, 1943, in a dispute over the finding of the graves of thousands of Polish officers in the forests near Smolensk. Russia accused the Germans of having killed the officers, but the London Poles asked the International Red Cross to investigate a counterclaim by the Germans that the Russians had committed the atrocity. ◆

JANUARY 9, 1945

Editorial
WINTER WARFARE

One of the outstanding characteristics of the war—and, as such, a token of its growing bitterness—has been the development of large-scale winter offensives on all fronts, to the complete abolition of the formerly customary winter pause. That winter pause was never certain in the east, as past invaders of Russia, including Napoleon, found out, and in this war the Russians developed the technique of winter warfare to a fine art. But "going into winter quarters" used to be a recognized rule of warfare in the west, and though the winter quarters of the last war were only muddy trenches, fighting died down during the winter months to a minimum. In fact, the German offensive against Verdun had to be postponed for ten days on account of a blizzard, which contributed to its failure. Even in this war, Hitler waited with his campaign against the west in 1940 till the balmy days of May.

This time, however, the Germans launched their most ambitious offensive in the west in the midst of winter, and at this very moment American and British troops are battling the enemy amid a raging snowstorm which would have made fighting unthinkable in the past. The great Battle of the Bulge is assuming more and more the aspect of the final stages of the Battle of Normandy, which led to the establishment of a huge pocket with a narrow opening at Falaise. Not only is the bulge shrinking which the Germans drove into our lines; it is assuming the contours of a sack which the British are holding tight at the western end and which the American First and Third Armies are trying to close farther east by concerted counter-offensives from the north and south. They have already succeeded in cutting one of the last two roads open to the Germans for supplies and retreat; they have brought the last remaining road under artillery fire from both sides; they have narrowed the remaining gap between them to less than ten miles. Within the sack thus forming are reported to be three German armored divisions and considerable numbers of other German troops.

It would be premature to expect too much, for the Germans are masters in escaping traps. Even in Normandy they slipped out most of their troops through the Falaise gap when it was only six miles wide. But the chance for great ▶

◀ success is there, and it appears unlikely that the Allies will permit themselves to be diverted from making the most of it by the German efforts around Strasbourg and Venlo. ◇

JANUARY 10, 1945

Yanks Land from 800 Ships; MacArthur Ashore With Men

By GEORGE E. JONES
By Wireless to The New York Times.

ABOARD AMPHIBIOUS FLAGSHIP, in Lingayen Gulf, Jan. 9—History's greatest overseas invasion is landing thousands of troops on the road to Manila today. American soldiers are pushing through marsh-studded beachlines, heading for the open country and near-by hills, from which the enemy can reinforce troops and support them with artillery.

More than 800 ships participated in this convoy, which traveled under constant surveillance from aircraft and submarines. Not a single troopship was damaged as the line of transports and escorts, stretching for eighty miles, threaded its way through the narrow channels and glassy open seas.

The climax of a hazardous voyage came west of Corregidor when a Japanese destroyer, putting out from Ma-nila Harbor, attempted to break into the troopships. The destroyer was sunk within our vision by American destroyers before it could do any damage.

In number of troops involved this invasion may not compare with Normandy, but that fact is offset by the long, hazardous journey of the Lingayen force under the over-all command of Vice Admiral Thomas C. Kinkaid. ◇

ON FIFTEEN-MILE BEACHHEAD
By WILLIAM C. DICKINSON
United Press Correspondent

WITH MacARTHUR'S FORCES, on Luzon, Wednesday, Jan. 10—American Sixth Army forces, completing under the personal direction of Gen. Douglas MacArthur the largest amphibious operation of the Pacific war, today held a fifteen-mile beachhead on Lingayen Gulf.

With almost no initial ground resistance and with but slight loss to our shipping despite fierce and fanatical Japanese air attacks, vast numbers of men and enormous quantities of guns, armored equipment and supplies have been placed ashore.

While no exact information was forthcoming from General MacArthur's advanced headquarters on Luzon as to the exact depth of our advances from the four landing beaches, it was known that deep penetrations had been made at some points and only scattered light resistance had been encountered anywhere.

It was believed that all units had reached or passed beyond their first day objectives in the daylight hours following our landing at 9:30 A.M. yesterday.

Battleships and other units of the Seventh Fleet began fierce preliminary bombardments which knocked out every Japanese shore battery which might have ranged on our vast armada of more than 800 vessels with their supporting and protecting hundreds of warships.

General MacArthur went ashore only a few hours behind his assault troops and only a short time after Lieut. Gen. Walter Krueger Sixth Army commander, had established headquarters ashore and taken over active command of the operations from Vice Admiral Thomas C. Kinkaid, Seventh Fleet commander.

General MacArthur waded ashore from his barge accompanied by Lieut. Gen. Richard K Sutherland, his chief of staff, and congratulated his leaders on the progress so far made. He urged them to keep driving ahead—no letting the Japanese get set in any position to bar our advance.

General MacArthur told correspondents that the entire Lingayen Gulf operation was progressing "better than could have been expected" and that all units were making good progress against little or no resistance.

"The Jap was apparently taken completely by surprise," he said "He apparently expected us from the south, and when we came in behind him he was caught off base. The entire operation so far had been a complete success."

He said it was not yet apparent where the Japanese would make their main defense stand, but that there "is no doubt that the battle for Manila and the entire Philippines will be fought and won on the great central plain north of Manila."

He was smoking a new corncob pipe and appeared bronzed and rested.

"I slept well last night," he said "in spite of some little disturbance created by the Japanese during the night."

Although our ground forces went ashore standing up with almost no opposition, we suffered some loss and damage to shipping en route here and during the preliminary bombardments and carrier activities.

The Japanese lost heavily, seventy-nine planes shot down, a midget submarine, two destroyers, one coastal vessel and many small craft sunk by our attacks. These losses are in addition to those inflicted by the Third Fleet forces of Admiral William F. Halsey which gave coordinated support to our landings.

A considerable measure of strategic surprise was attained through our recent feints in the direction of Batangas and other points.

The landing itself was completely uneventful. Not a shore battery fired as the hundreds of American vessels

Coast Guard landing ships carrying the first wave of American soldiers to invade the beaches of Luzon, Philippines, January 1945.

steamed into the gulf before dawn. After a shore bombardment of more than two hours, in which battleships—including restored pre–Pearl Harbor veterans—participated, in greater strength than in any previous Southwest Pacific operation, the swarms of amphibious tanks, alligators, buffaloes and larger landing craft moved in almost unmolested.

A little mortar fire at one point was quickly silenced. During S-day, as the landing date for this operation was named, only a few sneak raiders disturbed the routine of pouring in supplies and men.

The troops were still on the alert on the beach when General MacArthur waded ashore, but the general started

right off in a jeep to find the nearest divisional command post. When the jeep broke down, the general took off across the sand dunes on foot and in a few minutes was firing questions and nodding his head with very apparent satisfaction as the divisional commander reported the progress made ⌃

JANUARY 20, 1945

5 ARMIES ON MARCH
New Russian Offensive Scores 50-Mile Gain Above Carpathians

By The United Press.

LONDON, Jan. 20—The Red Army yesterday reached the border of German Silesia, captured the great Polish cities of Lodz, Cracow and Tarnow and hammered thirty-one miles inside East Prussia after advances of up to twenty-eight miles in one of two new offensives opened on the blazing Eastern Front.

Adding victory to victory, the Red Army was forging a great encirclement of East Prussia as it approached within three miles of the southern frontiers of the Junker stronghold on a sixty-mile front. Simultaneously, the Red Army opened another new offensive in southern Poland, driving fifty miles forward to outflank the city of Nowy Sacz.

Berlin said that almost 3,000,000 Soviet troops were on the march along a twisting 650-mile front from East Prussia to Czechoslovakia. In one of the greatest days in the Red Army's history Premier Stalin issued five orders of the day.

Five Soviet armies, carving out gains of up to thirty-one miles, seized 2,750 localities in East Prussia and Poland and killed thousands of enemy troops fleeing under the lashing blows of Soviet planes.

ENEMY DEFENSES OVERPOWERED
Every German river and railroad defense line was being shattered and Russia's eight-day-old offensive still was gathering momentum.

Giant Stalin tanks of Marshal Ivan S. Koneff's First Ukrainian Army reached the border of German Silesia in an unexpected area. Veering northwest from the Polish city of Czestochowa his forces followed the border line for twenty-

eight miles and reached the frontier at the Polish town of Praszka, 225 miles southeast of Berlin.

At the same time other spearheads advanced twenty-eight miles along the Radom-Breslau highway, cutting across the vital north-south railroad linking Danzig with Silesia to take Wielun, which in turn severed the rail line between Silesia and the great Polish city of Posen.

The Russians crossed the Warta River, a tributary of the Oder, and cut the Danzig-Silesia railroad along a twenty-mile front. A twelve-mile stretch of the Danzig-Posen railroad defense and supply line was shattered between Wielun and Rudniki.

STEEL CENTERS OUTFLANKED
The advance to Praszka outflanked by fifty-two miles on the northwest the great German coal and steel-producing centers of Beuthen, Hindenburg and Gleiwitz, the loss of which would be a heavy blow to the German war machine.

Koneff's troops approached the border of Germany and its rich Silesian cities along a fifty-five-mile front, and for thirty miles southeast of Praszka they were but three to five miles from the frontier.

It was troops of Koneff's army who captured Cracow, ancient capital of Poland Thirty-one miles northwest of the city, guarding the approaches is the Dabrowa coal-mining region, they seized Ogrodzieniec, sixteen miles northeast of Dabrowa and twenty-six miles from Beuthen.

Cracow, fourth largest city of Poland, with a pre-war population of 259,000 and former seat of the Nazi puppet Government General of Poland, was captured when Koneff's troops severed the city's connections with Silesia in an outflanking movement that won them the railroad stations of Zabierzow, Rudawa and Krzeszowice.

Forty-seven miles east of Cracow, other troops operating south of the Vistula River captured Tarnow.

South of the Tarnow-Cracow railroad and west of Sanok, Gen. Ivan I. Petroff's Fourth Ukrainian Army went over to the offensive and, breaking through powerful enemy fortifications,

advanced fifty miles along a thirty-seven-mile front in the Carpathian foothills.

LODZ BARRIER CONQUERED
Fifty-one miles northeast of the point where Koneff's army reached the Silesian border, Marshal Gregory K. Zhukoff's First White Russian Army advanced on an eighty-five-mile front south of the Vistula River and captured Lodz, Poland's second city and its largest industrial center.

Lodz, a pre-war city of 672,000 persons, was captured in a twenty-four-mile advance. Twenty-nine miles to the north the town of Kutno, on the Warsaw-Berlin railroad, was seized and, between Kutno and Lodz, Zhukoff's fast-moving spearheads captured Leczyca, 100 miles east of the Polish city of Poznan.

The capture of Lodz, a great twelve-way road and rail center, and of Cracow collapsed the so-called German "middle European Wall." The fall of Lodz also left western Poland wide open for rapid conquest by the Russian juggernaut.

TRANSIT CENTER SEIZED
Advancing along the south bank of the Vistula River, Zhukoff's northern wing seized Gostynin, fifty-three miles southeast of the great Polish city of Torun. It also outflanked the Vistula road and rail crossing town of Plock, ten miles to the northeast.

Plock, on the north bank of the Vistula, also was menaced by troops of Marshal Konstantin K. Rokossovsky's Second White Russian Army which was advancing westward north of the Vistula along a fifty-four-mile front. In a seven-mile gain his troops drove to within twenty-three miles northeast of Plock by capturing Raciaz, on the Warsaw-Torun railroad. A few miles to the north, Radzanow, sixty-one miles east of Torun, was taken in a nine-mile advance.

Other troops of Rokossovsky's army were advancing on East Prussia's southern borders along a sixty-mile front, and, in a twenty-one mile dash they seized the fortress transit hub of Mlawa, seven miles south of the border and pushed the Germans northward to take ⟩

◀ Dzialdowo, three miles from the frontier.

Berlin said that Marshal Rokossovsky was attempting to reach the Baltic Sea near Danzig and effect a huge encirclement of East Prussia in conjunction with Gen. Ivan D. Chernyakhovsky's Third White Russian Army pushing into the province from the east.

At Dzialdowo, Rokossovsky's troops were 75 miles south of the Baltic and ninety miles southeast of the former free city of Danzig.

TILSIT HIGHWAY CUT

Chernyakhovsky's army, Marshal Stalin revealed, launched a great offensive in east Prussia five days ago and, crashing through deep enemy fortifications, advanced up to twenty-eight miles along a thirty-seven-mile front.

Seizing more than 600 towns and villages, his troops cleared almost the entire northeastern corner of east Prussia—an area of about 750 square miles, and were thirty-one miles inside the frontier at the town of Breitenstein. While other spearheads pressed to within four miles southeast of the great rail center of Tilsit by winning Ragnit and cutting the Gumbinnen-Tilsit highway along a nineteen-mile front between Ragnit and Neusiedel, the troops who captured Breitenstein crossed the Inster River. ◆

Russian soldiers, with cases of explosives, meet German resistance and smoking ruins in Cracow, Poland, 1945.

JANUARY 21, 1945

RHINE PUSH BEGUN
U.S. 1st and 3d Armies Further Compress the Belgian Salient

By The Associated Press,

SUPREME HEADQUARTERS, Allied Expeditionary Force, Paris, Jan. 20—The French First Army struck a surprise blow for Alsace's liberation today with a new offensive on a twenty-five-mile front that rolled up three-mile gains seventy miles south of where American comrades-in-arms battled to save the imperiled capital of Strasbourg.

The French jumped into the mounting battle, with the fate of Alsace and Strasbourg in the balance, after tank-led German troops drove United States Seventh Army lines back five miles and threatened to undermine American positions in the northeast corner of France.

FRENCH SURPRISE GERMANS

The assault, rolling out under the cover of a blinding snowstorm from the Vosges eastward to the Rhine in the Mulhouse area, achieved complete surprise and still was pressing forward tonight against that tough German core known as the Colmar pocket from which the enemy was menacing Strasbourg from the south.

At the opposite end of the 300-mile western front, the British Second Army ran into enemy tanks for the first time, but plowed on three miles into western Germany and the Netherlands appendix, seizing at least six more towns.

The British cut off a German area five miles by three miles with a pincers movement of two armored columns northeast of Sittard. One British unit attacked eastward from Echt and the other pushed north from Hoengen until the junction was made. More than 400 prisoners were taken by the British.

The American First Army was methodically tightening the screws on St. Vith, the Belgian highway and rail center four miles from the Reich border through which the Germans must retire.

THIRD NEARS VIANDEN

The American Third Army was driving in from the west against stout resistance, and to the east was battling over northern Luxembourg's snow-clad hills within three miles of Vianden, on the Reich border where Hitler's legions swept across in the Ardennes offensive.

A dispatch from the front said there were signs that the Germans were withdrawing into the Siegfried Line as the Third Army pressed on a mile and a half, deepened its Sauer River bridgehead to three miles near the Reich border and moved up to the frontier along a three-mile front on the Our River.

In the Netherlands, British units of the Canadian First Army lifted the threat to Nijmegen by routing crack German parachute troops from the village of Zitten, six miles to the north.

TANKS ATTACK BRITISH

The attack by tanks came east of Echt, seven and a half miles southwest of the German Meuse River stronghold of Roermond.

While the British under Lieut. Gen. Miles C. Dempsey were slowed here in the push toward the Roer, they were lashing out aggressively to the east and west, using white camouflaged tanks in the snow that blanketed the battlefield.

They crossed the Meuse unopposed and captured Stevensweert, seven miles southwest of Roermond, as the Germans pulled out under the gathering threat of encirclement from the east. The small German panhandle jutting into the Netherland appendix a few miles to the south was virtually severed as Tommies struck nearly a mile through the fog and seized Saeffelen.

Two miles to the east another British column plowed a mile and a half through the slush and snow and captured Breberen, three miles inside the Reich. ◆

FIRST RED IN BERLIN TO GET $1,000 PRIZE
Native of Lublin, Now Citizen of U.S., Offers Reward— Also Wants to Aid Stalingrad

The rapid advance of the Russian armies has given David Kay no end of joy. Yesterday, Mr. Kay, a native of Lublin, Poland, and a businessman with offices at 450 Seventh Avenue, offered $1,000 to the first Russian soldier or unit to enter Berlin.

His offer was contained in a letter to the Russian Consul General's office in New York, and a spokesman of the Consul's office said that the offer would be "accepted as a token of appreciation." Mr. Kay also offered an extra $1,000 that would start a fund toward the rebuilding of Stalingrad. The spokesman, however, explained that a fund was being raised for that purpose in this country.

"This may appear to be a strange letter," Mr. Kay wrote, "but I should like to emphasize that it is written in all sincerity and with the hope that you will cooperate with me." The letter went on to mention the first offer of $1,000 to start the fund for the rebuilding of Stalingrad, "that it may be the start of a special fund, perhaps a memorial fund in grateful memory to the valiant and successful stand of the Soviet forces in that city." Then followed Mr. Kay's reference to the second offer of $1,000:

"The second check is a prize for the first Russian soldier to enter Berlin. Should it prove impossible to determine who that individual is, then I should like the money to be divided equally among the men comprising the first Russian unit to enter the German capital."

Soon after the Allied invasion of France, Mr. Kay offered a $1,000 War Bond to the first American soldier to reach Paris. Since the liberation of Paris, he explained, the authorities have not been able to determine the rightful recipient. ◆

LUFTWAFFE AGAIN A MENACE WITH ITS JET-DRIVEN PLANES
Allies Have No Fighters Which Can Deal With the Latest German Sky Raiders

By HARRY VOSSER
By Wireless to The New York Times.

LONDON, Jan. 27—Six months ago the Allied public, rejoicing over the successful achievements of their armed forces on the Continent, was indulging in the comfortable assumption that the much-vaunted German Air Force was no more. "Where is Goering's Luftwaffe now?" was the question, asked with some sarcasm.

Today the situation has changed once more. Not only is the Luftwaffe fighter-plane production on the increase, not only is it able to conduct an occasional mass attack such as the recent sortie against Allied airfields in Belgium and Holland, but there is a chance now that it may develop once more into a serious threat to the Allies.

Outnumbered and outmaneuvered, the Luftwaffe resorted to the employment of the unorthodox, and this, like so many of Germany's other innovations, has succeeded in temporarily nonplussing the Allies. The jet-propelled and rocket-assisted fighters and fighter-bombers with which the Germans are stiffening their air force are potentially a great danger to us. And if, in fact, the threat doesn't develop into something more than it is now before the end of the war, it will be only because the Germans have again started with too little and too late.

BUILT FOR QUICK WAR
In common with all German weapons, the Luftwaffe was built for a quick war. Design and production of aircraft were frozen to about six standard types to insure uninterrupted output. As the Allied forces grew in size and strength, it became clear to the Germans that they had no chance of ever regaining their lost numerical superiority. Technical superiority of their planes by the production of a revolutionary type of aircraft against which the Allies would at first be powerless was their only hope.

The Focke-Wulfe 190 was their first effort at gaining the technical lead, and for a while this machine did give them a slight technical advantage over the Allies. For many months, however, it has been clear that the Nazis have given up trying to achieve technical advantages over the Allies by improvements on their regular aircraft and are pinning their hopes on the revolutionary jet planes with hitherto unobtainable speeds of 500 miles an hour or more and rates of climb around 10,000 feet a minute.

By the end of 1944 the ME-163—the Comet—a rocket-assisted glider-fighter, and the ME-262—the Swallow, a twin-motored, jet-propelled reconnaissance fighter-bomber—were in operation over Germany and the Western Front. Other types of German jet-propelled planes are known to exist, but they do not seem yet to have progressed into the full operational stage.

Will the Luftwaffe be able to stage a real come-back with these new types? The answer depends to a large extent on whether the Germans will be allowed the time and the opportunities to develop their "jets." They are already appearing in gradually increasing numbers—mainly the ME-262 over the Low Countries, while the ME-163 is kept for the home defense forces and used for attacking heavy bomber formations.

It is no secret that we equally possess jet planes. Nevertheless, the Allies, so far as is known, are not producing them in sufficient quantity to provide an effective opposition to the enemy.

The Allies have successfully, but not generally, used jet planes in the battle against the V-1. Apart from that, we have no indication that Allied "jets" have been pitted against the enemy—or, that, in fact, ours are in any more than a purely experimental stage.

WHAT ALLIES ARE DOING
Are the Allies planning increased production of "jets" to fight the new German weapon? So far there is no known evidence that they are. What are the Allies doing then?

At present, our main defense seems to consist of attacks on the factories and machine shops engaged in production of jet planes.

At present, the jet and rocket types of aircraft are encountered only in twos and threes—not in formations—and experts think this method of attack is only a tryout for an entirely new technique of formation attacks on raiding bombers. One thing that pilots and experts are agreed upon is that at present the Allies have no motored plane that can successfully chase a jet.

Pilots who have succeeded in shooting down this type of plane report that they have caught the German pilot when he has been coasting—that is, between jet-driven bursts of speed—and have gone into action before he has had time to turn on his extra power. It seems to be generally agreed, too, that German pilots are not willing to enter into an air fight, probably because their missions are at present confined to reconnaissance and photographic work.

'JETS' POSE PROBLEMS

Of course, before the Germans can operate jet-propelled aircraft in any great numbers, they have many difficulties to overcome. Both the jet and rocket assisted types are difficult to fly and require specially trained top-category pilots. In addition, they are not as maneuverable as the orthodox fighter and have only a short flight duration.

Allied pilots have confirmed that these jet machines are not easily thrown about in the air and pilots who have found themselves placed in combat position with either the "Swallow" or the "Comet," say they can easily turn inside them, as they are no good at quick turns.

The Allies believe that the Germans have not been able to produce and bring into operation as many jet machines as they would like because their aircraft industry is so dispersed to avoid bomb damage. They are still in the position of being forced to rely on tried types because of the urgent requirements of the Luftwaffe on both home defense and tactical work. ◆

JANUARY 29, 1945

NEGRO UNIT AT BASTOGNE 969th Field Artillery Battalion Filled Heroic Role

WASHINGTON, Jan. 28 (AP)—The 969th Field Artillery Battalion, with Negro enlisted men manning its 155-mm. howitzers, has fought all the way from Normandy to Bastogne.

The War Department reported today that the battalion stuck to its guns and helped beat off waves of German attackers at Bastogne, where for a time American forces were isolated in the German breakthrough push.

In the heaviest fighting at Bastogne all except the actual cannoneers fought infantry fashion, taking thirty or forty prisoners.

The battalion set up its guns under the direction of the 101st Airborne Division, to which it was attached. Enemy tanks and infantry approached. With the help of a few scattered tanks, the battalion poured out fire that held the enemy at bay. Casualties became heavy before the tide turned with the appearance of supply planes and armored forces from the south. ◆

FEBRUARY 8, 1945

PATTON OVER RIVER; WIDE FRONT ABLAZE

By CLIFTON DANIEL
BY Wireless to The New York Times.

SUPREME HEADQUARTERS, Allied Expeditionary Force, Feb. 7—The coordinated attack by two American Armies against the Siegfried Line broadened to a front of seventy miles today when four divisions of Lieut. Gen. George S. Patton's Third Army renewed their eastward thrust and burst over the German border at ten places beyond the Luxembourg frontier.

American infantrymen, who had already been thrusting into the Siegfried Line to the north, meanwhile drove clean through the main permanent defenses of the last remaining zone of the Siegfried Line in two places, one on the Olef River southwest of Schleiden, the other only three miles from Pruem, vital road junction in Germany southeast of St. Vith.

Allied advances had left a fat salient bulging as much as fourteen miles into our lines along the Luxembourg frontier, and the Third Army forces struck a series of determined blows today to flatten that bulge. Striking across the distended Sauer and Our Rivers, which mark the German border, they pushed into Germany as much as a mile in one place and an average of a half mile elsewhere.

Broadening of the offensive brought a total of at least twelve divisions into the attack on the Siegfried zone between Echternach in the south and Schmidt in the north, a distance of seventy miles. Beyond Schmidt and around Aachen the Westwall has already been effectively reduced, and the American Ninth and British Second Armies are standing along the Roer River awaiting developments while the methodical attack proceeds toward the Siegfried Line and, incidentally, toward the dams that control the Roer's level.

Although a dozen divisions are now battering away at the Westwall or moving up to within range of it, these forces are only a token of the total that Gen. Dwight D. Eisenhower can swing into action at a chosen moment. This moment seems to await developments in the Siegfried Line battle.

In the interim the former German salient jutting into the high Vosges south of Mulhouse dwindled today until it was nothing but a slender bridgehead across the Rhine, east of Colmar and Mulhouse.

At the northern end of the front on which two American armies are attacking, the forces bearing south from Bergstein into one of the thickest parts of the Westwall are unable to move across the Kall River toward the biggest of the Roer dams because of mines and small-arms fire spewing out of Siegfried pillboxes.

To the south and west, however, the Seventy-eighth Division with the aid of tanks managed to drive 1,000 yards farther northeast along the valley floor toward Schmidt, stubborn strongpoint of the Siegfried system. Its infantry is now within rifle range of the village, which is 500 yards away.

Just a thousand yards northwest of Schmidt, which also guards Schwammenauel dam, other Seventy-eighth Division troops edged into the outskirts of Kommerscheid. How thickly studded the defenses are in this area was demonstrated by the fact that in its slight advances of the past few days the Seventy-eighth Division has already captured 159 pillboxes, most of them defended. In this area the pillboxes, painted green to match the evergreen woods, are blended into the terrain on twisting roads and steep valley walls.

The line of the new Third Army advance into Germany begins southwest of Brandscheid, at the northern side of Luxembourg, and stretches south to the Echternach area. Generally, the drive seems to be aimed not only at the Siegfried Line, but at a useful communications network lying beyond it and centered on the hubs of Pruem in the north and Bitburg, seventeen miles to the south. The attack went forward at points on a twenty-two-mile front.

Doughboys of the Sixth Armored Division, leaving the division's tanks on the west bank, crossed the Our River in three places two and a half miles northeast of Dasburg, which is due east of Clerf, and advanced a half mile beyond the river. The Seventeenth Airborne Division, spanning the river due east of Clerf, also advanced a half mile against small-arms fire from the Dasburg area.

At 3 A.M. the Eightieth Division, after an hour and a half of artillery preparation, moved over the Sauer River two

miles northwest of Bollendorf, which is four miles northwest of Echternach, and units of the same division crossed the Our at two points and speared forward a half mile due east of Diekirch, where the Our joins the Sauer. They entered Bettel, northeast of Diekirch.

FIFTH GETS OFF FIRST

The Fifth Division moved off earliest of all at 1 A.M. and caught the first counter-attack. Its thrust was made across the Sauer at three points northwest of Echternach. It extended into Germany for a mile after a counterblow against one of its crossings had been beaten off.

The crossings were accomplished despite the swift current and high water. Fire from the opposite bank, which was guarded by a thick tangle of barbed wire, sank some of the assault boats on swirling streams.

French First Army forces, including an American corps, meanwhile were making a clean sweep of the Colmar pocket south of Strasbourg. Remnants of the German forces in the Vosges were being swept into prisoner cages. Along the Rhine American forces overran Neuf-Brisach, on the northern side of the German bridgehead,

yesterday, and pushed five miles south of that town. All territory west of the Rhone-Rhine Canal, which parallels the Rhine, was cleared by the American Twenty-eighth Division and the French First Armored Division. A bridgehead established across the canal at Ile de Napoleon, in the south, by the French Ninth Colonial Division, was extended toward the Rhine today.

All that is left to the Germans west of the Rhine now is a strip five or six miles wide and ten miles long up to the Rhone-Rhine Canal. At the rate at which they are evacuating by ferry and pontoon bridges they will not hold that long.

The western zone along the German border has been effectively penetrated along a forty-five-mile stretch from a point north of Aachen to a point due east of Malmedy. The attack now proceeding is against the second zone, which is based roughly on the Olef River at Hellenthal, Schleiden and Gemuend and then continues north into Huertgen Forest along both sides of the Roer River, into which the Olef runs. The main part of this line was cracked, if not broken, today with the crossing of the Olef at Hellenthal. ◇

FEBRUARY 13, 1945

Text of the Big Three Announcement On the Crimea Conference

WASHINGTON, Feb. 12 (AP)—The text of the report on the Big Three conference in the Crimea, released at the White House today, follows:

REPORT OF CRIMEA CONFERENCE
For the past eight days, Winston S. Churchill, Prime Minister of Great Britain; Franklin D. Roosevelt, President of the United States of America, and Marshal J. V. Stalin, Chairman of the Council of People's Commissars of the Union of Soviet Socialist Republics, have met with the Foreign Secretaries, Chiefs of Staff and other advisers in the Crimea.

The following statement is made by

The "Big Three" at the Crimea Conference, 1945.

the Prime Minister of Great Britain, the President of the United States of America and the Chairman of the Council of People's Commissars of the Union of Soviet Socialist Republics on the results of the Crimean conference:

THE DEFEAT OF GERMANY
We have considered and determined the military plans of the three Allied powers

for the final defeat of the common enemy. The military staffs of the three Allied nations have met in daily meetings throughout the conference. These meetings have been most satisfactory from every point of view and have resulted in closer coordination of the military effort of the three Allies than ever before. The fullest information has been interchanged. The timing, scope and coordination of new ▸

❨ and even more powerful blows to be launched by our armies and air forces into the heart of Germany from the east, west, north and south have been fully agreed and planned in detail.

Our combined military plans will be made known only as we execute them, but we believe that the very close-working partnership among the three staffs attained at this conference will result in shortening the war. Meetings of the three staffs will be continued in the future whenever the need arises.

Nazi Germany is doomed. The German people will only make the cost of their defeat heavier to themselves by attempting to continue a hopeless resistance.

THE OCCUPATION AND CONTROL OF GERMANY

We have agreed on common policies and plans for enforcing the unconditional surrender terms which we shall impose together on Nazi Germany after German armed resistance has been finally crushed. These terms will not be made known until the final defeat of Germany has been accomplished. Under the agreed plan, the forces of the three powers will each occupy a separate zone of Germany. Coordinated administration and control have been provided for under the plan through a central control commission consisting of the Supreme Commanders of the three powers with headquarters in Berlin. It has been agreed that France should be invited by the three powers, if she should so desire, to take over a zone of occupation and to participate as a fourth member of the control commission. The limits of the French zone will be agreed by the four Governments concerned through their representatives on the European Advisory Commission.

It is our inflexible purpose to destroy German militarism and nazism and to insure that Germany will never again be able to disturb the peace of the world. We are determined to disarm and disband all German armed forces; break up for all time the German General Staff that has repeatedly contrived the resurgence of German militarism; remove or destroy all German military equipment; eliminate or control all German industry that could be used for military production; bring all war criminals to just and swift punishment and exact reparation in kind for the destruction wrought by the Germans; wipe out the Nazi party, Nazi laws, organizations and institutions, remove all Nazi and militarist influences from public office and from the cultural and economic life of the German people; and take in harmony such other measures in Germany as may be necessary to the future peace and safety of the world. It

is not our purpose to destroy the people of Germany, but only when nazism and militarism have been extirpated will there be hope for a decent life for Germans, and a place for them in the comity of nations.

REPARATION BY GERMANY

We have considered the question of the damage caused by Germany to the Allied Nations in this war and recognized it as just that Germany be obliged to make compensation for this damage in kind to the greatest extent possible. A commission for the compensation of damage will be established. The commission will be instructed to consider the question of the extent and methods for compensating damage caused by Germany to the Allied countries. The commission will work in Moscow.

UNITED NATIONS CONFERENCE

We are resolved upon the earliest possible establishment with our allies of a general international organization to maintain peace and security. We believe that this is essential, both to prevent aggression and to remove the political, economic and social causes of war through the close and continuing collaboration of all peace-loving peoples.

The foundations were laid at Dumbarton Oaks. On the important question of voting procedure, however, agreement was not there reached. The present conference has been able to resolve this difficulty.

We have agreed that a conference of the United Nations should be called to meet at San Francisco, in the United States, on April 25, 1945, to prepare the charter of such an organization, along the lines proposed in the informal conversations at Dumbarton Oaks.

The Government of China and the Provisional Government of France will be immediately consulted and invited to sponsor invitations to the conference jointly with the Governments of the United States, Great Britain and the Union of Soviet Socialist Republics. As soon as the consultation with China and France has been completed, the text of the proposals on voting procedure will be made public.

DECLARATION ON LIBERATED EUROPE

The Premier of the Union of Soviet Socialist Republics, the Prime Minister of the United Kingdom and the President of the United States of America have consulted with each other in the common interests of the peoples of their countries and those of liberated Europe. They jointly declare their mutual agreement to concert during the temporary period of instability in liberated Europe the policies

of their three Governments in assisting the peoples liberated from the domination of Nazi Germany and the peoples of the former Axis satellite states of Europe to solve by democratic means their pressing political and economic problems.

The establishment of order in Europe and the rebuilding of national economic life must be achieved by processes which will enable the liberated peoples to destroy the last vestiges of nazism and fascism and to create democratic institutions of their own choice. This is a principle of the Atlantic Charter—the right of all peoples to choose the form of government under which they will live—the restoration of sovereign rights and self-government to those peoples who have been forcibly deprived of them by the aggressor nations.

To foster the conditions in which the liberated peoples may exercise these rights, the three Governments will jointly assist the people in any European liberated state or former Axis satellite state in Europe where in their judgment conditions require (A) to establish conditions of internal peace; (B) to carry out emergency measures for the relief of distressed peoples; (C) to form interim governmental authorities broadly representative of all democratic elements in the population and pledged to the earliest possible establishment through free elections of governments responsive to the will of the people; and (D) to facilitate where necessary the holding of such elections.

By this declaration we reaffirm our faith in the principles of the Atlantic Charter, our pledge in the Declaration by the United Nations and our determination to build, in cooperation with other peace-loving nations, world order under law, dedicated to peace, security, freedom and the general well-being of all mankind.

A new situation has been created in Poland as a result of her complete liberation by the Red Army. This calls for the establishment of a Polish Provisional Government which can be more broadly based than was possible before the recent liberation of western Poland. The Provisional Government which is now functioning in Poland should therefore be reorganized on a broader democratic basis with the inclusion of democratic leaders from Poland itself and from Poles abroad. This new government should then be called the Polish Provisional Government of National Unity.

M. Molotoff, Mr. Harriman and Sir A. Clark Kerr are authorized as a commission to consult in the first instance in Moscow with members of the present Provisional Government and with other Polish democratic leaders from within Poland and from abroad, with a view to the reorganization of the present Government along the above lines. This Polish Provisional Government of National Unity shall be pledged to the holding of free and unfettered elections as soon as possible on the basis of universal suffrage and secret ballot. In these elections all democratic and anti-Nazi parties shall have the right to take part and to put forward candidates.

When a Polish Provisional Government of National Unity has been properly formed in conformity with the above, the Government of the U.S.S.R., which now maintains diplomatic relations with the present Provisional Government of Poland, and the Government of the United Kingdom and the Government of the United States of America will establish diplomatic relations with the new Polish Provisional Government of National Unity and will exchange Ambassadors, by whose reports the respective Governments will be kept informed about the situation in Poland.

The three heads of Government consider that the eastern frontier of Poland should follow the Curzon Line, with digressions from it in some regions of five to eight kilometers in favor of Poland. They recognize that Poland must receive substantial accessions of territory in the north and west. They feel that the opinion of the new Polish Provisional Government of National Unity should be sought in due course on the extent of these accessions and that the final delimitation of the western frontier of Poland should thereafter await the peace conference. ◇

FEBRUARY 14, 1945

Editorial
THE CASE OF POLAND

Until the spokesmen of the Big Three Powers met at Yalta the outlook was bleak for any satisfactory, or even acceptable, settlement of the controversy over Poland. The Russians, who had twice within one generation been invaded by the Germans across the Polish plains, insisted upon a new strategic frontier farther west, along the so-called Curzon Line. Their claim for such a frontier was buttressed by the fact that east of the Curzon Line there are fewer Poles than non-Poles, and by the further fact that the old frontier had been established at the end of the last war by force of Polish arms. Meanwhile, in opposition to this view, the Polish Government-in-Exile, functioning in London, insisted that it had no mandate from the Polish people to surrender any part of Polish territory and that Russia was attempting to force a settlement of the whole question by unilateral action.

That was true before the Yalta conference met. It is now no longer true. The solution proposed at Yalta is a three-Power plan, supported not only by Russia but by Britain and the United States. To be sure, the Polish Government-in-Exile had no hand in this decision. But the fact remains that the decision was made in the name of the three Powers which alone are capable of defending the integrity of Poland against a renewal of German aggression, and by the three Powers which will once more have to bear the brunt of the fighting in case such a threat develops.

Moreover, the solution has much to commend it on other grounds than this vital one that it represents a decision which the Great Powers are prepared to defend in Poland's interest. For while Russia's claim to the Curzon Line is recognized, with certain minor digressions in Poland's favor, Poland is assured of "substantial accessions of territory in the north and west." Meanwhile, the present puppet Government set up in Warsaw by Russia's unilateral action is to be reorganized "on a broader democratic basis" under the aegis of an international commission of three members, in which Russia will have a minority of one, and the new provisional Government thus formed is to be "pledged to the holding of free and unfettered elections as soon as possible, on the basis of universal suffrage and secret ballot." In these elections "all democratic and anti-Nazi parties shall have the right to take part and to put forward candidates."

Because we believe that this plan offers the Polish people west of the Curzon Line an opportunity to choose ❯

FEBRUARY 14, 1945

RAF HITS DRESDEN HEAVY NIGHT BLOW

LONDON, Feb. 14 (AP)—The RAF, launching one of the greatest night attacks of the war, sent 1,400 aircraft over Germany last night and delivered a smashing blow to Dresden in support of the Red Army's drive on that city.

Attacks also were made on a synthetic oil plant at Bohlen, south of Leipzig, and on Magdeburg, seventy-five miles southwest of Berlin.

Dresden, however, was the main target, an Air Ministry announcement said.

"As the center of a railway network and a great industrial town, it has become of the greatest value for conducting any defense the Germans may organize against Marshal Koneff's armies," the announcement added. ◇

The devastation in Dresden after the Allied bombing in 1945.

their own Government by democratic methods; because we believe that the Curzon Line itself, judged historically, is not unfair or unreasonable; because we believe that, with the accession of some new territory in the west and north, there will be ample living space in which a sturdy Poland can prosper, and because we believe that the guarantee of Polish integrity implied in this three-Power decision is of great importance from the point of view of the long future, we regret the action of the Polish Government in London yesterday in flatly rejecting the Yalta plan. We think that history will say that it missed an opportunity. ◇

FEBRUARY 16, 1945

JAPANESE EXPECT TO WIN, POLL FINDS
Concede Our Industrial Might But Put Faith in Japan's 'Spiritual Superiority'

By ROBERT TRUMBULL
By Wireless to The New York Times.

SAIPAN, Feb. 15—What does the average Japanese feel and think—about the war, about the United States, about democracy?

How well informed is he on the progress of the war? Does he still believe after having seen some of America's armed might that Japan will win? To get the answers to questions such as these, language officers on Saipan conducted a poll, in Camp Suspe, where 13,243 Japanese on Saipan are housed.

The poll was limited to 500 Japanese civilians selected according to education, station in life and sex so as to give the nearest possible cross section of civilian Japanese opinion as it might exist in the homeland. The results are admittedly inconclusive in some respects—for instance in evaluating the answer to the question whether Japanese civilians will fight to the death if Japan is invaded it must be borne in mind that those answering were Japanese who did fight.

However, the poll does lift a small corner of the veil that has hidden the average Japanese mind since the outbreak of the war. It disproves a few fallacies—such as the American belief that hara-kiri is widespread—and something of the attitude of the average Japanese toward his Emperor. It also discloses contradictory habits of thought that American officers have found to be characteristic of the Oriental enemy here and elsewhere.

SOME NEVER HEARD OF U.S.

The officers taking the poll chose the 500 civilians with care for the preservation of a proper ratio between Oki-nawans, who make up the bulk of the Japanese population on Saipan and Japanese from the home islands. It was noted, incidentally, that 5 per cent of the homeland Japanese considered the Okinawans inferior people but the Okinawans themselves were practically unanimous in their belief that there is no difference between themselves and other Japanese. The only actual difference in the poll as found between the two groups was that the Okinawans were less educated. Some had never heard of America.

Another factor considered in evaluating the answers was that the Saipan Japanese have received considerable information about the war since their capture. The Chamorro natives in Camp Suspe who hear of American victories from their soldier guards take delight in carrying this news to their Japanese fellow refugees. Also the Japanese on Saipan have seen with their own eyes considerable evidence of American strength. In this respect they have an advantage over their countrymen at home.

Fewer than 40 per cent of the Japanese in Suspe surrendered voluntarily; of the 500 queried 309 had been captured while only 191 gave up. Many said they would have surrendered had they not believed they would be tortured. This belief was based on horror stories disseminated by the Japanese army.

FEAR A MAJOR FACTOR

The Japanese encountered canards emanating from Guadalcanal that captured Japanese men and children would be run over by tanks while the women would be removed to ships and despoiled. Some of these stories were put into Japanese newspapers and magazines but most had been told by soldiers. Some civilians said they would have surrendered but were prevented by soldiers.

Answers to the "How did you feel when you were captured?" bore out a growing belief here that fear rather than fanatic patriotism ruled the Japanese civilians in resistance to capture. Only seventy-nine said they were "ashamed" while 348 admitted fright was the dominant emotion.

Incidentally, officers here believe that stories of civilian suicides on Saipan were greatly exaggerated; it is doubtful if the suicides exceeded 200, or 1 per cent of the population.

"If the Japanese homeland is invaded what do you think that the civilians will do?" Fight to the last, said 281; fight until it looks hopeless, said twenty-seven; the civilians won't fight, said seventy-nine. (Half of these said "it will be like Saipan.") About a quarter of those questioned had no opinion.

Three-fifths to four-fifths of the Japanese queried had the correct answers to questions on the progress of the war. They knew that Japan had been bombed, they didn't believe that Japan had invaded Australia or bombed California or occupied a large part of India. It is possible, however, that they had obtained much of this information since their capture.

Of the 500, 412 believed United States was more powerful industrially than Japan, and this was surprising to the interrogators. However, many qualified their answers, saying "but Japan is more powerful spiritually," and a number believe Japan will equal or surpass us in production when full use can be made of the resources in occupied countries.

Now comes a contradiction. Despite what they can see with their own eyes as great numbers of American ships moving in and out of Saipan harbor, more than half the group still believes Japan has the strongest navy in the world. Some confessed that their faith in the Japanese Navy was shaken by events in Saipan but others insisted that the Japanese Navy was still superior by some mysterious "spiritual power." Only 100 think the United States Navy has been sunk, however.

LONG WAR PREDICTED

As to who will win the war, a majority believe Japan will. Significantly these same persons think it will be a very long war. Frequently those answering revealed that their confidence in Japan was based on national pride. Many said something like this: "I think Japan will win, since I am a Japanese." It was evident that the Battle of Saipan had given many Japanese here a more realistic outlook on the facts of this war than they had had before.

More results of the questionnaire add no hope to any plans being held for a democratization of Japan after the war. There was a division of opinion as to actions of Japanese leaders, only 185 backing army and navy policies while seventy-four were opposed and 241 offered no opinion. Here an inconsistency appears. Asked if the Emperor favored the war 138 said "no," yet half of this group when asked the question, who actually controls the Japanese Government, answered "the Emperor."

There was little desire shown for a democratic form of government and three-fifths of those who wanted it did not think it would work if they got it.

Japanese opinion of American troops differed sharply before and after capture. Whereas 376 had thought American soldiers "barbarous and cruel" before capture, 422 now think them "kind, generous and friendly."

The Japanese here hold, however, to their previously inculcated opinions of the American people in general as distinct from the soldiery. Of the 500, a total of 330 think we are "soft, luxury loving, rich, spiritually weak"; 139 had no opinion. ◇

FEBRUARY 17, 1945

Dresden Dead Put At 70,000

STOCKHOLM, Sweden, Feb. 16 (AP)— The German-controlled Scandinavian Telegraph Bureau said today that 70,000 persons had been killed in this week's Allied bombings of Dresden. The city has been cut off from all communication with the rest of Germany as a result of destruction of the telegraph station, post office, railroad station and high command headquarters, the report said. ◇

FEBRUARY 19, 1945

GERMAN LINER SEEN SUNK
Finnish Radio Says Only 1,000 of 8,700 Aboard Were Saved

LONDON, Feb. 18 (AP)—The Finnish radio reported tonight the sinking of the 25,000-ton German liner Wilhelm Gustloff with the loss of 7,700 persons while she was evacuating refugees and sailors from Danzig.

[The Wilhelm Gustloff, a passenger liner before the war, had been converted into a troop transport.]

The broadcast did not state how or when the German ship was sunk, but said that of the 3,700 naval personnel and 5,000 refugees aboard only 1,000 were saved. ◇

FEBRUARY 22, 1945

Windbreaker Jacket Named For Eisenhower Is A Feature in Spring Style Collection

By VIRGINIA POPE

A complete review of the spring collection of one house of design was shown yesterday noon in the Cotillion Room of the Hotel Pierre, by Sada Saks, specialty shop of 671 Madison Avenue. It is usually the custom of stores to show styles from many houses. Yesterday's collection was from Anna Miller and designed by Henry Patrick.

Several main lines ran throughout. One of the most attractive was the windbreaker jacket used as the blouse of two-piece dresses. In honor of the Commander in Chief of the Allies' European armies it was called the Eisenhower. The feminine version was developed in crepes, sometimes in monotone effect and again in a two-color scheme. To soften it it was gathered into the waistline. Appliques on the sleeve or a bit of jeweled embroidery at the front added decorative interest.

Applause greeted dresses made with long gathered tunic tops. These came in prints or plain crepes. Large square-cut topaz-tinted stones made the buttons on one such model of banana-yellow rayon crepe. The chic look that one associates with New York women in the spring and summer was seen in simple crepes made on shirtwaist lines fastened with pearl or jeweled buttons. Stripes were used to their best advantage. A black and white dress had a wide cummerbund of red that tied at the side. Suits were made with hipbone length or bolero jackets.

There were refreshing black crepes for restaurant dining. Here the trump was a crepe with a tunic top of net. The lower portion was gathered full, ballerina style. Less formal was a frock with a Mexican pink skirt and a black bodice. ◇

FEBRUARY 25, 1945

JAPANESE OVERRUN
Marines Smash Through Maze Of Defenses in Bloody Iwo Battle

By WARREN MOSCOW
By Wireless to The New York Times.

ADVANCED HEADQUARTERS. Guam, Feb. 25—Despite bazooka-type weapons and new 1,100-pound rocket bombs used by fiercely fighting Japanese in a mass of powerful interlocking defenses, the marines on Iwo Island pushed northward 300 to 500 yards to overrun half of the fighter airstrip in the center of the ❯

(island on Saturday.

In a general push they widened the beachhead on the eastern coast by 600 yards, overcoming a maze of connecting pillboxes, blockhouses and fortified caves. They passed through heavily mined areas to make the advances, the greatest in one day since the landing on Monday.

In a single area of 400 by 600 yards on the east coast, the marines had to neutralize about 100 caves, thirty to forty feet deep, indicating clearly why the seventy-four-day aerial bombardment of the island and the three-day ship shelling prior to our landing failed to decimate the garrison or its supplies.

SUPPLIES POURING ASHORE
The marines are benefiting from the capture of Mount Suribachi, volcano at the southern end of the island, and the advance northward. Enemy artillery fire

no longer is dominating the interior area under American control. The mortar fire on the marines' landing places has been reduced and supplies are pouring ashore.

Apparently the Japanese on Iwo are using new techniques developed from lessons of previous American landings, making our advances more costly.

While there is no recent report on American casualties, this morning's communiqué reported a total of 2,799 enemy dead had been counted.

Something less than half of Iwo now is in our possession. Many Japanese strong points and small groups probably have been bypassed in the drive.

Mopping-up operations continued on Mount Suribachi. The marines reported 115 enemy emplacements destroyed in that area while squads of Leathernecks picked their way up and down the volcanic slopes. The planting

of the American flag on Suribachi two days ago marked a definite change in American fortunes on Iwo.

Meanwhile the fleet units continued furnishing aerial support while Seventh Army Air Force Liberators worked away neutralizing Japanese bases on Chichi and Haha Islands in the near-by Bonins.

A previous communiqué issued last midnight covering operations up to noon reported the start of the general marine attack now paying dividends. American tanks are leading the way.

TOKYO'S VERSION OF IWO BATTLE
An unsupported claim that American casualties on Iwo Island up to Friday night "totaled 17,000" was broadcast by the Tokyo radio yesterday, The Associated Press reported.

The broadcast, beamed to North America and recorded by the Federal

---

MARCH 6, 1945

39 NATIONS INVITED TO SECURITY PARLEY AT SAN FRANCISCO
Poles Are Omitted Until New Government Is Set Up as Proposed at Yalta

By LANSING WARREN
Special to The New York Times.

WASHINGTON, March 5—Invitations to attend the security conference in San Francisco April 25 were conveyed today by United States diplomatic representatives to the governments of thirty-nine nations, the State Department announced.

In extending the invitations to the conference, which was decided on at Yalta as a sequel to the Dumbarton Oaks meeting, this country was acting on behalf of the other sponsoring powers, the United Kingdom, Russia and China.

Included in or accompanying the announcement were these other four major developments in the preparations for the San Francisco meeting: Secretary of State Edward R. Stettinius Jr., in a statement issued here and in Mexico City, where he is attending the meeting of Inter-American States, gave a detailed explanation of the settlement at Yalta on the voting procedure in the proposed Security Council. Under this compro-

mise, the unanimous consent of the Big Five would be required in deciding certain questions involving the use of force, and any one of the five could veto a move to enforce peace.

FRANCE WILL ATTEND PARLEY
France, while agreeing to participate in the conference, declined to serve as an inviting power, owing to the fact that she made this contingent on conditions which the other major powers could not agree to approve, but it was learned that France's status as a permanent member of the security council would not be affected by her refusal to be an inviting power.

Poland was temporarily not invited, and her invitation was made conditional on the reorganization of her Provisional Government in conformity with the provisions of the Crimea Conference.

Senator Arthur H. Vandenberg of Michigan, the only one of the Republicans on the American delegation

who had not already accepted, announced that he had agreed to be a delegate. He said that an exchange of letters with President Roosevelt had convinced him of his right of free action, adding that he would exercise it to insure that "justice" should be made the "guiding objective" of the peace.

The invitations issued today, besides the omission of Poland, showed several divergences from the lists of countries previously invited to United Nations conferences. It was explained that since Jan. 1 eight countries had signed the United Nations declaration. It was decided to invite all signatory powers to the declaration as of Feb. 5, 1945, as well as Turkey and any country which had declared war on an Axis power up to March 1.

A special invitation was decided later in the case of Saudi Arabia, following the conference between Mr. Roosevelt and King Ibn Saud on a warship near Cairo.

NEUTRALS NOT INVITED
Syria and Lebanon, Iceland and Denmark, which had sent representatives to previous gatherings, were omitted from the conference, as were such neutral countries as Switzerland, Spain, Sweden, Portugal, Ireland and Argentina. Liberated countries, such as Italy, Rumania, Hungary, Bulgaria and the Baltic nations, several of which under new governments have declared war on Germany, also were excluded.

Neutral countries, it was explained,

Communications Commission, said that "the enemy's advance has been stemmed—as a matter of fact, the enemy has had to withdraw his line somewhat."

The Japanese radio had nothing to say about the American capture of Mount Suribachi, claiming instead that fighting continues there "without distinction to day or night, as our matchless drawn-swords continue to penetrate into the enemy midst."

"More than 40,000 enemy troops are caught and. unable to move in a small area about three kilometers in length running from the south dock toward the west, and one kilometer deep from the coastal area to Sunajigahara," Tokyo said. "With this concentration of enemy men as a target, our shells are being well aimed, and not one shell explodes but that it makes its mark." ◆

---

cannot share in the peace settlement, and the former enemy countries, even though now recognized diplomatically, cannot be admitted to the security negotiations until after the organization has been set up. There was no explanation of the omission of Syria, Lebanon, Iceland and Denmark.

FRANCE RAISES PROBLEM

One of the problems disclosed in today's announcement is the defection of France, widening the rift caused by General de Gaulle's recent refusal to meet Mr. Roosevelt in Algiers. The French leader has complained that France was not informed sufficiently of the Crimea decisions, and not having been represented at Yalta had framed several objections and suggestions which it desired to make.

After study of the French propositions and consultation among the inviting powers, it was found impossible to accept her proposals and France was so informed. Her reply was to agree to attend the conference, but to refuse to be a sponsor. The action is equivalent to serving notice that France intends to defend her proposals to amend the Yalta and Dumbarton Oaks decisions in conformity with French views.

Although nothing was disclosed officially on the proposals, it is known the French Government is especially interested in the peace settlement with Germany and the disposition of the Rhineland. ◆

MARCH 6, 1945

TITO IS BELGRADE PREMIER

BELGRADE, Yugoslavia, March 5 (Reuter)—After the formation of the Regency Council here at noon today, Marshal Tito and Premier Ivan Subasitch of the Yugoslav Royal Government conferred.

In the afternoon Dr. Subasitch handed the resignation of the Royal Government to the Regency and later Marshal Tito presented to the President of the National Liberation Assembly, Dr. Ivan Ri-bar, the resignation of the whole National Committee, which for the last two years has acted as a Government and carried on the war.

The Regents, on the advice of Dr. Ribar and Dr. Subasitch, then entrusted the Marshal with the mandate to form a united Yugoslav Government, which is expected to be completed by tomorrow. ◆

MARCH 11, 1945

FURIOUS FIGHTING RAGES AT BRIDGE
Germans Pour Shells On U.S. Forces—Air Attack Fails—Men Pour Over Rhine

By GLADWIN HILL
By Wireless to The New York Times.

AT THE RHINE BRIDGEHEAD, March 10—While American forces pressed steadily east of the Rhine under the secrecy of a blackout, a furious many-sided battle raged all day at the Remagen bridgehead today.

German guns shelled the bridge and both banks of the river from lateral positions on the east bank outside the bridgehead. German bombing planes came over at scarcely more than ten-minute intervals from noon on, evoking flaming barrages from hundreds of American anti-aircraft guns on the hills around and even from pistol-packing GI's, who cheered our ack-ack blasts and blazed away from the ground with their own small arms.

But at the end of the day, our reinforcements were still pouring across into the growing piece we are biting out of Germany's interior fortress.

American engineers worked on the more vulnerable west bank— because it is not protected by bluffs such as those that overhang the east side—under a succession of screaming shells that, as this correspondent can testify, were far from reassuring. Some hit vehicles and other equipment on the river bank, starting fires that roared for hours, and sent up great columns of smoke.

Against an obligato of shell whines and the tat-tat-tat of ack-ack fire, Brig. Gen. William T. Hoge, who directed the original coup of capturing the bridge, coolly continued in his temporary command post in a dark cellar on the east bank the supervision of his forces in the exploitation of the break.

GERMAN AIR BLOW SMASHED

A special squadron of eleven German fighter planes made a desperate attempt late today to bomb the Remagen Bridge leading to American positions across the Rhine, but a United States Thunderbolt squadron stopped them before they could reach their objective.

Six Messerschmitt 109's, carrying "heavy bombs," escorted by five Focke-Wulf 190's, made the attempt. The Thunderbolts intercepted them above the town of Linz and a spectacular dogfight developed in which two of the German planes were shot down and the others were forced to jettison their bombs and scurry for inner Germany.

Two American fighters were lost but the vital bridge, feeding Lieut. Gen. Courtney H. Hodges' First Army troops, suffered not the slightest damage.

First Lieut. Norman D. Gould of Erie, Pa., shot down one of the bomb-carrying Messerschmitts and two other Thunderbolts shot down one of the escorting Focke-Wulfs. Another Messerschmitt was damaged.

U.S. GUNS HIT AMERICAN

The some 100 American fighters patrolling the bridgehead throughout the day had to brave both their own and enemy antiaircraft fire and a solid cloud formed a 2,500-foot ceiling over the sector. United States gunners clustered around the bridge itself were firing at every ❱

‹ plane that appeared without taking time to determine its identity.

One of the Eighth Air Force's leading aces, Capt. Ray Wetmore of Kerman, Calif., narrowly escaped when gunfire from United States batteries crippled his fighter plane and forced him to make an emergency landing.

His plane was set afire by flak, which also crippled his hydraulic system. But Captain Wetmore made a successful belly landing and reported by radio that he was not hurt.

He holds a record of twenty-one planes shot down in combat in addition to two destroyed on the ground. ◇

A First U.S. Army tank rolls off the east end of the Rhine River bridge at Remagen, Germany as U.S. infantrymen advance to consolidate and expand the east bank bridgehead in March 1945.

MARCH 11, 1945

GIANT TOKYO FIRES BLACKENED B-29'S
Correspondent in One Reports Soot and Smoke Reached Planes High in Skies

By MARTIN SHERIDAN
Boston Globe Correspondent for the Combined American Press.

OVER TOKYO, March 10—I not only saw Tokyo burning furiously in many sections, but I smelled it. Huge clouds of smoke billowed high above the city. The conflagration was so great that the bomb bay doors of this Superfortress, the underside of the fuselage and the gun blisters were blackened with soot.

This bomber was one of more than 300 from American bases in the Marianas—forming the greatest fleet of Superfortresses ever put in the air—which gave the Japanese capital the hotfoot early today.

Our navigator didn't have to give the pilot a bearing on Tokyo. Other bombers were ahead of us and forty miles from the city we could see the reddish glow of fires already started.

As soon as we reached the Japanese mainland we saw scores of smaller fires, en route to Tokyo, and possibly set by the Japanese as diversionary ruses.

The Superfortresses went in singly, a complete change from their previous formation tactics.

Over the outskirts of Tokyo our plane tore through high, somber clouds of smoke and fires. The smoke seemed inside the plane. It smelled like the interior of a long burnt building.

A DISPLAY OF DESTRUCTION

Suddenly there was an opening through the pall of clouds, and there was Tokyo.

I have never seen such a display of destruction, nor had such an experience.

Fires were raging in several multi-block areas and creating almost daylight conditions. In addition, there were hundreds of blazes throughout the waterfront area, the most densely populated section in the world.

Another indication of the conflagration's intensity was the turbulent air conditions we encountered over the target. Our plane named Patches and bearing a semi-nude painting on its nose struck down and up drafts and bounced 2,000 feet in split seconds. Crewmen were tossed from their seats. Several struck their heads violently against the top of the plane. They were protected from injury by helmets.

Maj. Walter F. Todd of Ogden, Utah, operations officer and command pilot, said he thought we were hit by anti-aircraft fire, but speeedy examination proved everything was operating satisfactorily.

A moment later Second Lieut. Lee P. Ziemiansky of Buffalo, N.Y. navigator, sang out: "Three, two, one, mark!" At the last word of the count the bombardier, Second Lieut. Thomas C. Moss of Aurora Ill., dropped the "eggs" in the target area.

SEARCHLIGHTS FINGER PLANE

As a civilian noncombatant, my contribution was limited to a brown beer bottle—empty, of course. Several searchlights played on the plane a few moments, but we saw no interceptors and only a few scattered anti-aircraft shell bursts.

We did see the city getting a terrific plastering and they'll need a highly efficient fire department to put out the blazes.

During the night trip out, the plane passed through several sharp squalls which would pass quickly and then the sky would be full of lights of other bombers.

We passed too close to Raha Island, north of Iwo. The Japanese probed the sky with searchlights.

Second Lieut. Richard W. Metcalfe of Chicago, flight engineer, at midnight broke out a cart containing sandwiches, a few oranges and several cans of grapefruit juice.

The crew was perturbed about "stateside" stories describing facilities on a bomber for keeping chow hot and other stories of fabulous meals. "That doesn't happen in the Pacific," they said.

WORRY OVER GASOLINE SUPPLY

The plane commander, Second Lieut. Leon L. Ballard of Houston, Tex., has been a second lieutenant for twenty-one months. The copilot, Second Lieut. Melvin Barnes of Blackfoot, Idaho, has gone

MARCH 17, 1945

3D CUTS FOE APART
Armor Slashes Up Links of the Enemy —Others Flank Him on Saar

By DREW MIDDLETON
By Wireless to The New York Times.

PARIS, March 16—The battle for the rich Saar Basin has been won almost before it got well under way. The Fourth Armored Division of Lieut. Gen. George S. Patton's United States Third Army has dashed from the Moselle to beyond Simmern, only sixteen miles from the Rhine at Bingen, according to front-line reports, while along the Saar River itself other Third Army forces have turned the right flank of the German defenses and the United States Seventh Army, attacking frontally, has driven through German positions for substantial gains on a front of sixty miles.

The tactics of envelopment that General Patton and Lieut. Gen. Courtney H. Hodges, commander of the United States First Army, practiced north of the Moselle are being brought to perfection south of the river by General Patton and Lieut Gen. Alexander M. Patch, commander of the United States Seventh-Army. Already Allied air forces report German withdrawals eastward toward the Rhine from the great quadrilateral whose corners rest on Coblenz, Mainz, Karlsruhe and Merzig.

KAISER'S STATUE SMASHED
Coblenz itself, standing at the confluence of the Moselle and the Rhine, should fall in a matter of hours. General Patton slipped strong forces across the Moselle six miles south of Coblenz at 3 A.M. today. After a terse "surrender or die" ultimatum was broadcast to the German garrison, Third Army artillery hammered the city with 5,000 shells, which, according to one report from the front, destroyed 75 per cent of the city. One shell blew the famous statue of Kaiser Wilhelm I, symbol of German imperial militarism, to bits.

But Coblenz is only a minor prize compared to the great victory that has been won generally throughout the area. The Germans may fight a number of stiff defensive actions. But the tactical decision has been made by General Patton's armor. The Germans now must either get out of the Saar, withdrawing eastward across the Rhine, or be surrounded and chopped up.

Elsewhere on the front the most important news was the northern thrust of the United States First Army forces in the Remagen bridgehead, which have pushed troops through Koenigswinter on the left and across the Autobahn in the center, bringing the latter forces onto the edge of the flat plain that extends northward. General Hodges has now developed the bridgehead, despite stout opposition, to a point from which a really damaging offensive can be launched.

BITCHE CAPTURED EASILY
The capture of Bitche, long a German stronghold barring the Americans' path into the eastern edge of the Saar Basin, was the outstanding feat of the Seventh Army front today. It fell to the 100th Infantry Division without much of a fight, and only fifty-eight German soldiers were found in the city, according to reports from the front.

Apparently there has not yet been any effort to take Saarbruecken, for the only action mentioned in that sector was around Feschingen, where infantry of the Sixty-third Infantry Division advanced several thousand yards to the north, after having cleared a town that lies four miles Southeast of Saarbruecken.

Habkirchen was cleared and troops advanced two miles to the north into Pebelsheim. Other elements of the Sixty-third entered Ensheim yesterday and cleared the woods southwest of Omersheim.

The battle line is now two miles from Saarbruecken at the nearest point. Patrols have advanced to within 1,000 yards of the town. ◆

---

fifteen months without a promotion. Moss, the bombardier, has been "frozen" sixteen months as a second lieutenant. The flight engineer, Metcalfe, hasn't been promoted for nineteen months and Lieutenant Zlemianski has not progressed in seventeen months.

Others in the crew were: S/ Sgt.1 Frank A. Gish of Chicago, Ill.; S/ Sgt. Elmo G. Hodges of Smithville, Tex.; Sgt. Joseph F. Kelly (address not included), and Cpl. Emerson B. Burke of Sapulpa, Okla.

These men and their enlisted mates sleep on cots in Quonset huts and tents at their base, eat mediocre chow and yet fly one of the Army's most difficult missions without complaints. They have had twelve Superfortress missions.

They have been flying through miserable weather, minus fighter escorts and without complete weather and navigational aids. I saw them in action this morning. under completely new conditions, and a crew couldn't have looked better.

The greatest worry after the target is left behind is stretching the gasoline supply over 3,300 miles (the round trip) and making it despite head winds and squally weather.

The hardest worker is the navigator, who fiddles with his instruments and charts every moment. His computation was on the nose and I can see Saipan again. After Tokyo, Saipan appears beautiful. ◆

German Army medics surrendering to American troops in Coblenz, Germany, 1945.

Chapter 23
"GERMANS CAPITULATE ON ALL FRONTS"
April–May 1945

The end of the war in Europe came suddenly, though not unexpectedly. The man who had contributed a great deal to the achievement, President Franklin Roosevelt, was not to witness the final hour of victory. At 3:30 p.m. on April 12 he died of a cerebral hemorrhage at the age of sixty-three at the Warm Springs spa in Georgia, where he was staying. He had been sitting for an artist's preliminary sketches when he suddenly collapsed. He lost consciousness shortly afterward and died without regaining it.

The entire Allied world was shocked by the news. The Times carried dignified and straightforward accounts of the story, including Roosevelt's last words: "I have a terrific headache." The vice president, Harry S. Truman, using Roosevelt's Bible from the White House, was sworn in by the Chief Justice, Harlan Stone, who recited the oath from memory. All around the world there were tributes, including Soviet flags in Moscow with a mourning border.

Only in Berlin was there rejoicing. Hitler and Goebbels, sealed inside the capital, thought this might be a sign that Destiny had not yet abandoned the German war effort and that there was now a chance to break Stalin's alliance with the Western powers. This was a fantasy, since Allied armies were now within days of capturing Germany.

Truman's first announcement was to confirm that nothing would change in American foreign policy. A week later American opinion was shocked again by the death of the correspondent Ernie Pyle on the Pacific island of Ie Shima, where a Japanese sniper machine-gunned him as he covered the action. Truman found himself giving a second eulogy, this time for a man who told the story of the American fighting man "as American fighting men wanted it told."

By April 21 the German Army in the west, cooped up in the Ruhr pocket, had surrendered. The Soviet assault on Berlin began on April 16 and ended with German surrender of the city on May 2. On April 25 soldiers of Lt. General Courtney Hodge's First Army met troops from Konev's First Ukrainian Army near the town of Torgau on the River Elbe. Over the following two weeks, remaining pockets of German resistance were cleared. The concentration camps were liberated and the full horror of the system the Allies had been fighting was revealed to the occupation armies. Estimates of four million deaths at Auschwitz were published. At Dachau concentration camp in Bavaria, the American troops who liberated it could not be restrained from killing the guards.

In Italy the long and difficult campaign up the peninsula also ended with a sudden Axis collapse. After building up his forces, the Allied commander in Italy, General Harold Alexander, launched the final campaign on April 9 and within three weeks had defeated what remained of Axis resistance, aided by Italian partisans who wanted to be seen as liberating their cities before the advancing Allied armies. On May 2 all Axis forces surrendered. The final collapse brought a violent end to Europe's Fascist dictators. On April 28 Mussolini, together with his mistress, Clara Petacci, and other leading Fascists, tried to escape into Switzerland but they were caught by partisans, summarily tried and executed. Their bodies were taken to the Piazzale Loreto in Milan and strung up by their feet. A Times reporter, Milton Bracker, watched as the local population kicked and slashed the bodies. An Italian photographer took pictures and offered them to The Times office in Switzerland but they were sent from Geneva by the new radiophoto technique and published at once in New York, one of the major scoops of the war's end.

Hitler and his mistress, Eva Braun, whom he married on April 28, committed suicide in his Berlin bunker on April 30, though Soviet officials claimed on May 4 that they could find no sign of the corpses. The evidence was good enough for the rest of the world, however. "Deep Satisfaction Is Felt by US Troops at Death" ran The Times headline. On May 7 German forces unconditionally surrendered to Eisenhower in a schoolhouse in the French city of Reims. Stalin wanted the ceremony in Berlin and on May 8 a second surrender document was signed there. On that day the American and British people celebrated victory in Europe. In New York, The Times's electric newsboard carried the message "The War in Europe Is Ended."

APRIL 1, 1945

U.S. AND BRITAIN REBUFF MOSCOW ON LUBLIN POLES

By BERTRAM D. HULEN
Special to The New York Times.

WASHINGTON, March 31—The United States and Great Britain have refused a Russian appeal that the Soviet-supported Lublin Provisional Government in Warsaw be invited to the San Francisco conference of the United Nations on world security.

It was revealed at the State Department today that the United States has joined the British in rejecting the appeal and in insisting on standing on the Yalta decision to broaden the base of the Warsaw Government by including democratic elements of many Polish groups in a new government.

When asked concerning the matter, a State Department spokesman said that it was the hope of the American Government that the formation of the new provisional Polish Government of National Unity in conformity with the decisions of the Crimean conference would be completed in time to send a delegation to the San Francisco conference.

In view of the current consultations respecting the formation of this new government, reorganized on a broader democratic basis with the inclusion of democratic leaders from Poland itself and from Poles abroad in accordance with the Crimean agreement, he added, the United States Government did not agree to the extension of an invitation to the present provisional government now functioning at Warsaw.

SOVIET GOVERNMENT INFORMED

The Soviet Government was informed of our position along these lines after its appeal was received here. It is understood that we consulted with the British before sending our reply to Moscow.

When Premier Stalin agreed at Yalta to the formation of a new Polish Government on broad lines inclusive of many Polish elements, it was felt that he had made an important concession to the United States, Great Britain and many Polish groups, and it was felt that he had made the concession in good faith.

It was in that spirit that, after the Crimean conference, discussions were immediately begun in Moscow looking to the formation of a new, fully representative and democratic Polish Government, but the negotiations have dragged along and have bogged down over what is described as procedural details.

In these circumstances and with the date of the San Francisco conference approaching, Premier Stalin made his appeal for the Lublin government to sit at San Francisco, it was stated.

Previously the United States had refused a plea of the Polish Government-in-exile in London, which we and the British still recognize, to attend the San Francisco conference.

Our position has been that the contemplated new Polish Government would attend that conference. For us to accept the Lublin Government now, it is felt, would mean the upsetting of the Yalta agreement on Poland. ◊

APRIL 2, 1945

Heads of States Will Not Escape War Crime Penalties, Allies Decide

United Nations Commission Puts Hitler At Top of First of Five Lists Now Ready— Plea of 'Superior Orders' to Be Insufficient

By CLIFTON DANIEL
By Cable to The New York Times.

LONDON, April 1—The United Nations War Crimes Commission announced today that Adolf Hitler's name headed one of five lists of war criminals that it had compiled and that enemy governmental leaders would not be immune from prosecution for war crimes.

Another of the lists is devoted entirely to the Japanese. A sub-commission in Chungking is preparing a further list of Japanese suspects.

As the liberation armies have marched forward, the commission reported, the number of cases that it has received from the war-crimes offices of individual countries has increased steadily with the flow of information. In announcing that the "names of major and obvious war criminals such as Hitler" were included in its first list, the commission officially refuted allegations that political personages would not be treated as criminals like their subordinates.

"The commission early in its work assumed that no immunity attached to heads of States," this statement said, "and it decided that the plea of superior orders of itself did not constitute justification for a war crime." The latter question has long been a disputed point about the treatment of war criminals. The dispute whether heads of States could be tried as common criminals was reported to have led to the resignation of Herbert C. Pell as the American representative on the commission.

At the same time the commission pointed out that under the Moscow declaration on the punishment of war criminals, the treatment of major criminals was reserved for future decision. Lesser criminals will be returned to the countries that were the scenes of their crimes to be judged by national courts.

The commission did not disclose any names on the lists except Hitler's, on the ground that publication of them would forewarn the wanted men. However, their names will be announced later.

The first list catalogues German war criminals; the second, Italians; the third, Germans; the fourth, Japanese; the fifth, Albanians, Bulgarians, Hungarians and Rumanians. Further lists are being prepared and will be forwarded to the sixteen nations represented on the commission. ◊

APRIL 6, 1945

KOISO CABINET OUT IN JAPANESE CRISIS
Hirohito Asks Admiral Suzuki, Known as a 'Moderate,' to Form Government

Racked by military defeats and a rising storm of criticism at home, Premier Kuniaki Koiso's Cabinet resigned en masse yesterday and Emperor Hirohito called on an elder statesman, Admiral Baron Kantaro Suzuki, to form Japan's third wartime government, the Tokyo radio announced in a broadcast recorded by the Federal Communications Commission, The Associated Press reported.

In facing the "gravity of the situation," which Tokyo said forced Koiso and his Ministers to step down, Japan turned to a 77-year-old veteran of public service who had been considered a "moderate" in pre-war years. Suzuki, president of the Privy Council, has been looked upon as an opponent of the extreme Army clique's program of conquest.

The Japanese news agency Domei reported later that on Friday morning (Japanese time) Suzuki established his "Cabinet organization headquarters" at his Tokyo residence and set to work to form the new Cabinet.

At 8 A.M., Domei said, former Premier Admiral Keisuke Okada called at Suzuki's residence. An hour and a half later, the dispatch said, Admiral Koshiro Oikawa, Chief of the Naval General Staff, conferred with the new Premier and at 9:40 A.M., Field Marshal General Sugiyama, who resigned as War Minister in Koiso's Cabinet, called on Suzuki to "confer on important matters."

The military disasters in the field and on the seas that have harassed Koiso since he took over the reins of the government from Premier Gen. Hideki Tojo nearly nine months ago made certain that his downfall was not far off.

"In view of the gravity of the situation the Cabinet has decided to resign en bloc to open the way for a far more powerful administration," a Tokyo communiqué said in announcing the fall of the Cabinet. "Premier Koiso accordingly tendered the collective resignation of his Cabinet to the throne today."

Close students of Japan predicted the succeeding Government would be a "moderate" one that might project peace feelers to the United States and its allies.

Suzuki has been in retirement since he was wounded in the revolt by young Japanese Army officers in 1936.

The collapse of the Koiso regime had been staved off for a time by his promise, fulfilled only last week, of forming a new "Sure Victory" political party that would include leading figures from all of Japan. Koiso's downfall came at a time when Japan was faced with the most critical war situation it had known.

American forces have secured footholds in the Volcano Islands, only 750 miles from Tokyo, and on Okinawa in the Ryukyus, closer yet, and remnants of the once mighty Imperial fleet are forced to hide out in home waters, subject to American air attacks. ◊

APRIL 7, 1945

EPIDEMICS IMPERIL EUROPE, UNRRA SAYS
Reports a Steady Rise In Diseases, With Typhus Presenting a 'Grave Danger'

Special to The New York Times.

WASHINGTON, April 6—Although there has been no disastrous epidemic thus far in the war, the situation in Europe is regarded as threatening, says a report of the United Nations Relief and Rehabilitation Administration's Health Division.

Absence of real disasters, says the report signed by Knud Stowman, chief of the Epidemiological Information Service, may be traced to the low endemic level of most diseases preceding the war and to the advance of preventive medicine.

The report warns, however, that

A medical van in the London area is set-up to immunize children against diphtheria.

there are "grave potentialities" for epidemics because of the debilitated condition of peoples in many countries, the increase in refugee movements and the fluid state of civil administration.

It says that "louse-borne typhus presents an immediate and grave danger for Europe," causing severe epidemics in some areas; that diphtheria has become a "leading disease of the war" on that Continent, and that there also has been a steady increase in infantile paralysis, dysentery, tuberculosis, malaria and syphilis.

The "new" disease of this war has been epidemic jaundice, the report says, adding:

"From an obscure existence ▶

among the garrison of Malta and in a few German Army units, it assumed proportions to interfere occasionally with military operations and spread among the civilian population from the Libyan Desert to North Cape.

"The disease is not really new, but was known in World War I, when at times it was confused with Weil's disease. It occurred also among civilians in various countries, but had never been considered capable of setting up veritable epidemics.

"Epidemic jaundice is clearly a virus disease of an extremely high degree of infectivity and capacity for covering distances. Since its potentialities are unknown and means of combating it have not so far been devised, this disease deserves to be closely watched."

The mortality rate has not been high so far, ranging from one a thousand to one a hundred.

"The number of tuberculosis cases," the report says, "has increased greatly in France, Belgium, the Netherlands, Germany, Austria, Czechoslovakia and Hungary, and it has doubled in many parts of this area. Among these countries the Netherlands is undoubtedly the worst sufferer. In Italy the situation is likely to become worse than ever before and Poland faces an unprecedented calamity."

"In several ways," the report concludes, "the outlook is darker than in 1918 because the destruction of buildings and displacement of persons is far more widespread than during World War I. But on the other hand, the endemic level was lower to start with in 1939 than in 1914, and the world is now better equipped to deal with many of the important infectious diseases." ◇

APRIL 9, 1945

3D ARMY OVERRUNS REICH 'DEATH CAMP'
4,000 at Extermination Center Slain

WITH THE UNITED STATES THIRD ARMY, April 8 (AP)—A ghastly extermination center where prisoners said the Germans starved, clubbed and burned to death more than 4,000 European captives in the last eight months has been overrun by the Fourth Armored Division. The Americans seized the camp near Ohrdruf, nine miles south of Gotha, on April 4.

Seventy-seven bodies of victims, said by prisoners to have been killed on April 2, the day before the Americans arrived, were found by Brig. Gen. William M. Hoge's tankmen. The bodies included one of a man the prisoners said was a naturalized American flier of Polish extraction. He had been shot through the neck.

Ashes and arms and legs of other victims were found around a crude woodland crematory two miles from the concentration camp.

[The crematory consisted of railway tracks over a big pit, a Reuter dispatch said. Charred remains of ten bodies still lay heaped on top of the grill, and the pit below where a fire still was burning, was deep in human ashes. The United Press reported that surviving prisoners said some 2,000 of the captives were buried in a huge pit a mile from the camp.]

Eighty prisoners who were liberated said those killed by the German SS [Elite Guard] troops operating the camp included Poles, Czechs, Russians, Belgians, Frenchmen, German Jews and German political prisoners.

BUERGERMEISTER A SUICIDE
Twenty-eight German civilians from the area were taken on a tour of the camp site by Col. Hayden Sears of Boston, commander of the Fourth Armored Division's Combat Command A, which captured Ohrdruf. All denied knowledge of what had taken place at the camp. The Buergermeister of the town and his wife were found slashed to death—apparently suicides—after a similar tour yesterday.

Liberated prisoners who hid in the woods said the last batch of victims numbering 150 was executed less than twenty-four hours before the Fourth Armored Division arrived. The bodies were stacked under a shed or left where they fell.

'INHUMAN TREATMENT' CHARGED

WITH THE UNITED STATES SEVENTH ARMY, April 8 (AP)—Two United States Army lieutenants, who survived the horrors of the Gerolstein and Hammelburg prisoner-of-war camps in Germany, escaped in their fourth attempt and reached the American lines east of the Main River today, declaring they had been subjected to "utterly inhuman treatment" by their captors.

One, a young West Point graduate of the class of 1943, and the other, an Arlington, Va., youth, broke away from their guards on a forced march toward a new prison camp at Nuremberg as advancing American troops approached the older camps.

French slave laborers supplied them with food as they made their way to the American lines. The West Pointer punctuated his story with the grim statement that the treatment they had received was "utterly inhuman" and he longed to get back into the lines to "kill Germans for what they did to our men."

PACKAGES USED AS BRIBES

"The Germans even tried to use Red Cross packages addressed to us as bribes—holding them back from us, then offering us something from them to try to get us to talk. Not one American officer or man in any prison I have been in ever talked.

"The Germans put me in solitary confinement for thirteen days trying to make me tell them who I was. They had a suspicion who my dad was, and his outfit, on which they had all the information, but I refused to tell them anything. I lost forty pounds." The other lieutenant said he had lost thirty pounds.

The names of the men who escaped could not be disclosed.

"This is the happiest day of my life," the escaped lieutenant said. "But we can never forget the horrors of those prison camps. Gerolstein should go down in history as a blot of shame on humanity."

The other lieutenant said, "What left searing scars on both of us was knowledge of the way our wounded prisoners lay untreated in hospitals." Paper bandages but no drugs or antiseptics were used, both men said. ◇

American soldiers and survivors looking at the last victims of the Ohrdruf concentration camp.

PRESIDENT ROOSEVELT IS DEAD
LAST WORDS. 'I HAVE TERRIFIC HEADACHE'

By The Associated Press.

WARM SPRINGS, Ga., April 12—President Franklin D. Roosevelt's last words were:

"I have a terrific headache."

He spoke them to Comdr. Howard G. Bruenn, naval physician.

Mr. Roosevelt was sitting in front of a fireplace in the Little White House here atop Pine Mountain when what was described as a massive cerebral hemorrhage struck him.

The President's Negro valet, Arthur Prettyman, and a Filipino messboy carried him to his bedroom. He was unconscious at the end. It came without pain.

Dr. Bruenn said that he saw the President this morning and he was in excellent spirits at 9:30 A.M.

"At 1 o'clock," Dr. Bruenn added, "he was sitting in a chair while sketches were being made of him by an artist. He suddenly complained of a very severe occipital headache (back of the head).

"Within a very few minutes he lost consciousness. He was seen by me at 1:30 P.M. fifteen minutes after the episode had started.

"He did not regain consciousness, and he died at 3:35 P. M. (Georgia time)."

NEEDED MORE WEIGHT

Mr. Roosevelt arrived at Warm Springs March 30. He had been underweight and his doctors wanted him to take it easy to see if he could regain the poundage at which he felt comfortable.

Rumors had been heard the last few days that the President was not picking up as much as his doctors would have liked.

He received reporters last Thursday and, in the presence of Sergio Osmena, president of the Philippine Commonwealth, told of his desire to grant full independence to the islands by autumn.

Mr. Roosevelt also outlined ambitious post-war plans for American participation in the Western Pacific to prevent further Japanese aggression.

He said that the United States and the other United Nations must accept trusteeships over Japanese-mandated islands, build new naval and air bases and help the Philippines rebuild, economically, after the commonwealth becomes a self-governing nation.

REPORT WAS TO BE HELD UP

Reports of this news conference were to have been withheld for security reasons until Mr. Roosevelt returned to Washington.

The President had planned to stay here another week, then he was to return to the Capital and spend one day before taking a train to San Francisco to open the United Nations Conference on International Organization.

This was Mr. Roosevelt's second stay here in four months. He spent nineteen days here only last November–December.

White House reporters had recently noticed his gray pallor, and it had caused considerable comment among them.

Mr. Roosevelt's voice also had become weak in recent months, and he frequently asked reporters to repeat their questions.

This was attributable, according to those close to him, to a sinus leakage into the throat which caused slight constrictions.

The death announcement was made in the center of the 2,000-acre foundation for polio treatment which the President helped found more than twenty years ago. That was before he began serving his first term as Governor of New York. ◇

APRIL 13, 1945

Franklin Delano Roosevelt
END COMES SUDDENLY AT WARM SPRINGS

By ARTHUR KROCK
Special to The New York Times

WASHINGTON, April 12—Franklin Delano Roosevelt, War President of the United States and the only Chief Executive in history who was chosen for more than two terms, died suddenly and unexpectedly at 4:35 P.M. today at Warm Springs, Ga. and the White House announced his death at 5:48 o'clock. He was 63.

The President, stricken by a cerebral hemorrhage, passed from unconsciousness to death on the eighty-third day of his fourth term and in an hour of high triumph. The armies and fleets under his direction as Commander in Chief were at the gates of Berlin and the shores of Japan's home islands as Mr. Roosevelt died, and the cause he represented and led was nearing the conclusive phase of success.

Less than two hours after the official announcement, Harry S. Truman of Missouri, the Vice President, took the oath as the thirty-second President. The oath was administered by the Chief Justice of the United States, Harlan F. Stone, in a one-minute ceremony at the White House. Mr. Truman immediately let it be known that Mr. Roosevelt's Cabinet is remaining in office at his request, and that he had authorized Secretary of State Edward R. Stettinius Jr. to proceed with plans for the United Nations Conference on international organization at San Francisco, scheduled to begin April 25. A report was circulated that he leans somewhat to the idea of a coalition Cabinet, but this is unsubstantiated.

FUNERAL TOMORROW AFTERNOON

It was disclosed by the White House that funeral services for Mr. Roosevelt would take place at 4 P.M. (E.W.T.) Saturday in the East Room of the Executive Mansion. The Rev. Angus Dun, Episcopal Bishop of Washington; the Rev. Howard S. Wilkinson of St. Thomas's Church in Washington and the Rev. John G. McGee of St. John's in Washington will conduct the services.

The body will be interred at Hyde Park, N.Y., Sunday, with the Rev. George W. Anthony of St. James Church officiating. The time has not yet been fixed.

Jonathan Daniels, White House secretary, said Mr. Roosevelt's body would not lie in state. He added that, in view of the limited size of the East Room, which holds only about 200 persons, the list of those attending the funeral services would be limited to high Government officials, representatives of the membership of both houses of Congress, heads of foreign missions, and friends of the family.

President Truman, in his first official pronouncement, pledged prosecution of the war to a successful conclusion. His statement, issued for him at the White House by press secretary Jonathan Daniels, said:

"The world may be sure that we will prosecute the war on both fronts, East and West, with all the vigor we possess to a successful conclusion."

NEWS OF DEATH STUNS CAPITAL

The impact of the news of the President's death on the capital was tremendous. Although rumor and a marked change in Mr. Roosevelt's appearance and manner had brought anxiety to many regarding his health, and there had been increasing speculation as to the effects his death would have on the national and world situation, the fact stunned the Government and the citizens of the capital.

It was not long, however, before the wheels of Government began once more to turn. Mr. Stettinius, the first of

Harry S. Truman being sworn in as president of the United States by Supreme Court Chief Justice Harlan F. Stone less than two hours after President Roosevelt's death.

the late President's Ministers to arrive at the White House, summoned the Cabinet to meet at once. Mr. Truman, his face gray and drawn, responded to the first summons given to any outside Mr. Roosevelt's family and official intimates by rushing from the Capitol.

Mrs. Roosevelt had immediately given voice to the spirit that animated the entire Government, once the first shock of the news had passed. She cabled to her four sons, all on active service:

"He did his job to the end as he would want you to do. Bless you all and all our love. Mother."

Those who have served with the late President in peace and in war accepted that as their obligation. The comment of members of Congress unanimously reflected this spirit. Those who supported or opposed Mr. Roosevelt during his long and controversial years as President did not deviate in this. And all hailed him as the greatest leader of his time.

FLAG AT CAPITOL LOWERED

As soon as the news became a certainty the White House flag was lowered to half-staff—the first time marking the death of an occupant since Warren G. Harding died at the Palace Hotel in San Francisco, Aug. 2, 1923, following a heart attack that succeeded pneumonia. The flag over the Capitol was lowered at 6:30 P.M. Between these two manifestations of the blow that had befallen the nation and the world, the news had spread throughout the city and respectful crowds gathered on the Lafayette Square pavement across from the executive mansion. They made no demonstration. But the men's hats were off, and the tears that were shed were not to be seen only on the cheeks of women. Some Presidents have been held in lukewarm esteem here, and some have been disliked by the local population, but Mr. Roosevelt held a high place in the rare affections of the capital.

The spoken tributes paid by members of Congress, a body with which the late President had many encounters, also testified to the extraordinary impression Mr. Roosevelt made on his times and the unparalleled position in the world he had attained. The comment of Senator Robert A. Taft of Ohio, a constant adversary on policy, was typical. "The greatest figure of our time," he called him, who had been removed "at the very climax of his career," who died "a

hero of the war, for he literally worked himself to death in the service of the American people." And Senator Arthur H. Vandenberg of Michigan, another Republican and frequent critic, said that the late President has "left an imperishable imprint on the history of America and of the world."

MORE THAN MERE WORDS

These were not mere words, uttered in conformity to the rule of "nil nisi bonum." Mr. Roosevelt's political opponents did what they could to retire him to private life, and their concern over his long tenure was real and grew as the tenure increased. But ever since his fourth-term victory in 1944 they have felt sincerely that it would be best for the country if he were spared to finish the great enterprises of war and peace which the country had commissioned him to carry through. And when they called his death a national and international tragedy they meant it.

But this tribute paid, this anxiety expressed, they and the late President's political supporters and official aides turned their hearts and minds again to the tasks before the nation. No one said "On to Berlin and Tokyo!" For Americans do not speak dramatically. But that is what everyone meant, and it was the gist of what President Truman said and did after the homely ceremony that made him the head of the State.

When the dignitaries were assembled with Mr. Truman for this solemn purpose, there was a slight delay until his wife and daughter should arrive. Then the Chief Justice, using a Bible borrowed from Mr. Roosevelt's office and speaking from memory, read the oath and the new President repeated it after him. Then he and Mrs. Truman called on Mrs. Roosevelt and, as the President said, went "home to bed."

He wore a gray suit, a white shirt and a polka-dot tie. His face was grave but his lips were firm and his voice was strong. He said through Mr. Early that his effort will be "to carry on as he believed the President would have done." And he arranged to meet with the Army and Navy chiefs tomorrow, to assure them as tonight he did the people that his purpose is to continue the conduct of the war with the utmost vigor and to the earliest possible and successful conclusion. ◆

BRITAIN MOURNS AS FOR HER OWN
People Feel They Have Lost A Personal Friend

By CLIFTON DANIEL
Special to The New York Times.

LONDON, April 13—Great Britain mourned for President Roosevelt today as deeply as if he had been one of her own great sons.

Shock, sorrow and fear were mingled in the faces of those who heard the news at midnight and afterward.

With Prime Minister Churchill, who was deeply affected, the people of Britain felt that they had lost a gallant personal friend. In the coming days this country will do honor to his memory in a way that will leave no doubt of her gratitude. It is the gratitude of a people who feel that the President was, in spirit and in fact, one of their saviors.

A great measure of the glory that Britain has felt in recent weeks in the triumph of Allied arms died with Mr. Roosevelt. No event since the military reverses of the summer of 1942 has left such a deep mark of depression on this country.

FAITH PUT IN TRIUMVIRATE

Ever since the catastrophe of Pearl Harbor, which caused scarcely more pain in London than the news of the President's death, the British masses have put their faith and trust in the Allied triumvirate in which he was a partner.

By contrast with the high hopes raised by Yalta, doubts have been assailing people and politicians of Britain in the past few weeks—doubts especially about the ability of the United Nations to insure future peace.

As always, the people were beginning to turn again toward the "Big Three" to guide them out of their bewilderment. The loss of Mr. Roosevelt can, for the moment at least, only increase their concern.

It had been hoped by many in this country that Mr. Roosevelt, in his projected address to the San Francisco World Conference would have breathed inspiration into an assembly the value of which is now questioned by many.   ❯

‹ Prime Minister Churchill had not retired when the news reached London just before last midnight. He had returned to No. 10 Downing Street only a short while earlier from a dinner party with British and Commonwealth delegates to the San Francisco conference.

There was no immediate statement from No. 10 Downing Street. It was explained that the Prime Minister, as was customary, would speak from the Commons and that, moreover, Mr. Roosevelt was his personal friend.

There was no doubt of the sadness which had fallen on the Prime Minister's residence.

HIS POPULARITY WAS WIDE

His popularity as a war leader and statesman was second only to that of Mr. Churchill. His speeches were read and heard here with profound interest. The British people had faith in him as a defender of the oppressed, the inspiration of American military prowess, and the architect of the future.

There was a genuine and widespread wish in this country to see the President here at the end of the war. There is no doubt that he would have received a public ovation the like of which no other man before him had ever received.

Although the British have had their tiffs with their American Allies throughout the war, they never doubted that the President personally was their friend.

They remembered tonight that it was he who sent British soldiers and Home Guards rifles with which to defend these islands in the grim hour when Britain stood unarmed against Germany in the summer of 1940.

They felt that to him, as much as to any man, they owed such measures as the Lend-Lease Act which kept Britain from going hungry and unprotected in the direst period of her struggle to regain her strength.

VICTORY SPIRIT DAMPENED

Not only was Britain's victory spirit dampened by the news of the President's death, but also its hopes for the future were affected. Great reliance had been placed in Mr. Roosevelt, and his skill as an international negotiator as demonstrated so often in his meetings with Mr. Churchill and Marshal Stalin to help bring the world through the agony of reconstruction.

Recalling the miracle whereby a peaceful nation was turned almost overnight into a great "arsenal for democracy," the British had been hoping that the same genius would help bring order and assurance of future peace out of the chaos of a war-rent world.

The British people do not know President Truman. They not only knew Mr. Roosevelt but felt that through Mr. Churchill, who called Mr. Roosevelt by his first name, they shared a personal friendship. ◆

APRIL 13, 1945

Men at the Front Are Shocked by News

By RICHARD J. H. JOHNSTON
By Wireless to The New York Times.

WITH THE SEVENTH ARMY, April 13—Profound shock and deep concern for the strength of the United States position at the peace table were expressed by our troops along this front in the early hours this morning when the news of President Roosevelt's death was brought to them. It was with disbelief that many received the shocking report which was picked up on the radios and relayed by word of mouth from unit to unit up and down this front.

"This is a great tragedy and it will put a new slant on the peace conference," said Sgt. George Markel of Santa Ana, Calif.

Expressing disbelief, Corp. Israel Goldberg of St. Louis declared:

"I can't believe it. Were people at home prepared for this or told about it?"

"We are so close to victory it is a terrible time for this to happen," said Corp. Robert E. Viedt of South Dakota.

Pfc. John Lynch, Brooklyn, declared:

American Soldiers in London read about the death of President Roosevelt.

"I couldn't believe such a thing could happen.

"President Roosevelt was so important to us I can hardly believe he is gone."

By Wireless to The New York Times

GUAM, April 13—The deepest gloom settled over this advance headquarters of the Pacific Fleet as the word spread among Navy men that President Roosevelt had died suddenly at Warm Springs.

The men of the fleet knew that they had lost not only their Commander in Chief but a good friend—because the Navy always was close to Franklin Roosevelt's heart from his earliest years.

Officers who heard the news from correspondents who had received the Army news flash by radio could scarcely believe it.

"My God!" was the immediate and almost universal reaction, and most of them could say no more.

The President had been expected to come to the Pacific war theatre next summer on one of his periodic war inspection visits. ◆

APRIL 14, 1945

ORDERS 'NO CHANGE' IN FOREIGN POLICY

President Promises There Will 'Be No Break Of Continuity'

By JAMES B. RESTON
Special to The New York Times.

WASHINGTON, April 13—President Truman authorized Secretary of State Stettinius to say today that there would "be no change of purpose or break of continuity in the foreign policy of the United States Government."

In a statement issued at the State Department less than twenty-four hours after the death of Mr. Roosevelt, and only a few hours after reports from Europe had indicated some anxiety over the future course of American foreign policy, Secretary Stettinius declared:

"We shall press forward with the other United Nations toward a victory whose terms will deprive Germany and Japan of the means with which to commit aggression ever again, and toward the establishment of a world organization endowed with strength to keep the peace for generations and to give security and wider opportunity to all men."

COMMANDS UNUSUAL SUPPORT

It was admitted by those Senators who have followed foreign affairs closely that the death of Mr. Roosevelt would undoubtedly raise some questions in the minds of Prime Minister Churchill and Marshal Stalin as to what policy President Truman would follow, but the general opinion expressed was first, that the new President would carry through the international policies of President Roosevelt, not only because of a sense of obligation, but because of a sense of conviction that they were right, and second, that he would be able to command unusual support on Capitol Hill for this policy.

The President will not go to the San Francisco conference. He indicated to his associates today that he would probably address the conference by radio. Consequently, it is assumed that he will give considerable leeway to the members of the delegation in drafting our national policy.

If there were any doubts about Mr. Truman's desire to see the United States not only participate but assume a leading part in a world security organization, these doubts would undoubtedly be found among those Senators who have led the fight for such a policy and who have discussed it at great length with him.

REACTION OF SENATORS

The reaction of these Senators, however, was not only that he would maintain the continuity of the Roosevelt foreign policy but that he would "in some respects go further" than the late President.

It was recalled, for example, that Mr. Truman participated with Senators, Ball, Burton, Hatch and Hill in the campaign centering around the resolution to force the Administration to take the lead in establishing an international security organization.

That campaign, in fact, was planned at a luncheon called by Mr. Truman, who discussed it on a number of occasions with Senator Hatch and supported the campaign whenever he could.

At the same time, however, Mr. Truman did not at any time go far enough with this group to become vulnerable to criticism from other groups who did not favor such an advanced position.

The quality which contributed so much to his nomination as Vice President, his ability to keep out of serious trouble with almost every group on Capitol Hill, is thus thought to be of great value to him in gaining the support necessary for ratification of whatever treaty is approved by the American delegation and proposed by the San Francisco conference.

That the President recognizes this support on Capitol Hill as one of the main sources of his strength and that he intends to do everything he can to narrow the gulf between the legislative and executive branches of the Government, was indicated today by his decision to go to Capitol Hill to have luncheon with some of his former colleagues there.

Throughout his stay there he kept saying to his friends:

"We must stay together; we must see this thing through together." This frank and friendly attempt to carry the White House to Capitol Hill was the first clear theme of the new Administration and those Senators, who have been seeking most avidly for American leadership in world affairs, consider it a good and important augury for the success of the policy they favor. ◈

APRIL 14, 1945

ROOSEVELT DEATH ENCOURAGES NAZIS

By Wireless to The New York Times.

PARIS, April 13—The German strategy of withdrawing what forces are left into two national redoubts in the north and south of the Reich, which has been evident for some weeks, has undoubtedly been encouraged by the death of President Roosevelt, one of Nazi Germany's most implacable enemies, according to a senior officer at Supreme Headquarters.

German strategists have gambled on the chances of a disagreement between the three leading Allied powers and this source believed that Hitler's political and military strategists would view the President's death as weakening the ties between the United States and Britain on the one hand and the Soviet Union on the other.

In the past the enemy has paid Mr. Roosevelt the compliment of naming him as the man who roused the Western World to action against fascism. Berlin has regarded his powerful personality as the chief element in welding Russian and western strategy for the final phase of the conflict in the west.

The Germans undoubtedly will redouble their efforts to construct a strong defensive position across north Germany, probably from Luebeck on the east to Emden on the west, with Kiel, the former headquarters of the German fleet, as "capital" of this northern redoubt.

HEAVIEST DEFENSE IN NORTH

The heaviest opposition met by Allied forces north of the Harz Mountains has been on the front of the British Second Army, where yesterday elements of the Seventh Infantry and the Twenty-first Parachute Divisions, the former one of the finest remaining in the German Army, were pivoting northward on Bremen.

The western end of the German line evidently is intended to extend from Bremen west to the mouth of the Ems, while the eastern sector will run from Bremen eastward, crossing the Elbe south of Hamburg, and then extending northeastward to reach the Baltic east of Luebeck.

Today pilots of the British Second Tactical Air Force sighted large convoys of German troops, guns and trucks streaming into the area east of the ❯

◄ Elbe and southeast of Hamburg. Other convoys were moving into the area of Cuxhaven on the North Sea and Wilhelmshaven, another German naval base.

The northern redoubt has one purpose and one advantage. The purpose is to deny the use of the great ports of the northern Reich to the Allies in a bitter defensive action that will postpone the moment when the Allies' full might can be directed against the redoubt in southeastern Germany. The advantage is that it is one of two areas in the Reich that can be reinforced from the outside. Troops can move in from Denmark or the ports of Norway. That will be difficult in view of the Allies' sea and air supremacy, but granted the fanatic valor of the SS troops, it is not impossible.

Meanwhile, the Germans will move troops and supplies southeastward into the larger redoubt in the mountains east of Lake Constance, in which Nazi leaders hope to hold out for months waiting for a split between the western Allies and the Soviet Union, which they believe to be inevitable.

This redoubt, too, can be reinforced from the outside. There already are some indications from Italy that some of the best troops of the German armies there are moving northward toward the Alps and the southern perimeter of the redoubt.

The forces from Italy, which the Germans regard as unbeaten, will probably form a considerable percentage of the defenders of the southern redoubt. They have a high propaganda value

for whoever directs the German radio broadcasts from the redoubt to the people of Germany because the propagandists undoubtedly will refer to the forces there as still unbeaten.

The Germans have gone to a great length to protect the routes into the southern redoubt. Resistance on the front of Lieut. Gen. Alexander M. Patch's United States Seventh Army in western Bavaria has been extremely fierce. The Germans have committed to battle in that area reinforcements that could have been more usefully employed on the central front were it not for the necessity of defending the highways and railroads running from western Czechoslovakia into the redoubt.

It is from the forges of the great Skoda

SOVIET FLAGS SHOW MOURNING BORDER
Tributes Never Before Paid To Foreigner Honor Roosevelt As Friend of Peace

By C. L. SULZBERGER
By Wireless to The New York Times.

MOSCOW, April 14—The official black-fringed red banner of national mourning was raised over the Kremlin early today as the Russian people and their Government grieved for their friend Franklin D. Roosevelt and did him honors such as no foreigner has ever received in the history of the Soviet Union.

The President's death is, one might hazard, almost as keenly felt here as in America. Among Government leaders who had the privilege of meeting him and among the great mass of the people who knew him only as a true friend of Russia and of peace, an enemy of fascism and of war, and a venturesome, smiling liberal whose face had won him sympathy and liking in many newsreels, his loss is regarded as a personal blow on the eve of this war's end.

One can detect this feeling in all quarters. Premier Stalin received United States Ambassador W. Averell Harriman last night to express his condolences. So many Russians, both officials and little people, have been telephoning the American Embassy to voice their sympathy that extra operators have been taken on. Huge crowds form queues at movie the-

atres for a glimpse of the late President in newsreels of the Yalta Conference, which have already been on view for many days.

The black-bordered red flag which the Union of Socialist Soviet Republics employs to honor and mourn its own great dead was flapping this chill spring day not only over Marshal Stalin's residence but on all Government and many private buildings. People traveling about their affairs in the subway are still talking about what President Roosevelt meant.

MANY RUSSIANS WEEP AT LOSS
It may seem strange to Americans that many, many people here who never even saw Mr. Roosevelt with their own eyes have wept and are weeping over what they feel is a personal tragedy. This bereavement has apparently brought the Soviet and the American people psychologically closer at this moment than at any time in the personal knowledge of this correspondent.

Coupled with this moving, emotional phenomenon is a keen intellectual interest in American politics and in everything concerning President Truman, past, present and future. This earnest curiosity is exhibited from the very top to the very bottom of the social structure.

In all possible ways, however, the Government is encouraging the population to honor the memory of their friend who first brought diplomatic recognition of the U.S.S.R., and then stood by it during its blackest moments. In Leningrad, a public library memorial exhibition dedicated to Mr. Roosevelt has been opened. At an All-Slav reception for Marshal Tito, a minute of silence was observed for the dead leader.

TITO CABLES HIS SYMPATHY
Marshal Tito cabled to President Truman

that he considered that this was "a tremendous loss for all the United Nations."

Alexander Troyanovsky, first Soviet Ambassador to Washington, wrote a tribute to Mr. Roosevelt in Red Star, the Army newspaper. He said that Mr. Roosevelt's prewar political life "was a preparation for the outstanding role which he played during the Second World War as a leader in the cause of guaranteeing security to the world" and that he often swam against the current and was proved right. Calling him an outstanding statesman, the former Ambassador said that the present grand alliance would have been impossible without the establishment of diplomatic relations between the two countries twelve years ago.

Mr. Troyanovsky said that Mr. Roosevelt had bequeathed to President Truman "a rich heritage in the form of a militant commonwealth of freedom-loving peoples, huge armed forces, successful military operations on all fronts to the glory of the United Nations now killing the Fascists."

The Soviet-recognized Polish Provisional Government declared yesterday, in a broadcast over the Moscow radio, as reported by the Federal Communications Commission to the Office of War Information:

"Roosevelt is dead.

"This tragic news has profoundly shaken all Poland. It seems as if we could hear the rustling of pages of history. One of the greatest men of America has entered the Pantheon.

"A gigantic personality who, in the history of America, will take his place next to Washington, Franklin and Lincoln. We have lived in Roosevelt's times and so have lived in great times." ◊

Works and other industrial plants in the Prague area that the enemy is creating stocks of arms and ammunition in the redoubt.

According to Swiss reports, some small factories already have been moved in the redoubt into which stocks of food have been pouring since late last summer.

These, briefly, are the outlines of the German strategy, a plan that relies on a split between the Allies to allow the Nazi gang to escape with their lives and perhaps even with some semblance of power. The enemy, although he has convinced no one else, has convinced himself that such a split was inevitable and that it would be hastened by the death of Mr. Roosevelt.

Until it appears, they intend to hold on, first in the north and finally in the south. ◇

Ernie Pyle, chronicler of the American soldier, filing a story from the Anzio Beachhead, Italy, March 18, 1944.

APRIL 19, 1945

Ernie Pyle Is Killed on Ie Island; Foe Fired When All Seemed Safe

By Wireless to The New York Times.

GUAM, April 18—Ernie Pyle died today on Ie Island, just west of Okinawa, like so many of the doughboys he had written about. The nationally known war correspondent was killed instantly by Japanese machine-gun fire.

The slight, graying newspaper man, chronicler of the average American soldier's daily round, in and out of foxholes in many war theatres, had gone forward early this morning to observe the advance of a well-known division of the Twenty-fourth Army Corps.

He joined headquarters troops in the outskirts of the island's chief town, Tegusugu. Our men had seemingly ironed out minor opposition at this point, and Mr. Pyle went over to talk to a regimental commanding officer. Suddenly enemy machine gunners opened fire at about 10:15 A.M. (9:15 P.M., Tuesday, Eastern war time). The war correspondent fell in the first burst.

The commanding general of the troops on the island reported the death to headquarters as follows:

"I regret to report that War Correspondent Ernie Pyle, who made such a great contribution to the morale of our foot soldier, was killed in the battle of Ie Shima today."

AT A COMMAND POST, Ie Island, Ryukyus, April 18 (AP)—Ernie Pyle, the famed columnist who had reported the wars from Africa to Okinawa, met his death about a mile forward of this command post. Mr. Pyle had just talked with a general commanding Army troops and Lieut. Col. James E. Landrum, executive officer of an infantry regiment, before "jeeping" to a forward command post with Lieut. Col. Joseph B. Coolidge of Helena, Ark., commanding officer of the regiment, to watch front-line action.

Colonel Coolidge was alongside Mr. Pyle when he was killed. "We were moving down the road in our jeep," related Colonel Coolidge. "Ernie was going with me to my new command post. At 10 o'clock we were fired on by a Jap machine gun on a ridge above us. We all jumped out of the jeep and dived into a roadside ditch.

MAY BE BURIED WHERE HE FELL

"A little later Pyle and I raised up to look around. Another burst hit the road over our heads and I fell back into the ditch. I looked at Ernie and saw he had been hit.

"He was killed almost instantly, the bullet entering his left temple just under his helmet.

"I crawled back to report the tragedy, leaving a man to watch the body. Ernie's body will be brought back to Army grave registration officers. He will be buried here on Ie Jima unless we are notified otherwise."

"I was so impressed with Pyle's coolness, calmness and his deep interest in enlisted men. They have lost their best friend."

Colonel Coolidge was visibly shaken as he told the facts of the columnist's death. Almost tearfully, he described the tragedy. He said he knew the news would spread swiftly over the island.

FEARED BEING DISLIKED

Ernie Pyle was haunted all his life by an obsession. He said over and over again, "I suffer agony in anticipation of meeting people for fear they won't like me."

No man could have been less justified in such a fear. Word of Pyle's death started tears in the eyes of millions, from the White House to the poorest dwellings in the country.

President Truman and Mrs. Eleanor Roosevelt followed his writings as avidly as any farmer's wife or city tenement mother with sons in service.

Mrs. Roosevelt once wrote in her column "I have read everything he has sent from overseas," and recommended his writings to all Americans.

For three years these writings had entered some 14,000,000 homes almost as personal letters from the front. Soldiers' kin prayed for Ernie Pyle as they prayed for their own sons.

In the Eighth Avenue subway yesterday a gray-haired woman looked up, wet-eyed, from the headline "Ernie Pyle Killed in Action" and murmured ▶

"May God rest his soul" and other women, and men, around her took up the words. This was typical.

It was rather curious that a nation should have worked up such affection for a timid little man whose greatest fear was "Maybe they won't like me."

He wrote simple, gripping pieces about five days spent with the lepers at Molokai, and put his feeling on paper: "I felt unrighteous at being whole and clean," he told his readers when he came away.

He wrote of Devil's Island, of all South America, which he toured by plane. He covered some 150,000 miles of Western Hemisphere wearing out three cars, three typewriters; crossed the United States thirty-five times.

MAGNET PULLS HIM TO LONDON

In the fall of 1940 he started for unhappy London. "A small voice came in the night and said go" was the way he put it, and his writings on London under Nazi bombings tore at his readers' hearts.

He lived with Yank troops in Ireland and his descriptions of their day-by-day living brought wider reception. When he went into action with the Yanks in Africa, the Pyle legend burst into flower.

His columns, done in foxholes, brought home all the hurt, horror, loneliness and homesickness that every soldier felt. They were the perfect supplement to the soldiers' own letters.

Though he wrote of his own feelings and his own emotions as he watched men wounded, and saw the wounded die, he was merely interpreting the scene for the soldier.

He got people at home to understand that life at the front "works itself into an emotional tapestry of one dull dead pattern—yesterday is tomorrow and Troiano is Randozzo and, O God, I'm so tired."

He never made war look glamorous. He hated it and feared it. Blown out of press headquarters at Anzio, almost killed by our own planes at St. Lô, he told of the death, the heartache and the agony about him and always he named names of the kids around him, and got in their home town addresses.

By September, 1944, he was a thin, sad-eyed little man gone gray at the temples, his face seamed, his reddish hair thinned. "I don't think I could go on and keep sane," he confided to his millions of readers.

He started home, with abject apologies. The doughfoots had come to love him. Hundreds of thousands of combat troops, from star-sprinkled generals to lowly infantrymen, knew him by sight, called "H'ya, Ernie?" when he passed.

He wrote, "I am leaving for just one reason . . . because I have just got to stop. I have had all I can take for a while." Yet the doughfoots understood. They wrote him sincere farewells and wished him luck.

PACIFIC FOXHOLES CALLED

His books "Here Is Your War" and "Brave Men," made up from his columns, hit the high spots on best-seller lists, made Hollywood. He was acclaimed wherever he dared show himself in public.

He loafed a while in his humble white clapboard cottage in Albuquerque, N.M.

He would sit there with "That Girl" and stare for hours across the lonely mesa, but the front still haunted him. He had to go back.

He journeyed to Hollywood to watch Burgess Meredith impersonate him in the film version of his books and last January he left for San Francisco, bound for the wars again—the Pacific this time.

He had frequent premonitions of death. He said: "You begin to feel that you can't go on forever without being hit. I feel that I've used up all my chances, and I hate it. I don't want to be killed."

Fortune had come to Ernie Pyle—something well over a half-million dollars the past two years—and his name was a household word. He might have rested with that.

"But I can't," he wrote. "I'm going simply because there's a war on and I'm part of it, and I've known all the time I was going back. I'm going simply because I've got to—and I hate it."

So he went, and in the endless hours over the Pacific, in great service planes, he wrote with a soft touch of glorious Pacific dawns and sunsets at sea, of green islands and tremendous expanses of blue water.

SHARED GI'S POST-WAR HOPES

He journeyed to Iwo on a small carrier and wrote about the carrier crew. Then he moved on to Okinawa and went in with the marines, and there were homely pieces about that.

He had post-war plans. He thought he would take to the white clean roads

---

APRIL 19, 1945

BOTH ARMIES GAIN IN BOLOGNA DRIVE
British Capture Argenta and Battle Toward Ferrara as Poles Push Westward

By MILTON BRACKER
By Wireless to The New York Times.

FIFTEENTH ARMY HEADQUARTERS, Italy, April 18—British troops of the Eighth Army, slashing toward the main escape routes from Bologna on the northeast, have captured Argenta and are battling through the flood-flanked gap toward Ferrara, barely fifteen miles away, and the Po River, some three miles farther along Highway 16.

The latest reports emphasized that

again with "That Girl" and write beside still ponds in the wilderness, on blue mountains, in country lanes, in a world returned to peace and quiet. And these were the dreams of the doughfoot in the foxhole as much as they were his own.

But he knew that death would reach for him. In his last letter to George A. Carlin, head of the United Feature Syndicate which employed him, he wrote:

"I was completely amazed to find that I'm as well known out here as I was in the European Theatre. The men are depending on me, so I'll have to try and stick it out for a long time.

"I expect to be out a year on this trip, if I don't bog down inside again, and if I don't get sick or hurt. If I could be fortunate enough to hang on until the spring of 1946, I think I'll come home for the last time. I don't believe I have the strength ever to leave home and go back to war again."

But yesterday Ernie Pyle came to the end of the road on tiny Ie, some 10,000 miles from his own white cottage and from "That Girl."

In one of his first columns from Africa he had told how he'd sought shelter in a ditch with a frightened Yank when a Stuka dived and strafed, and how he tapped the soldier's shoulder when the Stuka had gone and said, "Whew, that was close, eh?" and the soldier did not answer. He was dead.

So yesterday on Ie a doughfoot, white and tense, looked up from a thin-faced, gray-haired figure prone beside him. Ernie Pyle had written his last letter home.

◆

CONGRESS, PRESS TO VIEW HORRORS
Eisenhower Asks Delegations of Both To See German Concentration Camps

By WILLIAM S. WHITE
Special to The New York Times.

WASHINGTON, April 21—A Congressional delegation of twelve and a group of seventeen editors and publishers were formed tonight, at Gen. Dwight D. Eisenhower's request, to go overseas by air to inspect German concentration camps for political prisoners, conditions that the general had termed almost indescribably horrible.

The findings of these groups will be available to the world and to the United Nations Conference on International Organization in San Francisco. The gravity of approach to this extraordinary mission— which could have a profound effect on the kind of peace eventually granted to the Germans—was illustrated in the fact that Senator Alben Barkley of Kentucky, the majority leader, accepted a place on the Congressional delegation, although he will of necessity leave important pending legislation behind him.

DELEGATION IS BIPARTISAN
The Congressional delegation is bipartisan and includes members of the Military,

Naval and Foreign Affairs Committees of both houses. Its membership follows:

Senators Barkley, Democrat, of Kentucky; Kenneth S. Wherry, Republican, of Nebraska; Walter F. George, Democrat, of Georgia; C. Wayland Brooks, Republican, of Illinois: Elbert D. Thomas, Democrat, of Utah, and Leverett P. Saltonstall, Republican, of Massachusetts; and Representatives R, Ewing Thomason, Democrat, of Texas; James P. Richards, Democrat, of South Carolina; Edward V. Izak, Democrat, of California; James W. Mott, Republican, of Oregon; Dewey Short, Republican, of Missouri, and John M. Vorys, Republican, of Ohio.

Messrs. Brooks, Vorys and Short have been among the most active men in Congress against internationalism.

JOURNALISTS LISTED
The delegation of editors and publishers includes:

Brig. Gen. Julius Ochs Adler, vice president and general manager, The New York Times.

⟩

Allies Close in on Bologna from two sides: British troops of the Eighth Army (1) took Argenta and battled along Highway 16, while Polish units (2) drove beyond Castel San Pietro to points within nine miles of Bologna. In the central sector (3) Americans of the Fifth Army reached the outskirts of Pianoro, while other forces of the same army took Mount Tramanto and San Propsero. On the Lingurian coast (4) the Americans advanced a mile northwest of Ortonovo and were ten miles from La Spezia.

the mountains south and southwest of Bologna were slowing the Fifth Army's main push. But the Poles on Highway 9 crashed two miles beyond Castel San Pietro to a point within nine miles of Bologna and the Americans cutting their way through the gorges of Highway 65 from the south eked out gains that brought them to the outskirts of Pianoro.

This is two miles beyond what is left of Livergnano. Even in this toughest of all sectors on the Italian front, the Allies'

forces are on the move under continuing air support by heavy bombers on tactical missions.

STAND ON IDICE SEEN
All signs pointed to a crucial German stand along the general line of the Idice River, which cuts Highway 9 four miles outside Bologna and curves up toward Argenta to form what has been dubbed the enemy's Genghis Khan line. The Germans are believed to have staked the final defense of Bologna and the most vulnerable approaches to the Po on the holding of this line. New Zealand, Indian, Polish and Italian troops made notable gains toward it during the day, crossing the Gaiana Canal and extending the penetration since the Senio River crossings to almost twenty miles.

But there was still no sign of a breakthrough. Although the Eighth Army

took 1,000 more prisoners, the Germans continued to fight back with all the fury of which they have long been capaable.

AMERICANS 8 MILES FROM CITY
The Fifth Army's central drive down the "main line" to Bologna lowered the distance to that great objective to the shortest that it has ever been. Pianoro is between seven and eight miles from that city and the Americans have now fought through the mountain rimming the highway to a point within 1,000 yards of Pianoro. Tanks were able to grind onto Highway 65 at Zula, between Livergnano and Pianoro. Zula was entered after a terrible day during which one American unit on the most forward peak was inadvertently shelled by our own artillery. ◆

◀ Malcolmn Bingay, editor, Detroit Free Press.

Norman Chandler, general manager, Los Angeles Times.

William L. Chenery, publisher, Collier's Magazine.

E. Z. Dimitman, executive editor, Chicago Sun.

Ben Hibbs, editor, Saturday Evening Post.

Stanley High, associate editor, Reader's Digest.

Ben McKelway, editor, Washington Star.

Glenn Neville, executive editor, New York Daily Mirror.

William I. Nichols, editor, This Week.

L. K. Nicholson, president and editor, New Orleans Times-Picayune,

Joseph Pulitzer, editor and publisher, St. Louis Post-Dispatch.

Gideon Seymour, executive editor, Minneapolis Star-Journal.

Duke Shoop, Washington correspondent, Kansas City Star.

Beverly Smith, associate editor, American Magazine.

Walker Stone, editor, Scripps-Howard Newspaper Alliance.

M. E. Walter, managing editor, Houston Chronicle.

CONGRESSMEN SEE BUCHENWALD

WEIMAR, Germany, April 21 (AP)— Republican Representative Clare Boothe Luce of Connecticut, John Kunkel of Pennsylvania and Leonard Hall of New York visited the Buchenwald concentration camp today.

Mrs. Luce spared herself none of the grisly spectacles. She said that she hoped that the people of the United States would see motion-picture records that have been made there. She visited the basement crematorium where, in a white-walled room, thousands had been hanged from iron hooks.

Her prisoner guide told her how the executioner had used clubs shaped like potato mashers to kill victims who did not die quickly enough in the noose. She saw the elevator that carried the bodies upstairs to the furnaces. Outside the crematorium she saw a wagon stacked high with shriveled bodies. She did not remain long, saying: "It's just too horrible."

In the barracks she saw prisoners too weak to move from the tiered shelves on which they lay. Six had been forced to lie on the shelves in a space big enough only for three. She talked to many patients in the hospital—once a brothel—getting

first-hand information about Buchenwald's brutalities.

Among the emaciated prisoners was a 6½-year-old boy who had been imprisoned two and one-half years. "He was picked up in Paris because he was out after the curfew," Mrs. Luce said. "No one wants to believe these things, but it is important that people know they're true."

She asked several of the former prisoners what should be done with Germans responsible for the atrocities, and they replied: "The same as they did to us."

"That's no answer," Mrs. Luce said, but she did not amplify.

Mr. Kunkel declared: "No one could visualize these horrors without seeing them. It is hard to believe that such brutality existed anywhere in the world, but it certainly did here. It is incredible that some of the people were able to survive such an awful ordeal. This is a sight I hope never to see again."

After a half-hour tour, Mr. Hall said: "You have to see Buchenwald to realize fully what debased beasts the Germans are. There is nothing here except brutality; corpses by the wagon loads. It certainly points up the question as to what should be done with Germany after the war." ◆

APRIL 23, 1945

7 MILES INSIDE CITY Defenses Overrun On 3 Sides— Resistance Is Mounting in Fury

By C. L. SULZBERGER
By Wireless to The New York Times.

MOSCOW, April 23—Despite bitter German resistance on both the Berlin and Dresden sectors, Soviet troops shoved forward again yesterday, capturing sixteen suburbs of Hitler's dying capital of Greater Berlin and driving a salient across the main highway linking it with the Saxon citadel of Dresden, thus effectively narrowing the escape gap leading to the south. In addition to the suburbs, the Soviet High Command announced the capture of five towns on the approaches to Berlin.

[The Red Army has already seized one-sixth of Berlin in penetrations that total seven miles. A Stockholm report received from Berlin said that Soviet tanks had already thrust to within a mile of the center of the city at the intersection of Unter den Linden and Friedrichstrasse, according to The Associated Press.]

Official Soviet gains were reported early this morning in a restrained communiqué, which indicated that Marshal Gregory K. Zhukoff was driving hard on Berlin from the northeast, east and southeast. He solidified his positions by capturing the isolated towns of Biesenthal and Fuerstenwalde and then drove deeper into the thick cluster of suburbs ringing the city itself.

KONEFF STRIKES TOWARD DRESDEN

Marshal Ivan D. Koneff would appear to be by-passing Dresden farther to the south after having severed its principal link with the capital. His troops this morning were pushing hard for the Elbe River and Dessau, where the Americans are now battling German units striving to hold the flank of the last escape avenue for the besieged Berlin armies.

There has been no let-up in this shattering battle. Thirteen thousand prisoners have been taken in the Berlin sector alone, plus 500 artillery pieces. That Marshal Zhukoff has been able to seize more airfields is confirmed by the announcement that he captured sixty planes.

Marshal Koneff also overran some Luftwaffe bases and took 10,000 prisoners. The two army groups between them have taken 250 tanks and destroyed 156 others.

Edging like an inevitable juggernaut toward the city's heart, concentric rings of rocket-firing Katusha trucks and line upon line of artillery—76 mm., 85's, 122's, 152's, 203's—hurled thousands of rounds into the crumbling citadel and were pulverizing it into that Goetterdaemmerung that haunts every German mind.

SOVIET FLIERS SIGHT AMERICANS

Overhead, wheeling and banking and virtually ignoring the last fanatic waves of fighters mustered by Reich Marshal Goering's atrophied Luftwaffe, hundreds and hundreds of Soviet bombers, fighters and Stormovik attack planes bombed, strafed and rocketed to death the heart of "Festung Germania."

As the political and military for-

German soldier surrendering during the Allied drive toward Berlin, 1945.

tress of Nazidom disintegrated beneath this assault other Russian forces poured through the woods north of Dresden and east of Leipzig toward the advancing allies of Gen. Dwight D. Eisenhower's command.

Soviet pilots in the south reported sighting the Americans at several spots, and some estimate the distance separating the advancing armies at no more than fifteen miles.

As this dramatic meeting impends, signalizing the ultimate strategical conclusion of the plans conceived in Moscow, London and Washington, Berlin's doom was virtually sealed.

At this writing the furious battle is still raging, but fierce German resistance by regular units was being firmly compressed into an ever-smaller area. Resistance was being met from storm troopers, the Volkssturm and hastily mobilized groups of retired reservists and civilians. They were using vast tank and tank-destroyer concentrations and withdrawing into the burning recesses of the city. The Russians also faced masses of artillery, including flak batteries hastily redisposed against the advancing Soviet armor.

Pushing strenuously forward from suburbs to the east, northeast and southeast, which they had already gained Saturday night, Russian forces pierced at several points the ring of boulevards surrounding Berlin.

Soviet tanks picked up on their radios the frantic German messages—"They are blasting us hellishly"—and the eleventh-hour orders to "halt them at any price." But the Russians kept on going. Working in individual combat teams, tanks, infantry and Cossack horsemen

poured into Berlin while Russian shells strode up Kaiser Wilhelmstrasse with deadly, explosive steps.

RUSSIANS LAST IN BERLIN IN 1760
To the southeast the Russians had established themselves on the Spree River near the Lichtenberg railway station. Thousands, and more thousands, of troops kept pouring across the Spree, washing their grimy faces in its waters and shouting, "The war is coming to its end!" Others were driving westward toward Berlin, the Elbe and their Allies.

To the south they drove toward Tempelhof airdrome, to which at the zenith of his career the Fuehrer had summoned Europe's statesmen to listen to his orders. Now the huge airfield is a pock-marked waste, plastered by shells, bombs and Stormovik rockets.

Russian troops had not been inside Berlin since Oct. 9, 1760, when General Totleben accepted the capital's surrender for his Empress Elizabeth and took its city keys, which to this day repose in the Kremlin.

At that time another German conquerer, Frederick the Great, wrote in his diary words that might well serve for Hitler: "I have no more authority over the Army. In these days of despair, they will do well in Berlin to think of their safety. It is a cruel misfortune . . . I have no resources left, and to tell the truth, I count everything lost."

Then, as now, the Russian attack spearheads included Cossacks from the Don and the wide Kuban then, as now, Russian guns—although Totleben had only nineteen—sealed the city's doom. Totleben demolished Berlin's gun foundry, powder mills and the Potsdam and Spandau munitions factories. Berlin today is being ground to death in like manner. ◆

APRIL 26, 1945

WEREWOLF THREAT ONLY PROPAGANDA

By GLADWIN HILL
By Wireless to The New York Times.

PARIS, April 25—The German Werewolf underground menace has turned out so far over considerable areas of conquered territory to be only propaganda, it was learned from high Allied officers today, but possible trouble from un-uniformed Germans in the near future is not being discounted and is being prepared for.

The effectiveness of the handling of the initial instances of resistance will probably be to a considerable degree the key to the success of the Allies' whole administration of conquered Germany and its neutralization as a chronic disrupter of International peace. There have been plenty of small individual cases of resistance by Germans behind the front lines. American soldiers have been shot in the dark. Army wires have been cut. Tires have been stabbed. Explosive charges have been set.

There have also been active battling and sniping as much as thirty miles behind our advance. But few if any of these instances have been traced to anything but individual impulses. The notable instances of battling and sniping generally turned out to have been the work of isolated German regular forces.

One whole Army group whose territory covers thousands of square miles has not had a single confirmed instance of Werewolf activity. The Germans' Werewolf campaign, many responsible officers believe, was essentially another eleventh-hour propaganda shot in the dark—although, by the very nature of the situation, almost inevitably bound to bear fruit eventually.

Thus far the German civilians generally have been docile and obedient. But it is not an informed docility growing out of respect for and understanding of the Allies' conquest. It is the docility of benumbed, browbeaten people habituated to following orders with little consideration for their origin, lest they be dealt with summarily and fatally by the Gestapo. The time is bound to come, it is realized, when the Germans will become aware that the Gestapo is no longer on their backs and they are dealing with a different authority. They will naturally try to see what they can get away with. ◆

GOERING 'RESIGNS' AS NAZIDOM CRACKS

By SYDNEY GRUSON
By Wireless to The New York Times.

LONDON, April 26—Reich Marshal Hermann Goering, founder and commander of the Luftwaffe and second only to Martin Bormann in the plan of leadership under Adolf Hitler, has been relieved of his command, the first of the Nazi hierarchy to fall under the pressure of Germany's defeat.

With his air force virtually wiped out, the rotund marshal who once boasted that enemy planes never would fly over Germany has been succeeded by Col. Gen. Robert Ritter von Greim, a 53-year-old senior officer of the Luftwaffe since the beginning of the war. Von Greim was promoted to field marshal on taking over.

Announcing the news of Goering's "retirement" tonight, the Hamburg radio said he had asked Hitler to be relieved and that the Fuehrer had granted the request because Goering was suffering from a heart disease that had become acute. Goering, who is 52, had been noticeably out of the German news for the last several months. None of the German broadcasts declaring that Hitler and Propaganda Minister Joseph Goebbels remained in besieged Berlin had mentioned his whereabouts and he was believed to have fallen into disfavor because of the Luftwaffe's annihilation.

A German ace in World War I, Goering was one of the original old guard of Nazism that took part with Hitler in the abortive Munich putsch. When the Nazis came to power, Hitler gave him the job of reviving the German air force. He founded thousands of glider clubs as the first step in building the Luftwaffe, with which he eventually razed Warsaw and ravaged Rotterdam and tried to blast Britain into submission for the Wehrmacht.

At the height of the German blitz in 1940 the Germans said that Goering personally led one bombing attack on London. His decision to switch suddenly from destroying Royal Air Force airfields to burn down London is credited with a large part in the saving of Britain. London survived and the RAF, using the fields Goering let alone, inflicted such heavy losses that he called off daylight bombing.

Goering's prestige had been declining since the Luftwaffe failed to halt the Allied bombing of Germany. For all purposes it was wiped out two weeks ago when, during a ten-day period, the United States Eighth Air Force destroyed more than 1,700 planes on the ground. It has hardly been evident in the German sky since.

A familiar subject of cartoonists because of his girth and his love for medals and fancy uniforms, Goering nevertheless was one of Nazism's best ambassadors among foreigners before the war. ◊

First Link Made Wednesday By Four Americans On Patrol

By HAROLD DENNY
By Wireless to The New York Times.

AT A RED ARMY OUTPOST, on the Elbe, April 27—The United States and Russian armies have met on the Elbe. The Western and Eastern fronts are at last linked up and Germany is cut in two. First contact was made two days ago—at 4:40 P.M., April 25, by a four-man patrol of the 273d Infantry Regiment of the Sixty-ninth Infantry Division and a Russian outpost at the sizable town of Torgau, twenty miles west of our then most advanced forces.

On the American side the honor of making this historic junction goes to Gen. Courtney H. Hodges' United States First Army, which forced the Normandy beaches last June and has advanced 700 miles through France, Belgium and Germany to this spot. On the Russian side it goes to Marshal Ivan S. Koneff's First Ukrainian Army, which has fought its way 1,400 miles from Stalingrad in one of the greatest marches against bitter opposition in all history.

MEETING SCENE OF JOY

The spirit in which the American and Russian troops and their local commanders met was worthy of great occasion.

The Russians received us with open-handed hospitality and our men have responded in kind. From the moment the first American patrol was taken into a Russian forward command post, it has been almost a continuous party.

There was handshaking and backslapping among the troops who made the first contacts.

The Russians laid out front-line banquets of food and vodka and the Americans produced brandy and champagne "liberated" from German Army stores and there were toasts and songs and expressions of hope for the future in which America, Russia and Britain would stand together for enduring peace.

There is something kindred in the warm-hearted, uninhibited cordiality of the Russians, such as we have met these past three days, and the hearty friendliness of the average GI. Our soldiers and the Russians have got along beautifully thus far. The American attitude in the front line might be summed up in the remark of one jeep driver: "These Russkys are pretty good boys."

BRONX SOLDIER IN GROUP

When our forces and the Russians did meet it was largely accidental—so accidental, indeed, that there was a bit of shooting before the groups that made contact were sure the others were friends and not Germans.

The American patrol officially credited now by American Army authorities with the first meeting was headed by dusty, young Second Lieut. William D. Robertson of Los Angeles, Calif. He is a rather short but well-built and good-looking lad who before he joined the army was a pre-medical student at the University of California in Los Angeles. With him, and all traveling in one jeep, were Corp. James G. McDonnell of Peabody, Mass.; Pfc. Paul Staub of the Bronx, New York City, and Pfc. Frank P. Huff of Washington, Va.

The race for the honor of the first meeting was close. Lieut. Albert Kotzebue of Houston, Tex., was first reported unofficially to have reached the Russians near Reisa with a reconnaissance patrol of twenty men in six jeeps at 3 o'clock Wednesday afternoon and to have remained with them. But whoever was the first, Lieutenant Robertson and his three men had a first-class adventure greeting the Russians.

Lieutenant Robertson and his one-jeep army were on duty Wednesday around Wurzen. The Germans had given up without fighting, but fleeing German civilians, liberated prisoners of war and slave laborers were milling about in such numbers that they clogged the roads. Lieutenant Robertson's captain suggested that he head off the civilians beyond Wurzen to prevent them from entering the town.

So Lieutenant Robertson set out to clear roads at 10:30 Wednesday morning and went on and on. Fifteen miles north of Wurzen his patrol met thirty freed

Soviet soldiers from the Fifth Guards Army and U.S. soldiers from the First Army meet on April 25, 1945 in Torgau, on the Elbe River in Germany.

British prisoners of war who said there were more British prisoners and some Americans up the road. Their hunt for these took Lieutenant Robertson and his men to the substantial town of Torgau on the Elbe. Lieutenant Robertson liberated a number of people in the town, including some who he was told were to have been shot on trumped-up charges of espionage. Thirty of these were found in a German barracks.

While Lieutenant Robertson was talking with them he heard small-arms fire near by. The town previously had been heavily shelled by the Russians and the civilians told Lieutenant Robertson that the Russians were just across the river, which at that point is about 150 yards wide.

Not sure of what reception he might get, Lieutenant Robertson rigged up a flag, attaching it to his jeep on a pole cut from a tree. He got out of the jeep to seek contact with the Russians and then had a brilliant idea. He broke into a German drugstore, got dyes and crudely painted red stripes and a blue field on his flag. Near the river was a castle-like building surmounted by a tower. Lieutenant Robertson and his men climbed to the top of the tower and waved the flag. "Tovarisch!" Lieutenant Robertson shouted— the only Russian he knew—and he waved the flag.

Lieutenant Robertson could see the Russians with an armored car in the woods opposite. They called something he did not understand and fired colored flares—the prearranged Russo-American recognition signal. The American reply was to have been colored flares, but Lieutenant Robertson had none.

He tried to explain this in English to the Russians and waved his home made flag again. The Russians then fired two rounds of anti-tank ammunition at the tower. It seems the Germans recently had tried to trick the Russians with an American flag and the Russians were suspicious. Lieutenant Robertson left his flag flying and he and his men hurried out of the tower. Down in the town he found an English-speaking liberated Russian and got him to return with him to the tower and explain to the Russian soldiers they were friends.

This worked. The Russians came out of the woods and ran down the bank onto a blown-up bridge, whose central spans sagged to the river. Lieutenant Robertson and his men swarmed onto the bridge also and slid down the slanting girders and were the first actually to touch the Russians. A Russian soldier— Pvt. Nikolai Ivanovich Andreeff—got down first from the Russian side, followed by Lieut. Alexander Sylvachko.

The Americans and Russians pounded each other on the back and shouted "Hello" at each other in the beginning of a celebration of the junction of the two armies, which became uproarious as meeting expanded Thursday,

Lieutenant Robertson and his men were led to the east side of the Elbe where they were joined by Capt. Vassili Petrovich Nyedoff and in a few minutes by Maj. Anaphim Larionoff, commanding the river post.

RUSSIANS MAKE A PARTY

The Russians immediately made it a party. They got out wine, sardines, biscuits and chocolate captured from the Germans. They toasted everybody bottoms up and the Americans and Russians smiled and laughed at each other.

After an hour or so of this Lieutenant Robertson and his party started back, taking the Russians with them—all eight piled on the jeep. They made the long trip back to the headquarters of the American 273d Infantry Regiment at Trebsen and reported to Colonel Adams.

Colonel Adams led the whole group back to division headquarters across the Mulde River and introduced the Russians to General Reinhardt. They all conferred far into the night, exchanged information about the disposition of their troops and arranged for General Reinhardt to visit the Russian division commander Thursday afternoon. And meantime they exchanged innumerable more toasts to Premier Stalin, to the President of the United States, to the Red Army and to the American, to the happy Russo-American relationship, to the destruction of fascism and to the lasting peace of the world.

Meanwhile it had been arranged for the American correspondents—most of whom had had little sleep Wednesday night and little rest for days in which they hunted for the expected junction of the American and Red Armies—to visit the Russian lines. We left regimental headquarters in a long convoy guarded by a jeep mounting machine guns shortly before 8 o'clock Thursday morning and struck out across this No Man's Land.

We found a town badly battered, some of its buildings still burning but no Russian troops. We circled the town cautiously and then entered it past a slave labor camp whose inmates waved at us.

SINGING ONLY SOCIAL SUCCESS

We drove through a square past a statue of Frederick the Great and stopped in another large square. Then someone shouted and we saw walking almost majestically from the archway of a building a tall young Russian who turned out to be Lieut. Ivan Feodorovich Kuzminski of Kirovograd, commanding the outpost in the city. His men followed him. The American soldiers accompanying us made a rush for them, and in seconds the Russians and Americans were clasping hands, exchanging names and trying to express mutual gratification.

A score or so of Russian soldiers strolled up and were friends with the Americans instantly. They produced bottles of cognac and champagne "liberated" from German Army stores and rolled out a barrel of German beer ❯

and treated the Americans. Several Russian soldiers had accordions and they and our GI's joined in a songfest — which was a greater social than a musical success, inasmuch as the Americans sang "Swanee River" while the Russians rendered "If There Should Be War

Tomorrow," a Soviet patriotic ballad.

A Red Army "Wac" walked down the street to join us—Sgt. Anna Konstantivovna Eugenia of Kharkov—and sang another Russian patriotic song of Soviet greetings to the English and American peoples. ◊

MAY 1, 1945

Dachau Captured By Americans Who Kill Guards, Liberate 32,000

By The Associated Press.

DACHAU, Germany, April 30— Dachau, Germany's most dreaded extermination camp, has been captured and its surviving 32,000 tortured inmates have been freed by outraged American troops who killed or captured its brutal garrison in a furious battle.

Dashing to the camp atop tanks, bulldozers, self-propelled guns—anything with wheels—the Forty-second and Forty-fifth Divisions hit the notorious prison northwest of Munich soon after the lunch hour yesterday. Dozens of German guards fell under withering blasts of rifle and carbine fire as the soldiers, catching glimpses of the horrors within the camp, raged through its barracks for a quick clean-up.

The troops were joined by trusty prisoners working outside the barbed-wire enclosures. Frenchmen and Russians, grabbing weapons dropped by slain guards, acted swiftly on their own to exact full revenge from their tormentors.

The sorting of the liberated prisoners was still under way today but the Americans learned from camp officials that some of the more important captives had been transferred recently to a new hideout, probably in the Tyrol. These were said to have included Premier Stalin's son, Jacob, who was captured in 1941; the former Austrian Chancellor, Kurt Schuschnigg, and his wife; Prince Frederick Leopold of Prussia, Prince Xavier de Bourbon de Parme and the Rev. Martin Niemoeller, the German Lutheran, who was arrested when he defied German attempts to control his preaching. [Prisoners at another camp liberated by the Americans recently reported that Dr. Schuschnigg had been executed by his guards earlier this month.] One of the prisoners remaining here said that he was the son of Leon Blum, former French Premier.

Prisoners with access to records said that 9,000 captives had died of hunger

and disease or been shot in the past three months and 14,000 more had perished during the winter. Typhus was prevalent in the camp and the city's water supply was reported to have been contaminated by drainage from 6,000 graves near the prison.

39 CARS FULL OF BODIES

A short time after the battle there was a train of thirty-nine coal cars on a siding. The cars were loaded with hundreds of bodies and from them was removed at least one pitiful human wreck that still clung to life. These victims were mostly Poles and most of them had starved to death as the train stood there idle for several days. Lying alongside a busy road near by were the murdered bodies of those who had tried to escape.

Bavarian peasants—who traveled this road daily—ignored both the bodies and the horrors inside the camp to turn the American seizure of their city into an orgy of looting. Even German children rode by the bodies without a glance, carrying stolen clothing.

In the wake of the storming Americans the bodies of the trimly-clad German guards lay scattered like tenpins, bowled over as they sought to flee. The highest officers surrendered, waving a white flag, but a Red Cross representative said that the real executives of the camp had escaped the night before.

The camp held 32,000 emaciated, unshaven men and 350 women, jammed in the wooden barracks. Prisoners said that 7,000 others had been marched away on foot during the past few days. The survivors went wild with joy as the Americans broke open their pens, smothering their liberators with embraces.

Bodies were found in many places. Here also were the gas chambers—camouflaged as "showers" into which prisoners were herded under the pretext of bathing—and the cremation ovens. Huge stacks of clothing bore mute testimony to the fate of their owners.

A French general was slain last week as he walked toward a truck, believing that he was to be evacuated, prisoners reported. They said that Elite Guards had shot him in the back.

The Americans stormed through the camp with tor-

American troops discover the bodies of prisoners after liberating the Dachau concentration camp in Germany, 1945.

nadic fury. Not a stone's throw from a trainload of corpses lay the bleeding bodies of sixteen guards shot down as they fled.

In the mess hall of the guards' barracks, food was still cooking in the kitchen. One officer was slumped over a plate of beans, a bullet through his head. Nearby was a telephone with the receiver down and the busy signal still buzzing. Outside the power house were the bodies of two Germans slain by a Czech and a Pole working in the engine room.

The main part of the camp is surrounded by a fifteen-foot-wide moat through which a torrent of water circulates. Atop a ten-foot fence is charged barbed wire.

When Lieut. Col. Will Cowling of Leavenworth, Kan., slipped the lock in the main gate, there was still no sign of life inside this area. He looked around for a few seconds and then a tremendous human cry roared forth. A flood of humanity poured across the flat yard—which would hold a half dozen baseball diamonds—and Colonel Cowling was all but mobbed.

RESCUED BY SOLDIERS

He was hoisted to the shoulders of the seething, swaying crowd of Russians, Poles, Frenchmen, Czechs and Austrians, cheering the Americans in their native tongues. The American colonel was rescued by soldiers, but the din kept up.

Flags appeared and waved from the barracks. There was even an American flag, although only one American was held there. He is a major from Chicago captured behind the German lines when he was on special assignment for the Office of Strategic Services.

The joyous crowd pressed the weight of thousands of frail bodies against the wire, and it gave way at one point. Like a break in a dam, the prisoners rushed out, although still penned in by the moat. Three tried to climb over the fence, but were burned to death on the top wires, for the current still was on.

Two guards fired into the mass from a tower, betraying their presence. American infantrymen instantly riddled the Germans. Their bodies were hurled down into the moat amid a roar unlike anything ever heard from human throats.

Inside the barracks were more than 1,000 bodies—some shot by guards in a wild melee last night, others victims of disease and starvation. ◆

MAY 1, 1945

The bodies of Benito Mussolini and Clara Petacci (center), his mistress, hang from the roof of a gasoline station in Milan after they had been shot by anti-Fascist forces while attempting to escape to Switzerland.

Inglorious End of A Dictator

By Wireless to The New York Times.

MILAN, April 29 (Delayed)—The degradation to which the bodies of Mussolini, his mistress, Clara Petacci, and his fascist followers were subjected this morning did not end in the muddy gutter.

Soon after 10 A.M., six of the corpses, including Mussolini's and Signorina Petacci's, were hung by the feet with wire from an exposed steel girder of a former gasoline station a few yards from the original dumping point. Black-lettered white signs bearing their names were plastered above them. Later the bodies were cut down and taken to the morgue, where a crowd gathered all over again, and men, women and children climbed fences to get a final look.

An inspection of the bodies revealed a delicate square gold locket that Signorina Petacci had worn. Outside, in the lower right corner, it bore initials and the inscription: "Clara—io sono te, tu sei me [Clara—I am you, you are me]." It was signed "Ben" and dated April 4, 1939, and April 4, 1941—presumably when Mussolini met Signorina Petacci and when he gave her the locket.

No funeral plans had been set tonight and there was some talk of an autopsy on what was left of the dictator. Frankly, it was not much, for the crowd had kicked his face out of shape. ◆

MAY 3, 1945

GERMANS CAPITULATE IN ITALY AND AMERICAN FORCES ENTER CITY OF MILAN

2 GERMAN OFFICERS SIGN CAPITULATION

By Wireless to The New York Times.

ADVANCED ALLIED HEADQUARTERS, Italy, May 3—Among the six correspondents chosen by lot to record the ceremony of the Germans' surrender in Italy was Sgt. Howard Taubman of The Stars and Stripes, a former music critic for The New York Times. His description was printed in the Army newspaper as follows:

The signing of the surrender terms took exactly twelve minutes. Hundreds of thousands of enemy troops and ❯

thousands of enemy-held square miles were forfeited in a room 18x25 feet. The signing was conducted with rigorous simplicity and swift military precision.

The German lieutenant colonel, Col. Gen. Heinrich von Vietinghoff Scheel's representative, was tall and had blonde receding hair and a wisp of a moustache. His eyes were pale and he looked as if he were trying to mask all feeling. He looked like the Hollywood version of a Prussian officer.

The German major, Obergruppenfuhrer Karl Wolff's emissary, was short, dark and intense-looking. His face had a high color, as if he could be short-tempered. There was less cool dignity in him, but he had an air of more suppressed tension. Several times when a photographer came too close to him he waved his hand with an imperious gesture, but then hastily restrained himself. He looked his role, too—that of spokesman for the thoroughly Nazified Elite Guard troops.

BOTH SMARTLY DRESSED

Both Germans were in civilian clothes, smartly dressed as if outfitted on Bond Street or by Brooks Brothers, but even in these peaceable get-ups they did not seem like men who would win friends and influence people easily—with or without force.

Lieut. Gen. W. D. Morgan, standing behind a chair at one end of the conference table, began the proceedings by saying, "I understand that you are prepared and empowered to sign the terms of a surrender agreement. Is that correct?"

The tall Prussian colonel replied, "Ja."

General Morgan repeated the question to the major, who did not understand English. The translator put the question in German and the major said: "Jawohl."

General Morgan went on: "I have been empowered to sign this agreement on behalf of the Supreme Allied Commander—the terms to take effect by noon of May 2, Greenwich mean time. I now ask you to sign and I shall sign after you."

The Prussian colonel sat down and signed his name hastily on five copies. The major followed him. It took them two minutes to surrender for their commanders. General Morgan sat down at the other end of the table and signed as the Allies' officers standing near him looked on. It took him one minute. ◆

HITLER DEAD IN CHANCELLERY, NAZIS SAY ADMIRAL IN CHARGE

By SYDNEY GRUSON
By Cable to The New York Times

LONDON, May I—Adolf Hitler died this afternoon, the Hamburg radio announced tonight, and Grand Admiral Karl Doenitz, proclaiming himself the new Fuehrer by Hitler's appointment, said that the war would continue.

Crowning days of rumors about Hitler's health and whereabouts, the Hamburg radio said that Hitler had fallen in the battle of Berlin at his command post in the Chancellery just three days after Benito Mussolini, the first of the dictator, had been killed by Italian Partisans. Doenitz, a 53-year-old U-boat specialist, broadcast an address to the German people and the surviving armed forces immediately after the announcer had given the news of Hitler's death.

First addressing the German people, Doenitz said that they would continue to fight only to save themselves from the Russians but that they would oppose the western Allies as long as they helped the Russians. In an order of the day to the German forces he repeated his thinly veiled attempt to split the Allies.

RADIO PREPARES GERMANS

Early this evening the Germans were told that all important announcements would be broadcast tonight. There was no hint of what was coming. The standby announcement was repeated at 9:10 P. M., followed by the playing or excerpts from Wagner's "Goetterdaemmerung."

A few minutes later the announcer said: "Achtung! Achtung! In a few moments you will hear a serious and important message to the German people." Then the news was given to the Germans and the world after the playing of the slow movement from Bruckner's Seventh Symphony, commemorating Wagner's death.

Goebbels and Fuehrer Died By Own Hands, Aide Says

By Cable to The New York Times.

LONDON, May 3—A deposition by Joseph Goebbels' chief assistant that both the German propaganda chief and Adolf Hitler had committed suicide in Berlin was given to the world early today by Red Army forces after they had occupied the capital of the crumbling Reich. Hans Fritzsche, Goebbels' deputy, was quoted in the Soviet communiqué as having reported also the suicide of General Krebs, who was disclosed to have been appointed Chief of the German General Staff in place of Field Marshal Gen. Wilhelm Keitel, lately believed to have been backing Heinrich Himmler's peace bid to the Western Powers.

The statement of Fritzsche, who was captured in Berlin with a large assortment of defense chiefs, added another version of the Fuehrer's demise to two already given—that he had died in battle and that he had succumbed to cerebral hemorrhage.

Suicide seemed more in character for Goebbels, whose brilliant mind was as twisted as his club foot. Administrator for the defense of Berlin as well as Minister of Enlightenment and Propaganda, he had announced that he would remain in Berlin and kill himself rather than live in a Germany dominated by "Bolshevist terror."

A cynical propagandist who set out without scruple to warp the mind of a whole nation, he was the great intellect of the Nazi party, a Catholic-bred,

Adolf Hitler in Berlin, some ten days before he committed suicide in the last hours before the Russians captured the city.

APPEALS FOR COOPERATION

Appealing to the German people for help, order and discipline, Doenitz eulogized Hitler as the hero of a lifetime of service to the nation whose "fight against the Bolshevik storm flood concerned not only Europe but the entire civilized world... It is my first task," Doenitz added, "to save Germany from destruction by the advancing Bolshevist enemy. For this aim alone the military struggle continues."

Clinging to the line of all recent German propaganda, reflected in Heinrich Himmler's reported offer to surrender to the western Allies but not to Russia, Doenitz said that the British and Americans were fighting not for their own interests but for the spreading of Bolshevism. He demanded of the armed forces the same allegiance that they had pledged to Hitler and he assured them that he took supreme command "resolved to continue the struggle against the Bolsheviks until the fighting men, until the hundreds of thousands of German families of the German east are saved from bondage and extermination." To the armed forces he described· Hitler as "one of the greatest heroes of German history," who "gave his life and met a hero's death." ◇

---

university-trained Rhinelander. A Nazi since he first heard Hitler speak in 1922, he was largely responsible for the hypnotic hold his party fastened on Germany. There had been none of his finesse and assurance in the recent German propaganda broadcasts.

President Truman announced at his press conference today that Adolf Hitler was dead.

This Government, the President said, has received information to this effect on the best authority possible. He added that he personally was convinced it was true.

The President's announcement came unexpectedly. He was asked for comment on the death of Benito Mussolini and the reported death of Hitler.

It meant, of course, he replied, that the two principal war criminals would not have to come to trial, that this was now a fact.

"Does that mean that official confirmation has been received that Hitler is dead?" he was asked.

It was then that he made his announcement and said he was glad. He was next asked if Grand Admiral Karl Doenitz, who has proclaimed himself Hitler's successor, was on the list of war criminals. The President replied in the negative. He did not discuss the matter further. ◇

JACKSON WILL HEAD WAR CRIME COUNSEL BY LEWIS WOOD

By Lewis Wood
Special to The New York Times.

WASHINGTON, May 2—Associate Justice Robert H. Jackson of the Supreme Court has been appointed by President Truman as the chief counsel of the United States in preparing and prosecuting charges against the leading war criminals of the Axis powers. Already, President Truman stated in making the announcement, Justice Jackson has assembled a staff from the War, Navy and other departments and preparations are under way, although the details of the military court before which the criminals will appear have not yet been arranged.

The trials in which the associate justice will take part will be held before an international military tribunal to be set up by the Allies.

Justice Jackson accepted the assignment in a statement in which he promised "no delay" on the part of the United States in the prosecution of those "who have thought it safe to wage aggressive and ruthless war." However, he added that he would pursue his task in a way "consistent with our traditional insistence upon a fair trial for any accused."

Those who will face the court, the President indicated, will be the men primarily responsible for atrocities and war crimes, not the lesser officials who personally carried out orders.

Pursuant to the Moscow Declaration of Nov. 1, 1943, all war criminals against whom there was enough proof of specific atrocities would be tried in the countries where the crimes took place, the President stated. The persons to be taken before the international tribunal will be "major war criminals and their principal agents and accessories," whose offenses have no specific geographical base.

The President's statement indicated that this Government expected the court to complete its work between the prospective adjournment of the Supreme Court on May 28 and its resumption in October. ◇

U.S. LIEUTENANT TAKES RUNDSTEDT
Marshal, Called Ablest of Foe's Chiefs By Eisenhower, Urges Reich to Yield

By Wireless to The New York Times.

PARIS, May 2—Field Marshal Gen. Karl von Rundstedt, Germany's "high priest of strategy" whom Gen. Dwight D. Eisenhower considers the ablest German commander that he has encountered, has been captured by the American Seventh Army in Bad Tolz, twenty-three miles south of Munich, it was officially reported today.

[The Americans also captured Field Marshal General Hugo Sperrle, former commander of German air forces on the western front accused of directing the London blitz, and Field Marshal Gen. Maximilian von Weichs, commander of German armies in the Balkans, The Associated Press reported.]

Rundstedt, who has been an officer for fifty-three years, was captured by Second Lieut. Joseph Burke, a tank commander who was on his first battlefield assignment since receiving his commission in the field three weeks ago. Rundstedt's son and aide, Lieut. Hans Gerd von Rundstedt, was captured with him.

Rundstedt was under medical treatment in Bad Tolz when it was overrun by the 141st Regiment of the Thirty-sixth Infantry Division last night. The marshal, his wife and their son had finished dinner and were expecting the Americans in the morning. The retired German leader had been in Bad Tolz for some time undergoing treatment. He is 70 years old. ❯

◄ 'READY TO SURRENDER'

According to Herman Jobe, an American private who drove Rundtstedt away—preliminary reports did not give his destination—Rundstedt "seemed ready to surrender." Rundstedt retired on March 13, the day after he last saw Adolf Hitler, after one of the most remarkable military careers of modern times. An old man in the military sense and already retired at the outbreak of the war in 1939, he returned to uniform to lead Army groups to victory in Poland, France and Russia.

Even at the end he was dangerous. Less than five months ago he broke through the American lines in the Ardennes with two armies and smashed for the Meuse River. The offensive was halted after hard fighting, but von Rundstedt had succeeded in forcing General Eisenhower to divert the American Third Army from its assault on the Saar to the flank of the Ardennes bulge and thus brought the operations on the Cologne plain to a close.

Tall, erect and spare, von Rundstedt is a Hollywood casting office's dream of a Junker general. ◊

MAY 4, 1945

RANGOON CAPTURED IN LIGHTNING DRIVE
Capital's Fall Heralds Early Burma Liberation

By The United Press.

CALCUTTA, India, May 3—The capital city of Rangoon fell to the British Fourteenth Army today, and the three-year war to liberate Burma from the Japanese was virtually at an end.

A special communiqué early today announced that British forces who fought through hundreds of miles of steaming jungles and across rugged mountains from the India border were storming the ancient city from two sides. Its capture was announced a few hours later.

The Japanese defenders—once estimated at 30,000—were believed to have fled into the delta country around Rangoon or across the narrow Gulf of Martaban toward Indo-China. In recent days the Japanese military forces in South Burma have disintegrated and the British drive on Rangoon was made at lightning speed.

A British tank in Burma, 1945.

The southward drive by armored columns was supported by parachute troops who dropped between Rangoon and the coast and by British assault troops who poured ashore on both banks of the Rangoon River at a point twenty miles below the city of 400,000 in the largest amphibious operation in this war theatre.

Admiral Lord Louis Mountbatten was believed to have concentrated troops above Rangoon, ready for an immediate strike eastward into Thailand, French Indo-China and Malaya, with its great naval base at Singapore. Some units chasing fleeing Japanese troops have been reported only a few miles from the Thailand border.

The reconquest of Burma—now all but completed after three years of some of the most difficult fighting the world has ever known—was across country so difficult that the entire Fourteenth Army was supplied by air. During the campaign entire divisions were transported by plane in a new technique of aerial warfare.

Recapture of Rangoon, which fell to the Japanese on the Sunday of May 8, 1942, cuts off all supplies for the disintegrated Japanese troops in lower Burma. Except for mopping up these hopelessly trapped pockets of resistance, the heartbreaking campaign is over.

The recapture of all Burma except for the thin sliver paralleling Thailand to the south and east, was almost entirely carried out during the past year.

FOE AT IMPHAL A YEAR AGO

A year ago the Japanese opened an offensive toward New Delhi and reached the Indian border at Imphal and Kohima, while other forces from the mountainous Arakan region drove on to Calcutta along the Bay of Bengal. Both drives were stopped and British, American and Chinese forces began pushing south.

The drive has been made almost entirely by the Fourteenth Army, with American and Chinese forces participating in the early stages to open up the Stilwell Road to China. The Fifteenth Indian Corps meanwhile killed or trapped the few thousand enemy remaining in the Arakan, and provided additional airdromes for the air-supplied army.

British officers here disclosed meanwhile that the Burma National Army is operating with the British Fourteenth in blocking escape routes and sniping and ambushing Japanese troop concentrations. The announcement was the first that loyal Burmese are openly fighting the Japanese. ◊

MAY 4, 1945

Russians Find No Trace of Hitler In Berlin, Moscow Paper Reports

By Wireless to The New York Times.

MOSCOW, May 3—Soviet security troops and military police hunted hard through the wreckage of Berlin today for wanted war criminals and sought to check and double check the whereabouts of Adolf Hitler's body, not yet by any means convinced that he, Propaganda Minister Joseph Goebbels and other members of the Nazi hierarchy actually had committed suicide.

The skeptical view prevailing in Soviet circles, who are determined to give these top enemies no chance to escape through trickery, was expressed by the well-known Pravda writer Nikolai Tikhonoff, who wrote that in the devastated occupied capital "there is no

MAY 8, 1945

GERMANY SURRENDERS: NEW YORKERS MASSED UNDER SYMBOL OF LIBERTY

Thousands filling Times Square in spontaneous celebration yesterday

By FRANK S. ADAMS

New York City's millions reacted in two sharply contrasting ways yesterday to the news of the unconditional surrender of the German armies. A large and noisy minority greeted it with the turbulent enthusiasm of New Year's Eve and Election Night rolled into one. However, the great bulk of the city's population responded with quiet thanksgiving that the war in Europe was won, tempered by the realization that a grim and bitter struggle still was ahead in the Pacific and the fact that the nation is still in mourning for its fallen President and Commander in Chief.

Times Square, the financial section and the garment district were thronged from mid-morning on with wildly jubilant celebrators who tooted horns, staged impromptu parades and filled the canyons between the skyscrapers with fluttering scraps of paper. Elsewhere in the metropolitan area, however, war plants continued to hum, schools, offices and factories carried on their normal activities, and residential areas were calmly joyful.

One factor that helped to dampen the celebration was the bewilderment of large segments of the population at the absence of an official proclamation to back up the news contained in flaring headlines and radio bulletins. With the premature rumor of ten days ago fresh in everyone's mind, and millions still mindful of the false armistice of 1918, there was widespread skepticism over the authenticity of the news.

By mid-afternoon loudspeakers were blaring into the ears of the exulting thousands in the amusement district the news that President Truman's proclamation was being held up by the necessity of coordinating it with the announcements from London and Moscow, and that the formal celebration of the long-awaited V-E Day would be delayed until today. The news spread through these areas almost as rapidly as it did in the business centers of the city, but it brought a very different reaction. Residents smiled their happiness, but they were too keenly aware of the bereavements that many families had suffered in three years of war, and of the dangers that millions of our fighting men must still face in fighting the Japanese, for any great display of ardor.

Suburban communities seemed to share this sentiment. In northern New Jersey a few large war plants closed, but elsewhere most of them kept on working, in response to the Government's appeal stressing the urgent need of planes, guns and tanks in the Pacific. In New Jersey, Westchester and Long Island alike, schools and business establishments kept steadily at their tasks.

Thousands of men, women and children flocked to the churches and synagogues of the city for solemn prayers of thanksgiving at the news of the surrender. Many of the churches held special services, among them the Cathedral of St. John the Divine and St. Patrick's Cathedral. At the latter edifice two special services were held in the early afternoon, but others that had been planned for the remainder of the day were canceled when it was realized that V-E Day would not be proclaimed officially until today. Many churches announced they would repeat their special observances today.

The Associated Press flash at 9:35 A.M. had given the world its first news of the surrender. For six hours Times Square was closed to all vehicular traffic by a crowd that the police placed at 500,000 between noon and 1 P.M., but by 4:30 P.M. the police had cleared the streets sufficiently for street cars and buses to operate.

Jubilation in the other areas in which crowds gathered, such as the dis-)

Hitler himself."

Since Mr. Tikhonoff can have no special information on this subject that would not have been officially announced, it can be assumed that he means that no living Fuehrer dominates Berlin today. This he makes clear by promising that the riddle of Hitler's final fate will be ferreted out.

"Whether he escaped to hell, to the devil's paws or to the arms of some Fascist protectors, still he is no more," the Soviet writer says. "We shall see what has really happened to him. And if he escaped, we shall find him, no matter where he is."

STIMSON ACCEPTS DEATH STORY
Secretary of War Henry L. Stimson today followed the lead of President Truman in expressing the opinion that Hitler is dead. Referring at his press conference to the execution of Benito Mussolini and the "reported death" of Hitler, he observed:

"Since information indicates that the Nazi leader has in fact died, both men have escaped trial as war criminals. But they both stand convicted in the minds

of all peoples and in the annals of history as men with the blood of innocent millions on their hands."

He was asked if he could amplify this comment by saying whether the evidence had convinced him beyond doubt that Hitler no longer is alive.

"I have no more evidence than has been given from general sources," Mr. Stimson replied. "But that is my conclusion."

JAPANESE SEND CONDOLENCES
Japan, troubled by faulty communications with her dying Axis partner in Europe, has decided to accept the news of Hitler's death as certain, it was indicated when Foreign Minister Shigenori Togo called at the residence of Nazi Ambassador Heinrich Stahmer to express the condolences of the Japanese Government.

The Japanese Domei Agency, in a series of transmissions recorded by the Federal Communications Commission, reported Togo's visit and said Stahmer had issued a statement declaring that "the Fuehrer is dead, but his struggle continues." ◆

trict centering about Wall and Broad Streets, the Borough Hall section of Brooklyn, Union, Madison and Herald Squares, and the garment manufacturing center in the West Thirties, followed an almost identical pattern. Along Fifth Avenue, on the other hand, the excitement never attained the crescendo that it did elsewhere.

NEWS SPREADS RAPIDLY

Only the usual handful of morning idlers was watching The New York Times bulletins on Times Tower when the electrifying news was posted there. Their outward response was not spectacular, but from mouth to mouth the news spread with astonishing speed. Meanwhile, from offices and loft buildings, thousands who had heard it on the radio were pouring into the streets and the crowds grew steadily larger until the police estimated that 500,000 were in the Times Square area.

A few blocks to the south, in the garment district, the enthusiasm reached an even more ecstatic level. From their loft windows towering many stories above the street, workers threw odds and ends of brightly colored materials into the breeze. Then they dropped their work and rushed pell-mell into the sunshine to help celebrate.

Outside the New York Stock Exchange, where trading was continued, the crowd grew so thick that by 10:20 A.M. the police were forced to shut off vehicular traffic along Wall Street from Broad Street to Broadway. They also closed Broad Street from Wall Street to Exchange Place. Extra police details were sent into the area to handle the congestion. ◊

MAY 8, 1945

GERMANS CAPITULATE ON ALL FRONTS
American, Russian and French Generals Accept Surrender in Eisenhower Headquarters, a Reims School

By EDWARD KENNEDY
Associated Press Correspondent

REIMS, France, May 7—Germany surrendered unconditionally to the Western Allies and the Soviet Union at 2:41 A.M. French time today. [This was at 8:41 P.M.. Eastern Wartime Sunday.]

The surrender took place at a little red school-house that is the headquarters of Gen. Dwight D. Eisenhower.

The surrender, which brought the war in Europe to a formal end after five years, eight months and six days of bloodshed and destruction, was signed for Germany by Col. Gen. Gustav Jodl. General Jodl is the new Chief of Staff of the German Army.

The surrender was signed for the Supreme Allied Command by Lieut. Gen. Walter Bedell Smith, Chief of Staff for General Eisenhower.

It was also signed by Gen. Ivan Susloparoff for the Soviet Union and by Gen. François Sevez for France.

[The official Allied announcement will be made at 9 o'clock Tuesday morning when President Truman will broadcast a statement and Prime Minister Churchill will issue a V-E Day proclamation. Gen. Charles de Gaulle also will address the French at the same time.]

General Eisenhower was not present at the signing, but immediately afterward General Jodl and his fellow delegate, Gen. Admiral Hans Georg Friedeburg, were received by the Supreme Commander.

GERMANS SAY THEY UNDERSTAND TERMS

They were asked sternly if they understood the surrender terms imposed upon Germany and if they would be carried out by Germany.

They answered Yes.

Germany, which began the war with a ruthless attack upon Poland, followed by successive aggressions and brutality in internment camps, surrendered with an appeal to the victors for mercy toward the German people and armed forces.

After having signed the full surrender, General Jodl said he wanted to speak and received leave to do so.

"With this signature," he said in soft-spoken German, "the German people and armed forces are for better or worse delivered into the victors' hands.

"In this war, which has lasted more than five years, both have achieved and suffered more than perhaps any other people in the world." ◊

Crowds celebrate Victory in Europe day in Times Square, New York, on May 7, 1945.

MAY 8, 1945

OSWIECIM KILLINGS PLACED AT 4,000,000
Soviet Commission Reports Death Camp In Poland Was Founded by Himmler

By C. L. SULZBERGER
By Wireless to THE New York Times.

MOSCOW, May 7—More than 4,000,000 persons were systematically slaughtered in a single German concentration camp—that at Oswiecim in Poland, near Cracow—from 1939 to 1944. The Germans thus accomplished with scientific efficiency the greatest incidence of mass murder in recorded history.

This slaughter exceeds in barbaric intention and method not only the greatest brutalities of such infamous conquerors as Genghis Khan but also surpasses even Germany's own record in her previous prize exhibitions at Maidanek, Dachau and Buchenwald.

Such is the miserable tale made public today—on the eve of the official end of the European war—by the Soviet Union's Extraordinary State Commission investigating the extermination center at Oswiecim. For some time various Russians have had a pretty good idea of the abysmal tale of Oswiecim, especially those now working on a Black Book of German infamy, but these are the first statistical data of the horrible camp's record.

According to the Soviet commission, "more than 4,000,000 citizens" of the Soviet Union, Poland, France, Belgium, the Netherlands, Czechoslovakia, Yugoslavia and other countries, including the non-Allied lands of Hungary and Rumania, were exterminated in Oswiecim. The means used were "shooting, famine, poisoning and monstrous tortures."

The report states that gas chambers, crematoria, surgical wards, laboratories and clinics were erected around Oswiecim to accomplish this mass-production monstrosity.

Such a report would seem incredible to American readers, except that now they have been "conditioned" by the horrors of Buchenwald, which already have been fully investigated.

According to the Soviet report, which included interviews with 2,819 liberated prisoners at Oswiecim, German professors and doctors conducted their experiments on healthy persons,

Still shot from a film recorded by Alezandra Woroncewa after his release from Oswiecim (Auschwitz) concentration camp in January 1945.

including castration, sterilization of women, artificial infection with cancer, typhus and malaria germs, tests of the effects of poisons and the destruction of children by injections into the heart of carbolic acid or the simpler method of heaving them into furnaces.

The camp, it is charged, was organized by Heinrich Himmler, built in 1939 by his order and constructed in a huge series of buildings around the Oswiecim suburbs to house between 180,000 and 250,000 prisoners simultaneously.

The first crematorium was erected in 1941, but the next year, it is stated, Himmler inspected the camp and decided that "improvements" were necessary, so new furnaces were built by the German firm of Topf & Sons.

Public baths were installed for group cyanide poisoning, and because "the baths" output exceeded the crematoria's capacity, deep pits were dug where excess bodies were burned over huge fires.

The report states that in 1943 the frugal Germans decided to sell the unburned bones to the firm of Schterhm to be used for the production of superphosphates, which was done, and that, in addition to almost 113 tons of crushed bones, loads of women's hair were sold for industrial purposes.

Within twenty-four hours, each crematorium was able to consume more than 10,000 bodies, it is stated on the basis of information provided by Polish, Hungarian, French, Czechoslovak, Netherland, Yugoslav, Italian, Greek, Rumanian and Belgian survivors interviewed. ◇

MAY 10, 1945

KEITEL IS DEFIANT AT BERLIN RITUAL

RUSSIA RATIFIES THE UNCONDITIONAL SURRENDER OF GERMANY IN BERLIN

By JOSEPH W. GRIGG Jr.
United Press War Correspondent For the Combined Allied Press

MARSHAL ZHUKOFF'S HEADQUARTERS, Berlin, May 9—The final seal was set on the Wehrmacht's defeat and humiliation before the world ❯

when Field Marshal Wilhelm Keitel, titular head of the once proud Oberkommando der Wehrmacht, was brought to Marshal Gregory K. Zhukoff's headquarters in the devastated German capital early this morning to sign the formal ratification of Germany's unconditional surrender.

As one of the first two American newspaper men officially permitted to go to Berlin since the Russian occupation, I witnessed the signature in the large whitewashed hall of an army technical school in the eastern residential suburb of Karlshorst, now used by Marshal Zhukoff as his headquarters.

The document was more or less identical in terms with that signed at Reims Monday morning, with certain additions requested by the Russians defining more closely the details of the surrender of German troops and equipment.

KEITEL ARROGRANT TO END
On the Allied side it was signed by Marshal Zhukoff for the Russians and by Air Chief Marshal Sir Arthur W. Tedder on behalf of Gen. Dwight D. Eisenhower, and was witnessed by Gen. Carl A. Spaatz, commander of the United States Strategic Air Forces, and Gen. Jean de Lattre, commander of the First French Army. On the German side, Keitel, as Oberkommando der Wehrmaeht, signed together with Gen. Admiral Hans Georg von Friedeburg, Commander in Chief of the German Navy, and Col. Gen. Paul Stumpff, Commander in Chief of the Luftwaffe.

With the signatures of the heads of all the German armed forces appended, this historic document forestalls forever any future German claim that the German Army ended the war unbeaten.

Keitel, a tall, haughty, gray-haired figure wearing the full-dress uniform of a German field marshal, maintained his Prussian arrogance to the bitter end.

After he had signed the document and while the Allied chiefs were signing, Keitel made a last-minute attempt to play for time. He beckoned the Russian interpreter to him and began haranguing him, protesting that there was an insufficient time to notify the forces under his command of minor modifications in the capitulation text and asking for another twenty-four hours grace before it became effective.

He could clearly be heard repeatedly saying to the interpreter: "I insist that you go to the Colonel General—I mean Marshal Zhukoff—and tell him I must de-

mand another twenty-four hours' respite."

The interpreter hesitated and appeared uncertain what to do and finally went and consulted members of Marshal Zhukoff's staff. As no reply was conveyed back to Keitel, it appeared that the Russians ignored the request. Marshal Zhukoff, medium-sized and stocky, his hair close-cropped and thinning on top, wore a marshal's full-dress uniform and was a dignified soldierly figure throughout. He spoke only Russian and all the conversation between him and the SHAEF personnel had to be interpreted.

Keitel and the other Germans, meanwhile, had been escorted to a near-by villa to await the capitulation document. Marshal Zhukoff asked Marshal Tedder to stay behind and confer alone with him. The two remained closeted about a half hour while Marshal Tedder gave Marshal Zhukoff the draft of the capitulation terms, embodying certain changes that the Russians desired. At 5:30 P.M. they came out and Marshal Zhukoff asked Marshal Tedder to give him until 7 P.M. to consider the exact wording.

A long wait then began. At 8 P.M. Marshal Zhukoff and the SHAEF experts had not yet agreed on the final text. At one point Marshal Tedder was called away to confer again with Marshal Zhukoff. It was not until shortly before midnight that the document was finally completed, typed and presented to the Germans.

At midnight Marshal Zhukoff gave the word to the delegates to enter the hall for the signing.

The large, whitewashed hall was brilliantly lighted with Klieg lights, spotlighting the Soviet, American, British and French flags immediately behind the chief Allied delegates. The

long tables were arranged like a letter E. Marshal Zhukoff, stern-faced, took the middle seat, with Marshal Tedder and Soviet Assistant Foreign Commissar Andrei Y. Vishinsky and Admiral Sir Harold Burroughs, the Allied supreme naval commander, on his right, and General Spaatz followed by General de Lattre, who had arrived independently from the First French Army.

Other members of the Allied delegation included American Maj. Gen. Harold R. Bull, head of SHEAF's G-3, and British Maj. Gen. K. W. D. Strong, head of G-2. The newsmen were escorted by Capt. Harry Butcher, Brig. W. A. S. Turner and Col. Ernest Dupuy of SHEAF public relations.

The delegates spent several minutes posing for the Russian photographers, who swarmed all over the hall. At 12:07 Marshal Zhukoff arose and read the text of the capitulation document and then ordered the German delegation brought in.

At 12:10 Keitel walked in, followed by Friedeburg and Stumpff. Keitel, haughty and self-possessed, his face slightly flushed, slammed his marshal's baton down on the table and took a seat, looking straight ahead, ignoring the photographers. Once or twice he fingered his collar and nervously wetted his lips.

The Germans sat at a separate table near the door, with four uniformed aides and two Allied interpreters standing behind.

When Keitel was seated Marshal Tedder arose and said in a cold voice in English:

"I ask you: Have you read this document of unconditional surrender? Are you prepared to sign it?"

After the translation Keitel picked a copy of the document off the table and replied in harsh Prussian accent in German:

Field Marshal Wilhelm Keitel, Hitler's chief military adviser in World War II, signing the unconditional surrender to the Allies and Russians in Berlin May 10, 1945.

"Yes, I am ready."

Marshal Zhukoff then motioned to him to come over to the table. Keitel picked up his cap, his marshal's baton and gloves, slowly and carefully inserted his monocle in his right eye, walked over and sat down to sign in a long scrawling hand the single name "Keitel."

The first signature was appended at 12:15 A.M., central European time. There were nine copies to sign, three each in Russian, English and German, of which the Russian and English texts were official for the record.

As the signing was completed Marshal Zhukoff arose and said coldly in Russian: "I now request the German delegation to leave the room."

Keitel arose, snapped together the folder in which he was carrying his copy and marched out haughtily, followed by the other Germans. ◇

SHIFT TO ONE-FRONT WAR BIG PROBLEM FOR ARMY

By SIDNEY SHALETT

WASHINGTON, May 12—Now that R-Day—Redeployment Day—is approaching, the greatest movement of men in all military history, dwarfing even the colossal but more gradual build-up for D-Day in Europe, will be staged by the United States Army during the next twelve months.

On the basis of information made public by the Army since victory in Europe, it seems conservative to estimate that 5,000,000 men—and perhaps 500,000 more—will be on the high seas during the next year, streaming back to the United States from Europe and to a smaller degree from the Pacific, and then out to the Pacific again, with Tokyo their ultimate destination.

Gen. Brehon Somervell, commanding general of the vast Army Service Forces, has revealed that 3,100,000 men will be withdrawn from Europe in "less than one year." Some will go directly to the Pacific. Many already have been shipped from Italy to the new one-front war theatre—but the "great majority" will return to the United States for fur-loughs and then new assignments, or, if they are eligible, demobilization.

In addition to the 3,100,000 leaving Europe, several hundred thousand Pacific veterans should be returning to the United States for demobilization. While these movements are under way reinforcements for the Pacific, including European veterans, rested after their furloughs, will be going to the Orient.

'FULL SPEED AHEAD'

The Army has not disclosed how fast it hopes to transfer its complete forces to the Pacific, but our military leaders have indicated that "full speed ahead" will be the order of the day, limited only by shipping facilities and the availability of Far Eastern bases. We want to defeat Japan as quickly as possible, they grimly emphasize, and the way to do it is to follow Forrest's axiom of getting there "fu'stest with the mostest."

Here is the general pattern of both redeployment and demobilization, as revealed by War Department leaders at a series of conferences since V-E Day:

REDEPLOYMENT—To be moved from Europe, 3,100,000 troops (400,000 will remain as occupation forces). Movements will take place at this minimum schedule:

May, June and July—about 845,000 men, or more than 280,000 a month.

August, September, October—about 1,185,000, or 395,000 a month.

November, December, January—about 807,000, or 269,000 a month. ◇

JAPANESE FEELERS ON PEACE SPURNED

WASHINGTON, May 17 (AP)—Individual Japanese in neutral countries are fishing for signs of peace short of unconditional surrender, but thus far no official peace bid has been received from Japan, it was learned today.

Particularly since the fall of Manila, a number of Japanese have urged neutrals to learn the "real American attitude," but these Japanese specify only that unconditional surrender is impossible for Japan and suggest no definite terms.

Asked about reports that the Office of Strategic Services had received a definite Japanese peace bid, officials here familiar with Japanese affairs said they knew of nothing of that kind. They stressed the futility of informal, personal peace feelers, representing as they do no authority from the militarists who still control Japan's destiny.

REAL RULERS NOT INVOLVED

All the evidence in American hands indicates that this element has no self-interest in facing the prospect of unconditional surrender and probably will not face it until Japanese military pride has been brought considerably lower. The Cabinet of Admiral Kantaro Suzuki, the new Premier, is a strong one, composed of some of the empire's best production experts with emphasis on the development of the war potential in Korea and Manchuria.

Until a peace bid bears unmistakably the stamp of Japan's real rulers it means nothing except possibly to indicate factional and minority trends in Japan, according to the view here.

While one peace inquiry may have originated with the wealthy classes of Japan and another appeared to have been associated at one stage with the Japanese court, both fizzled out because there was no hint that they represented the intentions of the militarists who run the Government in Tokyo.

American policy, it is learned, is based on the idea that to give unmerited attention to such unofficial feelers would lead Japanese militarists to believe that this country would actually accept a peace short of unconditional surrender. ◇

Chapter 24
"NEW AGE USHERED..."
June–September 1945

The months after the German defeat left the world in limbo, hoping to build a new order out of the ruins of the most damaging war in history but still waiting for the conflict raging in Asia and the Pacific to end. Following the United Nations's founding conference in San Francisco in May, the participants moved toward full ratification. In Washington Congress approved the new structure on July 28 during the last of the major wartime summits between the three major Allies. It was held at Potsdam, just outside Berlin, from July 17 to August 2, 1945. Like the previous wartime summits, the Potsdam conference was conducted in complete secrecy, with no reporters present.

The Times speculated on the uncertainties now dividing the former wartime Allies over the future of Europe and Asia. The one certainty, The Times claimed, was Churchill's imminent reelection as Britain went to the polls; there was "little doubt" about the British election's outcome. When Churchill was defeated by Clement Attlee's Labour Party, The Times conceded some "deep-seated forces" underlying Churchill's ouster. With Roosevelt's death in April 1945, Stalin was the only head of state at Potsdam who had led his country through the whole war.

The principal concern at Potsdam was to finish the war. Despite Japanese peace feelers extended via Moscow (which the Soviets denied), those in Tokyo who favored surrender could not defy the die-hard militarists, and feared for the future of the emperor.

On August 6 the United States dropped the first atomic bomb on the Japanese port of Hiroshima. The Times had been given exceptional access to the last stages of the bomb's development. In April 1945 Times science correspondent William L. Laurence had been invited by Brig. General Leslie Groves, head of the Manhattan Project (the super-secret program to develop the bomb), to become the project historian. Laurence wrote plenty of newspaper copy, but it was locked in the safe at the Oak Ridge, Tennessee Air Force facility, where he was based. He watched the first atomic test at the Alamogordo, New Mexico airbase in July. On August 4 Groves told The Times

that the paper would be given exclusive access when a special, but still secret, event took place. Thus when the first bomb was dropped Times War Department reporter Sidney Shallett beat the rest of the press with a story headlined "New Age Ushered" on August 7. Two days later, Laurence rode in the B-29 that dropped the second bomb on Nagasaki.

Surrender followed quickly, though not only because of the atomic bombs. On September 2 aboard the battleship *Missouri*, Japanese representatives, some in tears, signed the surrender document. That same day the electric board on Times Square carried the message "Official * * * Truman Announces Japanese Surrender." The Times later wrote, "This was the hour free men had dreamed of, and for which they had strained and died."

Atomic weapons transformed the balance of power in America's favor overnight. On August 18 The Times announced the issue was how to use that power in a world reduced in many places to a ruined chaos. In Germany a program of "de-Nazification" was established, though it made slow progress. France under Charles de Gaulle's provisional rule moved toward a new democratic constitution.

But outside Europe, issues that had been suppressed by war blazed up again after 1945. In the Middle East Arab states sought complete independence and curbs on Jewish immigration; in India Gandhi called for Britain to honor its wartime pledges and grant the nation independence; in Indo-China (later known as Vietnam) nationalists and Communists resisted the return of French rule; China was faced with an incipient civil war once the Japanese Army left.

Relations between the Soviet Union and the West were still uncertain, but Stalin had ordered an immediate acceleration of the Soviet atomic program. On September 17 The Times reported that a B-29 bomber had been forced down by Soviet jets over Korea. Two days later Soviet ambitions for a controlling hand in North Africa were published. This was not yet the Cold War, but the new age of peace began in an atmosphere of distrust and crisis.

JUNE 27, 1945

20 NATIONS PLEDGE RATIFICATION IN '45

SAN FRANCISCO, June 26 (AP)—If given a quick start by the United States Senate, a sufficient number of the other United Nations might ratify the World Charter in time to put it into effect before the end of 1945.

This was the prospect shown today in a poll conducted at the Security Conference by The Associated Press. Out of the first twenty-six nations to reply to a questionnaire, twenty predicted ratification by their home Governments before the end of the year. None raised any bar to ratifications. Six declined to fix a probable date.

Assuming Senate approval, as indicated by Senators' replies to another canvass by The Associated Press in Washington, the feeling expressed by delegates here was that a real landslide of favorable votes by small nations would follow.

All of the major powers, the United States, Great Britain, Russia, France and China, plus twenty-three of the other forty-five members of the United Nations must ratify it before the Charter can become effective.

The United States, Britain and China, together with eighteen small nations replying to the current questionnaire, already have been placed on the line as probable signatories before Jan. 1, 1946.

If Russia and France completed the Big Five line-up quickly, the full force of the new world organization almost certainly would go into effect this year.

Ratification predictions ranged from a "few weeks" in the case of China to "the earliest practicable date" in the case of the Philippines.

In several instances, as in Britain, Norway, Belgium and Greece, the delegations said that pending elections would govern the date of ratification, but even in these instances a 1945 date usually was given.

The Australian delegation forecast, given as "unofficial," was ten weeks. Peru's prediction was "possibly August"; Cuba and Paraguay said approval would be "speedy"; Norway indicated November; Belgium, December; Honduras named this same month, as did South Africa, with a proviso that final action might go over to 1946; Bolivia said "August or September"; Haiti said "in the next three months"; Luxembourg said "autumn," and the Dominican Republic said "without delay." ◊

JULY 2, 1945

4,000 Tons of Fire Missiles Bring Ruin to 4 Enemy Cities

By WARREN MOSCOW
By Wireless to The New York Times.

GUAM, July 2—In the pre-dawn darkness, American Superfortresses filled the air over Japan this morning, bringing destruction and ruin to four more Japanese cities. The greatest number of B-29's ever put in the air, from 550 to 600, rained down approximately 4,000 tons of incendiaries on the industries of three cities on the main island of Honshu and one on Kyushu.

The targets were Kure, Shimonoseki and Ube on Honshu and Kumamoto on Kyushu, all tasting the incredible heat of the fire bombs for the first time as the B-29 high command went about its business of wrecking Japan's industrial machine, city by city and factory by factory. Last night, from their bases on Guam, Tinian and Saipan, the planes that took off outnumbered those that took part in the fire bomb attack on Tokyo on May 24. There was little left of the Tokyo target when that raid was over, and the four secondary cities that received the heavier load early this morning were in line for a similar fate.

There has been a continual stepping up of the number of planes taking part

JULY 17, 1945

Editorial
POTSDAM SECRECY

Like all its predecessors, the conference of the Big Three at Potsdam is surrounded by secrecy and a strict censorship which bars the press and severely censors whatever press representatives may learn at its fringes. President Truman has expressed himself in favor of brief and generalized reports on the progress of the meeting, But it is evident that such reports will be issued only by common agreement and that they will tell little about the actual negotiations. Since the conference is expected to last three weeks, the world's patience is likely to be tried as never before.

Yet, however much the world in general and the press representatives in particular may chafe under this secretiveness, it must be regarded as inevitable for this kind of meeting, and as part of the price for its success. For this is no San Francisco conference called upon to put the finishing touches to a blueprint already drafted. This conference, though it has a solid basis of commonly accepted principles to work upon, will involve some fundamental decisions out of which the blueprint for the new world is to emerge. These decisions will pertain to both war and peace.

They will pertain to war because it is now evident that the war against Japan will be one of the main topics on the agenda. The presence of President Truman's and Prime Minister Churchill's top military, naval and air advisers is proof of that. And any decision made regarding that war would automatically fall into the category of military secrets, to be disclosed only in future military action. Nobody except the enemy would want them announced in advance.

But to a large extent secrecy at this

JULY 19, 1945

TOKYO PEACE BID VIA STALIN DENIED

Special to The New York Times

WASHINGTON, July 18—Renewed reports of a Japanese peace offer met with denial today when a State Department spokesman declared that no official proposals of terms had been received from the Japanese Government.

When the spokesman was asked concerning reports that Marshal Stalin had gone to the Postdam Conference with terms that the Japanese were prepared to accept for the termination of the Pacific war, he indicated that the State Department had no knowledge of such an offer.

The statement issued by Acting Secretary of State Joseph C. Grew on July

in the attacks. Only a few months back 200 planes in the air set a record. Then came the 300-, 400- and 500-plane attacks. We have promised to the Japanese attacks by 1,000 planes, and once the new bases on Okinawa are in use those promises will become a reality.

This morning's attacks bring to twenty-two the number of Japanese cities attacked by the incendiary method. There have been thirty-three incendiary missions, exclusive of pin-point bombing attacks and mining missions. Of the twenty-two cities fired by incendiaries, fifteen are on Honshu and the others on Kyushu. ◈

U.S. soldiers examine the results of a B29 Superfortress bomb run on the streets of the Ginza district, Tokyo, July 1945.

stage is also justified in respect to the decisions regarding the future peace. For these decisions, even if they involve nothing more than the practical application of principles previously agreed upon, involve all the many difficult problems which have set Europe aflame for centuries. They involve the issue of borders over which any nation is ready to fight at the drop of a hat; they involve the heartbreaking problems of restoration and reconstruction, of millions of displaced persons and projected new expulsions, of staving off hunger and disease which must lead to chaos and anarchy. It is inevitable that the three countries should have differing views on many of these problems. But it is also evident that if these differences are to be reconciled, as they must be, it is far better to talk them over first in a confidential exchange of views than to blare them forth in a public meeting where any nation, once it has proclaimed its stand, can change it only with great difficulty, if at all. And since the discussions are likely to affect the interests of

many other nations, any premature publication would precipitate a storm of rival pressure propaganda which might make any agreement utterly impossible.

To some this will seem to smack of "secret diplomacy," contrary to the "shirt-sleeve diplomacy" of President Wilson and its motto of "open covenants openly arrived at." But even President Wilson never contemplated, as his own practice at Versailles showed, that every development at every phase of every conference should be immediately trumpeted to the world. Real secret diplomacy is based on secret agreements secretly arrived at and kept secret from the world. There is nothing secret about the fact that the Big Three are meeting to reach agreements, and President Truman has specifically announced that he will make no secret commitments and will report to Congress immediately upon his return. With that America will be satisfied. ◈

JULY 22, 1945

BIG THREE ACHIEVE MARKED PROGRESS TOWARD ACCORD ON PEACE IN EUROPE, U.S. DELEGATION AT POTSDAM REPORTS

By RAYMOND DANIELL
By Wireless to The New York Times.

BERLIN, July 21—The United States delegation at the tripartite conference let it be known today that Premier Stalin, Prime Minister Churchill and President Truman had made considerable progress toward agreement on how the peace of Europe, won at so great a cost to all three nations and many lesser ones, could be preserved.

Since the first formal session Tuesday the leaders of the three major powers have met every day, including today, notwithstanding a British victory parade, which Mr. Churchill reviewed this morning from a stand in the Charlottenburger Chaussee in the Tiergarten.

With the Prime Minister in the reviewing stand were Clement R. Attlee, Labor party chief; Foreign Secretary Anthony Eden and most of Britain's serving field marshals. Gen. George C. Marshall, Fleet Admiral Ernest J. King and Gen. Henry H. Arnold were among the Americans who attended ❯

10, in which he said no peace proposals directly or indirectly had been received from the Japanese Government "still stands," the spokesman said. On that occasion Mr. Grew declared that the United States would accept only unconditional surrender.

Advices from Germany reported that President Truman intended to return to this country almost immediately after the conclusion of the Potsdam conference, and that plans for extended trips to various European and Mediter-

raneon countries had been abandoned. Peace feelers by unauthenticated Japanese sources, mentioned by Mr. Grew in his previous statement, together with the expectation of Presiden Truman's early return are believed to account for the speculation on the possibilities of an early end to the war with Japan. ◈

⟨ what was primarily a British show.

UK Prime Minister Winston Churchill, U.S. President Harry Truman and Soviet Premier Josef Stalin at the Potsdam conference, July 1945.

YALTA POINT CITED

It is believed that one of the problems that have occupied considerable time of the Big Three conference is the question of how to integrate the economy of partitioned Germany, part of which has been opened to the Poles by the Russians without waiting for any clarification or implementation by the other Allies of the decision reached at Yalta to compensate Poland for the loss of her eastern marshes with territory in the West taken from Germany.

As a result, it is reported, hundreds of thousands of Germans from Pomerania and the land east of the Oder River are being evicted by the Poles before the creation of any machinery for the transfer of the population and are beginning a migration westward. About 9,000,000 Germans are said to be affected.

It was explained today that a large part of the work of the conference is done by experts and members of subcommittees who toil far into the night and report on their progress at the daily conference of Foreign Secretaries. The latter, Vyacheslaff M. Molotoff, Mr. Eden and James F. Byrnes, decide then which subjects are ready for discussion by the Big Three and prepare the agenda for the next meeting of their leaders. In this much time is saved and the Prime Minister, Premier and President are spared the wasted effort of discussions that could lead nowhere for lack of some pertinent facts.

Observers speculated on the effect of the British elections on the timing of the conference.

There is little doubt among British political observers here that Mr. Churchill's Conservative party will emerge from the election with a majority in the Commons. There is, however, some doubt among them whether British constitutional practice requires his presence in England the day election results are announced or immediately thereafter.

Of course, if Labor won the election, both he and Mr. Attlee would probably have to return to England, Mr. Churchill to hand in the seals of office as the King's First Minister and Mr. Attlee to attempt to form a Government. There are some who hold that the Prime Minister will have to be back in London anyway to go through the formalities of re-forming his Government, and for that reason today's statement that much of the serious business of the conference had already been done was noted with interest. ◇

JULY 27, 1945

VOTE LEAVES STALIN LAST OF INITIAL BIG 3

POTSDAM, Germany, July 27 (AP)— News of the British Labor party's election triumph produced the political sensation of the year among delegations of the three great Allied powers in Potsdam today.

The defeat of Prime Minister Churchill's Government apparently marks the second break in the original Big Three and leaves Premier Stalin as the only member of that triumvirate.

The first break was the death April 12 of President Roosevelt, whose place was filled by President Truman.

Clement R. Attlee has been attending the Potsdam conference with Mr. Churchill and thus is fully informed on the discussions.

The first impression here this afternoon was that Mr. Attlee would extend Mr. Churchill the courtesy of an invitation to return to Potsdam as a member of his delegation. But it was only a guess and few appeared to believe that Mr. Churchill would accept in view of the British voters' verdict.

There was no authoritative information at once available to clarify the question as to how soon Mr. Attlee himself might be able to come back, but in most quarters it was believed that this would be within two or three days at most or the conference recess would become a formal adjournment.

There was no comment from President Truman and Premier Stalin.

The presumption was that plans were being made for continuance of the conferences here with Mr. Attlee. ◇

CHURCHILL IS DEFEATED IN LABOR LANDSLIDE

BRITISH TURN LEFT

War Regime Swept Out as Laborites Win 390 of 640 Seats

CHURCHILL BIDS ADIEU

By HERBERT L. MATTIEWS
By Cable to The New York Times

LONDON, July 26—In one of the most stunning election surprises in the history of democracy, Great Britain swung to the Left today in a landslide that smothered the Conservatives and put Labor into power with a great majority.

Winston Churchill has resigned as Prime Minister and Clement R. Attlee has accepted the King's invitation to form a Laborite Government. The Liberals went down to an equally surprising defeat. The world, which lookcd to Britain for a guiding trend, has had its tremendous answer. Today and tomorrow and for months or years to come, the Left is the dominating power in global politics.

When the final result came in from the constituency of Hornchurch at 10:30 P. M., Labor had a staggering total of 390 scats out of a Parliament of 640, of which the holders of thirteen seats will not be known until early in August.

In the last Parliament, Labor had only 163 and in its greatest previous triumph, in 1929, it had 288.

CONSERVATIVES CUT TO J95 SCATS

The Conservatives had fallen from 358 seals to 195. The Liberals, too, lost seven seals and now have only eleven members in Parliament.

Adding fourteen Liberal Nationals and one National, the former Government is down to 210 seats, whereas if the Liberals, Independent Labor with three seats, the Commonwealth with one, the Communists with two and the Independents with ten are added to Labor, one gets a total of 417.

Such a tremendous majority means that the Labor party can confidently count on a full five year tenure of office, for it cannot be beaten on any vote of confidence.

Winston Churchill at the rear of Downing Street on his way to hand in his resignation to King George VI, July 26, 1945.

Out of nearly 25,000,000 votes, Labor alone won nearly 12,000,000. The Conservatives got a little more than 9,000,000 votes. The Labor party did not lose a single seat to the Conservatives, although it gained 130 from that party.

The results were a personal, decisive repudiation of Mr. Churchill as a peacetime leader. He himself personalized the election; he had asked that votes be cast for him so that he would be returned to power. The answer came not only in an overwhelming defeat for his party but even in his constituency of Woodford, where he was opposed only by a candidate whom he called "Tomfool" Hancock, 10,500 persons out of 38,000 voted against him. His son, Maj. Randolph Churchill, and his son-in-law, Duncan Sandys were defeated. ◊

BRITISH VOTE REFLECTS DEEP-SEATED FORCES

By CLIFTON DANIEL
By Wireless to The New York Times.

LONDON, July 28—British voters had a choice between Churchill and change. When the ballot boxes were opened this week they had chosen change and Britain had joined the European swing to the Left. Britain had been in the swing all along, but during ten years without a general election no one had been able to gauge the extent of the fact.

If Americans now wish to understand why the British people with seeming ingratitude turned Winston Churchill out of office, they must first appreciate the depth of the yearning here for a change in the conception, functions and performance of government. That urge overrode all other considerations.

BREAK WITH PAST

To its own undoing the Conservative party underestimated the popular impulse. Beguiled by the personality of Mr. Churchill and deceived by the outward apathy of the voters, disinterested observers, including this writer, failed to perceive the irresistibility of that impulse in the English people.

But it is now apparent that by installing a Labor Government at Westminster the British people intended to make a clean break with the past the past of unemployment and doles, the past of appeasement and unpreparedness, the past of war and suffering, the past of unfulfilled promises and national frustration.

Whatever they may have gained or failed to gain by their votes, it is plain ❯

most of the British people were seeking somehow a guarantee for the future, a guarantee for the fulfillment of postwar hopes and schemes that have no relation to the muddling uncertainty that characterized years between the wars.

ALLIED PLEDGES ARE FIRM

There is no question of the new Attlee Government's repudiating any of the broad international agreements undertaken by Britain in the five war years under Mr. Churchill, for the leaders of the Labor party participated in them all, as they have participated in the San Francisco and Potsdam conferences.

The victorious Labor party, which its opponents try to stigmatize with the label of "socialist," is by no means a party of working-class revolution. Its domestic and foreign policies are not so alien to the modern British mind as the Conservatives would have had the voters believe.

But the British vote for Labor does represent a profound and fundamental change in political trends. For the ballots cast have turned out of office not only a party but a class. ◊

FIRST ATOMIC BOMB DROPPED ON JAPAN

By SIDNEY SHALETT
Special to The New York Times.

WASHINGTON, Aug. 6—The White House and War Department announced today that an atomic bomb, possessing more power than 20,000 tons of TNT, a destructive force equal to the load of 2,000 B-29's and more than 2,000 times the blast power of what previously was the world's most devastating bomb, had been dropped on Japan

The announcement, first given to the world in utmost solemnity by President Truman, made it plain that one of the scientific landmarks of the century had been passed, and that the "age of atomic energy," which can be a tremendous force for the advancement of civilization as well as for destruction, was at hand.

At 10:45 o'clock this morning, a statement by the President was issued at the White House that sixteen hours earlier—about the time that citizens on the Eastern seaboard were sitting down to their Sunday suppers—an American plane had dropped the single atomic bomb on the Japanese city of Hiroshima, an important army center.

JAPANESE SOLEMNLY WARNED

What happened at Hiroshima is not yet known. The War Department said it "as yet was unable to make an accurate report" because "an impenetrable cloud of dust and smoke" masked the target area from reconnaissance planes. The Secretary of War will release the story "as soon as accurate details of the results of the bombing become available."

But in a statement vividly describing

Editorial
THE CONFERENCE ENDS

After three weeks of deliberations, the momentous Conference of Potsdam, which met to liquidate Hitler's ghastly heritage and to lay the cornerstone for the new world of tomorrow, has come to its end. The Big Three, on whose shoulders rested perhaps greater responsibility this time than ever in the past because victory in Europe enlarged their freedom of choice, are homeward bound to put their decisions into effect.

Nearly three months have passed since V-E Day, and a distraught and devastated Europe looks with dread to the approaching winter, which promises to be the hardest in its history, but against which it can do little until peace succeeds war. And that peace, for the first time since Europe beat off the invasions from Asia and Africa, is now in the keeping of the three chiefly extra-European Powers which met in Potsdam. Time presses, therefore, and it is quite in order that President Truman should have declined the numerous invitations to visit other countries in favor of a brief visit to the King of England aboard a battle cruiser at Plymouth. It is a welcome and a graceful gesture which not only returns the King's visit to the United States just prior to the war, but also demonstrates the enduring friendship between our two countries beyond all changes in national and international politics.

What decisions the Conference has made will not be revealed until its final communiqué is published. It would be useless to speculate on them. But one can take hope from the repeated interim reports that progress was being made. The alternative to agreement, in fact, would be too grim to contemplate. At the same time, the change in the personnel of the Big Three since their previous meetings, and even in the midst of this conference, has demonstrated that this was a meeting, not of three men, but of three nations with specific problems and interests to reconcile. And the further fact that the United States not only played the decisive role in the victory, but that its President also presided over the conference to gather its fruits, has put a particularly large share of responsibility on America.

In a sense, the Potsdam Conference was in the nature of a preliminary peace conference at which the Big Three sought to agree among themselves on the framework of a peace that will so much depend on their support. In such a preliminary gathering, secrecy is unavoidable if results are to be achieved. Not even the most enthusiastic exponents of open diplomacy will cavil as long as the full results are published at its conclusion. And it is inevitable that its decisions will go far to determine the shape of things to come. But it will be well to bear in mind that in the last analysis even its decisions can only be provisional—a basis of procedure, not a dictate to be blindly accepted by the rest of the world. They must still remain subject to ratification—by one or more peace conferences in which all affected nations must have a voice, by the individual Governments of the Big Three themselves, and in the end by the conscience of the world. For unless they are so ratified, they will not endure. The development of the United Nations Charter, from the Atlantic Charter, through Dumbarton Oaks, through the San Francisco Conference, to the final ratification by the United States Senate, with its successive stages of increasing publicity, debate and improvement, has set the precedent and the moral for the peace treaties to come. ◊

the results of the first test of the atomic bomb in New Mexico, the War Department told how an immense steel tower had been "vaporized" by the tremendous explosion, how a 40,000-foot cloud rushed into the sky, and two observers were knocked down at a point 10,000 yards away. And President Truman solemnly warned:

"It was to spare the Japanese people from utter destruction that the ultimatum of July 26 was issued at Postdam. Their leaders promptly rejected that ultimatum. If they do not now accept our terms, they may expect a rain of ruin from the air the like of which has never been seen on this earth."

MOST CLOSELY GUARDED SECRET

The President referred to the joint statement issued by the heads of the American, British and Chinese Governments, in which terms of surrender were outlined to the Japanese and warning given that rejection would mean complete destruction of Japan's power to make war.

What is this terrible new weapon, which the War Department also calls the "Cosmic Bomb"? It is the harnessing of the energy of the atom, which is the basic power of the universe. As President Truman said, "The force from

The mushroom cloud at the time of the explosion, 1,640 feet above Hiroshima, Japan, on August 6, 1945.

which the sun draws its power has been loosed against those who brought war to the Far East." "Atomic fission"—in other words, the scientists' long-held dream of splitting the atom—is the secret of the atomic bomb. Uranium, a rare, heavy metallic element, which is radioactive and akin to radium, is the source essential to its production. Secretary of War Henry L. Stimson, in a statement closely following that of the President, promised that "steps have been taken, and continue to be taken, to assure us of adequate supplies of this mineral."

The imagination-sweeping experiment in harnessing the power of the atom has been the most closely guarded secret of the war. America to date has spent nearly $2,000,000,000 in advancing its research. Since 1939, American, British and Canadian scientists have worked on it. The experiments have been conducted in the United States, both for reasons of achieving concentrated efficiency and for security; the consequences of having the material fall into the hands of the enemy, in case Great Britain should have been successfully invaded, were too awful for the Allies to risk.

All along, it has been a race with the enemy. Ironically enough, Germany started the experiments, but we finished them. Germany made the mistake of expelling, because she was a "non-Aryan," a woman scientist who held one of the keys

to the mystery, and she made her knowledge available to those who brought it to the United States. Germany never quite mastered the riddle, and the United States, Secretary Stimson declared, is "convinced that Japan will not be in a position to use an atomic bomb in this war."

A SOBERING AWARENESS OF POWER

Not the slightest spirit of braggadocio is discernable either in the wording of the official announcements or in the mien of the officials who gave out the news. There was an element of elation in the realization that we had perfected this devastating weapon for employment against an enemy who started the war and has told us she would rather be destroyed than surrender, but it was grim elation. There was sobering awareness of the tremendous responsibility involved.

Secretary Stimson said that this new weapon "should prove a tremendous aid in the shortening of the war against Japan," and there were other responsible officials who privately thought that this was an extreme understatement, and that Japan might find herself unable to stay in the war under the coming rain of atom bombs.

The first news came from President Truman's office. Newsmen were summoned and the historic statement from the Chief Executive, who still is on

the high seas, was given to them.

"That bomb," Mr. Truman said, "had more power than 20,000 tons of TNT. It had more than 2,000 times the blast power of the British 'Grand Slam,' which is the largest bomb (22,000 pounds) ever yet used in the history of warfare."

EXPLOSIVE CHARGE IS SMALL

No details were given on the plane that carried the bomb. Nor was it stated whether the bomb was large or small. The President, however, said the explosive charge was "exceedingly small." It is known that tremendous force is packed into tiny quantities of the element that constitutes these bombs. Scientists, looking to the peacetime uses of atomic power, envisage submarines, ocean liners and

planes traveling around the world on a few pounds of the element. Yet, for various reasons, the bomb used against Japan could have been extremely large.

Hiroshima, first city on earth to be the target of the "Cosmic Bomb," is a city of 318,000, which is—or was—a major quartermaster depot and port of embarkation for the Japanese. In addition to large military supply depots, it manufactured ordnance, mainly large guns and tanks, and machine tools and aircraft-ordnance parts.

President Truman grimly told the Japanese that "the end is not yet."

"In their present form these bombs are now in production," he said, "and even more powerful forms are in development."

He sketched the story of how the late President Roosevelt and Prime Minis-

ter Churchill agreed that it was wise to concentrate research in America, and how great, secret cities sprang up in this country, where, at one time, 125,000 men and women labored to harness the atom. Even today more than 65,000 workers are employed.

"What has been done," he said, "is the greatest achievement of organized science in history.

"We are now prepared to obliterate more rapidly and completely every productive enterprise the Japanese have above ground in any city. We shall destroy their docks, their factories and their communications. Let there be no mistake; we shall completely destroy Japan's power to make war." ◆

AUGUST 10, 1945

TRUMAN WARNS JAPAN: QUIT OR BE DESTROYED

SECOND BIG AERIAL BLOW

Japanese Port of Nagasaki Is Target In Devastating New Midday Assault

By W. H. LAWRENCE
By Wireless to The New York Times.

GUAM, Aug. 9—Gen. Carl A. Spaatz announced today that a second atomic bomb had been dropped, this time on the city of Nagasaki, and that crew members reported "good results."

The second use of the new and terrifying secret weapon which wiped out more than 60 per cent of the city of Hiroshima and, according to the Japanese radio, killed nearly every resident of that town, occurred at noon today, Japanese time. The target today was an important industrial and shipping area with a population of about 253,000.

The great bomb, which harnesses the power of the universe to destroy the enemy by concussion, blast and fire, was dropped on the second enemy city about seven hours after the Japanese had received a political "roundhouse punch" in the form of a declaration of war by the Soviet Union.

VITAL TRANSSHIPMENT POINT

GUAM, Aug, 9 (AP)—Nagasaki is vitally important as a port for transshipment of military supplies and the embarkation of troops in support of Japan's operations in China, Formosa, Southeast Asia and the Southwest Pacific. It was highly important as a major shipbuilding and repair center for both naval and merchantmen.

The city also included industrial suburbs of Inase and Akinoura on the western side of the harbor, and Urakami. The combined area is nearly double Hiroshima's.

Nagasaki, although only two-thirds as large as Hiroshima in population, is considered more important industrially. With a population now estimated at 253,000, its twelve square miles are jam-packed with the eave-to-eave buildings that won it the name of "sea of roofs."

General Spaatz' communiqué reporting the bombing did not say whether one or more than one "mighty atom" was dropped.

HIROSHIMA A 'CITY OF DEAD'

The Tokyo radio yesterday described Hiroshima as a city of ruins and dead "too numerous to be counted," and put forth the claim that the use of the atomic bomb was a violation of international law.

The broadcast, made in French and directed to Europe, came several hours after Tokyo had directed a report to the Western Hemisphere for consumption in America asserting that "practically all living things, human and animal, were literally seared to death" Monday, when the single bomb was dropped on the southern Honshu city.

The two broadcasts, recorded by the Federal Communications Commission, stressed the terrible effect of the bomb on life and property.

European listeners were told that "as a consequence of the use of the new bomb against the town of Hiroshima on Aug. 6, most of the town has been completely destroyed and there are numerous dead and wounded among the population."

[The United States Strategic Air Forces reported yesterday that 60 per cent of the city had been destroyed.]

"The destructive power of the bombs is indescribable," the broadcast continued, "and the cruel sight resulting from the attack is so impressive that one cannot distinguish between men and women killed by the fire. The corpses are too numerous to be counted.

"The destructive power of this new bomb spreads over a large area. People who were outdoors at the time of the explosion were burned alive by high temperature while those who were indoors were crushed by falling buildings."

Authorities still were "unable to obtain a definite check-up on the extent of the casualties" and "authorities were having their hands full in giving every available relief possible under the circumstances," the broadcast continued.

In the destruction of property even emergency medical facilities were burned out, Tokyo said, and relief squads were rushed into the area from all surrounding districts.

The Tokyo radio also reported that the Asahi Shimbun had made "a strong editorial appeal" to the people of Japan to remain calm in facing the use of the new type bomb and renew pledges to continue to fight.

[A special meeting of the Japanese Cabinet was called at the residence of Premier Kantaro Suzuki to hear a preliminary report on the damage, The United Press said.] ◆

AUGUST 15, 1945

PRESIDENT ANNOUNCING SURRENDER OF JAPAN

YIELDING UNQUALIFIED, TRUMAN SAYS MAC ARTHUR TO RECEIVE SURRENDER

By ARTHUR KROCK
Special to The New York Times.

WASHINGTON, Aug. 14—Japan today unconditionally surrendered the hemispheric empire taken by force and held almost intact for more than two years against the rising power of the United States and its Allies in the Pacific war.

The bloody dream of the Japanese military caste vanished in the text of a note to the Four Powers accepting the terms of the Potsdam Declaration of July 26, 1945, which amplified the Cairo Declaration of 1943.

Like the previous items in the surrender correspondence, today's Japanese document was forwarded through the Swiss Foreign Office at Berne and the Swiss Legation in Washington. The note of total capitulation was delivered to the State Department by the Legation Charge d'Affaires at 6:10 P.M., after the third and most anxious day of waiting on Tokyo, the anxiety intensified by several premature or false reports of the finale of World War II.

ORDERS GIVEN TO THE JAPANESE

The Department responded with a note to Tokyo through the same channel, ordering the immediate end of hostilities by the Japanese, requiring that the Supreme Allied Commander—who, the President announced, will be Gen. Douglas MacArthur—be notified of the date and hour of the order, and instructing that emissaries of Japan be sent to him at once—at the time and place selected by him—with full information of the disposition of the Japanese forces and commanders."

President Truman summoned a special press conference in the Executive offices at 7 P.M. He handed to the reporters three texts.

The first—the only one he read aloud—was that he had received the Japanese note and deemed it full acceptance of the Potsdam Declaration, containing no qualification whatsoever; that arrangements for the formal signing of the peace would be made for the "earliest possible moment"; that the Japanese surrender would be made to General MacArthur in his capacity as Supreme Allied Commander in Chief; that Allied military commanders had been instructed to cease hostilities, but that the formal proclamation of V-J Day must await the formal signing.

The text ended with the Japanese note, in which the Four Powers (the United States, Great Britain, China and Russia) were officially informed that the Emperor of Japan had issued an imperial rescript of surrender, was prepared to guarantee the necessary signatures to the terms as prescribed by the Allies, and had instructed all his commanders to cease active operations, to surrender all arms and to disband all forces under their control and within their reach.

PRESIDENT ADDRESSES CROWD

After the press conference, while usually bored Washington launched upon a noisy victory demonstration, the President with Mrs. Truman walked out to the fountain in the White House grounds that face on Pennsylvania Avenue and made the V sign to the shouting crowds.

But this did not satisfy the growing assemblage, or probably the President either, for, in response to clamor, he came back and made a speech from the north portico, in which he said that the present emergency was as great as that of Pearl Harbor Day and must and would be met in the same spirit. Later in the evening he appeared to the crowds and spoke again.

He then returned to the executive mansion to begin work at once on problems of peace, including domestic ones affecting reconversion, unemployment, wage-and-hour scales and industrial cut-backs, which are more complex and difficult than any he has faced and call for plans and measures that were necessarily held in abeyance by the exacting fact of war.

But certain immediate steps to deal with these problems and restore peacetime conditions were taken or announced as follows:

1. The War Manpower Commission abolished all controls, effective immediately, creating a free labor market for the first time in three years. The commission also set up a plan to help displaced workers and veterans find jobs.

2. The Navy canceled nearly $6,000,000,000 of prime contracts.

The Japanese offer to surrender, confirmed by the note received through Switzerland today, came in the week after the United States Air Forces obliterated Hiroshima with the first atomic bomb in history and the Union of Soviet Socialist Republics declared war on Japan. At the time the document was received in Washington Russian armies were pushing back the Japanese armies in Asia and on Sakhalin Island, and the Army and Navy of the United States with their air forces—aided by the British—were relentlessly bombarding the home islands.

When the President made his announcements tonight it was three years and 250 days after the bombing of Pearl Harbor, which put the United States ❯

President Harry S. Truman announces the surrender of Japan to the White House Press Corps, August 15, 1945.

at war with Japan. This was followed immediately by the declarations of war on this country by Germany and Italy, the other Axis partners, which engaged the United States in the global conflict that now, in its military phases, is wholly won.

If the note had not come today the President was ready, though reluctant, to give the order that would have spread throughout Japan the hideous death and destruction that are the toll of the atomic bomb.

These are a few highlights in the violent chapter of unprecedented war that ended today with the receipt of the note from Tokyo. It is not strange that, remembering all these things, the President and high officials were under a strain as acute as any mother, father or wife of a man in the Pacific combat could have been while waiting for the words that would bring the chapter to a present close.

The alternative for the Japanese would, of course, have been national suicide. But there are many in Washington, students of this strange race or baffled by the ways of the Orient, who have predicted that such would be the decision of the Japanese military leaders to which the people would submit. The Japanese, they contended, would commit mass suicide before they would yield their god, the Emperor, to an alien enemy as his overlord.

But now this god, in the person of an ordinary human being, representative of other human beings who were vanquished with him, is to take his orders from a mortal man who, above all others, symbolizes the spirit of the alien enemy that was foremost in crushing the myth of divinity and shattering the imperial dream. And the Emperor, with his Ministers and commanders, has been obliged to accept the condition that disproves the fanatical concept used by the militarists of Japan to produce unquestioned obedience to orders issued in the Emperor's name, however much or little he may have had to do with them. ◆

AUGUST 19, 1945

Editorial
EIGHTEEN FATEFUL DAYS

The first eighteen days of August, 1945, can be set down as the most nerve-racking in modern history. Whether they are also the most auspicious depends on what we do with their results. So fast have events moved that the situation of three weeks ago seems like ancient history. First, on Aug. 2, we had the Potsdam communiqué, with its hopeful promise of the restoration of democracy and civil liberties in Europe and its practical economic and political proposals, not all of which could be accepted without reservations.

Second, on Aug. 6, we had the announcement of the first atomic bomb. One could accept this horrible weapon because it would shorten a bloody war and because the knowledge on which it was based might some day ease the burdens of all humanity. But the indiscriminate slaughter which it caused did not lie easily on American consciences, and the problem of its future control was, and is, appalling.

Third, on Aug. 8, Russia made her long-expected declaration of war and immediately moved into Manchuria. Her swift gains confirmed other evidences of Japanese weakness and the surrender offer of Aug. 10 was not a surprise. The surprise—and the nervous strain—lay in the arrogance, the defiant propaganda and the unaccountable delays which characterized the last days and hours of the Japanese Empire.

The jubilant and in some cities riotous celebrations of the coming of peace will cause Tuesday and Wednesday of last week to be long remembered. Less dramatic were the quiet people, probably all over the country, who came out to their front porches to breathe the air of peace again, or offered up prayers in their homes or in their churches, or felt in their hearts, as so many millions of wives and parents must have done, a thankfulness too deep for words. Not since the ending of the war of 1861–65 has this nation been through such a moving experience.

Yet there was evident, both in the noisy celebrations and in the quietness that followed. an element of apprehension as to the future. The goal toward which free humanity had been struggling for so long, at such terrible cost, had at last been attained, but with it there came a realization of the nature of victory in war. Victory is a negative thing at best. It merely ends the dangers and horrors of war. It does not give back the lives that were lost, or restore those that were broken, or reestablish the conditions that existed before war broke out. It does not, in itself, establish a lasting peace.

The morning after victory must, therefore, be sober indeed. New problems rise. In our own country we face immediately the tremendous task of turning our production from war to peace. No war worker could wish to keep his job at the expense of other people's lives, yet he cannot help concern as to his personal future. Most soldiers, sailors and marines want their discharges at the earliest possible moment, but now they must ask themselves what are their opportunities in civilian life.

In the countries which have borne the brunt of battle, from Russia, France and the Balkans to China, the immediate outlook is worse. Security and prosperity are plants that grow very slowly amid the ruins. Liberty is sweet, but it is not food, clothing, fuel and shelter. It will in time produce them or all our hopes are vain, but the time is necessary and there are countless millions who will find it hard to wait.

Thus these days of new-born peace are also days of crisis. We have to see that relief goes swiftly to those who need it most, at home and abroad. We have to see that economic and political reconstruction is of such a sort as to perpetuate peace, in the light that glared over Hiroshima and Nagasaki we have to reconsider the obligations assumed under the United Nations Charter, and ask ourselves whether we have gone far enough in the new machinery for the amicable settlement of international disputes. Two atomic explosions have been sufficient to make peace more than a desirable objective. It is now a necessity to the survival of civilization.

Much of the burden of the new tasks imposed on humanity by these fateful days of August, 1945, rest upon the United States. We have become the most powerful nation in the world. Five years ago honest, if mistaken, Americans could talk of a policy of isolation. Now we are the center and focus of a new fear and a new hope. And a center cannot be isolated. ◆

SEPTEMBER 1, 1945

Japanese Bitter In Defeat; Angered By Raids on Tokyo

By FRANK L. KLUCKHOHN
By Wireless to The New York Times.

TOKYO, Aug. 31—This nation in defeat is bitter. Everyone is "so sorry." The Japanese did not lose the war. That nasty contraption, the atomic bomb, did the job. They want to know why we ripped Tokyo to pieces. They even want to take us on sightseeing trips to show us how unsportsmanlike we are.

If you ask why they attacked Pearl Harbor on Dec. 7, 1941, they are embarrassed. If you answer, "Manila is worse," to their queries as to why Tokyo is so severely mauled you have attacked Oriental "face."

I found that out after being one of the first correspondents into Yokohoma and after riding in a packed train into Tokyo.

Riding from Atsugi Airdrome into Yokohama, we saw peasants turn their backs to ignore us. We saw a soldier chase three women who wanted to look at us

and force them to hide. We saw the destruction that had been visited on Yokohama, one of Japan's major ports and chief industrial centers, and saw people living in corrugated tin huts as a substitute for homes. We watched curiosity almost overcome discipline as children grinned at us before dodging into doorways.

We saw a badly beaten people.

With Gordon Walker of the American Broadcasting Company I made the trip into the capital of a defeated empire on an ordinary commuter train. It was a trip not without strain, but as it turned out nothing unfortunate happened.

All during the drive into Yokohama from Atsugi Airdrome we were struck by the unfriendly, even hostile, attitude of the populace. As we entered Yokohama, we again received stony stares that made it evident that this nation is suffering deeply under the lash of defeat.

At the railway station we encountered two nuns—one English and one French—who had just arrived together from the capital. They told us they did not know whether it was safe for us to travel in a United States uniform there. But when we insisted they helped us buy rail tickets.

We went out on to a wooden platform like that at Rye, N.Y., and boarded an all-third-class train. Aboard our car

were mostly Japanese soldiers being dropped by the army, in full or part uniform, and a few women wearing trousers and shirts, which have been the wartime dress of the women, who used to wear kimonos.

The hostility was thick. It gave a peculiar feeling to be among people we had fought so long. As the train halted at each of the five or six stations on the fifty-minute trip, we both became more and more tense. The coach became as crowded as a New York subway coach at a rush hour.

We tried to break the tension by asking what time the train would arrive. We obtained curt answers. The first soldier we approached even refused to speak to us.

FACTORY AREA LEVELED

We gazed through the window at the completely destroyed factory area between the port and the capital. Once one of the most densely populated areas of the world, it is now a conglomerate of corrugated tin huts where people live in worse conditions than the Oakies in California at the depth of the depression in the Nineteen Thirties. Then we looked back at hostile eyes. Mr. Walker and I tried to talk with each other but this seemed to annoy the Japanese so we gave it up.

Finally we stepped out at an undestroyed station and walked past a thousand glaring soldiers by a subway onto the street. We tried to hail several cabs but were ignored. Finally we walked into a bank, where we asked if anyone spoke English. We received more glares and were ignored. We walked about a block and then saw a man just entering a small car with a chauffeur. We requested, with as much an air of authority as we could muster, that he drive us to the Imperial Hotel. He acceded but refused to talk with us.

The "cold treatment" thereafter alternated during the long day with complaints as to the way our bombers had acted.

Few we met failed to mention the complete destruction of the Yokohama-Tokyo industrial area by superfortresses. They wanted to know why we had bombed Tokyo and how we reconciled that with "civilization."

They said that only Emperor Hirohito's order had made them stop fighting and that if this had not been issued they could have resisted an invasion.

There were serious complaints over the fact that United States planes were still flying over the Imperial Palace—a practice characterized as a "direct insult" by those we met. We saw in the five-minute drive to the Imperial Hotel ❯

Scorched ruins of Tokyo, a result of massive Allied air raid attacks in 1945.

that many of Tokyo's leading buildings were still standing, although we had observed that the factory and residential sections were largely destroyed. At the desk of the hotel we were greeted by an English-speaking Japanese, who said "How do you do, Mr. Kluckhohn?" as if there had never been a war. He pushed out the register, which I signed, and then he asked about Otto D. Tolischus, who was Tokyo correspondent of The New York Times at the outbreak of the war. The nuns in Yokohama had suggested that we ask for the Rev. Patrick Byrne of Washington, and we did so. He came down, shook hands delightedly and took us to his room, where he introduced us to a member of the secret police who had guarded him throughout the war.

Toshiyuki Myamoto, a reporter for the newspaper Asahi, was there and proceeded to try to interview us. He called the Asahi and within a few moments a photographer and a man whom we took to be of the secret police arrived. The unidentified arrival questioned us as, to the United States attitude toward Japan, why we had bombed Tokyo, what we thought of the effect of the bombing. We said it was "not so bad as Manila" as far as complete destruction went. He looked at us with pain and quickly left.

Although the Asahi man insisted that it was dangerous for us to be in the streets, we wandered through the park opposite the hotel. We again got cold glances. ◆

TOKYO AIDES WEEP AS GENERAL SIGNS

By The Associated Press

ABOARD U.S.S. MISSOURI in Tokyo Bay, Sept. 2—The solemn surrender ceremony, on this battleship today, marking the first defeat in Japan's 2,600-year-old semi-legendary history, required only a few minutes as twelve signatures were

---

AMERICANS ENTERING JAPAN SEE ENTIRELY ALIEN LAND
Here Are Some Characteristic Features of the Enemy Homeland

By HENRY C. WOLFE

American occupation forces in Japan are seeing a land and a people very different from what the movies and popular fiction have led them to expect. They probably feel let down. Here is what they are finding:

Country and Climate—All four of Japan's main islands together have an area smaller than the State of California. Nippon (Honshu), is the main island, with almost twice the area of the other three. Much of the land is mountainous. Only one-eighth is arable. Earthquakes are commonplace. The islands have a temperate climate, with rather extreme variations. Kyushu and Shikoku have mild winters. On the east coast of Honshu the winters are apt to be mild, but on its west coast there is deep snow and bitter cold. Hokkaido, the northern island, has a cold and inhospitable winter climate. On the whole, Japan has short, hot, humid summers and long, cold, clear winters.

Population—Japan's 75,000,000 people are largely concentrated in the coastal areas, the Tokyo-Yokohama region, the Kobe-Osaka-Kyoto district, Nagoya and Nagasaki. About half of the Mikado's subjects live in villages or on individual farms. There are, however, large tracts, especially in western Honshu and in Hokkaido, where there are no people at all, for the terrain is mountainous or the winters extremely cold.

Natural resources—One of the principal reasons for Japan's drive to the South Seas was to obtain raw materials in which she was deficient. There are some natural resources in Nippon— coal, petroleum, sulphur, salt, iron, copper, lead, zinc, chromite, white arsenic, gold and silver. A few years ago Japan was almost self-sufficient in copper. With the rise of war industries, however, the exports required to pay for raw materials imports and the heavy drain of the long conflict in China made copper importation essential. In terms of yen value, gold was the second most valuable metal produced in Japan before the war. Japan is fairly well situated so far as coal is concerned, but she must import coking coal and anthracite.

RULERS OF JAPAN

Government—The Japanese Government has been representative only in theory. Actually it is an oligarchy. At the head is the Emperor, at least in name. Below him is the Imperial Diet, consisting of the House of Representatives and the House of Peers. But somewhere between the Emperor and the Diet come the Imperial Household Ministry, the Privy Council, the Genro (Elder Statesmen), the Prime Minister and the army and navy chiefs. This has made the real source of Japan's governing power a kind of political shell game for foreigners.

Autocrats—Japan's two greatest business houses are the Mitsui and the Mitsubishi interests. Their commercial ramifications were worldwide and brought vast wealth and power to their concerns. The house of Mitsui, for example, owns or controls banks, department stores, shipping, factories, international trading offices, newspapers and pulp paper companies. Because the little people had virtually no purchasing power in the Western sense, the Mitsuis and the Mitsubishis were dependent for profits on international trade.

LANGUAGE DIFFICULTIES

Language—Spoken Japanese will not prove an insuperable difficulty, but it is to be doubted that many of our men will get far with the written language. Japanese words are not hard to pronounce. Moreover, they are rather easy to understand, with their generous use of vowels. But the written language, a language of ideographs, is extremely difficult. In the great coastal cities, especially the Tokyo-Yokohama area, Osaka and Kobe, many Japanese speak, or at any rate read, some English. English is the most widely understood foreign language in Japan; it is the great commercial speech of the Far East. Nearly all Japanese engaged in international trade understand it.

Amusement—Our service men in Japan will have to bring their own amusements with them. Their sight-seeing will, of course, include Mount Fuji and the Shinto shrines of Ise. The Japanese theatre—the serious No plays and the Kabuki farces—will be unintelligible to all but

affixed to the articles.

Surrounded by the might of the United States Navy and Army, and under the eyes of the American and British commanders they so ruthlessly defeated in the Philippines and Malaya, the Japanese representatives quietly made the marks on paper that ended the bloody Pacific conflict.

The Japanese delegation came aboard at 8:55 A.M., 7:55 P.M. Saturday, E.W.T., as scheduled. They reached the Missouri in personnel speed boats flying the American flag.

Foreign Minister Mamoru Shigemitsu led the delegation. He climbed stiffly up the ladder and limped forward on his right leg, which is artificial. He was wounded by a bomb tossed by a Korean terrorist in Shanghai many years ago.

On behalf of Emperor Hirohito, Mr. Shigemitsu signed first for Japan. He doffed his top hat, tinkered with the pen and then firmly affixed his signature to the surrender document, a paper about twelve by eighteen inches. Mr. Shigemitsu carefully signed the American copy first, then affixed his name to a duplicate copy to be retained by Japan.

Following him, Gen. Yoshijiro Umezu, chief of the Imperial General Staff sat down resolutely and scrawled his name on the documents as if in a tremendous hurry. A Japanese colonel present was seen to wipe tears from his eyes as the general signed. All the Japanese looked tense and weary. Mr. Shigemitsu looked on anxiously as General Umezu signed.

Gen. Douglas MacArthur was next to sign, as Supreme Commander for the Allies, on behalf of all the victorious Allied Powers. General MacArthur immediately called for Lieut. Gen. Jonathan M. Wainwright of Bataan and Coregidor and Lieut. Gen. Arthur E. Percival of Singapore to step forward. These two defeated Allied commanders, now savoring their hour of triumph, stepped up, and General Wainwright helped General MacArthur to take his seat.

General MacArthur signed the documents with five pens. The first he handed immediately to General Wainwright, the second to General Percival. The third was an ordinary shipboard Navy issue pen.

General MacArthur then produced a fourth pen, presumably to be sent to President Truman. Then he completed his signatures with still a fifth, possibly a trophy to be retained by himself.

Generals Wainright and Percival, both obviously happy, saluted snappily. They were followed by serene-faced Admiral Chester W. Nimitz, who signed on behalf of the United States. Next came China's representative.

General MacArthur acted as a brisk master of ceremonies. He made a brief introductory statement before the Japanese signed, then called upon each nation's signer in turn to step forward. The United Kingdom's signature was followed by that of the Soviet Union.

The Russian staff officer signed quickly, scooting his chair into a more comfortable position even as he was signing. General MacArthur smiled approvingly as the Russian rose and saluted. Quickly in turn, Australian, Canadian, French, Netherlands and New Zealand representatives signed in that order. The Australian, Gen. Sir Thomas Blamey, happened to sign the Japanese copy first, with an expression that denoted that it did not make any difference.

Finally, after New Zealand's signature, less than twenty minutes from the start of the ceremony, General Mac Arthur formally and in a firm voice declared the proceedings closed.

The Japanese prepared to depart immediately, their bitter chore accomplished.

The historic signing took place on a long table on the gallery deck. All Allied representatives were sober-faced, but obviously glad it was over. Soldiers, sailors and marines, some of whom had fought their way across the Pacific, hardly could hide a trace of exuberance on their serious faces. ◆

---

the few who may be interested in Japanese culture for its own sake. Dance halls and cabarets were closed before Pearl Harbor, when the empire began to feel the heavy economic and social pressures of the long-drawn-out "China incident."

EATING AND SPORTS

Food—Tokyo had plenty of small restaurants and tea rooms before the war. Today, quite aside from air raid damage, the food situation is undoubtedly very bad. Meat-eating Americans will probably not enthuse over Japanese cooking with its emphasis on rice and fish. But the newcomers may enjoy the experience of eating sukiyaki or tempura, with a glass of rice liquor called saki.

Sports—Baseball is the favorite sport of Japan, so much so that before the war American ball players were heroes of the Japanese fans. This is a far from insignificant fact in our relations with the Japanese. It helps explain the seemingly inexplicable spectacle of a banzai charge in which Nippon's soldiers were shot down screaming "To hell with Babe Ruth!" Now that the war is over, baseball may actually prove a psychological factor with which to win Japanese youth over to our way of thinking. ◆

Japanese Minister of Foreign Affairs, Mamoru Shigemitsu signing the surrender of Japan aboard the USS *Missouri* in Tokyo Bay on September 2, 1945. General Douglas MacArthur is at the microphone.

SEPTEMBER 2, 1945

Text of the Address by Truman Proclaiming V-J Day

The complete text of President Truman's V-J Day speech, as recorded and transcribed in the recording room of The New York Times follows:

My Fellow Americans, Supreme Allied Commander General MacArthur and Allied representatives on the Battleship Missouri in Tokyo Bay:

The thoughts and hopes of all America—indeed of all the civilized world—are centered tonight on the battleship Missouri. There on that small piece of American soil anchored in Tokyo harbor the Japanese have just officially laid down their arms. They have signed terms of unconditional surrender.

Four years ago the thoughts and fears of the whole civilized world were centered on another piece of American soil—Pearl Harbor. The mighty threat to civilization which began there is now laid at rest. It was a long road to Tokyo—and a bloody one.

We shall not forget Pearl Harbor.

The Japanese militarists will not forget the U.S.S. Missouri.

The evil done by the Japanese war lords can never be repaired or forgotten. But their power to destroy and kill has been taken from them. Their armies and what is left of their Navy are now impotent.

To all of us there comes first a sense of gratitude to Almighty God Who sustained us and our Allies in the dark days of grave danger, Who made us to grow from weakness into the strongest fighting force in history, and Who has now seen us overcome the forces of tyranny that sought to destroy His civilization

God grant that in our pride of this hour we may not forget the hard tasks that are still before us; that we may approach these with the same courage, zeal and patience with which we faced the trials and problems of the past four years.

Our first thoughts, of course—thoughts of gratefulness and deep obligation—go out to those of our loved ones who have been killed or maimed in this terrible war. On land and sea and in the air American men and women have given their lives so that this day of ultimate victory might come and assure the survival of a civilized world. No victory can make good their loss.

We think of those whom death in this war has hurt, taking from them fathers, husbands, sons, brothers and sisters whom they loved. No victory can bring back the faces they long to see.

Only the knowledge that the victory, which these sacrifices have made possible, will be wisely used, can give them any comfort. It is our responsibility—ours, the living—to see to it that this victory shall be a monument worthy of the dead who died to win it.

We think of all the millions of men and women in our armed forces and merchant marine all over the world who, after years of sacrifice and hardship and peril, have been spared by Providence from harm.

We think of all the men and women and children who during these years have carried on at home, in lonesomeness and anxiety and fear.

Our thoughts go out to the millions of American workers and business men, to our farmers and miners—to all those who have built up this country's fighting strength and who have shipped to our Allies the means to resist and overcome the enemy.

Our thoughts go out to our civil servants and to the thousands of Americans who, at personal sacrifice, have come to serve in our Government during these trying years; to the members of the Selective Service Boards and ration boards; to the civilian defense and Red Cross workers; to the men and women in the USO and in the entertainment world—to all those who have helped in this cooperative struggle to preserve liberty and decency in the world.

We think of our departed gallant leader, Franklin D. Roosevelt, defender of democracy, architect of world peace and cooperation.

And our thoughts go out to our gallant Allies in this war; to those who resisted the invaders; to those who were not strong enough to hold out but who nevertheless kept the fires of resistance alive within the souls of their people; to those who stood up against great odds and held the line until the United Nations together were able to supply the arms and the men with which to overcome the forces of evil.

This is a victory of more than arms alone. This is a victory of liberty over tyranny.

From our war plants rolled the tanks and planes which blasted their way to the heart of our enemies; from our shipyards sprang the ships which bridged all the oceans of the world for our weapons and supplies; from our farms came the food and fiber for our armies and navies and for all our allies in all the corners of the earth; from our mines and factories came the raw materials and the finished products which gave us the equipment to overcome our enemies.

But back of it all were the will and spirit and determination of a free people—who know what freedom is, and who know that it is worth whatever price they had to pay to preserve it.

It was the spirit of liberty which gave us our armed strength and which made our men invincible in battle. We now know that that spirit of liberty, the freedom of the individual and the personal dignity of man are the strongest and toughest and most enduring forces in all the world.

And so on V-J Day, we take renewed faith and pride in our own way of life. We have had our day of rejoicing over this victory. We have had our day of prayer and devotion. Now let us set aside V-J Day as one of renewed consecration to the principles which have made us the strongest nation on earth and which, in this war, we have striven so mightily to preserve.

Those principles provide the faith, the hope and the opportunity which helped men to improve themselves and their lot. Liberty does not make all men perfect nor all society secure. But it has provided more solid progress and happiness and decency for more people than any other philosophy of government in history. And this day has shown again that it provides the greatest strength and the greatest power which man has ever reached.

We know that under it we can meet the hard problems of peace which have come upon us. A free people with free Allies, who can develop an atomic bomb, can use the same skill and energy and determination to overcome all the difficulties ahead.

Victory always has its burdens and its responsibilities as well as its rejoicing.

But we face the future and all its dangers with great confidence and great hope. America can build for itself a future of employment and security. Together with the United Nations it can build a world of peace founded on justice and fair dealing and tolerance.

As President of the United States I proclaim Sunday, Sept. 2, 1945, to be V-J Day—the day of the formal surrender of Japan. It is not yet the day for the formal proclamation of the end of the war nor of the cessation of hostilities. But it is a day which we Americans shall always remember as a day of retribution—as we remember that other day, the day of infamy.

From this day we move forward. We move toward a new era of security at home. With the other United Nations we move toward a new and better world of cooperation, of peace and international good-will.

God's help has brought us to this day of victory. With His help we will attain that peace and prosperity for ourselves and all the world in the years ahead. ◇

SEPTEMBER 4, 1945

Attlee, Citing Occupation Rote, Dashes Demobilization Hopes

By HERBERT L. MATTHEWS
By Wireless to The New York Times

LONDON, Sept. 3—The British people heard some plain and courageous speaking tonight from the Prime Minister, Clement R. Attlee who told them in a broadcast the demobilization could not be speedy and that Britain's responsibilities required the maintenance of great forces for some time to come.

It has fallen to the lot of the Labor Government to tell the people some unpleasant truths and to take unpopular measures, like further cuts in clothing and food rations just as everyone expected relief from the end of war. Now comes the bad news about demobilization.

Britain's position as a world power, her duties in the future maintenance of world peace and her policy of fostering popular democratic governments in Europe all made demands of manpower that could not be shirked, Mr. Attlee declared. He had to tell this to the British people on the sixth anniversary of the day when the sirens first sounded in London, and his plea was for renewed patience.

The lesson that peace was indivisible, which should have been learned in 1918, must be learned today, he said, and there must be established "a world order in which war shall ever be banished."

NO TIME FOR RELAXATION

The development of the atomic bomb had made this "vital for the future of civilization," Mr. Attlee continued.

"This is no time for relaxation, tempting as this is after years of strain," he added.

So he went on to tell them of the responsibilities that Great Britain must shoulder and he recalled that he had never encouraged them to think that the war's end would mean the immediate release of all the men and women in the armed forces.

Announcing that men between the ages of 18 and 30 would continue to be called up to meet the continuing needs of the services, he explained that large occupation forces would be required in Germany, southeastern Europe, the Mediterranean and Middle East where they would have to carry out "the difficult and perhaps thankless task" of helping to establish "governments resting on popular consent."

"Those of you who remember the disturbed period at the end of the last war," Mr. Attlee said later, "will remember that one of the prime difficulties of the situation was the inability of the powers which had won the war to provide the necessary forces for the prevention of violent action by sectional interests pending completion of negotiations for world peace."

STRESSES ROLE IN JAPAN

Mr. Attlee showed the extent to which his Government is continuing traditional British foreign policy by discussing "the establishment of order in Burma" and the necessity for using large forces to maintain empire life lines. Aside from that, he called attention to the obvious need of men to help in the occupation of Japan.

The sum total of all this, he indicated, was that Britain, which mobilized literally all her manpower and which was desperately short of it for industrial labor, must still keep large forces under arms and away from home. ◇

SEPTEMBER 4, 1945

INDUSTRY SPEEDS RECONVERSION JOB
Reports Throughout Country Found Encouraging as the Plants Shift Rapidly

By RUSSELL PORTER

Highly encouraging reports on the progress of reconversion have been received over the weekend from scattered industrial centers throughout the country by the Committee for Economic Development, an organization of business and industrial leaders who have been formulating plans during the last three years to stimulate postwar production and employment.

The reports indicate that industry is reconverting its plants from war to peace production much more quickly and easily, and that reconversion unemployment is much smaller than anticipated. Many industries have no problem at all, simply making the same goods in peace they did in war, and others require only a few weeks to reconvert.

Workers laid off by war plants are being absorbed rapidly in the plants that have already reconverted, in companies making new products developed by wartime research, or in other industries, considered unessential during the war, that have hitherto been short of labor. Agriculture, distribution, construction, transportation and communications, and services of all kinds that were curtailed or abandoned during the war are also offering many job opportunities.

Some ex-war workers are opening small business ventures for themselves.

The situation is also being eased by the fact that many women and other workers, including the overage and the underage, who were employed in the war plants but normally would not have been considered part of the industrial labor force, are quitting for their homes, farms, schools or jobs outside industry.

So far war veterans have been absorbed by business and industry, in accordance with their veterans' and seniority rights, and indications are that by the time they are discharged in large numbers reconversion will have progressed far enough to take care of them without serious difficulty.

The chief bottleneck seems to be delay in getting raw materials in some industries, notably in the textile and hosiery mills. Achievement of full employment in some other industries, including the printing and mechanical trades, has been slowed down by a shortage of skilled labor, and the need of long training periods for apprentices. A "back to normalcy" psychology on the part of some small employers has also been a brake on the movement for an expanding economy. ◇

SEPTEMBER 4, 1945

Soviet Hints Race For Atom Bomb; Pooling of Data For Peace Urged

By The United Press.

MOSCOW, Sept. 3—The magazine New Times assailed today some sections of the American press for allegedly advocating that the United States "secure world ▶

{ mastery by threatening use of the atomic bomb," and warned that other nations would soon invent weapons equally potent.

The article, the first detailed analysis of the atomic bomb's significance to appear thus far in the Soviet press, said that the missile's development made lasting peace and security imperative. It urged international pooling of atomic knowledge as "the most effective method of mutual understanding of all freedom-loving nations."

Characterizing the bomb as "one of the greatest inventions of modern science, fraught with enormous consequences in all fields of human life," the article, by M. Rubinstein, said:

"At the same time, it is clear to all right-thinking men that the discovery does not solve any political problems internationally or inside individual countries. Those who cherish illusions in this respect will suffer inevitable disappointment."

The article bitterly attacked the "Hearst-Patterson-McCormick press" for its alleged arguments that the United States use the threat of the atomic bomb to enforce its will in international affairs, and said:

"These flagrant imperialists forget history's lessons. They ignore the collapse of Hitlerite plans for world hegemony, which were based on intended utilization of temporary superiority in technical development."

The article said that "many other countries have scientists who studied the problem of splitting the atom and who will work with redoubled energy to invent weapons as good or better." It approved suggestions to vest the control of atomic energy in an international body, "since the fundamental principles are well known and henceforth it is simply a question of time before any country will be able to produce atomic bombs."

In addition to the gravest danger threatening humanity, "should aggressors seize control of this terrible weapon" Mr. Rubinstein said that unlimited economic abuses were possible by exploitation of atomic energy productively under conditions of "capitalist monopoly."

He said that the latter would cause "monstrous mass unemployment and permanent elimination of millions of miners and other industrial workers and intensification of monopoly rule." ◊

SEPTEMBER 5, 1945

DE GAULLE INSISTS ON 4TH REPUBLIC

By G. H. ARCHAMBAULT
By Wireless to The New York Times.

PARIS, Sept. 4—Gen. Charles de Gaulle, President of the Provisional Government, indicated tonight in a broadcast marking the seventy-fifth anniversary of the proclamation of the Third Republic, that he stood by the referendum that will accompany the elections next October.

In his address he emphasized the democratic principles—"liberty, justice and sovereignty of the people, without which there can be no lasting force, no solidity and no light."

He pointed out, however, that the Third Republic had inherent defects that eventually brought about "conditions of permanent political crisis" resulting in twenty different Prime Ministers in the twenty-one-year period between the two world wars.

To avoid a recurrence of such conditions, General de Gaulle explained, he wished the nation itself to decide the character of the Fourth Republic.

"Through a capital innovation known as the referendum the French people, at the same time as they will elect their representatives, will indicate the nature of the institutions they have chosen for themselves. ... I am convinced that the immense majority will receive these proposals with favor. ... Frenchmen and Frenchwomen, you will soon launch the Fourth Republic."

Thus it was revealed that General de Gaulle had not budged tonight from the stand taken yesterday when he refused to meet Leon Jouhaux, secretary general of General Labor Confederation, heading a delegation of Leftist parties desirous of obtaining modifications in the methods of voting to be applied next October.

CABINET POSTPONES MEETING

Leftist newspapers this morning were very critical of General de Gaulle's refusal to receive the delegation, and rumors spread of possible resignations among his Ministers. These rumors increased when it was learned that the regular Cabinet meeting scheduled for today would be postponed "to enable General de Gaulle to prepare his broadcast address."

It was recalled that the President of the Provisional Government had said on several occasions that he was prepared to go should his task be deliberately complicated.

Various Leftist groups met during the day. The Central Council of French Renaissance, consisting of members of the National Resistance Council and of the departmental liberation committees, passed a resolution condemning the Government's election plan as "not conforming with true proportional representation."

The National Committee of the General Labor Confederation protested against what it described as General de Gaulle's "authoritarian" refusal to receive the delegation and recalled the extent of the confederation's participation in the resistance movement.

After Gen. Charles de Gaulle had seen Leon Blum, leader of the Socialist party, for three-quarters of an hour this evening the political storm that raged all day seemed ended. M. Blum was pledged to secrecy regarding the nature of the conversation, but it is understood that his part was that of a peacemaker.

SURPRISES HELD POSSIBLE

General de Gaulle also received Dr. Pierre Maze, secretary general of the Radical party. He received no Communist.

With the national elections scarcely more than six weeks off, more storms of this nature may be expected and surprises are always possible.

Late tonight representatives of the five groups that had asked General de Gaulle to receive a deputation—the League of the Rights of Man, the Radical party, the Communist party, the Socialist party and the General Labor Confederation—met again and decided to send to the President of Provisional Government a memorandum in which they would outline criticism of his election plan, which he declined to discuss in conference with them.

The seventy-fifth anniversary of the proclamation of the Third Republic was marked by a parade of citizens organized by the Leftist parties. The paraders marched round a monument in the Place de la Republique, the base of which was heaped with flowers. ◊

SEPTEMBER 9, 1945

REMAKING OF GERMANY IS PROVING SLOW WORK

By GLADWIN HILL
By Wireless to The New York Times

BERLIN, Sept. 8—While the eyes of the world have been turned during the past month on the war's finale in the East, the great practical experiment in international collaboration growing out of the war, the four-power occupation of Germany has been making laborious but tangible progress. The most significant progress has been made not with the Germans but among the Allies themselves in feeling out a technique of international management. Each day has brought forth new hitches and in advertent frictions in the joint effort, but each day also has brought broadening tolerance and patience to a remarkable degree.

The approaching winter, with its problems of food, fuel and shelter, is the prime concern at present of the occupation authorities and of all Germany. General Eisenhower has announced flatly that it will be "inescapable" to import food from the United States to feed the Germans, since our policy of just retribution to the Germans does not extend to killing them off by starvation or by the gunfire which unquestionably would be necessary if widespread starvation set in. With Germany's main coal fields producing only 15 per cent of normal and most of that earmarked for the Army and public utilities, the fuel problem is not so easily solved and large numbers of Germans are going to suffer from exposure this winter.

PROGRESS REPORT

In less urgent fields of rehabilitation Germany has made marked progress in the last few weeks. Eight thousand miles of railroad now are operating in the British zone and around 6,500 in the American zone. The latter is about 78 per cent of the normal trackage. Traffic amounts to 15 per cent of pre-war. The Rhine, one of Germany's most important transport arteries, is scheduled to he cleared northward from the Ruhr to the coast this month and also upstream for an indefinite distance.

The Military Government reports that German civil administration in the American zone is about one-third re-created. Democratic elections of certain

Bucket brigades of mostly women working to clear rubble in Berlin, September 1945.

officials at the city and county level are planned for this winter.

In Berlin, where the Russians re-opened the schools before we arrived, 225,000 pupils—out of a 3,000,000 population—now are attending classes, 70,000 of them in the American sector.

In the rest of the American zone revival of education is being pursued more slowly on a local basis. Half of the 5,000,000 textbooks, which will be needed when the schools are reopened generally, have been printed.

Americans licensed the first private book publisher, a Heidelberg anti-Nazi who is going to print pocket classics, including Emerson and Poe. One hundred and fifty thousand copies of a new American literary review in Germany are being distributed in the American and British zones.

A number of American movies of the "Young Tom Edison" vintage with German dialogue are now being shown in the American zone.

Displaced persons, initially the Allies' greatest problem, have been reduced by repatriations from 6,000,000 to a "hard core" of 1,748,000. About half those remaining are Poles. Other main groups are Russians, Italians and Hungarians. Most of them are settled in orderly camps managed by UNRRA.

OUSTED NAZIS

Denazification is being pursued. Seventy-four Mayors in the Munich area were ousted recently along with 4,300 city employees, and Bavaria's purge total was due to reach around 100,000 by the end of August. In Franconia 5,363 Nazis have been ousted. In Wiesbaden thirty-eight members of the police department and twenty-six banking and insurance

officials were dismissed. The Bremen Burgomeister was fired for disobeying the Military Government.

The Allies' major punitive effort, the international war criminal trials at Nuremberg of Goering and other members of the Hitler gang and the military leaders who for the first time in history will be called to account for promoting a war, has been put off to mid-October for the stated reason of the difficulty of arranging the court facilities. British trials of the Belsen concentration camp officials are scheduled to start in a few days at Luneberg.

The Allied Control Council, composed of General Eisenhower, Marshal Montgomery, Marshal Zhukoff, General Koenig and their assistants, which meets every ten days, has held its fourth meeting. While the sessions have been milestones in international harmony, they have not yet yielded much in tangible legislation because the council is just emerging from the organizational stage.

JOB FOR THE COUNCIL

The council's primary task is establishment of central German administrations of finance, transport, communications, industry and foreign trade as authorized in the Potsdam agreement. This will be a major step toward restoring Germany to a workable basis of self-support. After that is likely to come the matter of establishing a centralized administration in food and agriculture which was not specified in the Potsdam agreement but which American officials believe was not precluded and is desirable.

More and more American officials ▸

are coming to the view that we have been spending too much time juggling theories when we were confronted by conditions, and that we could use a little more Russian decisiveness. This is valuable because even within American councils there is a lot of bewilderment and disagreement about the practical application of broad directives. Even hard-peace exponents are realizing that many principles originally laid down on paper are in some applications merely unworkable rather than hard—that, to take a simple example, regardless of your desire to decentralize, you cannot run the railroads in a big country on a county basis, and that in carrying too far our basic policy of re-creating Germany from the bottom up by local units we sometimes are hamstringing ourselves as much as the Germans.

THEORY VS. PRACTICE

When the Russians drew attention by installing twelve German subordinate officials in their zonal administrative sections while Americans still were working at local and county levels, a number of American officers opined that we might better be doing the same thing. The Russians are working on the principle that outward forms don't mean so much when you have police power. Thus while the Americans were working out the fine points of a long-range program to provide Germans with non-Nazi movies, the Russians blandly authorized German movie houses to re-open, with the implicit warning for every German exhibitor that if he peddled any nazism he might turn up missing.

What it boils down to is that an authoritarian Government of the Russian sort is more suited to a lot of immediate problems of an occupation than a democratic regime, and in coping with immediate problems of a chaotic Germany Americans have been learning something from the Russians. ◆

SEPTEMBER 12, 1945

CHINA REDS OFFER DIVISION OF POWER

But Firmness of Both Sides at Chungking Parley Causes Hope Of Accord to Wane

By TILLMAN DURDIN
By Wireless to The New York Times.

CHUNGKING, China, Sept. 11—Talks for the settlement of Communist-Kuomintang differences are continuing here between Central Government representatives and the Communist leaders, Mao Tze-Tung, Gen. Chou En-lai and Wang Jo-fei.

Progress is reported to have been limited and there is less optimism over the outcome of the discussions although the spokesmen of both sides still maintain they are hopeful of agreement.

The Communists are said to be still holding out for extensive reforms in the Central Government and the formation of a coalition government of all parties before the Communists yield any degree of control over their armies.

The Communists are reported to be prepared to concede Kuomintang domi-

nation of the Yangtze valley but want predominance in the governments of the provinces in which their influence is greatest, such as Shantung, Hopei, Shanghai, Chahar and Shensi. The Central Government representatives are said to object to the Communists' retaining any special area of influence as well as separate military forces on the grounds that this would not create real national unity.

The Communists fear eventual liquidation if their military and political strength is too widely dispersed.

CHINESE MARCH INTO HANKOW

CHUNGKING, Sept. 11 (AP)—The Chinese High Command announced today that troops had entered Hankow on the Yangtze; Nanchang, the capital of Kiangsi Province; Kaifeng, capital of Hunan; Hingho, on the Charhar-Sui-yuan border, and Suikai on the Luichow peninsula in South China.

Other forces assigned to occupation of northern Indo-China have entered Hanoi, an official announcement said.

An OWI correspondent reported that Hankow was economically dead after repeated air raids and Japanese looting. Only in the former French concession was business being transacted, he said.

Chinese who have flocked into the ruined city since the surrender were reported to have mobbed Japanese trucks that were making off with the last remaining supplies of soap, sugar, salt and other commodities. ◆

SEPTEMBER 10, 1945

ARABS PUBLISH DEMANDS
Want Sales of Land To Jews in Palestine Barred

By Wireless to The New York Times.

CAIRO, Egypt, Sept. 9—Demands by the economic commission of the Arab League, including the prohibition of further sales of Arab lands to Palestine Jews, were disclosed here today, with proposed legislation, to take immediate effect, against further alleged illegal Jewish immigration into Palestine and a request for tariff protection of Arab products. ◆

SEPTEMBER 16, 1945

INDIAN PARTY WARNS THE UNITED NATIONS

POONA, India, Sept 15 (AP)—The Indian Congress party working committee informed the United Nations today that the people of India would not be bound by any international commitments made by India's "present unrepresentative and irresponsible Government."

The committee adopted a resolution, which said: "It appears to be the policy of the British Government to obstruct and delay formation of a people's national government of India."

Conceding that "it may take some time" for such a national government to function, the resolution said that in the intervening period "the present unrepresentative and irresponsible Government may enter into various kinds of commitments on behalf of the Indian people, which may create shackles preventing growth and development." ◆

SEPTEMBER 16, 1945

IS HITLER DEAD OR ALIVE?
Nobody Knows for Sure, and the Basis For a Disturbing Legend Has Been Laid

By HARRY COLLINS
By Wireless to The New York Times.

LONDON, Sept. 15—The sigh of relief that echoed around the world with the report that the charred body of Adolf Hitler had been found by the Russians in the Berlin Chancellery may have been breathed too soon. The name of the man who hypnotized and blighted Europe for a decade is again in the headlines.

Is Hitler alive? The welter of speculation grows with each new "clue" and "disclosure." The answer is simple—his conquerors do not know.

The Russians have never accepted as proved that the body they found in the Chancellery grounds was Hitler's. The Chancellery is in the Russian-controlled section of Berlin, and with great thoroughness the Soviet authorities have pursued their investigation independently. Although the result of the Russian sleuthing is secret, it would seem the mystery is no nearer solution.

BRITISH VIEW

British Army authorities have declared that the latest rumor that Hitler was seen in Hamburg is "completely unfounded." They also deny that British security police are searching for him. Yet it is known that British intelligence is far from convinced that Hitler is dead.

A Foreign Office spokesman pointed out that the omission of Hitler's name from the war criminals' list did not indicate that the British Government felt certain he was beyond earthly justice.

If Hitler could be brought to trial and dispassionately judged for his crime against humanity, there would be no Hitler legend to inspire the hard core of fanatical youth whose sole complaint against the Nazi regime is that it failed to win the world for Germany.

For years to come there will be Germans ready to obey to the death the "Fueher's" commands. Any bogus message purporting to come from their leader, issued from an underground cell, could be one technique for stirring up trouble. Already Nazi underground radio broadcasts picked up in Sweden have said that Hitler is alive and in Germany. "Hitler will return" is the constant theme of these broadcasts.

It is not overstating matters to say that one of the greatest single factors in the regeneration of German youth is the solution of the Hitler mystery. ◆

SEPTEMBER 17, 1945

RUSSIANS FIRE B-29 BY 'ERROR' IN KOREA

By The United Press.

TOKYO, Sept. 16—Four Russian fighter planes shot down an American B-29 which was on a mercy mission over Korea on Aug. 29, it was disclosed today. The incident brought a "strong and vigorous" protest from Gen. Douglas MacArthur to the Soviet High Command.

Red Army officials promptly replied, regretting the "mistake."

None of the thirteen Americans aboard the Superfortress was injured, although six bailed out into the sea after a burst from the Russian guns had set afire one of the bomber's four engines. One airman reported that he was strafed by a Russian plane after he had hit the sea.

The incident occurred at 2:30 P.M. off the west coast of Korea. The B-29, loaded with food and medical supplies to be dropped at an Allied war prisoner camp in Konan, just inside Soviet-occupied Korea, was "boxed in" by four Yak fighter planes over the near-by Hammung airfield.

The Soviet planes indicated by "buzzing" the field and lowering their landing gear that the B-29 was to land there at once. Lieut. Joseph Queen of Ashland, Ky., refused to land the B-29 because the field was too small, and headed out to sea, intending to return to his Saipan base "until things got straightened out with the Russians."

"About ten miles off the west coast of Korea the Yaks started making passes," Lieutenant Queen told a United Press correspondent. "First they fired across our bow.

"Our guns were loaded and ready to talk, but I told the crew to hold fire.

"Then the Yaks made another pass and hit the No. 1 engine. It burst into flames and a few minutes later I gave the order to bail out. Six of the men jumped, but I got the fire under control and told the rest of the men to stay in the plane for a crash landing."

Lieutenant Queen made a crash landing on the Hammung field. He and the crew removed all instruments and spent the night on the field with the Russians.

"The Russians told us they saw he American markings, but weren't sure because sometimes the Germans used American markings and they thought the Japs might, too," the pilot said.

The next morning Lieutenant Queen went to the prisoner camp. The six men who had bailed out were there. The plane's radio operator, Douglas Arthur of Millersburg, Pa., who jumped, said that the men were in the sea a half hour to four hours before a Korean fishing boat picked them up.

Arthur said that it was he who was strafed.

"The Korean fishermen took us to a village where the head man prepared a big feast," he continued. "The dancing girls were just about to appear when two Russian captains and a major showed up. We asked to be taken to the prison camp. They were nice about that and took us there."

All twelve were taken to Seoul in a C-46 transport plane. ◆

SOVIET SEEKS HOLD IN NORTH AFRICA BY A TRUSTEESHIP

ERITREA IN SOVIET SCOPE
Big Five Council Startled by Bid for North Africa Area— Molotoff Explains Aims

By C. L. SULZBERGER

By Council to The New York Times,
LONDON, Sept. 18—The Soviet Union has formally advised the Big Five Council of Foreign Ministers that it considers that the former Italian domain of Tripolitania should be administered under an individual trusteeship for the United Nations organization and that the U.S.S.R. would like to assume that role.

Foreign Commissar Vyacheslaft M. Molotoff in placing this suggestion before a slightly startled council, pointed out that the Soviet Union was extremely interested in the future development of the Mediterranean and Africa and believed that with the modernization of communications it was fully qualified to undertake this job.

This information was entirely confirmed today by responsible persons and even partly confirmed by Mr. Molotoff himself at a conference, where he said there was "a grain of truth" in reports of Russian interest in Tripolitania and. furthermore, that Moscow was directly interested in the future of Italy's Red Sea colony Eritrea.

ERITREAN BID LIKELY
So far however, Mr. Molotoff has not yet informed the Big Five that the U.S.S.R. wants individual administrative rights in Eritrea. But from what the Foreign Commissar said today that cannot be far in the offing.

Soviet interest in the Mediterranean area is not limited to these two ideas on Tripolitania and Eritrea. The U.S.S.R. has made no request for any bases or administrative rights in the Dodecanese Islands. However, while admitting that these are colonies and, therefore, not subject to the trusteeship formula and furthermore, that the islands should not be returned to Italy, the Russians have failed to agree with the other four powers in the Council that they should be awarded to Greece with the possible exception of Castclorixzo. which might be given to Turkey.

This has led some of the delegates to suspect—perhaps erroneously but nevertheless very earnestly—that Mr. Molotoff is preparing the background for a Soviet demand for a Dodecanese base. At San Francisco it was agreed that the Allied powers would not seek territorial gains in peace. However, when Secretary of State James F. Byrnes mentioned this casually in a reference to the Dodecanese Mr. Molotoff dodged the issue.

The British are worried about collective trusteeships, because they would put Russia into the Mediterranean. Now the individual trusteeship plan is equally disturbing to them because of Soviet interest in Tripolittania and Eritrea as wall as possibly, in the future, in the Dodecanese. They also are concerned about Cyprus and the status of Hong Kong, if the former is placed under the United Nations or given to Greece.

The Chinese favor collective trusteeships but with a maximum time limitation of ten or fifteen years. The French want individual trusteeships—clearly thinking of Indo-china—with no time limitation at all.

The subject of Italian colonies was raised at Mr. Molotoff's conference when he was asked what was the Soviet attitude on Eritrea. He replied:

"The question is under discussion. I shall not conceal that the Soviet Union has an interest in this question and can be helpful in deciding it."

He was then asked whether there was any truth in newspaper reports concerning Soviet interest in Tripolitania. He replied:

"There is a grain of truth in this, but I shall defer my comments. The question has not yet been settled." ◆

Truman Statement on Aid To Europe

By The Associated Press.

WASHINGTON, Sept. 17—The text of a statement by President Truman in connection with the European relief and rehabilitation program follows:

The United States Government is now in a position to fulfill the main requests of Europe—with the exception of sugar, fats and oils—from this date until Jan. 1 as these requests have been stated to it by the governments of the liberated countries and by UNRRA.

Provision of the supplies thus requested does not, however, mean that the civilian populations of Europe will reach even a minimum level of subsistence, and much suffering may be expected during the coming winter in certain areas of the Continent.

The limiting factor in meeting the minimum needs of the liberated peoples is no longer one of shipping. For the moment, in the case of most commodities, it is no longer a problem of supply. Today it is primarily a twofold financial problem; first, to work out credits or other financial arrangements with the European governments; second, to make additional funds available to UNRRA for emergency relief.

When I returned from Potsdam I said, "If we let Europe go cold and hungry, we may lose some of the foundations of order on which the hoped for worldwide peace must rest. We must help to the limits of our strength. And we will." That pledge, made not only to our Allies but to the American people, must be kept. It should be made perfectly clear that, contrary to the belief of many, relaxation of rationing on the home front is not a factor in the allocation of relief supplies to Europe. The Department of Agriculture reports that, despite the release of cheese from rationing controls, and the possible relaxation of domestic meat rationing, we have sufficient quantities of meat and dairy products to fulfill the requirements placed upon us by UNRRA and the paying governments for the last quarter of the year.

The most desperate needs of the liberated people are for coal, transportation and food, in that order of priority. Other commodities urgently required include hides and leather, cotton, wool, textiles,

German housewives waiting in line for food in post-war Berlin, 1945.

soap, farm equipment, including fertilizer and seeds; repair parts and machinery, medical supplies, and a general list of raw materials. The items which are causing major concern because of worldwide shortages are coal, sugar and fats, hides and leather, textiles, and a few of the raw materials, in minor quantities. Locomotives constitute a special and acute problem because of the time factor involved in their manufacture.

Coal presents not only the most serious but the most complicated problem. Once self-sufficient in this commodity, Europe is now without the labor, the food, the transportation, the housing and the machinery needed to restore production quickly to its pre-war level. The Allied Control Commission is making every effort to speed the resumption of German production in order to supply the liberated areas, but despite considerable progress, the people of these areas face a winter of extreme hardship.

The United States is now shipping approximately 1,400,000 tons of coal to Europe a month. For the period ending Jan. 1 the goal is 8,000,000 tons, or slightly more than 1 per cent of our domestic production. The limiting factor is not primarily one of supply, but of inland transportation facilities both here and abroad.

The Department of Agriculture reports that shipments of food to the paying Governments and UNRRA during the last quarter of this year will include approximately these quantities:

One hundred and fifty million pounds of meat and meat products;

Seventy million bushels of wheat;

Twenty-eight thousand short tons of raw sugar;

Ninety million pounds of dried peas and beans;

Thirteen million pounds of lard.

In addition, the Department of Agriculture is prepared to ship the following supplies of dairy products, in at least these quantities, as soon as financial arrangements have been satisfactorily completed:

Sixty million pounds of cheese;

Two hundred million pounds of evaporated milk;

Twenty-five million pounds of dry whole milk powder;

Eighty million pounds of dry skim milk powder;

Fifteen million pounds of condensed milk.

It should be remembered that these supplies will serve not to improve, but only to sustain the diet of the liberated peoples, which remains below the minimum level of subsistence. In some cases the doubling of these food shipments waits only upon the conclusion of satisfactory financial arrangements.

This Government has abundant evidence that the American people are aware of the suffering among our Allies. They have also made plain their determination that this country shall do its full part, along with other supplying nations, in helping to restore health and strength to those who fought at our side both in Europe and in the Far East. It is an American responsibility not only to our friends, but to ourselves, to see that this job is done and done quickly. ◇

STIMSON PRAISED

Truman Says That He Accepted Resignation Very Reluctantly

By SIDNEY M. SHALETT
Special to The New York Times.

WASHINGTON, Sept. 18—Secretary Stimson, who, since July, 1940, headed the War Department through the mobilization, war and victory years, resigned today, and President Truman nominated Robert P. Patterson, Under-Secretary of War, as his successor.

Mr. Truman hailed Mr. Stimson as one of the country's truly great public servants and told his news conference that he accepted the resignation very reluctantly.

Mr. Stimson's immediate plans were not disclosed. He will be 78 years old Friday. Mr. Stimson will hold his final news conference at 10:30 A.M. tomorrow, and the War Department will honor him at a reception from 5 to 7 P.M. at Dumbarton Oaks.

The Senate must confirm the nomination of Mr. Patterson, a Republican, who has supervised the Army's $100,000,000,000 procurement program. Approval is expected, but not without some discussion, for Mr. Patterson's outspoken views frequently have brought him into sharp conflict with Congress.

It was recalled that he and Mr. Truman, when the latter headed the Senate War Investigating Committee, occasionally were at odds, but today Mr. Patterson also received the Distinguished Service Medal by direction of the President.

DECLINES OTHER RESIGNATIONS

Mr. Truman disclosed that he also had received the resignation of John J. McCloy, assistant Secretary of War, and Robert A. Lovett, assistant Secretary of War for Air, but would not accept them at this time.

However, it is authoritatively reported that Mr. McCloy and Mr. Lovett wish to return to private life. Their present plans are to stay on so long as they can be useful to Mr. Patterson in setting up his departmental organization, then they would like to step out.

Harvey H. Bundy Sr., a special assistant to Mr. Stimson since he took office, also will retire. Mr. Bundy, who ▸

served under Mr. Stimson when he was Secretary of State from 1929 to 1933, will return to his law firm, Choate, Hall & Stewart in Boston.

Mr. Patterson is a champion of the merger of the War and Navy Departments into a single Department of National Defense, a move which the President favors and for which there is considerable Congressional sentiment. ◊

U.S. President Harry S. Truman with American diplomat Henry Stimson after Stimson received a Distinguished Service Medal.

SEPTEMBER 22, 1945

INDO-CHINA FIGHTS RETURN OF FRENCH

By Wireless to The New York Times.

PARIS, Sept 21—"Only France menaces the independence of IndoChina," Prof. Tran Due Thao, vice president of the Indo-Chinese general delegation representing 25,000 Indo-Chinese laborers in France, told the press here today.

"Our object is to let the French people know what the effect of the arrival of the forces of General Leclerc [Maj. Gen. Jacques-Philippe Leclere de Hauteclo-que] is going to be," he declared. "We will resist the French. Admiral d'Argen-lieu [Vice Admiral Georges Thierry d'Argenlieu, High Commissioner in In-do-China] can expect to be shot at when he reaches Hanoi."

The little Indo-Chinese professor had difficulty getting a word in during the ensuing hubbub among Frenchmen present, but he made his points.

Viet Nam, the Indo-Chinese resistance movement, already has set up a government in Hanoi, he said. It demands total independence, and the

SEPTEMBER 21, 1945

KOREANS PROTEST TWO-ZONE CONTROL

SEOUL, Korea, Sept. 19 (Delayed) (U.P.)—Korean leaders protested today that the division of Korea into a Russian-occupied industrial zone and an American-occupied agricultural zone had been made without consideration of Korea's dove-tailed economy and said the existence of two separate occupation governments would hamper the establishment of an independent Korean government.

The Koreans pointed out that the arbitrary division line—the thirty-eighth parallel—which gave the Russians the northern half of the country was so shortsighted that it split three of Korea's thirteen provinces and that the Governors of these provinces were under both Russian and American influence.

There is little similarity between the two occupation governments and virtually no liaison, they declared, adding that military government still continues in the Russian zone.

The Koreans said the Russian zone contained virtually all of Korea's hydro-electric power and much of her heavy industry, while the southern zone largely supplied the north with rice, fish and other food. The economy of the country was established by the Japanese over a period of thirty years and was functioning efficiently when it was chopped in two, they said.

'BROKEN FAITH' CHARGED

The Koreans asserted that the "crime of the occupation set-up" was that the Allies had "broken faith" with small countries in the Far East. They said President Truman, Prime Minister Winston Churchill and Generalissimo Chiang Kai-shek had declared at Cairo that Korea would become free and independent in "due course."

Korean nationalists said they could not see how bisecting the country could do anything but hinder Korean independence and some said they believed it was done deliberately to prevent Korea from becoming integrated.

The division of the country's economy is the hardest blow, they said, for under Japan—as much as the Japanese rule was disliked—the country became nearly self-sufficient while the rich provinces in northeast Korea contained one of Japan's heaviest concentrations of industry, including integrated iron and steel mills.

Government officials said the Japanese-built industrial empire should be turned over to them in payment for the years when the Japanese bled the country of its wealth, but said that first there must be a government by Koreans and asserted "when the Russians and the Americans leave—if you do leave"—Korea "will have two governments. It's like drawing a line down the center of the United States with the western half a communistic government and the eastern half a democracy." ◊

withdrawal of French troops and officials. A treaty might be made permitting French technicians, industrialists and others to work in Indo-China on the same basis as other foreigners. Since a Government already is established, he declared, there no longer is any question of granting Indo-China independence by stages, as in the Philippines.

FRENCH RECORD DENOUNCED

"We do not fear the Chinese or the British because they intend to withdraw," the professor explained, "but the French intend to stay."

He denounced France's record, alleging that old elite had been destroyed and replaced by servile nouveaux riches, that the old culture had been destroyed and replaced by an illiteracy rate of 89 per cent and that industry had been suppressed to safeguard French markets.

GERMAN BACKING SEEN

SAIGON, Indo-China, Sept. 20 (Delayed) (UP)—Reports from Tongking, in northeast Indo-China, said today that fighting had broken out there between the French and Annamite nationalists. Tension here was increased by an Annamite boycott against the French.

French representatives here indicated that the disturbances, which have been reported from all over Indo-China in recent weeks, may have been inspired by Germans as well as by Japanese. The Japanese last March proclaimed an independent puppet state of Viet Nam.

It was announced that a Dr. Nochte, leader of the German mission to Saigon, had been interned in his own house. He formerly was a specialist in espionage in Mexico and arrived here in 1942. Well-informed French quarters believed he was the leading brain behind the Annamite anti-French movement.

The Tongking reports—which did not indicate the scale of the disturbances—said fighting began when some of the 1,500 French troops interned with 3,500 other Europeans escaped to China and then came back.

Saigon remained tense and newspapers were suspended for printing false and alarmist news. Members of the Viet Nam [the Annamite nationalist party] began a policy of passive resistance following the establishment of virtual martial law here.

DR. SUN URGES TRUSTEESHIP

CHUNGKING, China, Sept. 21 (UP)—Dr. Sun Fo, President of the Legislative Yuan of China, said today the best disposition of the French Indo-Chinese protectorate of Annam would be to place it under the trusteeship of the United Nations. He foresaw perpetual internal strife if the French attempted to retain power. "Although the French pushed economic development, their rule was despotic and Indo-China was the worst government colony in the Far East," he said. ◊

SEPTEMBER 30, 1945

'AXIS SALLY' GETS JAIL TERM IN ITALY
Woman Who Renounced U.S. and Broadcast For Nazis Will Serve 4 Years

ROME, Sept. 29 (AP)—Rita Louisa Zucca, an "Axis Sally" broadcaster of Nazi radio propaganda to United States troops in the Mediterranean area, was sent to prison today by an Italian military tribunal for four years and five months.

The court required only fifteen minutes to convict the 33-year-old, American-born daughter of a New York restaurateur of a charge that she had intelligence with the enemy. However, it found "extenuating circumstances" and declined to impose the ten-year sentence asked by the prosecution.

Miss Zucca, who renounced her United States citizenship in 1941 because she "liked to live in Italy," took her sentence calmly and with only a blinking of her eyes. Before she was led away by a British guard she smiled broadly at the German, Karl Goedel, who played "George" in the propaganda skit "Sally and George."

"Sally" testified that she had taken the job with the German-controlled Rome radio only because she needed the money for her Italian lover; that she never organized or wrote the scripts for the propaganda programs but merely read prepared dialogues.

Just before the court returned its verdict her Italian attorney, Ottavio Libotte, received a cable from the United States asking postponement of the trial and saying the defendant's mother, Mrs. Edvina Zucca, was sailing for Italy "with important documents." It came too late, however.

Signor Libotte announced he would appeal the sentence to the Supreme Military Tribunal.

Three American soldiers testified briefly that they had heard "Sally's" broadcasts. Statements of each of the three that the program was designed to demoralize American troops also were read.

SALLY'S PARENTS NOT AVAILABLE

"Axis Sally's" father is Louis Zucca, owner of Zucca's Italian Garden at 118 West Forty-ninth Street. At the restaurant last night it was said that Mr. and Mrs. Zucca were out of town.

A cousin, Tino Zucca, who acted as spokesman, said: "There is nothing that we can say. The whole thing has been a terrible shock to the family." ◊

Epilogue
"ATOM BLAST IN RUSSIA DISCLOSED"
1945–1949

The four years that followed the end of World War II decisively shaped world politics for the next fifty years. The immediate task in 1945, however, was to complete the business left over from the conflict. War crimes trials in Nuremberg, and later in Tokyo, exposed the guilty and assuaged for many the thirst for revenge. Oppressed populations exacted retribution from those regarded as traitors. For the major victors, the end of the war brought on rapid demobilization from the extraordinary conditions of war. Armies were sent home, prisoners released and repatriated, industry retooled for civilian production and trade resumed. This proved a difficult transition as men replaced women who had gotten used to wartime wages and independence, businesses tried to compensate for the sudden loss of military orders, and nations bankrupted by war and occupation tried to address the pressing issues of food, fuel and work for their impoverished populations.

By 1947 it was evident that the post-war world could not be remade easily and on June 6, at Harvard, Truman's secretary of state, George Marshall, announced what was to become the European Recovery Program, or, more simply, the Marshall Plan. "This project fires the imagination as nothing has done since the end of the war," The Times declared. Nevertheless, the Marshall Plan exacerbated the widening rift between the West and the Soviet Union. People in areas now under Communist domination in Europe were not permitted to apply for American assistance. When the Czechs thought about doing so, a Communist coup removed the last hope of a genuinely democratic system in the bloc now dominated from Moscow.

The Cold War, a term coined by the correspondent Walter Lipmann, was taking shape by the end of 1945, with ongoing arguments over the future of Germany and Soviet input in the areas liberated by the Western Allies. Churchill addressed this issue on March 5, 1946, at a small college in Fulton, Missouri. While on a speaking tour, he took the opportunity to denounce the Communist construction of what he called an "Iron Curtain" across Europe. The Times did not immediately endorse the speech and the Soviet leadership interpreted it as an attempt to torpedo collaboration between the former wartime allies. But Churchill was not wrong in describing what became by 1949 international reality—a world divided along ideological lines between a democratic, capitalist West and an area from East Germany to North Korea, dominated by Communist dictatorships.

Civil wars in Greece and China exposed the wider battle lines of the Cold War. In Greece, Truman finally intervened, offering American assistance after declaring what became known as the "Truman Doctrine" which supported democratic freedoms in the face of authoritarian threat. In practice, the doctrine could only be applied selectively. Greece remained outside the Soviet bloc, but China, where Mao Zedong's armies finally routed the nationalist forces of Chiang Kai-shek, became a second Communist power.

In Germany the issue remained finely balanced, since the Soviet Union wanted a unitary, but pro-Soviet German state. When the United States and Britain predictably rejected the Soviet ambition, Moscow blockaded the western zones of Berlin in hopes that the former German capital would become a Soviet city. The West responded by initiating an airlift that supplied Berliners long enough to persuade Moscow to call off the blockade, but the result was two separate German states, which remained separate until their reunification in 1990 after the Berlin Wall was toppled. Western nations, meanwhile, moved toward creating a military alliance, which The Times strongly favored long before NATO (the North Atlantic Treaty Organization) was organized.

On August 29 a Soviet atomic bomb was tested at a remote site in Kazakhstan, launching a nuclear arms race and dividing the world clearly into two superpower blocs. A month later The Times announced, "Atom Blast in Russia Disclosed." A new and even more dangerous world had been born out of the ruins of World War II.

90% CUT IN OUTPUT HITS PLANE PLANTS

By RUSSELL PORTER
Special to The New York Times.

SAN DIEGO, Oct. 6—One of the most serious problems of the postwar period—the future of the aircraft industry—was spotlighted today for the group of newspaper men who are making a month's tour of the country's industrial centers to report on the progress of reconversion.

I. M. Laddon, executive vice president of the Consolidated Vultee Corporation, made it clear that in his industry the problem is really not reconversion but contraction. He cited the experience of his company as typical of the industry.

The company's wartime sales peak, in 1944, totaled $990,000,000 in its plants throughout the country, about half of which was represented by San Diego production, whereas the 1946 country-wide estimate is $90,000,000, according to Mr. Laddon.

DESCRIBES DOUBLE JOLT

Mr. Laddon added that during the war the industry as a whole reached a production peak of $20,000,000,000 a year, which is expected to come down to 5 or 10 per cent after reconversion.

Although that would be five to ten times as large as pre-war production, he said, it still leaves unsolved the problem of finding new jobs for a great many of the hundreds of thousands of men and women who worked in the aircraft plants during the war. He continued:

"Probably no other industry received a greater double jolt than aircraft. It did not have large peacetime plants and payrolls which could be converted to war and it did not have a large normal peacetime market to which it could turn at the end of the war."

The company's country-wide payroll increased from 5,338 at the beginning of 1940 to a wartime peak of 93,000 in 1944, as its production grew from 580 planes to 7,960 in the same two years. Today it is down to 17,000 employees and has closed down a number of its plants throughout the country. For the future the company is trying to develop commercial and private airplane markets in addition to whatever military planes are needed for the Government's post-war aviation program.

The press group was taken inside the fuselage of the XC-99, the 400-passenger Army transport now being built here. Climbing up the ladders of the two decks reminded one of going aboard an ocean liner. It is the largest land plane under construction and today was the first time, according to the company, that the Government has permitted a press preview.

CARRY FIFTY-TON PAY LOAD

A fleet of these planes in their commercial version—a 240-passenger ocean airliner—has been ordered by Pan American World Airways. They will carry a pay load of fifty tons 1,500 miles and have a range of 8,000 miles with a reduced pay load. There are six pusher-type engines. The length is 183 feet and the wing spread 230 feet.

The reporters were also taken through a wooden replica of a new thirty-passenger domestic transport, a low-wing, twin-engine monoplane with a cruising speed of 275 miles an hour. It has luxurious passenger accommodations.

A demonstration was given of "Jato" a jet-assisted take-off of a Coast Guard flying boat. This has greatly facilitated rescue work in high seas and is expected to find new applications in post-war commercial and private flying.

Albert J. Reader, president, and E. F. Johnstone Jr., industrial consultant, of the San Diego Chamber of Commerce, explained the city's plans to meet its reconversion problems, and said the city was taking the shrinkage in aircraft employment in its stride as a result of post-war planning done over the past three years.

From 1940 to 1944 the city's population grew from 203,000 to 286,000 and is expected to level off at 280,000.

JOBS FOR 23,500 EXPECTED

Pre-war industrial employment was 12,000. The wartime peak was 65,000, the present figure is 16,000. And the estimate after reconversion is completed is 23,500, or about double pre-war.

Most of those laid off seem to have remained in the city, some have been absorbed by other industries, trades and services that have been short of help. Some have gone back to the farm, the kitchen, the school and the retirement list. ◊

PATTON INCIDENT SERVES TO SPEED DENAZIFICATION
His Attitude Focused Attention on Mistakes Now Being Corrected

By RAYMOND DANIELL
BY Wireless to The New York Times

BERLIN, Oct. 6—In his own inimitable fashion Gen. George S. Patton has rendered still another service to his country. It is his misfortune that this time it took such form that it won him banishment to an obscure command instead of another decoration to add to his five rows of ribbons. But by voicing frankly some of the doubts and reservations in the minds of many American officers regarding the denazification program laid down by the heads of State at Potsdam and implemented by General Eisenhower in a clear-cut directive, he helped dramatize an issue, which was stultifying one of the primary steps toward the reorientation of Germany.

By his ill-timed, ill-chosen phrases, likening the situation in the defeated Reich to the aftermath of a Democratic-Republican election fight, he drew clearly the issue between himself and Eisenhower, which could not be ignored.

As Lieut. Gen. Walter Bedell Smith, Chief of Staff to Eisenhower, phrased it, the real danger of the situation that resulted was not that Patton would fail to carry out his superior's orders but that his remarks would be misunderstood and misconstrued by junior officers throughout the whole American zone by creating doubt regarding the real purpose of American occupation. As Patton saw it, the purpose was to "show the Germans what grand fellows we are."

A DANGER REMAINS

Eisenhower's action in forcing Patton to remove the reactionary Bavarian Government, which the former Third Army commander was propping up in office long after it had lost all usefulness to us, and the subsequent transfer of Patton from the role of military governor of Bavaria to a purely literary role of directing compilation of a tactical history of the war he fought so well in the field, should end all danger of such misconceptions. One danger remains, however, and that is that the drastic action taken against General Patton will be mistaken for a cure of the fundamental cleavage between promise and performance in occupation policy, instead of the purely disciplinary action that it was. .

Yet it cannot be denied that General Patton's interview and its aftermath have had a healthful effect upon the execution of our declared policy of ridding Germany's economic as well as her political life of a Nazi nucleus which might seize control after our occupation ends. If it did nothing more than remind the officers in the field—many of whom were drawn from civilian life where the tradition of obedience is less ingrained than among the Regular Army officers—that their role is to enforce and not to make policy, it would have been a net gain.

But it did more. It led to the overthrow of the ultra-conservative, one-sided German Government in Bavaria, support of which had begun to arouse skepticism in Bavaria regarding our sincerity in advocating democratic principles. It has brought a showdown on the denazification order which was being evaded and avoided in the name of expediency and efficiency.

But denazification is only one phase of our occupation program. There may have to be a large number of similar showdowns before the policies as laid down at Potsdam, envisaging a disarmed Germany limited to a standard of living not to exceed that of her European neighbors, are realized. For in all phases of the occupation machinery cleavages are developing between those ready to enforce peace terms as stringent as those laid down at Potsdam, and those who would soften them by closing an eye here and cutting a corner there.

It was Patton who dramatized and crystallized an issue which might have dragged along indecisively for an indefinite period. He is the one who has felt the brunt of punishment. But it would be a mistake to regard him as the only sinner. There are scores, perhaps hundreds of lesser figures who feel as he did but who now can be expected to carry out orders as issued on denazification at least because they know now it isn't healthy to disobey.

The lackadaisical attitude that prevailed in the American zone toward denazificaion is not, however, limited to that part of Germany. Its counterpart is to be found in the British-occupied Ruhr where old managers of industries which played the Nazi game have still to be removed from their lucrative and influential positions. ◊

Editorial
UNREST IN INDONESIA

In the Netherlands East Indies, as elsewhere in what the Japanese used to call their "Co-Prosperity Sphere," the end of the war has not restored the conditions existing in December, 1941. The Japanese rebellion may not be serious in the military sense, but it suggests wide discontent. And discontent among a total population in the Indies of nearly 75,000,000, gathered into an area about one-fourth that of the United States, with some regions, as in Java itself, of intense congestion, could be extremely significant.

The East Indies under Dutch rule have had an enormous population increase—about 100 per cent since 1905. This population, about eight times that of the mother country, is 85 per cent Moslem. Twenty years ago it had a strong independence movement, with a religious basis. Under the Japanese threat and later under actual Japanese occupation this movement lost ground. The East Indians did not like European imperialism, but they liked the Japanese variety still less. But like other East Asiatics, they have been influenced by the democratic professions of the Allies, and presumably what they are after is greater political and economic freedom without the complete withdrawal of European protection.

No doubt the root grievance is that the native continues to occupy an inferior position and does not have the first claim on the exportable natural resources of his own country. He wants a higher standard of living and a say as to his own destiny. In the Philippines the native is soon to achieve the latter, whatever may happen to the former. The Indonesian, looking northward, may wonder why he should not be equally fortunate. ◊

ARMY TO DISCHARGE MILLION A MONTH

Special to The New York Times.

WASHINGTON, Oct. 9—The Army and the Navy announced today that their respective demobilization programs were being accelerated. An Army spokesman stated that the present tempo of discharges would mean that men would be leaving for civilian life at the rate of 1,000,000 men a month.

The Army expects to reach the 1,000,000 rate by the end of October. The number of men discharged from the Army in September was 597,302, far beyond the goal of 450,000 estimated by General Marshall on Sept. 20 in a talk with members of Congress.

The Navy announced today that its critical score for medical officers had been reduced from 60 to 53, which means that 4,000 doctors will return to civilian life by Jan. 1.

Possible further reduction of the score will depend on the rate of general demobilization. Medical officers are being discharged at present at the rate of three doctors for each 1,000 men demobilized.

REPORTS 208,000 DEMOBILIZED

As for general demobilization, the Navy stated that in the six days ending Oct. 6, 60,000 men had been discharged, bringing the Navy's total demobilized to 208,000 men.

On the incoming side, the Navy reported that 16,000 men had voluntarily enlisted in the Navy during September, including 11,800 who joined the Regular Navy.

Consequently, the Navy Department will reduce its draft request for November from 5,000 to 1,000 men.

On Oct. 1 there were 539,000 men with points to qualify for discharge, and 335,000 of these were at sea or overseas. ◊

OCTOBER 14, 1945

WASHINGTON BACKS A 'HARD APPROACH' TO RUSSIA

By JAMES B. RESTON

WASHINGTON, Oct. 13—The current trend at the State Department is to be firm with Russia. The purpose is not to minimize our cooperation with Moscow but to increase it. The theory is that the "soft approach" has failed and the "hard approach" will put our cooperation on a sounder basis.

This is presently a popular thesis in Washington, particularly on Capitol Hill. When Secretary of State Byrnes came back from the London conference and developed it before the Senate Foreign Relations Committee he was generally well received. The main questions raised by the committee, in fact, were not whether the tough line was right but whether it was tough enough and whether it was his intention to "be tough" or only to "act tough."

For example, while applauding the Secretary's tactics of standing up to the Russian Commissar in London on the question of letting France and China participate in the preliminary peace treaty discussions, the committee criticized him adversely for letting Russia in on an advisory committee for Japan.

Several members of the committee argued that he never should have suggested the creation of a Japanese advisory committee in the first place, and proposed that, in view of Russia's insistence that the committee should "control" Japanese policy instead of merely advising on it, the United States should forget the whole thing and continue to govern Japan unilaterally, as we are now doing.

PRESSURE ON BYRNES

Therefore, it is fair to say that the Secretary is under considerable pressure to "be tough" with Moscow, but his new line, like all other possible policies toward the Soviet Union, is controversial and has produced mixed reactions.

In the first place there are some officials in Mr. Byrnes' own department who do not concede the premise that our policy toward Russia has either been "soft" or has "failed." This group points out that the Roosevelt Administration did not accede to Russia's demands for a "second front" in 1942 and 1943, that neither Mr. Roosevelt nor Mr. Truman acceded to their requests for heavy machinery

under lend-lease, that both Democratic Presidents refused their request for a $10,000,000,000 postwar credit, and that both consistently opposed attempts to keep us out of Eastern Europe.

Moreover, this faction contends that, as a result of a persistent American policy, the wartime coalition has been kept in being and an international organization has been established which is much nearer to the American blueprint than the Russian. This, they argue, is not "failure" but as much success as can be expected in negotiations between such vastly different nations as the United States and the Soviet Union.

There is no tendency in the capital to condone Soviet Russia's tendency to insist that military power is the only basis of authority in the world and that the Big Three should, therefore, make the peace. Nor is there anything but apprehension at the sight of Soviet power moving like a great cloud across the face of Europe and blotting out all information as it goes.

Consequently, Mr. Byrnes has found very little opposition in the capital to his firmness in opposing the Russian Foreign Commissar in London on these points. But few observers here believe that more progress is to be made in the peace negotiations by stopping bad things than by thinking through and defining good and positive things, and the charge is definitely being made here that we have been in opposition most of the time sometimes against policies we ourselves seemed to be employing in other parts of the world.

CLAIMS AND COUNTER-CLAIMS

For example, the Administration insisted again this week that in the event of any disagreement among the Allies about policy in Japan, the will of the United States should govern. This principle is undoubtedly supported in Congress and is justified by the fact that the United States, almost alone, achieved the conquest of the Japanese islands.

But in response to our claim for an equal voice in the Allied administration of Bulgaria and Rumania, the Russians say they conquered these countries and insist that like the United States in Japan their policy should govern. Admittedly, they restrict us much more in these countries than we restrict them in Japan, but the controversy raises the point whether we are strengthening the principle of equal control among the Allies by insisting on it in Eastern Europe

Secretary of State James F. Byrnes arriving in Washington, D.C. after the London Conference, 1945.

and denying it in Japan.

Similarly the Administration insisted on the acquisition of bases in the Pacific islands but opposed attempts by Russia to gain a sole trusteeship over Eritrea, and originally we suggested that the Dardenelles be put under an international commission, though we would hesitate to accept a similar device for the Panama Canal.

It cannot be argued that these are exact parallels, but it is being argued both within the Administration and within the ranks of the United Nations, that American foreign policy is liberal, if not radical, in its proposals for other countries and generally conservative where our own vital interests are concerned.

On the one hand, it is argued against us, we exclaim against Russia's exercise of national power and on the other insist on our exclusive rights to the atomic bomb. In one case we put pressure on Britain to admit thousands of Jews into Palestine and put restrictions on their entrance into the United States. At the Mexico City conference we sought to strengthen the idea of joint action by the Americas on hemisphere problems and we supported the principles of nonintervention in the affairs of other nations, and in practice we managed to call off the Rio de Janeiro conference without consulting all the Latin-American nations.

CAPITOL HILL TALK

If these problems could be solved with casual conversation, the United Nations would really be united in a hurry, for "the Russian problem" has replaced Franklin D. Roosevelt as the chief topic of discussion in the capital.

Most of the talk on Capitol Hill at the moment, however, deals with the shortcomings of our Allies and the complexity of the problems. Here and there in Congress, and in the executive branch of the Government, there are men who start from the premise that they can do very little to change the policies of foreign governments, but might have some effect on the future actions of their own Government, but they are definitely in a minority.

Even in the State Department itself the tendency is to say merely that we must now be "firm with the Russians" and "stand up for our principles," but Mr. Byrnes and his new team have been so busy negotiating on urgent questions that they have not had time to see each other long enough to find out whether they agree on what our principles are. ◊

RUSSIA'S DISPUTED "ZONE OF INFLUENCE" IN MIDDLE EUROPE

POLITICAL STRUGGLE STIRS WHOLE OF EASTERN EUROPE

By C. L. SULZBERGER
By Wireless to The New York Times.

LONDON, Oct. 13—Eastern Europe from the Baltic to the Aegean is still, as it has been intermittently throughout the last century, the most troublesome area of the Continent, diplomatically speaking. This was conclusively proved at the Foreign Ministers' Council.

This Eastern group of countries could scarcely be called a coalition today despite the fact that Russian influence predominates in all of them, except Greece and European Turkey. On the Thracian-Macedonian boundary British influence begins.

Broadly speaking, the U.S.S.R. considers that its victory in this war justifies the assumption of special privileges in Eastern Europe for security reasons.

In all the countries within the broad Russian sphere the Communist party is the dominating and controlling force, although it is neither the majority party nor does it hold a majority of Cabinet posts—rather the key Ministries.

POLISH COALITION

In Poland the Beirut Government is a coalition of Communists, Socialists, Peasant party and Democrats. The Christian Democrats are trying to chisel their way in.

Communist influence is predominant. President Boleslaw Beirut, who calls himself a non-party man, is to all intents and purposes a Communist. A Communist heads the Ministry of Security, another really runs the Foreign Office (Zygmunt Modze Ewaki), and another—Hilary Mine—is virtual economic dictator.

Economically, Poland's main job is reconstruction. There should be enough food to go around but transport is very bad.

Socially, the greatest problem, agrarian reform and land distribution, has been ruthlessly but effectively solved.

All large factories have been nationalized.

Internally, anti-Semitism and guerrilla trouble with remnants of the old Home Army are the big headaches. Although there are not many more than 100,000 Jews left alive in Poland, they are still being persecuted, especially in provincial areas.

Expulsion of the Germans, relations with Russia and the Czechoslovak frontier are the main foreign problems. The first will be and is done, although in a pretty tough way. The second are bound to remain good because that is the way geography is. The third is something that will have to be solved by mutual agreement.

A BASIC PATTERN

Polish difficulties are in a sense a basic pattern for other lands in the eastern belt. They certainly want good relations with the U.S.S.R., but they want more democracy, according to the western interpretation of the disputed word.

Czechoslovakia has the same problem with the Red Army, with expelling Germans—and, in this case, also Hungarian minorities. She does not have the Polish headache of shifting borders westward while giving up areas in the east. She just did the latter—Ruthenia.

The Communist influence is not so strong as in Poland, but, especially in Slovakia, it is mighty powerful. President Eduard Benes has such prestige that he is a good figurehead for all the anti-Communist groups.

Country No. 3 in the Slavic alliance belt created last spring by Moscow is Yugoslavia. There the old guerrilla spirit of the Hajduks is very strong. A visitor recently returning from Belgrade said so many arms were buried beneath the soil that a magnet would point down all over the country.

Marshal Tito is a most popular figure, but some of his aides are not. The Tito-Subasich agreement has broken down with the resignation of Foreign Minister Ivan Subasich, Vice Premier Milan Grol and Minister without Portfolio Juras Sutej and there may be trouble during or after the elections.

YUGOSLAV CLAIMS

Yugoslavia's frontier claims against Italy—especially Trieste—and to a lesser degree those against Austria and probable eventual ones against Greece, are all of current interest. Tito has also become a kind of godfather to Enver Hoxhas' Communist Government in Albania, which is proving a useful anti-Greek irritant.

Austria and Hungary, among the ▸

defeated satellites, are in a special category. Their governments, being those nearest the western world—not bloc, as some propagandists would have it—are about to receive western recognition.

The West has a slightly better peephole into those lands. Freedom of the press is of a rather euphemistic sort in large belts of Eastern Europe. On the whole, London and Washington seem to feel that democracy in Austria and Hungary is not entirely a Molotoff cocktail. The land redistribution of Hungary certainly brought that country's social structure up from the Middle Ages in a hefty leap.

Rumania and Bulgaria, old enemies whom Hitler forced into a friendship that Stalin has managed to preserve, are the unwilling troublemakers between Russia and the West. The Communist toehold in both countries goes right up to the thigh.

GREECE'S MIDDLE WAY

Both are right next to the U.S.S.R., and do they know it! In each case the agrarian leaders—Dr. Juliu Maniu and George M. Dimitroff (the one Pravda calls a Fascist beast, not the party adherent)—are the propaganda targets every night.

Last on the list are Greece and Turkey. Since the latter is principally Asiatic, it can be skipped in this review. Greece is trying to get some sort of government going that represents the large but disorganized middle.

Neither the Right nor the Left is being very helpful in this process and the Left gets the old and curiously harmonious support of Sofia, Belgrade, Tirana and Moscow. ◇

OCTOBER 16, 1945

LAVAL IS EXECUTED

Prosecutor and Judges Find Him Stricken by Poison Smuggled Into Prison

By LANSING WARREN
By Wireless to The New York Times.

PARIS, Oct. 15—Pierre Laval, who led Vichy along the road of collaboration with the Germans, lies tonight in a traitor's grave in the potter's field of the Thiais Cemetery, south of Paris.

The last five hours of his life were as dramatic as any that he ever lived and were marked by a confusion bordering on consternation among the officials who had charge of his execution. When he was notified at 8:45 A.M. that he was about to be taken before the firing squad, Laval drank the contents of a vial of poison that he had kept secreted on his person for more than a year.

In the presence of prison officials he fell unconscious on the floor of his cell. After resuscitation by a stomach-pump and some hours of rest and formalities, he was taken just outside the prison and shot to death under circumstances unprecedented in French judicial history. The press and the public were kept out of range by a large detachment of police.

SAY HE DIED BRAVELY

According to his lawyers and the few officers who were the only witnesses, Laval died bravely. He explained in a letter that he had planned suicide "so that French soldiers should not be involved in a judicial crime." He said that he had wished to die as a Premier should and had chosen to execute himself as did the ancient Romans. He insisted on being allowed to wear the white tie that he had made famous. Wrapping his throat in a Tricolor scarf, he faced his executioners without a blindfold and died shouting: "Vive la France!"

It had been planned to execute Laval, as is customary in cases of treason, by a military squad at the Chatillon Fort, some distance from the prison. It was found impracticable to take him there and, after some discussion, the platoon of colonial troops charged with the execution was brought with a hearse to the Fresnes prison, where Laval had been confined. After a wait of an hour or more he was shot at a hastily erected stake in front of the prison's reservoir.

Tonight an official inquiry was ordered at Fresnes to determine how Laval had got the poison. He made a formal statement exculpating his lawyers and the prison personnel, declaring that the poison had been carried hidden in the fur collar of his overcoat ever since he left for Germany in August, 1944. His lawyers and his medical attendants expressed the opinion that the suicide attempt had failed because this poison had lost its effectiveness with time. ◇

OCTOBER 19, 1945

BIG FOUR INDICT 24 TOP NAZIS FOR PLOTTING AGAINST PEACE; ATROCITIES IN WAR CHARGED

Goering, Hess, 13 Others Accused On All Four Counts in Bill

By RAYMOND DANIELL
By Wireless to The New York Times.

BERLIN, Oct. 18—An indictment was presented today before the international military tribunal representing the United States, Russia, Britain and France to charge twenty-four of Germany's war leaders—all Nazi followers of Adolf Hitler—with participation in the bloodiest, blackest plot against peace and humanity that has ever stained history's pages.

It was an unparalleled proceeding and never before have men been called on to answer for such heinous crimes on so vast a scale. All the human and material loss that Europe has suffered since Hitler came to power, including the blood of 5,700,000 Jews who were systematically exterminated, was laid to their criminal machinations. They were charged, too, with the ultimate responsibility for forcing more than 5,000,000 Europeans into slavery to Germany's war machine and for crimes committed by the German armed forces on the battlefield and at sea.

The prosecution requested the tribunal, which holds the power of life and death over the accused Germans, to declare that the Cabinet and the military and semi-military organizations that helped them to subjugate first Germans and then Germany's European neighbors be declared "criminal in purpose." The seven organizations included the Leadership Corps of the Nazi party, the Elite Guard, the Storm Troops, the Gestapo and the General Staff and High Command of the German armed forces.

WOULD MINIMIZE LATER TRIALS

If this were done, it was pointed out, it would be unnecessary to hold any more protracted trials such as that to be held soon in Nuremberg. Such action by the court would relieve the prosecution of proving in each instance that the members of those organizations were war criminals and would transfer the burden of proof to thousands of defendants to show that they were unwilling or passive members of the outlawed bodies, thus reducing the proceedings in their cases to the level of magistrates' hearings.

The indictment contained four counts. The first traced the historical development of the plot to turn peaceful Germany into an instrument of aggressive war by submerging everything in the state to the Nazi will as personified by Hitler. All twenty-four defendants were accused under this count.

The second charged that under their leadership Germany had embarked on a series of aggressive wars in violation of her treaty obligations. The third charged that, in the prosecution of "total war," Germany had resorted to murder, pillage, torture and destruction in violation of the conventions of civilization and the penal laws of the countries where the crimes were committed.

The fourth count laid at the door of most of the defendants the responsibility for the extermination, enslavement and deportation of civilian populations before and during the war, and for the persecution, on political, racial and religious grounds, of all those who opposed them or threatened to do so. This count is entitled, "Crimes Against Humanity."

Fourteen of the prisoners now in the Nuremberg jail were made defendants on all four counts. Besides former Marshal Hermann Goering and Rudolf Hess, who were Deputy Fuehrers, these defendants were:

Joachim von Ribbentrop, former Foreign Minister.

Alfred Rosenberg, official "philosopher" of German racial theories and commissioner for occupied Russian territory.

Wilhelm Frick, Minister of the Interior.

Fritz Sauckel, commissioner for forced labor.

Albert Speer, Minister of Production.

Walther Funk, Minister of Economics.

Gustav Krupp von Bohlen und Halbach, armament manufacturer.

Baron Constantin von Neurath, "Protector" of Bohemia-Moravia.

Arthur Seyss-Inquart, commissioner for Austria and the Netherlands.

Field Marshal Gens. Wilhelm Keitel and Alfred Jodl as members of the General Staff.

Hans Fritzsche, arch-disseminator of German propaganda at home and abroad.

Four defendants—Ernst Kaltenbrunner, who helped to rule Austria; Hans Frank, Governor General of Poland; Robert Ley, leader of the Labor Front, and Martin Bormann, Deputy Fuehrer, still at large—were charged with complicity in the plot to wage aggressive war and with responsibility for war crimes and crimes against humanity, but their names were omitted from those who actually led Germany into war in violation of her treaties. Dr. Hjalmar Schacht, former president of the Reichsbank, and Franz von Papen, former Ambassador, were accused of plotting to wage aggressive war and doing so in violation of treaties, but they were not charged with any complicity in the commission of war crimes or crimes against humanity.

Grand Admiral Erich Raeder, former commander in chief of the navy, and his successor, Grand Admiral Karl Doenitz, who assumed succession to Hitler, were called on to answer all the counts, including responsibility for submarine warfare, but they were not held accountable for the wholesale extermination and enslavement of conquered peoples.

All the defendants will have at least thirty days to prepare their defense.

As the indictment was drawn it places the whole Nazi system, if not totalitarianism itself, on trial. ◈

Prosecutor Robert Jackson's opening statement at the beginning of the Nuremberg trials, 1945.

Germans Indicted In Massacre Of 11,000 Poles In Katyn Forest

Special to The New York Times.

BERLIN, Oct. 18—An indictment returned today before the International Tribunal holds the Germans responsible for the slaughter of 11,000 Polish officers in the Katyn forest near Smolensk.

This is but one of the many war crimes for which the majority of the German war leaders awaiting trial at Nuremberg will have to answer, but it is likely to prove by far the most controversial issue of the whole trial.

For the Germans have charged that the massacre was perpetrated by the Russians themselves before the German attack on the Soviet Union and the defense can hardly be expected to miss the opportunity to challenge the Russian prosecutors for proof of the charge.

The discovery of the bodies in mass graves in the Katyn Forest and its announcement by Germany marked one of the diplomatic crises of the war. The Polish Government in Exile in London immediately appealed to the International Red Cross to investigate and fix the responsibility. The Russians retorted by declaring this an unfriendly action by an ally and ultimately severed relations with the London Poles.

Later the Russians held a public exhumation of the bodies but the results were inconclusive.

Now for the first time the whole issue is thrown before a legal tribunal bound by the rules or evidence applying to military tribunals. Since it has been agreed that the Russian prosecutor, R. A. Rudenko, shall have charge of the presentation of proof relating to war crimes committed east of a line running north and south through the center of Berlin, it will fall to the lot of the Russians to prove their own charge that the Germans slaughtered the Poles and buried them in the Katyn forest.

It is an issue that the Germans are almost sure to challenge with all the documentation at their disposal.

The fate of these Polish officers was a mystery to Polish leaders for a long time before their bodies were found. It is said that the late former Premier, Gen. Wladislaw Sikorski, on his first visit to Moscow at Christmastime in 1941, ➤

❨ asked Premier Stalin about what had happened to them, and at first received satisfactory assurances regarding their safety.

Much of the proof of what really happened in the Katyn forest will devolve upon the date upon which these Polish officers were slaughtered; for if the crime was committed after the date when the Germans overran their last resting place it could not possibly have been committed by the Russians.

The Germans overran the Katyn Forest in July, 1941. ◇

OCTOBER 22, 1945

Atom Bomb And Politics

Despite Our New 'Bargaining' Power, Peace Is Seen as a Still Far-Off Goal

By HANSON W. BALDWIN

Eleven weeks have passed since the first atomic bomb in world history was dropped on Hiroshima, Japan.

They have been weeks in which the history of tomorrow has been shaped to the dangerous pattern of today; they have been weeks in which the world has made little progress toward either international security or international morality. They have been weeks of confusion and divided counsel, of lack of leadership, of claims and contradictions—and all the while the atomic bomb has clouded the skies of tomorrow.

In those weeks so many contradictory statements have been made about the atomic bomb—and incidentally about the technological revolution in war, of which the atomic bomb is only a part—that it is necessary to clear away some of the trees before we can see the woods.

First, in the field of atomic developments and manufacture:

Our monopoly of the "secret" of the atomic bomb is not a laboratory monopoly, not a monopoly in the field of physics. As Dr. J. Robert Oppenheimer has put it, "You cannot keep the nature of the world a secret; you cannot keep atoms secret." The data essential for atomic fission are known to all nations; indeed, our own nation did not originally lead in the laboratory and development race. We were able to manufacture the atomic bomb first, and we hold a head-start now, because of this country's unequaled industrial facilities, engineering and production "know-how" and power capacity. That is the real "secret" of the atomic bomb—America's engineering-industrial capacity.

RUSSIA A POTENTIAL PRODUCER

The present known methods of manufacturing the bomb require an industrial "know-how" so versatile, power resources so tremendous and an investment of plant and capital so great that it is probable that today only the United States is capable of manufacturing the atomic bomb. Until the processes are simplified, which they will be, not even Great Britain (which probably does not know the full secret of manufacture and detonation) has the capacity or the industrial economy to manufacture the bomb. Russia probably is the only other nation in the world, besides the United States, with sufficient potential to make the bomb by the processes now known. Russia must still develop that potential into actual manufacturing capacity. How long that will take no one knows, but it seems probable that non-Soviet physicists have misappraised the engineering problems involved and the present stage of development of Russian industry. But in any case, within two to fifteen years, conceivably less, improbably more, at least Russia, and quite possibly other powers, will be able to manufacture atomic bombs.

And they will have the raw material resources necessary to do it. At present uranium and thorium are the only practicable "atomic bomb" elements; in time, the energy in other elements will be tapped. Deposits of pitchblende or carnotite, from which uranium is derived; are known to exist in Canada, the United States, the Belgian Congo and Europe. At least one of the European sources is within the Russian sphere of influence, and there are believed to be sizable sources, unknown to us, in the Soviet Union.

Our own progress in atomic physics and engineering will not halt, but whether we can maintain our present lead and advance more rapidly than Russia is uncertain. Our best physicists and engineers are going back to civilian labo-

---

OCTOBER 21, 1945

DE GAULLE SCORES THREE-FOLD VICTORY IN FRENCH ELECTION

By LANSING WARREN
By Wireless to The New York Times.

PARIS, Monday, Oct. 22—Incomplete returns from more than half the departments of France early today continued to confirm the early indications of a threefold victory for Gen. Charles de Gaulle in yesterday's national elections.

On the issues of the referendum, an overwhelming vote in favor of framing a new constitution and a lesser yet still unexpectedly strong ballot in favor of giving the Constituent Assembly extended powers were piling up. Almost all the present Ministers—some of whom have been heavily attacked—have been victorious. The final returns are not expected before tomorrow morning, but the parties' standings on first examination appear to have closely repeated the indications of the cantonal elections.

[The count at 7:30 A.M., Paris time, reported by The United Press showed: 8,552,929 to 290,434 for a new constitution; 5,775,528 to 2,667,984 for the de Gaulle Assembly plan. The Socialists had elected seventy-eight candidates to the Assembly; the Mouvement Republicain Populaire, 64; Communists, 58; Radical Socialists, 17; other parties, 38.]

The Catholic-Socialist Mouvement Republicain Populaire appeared to be making even larger gains than it did then, and the Socialists were holding closely to their previous winnings and had every chance of being the most powerful party in the new Assembly. The Communists, with lesser successes than in the cantonal balloting, were nevertheless heading for a strong place. The Radical Socialists had even greater losses than before.

Government officials professed great satisfaction as the favorable results came in after midnight The official figures then showed the Socialists leading in sixteen departments, the Communists ahead in twelve, the MRP victorious in eleven and the Republican Entente ahead in ten.

Returns from more than half the departments showed 92 per cent of "Yes"

The ruins of Hiroshima two months after the atomic bomb was dropped, October, 1945.

ratories. Dr. Oppenheimer and others like him will be leaving the Government atomic bomb project early next year. The Russians, on the other hand, operating under a totalitarian system, will be able to concentrate just as much energy and capacity as they wish upon their project.

Second, in the political field:

The atomic bomb, it has been said, is giving us a great though admittedly a temporary advantage in our political negotiations with Russia and in settling the problems of the peace.

The past eleven weeks belie this statement. The problems of the peace are at stalemate. Moreover, the atomic bomb is of relatively little use to us in political bargaining, for the Russians are realists; they know we would not use the atomic bomb against them unless they used it first, or unless they attacked us suddenly and brutally by other means. In other words, in so far as the atomic bomb is

concerned we are not holding an ace; we are bluffing. Moreover, if Russia should say in a year or so, or even tomorrow, "We have made an atomic bomb"—the United States, given its present intelligence service, would not know whether the claim was true or not. Furthermore, put ourselves in the Russian position. If the Russians possessed the bomb and we did not, would we consider its possession conducive to peace; would we be disturbed or placid?

Where, then, is the political advantage to us of the atomic bomb ? It has given us no advantage so far; indeed, it seems to have forced thinking in Washington more strongly than ever before into the glib old pattern of dependence upon national power.

There are too little imagination and breadth of vision in the halls of Congress and the streets of America, and without them the people perish. ◇

replies on the first referendum question and 70 per cent "Yes" on the second suits meant a notable defeat for the Communists, who led a furious campaign for a "No" reply to the second question, and an even more notable one for the Radical-Socialists, who advocated "No" replies to both questions. The success of the Government's supporters unquestionably exceeded their expectations.

Because of the complicated system of voting and the restrictions against writing names or anything at all on the ballots, many were declared invalid. Abstentions were apparently not so great as in the cantonal elections and were larger in small rural communities than in cities and centers of industry. Some districts in Paris polled almost 90 per cent of the registered voters, but in war-torn centers the vote fell off.

The approval of the first question of the referendum meant that France had rejected the Constitution of 1875 and authorized the new Assembly to write a new constitution. The approval of the second question meant that France recognized the new Assembly as a sovereign body with power to overthrow the Government but limited in tenure to seven months.

At the end of seven months the new constitution must be submitted in another referendum, after which, if it is approved, a new Parliament will be elected under it. If the Assembly fails to complete a new constitution within seven months, as is possible, it will be dissolved and a similar Assembly will be elected to try again. ◇

OCTOBER 22, 1945

Poles Found Cowed by Fear into Submission To Regime

60,000 to 80,000 Prisoners Reported Held—Oswiecim Camp Reopened— Secret Police Watch Homes

By GLADWIN HILL
By Wireless to The New York Times.

WARSAW, Poland, Oct 12. (Delayed; via Berlin)—This is written in Warsaw, but it will not be committed to print until this correspondent is safely out of Poland.

Foreign correspondents at present are being allowed to circulate in Poland under the Potsdam Agreement and none so far has been harmed but a definite hostility toward foreign reporting of unquestionable facts already has been displayed.

There also exists throughout the war-torn country today a condition approaching a subtle reign of terror in which there is no assurance of what may happen to critics of the present regime.

There are, however, too many indications of what may happen. The official line advanced by some Government officers is that there are no more than 1,000 political prisoners in Poland today. However, other Government officials have acknowledged to me that there were between 60,000 and 80,000, with the stipulation that the bulk of them are "Volksdeutsch"—Polish Germans or Germanized Poles.

The belief is widespread in Warsaw that there are 10,000 at Cracow alone and some responsible observers think the total may be nearer 100,000.

The former German concentration camp at Oswiecim, whose name to any Pole is synonymous with horror, is operating again under Polish auspices and its wire fences have been charged with electricity.

The round-up of persons whose only evident offense was suspected opposition to the current Communist-dominated regime was in any case extensive enough to have netted in recent days a number of individuals with claims on American citizenship, most of whom are still locked up under no specific charges and without trial. ›

One institution in Warsaw and other cities these days is "The Well," a Gestapo-like operation in which the police keep a guard, for days on end if necessary, at a block, a building or part of a building, seizing indiscriminately anyone who visits the place. This might be excused as an ordinary manhunt except that it happens curiously often, involves the detention of innocent people and has spread such fear that I know of innocent people who have stayed away from home nights on end because they had been told that "The Well" was working in their neighborhood.

I will give other examples of incidents that have contributed to what I have been forced to describe—only after considerable thought and with considerable regret—as a near reign of terror in a country whose regime takes pride in being "democratic."

On Sept. 16 the Polish Peasants party, principal opposition threat to the present regime, held a rally at Cracow. One of its most prominent regional leaders was a man named Rjeszow Kojder. The day after the rally I was informed authoritatively that four uniformed men had appeared at M. Kojder's home and had taken him away.

Three days later he was found shot to death.

OFFICIALS FEARFUL AT NIGHT

What is the purpose of this reign of fear? There are two obvious possible answers. One is that the police measures were taken to preserve order. If this be the aim the measures are failing notably.

In Polish cities, with shooting a nightly occurrence, even Government officials are timid about traveling by night.

The conditions are openly admitted in the newly announced installation of units, headed by Russian generals, in each of the country's dozen regional divisions for the stated purpose of stopping "marauding."

The other obvious answer is that the present "provisional" regime is going to these extremes to suppress opposition and perpetuate itself. The official attitude is that sweeping measures were necessary against the "reactionary" and "Fascist" elements at large in Poland who jeopardized national unity—an argument curiously as old as authoritarianism itself.

To just what extent the Russians are immediately responsible for the undesirable conditions is debatable. There was fascism in Poland before the war. But the fact that Russian influence in Poland physically—with hundreds of thousands of Russian troops on Polish soil—economically and otherwise and the fact that the present Polish Government is largely a Russian creation cannot be gainsaid.

It is also unquestionable that along with the current situation in Poland there is a concerted effort to hamper the dissemination of details to the outside world. American and British correspondents have been in Poland only a few weeks but already there have been snide attacks on them in the press for their clothes, their dancing and even their cigarettes—as well as on their re-

---

OCTOBER 23, 1945

Quisling Executed by a Firing Squad

By The United Press.

OSLO, Norway, Oct 24—Vidkun Quisling, the traitor Premier of Norway under Nazi occupation, was executed early today by a firing squad at ancient Akershus Portress, where Quisling's German friends themselves killed many loyal Norwegians.

Quisling, 58, who helped the Germans to invade his country April 9, 1940, was sentenced to die last Sept. 10 by a Norwegian court. He was convicted of many charges, the greatest of which were treason and murder. His crimes ranged from sending thousands of Jews to their deaths to stealing King Haakon's silverware.

Quisling appealed to the Norwegian Supreme Court, but his defense availed him nothing and on Oct. 13 the Supreme Court said he must die. ◇

Vidkun Quisling, center, listening during the summation of his trial, 1945.

MARCH 12, 1946

PRAVDA DENOUNCES CHURCHILL'S SPEECH AS THREAT OF WAR

By BROOKS ATKINSON
By Wireless to The New York Times.

MOSCOW, March 11—Six days after Winston Churchill's speech in Fulton, Mo., Pravda, official organ of the Central Executive Committee of the Communist party, vigorously denounced Mr. Churchill as an anti-Soviet warmonger in a three-column front-page editorial today.

It accuses Mr. Churchill of trying to destroy the United Nations Organization and to establish a policy of force to control the world. Specifically Pravda declares:

"What does the proposal of Churchill come to? The formation of an Anglo-American military alliance that would assure Anglo-American rule throughout the world, the liquidation of the three-power coalition, also the UNO, and make a policy of force the dominant factor in the development of the world. All you need to complete the picture is

porting. Larry Allen's initial report to the Associated Press that there had been shooting in the streets of Warsaw was indignantly denied by Government officials until they were invited to see it for themselves almost any night from the balcony of the United States Embassy. Then they admitted it.

Charles Arnot of the United Press also has been criticized baselessly for his reports. This correspondent has been attacked in the Polish press for an alleged "report to The New York Times" which he did not write and, so far as he knows, never had been written by anyone.

The intensity of this campaign of defamation, before much really had been written about Poland, makes it look like a preparatory backfire to discredit correspondents' reports in advance and maintain a shroud of phony propaganda around the Poles, if not around the rest of the world. ◇

---

a frank formula for a 'cordon sanitaire' against the U.S.S.R."

The bold statements in Pravda aroused the greatest interest in Moscow today. On Friday all newspapers published a brief report that Mr. Churchill had made an anti-Soviet speech at the head of a column of unfavorable comments by United States Senators and British Labor party representatives.

Pravda today published a two and one-half column summary of the speech, containing many direct quotations. Today's editorial, coming on the eve of the first session of the new Supreme Soviet, is the first indication of the seriousness of the Churchill charges.

CHARGES SEEN CONFIRMED

It is regarded here as confirming many recent election speeches that stressed that the danger of capitalist encirclement of the Soviet Union was still present and increased the belief here that reactionaries in the West who are hostile to the Soviet Union are trying to split the UNO. In the circumstances Moscow people take the gravest view of Mr. Churchill's speech and wonder what it signifies.

Now that the war against Germany and Japan is finished, Pravda says Churchill is returning to his previous policy of shaking the scarecrow of "Bolshevik danger and Bolshevik expansion," dug out of his archives. It says the British people paid dearly for the old

---

MARCH 13, 1946

Editorial
ANSWERING MR. CHURCHILL

After six days of silence the entire Russian propaganda apparatus has now opened up a barrage against Winston Churchill as a warmonger who would disturb the friendship between Russia and the United States and align us with the British Empire in a war against the Soviets. That is poor recompense for a man who aligned himself with Russia the moment Hitler attacked. But this line has a familiar ring from the recent past. There are two things, we believe, that need be said about it.

The first is that if Russia interprets the hesitant reception accorded Mr. Churchill's speech as an opportunity to split the United States and Britain it is making the same grave mistake that oth-

---

"adventure of British reactionaries who tried by armed force to enforce their will on the young Soviet Republic."

Referring to the intervention after World War I, Pravda declares, "this adventure, as is known, fell with a crash despite all the efforts of the Churchills and Chamberlains." Discussing Mr. Churchill's statement that he does not think a new war is inevitable, Pravda says:

"He does not say what he thinks. In reality he tries to give the impression of an impending war. Moreover, he urges a new war, a war against the Soviet Union, when he makes a slander against the Soviet Union."

Pravda also points out that an Anglo-American military alliance would be directed "against that power which bore on its shoulders the main burden of the struggle and played a decisive role in the defeat of Hitlerite Germany." According to Pravda, Mr. Churchill knows he does not have sufficient strength to carry on a war against the Soviet Union and therefore is trying to enlist American support.

"Churchill convulsively grabs for the coat tails of Uncle Sam," it says, "in the hope that an Anglo-American military alliance would enable the British Empire, although in the role of a junior partner, to continue the policy of imperialist expansion." ◇

---

ers have made before it. To a degree which should give pause to Moscow, the American and the British people are in complete agreement on the causes of the present international tension, as analyzed by Mr. Churchill, and if they differ on the immediate means for meeting this tension it is chiefly because the American people are still more optimistic about Russian reasonableness and the possibility of agreement than either Mr. Churchill or large sections of British opinion appear to be.

The second observation is that both the American and the British people have a clear realization of what is cause and what is effect in the present situation. After going to the limit in tendering Russia both their friendship and their aid, and after making enormous concessions to Russia against the dictates of their own interests, their judgment and sometimes their consciences, they are now disturbed by the discovery that Russian appetites appear to grow upon what they feed, and that in satisfying these appetites Russia is inclined on occasion to make light of treaties and agreements on whose observance must rest world peace and order.

If Russia really desires to give an effective answer to Mr. Churchill there is a very simple way of doing this. All Moscow needs to do is to abide by the pledges, agreements and treaties it has made and the whole international tension will disappear overnight. ◇

MARCH 13, 1946

Truman on World Situation: 'We Will Work Out of It'

By FELIX BELAIR Jr.
Special to The New York Times.

WASHINGTON, March 14—President Truman said today that he saw no reason to become alarmed over the international situation and that "I do not think it is as fraught with danger as a lot of people seem to think it is." He was asked later if he would be willing to express his feelings about the situation in affirmative fashion.

"Would it help any if I said I am not alarmed about it?" he replied.

OPTIMISTIC ABOUT FUTURE

"Yes," said his questioner. "May we quote you on that?" "Of course you may," said Mr. Truman.

"You are optimistic that it will-work out?" the newspaper writer persisted.

"I am sure we will work out of it," the President replied.

The President showed more than usual reluctance to get into the field of international relations during his regular news conference and it was not until a reporter reminded him during the latter half of the session that some sort of statement was expected of him in view of widespread public concern that the Chief Executive would venture beyond his "no comment" replies.

SHUNS CHURCHILL-STALIN ISSUE

At the same time he steered entirely clear of questions calculated to place him on one or the other side of what one reporter termed the "world debate" between Winston Churchill and Premier Stalin.

Meanwhile, the President sought to spike rumors of a continuing rift between him and Secretary of State James F. Byrnes. He opened his news conference by volunteering the explanation that he wanted to make a strong and emphatic statement that there was no rift, never had been and never would be—he hoped—between him and the Secretary of State.

Reports had come to the President's attention, he said, that "gossip columns" had published rumors that Mr. Byrnes was on his way out. When a reporter suggested that the rumor might have been inspired and could not have come from mere spontaneous combustion, Mr. Truman said that such must have been the case unless somebody just wanted to tell a big lie.

Although he said there were no plans afoot for another meeting with Prime Minister Attlee and Premier Stalin, the President said that he confidently expected the scheduled opening meeting of the United Nations Organization Security Council to be held later this month as planned and with its full membership attending.

Mr. Truman said that he had not been advised officially or otherwise of the nature of Mr, Churchill's scheduled radio address Friday night beyond what had been published in the newspapers. Neither would the President comment on the "appropriateness" of the former British Prime Minister's "conducting his debate from this country," as a reporter described Mr. Churchill's speaking activities.

In much the same manner the President replied to a question whether he would comment on a published interview with Premier Stalin in the Moscow newspaper Pravda describing the British war leader as a "warmonger." Mr. Truman replied with a chuckle that since he could not read Russian he had no way of knowing whether the stories published in this country contained an accurate translation.

However, the President made it quite clear that he had had no communication of any kind with Mr. Stalin in the immediate past. ◇

OCTOBER 1, 1946

Germans Haggard Awaiting Fate; Only Goering Can Muster a Smile

By KATHLEEN McLAUGHLIN
Special to The New York Times

NUREMBERG, Germany, Sept. 30— Haggard of face and subdued of manner, the accused who expected to be the convicted were the most absorbed listeners throughout today's dramatic penultimate sequence in the war crimes trial here. With head sets clamped to their ears and tuned to German translations of the judgment of the International Military Tribunal, they missed no passing phrase in the measured reading of the decisions that might provide a clue to their individual life or death sentences tomorrow.

Their jauntiness and good humor had vanished, in contrast to the attitudes frequently exhibited during the last ten months.

Only Hermann Goering, former Reich Marshal and Luftwaffe commander, could summon a feeble smile at rare intervals. Only Rudolf Hess, the former deputy Nazi party leader—consistent to the end in his real or simulated role of a man of vacant mind—ignored the proceedings and sat oblivious to everything around him. Until early afternoon when he once more was escorted from the courtroom on a claim of illness, he sat with folded arms, now and then flinging up his head to stare fixedly at the occupants of the visitors' gallery.

Julius Streicher, the "Jew baiter," champed unceasingly on a wad of gum. Karl Doenitz, onetime Grand Admiral and Reichsfuehrer, wearing dark glasses, doodled idly on a scrap of paper. Dr. Wilhelm Frick, former Protector of Bohemia and Moravia, and Dr. Alfred Rosenberg, once occupation chief in Soviet territory, glowered steadily at those in the press section who were using opera glasses.

For the most part, the day passed with a minimum of flurry and without incident, except for the sudden slumping to the floor during the morning session of one of the white-helmeted military policemen ranged stiffly across the rear of the dock behind the defendants.

Sir Geoffrey Lawrence of Great Britain began the reading of the 260-page judgment and passed the task in turn to each of the other three judges and four alternates representing the United Kingdom, France, Russia and the United States. Meticulously and thoroughly, the document marshalled the details of the frightfulness of the war and its attendant crimes, of which the defendants stand accused.

OCTOBER 16, 1946

GEHRING ENDS LIFE BY POISON, TEN OTHERS HANGED

By DANA ADAMS SCHMIDT
Special to The New York Times.

NUREMBERG, Germany, Oct. 16—Ten Nazi war criminals were hanged in the prison here early today, but the eleventh, Hermann Wilhelm Goering, committed suicide by swallowing poison in his cell some two hours before he was to have gone to the gallows.

Goering, former No. 2 Nazi and chief of the Luftwaffe, took cyanide of potassium, which he somehow had succeeded in secreting, Col. Burton C. Andrus, commandant of the prison security detail, announced.

Factually, coolly, each of the judges in turn intoned the findings, evaluating the testimony submitted and disclosing gradually how effectively the prosecution had built its case on the archives of the Nazi regime itself. This time the grim, familiar chapters held a special significance for the score of men awaiting judgment. Yet only one revealed evidence of any particular emotion.

Ernst Kaltenbrunner, former head of the secret police, listening to the declaration that he, among others, had used the Gestapo for criminal purposes, and to a recital of those crimes, was visibly affected. His facial contortions, convincing some of those present that he was trying to smile but was about to weep instead, were so marked that the suspicion was generated that he might be about to suffer a recurrence of the cerebral hemorrhage that put him into the hospital for a time early in the trial.

No flicker of reaction crossed Goering's sober countenance as pointed references to his participation in the war conspiracy and war crimes underlined his scant chance of escaping with a light sentence. ◆

German war crimes defendants during the Nuremberg trials. Among them, from left to right, are Hermann Goering, Joachim Von Ribbentrop, Wilhelm Keitel, Alfred Rosenberg in the front row; Karl Doenitz, Erich Raeder, Baldor von Schirach, Fritz Sauchel, Alfred Jodl behind them.

Hermann Goering having a meal in Nuremberg prison, October 1946.

A guard saw Goering twitching on his cot at 10:45 o'clock last night and summoned aid, but Adolf Hitler's erstwhile heir-apparent could not be revived. Colonel Andrus said glass from a capsule containing the poison was found in Goering's mouth.

INTERVENTION TOO LATE

The guard did not see Goering put his hand under his blanket, and intervened the instant he saw the prisoner twitch, but it was too late.

[An envelope containing penciled notes and a small brass cartridge case that apparently had contained the poison vial were found on Goering's body, press services reported.]

Except for Goering, the executions then took place in the order of the indictment and in which the condemned men had sat in the prisoners' dock during the ten-month trial before the International Military Tribunal.

The Nazis walked to the gallows in this order:

Joachim von Ribbentrop, former Foreign Minister; Field Marshal Gen. Wilhelm Keitel, chief of the German High Command; Ernst Kaltenbrunner, head of the Gestapo; Alfred Rosenberg, Minister for Occupied Territories; Hans Frank, who led in the killing of thousands of Poles; Wilhelm Frick, former Minister of the Interior; Julius Streicher, leader of Nazi anti-Semitism; Fritz Sauckel, director of forced labor; Col. Gen. Alfred Jodl, head of the German General Staff, and Arthur Seyss-Inquart, who sold out Austria.

The condemned men were notified on two occasions of the date of the executions, authoritative sources said, but the ten who were hanged did not know the time until an hour before they began.

Repeated shouts as of the conclusion of frenzied speeches, followed by a thudding like the springing of a heavy trap door, were heard from a building at the rear of the prison courtyard between 2 and 3:15 A.M., according to the German News Agency.

DEFIANT TO THE LAST

NUREMBERG, Oct. 16 (U.P.)—While officials started an investigation into Goering's suicide, his ten fellow-criminals paraded to the gallows and were hanged. Goering was to have led the procession. The prison gymnasium was used as the execution chamber. Three gallows had been erected there under electric lights. Two of them were used.

Witnesses said the first execution took four minutes and that the hangings continued from 1:01 A.M. (7:01 P.M. Tuesday Eastern Standard Time) to 2:45 A.M.

Von Ribbentrop entered the execution chamber first.

"God save Germany! My last wish is that Germany rediscover her unity and that an alliance be made between East and West and that peace reign on earth," he shouted a moment before he died. The hangman's trap dropped him into space at 1:14 A.M. Seyss-Inquart, the Austrian traitor, was the last to be executed. He was pronounced dead at 2:57 A.M. (10:57 P.M., Eastern Standard Time.)

Sauckel shouted before he died: "I pay my respect to American officers and American soldiers but not to American justice." He had been trying to get President Truman to intercede for him.

Keitel called on God in a firm voice to protect Germany. He thanked the ▶

‹ priest who stood beside him for his offices. "I call on the Almighty to be considerate of the German people," Keitel said. "All for Germany. I thank you."

"Good luck to Germany," shouted Kaltenbrunner.

Rosenberg, atheist political philosopher of the Nazi party, said nothing. He merely cleared his throat.

"I am thankful for the kind treatment I have received," said Frank. "I pray to God to receive me mercifully."

Most of the executed men endeavored to show their bravery, said Kingsbury Smith of the International News Service, who was the representative of the American press. Most of them were bitterly defiant and some grimly resigned, while others begged the Almighty for mercy. All ten went with apparent stoicism; none collapsed.

The only one, however, to make any reference to Hitler or the Nazi ideology in the final moments, said Mr. Smith, was Streicher. He screamed "Heil Hitler" at the top of his lungs as he was about to mount the steps leading to the gallows.

[Each of the condemned was held steady by two United States Army guards from the time he left his cell until the time the trap was sprung, The Associated Press said. Their hands were tied behind them with black shoe laces and their feet were strapped with army belts.] ◆

Editorial
THE NAZI HERITAGE

In his report on the Nuremberg trial Justice Jackson rightly emphasizes that more important than the personal fate of the Nazi leaders, already broken and discredited men before they died, are the principles to which the great nations of the world have committed themselves by their participation in the trial and their execution of its judgment. These principles, now backed by the power of precedent, constitute the basic charter of international law and this law applies not only to the Nazi leaders but to all men everywhere.

This means, as Mr. Jackson points out, that many more Germans will have to be tried for crimes committed on a lower level, and preparations for such trials are already under way. Whether the method of trial by the individual occupying Powers suggested by Mr. Jackson best serves not only economy but also justice is another matter. Though the four Powers agreed on procedure at Nuremberg, they do not all subscribe to the same rules within their respective jurisdictions, and it would discredit the

Nuremberg judgment if it were used to sanction trials based on collective instead of individual guilt, or trials in which the prosecutor dominates the judge.

Beyond that, Mr. Jackson also emphasizes the unchallengeable maxim that the "standards by which the Germans have been condemned will become the condemnation of any nation that is faithless to them." There may have been some doubt in the first flush of victory as to what the obligations of the victors were. But there is no excuse for further uncertainty or indulgence. It is incumbent upon all victors to review their own policies and practices in the light of the new law.

For the Nazi leaders were convicted not only of waging aggressive war but also of many other deeds connected with that act. They were convicted of plundering and exploiting occupied territories and ill-treating and starving the civilian population. The victors have just claims against the Nazi regime and the German state; they can have no right to confiscate the property of individuals or to pursue policies which impose upon the conquered populations "needless aggravation or economic distress," for which the American Secretary of State himself holds the victors responsible.

The Nazis were also convicted of deporting civilian populations, but the victors themselves have not only decreed the deportation of even larger numbers but have, in some cases, carried these

---

Viceroy Gives British Plan For the Partition of India

By GEORGE E. JONES
Special to The New York Times.

NEW DELHI, India, June 2—The Viceroy, Viscount Mountbatten, informed Indian political leaders today of the British Government's plan to partition India into Hindu and Moslem states upon Britain's departure by June, 1948.

Tomorrow night the Viceroy will broadcast the text of the plan to India and the Empire and subsequently leaders of the three main political elements— Pandit Jawaharlal Nehru for the predominantly Hindu Congress party, Mohammed Ali Jinnah for the Moslem League, and Sardar Baldev Singh for the

Sikhs—will broadcast to the Indians.

The Viceroy will hold a press conference on Thursday.

Today's meeting lasted two hours. It adjourned until 10 o'clock tomorrow morning. This, according to a press communiqué from the Viceroy's House, will enable the Working Committees of the Congress party and the Moslem League to consider the plan.

From present indications the country's two largest parties will acquiesce to the British proposal, even though grudgingly, as the only practicable solution of

a political vacuum which means bloodshed and civil strife. Even as the leaders met today, military and police forces were alerted for possible outbreaks in strategic centers of India, particularly in Bengal, the Punjab and Delhi.

GAVE FULL ACCOUNT

The communiqué said that the "Viceroy gave the meeting a full account of his discussions both in India and in England which had led up to the formulation of His Majesty's Government's plan and of the arguments which had resulted in its adoption." Copies of the announcement were then handed round to the leaders.

"Mr. Jinnah remained for a brief interview with His Excellency after the meeting," the communiqué said.

The communiqué disclosed also that the Viceroy later met Mohandas K. Gandhi for forty-five minutes. It said also that tomorrow afternoon the Vice-

out without any regard for the "orderly and humane manner" which they themselves prescribed. The Nazis, again, were convicted of employing slave labor during the war, yet a year and a half after the cessation of hostilities some of the victors are still employing as slave laborers several million war prisoners, often under conditions no better than those provided by the Nazis.

Moreover, the Nazis were convicted of maintaining concentration camps for political opponents, but the concentration camps maintained by one of the victors, Russia, stretch from the Atlantic to the Bering Strait, and hold not merely persons suspected of criminal Nazism or collaboration, but many others also, including former political and economic leaders of "liberated" territories.

Finally, the Nazis were convicted of requisitioning agricultural products, raw materials and foreign securities without consideration of the local economy and of making their armies live on conquered lands. A mere glance at the daily press shows that this process is being continued in many parts of Eastern Europe.

The Nazis committed their deeds in pursuit of aggressive war. The victors may plead that what they are doing is just retribution upon the conquered peoples, but they cannot inflict such retribution without putting themselves above the law they have just imposed upon the vanquished. ◆

roy would meet the Chancellor of the Chamber of Princes and the Princely States Negotiating Committee to inform them of the plan.

The wording of the communiqué indicated that if the Congress party representatives this morning offered to Mr. Jinnah unqualified assurances of adhering to last year's British plan to preserve India's unity, he rejected the offer as too late.

Attending the round table conference with the Viceroy were Pandit Nehru, Acharya Kripalani and Sardar Vallabhbhai Patel for the Congress party; Mr. Jinnah, Liaqat Ali Khan and Sardar Abdur Rab Nishtar for the Moslem League and Sardar Baldev Singh for the Sikhs. ◆

JUNE 6, 1947

MARSHALL URGES UNITY IN EUROPE

He Tells Harvard Alumni Our Policy Is Not Set Against 'Any Country or Doctrine'

By FRANK L. KLUCKHOHN
Special to The New York Times.

CAMBRIDGE, Mass., June 5—The countries of Europe were called upon today by the Secretary of State, George C. Marshall, to get together and decide upon their needs for economic rehabilitation so that further United States aid could be provided upon an integrated instead of a "piecemeal" basis. This was important to make possible a real "cure" of Europe's critical economic difficulties, he asserted in an address to Harvard alumni this afternoon after he had received the honorary degree of Doctor of Laws at this morning's commencement exercises.

General Marshall supported President Truman's statements in Washington earlier today that United States aid abroad was necessary. He declared that Europe "must have substantial additional help or face economic, social and political deterioration of a very grave character."

"There must be some agreement among the countries of Europe as to the requirements of the situation," he warned, adding that no American aid would be given to "any government which maneuvers to block the recovery of other countries." The Secretary emphasized that governments or parties or groups, seeking

Secretary of State George Marshall in 1947.

to make political capital by perpetuating human misery, would encounter "the opposition of the United States."

General Marshall was the recipient of several ovations as he participated in Harvard's first fully normal post-war graduation exercises. The first came when he moved to the platform before Memorial Church in the procession of 2,185 undergraduates, graduate students and the honor group who were to receive degrees. The second ovation came when James B. Conant, president, conferred an honorary degree upon him.

The biggest ovations came just before and after he spoke, with applause interlarded when the Secretary said American help would be withheld from those making capital of trouble in Europe.

General Marshall was one of the last to speak this afternoon. Gen. Omar N. Bradley, administrator of veterans' affairs, who also received a Doctor of Laws degree, had asserted that the expenditure of $12,000,000,000 for veterans' education was a good investment for the United States and Dr. Conant had called for the raising of $90,000,000 to increase Harvard's activities.

"FRIENDLY AID" STRESSED
After asserting that no "assured peace" or political stability was possible without the aid of the United States in effecting a return to normal economic health in the world, General Marshall said that "the initiative, I think, should come from Europe." This country should restrict itself to "friendly aid" in the drafting of a European program and later in supporting this program "as far as it may be practical for us to do so," he added.

He held it to be essential that several and, if possible, all European states should effect what he termed a "joint" program. It would be neither "fitting nor efficacious" for us to draw up a unilateral program and then foist it upon possibly unwilling governments and nations, said the General.

Economic rehabilitation in Europe would require "a much longer time and greater effort" than had been officially foreseen, he continued. Then he stressed that the United States was willing to give "full cooperation" to countries willing to assist in steps toward European recovery, and denied that the policy of the United States was directed against "any country or doctrine."

FOR AMERICAN UNDERSTANDING
In a few brief words after his prepared talk, Secretary Marshall said that he

❨ regarded full understanding by the American people of foreign problems and the aims of American policy to be of high importance.

He already had expressed the fear that the enormous complexity of problems and the mass of facts available were confusing people.

The dislocation of the entire fabric of European economy through the breaking up of commercial ties and the elimination of private banks, insurance companies and the loss of capital, probably was even more serious than the destruction of physical property of all sorts and the losses in manpower, he explained.

The Secretary said that one important factor leading to the threat of a complete "breakdown" in Europe was the fact that the cities were no longer producing much that the farmers wanted and that, as a result, the farmers were making little effort to raise enough to feed the cities. Thus, with city people

short of food and fuel, he added, "the Governments are forced to use their foreign money and credits for necessities instead of reconstruction."

The Secretary, who was presented to the Harvard alumni by Gov. Robert F. Bradford, returned to Washington by air after the ceremonies.

General Bradley, in the uniform of a full general with four rows of ribbons, devoted himself largely to one facet of the country's program, his own.

"In the United States, of the 2,300,000 students in colleges, 1,200,000 are veterans, getting their education mostly at Government expense," he said. "Within twenty months after the close of the war, the American people had already invested nearly $2,500,000,000 in the (educational) program. By the time it is completed, the program may have cost a total of $12,000,000,000, or barely enough to have run the war for several weeks."

"There are times when it may be

more dangerous to spend too little than to spend too much," General Bradley continued. "For example, if ever we should expose our people to sickness, our resources to waste, our economy to depression and our nation to aggression in a panicky effort to save dollars, we may some day have to ask ourselves if such savings were worth the cost.

"If we offer youth a fair chance to make its way in the nation we need not fear political deflection to either the left or right. We cannot meet the challenge of rival ideologies with labels and reaction. We must offer these young veterans progress and the opportunity for constant self-betterment throughout their busy lives."

General Bradley obtained a laugh from his audience when, referring to his honorary degree, he said:

"Like thousands of other veterans, I appear to be getting my education as a result of the GI bill." ◊

JUNE 8, 1947

TRUMAN DOCTRINE UPHELD BY PORTER

Declaring that the Truman Doctrine of aid for Greece and Turkey was in line with the late President Roosevelt's "quarantine the aggressors" speech in 1937, Paul Porter, former head of the American Economic Mission to Greece yesterday said that he hoped to see American financial aid extended to other European countries to help in reconstruction of then economies.

Mr. Porter, who spoke at a luncheon of the New York County organization of the Liberal party in the Grand Ball Room of the Hotel Commodore, called for a liberal American foreign policy with the twin objectives of economic abundance and economic freedom for all.

"Greece, in my judgment, should be looked on as only the first item in a much broader program of European reconstruction," Mr. Porter said. "Our difficulties in Greece stem largely from the fact that we are entering the situation so late, after it had boiled up to crisis.

"Today we are faced with the symptoms of impending collapse in large areas of Western Europe. We are faced with the gradual shrinkage of the dollar

resources on which European countries must depend for the rehabilitation and modernization of their capital equipment. Europe cannot be on its feet politically because it is not yet on its feet economically, and an investment in European economic and political stability, no matter how large an investment that may be, will cost a good deal less than the cost of chaos and ware.

HEROIC EFFORT HELD NEEDED

"It will require a heroic effort on our part, but it is the only basis for a sound liberal policy. And it is the business of liberals to educate public opinion and rouse public demand so that the Administration may get the money and backing to carry out this policy.

"Food and fuel are our best weapons against totalitarianism. We will soon be throwing them into Greece. I hope that before long we will be throwing them in tremendous volume into other parts of Europe. We will use them in favor of economic security and of political liberty. We will not use them in an effort to impose laissez-faire capitalism upon Europe. We stand for expanding production and against social chaos, whatever the system. And we will not use food and fuel, I hope, in the service of reactionary government."

Mr. Porter said the purpose of the

loan to Greece was to secure that country from external aggression and make possible its economic reconstruction and political democratization. Conceding that the present government of Greece needed reform, Mr. Porter expressed confidence that we could work with this government and develop elements of the center and non-Communist left as a basis for peace within Greece. ◊

President Harry S. Truman signing the Foreign Aid Assistance Act, also known as the Truman Doctrine, which provided foreign aid to Greece and Turkey, 1947.

NANKING LEADERS PLAN ALL-OUT WAR
Government Is Expected to Call for 'Punitive Expedition' Against Reds as 'Rebels'

By TILLMAN DURDIN
Special to The New York Times.

NANKING, June 30—Meeting in a five-hour secret session, Kuomintang leaders prepared today to draw more sharply the lines of conflict with the Communists.

A joint session of the Kuomintang Central Political Council and the Standing Committee of the Central Executive Committee decided to "reinforce punitive action" against the Reds.

The decision is expected to result in the State Council's declaring that the Communists are rebels against the State and proclaiming the anti-Communist war to be a "punitive expedition."

Many Government leaders maintain that such a move would commit the Government more definitely in the public mind to a war to the finish with the Communists and would improve the morale of the army. They point out that such a step would remove the domestic strife from the category of civil war and change the conflict into a campaign against rebels.

MORE U.S. AID EXPECTED

It is argued that if the Government declared itself to be fighting Communist insurgents against recognized national authority there might be a better chance of obtaining American sympathy and support and more basis for countering any Russian move to assist the Communists.

Saturday's Supreme Court order, branding Mao Tze-tung as the rebel leader of an illegal party and directing his arrest, is seen as fitting in with the new Government line regarding the Communists.

Today's conclave of more than fifty high Kuomintang officials, including most Government Ministers, was the most important held in Nanking since the sessions that led to the Government reorganization in March. Generalissimo Chiang Kai-shek presided during the first stages of the session. Information Minister Peng Hsueh-pei denied after the meeting that Russian or American angles were discussed. It is assumed, however, that Washington's decision to sell ammunition to Nanking and to give the Chinese access to commercial supplies of military equipment in the United States was in the background of the discussion. It is likely the Washington move encouraged the meeting to take a firmer anti-Communist stand.

Mr. Peng said the recent Government victories over the Communists in Manchuria and Shantung contributed to the confidence at the session. He announced that the consensus was that the Communists were not as strong militarily as their propaganda made them appear and that resolute Government action would insure victory over the Reds. ◆

CZECHS, IN DILEMMA, SEEK MOSCOW CUE

By The Associated Press.

PRAGUE July 4—Czechoslovak leaders hurriedly scheduled a trip to Moscow tonight, undoubtedly in the hope of conferring with the Russians about the serious economic situation created here by Soviet rejection of the French plan for implementing the Marshall proposals for aiding Europe.

Premier Klement Gottwald, a Communist, and Foreign Minister Jan Masaryk decided on the Moscow trip after day-long discussion in Parliamentary circles of the new complications arising from the recent three-power conference in Paris.

They arranged to ride as far as Warsaw with Premier Josef Cyrankiewicz of Poland and nine of his Ministers, who had signed a treaty forging the last link in a Slav network of cultural and trade pacts. These could conceivably form the basis of a separate eastern European economy. Many persons here feel that Soviet Foreign Minister Molotov's refusal in Paris on Wednesday to go along with British and French ideas on the Marshall plan may have been the first phase of an outright division of Europe into two camps, at least economically.

CZECH POSITION NOT CLEAR

The Czechs—the hurried trip by their leaders to Moscow underscores this—are unable to foresee which camp they will join or whether it will be possible to straddle.

There has been no official announcement here whether the British-French note inviting Czech participation in a twenty-four-nation economic parley in Paris on July 12 has been received. It appeared certain that no answer would be forthcoming until Messrs. Gottwald and Masaryk returned. Prague's Communist daily newspaper described the new Paris bid as "an invitation to participate in a Western bloc." If this turns out to be the view of the Government, it will be hard for it to accept the invitation, especially in the light of Mr. Molotov's statement that the sovereignty of countries participating in a program under the Marshall suggestions would be sacrificed to the Western powers.

However, Czechoslovakia's economy urgently needs in the West markets, raw materials and financial credits. She has credit now only with Britain, Canada and Argentina.

TRADE LINKS ARE STRONG

Trade alliances and other ties with her Eastern Slav neighbors are strong, but none of these countries has foreign credit, cash markets or substantial exportable goods.

While the treaties signed today are regarded in most of eastern Europe as a pan-Slav alliance, Czechoslovakia takes a different view. The Czechs are trying hard to maintain cordial ties with both the East and the West. ◆

JANUARY 31, 1948

GANDHI IS KILLED BY A HINDU; INDIA SHAKEN, WORLD MOURNS; 15 DIE IN RIOTING IN BOMBAY

DOMINION IS BEWILDERED
Nehru Appeals to the Nation to Keep Peace— U.S. Consul Assisted in Capture

By ROBERT TRUMBULL
Special to The New York Times.

NEW DELHI, India, Jan. 30—Mohandas K. Gandhi was killed by an assassin's bullet today. The assassin was a Hindu who fired three shots from a pistol at a range of three feet.

The 78-year-old Gandhi, who was the one person who held discordant elements together and kept some sort of unity in this turbulent land, was shot down at 5:15 P.M. as he was proceeding through the Birla House gardens to the pergola from which he was to deliver his daily prayer meeting message.

The assassin was immediately seized.

He later identified himself as Nathuran Vinayak Godse, 36, a Hindu of the Mahratta tribes in Poona. This has been a center of resistance to Gandhi's ideology.

Mr. Gandhi died twenty-five minutes later. His death left all India stunned and bewildered as to the direction that this newly independent. nation would take without its "Mahatma" (Great Teacher).

The loss of Mr. Gandhi brings this country of 300,000,000 abruptly to a crossroads. Mingled with the sadness in this capital tonight was an undercurrent of fear and uncertainty, for now the strongest influence for peace in India that this generation has known is gone. [Communal riots quickly swept Bombay when news of Mr. Gandhi's death was received. The Associated Press reported that fifteen persons were killed and more than fifty injured before an uneasy peace was established.]

APPEAL MADE BY NEHRU

Prime Minister Pandit Jawaharlal Nehru, in a voice choked with emotion, appealed in a radio address tonight for a sane approach to the future. He asked that India's path be turned away from violence in memory of the great peacemaker who had departed,

Mr. Gandhi's body will be cremated in the orthodox Hindu fashion according to his often expressed wishes. His body will be carried from his New Delhi residence on a simple wooden cot covered with a sheet at 11:30 tomorrow morning. The funeral procession will wind through every principal street of the two cities of New and Old Delhi and reach the burning ghats on the bank of

the sacred Jumna River at about 4 P.M. There the remains of the greatest Indian since Gautama Buddha will be wrapped in a sheet, laid on a pyre of wood and burned. His ashes will be scattered on the Jumna's waters, eventually to mingle with the Ganges where the two holy rivers meet at the temple city of Allahabad.

These simple ceremonies were announced tonight by Pandit Nehru in respect to Mr. Gandhi's wishes, although many of the leaders desired that his body be embalmed and exhibited in state. India will see the last of Mr. Gandhi as it saw him when he lived—a humble and unassuming Hindu.

NEWS SPREADS QUICKLY

News of the assassination of Mr. Gandhi—only a few days after he had finished a five-day fast to bring about communal friendship—spread quickly through New Delhi. Immediately there was spontaneous movement of thousands to Birla House, home of G. D. Birla, the millionaire industrialist, where Mr. Gandhi and his six secretaries had been guests since he came to New Delhi in the midst of the disturbances in India's capital.

While walking through the gardens to this evening's prayer meeting Mr. Gandhi had just reached the top of a short flight of brick steps, his slender brown arms around the shoulders of his granddaughters, Manu, 17, and Ava, 20,

Someone spoke to him and he turned from his granddaughters and gave the appealing Hindu salute—palms, together and the points of the fingers brought to the chin as in a Christian attitude of prayer.

At once a youngish Indian stepped from the crowd—which had opened to form a pathway for Mr. Gandhi's walk to the pergola—and fired the fatal shots from a European-made pistol. One bullet struck Mr. Gandhi in the chest and two in the abdomen on the right side. He seemed to lean forward and then crumpled to the ground. His two granddaughters fell beside him in tears.

CROWD IS STUNNED

A crowd of about 500, ac-

Members of the ashram of Mohandas Gandhi gather around his body as it lies in the stateroom in Birla House shortly after his assassination, India, 1948.

cording to witnesses, was stunned. There was no outcry or excitement for a second or two. Then the onlookers began to push the assassin more as if in bewilderment than in anger.

The assassin was seized by Tom Reiner of Lancaster, Mass., a vice consul attached to the American Embassy and a recent arrival in India. He was attending Mr. Gandhi's prayer meeting out of curiosity, as most visitors to New Delhi do at least once.

Mr. Reiner grasped the assailant by the shoulders and shoved him toward several police guards. Only then did the crowd begin to grasp what had happened and a forest of fists belabored the assassin as he was dragged toward the pergola where Mr. Gandhi was to have prayed. He left a trail of blood.

Mr. Gandhi was picked up by attendants and carried rapidly back to the unpretentious bedroom where he had passed most of his working and sleeping hours. As he was taken through the door Hindu onlookers who could see him began to wail and beat their breasts.

Less than half an hour later a member of Mr. Gandhi's entourage came out of the room and said to those about the door:

"Bapu (father) is finished." ◇

MARCH 20, 1948

GREEK, U.S. CHIEFS SPEED ATTACK PLAN

ATHENS, March 19 (AP) — Senior Greek and United States Army officers have mapped plans for stepped-up Greek operations against the Communist-led guerrillas, it was learned tonight.

The Greek Government has ordered the evacuation of all children from northern Greece, the main battleground in the civil war.

The military plans were developed during the past forty-eight hours. Greek commanders of the First, Second and Third Corps and division heads met with the Greek Chief of Staff, Lieut. Gen. Demitrios Yantzis. United States military observers from Larissa, Trikkala, Yanina, Salonika, Kavalla and other points in northern Greece held discussions with Lieut. Gen. James A. Van Fleet, chief of the military section of the American Aid Mission. The American and Greek viewpoints then were coordinated.

The Government acted under powers of the new civilian mobilization measure in ordering the evacuation of children. The Welfare Ministry sent telegrams to officials of northern Greece telling them to use all available facilities to carry the movement out immediately.

Gen. Markos Vafiades' guerrillas have been taking children from villages in their hands and sending them northward to countries in the Soviet sphere of influence.

The Greek General Staff has agreed to assist in the evacuation of the children. Some observers suggested the area was being cleared for large-scale military operations.

Gen. Alexander Tsingounis, commander of the Second Division with headquarters in Larissa, has been appointed commander of the Government forces in the Peloponnesus, succeeding Gen. Christos Mandas. The military situation in the Peloponnesus has deteriorated. Recently two National Guard companies were ambushed and wiped out west of Tripolis. The General Staff said forty-five guerrillas were killed during recent fighting in a southwestern region of the Peloponnesus. ◇

MARCH 21, 1948

JEWS AND ARABS PLAN FOR A FULL-SCALE WAR

By DANA ADAMS SCHMIDT
Special to The New York Times.

JERUSALEM, March 20—Even though the United States has officially abandoned partition and the whole question of Palestine's future will probably have to be reconsidered by the United Nations Assembly, Jews and Arabs are going right ahead with plans for a battle for Palestine. For the Jews declare they will proclaim a sovereign Jewish state, regardless. and the Arabs say they will destroy it, regardless.

The feeling is that the future of Palestine will be decided not by the diplomats at Lake Success but by the relative strengths of Jews and Arabs in Palestine.

Both sides are looking to May 15 as the critical date. Then British efforts to hold Jews and Arabs apart, however ineffective they may have been, are expected to end and both sides may launch operations without interference.

The Arabs are in a hurry. They must try to get in decisive blows as soon as possible after May 15, which, if the present British schedule is adhered to, will mark the end of the blockade of the coast and the beginning of a heavy influx of Jewish arms and men.

For both, the problem is more one of arms than men—especially heavy arms. Here the Jews hold the advantage because they have perhaps ten times as many men as the Arabs who fought in the last war and who know how to use mechanized equipment, heavy machine guns, artillery, mines, barbed wire or aircraft.

POSITIONS UNCHANGED

A spokesman of the Jewish Agency for Palestine said the other day that "if the United States arms embargo is lifted we can take care of ourselves without international forces." Even if the embargo remained he was hopeful, considering large quantities of equipment already stored in Mediterranean ports ready for shipment to Palestine.

It is a striking fact that all the shooting, bombing and bloodshed since Nov. 30 has caused death or injury to some 5,000 persons and incalculable material loss, but has left the positions of Jews and Arabs practically unchanged.

But after the British leave, considerable movement may be expected. Responsible Arab leaders indicate their strategy will continue to be directed mainly against Jewish communications. Once the Jews lose the protection of British convoys and road patrols, the Arabs believe it will not be difficult to isolate and eventually starve out or reduce more remote sections of the Jewish community.

Arab objectives will be to isolate the 100,000 Jews living in Jerusalem, the twenty-five little settlements below Gaza on the edge of the Negev Desert and some 15,000 Jews in colonies in northern Galilee, which extends like a finger between Lebanon and Syria.

In many cases the Arabs are convinced that shooting will scarcely be necessary, that it will be sufficient to blockade roads in Arab territory over which Jews must pass, as on the route from Jerusalem to the coast. The coastal plain of Sharon from Haifa to Tel Aviv, it is conceded, will be a tougher proposition. Arab sources nonetheless speak of driving spearheads into the coastal plain. One might be ▸

A Jewish militia during secret training in Palestine, 1948.

◀ launched from Tulkarm at the westernmost extremity of the so-called "triangle of terror" where Fawzi el-Kawukji has set up headquarters.

ARAB STRENGTH

A great deal less is known about Arab forces than about Jewish. Far less highly organized than the Jews, they are thought to have thus far raised a national guard of some 30,000 men among 1,200,000 Palestinian Arabs, primarily for defensive purposes. For offensive, they have Fawzi Bey's lightly armed volunteer "liberation army" of 6,000 to 7,000 Arabs, most of whom come from Syria and Iraq.

This volunteer force may well be doubled by May 15. Its armament is also likely to improve—possibly French 75's from Syria, Lebanon aircraft from Egypt, and more automatic weapons through orders placed by the Syrian Government in Czechoslovakia, if King Abdullah and his mechanized Arab Legion can be induced to cooperate. Arab armored cars (other than those already filched from the British) and light tanks may put in an appearance.

A Jewish Agency official told this correspondent, "We are preparing psychologically for defeat at the beginning."

The Jews are now mobilizing their manpower, combing out the community for slackers, and transforming Haganah from an underground force to a fighting machine. The Jewish Agency has stated that Haganah, drawn from the population of 700,000 Jews, has 85,000 men. Among these 30,000 are on full-time duty and 20,000 are ready for combat. ◊

MARSHALL INSISTS ON URGENT ACTION TO CHECK TYRANNY
He Says Experience Proves That Democracies, Once Alert, Can Defeat Dictatorships

By GLADWIN HILL
Special to The New York Times.

LOS ANGELES, March 20—Underscoring for a third time President Truman's message of Wednesday on the seriousness of the international situation, George C. Marshall, Secretary of State, said today that "urgent and resolute action by the United States is necessary if we are to safeguard our own security and protect the civilization of which we are a part."

Acknowledging that "the initial ad-

TRIESTE PROPOSAL ADDS TO U.N. GLOOM

By GEORGE BARRETT
Special to The New York Times.

LAKE SUCCESS, N.Y., March 20—The three-power declaration by the United States, Britain and France calling for the return of Trieste to Italy was interpreted here today by disheartened officials as another sharp slap at the much-buffeted prestige of the United Nations.

The joint request to have the troubled Trieste area taken from the protection of the United Nations was deposited with Secretary General Trygve Lie this afternoon under gloomy circumstances arising from the series of crucial issues the international peace organization had faced during the past ten days.

The latest attack on the usefulness of the United Nations comes only twenty-four hours after the United States had abandoned the Palestine partition plan and only a few days after Chile had brought up before the Security Council a request to investigate the Communist coup in Czechoslovakia as a threat to world peace.

The rapid-fire sequence of events is giving the United Nations its severest test and has produced an atmosphere of dejection. The gloom is increasing as each day passes and brings new evidence of an ever-widening split between the United States and the Soviet Union, a split that underlines and consequently hampers virtually every important step the United Nations tries to take.

The Trieste declaration is especially disheartening to many officials here, for under the terms of the Italian peace treaty the Council-appointed Governor was to have very broad powers in administering the international zone and the Council itself was to have the important task of assuring Trieste's "integrity and independence."

While the declaration on Trieste stressed that discussion in the Security Council had shown that agreements on the selection of a Governor were impossible, some observers said the Big Four were responsible for the failure of the fifteen-month search for a suitable candidate. Britain and the United States rejected ten days ago three names submitted by the Soviet Union, and before that the Soviet Union rejected a long list of suggestions made by the other powers.

One of the few delegates who would comment on the Trieste declaration was Faris el-Khoury of Syria, who said that he thought it was a "very good idea" to return Trieste to Italy but that he was afraid the suggestion might lead to another opening of the conflict between the Western powers and the Soviet Union. ◊

vantage lies with the dictators" because of their machinery for quick action, the Secretary, on a note of confidence, declared:

"Experience has proved that the democracies, once aroused to concerted action, possess the material and spiritual strength to overcome the initial advantage of the dictator."

But, he warned, "a late awakening to danger, failure to act promptly, add immeasurably to the costs of ultimate success."

Mr. Marshall spoke favorably of the legislative progress of the European Recovery Program, observing:

"The present indications are that the House of Representatives intends to move rapidly to a decision."

"We know here and abroad," he said "that the Soviet Union and the Communist parties of Europe will go to extreme lengths to defeat the recovery and the revival of a strong, democratic and independent Europe.

"Despite their aggressive opposition, we and the Western nations of Europe are determined that recovery shall be achieved, that tyranny of government shall be checked, and that the people who wish to govern themselves shall remain free to do so."

In an apparent rejoinder to the numerous proposals for extension of United States economic aid beyond the bounds of ERP, the Secretary took cognizance of "situations" in other parts of the world.

"The critical problem for us," he said, "is just where and how we should exert our influence. In Europe, in the Middle East, in Indonesia, in China? What about Latin America and our direct responsibilities in Japan and Korea?

"Very important decisions must be made by this government as to exactly what we should do to meet these various situations."

Remarking that the problem was parallel to that with which he had "labored" as Chief of Staff, Mr. Marshall continued:

"We must keep in mind that, rich and powerful as we are, we cannot afford to disperse our efforts to a degree which not only might seriously weaken us but would render all our efforts ineffective.

"Every region has its claims and, its proponents and it is therefore necessary to reach a firm decision on the general strategy to be employed, economic or otherwise, having in mind the entire situation."

"The unity of our people at this time," the Secretary summarized, "is of the greatest importance. The President has made his appeal. The Senate has pointed the way. Let every American do his part to demonstrate in this great crisis that we are truly a great people, citizens of the world." ◆

RED MOVES IN ASIA SEEN IN A PATTERN

By ROBERT TRUMBULL
Special to The New York Times.

NEW DELHI, India, March 22—Certain well-informed quarters here understand that Communist activity throughout Asia is coordinated from Moscow through agents who meet in several Asiatic ports, principally Bangkok and Hong Kong.

The pattern of Communist infiltration in Asia was established by observers for interested powers who kept a close watch on the movement of known Communist leaders. An intensive check on radio communications and on the activities of certain travelers tended to confirm the belief that a solid front was maintained by the Communists in all the Asiatic countries.

The central direction for the advance of communism in Asia is said to come from the "Eastern Political Department" in Moscow, headed by a former North China Communist leader named Wong Min. Closer centers are said to be maintained in Harbin and Vladivostok. Headquarters for China, formerly in Yenan, are thought to move about with the Communist army command.

One report from an informed source says that Communist agents and agitators—mostly Chinese—are dispersed through Southeast Asia via Hong Kong, where they are brought by the Russian ship Smolny, which operates between Vladivostok, Shanghai and Hong Kong. Other ships that regularly change crews at Hong Kong are also watched as possible carriers of Communist infiltrators.

Singapore, where the Communists are powerful in a strong trade union movement, is cited as another clearing house for Communist agents in Southeast Asia. Although few Russians have been noticed among Communist workers in Asia, some significance was attached by foreign observers and British authorities to the visit to Singapore and then Bangkok last autumn by a Soviet trade representative, Nicolai Plavin. The British refused to extend his visa for Malaya on its expiration.

Dutch sources believe that the Indonesian Communists maintain direct radio contact with Moscow. They cite as proof that the speeches of the Indonesian Communist leader Alimin are frequently quoted word for word a few days later by the Moscow radio.

The chief correspondent in India for Tass, official Soviet news agency, Oleg Orestov, has applied to the Netherlands Embassy here for a visa to the Dutch East Indies. Another Tass correspondent, Georgi Afrin, recently left Batavia, Java.

Bangkok as a center of Communist activity in Asia has assumed a new importance with the opening of a Soviet Embassy. The embassy staff is said to number about 200 while some 2,000 Russians are understood to have applied for permission to enter Siam as "merchants" or "traders."

Observers here accuse Moscow of seeking to influence the Asiatic masses through numerous international organizations such as trade union federations, the World Federation of Democratic Youth and women's and students' organizations.

Moscow's contact with the Communists in India is believed to come through Afghanistan rather than through China. The Communist cell in New Delhi is said to be the source for agitation in Ceylon and Burma. The Soviet Union recently opened an embassy in New Delhi.

Since the end of the war conferences of Communists from every country in Asia have been held at Dairen, Bangkok, Hong Kong and Vladivostok. From the Bangkok meeting held last September there emerged the "Southeast Asia League," which gave as its objective the independence of the Southeast Asiatic peoples, the furtherance of world peace and the advancement of a Southeast Asia federation. This campaign appeals to nationalism, a racialism somewhat after the manner of Japan's pre-war "Asia for the Asiatics" agitation. ◆

TRUMAN ASSAILED BY RUSSIAN PRESS

MOSCOW, March 24 (UP)—Moscow publications today denounced President Truman's "hysterical screams," discounted the effectiveness of germ warfare and hinted anew at Russian progress in making atomic bombs in a major blast against the United States.

Basing its charges largely on President Truman's recent message to Congress, the Literary Gazette, organal of ❯

‹   the Union of Soviet Writers, led the attack. It devoted nearly half its space to articles criticizing the United States. Izvestia, the Government newspaper, and Red Star, organ of the Ministry of the Armed Forces, joined in.

"The hysterical screams of Truman and Co. have exposed the aggressors completely," one Literary Gazette article said. "Simultaneously they have exposed their weakness and fear.

"American imperialism wants to repeat Hitler's game. Already it is selecting its Goebbelses and Goerings, its Himmlers and Ribbentrops. It selects its Quislings and forms its SS men."

A cartoon depicted a wild-looking President Truman sitting before a set of trap drums in such a position that the shadow thrown on a wall behind him resembled Adolf Hitler with his arm out stretched in a Nazi salute.

"Truman—Hysterical Drummer of war," the caption said.

The Literary Gazette said also that the United States was making exaggerated claims of the effectiveness of bacteriological warfare in an attempt to frighten other nations.

"The world's progressive public must nail to the pole of shame the American scientist-poisoners and their militarist lackeys who are trying at all cost to utilize the mighty forces of science for the development of a new world war," the article said.

Red Star recalled a book in which Maj. Gen. John R. Deane, head of a wartime mission to Moscow, expressed doubt of Russia's ability quickly to make an atomic bomb.

General Deane, Red Star said, wrote that when he was asked about Russia's ability to make such a bomb he thought about a Moscow tire factory where technique and production were bad, and that he drew "definite conclusions" from it. This factory, Red Star said, will turn out its 1,000,000th tire about May 1.

"Let the Deanes draw their definite conclusions," Red Star said.

Izvestia said, in commenting on President Truman's message, that the danger of war existed in the actions of American "ruling circles." But to such actions, Izvestia said, "there is opposed the peace policy of the Soviet Union." ◇

PARLIAMENT BACKS BRITISH RED PURGE

By HERBERT L. MATTHEWS
Special to The New York Times

LONDON, March 25—Britain's Parliament gave its blessing today to the Labor Government's policy of weeding Communists and Fascists out of civil service positions involving the security of the state.

There was no vote but a tense and vehement House of Commons showed its overwhelming support for Prime Minister Attlee. William Gallacher, Communist member, fought the Government's move bitterly in one of the most powerful speeches of his career, but he had few friends. However, all members showed their anxiety to have every possible safeguard for those accused and to avoid the sort of witch hunt that Britons believe the United States Congress sometimes conducts.

Mr. Attlee apparently set most fears at rest in winding up the debate.

If a civil servant is a suspect, Mr. Attlee explained, he will not only be informed but will be told the specific reasons for the suspicion. He will have full opportunity to study the information and reply to it.

The matter will then go to his departmental head, and if the latter decides that action should be taken it will be passed on to the Minister. The Minister can then consult an advisory board of three retired civil servants, if he considers that there is a prima-facie case. The accused person will be allowed to appear before this board and bring other persons to support him.

It is only then that the Minister will make his decision and, whenever possible, the suspect will be transferred, not dismissed.

Mr. Attlee expressed the belief that there would be few dismissals and the House clearly approved his mixture of firmness and fairness.

It was a Liberal party member who appropriately lamented the fact that the "tragedy of tyrannies is that they impose tyranny on the democracies" and it was a Conservative who posed the great problem that is facing all democracies—whether to permit the "liberty of the Communist to take other people's liberties away."

If they all spoke in sorrow, "Willie" Gallacher spoke in anger and even in religious fervor.

He launched into a most vicious personal attack on the Government leaders yet heard in the House while the Conservatives sat in obvious glee watching dirty linen being washed in public.

Mr. Gallacher, among other things, accused Herbert Morrison, Lord President of the Council, of dodging the Army in the first World War and then dodging jail by taking a job as a market gardener. He also said that Mr. Morrison tried to foment a strike against conscription in 1916. Mr. Morrison got up and denied this.

Mr. Gallacher blamed the "multimillionaires of America" whom he referred to as "typical" gangsters for what he termed a slander campaign leading to the present measure.

He aroused a storm of protest when he said:

"America wants to make war against the Soviet Union and use this country as a forward base.

The Government will then go away and the royal family will probably go to Ottawa and the people will be left to perish and by the time it is finished this Britain will be a mass of radioactive mud, if such a war develops."

Most speakers agreed with Mr. Attlee in considering Mr. Gallacher's tirade as somewhat beside the point. The Prime Minister brought the debate back to its central theme of the necessity for loyalty to the state by members of the civil service. The Communists, he said, "hold loyalty to another power."

"As long as we are in a world where there is the possibility of war," continued Mr. Attlee, "we must have defense and its secrets must be preserved." ◇

MAY 15, 1948

ZIONISTS PROCLAIM NEW STATE OF ISRAEL

THE JEWS REJOICE
Some Weep As Quest for Statehood Ends

By GENE CURRIVAN
Special to The New York Times.

TEL AVIV, Palestine, May 15—The Jewish state, the world's newest sovereignty, to be known as the State of Israel, came into being in Palestine at midnight upon termination of the British mandate.

Recognition of the state by the United States, which had opposed its establishment at this time, came as a complete surprise to the people, who were tense and ready for the threatened invasion by Arab forces and appealed for help by the United Nations.

In one of the most hopeful periods of their troubled history the Jewish people here gave a sigh of relief and took a new hold on life when they learned that the greatest national power had accepted them into the international fraternity.

CEREMONY SIMPLE AND SOLEMN

The declaration of the new state by David Ben-Gurion, chairman of the National Council and the first Premier of reborn Israel, was delivered during a simple and solemn ceremony at 4 P.M., and new life was instilled into his people, but from without there was the rumbling of guns, a flashback to other

declarations of independence that had not been easily achieved.

The first action of the new Government was to revoke the Palestine White Paper of 1939, which restricted Jewish immigration and land purchase.

In the proclamation of the new state the Government appealed to the United Nations "to assist the Jewish people in the building of its state and to admit Israel into the family of nations."

The proclamation added:

"We offer peace and amity to all neighboring states and their peoples, and invite them to cooperate with the independent Jewish nation for the common good of all. The State of Israel is ready to contribute its full share to the peaceful progress and reconstitution of the Middle East."

WORLD JEWS ASKED TO AID

The statement appealed to Jews throughout the world to assist in the task of immigration and development and in the "struggle for the fulfillment of the dream of generations—the redemption of Israel."

Plans for the ceremony had been laid with great secrecy. None but the hundred or more invited guests and journalists was aware of the meeting until it started, and even the guests learned of the site only ten minutes before. It was held in the Tel Aviv Museum of Art, a white, modern-design two-story building. Above it flew the Star of David, which is the state's flag, and below, on the sidewalk, was a guard of honor of the Haganah, the army of the Jewish Agency for Palestine.

As photographers' bulbs flashed and movie cameras ground out reels of the scene, great crowds gathered and cheered the Ministers and other members of the Government as they entered the building. The security arrangements were perfect. Sten guns were brandished in every direction and even the roofs bristled with them.

The setting for the reading of the proclamation was a dropped gallery whose hall held paintings by prominent Jewish artists. Many of them depicted the sufferings and joys of the people of the Diaspora, the dispersal of the Jews.

The thirteen Ministers of the Government Council sat at a long dais beneath the photograph of Theodor Harzi, who in 1897 envisaged a Jewish state. Vertical pale blue and white flags of the state hung on both sides. To the left of the ministers and below them sat other

Young Jews celebrate the proclamation of a new state of Israel, Tel Aviv, May 14, 1948

members of the national administration. There are thirty-seven in all, but some were unable to get here from Jerusalem.

At 4 P.M. sharp the assemblage rose and sang the Hatikvah, the national anthem. The participants seemed to sing with unusual gusto and inspiration. The voices had hardly subsided when the squat, white-haired chairman, Mr. Ben-Gurion, started to read the proclamation, which in a few hours was to transform most of those present from persons without a country to proud nationals. When he pronounced the words "We hereby proclaim the establishment of the Jewish state in Palestine, to be called Israel," there was thunderous applause and not a few damp eyes.

After the proclamation had been read and the end of the White Paper and of its land laws pronounced, Mr. Ben-Gurion signed the document and was followed by all the other members of the administration, some by proxy. The last to sign was Moshe Shertok, the new Foreign Minister and the Jewish Agency's delegate to the United Nations. He was roundly applauded and almost mobbed by photographers.

The ceremony ended with everyone standing silently while the orchestral strains of the Hatikvah filled the room. Outside, the fever of nationalism was spreading with fond embraces, warm handshakes and kisses. Street vendors were selling flags, crowds gathered to read posted bulletins, and newspapers were being sold everywhere.

As the Sabbath had started, there was not the degree of public rejoicing that there would have been any other day.

The proclamation was to have been read at 11 P.M. but was advanced to 4 because of the Sabbath. Mr. Shertok explained that the proclamation had to be made yesterday because the mandate was to end at midnight and the Zionists did not want a split second to intervene between that time and the formal establishment of the state.

In the preamble to the declaration of independence the history of the Jewish people was traced briefly from its birth in the Land of Israel to this day. The preamble touched on the more modern highlights, including Herzi's vision of a state, acknowledgment of the Jewish national homeland by the Balfour Declaration in 1917 and its reaffirmation by the League of Nations mandate and by the United Nations General Assembly resolution of Nov. 29, 1947.

It asserted that this recognition by the United Nations of the right of the Jewish people to establish an independent state could not be revoked and ▸

added that it was the "self-evident right of the Jewish people to be a nation, as all other nations, in its own sovereign state."

The proclamation stated that as of midnight the National Council would act as a Provisional State Council and that its executive organ, the National Administration, would constitute a provisional government until elected bodies could be set up before Oct. 1.

Israel, the proclamation went on, will be open to immigration by Jews from all countries "of their dispersion." She will

develop the country for the benefit of all its inhabitants, it added, and will be based on precepts of liberty, justice and peace taught by the Hebrew prophets.

The new state, according to the proclamation, will uphold the "social and political equality of all its citizens without distinction of race, creed or sex" and "will guarantee full freedom of conscience, worship, education and culture."

The statement pledged safeguarding of the sanctity and inviolability of

shrines and holy places of all religions. It also contained a promise to uphold the principles of the United Nations.

There was great cheering and drinking of toasts in this blacked-out city when word was received that the United States had recognized the provincial Government. The effect on the people, especially those drinking late in Tel Aviv's coffee houses, was electric. They even ran into the blackness of the streets shouting, cheering and toasting the United States.

MAY 17, 1948

5 ARMIES ADVANCE
Some Arab Units Said to Be In Israel—Jerusalem Battle Growing

AIR RAIDS KILL FIVE JEWS
Reprisals on Cairo Threatened— Haganah Captures Latrun, Pushes Ahead in Nort

By The Associated Press.

CAIRO, Egypt, May 16—The invasion armies of five Arab nations hammered away with air and artillery attacks today at outlying Jewish settlements in Palestine, dispatches from Arab capitals said. [Tel Aviv, the provisional capital of Israel, was bombed again, and violent fighting continued in Jerusalem. The Haganah reported the capture of Lat-run, on the Tel Aviv–Jerusalem highway, and an Arab Legion communiqué announced the capture of Lydda airfield.] An official Arab military source in Amman, capital of Trans-Jordan, said that the Egyptian army had occupied the town of Majdal, fourteen miles north of Caza on the Palestine coastal plain. This source also said that Syrian forces had occupied Samakh, south of Galilee, on the southern lip of Lake Tiberias.

The Egyptians were reported to be setting up civil administrations in all occupied areas.

Syrian troops, according to dispatches, also occupied a camp adjoining Samakh and shelled two Jewish settlements—Masada and Sarajulean. Nuqeib, on the eastern shore of Galilee, was encircled, shelled and bombed by planes.

SYRIAN LOSSES REPORTED

A Syrian Air Force squadron was reported to have been supporting Lebanese troops in their advance. Syrian losses were given as one killed and wounded, with seven Jews reported killed.

An Iraqi motorized force was reported attacking Tiberias on the western shore of Galilee. The town was recently occupied by the Jews.

Fadl tribal warriors supported by Syrian armor were said to be moving in the lush Hule Valley, part of Israel under the boundaries set in the United Nation's decision on partition.

A combined Syrian and Lebanese striking force was moving into the northern coastal area from the Lebanese frontier, a Damascus dispatch said.

An Arab Legion communiqué said that Legion troops that had recently accepted the surrender of the Jewish settlement of Kfar Etzion had taken over the colonies of Naureen, Bayaun, Rifodina and Sacara as well.

The Legion declared that it had taken 300 prisoners, including eighty-six women and children. The communiqué said that the women and children had been turned over to the Red Cross in Jerusalem while the male prisoners had been interned. Captured supplies and ammunition were distributed among local Arab volunteers, the communiqué said.

LYDDA'S CAPTURE REPORTED

It added that Lydda airfield was captured yesterday by the Arab Liberation Army, along with Kalandiya colony and an adjoining airfield between Jerusalem and Ranullah.

In Amman an Arab source said that heavy artillery of the Iraqi Army had reached the upper Jordan valley.

Iraqi infantry crossed the Jordan at Jisr al Majami and captured the Rutenburg hydroelectric station at the junction of the Yarmuk and Jordan Rivers.

The heavy artillery units crossed a temporary bridge erected to take the place of one dynamited by the Jews, advanced west and captured Geaher, nine miles north of Beisan, Haganah-held communications center for northeastern Palestine.

A published communiqué of the Egyptian volunteer forces in southern Palestine stated that it had wiped out a Haganah convoy yesterday near Dei el Ublah on the coast nine miles southwest of Gaza. Regular Egyptian Army troops have reached Gaza, it said. ◆

JUNE 21, 1948

Editorial
THE BATTLE FOR GREECE

What looks like a determined and perhaps final effort to end the Greek civil war was launched yesterday on the rugged mountain sector around Mount Grammos. There General Markos' depleted guerrilla forces are facing 70,000 royal troops advancing from three sides. The Greek Army, equipped with modern American weapons and advised by top American field officers, is now a formidable body. If it can overrun the entrenched rebels the long blood-letting may cease at last.

Greece is the one front in Europe where Russia, masked by her Balkan satellites, has dared to foment actual warfare. Elsewhere she has relied on infiltration, falsehood, sabotage and treason. For a while her bold venture prospered. Northern Greece, except for a few cities, was a shambles or a wilderness. Russia's longed-for window on the Mediterranean appeared about to open. When the British pulled out and the Americans took over, the Greek state

Greek government commandos equipped with British berets and American fur-trimmed jackets, 1948.

seemed tottering into chaos. Now much has changed. Greece is rising once more from the ashes of desolation and despair. For the first time since the Great War she is able to organize the inherent power of her people to crush an alien-born rebellion.

There have been many signs lately that Russia may be trying to devise some face-saving formula to liquidate her Greek commitments. Bulgaria is seeking to renew diplomatic relations with Athens, which she could not do without Moscow's consent. Marshal Tito, fail-

ing to obtain Trieste or Carinthia, has toned down Yugoslav aggressiveness, and disillusion over the Greek venture is spreading. General Markos has already lost a third of his forces, and his men are surrendering at an increasing rate. The Congress of the United States has just voted further financial aid for Greece. The barrier against Russia's drive for the Mediterranean is stronger today than it has ever been. ◆

JUNE 24, 1948

U. S. TO OPEN TALKS ON WESTERN PACT

By BERTRAM D. HULEN
Special to The New York Times.

WASHINGTON, June 23—Under-Secretary of State Robert A. Lovett forecast at a news conference today that the State Department would soon begin discussions through diplomatic channels with the nations belonging to the Western European Union.

These discussions will be based on the Vandenberg resolution, adopted by the Senate, which proposes strengthening the United Nations and developing regional defense organizations within the world organization, and includes the possibility of military support by the United States.

This diplomatic development today was one of two regarded here as point-

ing to a clearer insight into relations between Russia and the Western world. The other was the surprise conference in Warsaw by representatives of the Soviet and its Eastern European satellites.

The Warsaw meeting was called to consider the plan of the London conference of six Western states for the organization of Western Germany, and presumably the probable impact of the European Recovery Program and other questions.

CALLED REASONABLE EXPECTATION

It was reasonable to expect, Mr. Lovett added, that such a conference would be called after Congress had passed the European Recovery Program and the plan for a Western German state had been developed.

It is believed that indications of which way the wind is blowing may become discernible when the Big Four and the Danubian countries meet in Belgrade on July 30 in an effort to agree upon freedom of navigation for the Danube.

Because of the importance of the river to East-West commerce, it is felt that this conference will demonstrate whether Russia and the West can negotiate. If

the conference should be successful, according to some forecasts, it might well turn out to be the opening wedge for the resumption of negotiations on other outstanding problems. While the approach to the members of the Western Union—Great Britain, France, the Netherlands, Belgium and Luxembourg, which are cooperating under the Brussels pact—will be preliminary, the ultimate objective will be to carry out the terms of the Vandenberg resolution, Mr. Lovett said.

GIVES BASIS FOR ASSOCIATION

This resolution declares that the basis for association by the United States with regional defense pacts is that they must be important to this country, that the other countries involved agree to help themselves and that provision should be made for continuing effective cooperation among the countries.

While Mr. Lovett was not prepared to discuss the prospect of United States military support for the Western Union, it was predicted in other circles that military conversations would follow promptly the preliminary diplomatic discussions. ◆

JUNE 25, 1948

ARABS FORMULATE POSITION ON PEACE

Formal Agreement with Israel Held Unlikely But Long Halt in Hostilities Is Seen

By DANA ADAMS SCHMIDT
Special to The New York Times.

BEIRUT, Lebanon, June 24—King Abdullah's trip to Cairo and Riyadh, Saudi Arabia, and Abdul Rahman Azzam Pasha's visit to Beirut and Damascus, Syria, have set in motion a round of intensive diplomatic activity that is expected to culminate in formulation of the Arab attitude toward Count Folke Bernadotte's mediation efforts. This is due to come at a meeting of the Arab League political commission, beginning Saturday.

Lebanon and Syria were opposed from the start to the acceptance of the Palestine cease-fire. Their leaders in public statements have shown more reluctance than those of any other Arab state to transforming the truce into a peace.

Iraq's forces had only just begun to go into action at the time of the cease-fire, and Egypt's had been by no means fully committed. But the last word in the Arab consultations is likely to be up to King Abdullah, whose Arab Legion has achieved the principal Arab military successes and is best equipped to occupy Palestinian territory.

FORMAL PEACE NOT EXPECTED

Many neutral observers who have had access to both Arab and Israeli areas in recent weeks believe that a clear-cut formal peace between Jews and Arabs is most improbable. In principle, Arab and Israeli objectives remain as irreconcilable as ever. No Arab statesman is going to sign an agreement recognizing Israel's sovereignty and the right to unlimited immigration and none of the Israeli leaders is prepared to sign an agreement for anything less.

But such observers also believe that if, as reportedly stated by a London Foreign Office spokesman, a tacit understanding on Middle Eastern questions has been reached between Britain and the United States and if Count Bernadotte avoids confronting Jews and Arabs with hard yes or no questions, the fighting in Palestine may be ended for some time to come.

JUNE 26, 1948

BERLIN SIEGE ON AS SOVIET BLOCKS FOOD

Clay Declares Three-Zone Regime Is Near— London Cabinet Discusses Issue

By DREW MIDDLETON
Special to The New York Times.

BERLIN, June 25—About 2,250,000 Germans in the Western sectors of Berlin came face to face with the grim specter of starvation today as the siege of those sectors began in earnest.

The Soviet Military Administration banned all food shipments from the Soviet-controlled areas into Berlin as part of its calculated policy of starving the people of the Western sectors into the acceptance of the Communist demand for the withdrawal of the Western powers.

Although they see dark days ahead, the Berliners remained calm. Those in the Western sectors changed their marks for the new Deutsche mark of the Western powers with a minimum of disturbance.

Straightaway a brisk black Bourse developed in which one Deutsche mark was sold for up to thirty of the new Russian-sponsored marks, which the Germans call "tapetengeld," or wall paper money.

CLAY AND ROBERTSON MEET

Although Generals Clay and Sir Brian Robertson, British Military Governor, conferred this afternoon, no announcement of policy toward the Russian siege was made after their conference.

The desperate situation in which the strategy of starvation is being exerted ruthlessly by the Russians for political ends, has been lifted out of the hands of the Military Governors to Washington, London and Paris.

According to official figures sent to London yesterday the present food situation in the Western sectors is more serious than has been admitted.

These figures were based on the food supplies available for all of Berlin June 15. Since then there has been very little addition to the existing stocks because of the increasing severity of the Soviet blockade and, of course, constant consumption.

It is estimated that the following food stocks are on hand today for all Berlin, including the Soviet sector: Seventeen days' supply of bread grains and flour, thirty-two days' supply of cereals, forty-eight days' supply of fats, twenty-five days' supply of meat and fish, forty-two days' supply of potatoes and twenty-six days' supply of skimmed and dried milk.

FOODSTUFF STORES SCATTERED

These foodstuffs are scattered throughout the city in warehouses. Most of those containing bread grains and flour stocks are in the Soviet sector and henceforth the stocks will not be available to the Western sectors.

The commandants of the three Western sectors have replied to the Soviet ban by forbidding the shipment of any food from their sectors into the Russian sector. Since the people of the Soviet sector can be supplied by the entire Soviet zone, the order, although impressive in tone, means little.

A more telling blow at the economy of the Soviet zone was leveled by the bipartite Economic Commission of the United States and British zones in Frankfort on the Main, which suspended "indefinitely" the shipment of all classes of goods from coal to fountain pens into the Soviet zone. This embargo was added to that imposed by the British authorities last night on Ruhr coal and steel for the Soviet zone.

There was no indication that these measures had affected the Soviet blockade, which became more complete today when six barges from Hamburg, five of them carrying food, were stopped outside Berlin. Thus the Russians have added the blockade of incoming canal traffic to those already existing for railroads and highways.

The only manner in which the West-

With every day that the fighting is postponed its resumption becomes psychologically more difficult. In some places refugees are returning home. In Jerusalem the security Council's Truce Commission is working on plans to give the Arabs access to their homes in the Jewish-held new city and to give the Jews access to the Walling Wall.

It is planning a resumption of the water supply to Arab and Jewish parts of the town. Local arrangements have been made to permit Arabs and Jews to harvest their crops. United Nations observers are on the spot at the most critical points.

Latest indications reaching diplomatic quarters are that King Abdullah would accept the internationalization of Jerusalem if the Jews agreed to internationalize Haifa and give up their claim to most of the Negeb. On these points the prospects for agreement seem brightest.

Most of the Arab countries appeared determined to maintain some form of economic blockade of Israel whatever other arrangements may be made. ◇

Berliners buying goods on the city's market, during the occidental zone blockade by Russia, June 1948.

JUNE 27, 1948

EAST AND WEST HEADING FOR GERMAN SHOWDOWN
Russians Threaten to Starve People Of Berlin in Order to Gain Their Ends

By DREW MIDDLETON
Special to The New York Times.

BERLIN, June 26—Storm signals are flying in Berlin. Political thunderheads which have been piling up since the breakdown of the Council of Foreign Ministers meeting last December have burst and all Germany and Berlin in particular is lashed by a major political struggle. Today the two great power groups of the West and East are moving toward a showdown across the shattered capital of the enemy they joined to defeat.

The gravity of the situation rests not only on the importance of Germany's future political coloration in relation to Europe but on the fact that Germany and specifically Berlin, the focal point for the political battle, are occupied by troops of the Soviet Union, the United States, the United Kingdom and France. Where troops of two antagonistic power groups are in close contact as they are in Berlin, the possibility of the type of "incidents" which lead to war is always present. Intemperate words of statesmen and generals can be discounted by skillful diplomacy. But not bullets and death.

The immediate struggle in Germany stems from the effort, planned by political advisers to Marshal Vassily D. Sokolovsky, Soviet Commander in Chief, to starve the people of the three sectors of Berlin occupied by the Western Powers into a state of political submission, so that they will demand withdrawal of the Allied occupation forces as the price of food and the end of the period of economic chaos which the Russians through their control of the utilities will force upon them.

POLITICAL WEAPON
In another era, the idea that one of the most powerful nations in the world would consciously plan and carry out starvation of two and a quarter million people to gain its political ends would have been unthinkable. Nevertheless, that is the brutal truth about what is going on in Berlin.

Conditions in Western sectors of the city are bound to deteriorate daily. The Russians have shut off all food supply to those areas. They gave as an excuse for the blockade introduction of the new currency in the Western zones of occupation and then in the Western sectors of Berlin. But there is no indication that when bilateral currency is circulating in the city, the blockade will be lifted.

It will take all the stamina and courage that Berliners can muster after five years of war and three years of occupation to face these conditions. There are many stouthearted enough to defy ❯

ern powers can save the food situation is to fly in additional supplies when it becomes serious. A daily lift of about 2,500 tons of food would be necessary to feed the people of the Western zones and capacity of the present United States–British air transport commands is already filled with the task of supplying the military personnel and the civilian military government employes of the two powers.

The morale within the Western sectors continues to be fairly good, but the Berliners of 1948 are not equipped physically or emotionally to withstand the sort of siege that the Soviet measures foreshadow without some indication of outside assistance.

There were a few incidents during the daylight hours. Two truckloads of Germans distributing anti-Western leaflets were chased unsuccessfully by United States constabulary patrols this morning. German policemen reported that the leaflets contained a long attack on General Clay for his part in the so-called "the rape of Germany." ◇

❪ the Soviet military administration. But there are many, too, who want an end to discord and want.

But there is a larger struggle for Germany in which the battle of Berlin is only one of a series of political frays, although at the moment it is the most important single battle. This general struggle is the ultimate result of that division of Germany made inevitable by the failure last year of two successive meetings of the Council of Foreign Ministers to find a formula for four-power rule of the Reich and eventual establishment of an all-German Government.

The event which has pushed the Russians headlong into their present offensive is approval by the Western Powers of agreements on the Western German state and control of the Ruhr reached at London early this month. And the single point which has aroused the greatest anger in Moscow is the fact that these agreements remove from the sphere of Soviet influence the Ruhr, richest industrial prize in Europe.

IMPORTANCE OF RUHR

For in contrast to some doubting Thomases in the West, the realists of the Kremlin know that the Ruhr can be made to work as part of a new German state to the extent that it will slowly fulfill its maximum contribution to the reconstruction of Western Europe and a power group that will balance the new Soviet empire to the East.

Loss of any hope of either sharing in this production or in hampering it by their tested political means of disruption so that it cannot be used as it should be used is the mainspring of the present Soviet political offensive in Germany. Hence, emphasis on the Ruhr in the Declaration of Warsaw published by the foreign ministers of the Soviet Union and its satellite countries of the East and the very evident bid within the body of the communiqué for another meeting of the Council of Foreign Ministers. At such a meeting Molotov could try once more to win a Russian foothold in Western Germany through establishment of an all-German Government eventually to be dominated by Communists.

What do the Russians want? It is obvious that under any conditions they want the Western powers out of Berlin.

But this correspondent believes that the Russians are also seeking, and have been seeking since April, a meeting of the Council of Foreign Ministers at which they will make one more attempt to win an all-German Government in some form under the aegis of the four occupying powers.

For in the Russian case half a loaf, Eastern Germany, is not better than none. The Russians want all Germany. And since the Russians think in terms of decades and centuries it is quite possible that Molotov would come to a Foreign Ministers' conference prepared to make concessions on the structure of an all-German Government in return for knowledge that such a Government would exist ten years from now as a prey to Communist infiltration.

BALANCE OF FORCES

What are the strengths and weaknesses of the two groups in the present struggle for Germany? First and most obvious is the fact that there are three powers in the Western grouping and only one in the Eastern grouping. Soviet policy in Germany has often revealed its inflexibility but it is much easier to carry out one policy than three through one Military Government administration rather than three, no matter how closely they are allied.

But the principal advantage of the Russians is that enjoyed in this sort of struggle by any totalitarian state. The Russians can do as they please in Berlin and their zone within the limits imposed by their present unpreparedness for a long-term war.

The alliance between the Western powers and the democratic parties of Berlin and Germany has closed the ranks to some extent in the face of the new Russian offensive. Yet differences of opinion exist, notably over control of the Ruhr, and during the present stage the Russians are making every effort to capitalize on those differences and widen any splits between the Western powers and the Germans and lessen the effect of this alliance.

The greatest advantage on the side of the Western powers here in Germany, as it has been all through Western Europe, is the combination of economic strength and political tolerance. ◇

Marshall Plan Cracks Bloc in East, Washington Holds

By JAMES RESTON
Special to The New York Times.

WASHINGTON, June 28—The general reaction in Washington today to the Communist Information Bureau's split with Marshal Tito of Yugoslavia was much like the reaction of Winston Churchill to the sudden arrival of Rudolf Hess in Scotland during the war.

"It would appear," said Mr. Churchill, "that there is a maggot in the apple."

TOJO AND 6 OTHERS HANGED BY ALLIES AS WAR CRIMINALS

Four Japanese Leaders Are Executed Simultaneously In Prison

By LINDESAY PARROTT
Special to The New York Times.

TOKYO, Dec. 23—Hideki Tojo, former dictator of Japan, and six of his most prominent collaborators in the war against the Allied powers, were hanged this morning at Sugamo Prison on the outskirts of Tokyo as criminals against international law. The death sentences against them, imposed by the International Military Tribunal after about two and a half years of trial, were carried out by the United States Eighth Army.

This was announced officially by Gen. Douglas MacArthur's public information office in a very brief statement handed to waiting correspondents at 1 o'clock this morning. The official announcement said:

"Between 12:01 and 12:35 A.M., Dec. 23, all seven of the war criminals that were condemned by the International Military Tribunal in the Far East were hanged."

[The seven bodies were taken to

Officially, the Truman Administration said nothing, but informed persons made these observations:

1. It is unlikely that there will be any complete break between Belgrade and Moscow. Marshal Tito will either satisfy the will of the Kremlin or be replaced, these sources suggested.

2. The Marshall Plan has been more of a thunderbolt in Eastern Europe than the United States realized. It has cracked the smooth facade of the Communist world by demonstrating that the interests of the Soviet satellites are not necessarily identical to the interests of the Soviet Union.

3. These circles said that the Yugoslav crack would undoubtedly be smoothed over but that meanwhile it had confirmed an important fact: that even in Eastern Europe the foundation of communism is not secure and that nationalism is still a force capable of challenging communism.

4. The cleavage has come at a critical time in the relations between East and West and will stiffen the opposition to the Soviet efforts to drive the United States, Britain and France out of Berlin.

5. Finally, reliable official reports suggest that the action by the Cominform may be Moscow's reaction to the recent purge by Marshal Tito of several prominent Communists who opposed what they felt were his half-measures in the organization of the state.

At the end of April, according to these reports, about fifteen Communists who held responsible Government positions were condemned to death or long terms in prison at Ljubljana. Shortly thereafter two Communists who had been active with Marshal Tito in the Partisan fight during the war were arrested.

These diplomatic reports, which also spoke of further purges in the Yugoslav Army, indicated that the reason for the replacement of Sreten Zujovitch and Andrija Helbrang, high Government officials, was that they had opposed a form of economic planning that would leave Yugoslavia free to trade where she liked, rather than to follow the Soviet and Cominform efforts to make every sacrifice to beat the Marshall Plan.

The tendency in the capital is not to make too much now of the Tito incident. What the incident has done, however, is to confirm a belief of the leaders of both parties that the policy of economic and political assistance to Western and Southern Europe, and of stern resistance to Soviet pressure is the right one and is showing results. ◆

---

the Yokohama crematory in American Army trucks escorted by military police, the United Press reported. Soldiers with fixed bayonets stood in a light drizzle, barring the way to newsmen, as the trucks sped through the gates. The cremations began at 8:10 A.M. in a square stucco building that contains fourteen ovens. An hour and twenty minutes later all had been burned to ashes.]

Those executed were Tojo; former Premier Koki Hirota; Gen. Kenji Doihara, variously called the "Tiger," the "Terror" and the "Lawrence" of Manchuria; Gen. Iwane Matsui, protagonist of the rape of Nanking; Gen. Akira Muto, chief of staff in Sumatra and then in the Philippines when the captured United States forces were compelled to walk in the Bataan Death March; former War Minister Seishiro Itagaki; and Gen. Hitaro Kimura, former chief of staff in Burma and one of those held most responsible for the maltreatment of war prisoners.

Later, General MacArthur's public relations office, in what it called "a factual report of the executions," revealed that there were several witnesses at the executions from nations that shared in the trial.

In addition to "doctors and essential prison personnel," those present included William J. Sebald, United States member of the Allied council, Gen. Shang Chen for China, Patrick Shaw for the British Commonwealth and Lieut. Gen. Kuzma Derevyanko for the Soviet Union.

It was announced that they had been invited to attend by General MacArthur by a message that said:

"Inasmuch as the execution will carry out the pertinent part of the judgment of the Allied powers represented on the tribunal, I request your attendance thereat as witnesses in order that you may thereafter certify to the execution of that phase of the tribunal's judgment."

It was announced that the time of execution had been told to the prisoners two hours in advance and that each had had an interview with the prison's Buddhist priest, Nobukatsu Hanayama. Then services were held in a specially constructed shrine in the cellblock where the prisoners had lived.

The first to die, it was stated, were Doihara, Matsui, Tojo and Muto, who fell simultaneously from four gallows erected in the death-house. Itagaki, Hirota and Kimura were hanged in the second group. All had black hoods placed over their heads as the trap was sprung, it was stated, and none needed assistance as he walked up the thirteen steps to the gallows.

The ashes of all will be scattered, it was stated. This is to minimize, as much as possible, the chance of the worship of the prisoners' remains.

It is understood that the others of the Japanese war criminals will remain in Sugamo Prison under guard of United States soldiers as jailers for the eleven Allied nations, at least until a peace treaty is signed or arrangements are made with other powers to remove them elsewhere.

Two of those sentenced to life imprisonment are at present in the United States Army hospital. They are Mitsujiro Umezi, former Chief of the General Staff, and Toshio Shiratori, Ambassador to Rome and signer of the Tripartite Axis pact.

The executions were carried out with the same secrecy with which the Army has surrounded the prisoners since they were sentenced by the international court last Nov. 12 after a trial that opened June 3, 1946. American, British and French correspondents waited for hours in the public relations office for a formal announcement after being told that they would not under any circumstances be permitted to enter Sugamo Prison, from which all unofficial witnesses were excluded.

The date and the time of hangings also had been well concealed. An automobile tour around the prison's long concrete wall just after the executions revealed nobody at the gates and nobody waiting. The whole district, in fact, one of small shops, and flimsy post-war homes, was asleep.

The Japanese press pledged this morning that General MacArthur's suggestion that a day of prayer be held nationally after the executions would be observed. The newspaper Asahi said editorially:

"All sects, Buddhists, Christians, Shintoists and others will offer a prayer for peace today and spend a moment of solemn silence.

"Whatever crimes these seven men committed it is a tragedy for the human race to be compelled to carry out such sentences. We must see that this tragedy does not end meaninglessly.

"These prayers for peace must not end after a moment, but should become a milestone for Japan while the Japanese carry out their mission of seeking permanent peace for the world.

"If the Japanese people now fail to reflect on their moral responsibility for the war and the execution of these seven criminals the long trial by the International Tribunal will have gone in vain." ◆

MARCH 9, 1949

INDO-CHINA ACCORD SIGNED BY BAO DAI

By LANSING WARREN
Special to The New York Times

PARIS, March 8—Letters approving the accord establishing "an independent Viet Nam within the French Commonwealth" were signed at Elysée Palace today by French President Vincent Auriol and the Emperor of Annam, Boa Dai.

Soon after the ceremony the former Emperor announced at a press conference that he would "return to his ancestral soil on April 25" to bring back peace and to establish the democratic institutions of a new government in Indochina.

It was learned that the accord would not become effective until after the former Emperor's arrival in Indo-China as the result of a formal agreement between the former Emperor and Leon Pignon, French High Commissioner.

This step removes the immediate necessity of submitting the accord to ratification of the French National Assembly and it was asserted that the text of the accord would not be made public until it became effective.

SOCIALISTS ASKED TO CHANGE

Premier Henri Queuille today had leaders of the Socialist party to lunch and tried to get them to lift their opposition to the present policy of the Government in Indo-China. It was understood that the Assembly would be asked to give approval only to an accord changing Cochin-China from a colony to an independent state and giving it an Assembly as a preparatory measure for the setting up of the Viet Nam state combining Cochin-China, Tongking and Annam and providing for cooperation with the states of Cambodia and Laos.

[The Associated Press reported that, under the tentative accord, the three states of Annam, Tongking and Cochin-China could merge, either into a Viet Namese monarchy or a republic.]

The Socialists can with difficulty reverse the position that they took at a party congress early in the year after which General Secretary Guy Mollet wrote to Premier Queuille opposing any accord with Bao Dai and asking for an understanding with dissident leader Ho Chi Minh.

Of Bao Dai, M. Mollet stated, it was learned tonight, that "he enjoys no authority in the country—armed forces of Viet Nam do not obey him."

BEDS IN CHINA CITED

"Events," M. Mollet continued, "are moving rapidly in Indo-China. In a few months the so-called Chinese Communist troops may be on the frontier of Viet Nam and offer their military aid, official or unofficial, to the Government of Ho Chi Minh.

"At that moment nothing could save France from disaster and separation from all Indo-China. The Socialist party believes that an accord can still be made with Ho Chi Minh."

The Socialists now are being asked to reverse this stand to maintain the Government coalition and to at least suspend their opposition to an accord with Bao Dai.

In French quarters the accord was said to define details of a general understanding reached last June in conference with Bao Dai and include every essential provision for the independence formerly asked by Ho Chi Minh. It was understood that the latter condemns the agreement approved here today. ◇

MARCH 11, 1949

CLEAN-UP IS NEAR IN PELOPONNESUS
Greek Army, Winning Villagers to It, Forces Rebel Remnants Into Last Stand in South

By A. C. SEDGWICK
Special to The New York Times

TRIPOLIS, Greece, March 10—Things are looking up in the Peloponnesus. Here in this agricultural center, the capital of Arcadia and the largest inland town on the peninsula, the very faces of the people reflect a change that has taken place since the Greek Army started its major offensive against the Communist-led rebel bands last Christmas week.

Then the guerrillas were increasing their strength in the area. The Army seemed powerless and the people were downcast and sullen. The Communist underground organization, which recruits for the rebels, spies for them and commits acts of sabotage, was growing.

Today, according to every indication, the underground is completely disrupted and possibly destroyed.

A major result of this is that, with fear of reprisal removed, the townsfolk and peasants dare to support the National forces openly. They now come forward with intelligence concerning movements of rebel forces and inform on Communist agents.

The military authorities estimate that another two weeks will see the end of the Peloponnesian campaign and the beginning of civil recontruction. Already all the main roads, over which one could not go in safety a month ago, are deemed safe for civilian traffic. In many villages, gendarmes have relieved Greek Army units.

The fighting still goes on, mostly among the barren peaks of the Parnon and Taygetos ranges. But according to reports received from those areas rebel forces are virtually beaten. A spell of unprecedentedly cold winter weather has further worked against the guerrillas.

When the Army's Peloponnesian operations began, the rebel fighting force of men well armed and equipped numbered about 3,860, according to Army estimates. Subsequently more than 1,000 men had been added to the rebel strength.

The Army asserts that it has put out of action about 4,500 guerrillas in the campaign. During the first week of March, the bodies of 211 rebels killed in action were recovered on various fields of conflict, and 593 guerrillas either gave themselves up or were captured.

According to the statements of rebels captured within the last couple of days, it have been not only cold and hunger that has impelled them to abandon the struggle, but also disillusionment that has come, they say, from recent reports that Communist party policy was favoring the separation of Greek Macedonia from Greece and its incorporation into the Slav Macedonian Organization, the NOF. ◇

MARCH 11, 1949

U.S. C-47 cargo plane approaching Tempelhof Airport in Berlin with food and other relief supplies, 1948.

U.S. Crews on Berlin Lift To Fly On Regular Basis

By The Associated Press.

BERLIN, March 10—The United States Air Force today announced plans for personnel replacements that would facilitate carrying on the airlift to Soviet-blockaded Berlin for years, if necessary.

United States taxpayers are paying almost $500,000 a day to maintain the United States end of the U.S.-British operation, which began last June 26.

The Air Force announced in Wies-baden today that, beginning May 1, replacements of airlift personnel from the Great Falls, Mont., training school would be placed on a regular instead of temporary duty status.

Airmen who bring families with them overseas will serve three years on the lift. Those without families in Germany will serve two years. Under the present system the men flying in the food, fuel and essential supplies from Western Germany to Berlin are rotated to their home bases in the United States every six months.

The airlift is moving about 7,000 tons of supplies to Berlin daily in good weather. ◆

MAY 4, 1949

HANGCHOW FALLS TO COMMUNISTS
Loss of Port Completes Red Entrapment of Nationalist Forces in Huge Triangle

SHANGHAI, May 4 (AP)—The Shanghai garrison command today admitted the loss of Hangchow, Nationalist escape port 100 miles southwest of Shanghai. [Communist control of Hangchow seals off Shanghai by land from the rest of China and closes the trap on Nationalist forces remaining in the Nanking-Shanghai Hangchow triangle. Their only exit now is by sea.] The garrison command communiqué said the Cheki-ang Provincial Peace Preservation Corps had evacuated Hangchow at noon yesterday after completing a delaying action. This force was all that was left for the defense of Hangchow. ◆

MAY 5, 1949

U.S. AIRLIFT PILOTS 'JUMPING FOR JOY'

By SYDNEY GRUSON
Special to The New York Times.

BERLIN, May 4—The boys who held Berlin for the West during 320 days of the Russian blockade were "jumping up and down for joy" tonight

That was the way Private Louis N. Wagner of Freehold, N.J., described the reaction of United States airlift fliers to the news that the blockade was ending.

Private Wagner was on duty in the Operations Room at Tempelhof Airfield when the flash of the Russian agreement came through. Minutes later, he said, "the airways were buzzing with the news" as the flash was repeated over the radios of planes still lugging coal, flour and other supplies to the besieged city.

The tower at Tempelhof, busy enough bringing in planes at the now familiar rate of one every three minutes, was flooded with calls from fliers seeking confirmation. On the 320th day of the blockade they along with their British buddies had brought another 8,900 short tons of supplies into Berlin.

It was a job they were prepared to continue indefinitely. But they were not sorry that the end of it was now possible.

"We've shown them we can do it," said a husky flight engineer sergeant. "They'll think twice about trying us out on this one again."

The news spread through the city with the effect of an electric shock. It bounced off skeptics into delighted groups of Berliners who have scarcely considered any other subject since the first announcement was made that Russo-American negotiations to end the blockade were under way.

Under the impact of the official announcement most Berliners on the streets tonight momentarily forgot their fears of what might come out of the Foreign Ministers' meeting to dwell delightedly on the prospects of renewed normal contact between Western Germany and the food-producing Eastern zone.

"What can we be expected to think of after living for ten months under blockade conditions?" said a policeman walking his beat. "We want life to be a little easier. We want more light, more gas and perhaps, most important of all, an end to dehydrated potatoes." ▸

◀ To a girl secretary the news meant "prices will come down. I can buy some clothes again."

To a GI on guard at Headquarters Company barracks it meant "better times, better chow and a chance to get out of here on leave."

To Wilhelm Zapf, radio salesman, it meant "business will boom again, people will have money."

For thousands of Berliners it will mean a chance to go back to work to earn a decent wage and to settle back in the stride of recovery that the imposition of blockade so abruptly shattered last June. ◇

Russian border crossing barrier was opened to allow access to Berlin after the end of the blockade, 1949.

MAY 5, 1949

TEN NATIONS ADOPT STATUTE OF EUROPE

By BENJAMIN WELLES
Special to The New York Times.

LONDON, May 4—Nine Foreign Ministers and the Belgian Ambassador reached full agreement here today on a Statute of the Council of Europe, which will now carry into effect the long-cherished ideal of a democratic European Parliament.

A three-hour session was held this morning in St. James's Palace by the representatives of Britain, France, Belgium, the Netherlands, Luxembourg, Italy, Ireland, Norway, Denmark and Sweden. They completed the review of the draft Statute, which had been laboriously hammered out during the past months by a diplomatic working party here. The draft was turned over to a technical drafting committee at midday and the Foreign Ministers and the Belgian envoy, acting for Premier-Foreign Minister Paul-Henri Spaak, re-assembled in a special session at night and gave it their final approval. M. Spaak was unable to come to London because of illness.

The signing is to take place tomorrow afternoon. The ceremony will be attended by leading officials of the British Government headed by Foreign Minister Bevin and the Foreign Ministers and diplomats of the participating nations.

Although no communiqué was issued, it is understood the British Government has finally decided that its delegation to the Consultative Assembly of the Council of Europe (the Parliament) will include representatives of the opposition parties. The Conservative and Liberal parties will be allowed to name representatives from the House of Commons and the House of Lords and thus, it is remarked, Winston Churchill might attend meetings of the Parliament of Europe as a member of Britain's delegation.

Strasbourg, France, has been definitely chosen as the seat of the Council of Europe, although the Scandinavian representatives had proposed that a site be chosen in the Netherlands. It is also learned that the Secretary General of the Council, who has yet to be selected, will be a Frenchman.

The Foreign Ministers are reported to have agreed that Greece and Turkey should be invited to join the Council of Europe before its first meeting in July or August. However, no decision was taken as to whether a future West German Government would be invited to associate itself with the organization.

Chief debate in the morning session arose over rival Swedish and British proposals as to voting procedure in the Consultative Assembly. Sweden proposed that Assembly resolutions be adopted only by unanimous vote, while Britain suggested a two-thirds majority. The issue was compromised by a decision that full resolutions would require a unanimous vote and expressions of the Assembly's "wish" would go through by two-thirds vote.

Another discussion took place over a wording in the Preamble of the Statute. The Dutch delegation urged that the term "Christian" democratic countries of Western Europe be used, but in the face of considerable opposition the Dutch agreed to the substitution of the word "spiritual." ◇

ATOM BLAST IN RUSSIA DISCLOSED

TRUMAN AGAIN ASKS U. N. CONTROL

By ANTHONY LEVIERO

WASHINGTON, Sept. 23—President Truman announced this morning that an atomic explosion had occurred in Russia within recent weeks. This statement implied that the absolute dominance of the United States in atomic weapons had virtually ended.

"We have evidence that within recent weeks an atomic explosion occurred in the U.S.S.R.," President Truman said.

These words stood out in red-letter vividness in a brief undramatic statement in which the Chief Executive said that the United States always had taken into account the probability that other nations would develop "this new force."

He pleaded once again for adoption of the system of international control of atomic energy promulgated by the United States and supported by the large majority of countries now assembled in the United Nations General Assembly at Flushing Meadow.

MCMAHON REVEALS NEWS

Mr. Truman announced the discovery to the Cabinet, assembled in the White House at 11 A. M. for the usual Friday meeting.

White House correspondents had their usual conference with Charles G. Ross, the President's secretary, at 10:30 A. M. It was routine, but as they filed out his secretary, Miss Myrtle Bergheim, advised them not to go away. A moment before 11 A. M. Miss Bergheim entered the press room and said:

"Press!"

The news men filed into Mr. Ross' office. He said he wished the door closed, and a secret service man took his post there. Then Mr. Ross said that he would pass out an announcement and that nobody was to leave the room until everyone present had a copy. Then he began passing around the President's mimeographed statement.

One of the first reporters to scan his copy exclaimed, "Russia has the atomic bomb!" There was a wild rush through the door and to the telephones in the nearby press room. One of the news men who sprinted out was the correspondent of Tass, the official Soviet news agency.

ACHESON MENTIONS WEAPON

President Truman did not say that Russia had an atomic bomb. Only Secretary of State Dean Acheson, who was at the United Nations General Assembly in New York, went so far as to say he assumed that a "weapon" had caused the explosion. Other Cabinet members and lower officials neither privately nor publicly would go behind Mr. Truman's phrase—"atomic explosion occurred"—to indicate precisely what had caused it.

Mr. Truman's use of that phrase was studied and premeditated, it was learned, and led certain officials to suggest that Russia might have been getting to the point of testing a bomb that might be neither so practicable nor so effective as that of the United States.

There was also some doubt that Russia had been able to begin stockpiling numbers of the so-called absolute weapon, as the United States has been doing since the explosion over Hiroshima.

Nevertheless it was obvious that the force and the magnitude of the explosion had been comparable to the deadly effect of the United States atomic bombs, else its positive detection and evaluation by this country would not have been possible.

The Russian development, consequently, was bound to have a profound effect, ultimately, on international relations, and particularly on the balance of power between the democracies and Russia and her satellites. It appeared to have reduced this country's absolute dominance in atomic weapons to a relative superiority that would gradually diminish. ◆

Glossary

PEOPLE

HAROLD ALEXANDER *(1891–1969)*: After commanding the Dunkirk evacuation in 1940, he was appointed commander-in-chief in the Middle East in August 1942. As Eisenhower's deputy, he commanded the invasion of Sicily and then Italy and became supreme commander in the Mediterranean in November 1944.

CLEMENT ATTLEE *(1883–1967)*: The leader of the British Labour Party, he joined the War Cabinet in May 1940 under Churchill. He took responsibility for home affairs and from 1942 was deputy prime minister. He succeeded Churchill in July 1945 following Labor's election victory.

PIETRO BADOGLIO *(1871–1956)*: Italian marshal who was head of the Supreme Command in 1940 and succeeded Mussolini as premier in July 1943. He negotiated an armistice in September 1943 and then left Rome for Salerno. He was replaced as premier in June 1944.

OMAR BRADLEY *(1893–1981)*: He was appointed deputy to Patton in the Operation Torch campaign, but by May 1943 he was commander of the Second U.S. Army Corps, which he led into Sicily. He commanded the First U.S. Army for the Normandy invasion, then the Twelfth U.S. Army Group, which he led to the end of the war in the final battles in Germany.

NEVILLE CHAMBERLAIN *(1869–1940)*: British prime minister from May 1937, Chamberlain was responsible for organizing the Munich Conference in September 1938 but then took Britain into war a year later after Germany's invasion of Poland. He resigned on May 10, 1940 and died a few months later.

CHIANG KAI-SHEK *(1887–1975)*: Leader of the Guomindang Party in China, Chiang tried to unite the nation in the 1930s in the face of Japanese aggression. He was defeated in the post-1945 civil war with the Communists and ended up as ruler of Taiwan, where he retreated in 1949.

WINSTON SPENCER CHURCHILL *(1874–1965)*: Britain's wartime prime minister from May 1940 to July 1945 and also minister of defense, he played a central part in sustaining British belligerency in 1940 and in forging links with Stalin and Roosevelt in the wartime "Grand Alliance." He strongly supported bombing the European Axis, and favored a Mediterranean strategy over a frontal assault on Hitler's European fortress. Churchill's influence began to decline as the war continued, but post-war he became a prominent Cold Warrior, hostile to Communist expansionism.

MARK CLARK *(1896–1984)*: Following a rapid promotion from a pre-war major to chief of staff of U.S. Army Ground Forces in 1942, Clark went on to command the U.S. Fifth Army in the invasion of Italy. In December 1944 he became commander-in-chief of Allied ground forces in Italy.

KARL DÖNITZ *(1891–1980)*: Grand admiral of the German Fleet from January 1943 until April 1945, when he succeeded Hitler as head of the German state. From 1939 to 1943 he headed the German submarine arm and was responsible for waging the Battle of the Atlantic. He was condemned to ten years in jail at the Nuremberg Trials.

ANTHONY EDEN *(1897–1977)*: British minister of war in 1940 after Churchill's appointment as prime minister, and then, from December 1940, foreign secretary, succeeding Lord Halifax. Eden played an important part in Britain's war effort and helped to see the United Nations Organization through to its inception in May 1945.

DWIGHT D. EISENHOWER *(1890–1969)*: Appointed head of the Army Operations Division after the Japanese attack on Pearl Harbor, Eisenhower was chosen to lead the Operation Torch landings in North Africa in November 1942. He was appointed supreme commander in the Mediterranean and then for the Allied invasion of France in 1944, a position he retained to the end of the war.

CHARLES DE GAULLE *(1890–1970)*: A brigadier general in 1940, de Gaulle was a pioneer of armored warfare and commander of the French Fourth Armored Division in the Battle of France. In June 1940 he moved to London where he declared the Free French movement, which he led through the liberation of France in 1944 despite the hostility of U.S. President Franklin D. Roosevelt. In May 1943 he was co-chair of the Committee of National Liberation with Henri-Honoré Giraud, but by 1944 he was the dominant figure. He helped to construct a new democratic order in France after the liberation.

HENRI-HONORÉ GIRAUD *(1879–1949)*: A French general who commanded the French Seventh Army in the Battle of France. He escaped from German captivity in 1942 and established close contact with the Americans. He was made commander-in-chief of all French forces in North Africa and then French high commissioner in the region. He worked with de Gaulle to found the French Committee of National Liberation, but was ousted from the committee in November 1943 and in April 1944 resigned, to disappear as a political figure.

JOSEPH GOEBBELS *(1897–1945)*: A prominent German National Socialist politician, Goebbels headed both the Party Propaganda Office and the Ministry of Popular Enlightenment and Propaganda. In 1942 he was made a commissar for civil defense and in July 1944 was named Reich plenipotentiary for total war. He committed suicide in Hitler's bunker on May 1, 1945.

HERMANN WILHELM GOERING *(1893–1946)*: Commander-in-chief of the Luftwaffe and air minister, he was named Hitler's successor in 1939 and given the supreme rank of Reich marshal after the defeat of France in 1940. His political stock declined during the war, but was revived briefly when he was considered the most important Nazi on trial at Nuremberg. He committed suicide on the night before his scheduled execution.

RODOLFO GRAZIANI *(1882–1955)*: Italian general who was governor of Ethiopia from 1936–1937 and then commander of Italian forces in Libya. He resigned after defeat in the desert in early 1941, but returned as Mussolini's defense minister from 1943–1945. He was condemned in 1948 to nineteen years in jail but served only a few months.

ARTHUR HARRIS *(1892–1984)*: Named marshal of the British Royal Air Force in 1945, Harris masterminded the bombing assault on Germany after becoming commander-in-chief of the RAF Bomber Command in February 1942.

HEINRICH HIMMLER *(1900–1945)*: Head of the SS (*Schutzstaffel*) security force of the National Socialist Party, Himmler was appointed Reich chief of police in June 1936. In 1939 he set up the Reich Security Main Office under Reinhard Heydrich. Himmler was responsible for the genocide of the European Jews and the system of concentration camps. In August 1943 he was made interior minister and in July 1944 commander of the German Reserve Army. He committed suicide in May 1945 after he was captured by British soldiers.

ADOLF HITLER *(1889–1945)*: Leader of the National Socialist Party in Germany and German head of state from 1934, Hitler led his nation into war in 1939 as supreme commander of the armed forces. A dictator who made himself commander of the German Army in December 1941. Hitler led his forces to complete defeat. He committed suicide in Berlin on April 30, 1945.

CORDELL HULL *(1871–1955)*: Roosevelt's secretary of state from March 1933 to October 1944, Hull played an important part in drafting the United Nations Declaration on January 1, 1942 and, later on, creating the United Nations Organization. He was tough on Japan in the negotiations in 1941 and his stance accelerated the Japanese decision for war.

ALBERT KESSELRING *(1885–1960)*: German field marshal and air force commander, Kesselring was appointed commander-in-chief of Axis forces in the Mediterranean theater in November 1941. At the end of the war he was commander-in-chief in Western Europe. Tried for war crimes, he was condemned to death, but his sentence was commuted.

ERNEST KING *(1878–1956)*: In 1941 he became admiral of the U.S. Atlantic Fleet, where his success in the anti-submarine war persuaded Roosevelt to make him commander-in-chief of the U.S. Fleet and in March 1942 also chief of naval operations.

FUMIMARO KONOYE *(1891–1945)*: A Japanese prince who served as prime minister on three occasions between 1937 and 1941, failing to bring the war with China to a conclusion or to negotiate agreement with the United States in 1941. He was a champion of a Japanese "New Order" but played little part in the politics of the Pacific war. He committed suicide in prison in December 1945.

WILLIAM LEAHY *(1875–1959)*: A chief of U.S. naval operations in the 1930s, Leahy was a close confidant of President Roosevelt. He was U.S. ambassador to Vichy France in 1941–1942, but then became Roosevelt's personal chief of staff and chair of the U.S. Joint Chiefs of Staff.

DOUGLAS MACARTHUR *(1880–1964)*: A former U.S. Army chief of staff, MacArthur was military adviser in the Philippines when war broke out and commander of U.S. forces there. He was appointed commander in chief in the Southwest Pacific in April 1942, and later became supreme commander of the Allied Powers for the occupation of Japan in August 1945.

MAO ZEDONG *(1893–1976)*: The Chinese Communist leader who led a long march to Shaanzi province to escape Chiang Kai-shek's forces in 1934. Mao helped to establish a Red Army to fight the Japanese and resist Chiang, and in the post-war civil war this army formed the core of the successful Communist takeover of the country in 1949.

GEORGE C. MARSHALL *(1880–1959)*: Chief of the War Plans Division in Washington in the late 1930s, Marshall was chosen as army chief of staff in 1939, a post he held to the end of the war. In 1947, as secretary of state, he launched the European Recovery Program, known as the Marshall Plan.

CHARLES MERZ *(1893–1977)*: A journalist on a number of papers before joining The New York Times editorial board in 1931. In November 1938 he was appointed editor of the paper and held that post through 1961.

VYACHESLAV MOLOTOV *(1890–1986)*: One of the favored inner circle around the Soviet dictator Joseph Stalin, Molotov was Soviet premier in the 1930s and foreign minister from March 1939, a post he held throughout the war. He negotiated Soviet participation in the United Nations Organization.

BERNARD LAW MONTGOMERY *(1887–1976)*: The British field marshal who achieved Britain's first major land victory at El Alamein in November 1942. He led the Eighth Army into Italy and was then appointed commander of the land campaign in the Normandy invasion. He ended the war in command of the Twenty-First Army Group.

BENITO MUSSOLINI *(1883–1945)*: Leader of the Italian Fascist Party and Italian prime minister from October 1922 to July 1943. Mussolini had ambitions to create a new Roman Empire in the Mediterranean and Africa, and launched a war against Ethiopia in October 1935. The war was won and Mussolini forged a close "Axis" partnership with Hitler. He launched war against Britain and France on June 10, 1940 and against Greece in October 1940. Popular support for Mussolini declined as Italian forces were defeated on all fronts, and he was overthrown by a coup in July 1943. Rescued by German special forces, he headed a new Italian Social Republic in German-occupied Italy. He was killed by partisans on April 28, 1945, trying to flee to Switzerland.

CHESTER NIMITZ *(1885–1966)*: Appointed commander of the U.S. Pacific Fleet in December 1941, he became overall commander-in-chief of U.S. Pacific forces in March 1942. In 1944 he was made fleet admiral in recognition of his role in the island-hopping campaign against Japan.

GEORGE PATTON *(1885–1945)*: A career cavalry officer, Patton became commander of the First Armored Corps in 1942, and then, for Operation Torch, commanded the Second U.S. Army Corps. He was commander of the Third U.S. Army in France in 1944 and played a spectacular part in driving the Germans back to their frontier. He died in a car accident in 1945.

JOACHIM VON RIBBENTROP *(1893–1946)*: Hitler's foreign policy adviser and, from February 1938, German foreign minister. He signed the pact with the Soviet Union in August 1939 but played a role throughout the war as Germany's leading diplomat. He was executed after the Nuremberg Trials for crimes against peace.

ERWIN ROMMEL *(1891–1944)*: The German field marshal who led the Afrika Korps in the North African campaign from 1941 to 1943, and then became responsible for building up the defenses against the D-Day invasion. He committed suicide after the July plot to assassinate Hitler in 1944.

FRANKLIN DELANO ROOSEVELT *(1882–1945)*: U.S. president for most of the war years, Roosevelt was elected for unprecedented third and fourth terms in 1940 and 1944. He helped steer America through the economic crisis of the 1930s with his New Deal strategies and pressed for U.S. rearmament at the end of the decade. He threw the United States behind the Allied war effort in everything short of war. After the surprise Japanese attack on Pearl Harbor, Roosevelt insisted on a Germany-first strategy and was generous in making U.S. resources available to the rest of the Allied nations through the Lend-Lease program.

CARL SPAATZ *(1891–1974)*: Overall commander-in-chief of U.S. Strategic and Tactical Air Forces in Europe in December 1943, Spaatz built up the Eighth Air Force in England in 1942 and then went to the Mediterranean theater as Eisenhower's commander of Allied Air Forces. He was the architect of the strategy to defeat the Luftwaffe and to destroy German oil supplies in 1944.

JOSEPH STALIN *(1878–1953)*: Stalin was appointed general secretary to the Central Committee of the Soviet Communist Party in 1922 and in 1941 became chairman of the Council of Commissars (that is, Soviet premier). During the war he was also chair of the Soviet Defense Committee and in this role he supervised the whole Soviet war effort.

EDWARD STETTINIUS *(1900–1949)*: In January 1941, Stettinius was appointed director of the Office of Production Management and in August 1941 administrator of the Lend-Lease Program. He became secretary of state in November 1944 and represented the United States at the founding conference of the United Nations at San Francisco in May 1945.

ARTHUR HAYS SULZBERGER *(1891–1968)*: Publisher of The New York Times from 1935 to 1961, succeeding his father-in-law, Adolph Ochs. Hostile to U.S. isolationism in the pre-war period, he also disliked the new powers acquired by Roosevelt to push through his legislation. During the war, Sulzberger championed a post-war order in which the United States would play a major part. He was concerned that his Jewishness might give rise to charges of bias, so he failed to give Nazi persecution of the European Jews prominent news coverage in The Times before and during the war.

HIDEKI TOJO *(1884–1948)*: Japanese prime minister from 1941, he led Japan into war with the United States. Military reverses forced his resignation in July 1944 and he was hanged as a war criminal in 1948.

HARRY S. TRUMAN *(1884–1972)*: Vice president of the United States in 1944 and then U.S. president following Roosevelt's death in April 1945. He led the Senate Special Committee that investigated war contracts, and saved millions of dollars of federal expenditure. He made the fateful decision to approve the atomic bombing of Japan and, post-war, played a leading role in containing the spread of Communism in Europe.

ALEXANDER VANDERGRIFT *(1887–1973)*: A senior Marine Corps officer, Vandergrift was given command of the First Marine Division for the invasion of Guadalcanal. In January 1944 he was promoted to lieutenant general and became commandant of the Marine Corps in Washington.

ISORUKU YAMAMOTO *(1884–1943)*: In 1939 he was appointed commander-in-chief of the Japanese Combined Fleet and organized the assault on Pearl Harbor. In 1943, intercepted messages allowed U.S. fighter aircraft to shoot down the plane in which he was flying.

GEORGI ZHUKOV *(1896–1974)*: The Soviet marshal who saved Moscow from capture in 1941, Zhukov became Stalin's deputy supreme commander in August 1942, and masterminded the capture of Berlin in April 1945.

EVENTS

ARNHEM *(September 17–26, 1944)*: Operation Market Garden was a British paratroop operation designed to seize a crossing on the lower Rhine around the Dutch town of Arnhem to create a salient for the invasion of Germany. Heavy German resistance led to the collapse of the operation with heavy British losses.

ATLANTIC CHARTER *(August 9–12, 1941)*: The document agreed to by Churchill and Roosevelt at a meeting in Placentia Bay, Newfoundland. The eight-point charter committed the two nations to establishing free trade and democratic government worldwide after the war.

BARBAROSSA CAMPAIGN *(June 22–December 5, 1941)*: The German campaign to destroy the Soviet forces in a quick strike in the summer of 1941. Despite rapid progress toward Moscow, Kiev and Leningrad the campaign bogged down into a war of attrition by the winter of 1941.

BATTLE OF BERLIN *(April 16–May 2, 1945)*: The last great offensive campaign by the Red Army drove deep into Germany and captured the German capital. Marshals Zhukov and Ivan Konev competed to be the first to get to the center of Berlin; Zhukov won the race. Hitler and Goebbels committed suicide rather than face capture. On May 2 the city was surrendered.

BATTLE OF BRITAIN *(July–October 1940)*: A series of air battles fought over southern Britain between the British RAF Fighter Command and the Second and Third German Air Fleets, stationed in northern France. The RAF lost 915 aircraft; the Luftwaffe 1,733.

BATTLE OF THE BULGE *(December 16, 1944–February 7, 1945)*: The German Operation Autumn Mist was a surprise assault against the advancing Allied line to try to reach the port of Antwerp and divide Allied forces. Despite early advances, Allied air power and resources were too great and in February 1945 the German Army ended up right where it had started.

BATTLE OF FRANCE *(May 10–June 17, 1940)*: German armies invaded the Low Countries and France on May 10, achieving a rapid breakthrough and dividing the Allied line. The Netherlands surrendered on May 15, Belgium on May 28, and France sought an armistice on June 17 after the German capture of Paris.

BATTLE OF KURSK *(July 5–13, 1943)*: One of the largest set-piece battles on the Eastern Front, Operation Citadel was launched by Hitler to try to eliminate a large Red Army salient around the city of Kursk. After a massive tank attack, the operation bogged down and German forces were then hit by a major Soviet counteroffensive that forced a rapid German retreat.

BATTLE OF LEYTE GULF *(October 23–26, 1944)*: The last fling of the Japanese Navy. The Japanese naval force was divided in three to try to reach the American invasion of the Philippines at Leyte from a number of routes. In the battles that followed, the Japanese lost 24 warships, the U.S. Navy 6.

BATTLE OF MIDWAY *(June 4–5, 1942)*: A decisive encounter between the Japanese main fleet and a U.S. naval force under Admiral Frank Fletcher. Four Japanese carriers were sunk and one-third of Japan's elite naval aviators lost, at the cost of the U.S. carrier *Yorktown*.

BATTLE OF THE PHILIPPINE SEA *(June 19–21, 1944)*: The largest carrier battle of World War II (24 carriers in all) resulted in a decisive defeat for Admiral Jisaburo Ozawa's fleet and the loss of over 400 aircraft in what American naval aviators called the "Great Marianas Turkey Shoot."

BISMARCK **SINKING** *(May 24–27, 1941)*: The largest German battleship, *Bismarck,* tried to escape into the Atlantic to prey on Allied shipping. Crippled by a British naval air attack on May 26, the battleship was sunk by naval fire and torpedoes.

BLITZ *(September 7, 1940–May 16, 1941)*: Beginning with the bombing of the London docks on September 7, the German Second and Third Air Fleets kept up continuous bombing of British ports, food stocks, oil, and the aero-engine industry. More than 43,000 Britons were killed, but the economic effects were limited.

CASABLANCA CONFERENCE *(January 14–24, 1943)*: A gathering of Churchill, Roosevelt and their military staffs at which it was decided to invade Sicily and Italy before opening a second front in France. The Combined Bomber Offensive was also approved at the Conference.

CRETE *(May 20–June 3, 1941)*: The Greek island was occupied by British Commonwealth forces as they retreated from mainland Greece. German paratroopers attacked them and captured the main airfield. Although outnumbered, the German troops forced a British evacuation by late May, leaving behind 5,000 prisoners of war.

DRESDEN BOMBING *(February 13–14, 1945)*: A raid by RAF Bomber Command that created a firestorm and killed an estimated 25,000 people, including German refugees.

DUMBARTON OAKS *(August 21–October 7, 1944)*: The conference where the groundwork was laid for the United Nations Organization; held outside Washington with representatives of 39 nations. The idea of a General Assembly and a Security Council was approved, but the issue of a veto for Council members was left unresolved.

EL ALAMEIN *(October 23–November 4, 1942)*: A decisive battle in North Africa in which Axis forces were driven back from the Egyptian frontier after a massive tank battle in the desert. The Axis forces retreated back to Tunisia, where they surrendered on May 13, 1943.

FALL OF ROME *(June 4–5, 1944)*: The Italian capital fell to an operation by General Mark Clark's U.S. Fifth Army after long months of stalemate around Monte Cassino.

GERMAN-POLISH WAR *(September 1–27, 1939)*: The German Army and Air Force invasion of Poland resulted in a rapid Polish retreat and a final defense around Warsaw. On September 17 Soviet troops entered and occupied eastern Poland. Poland surrendered on September 27.

GREEK CIVIL WAR *(1946–1949)*: After the liberation of Greece, wartime tensions between Nationalist and Communist resistance movements flared into open civil war between the new Greek Army and ELAS, the Greek People's Liberation Army, dominated by the Communist-backed Democratic Army of Greece. With British and U.S. military backing, the pro-Communist forces were finally defeated in 1949.

GUADALCANAL *(August 7, 1942–February 8, 1943)*: An island in the South Pacific Solomon Islands, occupied by the Japanese, where the first U.S. counterattack took place. After fierce and prolonged fighting, the Japanese garrison abandoned the island in February 1943.

HAMBURG BOMBING *(July 24–August 1943)*: Hamburg was hit by repeated raids in Operation Gomorrah, which destroyed more than twelve square miles of the urban area and killed an estimated 34,000–37,000 people, half of them in a firestorm on the night of July 27–28.

HIROSHIMA-NAGASAKI *(August 6 and 9, 1945)*: These two Japanese cities were the targets of the atomic bombs dropped by the USAAF 20th Bomber Command. At least 200,000 people were killed as a result of the explosions and subsequent radiation exposure.

IMPHAL-KOHIMA *(March 7–July 18, 1944)*: Japan's last major offensive against the Indian border towns of Imphal and Kohima. Imphal was besieged for four months, but held out until Allied reinforcements drove back the Japanese and opened the way for the reconquest of Burma.

INDIAN INDEPENDENCE *(August 15, 1947)*: After years of agitation for independence for India, led by Mohandas Gandhi, the post-1945 British Labour government agreed in early 1947 to grant independence and to divide India between a Hindu India and a Muslim Pakistan. Jawaharlal Nehru became prime minister of India and Muhammad Ali Jinnah became governor-general of Pakistan. Independence brought civil war and up to one million deaths in religious clashes. On January 30, 1948 Gandhi was assassinated.

INVASION OF SICILY *(July 9–August 17, 1943)*: Operation Husky, the invasion of the southern coast of Sicily, was a major amphibious operation involving soldiers and ships from the United States and Britain. The German defenders retreated in good order and largely escaped across the Straits of Messina, but the Italian soldiers surrendered in large numbers.

IWO JIMA *(February 19–March 26, 1945)*: One of the toughest island battles against Japanese defenders dug into caves and hideouts. Massive U.S. firepower eventually overcame resistance but at a cost of one-third of the U.S. force as casualties. Almost the entire Japanese garrison was killed.

July plot *(July 20, 1944)*: The failed attempt by senior German officers to assassinate Hitler at his headquarters. The organizer, Claus von Stauffenberg was shot that same night in Berlin and hundreds of other conspirators were rounded up and executed or sent to camps.

Kristallnacht *(November 8, 1938)*: Anti-Semitic riots in Germany directed against Jewish shops and synagogues, orchestrated by Joseph Goebbels with Hitler's tacit approval in revenge for the assassination of a German diplomat in Paris by a Jewish protester.

Lend-Lease program *(March 11, 1941–August 15, 1945)*: A plan to provide food, materials and weapons to the nations fighting against the Axis, without an immediate requirement for repayment. The United States aided 38 nations through this program but the bulk of aid went to Britain and the Soviet Union. Over the course of the war $42 billion in aid was granted, including $20.6 billion worth of munitions.

Liberation of Paris *(August 19–24, 1944)*: As Allied forces raced toward Paris, the French resistance began its own uprising. The German commander eventually abandoned suppression and a day after a French armored division entered the capital on August 24 the Germans surrendered the city.

Monte Cassino *(January 17–May 18, 1944)*: A mountain overlooking the small town of Cassino in Italy, on which stood an ancient monastery. Repeated Allied failure to break the German line around Cassino led to the bombing of the monastery on February 15. The mountaintop was eventually captured by the Polish Second Corps.

Munich Conference *(September 30, 1938)*: The conference at which the leaders of Germany, Italy, Great Britain and France agreed to the territorial division of Czechoslovakia, granting Germany the German-speaking areas of the Sudetenland, which were occupied from October 1 through the end of the war.

Normandy invasion *(June 6–July 24, 1944)*: Operation Overlord was the planned invasion of Normandy, designed to place the main Allied ground armies in northern Europe to drive the Germans from France. The landing was successful but got bogged down against tough German resistance. Not until late July was the balance sufficiently in the Allies' favor to permit a breakout from Normandy and a rapid defeat of German forces in the month that followed.

Nuremberg Trials *(November 20, 1945–October 14, 1946)*: The first trials of German leaders (the major war criminals) were held in the main courtroom in Nuremberg. Twenty-two were tried (Martin Bormann in absentia) and twelve were condemned to death for crimes against peace, crimes against humanity, war crimes and conspiracy to launch aggressive war.

Okinawa *(March 23–June 30, 1945)*: Operation Iceberg was designed to capture a major island close to Japan's home islands. The invasion was on a vast scale, with half a million U.S. forces pitted against 100,000 Japanese, dug into defensive positions. The high cost of this operation (12,520 U.S. dead) boosted support for the argument that the atomic bombing of Japan would save American lives.

Operation Torch *(November 8–10, 1942)*: This was the first major amphibious operation in Europe, a landing of U.S. and British forces in French Northwest Africa, in Morocco and Algeria. After brief resistance the French garrisons surrendered and the Allied force pressed east toward Tunisia, where Rommel led Axis resistance until May 1943.

Pearl Harbor *(December 7, 1941)*: The attack by the Japanese Combined Fleet on the U.S. Pacific Fleet base at Pearl Harbor brought the United States into World War II. Eighteen American ships were sunk or damaged and 347 aircraft lost in the surprise attack.

Potsdam Conference *(July 17–August 2, 1945)*: The last of the major wartime conferences between leaders of the three principal nations. By this time, Truman had replaced Roosevelt and midway through the talks, Clement Attlee replaced Churchill after defeating him in the British election. The Allies discussed Japanese surrender, the future of Europe and the issue of Polish territory. They also approved the terms of the major war crimes trials in Europe.

Soviet-Finnish winter war *(November 30, 1939–March 12, 1940)*: The Soviet Union launched a war against Finland for refusing to cede territory and bases, demanded to improve Soviet security in the Baltic Sea. Despite heroic resistance, the Finns were worn down by the greater numbers of Soviet forces and sued for an armistice in March 1940.

Stalingrad *(August 19, 1942–February 2, 1943)*: The city became a battleground during the German Operation Blue. Fierce Soviet defense prevented the capture of the city and on November 19, 1942 the Germans were encircled and cut off, eventually surrendering at the end of January 1943, although resistance continued in some places for two more days.

Teheran Conference *(November 20–December 1, 1943)*: The first major conference between the three main Allied leaders took place in the capital of Iran. The key issue for Stalin was obtaining a commitment from the West to open a major second front. It was agreed that invasion of northern France would occur in May 1944.

Warsaw uprising *(August 1–October 2, 1944)*: Polish nationalists organized in the Polish Home Army launched an uprising against the German occupiers as the Red Army approached. The timing was misjudged and no effective help came from the Allies. The uprising was defeated and the Germans took revenge on Warsaw by destroying whatever was still standing.

Yalta Conference *(February 5–11, 1945)*: The second of the major summits between the three wartime leaders, Yalta saw Stalin commit to fighting Japan when Germany was defeated, while Roosevelt and Churchill approved the Soviet territorial gains in Poland, which was to be compensated with former German territory.

Index

Illustrations are in BOLD

Acknowledgments

The editor would like to gratefully acknowledge all the help in preparing the manuscript from the team at Black Dog Leventhal: JP Leventhal, Lisa Tenaglia and Pamela Schechter.

The publisher would like to thank Richard Overy for taking on this enormous project, Dwight Zimmerman for his thorough research, Sheila Hart for the wonderful design and all the hard work she put into it, and everyone at The New York Times who worked on this book, particularly Alex Ward and Mitchel Levitas.

The New York Times would like to thank Susan Beachy, Kristi Reilly, James Boehmer, Robert B. Larson, Barbara Gray, Jack Begg, Alain Delaqueriere and Heidi Giovine for their research and technological contributions, as well as Kenneth A. Richieri and Lee Riffaterre of The Times and Anthony Brito and Jonathan Fuhrman of The Associated Press for their advice and assistance.